THE ULTIMATE ENCYCLOPEDIA OF
BOXING

DEDICATION

To Miguel Matthews, Seamus Casey and their blood brothers: journeymen fighters who will never feature in any encyclopedia of boxing, but without whose honest professionalism the game could not flourish.

Publisher's Note

During the preparations for the second edition, in 1999, to the great sadness of his wife and family and the heartfelt regret of the boxing fraternity, Harry Mullan died. At Harry's request, the updating work was carried out by friend and fellow boxing writer Bob Mee.

This edition published in 2018 by Sevenoaks
an imprint of the Carlton Publishing Group
20 Mortimer Street, London W1T 3JW

A CIP catalogue record for this book is available from the British Library

ISBN 978-1-78177-880-7

Project Editor: Martin Corteel
Production: Lisa Cook
Designer: Luke Griffin
Picture Research: Paul Langan

Printed and bound in Dubai

(OPPOSITE) ANTHONY JOSHUA: *stopped Wladimir Klitschko in 11 rounds at Wembley on April 29, 2017 in what many deem to have been the best heavyweight fight in years*

(FACING CONTENTS) FLOYD MAYWEATHER: *had far too much know-how for MMA star Conor McGregor in their much-hyped fight in Las Vegas on August 26, 2017*

LIST OF ABBREVIATIONS

Alg Algeria
Arg Argentina
Arm Armenia
Aus Australia
Aut Austria
Bah Bahamas
Bel Belgium
Blr Belarus
Bop Bophuthatswana
Bra Brazil
Cam Cambodia
Can Canada
Ch China
Cmr Cameroon
Col Colombia
Cub Cuba
Den Denmark
DR Dominican Republic
Ecu Ecuador
Egy Egypt
El Sal El Salvador
Eng England
Eth Ethiopia
Fra France
Ger Germany
Gha Ghana
Gre Greece
Guad Guadaloupe
Guy Guyana
Hai Haiti
Haw Hawaii
Hol Holland
Hon Honduras
Hun Hungary
IC Ivory Coast
Indo Indonesia
Ire Ireland
Irn Iran
Is Israel
Ita Italy
Jam Jamaica
Jap Japan
Kaz Kazakhstan
Ken Kenya
Kor South Korea
Ku Kuwait
Lib Liberia
Mlw Malawi
Mex Mexico
Mon Monaco
Mor Morocco
Mng Mongolia
N. Ire Northern Ireland
Neth Ant Netherlands Antilles
Nic Nicaragua
Nig Nigeria
Nor Norway
NZ New Zealand
Pan Panama
Par Paraguay
Phi Philippines
Pol Poland
Por Portugal
PR Puerto Rico
Rom Romania
SA South Africa
Sco Scotland
Sp Spain
Svk Slovakia
Swe Sweden
Swi Switzerland
Tha Thailand
Ton Tonga
Tr Trinidad
Tun Tunisia
Ug Uganda
Ukr Ukraine
Ur Uruguay
US United States
Uzb Uzbekistan
Ven Venezuela
Wal Wales
Yug Yugoslavia
Zai Zaire
Zam Zambia
Zim Zimbabwe

CHAMPIONSHIP WEIGHT LIMITS

Category	*American*	*British*	*Metric*
Minimumweight	105 lb	7 st 7 lb	47.627 kg
Light-flyweight	108 lb	7 st 10 lb	48.988 kg
Flyweight	112 lb	8 st	50.802 kg
Super-flyweight	115 lb	8 st 3 lb	52.163 kg
Bantamweight	118 lb	8 st 6 lb	53.524 kg
Super-bantamweight	122 lb	8 st 10 lb	55.338 kg
Featherweight	126 lb	9 st	57.153 kg
Super-featherweight	130 lb	9 st 4 lb	58.967 kg
Lightweight	135 lb	9 st 9 lb	61.235 kg
Light-welterweight	140 lb	10 st	63.503 kg
Welterweight	147 lb	10 st 7 lb	66.678 kg
Light-middleweight	154 lb	11 st	69.853 kg
Middleweight	160 lb	11 st 6 lb	72.575 kg
Super-middleweight	168 lb	12 st	76.203 kg
Light-heavyweight	175 lb	12 st 7 lb	79,379 kg
Cruiserweight	200 lb	14 st 4 lb	90.718 kg
Heavyweight	*any weight above the cruiserweight limit*		

THE ULTIMATE ENCYCLOPEDIA OF BOXING

NINTH EDITION

HARRY MULLAN

WITH BOB MEE & MATT BOZEAT

SEVENOAKS

Corona
MGM RESORTS

CONTENTS

CLOWN PRINCE *Max Baer*

GOLDEN BOY *Oscar De La Hoya*

AGELESS *Bernard Hopkins*

CLETO REYES
HUBLOT
FanDuel

INTRODUCTION

Welcome to this the ninth edition of this, *The Ultimate Encyclopedia of Boxing*.

Much has happened in the world of boxing in recent times. That fight between Floyd Mayweather Jr. and Manny Pacquiao – covered in the Great Fights section – showed what a great fighter Mayweather is, even if some of the casual fans didn't fully appreciate what they were watching. And then the sport has seen the emergence of Anthony Joshua – the British heavyweight is seen as one of the brightest stars the sport has seen for years.

In years to come, Mayweather, Pacquiao, Bernard Hopkins, Wladimir and Vitali Klitschko, and more, are sure to be fondly remembered – along with a night at Wembley Stadium when 80,000 fans saw Joshua prevail against Wladimir Klitschko.

This truly is a golden age for boxing – and it should be appreciated as such. It is reflected in the amount of televised interest in the sport. In America, boxing is being shown on free-to-air television again and in Britain, Channel Five and ITV are doing the same and providing competition for Sky Sports and Box Nation, the latter a station dedicated entirely to boxing. So the next time someone tells you boxing isn't the sport it was, remind them of the above.

Of course, there are reasons why boxing is unrecognisable from the sport our fathers and grandfathers watched and took part in. As the expanding record section shows, the world championships are becoming far more fragmented. There are more and more interim world title fights being held, along with Silver title fights.

That looks set to continue. Because boxing is such a maverick sport, in that it has very little government backing around the world, it is very hard for an overall umbrella organization to exist. There is not enough political will to make it happen, nor unity of spirit or purpose, were that miracle to occur, for it to survive. The current situation benefits many people, so why would anyone change it?

Having a plethora of titles is good for the finances of the governing bodies, but not so good for those trying to follow the sport – or those trying to update encyclopedias! The linear champions are still there, but they are harder to find these days.

The hardcore boxing fans know who the real champions are, but for casual fans, it's confusing. For them, possibly the best sources of information are The International Boxing Organization's computerized rankings and also *The Ring* and *Boxing Monthly* magazines.

The latter lost its editor when Glyn Leach died in August, 2014. A true boxing man, he was editor of the magazine for 22 years.

I never worked for Glyn, but instead served my apprenticeship in local newspapers and covering amateur and professional shows around the Midlands for *Boxing News*. That was the same path taken by Bob Mee before me.

It was Bob who asked me to take on the job of updating this Encyclopedia a couple of years ago, to carry on the good work he and Harry Mullan had started. I considered it an honour and I was honoured again when the publishers contacted me and asked me to update this edition.

(OPPOSITE) FLOYD MAYWEATHER JR.: *was far too good for Manny Pacquiao in what was dubbed the "Fight of the Century" in May 2015, retaining his three welterweight titles with a unanimous points verdict*

THE ORIGINS OF BOXING

Prizefighting reached its peak in eighteenth- and nineteenth-century England, when champions were recognized and kings, poets and statesmen patronized a sport which the law nevertheless prohibited. By the time modern boxing began to take over from bare-knuckle savagery, the centre of activity was switching to America.

Perhaps the one incontrovertible piece of evidence boxing's abolitionists can never deny is that it has been with us for as long as man can remember. Fist-fighting, as sporting competition, has been a part of us for thousands of years. It was certainly practised during the original Olympic Games in ancient Greece. Homer refers to it in the *Iliad*. It was a regular entertainment in Roman times too, and possibly existed in Britain during the centuries of Roman occupation. However, the first vague references do not emerge until the late seventeenth century. In January 1681, the *Protestant Mercury* recorded "a match of boxing before His Grace, the Duke of Albemarle, between the Duke's footman and a butcher". The latter, apparently, was a small but experienced boxer, and he won. How and where, we know not.

JAMES FIGG *Prize fighter, swordsman and bear baiter*

The first English champion of record was James Figg, from Thame in Oxfordshire, who was brought to London by a patron who saw him performing on the village green and set him up in a boxing "academy". Figg was illiterate, but a cunning businessman and the most celebrated teacher of the 1720s. Boxing was so popular King George I ordered a ring to be erected in Hyde Park for public use. Figg taught the use of sword, broadsword, cudgel and fist in premises at the Adam and Eve pub between what is now Tottenham Court Road and Oxford Street.

Boxing was only loosely related to the art we see today, but then so were other fledgling sports – cricket, for example, bore only rough comparison to the complex game now laid before us. Wrestling was accepted as a proper part of boxing, and so were blatant fouls, such as gouging and "purring" – the raking of the spiked boot across a fallen man. These were outlawed only by the rules introduced in 1743 by Figg's successor, John Broughton, which laid the broad foundation for the way boxing was run for almost 100 years until the establishment of the London Prize Ring Rules in 1838.

But it took the first major ring tragedy for the atmosphere to be created whereby such regulations could be enforced. Broughton beat the inexperienced George Stevenson of Hull in his own booth, close to Figg's old premises, in February 1741. It was a brutal bout which lasted almost 40 minutes before Broughton drove in a punch beneath the heart that forced Stevenson's collapse. He recovered consciousness, only to linger a few weeks in the Adam and Eve before dying in Broughton's arms. The champion was so affected that he used his influence and status to

BROOME VS. HANNAR *was for a £1,000 purse and took place at New Farm Park, near Bicester, in England's South Midlands*

introduce this first attempt to regulate boxing and to lessen the possibility of tragedy in the ring.

Royal Patronage

Aside from his rules, Broughton made boxing acceptable to the gentry, providing lessons and sparring sessions with "mufflers" to minimize the risk of damage to a man's looks. His career was enhanced by the patronage of the Duke of Cumberland, the notorious Butcher of Culloden, whom he beat in a "small sword" match held at the academy, which Cumberland had visited as an exercise.

This victory was important in that it persuaded the gentry and aristocracy that there was something to be learned from "academies" where "the science of defence" was taught. It also helped enormously that John Broughton's personality was unusually cultured for a man who made his living in the way that he did. This enabled him to make influential friends who helped him even when Cumberland's patronage ended, following his shock defeat by Jack Slack in 1750. Cumberland made a crazy bet of £10,000 to win £400 from a lesser crony, then blamed Broughton when a surprise punch from Slack blinded him temporarily and rendered him unable to fight.

The undiluted anguish of Broughton's plaintive: "By God, I'm done!" passes down the centuries, but Cumberland was unimpressed, claimed he had been double-crossed and promptly closed down the academy and had boxing outlawed from civilized society. Broughton, however, knew enough people to survive, turned his academy into what amounts now to a furniture warehouse, made a fortune on the stock market and lived to the age of 84. He was buried in Lambeth and a tablet was erected in his memory in Westminster Abbey.

Slack is largely blamed for pugilism's demise in the middle years of the eighteenth century, but then he lacked Broughton's towering personality, his business acumen – and royal patronage. He was a butcher by trade, who travelled to London from Norwich to find his fortune. He did draw some fame from a victory over a 6ft 4in Frenchman known only as "Petit", presumably a nickname, at Harleston in Norfolk in July 1751. A defeat of a foreigner always went down well. Slack based himself in London where he gave lessons. But he was a rugged fighter with a huge heart and big punch … and that doesn't necessarily make for a good teacher.

RULES

TO BE OBSERVED IN ALL BATTLES ON THE STAGE

THE FIRST PRIZE-RING RULES *were drawn up in London in 1743*

John Broughton opened the "Tennis Court" in London's Haymarket, which housed a fight between Slack and William Stevens of Birmingham in 1760. Cumberland, by now a man of declining fortunes, returned to his old habits and gambled on this fight again … on Slack, who lost the championship when Stevens landed his "chopper blow" and threw him heavily, his head smacking on the wooden boards. This time Cumberland broke all ties with pugilism. Within nine months Stevens had taken a dive against one George Meggs of Bristol and the decline of boxing was set.

After a run of ordinary champions, boxing was effectively rescued by a former corn porter from Derby, Thomas Jackling, who took the ring name Johnson. He drew crowds on a regular basis, and eventually royal interest returned – most notably the young Prince of Wales, the future George IV. Peers of the realm began to sponsor fighters and once more boxing became an activity on which large sums could be won and lost. By using his fists a man could escape poverty and, while he could never traverse the boundaries of class, he could at least appear to do so by association.

The greatest star to emerge since Broughton was Daniel Mendoza, born in Aldgate in the east end of London of Jewish descent. Mendoza was one of the cleverest boxers in history, who had a celebrated series of bouts with Richard "The Gentleman" Humphries between 1788 and 1790, which captured the imagination of the nation. Humphries won the first, after which he sent a message to his patron that read simply: "Sir, I have done the Jew and am in good health," but Mendoza won the second and third battles.

Their third encounter was in Doncaster and was important enough to persuade men to travel nearly 200 miles from London to see it – no easy journey when roads were often no more than mudtracks. Humphries was beaten after 73 minutes, retired and made good money as a coal merchant, while Mendoza lived on his wits, touring with a circus, mixing with royalty, giving public sparring tours, and even writing his autobiography. He also found himself in debtors' prison more than once, but his friends usually bailed him out.

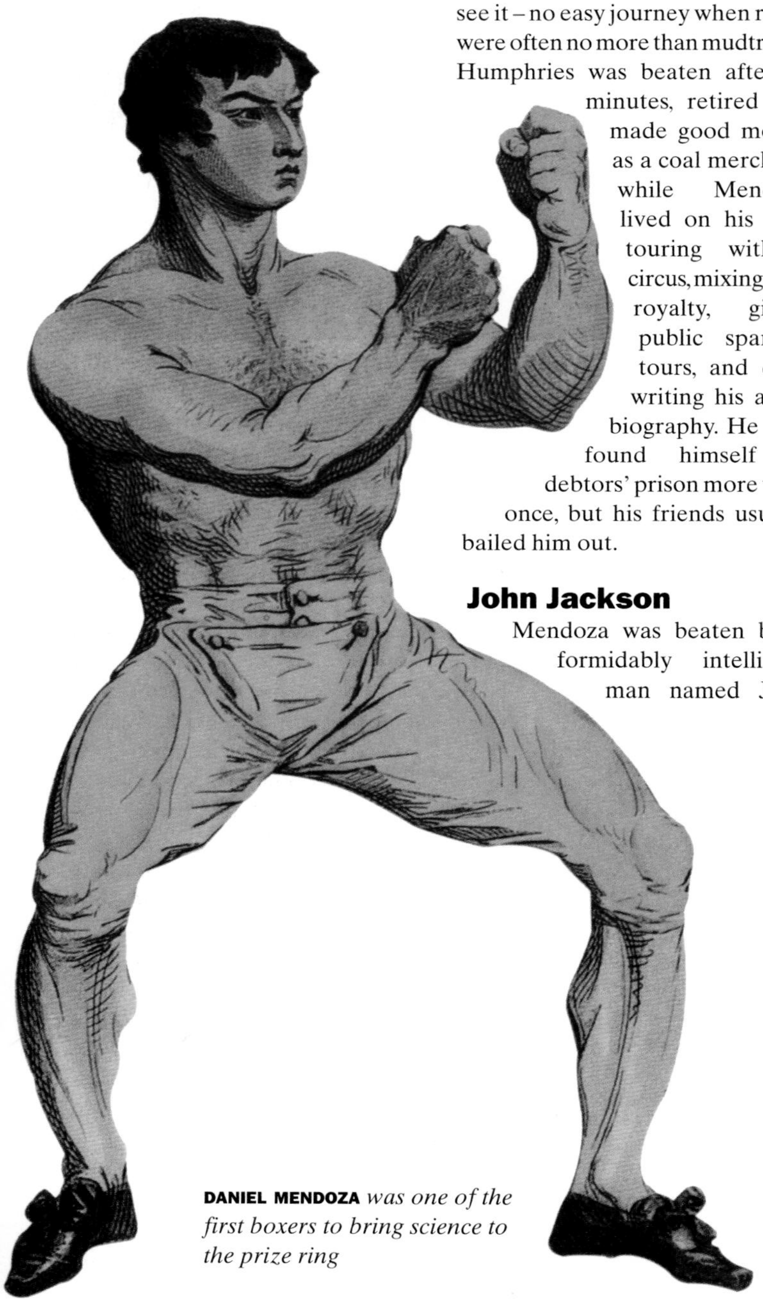

DANIEL MENDOZA *was one of the first boxers to bring science to the prize ring*

John Jackson

Mendoza was beaten by a formidably intelligent man named John Jackson, who was known as "Gentleman", and who was perhaps the most complete "heir" to Broughton. Like the old hero he was a tremendous technical boxer, a thinking man and a genius in business. He thrashed the smaller Mendoza in little more than 10 minutes near Hornchurch in Essex in April 1795. He had worked hard for his success – the only bout he lost was when he broke an ankle and yet he still offered to fight on if he could be strapped to a chair! – and after defeating Mendoza he cashed in, retiring to open what became a busy and thriving business at 13 Old Bond Street in the centre of London. It was there that the rich and famous flocked to be taught the "noble art" and Jackson became one of the most celebrated figures of his day. Lord Byron was a pupil and once grandly labelled Jackson "The Emperor of Pugilism". Through Jackson's influence, boxing became fashionable once more, and moved into perhaps its grandest age. Jackson himself lived on into old age in comfort, dying in 1845 at the age of 76.

The supremacy of the Bristol "school" of pugilism reached its height at the turn of the nineteenth century with the arrival of Jem Belcher, a precocious young man who astonished London society with his brilliance and who was called "Napoleon of the Ring". He was barely 19 when he beat Jack Bartholomew, a man who laid good claim to be champion. Belcher was acknowledged beyond dispute as the champion when he defeated Andrew Gamble, a stonemason who was the Irish champion, on Wimbledon Common in December 1800. It is said that the roar of the crowd could be heard ten miles away, and pigeons carrying news of his victory were sent back to Bristol, where church bells were rung in celebration.

After that Belcher defeated a tough Shropshireman named Joe Berks three times and then Jack Fearby. Still only 22, Belcher had the world at his feet. But in July 1803, he was struck in the eye by a ball while playing racquets and maimed permanently. He retired to run a pub in Wardour Street in Soho, inviting another Bristol man, Henry Pearce, to London to assume his championship status. Pearce did so well enough, beating Jack Fearby in a ten-foot square taproom in a pub in Windmill Street so badly that a woman had to be hired to clean the blood from the walls.

Pearce quickly established his supremacy, but then had the unpleasant task of dealing with a challenge from the one-eyed and by now bitter Belcher, who had lost his money and was old before his time. They drew a crowd of 25,000 people to Blyth, south of Doncaster, on December 6, 1805. Belcher boxed well for a time before Pearce took over. After 35 minutes Belcher was tottering pathetically, unable to see, and with one arm hanging uselessly by his side. Pearce called out: "I'll take no advantage of thee, Jem. I'll not strike thee, lest I hurt thy other eye."

As astonishing as it seems to us now, Belcher fought twice more, losing to a new champion, Tom Cribb, in 1807 and 1809. He lost all his money, and with it his health, eventually dying in July 1811 at the age of 30. Henry Pearce, who was called "The Game Chicken", also died young. After beating Belcher, he lost his way, giving exhibitions in various towns and living on his wits and what was left of the fortune he had amassed and somehow blown. By 1808 he had tuberculosis. And after watching Belcher fight Tom Cribb for the second time, he was taken ill on the way back to London and died, aged 32, in April 1809.

The most gruelling fight Pearce had was a remarkable encounter with John Gully, whom he had known in his youth in Bristol, and whom he found languishing in the debtors' prison at Fleet. These were wild times in which men could lose everything and find themselves rotting away in jail, in the vague hope that somehow their debts could be cleared. Gambling, not only on boxing, was a national habit. The Duchess of Bedford was once forced to admit to her husband that she had lost a little matter of £176,000 playing cards!

TOM CRIBB *(of England, left) beat American Tom Molineaux in the first international contest of note at Copthall Common, south of London*

Because of the readiness of the people who travelled miles in often appalling conditions to witness and gamble large sums of money on their fights, the rewards for pugilists increased dramatically. And because of that, Pearce was able to entice young, wretched Gully into a prize fight after a "sporting gentleman" named Fletcher Reid had cleared the debts that had put him inside. Gully could fight – and proved it by extending Pearce for 64 rounds at Hailsham in Sussex in October 1805. Pearce eventually knocked him out with a blow to the throat.

Upon Pearce's retirement Gully was considered the best man in the country, purely because of that single epic battle. He proved his ability when he defeated a Lancastrian rogue named Bob Gregson in front of a crowd that included dukes, marquises and lords, at Six Mile Bottom near Newmarket in 1807. They were matched again the following year and once more Gully triumphed, in 28 rounds lasting an hour and a quarter in front of a crowd of more than 20,000 near Woburn. Gully had the good sense to announce his retirement and, unlike so many, stuck to his decision. He took over a pub, ran with a disreputable crowd and made more money from bookmaking, and eventually won a £40,000 fortune by betting on horses he owned. He built himself a house in Yorkshire, owned three Derby winners and became MP for Pontefract in 1832! He lived to be 80 years old.

An American Challenge

Tom Cribb, from Hanham near Bristol, succeeded Gully and became one of the greatest sporting heroes England has ever known. He was not particularly skilful, but his courage – known then as "bottom" – was magnificent, and he was a man of the people. He had charisma. He beat Gregson, Belcher twice (as he should have done) and the 42-year-old American Bill Richmond, who was the first black fighter of note. But it was Richmond's acquaintance and protégé, Tom Molineaux, another black American and a former slave, who made Cribb into a national star. Molineaux was a talented fighter, but Cribb beat him in a vicious fight that lasted 55 minutes on Copthall Common south of London in December 1810. Molineaux seemed on the way to victory when Cribb's second, Joe Ward, accused the American of carrying bullets in his hands. The ensuing row bought Cribb time – and the freezing English winter did the rest. Cribb recovered and slowly broke Molineaux down, fouling as he pleased without restraint from the referee. In the end, frozen stiff and thoroughly discouraged, Molineaux quit.

Cribb retired but returned when Molineaux claimed the championship. England considered this an affront – and Cribb fought him again at Thistleton Gap, Rutland, in September 1811. Molineaux wasn't the brightest man boxing has ever embraced – he devoured a whole chicken, an apple pie and four pints of beer before the fight! He managed to close Cribb's eye, but couldn't fight for long and Cribb prolonged it into the 11th round because he was enjoying himself.

Cribb's successor was the more talented Tom Spring from Townhope near Hereford. Like so many who follow great sporting heroes, he was overshadowed. Nevertheless, his fights drew enormous crowds as pugilism's popularity soared. More than 30,000 saw him beat Bill Neat near Andover in Hampshire in 1823 and a similar number turned up at Worcester racecourse to watch his incredible 149-minute epic with the Irishman, Jack Langan, in 1824. Before the Langan fight, part of the grandstand collapsed under the weight of humanity – one person was killed and several injured. A return with Langan five months later lasted a mere 76 rounds and 108 minutes! By the end Langan was so exhausted he went down from a push and couldn't get up.

Prizefighting in Decline

Both men retired to run pubs, their fortunes intact, and with their exit boxing began to fade. Tom Cannon, nicknamed The Great Gun of Windsor, followed Spring, but lost to Jem Ward at Warwick in 1825. Ward was a rogue, brilliantly gifted as an artist and musician as well as a fighter, but was also known to throw the odd fight or two. Ward somehow lost to Peter Crawley, who was suffering from a hernia at the time of the fight, and who retired immediately afterwards to invest his £530 purse in a butcher's shop, leaving Ward to continue his reign as champion.

England was changing. George IV died, to be followed by the colourless William and, in 1837, Queen Victoria. The new morality of the Victorian era is often considered a product of the lady herself, but this is probably unfair: the influence of the new evangelical movement, the new Protestantism of the Wesleyans and Baptists, was already set when Victoria took the throne. However, it must be admitted that she did fit the mood perfectly. Disapproval was rife. Boxing declined, just as other sports and pastimes did.

James "Deaf 'Un" Burke claimed the championship, but killed a man, Simon Byrne, at Ascot in 1833 and subsequently became the first English pugilist to try his luck in America. He didn't have much. He was beating Sam O'Rourke in New Orleans when the mob, O'Rourke's fans to a man, broke up the ring. Burke very narrowly escaped being lynched.

Bendigo, alias William Thompson, was a southpaw from Nottingham who conceded 5in in height and more than three stones to Ben Caunt in 1835 yet beat him after 22 rounds in which he had sensibly refused to stand and trade punches with the big man. Finally Caunt lost his temper, ran over to Bendigo's corner and hit him as he sat enjoying his rest. Caunt was disqualified.

Disqualifications were a common result as men toiled for hours, often manipulating the rules by dropping when tapped or cuffed, simply to get out of tough situations or when they wanted a rest. In the first rematch, Caunt beat Bendigo on a foul in 75 rounds, a decision which caused a riot. A third fight, in 1845, saw the third disqualification result between them – Bendigo winning this time in the 93rd round for a purse of £400.

Bendigo was a larger than life figure who was converted to the ministry when in prison for what was described as his "28th breach of the peace". Apparently he gave well-attended sermons on the evils of drink. This sort of thing was popular entertainment in its own right. Bendigo died at the age of 68 in August 1880 after a fall at his Nottingham home.

Boxing has a way of surviving, but by the middle years of the century was in steep decline. Old men remembered its glory days, but fights were now poorly attended and not especially well paid. One of the better-known champions was William Perry, the "Tipton Slasher". He had fought Ben Caunt's giant American protégé Charles Freeman in a marathon that spread over three days before Freeman was given the verdict on a foul. Perry beat Tom Paddock, but lost to Harry Broome of Birmingham. And in 1857 the poor old Slasher gambled every penny he had on himself against the young, rising Tom Sayers, who beat him in ten rounds that lasted 102 minutes on a boat moored on the Thames.

Sayers, a cobbler's son from Brighton, stood only 5ft 8in and scaled 147lb … a welterweight by modern standards … yet was one of the greatest boxers Britain has ever produced. He learned the hard way, inevitably giving away weight to stronger, bigger men, but progressed to become the best in England.

Sayers vs. Heenan

Then, on April 17, 1860, Sayers fought John Heenan from West Troy, New York, at Farnborough in Hampshire. Historians hail this as the last great prizefight staged in Britain and through this single meeting boxing had a sudden resurgence. The police virtually stood aside to let it happen – they didn't really have much choice in the matter as hordes left on trains out of London clutching tickets with "To Nowhere" printed on them. Included in the throng were Members of Parliament and writers Charles Dickens and William Thackeray.

Sayers found the big man easy to hit, and cut him in the opening round, but Heenan got on top and in the sixth landed a heavy punch on Sayers' right arm, rendering it useless. Sayers boxed one-handed from then on, chipping away at Heenan's face and closing his right eye in the seventh. Heenan hurt his left hand, which was swollen and puffy … and so it went on, round after round, with Sayers "weak but cheerful" by the 25th round. Heenan was suddenly tiring in the 29th and his left eye seemed to be closing too. By the 36th his face was in a terrible mess, but he still had the strength to pin Sayers against the ropes and put all his weight on the little man's throat. He applied the same tactic in round 37, at which point the police finally closed in to stop the fight, only to find the crowd close in even further.

The ring was now only a few feet wide, but the two men fought on for five more so-called rounds before the officials finally had their way and called a halt. Heenan ran away but within minutes was unable to see, while Sayers, his arm feared broken, and desperately tired, was helped to his carriage. Both received commemorative belts and Sayers also had a payout of £3,000, raised by the public in appreciation of his effort, on the promise that he never boxed again. He didn't, but the combined effects of alcohol and tuberculosis drove him into an early grave, at the age of 39, in November 1865. Heenan returned to England to fight Tom King but lost in 24 rounds and was himself only 38 when he died penniless in Wyoming in 1873.

After Sayers came a string of unremarkable men, punctuated only by Jem Mace, who allowed himself to be called the Swaffham Gypsy even though he had no gypsy blood. Mace was a man of marvellous skill, like Sayers, small and tough, who happily took on opponents weighing dozens of pounds more. He was an innovator, a ring artist completely at home when involved in the toughest of fights. But the pickings for a pugilist were becoming so poor in England that he took his craft abroad, first to the USA, then to Australia and New Zealand, where he taught from his own booth. Among his pupils were the early glove heroes Bob Fitzsimmons and Peter Jackson.

Sayers and Heenan in a Great Fight for the Championship

They fought like lions in the ring,
Both men did boldly stand,
They two hours and six minutes fought,
And neither beat his man.

POPULAR BALLAD OF 1860

When Mace retired, the title was claimed by Tom Allen, Birmingham-born but by now an American citizen. He lost to the 37-year-old, Northampton-born Joe Goss in 1876. By now the boxing scene had well and truly shifted to the USA.

Queensberry Rules

Bare-knuckle fighting was declining rapidly in Britain as, with the introduction of the Queensberry Rules in 1867, amateur and glove fighting was generally thought to be more in keeping with the times. The Queensberry Rules banned wrestling, changed the length of rounds to three minutes with a one-minute rest in between, and ruled that the contestants had to wear "fair-sized boxing gloves of the best quality and new".

The old habits still died hard. There were still fights to a finish, but gradually promoters saw the commercial sense in using a maximum number of rounds and, if no knockout had been achieved, having a points verdict based on which man had done the better work over the whole of the fight.

For some time the bare-knuckle and gloved codes existed side by side, but it was boxing with gloves which prevailed. The title in America passed from Goss to Paddy Ryan, a raw, unskilled Irishman, in 1880 ... and on to the last and one of the greatest of all bare-knuckle legends, the immortal John L. Sullivan, who thrashed Ryan in nine rounds, lasting only ten-and-a-half minutes, in Mississippi City in February 1882.

Sullivan, the "Boston Strong Boy", was only 23 and as good as anybody had been for years. Sullivan, who would walk into a bar and boast "My name is John L. Sullivan and I can lick any son-of-a-bitch in this house", was adored by the multitudes and loathed by the moralists. But he walked his own path for ten long years, his supremacy only rarely challenged.

Emotionally Sullivan was the heir of James Figg, not Jack Broughton. There was nothing cerebral or slick about him, but his attraction was that he could fight and loved to do so.

Sullivan took part in the last bare-knuckle championship contest in history when he outlasted Jake Kilrain for a stoppage in the 75th round at Richburg, Mississippi, in July 1889. Afterwards, he vowed he would never take a bare-knuckle fight again.

However, in September 1892, in New Orleans, Sullivan fitted his new-fangled gloves and was thoroughly beaten in 21 one-sided rounds by the princely, pompadoured artist of the ring James J. Corbett otherwise known as "Gentleman Jim".

Corbett belonged to a new era, a new world where practiced skill, physical conditioning and well-drilled technique would always overcome heart, toughness and desire. Those privileged few who saw John L. fall into the resin saw the passing, not just of a great champion, but of a way of life.

TOM SAYERS *and John Heenan were the combatants in the last great prizefight to be staged in England, at Farnborough, Hampshire, in 1860*

THE GREAT BOXERS

Boxing has had more than its share of heroes, and it is not an easy task to whittle them down to the 225 who were the most outstanding performers in the history of the modern, gloved game. These are the men who created their own legends, and whose memories are cherished by fans around the world. They are, by any definition, the game's greats.

Arthur Abraham

Born: *Yerevan, Armenia, February 20, 1980*
Titles: *IBF middleweight champion 2005–09, WBO super-middleweight champion 2012–13 & 2014–16*
Record: *52 contests, 46 wins, 6 defeats*

Arthur Abraham became a two-weight world champion when he took the WBO super-middleweight title from Robert Stieglitz in August 2012, but lost it in the rematch. Stieglitz retired Abraham after three one-sided rounds, having ambushed him with non-stop punches and leaving his left eye swollen shut. A third meeting saw Abraham turn back the clock to reclaim the WBO belt on a split decision.

His first defeat, after 31 wins, was to Andre Dirrell, in March 2010. Behind on points, Abraham was disqualified in the 11th. Abraham was unbeaten at middleweight – relinquishing the IBF title after 10 defences – but he had previously lost world-title challenges at 168lbs to Andre Ward and Carl Froch before beating Stieglitz.

The Armenian is a supremely smart fighter. He can control a fight's pace, moving up and down the gears, and is a strong and accurate, heavy puncher.

In 2006, Abraham outpointed Colombia's Edison Miranda despite suffering a badly broken jaw that needed two steel rods to repair. Bizarrely, his trainer Ulli Wegner was threatened with prosecution for allowing the fight to continue. The rematch was at super-middleweight and Abraham, after being outhustled in the first three rounds, floored Miranda three times to win in the fourth round.

Muhammad Ali

see Legends of the Ring (pp 74–75)

Saul Alvarez

Born: *Tlajomulco, Mexico, July 18, 1990*
Titles: *WBC light-middleweight title 2011–13, WBC middleweight title 2015–, WBA light-middleweight title 2016*
Record: *52 contests, 49 wins, 2 draw, 1 defeat*

Known as "El Canelo" – Spanish for cinnamon – Alvarez turned pro when he was 15 years old.

He made the step up to 12-round level just a month after his 17th birthday and, while still in his teens, he spelled out his ambition to oust Floyd Mayweather Jr. and Manny Pacquiao from the top of the pound-for-pound rankings. He got his chance in September, 2013, but was well beaten on points by Mayweather.

That cost Alvarez the WBC light-middleweight title he had won by punishing Matthew Hatton – brother of Ricky – throughout their 12-round clash for the vacant belt. Following the loss to Maywweather, Alvarez rebuilt his reputation with wins over Alfredo Angulo and Erislandy Lara. He became world champion again in November 2015 with a unanimous points decision over Miguel Cotto and then drew with Gennady Golovkin in what many thought was the best fight of 2017.

SAUL ALVAREZ *lands a punishing right hand on Carlos Baldomir*

Dennis Andries

Born: *Buxton, Guyana, November 5, 1953*
Titles: *WBC light-heavyweight champion 1986–1987, 1989, 1990–91; British light-heavyweight champion 1984–86; WBC Continental Americas champion 1990; British cruiserweight champion 1995*
Record: *65 contests, 49 wins, 2 draws, 14 defeats*

The date of birth is debatable, since Andries has always claimed to be considerably older, but whatever the truth, he is a remarkable character. From the most unpromising raw material, he became WBC light-heavyweight champion three times, and won the British cruiserweight title when he was officially past 40.

After an undistinguished amateur career he turned pro in May 1976, and his crude but powerful style quickly made him a man to avoid. He was jeered from the ring after his first British title fight, a points loss to Bunny Johnson in 1980, but ignored the jibes and worked his way back. Tom Collins outpointed him for the British title in 1982, but he finally claimed it two years later, winning a Lonsdale Belt outright.

In April 1986 he became an improbable WBC champion, beating J. B. Williamson in London, but lost the title on his first defence to Thomas Hearns. He promptly joined the Hearns camp and, basing himself in Detroit, won the title twice more, including a memorable three-fight series with the Australian, Jeff Harding, before moving up to win and lose the British cruiserweight crown in 1995.

Alexis Arguello

Born: *Managua, Nicaragua, April 19, 1952*
Titles: *WBA featherweight champion 1974–77, WBC super-featherweight champion 1978–80, WBC lightweight champion 1981–82*
Record: *85 contests, 77 wins, 8 defeats*

The stylish, handsome Arguello was a major star in the 1970s and early 1980s, winning titles at three weights and becoming a favourite with American TV viewers, who were enjoying a glut of live networked boxing during that period. Like so many of the great Latin fighters, he started young: he lost his professional debut when he was only 16.

A JUBILANT *Alexis Arguello, after claiming his third world title*

Ernesto Marcel outpointed him in his first bid for the WBA featherweight title in 1974, but nine months later he knocked out Marcel's successor Ruben Olivares in 13 rounds. He relinquished the title two years later and promptly won the WBC super-featherweight championship, retaining it eight times.

British fans saw him in action in June 1981 when he took the WBC lightweight title from Scotland's Jim Watt. He came close to a fourth title in July 1982, when he battled Aaron Pryor for 14 unforgettable rounds for the WBA light-welterweight title, but retired after Pryor knocked him out in a rematch. He made a short-lived comeback in 1995 and then entered politics but, sadly, died in 2009.

Henry Armstrong

see Legends of the Ring (pp76–77)

Abe Attell

Born: *San Francisco, California, February 22, 1884*
Titles: *World featherweight title claimant 1904–12*
Record: *(approx.) 172 contests, 91 wins, 18 draws, 2 No Contests, 50 No Decisions, 11 defeats*

The clever Californian became accepted as the best man in the featherweight division after the champion, Young Corbett II, announced that he could no longer make the weight. Attell – still only 17 – had drawn with and beaten the great George Dixon in 1901, and on that basis proclaimed himself champion.

He consolidated his position with an unbeaten run of 18, against the era's outstanding featherweights. Owen Moran from Birmingham held him to a draw in 1908, and was given a rematch eight months later. Attell wanted 20 rounds, the Englishman 25, so they compromised and, for the only time in history, a championship was contested over 23 rounds. Again, they drew.

Jim Driscoll easily outboxed Attell in 1909, but because it was a "No Decision" contest the American continued to claim the title until he was outpointed by Johnny Kilbane in 1912. His career virtually ended in 1913, as he boxed only twice between then and his farewell appearance in 1917. He was implicated in the notorious 1919 World Series "Black Sox" betting scandal, but was never charged and later ran a bar in New York. He died on February 7, 1970.

Max Baer

Born: *Omaha, Nebraska, February 11, 1909*
Titles: *World heavyweight champion 1934–35*
Record: *84 contests, 71 wins, 13 defeats*

Had Max Baer been able to take boxing seriously, his ferocious hitting could have made him an outstanding heavyweight champion. Instead, he lost the title in his first defence against James J. Braddock, in what remained the biggest upset in history until Buster Douglas dethroned Mike Tyson in 1990. Baer loved to clown and wisecrack, which, while it endeared him to the fans, prevented him achieving his full potential.

But he could fight when he chose to, and wins over contenders Tom Heeney, King Levinsky and ex-champion Max Schmeling earned him a title fight with the Italian giant Primo Carnera in June 1934. The unfortunate Carnera took a brutal beating, being floored 12 times in 11 rounds.

Baer was humiliated in four rounds by Joe Louis in his first fight after losing to Braddock, a defeat which removed him from the title picture. He fought on until 1941, but retired after Lou Nova knocked him out. He died in a Hollywood hotel room on November 21, 1959: his last words, to the hotel operator who asked if he wanted the house doctor, were "No – I need a people doctor."

Marco Antonio Barrera

Born: *Mexico City, Mexico, January 17, 1974*
Titles: *WBO super-bantamweight champion 1995–96, 1998–2000, 2000–01, WBC super-featherweight 2004–07. Won WBC featherweight title in 2002, but did not accept the belt.*
Record: *75 contests, 67 wins, 7 defeats, 1 No Contest*

Great fighters are made by great rivalries. Marco Antonio Barrera's place as one of the modern ring giants was cemented by his bitter three-fight series with Erik Morales. Barrera also destroyed the pretensions to greatness of the best British featherweight of the era, Naseem Hamed, when he handed the self-styled Prince from Sheffield an emphatic boxing lesson in April 2001.

However, Barrera's first fight with Morales, a unification bout at

PLAYBOY CHAMPION *Max Baer*

super-bantamweight at the Mandalay Bay hotel on the Vegas Strip, will be remembered as one of the greatest contests of all time. It was a marvellous 12-round exhibition of everything that is good about this business. The majority of ringside press felt Barrera won. The judges had Morales ahead by a 2–1 split vote. If the rematch at the MGM Grand, for the featherweight title, did not live up to the breathtaking heights of the first meeting, it was still a compelling spectacle, and equally controversial. A draw, so often an unsatisfactory outcome, would not have been unfair. In fact, Barrera was awarded a surprisingly clear unanimous verdict.

The third fight took time to arrange, but eventually went ahead at super-featherweight in 2004. Barrera began as an outsider, as he had been stopped in the 11th round by the Filipino southpaw Manny Pacquiao in an upset the previous year. However, he produced an educated, cunning tactical display to outpunch Morales early and won a majority verdict. That victory made him, along with Morales and Julio Cesar Chavez, one of the only Mexican boxers to hold world titles in three separate weight divisions.

For some years Barrera had ignored the various sanctioning bodies and, following his win over Hamed, had been happy to be acknowledged as the best featherweight in the world without bothering to pay fees to those who purported to govern the sport. Even so, by the end of 2006, Barrera had taken part in 24 world championship contests sanctioned by the "big four" organizations. Barrera was a professional boxer in his mid-teens and won his first world title at 21, when he defeated Daniel Jimenez of Puerto Rico for the WBO super-bantamweight crown in 1995. Two defeats by Junior Jones seemed to have sent him into decline, but he came back even better. Before his defeat by Pacquiao, it was revealed that he had been boxing for some time with a metal plate in the top of his skull after repair work to blood vessels in the brain. He insisted he was fit to box but the ensuing controversy, plus disruption to training when forest fires forced him out of his training camp, may have had a negative effect on him.

He came back from that and at the end of 2006 was still putting young pretenders like Robbie Peden, who held the IBF super-featherweight title, and Rocky Juarez in their place. Defeats by Juan Manuel Marquez and Manny Pacquiao and, in 2009, Amir Khan, suggested the end of his great career was near and he fought his final bout in 2011.

Carmen Basilio

Born: *Canastota, New York, April 2, 1927*
Titles: *World welterweight champion 1955–56, 1956–57, world middleweight champion 1957–58*
Record: *79 contests, 56 wins, 7 draws, 16 defeats*

Carmen Basilio's rugged fighting philosophy was shaped in the onion fields around Canastota, New York, where he worked alongside his nine brothers and sisters. After that, he reckoned, boxing was easy. He learned the business as he went along, and his early record was littered with defeats and draws. But through sheer hard work and persistence he developed into a contender for the welterweight title, losing to Kid Gavilan in his first title bid in 1953.

Two years later he knocked out Tony DeMarco in the 12th round of a wildly exciting championship battle, and repeated the result in a rematch before losing to Johnny Saxton on a shockingly bad verdict. He took no chances in the rematch, knocking Saxton out in nine rounds. In September 1957 he scored his most famous victory, taking the middleweight title from Ray Robinson after 15 thrilling rounds. The rematch was just as exciting, though Robinson won.

Basilio tried three times to regain the title, being stopped twice by Gene Fullmer and, in his last fight, losing on points to Paul Pender in April 1961.

Hogan Bassey

Real name: *Okon Bassey Asuguo*
Born: *Calibar, Nigeria, June 3, 1932*
Titles: *British Empire featherweight champion 1955–57, world featherweight champion 1957–59*
Record: *86 contests, 69 wins, 4 draws, 13 defeats*

Bassey was the first Nigerian boxer to hold a world championship – under English manager George Biddles he was featherweight champion for two years. By the time he came to Britain in late 1951 he had won the Nigerian and West African bantamweight titles, but found the going harder against the higher standard of competition.

It took him four years and 43 fights to become a champion again, knocking out Billy Kelly – who had previously beaten him – for the Empire featherweight title. When Sandy Saddler relinquished the world title, Bassey became Nigeria's first world champion by stopping Cherif Hamia for the vacant title in Paris on June 24, 1957.

He retained it with a stunning knockout of Ricardo Moreno, a fierce-hitting Mexican who had been widely expected to dethrone him, but then found the stylish Davey Moore too good for him. Moore took his title in 13 rounds in March 1959, and when he repeated the result in a rematch, Bassey quit the ring. He later trained the Nigerian Olympic boxing team. He died on 20 January 1998, aged 65.

Wilfred Benitez

Born: *Bronx, New York, September 12, 1958*
Titles: *WBA light-welterweight champion 1976–77, WBC welterweight champion 1979, WBC light-middleweight champion 1981–82*
Record: *62 contests, 53 wins, 1 draw, 8 defeats*

The flashy Benitez, of Puerto Rican parentage, was a true prodigy of the ring. Managed by his volatile father Gregorio, he became the youngest-ever world champion when, on March 6, 1976, he ended Antonio Cervantes's long reign as WBA light-welterweight champion. The WBA stripped him of the title after two defences when he refused to give Cervantes a rematch, so he moved up to welterweight and took that title from Carlos Palomino.

He defended it against Harold Weston, but, in November 1979, Ray Leonard stopped him in the 15th and final round. Still only 22, Benitez won his third title in May 1981, knocking out Britain's Maurice Hope with a crushing right in the 12th round in Las Vegas for the WBC light-middleweight belt. He retained it against Carlos Santos and Roberto Duran, but after Thomas Hearns outpointed him in December 1982, Benitez's career went into an abrupt and steep decline.

A combination of management problems, ill-discipline and high living soon took care of the substantial fortune he had earned, and the career which had once promised so much petered out in a sad series of unsuccessful comebacks. In his early 40s Benitez was a shell of his old self, suffering the effects of his boxing career and cared for by his family.

Nigel Benn

Born: *Ilford, England, January 26, 1964*
Titles: *Commonwealth middleweight champion 1988–89, WBO middleweight champion 1990, WBC super-middleweight champion 1992–96*
Record: *48 contests, 42 wins, 1 draw, 5 defeats*

The former soldier, nicknamed "The Dark Destroyer", became one of Britain's most successful and popular champions with a style based on relentless aggression, hard punching and an indomitable will to win. He won the ABA middleweight title in 1986, and turned pro in disgust when Rod Douglas, whom he had beaten, was selected ahead of him for the Commonwealth Games team.

He was an instant sensation, and flattened his first 21 opponents, 11 in the first round, winning the vacant Commonwealth title in April 1988. Michael Watson brought him down to earth by knocking him out in six rounds in May 1989, but Benn re-established himself in America where he won the WBO title from Doug DeWitt and retained it sensationally against Iran Barkley.

NIGEL BENN *"The Dark Destroyer"*

Arch-rival Chris Eubank stopped him in a nine-round thriller in 1990, but Benn stepped up to super-middleweight and won the WBC version of the title. His knockout of Gerald McClellan in 1995 deserves to be remembered as a classic of the British ring, despite its tragic aftermath which saw the American suffer permanent damage. A hot favourite to retain his crown against the South African Sugar Boy Malinga in March 1996, Benn lost on points. He retired after two WBO title fight losses against Steve Collins.

Nino Benvenuti

Born: *Trieste, Italy, April 26, 1938*
Titles: *European middleweight champion 1965–66, world light-middleweight champion 1965–66, world middleweight champion 1967, 1968–70*
Record: *90 contests, 82 wins, 1 draw, 7 defeats*

Benvenuti was always a winner. He was a gold medallist at the 1960 Rome Olympics – beating Cassius Clay in the voting for the Val Barker trophy as the Games' best stylist – and went undefeated in his first 65 fights, winning the Italian middleweight title in 1963. By 1965 he was a contender for the world middleweight title, but instead dropped down a division to knock out his compatriot Sandro Mazzinghi for the light-middleweight championship.

He lost it in his first defence to Ki-Soo Kim of Korea, who became his country's first world champion by outpointing the elegant Italian in Seoul in June 1966, but Benvenuti came back as a middleweight to beat Emile Griffith in two of their three clashes for the 160-lb title. He retained it four times before Carlos Monzon stopped him in 12 rounds, and retired after Monzon knocked him out in three in a rematch.

He entered politics, and built a successful business career before, in 1995, he turned his back on material rewards to become a volunteer in Mother Teresa's hospice in Calcutta. He then returned to Italy and in his late 60s worked as a boxing analyst for Italian television.

Jack "Kid" Berg

Real name: *Judah Bergman*
Born: *London, England, June 28, 1909*
Titles: *World light-welterweight champion 1930–31, British lightweight champion 1934–36*
Record: *(approx.) 192 contests, 157 wins, 9 draws, 26 defeats*

Berg, a product of the East London Jewish community, was boxing professionally at 14, his all-action style earning him the nickname "The Whitechapel Whirlwind". He boxed all-comers in a hectic few years between 1924 and 1927 before moving to New York, where he became hugely popular. He returned briefly in February 1930 to beat Mushy Callahan for the junior-welterweight title at the Albert Hall in London, an event notable for the pre-fight intervention of Lord Lonsdale who, waving his walking stick, announced that no such title existed.

Nevertheless, Berg made a career out of defending the championship throughout 1930 and 1931, and even after Tony Canzoneri knocked him out in April 1931 he continued to claim the title on the grounds that their fight had involved Canzoneri's lightweight belt rather than his own championship.

He boxed in the top class for another five years, but his career wound down to the eight-rounds class. He returned to England in 1939, and boxed sporadically until 1945, enjoying a second career as a film stuntman. He died on April 22, 1991.

Riddick Bowe

Born: *New York, NY, August 10, 1967*
Titles: *WBC, WBA and IBF heavyweight champion 1992, WBA and IBF champion 1993, WBO champion 1995*
Record: *42 contests, 40 wins, 1 No Contest, 1 defeat*

The amiable Bowe, nicknamed "Big Daddy", was the dominant figure in world heavyweight boxing during the years of Mike Tyson's absence. Bowe, from the same Brownsville district as Tyson, was beaten by Lennox Lewis in the 1988 Olympic final, one of only eight defeats he sustained in 112 amateur fights. He turned pro after the Games and, guided by the independent-minded Rock Newman, made rapid progress, including wins over Pinklon Thomas and Tony Tubbs.

By 1992 he was the leading contender for Evander Holyfield's championship, which he won in November 1992 in the first of their three epic meetings. Their second fight, a year later in the same outdoor arena at Caesars Palace, Las Vegas, featured a truly bizarre incident when the action was interrupted by the arrival in the ring of a publicity-seeking paraglider. Bowe lost the decision in this exciting contest, but was a champion again by 1995, beating Britain's Herbie Hide to capture the WBO title.

He retained that title against the dangerous Cuban Jorge Luis Gonzalez, and then survived the first knockdown of his career to stop Holyfield in the final instalment of their memorable series. Bowe retired after two disqualification wins in fights he was losing against the Pole Andrew Golota.

Bowe's personal life became chaotic. A spell in the US marines lasted a matter of days, and he served jail time for the bizarre kidnap of his estranged wife, at which point doctors said he had been damaged by his career. He later refuted those claims and made a brief, very sad comeback in 2004.

Cornelius Boza-Edwards

Born: *Kampala, Uganda, May 27, 1956*
Titles: *WBC super-featherweight champion 1981, European super-featherweight champion 1982*
Record: *53 contests, 45 wins, 1 draw, 7 defeats*

The Ugandan southpaw was brought to England as a boy by a Londoner, Jack Edwards, and adopted his surname in appreciation. An outstanding amateur before turning professional in December 1976, he served an exotic apprenticeship with fights in Italy, Zambia and Monte Carlo.

But his career did not take off until he faced WBC super-featherweight champion Alexis Arguello in a non-title match in his American debut in 1980. He lost, but performed so well that he was rewarded seven months later with a crack at Arguello's successor, Rafael Limon. Boza won a thriller on points, and retained the title in another epic against Bobby Chacon before he was surprisingly knocked out by Rolando Navarette in August 1981.

He came back to win the European title, but was outpointed by Chacon when he tried to regain his WBC title. His popularity with American TV viewers ensured other opportunities, and he made two losing bids for the WBC lightweight title before retiring in 1987. His first wife died tragically, but he remarried and now lives in Las Vegas where he trains fighters.

James J. Braddock

Born: *New York, NY, June 7, 1906*
Titles: *World heavyweight champion 1935–37*
Record: *86 contests, 46 wins, 4 draws, 11 No Decisions, 2 No Contests, 23 defeats*

Braddock's late-career success is one of the ring's heart-warming stories. He had been a mediocre light-heavyweight, whose career highlight was a points defeat by Tommy Loughran for the world title in 1929. Losses wer¡e as numerous as wins after that, and by 1933 Braddock was so down on his luck that he had to apply for welfare payments to keep his family together.

In June 1934 he was engaged as an "opponent" for Corn Griffin, a bright young heavyweight prospect, but upset the script by winning in three rounds. When he outpointed future light-heavyweight champion John Henry Lewis – who had beaten him in 1932 – the business began to take note of him, but even so he was regarded as a soft touch for Max Baer when they met for Baer's heavyweight title in June 1935.

It was said an ambulance waited discreetly outside the arena ready to take Braddock away. Instead Braddock boxed steadily to outpoint the erratic champion, and earn himself the nickname of "The Cinderella Man". In his only defence, Braddock had the satisfaction of flooring Joe Louis before Louis took his title on an eighth-round knockout two years later. Braddock died on November 29, 1974, aged 69, and his legend was immortalized by the 2005 movie of his story, *Cinderella Man*, starring Russell Crowe.

Jack Britton

Real name: *William J. Breslin*
Born: *Clinton, New York, October 14, 1885*
Titles: *World welterweight champion 1915, 1916–17, 1919–22*
Record: *(approx.) 349 contests, 107 wins, 19 draws, 2 No Contests, 194 No Decisions, 27 defeats*

Britton enjoyed one of the longest careers of any world champion: he had his first pro fight in 1904 and his last in 1930, when he was almost 45. He was already a veteran when he won the welterweight title in 1915, and he and arch-rival Ted "Kid" Lewis alternated the title between them until 1921. They met at least 20 times, of which Britton won four, Lewis three, one was drawn and the other 12 were No Decision affairs.

He featured in a controversial defence against lightweight champion Benny Leonard, who was well on the way to victory when he floored Britton and then deliberately hit him while he was down, earning instant disqualification. His reign was finally ended by Mickey Walker, who beat him on points in November 1921. Walker was 20, Britton 36, but the cagey Irish-American made Walker work hard for his win. Britton boxed on for another eight years, and finished his career on a downbeat note by winning only three of his final 12 fights.

Kell Brook

Born: *Sheffield, England, May 3, 1986*
Titles: *IBF welterweight champion 2015–17*
Record: *39 contests, 37 wins, 2 defeats*

Kell Brook became the fourth fighter from the Ingles' gym in Sheffield to win world honours when, in August 2014, he took the IBF welterweight title from Shawn Porter on a majority decision in Carson, California.

Brook landed enough clean punches and finished the fight well enough to impress two of the judges. Nineteen days later, on holiday in Tenerife, Brook was close to death having been stabbed. After life-saving surgery, he returned to the ring in March 2015.

He stepped up to middleweight in an attempt to wrest the world title from Gennady Golovkin in London in September 2016, but lost by TKO in the fifth round – his first defeat as a professional. His second followed in his next bout, when he was knocked out by Errol Spence Jr in the 11th round.

As a boy his stepfather first took Brook to a boxing gym and, from an early age, trainer Brendan Ingle predicted he would one day be as good as Prince Naseem Hamed.

He won the Lonsdale belt outright before finally getting his world-title chance after a long time

KELL BROOK *recovered from a stabbing to become a world champion*

as No 1 in the WBO rankings and three times an IBF title fight against Devon Alexander fell through.

Adrien Broner

Born: *Cincinnati, Ohio, July 28, 1989*
Titles: *WBO super-featherweight champion 2011–12, WBC lightweight champion 2012–13, WBA welterweight champion 2013, WBA Super lightweight champion 2015–*
Record: *36 contests, 33 wins, 3 defeats*

There were few tears when Adrien Broner had his bubble burst by Marcos Maidana in 2013's upset of the year. Quite the opposite in fact. News of his defeat produced an outpouring of *schadenfreude.*

Tim Smith wrote in *The Ring* that Broner's defeat "sent waves of euphoric joy through much of the boxing world." Why? He may have captured world titles at three weights, but his actions outside the ring have alienated many.

Known as "The Problem", Broner was a good amateur, winning bronze at the 2005 Junior Olympics and, as a professional, claimed the vacant WBO super-featherweight title by knocking out Vicento Martin Rodriguez and thrashing Eloy Perez in his first defence.

Broner lost the title on the scales before he defended against Vicente Escobedo and went on to take the WBC lightweight title from Antonio DeMarco. He added the WBA welterweight title with a points win over Paulie Malignaggi, before suffering losses to Maidana and Shawn Porter. He beat Khabib Allakhverdiev with a 12th-round TKO to claim the WBA Super welterweight title in October 2015 and made a successful defence against Ashley Thompson (TKO, round 9) in April 2016.

Frank Bruno

Born: *London, England, November 16, 1961*
Titles: *WBC heavyweight champion 1995–96*
Record: *45 contests, 40 wins, 5 defeats*

Bruno's career was a model of persistence and hard work. He took up boxing as an outlet for the energy which had made him a difficult boy to handle, and responded so well to its disciplines that he became, in 1980, the youngest-ever ABA heavyweight champion. He had to wait almost two years before launching his pro career, because of managerial disputes and an eye problem which necessitated surgery, but his rise was meteoric.

Managed by Terry Lawless and promoted by Mickey Duff and his associates, he scored 21 straight knock outs before James "Bonecrusher" Smith, then unknown, knocked him out in ten rounds at Wembley in May 1984. He was re-established via the European championship, but failed in 11 rounds against Tim Witherspoon for the WBA title in 1986.

Astonishingly, he secured two more title fights, losing in five rounds to Mike Tyson in 1989 and in seven to Lennox Lewis in 1993, but just when his career looked to be virtually over, his new promoter Frank Warren presented him with one last chance and this time Bruno outpointed Oliver McCall to win the WBC title in front of an ecstatic home crowd at Wembley in September 1995. His glory lasted barely six months, however, as Tyson stopped him in three rounds in March 1996 in Las Vegas.

Ken Buchanan

Born: *Edinburgh, Scotland, January 28, 1945*
Titles: *WBA lightweight champion 1970, world champion 1971–72, European champion 1974–75, British champion 1968–70, 1973–74*
Record: *69 contests, 61 wins, 8 defeats*

Buchanan was probably Britain's best-ever lightweight, but this one-time carpenter was always more respected in America than at home. Most of his early fights were in sporting clubs, so that by the time he became British champion in 1968 he was barely known outside the game's hard-core followers.

Manager Eddie Thomas manoeuvred him into a challenge for Ismael Laguna's WBA title in September 1970. Few gave him a chance, but he boxed brilliantly to take the title. He became undisputed champion in February 1971, but was then stripped by the WBC for meeting Laguna in a rematch. In June 1972 he lost the title to Roberto Duran in 13 brutal rounds, and Duran always refused to face him again. Wins over Jim Watt (which won him a Lonsdale Belt outright) for the British title and Antonio Puddu for the European championship brought a crack at Guts Ishimatsu's WBC title in 1975, but the Scot lost on points. He boxed on, but with only limited success until 1982. His money gone, Buchanan made a comeback on the unlicensed circuit to clear his debts, then retired for good.

Ricky Burns

Born: *Belshill, Scotland, April 13, 1983*
Titles: *WBO super-featherweight champion 2010–11, WBO lightweight champion 2012–14, WBA light-welterweight champion 2015–17*
Record: *49 contests, 41 wins, 7 defeats, 1 draw*

A British-title defeat to Carl Johanneson indicated Burns had found his level, but he retained his self-belief and a switch to trainer Billy Nelson brought out the best in him.

Burns, from near Glasgow, won the Commonwealth super-featherweight title and to the surprise of just about everyone outside his camp, took the WBO super-featherweight title from Roman Martinez in a fight rated the best of 2010 by both *Boxing Monthly* and the WBO.

Burns made three low-key defences. He claimed the interim WBO belt with a unanimous points win over tough Aussie Michael Katsidis and, after being upgraded to full champion, he successfully defended against Paulus Moses, Kevin Mitchell and Jose A Gonzalez.

Burns was fortunate to keep the belt following a draw with Raymundo Beltran, and was outboxed and outpointed by Terence Crawford. He became WBA Super light-welterweight champion after knocking out Michele di Rocco for the vacant belt in May 2016, made a successful defence five months later, but the lost a unification bout (on points) against Julius Indongo in April 2017.

RICKY BURNS *came from nowhere to become a three-weight world champion*

Celestino Caballero

Born: *Colon, Panama, June 21, 1976*
Titles: *WBA super-bantamweight champion 2006–10, IBF super-bantamweight champion 2008–10, WBA featherweight 2011–12*
Record: *43 contests, 37 wins, 6 defeats*

Formerly the best super-bantamweight in the world, Caballero claimed the WBA featherweight title in October 2011. At the age of 35, he reversed a previous points loss to Jonathon Victor Barros to win the belt. The following year, he vacated the title and, after two defeats in three fights, he retired.

At 5ft 11ins tall, Caballero – who grew up scrapping on the same Panama City streets that spawned Roberto Duran – was a wiry, intelligent boxer with a stiff punch. A slow developer, he was 30 years old when he became WBA super-bantamweight champion in 2006, stopping Somsak Sithchatchawai, in three rounds in Thailand – Somsak's second defeat in 49 fights. A year earlier, Caballero had won a clear points decision over future WBO champion Daniel Ponce de Leon, and so had the full respect of the aficionados.

When he unified the WBA and IBF belts in November 2008 with an emphatic fourth-round stoppage of Canadian southpaw Steve Molitor, he was acknowledged as not only the best 122-lb fighter in the world but also probably the best for some considerable time.

Perhaps as a reaction to that, Caballero suffered a dip in form next time out when he needed a split decision to beat South African Jeffrey Mathebula, but then he defended his titles against Francisco Leal, before the IBF stripped him on a technicality.

Caballero admitted defeat in his battle with the scales, moved up to 126lb and was handed his first defeat for more than six years by Jason Litzau. He went on to capture the WBA title at the second attempt.

Joe Calzaghe

Born: *Hammersmith, London, England, March 23, 1972*
Titles: *WBO super-middleweight 1997–2008, IBF super-middleweight 2006, WBC & WBA super-middleweight champion 2007–2008*
Record: *46 contests, 46 wins*

Calzaghe's clever, quick-handed southpaw style made him the best super-middleweight in the world and, when he retired at the end of 2008, he walked away with a perfect record of 46 consecutive wins. He had taken his career to a new level in 2006 when, after a multitude of defences of the World Boxing Organization title, he handed out a drubbing to highly regarded Jeff Lacy, the International Boxing Federation champion.

Calzaghe, born in London to a Welsh mother and Italian father, was raised from infancy in Newbridge, South Wales. His father Enzo, a former musician, learned how to train him and together they made an unorthodox but formidable partnership. He won three consecutive British amateur titles as a teenager, then turned pro at Cardiff Arms Park on the undercard of the world heavyweight title fight between Lennox Lewis and Frank Bruno in 1993. Way down the bill, Calzaghe won his contest in the first round.

He won the British title, and then in 1997 was ready to challenge the WBO super-middleweight champion Steve Collins. Sadly, injuries forced Collins to retire, and instead Calzaghe beat Chris Eubank, Collins' predecessor as champion, on points in Sheffield. Eubank was knocked down twice.

For the next decade, in spite of persistent hand problems, Calzaghe was unbeatable. He did not let his frustrations at not boxing one of the major names in the business get him down. At one point promoter Frank Warren thought he had a career-defining fight with Bernard Hopkins, the long-serving middleweight champion, only for Hopkins to change his mind. Calzaghe's career might have gone on to a new level had he taken a big-money fight in the United States, too, but in the end he settled for defending his title in Britain and, occasionally, Europe.

He beat former champions Robin Reid, Charles Brewer and Richie Woodhall and eventually unified the WBO and IBF belts when he floored and outpointed Florida's Jeff Lacy over 12 rounds. Lacy, so confident before the fight, was given a boxing lesson. He retained both belts against Sakio Bika the following September, then gave back the IBF championship when ordered to box German Robert Stieglitz, a match in which he saw no point. Instead he took on Peter Manfredo, who had taken part in the popular American television boxing series *Contender,* in a fight that attracted the backing of HBO.

Calzaghe beat Manfredo inside three rounds and then attracted a fantastic crowd of 52,000 to the Millennium Stadium, Cardiff, for a unification fight with the WBA and WBC champion Mikkel Kessler of Denmark. Calzaghe won a good fight on points, which earned him the BBC Sports Personality of the Year award. Calzaghe rounded off his career by fulfilling a dream to box in Las Vegas and New York with points wins over veteran greats Bernard Hopkins and Roy Jones Jr.

Hector Camacho

Born: *Bayamon, Puerto Rico, May 24, 1962*
Titles: *WBC super-featherweight champion 1983, WBC lightweight champion 1985, WBO light-welterweight champion 1989–91, 1991–92*
Record: *88 contests, 79 wins, 3 draws, 6 defeats*

Camacho won his first title – the NABF super-featherweight belt – in 1981, and was still a world-class performer 17 years on, his capacity to shock and entertain undiminished by the years. He held the WBC super-featherweight and lightweight championships (1983 and 1985 respectively) and the WBO light-welterweight title, maturing into a cagey and seasoned campaigner.

The self-styled "Macho Man" cornered the market in frills, skirts and loin-cloths, and his capacity to shock extended far beyond the ring. But he could really fight, for all the corny showmanship, and when he took a painful beating from Julio Cesar Chavez in a losing bid for the WBC light-welterweight title in 1992, he proved he had heart to match his gimmickry.

Increasing weight caused him to give up his super-featherweight title after one defence, and his lightweight crown after two. He won the WBO light-welterweight title by beating Ray Mancini in 1989, lost and regained it against Greg Haugen, but was stripped in 1992 for failing to defend it. Camacho won IBC titles at welterweight and middleweight, beating Roberto Duran and Sugar Ray Leonard, but was well beaten when he took on WBC welterweight champion, Oscar De La Hoya, in September 1997. He was, however, still standing at the final bell. Astonishingly, he was still competitive as he approached his late 40s, when he drew with another veteran world champion, Yory Boy Campas, in 2009. Camacho's last fight was in May 2010 and he was shot in the face and killed outside a bar in Bayamon in November 2012.

Orlando Canizales

Born: *Laredo, Texas, November 25, 1965*
Titles: *NABF flyweight champion 1987, USBA super-flyweight champion 1988, IBF bantamweight champion 1988–94*
Record: *57 contests, 50 wins, 1 draw, 1 No Contest, 5 defeats*

This busy performer was an outstanding bantamweight champion between July 1988, when he stopped Kelvin Seabrooks in the 15th and final round of a rare all-American bantamweight title fight to win the IBF version, and December 1994, when he relinquished it because of weight-making problems. In between, he made 16 defences, which included a two-round stoppage of the only man to have beaten him, the former Olympic champion Paul Gonzalez. That loss came in a 1986 challenge for the NABF flyweight title, which he eventually won by stopping Armando Velasquez for the vacant title a year later. He moved up to super-flyweight, winning the USBA title in 1988 in his last fight before beating Seabrooks on his bantamweight debut.

He defended his IBF title in Europe and South Africa, and at one time shared the bantamweight championship with his elder brother Gaby, the former WBA champion, whose brief three-month reign as WBO champion coincided with his brother's IBF tenure. Wilfredo Vazquez beat Orlando in a WBA super-bantamweight title fight in 1995, but the tough Texan boxed on for another four years. His last contest was a close points defeat to a future champion, Frankie Toledo, in 1999.

Tony Canzoneri

Born: *Slidell, Louisiana, November 6, 1908*
Titles: *World featherweight champion 1928, world lightweight champion 1930–33, 1935–36, world light-welterweight champion 1931–32, 1933*
Record: *175 contests, 141 wins, 10 draws, 24 defeats*

In the days when there were only ten weight divisions and (usually) one champion per division, Canzoneri achieved the astonishing feat of contesting four titles and winning three of them. He turned pro at 16 in 1925, and lost only once in 39 fights before being matched with Bud Taylor for the vacant NBA title in March 1927. They drew, and Taylor won the rematch.

He moved up to featherweight, beating Benny Bass for the title in February 1928. Andre Routis took his championship seven months later, but Canzoneri stepped up again to beat Sammy Mandell for the lightweight title in August 1929. His win over Jack "Kid" Berg in 1931, although officially a lightweight match, also gave him the Englishman's junior-welterweight title since both were inside that division's limit, and Canzoneri continued to defend both titles. He lost the 140-lb title to Johnny Jadick and regained it from Battling Shaw before losing both titles to Barney Ross in June 1933.

He enjoyed one last spell as lightweight champion in 1935–36, retiring in November 1939 to become an actor and restaurateur. He died in New York on December 9, 1959.

Primo Carnera

Born: *Sequals, Italy, October 26, 1906*
Titles: *World heavyweight champion 1933–34*
Record: *104 contests, 89 wins, 1 No Decision, 14 defeats*

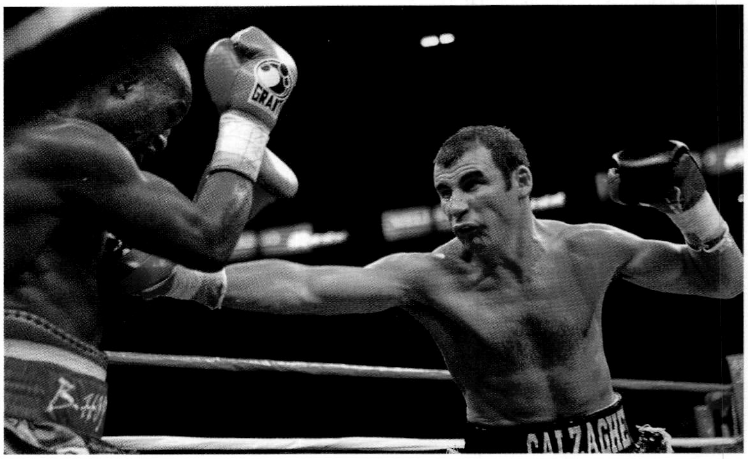

JOE CALZAGHE, *the Pride of Wales, had an unblemished career in the super middleweight division, winning all 46 of his fights*

The exploitation of the giant Carnera, who stood 6ft 5¾in and weighed 270lb, says much about the way boxing operated in the 1930s. He was discovered working as a circus strongman, and his manager, Leon See, launched him as a professional in September 1928.

Virtually all his early fights were fixed, although Carnera may have been unaware of this. When See took him to America in 1930 the manager was quickly pushed aside by much more sinister figures, who provided Carnera with a long series of "knockovers" on the way to a title fight. Occasionally, they made mistakes, but by June 1933 he was judged ready to challenge Jack Sharkey for the title.

The American succumbed in six rounds, a result which remains unconvincing, and although Carnera managed two successful defences, he was then badly beaten by Max Baer in June 1934. The Mob did get one more payday out of him, feeding him to Joe Louis in June 1935, but that beating effectively ended his career. He retired in December 1937, making a brief comeback in 1945–46. He later enjoyed a second lucrative career as a wrestler in America, and died in Sequals, Italy, on June 29, 1967.

Georges Carpentier

Born: *Lens, France, January 12, 1894*
Titles: *European welterweight champion 1911, middleweight champion 1912, light-heavyweight champion 1913, heavyweight champion 1913–19, world light-heavyweight champion 1920–22*
Record: *110 contests, 88 wins, 6 draws, 1 No Decision, 15 defeats*

Carpentier boxed professionally in each of the (then) eight weight divisions, starting as a 13-year-old flyweight in 1908. He won the French lightweight title at 15, and was welterweight champion of France and Europe at 17. His combination of stylish boxing, heavy hitting and good looks made him a major attraction, and for the first time women began to attend fights in significant numbers.

He progressed through the divisions, winning European titles at welterweight (1911), middleweight (1912), light-heavyweight and heavyweight (both in 1913), knocking out the English star Bombardier Billy Wells twice in heavyweight title fights. When the War broke out he joined the French Air Force, and was awarded the Croix De Guerre and the Medaille Militaire. He resumed his career in 1917, and by 1919 was world light-heavyweight champion.

He used that title as a stepping stone to a heavyweight title clash with Jack Dempsey in 1921, but was knocked out in four rounds. Battling Siki took his light-heavyweight title in 1922, and he boxed infrequently from then until his retirement in 1927. Carpentier remained immensely popular until his death in Paris on October 28, 1975.

Jimmy Carruthers

Born: *Paddington, Australia, July 5, 1929*
Titles: *World bantamweight champion 1952–54*
Record: *25 contests, 21 wins, 4 defeats*

This hard-punching southpaw was Australia's first undisputed world champion, knocking out the South African Vic Toweel in the first round in November 1952, and again in the tenth round four months later. Ironically, he had been inspired to turn pro by the success of Toweel, whom he had watched in the 1948 Olympic Games in London, in which they both competed.

He took the national title from Elley Bennett in his ninth fight, but despite being unbeaten in 14 fights he had no international pedigree to speak of when he challenged Toweel, and his win was a major upset. He retained the title against Henry "Pappy" Gault of America and Thailand's Chamrern Songkitrat in a match that was remarkable for two reasons: they fought in bare feet, during a rain storm in the open-air arena, and the fight was over the unusual – at that time – distance of 12 rounds.

Carruthers retired after that to run a pub and become a referee, but was tempted into an ill-advised comeback in 1961 and lost four of his six fights. He died of cancer in 1990.

Joel Casamayor

Born: *Guantanamo, Cuba, July 12, 1971*
Titles: *WBA super-featherweight champion 2000–02, WBC lightweight champion 2006–07*
Record: *45 contests, 38 wins, 1 draw, 6 defeats*

When Joel Casamayor returned from the Barcelona Olympics with the bantamweight gold medal, he was given a present by the Cuban government…a bicycle. He exchanged it for a pig to help feed his family. The workmanlike, slippery southpaw continued to represent his country, but disenchantment set in before the 1996 Olympics and, while in a training camp in Mexico, Casamayor slipped away, crossed the border and sought asylum in the United States.

He settled in Miami, where there is a large Cuban population, and understandably took some time to adjust to his new life. He also left his wife and family in Cuba. Inevitably, he boxed professionally and unlike many Cubans who try their luck in US rings, he managed to transfer his style. Eventually he became an accomplished 12-round operator, seasoned and capable of pacing himself perfectly.

Casamayor won the WBA super-featherweight title in May 2000 in Kansas City, stopping Korea's Jong-kwon Baek on cuts in five rounds and defended his title four times, losing a close unanimous decision to Acelino Freitas in a unification fight in Las Vegas in January 2002.

For a while, he was frustrated. He won an eliminator with Diego Corrales in the sixth round of a war, in which both men were down, the end coming because the Californian had a horrible gash in his mouth. However, when they boxed again in March 2004 for the vacant WBO lightweight title, Corrales pulled off an upset split decision. Casamayor had similar ill luck when he challenged Jose Luis Castillo for the WBC title in Las Vegas the following December.

When weight problems eventually forced Castillo out of the division, Casamayor had a third fight with Corrales for the vacant WBC belt and this time, at the Mandalay Bay, Las Vegas, he won a split decision to become a two-weight world champion at the third time of asking.

His bid to take the WBO light-welterweight title from Timothy Bradley in 2011 ended in an eighth-round defeat and Casamayor tested positive for marijuana and stimulants.

Jose Luis Castillo

Born: *Empalme, Mexico, December 14, 1973*
Titles: *WBC lightweight champion 2000–02, 2004–05*
Record: *77 contests, 64 wins, 1 draw, 12 defeats*

Castillo learned his trade as a long-time sparring partner of the great Julio Cesar Chavez and eventually developed into a strong, persistent lightweight champion. He made his debut in 1990 when he was only 16, and took four attempts to win a Mexican title. He improved, however, and in June 2000 upset the crafty southpaw Stevie Johnston to win the WBC title on a majority decision on a boiling hot afternoon in the California desert. A rematch ended in a controversial draw in Johnston's home city of Denver – the decision was originally announced as a win for Johnston, but a mathematical error was discovered on the cards and the result changed.

Castillo lost his title on points to Floyd Mayweather in a close, tough fight in Las Vegas in 2002. Mayweather put his laboured display down to a shoulder injury, and there were those who felt Castillo was "robbed". However, in a rematch, Mayweather defused the Mexican and won clearly, again over 12 rounds. Castillo slogged away and, when Mayweather moved up, he regained his old title by outpointing Juan Lazcano in June 2004. After good wins over Joel Casamayor and Julio Diaz, Castillo lost a sensational, epic struggle with Diego Corrales in

May 2005. He had Corrales down and apparently out with two heavy knockdowns, but Corrales somehow rallied and rocked him. Castillo looked out on his feet and the fight, which he had in the bag only seconds before, was lost. A return went on as a non-title bout when Castillo couldn't get near the lightweight limit. Then a third fight in June 2006 was scrapped at the scales when Castillo came in five pounds too heavy. He was fined and suspended by the Nevada Commission.

In 2007 Castillo beat Herman Ngoudjo to set up a showdown with Ricky Hatton – but a fourth-round, body-shot knockout suggested it was the end, at least in the top class, but he continued to box until 2016.

Marcel Cerdan

Born: *Sidi Bel-Abbes, Algeria, July 22, 1916*
Titles: *European welterweight champion 1939–42, middleweight champion 1947–48, world middleweight champion 1948–49*
Record: *123 contests, 119 wins, 4 defeats*

Two of Cerdan's four defeats were on disqualification, another on a bitterly disputed decision and the last on injury. He was never beaten on merit. That is a true measure of the ability of this extraordinary fighter, who won French and European welterweight titles before moving up to middleweight and doing the same again.

Had the Second World War not retarded his career he would surely have won world titles in both divisions, but instead he had to wait until 1946, when he made his American debut, to be taken seriously as a contender. Cyrille Delannoit looked to have wrecked his dream when he outpointed him for the European title in May 1948, but the handsome Algerian reversed the result two months later and then, in September that year, battered Tony Zale into a 12th-round defeat to become world middleweight champion.

He lost the title to Jake LaMotta on a shoulder injury in June 1949, and was killed on October 27, 1949, when the plane carrying him back to America for the LaMotta rematch crashed in the Azores. Cerdan's place in the romantic affections of the French was cemented by his long-running affair with the singing star Edith Piaf.

Bobby Chacon

Born: *Los Angeles, California, November 28, 1951*
Titles: *WBC featherweight champion 1974–75, WBC super-featherweight champion 1982–83*
Record: *67 contests, 59 wins, 1 draw, 7 defeats*

Chacon's explosive style made him a huge drawing card in his home town of Los Angeles. Only two of his 26 fights on the way to his first world title went the distance, with the solitary loss coming on a ninth-round knockout by the Mexican Ruben Olivares in June 1973. He knocked out Alfredo Marcano to win the WBC featherweight title in September 1974, but lost it in his second defence to Olivares, this time in two rounds. He finally beat Olivares in a ten-rounder in August 1977, and then moved up to super-feather. Alexis Arguello turned back his first title bid, and Cornelius Boza-Edwards stopped him in a 13-round thriller in May 1981, but he won the WBC belt at the third attempt, outpointing Rafael Limon in December 1982.

The WBC stripped him six months later when he refused to fight Hector Camacho on a Don King promotion for $450,000 when he had been offered $1m by another promoter for the same fight. He was stopped in three rounds by Ray Mancini in a WBA lightweight challenge in 1984, and retired in 1985.

Jeff Chandler

Born: *Philadelphia, Pennsylvania, September 3, 1956*
Titles: *USBA bantamweight champion 1979–80, NABF bantamweight champion 1980, WBA bantamweight champion 1980–84*
Record: *37 contests, 33 wins, 2 draws, 2 defeats*

Until Chandler took the WBA title from Julian Solis in November 1980, no American had been bantamweight champion since Harold Dade reigned for just two months in 1947. The classy Philadelphian proved rather more durable, turning back nine challengers in over three years before losing to compatriot Richard Sandoval. Chandler was not the usual Philadelphia fighter, all left hooks and snarling aggression *à la* Joe Frazier. He was a stylish boxer and an excellent counter-puncher, and achieved a respectable 18 wins in his 33 victories.

There has never been a great market for bantamweights on the Eastern side of America, since they are considered more the province of the Mexican border states like Texas and California. Consequently Chandler managed only 15 fights in three years, and the first six were four-rounders. But by 1979 he had moved up to main-event status, winning the USBA title and adding the NABF championship the following February, before taking the WBA belt from Solis in November.

His ten challengers included four Americans, clear evidence of the division's growing popularity there. Chandler retired after losing to Sandoval in April 1984.

Ezzard Charles

Born: *Lawrenceville, Georgia, July 7, 1921*
Titles: *NBA heavyweight champion 1949–50, world heavyweight champion 1950–51*
Record: *122 contests, 96 wins, 1 draw, 25 defeats*

Many of those who saw him in action maintain that Charles was a better middleweight and light-heavyweight than he was a heavyweight. He beat Joey Maxim and Archie Moore three times apiece, knocked out former light-heavyweight champion Anton Christoforodis, beat Teddy Yarosz, and drew with Ken Overlin, both ex-middleweight champions.

But he could not secure a title chance, and so moved up to heavyweight where, despite weighing no more than the modern cruiserweight limit of 190lb, he scored a string of wins which culminated in him beating Jersey Joe Walcott for the NBA title left vacant by Joe Louis' retirement. He retained it three times before beating Louis in September 1950 to earn undisputed recognition, and made a further four defences before Walcott knocked him out in July 1951.

He made two heroic efforts to regain the title from Rocky Marciano in 1954, but then disappointingly had only ten wins in 23 fights. He retired in 1959, and died from multiple sclerosis in Chicago on May 27, 1975.

Julio Cesar Chavez

Born: *Ciudad Obregon, Mexico, July 12, 1962*
Titles: *WBC super-featherweight champion 1984–87, WBA lightweight 1987–89, WBC lightweight champion 1988–89, WBC light-welterweight champion 1989–94, 1995–96, IBF light-welterweight champion 1990–91*
Record: *116 contests, 108 wins, 2 draws, 6 defeats*

Chavez wanted to go 100 fights without a loss, and he almost made it: his first defeat, by Frankie Randall for the WBC light-welterweight title in January 1994, came after 91 fights. He is generally accepted as the greatest fighter of his generation.

His explosive short hooks and body punches brought him the WBC super-featherweight crown in September 1984, and he retained it nine times before moving up to lightweight in 1987. He completed the WBA/WBC double there, then stepped up to light-welterweight, where he achieved his greatest fame. He won the WBC title in May 1989, and added the IBF championship in the most dramatic ending imaginable when, trailing on points, he produced a blistering attack to stop Meldrick Taylor with just two seconds left in the final round.

His reputation was dented when he was given a fortunate draw in a challenge for Pernell Whitaker's WBC welterweight title in 1993, but he regained his light-welterweight title from Randall in May 1994 and held it for two years before Oscar De La Hoya ended his reign. De La Hoya beat him in a rematch in eight rounds in 1998, but the last of his record 37 world title fights was when the WBC approved an odious match against Kostya Tszyu in Arizona in July 2000. The 38-year-old Chavez lost in six rounds. He continued boxing until 2005.

Kid Chocolate

Real name: *Eligio Sardinias*
Born: *Cerro, Cuba, January 6, 1910*
Titles: *World junior-lightweight (super-featherweight) champion 1931–33, NY-recognized world featherweight champion 1932–34*
Record: *152 contests, 136 wins, 6 draws, 10 defeats*

The hard-punching "Cuban Bon Bon" knocked out 86 of his 100 amateur opponents, and all 21 as a pro in Cuba before trying his luck in America in 1928. He was unbeaten in a further 45 fights, mainly in New York, before his record was spoilt by Jack "Kid" Berg, who outpointed him over ten rounds in August 1930.

It was the first of three defeats that year, including a points loss to Bat Battalino for the featherweight title. Seven months later, in July 1931, he knocked out Benny Bass for the junior-lightweight championship, but was outscored by Tony Canzoneri in November 1931 when he tried for the lightweight title. He dropped down to featherweight and won the New York version of the world title in October 1932, defending it twice before outgrowing the division.

Frankie Klick took his junior-lightweight title in December 1933, and despite losing only three of his subsequent 50 fights he was unable to land another title chance. The Cuban government awarded him a pension when he retired in 1938, in recognition of his services both to the country and the sport. He died in 1988.

Steve Collins

Born: *Dublin, July 21, 1964*
Titles: *WBO middleweight champion 1994–95, WBO super-middleweight champion 1995–97*
Record: *39 contests, 36 wins, 3 defeats*

The tough Dubliner made his name in America, but enjoyed his greatest success when he returned home to become the first Irishman to win versions of the world title at two weights.

It was a deserved late-career bonus for the single-minded professional who never lost faith in his own ability. After winning the Irish amateur middleweight title in 1986, Collins emigrated to Boston and joined the Petronelli brothers' gym at the end of Marvin Hagler's career. He won the Irish and USBA titles before losing on points to Mike McCallum in a gallant bid for the WBA championship.

This and close points losses to Reggie Johnson – for the vacant WBA title after McCallum had relinquished it – and to Sumbu Kalambay for the European crown, were good learning experiences. Collins became WBO middleweight champion by stopping Chris Pyatt in four rounds in 1994, then stepped up to 168lb and beat the previously undefeated Chris Eubank for the WBO super-middleweight belt on a great night in Millstreet, Cork.

Collins outpointed Eubank again, Nigel Benn twice and made a total of seven successful defences before he retired as undefeated champion in 1997.

Billy Conn

Born: *East Liberty, Pennsylvania, October 8, 1917*
Titles: *World light-heavyweight champion 1939–41*
Record: *77 contests, 64 wins, 1 draw, 12 defeats*

Billy Conn gained immortality for a fight he lost, his bid for Joe Louis' world heavyweight title in June 1941. He was ahead on points after 12 rounds, boxing brilliantly and staying away from Louis' powerful punches, but in the 13th he had a rush of blood to the head and decided to go for the big finish and was flattened. His defeat fulfilled Louis' prediction: "He can run, but he can't hide."

Conn, an Irish-American, started as a welterweight in 1935. He was hardly an overnight sensation, losing six of his first 14 fights, but he persevered and was soon a contender for the middleweight title, beating champions like Fritzie Zivic, Vince Dundee, Teddy Yarosz, Solly Krieger and Fred Apostoli. But his chance came at light-heavyweight, when he beat Melio Bettina for the vacant championship in 1939.

He made three defences, then relinquished the title to challenge Louis. Like Louis, he joined the US Army in 1942, and was inactive from then until June 1946, when Louis knocked him out in eight one-sided rounds. He retired in 1948, and died on May 29, 1993.

THE END *of the line nears for Billy Conn as he prepares for his last fight, in 1948*

John Conteh

Born: *Liverpool, England, May 27, 1951*
Titles: *European light-heavyweight champion 1973–74, British and Commonwealth champion 1973–74, WBC world champion 1974–77*
Record: *39 contests, 34 wins, 1 draw, 4 defeats*

Had it not been for managerial disputes and injury problems, Conteh would surely have earned a place with Britain's all-time greats. As it was, he compiled a record of which he could be proud and won every championship open to him A brilliant amateur, he took the European title in his 19th fight and the British and Commonwealth in his 20th, beating arch-rival Chris Finnegan for the latter two. When Bob Foster was stripped by the WBC in August 1974 for failing to defend against either Conteh or Jorge Ahumada of Argentina, Conteh outpointed Ahumada in London for the vacant championship.

He made three successful defences, but a serious hand injury restricted his activity. He gave up the title on a point of principle a couple of days before he was due to defend against Miguel Cuello, and then failed in three bids to regain it, losing to Mate Parlov in Belgrade and being beaten twice by Matthew Saad Muhammad in Atlantic City. The first Muhammad fight was desperately close, but he lost badly in the second and retired after just one more fight.

Henry Cooper

Born: *Westminster, London, May 3, 1934*
Titles: *British and Empire (later Commonwealth) heavyweight champion 1959–69 and 1970–71, European champion 1964, 1968–69, 1970–71*
Record: *55 contests, 40 wins, 1 draw, 14 defeats*

Cooper's amiable disposition and sportsmanship earned him a unique place in the affections of the British public, based largely on his two most famous defeats, by Cassius Clay in 1963 and Joe Bugner in 1971. Cooper

HENRY COOPER *National hero, in 1966*

floored Clay with a perfect left hook at the end of the fourth round, and trainer Angelo Dundee gained his dazed man more invaluable recovery time between the rounds by drawing the referee's attention to Clay's burst glove.

Clay won on cuts in the next round, but the myth grew that somehow the gallant British loser had been given a raw deal. They met again for the title in 1966, but Cooper's vulnerable eyebrows let him down, as they often did.

He was European champion three times and was Britain's longest-serving heavyweight champion, reigning from 1959 to 1971 with only a short break when he relinquished the title because the British Board would not allow him to contest the WBA title. Cooper won three Lonsdale Belts outright, a record, and retired on a wave of sympathy after Bugner won a controversial verdict over him. His charity work brought him a Papal knighthood, and he remained hugely popular until his death on May 1, 2011.

James J. Corbett

Born: *San Francisco, California, September 1, 1866*
Titles: *World heavyweight champion 1892–97*
Record: *30 contests, 20 wins, 5 draws, 5 defeats*

The elegant Corbett rewrote the textbooks as well as the history books. He was the first heavyweight champion of the gloved era, and the first to use speed, accuracy of punch and deft footwork in preference to the raw strength personified by John L. Sullivan, from whom he took the title in September 1892.

Unusually for boxers then, he was an educated man who was a bank clerk in San Francisco before taking up boxing. He made his name in a famous fight with local rival Joe Choynski, staged on a barge in June 1889. Corbett won in 27 rounds, and earned a title chance by beating Jake Kilrain and fighting a 61-round "No Contest" with Peter Jackson.

Corbett outboxed Sullivan effortlessly before knocking him out in the 25th, sending the old champion into retirement. He defended the title only once in five years, against Charlie Mitchell, and was dethroned by Bob Fitzsimmons in March 1897. Corbett tried twice to regain the title from James J. Jeffries in 1900 and again in 1903, but was knocked out each time. He died in Bayside, New York on February 18, 1933.

Diego Corrales

Born: *Sacramento, California, August 25, 1977*
Titles: *IBF super-featherweight champion 1999–2000, WBO super-featherweight champion 2004, WBO lightweight champion 2004–05, WBC lightweight champion 2005-06*
Record: *44 contests, 40 wins, 4 defeats*

For a warrior's spirit, fight fans of the first years of the 21st century need look no further than Diego "Chico" Corrales. A tough background in California gave Corrales a ruthless streak and a stubbornness that was hard to break down and, in a career filled with hard fights, only the very best could beat him.

Corrales won the IBF super-featherweight title, stopping Robert Garcia in seven rounds in Las Vegas in October 1999. During his days as a tall, almost impossibly lean super-featherweight, he dealt with men as respected as Derrick Gainer and Angel Manfredy in three rounds apiece.

He gave up the IBF belt because of weight-making nightmares, then agreed to try one last time to challenge WBC champion Floyd Mayweather for a substantial purse. It was a mistake. Mayweather, a brilliant boxer but not a heavy hitter, floored him five times before it was called off in the tenth. After that Corrales went off the rails and spent time in jail for domestic violence offences, but served his time, put his life back together and returned to world class. In October 2003 he lost a thunderous battle with Joel Casamayor: Corrales was floored twice, Casamayor once, and then the doctor intervened because of a gory cut in Corrales' mouth in round six. He was furious. In a rematch, Corrales upset the odds to win a split decision, and then, at lightweight, he stopped the Brazilian Acelino Freitas in ten rounds. In May 2005 he recovered from two shockingly heavy knockdowns to turn the sensational fight with Jose Luis Castillo on its head and win by a tenth-round stoppage. A rematch was inevitable, in spite of some misgivings because of the brutal nature of the first fight. This time Castillo could not make the weight, Corrales agreed to box anyway – and was flattened by a left hook in round four.

A third meeting was called off at the weigh-in because Castillo was too heavy, but the same fate struck Corrales next time out – he forfeited his lightweight title on the scales before a third fight with Casamayor. The Cuban went on to win a split decision. Corrales died in a motorcycle accident in Las Vegas on May 7, 2007.

PREDATOR SUPREME: *Miguel Angel Cotto was described as "the toughest guy I fought" by Floyd Mayweather Jr*

Miguel Angel Cotto

Born: *Caguas, Puerto Rico, October 29, 1980*
Titles: *WBO light-welterweight champion 2004–06, WBA welterweight champion 2006–08, WBA light-middleweight champion 2010–12, WBC middleweight champion 2014–15, WBO Super welterweight champion 2017*
Record: *47 contests, 41 wins, 6 defeats*

Cotto became a five-weight world champion in August 2017 when he beat Yoshihiro Kamegai on points for the vacant WBO Super welterweight title, only to lose it (on points) to Sadam Ali in his first defence.

A compact, organised and predatory fighter, Cotto had "champion" stamped all over him almost from the moment he turned professional. The Puerto Rican boxed in the Sydney Olympics, but his style was not for the amateur sport and he lost a contentious decision to the Uzbek Mahatkadir – later Mohamed – Abdullaev.

He signed a contract with Bob Arum's Top Rank organization

and rose steadily through the light-welterweight ranks, despite a spell out caused by a car accident. On the way to the gym in Puerto Rico, he fell asleep, drove into a concrete wall and needed titanium rods in a broken arm.

Cotto won WBO recognition as 140-lb champion with a sixth-round stoppage of Kelson Pinto of Brazil and made six defences, including a satisfying defeat of his Olympic conqueror, Abdullaev. Weight-making difficulties increased, and he was in momentary trouble before stopping former champion DeMarcus Corley, then survived a knockdown to beat Colombian Ricardo Torres in a thrilling fight. His last defence at light-welter was a one-sided decision over Paul Malignaggi in New York.

In December 2006 he made the inevitable move up to welterweight and won the vacant WBA crown by forcing Carlos Quintana to retire after five rounds. Wins over Zab Judah and Shane Mosley confirmed his reputation as one of the best pound-for-pound fighters in the world, but a controversial stoppage by Antonio Margarito in 2008 cost him the WBA belt.

However, Margarito was suspended for tampered hand wrappings and Cotto won the WBO version instead, but Manny Pacquiao handed him a 12-round defeat in 2009. Cotto avenged the Margarito defeat and became a three-weight world champion when he took the WBA light-middleweight title from Yuri Foreman and became a four-weight champion in June 2014 when he took the WBC middleweight title from Sergio Martinez following a tenth-round retirement.

Terence Crawford

Born: *Omaha, Nebraska, September 28, 1987*
Titles: *WBO lightweight champion 2014–15, WBO light-welterweight champion 2015–, WBC light-welterweight champion 2016–*
Record: *32 contests, 32 wins*

Skilled switch-hitter Terence Crawford became WBO lightweight champion when he outpointed Ricky Burns in Scotland in March 2014.

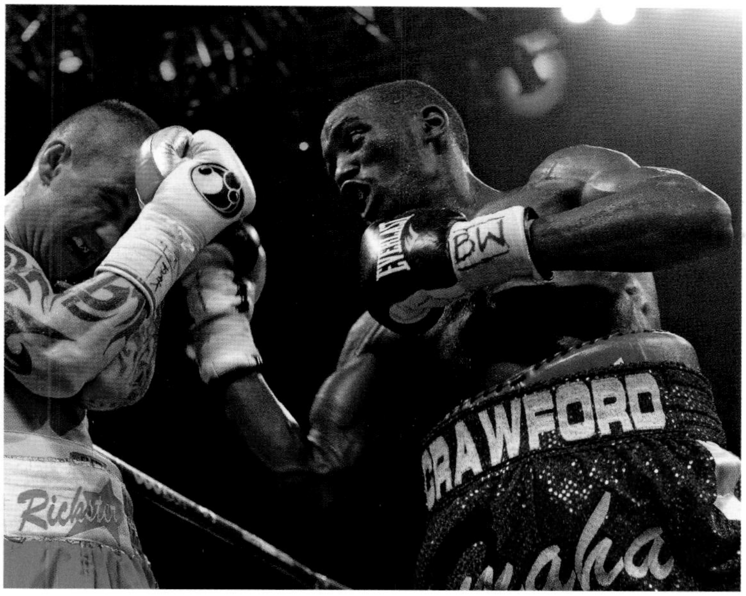

TERENCE CRAWFORD *outpointed Ricky Burns for the WBO lightweight title*

Burns had looked vulnerable in his two previous fights, but the way Crawford dominated while still appearing to have plenty in reserve marked him out as a special talent.

He coolly boxed to instructions to win clearly on all the cards.

Crawford made his first defence against ex-WBA and IBF featherweight champion Yuriorkis Gamboa and came through what he regarded as his toughest fight in nine rounds.

He stepped up a weight in June 2015 to beat Thomas Dulorme in six rounds for the vacant WBO light-welterweight title and added the WBC title to his haul with a points victory over Viktor Postol a year later.

Pipino Cuevas

Born: *Mexico City, Mexico, December 27, 1957*
Titles: *WBA welterweight champion 1976–80*
Record: *50 contests, 35 wins, 15 defeats*

Cuevas was the archetypal Mexican fighter: an explosive puncher, particularly with the left hook, but short on defence. He turned pro at 14, and was outpointed in four of his first 11 fights, but he won the rest by knockout. Aged 17 he won the Mexican welterweight title from world-ranked Jose Palacios.

That win brought him international attention, but when the clever American Andy Price outscored him two fights later, WBA champion Angel Espada was fooled into thinking that the Mexican, still five months away from his 19th birthday, would be an easy defence. He lasted less than two rounds, and Cuevas' spectacular reign was under way.

His fierce punching accounted for 11 challengers, many of them high-quality contenders, and only Randy Shields took him the distance. But, like an old-time gunfighter, Cuevas eventually met someone faster and harder than himself: Thomas Hearns, who knocked him out with one punch in August 1980. He boxed on until 1989, but a fourth-round stoppage by Roberto Duran in 1983 ended his hopes of regaining the title.

Vic Darchinyan

Born: *Vanadadzor, Armenia, January 7, 1976*
Titles: *IBF flyweight champion 2004–07, IBF super-flyweight 2008–09, WBC super-flyweight champion 2008–10, WBA super-flyweight champion 2008–09*
Record: *54 contests, 43 wins, 1 draw, 9 defeats*

Darchinyan created history by becoming the first Armenian to hold a world title when he upset the highly respected, unbeaten IBF flyweight champion Irene Pacheco in Florida in December 2004. Darchinyan's heavy-handed, somewhat wild southpaw style brought him an 11th-round stoppage win.

After boxing in the Sydney Olympics, Darchinyan stayed on to turn professional and four years later became an Australian citizen, while remaining a hero in Armenia. He held the IBF title until July 2007, when he was surprisingly picked apart in five rounds by the clever, straight punching Filipino, Nonito Donaire.

Darchinyan moved up to super-flyweight and became champion at a second weight when knocking out Russian Dmitry Kirilov in five rounds in New York. He unified three of the titles with his finest win, a ninth-round knockout of Mexican Cristian Mijares in November 2008.

His attempt to win a world title at bantamweight met with a setback. By his own admission, Darchinyan tried too hard to knock out Ghana's IBF champion, Joseph Agbeko, and lost a narrow decision in July 2009. He failed in further world-title bids at 118lb to Anselmo Moreno and Shinsuke Yamanaka, then lost for the WBA featherweight title to Nicholas Walters and Jesus Marcelo Andres Cuellar.

James DeGale

Born: *London, England, February 3, 1986*
Titles: *IBF super-middleweight champion 2015–17*
Record: *26 contests, 23 wins, 1 draw, 2 defeats*

In May 2015, James DeGale became the first British boxer to win both Olympic gold and world professional honours when he claimed the vacant IBF super-middleweight title with a points win over Andre Dirrell in Boston.

DeGale, a skilled, fast-fisted southpaw, downed Dirrell twice in the second, but the job wasn't done. Dirrell clawed his way back into the fight and it took a big effort from the Londoner in the championship rounds to make sure of the unanimous decision.

His path to the world title was far from smooth. He had become Britain's first Olympic middleweight champion for 40 years when he struck gold in Beijing in 2008.

He turned professional with Frank Warren, lost a grudge fight to George Groves on a close, majority verdict and although Warren secured him a European-title shot in his next fight, fighter and promoter fell out.

DeGale joined Mick Hennessy and despite a groin injury and growing disillusionment with boxing politics, "Chunky" kept winning.

Again, his relationship with the promoter broke down and he switched to Eddie Hearn. However, his career suffered a major setback when he lost his world title on a split decision to Caleb Truax in December 2017.

Esteban DeJesus

Born: *Carolina, Puerto Rico, August 2, 1951*
Titles: *WBC lightweight champion 1976–78*
Record: *62 contests, 57 wins, 5 defeats*

DeJesus claimed his own little piece of boxing history on November 17, 1972, when he became the first man to beat Roberto Duran, winning their non-title ten-round bout in New York on points. It had been a brave match for Duran to take: DeJesus had lost only once in 33 fights, and was clearly a rising star. He won the NABF title in his next fight, but then lost to Duran in a lightweight championship bid, and to Antonio Cervantes for the WBA light-welterweight crown, before finally taking the WBC lightweight title from Guts Ishimatsu in May 1976. He made three successful defences, but was then knocked out in 12 by Duran in a championship unification match.

He boxed until 1980, being stopped in the 13th by Jamaican Saoul Mamby for the WBC light-welterweight title in his last fight. After boxing drugs took over his life, and while in jail for a drug-related killing he contracted AIDS, from which he died on May 11, 1989. His old rival, Duran, visited him in hospital in the last days of his life.

Oscar De La Hoya

Born: *Montebello, California, February 4, 1973*
Titles: *WBO super-featherweight champion 1994, WBO lightweight champion 1994–96, IBF lightweight champion 1995, WBC light-welterweight champion 1996–97, WBC welterweight champion 1997–99 and 2000, WBC light-middleweight champion 2001–03 and 2006–07, WBO middleweight champion 2004*
Record: *45 contests 39 wins 6 defeats*

Oscar De La Hoya was one of the superstars of the 1990s. His flashing smile and ease with media and fans alike justified the Golden Boy tag given to him after his success in the 1992 Olympic Games in Barcelona. While a schoolboy, Oscar regularly sent his coursework to school when he was away on international duty. If boxing had not worked out, he planned to be an architect. As it was, his fists secured his future. When he stopped Oba Carr in Las Vegas in May 1999 he took his career past the $100 million mark: a phenomenal sum for a man who had even two years later never boxed above 154lb.

GOLDEN GREAT *Oscar De La Hoya outclasses Ricardo Mayorga in 2006*

Within two years of winning the USA's only boxing gold in Barcelona, he won the WBO super-featherweight championship by stopping Jimmi Bredahl of Denmark. He went on to hold world titles at lightweight, light-welterweight, welterweight and light-middleweight. When he outpointed Javier Castillejo of Spain for the WBC light-middleweight crown in 2001, he joined the elite band of men who have won world championships in five weight divisions. De La Hoya twice stopped the legendary Julio Cesar Chavez, and also outpointed Pernell Whitaker, Ike Quartey and Hector Camacho. He lost split decisions to Felix Trinidad, which he disputed, and Shane Mosley, which he did not, but was still a world champion in 2002 at the age of 29.

De La Hoya, whose father and grandfather were professionals in Mexico, had a tough streak that belied his looks. He was vastly wealthy but continued to box, even after setting up his successful promotional company Golden Boy Promotions. In the first decade of the 21st century it looked as if he would one day take over as the leading promoter in the sport from Bob Arum, who had once promoted him, and Don King.

In the ring De La Hoya looked to have beaten Mosley in a return, and was shocked when all three judges voted against him by an identical score of 115–113. That said, he was fortunate to win a world title in a sixth weight division when he beat German Felix Sturm on points for the WBO middleweight belt in June 2004. Three months later his middleweight experiment ended with a ninth-round defeat by Bernard Hopkins in a huge-money fight in Las Vegas.

After a 19-month break, De La Hoya proved he had plenty left by regaining his old WBC light-middleweight crown with a classy sixth-round stoppage of Ricardo Mayorga, which set up another big box-office fight with Floyd Mayweather in 2007.

On one of the fighting occasions of the decade, De La Hoya and Mayweather attracted a huge pay-per-view audience as well as a full-house at the MGM Grand. There were those who felt De La Hoya's educated pressure had earned him the decision – among them the lone "out-of-town" judge, Tom Kaczmarek. However, the two Las Vegas judges, Duane Ford and Chuck Giampa, rewarded Mayweather's clever countering to give the "Pretty Boy" a split-decision win. De La Hoya retired after draining himself to make 145lb against Manny Pacquiao in 2008 and losing in eight one-sided rounds.

"Nonpareil" Jack Dempsey

Real name: *John Kelly*
Born: *Kildare, Ireland, December 15, 1862*
Titles: *World middleweight champion 1884–91*
Record: *65 contests, 45 wins, 10 draws, 7 No Contests, 3 defeats*

The most impressive evidence of Dempsey's ability in the ring is the fact that William Harrison Dempsey chose to borrow his *nom du ring* from the Irishman. The original Jack Dempsey was known as "Nonpareil" because he was precisely that: without peer among his contemporaries. Unbeaten for the first six years of his career, he staked a claim to the middleweight championship in 1884, when he beat George Fulljames.

He was not generally accepted as champion, however, until a 27-round win over Jack Fogarty in 1886, and he defended the title twice before controversially being knocked out by George LaBlanche, whom he had beaten in an 1886 title defence. LaBlanche used the so-called "pivot punch", a back-handed blow, to do the damage. The punch was subsequently declared illegal, and Dempsey continued as champion until Bob Fitzsimmons knocked him out in 1891.

He boxed only three more times, and in his last fight, in January 1895, was knocked out in three rounds by Tommy Ryan for the welterweight title. Dempsey died in Portland, Oregon, that same year, on November 2.

Jack Dempsey

see Legends of the Ring (pp 78–79)

Juan Diaz

Born: *Houston, Texas, September 17, 1983*
Titles: *WBA lightweight champion 2004–08, WBO & IBF lightweight champion 2007–08*
Record: *46 contests, 42 wins, 4 defeats*

At 16, after winning 105 and losing only five amateur bouts, Juan Diaz expected to be selected for Mexico's team for the Sydney Olympics, but was told he was too young. Instead, he turned pro, combining his schoolwork – he studied political science at university – with training. Diaz went on to become the best lightweight in the world in the first decade of the 21st century and unified three of the "big four" titles.

He won the WBA lightweight title at the age of 20 in 2004, outpointing Mongolia's Lavka Sim. In 2006, Diaz put his name forward to box Ricky Hatton, who was then the world's top light-welterweight. Nothing came of it, but it was typical of his fearless self-belief that he was prepared to concede weight and natural strength to a man in a higher weight division with a style similar to his.

He forced heavy-handed Brazilian Acelino Freitas to retire in eight rounds to add the WBO belt in 2007, and then stopped the IBF champ Julio Diaz in nine for all three titles.

He took a break after failing to reverse a previous points loss to Juan Manuel Marquez in July 2010. Twelve months later, he was set to return against David Torres, but instead accepted an offer to study at University of Masscchussetts Dartmouth Law School.

Diaz returned in 2013, after three years away, and set about climbing back into world-title contention. However, after a fall-out with promoter Don King, he lost a surprise split decision to Nate Campbell and struggled thereafter to regain his momentum. He beat Michael Katsidis, lost to Juan Manuel Marquez, and then won and lost against the clever light-welter Paulie Malignaggi.

Nonito Donaire

Born: *Talibon, Philippines, November 16, 1982*
Titles: *IBF flyweight champion 2007–09, WBC & WBO bantamweight title 2011–12, WBO & IBF super-bantamweight champion 2012–13, WBA Super world featherweight champion 2014, WBO Super world bantamweight champion 2016–*
Record: *42 contests, 38 wins, 4 defeats*

NONITO DONAIRE*'s skills and punching power made him unbeatable for more than a decade*

Donaire, a supremely skilled, fast-fisted boxer-fighter with a lights-out left hook he learned watching hours of Alex Arguello videos, has been – like his boyhood hero – a multi-weight world champion.

"The Filipino Flash" was unbeaten for 12 years, including wins over ten fighters who have held world titles, before running into Guillermo Rigondeaux. Although Donaire had the Cuban on the floor with a left hook, he was otherwise outboxed and lost his IBF super-bantamweight title on a unanimous decision.

He went on to take the WBA Super world featherweight title from Simpiwe Vetyeka on an unsatisfactory technical points verdict, but then lost to Nicholas Walters. Donaire showed he still had skills, but Walters was too fresh, too big, hit too hard and won in six rounds.

Donaire, who went to the same school as Manny Pacquiao, announced his arrival at world level by upsetting unbeaten IBF flyweight champion Vic Darchinyan in July 2007, plunging the Armenian into a fifth-round daze. He made three defences before winning interim WBA honours at 115lb and went on to take the WBC and WBO bantamweight titles from Fernando Montiel, flattening him in the second round. He then proved he was the best at 122lb by sending both Tishioka Nishioka and Jorge Arce into retirement. In 2016, he won the WBO World super bantamweight title by knocking out Zsolt Bedak in the third round.

James "Buster" Douglas

Born: *Columbus, Ohio, April 7, 1960*
Titles: *WBC, WBA and IBF heavyweight champion 1990*
Record: *46 contests, 38 wins, 1 draw, 6 defeats*

Douglas was on the road to obscurity when, on February 11, 1990, he scored the biggest upset in boxing history by knocking out Mike Tyson for the world title in Tokyo. A huge outsider in the betting, Douglas made the most of his opportunity: he was superbly conditioned, for almost the only time in his career, and he outboxed and outpunched the hitherto unbeatable Tyson, surviving an eighth-round knockdown to knock him out in the tenth.

Managed by his father Billy, a former pro boxer at middleweight, Douglas had his first fight in 1981. He had plenty of natural talent but little discipline, and when he flopped in the tenth round of a fight with Tony Tucker for the vacant IBF title, critics also questioned his heart. But he had the last laugh in Tokyo, even if his reign was short, ending in a third-round humiliation by Evander Holyfield eight months later.

He retired financially secure, but let his weight balloon and collapsed in a diabetic coma. In 1996, after dieting and training hard, Douglas made a comeback. After six wins, he lost to Lou Savarese, ending his dreams of a Holyfield rematch.

Terry Downes

Born: *London, England, May 9, 1936*
Titles: *British middleweight champion 1958–59, 1959–62, New York and European recognition as world middle-weight champion 1961–62*
Record: *44 contests, 35 wins, 9 defeats*

Terry Downes learned his boxing in the US Marines. He won the All-Services title and qualified for the American team for the 1956 Olympics, before his true nationality was discovered. On his return to Britain he turned professional and, despite a tendency to cut, became British middleweight champion after only 17 months. A points win over Joey Giardello earned him a challenge for Paul Pender's championship, but the Bostonian stopped him on cuts in seven rounds in January 1961. There was a rematch at Wembley six months later, and this time the American retired exhausted at the end of the ninth round. They met for the third time in Boston in April 1962, Pender winnning on points. Downes was already a wealthy man, having capitalized on the legalization of bookmaking by opening a string of betting shops, but he boxed on in the hope of another world title opportunity.

He beat the fading Sugar Ray Robinson in September 1962, and then moved up to light-heavyweight, making a brave bid for Willie Pastrano's world title in his last fight, in November 1964. He died, aged 81, in October 2017.

"Peerless" Jim Driscoll

Born: *Cardiff, Wales, December 15, 1880*
Titles: *British featherweight champion 1906–1913, Empire champion 1908–13, European champion 1912–13, British and IBU recognition as world champion 1909–13*
Record: *77 contests, 58 wins, 6 draws, 10 No Decisions, 3 defeats*

Driscoll was a classic exponent of the "British style" of boxing, built around a fast straight left and deft footwork. He took up the sport professionally in 1899: according to legend, he had taught himself to box using wastepaper wrapped around his hands.

By 1906 he was British featherweight champion, though that status was not officially recognized until 1910, when he won the first Lonsdale Belt contest at that division. He made the Belt his own property in 1911 and added the European title a year later. But his career peaked in 1909, when he faced Abe Attell, the world champion, in New York. Attell would only agree to a "No Decision" contest, but Driscoll won each of the ten rounds and was accepted as world champion by Britain and the IBU.

He retired in 1913, after an epic 20-round draw with Owen Moran at the NSC. Six years later, he made a three-fight comeback aged 38, which ended when he outboxed the dangerous Frenchman Charles Ledoux for 16 rounds before being beaten by a body punch. He died on January 31, 1925.

Johnny Dundee

Real name: *Giuseppe Corrara*
Born: *Sciacca, Sicily, Italy, November 22, 1893*
Titles: *World junior-lightweight champion 1921–23, 1923–24, world featherweight champion 1923–24*
Record: *342 contests, 89 wins, 20 draws, 1 No Contest, 202 No Decisions, 30 defeats*

Dundee, a Sicilian known with due insensitivity as "The Scotch Wop" when he was one of the best fighters in the world in the 1920s, held both the world feather and super-featherweight (then called junior-lightweight) titles. His record is still being discovered as researchers dig out previously unseen results from the newspapers of the day. Like so many boxers of that era, Dundee fought whenever and wherever he could and it is possible the true statistics will never be known. Even more remarkably, the overwhelming majority went the full distance. He scored just 22 inside-schedule wins, and was knocked out only twice.

His career spanned 22 years, from 1910 to 1932, and his first title chance came in 1913 when he drew with Johnny Kilbane for the featherweight title. Despite meeting all the top featherweights and lightweights of the time, he had to wait until 1921 for a second chance, beating George Chaney on disqualification in the first-ever junior-lightweight title fight. After two defences he lost the championship to Jack Bernstein in May 1923, but two months later won the featherweight title from the French war hero Eugene Criqui and then, in December that year, regained the junior-lightweight title from Bernstein. He never defended the featherweight title, and lost the junior-lightweight championship to Kid Sullivan in June 1924.

Roberto Duran

see Legends of the Ring (pp 80–81)

Gabriel "Flash" Elorde

Born: *Bogo, Philippines, March 22, 1935*
Titles: *World junior-lightweight champion 1960–67*
Record: *117 contests, 88 wins, 2 draws, 27 defeats*

The colourful Filipino deserves to be remembered as the man who, single-handedly, gave credibility to the super-featherweight (or junior-lightweight, as it was then known) division. He won the recently revived title from Harold Gomes in March 1960, and his ten successful defences, most of them against top-quality challengers from around the world, established the 130-lb division in the public mind.

Elorde was already a national hero in the Philippines before then, having won national and Oriental titles from bantamweight to lightweight and battled for 13 rounds with Sandy Saddler in a tremendous world featherweight title challenge in 1956. He also tried twice to become lightweight champion, but each time Carlos Ortiz turned him back in 14 rounds, in 1964 and 1966.

He finally lost his junior lightweight title to Yoshiaki Numata in June 1967, and retired after an unsuccessful comeback in 1969–71. He later became a leading promoter, working with his father-in-law Lope Sarreal (who had also been his manager), before his death from cancer on January 2, 1985.

ZSOLT ERDEI *A brilliant amateur who made the transition to professional world champion*

Zsolt Erdei

Born: *Budapest, Hungary, May 31, 1974*
Titles: *WBO light-heavyweight champion 2004–09, WBC cruiserweight champion 2009*
Record: *35 contests, 34 wins, 1 defeat*

A clever, methodical boxer, Zsolt Erdei developed into a cunning ring general who won world titles at two weights before retiring in 2011. He returned two years later, lost to Denis Grachev, but decided to continue fighting.

Erdei made 11 defences of the WBO light-heavyweight championship he won by outboxing Julio Cesar Gonzalez in 2004. Needing a new challenge, he moved up to cruiserweight in 2009 and won the WBC version of the title by outpointing the rugged, ageing Italian, Giacobbe Fragomeni.

One of the most successful amateurs in Hungary's long, top-class tradition, he fought at both the 1996 and 2000 Olympics, winning a bronze medal at Sydney, Erdei also was world champion in 1997 and European champion in 1998 and 2000. In all, he won 212 of 232 amateur bouts.

To turn pro he moved to Germany and joined Klaus Peter Kohl's Universum operation. It paid off when, aged 29, he won the WBO light-heavyweight title. While his opposition was not always top-bracket, he made his championship pay. When unification fights eluded him, he moved up in weight to beat Fragomeni, but decided to return to the light-heavyweight division.

Alfredo Escalera

Born: *Carolina, Puerto Rico, March 21, 1952*
Titles: *WBC super-featherweight champion 1975–78*
Record: *70 contests, 53 wins, 3 draws, 14 defeats*

Few fighters have employed as colourful a gimmick as Alfredo "Snake Man" Escalera, who used to enter the ring with a serpent or two wrapped around his neck and limbs. He was a capable if unspectacular performer in the early years of his career which began in September 1970, and he had won only two of the five fights which preceded his WBC super-featherweight championship win over Kuniaki Shibata in July 1975.

His championship reign began equally uncertainly with a disputed 15-round draw with Venezuelan Leonel Hernandez in Caracas, but he settled down to become one of the better 130-lb champions, making ten successful defences in five countries (Finland, Japan, America, Puerto Rico and Venezuela) before Alexis Arguello took his title in 13 rounds in January 1978. His points win over the flashy Philadelphian Tyrone Everett in November 1976 is remembered as an outrageously unjust verdict, and he was careful not to give the American a second chance.

He had only a handful of fights after losing his title, and was beaten in 13 rounds again when he tried to regain the championship from Arguello in February 1979.

Sixto Escobar

Born: *Barcelona, Puerto Rico, March 23, 1913*
Titles: *NBA bantamweight champion 1934–35, 1935, New York champion 1935–36, world champion 1936–37, 1938, 1939*
Record: *72 contests, 45 wins, 4 draws, 23 defeats*

The host of champions who have come out of Puerto Rico in the last few decades owe a debt to Escobar, who won the bantamweight title three times and was one of that tiny country's early success stories in the ring.

Escobar came to America in 1934 via Canada and Venezuela, where he had most of his early fights. He won the vacant NBA title by knocking out Baby Casanova in Montreal, retained it against Eugene Huat, then lost to Lou Salica in the first of three championship meetings. Less than three months later he was champion again, and went on to become the undisputed title-holder in August 1936 by beating the ill-fated Tony Marino (who collapsed and died after a fight in January 1937).

Escobar lost the title in his third defence, to Harry Jeffra, but regained it in February 1938. It was the only time in five fights that he got the better of Jeffra. He relinquished the title in October 1939 because of his inability to make the weight, and retired the following year after losing five of his last six fights.

Luis Estaba

Born: *Guiria Sucre, Venezuela, August 13, 1941*
Titles: *WBC light-flyweight champion 1975–78*
Record: *52 contests, 41 wins, 2 draws, 9 defeats*

Luis "Lumumba" Estaba made full use of the World Boxing Council's decision to introduce the 7st 10lb light-flyweight division in the mid-1970s. The first WBC champion was Italian Franco Udella, but he relinquished it without defending it within four months.

Estaba then won it, with a fourth-round knockout of Rafael Lovera in Caracas in September 1975. It was later revealed that Lovera's claimed record was entirely false, and he was making his professional debut. But Estaba, who was already aged 34, put that fiasco behind him and became a very accomplished champion. Although it had taken him eight years to break through he established a seemingly iron grip on the belt.

One of his challengers was the former champion Udella, but the Italian lasted only three rounds in Caracas in July 1976. Estaba also beat the future champion Netrnoi Vorasingh of Thailand over the full 15 rounds in Caracas in October 1977.

That was the last of his 11 successful defences. In February 1978 his reign ended when, aged 36, he was knocked out in the 14th round by Mexican Freddie Castillo. The defeat took his hunger away. Castillo quickly lost the title to Vorasingh, and Estaba challenged the Thai in Caracas in July 1978, but lost in five rounds.

Chris Eubank

Born: *London, England, August 8, 1966*
Titles: *WBC International middleweight champion 1990, WBO middleweight champion 1990–91, WBO super-middleweight champion 1991–95*
Record: *52 contests, 45 wins, 2 draws, 5 defeats*

The flamboyant and frequently outrageous Eubank professed to despise boxing, yet made a fortune from the sport and, with 24 WBO title fights, engaged in more so-called world title fights than any other British boxer. A troubled and difficult youth, he was sent to New York to join his mother, and it was there that he took up amateur boxing seriously. He turned professional in October 1985, winning five four-rounders in Atlantic City before returning to Britain in 1987. His career really took off when he joined promoter Barry Hearn, who steered him to the WBO middleweight title, won in a heroic battle with Nigel Benn.

He defended that three times, the last a disputed win over Michael Watson, then moved up to super-middleweight and captured the vacant WBO title in a dramatic and tragic rematch with Watson, who was left permanently disabled. That experience seemed to affect Eubank, as he repeatedly settled for points decisions when he could have won by stoppage. He retired briefly after a second loss to Steve Collins in September 1995, but returned to action in October 1996. However, further WBO title defeats by Joe Calzaghe and Carl Thompson led to his retirement at the age of 32.

Johnny Famechon

Born: *Paris, France, March 28, 1945*
Titles: *Empire (Commonwealth) featherweight champion 1967–69, WBC champion 1969–70*
Record: *67 contests, 56 wins, 6 draws, 5 defeats*

Famechon was born into the aristocracy of French boxing. His uncle Ray was an outstanding European featherweight champion who fought for the world title, while his father Andre and uncle Emile were both champions. When Andre divorced he moved to Australia, taking Johnny with him.

The youngster never boxed as an amateur, turning pro at 16 in June 1961. He won the Australian featherweight title after 22 fights and the Commonwealth belt in his 49th. In January 1969 he took the WBC title from Jose Legra in London, giving a dazzling display of quickfire boxing to outscore the Cuban. British fans liked his style, and he had a series of non-title fights there.

He retained his title twice, each time against former flyweight and bantamweight champion Fighting Harada of Japan. Famechon was floored three times in their first meeting, but knocked out Harada in the 14th round of their rematch in Tokyo. He lost the title to Vicente Saldivar in Rome in May 1970, and never fought again. In 1995 he was critically injured in a car accident, spending some time on a life support machine, but he made a good recovery.

Tommy Farr

Born: *Tonypandy, Wales, March 12, 1913*
Titles: *British heavyweight champion 1937–38*
Record: *126 contests, 81 wins, 13 draws, 2 No Contests, 30 defeats*

The rugged Welshman will always be remembered for his stirring 15-round challenge for Joe Louis' heavyweight title in August 1937. It was Louis' first defence, and he was confidently expected to dismiss the little-known British champion without much difficulty. Instead Farr, fighting bravely and stubbornly, defied Louis for the full distance of a fight to which millions at home listened on BBC radio.

Farr came from a tough school, having learned his boxing on the booths from the age of 13. He started as a middleweight in 1926 and progressed to the Welsh light-heavyweight title, which he won in 1933, but after a string of defeats he moved up to heavyweight and started a long winning run which carried him to the British title in March 1937. Victories over former champion Max Baer and the German star Walter Neusel earned him the fight with Louis.

He stayed on in America hoping for a second chance, but lost four bad verdicts, including a return with Baer, and came home to find that the Board had stripped him of the British title. Farr retired in 1940, but made a reasonably successful comeback ten years later before quitting for good in 1953. He died in Brighton on March 1, 1986.

Jeff Fenech

Born: *Sydney, Australia, May 28, 1964*
Titles: *IBF bantamweight champion 1985–87, WBC super-bantamweight champion 1987–88, WBC featherweight champion 1988–89*
Record: *32 contests, 28 wins, 1 draw, 3 defeats*

Fenech was a rough handful in or out of the ring, a delinquent tearaway who successfully channelled his aggression into boxing. The son of Maltese immigrants, he represented Australia at the 1984 Olympic Games and turned professional on his return, winning the national super-flyweight title in his third bout.

Just four fights later, after a grand total of 24 rounds as a professional, he was a world champion, after knocking out Satoshi Shingaki for the IBF bantamweight title in Sydney. He made three defences before moving up to super-bantamweight to win the WBC title from Thailand's Samart Payakarun, with a surprise fourth-round knockout in May 1987. He retained that against former world champions Greg Richardson and Carlos Zarate, then stepped up again to featherweight to become WBC champion by stopping Victor Callejas in March 1988.

After three defences he retired because of hand trouble, then returned to fight a bitterly disputed draw with Azumah Nelson. He was expected to win the return, but Nelson outclassed him in eight rounds. He retired again, returned and then quit for good after South African Philip Holiday defeated him in two rounds in 1996. In retirement he became a respected manager and trainer in Sydney.

Bob Fitzsimmons

Born: *Helston, England, May 26, 1863*
Titles: *World middleweight champion 1891–94, heavyweight champion 1897–99, light-heavyweight champion 1903–05*
Record: *84 contests, 50 wins, 5 draws, 21 No Decisions, 8 defeats*

The spindly, unathletic-looking Fitzsimmons, who never scaled more than 175lb, was a true cosmopolitan. He was born in Cornwall, England, raised in New Zealand, spent the first seven years of his career in Australia, and won two of his three world titles as an American citizen. His career started when, as an apprentice blacksmith, he won a competition organized by the old bare-knuckle champion Jem Mace.

He took the middleweight title from "Nonpareil" Jack Dempsey in 13 rounds in January 1891, retaining it twice before moving up to heavyweight. Challenging James J. Corbett on St Patrick's Day, 1897, Fitzsimmons was comprehensively outboxed for 13 rounds before landing a left to the stomach which left Corbett on his knees, gasping for breath.

He lost in his first defence to James J. Jeffries, who outweighed him by 50lb, and Jeffries knocked him out again in 1902. Fitzsimmons bounced back once more, this time in the newly created light-heavyweight division, and won his third world title in 1903, by outpointing George Gardner, holding it for two years. He finally retired in 1914, aged 52, and died in Chicago on October 22, 1917.

Tiger Flowers

Real name: *Theodore Flowers*
Born: *Camile, Georgia, August 5, 1895*
Titles: *World middleweight champion 1926*
Record: *161 contests, 119 wins, 7 draws, 20 No Decisions, 15 defeats*

Flowers was a thoughtful and religious man, a rarity in an era of hellraising middleweights like Harry Greb and Mickey Walker, so he was known as the "Georgia Deacon". A southpaw, he started boxing in 1918 and maintained a prodigious work rate, having 36 fights in 1924 alone.

He was a cagey boxer with a stiff punch, but frequently had to fight out of his weight class, losing to light-heavyweight champions Jack Delaney (twice), Mike McTigue and Maxie Rosenbloom. He finally got a world title chance in February 1926, and outpointed Greb (who by then was blind in one eye) over 15 rounds to become the first black middleweight champion.

Flowers fought Mickey Walker in Chicago in December that year, under the impression that it would be a No Decision affair, only to hear Walker proclaimed champion at the end of their ten-rounder. He campaigned for a rematch, and lost only one of his 18 fights in 1927. But on November 16, 1927, Flowers died in New York following a routine eye operation.

George Foreman

Born: *Marshall, Texas, January 10, 1949*
Titles: *World heavyweight champion 1973–74, WBA and IBF champion 1994–95*
Record: *81 contests, 76 wins, 5 defeats*

Foreman took up boxing as a rebellious teenager, winning the heavyweight gold medal at the 1968 Olympics before launching a spectacular pro career. He had won 37 in a row, 34 by knockout, when he faced the formidable Joe Frazier for the title in Kingston, Jamaica, on Foreman's 25th birthday. Despite his KO record, Foreman was a big outsider, but he floored Frazier six times to force a second-round stoppage. Chilling defences against Joe Roman and Ken Norton made him seem invincible, and there were fears for Muhammad Ali's safety when the ex-champion challenged him in Zaire in October 1974. Instead, Ali flattened the Texan in the eighth.

Foreman drifted away from boxing, becoming a minister before, after a ten-year layoff, he started an improbable comeback. He worked his way into contention, and lost honourably to Evander Holyfield in his first attempt to regain the title. In November 1994, he knocked out WBA and IBF champion Michael Moorer to become the oldest-ever heavyweight champion. The WBA later stripped him, and he relinquished the IBF title after one unimpressive defence in April 1995. Foreman retired for good after losing a much-criticized decision to Shannon Briggs. In retirement he made another fortune marketing a grill named after him and was a regular broadcaster with HBO.

Joe Frazier

Born: *Beaufort, South Carolina, January 12, 1944*
Titles: *New York heavyweight champion 1968–1970, world heavyweight champion 1970–73*
Record: *37 contests, 32 wins, 1 draw, 4 defeats*

Despite his Southern origins, "Smokin' Joe" Frazier came to personify the left-hooking, aggressive Philadelphia style of fighting. His family had moved north when Joe was a boy, and he turned professional in August 1965 after winning the 1964 Olympic heavyweight gold medal, replacing the injured Buster Mathis.

He was managed by a syndicate of mainly white businessmen, calling themselves Cloverlay Inc., but the training and match-making decisions were made first by Yank Durham and later by Eddie Futch. Frazier surged up the rankings with important wins over men like Oscar Bonavena, Doug Jones, Eddie Machen and George Chuvalo, and in 1968 he stopped his old amateur rival Mathis to win the New York version of the world title which had been stripped from Muhammad Ali.

Two years later he stopped WBA champion Jimmy Ellis to unify the title, and removed all doubts about his right to be champion when he knocked down and outpointed Ali in March 1971.

Frazier lost the title to George Foreman in Kingston, Jamaica, in 1973, and failed in a magnificent effort to regain it from Ali in the "Thrilla in Manila" in October 1975, retiring a year later. His last fight was a draw with Floyd Cummings in a brief comeback in 1981. He died from cancer in September 2011.

Acelino Freitas

Born: *Salvador, Bahia, Brazil, September 21, 1975*
Titles: *WBO super-featherweight champion 1999–2003, WBA super-featherweight champion 2002–03, WBO lightweight champion 2004 and 2006–07*
Record: *41 contests, 39 wins, 2 defeats*

Freitas was a Brazilian hero: when he returned to Salvador to defend his WBO super-featherweight title in 1999, more than 60,000 people saw him demolish Anthony Martinez in the second round.

In his youth, Freitas kept fans on the edge of their seats as a scary lack of attention to his own defence gave him an air of vulnerability. But he could punch so hard that super-featherweights couldn't stay with him. He won his first world title in 101 seconds, leaving Anatoly Alexandrov on the canvas for five minutes and he never boxed again. Title defences against the Mexican Javier Jauregui and Orlando Soto from Panama both ended in round one.

Freitas unified the WBO and WBA titles with a narrow win over Joel Casamayor in January 2002 and came through a brutal fight with Argentina's Jorge Barrios the following August. Freitas was down in the eighth, and both men were on the floor in round 11, before the Brazilian finished off Barrios in the 12th.

In January 2004 Freitas moved up to lightweight and ended the long reign of WBO champion Artur Grigorian on points. He then faced a fired-up Diego Corrales but lost in the tenth round, with critics saying he quit.

Freitas regained the WBO title with a split-decision win over Zahir Raheem – but retired after losing in eight rounds to WBA champion Juan Diaz in a unification fight. After more than five years away, Freitas returned to knock out unbeaten Michael Oliveira in nine rounds, but retired for good in 2017.

CARL FROCH *Grit and fitness brought WBC super-middleweight champ Froch through to a last-round stoppage of Jermain Taylor in his American debut*

Carl Froch

Born: *Nottingham, England, July 2, 1977*
Titles: *WBC super-middleweight champion 2008–10 and 2010–11, IBF super-middleweight champion 2012–14*
Record: *35 contests, 33 wins, 2 defeats*

Carl Froch did things his own way. The World Amateur Championships bronze medallist did not want meaningless "trinket titles"; he took the traditional route, from British and Commonwealth to recognized world championships. It took him time to make the breakthrough because the fight he wanted, against world champion Joe Calzaghe, did not materialize.

By the time Calzaghe had vacated, Froch was past his 30th birthday, but when he got the chance, against the Canadian Jean Pascal, in December 2008, he took it. In a gruelling 12 rounder, the man from Nottingham won on points to become WBC super-middleweight champion.

Froch signed up for the Showtime-backed "Super Six" tournament, featuring the world's top super-middleweights. In the event's first fight, he went to Connecticut to box former world middleweight champion Jermain Taylor. Knocked down early on, it seemed Froch would not do enough, but a sensational surge in the last round gave him a stoppage victory.

His second defence was against spoiling, counter-punching American Andre Dirrell and the split decision in Froch's favour after 12 messy rounds did not please everyone, but he would argue that he was the only one trying to make the fight.

Froch's unbeaten run ended in his 27th fight when he lost a unanimous decision to Mikkel Kessler in another hard, uncompromising fight in Denmark in April 2010. An eye injury forced Kessler to vacate the WBC title and Froch regained the belt by outboxing Arthur Abraham, but Andre Ward handed him a points defeat in the final of the "Super Six" tournament.

Typically, Froch responded with arguably his career-best performance. He thrashed Lucian Bute in five rounds to take the IBF super-middleweight title and become a three-time world champion. He picked himself off the floor to beat Londoner George Groves and won the rematch more convincingly in front of 80,000 fans at Wembley Stadium, in what proved to be his final fight, laying him out with an eighth-round right hand.

Gene Fullmer

Born: *West Jordan, Utah, July 21, 1931*
Titles: *World middleweight champion 1957, NBA champion 1959–62*
Record: *64 contests, 55 wins, 3 draws, 6 defeats*

One of a family of boxing brothers, the crude, brawling Fullmer had his first pro fight in June 1951 under the management of Utah mink farmer, Marv Jensen, who guided him throughout his career. He knocked out his first 11 opponents, six in the first round, and before the end of 1951 had established himself by beating the respected Garth Panter.

By 1957, having lost only three times in 40 fights, he was a leading contender and, on January 2, 1957, shocked Ray Robinson by outpointing him in New York. Robinson reclaimed the title four months later with a perfect, one-punch knockout, but Fullmer fought on and, in August 1959, stopped Carmen Basilio to win the vacant NBA title.

He retained it seven times, including a repeat stoppage of Basilio and a draw and points win in further meetings with Robinson. Dick Tiger outpointed him in October 1962, and although Fullmer held him to a draw in a rematch he was on borrowed time. Tiger stopped him in seven rounds in their third fight, and Fullmer never fought again. He died aged 83 in April 2015.

Victor Galindez

Born: *Buenos Aires, Argentina November 2, 1948*
Titles: *WBA light-heavyweight champion 1974–78, 1979*
Record: *70 contests, 55 wins, 4 draws, 2 No Contests, 9 defeats*

Although Victor Galindez held only the WBA version of the light-heavyweight title, he was good enough to have been a world champion in any era. Yet he made an indifferent start, winning only half of his first 22 fights. After that, he never looked back. An unbeaten run of 23 brought him the Argentine title and a match with Len Hutchins of America for the WBA title, which had been stripped from Bob Foster. Galindez won in 13 rounds and proved a busy champion, willing to go anywhere for a payday. He retained the title ten times against outstanding challengers like Alvaro Lopez, Pierre Fourie, Jorge Ahumada, Richie Kates and Eddie Gregory. He was especially popular in Italy, where he defended four times, and in South Africa, where his four defences included a last-round knockout of Kates in a dramatic and bloody battle.

Mike Rossman took the title with a surprise 13th-round stoppage in New Orleans in September 1978, but Galindez regained it in April 1979 before losing it to Marvin Johnson seven months later. He boxed just once more, before he was killed in a car accident on October 26, 1980.

Joe Gans

Real name: *Joseph Gaines*
Born: *Baltimore, Maryland, November 25, 1874*
Titles: *World lightweight champion 1902–04, 1906–08*
Record: *161 contests, 123 wins, 11 draws, 19 No Decisions, 8 defeats*

Gans, a classy counter-puncher, was one of the best lightweights in history, but the suspicion attached to several of his defeats tainted his reputation. He began boxing in 1891, and was beaten only three times on the way to his first world title bid, against Frank Erne in 1900. He was comfortably ahead when, in the 12th round, he sustained a cut eye and suddenly quit.

In December of that year he performed so poorly in losing in two rounds to Terry McGovern that the fight could scarcely have been on the level, but despite these scandals he was given a rematch with Erne in May 1902 and this time won on a first-round knockout – which served only to strengthen the doubts about the previous result.

He retained the title six times between 1902 and 1908, when he lost it to Battling Nelson, and fought a 20-round draw with Joe Walcott for the welterweight title in 1904. Nelson knocked him out in a rematch, and Gans boxed only once more, retiring in 1909. He died of tuberculosis in Baltimore on August 10, 1910.

Danny Garcia

Born: *Philadelphia, March 20, 1988*
Titles: *WBC light-welterweight title 2012–, WBA Super world light-welterweight title 2012–, WBC welterweight title 2016–17*
Record: *34 contests, 33 wins, 1 defeat*

Danny Garcia claimed the vacant WBC light-welterweight title by outpointing 35 year-old Erik Morales in March 2012 and what happened next propelled him into boxing's elite. Pre-fight provocation from father Angel – a former professional boxer and Garcia's trainer from the start – appeared to unsettle Amir Khan before their unification match in Las Vegas.

Whatever the reason, Khan strayed from the hit-and-move game plan drawn up by trainer Freddie Roach, traded punches and ended up flat on his back in the third. Khan picked himself up, tried to fight back, but Garcia grabbed his chance to claim the best win of his career. He kept punching to floor Khan twice more before the referee waved the fight off in the fourth round.

Garcia was ven more spectacular when laying out Morales in the fourth round of their October 2012 rematch with another left hook, then claimed a career-best win outpointing feared Argentine puncher Lucas Matthysse. He lost his WBC world welterweight title to Keith Thurman in March 2017 on a split decision.

DANNY GARCIA *hit too hard for Erik Morales and Amir Khan*

Arturo Gatti

Born: *Montreal, Canada, April 15, 1972*
Titles: *IBF super-featherweight champion 1995–97, WBC light-welterweight champion 2004–05*
Record: *49 contests, 40 wins, 9 defeats*

Arturo "Thunder" Gatti's blazing, hit-or-be-hit style made the old purists turn in their graves, but he had spirit in abundance and towards the end of his career could fill the 12,000-seat Boardwalk Hall in Atlantic City whenever he fought. Born in Montreal of Italian parents and raised in Jersey City, he won the IBF super-featherweight title by dominating Tracy Harris Patterson, the adopted son of former heavyweight champion Floyd, in Madison Square Garden in December 1995.

His first defence was a typical Gatti war: down, cut and almost out against Wilson Rodriguez in New York, he turned it all around and knocked him out in round six. He went on to become one of the stars of east coast boxing over the next decade. He beat Patterson again, and then in October 1997 won a brutal war with Gabriel Ruelas in Atlantic City. When he relinquished his world crown and moved up to lightweight, he hit a bad patch: three defeats in a row, on cuts to Angel Manfredy and two decisions in gruelling fights with Ivan Robinson. Then an eccentric attempt to try his luck at welterweight led to a five-round hammering from Oscar De La Hoya.

His reputation was cemented, not by a world title win, but by three amazing non-title ten rounders with "Irish" Micky Ward: the first, in Connecticut, was an incredible toe-to-toe war which Ward won on a majority decision. For the rematch, Gatti hired rising trainer Buddy McGirt – and stunned critics by getting on his toes and outboxing Ward for a deserved decision. The third fight, in June 2003, saw Gatti come out of another exciting contest with a unanimous decision.

When the WBC stripped Kostya Tszyu, they paired Gatti with the Italian Gianluca Brano and, in Atlantic City, Arturo delighted his fans once again by winning his second world title. Again, it went 12 hard rounds. After one defence, he lost it to Floyd Mayweather, who was just too quick and too young. Gatti retired after the sixth. Two fights later, up at welterweight, he was stopped in the ninth by WBC welterweight champion Carlos Baldomir and, at long last, it seemed the years of wars had finally caught up with him. Gatti died in mysterious circumstances in a Brazilian hotel room in July 2009.

Kid Gavilan

Real name: *Gerardo Gonzalez*
Born: *Camaguey, Cuba, January 6, 1926*
Titles: *World welterweight champion 1951–54*
Record: *143 contests, 107 wins, 6 draws, 30 defeats*

Known as the "Cuban Hawk", Gavilan's trademark was a whipping half-hook, half-uppercut called the bolo punch, which he claimed to have perfected during his years of using a machete in the sugar fields where he worked before becoming a pro fighter in 1943. He had lost only twice in 27 fights when he moved to America in 1946, where his all-action style proved immensely popular.

Although not a heavy puncher – only 27 of his 107 victories were inside the distance – he was never in a bad fight. Sugar Ray Robinson outpointed him in his first world title bid in 1949, but he became champion two years later when he outscored NBA champion Johnny Bratton for the vacant undisputed title. He held it for three years and seven successful defences, until Johnny Saxton outpointed him in October 1954.

He tried for the middleweight title in April 1954, losing to Carl "Bobo" Olson, and continued boxing in top class, though with scant success, right up to his retirement in September 1958. Sadly, his eyesight had been affected by his punishing 143-fight career, and he later went blind. He died in Miami on February 13, 2003.

Joey Giardello

Real name: *Carmine Tilelli*
Born: *Brooklyn, New York, July 16, 1930*
Titles: *World middleweight champion 1963–65*
Record: *133 contests, 100 wins, 7 draws, 1 No Decision, 25 defeats*

Joey Giardello was already a veteran of 123 fights and 15 years in the ring business when he finally became world middleweight champion in December 1963, outsmarting Dick Tiger in a cagey, 15-round tactical battle in Atlantic City. It was Giardello's second title challenge, having fought a bruising draw with Gene Fullmer for the NBA championship three years earlier.

Based in Philadelphia, Giardello had been boxing in top class from an early stage of his career, but he tended to win a series of important fights and then lose just when he was on the point of a title fight. He fought all the stars of the 1950s – the golden years of the middleweight division – and beat most of them, but his career looked to be winding down when Tiger gave him his chance.

It was their third meeting, having split a pair of ten-rounders in 1959. Giardello managed one defence, outpointing Rubin "Hurricane" Carter, but then lost the title back to Tiger in October 1965. He made a brief comeback as a light-heavyweight, having the last of his 133 fights in 1967.

Gennady Golovkin

Born: *Karaganda, Kazakhstan, April 8, 1982*
Titles: *WBA middleweight champion 2010–, IBO world middleweight champion 2012–, WBC world middleweight champion 2016–*
Record: *38 contests, 37 wins, 1 draw*

Only Bernard Hopkins (20) has made more world middleweight title defences than Gennady Gennayevich Golovkin, aka "GGG". His 14th defence of the WBA title – a six-round mauling of American Willie Monroe Jr – brought him level with Carlos Monzon, who ruled the division in the 1970s.

Born in Kazakhstan, Gennady soon learned how to fight on the insistence of older brothers Sergey and Vadim. Their deaths while serving with the Russian army hit him hard, but he persevered with boxing and compiled a 345–5 amateur record that included silver at the 2004 Olympics in Athens.

He turned professional in 2006 and, four years later, linked up with trainer Abel Sanchez, who promised to make Golovkin an all-time great. While it remains to be seen if that will happen, he is the most feared and devastating middleweight of his era.

His footwork and strength keep opponents under pressure. One commentator put it: "He makes the ring smaller and smaller," and his fists punish every mistake.

Possibly Golovkin's best win was in July 2014, a third-round knock-out of ex-WBA Super and IBF champion Daniel Geale.

GENNADY GOLOVKIN *has ruled the middleweight division since 2010*

Wilfredo Gomez

Born: *Las Monjas, Puerto Rico, October 29, 1956*
Titles: *WBC super-bantamweight champion 1977–83, WBC featherweight champion 1984, WBA junior-lightweight champion 1985–86*
Record: *48 contests, 44 wins, 1 draw, 3 defeats*

The hard-punching Gomez compiled a remarkable championship record. He drew his first pro fight, in November 1974, but won the next 32 inside the distance, including 14 for the WBC super-bantamweight title which he won in May 1977. He had been a brilliant amateur, and would almost certainly have taken a gold medal in the 1976 Olympics had he waited that long.

The highlights of his super-bantamweight reign were stoppages of the Mexican pair Carlos Zarate and Lupe Pintor, who had both been outstanding bantamweight champions. Gomez relinquished the title in April 1983 after 17 defences, all by knockout or stoppage, and won the WBC featherweight title in March 1984. It was his second attempt, having been stopped in eight rounds by Salvador Sanchez in August 1981.

Azumah Nelson knocked him out in 11 rounds in August 1984, but Gomez bounced back to win his third title, taking the WBA junior-lightweight championship from Rocky Lockridge in May 1985. Alfredo Layne ended his championship career with a ninth-round stoppage a year later, and Gomez retired in 1989. He was jailed for drug-related offences while living in Venezuela in 1994, but recovered in a rehabilitation unit and rebuilt his life back in Puerto Rico.

Miguel Angel Gonzalez

Born: *Ensenada, Mexico, November 15, 1970*
Titles: *WBC International lightweight champion 1992, WBC lightweight champion 1992–95*
Record: *63 contests, 57 wins, 1 draw, 5 defeats*

The tall, stylish Gonzalez defied tradition by coming from a comfortable middle-class background rather than the grinding poverty which has spawned so many of the great Mexican champions. He was educated to university level and represented Mexico at the 1988 Olympics in Seoul at 17. He lost only two of his 65 bouts as an amateur, before turning professional in January 1989.

In 1990 Gonzalez had a spell in Japan, winning five in a row under the name of Santa Tokyo! In early 1992, having returned to Mexico, he won the WBC International lightweight title and in August of the same year he won the vacant WBC lightweight championship, climbing off the floor to stop Wilfredo Rocha of Colombia in nine rounds.

Gonzalez defended the title ten times in three years, his last defence a criticized points win over American Lamar Murphy in Las Vegas in August 1995. Weight troubles forced him up to light-welterweight, where he was outpointed by Oscar De La Hoya in a hard fight in January 1997, and then unluckily held to a draw by Julio Cesar Chavez in Mexico in March 1998. Gonzalez continued to operate at world level into his mid-30s and lost in world title bids to Kostya Tszyu, Cory Spinks and Luis Collazo.

ROMAN GONZALEZ *won world titles at three weights*

Roman Gonzalez

Born: *Managua, Nicaragua, June 17, 1987*
Titles: *WBA minimumweight champion 2008–10, WBA light-flyweight champion 2011–12, WBC flyweight champion 2014–16*
Record: *48 contests, 46 wins, 2 defeats*

Roman Gonzalez, nicknamed "Chocolatito", emulated boyhood hero Alexis Arguello by winning world titles at three weights.

From a fighting family – Gonzalez's father, uncle and grandfather all boxed – as a boy, he fought for food at amateur tournaments organized by Arguello, who was the mayor of Managua. Gonzalez claims he was beaten only once in 89 amateur bouts and was only 21 years old when he won his first world title, taking the WBA minimumweight belt from Yutaka Niida in Japan with a fourth-round stoppage.

A compact box-fighter with good shot selection and power, Gonzalez made three defences before stepping up to win WBA light-flyweight honours. He went on to claim the WBC flyweight title with what he rates his best performance, a nine-round stoppage of Akira Yaegashi in Japan in September 2014.

In May, 2015, Edgar Sosa became the seventh world champion Gonzalez has beaten when he was overpowered inside a couple of rounds. However, back-to-back defeats to Wasaksil Wangek has left his career in the balance.

Rocky Graziano

Real name: *Thomas Rocco Barbella*
Born: *New York, NY, January 1, 1922*
Titles: *World middleweight champion 1947–48*
Record: *83 contests, 67 wins, 6 draws, 10 defeats*

Graziano, the son of an old fighter, was in constant trouble with the law. He was drafted into the US Army, but was given a dishonourable discharge for striking an officer and after serving time in an Army prison he turned professional in March 1942.

His brawling style made him a popular attraction, although his crude technique meant that he could often be outboxed: he lost six decisions in his first three years. 1945 was his breakthrough year, with big wins over Al Davis, welterweight champion Freddie Cochrane (twice), and Harold Green, who had outpointed him twice in 1944. A two-round knockout of former welterweight champion Marty Servo brought him a crack at middleweight champion Tony Zale in 1946, but Graziano was knocked out in the sixth round of a classic encounter.

The rematch a year later was a carbon copy, except this time Graziano won, but Zale regained the title in three rounds in 1948. Graziano compiled an unbeaten run of 21 as he sought another chance, but when it came Ray Robinson knocked him out in three rounds. He retired in 1952 and became a much-loved entertainer and TV personality. His story was made into a successful movie, *Somebody Up There Likes Me*, starring Paul Newman. He died on May 22, 1990, aged 68.

Harry Greb

Born: *Pittsburgh, Pennsylvania, June 6, 1894*
Titles: *American light-heavyweight champion 1922–23, world middleweight champion 1923–26*
Record: *305 contests, 115 wins, 3 draws, 179 No Decisions, 8 defeats*

Greb broke all the rules, in every sense: he was a rough and dirty fighter, and his lifestyle was the antithesis of a professional athlete's. He was a drinker and a prodigious womanizer, yet compiled an astonishing record of almost 300 fights in a hectic 13-year career. He scorned training, arguing that fighting so often kept him fit enough.

His most famous victory came in May 1922, when he battered Gene Tunney over 15 rounds. It was Tunney's sole defeat, and he trounced Greb in a rematch in February 1923. Greb won the middleweight title from Johnny Wilson in his next fight, and his five successful defences included a ferocious battle with Mickey Walker which, reportedly, was continued later that evening when the pair met outside a nightclub.

He lost the title to Tiger Flowers in February 1926, and Flowers beat him again six months later. It was Greb's last fight: he died on October 22, 1926 following a nose operation.

Robert Guerrero

Born: *Gilroy, California, March 27, 1983*
Titles: *IBF featherweight champion 2006–08, IBF super-featherweight title 2009–10*
Record: *42 contests, 33 wins, 1 draw, 2 no contests, 6 defeats*

ROBERT GUERRERO *is a good advert for boxing. A fearless fighter and decent family man*

A pro at 18 years old, Guerrero is a fast-fisted southpaw who lets his hands go. Ringsiders recorded him throwing 1,200 punches at Malcolm Klassen when he won the IBF super-featherweight title in August 2009.

Guerrero vacated to spend time with wife Casey, who was battling cancer. Casey found a bone marrow donor – and her life was saved. Guerrero is a decent family man. He's been with Casey since they were 14 years old and he's trained by father Rubin.

Known as "The Ghost", he took the IBF featherweight title from Eric Aiken in September 2006, but lost a defence against Orlando Salido, though the title was declared vacant after Salido failed a drugs test. Guerrero regained the belt with a nine-round stoppage of Spend Abazi, moved up to win IBF honours at 130lbs, then claimed the interim WBA and WBO lightweight titles by punishing Aussie Michael Katsidis in April 2011. Guerrero won the interim WBC welterweight title by outpointing Turkish hot-head Selcuk Aydin, then beat Andre Berto after a breath-taking last round.

Guerrero couldn't solve the riddle that is Floyd Mayweather Jr., losing on points, and then age seemed to catch up with him as he lost three of his next four fights.

Emile Griffith

Born: *St Thomas, Virgin Islands, February 3, 1938*
Titles: *World welterweight champion 1961, 1962–63, 1963–66, world middleweight champion 1966–67, 1967–68*
Record: *112 contests, 85 wins, 2 draws, 1 No Contest, 24 defeats*

The colourful Griffith worked in a New York milliner's before turning pro in June 1958, and by 1960 had beaten top contenders like Gaspar Ortega, Denny Moyer, Jorge and Florentino Fernandez and Luis Rodriguez to earn a crack at Benny Paret's welterweight title. He knocked Paret out in 13 rounds in April 1961, but lost the title back to him in September before stopping the Cuban in 12 rounds in their rubber match in March 1962. Paret never regained consciousness.

Griffith was dethroned by Luis Rodriguez in March 1963, but regained the crown three months later and then won their third meeting in June 1964. In total, he won ten and lost two welterweight title fights before taking the middleweight title from Dick Tiger in April 1966. He retained it twice against New York rival Joey Archer, then lost two out of three clashes with Nino Benvenuti.

Jose Napoles outpointed him when he tried to regain the welterweight title in 1969, and Carlos Monzon defeated him twice in middleweight title bids. Griffith also lost a 1976 challenge for the WBC light-middleweight title, and retired the following year after 112 fights. He died aged 75 in July 2013.

Marvin Hagler

Born: *Newark, New Jersey, May 23, 1952*
Titles: *World middleweight champion 1980–87, WBA and IBF champion 1987*
Record: *67 contests, 62 wins, 2 draws, 3 defeats*

Marvin Hagler added the word "Marvelous" to his name by deed poll, and nobody argued. For the best part of a decade, he was the king of the middleweights, who should already have been champion for a couple of years before he eventually won it.

The shaven-skulled switch-hitter, equally at home in southpaw or orthodox stances, moved with his family to Brockton, Mass., after the race riots in Newark in 1967, and turned professional after winning the AAU title in 1973. When he beat former Olympic champion Ray Seales in only his 15th fight, he gained the reputation as a man to avoid. Despite losing only two of his first 50 fights, he had to wait until 1979 for a title chance, when a draw allowed Vito Antuofermo to keep the title.

But he made no mistake next time, stopping Alan Minter in three rounds and going on to retain the title 12 times, including classic fights with Thomas Hearns and John Mugabi. When Ray Leonard won a controversial verdict over him, in April 1987, Hagler walked away from boxing to begin a new career in films.

Mashiko "Fighting" Harada

Born: *Tokyo, Japan, April 5, 1943*
Titles: *World flyweight champion 1962–63, world bantamweight champion 1965–68*
Record: *62 contests, 55 wins, 7 defeats*

The rugged Harada won world titles at flyweight and bantamweight and only narrowly failed to add the featherweight crown as well. He knocked out Thailand's Pone Kingpetch in 11 rounds to claim the flyweight title in October 1962, in his 28th professional fight, but Kingpetch regained it a few months later and Harada moved up to bantamweight.

A stoppage loss to the dangerous Mexican Joe Medel in September 1963 hindered his progress, but he came back strongly and, in May 1965, took the world title from the brilliant Brazilian Eder Jofre, who had not been beaten in 50 fights. He made four successful defences, including a revenge win over Medel, then lost it on points to Lionel Rose.

Harada was involved in a bizarre featherweight title fight in Sydney in July 1969 against Johnny Famechon, whom he floored three times and appeared to have outpointed. Referee Willie Pep, himself a former featherweight champion, at first declared it a draw, but then said he had found an error in his arithmetic, and gave Famechon the decision. Famechon won a rematch decisively, and Harada retired. He is now a respected TV boxing commentator in Japan.

Marvin Hart

Born: *Jefferson County, Kentucky, September 16, 1876*
Titles: *World heavyweight champion 1905–06*
Record: *48 contests, 29 wins, 4 draws, 10 No Decisions, 7 defeats*

Nowadays if Marvin Hart is remembered at all it is usually as the other world heavyweight champion to come from Louisville, Kentucky, or else as an undeserving stop-gap champion who bridged the reigns of James J. Jeffries and Tommy Burns. While he certainly was not one of the better champions, Hart was not as bad a fighter as unkind historians have depicted: he outpointed Jack Johnson over 20 rounds in 1905, one of only two verdicts Johnson lost in 112 fights, and he also fought draws against George Gardner and Gus Ruhlin, both well-respected performers.

But he was basically a light-heavyweight, as was Jack Root, the man he beat to win the vacant heavyweight title at Reno in July 1905. Jeffries had retired, and acting as referee as well as promoter, the former champion staged the Hart vs. Root match and "awarded" his title to the winner. Hart's short and undistinguished reign as champion was ended by Tommy Burns over 20 rounds in February 1906, and he never came close to another championship opportunity. He had the last of his 47 fights in December 1910.

Hart died at Fern Creek, Kentucky on September 17, 1931.

Len Harvey

Born: *Stoke Climsland, England, July 11, 1907*
Titles: *British middleweight champion 1929–33, light-heavyweight champion 1933–34, 1938–42, heavyweight champion 1933–34, 1938–42, Empire heavyweight champion 1934, 1939–42, Empire light-heavyweight champion 1939–42, British recognition as world light-heavyweight champion 1939–42*
Record: *133 contests, 111 wins, 9 draws, 13 defeats*

The Cornishman, a master tactician, collected championships like parking tickets. He fought a draw for the British welterweight title in 1926, won the middleweight and light-heavyweight titles in 1929, and completed a unique treble of British titles by becoming heavyweight champion in 1933. He also won the Empire heavyweight title and a version of the world light-heavyweight title which was only recognized in Britain, as well as challenging for the world middleweight title in 1932. Modern regulations mean that his feat will never be emulated.

Harvey started boxing professionally at 12, and the precise number of his contests is unknown. He claimed 418, but was surely including booth fights, as the most that record-compilers have been able to trace is 133, spread over 22 years.

His ring achievements and gentlemanly bearing made him a national idol, and it is significant that when he joined the forces on the outbreak of the Second World War he was given officer rank. He retired after losing his "world" title to Freddie Mills in June 1942, the only knockout defeat of his long career, and died in London on November 28, 1976.

Hozumi Hasegawa

Born: *Nishiwaki, Japan, December 16, 1980*
Titles: *WBC bantamweight champion 2005–10, WBC featherweight title 2010–11*
Record: *39 contests, 34 wins, 5 defeats*

Japan's most successful boxer ever in terms of world-title defences, Hasegawa was firmly established as the best bantamweight in the world at the end of 2009.

The 5ft 5in southpaw upset the tough Thai, Veerapol Sahaprom, on a 12-round decision in Tokyo to win the WBC bantamweight title in April 2005. It was only Veerapol's second defeat in more than 50 fights, and Hasegawa proved it was no fluke by stopping him in nine rounds when they met again in Kobe, his home city, in March 2006.

When he scored a wide points win over Italy's Simone Maludrottu in January 2008, Hasegawa became the first Japanese boxer to defend a world title more than four times. That seemed to spur him on and he became increasingly destructive in terms of punching power, with his next five challengers folding inside two rounds. Nicaragua's Alvaro Perez broke the run by lasting into the fourth round in December 2009. He lost the title in his 11th defence, to Mexico's Fernando Montiel in April 2010 – a shock fourth-round stoppage – but then claimed the vacant WBC featherweight title by outpointing Juan Carlos Burgos. Hasegawa lost the title in his first defence to Jhonny Gonzalez, then went on to lose to Kiko Martinez in a challenge for the IBF super-bantamweight title.

Ricky Hatton

Born: *Manchester, England, October 6, 1978*
Titles: *IBF and WBA light-welterweight champion 2005–06, WBA welterweight champion 2006, IBF light-welterweight champion 2007*
Record: *48 contests, 45 wins, 3 defeats*

Hatton, surely one of Britain's most popular boxers ever, battled drugs, drink and depression following his crushing two-round loss to Manny Pacquiao in May 2009. In interviews, Hatton said he had considered suicide in the aftermath of his second defeat and after three-and-a-half years of turmoil without boxing, "The Hitman" was back in the ring to face former WBA welterweight champion Vyacheslav Senchenko.

He sent Hatton into permanent retirement with a ninth-round body shot and "The Hitman" left the ring at the MEN Arena in tears.

Better to remember him for another night at the same venue in June 2005 when he pummelled Kostya Tszyu to defeat in 11 rounds to take his IBF title and position at the top of the 140lb division.

Hatton parted company with promoter Frank Warren, who controlled the MEN Arena, after that, so Hatton had to look elsewhere to fight. In Sheffield in November 2005 he knocked out the WBA champion Carlos Maussa in the ninth round, but gave up both belts, opting for a move up to welterweight, following a lucrative three-fight deal in the United States.

He joined the elite band of British boxers to have won world titles in America, and in two separate weight divisions, when he edged out Brooklyn southpaw Luis Collazo over 12 rounds for the WBA welterweight belt in Boston in May 2006. Hatton's trainer, Billy Graham, believed his man should boil back down to light-welterweight and they returned to the USA, this time to Las Vegas, where Hatton regained the IBF belt with a decision over Juan Urango.

THE PEOPLE'S CHAMPION *Ricky Hatton*

HBO, who paid the bulk of his wages, were not interested in the IBF mandatory challenger, Lovemore Ndou, and so Hatton gave up the belt and knocked out Mexico's Jose Luis Castillo with a body shot. He then signed for his dream fight, a huge payday against Floyd Mayweather Jr. in Las Vegas in December 2007.

Mayweather knew too much and stopped him in ten rounds, but Hatton opted to continue his career, while parting company from Graham. He won his next two fights, then ran into Pacquiao.

David Haye

Born: *London, England, October 13, 1980*
Titles: *WBC & WBA cruiserweight champion 2007–08, WBO cruiserweight champion 2008, WBA heavyweight champion 2009–11*
Record: *31 contests, 28 wins, 3 defeats*

Haye captured the imagination of the British public in November 2009 when he outwitted the huge Russian, Nikolay Valuev, to win the WBA heavyweight championship. He triumphed despite being 11 inches shorter and conceding 99lb in weight. Trainer Adam Booth's instructions were "sting and be gone" and throughout the fight, Haye beat Valuev to the punch, then moved clear of danger.

He made sure of victory by rocking Valuev in the 12th round and later revealed he broke his right hand during the fight. The defeat of Valuev made made him Britain's first world champion at both cruiserweight and heavyweight – and he won both titles away from home.

Haye made successful defences against former champion John Ruiz and Audley Harrison, in a grudge fight, but lost his belt in a disappointing unification match with WBO and IBF champion Wladimir Klitschko in July 2011, later blaming a broken toe for his inability to cut the ring off and let his hands go.

He looked set to keep his promise to quit boxing on his 31st birthday in October 2011, but became restless in retirement and attempted to secure a match with WBC champion Vitali Klitschko. He attended the press conference after Klitschko had outpointed Dereck Chisora in Munich in February 2012 and became involved in a brawl with his fellow Londoner. Haye and Chisora met in the ring, controversially under the jurisdiction of the Luxembourg Boxing Federation in East London, Haye winning the grudge fight in five exciting rounds. Two scheduled fights with Tyson Fury were cancelled when Haye pulled out through injury.

Previously, Haye had proved he was the world's best cruiserweight with dramatic knockouts of Jean-Marc Mormeck and Enzo Maccarinelli. His blend of smart boxing, powerful punching and vulnerability made him a big attraction. At a London press conference in 2006 he talked of his heavyweight ambitions – and the perils of his profession. "I can outbox them all," he said, "but then I could get knocked out and the next time you come here I might be serving the drinks instead of talking to you!"

Haye won a silver medal at the 2001 World Amateur Championships, but early in his pro career had to rebound from a five-round defeat by Carl Thompson. His independence and insistence on training away from the spotlight in Miami made purists suspicious, but his dynamism was evident when he destroyed Alexander Gurov in 45 seconds to win the European belt in 2005. He built on his reputation with three defences, the most exciting of which was a ninth-round stoppage of Giacobbe Fragomeni, and won the WBA and WBC titles by knocking out Jean-Marc Mormeck in Paris in 2007. That set up a unification match against WBO champion Maccarinelli that Haye won inside two rounds.

Thomas Hearns

Born: *Memphis, Tennessee, October 18, 1958*
Titles: *WBA welterweight champion 1980–81, WBC light-middleweight champion 1982–86, WBC light-heavyweight champion 1987, WBC middle-weight champion 1987–88, WBO super-middleweight champion 1988–91, WBA light-heavyweight champion 1991–92*
Record: *67 contests, 61 wins, 1 draw, 5 defeats*

Although born in Tennessee, Hearns will always be associated with his adopted hometown of Detroit, where he became the most famous product of Emanuel Steward's Kronk gym. He represented America as an amateur, but had a low knockout percentage. Yet under Steward's coaching, Hearns developed into the most feared hitter of his era.

He became the first boxer to win championships at five weights, starting with the WBA welterweight crown which he took from Pipino Cuevas in 1980. That led to a unification match with Ray Leonard, which proved a classic. Leonard was trailing on points when he launched a desperate rally in the 14th, flooring Hearns to force a stoppage.

Hearns also figured in perhaps the most thrilling middleweight title fight of all, when Marvin Hagler stopped him in three dramatic rounds in 1985. The Hitman took the WBC light-middleweight title from Wilfred Benitez in 1982, the WBC light-heavyweight crown from Dennis Andries in 1987, the vacant WBC middleweight title later that year and then completed the five-timer by winning the vacant WBO super-middleweight title in 1988 – just three days before arch-rival Leonard duplicated the feat.

Amazingly, Hearns continued to box on into the 21st century, primarily because he still enjoyed it. He won what seemed to be his final fight at the age of 47 in 2006... but nobody put any money down on his settling down with the pipe and slippers.

Virgil Hill

Born: *Clinton, Missouri, January 18, 1964*
Titles: *WBA light-heavyweight champion 1987–91, 1992–97, IBF light-heavyweight champion 1996–97, WBA cruiserweight champion 2000–02 and 2006–07*
Record: *57 contests, 50 wins, 7 defeats*

The neat-boxing Hill, of Native American extraction, was beaten only twice in 24 WBA light-heavyweight title fights spread over ten years. In his home town of Bismarck, North Dakota, he drew huge crowds, in spite of a cautious, light-punching style. An outstanding amateur, he lost only 11 of 261 contests, the crowning moment coming when he won a silver medal at the 1984 Olympic Games in Los Angeles. After leaving the Main Events team early in his professional life, he developed a huge support base at home and won the WBA title for the first time in 1987 by knocking out Trinidad's Leslie Stewart in four rounds in Atlantic City.

Over the next four years he made ten successful defences – and it took a boxer as good as Thomas Hearns to dethrone him, on points in Las Vegas in 1991. Hill overcame personal problems to get his career back on track, and regained the WBA belt in September 1992 with an emphatic points win over former middleweight champion Frank Tate.

In his tenth defence, in November 1996, also a unification fight – Hill shocked the long-serving IBF champion Henry Maske, outpointing the German on a split decision. But he lost the titles when a German-based Pole, Dariusz Michalczewski, outscored him seven months later. Though he lost to Roy Jones in 1998, he became the oldest cruiserweight champion in history by winning the WBA belt twice, the first time against Fabrice Tiozzo, at the age of 36 and the second time when he was 42 against Valery Brudov.

Larry Holmes

Born: *Cuthbert, Georgia, November 3, 1949*
Titles: *WBC heavyweight champion 1978–83, IBF heavyweight champion 1983–85*
Record: *75 contests, 69 wins, 6 defeats*

Like so many who succeed idols such as Muhammad Ali, Larry Holmes was doomed to suffer by comparison with his predecessor. Yet the stylish Holmes, who once earned a living as Ali's sparring partner, was a fine fighter in his own right.

Although he had been a top-flight amateur, Holmes had to struggle for recognition when he turned professional in 1973, and found it difficult to get significant matches, until he beat the fearsome-punching Earnie Shavers in March 1978. That brought him a fight with Ken Norton for the WBC title, which Holmes won after a superb 15-rounder. He retained the title 16 times, including a highly publicized encounter with "White Hope" Gerry Cooney, and then relinquished the WBC belt in December 1983 to accept recognition from the newly formed IBF.

He lost the IBF belt in his fourth defence and 48th fight to Mike Spinks, a defeat which ruined his ambition to emulate Rocky Marciano's record of 49 unbeaten fights, and Spinks was given another dubious verdict in the rematch. Holmes tried unsuccessfully to regain the title from Mike Tyson (1988), Evander Holyfield (1992) and Oliver McCall (1995).

Evander Holyfield

Born: *Atmore, Alabama, October 19, 1962*
Titles: *WBA cruiserweight champion 1987–88, IBF cruiserweight champion 1987–88, WBC cruiserweight champion 1988, WBC, WBA and IBF heavyweight champion 1990–92, WBA heavyweight champion 1996–99, 2000–01, IBF heavyweight champion 1993–94, 1997–99*
Record: *57 contests, 44 wins, 2 draws, 10 defeats, 1 No Contest*

Holyfield is the only man to have unified the cruiserweight division, but will be best remembered for his heavyweight exploits, notably sensational wins over Mike Tyson in 1996 and 1997. In the first he was a huge underdog, but floored Tyson before stopping him in the 11th round. In the rematch, Tyson was disqualified in round three for biting Holyfield's ear.

Evander won a bronze medal at the 1984 Olympic Games, and won his first pro title in a 15-round classic with Dwight Muhammad Qawi in Atlanta in 1986. By 1988, Holyfield was the undisputed cruiserweight champion, and moved up to heavyweight in search of Tyson. Buster Douglas had dethroned Tyson, but Holyfield knocked out Douglas in three rounds in October 1990. After three defences, Holyfield lost a classic 12-rounder with Riddick Bowe in November 1992. A rematch with Bowe saw Holyfield pull off a shock win to regain the WBA and IBF belts, but in 1994 Michael Moorer outpointed him and 19 months later Bowe stopped him in eight rounds.

Holyfield proved his superiority over Tyson and established his place in history. However, a lucky draw with Lennox Lewis in March 1999 suggested age might finally have caught up with him. He lost a rematch with Lewis that November, but held the WBA title again briefly when, after Lewis had been stripped following a court order Holyfield had a trio of fights with John Ruiz of Massachusetts. Holyfield, won the first, lost the second and drew the third. After losing to Larry Donald in 2004, the New York State Athletic Commission were so concerned about

Holyfield that they suspended his licence on medical grounds.

He managed to get it overturned and came back again in 2006, even forcing his way to title shots against, first, Sultan Ibragimov, then Nikolay Valuev, but lost the decision to both. Financial problems meant Holyfield carried on fighting and he won the lightly-regarded WBF belt with a win over fellow veteran Frans Botha.

Lloyd Honeyghan

Born: *Jamaica, April 22, 1960*
Titles: *British welterweight champion 1983–86, European champion 1985–86, Commonwealth champion champion 1985–86, world welterweight champion 1986, WBC and IBF champion 1986–87, WBC champion 1988–89, Commonwealth light-middleweight champion 1993–94*
Record: *48 contests, 43 wins, 5 defeats*

When he faced Don Curry for the undisputed welterweight championship on September 27, 1986, virtually no one apart from Lloyd Honeyghan (who had backed himself to win $25,000) and his manager Mickey Duff gave the challenger a realistic chance. Yet six rounds later Honeyghan was world champion, as the demoralized American, hitherto regarded as the world's best pound-for-pound fighter, retired. It was the summit of Honeyghan's career.

He learned his boxing in Bermondsey's Fisher Club, after the family had moved to London when he was a youngster. He represented England and won the London championship before turning professional under Terry Lawless, who guided him to the British and European titles before they split acrimoniously.

Honeyghan relinquished the WBA title in December 1986, and lost his WBC championship to Jorge Vaca on a technical decision in October 1987, when the IBF also stripped him. He regained the WBC title from Vaca in March 1988, holding it for a year until Marlon Starling stopped him in nine rounds. He was outclassed by Mark Breland for the WBA title, but made a moderately successful comeback, winning the Commonwealth light-middleweight title. He retired in 1995.

Bernard Hopkins

Born: *Philadelphia, PA, January 15, 1965*
Titles: *IBF middleweight champion 1995–2005, WBA and WBC middleweight champion 2001–05, WBO middleweight champion 2004–05, WBC light-heavyweight title 2011–12, IBF light-heavyweight champion 2013–14, WBA Super light-heavyweight champion 2014*
Record: *67 contests, 55 wins, 2 draws, 2 no contests, 8 defeats*

In May 2011, Hopkins became the oldest boxer to win a world title when, aged 46 years four months and six days, he took the WBC light-heavyweight championship from Jean Pascal in Montreal. Two years later, he broke his own record by outpointing Tavoris Cloud for the IBF light-heavyweight title, having lost the WBC belt to Chad Dawson.

Hopkins added the WBA Super belt with a points win over Beibut Shumenov before, in 2014, he took an ambitious match with WBO champion Sergey Kovalev. That proved to be a miracle even beyond "The Alien" and he lost a wide points decision after being dropped in the first.

Fiercely competitive, independent and eccentric, Hopkins had to wait for full acknowledgement of his talents, but eventually, at the age of 36, proved his right to be called the genuine, undisputed world middleweight champion. A product of the Philadelphia streets, he served five years in jail before making a career out of boxing. After losing his debut in October 1988, only Roy Jones beat him in the next 17 years. That was in 1993, when Jones outboxed him over 12 rounds for the IBF middleweight crown.

When Jones moved up, Hopkins took over – and eventually unified the three major titles in 2001 when he outpointed WBC champion Keith Holmes and stopped the undefeated WBA holder Felix Trinidad in the 12th round. Hopkins then put WBO champion Oscar De La Hoya in his place in Las Vegas in September 2004 to complete a clean sweep of the belts, knocking out "The Golden Boy" with a ninth-round left hook.

After 20 successful defences in ten years, Hopkins lost the world title on a close, disputed decision to Jermain Taylor. The rematch, equally close, also went against him. After toying with retirement, Hopkins cemented links with De La Hoya as a part of the Golden Boy promotional operation and, in 2006, outboxed the world's best light-heavyweight, Antonio Tarver. In 2008, Hopkins, aged 43, lost a split decision to Joe Calzaghe, but then outpointed unbeaten middleweight champion Kelly Pavlik.

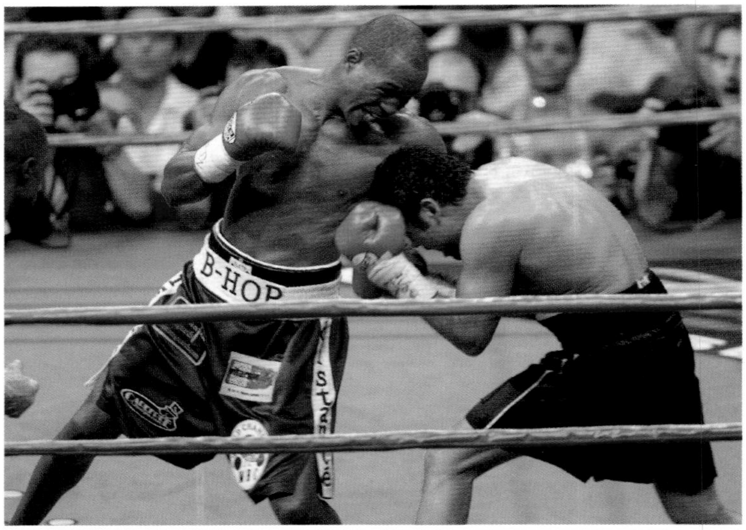

BERNHARD HOPKINS *is a rock-chinned, iron-willed fans' favourite who doesn't seem to understand the idea of taking a step backwards*

Marco Huck

Born: *Ugao, Serbia, November 11, 1984*
Titles: *WBO cruiserweight champion 2009–15, IBO cruiser-weight champion 2016–17*
Record: *41 contests, 38 wins, 1 draw, 2 defeats*

In August, 2014, Marco Huck outpointed Mirko Larghetii to defend his WBO cruiserweight title for the 14th time and equal Johnny Nelson's record for cruiserweight-title defences. But he lost in his next fight, knocked out in the 11th round by Pole Krzysztov Glowacki. He took the IBO version of the belt in his next fight, against Ola Apolabi, before losing it to Mairis Briedis in April 2017.

Coming from a kickboxing background, Huck at times appears to have little knowledge of boxing's fundamentals. He compensates for that with an unbreakable will to win. Alexander Alexeev, the European champion, described him as "a hurricane in the ring."

Huck, who fled war-torn Yugoslavia with his family when he was eight years old and settled in Germany, took the WBO cruiserweight title from Victor Emilio Ramirez in August 2009 and proved he was the division's best by out-toughing Ola Afolabi and Denis Lebedev in title defences.

In need of a new challenge, Huck met Alexander Povetkin for the WBA heavyweight title in February 2012 and given little chance before the fight, he was afterwards considered unlucky to drop a majority points decision.

Naoya Inoue

Born: *Yokohama, Japan, April 10, 1993*
Titles: *WBA light-flyweight champion 2014, WBO super-flyweight champion 2014–*
Record: *15 contests, 15 wins*

Good enough to reach the last 16 of the world amateur championships at 18 years old, Naoya Inoue captured world titles at two weights within his first eight professional fights.

He took the WBC light-flyweight title from Adrian Hernandez with a

NAOYA INOUE *celebrates another win*

sixth-round stoppage, made a successful defence against Samartlek Kokietgym, then jumped up two weight divisions to challenge Omar Narvaez for the WBO super-flyweight title.

Thirty-nine-year-old Narvaez was making his 12th title defence and Inoue dropped him four times inside two rounds, the final knockdown coming from a left hook to the body that left the Argentine on his knees for the full count.

By 2017, he had won all 15 of his professional fights.

James J. Jeffries

Born: *Carroll, Ohio, April 15, 1875*
Titles: *World heavyweight champion 1899–1905*
Record: *21 contests, 18 wins, 2 draws, 1 defeat*

By modern standards, Jeffries was not a big heavyweight, weighing around 220lb and standing 6ft $2\frac{1}{2}$in tall, but in his time he was considered a giant. Because of his bulk and his ability to absorb punishment, he was a popular choice as sparring partner for the leading heavyweights, but he soon established his worth as a contender and, in 1899, knocked out Bob Fitzsimmons to become champion after only 13 fights.

He made seven defences, including a 23-round knockout of his former employer James J. Corbett. He retired in August 1910, undefeated in 20 fights, of which he had won 15 by knockout and drawn two. But the eventual succession of Jack Johnson to the championship sparked a wave of racist feeling in America and Jeffries, by then a 35-year-old farmer, was persuaded to return to the ring in order, as novelist Jack London infamously phrased it, "to wipe the smile off the nigger's face".

They met in Reno on July 4, 1910, and Johnson administered a painful beating before stopping him in the 15th round. Jeffries died in Burbank, California on March 3, 1953.

Eder Jofre

Born: *Sao Paulo, Brazil, March 26, 1936*
Titles: *NBA bantamweight champion 1960–62, world bantamweight champion 1962–65, WBC featherweight champion 1973–74*
Record: *78 contests, 72 wins, 4 draws, 2 defeats*

One of the few vegetarians ever to win a world boxing title, Jofre turned professional in March 1957. His heavy punching soon made him a championship contender, and wins over top men like Danny Kid, Ernesto Miranda (for the South American title) and Mexico's perennial contender Joe Medel brought him a match with Eloy Sanchez for the vacant NBA bantamweight title, Jofre winning in six rounds.

He defeated Europe's representative John Caldwell to become undisputed champion in January 1962, and went on to compile an undefeated record of 50 fights (including three draws) until the tough Japanese slugger Fighting Harada took his title in May 1965. He retired after an unsuccessful attempt to regain the championship from Harada, but returned as a featherweight in 1969 after a three-year layoff and over the next three years fought his way to the WBC title, which he won from Jose Legra in May 1973.

The WBC stripped him in June 1974 for failing to meet their leading contender, and he retired for good after seven more fights. He later became a successful businessman and politician.

Ingemar Johansson

Born: *Gothenburg, Sweden, October 16, 1932*
Titles: *European heavyweight champion 1956–59, 1962–63, world champion 1959–60*
Record: *28 contests, 26 wins, 2 defeats*

The Swede had the unusual experience of going from national disgrace to national hero. He was disqualified for "not trying" against Ed Sanders in the 1952 Olympic final in Helsinki, but laid that ghost by knocking out Floyd Patterson to become the world heavyweight champion in 1959. He had a stunning right-hand punch, which the press nicknamed "Ingo's Bingo" when he started to build a knockout record after turning professional in December 1952.

He took the European title from Franco Cavicchi, and retained it with knockouts of British challengers Henry Cooper and Joe Erskine. But it was his first-round knockout of the classy American Eddie Machen which brought him his big chance. Patterson was floored seven times before the referee intervened in the third round. Johansson held on to his championship crown for less than a year before Patterson knocked him cold in the rematch and then flattened him again in their third meeting. They were the only losses in his professional career.

He won back the European title from Dick Richardson, but retired after one more fight. In retirement Johansson reaped the rewards of some sound business investments, lived in Miami for some time and then returned to Sweden. Before the onset of dementia in the 1990s, he became a succcessful big-fight analyst on Scandinavian television. Johannson died on January 30, 2009.

Chris John

Born: *Banjarnegara, Java, Indonesia, September 14, 1979*
Titles: *WBA featherweight champion 2004–13*
Record: *51 contests, 48 wins, 2 draws, 1 defeat*

John became one of the comparatively few champions from the Far East to break into the American market when he defended his WBA featherweight crown against Texan Rocky Juarez in Houston in February 2009. After 12 rounds, all three judges scored it level at 114–114, making a rematch inevitable. This time, on the bigger stage of the MGM Grand, Las Vegas, the long-reigning Indonesian proved his class, scoring a unanimous decision.

POWER-PUNCHER *Ingemar Johansson tunes up for a 1962 European title bid*

John began boxing as a child, taught by his father, and also learned the martial art of wushu. He turned professional in 1998, and held the WBA-backed Pan Asian Boxing Association belt for some time before a shot at the interim world belt brought him wider recognition, courtesy of a 12-round split decision over Oscar Leon in 2003.

He was recognized as the full WBA champion in 2004, and, the following year, switched his training base from Indonesia to Perth, Australia. Wins at home over established stars Derrick Gainer and Juan Manuel Marquez gave him greater credibility, though the rumblings that his successes were somehow merely a result of fighting at home continued.

He shook off those criticisms in 2009 with his performances against Juarez and the featherweight title was finally lost in his 19th defence – a record for the division bettered only by Eusebio Pedroza – to Simpiwe Vetyeka. John announced his retirement afterwards.

Jack Johnson

see Legends of the Ring (pp 82–83)

Marvin Johnson

Born: *Indianapolis, Indiana, April 12, 1954*
Titles: *WBC light-heavyweight champion 1978–79, WBA light-heavyweight champion 1979–80, 1986–87*
Record: *49 contests, 43 wins, 6 defeats*

The balding Johnson became a byword for courage, featuring in some of the toughest light-heavyweight battles of recent times. He won the 1972 Golden Gloves and took a bronze medal in the same year's Munich Olympics, turning professional in 1973. His early progress was slow, managing only 13 fights in four years, but the turning point was his first defeat, a 12th-round stoppage by Matthew Saad Muhammad in a titanic battle for the NABF title.

Wins over Billy Douglas (Buster's father), Eddie Davis and Jerry Celestine earned him a fight with Mate Parlov in December 1978 for the WBC title, and Johnson won in ten rounds. Franklin dethroned him only four months later, but Johnson was a champion again before 1979 was out, stopping Victor Galindez in 11 rounds for the WBA belt. Once more, his reign was short: Eddie Gregory stopped him three months later, and then Mike Spinks knocked him out.

It looked like the end, but in February 1986 he stopped Leslie Stewart for the vacant WBA title, losing it in a rematch a year later.

Junior Jones

Born: *Brooklyn, New York, December 19, 1970*
Titles: *WBA bantamweight champion 1993–94, WBO super-bantamweight champion 1996–97*
Record: *56 contests, 50 wins, 6 defeats*

Junior Jones' recovery from has-been to world champion was one of the success stories of the mid-1990s. The smooth-boxing New Yorker looked set for greatness as he won the WBA bantamweight title in his 31st unbeaten fight, 22 of which he had won inside the distance. He retained it once, then took a shocking beating as the unheralded John Johnson stopped him in 11 rounds in Las Vegas in 1994.

He moved up to super-bantam, blaming his defeat on weight-making, but a third-round loss to the unranked Darryl Pinkney in October 1994 seemed to spell the end. Instead, he put together a winning run of nine, including a 12-round points win over former bantamweight great Orlando Canizales for the IBC title, to earn a crack at Marco Antonio Barrera's WBO super-bantamweight title. Jones blasted the Mexican in five rounds, then outscored him in a rematch in 1997.

Dramatic defeats by Kennedy McKinney and Erik Morales clouded his reputation and his last world title shot brought an 11th-round defeat by Paul Ingle in New York in April 2000. Jones retired two years later and became a trainer.

Roy Jones Jr

Born: *Pensacola, Florida, January 16, 1969*
Titles: *IBF middleweight champion 1993–94, IBF super-middleweight champion 1994–96, WBC light-heavyweight champion 1997–2003 and 2003–04, WBA light-heavyweight champion 1998–2003, WBA heavyweight champion 2003*
Record: *75 contests, 66 wins, 9 defeats*

Jones's father, Roy Sr, was a competent professional middleweight who fought Marvin Hagler in 1977. Jones Jr. won the National Golden Gloves at light-welterweight in 1986, aged 17, and at light-middleweight in 1987, going on to take a silver medal in the 1988 Olympics where a scandalously unjust verdict robbed him of victory.

He turned professional under his father's cautious management, but eventually won the IBF middleweight title with a safety-first points win over Bernard Hopkins in 1993. In 1994 he moved up to 168lb and dethroned IBF super-middleweight champion James Toney. After five defences he moved on to the light-heavyweight division, outpointing Mike McCallum to become a three-weight world champion.

A disqualification defeat against Montell Griffin was a momentary hiccup, but Jones blasted him out in the rematch and won a unification fight with WBA champion Lou Del Valle on points in New York in July 1998. In spite of his no-risk attitude, Jones was widely acknowledged as the best pound-for-pound fighter in the business.

He took his career to a new level when he moved up to heavyweight and outboxed WBA heavyweight champion John Ruiz in March 2003, but it seemed to take something out of him. He barely beat Florida rival Antonio Tarver and in a sensational rematch was knocked out in the second round.

Defeats by Glen Johnson and Tarver in a decider seemed to finish him, but he refused to quit. He beat fellow old-timer Felix Trinidad, but lost to Joe Calzaghe – both fights at Madison Square Garden – beat former champ Jeff Lacy, but then lost in one to Danny Green, a result he protested bitterly. More decisive was the April 2010 rematch defeat to Hopkins on points and a 10-round knock-out loss to Denis Lebedev. Still Jones carried on fighting.

Anthony Joshua

Real name: *Anthony Joshua*
Born: *Watford, Hertfordshire, England, October 15, 1989*
Titles: *IBF heavyweight champion 2016–, WBA heavyweight champion 2017–, IBO heavyweight champion 2017–*
Record: *20 contests, 20 wins*

Blessed with a powerful, athletic frame, Anthony Joshua turned to boxing aged 18 to put a troubled childhood behind him and carved out a successful amateur career. He was a silver medallist at the 2011 World Championships, and then went on to become a gold medallist at the 2012 Olympic Games.

He turned professional in 2013, and the boxing world eagerly kept an eye on his progress. The excitement rose when he won his first professional fight with a first-round knockout. The boy could punch. Fifteen fights and 15 knockouts later, his meteoric rise (and spectacular style) brought him a world title shot against Charles Martin, the reigning IBF heavyweight champion who had won 23 of his 24 professional fights (18 of them by knockout). Joshua sent him sprawling to the canvas in the first round and again in the second – he had become world champion.

Impressive title defences followed against Dominic Breazedale and Eric Mollina, before Joshua faced the biggest challenge of his career: Wladimir Klitschko at Wembley Stadium, with his IBF title and the vacant WBA and IBO titles at stake. The fight was a modern-day classic: roared on by an 85,000-strong crowd, both men ended up on the canvas before Joshua landed the bout-winning punch in the 11th round. Victory brought him the chance to unify the heavyweight division in a bout against New Zealand's Joseph Parker.

Stanley Ketchel

Real name: *Stanislaus Kiecal*
Born: *Grand Rapids, Michigan, September 14, 1886*
Titles: *World middleweight champion 1906–08, 1908–09*
Record: *64 contests, 52 wins, 4 draws, 4 No Decisions, 4 defeats*

The son of a Russian father and Polish mother, Ketchel's heavy punching and non-stop aggression soon gained him a reputation, and by 1906 he was already claiming the middleweight title vacated by Tommy Ryan. He beat all three rival claimants in 1908, but lost in bizarre circumstances in a rematch with one of them, Billy Papke, in September 1908. Papke punched him in the throat before the first bell, and Ketchel was so dazed that he took four counts in the first round before losing in the 12th.

He beat Papke mercilessly in the return, and then faced heavyweight champion Jack Johnson. Johnson had agreed to "carry" Ketchel, whom he outweighed by 35lb, but in the 12th round Ketchel tried to double-cross the champion and knocked him down. Johnson got straight up and flattened Ketchel with the next punch.

Ketchel stuck to the middle-weights after that, and was still champion when he was shot dead in a dispute over a woman at Conway, Missouri on October 15, 1910.

Amir Khan

Born: *Bolton, England, December 8, 1986*
Titles: *WBA light-welterweight champion 2009–12, IBF light-welterweight champion 2011*
Record: *35 contests, 31 wins, 4 defeats*

Khan never boxed better than he did when outpointing Devon Alexander in December 2014. He won unanimously on the scorecards. That was his fourth fight with trainer Virgil Hunter, who first saw Khan when, as a 17 year-old, he won silver at the 2004 Athens Olympics.

Khan has electrifying hand speed and skills – but his chin has let him down. He repaired the damage done by a 54-second loss to heavy-handed Colombian Breidis Prescott with a cuts points win over faded Mexican legend Marco Antonio Barrera, then took the WBA light-welterweight title from Andriy Kotelnik with a clear-cut points win in Manchester in July 2009.

He blew away Dmitry Salita in just 76 seconds, then marked his American debut with an 11-round stoppage of Paul Malignaggi at Madison Square Garden. Then-trainer Freddie Roach reportedly advised Khan against meeting mandatory challenger Marcos Maidana, but Khan went ahead with the fight and got through a tough 10th round to hang on to his belt.

He added the IBF belt by knocking out Zab Judah, then lost both titles to Lamont Peterson, but was reinstated as champion by the WBA after the American failed a drugs test. The title was lost to WBC champion Danny Garcia in five rounds in July 2012 and a further defeat to Saul Alvarez in May 2016 left his career in the balance.

Johnny Kilbane

Born: *Cleveland, Ohio, April 18, 1889*
Titles: *World featherweight champion 1912–23*
Record: *142 contests, 51 wins, 7 draws, 78 No Decisions, 2 No Contests, 4 defeats*

Kilbane first fought in 1907, but became one of the most reluctant world champions in history. He won the featherweight title in 1912, but defended it only four times in 11 years. An artful fighter, he scored 21 inside-the-distance wins in a 16-year career, but was as much at ease against top lightweights like Benny Leonard as against men his own size.

He dethroned Abe Attell in 1912, and drew with future champion Johnny Dundee in his first defence in 1913. But despite a busy schedule of No Decision contests he did not defend again for three years, or for a further five years after that. The New York Commission finally stripped him of their version of the title, but Kilbane was tempted out of semi-retirement to face French war hero Eugene Criqui, who finished his career with a sixth-round knockout. Kilbane later became a State Senator, and died in Cleveland on May 31, 1957.

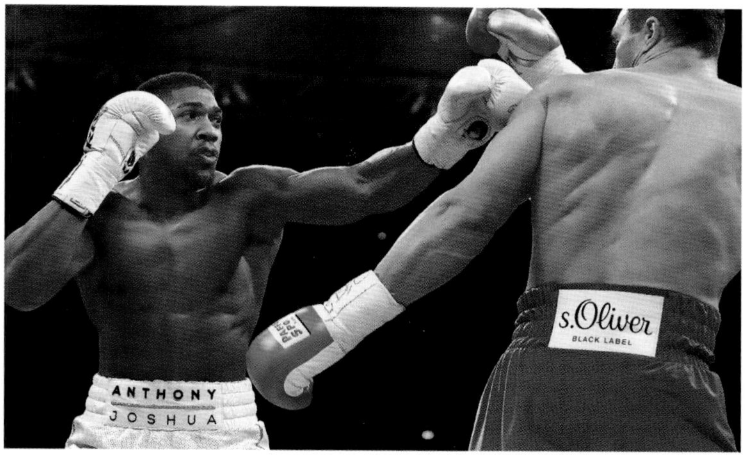

ANTHONY JOSHUA *is the bright new thing on the heavyweight block*

Pone Kingpetch

Born: *Hui Hui Province, Thailand, February 12, 1936*
Titles: *World flyweight champion 1960–62, 1963, 1964–65*
Record: *40 contests, 33 wins, 7 defeats*

Thailand's first world champion started boxing in 1955. He entered the world ratings when he took the Orient flyweight title from the tough Filipino Danny Kid in 1957, lost to Leo Espinosa in his first defence but regained it from Hitoshi Misako.

His career faltered in 1958–59, when he had only five fights, but in April 1960 he fought Pascual Perez, who had been world champion for five years. The champion could never get to grips with a challenger who was seven inches taller, and was soundly outpointed. Kingpetch went to Los Angeles for a rematch in September 1960, and knocked him out in the eighth round.

He retained the title twice, but then Japan's Fighting Harada knocked him out in October 1962. Three months later, Kingpetch outscored Harada to become the first man to regain the flyweight title, but he lost it again on a first-round knockout to Hiroyuki Ebihara. He became champion for the third time by outpointing Ebihara in January 1964, but lost it to Salvatore Burruni the following year. He died in 1982.

Vitali Klitschko

Born: *Belovodsk, Kyrgyzstan, July 19, 1971*
Titles: *WBO heavyweight champion 1999–2000, WBC heavyweight champion 2004–05, 2008–*
Record: *47 contests, 45 wins, 2 draws*

In December, 2013, Vitali Klitschko announced he was vacating the WBC heavyweight title and didn't expect to fight again. He was set to pursue a career in politics and anyway, he had run out of meaningful challengers. He made 11 defences in his second reign as champion – and had outclassed unbeatens Chris Arreola, Kevin Johnson and Odlanier Solis and Manuel Charr.

Nicknamed "Dr Ironfist", Vitali Klitschko was considered far more robotic and less talented than his brother Wladimir, yet it was Vitali who emerged as the natural successor to Lennox Lewis.

Vitali fought Lewis in Los Angeles in June 2003, replacing the injured Kirk Johnson, whom Lewis had taken lightly. The substitution caused more problems for Lewis as Klitschko had already prepared well for a fight on the undercard. When Lewis came in too heavy, the signs were plain to see – and Klitschko more than stood up to the champion. After six rounds, Klitschko was ahead on the scorecards, but two dreadful cuts over his left eye meant the ringside doctor ruled him out. A rematch was suggested in December 2003, but Lewis announced his retirement.

Klitschko became WBC champion by stopping South African southpaw Corrie Sanders in eight rounds in Los Angeles, then disposed of British challenger, Danny Williams. Repeated injuries forced him to retire briefly, but after considering a career in politics in Ukraine, he returned in 2008. He surprised many by electing to go straight for a shot at his old WBC title, but his judgement proved sound: at the age of 37 he still knew way too much for Nigeria's Samuel Peter, who retired at the end of eight one-sided rounds.

Vitali and his brother were from a middle-class family. Their father was a colonel in the Soviet airforce and their mother a teacher. As children, they moved around wherever their father was posted. Thus, Vitali was born in Kyrgyzstan and Wladimir in Kazakhstan. Vitali was in line to box in the Olympics, until a Ukrainian doctor gave him ointment for a leg injury that contained a banned substance. He was suspended and so turned to the professional business in Germany.

He won the minor WBO title with a second round knockout of Herbie Hide in London in 1999, but lost it when he elected to retire after the ninth round against Chris Byrd in a fight he was winning comfortably. He explained that he had a shoulder injury and felt it stupid to go on and risk a chronic injury. This did not endear him to American television critics, and it took until the Lewis fight in 2003, when he boxed with such grim determination, to persuade them of his world-class abilities and ambitions

Wladimir Klitschko

Born: *Semipalatansk, Kazakhstan, March 25, 1976*
Titles: *WBO heavyweight champion 2000–03 and 2008–15, IBF heavyweight champion 2006–15*
Record: *69 contests, 64 wins, 5 defeats*

Wladimir Klitschko held a version of the world heavyweight title between 2006 and 2015 and only Joe Louis has held the title for longer. Klitschko beat Chris Byrd to win the IBF heavyweight title and his points win over Bryant Jennings in November 2014 was his 18th successful world-title defence.

Five months earlier, Klitschko had handed a five-round knock-out to Kubrat Pulev at Madison Square Garden. Though not fancied to win, Pulev was expected to give Klitschko as much trouble as anyone, but instead was blasted out by left hooks. For a while at least, that helped Klitschko shed his safety-first, negative reputation.

His career-best performances were his rematch against Samuel Peter and the unification fight against David Haye. In September 2005, Klitschko decisioned Peter after being floored three times. Five years later he punished Peter and the fight could have been stopped long before the 10th-round ending.

His clash with Haye in July 2011 was hyped as the biggest heavyweight fight for years and although Klitschko was a clear points winner, it was a disappointing spectacle for the thousands of fans who sat through the rain in Hamburg.

Eight title defences followed over the next four years… and then Wladimir ran into Tyson Fury. He could not deal with the Englishman's size and tactics and lost a unanimous points decision. His swansong came against hard-hitting Anthony Joshua at Wembley in April 2017, which ended when he was knocked down in the 11th round.

Wladimir replaced elder brother Vitali at super-heavyweight in the Ukrainian team for the Atlanta Olympics in 1996. He had planned to grind himself down to the amateur heavyweight limit until Vitali tested positive for steroids and was barred. Wladimir won the gold medal.

He turned pro alongside Vitali in Germany under promoter Klaus Peter Kohl in 1996. In spite of losing to Ross Purrity in Kiev in 1998, when he ran out of stamina in the 11th round, he went on to win the European title and then, in October 2000, beat Chris Byrd to win the WBO heavyweight title. Byrd had been lucky to take the title from Vitali because of a shoulder injury, but was never in the fight against Wladimir, who knocked him down twice and outpointed him.

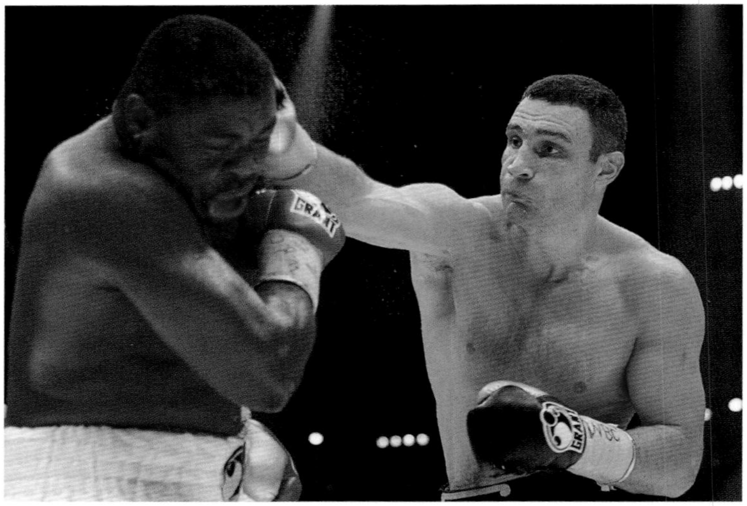

VITALI KLITSCHKO *ruled the heavyweight division between 2006 and 2015*

Wladimir turned down a string of challenges for the WBO belt, but then lost sensationally against heavy-handed South African southpaw Corrie Sanders in Hannover in March 2003. Sanders seemed to have taken the fight for some retirement money, but nailed Klitschko in the first round and finished him off in the second. A year later, he boxed for the vacant WBO belt, seemed to be doing as he pleased against Lamon Brewster, but came apart and was stopped in five.

It seemed all over, but Klitschko kept his career going by outpointing Peter and then beat Byrd in seven rounds to earn IBF recognition as champion in April 2006. A seventh-round stoppage of Calvin Brock seemed to prove Klitschko was the best in the world, but he disappointed when adding Sultan Ibragimov's WBO title in a unification fight at Madison Square Garden.

Sergey Kovalev

Born: *Kopeysk, Russia, February 4, 1983*
Titles: *WBO light-heavyweight champion 2013–17, WBA Super, IBF and WBO light-heavyweight champion 2014–17*
Record: *34 contests, 31 wins, 2 defeats, 1 draw*

Sergey "Krusher" Kovalev took the WBO light-heavyweight title from Nathan Cleverly in August 2013, coolly dismantling the Welshman and dropping him three times on the way to a fourth-round stoppage.

He described the belt as "the first in my collection" and, 15 months later, added the WBA Super and IBF titles with a unanimous points win over 49 year-old Bernard Hopkins.

Kovalev dropped Hopkins in the first, more than matched him for ring craft and went on to gain a unanimous points decision.

He grew up in poverty in the Ural Mountains after his parents separated and started boxing aged 11. Kovalev took a break from boxing, following his stepfather's death, until his amateur coach convinced him to return. He twice won gold at the World Military Games before heading to America to turn professional.

Kovalev found it hard to get fights, and was devastated when

SERGEY KOVALEV *held three belts at 32*

Roman Simakov died three days after they fought. After considering retirement, a two-round stoppage of Darnell Boone, in a rematch, led to a deal with Main Events.

He lost his belts following back-to-back defeats against Andre Ward in 2016 and 2017, the first on points and the second an eighth-round kockout.

Jake LaMotta

Real name: *Giacobe LaMotta*
Born: *Bronx, NY, July 10, 1921*
Titles: *World middleweight champion 1949–51*
Record: *106 contests, 83 wins, 4 draws, 19 defeats*

LaMotta gloried in his well-deserved reputation as a tough guy, and indeed the crude but immensely strong New Yorker – immortalized in the film *Raging Bull* – had almost super-human endurance in the ring.

He scored his most famous victory in February 1943 when he became the first man to beat Sugar Ray Robinson, but it was the only time he got the better of Robinson in six meetings. He also had a four-fight series with former welterweight champion Fritzie Zivic, winning that three to one, but successive champions declined to give him a title shot. Finally, he did a deal with the gangsters who ran the sport at the time: he would take a dive against Blackjack Billy Fox, a light-heavyweight they were promoting, in return for a title fight.

LaMotta duly obliged against Fox, but had to wait two years to get his reward, when Marcel Cerdan retired with an injured shoulder after nine rounds of their title fight. He retained the crown with a last-gasp knockout of Laurent Dauthuille, but then lost it to Robinson in February 1951. He died aged 95 in September 2017.

Sam Langford

Born: *Weymouth, Canada, February 12, 1880*
Titles: *None*
Record: *314 contests, 181 wins, 33 draws, 66 No Decisions, 34 defeats*

Had Langford been white, he would have been one of the great champions of the early century at any weight from middleweight upwards, but in those days opportunities were rare for good black fighters and so he spent much of his career having a long series of fights with others in the same predicament. He faced Harry Wills 18 times, Sam McVey 15, Joe Jeanette 14, Jeff Clark 13 and Jim Barry 12: a total of 72 fights against just five opponents. Known as "The Boston Tar Baby", Langford was only 5ft 7in tall and rarely scaled more than the middleweight limit, but he routinely gave away chunks of weight to genuine heavyweights just in order to keep busy.

Despite his fine record of almost 300 fights, he was never given a crack at a world title, although he faced many men who were or became champions. His career lasted until 1924, when he was virtually blind. He later went completely blind and lived in poverty until a newspaper highlighted his plight and raised enough money to keep him in modest comfort until his death in Cambridge, Mass, on January 12, 1956, aged 75.

Jose Legra

Born: *Baracoa, Cuba, April 19, 1943*
Titles: *European featherweight champion 1967–68, 1970–72, WBC featherweight champion 1968–69, 1972–73*
Record: *150 contests, 134 wins, 4 draws, 12 defeats*

The flashy, long-armed Legra, who favoured the "bolo punch" popularized by fellow-Cuban Kid Gavilan, was the busiest top-class fighter of his era, packing 150 fights into a 13-year career which began in Havana in 1960. He moved to Spain in 1963, and compiled an astonishing run of 83 fights with just one defeat, on points to Howard Winstone, between his European debut and his revenge win over Winstone for the WBC featherweight title in July 1968.

He had earlier knocked out Yves Desmarets to become European champion in December 1967, having taken out Spanish citizenship. He was surprisingly outpointed in his first WBC title defence by Johnny Famechon of Australia, and a later points loss to Vicente Saldivar seemed to rule him out of contention. But he carried on at European level, regaining and defending the continental title.

In December 1972 he finally got another world title chance and he took it, stopping Clemente Sanchez in ten rounds in Monterrey, Mexico. Sanchez was overweight, but the WBC agreed to recognize Legra as the new champion. He was dethroned in his next fight by Eder Jofre, then retired soon afterwards.

Benny Leonard

Real name: *Benjamin Leiner*
Born: *New York, NY, April 7, 1896*
Titles: *World lightweight champion 1917–25*
Record: *217 contests, 90 wins, 1 draw, 121 No Decisions, 5 defeats*

Leonard began and ended his career with knockout defeats, but in between compiled a remarkable record and reigned for seven years as world lightweight champion. More than half his contests were No Decision affairs, but his inside-schedule victories over boxers of the quality of Freddie Welsh, Johnny Kilbane, Charlie White and Richie Mitchell show that he must have been an impressive performer.

He won the title in disputed circumstances from Welsh, after flooring him three times to force a ninth-round stoppage. The fight was a No Decision match and Welsh was over the weight limit anyway, but his protests went unheeded and Leonard was accepted as the new champion.

His reputation was tarnished by a curious disqualification in a welterweight title bid against Jack Britton, when he deliberately struck Britton on the ground after flooring him. He retired as undefeated champion in 1924, but lost his savings in the Wall Street Crash of 1929 and returned to the ring, quitting for good in 1932. He died of a heart attack in New York on April 18, 1947, while refereeing a fight.

Sugar Ray Leonard

see Legends of the Ring (pp 84–85)

Gus Lesnevich

Born: *Cliffside Park, New Jersey, February 22, 1915*
Titles: *World light-heavyweight champion 1941–46*
Record: *79 contests, 60 wins, 5 draws, 14 defeats*

Lesnevich was one of those unfortunate champions who lost the best years of his career to the Second World War, which America joined shortly after he had won the light-heavyweight title in May 1941. He was out of the ring from March 1942 to January 1946.

Of Russian stock, he started boxing professionally in 1934 after winning the National Golden Gloves, and his only defeats in five years were to sometime world champions Freddie Steele and Young Corbett III, and to the Australian Ron Richards. He moved up to light-heavyweight after a four-fight trip to Australia in 1938–39, and lost twice in bids for Billy Conn's title before beating Anton Christoforodis to become champion at last.

Lesnevich made five defences, including a famous victory over Freddie Mills, but was outscored by Mills in a return fight in July 1948. Joey Maxim beat him for the American title in May 1949, and when Ezzard Charles knocked him out in his next fight, a challenge for Charles' NBA heavyweight crown, Lesnevich retired. He died at his Cliffside home on February 28, 1964.

John Henry Lewis

Born: *Los Angeles, California, May 1, 1914*
Titles: *World light-heavyweight champion 1935–39*
Record: *117 contests, 103 wins, 6 draws, 8 defeats*

Lewis dominated the light-heavyweight division from 1935 until his retirement as undefeated champion four years later. A stylish and hard-punching boxer, he lost only two of his first 56 fights, both to sometime world champions Maxie Rosenbloom and James J. Braddock, whom he had previously outscored.

Oddly, he lost both his fights immediately before challenging Bob Olin for the world title: Rosenbloom outpointed him to level their series at 2–2, and the relatively obscure Abe Feldman also beat him on points. His win over Olin was a hard-fought affair, and when he boxed again only four weeks later against his perennial rival Rosenbloom, he lost their non-title fight on points.

Lewis defended the championship five times, and kept busy on the non-title circuit with a total of 51 appearances, which today's champions would find unthinkable. But he developed eye problems, and by late 1938 his sight was failing fast. Heavyweight king Joe Louis, a close friend, agreed to give him a title shot, and some welcome retirement money, on condition that Lewis never boxed again. Louis won in the first round, and Lewis kept his word.

Lennox Lewis

see Legends of the Ring (pp 86–87)

Ted "Kid" Lewis

Real name: *Gershon Mendeloff*
Born: *London, England, October 24, 1893*
Titles: *British featherweight champion 1913, European featherweight champion 1914, world welterweight champion 1915–16, 1917–19, British and European welterweight champion 1920, British & European middleweight champion 1921–23, Empire middleweight champion 1922–23, Empire welterweight champion 1924*
Record: *300 contests, 193 wins, 13 draws, 65 No Decisions, 29 defeats*

GLOBETROTTER *Kid Lewis fought anywhere*

The indefatigable Lewis had 48 fights in 1911 alone, more than Ray Leonard had in his entire career. Starting at 14 in 1909, he thought nothing of boxing three or four times a week, and by the time he won the British featherweight title in October 1913, three weeks before his 19th birthday, he was already a veteran of 115 contests. He added the European title, then toured Australia before heading for America where he twice won and lost the welterweight title in a famous 20-fight series with Jack Britton.

He returned to Britain in 1919, and in five years won British, Empire and European titles at welterweight and middleweight, claimed the British light-heavyweight title, and fought for Georges Carpentier's world light-heavyweight title, being knocked out in the opening round. His last title went in 1924, but he boxed until 1929 with appearances in America (where he remains the most popular British fighter ever to box there), Canada and South Africa. He died in London on October 20, 1970.

Charles "Sonny" Liston

Born: *St Francis, Arkansas, May 8, 1932*
Titles: *World heavyweight champion 1962–64*
Record: *54 contests, 50 wins, 4 defeats*

The brooding figure of Sonny Liston cast a shadow over the heavyweight division for years before he became champion in 1962. He deserved the chance much earlier, but his background, which included jail terms, saddled him with an unsavoury image which he never could shake off.

Cus D'Amato, manager of champion Floyd Patterson, refused to allow him to defend against Liston, but Patterson took the match against D'Amato's advice. He was knocked out in two minutes six seconds, and lasted four seconds longer in the rematch. Liston looked unbeatable, but Cassius Clay thought otherwise, harrassing Liston into giving him a title fight, which took place in February 1964. Liston retired after six rounds, claiming a damaged shoulder. The return was even less satisfactory, Liston going down for the count in the first round from a "phantom" punch.

He won 15 fights on a comeback, then was knocked out by former sparring partner Leotis Martin. Liston won his last fight against Chuck Wepner, but was found dead in his Las Vegas home by his wife in January 1971.

Duilio Loi

Born: *Trieste, Italy, April 19, 1929*
Titles: *European lightweight champion 1954–58, European welterweight champion 1959–63, world light-welterweight champion 1960–62, 1962–63*
Record: *126 contests, 115 wins, 8 draws, 3 defeats*

Loi was a phenomenally successful performer. He lost only one of his first 110 fights, on points to Dane Jorgen Johansen in his first attempt on the European lightweight title. Loi took his revenge in 1954, and went on to retain the championship eight times until he relinquished it four years later.

Loi moved up to welterweight and took the European title from fellow-Italian Emilio Marconi in 1959. The light-welterweight division had recently been resurrected, and Loi, never a natural welterweight, saw an opportunity to fulfil his world championship dream. Carlos Ortiz turned back his first challenge, in San Francisco in June 1960, but Loi finally made it by outpointing Ortiz three months later.

He defended both his world and European titles for two years. The stylish American Eddie Perkins, who had previously held him to a draw, took the light-welterweight belt with a points win in September 1962, but Loi regained it in December that year and, the following month, announced his retirement. Loi died at the age of 79 in January 2008.

VASYL LOMACHENKO *won a world title in his third fight*

Vasyl Lomachenko

Born: *Bichorod-Dnistrovskyi, Ukraine, February 17, 1988*
Titles: *WBO featherweight champion 2014–*
Record: *11 contests, 10 wins, 1 defeat*

Vasyl Lomachenko won Olympic gold at two weights – at featherweight in Beijing in 2008 and up at lightweight in London four years later He turned professional after winning an astonishing 396 of his 397 amateur bouts – and he avenged the sole loss, to Albert Selimov, twice – and fought for a world title in just his second pro contest.

Orlando Salido weighed in too heavy for the WBO featherweight title fight, but roughed up Lomachenko and beat him on a split points vote. However, because Salido was overweight and won, the title was declared vacant and in his third professional fight, Lomachenko outpointed Gary Russell Jr. for the belt.

That proved to be the only loss of his career to date, and he has held on to defend his title on nine occasions.

Juan Manuel Lopez

Born: *Rio Piedras, Puerto Rico, June 30, 1983*
Titles: *WBO super-bantamweight champion 2008–10, WBO*

featherweight champion 2010–11, 2013–14
Record: *40 contests, 35 wins, 5 defeats*

Lopez's brand of explosive punching excited fans the world over and his outgoing personality made him a mainstream star in Puerto Rico.

He began boxing at the age of ten, represented his country at the 2004 Olympic Games in Athens aged 21 and announced his arrival on the professional scene with a sensational first-round demolition of defending WBO super-bantamweight champion Daniel Ponce De Leon in June 2008. His first two challengers, Cesar Figueroa and Sergio Medina, were also wiped out inside a round, then he forced veteran former champion Gerry Penalosa to retire in 10 rounds in April 2009.

Lopez made two more defences, then moved up to featherweight and in his debut at 122lb, he took the WBO belt from Steven Luevano in seven rounds in Madison Square Garden. The belt was lost to Mexican hard man Orlando Salido in eight rounds in April, 2011. Lopez led after nine rounds in the rematch but was stopped in the tenth. He won and lost the WBO featherweight title in 2013 and 2014.

Tommy Loughran

Born: *Philadelphia, Pennsylvania, November 29, 1902*
Titles: *New York recognition as world world light-heavyweight champion 1927, world champion 1927–29*
Record: *175 contests, 96 wins, 9 draws, 45 No Decisions, 1 No Contest, 24 defeats*

The career of the stylish Irish-American spanned 18 years, during which he was world light-heavyweight champion, challenged for the heavyweight title, and fought 14 men who were, or became, world champions from welter- to heavyweight. His victims included Harry Greb, Mickey Walker, Max Baer, Georges Carpentier and James J. Braddock, and he faced many other stars in no-decision bouts.

A master boxer who worked behind a stinging left jab, Loughran's lack of a telling punch meant that only 18 of his 173 fights ended inside the distance. He started fighting for a living at 17, but despite being good enough to face Greb and Gene Tunney in successive bouts before his 20th birthday, it took him 102 fights to become world champion, outpointing Mike McTigue in October 1927 for the New York version and then beating Jimmy Slattery to become undisputed champion.

He moved up to heavyweight in 1929 after five defences, but found title-holder Primo Carnera just too big for him (he was conceding 86lb) and lost on points. He died in Pennsylvania on July 7, 1982.

Joe Louis

see Legends of the Ring (pp 80–81)

Benny Lynch

Born: *Clydesdale, Scotland, April 12, 1913*
Titles: *British flyweight champion 1935–38, NBA & IBU champion 1935–37, world champion 1937–38*
Record: *122 contests, 90 wins, 17 draws, 15 defeats*

Drink destroyed Benny Lynch, who went from being a brilliant world flyweight champion to the scrapheap in a year, and died of malnutrition at 33. Yet, in his brief prime, Lynch was arguably the best flyweight in history, a stiff puncher with a shrewd tactical brain and the charisma of a great champion.

He learned his trade on the booths and turned pro at 18, often boxing every week. He won the Scottish title in 1934, and in 1935 destroyed world and British champion Jackie Brown in two rounds. They had boxed a draw earlier in the year and Lynch learned from the experience.

A points defeat of Small Montana made him undisputed champion, and he retained the title in an epic clash with Peter Kane, but his drinking was now out of control and he was stripped of the championship when he weighed in almost seven pounds overweight for a defence against Jackie Jurich in June 1938. He retired later that year, after suffering his only knockout, and died in Glasgow on August 6, 1946.

Jock McAvoy

Real name: *Joseph Bamford*
Born: *Burnley, England, November 20, 1908*
Titles: *British and Empire middleweight champion 1933–39, British light-heavyweight champion 1937*
Record: *148 contests, 133 wins, 1 draw, 14 defeats*

McAvoy was a fierce-punching, very aggressive character who started boxing in 1927 to help supplement the family income, adopting a *nom du ring* to keep his occupation a secret from his widowed mother.

His heavy hitting made him a big attraction, but competition was strong in those days and it took him five years to land a title chance, losing to Len Harvey for the British middleweight title. He reversed the result a year later, and won a Lonsdale Belt outright before going to America to knock out world title claimant Ed "Babe" Risko in an overweight match.

He was outpointed by John Henry Lewis for the world light-heavyweight title, and by Jack Petersen when he tried for the British heavyweight title. But he won the British light-heavyweight championship, only to lose it to Harvey, who beat him again in 1939 in a fight recognized in Britain as being for the vacant world title. McAvoy had his last fight in 1945 and later became a polio victim. He spent 20 years confined to a wheelchair before dying in Rochdale on November 20, 1971.

Mike McCallum

Born: *Kingston, Jamaica, December 7, 1956*
Titles: *WBA light-middleweight champion 1984–87, WBA middleweight champion 1989–91, WBC light-heavyweight champion 1994–95*
Record: *55 contests, 49 wins, 1 draw, 5 defeats*

Known as "The Bodysnatcher", thanks to his ferocious body punching, McCallum was one of a rare breed that improves with age. He won a Commonwealth Games gold medal, turning pro in 1981 and winning 21 in a row, 19 inside schedule, to earn a match with the durable Irishman Sean Mannion for the vacant WBA light-middleweight title.

McCallum won a dour battle on points, and retained the title six times with some memorable performances, such as his stoppages of Julian Jackson and Milton McCrory, and his one-punch knockout of Don Curry. He relinquished it in September 1987 to go after the middleweight title, but failed in his first attempt when Sumbu Kalambay outpointed him for the WBA belt in 1988. He became WBA champion a year later, and his three defences included a revenge win over Kalambay.

He was stripped of the title in December 1991 for agreeing to fight IBF champion James Toney, with whom he boxed a draw, and then stepped up to light-heavyweight to take the WBC title from Jeff Harding in July 1994. This time, he managed only one successful defence before losing to Fabrice Tiozzo in June 1995. He retired two years later after back-to-back points defeats to Roy Jones and James Toney. He was still competing at the highest level, but by then was past his 40th birthday.

Al McCoy

Real name: *Al Rudolph*
Born: *Rosenhayn, New Jersey, October 23, 1894*
Titles: *World middleweight champion 1914–17*
Record: *156 contests, 43 wins, 13 draws, 92 No Decisions, 8 defeats*

Al McCoy became world middleweight champion almost by accident. He had been due to fight Joe Chip, George's brother, who held the title at the time, but Joe pulled out and George, sniffing some easy money, agreed to substitute in a No Decision match, a contest in which his title could only change hands on a knockout. McCoy's father, a poultry farmer, bet 100 chickens to a cigar that his son would lose, but had to pay out when Chip was flattened in 111 seconds of the opening round on April 6, 1914.

His surprise win made him the first southpaw champion at any weight, and he held onto the title for over four years, fighting mainly No Decision contests in New York and Pennsylvania. His reluctance to make a "proper" defence earned him the sneering nickname of "Cheese Champion", yet his title was always at risk – as Chip's had been – were he to be knocked out. He stayed champion until Mike O'Dowd did just that in November 1917, and when O'Dowd beat him again in a rematch, McCoy retired. He died in Los Angeles on August 22, 1966.

Charles "Kid" McCoy

Real name: *Norman Selby*
Born: *Rush County, Indiana, October 13, 1872*
Titles: *World middleweight title claimant 1896–97*
Record: *116 contests, 84 wins, 9 draws, 16 No Decisions, 7 defeats*

The adjective "controversial" is barely adequate when applied to Kid McCoy, an extraordinary rascal who conned a champion out of his title, was involved in a fixed fight with James J. Corbett, became a film actor on retirement from the ring, murdered his seventh wife and committed suicide after his release from jail. As a role model, he left a lot to be desired.

His erratic performances led fans to wonder which McCoy would turn up... the fraudster or "the real McCoy", an accomplished fighter who won more than half his 107 fights by knockout. When he persuaded middleweight champion Tommy Ryan (who had formerly employed him as a sparring partner) that he was dying of consumption and needed cash to pay doctors' bills, the gullible Ryan did not even bother to train and was duly knocked out by a perfectly conditioned challenger in 15 rounds in March 1896.

He later moved up to heavyweight with mixed success, then lost on points to Jack Root for the light-heavyweight title in 1903. He had his last fight in 1916, and died on April 18, 1940.

Wayne McCullough

Born: *Belfast, Ireland, July 7, 1970*
Titles: *WBC bantamweight champion 1995–97*
Record: *34 contests, 27 wins, 7 defeats*

Belfast's "Pocket Rocket" ignored conventional routes to professional success when he returned from the 1992 Olympic Games a national hero, having won a silver medal to go with his 1990 Commonwealth Games gold medal and a pair of Irish championships. He opted for a move to Las Vegas, under the management of Mat Tinley, a young TV executive who had no boxing experience or background. The attractions (apart from a sweet financial deal) were guaranteed TV exposure through Tinley's Prime Network channel, and the chance to work with trainer Eddie Futch, the game's most respected guru.

The move paid off when, barely two years after his professional debut in February 1993, and following victories over former champions Victor Rabanales and Fabrice Benichou, he travelled to Japan and dethroned WBC bantamweight champion Yasuei Yakshiji. Almost immediately he was beset by weight troubles. He stopped Johnny Bredahl in Belfast, then struggled to a split decision over Jose Luis Bueno in Dublin.

His unbeaten record went on a split decision when challenging Mexican Daniel Zaragoza for the WBC super-bantamweight title in Boston and McCullough officially gave up the bantamweight belt. After business problems with Tinley and the retirement of Futch, he was outpointed by Naseem Hamed and Erik Morales in world title challenges in 1998 and 1999. McCullough lost two years of his career when a cyst was discovered on his brain. He had three further world title challenges, one against Scott Harrison in Scotland and two against the rugged Mexican Oscar Larios who, in the last of those, inflicted his first-ever stoppage loss in July 2005. His licence was suspended. McCullough had one more fight, which he lost, in the Cayman Islands in 2008.

Terry McGovern

Born: *Johnstown, Pennsylvania, March 9, 1880*
Titles: *World bantamweight champion 1899, world featherweight champion 1900–01*
Record: *80 contests, 60 wins, 4 draws, 11 No Decisions, 5 defeats*

The Irish-American turned professional at 17 in 1897, and was not yet 20 when he flattened England's Pedlar Palmer in 75 seconds to win the bantamweight title in September 1899. His solitary defeat in 35 fights had been on a disqualification, and he rattled off another nine wins (eight by knockout) in 1899 before moving up to featherweight. The champion there was George Dixon, but McGovern gave him a fearful beating and won his second title on an eighth-round stoppage. He retained it three times in 1900, with knockouts of Eddie Santry, Frank Erne and Joe Gans, respectively, although there was an unpleasant aroma attached to the Gans result.

Still only 21, McGovern's future seemed bright, yet all turned sour when Young Corbett took his title in two rounds in November 1901. McGovern gave a feeble showing, and fared little better in a rematch two years later. His career ended in 1908, and he died in Brooklyn on February 26, 1918.

Barry McGuigan

Born: *Clones, Ireland, February 28, 1961*
Titles: *British and European featherweight champion 1983–85, WBA featherweight champion 1985–86*
Record: *35 contests, 32 wins, 3 defeats*

The charismatic McGuigan boxed for Ireland in the 1980 Olympic Games in Moscow, won a Commonwealth Games gold medal for Northern Ireland, and took out naturalization papers in order to compete for the British title, which he won in April 1983. Under Barney Eastwood's management and promotion, he drew huge TV audiences and capacity crowds to Belfast's atmospheric Kings Hall.

He was projected as a symbol of unity in a divided society, helped by the fact that he was a Catholic married to a Protestant. He was an obsessive trainer, always working on refinements to his thrillingly aggressive style. McGuigan's body punching was, in all senses, breath-taking, and he looked irresistible as he moved towards a shot at Eusebio Pedroza's WBA featherweight title. He became European champion in 1983, and by 1985 was ready for the veteran Panamanian.

Their 15-rounder, watched by a crowd of 25,000 at QPR football ground in London, was utterly absorbing, but McGuigan won clearly. He made two defences, then surprisingly lost to Steve Cruz in 1986, in unbearable heat in Las Vegas. He returned at super-feather, but retired after losing on a cut to Jim McDonnell. He has became an accomplished television performer, serving as a commentator and summarizer.

Duke McKenzie

Born: *Croydon, England, May 5, 1963*
Titles: *British flyweight champion 1985–86, European flyweight champion 1986–88, IBF flyweight champion 1988–89, WBO bantamweight champion 1991–92, WBO super-bantamweight champion 1992–93, British featherweight champion 1993–94*
Record: *46 contests, 39 wins, 7 defeats*

The McKenzies of Croydon are one of Britain's most famous fighting families, but none of them can match Duke's achievements. He started in 1985 with the British flyweight title, and in May 1986 added the European title by sending former WBC champion Charlie Magri into retirement.

The first of his three world titles came in October 1988, when he knocked out Rolando Bohol for the

IBF title, which he retained once but lost to Dave McAuley in 1989. He moved up to bantamweight, and a points defeat by Thierry Jacob in a European title bid proved only a temporary setback, as in June 1991 he outscored the respected Gaby Canizales to become WBO champion. Rafael del Valle knocked him out in a round in May 1992, his third defence, but before the year ended he had taken the WBO super-bantamweight crown from another top-flight American, Jesse Benavides.

He lost it in his next fight, but stepped up again to win the British featherweight title in December 1993. A knockout by Steve Robinson in October 1994, when he tried for the WBO featherweight title, ended his dreams of a fourth world title.

Jimmy McLarnin

Born: *Hillsborough, Ireland, December 19, 1907*
Titles: *World welterweight champion 1933–34, 1934–35*
Record: *77 contests, 63 wins, 3 draws, 11 defeats*

McLarnin was one of the game's success stories, who had a brilliant ring career and kept his considerable fortune to the end of his life. He was taken to Canada as a child, and started boxing professionally as a 17-year-old bantamweight in 1923, soon acquiring the nickname of "Babyface". His manager throughout his career was "Pop" Foster, and the pair were so close that when Foster died in 1956 he left everything to his former fighter.

McLarnin soon reached top class, and challenged Sammy Mandell for the lightweight title in 1928, losing on points. Foster regarded that as merely a learning experience, and manoeuvred his man into a shot at the welterweight title, while avoiding promotional tie-ups. Considering the way boxing was run in those days, that was a considerable achievement.

In 1933, McLarnin knocked out Young Corbett III to become champion, and then engaged in a classic three-fight series with Barney Ross, winning one. He lost and won against Tony Canzoneri, and quit on a high note by beating another champion, Lou Ambers, in November 1936. In all, he beat 13 men who held world titles. He died, aged 96, on October 28, 2004.

Sam McVey

Born: *Oxnard, California, May 17, 1885*
Titles: *none*
Record: *96 contests, 61 wins, 8 draws, 15 No Decisions, 12 defeats*

Like his famous contemporaries Joe Jeanette, Sam Langford and Jack Johnson, Sam McVey suffered cruel discrimination that prevented him achieving his full potential. He was restricted to meeting his fellow-blacks in endless round robins – for example, he fought Langford 15 times in nine years in France, Australia, America and Argentina. He met Jeanette four times, with their best-known being a brutal battle in Paris in April 1909.

Jeanette was floored 22 times in the first 37 rounds, but showed exceptional endurance to keep going and finally, in the 39th round, he put McVey down. But McVey could match him for courage, and although Sam was knocked down a further 18 times, he scored six more knockdowns himself. By the time the fight ended in the 49th round when the exhausted McVey got off his stool at the start of the round and collapsed without a punch being struck, the knockdown total was 46! They had been fighting for three hours and 12 minutes.

He boxed twice in England in 1911, beating the Boer George Rodel in a round and Alf Langford in seven. McVey died in New York in 1921.

Charlie Magri

Born: *Tunisia, July 20, 1956*
Titles: *British flyweight champion 1977–81, European champion 1979–82, 1984, 1985–86, WBC champion 1983*
Record: *35 contests, 30 wins, 5 defeats*

Magri can claim to have rescued the British flyweight division from extinction. Prior to his emergence after a dazzling amateur career, which included three ABA titles and an Olympic vest, the division was virtually dormant and there were serious proposals for its abolition. But the colourful Magri, raised in London, was a star from the start and won the British title in only his third fight. He raced through 23 wins in a row, and outscored the former WBC light-flyweight champion Franco Udella to win the European title in 1979. But then the vulnerability which, combined with his own heavy punching made him such an exciting performer to watch, let him down. He was stopped twice, by Juan Diaz and Jose Torres, but somehow was steered back into the world title picture.

He finally became WBC champion on March 15, 1983, stopping Eleoncio Mercedes on a cut, but lost the title on his first defence to Frank Cedeno. He twice regained and relinquished the European title, and made a brave bid for Sot Chitalada's WBC title before retiring after losing his European crown to Duke McKenzie.

Saoul Mamby

Born: *Bronx, New York, June 4, 1947*
Titles: *WBC light-welterweight champion 1980–82*
Record: *84 contests, 45 wins, 6 draws, 33 defeats*

Mamby had his first pro fight in September 1969 and his 79th and last 24 years later, when he was 46. It is one of the longest careers of modern times. He spent most of it in top class, boxed in 14 countries and failed to go the distance only once, in his final fight.

He made his debut in Jamaica, but moved to New York immediately afterwards, basing himself there for the rest of his busy career. His crafty style and durability earned him respect as "a good opponent", who could be relied on to lose on points to top names. He filled this role perfectly, proving his worth in ten-rounders against world champions Antonio Cervantes and Roberto Duran and, in 1977, giving Saensak Muangsurin a tough fight in his first WBC title bid.

He won the title at the second attempt, stopping Kim-Sang Hyun in 1980, and proved an efficient champion with five successful defences before Leroy Haley dethroned him in 1982. He failed to regain it from Billy Costello in 1984, and later became a high-quality journeyman, subsidizing his income by driving a yellow cab. When he finally retired, aged 52, in 2000, he had boxed in five decades.

Sammy Mandell

Real name: *Samuel Mandella*
Born: *Rockford, Illinois, February 5, 1904*
Titles: *World lightweight champion 1926–30*
Record: *188 contests, 85 wins, 9 draws, 73 No Decisions, 21 defeats*

It is one of history's ironies that, while Jimmy McLarnin and Tony Canzoneri are honoured as two of the greatest lightweights of all time, Sammy Mandell is known today only to the game's obsessives – yet he beat them both, in title fights. Perhaps because Mandell was not a big puncher – only 33 quick wins in 187 fights – he never captured the public's affections as the other two did, but he was a tough and competent battler who fought the best men of his era.

Of Italian-Albanian extraction, Mandell began boxing in 1920. He beat the popular Sid Terris in 1925 to earn a place in the elimination tournament to find a new champion following Benny Leonard's retirement. Mandell missed his chance, losing on a foul to Jimmy Goodrich, but stayed unbeaten to earn a crack at Rocky Kansas' title in July 1926 and this time made no mistake, winning on points.

He retained it against McLarnin and Canzoneri, then lost on a first-round knockout to Al Singer in July 1930. Mandell boxed for another four years. He died in Oak Park, Illinois, on November 7, 1967.

Rocky Marciano

see Legends of the Ring (pp 90–91)

Juan Manuel Marquez

Born: *Mexico City, August 23, 1973*
Titles: *IBF & WBA featherweight champion 2003–05, WBO featherweight champion 2006–07, WBC super-featherweight champion 2007–08, WBO lightweight champion 2009, WBO lightweight and WBA Super lightweight champion 2010*
Record: *64 contests, 56 wins, 1 draw, 7 defeats*

An accountant by trade, Marquez brought a mathematical, logical brain to the raw business of boxing, but he needed a big punch to claim the scalp he wanted most of all. In three previous fights with Manny Pacquiao, Marquez had drawn and twice lost razor-thin decisions. After five rounds of their fourth meeting, in December 2012, Pacquiao was one point ahead on all three cards, but Marquez landed a right hand in the sixth round that wiped out the deficit.

He lost a split decision to Timothy Bradley for the WBO welterweight title in 2013, but went on to win an up-and-down fight with Mike Alvarado in 2014.

Marquez was disqualified in his pro debut, but that was nothing compared to the frustration he suffered when attempting to break into world class. For two years he was the WBO No 1 contender, but champion Naseem Hamed was disinclined to box him.

In September 1999 Marquez took a chance to fight WBA champion Freddie Norwood, only to lose a poor fight on points. It was four years before he had another chance. When it came, he grabbed it, destroying Manuel Medina in seven rounds for the IBF title. He added the WBA belt, beating the exceedingly reluctant Derrick Gainer. Boxing politics robbed him of the titles, before a strange business decision took him to Indonesia in March 2006, where he lost to his successor as WBA champion, Chris John. A fight with WBO champion Scott Harrison fell through because of the Scot's troubles out of the ring.

Harrison was stripped of the title and Marquez was awarded it, but the Mexican moved up to super-featherweight and beat Marco Antonio Barrera for the WBC belt in a splendid 12-rounder that gave him his second championship. He lost it on points in a rematch with Pacquiao, and went up in weight again, to lightweight. Wins over Joel Casamayor and Juan Diaz, the latter for the WBO crown, set him up for a big-money fight with Floyd Mayweather Jr. Marquez lacked the size and snap to trouble Mayweather, but still went the full 12 rounds.

Sergio Martinez

Born: *Buenos Aries, Argentina, February 21, 1975*
Titles: *WBC middleweight champion 2010–14, WBO middleweight champion 2010*
Record: *56 contests, 51 wins, 2 draws, 3 defeats*

His points win over Kelly Pavlik and a jaw-dropping, one-punch knock-out of Paul Williams propelled Martinez into the pound-for-pound lists. A pro since 1997, he took the WBC and WBO middleweight titles from Pavlik in April 2010 and wiped out Williams in a rematch. For some, Williams was a new Thomas Hearns – a tall, long-limbed puncher – and he had previously outpointed Martinez.

The Argentine claimed his violent revenge in November 2010. Both put everything behind southpaw lefts in the second round – and Martinez landed first. It was the best knockout of the year. Martinez then handed Serhiy Dzinziruk his first defeat. Dzinziruk had previously made six defences of the WBO light-middleweight title and Martinez dropped him five times in an eight-round thrashing.

His defence of the WBC Diamond belt against Julio Cesar Chavez Jr. in September 2012 was tougher. Martinez was on the floor and did well to survive a last-round onslaught. Hampered by a knee operation, he then struggled to outpoint Martin Murray – some thought the Brit was unlucky – but was well beaten by Miguel Cotto in what proved to be his final fight. He retired in June 2015.

SERGIO MARTINEZ *celebrates beating Julio Cesar Chavez Jr. in September 2012*

Henry Maske

Born: *Trevenbrietzen, Germany, January 6, 1964*
Titles: *IBF light-heavyweight champion 1993–96*
Record: *32 contests, 31 wins, 1 defeat*

This tall (6ft 3in) southpaw is one of the few men who have become world champion without needing to adapt the style learned as an amateur. In his case, as a product of the former East Germany, that meant a rigid concentration on the basic jab-and-cross routine, while utilizing his height and long reach to make himself an inaccessible target. It carried him to world, Olympic and European gold medals and enabled him to win and keep the IBF light-heavyweight title for three years. Maske was an undramatic personality but extremely popular in Germany, where he drew huge crowds.

He won the IBF title with a clear points win over long- serving champion Charles Williams in March 1993, and made ten successful defences. He had trouble with only one opponent in that time, compatriot Graciano Rocchigiani. They fought twice in 1995, and both times Rocchigiani and his fans thought he had done enough to win. The judges, however, disagreed. A symbol of the new, unified Germany, Maske earned well out of boxing and TV appearances, but lost his title in a unification fight with Virgil Hill in 1996, after which he retired. Ten years on he came back for a one-off rematch against Virgil Hill, won to avenge his only defeat, and retired for good.

Joey Maxim

Real name: *Giuseppe Antonio Berardinelli*
Born: *Cleveland, Ohio, March 28, 1922*
Titles: *World light-heavyweight champion 1950–52*
Record: *115 contests, 82 wins, 4 draws, 29 defeats*

The former light-heavyweight champion took his ring name from the Maxim gun, his hyperbolic manager Doc Kearns claiming that his boy could fire left jabs at machine-gun speed. A former Golden Gloves champion, Maxim competed in top class from virtually the start of his pro career in 1941. He was mixing with the likes of Jimmy Bivins and Ezzard Charles by 1942, and beat Jersey Joe Walcott in 1946, losing a rematch.

In May 1949 he outscored ex-champ Gus Lesnevich for the American title, and the following January trounced Britain's Freddie Mills to win the world title. Two years later he had the last of his four-fight series with Ezzard Charles, who won on points to retain the NBA heavyweight title.

He scored a famous victory in a 1952 defence against Sugar Ray Robinson, who was overcome by heat exhaustion after 13 rounds. Archie Moore took Maxim's title in December 1952, but Kearns (who managed them both) secured him two unsuccessful rematches. But he had one more significant win, when he outpointed Floyd Patterson in 1954, and he boxed on until 1958. He died, aged 79, on June 2, 2001, amazingly survived by his mother.

Floyd Mayweather Jr.

Born: *Grand Rapids, Michigan, 24 February, 1977*
Titles: *WBC super-featherweight champion 1998–2002, WBC lightweight champion 2002–04, WBC light-welterweight champion 2005–06, IBF welterweight champion 2006, WBC welterweight champion 2006–08 & 2011–, WBC light-middleweight champion 2007, WBA super light-middleweight champion 2011–, WBO welterweight champion 2015–*
Record: *50 contests, 50 wins*

A fluid, beautifully balanced boxer with amazing speed and reflexes, Floyd Mayweather is from a talented boxing family. His father, Floyd Sr., fought Ray Leonard and Marlon Starling, his uncle Jeff was one of Oscar De La Hoya's early opponents and uncle Roger was a two-weight world champion.

A bronze medallist in the 1996 Olympics, Floyd Jr. turned pro while his father was in jail. They were reunited when Floyd Sr. was released, but then parted again.

Floyd Jr. won the WBC super-featherweight title at 21, outclassing champion Genaro Hernandez in eight rounds in October 1998. Despite trouble with brittle hands, Mayweather made eight defences of the WBC super-featherweight title until moving up to lightweight and squeezing past Jose Luis Castillo in Mexico in a hard fight for the WBC crown. Mayweather won a rematch more easily, then moved up to win further world titles at light-welterweight, where he outclassed Arturo Gatti in six rounds, and welterweight, outpointing both Zab Judah and Carlos Baldomir 2006.

Mayweather won the two biggest fights of 2007, edging out Oscar De La Hoya to become a five-weight champion, then returned to welterweight to beat Ricky Hatton in ten rounds. After a 21-month retirement, Mayweather outpointed Juan Manuel Marquez and pounded out a one-sided decision over Shane Mosley. He went on to outclass Victor Ortiz and unanimously outpoint Miguel Cotto over 12 hard rounds. In January 2012 Mayweather was sentenced to a 90-day prison term after being found guilty of a domestic violence charge. He returned to beat rising star Saul Alvarez, won a couple of fights with Marcos Maidana and beat Manny Pacquiao in a fight that predictably didn't live up to its "fight of the century" billing. He then beat Andre Berto on a unanimous points decision and outsmarted Conor McGregor in a much-hyped title clash to maintain his perfect record – 50 fights, 50 wins.

FLOYD MAYWEATHER JR. *unbeaten in 50 fights*

Freddie Miller

Born: *Cincinnati, April 3, 1911*
Titles: *NBA featherweight champion 1933–36*
Record: *251 contests, 209 wins, 7 draws, 4 No Decisions, 31 defeats*

Miller was a prodigiously busy performer who crammed 251 fights into his 13-year career. He won the world title in his first fight of 1933, yet had a further 18 contests that year, followed by 28 in 1934 and a remarkable 35 in 1935.

His first title chance came against stablemate Bat Battalino in July 1931, Battalino winning on points. They were rematched in January 1932. The deal was that the title would change hands. However, Battalino came in three pounds overweight and, when the fight went ahead as a non-title match, the champion went down in the third from a harmless-looking punch and the referee stopped it. The NBA and the New York Commission both ruled a "No Contest" and declared the title vacant.

Surprisingly, Miller got a second chance less than a year later, outpointing Tommy Paul for the NBA version. He retained it 11 times, including trips to England and Spain as well as non-title appearances in France, Belgium and Cuba, but was finally dethroned by Petey Sarron, a veteran whom he had already beaten three times. Sarron won their rematch in 1937, and Miller retired in 1940. He died on May 8, 1962.

Freddie Mills

Born: *Parkstone, England, June 26, 1919*
Titles: *British and Empire light-heavyweight champion 1942–50, European champion 1947–50, world champion 1948–50*
Record: *101 contests, 76 wins, 7 draws, 18 defeats*

Mills' courage and dogged determination was legendary. He could absorb endless batterings yet come back to win, even if the unseen toll was heavy. Mills learned his boxing in a West Country touring booth, turning professional at 16.

His brawling style and heavy punching made him a crowd-puller, although he lost ten times on the way up. By 1942 he was a contender from middleweight to heavyweight, but his big chance came at light-heavyweight, and he knocked out Len Harvey to win the British and Empire titles and the domestic version of the world title.

Jack London beat him in a brutal 15-rounder for the British and Empire heavyweight titles in 1944, and he took another pummelling from Gus Lesnevich for the world title in 1946. He also lost painfully to Bruce Woodcock, Joe Baksi and Lloyd Marshall, but rebounded to win the European title and take revenge over Lesnevich for the world title in 1948. Woodcock hammered him again in 1949, and he retired after losing his world title to Joey Maxim in 1950. He was found shot outside his London nightclub on July 25, 1965, apparently a suicide.

BULLDOG BREED *Freddie Mills*

Alan Minter

Born: *Crawley, England, August 17, 1951*
Titles: *British middleweight champion 1975–77, 1977–78, European champion 1977, 1978–79, world champion 1980*
Record: *49 contests, 39 wins, 1 No Contest, 9 defeats*

An unfortunate tendency to cut caused six of the eight inside-schedule defeats on the otherwise impressive record of this rangy southpaw, Britain's most successful middleweight of the 1970s. Minter won a bronze medal at the Munich Olympics and turned professional in October 1972. He started well, then hit a disastrous spell in 1973–74 when he won only three out of eight fights. But he kept his nerve and, in November 1975, won the British title by outpointing Kevin Finnegan in the first of their epic three-fight series, all of which Minter won.

He gained a Lonsdale Belt outright, and won, lost and regained the European title that he relinquished in December 1979 to go after the world championship. That meant a trip to Las Vegas in March 1980, where he scored a rare British "away" victory by outpointing Vito Antuofermo for the undisputed title. He retained the belts once, but then was stopped in three by Marvin Hagler in a fight that provoked disgraceful scenes at Wembley. Minter retired after Tony Sibson floored him in September 1981.

Brian Mitchell

Born: *Johannesburg, South Africa, August 30, 1961*
Titles: *WBA junior-lightweight champion 1986–91, IBF champion 1991–92*
Record: *49 contests, 45 wins, 3 draws, 1 defeat*

His country's loathsome apartheid policy meant that Mitchell could not defend his WBA junior-lightweight belt at home, which makes his achievement in retaining it 12 times all the more praiseworthy. He was the ultimate professional, unperturbed by risking his title in the challenger's country and ready to go wherever there was a payday.

Yet, ironically, almost all Mitchell's early opponents were black South Africans, and he boxed in the townships around Durban and Johannesburg. He won the South African 130-lb title in 1983, and made seven successful defences before crossing the border into Bophutaswana to take the WBA title from Alfredo Layne in September 1986. He defended it in Puerto Rico, Panama, France, Italy, Spain, England and America, and in March 1991 drew with IBF champion Tony Lopez in a unification match staged in Sacramento, Lopez's home town.

The verdict outraged Mitchell, and he gave up the WBA belt to force a rematch for the IBF title in September 1991. He was vindicated when the judges gave him the verdict this time, and announced his retirement. After a brief, winning comeback in the mid-1990s, he became a highly respected trainer in South Africa.

Bob Montgomery

Born: *Sumter, South Carolina, February 10, 1919*
Titles: *New York recognition as world lightweight champion 1943, 1944–47*
Record: *97 contests, 75 wins, 3 draws, 19 defeats*

Montgomery's break came in May 1941 when he outpointed lightweight champion Lew Jenkins in a non-title ten-rounder. It was their second meeting, Jenkins having outscored him the previous year, but the result established the hard-punching Southerner as a contender.

He could never get the better of Sammy Angott, who outpointed him in their three meetings, but the only other men to beat him in 69 fights on his way to the title were Tommy Spiegel in 1939 and Maxie Shapiro in 1942, a result Montgomery reversed in his next fight.

He outpointed the colourful Beau Jack to win the New York version of the title in May 1943, but lost it back to him six months later. He went 2–1 ahead in their entertaining series in March 1944, and made two defences before NBA champion Ike Williams knocked him out to unify the title in August 1947.

Montgomery never won another fight, losing seven in a row and retiring in March 1950. He died, aged 79, on August 25, 1998.

Carlos Monzon

Born: *Santa Fe, Argentina, August 7, 1942*
Titles: *World middleweight champion 1970–74, WBA champion 1974–77, world champion 1977*
Record: *101 contests, 89 wins, 8 draws, 1 No Contest, 3 defeats*

For 13 years between 1964 and 1977, Monzon was unbeatable. He compiled an amazing undefeated run of 82 fights, and set a new record for the middleweight division by making 14 defences of the title he took from Nino Benvenuti in 1970.

The handsome Argentinean was as close to the perfect fighting machine as anyone has ever come. Tall and rangy, with a long reach and a rock-hard chin, his left jab would soften up his opponents for the heavy hooks and uppercuts which brought him 61 inside-schedule victories in 101 fights. He won the Argentinean title in 1967, but did not attract international attention until he held Bennie Briscoe to a draw over ten rounds later the same year.

Despite his record Monzon was still the underdog when he challenged Benvenuti in November 1977. He knocked the Italian out in 12 rounds, stopped him in three rounds in a return, and embarked on his spectacular reign. His contenders were all top-drawer, and he retired in 1977 when he ran out of opposition. He was later jailed for killing his mistress, and died in a car crash on January 8, 1995, while on parole.

Archie Moore

Real name: *Archibald Lee Wright*
Born: *Benoit, Mississippi, December 13, 1916*
Titles: *World light-heavyweight champion 1952–62*
Record: *229 contests, 194 wins, 8 draws, 1 No Contest, 26 defeats*

It took Archie Moore 16 years to win the world light-heavyweight title, and ten years to lose it. Self-belief, and a stubborn streak of independence, kept him going during the scandalously long time he had to wait for his chance, despite being commonly accepted as the best man at the weight for years.

Moore's exact age was an open question for years, but the 1920 US census reveals that he was then a three-year-old living with his uncle Cleveland Moore, which fits with a birthdate of December 1916. He had extraordinary punching ability, had grace and timing in the ring, but also earned a reputation for being a hard man to deal with, perhaps because he rarely stayed with the same manager for very long. On the way up he lost three times to the future heavyweight champion Ezzard Charles, but was too good for almost everyone else around his weight in the late 1940s.

He won the light-heavyweight title in his 175th fight, dethroning his stablemate Joey Maxim in 1952, and over the next ten years he defended it nine times, including a modern classic against the Canadian Yvon Durelle in 1958. He challenged twice for the heavyweight title, losing to Rocky Marciano in nine rounds and Floyd Patterson in five, and retired in 1963. Moore trained boxers, worked with heavyweight champion George Foreman, and remained close to the sport up to his death on December 9, 1998, aged 81.

Davey Moore

Born: *Lexington, Kentucky, November 1, 1933*
Titles: *World featherweight champion 1959–63*
Record: *68 contests, 59 wins, 1 draw, 1 No Contest, 7 defeats*

The ill-fated Moore, known as "The Springfield Rifle" in honour of his adopted hometown, was a compact and precise boxer who won the 1952 AAU bantamweight title before turning professional the following year. He had some early setbacks, but then hit a 13-fight winning run that carried him to the world featherweight championship.

A first-round blitz of Mexican contender Ricardo Moreno brought him a match with champion Hogan Bassey in Los Angeles in March 1959, and Moore forced the Nigerian to retire after 13 rounds, his face a mess of cuts and swellings. He did the job in 11 rounds in the rematch, and then became a globe-trotter, with appearances in England, Venezuela, Mexico, France, Spain, Italy, Japan and even Finland.

He notched up five successful defences, and his only defeat in 24 fights as champion was when Carlos Hernandez, a heavy hitter who later won the light-welterweight title, broke his jaw. But then Cuba's Sugar Ramos surprisingly took his title in ten rounds in Los Angeles on March 21, 1963. Tragically, Moore collapsed in the dressing room, and died two days later.

Michael Moorer

Born: *Monessen, Pennsylvania, November 12, 1967*
Titles: *WBO light-heavyweight champion 1988–91, WBO heavyweight champion 1992–93, WBA and IBF champion 1994, IBF champion 1996–97*
Record: *57 contests, 52 wins, 1 draw, 4 defeats*

Moorer merits several footnotes in boxing history, as the WBO's first light-heavyweight champion and, more significantly, as the first southpaw to win the heavyweight championship. He profited from the close association his then manager Emanuel Steward had with the WBO, and stopped Ramzi Hassan for their inaugural light-heavyweight title in December 1988, seven months after turning professional. Moorer made nine successful defences of his title, none of them lasting more than nine rounds, then relinquished it in April 1991 to box at heavyweight and won a wildly exciting brawl with Bert Cooper for the vacant WBO title. He gave up his title in February 1993.

He took the heavyweight championship from Evander Holyfield on a points verdict in April 1994, a fight remembered for the inspirational corner work of his trainer Teddy Atlas, but then gave a disappointing performance to lose to George Foreman, who scored a surprise one-punch knockout in the tenth round in Las Vegas in November 1994. Moorer regained the vacant IBF title in 1996 against Axel Schulz, but lost a unification fight with Evander Holyfield in eight rounds in 1997. After a three-year retirement, Moorer came back. A quick knockout at the hands of David Tua wrecked any thoughts of another world title shot, but he carried on boxing until 2008.

Erik Morales

Born: *Valle de Santiago Guanajuato, Mexico, September 1, 1976*
Titles: *WBC super-bantamweight champion 1997–2000, WBC featherweight champion 2001–02, WBC super-featherweight champion 2004, WBC light-welterweight champion 2011–12*
Record: *61 contests, 52 wins, 9 defeats*

Erik "El Terrible" Morales became the first Mexican boxer to win world titles at four weights when he outpointed Pablo Cesar Cano for the vacant WBC light-welterweight title in September 2011. Six months later, he lost the belt on the scales before his defence against Danny Garcia after he weighed in heavy. Morales was then beaten on points after being dropped in the 11th round. The rematch ended in an emphatic four-round defeat. Morales was laid out by a left hook.

He will always be remembered for his bitter, smouldering rivalry with Marco Antonio Barrera, which produced their epic first meeting in Las Vegas in February 2000, and their compelling but less dramatic rematch two years later. Morales won the first, Barrera the second. Barrera won the decider on a very close majority decision in 2004.

Morales, from the rough North Zone of the border city Tijuana, turned pro when still a schoolboy. His parents insisted he continue with his education, until his father realized how good he was, by which time he was Mexican champion – and still a teenager.

He was only 21 when he beat Mexican veteran southpaw Daniel Zaragoza in 11 rounds for the WBC super-bantamweight title in 1997. He defended it nine times, including the first unification fight with Barrera, then moved up to the featherweights in 2000.

The following year, he won the WBC belt with a close decision over Guty Espadas Jr. The title was declared vacant after he lost to Barrera in June 2002, but Morales regained the crown with a clear points win over Paulie Ayala, then emulated Mexican legend Julio Cesar Chavez as a three-weight world champion by winning the WBC super-featherweight title with a points win over Jesus Chavez in Las Vegas in February 2004.

After Barrera beat Morales in their third meeting, Erik outboxed Manny Pacquiao, but a shock loss to Zahir Raheem and two stoppage defeats to Pacquiao sent him into retirement. Morales made a comeback in 2010, but a two-year ban in March 2013 for a doping offence ended his career.

Shane Mosley

Born: *Lynwood, California, September 7, 1971*
Titles: *IBF lightweight champion 1997–99, WBC welterweight champion 2000–02, WBA welterweight champion 2009–10, WBC & WBA light-middleweight champion 2003–04*
Record: *60 contests, 49 wins, 1 draw, 10 defeats*

You can't call yourself "Sugar" if you can't fight. After Sugar Ray Robinson and Sugar Ray Leonard, Shane Mosley had a lot to live up to from the day he decided to use their nickname. As an amateur in California, Mosley was top class. When he failed to make the Barcelona Olympic team, the disappointment was obvious, but it might have been the making of him. While his boyhood rival Oscar De La Hoya – Mosley won their only competitive match when they were very young – had every move scrutinized by the media, Shane was allowed to develop in his own time.

Trained by his father Jack, he turned professional in 1993. It took four years before Mosley reached world championship level, but when he got there, he was a hardened campaigner, with quick hands, a good defence and could hit. Mosley won the IBF lightweight title by outpointing Phillip Holiday over 12 rounds in August 1997. He had not been considered an exceptional fighter, but gradually, through eight defences, earned a reputation as one of the best of the world champions pound-for-pound.

By 2000 he had outgrown the division and, bypassing light-welterweight, moved up to challenge De La Hoya for the WBC welterweight title in Los Angeles. De La Hoya won the early rounds, but Mosley came on strongly over the second half. It was close – but the split decision went Mosley's way. De La Hoya had no complaints. Mosley was welterweight champion for only 16 months but, in that time, scored inside-the-distance wins in defences against Antonio Diaz, Shannon Taylor and Adrian Stone, none of whom were in his league. In January 2002, at Madison Square Garden, he lost for the first time. Vernon Forrest, another contemporary from his amateur days, dropped him twice and won a clear decision.

In the return six months later, in Indianapolis, Forrest beat him again. Mosley was out in the cold for more than a year, during which he was mentioned in the BALCO scandal, involving a Californian laboratory that distributed illegal substances to athletes in a range of sports. Mosley's name was on their list, but he was not prosecuted.

In September 2003 he took on De La Hoya in a return in Las Vegas, at light-middleweight for the WBC and WBA belts. After 12 rounds it looked as if De La Hoya had outboxed Mosley with something to spare. The jab that had worked so well for Mosley in their first meeting was barely in evidence. His punches fell short. Yet, after 12 rounds, all three judges scored 115–113 for Mosley. De La Hoya and his promoter Bob Arum were outraged.

Mosley's 154-lb reign did not last. He was twice outsmarted by Winky Wright, but then dropped back to welterweight, twice stopped Fernando Vargas, outclassed Luis Collazo, and was looking good until Miguel Angel Cotto was too sharp and young for him in a WBA title fight in November 2007. Mosley defied the years again, however, when he knocked out Ricardo Mayorga, in the 12th round, and then stopped Antonio Margarito in nine to win the WBA welterweight belt at the age of 37.

Mosley was 38 when he lost a decision to Floyd Mayweather Jr. in the spring of 2010. He drew with Sergio Mora, then lost world-title fights to Manny Pacquiao and Saul Alvarez. Mosley retired after the loss to Alvarez – then announced a comeback. He carried on fighting until 2016.

Jose Napoles

Born: *Oriente, Cuba, April 13, 1940*
Titles: *World welterweight champion 1969–70, 1971–76*
Record: *86 contests, 79 wins, 7 defeats*

His nickname, *Mantequilla* (butter – he was said to be as smooth as butter), suited the sleek Cuban, who moved to Mexico in 1962 and made boxing seem an effortless art. Napoles was a venomous puncher, but was also a thoughtful tactician. He first came to notice as a light-welterweight in 1963, and commanded a high ranking in that division. His only loss in 33 fights between May 1963 and April 1969, when he stopped Curtis Cokes for the welterweight title, was by L.C. Morgan, which he quickly avenged.

He retained his title 13 times and ducked nobody. Billy Backus stopped him in December 1970, but Napoles soon regained the title. However, he quit after six rounds of a middleweight challenge against Carlos Monzon in Paris in February 1974, relinquished the WBA title in May 1975, and lost the WBC belt to John H. Stracey in his final fight.

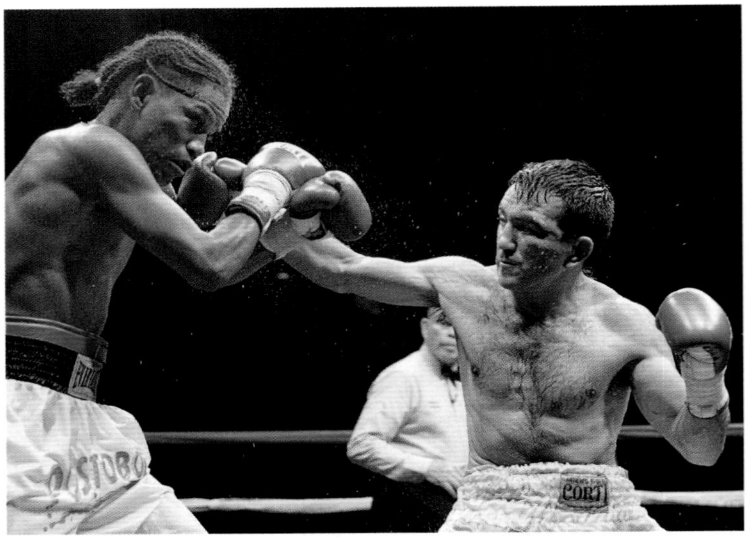

OMAR NARVAEZ *(right) the fiery WBO flyweight champion who calls himself El Hurrican*

Omar Narvaez

Born: *Trelew, Chubut, Argentina, July 10, 1975*
Titles: *WBO flyweight champion 2002–10, WBO super-flyweight champion 2010–14*
Record: *54 contests, 48 wins, 2 draws, 2 defeats*

A 5ft 3in southpaw who called himself "El Huracan", Narvaez won the WBO flyweight crown in only his 12th professional fight, a points decision over Nicaragua's Adonis Rivas in Buenos Aries. In doing so, Narvaez became the first boxer who competed at the Sydney Olympics to become a professional world champion.

He turned pro after another future world champion, Wladimir Sidorenko, had eliminated him from the competition. Narvaez was already 25, mature and strong, and adapted quickly to the rigours of the professional ring, winning his first world title in little more than 18 months. He was not a champion who confined himself to defending at home and was never afraid to travel into his challenger's territory.

Narvaez did that twice with the capable Sardinian, Andrea Sarritzu. The first time he retained his title with a split decision. The rematch was even closer – a draw – but Narvaez returned home with his belt. He also stopped Frenchman Bernard Inom in 11 and outpointed Brahim Asloum, a Sydney gold medallist, on points. The tough, veteran Russian Alexander Mahmutov also was beaten in 11 rounds.

After 16 title defences, Narvaez stepped up to super-flyweight and won the vacant WBO belt by outpointing Everth Briceno in May 2010. He made two defences and stepped up to bantamweight to challenge Nonito Donaire for his WBC and WBO belts. Outpointed by Donaire, Narvaez returned to 115lb to defend his WBO title. He finally lost the belt in December 2014, knocked out in two rounds by Japanese prodigy Naoya Inoue, but he was still fighting at the end of 2017.

Azumah Nelson

Born: *Accra, Ghana, July 19, 1958*
Titles: *Commonwealth featherweight champion 1981–83, WBC champion 1984–88, WBC super-featherweight champion 1988–94, 1995–97*
Record: *46 contests, 39 wins, 2 draws, 5 defeats*

The ageless African ended 1995 by battering Gabriel Ruelas to defeat to regain the WBC super-featherweight title, an astonishing performance by a man who had his first world title fight 13 years previously.

Nelson was a Commonwealth Games featherweight gold medallist in 1978 and had a meteoric rise as a pro, lifting the Ghanaian title in his second fight, the African title in his sixth, and the Commonwealth title in his tenth. He came in as a late substitute against WBC champion Salvador Sanchez in July 1982, and made his reputation by taking Sanchez into the 15th round.

Two years later, Nelson took the title, retaining it with six victories and then moving up to outpoint Mario Martinez for the vacant WBC super-featherweight title in 1988. He made nine successful defences until Jesse James Leija, who had held him to a draw in a 1993 challenge, outpointed him in May 1994, and when Nelson took 18 months out of the ring it was assumed he had retired... until that remarkable comeback against Ruelas. In March 1997, Nelson, aged 38, was outpointed by Genaro Hernandez for the WBC title and he retired in 1998.

Terry Norris

Born: *Lubbock, Texas, June 17, 1967*
Titles: *WBC light-middleweight champion 1990–93, 1994, 1995–97, IBF champion 1995–97*
Record: *56 contests, 47 wins, 9 defeats*

The gifted but erratic Norris was prone to lapses of concentration and self-control. In 1987 he was disqualified for hitting Joe Walker when he was down; lost his WBC light-middleweight title in November 1994 to Luis Santana – who was lying on a stretcher at the time – for a rabbit punch; and, again against Santana, for hitting after the bell. But, in August 1995, he stopped Santana to become a three-time world champion.

A pro since August 1986, he challenged Julian Jackson for the WBA title in July 1989, hurting Jackson badly before being stopped in the second round. He succeeded at the second attempt, knocking out John Mugabi in a round for the WBC title in March 1990, and made ten defences – including a win over Ray Leonard –

before Simon Brown knocked him out in December 1993. He beat Brown in a return in May 1994, and then came his three-fight series with Santana.

Norris took the IBF title from Paul Vaden in December 1995. He lost the WBC title when Keith Mullings beat him in nine rounds in December 1997 and should have retired then, but his 25th – and last – world title fight was in November 1998, a loss to WBA champion Laurent Boudouani.

Ken Norton

Born: *Jacksonville, Illinois, August 9, 1945*
Titles: *WBC heavyweight champion 1978*
Record: *50 contests, 42 wins, 1 draw, 7 defeats*

Even the greatest fighters have opponents who, while technically inferior, will give them trouble. In the case of Muhammad Ali, it was Ken Norton, who fought Ali three times. Even though Norton got only one verdict, the other two were very close.

A former US Marine, Norton won his first 16 in a row, 15 inside schedule, before Jose Luis Garcia beat him in July 1970. He put together a winning streak of 14, including breaking Ali's jaw in a points win for the NABF title in March 1973. Ali won the return six months later, and in his next outing, Norton was humiliated in two rounds going for George Foreman's world title. He rebounded with seven straight knockouts, then was outpointed by Ali in their 1976 title fight. When Leon Spinks was stripped of the WBC title in 1978, Norton was named champion. He lost the title in his first defence, to Larry Holmes, and boxed only five more times before retiring in 1981. He died, aged 70, on September 18, 2013.

Michael Nunn

Born: *Sherman Oaks, California, April 14, 1963*
Titles: *IBF middleweight champion 1988–91, WBA super-middleweight champion 1992–93*
Record: *62 contests, 58 wins, 4 defeats*

For a while in the late 1980s, this tall southpaw looked to have the potential to become one of the great middleweight champions. He won 168 out of 174 fights as an amateur, having been inspired to take up boxing by watching Ray Leonard in the 1976 Olympics.

He just missed out on an Olympic place in 1984 and turned pro in December that year, winning all 30 on the way to the IBF middleweight title which he took from Frank Tate in July 1988.

Nunn made five defences, until suffering a dramatic, 11th-round knockout by James "Lights Out" Toney. He stepped up to win the NABF super-middleweight title, and took the WBA title from tough Panamanian Victor Cordoba in September 1992. He made four winning defences to bring his record to 42 wins in 43 fights, but then performed lethargically to lose on points to American Steve Little in London in February 1994. Nunn lost a decision to Frankie Liles at the end of 1994, and although his weight sometimes ballooned to cruiser, he lost a split decision in a WBC Interim light-heavyweight title bout against Graciano Rocchigiani in Germany in 1998. Nunn retired, then in 2004 was sentenced to at least 24 years in jail for a serious drug offence. Witnesses said he had been involved in the drug trade since the early 1990s.

Philadelphia Jack O'Brien

Real name: *Joseph Francis Hagen (O'Hagan)*
Born: *Philadelphia, Pennsylvania, January 17, 1878*
Titles: *World light-heavyweight champion 1905–06*
Record: *185 contests, 93 wins, 16 draws, 69 No Decisions, 7 defeats*

O'Brien's parents came from a small townland in County Derry, Ireland. Their son, who started boxing for a living in 1896, was an incorrigible and unrepentant rogue who figured in a host of fixed fights, including the one that made him world light-heavyweight champion. Only two years after he knocked out Bob Fitzsimmons to become champion in December 1905, O'Brien published a signed statement in a San Francisco newspaper revealing that the title fight, like most of his 150-odd contests up to then, had been a fraud.

He fought Tommy Burns twice for the heavyweight title, drawing with him in November 1906 and losing on points in May 1907. Both were set-ups, he cheerfully acknowledged. Oddly, O'Brien scaled under the modern light-middleweight limit in the first Burns fight, weighing in at 153½lb, while Burns himself was only 170lb.

O'Brien faced many champions and contenders in a career spanning 185 fights, 69 of them No Decision affairs, but his extraordinary admissions make it impossible to know from this distance in time whether he could really fight at all.

Ruben Olivares

Born: *Mexico City, Mexico, January 14, 1947*
Titles: *World bantamweight champion 1969–70, 1971–72, WBA featherweight champion 1974, WBC featherweight champion 1975*
Record: *104 contests, 88 wins, 3 draws, 13 defeats*

Genuine one-punch knockout hitters are rare, but Ruben Olivares certainly had the knack. The Mexican, unusually, came from a prosperous background: his father was a successful businessman, and Ruben boxed simply because he liked it. He was unbeaten in his first 60 fights after turning professional in February 1964, and only four of them went the distance.

An eighth-round win over perennial contender Joe Medel in 1968 earned him a crack at Lionel Rose's bantamweight title, and the thunderous hitting challenger won it at a canter in three rounds. He went on to retain it against respected opponents Alan Rudkin and Chuchu Castillo, but Castillo beat him on a 14th-round cuts stoppage in October 1970. It was the first defeat of his career. Olivares recaptured the title in 1971, losing it in his fourth defence to Rafael Herrera in March 1972.

He returned as a featherweight and fought his way to the WBA title, which he won in July 1974, but lost four months later to Alexis Arguello. Boxers as popular as Olivares never lack for opportunities, and he won the WBC featherweight crown from Bobby Chacon in June 1975. Again his reign was short, David Kotey outpointing him in a thriller three months later. He was stopped by Eusebio Pedroza for the WBA title in 1979, and retired shortly afterwards.

Carl "Bobo" Olson

Born: *Honolulu, Hawaii, July 11, 1928*
Titles: *World middleweight champion 1953–55*
Record: *117 contests, 99 wins, 2 draws, 16 defeats*

Tattooed and balding, Olson was a fixture in the world ratings from 1950 until his retirement in 1966, a real model of consistency. Olson, whose father was Swedish and mother Portuguese, was in such a hurry to box professionally that he lied about his age. When the authorities learned the truth, he left for San Francisco, and had his first seven fights there before returning home in 1946.

He progressed to fight Ray Robinson for a version of the middleweight title, but was knocked out in 12 rounds in 1950. Robinson outpointed him in 1952 for the real title but, when he retired, Olson beat Randy Turpin for the vacant championship in October 1953. He retained it against three tough challengers, but failed in a bid for Archie Moore's light-heavyweight title in 1955.

His old foe Robinson – now back out of retirement – reclaimed the title from him with a second-round knockout in December that year, and beat him again, in four rounds, the following year. Olson then moved up to light-heavyweight permanently, occasionally even taking on heavyweights, but he continued to campaign in the top class to the end of his long career. Olson died on January 16, 2002, after a battle with Alzheimer's Disease in his final years.

Carlos Ortiz

Born: *Ponce, Puerto Rico, September 9, 1936*
Titles: *World light-welterweight champion 1959–60, world lightweight champion 1962–65, 1965–68*
Record: *70 contests, 61 wins, 1 draw, 1 No Contest, 7 defeats*

The smooth-boxing Ortiz, who moved to New York at nine and represented America as an amateur, was the first champion of the revived 140-lb division, but he really made his mark as a two-time lightweight champion.

He turned pro in 1955 and was a contender by 1958, but when the chance came to contest the vacant light-welterweight title against Kenny Lane, he jumped at the opportunity. The fight, in New York in June 1959, ended disappointingly when Lane was stopped on a cut in the second round.

Ortiz defended against Battling Torres and Duilio Loi, then lost his next two title fights with the Italian and came back down to lightweight, outscoring long-serving champion Joe Brown in April 1962. He defended his crown in Tokyo, Puerto Rico (twice) and the Philippines, losing to Ismael Laguna in Panama in April 1965. Ortiz won the rematch and made a further five successful defences before Carlos Teo Cruz ended his reign in Santo Domingo in June 1968.

Down on his luck, he launched a comeback in 1971 that brought him nine more wins, but which finally ended in a defeat by Ken Buchanan in September 1972.

Manuel Ortiz

Born: *Corona, California, July 2, 1916*
Titles: *World bantamweght champion 1942–47, 1947–50*
Record: *130 contests, 98 wins, 3 draws, 29 defeats*

Manuel Ortiz, the son of Mexican immigrants, is deservedly remembered as one of the finest of all bantamweight champions. Yet there was little hint of future greatness as he lost nine of his first 23 fights after turning professional in 1938. It was hardly surprising, though, as he was facing world-class opponents, such as Richie Lemos, Small Montana and Lou Salica, all of whom would become world champions of one kind or another.

Three wins out of four against Jackie Jurich earned him a flyweight rating in 1940, and in August 1942 he outscored bantamweight champion Lou Salica to launch his phenomenal reign. Apart from a two-month break in 1947, when he lost the title to Harold Dade in January and regained it in March, he was champion for eight years and made 19 successful defences. Yet he could be an indifferent performer in non-title matches, and lost nine of them.

He faced nine world champions, at every weight from flyweight to lightweight. Ortiz was finally beaten by Vic Toweel in Johannesburg in May 1950, and he never got another chance to regain the title he had graced for so long. Ortiz was only 53 when he died on May 31, 1970.

SVEN OTTKE *(left) made 21 defences of his IBF super-middlweight title*

Sven Ottke

Born: *Berlin, Germany, June 3,1967*
Titles: *IBF super-middleweight champion 1998–2004, WBA super-middleweight champion 2003–04*
Record: *34 contests, 34 wins*

Ottke's cautious, economical style was not to everyone's taste, but nobody could argue with the success it brought him. After taking up the sport at the age of 14, he established himself as one of the leading amateurs in the world. In a career of more than 300 contests, he boxed in three consecutive Olympics – Seoul in 1988, Barcelona in 1992, and Atlanta in 1996 – won gold medals in two European championships, bronze in a third and also bronze in the 1989 world championships. His international career brought him wins over American trio Michael Moorer, Chris Byrd, and Antonio Tarver.

After turning professional, the one-time plasterer's apprentice took only 13 fights to win the IBF super-middleweight title with a disputed split decision over Charles Brewer in Germany. Some felt Ottke's home advantage helped him in close verdicts – and it is true opponents had cases for saying they outworked him – but at the end of his career he was still unbeaten. He beat Byron Mitchell on another split decision to become WBA as well as IBF champion. In the end he made 21 defences of the IBF belt, including wins over Robin Reid, Mads Larsen, Silvio Branco, Glen Johnson, and David Starie.

After a costly divorce Ottke contemplated a comeback at the age of 40, but the idea failed to attract TV interest and was dropped.

Manny Pacquiao

Born: *Bukidnon, Philippines, December 17, 1978*
Titles: *WBC flyweight champion 1998–99, IBF super-bantamweight champion 2001–03, WBC super-featherweight champion 2008, WBC lightweight champion 2008, WBO welterweight champion 2009–12 & 2014–15, 2016–17, WBC light-middleweight champion 2010–11*
Record: *65 contests, 57 wins, 2 draws, 6 defeats*

In his prime, Pacquiao, a fast, heavy-handed southpaw, topped the pound-for-pound lists along with Floyd Mayweather Jr. The fight the world wanted to see finally happened in May 2015. Pacquiao was well beaten on points, and explained that just before the fight he had injured a shoulder that required surgery.

Despite that, Pacquiao will be remembered as one of the finest fighters of his generation. In the Philippines he is an iconic figure.

He had held the WBC flyweight and IBF super-bantamweight titles on the way up, but it was in San Antonio, Texas, in November 2003 that he exploded on to the big stage when he dominated and demolished Marco Antonio Barrera in 11 rounds. In May 2004, he looked set for a sensational win over Juan Manuel Marquez when he floored him three times in the opening round, but the crafty, unerringly determined Mexican worked his way back to earn a 12-round draw.

When he met the third of that great trio of Mexicans, Erik Morales, in March 2005, Pacquiao was systematically outboxed and he lost the decision. However, he won the rematch on a tenth-round stoppage, and beat Morales in the decider in three rounds, though the Mexican had slid from his peak.

Pacquiao still lived in the Philippines, but then trained under Freddie Roach at the Wild Card gym in Los Angeles. Whenever he went home, he was mobbed as a national hero. He beat the faded Barrera again on points, and then fought Marquez again for the WBC super-featherweight crown in

ROBBED *Most fight fans believed Manny Pacquiao beat Timothy Bradley in June 2012, but the judges thought otherwise*

Las Vegas in March 2008. It was less spectacular this time, but very close again: Pacquiao won a split decision after 12 rounds.

He had begun his march through the divisions, beating David Diaz in nine rounds for the WBC lightweight belt, annihilating Ricky Hatton with a second-round knockout at light-welterweight, and handing out a sustained lesson to Miguel Angel Cotto for the WBO welterweight championship – the Puerto Rican finally rescued in the 12th round.

Pacquiao became a six-weight world champion with a points win over Antonio Margarito in November 2010 that brought the vacant WBC light-middleweight title. Timothy Bradley brought an end to Pacquiao's 15-fight, seven-year winning run with a controversial points win in June 2012 and, six months later, Marquez claimed victory in their fourth fight with a chilling six-round knockout. He beat Jessie Vargas to win the vacant WBO welterweight title in November 2016 but, surprisingly, lost his next fight, on points, to Australia's Jeff Horn.

Carlos Palomino

Born: *San Luis, Mexico, August 10, 1949*
Titles: *WBC welterweight champion 1976–79*
Record: *38 contests, 31 wins, 3 draws, 4 defeats*

The moustachioed Mexican, who did most of his fighting in Los Angeles, was a cool professional who was at his best when under pressure. He was a fine all-round technician with a particularly sharp left hook, equally effective to head or body, and he used the body punches to devastating effect when, after 22 fights (three draws, one defeat) he challenged John H. Stracey for the WBC welterweight title at Wembley in June 1976.

Stracey was rescued in the 12th round as he knelt on the ring canvas, gasping for breath. It was the start of Palomino's busy spell as champion. He stopped Armando Muniz with 36 seconds left in the final round, with the points exactly even, and had a hard struggle against Englishman Dave Green, but produced a great left hook to knock Green out cold in the 11th round.

He made five more successful defences, beating Muniz again in May 1978, but then lost the title to Wilfred Benitez in January 1979. Following a loss to Roberto Duran, he retired but, aged 47, returned to the ring, won four fights and then lost to Wilfredo Rivera, who was 17 years his junior.

Billy Papke

Born: *Spring Valley, Illinois, September 17, 1886*
Titles: *World middleweight champion 1908, 1910–13*
Record: *62 contests, 37 wins, 6 draws, 8 No Decisions, 11 defeats*

Papke was an unscrupulous fighter who would do anything to gain an edge, as he demonstrated by smashing Stanley Ketchel in the throat as the referee was completing his instructions before their middleweight title fight in September 1908. He was allowed to get away with it, and Ketchel, who had not recovered from the foul, was knocked out in the 12th round. It was their second meeting, Ketchel having ruined Papke's 29-fight unbeaten record by outpointing him three months earlier.

In their third meeting, Ketchel administered a savage beating, knocking him out in the 11th, and outpointed him again the following year. When Ketchel gave up the title in 1910, Papke regained it by knocking out Willie Lewis, but then Ketchel changed his mind and was once more regarded as champion until he was shot dead in October 1910.

Papke proclaimed himself champion again, and defended his version of the title three times, losing it, with poetic justice, on disqualification to Frank Klaus in 1913. He had just three more fights before his retirement in 1919. He murdered his wife and committed suicide in Newport, California, on November 26, 1936.

Laszlo Papp

Born: *Debrecan, Hungary, March 25, 1926*
Titles: *European middleweight champion 1962–65*
Record: *29 contests, 26 wins, 3 draws*

Considering that he did not have his first professional fight until he was 31, Papp's record is impressive. A power-hitting southpaw, he won three Olympic Games gold medals at middleweight (1948) and light-middleweight (1952 and 1956), a hitherto unmatched feat, which the Hungarian government rewarded by giving him permission to box for money. He was the only man to be given this concession until the collapse of the Communist system, decades after Papp's retirement.

They did not go so far as allowing him to box at home, so he fought mainly in Vienna against a string of Europeans and imported Americans. He moved steadily up the world ratings, but a recurring hand injury cost him vital time out of the ring and delayed a European title chance until May 1962, when he stopped the balding Dane Chris Christensen.

He defended the title six times around the continent, in Paris, Vienna, Dortmund, Madrid and Copenhagen, and by 1965 negotiations were under way for a world title challenge against Joey Giardello. But the government abruptly withdrew their permission for Papp to box for money and he was forced to retire undefeated. He later became the Hungarian team coach and was 77 when he died in Budapest, Hungary on October 16, 2003.

Willie Pastrano

Born: *New Orleans, Louisiana, November 27, 1935*
Titles: *World light-heavyweight champion 1963–65*
Record: *84 contests, 63 wins, 8 draws, 13 defeats*

The handsome Pastrano, an indefatigable womanizer, was never more than a natural light-heavyweight but he routinely fought full-blown heavyweights. His very "British" style of left-hand boxing was particularly appreciated in England, where he appeared five times between 1958 and 1959.

He was not a big puncher, scoring only 14 inside-schedule wins in 84 fights, but within two years of his pro debut, aged 16 in 1951, Pastrano was meeting rated opposition. He entered the world heavyweight ratings in 1955 with wins over Joey Maxim and Rex Layne but, according to trainer Angelo Dundee, he always preferred a pretty girl to a session in the gym. By the early 1960s, his ambition seemed to have evaporated.

Pastrano won only once in three meetings with Wayne Thornton in 1963, but that proved a blessing in disguise. Light-heavyweight champion Harold Johnson decided that Pastrano would make a safe defence, but came unstuck as the challenger was given a controversial points decision. He retained the title twice, and retired after Jose Torres stopped him in March 1965. He died on December 6, 1997, aged 62.

Jackie Paterson

Born: *Springfield, Scotland, September 5, 1920*
Titles: *British flyweight champion 1939–48, Empire flyweight champion 1940–48, world flyweight champion 1943–48, Empire bantamweight champion 1945–49, European bantamweight champion 1946, British bantamweight champion 1947–49*
Record: *92 contests, 64 wins, 3 draws, 25 defeats*

Weight-making ruined this hard-hitting southpaw, who struggled to make the flyweight limit. He had a meteoric rise, winning the vacant British and Empire titles at 19, but losing an early bantamweight foray when outpointed by Jim Brady in a thriller for the Empire title.

In June 1943 he flattened Peter Kane in 61 seconds to become world champion, but thereafter met bantams and even feathers. He reversed the Brady result in September 1945, adding the European bantamweight title by beating Theo Medina, and drew a Scottish record crowd of 50,000 for his first defence of the world title, a points win over Joe Curran in June 1946 (which levelled their series at 2–2).

Paterson promptly lost his European title to Medina, but took the British bantamweight championship from Johnny King in February 1947. Having already lost NBA recognition because of weight problems, he went through agonies to get down to 112lb for a world flyweight title defence against Rinty Monaghan, who had beaten him once already. This time, Paterson was knocked out in seven rounds. His remaining titles soon went, and he retired in 1951.

He emigrated to South Africa, where he was murdered in 1966.

Floyd Patterson

Born: *Waco, North Carolina, January 4, 1935*
Titles: *World heavyweight champion 1956–59, 1960–62*
Record: *64 contests, 55 wins, 1 draw, 8 defeats*

Boxing proved the making of Patterson. He was a disturbed youth, but his life changed when he met trainer Cus D'Amato. He became D'Amato's star pupil, winning the 1952 Olympic middleweight gold medal when he was just 17. He turned pro under D'Amato's fiercely independent management, losing only to Joey Maxim in his first 36 fights. When Rocky Marciano retired, Patterson became the youngest-ever heavyweight champion, knocking out Archie Moore in November 1956. But he was never more than a cruiserweight (190lb), and was always vulnerable against fully fledged heavyweights, taking a total of 17 counts in his championship reign.

D'Amato picked easy opponents (one, Pete Rademacher, was having his first pro fight!), but in his fifth defence Patterson was knocked down seven times by Sweden's Ingemar Johansson and was stopped in the third round. He regained the title a year later, the first to do so, but lost it in one round to Sonny Liston and failed in attempts to regain it from Liston, Muhammad Ali and Jimmy Ellis (for the WBA title). He retired in 1972, and served several terms as New York State Athletic Commissioner. He died on May 11, 2006, aged 71.

Eusebio Pedroza

Born: *Panama City, Panama, March 2, 1953*
Titles: *WBA featherweight champion 1978–85*
Record: *49 contests, 42 wins, 1 draw, 6 defeats*

The tall Panamanian was a true professional who faced every worthwhile contender and, in the course of a 20-defence tenure of the WBA featherweight title, gave new significance to the term "world champion". He risked his title in Puerto Rico, America, Japan, New Guinea, Korea, Venezuela, Italy, St Vincent and England, and proved unbeatable from 1978 until Ireland's Barry McGuigan outworked him in June 1985.

He began his career as a bantamweight, but was easily dismissed in two rounds by Alfonso Zamora when he tried for the WBA title in April 1978. That was his second knockout loss in 16 fights, and when it happened again two fights later Pedroza looked finished. Instead, he moved up to featherweight, and was instantly successful.

He took the WBA title from a moderate champion, Cecilio Lastra of Spain, but quickly proved his worth by defeating a host of outstanding challengers. Pedroza acquired a reputation as a dirty fighter, but performed impeccably when losing to McGuigan in a superb contest. He retired after it, before made a short comeback as a lightweight.

Paul Pender

Born: *Brookline, Massachusetts, June 20, 1930*
Titles: *New York and European recognition as world middleweight champion 1960–61, 1962*
Record: *48 contests, 40 wins, 2 draws, 6 defeats*

Few fans outside Boston had heard of Paul Pender when the news came through on January 23, 1960, that the one-time fireman had ended Sugar Ray Robinson's reign as middleweight champion the previous night. The Irish-American with the distinctively crooked nose had done nothing previously to suggest he was capable of such an upset, barely scraping into the world ratings.

His career had started promisingly enough in January 1949, and he went undefeated in 21 fights before a run of bad form that saw him win only twice in seven attempts. He was consistently handicapped by injuries to his brittle hands, and had only five contests between March 1952 and November 1958, one of them a points defeat by future champion Gene Fullmer.

Pender returned to regular action late in 1958 and, on the back of a winning run of nine fights, earned the shot at Robinson. The verdict in their first fight was close enough for argument, but Pender won the return convincingly and retained the championship against Terry Downes and Carmen Basilio before losing to Downes in a rematch. He regained

GENIUS *Willie Pep once won a round without throwing a punch!*

the title from the Englishman in April 1962. After the fight Pender retired and never boxed again. He died in Bedford, Massachusetts, on January 12, 2003, aged 72.

Willie Pep

Real name: *Guglielmo Papaleo*
Born: *Middletown, Connecticut, September 19, 1922*
Titles: *New York recognition as world featherweight champion, 1942–46, world champion 1946–48, 1949–50*
Record: *242 contests, 230 wins, 1 draw, 11 defeats*

The cleverest featherweight of them all, Pep's defensive wizardry earned him the nickname "Will O' The Wisp". He was introduced to boxing when his father took him to watch the state's earlier featherweight idol, Bat Battalino, and one of his only two amateur defeats was to Ray Robinson. He turned pro at 17 and reeled off 62 straight wins before lightweight champion Sammy Angott outpointed him in March 1943, but then put together another amazing run of 73 victories.

He became the youngest world champion in 40 years by outpointing Chalky Wright for the New York title in November 1942, but the war restricted him to three defences between then and June 1946, when he knocked out NBA champion Sal Bartolo for the undisputed title.

He was dethroned in October 1948 by his great rival Sandy Saddler, but gave his finest display to outscore Saddler in a rematch in February 1949. He then made three more defences before Saddler took the title back in seven rounds and retained it in nine. Pep boxed on until 1959, and staged a brief comeback in 1965–66. He was 84 when he died in Connecticut on November 23, 2006.

Pascual Perez

Born: *Tupungate, Argentina, March 4, 1926*
Titles: *World flyweight champion 1954–60*
Record: *92 contests, 84 wins, 1 draw, 7 defeats*

The diminutive Argentinean stood only 4ft 10½in, but is a giant in the history of the flyweight division. He won the 1948 Olympic gold medal, but did not turn professional for another four years, by which time he was 26. Despite the late start he was an instant success, taking the Argentine title in only his seventh fight and winning the world championship from Yoshio Shirai in November 1954.

He extended his unbeaten run to 51, including seven defences in Japan, Argentina and the Philippines before Sadao Yaoita outpointed him in a non-title match in Tokyo in January 1959. Perez knocked him out in a championship rematch in November 1959, but then lost the title to Pone Kingpetch in April 1960. It was only his second loss in 56 fights. Kingpetch stopped him in eight rounds in a return in Los Angeles, the first time in 25 years that the flyweight title had been contested in America. Perez retired in 1964, and died in Argentina on January 22, 1977.

Lupe Pintor

Real name: *Jose Guadalupe Pintor*
Born: *Cuajimalpa, Mexico, April 13, 1955*
Titles: *WBC bantamweight champion 1979–83, WBC super-bantamweight champion 1985–86*
Record: *72 contests, 56 wins, 2 draws, 14 defeats*

Pintor won the WBC bantamweight title on a highly debatable split decision from his stablemate Carlos Zarate in June 1979: two judges had Pintor ahead by a solitary point, 143–142, but the third gave it to Zarate by a huge margin, 145–133. It was an unconvincing start, but the hard-punching Mexican developed into a solid champion, proving himself with eight successful defences. One, against the Welshman Johnny Owen, ended in tragedy. Owen was knocked out in the 12th round and died, after weeks in a coma, on November 4, 1980.

Pintor tried for Wilfredo Gomez's WBC super-bantamweight title in 1982, but the brilliant Puerto Rican was too big for him and stopped him in 14 rounds. In 1983, Pintor suffered serious injuries in a motorbike accident, and his title was declared vacant because of his inability to defend it.

He returned to action as a super-bantamweight, and took the WBC title from Juan Meza in Mexico City in 1985, but forfeited the title on the scales when he turned up three pounds overweight for his first defence, against Samart Payakarun. Pintor made an unsuccessful comeback in the 1990s.

Aaron Pryor

Born: *Cincinnati, Ohio, October 20, 1955*
Titles: *WBA light-welterweight champion 1980–83, IBF light-welterweight champion 1983–85*
Record: *40 contests, 39 wins, 1 defeat*

Yet another victim of America's drug culture, Pryor could have become the greatest of all the light-welterweight champions. Known as "The Hawk" because of the speed and ferocity of his attacks, he even rated comparison with Henry Armstrong, one of the few champions who could have matched his prodigious work-rate.

He was unstoppable as an amateur, winning the AAU title and boxing for his country before turning professional in November 1976. He was very much a hometown boy, most of his fights taking place in Cincinnati, and his reluctance to move to more glamorous venues probably prevented him becoming champion earlier. His chance finally came in Cincinnati in August 1980, when he knocked out Antonio Cervantes in four round.

Pryor made eight defences before relinquishing the title to accept recognition by the newly formed IBF. But he was already hooked on drugs, and drifted away from the sport after two IBF defences. When Pryor first retired, he had a perfect 36–0 record, but, blind in one eye and financially ruined, he made a bizarre comeback attempt some years later and was knocked out.

Dwight Muhammad Qawi

Formerly known as Dwight Braxton
Born: *Baltimore, Maryland, January 5, 1953*
Titles: *WBC light-heavyweight champion 1981–83, WBA cruiserweight champion 1985–86*
Record: *53 contests, 41 wins, 1 draw, 11 defeats*

This busy, aggressive fighter, known as "The Camden Buzzsaw", learned his boxing in the toughest school imaginable – Rahway State Penitentiary, New Jersey. He had never boxed as an amateur, but joined the boxing programme to relieve the frustrations of jail life.

He became a professional upon his release in 1978, managed by a former lightweight challenger, Wesley Mouzon, and not surprisingly won only once in his first three starts. But he learned quickly, and a run of 15 straight wins carried him to the WBC light-heavyweight title, which he took from another tough warrior, Matthew Saad Muhammad in December 1981. Curiously, one of his major wins was over a long-term inmate at Rahway, James Scott, and because all of Scott's fights had to be staged inside the prison, Braxton went back to fight there.

Braxton converted to Islam in 1982, following his second victory over Matthew Saad Muhammad. Boxing as Qawi, he lost to Mike Spinks in a unification match in 1983, but won the WBA cruiserweight title two years later and retained it against Mike's brother Leon before being knocked out by IBF champion Evander Holyfield. Robert Daniels beat him in a WBA title bid in 1989. He retired in 1992, had a brief comeback five years on and retired for good at the age of 45.

GUILLERMO RIGONDEAUX *took his slick amateur skills into the professional ring and won a world title in just his ninth fight*

Ike Quartey

Real name: *Issifu Quartey*
Born: *Accra, Ghana, Nov 27, 1969*
Titles: *WBC International welterweight champion 1992, WBA welterweight champion 1994–98*
Record: *42 contests, 37 wins, 1 draw, 4 defeats*

Ike "Bazooka" Quartey was one of the hardest hitting welterweights of the 1990s. He came desperately close to dethroning Oscar De La Hoya, in a tense WBC title fight in February 1999. Both were down in round six, but De La Hoya produced a last-round knockdown to clinch a split decision.

Quartey's elder brother Clement won a boxing medal in the Commonwealth Games. Ike was only 17 when he boxed in the 1988 Seoul Olympics, before turning professional. After taking the Ghanaian, African and WBC International titles at light-welterweight, he knocked out Venezuela's Crisanto Espana to win the WBA welterweight crown in 1994. Over the next few years he developed into one of the most dangerous fighters in world boxing.

Vincent Phillips, who became IBF champion, was destroyed in three rounds. Oba Carr did take him the distance in New York, and his final defence suggested he was getting bored: a 12-round draw against former WBO champion José Luis Lopez. The WBA stripped him in 1998, when he was inactive for the whole year, and then came the defeat by De La Hoya, a fight Quartey believed he had won. After losing to Fernando Vargas he retired to Ghana, but made a comeback and even in defeat showed he still had his old skills.

Frankie Randall

Born: *Birmingham, Alabama, September 25, 1961*
Titles: *WBC light-welterweight champion 1994, WBA light-welterweight champion 1994–96, 1996–97*
Record: *78 contests, 59 wins, 1 draw, 18 defeats*

Frankie "The Surgeon" Randall overcame drugs and alcohol addiction, endured a jail sentence, and beat odds of 15–1 to inflict a first defeat on WBC light-welterweight king Julio Cesar Chavez. Randall started boxing aged nine after moving to Morristown, Tennessee, and one of his rare defeats in 236 fights was to future IBF champion Joe Louis Manley in trials for the 1980 Olympics.

He turned pro in 1983, winning 23 straight before ex-champ Edwin Rosario outscored him in London in 1985. He came back strongly with a stoppage of Sammy Fuentes and a draw with Freddie Pendleton, both future world champions, but then, on the verge of a title shot, he was jailed for dealing in drugs in 1990.

By 1993, he was a top contender again and in January 1994 he floored Chavez and took a deserved points win. Chavez won a controversial technical decision in the rematch, but Randall rebounded to beat WBA champion Juan Martin Coggi in September 1994 for his second world title. He lost and regained the belt against Coggi in January and August 1996 respectively, but was finally dethroned by France's Khalid Rahilou in January 1997. Randall boxed on far too long, into his mid-40s, when he was a shell of the fighter he once was.

Guillermo Rigondeaux

Born: *Santiago de Cuba, Cuba, September 30, 1980*
Titles: *WBA super-bantamweight champion 2012–17, WBO super-bantamweight champion 2013–17*
Record: *18 contests, 17 wins, 1 defeat*

Until he ran into Hisashi Amagasha in December 2014, Rigondeaux was looking unbeatable. The Cuban southpaw still won, but survived two knockdowns to do it. He was also on the floor against Nonito Donaire in April 2013, but again picked himself up to add the WBO title to his WBA belt.

That should have been a breakthrough for Rigondeaux, but audiences in America didn't like his skilful performances, and promoters Top Rank dropped him.

An all-time amateur great, of his reported 477 bouts, he lost only 12, won back-to-back Olympic gold medals at bantamweight in 2000 and 2004 and was the 2001 world amateur champion.

Rigondeaux defected – at the second attempt – and was fast-tracked after turning professional aged 28. He stepped up to world level after just six fights and 23 rounds in 18 months as a pro. In his seventh fight, he won the WBA interim world title by outpointing Ricardo Cordoba for title in November 2010. Two fights later, in January 2012, Rigondeaux took the full title, overwhelming previously unbeaten Rico Ramos in six rounds.

He lost his IBO belt in controversial circumstances in June 2017, knocking out Moises Flores after the bell had rung at the end of the first round and, in his next fight, was stopped in six rounds by Vasyl Lomachenko to lose his WBO title.

Sugar Ray Robinson

see Legends of the Ring (pp 92–93)

Maxie Rosenbloom

Born: *New York, New York, September 6, 1904*
Titles: *World light-heavyweight champion 1930–34*
Record: *299 contests, 210 wins, 26 draws, 23 No Decisions, 2 No Contests, 38 defeats*

Rosenbloom's nickname of "Slapsie Maxie" derived from his tendency to hit with the open glove, which resulted in him winning only 19 of his fights inside schedule. But he was a cagey boxer who knew how to avoid trouble, and was himself only stopped twice.

He was a clown in the ring, and because he was an entertainer, Rosenbloom never lacked work. For nearly five years he averaged a fight every fortnight, having 30 in 1932. When Tommy Loughran retired as light-heavyweight champion in September 1929, Jimmy Slattery, an old rival of Rosenbloom's, won New York recognition but lost that to Rosenbloom in June 1930, the NBA subsequently also recognizing Maxie as champion.

The NBA stripped him in June 1931 for failing to defend on time, and their title eventually passed to Bob Godwin on March 1, 1933. Three weeks later Rosenbloom knocked him out to become undisputed king again, a distinction he held until a disputed points loss to Bob Olin in November 1934. He became a well-known character actor after his retirement in 1939, and died in Los Angeles on March 6, 1976.

Gianfranco Rosi

Born: *Perugia, Italy, August 5, 1957*
Titles: *European welterweight champion 1984–85, WBC light-middleweight champion 1987– 88, IBF champion 1989–94, WBO champion 1995*
Record: *70 contests, 62 wins, 1 draw, 1 No Contest, 6 defeats*

The awkward Italian spoiler was a significant figure in light-middleweight affairs between 1987, when he won the WBC title, and 1995, when, after a long spell as IBF title-holder, he won the WBO championship, only to be stripped of this title for failing a post-fight drug test.

Rosi won national titles at light-welterweight and welterweight as an amateur, turning professional in 1979. He lost only one of his first 33 fights, lifting the Italian and European welterweight titles, but moved up to light-middleweight soon after losing the European belt to Lloyd Honeyghan on a third-round knockout. After taking his second European title from Chris Pyatt, he outpointed Lupe Aquino for the WBC title, which he held for only nine months until Don Curry knocked him out.

He took the IBF version from Darrin Van Horn in February 1989, retaining it 11 times before Vincent Pettway beat him easily in four rounds in September 1994. Surprisingly, the WBO gave him yet another chance, which he seemed to have taken in style by outpointing Verno Phillips in his hometown of Perugia. A few days later, though, he was a disgraced ex-champion.

Rosi came out of a six-year retirement to compete on the European circuit and was 49 years old when he was badly knocked out and hospitalized by France's Robert Roselia in San Marino in 2006. This time it he quit permanently.

Barney Ross

Real name: *Beryl David Rosofsky*
Born: *New York, December 23, 1909*
Titles: *World lightweight and light-welterweight champion 1933–35, world welterweight champion 1934, 1935–38*
Record: *81 contests, 73 wins, 3 draws, 1 No Decision, 4 defeats*

The stylish Ross was a three-weight world champion in the days when that feat was infinitely harder to accomplish than it is today. He was raised in Chicago, turning professional in 1929 after robbers murdered his father, a grocer. He quickly became popular and Al Capone was a regular ringsider, although there was no suggestion that he ever "helped" Ross.

A points win over Tony Canzoneri in 1933 made him champion at lightweight and light-welterweight, but he relinquished the former after beating Canzoneri in a rematch. He held on to the heavier title, defending that nine times until giving it up in June 1935. He had become a double champion once again in May 1934 when he took the welterweight title from Jimmy McLarnin in the first of three famous meetings, losing to him four months later and then regaining it in May 1935. He finally lost the championship to Henry Armstrong, and immediately retired.

Ross was a much-decorated war hero, and won a long battle against drug addiction caused by medical treatment for his wounds. He died in Chicago on January 17, 1967.

Tommy Ryan

Real name: *Joseph Youngs*
Born: *Redwood, New York, March 31, 1870*
Titles: *World welterweight champion 1891–95, world middleweight champion 1898–1902*
Record: *113 contests, 87 wins, 4 draws, 12 No Decisions, 10 defeats*

Ryan reflected the fashion of the time by choosing an Irish ring name, although his father was French and his mother English. He started boxing in 1887, and claimed the welterweight title after the untimely death of champion Paddy Duffy in July 1890.

Ryan's claim was disputed by Mysterious Billy Smith, but he settled the argument by outpointing Smith. He defended twice, including a stoppage of "Nonpareil" Jack Dempsey, but was subsequently unable to make the championship limit (then 142lb), even though he continued to style himself as champion until 1898.

Kid McCoy knocked him out in March 1896 to become recognized as middleweight champion following Bob Fitzsimmons's retirement, but when McCoy relinquished the title Ryan took it over and held it for four years until his retirement in 1904. He stayed inactive for two years, and made a brief comeback in 1907.

He lost only three fights, two to McCoy and one on a foul to George Green, which he avenged in his next fight. He died in Van Nuys, California, on August 3, 1948.

Joseph "Sandy" Saddler

Born: *Boston, Massachusetts, June 23, 1926*
Titles: *World featherweight champion 1948–49, 1950–57; limited recognition as world junior-lightweight champion 1949–51*
Record: *163 contests, 145 wins, 2 draws, 16 defeats*

Saddler's unusual punching power brought him 103 inside-schedule wins. Of West Indian parentage, Saddler was reared in New York and had only a few amateur fights before turning professional in March 1944.

He worked hard: 22 fights in 1944 and 24 unbeaten in 1945, including 14 consecutive knockouts. But it took him 94 fights before he was given a title shot, although he had been rated for three years. Champion Willie Pep performed pathetically when they met in October 1948, losing in four rounds, but the rematch set a new indoor attendance record of 19,097, and this time Pep won comfortably.

Saddler collected a version of the super-featherweight title while he waited for a third fight with Pep, which he won on an eight-round retirement in September 1950. Their fourth meeting a year later earned Saddler (a famously dirty fighter) a 30-day suspension for fouling Pep, who lost in nine rounds. He was still champion when, in 1957, he was forced to retire after being injured in a car crash, later becoming a respected trainer. He died on September 18, 2001, aged 75.

Vicente Saldivar

Real name: *Vicente Saldivar Garcia*
Born: *Mexico City, Mexico, May 3, 1943*
Titles: *World featherweight champion 1964–67, WBC champion 1970*
Record: *41 contests, 38 wins, 3 defeats*

Saldivar boasted an abnormally slow heart and pulse rate, which he claimed was the secret of the phenomenal pace he was able to maintain. One of a poor family of nine, he turned professional at 17 in 1961. His hard punching from a southpaw stance and relentless work-rate earned him the Mexican featherweight title in his 24th fight (23 wins).

A points defeat of future lightweight champion Ismael Laguna brought him a chance at the world title held by Mexican-based Cuban Sugar Ramos, and Saldivar won a bloody battle in 12 rounds in September 1964.

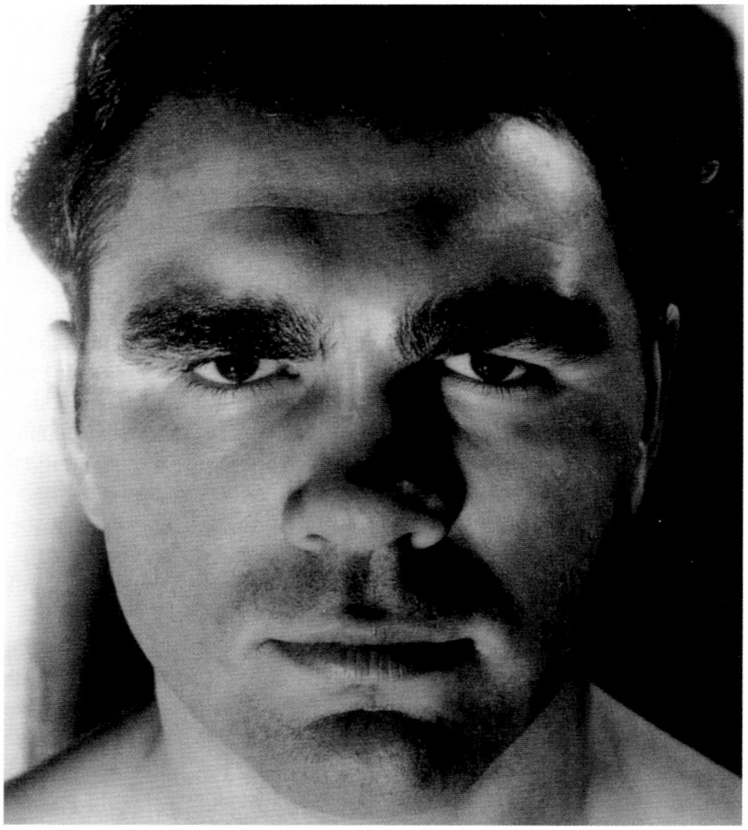

MAX SCHMELING *world heavyweight championship winner*

Eight defences followed in three years, three of them against brilliant Welshman Howard Winstone. Saldivar won the first two on razor-thin verdicts, but stopped Winstone in the 12th round of their third meeting in Mexico City and immediately announced his retirement. He was only 24 and had made eight successful defences.

He stayed out of the ring for almost two years, then beat Jose Legra to earn a title match with Johnny Famechon, whom he outpointed in Rome in May 1970 to win the WBC version of his former crown. Kuniaki Shibata dethroned him in December 1970, and he retired after failing to regain the title from Eder Jofre in 1973. He died on July 18, 1985.

Salvador Sanchez

Born: *Santiago, Mexico, February 3, 1958*
Titles: *WBC featherweight champion 1980–82*
Record: *46 contests, 44 wins, 1 draw, 1 defeat*

Salvador Sanchez's tragic death in a car accident robbed the boxing world of an extraordinary performer who may well have gone on to establish himself as the greatest featherweight in history. Three of the men against whom he defended the WBC title went on to win it after his death: Juan LaPorte, Wilfredo Gomez and Azumah Nelson.

The curly-haired Mexican won 17 of his first 18 fights inside the distance before suffering the only loss of his career when Antonio Becerra outpointed him in September 1977 for the vacant national title. He broke into the world ratings with a run of impressive results in 1979, and then battered Danny Lopez to a 13-round defeat in February 1980 to become WBC champion.

His challengers, without exception, were all top-drawer, five of them taking him the full 15 rounds. He stopped Nelson in the last round of a bruising fight in Madison Square Garden in July 1982 and, a few weeks later, on August 12, was killed at Queretaro, Mexico, in a high-speed, head-on crash in his Porsche.

Johnny Saxton

Born: *Newark, New Jersey, July 4, 1930*
Titles: *World welterweight champion 1954–55, 1956–57*
Record: *66 contests, 55 wins, 2 draws, 9 defeats*

Saxton may have been good enough to become world welterweight champion on his own, but given that his manager was Blinky Palermo, the notorious Mob figure who was the most significant of the underworld's links with boxing at the time, he simply could not miss.

He was an accomplished Golden Gloves and AAU champion before starting his paid career in 1949. More boxer than puncher, most of his victories at top level were on points. Saxton moved up the ratings in 1952–53, winning the title from Kid Gavilan in October 1954. The verdict was extremely controversial, but as the fight took place in Palermo's power-base, Philadelphia, that was hardly surprising.

He lost it on a 14th-round stoppage to Tony deMarco five months later, but regained it from Carmen Basilio in March 1956 on a verdict that was even worse than in the Gavilan fight. Public opinion forced a rematch, which Basilio won in nine rounds, and Basilio then removed all doubts by knocking him out in two rounds in February 1957. Saxton retired in 1958. He died on October 4, 2008, aged 78.

Max Schmeling

Born: *Klein Luckaw, Germany, September 28, 1905*
Titles: *European light-heavyweight champion 1927–28, world heavyweight champion 1930–32, European champion 1939*
Record: *70 contests, 56 wins, 4 draws, 10 defeats*

The heavy-browed German will always be remembered for his two fights with Joe Louis, one a glorious victory and the other an ignominious rout. Yet he was a major figure in the championship scene in the 1930s. His early career, which began in 1924, was spent in the light-heavyweight division, where he won the European championship in 1927. A first-round knockout by veteran Welshman Gypsy Daniels in February 1928 persuaded him to move up, and he became German heavyweight champion two months later before leaving for America.

When Gene Tunney retired, Schmeling was crowned champion in June 1930 while sitting on the canvas, having been fouled by Jack Sharkey. In the return, Sharkey was lucky to get the verdict. Losses to Max Baer and Steve Hamas pushed Schmeling down the list, and he seemed a safe match for the unbeaten Joe Louis in 1936 – but scored a shock, 12th-round knockout. The rematch, for Louis' title two years later, saw the German take a fearful one-round beating.

Schmeling staged a brief comeback after the war, and then made a fortune as a senior executive with Coca Cola. He retained his faculties and lived to be 99, dying on February 2, 2005.

Samuel Serrano

Born: *Toa Alto, Puerto Rico, November 17, 1952*
Titles: *WBA super-featherweight champion 1976–80, 1981–83*
Record: *57 contests, 52 wins, 1 draw, 4 defeats*

Samuel Serrano was one of those quietly effective, controlled boxers who are very hard to beat. Consequently, the Puerto Rican took part in 18 world title fights in a seven-year span during the 1970s and 1980s. He turned professional a week before his 17th birthday, in Puerto Rico in 1969, learned his trade slowly and by the middle of the next decade was accepted as one of the best 130-lb boxers in the world.

He was unlucky in his first title bout when he could only hold the defending WBA champion Ben Villaflor to a 15-round draw in Honolulu in April 1976, but made amends six months later when he beat Villaflor in a return in San Juan. Serrano was a crafty fighter who considered knockouts a bonus: most of his defences went the full 15 rounds. He had made ten when he was spectacularly upset by Japan's Yatsusune Uehara with a sixth-round knockout in the Joe Louis Arena in Detroit in August 1980. Serrano had won the first five rounds, then suffered a rare loss of concentration and was knocked out.

In the rematch in Japan the following year Serrano made light of being away from home and regained the championship by winning a close fight on points. This time he rolled out the defences until the young Roger Mayweather was just too fresh for him and stopped him in eight rounds.

Serrano quit the ring the following year, then, in his forties, decided to come back. He had two contests in Puerto Rico, won them both and, satisfied, retired for good.

Jack Sharkey

Real name: *Josef Paul Cukoschay*
Born: *Binghampton, New York, October 26, 1902*
Titles: *World heavyweight champion 1932–33*
Record: *55 contests, 38 wins, 3 draws, 1 No Decision, 13 defeats*

Doubts persist about the validity of Sharkey's defeat by Primo Carnera which cost him the heavyweight title in June 1933. The temperamental champion, a former sailor of Lithuanian extraction, had previously outpointed Carnera, yet made a feeble showing in the rematch and was knocked out in six rounds. Sharkey always refused to be drawn on the subject, but the rumours followed him to his grave.

At his best, though, Sharkey was a fine boxer who beat George Godfrey and Harry Wills to qualify for a championship eliminator with Jack Dempsey in 1927. He was clearly outboxing the former champion when, in the seventh round, he turned to complain to the referee and was knocked cold.

He fought against Max Schmeling for the vacant title in 1930, losing on a foul. He easily beat Carnera to earn another chance to fight for Schmeling's title, and this time was given a dubious verdict over the German. He enjoyed his title for a year, then lost it to Carnera and his career ended in a third-round humiliation by Joe Louis. In retirement Sharkey became a champion angler and died, aged 91, on August 17, 1994.

Battling Siki

Born: *St Louis, Senegal, September 16, 1897*
Titles: *World light-heavyweight champion 1922–23*
Record: *94 contests, 63 wins, 5 draws, 5 No Decisions, 21 defeats*

His real name will never be known, but when Siki was brought to France as a "toy boy" by a wealthy French woman she called him "Louis Phal" in joking tribute to his chief attribute, and that is what historians have solemnly recorded ever since. He had a few fights before the Great War, in which he earned the Croix De Guerre, and returned to the ring, as Battling Siki, in 1919.

He compiled an impressive record, losing only one of 45 fights, but was not considered a threat to Georges Carpentier when the French idol defended his light-heavyweight title in Paris in September 1922. Carpentier had sold the film rights for the fight, and to avoid an early finish he spurned repeated chances to win in the first round. But Siki floored him in the second and gave Carpentier a merciless beating, knocking him out in the sixth.

Siki lost the title to Mike McTigue in Dublin on St Patrick's Day, 1923, and moved to America later that year. His wild publicity stunts (he had a lion cub as a pet) kept him in the public. eye, but wins were scarce. He was found shot dead in a New York street on December 15, 1925.

Cory Spinks

Born: *St Louis, Missouri, February 20, 1978*
Titles: *IBF, WBC & WBA welterweight champion 2003–05, IBF light-middleweight champion 2006–08, 2009–10*
Record: *47 contests, 39 wins, 8 defeats*

Cory Spinks was born only five days after his father, Leon, beat Muhammad Ali for the world heavyweight title in Las Vegas. He was a boy of seven when his uncle Michael became champion by upsetting Larry Holmes. When he turned pro in 1997, few imagined he would come close to emulating them.

When he made his first bid for a world title, he had to travel to Italy to take on seasoned Michele Piccirillo for the IBF welterweight crown. Piccirillo knew too much for him and won on points. Spinks, promoted by Don King, worked his way back and almost 12 months later he returned to Italy and this time beat Piccirillo on a unanimous decision.

The fights that made Spinks were upset points wins over the marauding Nicaraguan Ricardo Mayorga and Brooklyn southpaw Zab Judah, both of whom were expected to beat him. The Mayorga fight, in Atlantic City in December 2003, was a unification: Spinks put his IBF belt on the line, Mayorga brought the WBC and WBA titles. The winner would be recognized as the world No.1. Most believed that would be Mayorga, who had knocked out Vernon Forrest to win his titles, but Spinks handled him well, boxing smoothly and winning a majority decision. Then Judah, moving up from light-welterweight, was expected to have too many skills and too much speed, but Spinks beat him even more clearly in another polished performance. A return, however, saw Judah upset Spinks in his home town of St Louis with a ninth-round stoppage in February 2005.

Spinks, with King's promotional backing, made amends when he returned to St Louis in July 2006 and became a two-weight champion by edging out Russia's Roman Karmazin on a majority decision for the IBF belt. By doing so, he matched his uncle Michael's achievement as a light-heavy and then heavyweight champion. In May 2007, Spinks lost a disputed split decision to Jermain Taylor in a bid for the world middleweight crown and returned to 154lb.

He lost the IBF title on a shock split decision to Verno Phillips, but regained it in April 2009, again on a split vote, this time against the less-experienced Deandre Latimore. The title was lost to Cornelius Bundrage via a five-round stoppage and Bundrage also won the rematch, this time in seven rounds.

Leon Spinks

Born: *St Louis, Missouri, July 11, 1953*
Titles: *World heavyweight champion 1978*
Record: *45 contests, 25 wins, 3 draws, 17 defeats*

It still seems unbelievable, but it happened in February 1978 in Las Vegas: Leon Spinks outpointed Muhammad Ali for the world heavyweight title, after only seven professional fights. There was nothing lucky about the verdict, either – Spinks won deservedly, but his tragedy was that the biggest triumph of his life would ultimately destroy him. The gap-toothed, almost illiterate Spinks was singularly ill-equipped to handle the money and the attention which that memorable victory brought him, and his life has been in a downward spiral ever since.

He had the pedigree to be champion, having won the light-heavyweight gold medal in the 1976 Olympics, but lacked the discipline and sophistication to go with it. Ali easily outpointed him in the rematch in September 1978, and then Gerrie Coetzee destroyed him in a round in a WBA eliminator.

Larry Holmes gave him a title shot in 1981, stopping him in three rounds, and Spinks dropped to cruiserweight to challenge Dwight Muhammad Qawi unsuccessfully for the WBA title in 1986. His money and his talent long gone, Spinks fought on. In 1995, he lost to a youngster making his pro debut – and retired the following year. A decade later, his son Cory became a world champion at welter and light-middleweight.

Michael Spinks

Born: *St Louis, Missouri, July 13, 1956*
Titles: *WBA light-heavyweight champion 1981–83, world light-heavyweight champion 1983–85, IBF heavyweight champion 1985–87*
Record: *32 contests, 31 wins, 1 defeat*

It would be hard to find two brothers less alike in nature than the Spinks. Michael had the qualities Leon lacked, and was able to retire as a wealthy and respected two-weight world champion, while his brother, to whom he remained devoted, unfortunately became a joke figure.

They both struck gold at the 1976 Olympics, Michael at middleweight, and when Leon found success so quickly, Michael selflessly put his own career on hold to help him. He resumed in 1980, and had won 16 in a row when he outpointed Eddie Mustafa Muhammad for the WBA light-heavyweight title in November 1981. He retained that five times, then beat WBC champion Dwight Muhammad Qawi for the undisputed title in March 1983.

He relinquished the title on becoming IBF heavyweight champion with a disputed points win over Larry Holmes in September 1985. He won an equally controversial verdict in the rematch, and defended the title only once before being stripped for fighting Gerry Cooney instead of Tony Tucker. A knockout of Cooney brought a match with Mike Tyson, but Spinks was annihilated inside a round and never boxed again.

Young Stribling

Real name: *William Lawrence Stribling*
Born: *Bainbridge, Georgia, December 26, 1904*
Titles: *none*
Record: *286 contests, 222 wins, 14 draws, 36 No Decisions, 2 No Contests, 12 defeats*

Known as "The Georgia Peach", Stribling is remembered for his colourful background and lifestyle as much as for his accomplishments in the ring. He won 222 out of 286 fights in a remarkably busy 12-year career, which would have easily topped 300 fights had he not been killed in a motorbike accident on October 2, 1933, returning from a fight in Houston where he had just beaten the light-heavyweight champion Maxie Rosenbloom in a non-title match.

His parents were circus acrobats, and Stribling and his brother worked as "midget boxers" in their boyhood. His formidable mother took over his management when he turned professional in January 1921, and worked him hard: he often had more than 30 fights a year.

Paul Berlenbach outpointed him in a light-heavyweight title bid in 1925, but Stribling took on heavyweights with such success that, after a triumphant tour of Europe under Jeff Dickson's promotion, he was given a crack at Max Schmeling's world title in 1931. But he fought an uncharacteristically negative battle, and was knocked out in the 15th.

John L. Sullivan

Born: *Roxbury, Massachusetts, October 15, 1858*
Titles: *World heavyweight champion 1882–1892*
Record: *45 contests, 41 wins, 3 draws, 1 defeat*

For ten years, John Lawrence Sullivan was the undisputed heavyweight champion of the world. And didn't everyone know it! His party piece was to march into a bar – and he visited many – and bellow: "I can lick any son-of-a-bitch in the house!"

While modern sensibilities may encourage us to disapprove of this boorish, overbearing champion, his impact on boxing as a sport was considerable. After a succession of dreary, ineffective titleholders, Sullivan's larger-than-life personality ensured the old bare-knuckle game was handed over to its glove-wearing successors with a swagger and a sense of purpose. Born of Irish parents, Sullivan won the bare-knuckle championship by demolishing Paddy Ryan from Troy, New York, in ten minutes in 1882. "I felt as if a telegraph pole had been shoved against me endways," complained the beaten Ryan. By then Sullivan was leaning out of his hotel windows, tossing dollar bills to the crowds paying homage below.

Sullivan's finest challengers were the crafty little Englishman, Charlie Mitchell, who held on for a draw in a 39-round marathon in Chantilly, north of Paris, and Jake Kilrain, who lasted 75 rounds in the last of the bare-knuckle championship bouts in Richburg, Mississippi, in 1889.

After that, Sullivan said he would never fight with knuckles again – and also, while he was thinking about principles, said he would never fight a black man, which coincidentally barred his major challenger, the great West Indian, Peter Jackson. In 1892, the ageing, fat champion lost the title in 21 rounds to James J. Corbett in New Orleans.

Ernie Terrell

Born: *Chicago, Illinois, April 4, 1939*
Titles: *WBA heavyweight champion 1965–67*
Record: *55 contests, 46 wins, 9 defeats*

His spoiling style meant that the 6ft 6in Terrell was never a real crowd-pleaser, but he certainly frustrated a lot of good fighters. Terrell did not attract much attention until 1963, nearly six years into his career, when he scored back-to-back wins over dangerous puncher Cleveland Williams and long-time contender Zora Folley.

By late 1964, heavyweight champion Muhammad Ali had become deeply unpopular with the American establishment because of his alignment with the so-called Black Muslims. So, when Ali signed for a rematch with Sonny Liston, the WBA used that as an excuse to strip him of their title, although return fights were commonplace. Terrell beat Eddie Machen for the vacant title in March 1965, and made some money defending it against George Chuvalo and Doug Jones. In all three fights Terrell took the decision on points.

A reunification match with Ali in Houston in February 1967 proved an unedifying spectacle. Terrell insisted on calling Ali by what Ali considered to be his "slave name", Cassius Clay, so Ali tormented him for 15 rounds, following every punch with the question "What's my name?" The beating finished Terrell as a fighter, and an attempted comeback was a failure. He later became a manager and promoter in Chicago.

Marcel Thil

Born: *Saint-Dizier, France, May 25, 1904*
Titles: *European middleweight champion 1929–30, 1934–38, and light-heavyweight champion 1934–35, IBU middleweight champion 1932–37*
Record: *149 contests, 113 wins, 14 draws, 22 defeats*

Unlike France's other boxing heroes Georges Carpentier and Marcel Cerdan, Marcel Thil was not the stuff of which young girls' dreams are made. He was prematurely bald, with a chest hairy enough to pass as a doormat. But he was a competent fighter who won 113 of his 148 fights, and for nearly five years the European-based IBU recognized him as world middleweight champion.

Thil won only 12 of his first 25 fights, but he hit form in 1928 and an unbeaten run of 15 contests carried him to the French and European titles, losing the latter to Mario Bosisio in November 1930. But his messy, brawling style brought him another 21 consecutive wins, including the 11th-round disqualification victory over the American NBA champion Gorilla Jones, which earned Thil IBU recognition.

He retained the championship nine times, including surprising points defeats of Len Harvey and Kid Tunero and a pair of disqualification wins over Lou Brouillard. In 1937, he went to New York in the hope of resolving the muddled championship position, but was stopped in ten rounds by Fred Apostoli and promptly retired. He died in Cannes on August 14, 1968.

Dick Tiger

Real name: *Richard Ihetu*
Born: *Amaigbo, Orlu, Nigeria, August 14, 1929*
Titles: *Empire middleweight champion 1958–60, 1960–62, WBA middleweight champion 1962, world champion 1962–63, 1965–66, world light-heavyweight champion 1966–68*
Record: *82 contests, 60 wins, 3 draws, 19 defeats*

The muscular Tiger lost only one of his 16 bouts in Nigeria, but found it a tougher game when he came to England in 1953 and lost his first four. But he was tough and determined. The breakthrough came when he stopped London favourite Terry Downes in five rounds. Downes earned £125, Tiger £75!

Tiger took the Empire title from Pat McAteer, then settled in New York, scoring a string of wins over the cream of a particularly tough division. The only real setback was the temporary loss of his Empire title to Wilf Greaves in June 1960: he regained it in November.

He outpointed Gene Fullmer for the WBA title, drew with him in a rematch, and then stopped him in seven to earn universal recognition. He lost and won in title fights with Joey Giardello, then lost the title again to Emile Griffith and moved up to become light-heavyweight champion by outpointing Jose Torres. He was beaten in his third defence by Bob Foster, retiring in July 1971. The Nigerian Civil War bankrupted him, and he died of liver cancer on December 14, 1971.

JAMES TONEY *was an intimidating fighter who went undefeated in his first 42 fights and went on to become a two-weight world champion*

James Toney

Born: *Grand Rapids, Michigan, August 24, 1968*
Titles: *IBF middleweight champion 1991–93, IBF super-middleweight champion 1993–94*
Record: *90 contests, 76 wins, 3 draws, 2 no contests, 9 defeats*

A truly intimidating fighter, Toney was undefeated in his first 42 fights before Roy Jones dazzled him to a points defeat in November 1994 to take his IBF super-middleweight title. It was an impressive record, considering Toney (whose hard punching earned him the nickname "Lights Out") had won no titles in his brief – 24-fight – amateur career.

But under the guidance of the glamorous Jackie Kallen, one of the few top-flight female managers, he made rapid progress after turning professional in October 1988, winning the Michigan State title and the IBC Americas championship. A victory over Merqui Sosa moved him to the top of the queue to face the unbeaten IBF middleweight champion Michael Nunn and he stunned the boxing world with an 11th-round, one-punch knockout in May 1991.

He proved less impressive as champion, struggling to retain the title against Reggie Johnson, Mike McCallum (twice) and David Tiberi, but he looked much more at home in the 168lb division when he took the IBF title from Iran Barkley in 1993 and retained it three times before losing to Jones.

Toney's weight troubles increased, but he kept fighting at a good level. He won a couple of minor titles, then upset Vassily Jirov to win the IBF cruiserweight title in 2003. He relinquished it immediately to box at heavyweight and in his debut in the division he stopped Evander Holyfield in the ninth round in Las Vegas. Toney beat defending WBA heavyweight champion John Ruiz only for the result to be wiped from the record books after Toney tested positive for a steroid.

After a short ban, he drew with WBC champion Hasim Rahman in March 2006. Then, aged 43, Toney fought Denis Lebedev for the interim WBA cruiserweight title, but was soundly outpointed in November 2011. Possibly his last chance at reaching world class again disappeared in April 2013 when Australian heavyweight Lucas Browne outpointed him in Melbourne. He has fought five times since, winning three and losing two of the bouts.

Felix Trinidad

Born: *Cupoy Alto, Puerto Rico, January 10, 1973*
Title: *IBF welterweight champion 1993–99, WBC welterweight champion 1999, WBA & IBF light-middleweight champion 2000–01, WBA middleweight champion 2001*
Record: *45 contests, 42 wins, 3 defeats*

Felix "Tito" Trinidad, a lethal puncher with a leaky defence, won world titles at three weights before surprising the boxing world by announcing his retirement in 2002 at the age of 29. Trinidad was only 20 when he won the IBF welterweight title with a second-round dismissal of the capable Maurice Blocker in San Diego in 1993. For the next six years the lean, organized Puerto Rican kept his championship and, coached by his father and promoted, for the most part, by Don King, he became a national hero in Puerto Rico.

His defining fight came in Las Vegas in September 1999 when he beat Oscar De La Hoya on a split decision – a verdict that upset many. A return was talked about but never materialized. Trinidad instead moved up to light-middleweight and outpointed 1996 Olympic gold medallist David Reid for the WBA belt. A 12th-round stoppage of the talented young IBF champion Fernando Vargas confirmed his class, and then he stopped William Joppy in five for the WBA middleweight title.

That win was a part of Don King's grand plan to unify the middleweight division, and in September 2001 Trinidad lost for the first time when Bernard Hopkins, the WBC and IBF champion, wore him down and stopped him in the last round at Madison Square Garden, New York. Trinidad retired after beating the former WBC champion Hassine Cherifi of France in a non-title fight. Trinidad couldn't resist the temptation to box again, however, and returned to stop the controversial Nicaraguan Ricardo Mayorga. Dreams of another world title were destroyed when Winky Wright handed him a boxing lesson in May 2005. He had one final payday, against Roy Jones Jr at Madison Square Garden in 2008, but lost the fight on points.

Konstantin Tszyu

Born: *Serov, Russia, September 19, 1969*
Titles: *IBF light-welterweight champion 1995–97, 2001–05, WBC light-welterweight champion 1999–2005, WBA light-welterweight champion 2001–05*
Record: *34 contests, 31 wins, 1 No Contest, 2 defeat*

When Konstantin Tszyu burst on to the professional world stage in 1995 by stopping highly respected IBF light-welterweight champion Jake Rodriguez, it seemed a new megastar had arrived. In fact it took the pig-tailed, Australian-based Russian six more years to prove his right to be considered the best 140-lb fighter of his generation.

Tszyu was a magnificent amateur – he was world champion in 1991 – and made such an impact at that event in Sydney that he turned professional in Australia. His family joined him and he settled down to fight his way to the top. After the win over Rodriguez, he held the IBF belt for two years but then lost to Vince Phillips on a shock tenth-round stoppage in May 1997. His doubters, who said he took too many punches for a top-level fighter, underestimated his resilience.

Two years later, he battered the resistance out of former lightweight champion Miguel Angel Gonzalez of Mexico, and this time there were no more mistakes on the way to establishing his supremacy. He stopped the WBA champion, Sharmba Mitchell, in seven and in a volatile fight hammered truculent Brooklyn southpaw Zab Judah in two. Judah attacked the referee afterwards and received a heavy fine. By then Tszyu was 32, but a year on he was still dominating decent challengers like Ben Tackie of Ghana.

Injuries sidelined Tszyu for more than a year, during which time the WBA and WBC withdrew recognition of him. He came back with an explosive three-round stoppage of Sharmba Mitchell, but then lost his title when trainer Johnny Lewis pulled him out after the 11th round against England's Ricky Hatton in Manchester in 2005.

Gene Tunney

Real name: *James Joseph Tunney*
Born: *New York, NY, May 25, 1897*
Titles: *American light-heavyweight champion 1922, 1923, world heavyweight champion 1926–28*
Record: *88 contests, 67 wins, 1 draw, 19 No Decisions, 1 defeats*

From the time Jack Dempsey became heavyweight champion in 1919, he was in Gene Tunney's sights. The former Marine, the son of a comfortably off family from Greenwich Village, always aspired to the championship and turned professional in 1915.

He was primarily a scientific boxer, but scored 42 inside-schedule wins in 87 fights. His career began in earnest on his return from wartime service in France in 1919, and an unbeaten run of 22 contests qualified him to challenge former world champion Battling Levinsky for the American light-heavyweight title. Tunney won, but then lost it to Harry Greb, from whom he took a fearful beating.

It proved to be the only defeat of his career, and he subsequently trounced Greb twice in title fights and in two No Decision matches. But Dempsey was always Tunney's real target, and when they met on a rainy afternoon in Philadelphia in September 1926, Tunney had his measure. He outpointed him again in the famous "Battle Of the Long Count", and defended the title only once more.

In retirement, Tunney became a wealthy businessman and father of a US Senator. He died in 1978.

Randolph Turpin

Born: *Leamington Spa, England, June 7, 1928*
Titles: *British middleweight champion 1950–54, European champion 1951–54, world champion 1951, Empire champion 1952–54, British light-heavyweight champion 1952, 1955, Empire champion 1952–55*
Record: *75 contests, 66 wins, 1 draw, 8 defeats*

For 64 glorious days in 1951, Randolph Turpin was a god. That was how long he reigned as world middleweight champion, and he was never able to recapture that glory. He began boxing while working as a Navy cook, and won ABA titles in 1945 and 1946, following his two brothers into the professional ranks later that year. His unorthodox style and powerful punches had brought him 40 wins in 43 fights (one draw) when, as British and European champion, he challenged Sugar Ray Robinson before an 18,000 crowd in London in July 1951. Robinson's preparations were casual, and he was outpointed.

The rematch in New York drew 61,370 to watch Robinson, badly cut, stop Turpin in the tenth with a desperation attack. Turpin won the British and Empire light-heavyweight titles in 1953, and was outpointed in a dull fight by Carl "Bobo" Olson for the vacant middleweight title after Robinson's retirement. He lost his European title in a round to Tibero Mitri, but won a Lonsdale Belt outright before his retirement in 1958. His money long gone, he shot himself in Leamington on May 17, 1966.

Mike Tyson

see Legends of the Ring (pp 94–95)

Rodrigo Valdes

Born: *Bolivar Colombia, Devember 22, 1946*
Titles: *WBC middleweight champion 1974–76, world champion 1977–78*
Record: *73 contests, 63 wins, 2 draws, 8 defeats*

Valdes would have made a fine world champion, had he not had the misfortune to be a contemporary of Carlos Monzon. Instead, he was obliged to be content with a spell as WBC champion after Monzon was stripped for failing to defend against him, and a five-month reign following Monzon's retirement. Valdes won 23 of 27 fights in Colombia (two draws) before moving to America in 1969.

He had some early setbacks, but entered the title picture in 1973 by outpointing Bennie Briscoe for the NABF title. They met again for the vacant WBC title in may 1974, Valdes winning in seven rounds, and the Colombian retained the title four times. Monzon outscored him in a reunification match in June 1976 and repeated the result a year later in his last fight, but Valdes snapped up the vacant title by beating Briscoe again. But he had little left, and Hugo Corro beat him twice before he retired in 1980.

Edwin Valero

Born: *Merida, Venezuela, December 3, 1981*
Titles: *WBA super-featherweight champion 2006-09, WBC lightweight champion 2009-10.*
Record: *27 contests, 27 wins*

The life of two-weight world champion Edwin Valero was cut short in horrible circumstances in April 2010, when he was still only 28.

Valero, the reigning WBC lightweight champion, was arrested for stabbing his wife to death in his home city of Merida in Venezuela. Before a case could be brought, he hanged himself in his prison cell.

Valero had a wild, tempestuous personality and a style to match: wrecking balls for fists, and the air of menace that could beat an opponent before the first bell sounds. He had the unquestioning authority of a man who did not believe he could lose. Outside the ring, his life was volatile: there was a drink-driving charge in Texas, alcohol and cocaine abuse, harassing his wife and assaulting personnel at the hospital. He had been in a psychiatric unit himself for nine days.

Valero won his first 18 professional fights in the first round, but showed he could box when he had to when taking until the tenth to stop Vicente Mosquera on the night he became WBA super-featherweight champion in Panama in August 2006.

He took out his first challenger, Michael Lozada, in 72 seconds in Tokyo, and after four defences, he moved up to win the vacant WBC lightweight championship by destroying Colombian Antonio Pitalua with three knockdowns in the second round. His reputation advanced further in February 2010 when he outgunned a slick, rising Mexican, Antonio DeMarco, in nine rounds in Monterrey.

As an amateur he won 86 of 92 contests, but in February 2001 at the age of 19, he fractured his skull in a motorbike accident. He needed surgery to remove a blood clot from his brain.

Nikolay Valuev

Born: *St Petersburg, Russia, August 21, 1973*
Titles: *WBA heavyweight champion 2005–07, 2008–09*
Record: *53 contests, 50 wins, 1 No Contest, 2 defeats*

The tallest and heaviest man to hold a version of the world heavyweight championship by some distance, Nikolay Valuev added some spice to the division just when it needed it.

After the retirement of Lennox Lewis, nobody dominated. The four main sanctioning bodies soon had their own champions, none of them demonstrably better than the other. Some felt Vitali Klitschko was Lewis' natural successor, but injuries forced his retirement. The heavyweight division was in a void when up stepped Valuev, nicknamed years before as "The Beast from the East" by Lewis' manager, Frank Maloney, who guided him for a while. Valuev, who had tried his luck at basketball and athletics (field events, naturally) before settling on boxing, had learned to fight in the pro ring after a brief amateur education. By the time he linked up with German promoter Wilfried Sauerland, he had paid his dues around the globe: in Australia, Japan, Korea and all over Europe.

Sauerland believed that, as well as being hard to beat because of his size, Valuev had an intelligence in and out of the ring that belied his "incredible hulk" image. When he set eyes on him, before they fought in Berlin in December 2005, defending WBA champion John Ruiz said: "I can't miss him. He's got a head the size of a Volkswagen." But at the end of 12 close rounds, Valuev was the new champion on a majority decision. At home in Russia, where he lived with his wife Galina and son Grigory, he was feted. "I train in Germany," he told his people, "but St Petersburg is where I belong." Away from the ring, he read Agatha Christie, Arthur Conan Doyle – even Tolstoy. His sheer size was enough to intimidate ordinary heavyweights. One American, after meeting him at the weigh-in, said: "Nobody told me I was fighting Big Foot," and headed straight for the hotel bar! Another, Larry Donald, said: "I never faced a man like him. In fact, I've never seen a man like him. He's like something from the Dark Ages."

After beating Ruiz, Valuev saw off second division heavyweights Owen Beck and Monte Barrett inside the distance and then won again when Jameel McCline was carried out of the ring after suffering a horrible knee injury in round three. Valuev and McCline set a new record for combined weight in a world championship boxing match – 590½lb! Valuev lost the WBA title when southpaw Ruslan Chagaev outsmarted him, but he worked his way back and regained it by outboxing John Ruiz for a second time in Berlin in August 2008. This time his reign lasted 15 months. He survived a close call with Evander Holyfield, then lost to David Haye in Nuremberg in November 2009 and, at 36, there was no coming back from the defeat.

Fernando Vargas

Born: *Oxnard, California, December 7, 1977*
Titles: *IBF light-middleweight champion 1998–2000, WBA light-middleweight champion 2001–02*
Record: *31 contests, 26 wins, 5 defeats*

Fernando Vargas was a precocious talent. He was only 18 when he lost a disputed 8–7 computer decision to Marian Simion at the Atlanta Olympics, and immediately turned professional with the powerful Main Events team. Only five days past his 21st birthday, Vargas was a world professional champion at light-middleweight thanks to a seven-rounds masterclass against the dangerous Mexican puncher "Yory Boy" Campas.

Vargas was not afraid of big fights, and while others have fought more, and rattled up longer unbeaten records, the Californian of Mexican extraction was fighting in the highest class almost from the start of his career. He turned back challenges from two of the best boxers of his era, southpaw Ronald "Winky" Wright and Ghana's Ike Quartey, both on points. His reign came to an end in December 2000 when he went in a bit too soon with Felix Trinidad and was stopped in the 12th.

But Vargas was not one to worry about setbacks like that and rallied to win the WBA light-middleweight title within nine months, thanks to a seventh-round knockout of Jose "Shibata" Flores. Vargas, who was rarely polite about any opponent, held a deep grudge towards Oscar De La Hoya, dating back to an early career incident – he said the Golden Boy laughed at him when he fell into a snow-drift on an early morning run. When they boxed in a light-middleweight unification fight in 2002, Vargas was stopped in the 11th round – and then tested positive for a steroid. Something had been knocked out of him, and he was twice beaten by Shane Mosley in 2006 and then retired after losing to Ricardo Mayorga in Los Angeles in 2007.

Pancho Villa

Real name: *Francisco Guilledo*
Born: *Illoilo, Philippines, August 1, 1901*
Titles: *American flyweight champion 1922–23, world champion 1923–25*
Record: *109 contests, 80 wins, 4 draws, 20 No Decisions, 5 defeats*

The busy little Filipino crammed 105 fights into a six-year career which began in 1919. He lost only twice in 56 fights before leaving for America in the spring of 1922, and promoter Tex Rickard developed him into a major attraction. Villa won the American title by knocking out Johnny Buff and retained it twice before losing to Frankie Genaro. But Rickard kept faith, and persuaded world champion Jimmy Wilde – by then retired – to face his protégé. Wilde was paid $65,000, a flyweight record, but was knocked out in seven rounds.

Villa made four defences, the one which gave him most pleasure being his defeat of Jose Sencio in Manila. Sadly, it was his last victory: in July 1925, two months after beating Sencio, Villa was outpointed over ten

NICHOLAS WALTERS *lands a power punch on Nonito Donaire during their 2014 WBA world featherweight title fight*

rounds by Jimmy McLarnin. He had had a wisdom tooth extracted the previous afternoon, and an abscess developed. Blood poisoning ensued, and Villa died on July 14, 1925.

Joe Walcott

Born: *Barbados, March 13, 1873*
Titles: *World welterweight champion 1897–98, 1901–06*
Record: *165 contests, 94 wins, 23 draws, 24 No Decisions, 24 defeats*

One of the better early welterweight champions, Walcott stood only 5ft 1½in but routinely gave weight away to middleweights and even heavyweights during his 21 years in the ring. Known as the "Barbados Demon", he settled in Boston in 1887, where he boxed and wrestled as an amateur until his professional boxing debut in February 1890. Boxing as a lightweight, he worked his way up to a match with champion George Lavigne, but lost the fight on a 12th-round retirement. He stepped up to welterweight, but was held to a draw and then outscored by Mysterious Billy Smith, their second clash involving Smith's title. They met six times, and their fights were so dirty that Smith had to lodge a "good behaviour" bond of $250 before one.

Walcott finally became champion in 1901 when he stopped Rube Ferns, and he retained the title four times before Honey Mellody stopped him in 12 rounds in September 1906. He retired in 1911 and died in a car crash near Massillon, Ohio, in 1935.

Jersey Joe Walcott

Real name: *Arnold Raymond Cream*
Born: *Merchantville, New Jersey, January 31, 1914*
Titles: *World heavyweight champion 1951–52*
Record: *72 contests, 53 wins, 1 draw, 18 defeats*

Walcott made his name in a spirited challenge for Joe Louis' heavyweight title in 1947, but the fight almost did not happen. The New York Commission were so unimpressed by Walcott's record that they demanded the fight be billed merely as an exhibition. They only relented under pressure from the champion.

The Commission's attitude was unfair to the challenger. In fact, Walcott floored Louis twice in the contest, but went on to lose an unpopular split decision.

That showing earned him three more title chances, one against Louis, which ended in an 11th-round knockout, and two against Ezzard Charles, both ending in losing decisions. Walcott was given a third shot against Charles in July 1951, and this time knocked him out in seven rounds to become, at 37, the oldest heavyweight champion.

He retained the title against Charles, but was then knocked out by Rocky Marciano in the 13th after outboxing the challenger. When Marciano flattened him in a round in the return in 1951, Walcott retired. He died, aged 80, on February 25, 1994.

Mickey Walker

Real name: *Edward Patrick Walker*
Born: *Elizabeth, New Jersey, July 13, 1901*
Titles: *World welterweight champion 1922–26, world middleweight champion 1926–31*
Record: *163 contests, 94 wins, 4 draws, 45 No Decisions, 1 No Contest, 19 defeats*

Mickey Walker was a relentless battler who loved to fight almost as much he enjoyed drinking and womanizing. He won world titles at welterweight and middleweight, fought twice for the light-heavyweight title and drew with future heavyweight champion Jack Sharkey. He faced 15 world champions in a 163-fight career and married four women, three of them twice.

Walker took the welterweight title from Jack Britton in November 1922, and made three defences before Pete Latzo outpointed him in May 1926. Joe Dundee knocked him out in eight rounds a few weeks later, prompting a move up to middleweight. He had already challenged Harry Greb in a famous 15-rounder for the middleweight title in July 1925, and he succeeded at the second attempt, outpointing Greb's conqueror Tiger Flowers.

He retained it three times, in between challenging for the light-heavyweight title, then relinquished the championship to box at heavyweight. His busy career ended in 1935, and he later became an internationally known painter. He died at Freehold, New Jersey, on April 28, 1981.

Nicholas Walters

Born: *Montego Bay, Jamaica, April 1, 1986*
Titles: *WBA featherweight champion 2012–15*
Record: *26 contests, 26 wins*

Known as "The Axeman", Nicholas Walters, the son of a former professional featherweight, Job, is a lean boxer-puncher with lights-out power.

Inspired by watching his father train, he took up boxing and had a reported 320 amateur bouts, and boxed in the 2007 world championships before turning pro the following year.

He got his chance to win the WBA featherweight title after Nonito Donaire was upgraded to Super champion – and became the first Jamaican to win world honours on home soil by stopping Daulis Prescott in seven rounds in December 2012.

His five-round knock-out of 38 year-old Vic Darchinyan in his second defence was brutal and Walters raised his profile further with a stoppage of four-weight world champion Donaire in October 2014.

Saved by the bell at the end of the second, after being badly shaken up, Walters dropped Donaire twice and stopped him in six. Walters lost the title on the scales in June 2015 before a defence against Miguel Marriaga.

Andre Ward

Born: *Oakland, California, February 23, 1984*
Titles: *WBA super world super-middleweight champion 2009–, WBC super-middleweight champion 2011–13, IBF light-heavyweight champion 2016–, WBO light-heavyweight champion 2016–*
Record: *32 contests, 32 wins*

As gold medallist in the 2004 Olympics, and with a 115–5 amateur record, much was expected of Ward when he turned professional. He has delivered.

Ward proved he was the world's best at 168lb – and entered the pound-for-pound rankings – by winning the Super Six tournament. Mikkel Kessler had been beaten just once in 43 fights, but Ward was too quick and slick, and was a clear points winner. He outclassed substitute Allan Green to set up a final against Carl Froch in December 2011. Ward banked the early rounds, held off a late-round surge and won on points.

No one wanted to face him, until Chad Dawson stepped down from light-heavyweight in December 2012, but he was thrashed in ten rounds and Ward's only fight in 2013 was a unanimous decision over Edwin Rodriguez. He didn't box in 2014, but returned in June 2015 to stop Paul Smith and continued to impress, notably with back-to-back victories over Sergey Kovalev.

Freddie Welsh

Real name: *Frederick Hall Thomas*
Born: *Pontypridd, Wales, March 5, 1886*
Titles: *European lightweight champion 1909–14, British lightweight champion 1909–11, 1912, Empire champion 1912, world champion 1914–17*
Record: *168 contests, 76 wins, 6 draws, 82 No Decisions, 4 defeats*

A sloppy MC was responsible for Freddie Thomas acquiring his ring name: he neglected to check the boy's name on his pro debut in Philadelphia and, hearing his accent, announced him as "Freddie Welsh". It stuck, and the clever-boxing Welshman soon became a star.

He won the British title from Johnny Summers in September 1909, a month after beating Henri Piet for the European title, and added the Empire championship by outpointing the Australian Hughie Mehegan in 1912. He also won a Lonsdale Belt outright by outpointing Matt Wells, having put his second notch on it in a bitter clash with his great Welsh contemporary Jim Driscoll.

Wins over top contenders Leach Cross and Joe Rivers earned him a world title chance against Willie Ritchie, although by the time Ritchie had been paid there was virtually nothing left for the challenger. But Welsh won on points and then toured America, boxing mostly No Decision matches. He made only one official defence, and Benny Leonard claimed the title after knocking Welsh out in an overweight fight in May 1917. He died in New York, penniless, on July 29, 1927.

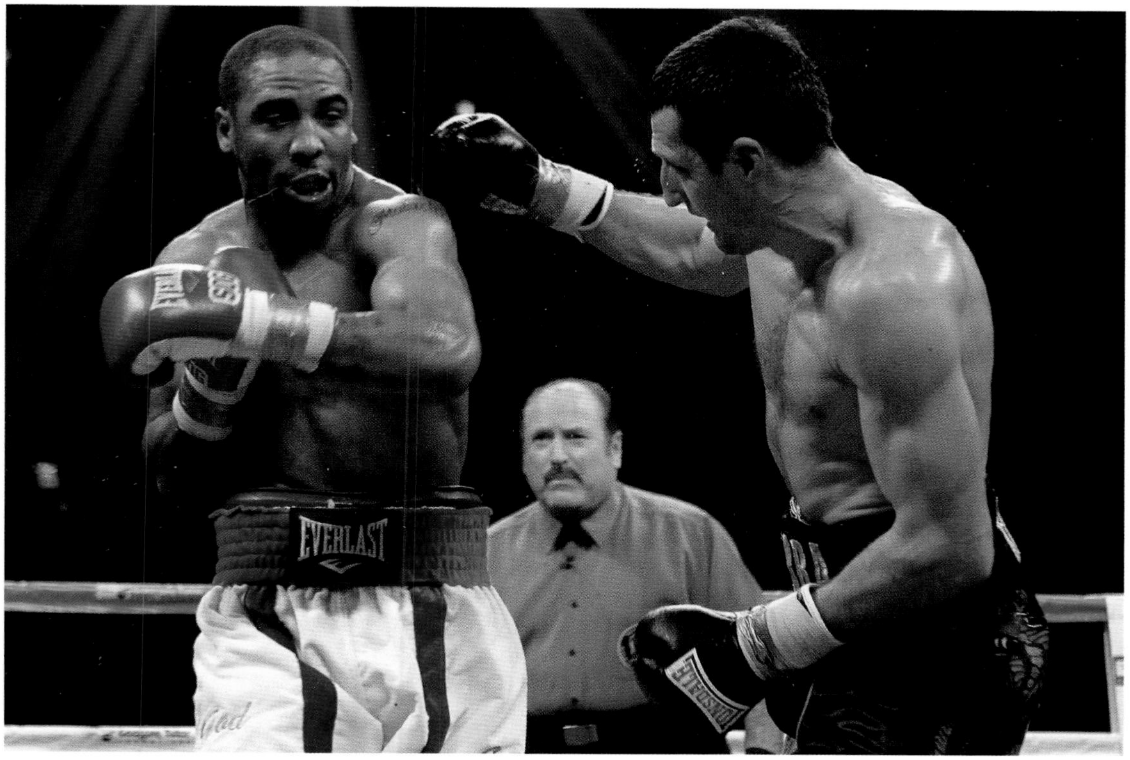

SENSATIONAL *Andre Ward outclassed Carl Froch in the final of the "Super Six"*

Pernell Whitaker

Born: *Norfolk, Virginia, January 2, 1964*
Titles: *IBF lightweight champion 1989–92, WBC champion 1989–92, WBA champion 1990–92, IBF light-welterweight champion 1992–93, WBC welterweight champion 1993–97, WBA light-middleweight champion 1995*
Record: *46 contests, 40 wins, 1 draw, 1 No Contest, 4 defeats*

World titles at every weight from lightweight to light-middleweight mark Whitaker as one of the era's foremost stars. In his peak years Whitaker's only setbacks were a points loss to Jose Luis Ramirez in his first lightweight title fight – a verdict generally considered to be a disgrace – and an equally controversial draw with Julio Cesar Chavez in San Antonio in 1993. Again, Whitaker was harshly treated.

He was America's top amateur, turning pro after taking a gold medal in the 1984 Olympics. The Ramirez "loss" in March 1988 snapped his winning run at 15, but he soon got back on course by taking the IBF title from Greg Haugen, the WBC belt in a rematch with Ramirez, and then the WBA title, which he won on a first-round knockout of Juan Nazario. He stepped up to win the IBF light-welter title from Rafael Pineda in July 1992, then took the WBC welterweight championship from Buddy McGirt. Whitaker completed the four-timer in March 1995 by outscoring Julio Cesar Vasquez for the WBA light-middleweight title – and immediately relinquished it to concentrate on the welterweight crown, which he lost to Oscar De La Hoya in April 1997. In February 1999, after a year's drug suspension, Whitaker was outpointed by IBF champion Felix Trinidad.

Jimmy Wilde

see Legends of the Ring (pp 96–97)

DEONTAY WILDER *won the heavyweight title America was waiting for*

Deontay Wilder

Born: *Tuscaloosa, Alabama, October 22, 1985*
Titles: *WBC heavyweight champion 2015–*
Record: *40 contests, 40 wins*

Deontay Wilder became the first American to hold a version of the world heavyweight title for more than seven years when outpointing Bermane Stiverne to win the WBC belt in January 2015.

He had won his first 32 fights inside four rounds, but after hurting his right hand in the fourth round, 6ft 7in Wilder used his physical advantages and athleticism to earn a unanimous points decision. He kept the belt with a nine-round knockout of Eric Molina. and has gone on to make six further successful defences – all inside the distance and two of them by knockout.

In his teens, Wilder, from Alabama, showed promise as a basketball player and American footballer, but quit collegiate sports aged 19, after his daughter Naieya was born with spina bifida.

He didn't start boxing until 2005 and, less than three years later, won bronze at the Beijing Olympics, the only American to come home with a boxing medal. Wilder turned professional and in his first 12 fights, he only went beyond the first round twice.

He picked himself off the floor to beat journeyman Harold Sconiers and climbed into world-title contention by blasting out ex-WBO champion Siarhei Laiakhovich and Malik Scott inside a round apiece with right hands

Jess Willard

Born: *Pottawatomie, Kansas, December 29, 1881*
Titles: *World heavyweight champion 1915–19*
Record: *35 contests, 23 wins, 1 draw, 5 No Decisions, 6 defeats*

By today's standards Willard would be considered a big heavyweight, standing 6ft 6½in tall and weighing around 230lb. But by the standards of his time he was a giant. He was a very late starter, his first fight coming when he was 29, but his sheer bulk was enough to intimidate most early opponents.

Significantly, though, he was unable to stop any of the higher-grade men he faced, like Gunboat Smith (who outpointed him). Perhaps because of his limitations, Jack Johnson selected him as his opponent in Havana in April 1915 in a fight scheduled for 45 rounds, the longest agreed distance under modern rules. In 103-degree heat, Willard lasted the pace better and Johnson was counted out in the 26th round. Johnson later claimed he had taken a dive, but this was never proven.

Willard was a poor champion: he boxed only once, a No Decision affair with Frank Moran, between winning the title and losing it to Jack Dempsey in July 1919. Dempsey gave him a bad beating, but Willard's bravery was memorable. He died, aged 86, in Los Angeles on December 15, 1968.

Ike Williams

Real name: *Isiah Williams*
Born: *Brunswick, Georgia, August 2, 1923*
Titles: *NBA lightweight champion 1945–47, world champion 1947–51*
Record: *154 contests, 126 wins, 4 draws, 24 defeats*

Ike Williams was born in Brunswick, Georgia, in 1923. He learned how to box as a means of defending the pitch on the street corner from where he sold newspapers. He turned professional in 1940, was drafted into the US Army in 1944, and put together an impressive string of 34 successive victories before being knocked out in the 12th round by Bob Montgomery in their fight in Philadephia in January 1944. He rallied with a pair of wins over former champion Sammy Angott, and in 1945 won the NBA lightweight title by knocking out the Mexican veteran Juan Zurita, who was having the last of his 130 fights. Williams defended it twice, against Enrique Bolanos in Los Angeles and Ronnie James in Cardiff. He then reunified the lightweight championship by beating his former conqueror Montgomery in six rounds.

Williams was a good champion, turning back five challengers before, drained by the effort of shedding 21lb, he was stopped in the 14th by Jimmy Carter in May 1951. He moved up to welterweight, and retired in 1955 after knocking out another ex-champion, Beau Jack. He died in Los Angeles on September 5, 1994

Howard Winstone

Born: *Merthyr Tydfil, Wales, April 15, 1939*
Titles: *British featherweight champion 1961–69, European champion 1963–66, WBC champion 1968*
Record: *67 contests, 61 wins, 6 defeats*

If Winstone had carried a worthwhile punch, it is doubtful if any featherweight in history could have beaten him. He had sublime skill, defensive artistry, a left jab of unerring accuracy and withering speed, but the loss of the tops of three fingers in an industrial accident meant that he could not punch his full weight. Despite the handicap, though, he stopped 27 of his 67 opponents.

A Commonwealth Games and ABA champion, he raced to 34 consecutive wins, including three for the British title, before an obscure American, Leroy Jeffrey, shocked him in two rounds. Winstone put that behind him by winning a second Lonsdale Belt in record time in 1963, and added the European title that July.

The first of three wonderful world title challenges came in September 1965, when Vicente Saldivar scraped home on points in London, and Saldivar edged another epic in Cardiff two years later before stopping Winstone in 12 rounds of their third fight.

The Mexican immediately retired, and Winstone stopped Mitsunori Seki for the vacant WBC title, which he lost in his first defence – and last fight – to Jose Legra. He died in the town of his birth, Merthyr Tydfil, on September 30, 2000, aged 61.

Tim Witherspoon

Born: *Pontiac, Michigan, December 27, 1957*
Titles: *WBC heavyweight champion 1984, WBA champion 1986*
Record: *69 contests, 55 wins, 1 draw, 13 defeats*

LITTLE BIG MAN *Flyweight star Pongsaklek Wonjongkam of Thailand bloodies the face of challenger Noriyuki Komatsu in 2005*

Lack of dedication prevented this talented heavyweight from achieving his full potential, but he still captured both the WBC and WBA titles. His family settled in Philadelphia, where Witherspoon learned his boxing. He had his first pro fight in 1979, after only seven amateur contests of which he had won six. Before long he was beating good opponents like local rival Marvin Stinson, Alfonzo Ratliff (who later won the WBC cruiserweight title) and Renaldo Snipes.

Larry Holmes inflicted his first defeat in a desperately tough battle to retain the WBC title in May 1983, and when Holmes relinquished the title Witherspoon beat Greg Page for the vacant championship. It should have been the start of a worthwhile reign, but Witherspoon was unsettled by managerial problems and lost to Pinklon Thomas in the first defence of his crown.

He worked his way back to the WBA championship, outpointing Tony Tubbs in January 1986 and retaining it in a thriller against Frank Bruno, but then flopped again as Bonecrusher Smith stopped him in the first round.

He came through a protracted legal battle with Don King but, although he campaigned for more than a decade and a half after losing to Smith, he was never given another world title chance.

Ad Wolgast

Real name: *Adolphus Wolgust*
Born: *Cadillac, Michigan, February 8, 1888*
Titles: *World lightweight champion 1910–12*
Record: *142 contests, 61 wins, 15 draws, 53 No Decisions, 13 defeats*

A lightweight of legendary ferocity and endurance, Wolgast paid a dreadful price for his hit-or-be-hit style: he became punch-drunk, and was confined to a sanatorium for many years before his death in 1955. Of German extraction, Wolgast had lost only once in 69 fights when he challenged Battling Nelson, the Durable Dane, for the world title in February 1910. They were due to go 45 rounds, but at the end of the 40th Nelson was in such bad shape that the referee stopped the fight.

Wolgast figured in another extraordinary championship fight, against Joe Rivers from Mexico at Vernon, California, on July 4, 1912. In the 13th round of a gruelling battle they landed simultaneous rights, and both went down. The referee, Jack Welch, started counting, then when it became obvious that neither could rise in time he tucked the champion under his arm and supported him while he counted Rivers out, justifying his action on the grounds that Wolgast's punch had landed first.

Wolgast lost the title on disqualification to Willie Ritchie in 1912, and retired in 1920. He died in California on April 14, 1955.

Pongsaklek Wonjongkam

Born: *Nakhon Ratchasina, Thailand, August 11, 1977*
Titles: *WBC flyweight title 2001–07, 2010–12*
Record: *97 contests, 90 wins, 2 draws, 5 defeats*

Wonjongkam was an outstanding world champion, but his skills and formidable power were seldom seen outside the Far East; his bouts were rarely even broadcast in America or Europe. In his first 12 years as a pro, only one man beat him: a journeyman from the Philippines, Jerry Pahayahay, who beat him twice when was learning the business. Pahayahay eventually lost more fights than he won.

The Thai won a third meeting and gave notice of the successes to come when he won the irrelevant WBU belt, blasting out the South African Mzukisi Sikali in 48 seconds in 1997. He didn't bother to defend the quasi-championship, moving on instead and waiting for one of the genuine sanctioning bodies to recognize his abilities.

As is sometimes the way with Thai boxers, he kept changing his ring name to suit his latest sponsor. Accordingly it was sometimes hard for international observers to keep up with his fight progress: at various times over the years he was Nakornthong Parkview and Nakornthong Sithkanongsak. His real name, for the record, is Dongskorn Wonjongkam.

He was finally granted a title fight by the WBC in 2001 – and he wasted no time in demonstrating his power, dropping the champion Malcolm Tunacao three times in the first round to score a sensational win. After that, although sometimes he had to go the full 12 rounds, including to defeat the tough Australian Hussein Hussein, nobody could push the 5ft 1in southpaw close. One challenger, Daisuke Naito, lasted a mere 34 seconds.

Wonjongkam outpointed Naito in a rematch, but lost his world title to him in his 18th defence in July 2007. He regained the WBC flyweight belt by handing Koki Kameda his first defeat in March 2010. Wonjongkam lost the belt to Sonny Boy Jaro, then retired after a shock three-round loss to Filipino journeyman Rey Megrino in November 2012. He returned to post three low-key wins.

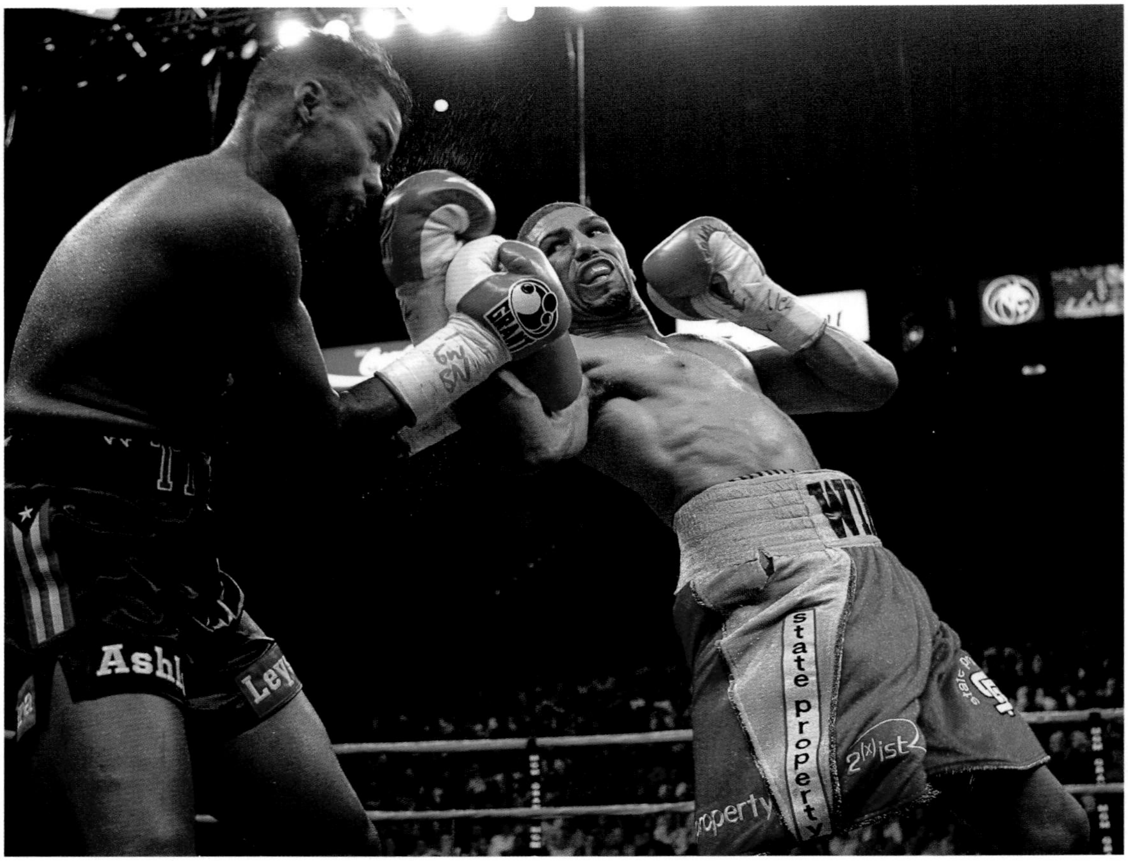

Ronald "Winky" Wright's *sharp stylish boxing was way too much for former champion Felix "Tito" Trinidad*

Ronald "Winky" Wright

Born: *Washington DC, November 26, 1971*
Titles: *WBO light-middleweight champion 1996–98, IBF light-middleweight champion 2001–05, WBC & WBA light-middleweight champion 2004–05*
Record: *58 contests, 51 wins, 1 draw, 6 defeats*

Ronald "Winky" Wright, a brilliant defensive southpaw, may have been forced to wait, but was eventually recognized as one of the expert ring technicians of his era. Born in Washington DC, as a child he was taken to St Petersburg, Florida, by his mother. From the moment he walked into the gym of life-long trainer Dan Birmingham, Wright proved he was tough enough to handle whatever the business could throw at him.

For years his style just made him an "unwanted" fighter. In frustration he went to Europe, to places, as he put it, he couldn't even pronounce, just to fight. One place was St Jean de Luz, in south-west France, where he fought for the WBA light-middleweight title held by the Argentine southpaw Julio Cesar Vasquez. Wright had trouble keeping his feet on a slippery canvas and eventually lost on points.

He returned to Florida and at short notice took a job in Monroe, Michigan, the hometown of WBO champion Bronco McKart. It was planned as a glorious home-coming for McKart, but Wright messed up the celebrations by outboxing him and winning a majority decision.

He defended his belt three times, all in Britain, against Ensley Bingham. twice, and Steve Foster, before losing it on a majority decision to the Namibian Harry Simon in South Africa When Wright lost a disputed challenge to the young IBF champion Fernando Vargas in Oregon in 1999, it seemed as if his career might peter out.

However, he won the vacant IBF title by outboxing Robert Frazier in October 2001, and then established himself, following a string of defences, as the best light-middleweight in the world when he handed Shane Mosley a comprehensive boxing lesson in Las Vegas in March 2004. Wright won 117–111 on two cards with 116–112 on the third. If anything, the judges were generous to Mosley. In a much closer return Wright won again, and then moved into the middleweight division in 2005, and staged a magnificent display to outbox Felix Trinidad over 12 rounds in Las Vegas.

However, when he challenged the world champion Jermain Taylor in Memphis in June 2006, bad luck returned – a big finish from Taylor salvaged a draw. Wright was furious, and turned down a return in spite of a big money offer. Instead, he out-boxed Ike Quartey, in a non-title fight in Florida, and then lost on points at 170lb to Bernard Hopkins in 2007. After more than three years away, Wright returned in June 2012 to box fast-rising Peter Quillin and announced his retirement after being outpointed over ten rounds.

Tony Zale

Real name: *Anthony Florian Zaleski*
Born: *Gary, Indiana, May 29, 1913*
Titles: *NBA middleweight champion 1940–41, world champion 1941–47, 1948*
Record: *87 contests, 67 wins, 2 draws, 18 defeats*

Zale lost the best four years of his career after joining the US Army in 1942, shortly after becoming middleweight champion, yet the fights that earned him boxing immortality all occurred after his return to the ring. He turned pro in 1934 to supplement his pay at a steel mill, but lost nine times in 29 fights and took a long break, returning in 1937.

This time, he fared better. A non-title win over NBA champion Al Hostak in January 1940 earned him a rematch for the title in July, and Zale won in 13 rounds. He defended it twice, then outpointed Georgie Abrams to become undisputed champion in 1941 and after one more fight, a points loss to Billy Conn, he joined the Forces.

He faced Graziano for the first time in September 1946, winning a wild battle in six rounds, but was knocked out by the New Yorker in the rematch, also in six rounds, before Zale settled the series with a third-round win. He lost the title in his next fight to Marcel Cerdan, and immediately retired. He died at the age of 82 on March 20, 1997.

Hilario Zapata

Born: *Panama City, Panama, August 19, 1958*
Titles: *WBC light-flyweight champion 1980–82, 1982–83, WBA flyweight champion 1985–87*
Record: *54 contests, 43 wins, 1 draw, 10 defeats*

A fast and stylish Panamanian, Zapata compiled an impressive championship record: he won 17 and drew one of the 23 world title fights he contested.

He was beaten by Alfonso Lopez, challenging for the Latin American title in his seventh professional fight, but a win over former champion Freddie Castle in June 1979 brought him a trip to Tokyo, where he dethroned WBC champion Shigeo Nakajima. He risked his title four times in 1980 and four more in 1981, boxing in Japan, Korea, Venezuela, Panama and America, but then lost in two rounds to Mexican Amado Ursua in February 1982. However, he was champion again before the end of the year, outpointing Tadashi Tomori in Japan.

Zapata won and lost in defences against Jung Koo-Chang, an outstanding champion, and moved up to flyweight. Santos Laciar foiled his first attempt for the WBA title, but he won the vacant championship when the Argentinean retired, and retained it five times, eventually losing it to Fidel Bassa, with whom he drew in a rematch. Sung-Kil Moon knocked him out in a round in his final fight, a bid for the WBC super-flyweight crown in 1993.

Carlos Zarate

Born: *Tepito, Mexico, May 23, 1951*
Titles: *WBC bantamweight champion 1976–79*
Record: *65 contests, 61 wins, 4 defeats*

It would have been a brave man who would have picked a winner between Carlos Zarate and Ruben Olivares, the two hardest-punching bantamweights in history, if they had met in their respective primes. Zarate's phenomenal record showed four losses in 65 fights, with three coming in bids for the super-bantamweight championship – the other was a split decision which cost him his bantamweight title against Lupe Pintor. And of Zarate's 61 career victories, 58 of them came inside the distance.

When Zarate knocked out his compatriot Rodolfo Martinez in five rounds in May 1976 to win the WBC title, it was his 39th inside-the-distance victory in 40 fights. Only Victor Martinez had heard the final bell in his first 24 fights, and he stopped his next 28 opponents. Zarate defended his title nine times against challengers from four continents – truly a world champion.

He stepped out of his division to challenge Wilfredo Gomez for the WBC super-bantamweight title in 1978, but was stopped in five rounds. Subsequent challenges against both Jeff Fenech and Daniel Zaragoza, who beat him for the vacant title, also failed and Zarate retired after the Zaragoza fight.

Fritzie Zivic

Born: *Pittsburgh, Pennsylvania, May 8, 1913*
Titles: *World welterweight champion 1940–41*
Record: *232 contests, 157 wins, 10 draws, 65 defeats*

In any poll to find the dirtiest fighter in history, Fritzie Zivic would come near the top. "Kids today think the laces are for tying up the gloves," he remarked once when asked his views on the current, more gentlemanly breed. Despite his reputation he was never disqualified in his 18-year, 232-fight career, but perhaps he always took his own advice: "Always work the ref's blind side."

One of five boxing brothers, Zivic averaged 18 fights a year between 1933 and 1946. He was already a grizzled veteran by the time he finally got a title chance, against Henry Armstrong in New York in October 1940. It was Armstrong's eighth defence that year, and Zivic gave him a severe beating, closing both his eyes and flooring him for the first time in 26 title bouts with the last punch of the fight. The rematch drew 23,306 New York fans to watch Armstrong take another pounding before being stopped in the 12th round. Zivic lost the title in his next defence, to Freddie Cochrane, an 8–1 outsider with 30 defeats on his record, but he did not retire until 1949, by which time he had faced 12 world champions.

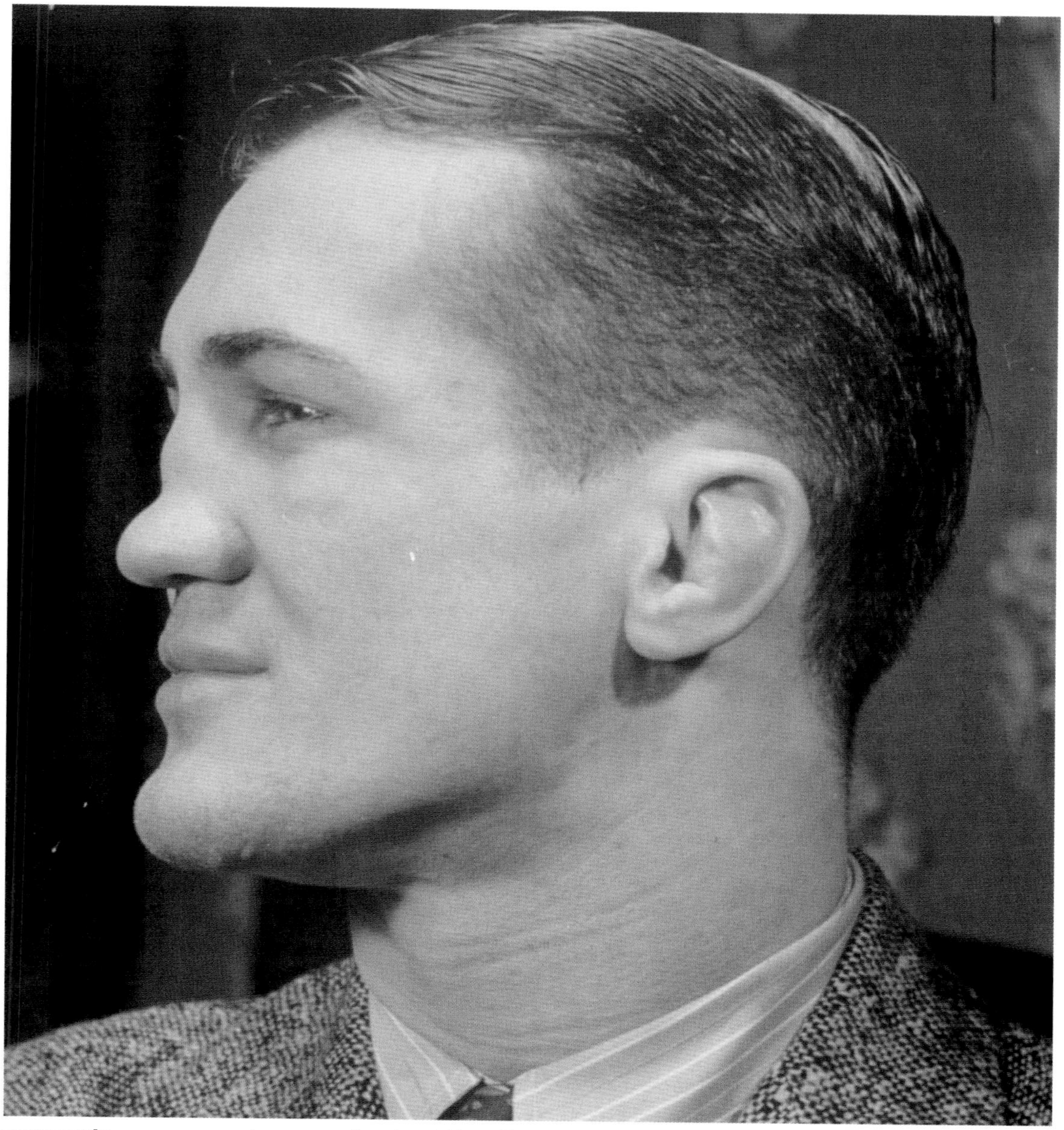

THEY DIDN'T *come any rougher or tougher than Fritzie Zivic*

THE LEGENDS OF THE RING

Fine champions like Wilfred Benitez, Carmen Basilio and Iran Barkley can win titles at more than one weight, but they still fail to attain that elusive and indefinable status of "legend". Others, such as Julio Cesar Chavez and Larry Holmes, can build long winning runs or, like Riddick Bowe and Evander Holyfield, earn prodigious amounts of money yet lack the mystique which separates the truly great from the very good. Any list of boxing legends must be arbitrary and personal, but the men featured here are surely very close to automatic selections. They bridge the decades and exemplify vastly different styles of boxing, but they are each landmark figures in the development and history of professional boxing.

MUHAMMAD ALI

The most graceful, original and entertaining heavyweight champion of them all, Ali revolutionized boxing in the 1960s and rewrote the history books by winning the title three times between 1964 and 1978. The impossible was his speciality and the standards he set will probably never be surpassed.

HENRY ARMSTRONG

Armstrong's claim to fame is unique: he was the only man in history to hold championships simultaneously at three different weights, a feat which modern regulations would not permit. His battles with Barney Ross, Lou Ambers and Fritzie Zivic are classics of the ring.

JACK DEMPSEY

The Manassa Mauler became a byword for ferocity, his ring style rooted in his hard and hungry teenage days when he battled in saloons and mining camps for a dollar. He went on to personify the Roaring Twenties, become the game's first million-dollar attraction and remains its most enduring symbol.

ROBERTO DURAN

Arguably the greatest lightweight the sport has seen, Duran moved on to win world titles at welterweight, light-middleweight and middleweight in a fabulous career which began in 1967 and was still going in 1999. He was the ultimate warrior, who fought for money but relished the thrill of combat almost as much.

LENNOX LEWIS

The last heavyweight champion of the 20th century, Lewis proved himself to be the finest heavyweight of his generation with comprehensive victories over Evander Holyfield and Mike Tyson.

SUGAR RAY ROBINSON

Robinson was the real Sugar Ray, the original and the best. His era spanned 25 years and 202 fights. He was welterweight champion for six years, and held the middleweight title five times. The Sugarman had style, glamour, charisma and class, and 14 of his victims were world champions.

JACK JOHNSON

In his time he was the most hated man in sport, perhaps even in the whole of American society, but by the sheer weight of his talent Johnson forced his way to the top despite every obstacle. He was the first black heavyweight champion, the forerunner of Muhammad Ali in style as well as spirit.

JOE LOUIS

Louis was one of that rare breed of athletes who transcend their sport to become figures of true international significance. He held the heavyweight title longer than anyone else, made a record number of defences, and became an icon and an inspiration for black Americans.

MIKE TYSON

In the second half of the 1980s, Mike Tyson was unbeatable. The youngest heavyweight champion in history, he swept contenders aside with an arrogant ease not seen since the prime of Joe Louis. But then it all went horribly wrong, inside and outside the ring, in an unparalleled fall from grace.

SUGAR RAY LEONARD

Leonard had a huge ego, but ability to match. He was world champion at five weights, from welter to light-heavy inclusive, and he beat magnificent champions like Marvin Hagler, Roberto Duran and Thomas Hearns. There have been few tougher ways to earn that "legend" status.

ROCKY MARCIANO

He was crude, stocky and unskilled – yet nobody beat Rocky Marciano in 49 fights. He had two natural assets: unlimited courage and a thunderous right, and they carried him to the heavyweight championship. He retired in his prime, the only heavyweight champion with a perfect record.

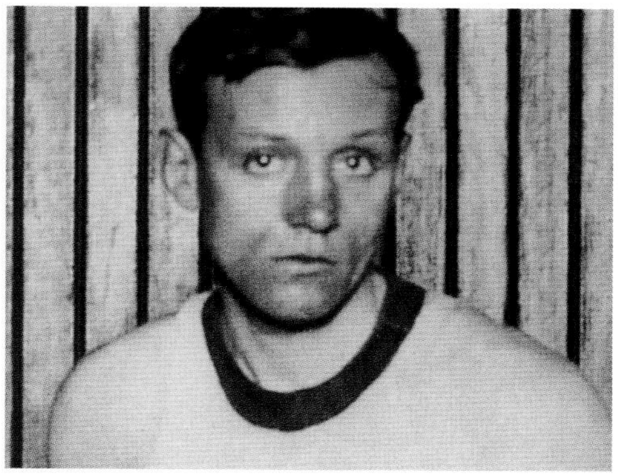

JIMMY WILDE

Wilde was the man who proved, once and for all, that size doesn't matter. He never scaled more than 102lb in his fighting prime, yet 101 of his 151 opponents failed to last the distance with this fierce-punching little Welshman, whose championship career stretched from 1914 to 1923.

ALI

"I'm so fast I can hit the light switch and be in bed before it's dark."

Ali, in his glorious prime.

"GET UP, YOU BUM" – *Muhammad Ali taunts Sonny Liston after his first-round "phantom punch" ended their world title rematch*

FLOATED LIKE A BUTTERFLY... STUNG LIKE A BEE

Muhammad Ali transcended sport. In purely boxing terms he was the most original and creative performer of his time, perhaps of all time, but his impact on the wider world was immense. He became a symbol of black pride, just as Joe Louis had been in the 1930s, and through his opposition to the Vietnam War, and the principled (and expensive) stand he took against it, he pricked America's conscience and contributed significantly towards the war's end.

In his own country he has been loved and hated in equal measure. But in Europe, and particularly in Britain, he has been a hero since he first exploded into our consciousness at the 1960 Rome Olympics, and the affection he has inspired is closer to real love than any other sportsman has known.

Boxing was in trouble when Ali – then known by his "slave name" Cassius Clay – came along. The small fight clubs which were the game's breeding ground had virtually gone out of business across America, and the major TV networks were not interested in promoting a sport which, only a few years previously, the Kefauver Commission inquiry into organized crime had shown to be riddled with corruption. Ali changed all that, taking the sport by the scruff of the neck and slapping it back into life with his outrageous mixture of bombast, comedy, innovation and, most of all, God-given talent. It took nerve to make the kind of boasts in which he specialized, but it took genius to make them come true, time after time.

At first, he played by white society's rules, even if privately he seethed, to the point where he threw his Olympic medal into a river in disgust after being refused service in a Southern diner a couple of weeks after his return from Rome. (He was given a replacement medal at the 1996 Olympic Games, where he lit the torch in the opening ceremony.) He signed with a consortium of white Kentucky businessmen, who engaged the respected trainer Angelo Dundee to work with him and select the opponents. Dundee, shrewdly, did not seek to impose conventional wisdom on such a free spirit. Instead, he took Ali's strengths and polished them to perfection, producing a superbly conditioned athlete whose grace and speed brought a whole new dimension to the sport.

Clay/Ali rewrote the textbooks with his hands-dangling, dancing style, and as he began to trounce men of significant reputation, the feeling grew that he was something special. He came off the floor to beat Henry Cooper, then took on the most feared heavyweight champion for years: the brooding, bullying Sonny Liston. Few gave Clay a chance, but Liston was bamboozled by the youngster's quicksilver attacks and retired, claiming a damaged shoulder, after six rounds. In the rematch, Liston went down and out in the first round from an unconvincing punch. The unsatisfactory nature of both fights helped turn American opinion against the new champion, especially when he announced that he had become a Muslim and changed his name.

He proved to be a truly international champion, defending the title three times in Europe, once in Canada and five times in the US as he battled conscription on the memorable grounds that, "I ain't got no quarrel with them Viet Cong." It was a fight he could not win, given the climate of the times, and when he was convicted the sport's governing bodies quickly disowned him. It took him three years to retrieve his boxing licence, by which time the majority of his compatriots shared his opposition to the war.

READY TO RUMBLE... *Ali prepares to face Henry Cooper in 1966*

Joe Frazier foiled his first attempt to regain the title, flooring and outpointing him in a 1971 classic, but Ali kept going and, in 1974, stunned the world when he knocked out the supposedly invincible George Foreman in Zaire. He reigned for three years and ten defences, then took Leon Spinks too lightly and was outpointed in February 1978. He put that right seven months later, and promptly retired. Financial pressures forced him back in October 1980 to challenge Larry Holmes, who pleaded with him to quit until Angelo Dundee signalled the finish after ten rounds.

There was one last, pathetic defeat by Trevor Berbick a year later, and then began the long, slow descent into illness and infirmity. How cruel that the game to which he gave so much should, in the end, have demanded so high a price from him. He died on June 3, 2016, aged 74.

MUHAMMAD ALI

BORN: January 17, 1942
Louisville, Kentucky

WORLD TITLE FIGHTS:

Feb 25, 1964, w ret 7
Sonny Liston, Miami Beach, FL

May 25, 1965, w ko 1
Sonny Liston, Lewiston, ME

Nov 22, 1965, w rsf 12
Floyd Patterson, Las Vegas, NV

Mar 29, 1966, w pts 15
George Chuvalo, Toronto (Can)

May 21, 1966, w rsf 6
Henry Cooper, London (Eng)

Aug 6, 1966, w ko 3
Brian London, London (Eng)

Sep 10, 1966, w rsf 12
Karl Mildenberger, Frankfurt (Ger)

Nov 14, 1966, w rsf 3
Cleveland Williams, Houston, TX

Feb 6, 1967, w pts 15
Ernie Terrell, Houston, TX
(undisputed)

Mar 22, 1967, w ko 7
Zora Folley, New York, NY

Mar 8, 1971, l pts 15
Joe Frazier, New York, NY

Oct 30, 1974, w ko 8
George Foreman, Kinshasa (Zai)

Mar 24, 1975, w rsf 15
Chuck Wepner, Cleveland, OH

May 16, 1975, w rsf 11
Ron Lyle, Las Vegas, NV

Jul 1, 1975, w pts 15
Joe Bugner, Kuala Lumpur (Mal)

Oct 1, 1975, w ret 14
Joe Frazier, Manila (Phi)

Feb 20, 1976, w ko 5
Jean Pierre Coopman, San Juan (PR)

Apr 30, 1976, w pts 15
Jimmy Young, Landover, MD

May 24, 1976, w rsf 5
Richard Dunn, Munich (Ger)

Sep 28, 1976, w pts 15
Ken Norton, New York, NY

May 16, 1977, w pts 15
Alfredo Evangelista, Landover, MD

Sep 29, 1977, w pts 15
Earnie Shavers, New York, NY

Feb 15, 1978, l pts 15
Leon Spinks, Las Vegas, NV

Sep 15, 1978, w pts 15
Leon Spinks, New Orleans, LA (WBA)

Oct 2, 1980, l ret 11
Larry Holmes, Las Vegas, NV (WBC)

OVERALL RECORD:
61 contests
56 wins
5 defeats

ARMSTRONG

TRIPLE HITTER *Henry Armstrong's record is unmatched*

THE HURRICANE THAT STRUCK THRICE

Can you imagine Naseem Hamed, weighing 126lb, defeating lightweight champion Oscar De La Hoya and welterweight king Pernell Whitaker – and then fighting a draw with Quincy Taylor for the middleweight championship? Hamed may have considered the feat well within his scope, but the rest of us would laugh at the absurdity of the notion. Yet that was what Henry Armstrong achieved in 1937–40, when he won world titles at featherweight, lightweight and welterweight and fought a draw with Ceferino Garcia for a version of the middleweight title. Even more remarkably, he won his three titles within a span of ten months, and for four glorious months in 1938 he held them simultaneously, something that can no longer happen under modern regulations.

Armstrong's real name was Henry Jackson, and like so many great champions he was born into appalling poverty, the youngest of 11 children. When he was four, the family moved north to St Louis after the local cotton crop failed, and his obsession with boxing began when he surprised himself with his performance in a playground fight at school.

After the briefest of amateur careers he turned professional under the name

ON THE BUTTON *B. Ross takes a right*

"Mellody Jackson", in tribute to the old welterweight champion Honey Mellody, but made a dismal start as he lost three of his first four fights. He rode the rails west to California, basing himself in Los Angeles where he re-entered the amateur ranks under the name he would make immortal – Henry Armstrong. The prodigious work-rate that was a feature of his later career was already in evidence: he travelled the length of California, sometimes boxing three or four times a week. In 1931, he was undefeated in 85 contests, 66 of them won inside the distance. His heart-rate was unusually slow, which allowed him to maintain a pace that would have been beyond normal fighters.

When he relaunched his pro career, his non-stop style brought him the nickname "Hurricane Hank", and he quickly built a large following. In August 1935, he was matched with Baby Arizmendi for the Californian version of the world featherweight title, but the cagey Mexican was too experienced for him and won on points. Armstrong reversed the result the following year, but his claim was not taken seriously outside California – although knockouts of champions Mike Belloise and Benny Bass showed that he belonged in championship class. In October 1937, he won the "real" featherweight title in six rounds from Petey Sarron, but never defended it.

Weight was becoming a problem, but instead of making the obvious move, from featherweight to lightweight, he skipped to welterweight and pounded champion Barney Ross into retirement, giving him a bad points beating. Three months later he was a triple champion, outpointing Lou Ambers in a fierce battle to take the lightweight crown. Ambers regained the lightweight title in August 1939, and Armstrong concentrated on defending his welterweight championship, which he did with amazing frequency. The indefatigable Armstrong found time to fit in a middleweight title challenge in March 1940, battling to a ten-round draw with Ceferino Garcia, whom he had already beaten in a welterweight defence. But the fighting machine was slowly winding down, and he finally lost the welterweight title in his seventh defence of the year in 1940, when Fritzie Zivic battered him for 15 rounds and then stopped him in 12 in a rematch.

He had the last of his 181 fights in February 1945 and, in retirement, successfully battled alcoholism and became a Baptist minister. He died in Los Angeles in October 1988.

HENRY ARMSTRONG

BORN: December 12, 1912
Columbus, Mississippi

WORLD TITLE FIGHTS:

Oct 29, 1937, w ko 6
Petey Sarron, New York, NY
(featherweight)

May 31, 1938, w pts 15
Barney Ross, Long Island, NY
(welterweight)

Aug 17, 1938, w pts 15
Lou Ambers, New York, NY (lightweight)

Nov 25, 1938, w pts 15
Ceferino Garcia, New York, NY
(welterweight)

Dec 5, 1938, w rsf 3
Al Manfredo, Cleveland, OH
(welterweight)

Jan 10, 1939, w pts 10
Baby Arizmendi, Los Angeles, LA
(welterweight)

Mar 4, 1939, w rsf 4
Bobby Pacho, Havana (Cub)
(welterweight)

Mar 16, 1939, w ko 1
Lew Feldman, St Louis, MO
(welterweight)

Mar 31, 1939, w ko 12
Davey Day, New York, NY (welterweight)

May 25, 1939, w pts 15
Ernie Roderick, London (Eng)
(welterweight)

Aug 22, 1939, l pts 15
Lou Ambers, New York, NY (lightweight)

Oct 9, 1939, w rsf 4
Al Manfredo, Des Moines, IA
(welterweight)

Oct 13, 1939, w ko 2
Howard Scott, Minneapolis, MN
(welterweight)

Oct 20, 1939, w ko 3
Ritchie Fontaine, Seattle, WA
(welterweight)

Oct 24, 1939, w pts 10
Jimmy Garrison, Los Angeles, CA
(welterweight)

Oct 30, 1939, w rsf 4
Bobby Pacho, Denver, CO (welterweight)

Dec 11, 1939, w ko 7
Jimmy Garrison, Cleveland, OH
(welterweight)

Jan 4, 1940, w ko 5
Joe Ghnouly, St Louis, MO (welterweight)

Jan 24, 1940, w rsf 9
Pedro Montanez, New York, NY
(welterweight)

Mar 1, 1940, drew 10
Ceferino Garcia, Los Angeles, CA
(middleweight)

(remainder all for welterweight title)
Apr 26, 1940, w rsf 7
Paul Junior, Boston, MA

May 24, 1940, w rsf 5
Ralph Zanelli, Boston, MA

Jun 21, 1940, w rsf 3
Paul Junior, Portland, ME

Sep 23, 1940, w ko 4
Phil Furr, Washington, DC

Oct 4, 1940, l pts 15
Fritzie Zivic, New York, NY

Jan 17, 1941, l rsf 12
Fritzie Zivic, New York, NY

OVERALL RECORD:
181 contests
152 wins
8 draws
21 defeats

"Henry, you're the greatest champ that ever walked."

Fritzie Zivic to Armstrong, after taking his welterweight title in January 1941.

DEMPSEY

JACK DEMPSEY *(behind) gave Jess Willard a fierce beating and took his title when Willard quit after three rounds*

THE MAULER WITH A KNOCKOUT PUNCH

Nobody remembers William Harrison Dempsey, but the whole world knows Jack Dempsey. He became part of the fabric of the 20th century, an original All-American hero whose progress from the hobo camps to the heavyweight championship inspired generations to rise above their background and environment. He won the title with a brand of ferocity and aggression that had rarely been seen before, and his colourful personality – and fondness for pretty women – perfectly captured the spirit of the Roaring Twenties.

He was one of nine children, born in Manassa, Colorado, on 24 June, 1895, to parents of exotically mixed ancestry: Irish, Scots, and Native American genes all went into the make-up of this formidable fighting man. His brother Bernie was a part-time professional boxer, taking the name "Jack Dempsey" after the famous middleweight champion, "Nonpareil" Jack. When William was old enough he started boxing as "Young Dempsey" until Bernie retired and he could take over the "Jack Dempsey" name.

Ring earnings were minimal, as he was fighting mainly in bare-knuckle matches in saloons for a share of the gambling winnings. Like thousands of his poor or dispossessed compatriots, he rode the rails across America seeking employment, sleeping in rough-and-ready "hobo camps" alongside railway tracks and, when he could, working in mining and timber camps.

He had virtually abandoned hope of making a living in the ring, and was working in a Seattle shipyard when news came that one of his brothers had died. Jack accepted another fight to pay for the funeral expenses, and this time he took it seriously. His formal career began in 1914, when he earned $3.50 for his first fight, but he did not break into the big-time until 1918, under the management of the shrewd Jack "Doc" Kearns. He boxed 21 times that year with only one defeat, to "Fat Willie" Meehan, whom Dempsey managed to beat just once in five meetings.

Doc Kearns eventually manoeuvred him into a world title fight with the giant Jess Willard at Toledo on July 4, 1919, confident that his man's ferocious punching would be too much for a champion who had not boxed competitively for over three years. Of Dempsey's previous 26 contests, all but three had ended inside six rounds, and an astonishing 17 had finished in the first. Kearns bet the challenger's entire purse on a first-round win, and Dempsey did his best to oblige. He floored Willard – who outweighed him by 56lb – seven times in the first round, but the champion's courage kept him going until the third.

Dempsey's reign began well, with three defences in ten months, including boxing's first million-dollar gate, his epic encounter with Georges Carpentier. But then his pace slowed appreciably, and he did not box again until 1923. The small town of Shelby, Montana, venue for his points win over Tommy Gibbons, was virtually bankrupted when its leading citizens bankrolled the flop, but nobody asked for their money back after his thrilling second-round defeat of Luis Firpo. Dempsey battered the challenger unmercifully, flooring him seven times in the first round before being knocked clean out of the ring in the second. He climbed back, aided by ringside reporters, and promptly flattened Firpo.

That fight was in September 1923, and he was not in serious action again until he faced Gene Tunney three years later. They fought in driving rain in Philadelphia, and Tunney comfortably outboxed him over ten rounds. The return, over the same distance in Chicago 364 days later, was the famous "Battle of the Long Count", in which Dempsey floored Tunney but the referee, Dave Barry, refused to take up the count until he had gone to a neutral corner. Tunney got up within Barry's count of ten, and won a deserved decision.

It was Dempsey's last fight, and the fifth time he had drawn a million-dollar gate. He had brought boxing from the backwoods into mainstream American life, and taken the sport onto a financial plane that would have been unimaginable only a decade earlier.

Dempsey opened a landmark bar/restaurant in New York after his retirement, but had to close it in the 1970s when the owner of the site, who wanted to redevelop it, took out a compulsory purchase order. The owner, it transpired, was Queen Elizabeth, who can thus claim to be the only woman to have knocked out Jack Dempsey. The old champion died on May 31, 1983.

> **"When I started I was really bad, and I never got any better."**
>
> *Dempsey, tongue in cheek.*

LEAN AND MEAN *Jack Dempsey at his fighting peak*

JACK DEMPSEY

BORN: June 24, 1895
Manassa, Colorado

WORLD TITLE FIGHTS:
Jul 4, 1919, w ret 3
Jess Willard, Toledo, OH
Sep 6, 1920, w ko 3
Billy Miske, Benton Harbor, MI
Dec 14, 1920, w ko 12
Bill Brennan, New York, NY
Jul 2, 1921, w ko 4
Georges Carpentier, Jersey City, NJ
Jul 4, 1923, w pts 15
Tommy Gibbons, Shelby, MT
Sep 14, 1923, w ko 2
Luis Angel Firpo, New York, NY
Sep 23, 1926, l pts 10
Gene Tunney, Philadelphia, PA
Sep 22, 1927, l pts 10
Gene Tunney, Chicago, IL

OVERALL RECORD:
83 contests
62 wins
9 draws
6 No Decisions
6 defeats

DURAN

“There’s no boxer in the world that doesn’t fight for money.”

Roberto Duran, on his motivation.

NICKNAMED “HANDS OF STONE”, *Roberto Duran was a four-weight world champion who fought in five separate decades*

FEROCIOUS SCRAPPER FROM PANAMA

For 30 crazy years Roberto Duran, *Manos de Piedra* (Hands of Stone), was the pure fighting animal, who loved the thrill of combat the way other men love sex or drugs. By the late 1990s, the contemporaries of his youth, the men he had been destroying more than 20 years earlier, had long since retired. Some, like the ill-fated Esteban DeJesus, were dead. But Duran fought on, still driven by his demons well into his 40s.

In August 1998 he was outclassed by WBA middleweight champion William Joppy, a man who wasn't even born when Roberto began his professional career. But the following March he was back in the ring in a ten-rounder in Argentina.

It was sad to see him fighting when he was such a shell of his old self, but there had been so many good times. Duran won four world titles, each of them taken from an outstanding champion, and by any standards he rates with the all-time best.

He personified the hungry fighter, clawing his way up from grinding poverty to financial security in the only way that was open to a *cholo*, a youngster of mixed Indian and Spanish blood. He was born in Guarare on June 16, 1951 and grew up in Chorillo, a disease-ridden slum on the east side of the Panama Canal. His father had long since absconded, leaving his wife to raise their nine children alone. By the time he was 13, Duran's schooling, such as it was, had ended and he was hustling money any way he could to support his family. He even stole fruit from an orchard owned by Carlos Eleta, who ironically was later to become his manager.

At 14, Roberto dabbled in amateur boxing, but after winning 13 of his 16 fights, he decided that he might as well be paid for doing what he enjoyed so much. His sheer ferocity in the professional ring was enough to intimidate his early opponents, and he breezed through 21 wins (16 by knockout) before Eleta became involved. The wealthy landowner bought his contract for a derisory $300, and then hired Ray Arcel and Freddie Brown – two of the game's legendary trainers – to hone and polish Duran's raw talent.

In his 29th fight, ten days after his 21st birthday, he faced WBA champion Ken Buchanan in Madison Square Garden, and won the title in a fight that illustrated his strengths as well as his dark side. He went on to equal the record for lightweight title defences, earning undisputed recognition in the 12th and last by knocking out Esteban DeJesus, the only man to have beaten him in 64 fights.

Increasing weight forced him to step up to welterweight, and he dethroned champion Ray Leonard in a memorable 15-rounder in June 1980. It was perhaps Duran's finest performance, yet in the rematch three months later he abruptly quit. His fighting reputation was in tatters, but he redeemed it on his 32nd birthday by stopping Davey Moore for the WBA light-middleweight title and then going the full 15 with Marvin Hagler in a middleweight title bid.

Ever unpredictable, Duran was flattened in two rounds by Thomas Hearns next time out, and when he lost to modestly talented Robbie Sims there seemed no way back. But this astonishing old warhorse had one great victory left. In February 1989, he took on the fearsome Iran Barkley, and outsmarted him in a spell-binding fight for the WBC middleweight title.

He lost a dreary third fight with Leonard at super-middleweight in 1989, gave up his middleweight belt and then drifted into a set pattern. He was good enough to beat most of his opponents, but lost the important fights, to Vinny Pazienza twice and Hector Camacho, as the 1990s wore on. He drew the crowds and always gave value, and at 47 fought his last world title fight against Joppy.

ROBERTO DURAN

BORN: June 16, 1951
Guarare, Panama

WORLD TITLE FIGHTS:

Jun 26, 1972, w rsf 13
Ken Buchanan, New York, NY
(WBA lightweight)

Jan 20, 1973, w ko 5
Jimmy Robertson, Panama City (Pan)

Jun 2, 1973, w rsf 8
Hector Thompson, Panama City (Pan)

Sep 8, 1973, w rsf 10
Ishimatsu Susuki, Panama City (Pan)

Mar 16, 1974, w ko 11
Esteban DeJesus, Panama City (Pan)

Dec 21, 1974, w rsf 1
Masataka Takayama, San Jose, CA

Mar 2, 1975, w ko 14
Ray Lampkin, Panama City (Pan)

Dec 14, 1975, w ko 15
Leoncio Ortiz, San Juan (PR)

May 22, 1976, w ko 14
Lou Bizzaro, Erie, PA

Oct 15, 1976, w ko 1
Alvaro Rojas, Hollywood, FL

Jan 29, 1977, w ko 13
Vilomar Fernandez, Miami Beach, FL

Sep 17, 1977, w pts 15
Edwin Viruet, Philadelphia, PA

Jan 21, 1978, w ko 12
Esteban DeJesus, Las Vegas, NV
(undisputed lightweight)

Jun 20, 1980, w pts 15
Sugar Ray Leonard, Montreal (Can)
(WBC welterweight)

Nov 25, 1980, l ret 8
Sugar Ray Leonard, New Orleans, NV
(WBC welterweight)

Jan 30, 1982, l pts 15
Wilfred Benitez, Las Vegas, NV
(WBC light-middleweight)

Jun 16, 1983, w rsf 8
Davey Moore, New York, NY
(WBA light-middleweight)

Nov 10, 1983, l pts 15
Marvin Hagler, Las Vegas, NV
(undisputed middleweight)

Jun 15, 1984, l ko 2
Thomas Hearns, Las Vegas, NV
(WBC light-middleweight)

Feb 24, 1989, w pts 15
Iran Barkley, Atlantic City, NJ
(WBC middleweight)

Dec 7, 1989, L pts 12
Sugar Ray Leonard, Las Vegas, NV
(WBC super-middleweight)

Aug 28, 1998, L rsf 3
William Joppy,, Las Vegas, NV
(WBA middleweight)

OVERALL RECORD:
119 contests
103 wins
16 defeats

HANDS OF STONE *Duran prepares for his 1986 encounter with Robbie Sims*

JOHNSON

JACK JOHNSON *(right) went to his grave insisting he threw this 1915 fight against Jess Willard*

CRUSHER OF "GREAT WHITE HOPES"

JACK JOHNSON

BORN: March 31, 1878
Galveston, Texas

WORLD TITLE FIGHTS:
Dec 26, 1908, w rsf 14
Tommy Burns, Sydney (Aus)
Oct 16, 1909, w ko 12
Stanley Ketchel, Colma, CA
Jul 4, 1910, w ko 15
James J. Jeffries, Reno, NV
Jul 4, 1912, w disq 9
Jim Flynn, Las Vegas NM
Dec 19, 1913, drew 10
Jim Johnson, Paris (Fra)
Jun 27, 1914, w pts 20
Frank Moran, Paris (Fra)
Apr 5, 1915, l ko 26
Jess Willard, Havana (Cub)

OVERALL RECORD:
126 contests
83 wins
11 draws
18 no decisions
14 defeats

With the possible exception of Primo Carnera, whose ascent to the title was shamelessly stage-managed, nobody has found it easy to become heavyweight champion of the world. Yet for Jack Johnson, the road was hardest of all.

He was a supremely gifted boxer, one of the handful from that era whose talent still shines through those flickering black-and-white images, yet because of his colour it took him 11 long years to be given the chance to prove himself. To become champion he had to chase the title-holder halfway around the world, finally catching up with him in Australia, and was then obliged to endure a campaign of hatred and vilification which defies the imagination of those born into more liberal times. In the end, he claimed, he was tricked into surrendering his title to a white man in exchange for the dropping of a prosecution that should never have been brought in the first place.

His long journey began in Galveston, Texas, where he was born on March 31, 1878 and where he started fighting for fun at 13 while working as a docker. He had his first professional fight in 1897, and over the next few years built a local reputation despite a third-round loss to the veteran Joe Choynski in 1901. Black vs white matches were not encouraged, unless the outcome was prearranged, so the top black boxers tended to fight each other, over and over again.

> **"No greater defensive fighter than Jack Johnson ever lived."**
>
> *Damon Runyon.*

PAPA JACK *a gifted boxer who would have thrived in any era*

Johnson joined that circuit, becoming recognized as the "Negro heavyweight champion" after beating Denver Ed Martin in 1903. He took them all on: Sam Langford, Black Bill, Joe Jeanette, Sam McVey, Frank Childs and a host of other, long-forgotten men who deserved a better deal. Yet despite his own difficulties, Johnson never tried to make life easier for other black fighters after he had become champion. "I won't box any of those coloured boys now," he was quoted as saying to an interviewer in 1913. "I have had a hard time to get a chance. I gave Langford, Jeanette and those boys a chance before I was champ. I'll retire still the only coloured heavyweight champion."

It was a hopeless ambition for him to entertain in those early years, when the "colour bar" raised by John L. Sullivan stayed firmly up. But gradually, as he began to beat white contenders like Jack Monroe, Bill Lang, Bob Fitzsimmons and Fireman Jim Flynn, the boxing world was forced to face up to the unpalatable fact that he would have to be accommodated, sooner or later.

He was kept waiting for as long as possible. Champions came and went; James J. Jeffries, Marvin Hart (who outscored Johnson in 1905) and Tommy Burns all had their day, and in the end it was Burns, the smallest heavyweight champion in history, who agreed to take him on after Johnson had pursued him across America, on to England and finally to Australia. They met at Rushcutter's Bay, Sydney, on December 26, 1908, and Johnson made Burns pay for every moment of frustration and discrimination he had endured over the years, taunting and tormenting the outclassed Canadian until the police intervened in the 14th round.

The search for a white challenger began immediately. Middleweight king Stanley Ketchel floored Johnson in the 12th round, but he got up to knockout Ketchel with the very next punch. The old champion Jeffries was next, tempted out of retirement to, as novelist Jack London exhorted him, "Wipe the smile off the nigger's face." Johnson was the one smiling when he stopped Jeffries in the 15th round.

He boxed only once more as champion in America, stopping Jim Flynn in a rematch in Las Vegas, and then defended twice in Paris. His penchant for white wives and girlfriends had finally got him into trouble as the Establishment seized on any excuse to bring him down. He was prosecuted under the Mann Act, prohibiting the transportation of women across state lines for immoral purposes, and was given a jail term. He fled to Europe, and, according to his story, worked out a deal to take a dive against Jess Willard if the case would be quashed. He was duly knocked out in Havana in 26 rounds on April 5, 1915, but if a deal had been done it was reneged upon.

He served his time and never got another chance, although he boxed sporadically until 1928. He died in a car crash in Raleigh, North Carolina, on June 10, 1946.

LEONARD

LOVE HIM *or hate him, there was no denying Sugar Ray Leonard's class in the ring*

MR COOL WITH A WILL TO WIN

RAY LEONARD'S *sweetest win, over Roberto Duran (left) in November 1980*

It was easy to dislike Ray Leonard for his arrogance, his manipulation of the public and the media, his cynical disregard for the rights of hard-working fellow-professionals whom he would routinely elbow aside from the queue for a title fight or browbeat into signing unfavourable contracts. But it was impossible not to admire Sugar Ray Leonard the fighter, a champion of sublime talent, invention and above all, fighting heart. He never commanded the affections of the public in the way that the original Sugar Ray did, but he is one of the handful who merit mention in the same breath as Robinson. His ego matched his genius... but, then, perhaps without the ego, the genius could never have flourished.

The natural, instinctive talent was there from the start, as he won 145 of 150 amateur fights in a career that peaked with a gold medal at the 1976 Olympic Games. Even then, Leonard knew how to market himself, enchanting middle America by boxing with a photo of Ray, his young son, tucked in his boot. When he came home from the Games, he approached the decision to turn professional with the icy calculation that marked everything he did. He engaged a lawyer, Mike Trainer, to handle the business deals, set up a company called Sugar Ray Leonard Inc. to ease the tax burdens, and hired Angelo Dundee, the world's best-known trainer, to fine-tune his preparations and select the opponents.

Too many boxers have been exploited, and Leonard was determined that he would never join the list. He negotiated lucrative deals with promoters and advertisers, even recruiting his son, Ray Jr, to appear with him in a TV commercial for the soft drink Seven-Up. He had banked $2m before he ever fought for a title, although there was a good reason for the near-three year gap between his pro debut in February 1977 and his WBC welterweight title win over Wilfred Benitez in November 1979: ever the egotist, he wanted to be the first non-heavyweight to command a $1m fee as challenger for a world title.

> **"Ray Leonard is the kind of guy who's always looking at the edge of the cliff, to see how close to the edge he can get."**
>
> *Mike Trainer, Leonard's adviser.*

He stopped Benitez in the final seconds of the 15th round, and fitted in a quick defence against England's Dave Green before taking on the man with whom his name will always be linked: Roberto Duran. The swaggering, uncouth Panamanian was the antithesis of Leonard, in ring style as much as personality, and he used the difference as a weapon. He taunted Leonard endlessly, questioning his masculinity and even insulting his wife – anything to goad Leonard into abandoning his boxing skills and brawling on Duran's terms. The strategy worked, as Duran won deservedly in an unforgettable fight.

Yet Leonard grew in defeat. He had lost for the first time in 28 fights, but he proved that he had a champion's heart. In the rematch, he used a similar strategy in reverse, confusing, bewildering and humiliating Duran.

After that, it was almost an anti-climax when Leonard won his second title, the WBA light-middleweight championship, which he immediately relinquished to concentrate on a welterweight unification match with WBA champion Thomas Hearns. They met in a marvellous contest in Las Vegas in September 1981, Leonard coming from behind to stop Hearns in the 14th. He defended the title once, then was forced into premature retirement because of a detached retina. He made an undistinguished, one-fight comeback two years later, and promptly retired again. But the lure of a fight with middleweight legend Marvin Hagler proved irresistible, and he won a bitterly disputed verdict in April 1987.

Nineteen months later, he was back in the Caesars Palace ring chasing two titles in one fight. WBC light-heavyweight champion Donny Lalonde was persuaded to come in under the super-middleweight limit so that Leonard would be able to claim both titles, which he duly did by stopping the Canadian in nine rounds. He relinquished the 175-lb title but defended the super-middleweight crown twice, getting a lucky draw in a rematch with Hearns and outpointing Duran in a dull 12-rounder.

Leonard quit after being floored and outpointed fighting for Terry Norris' WBC light-middleweight belt in 1991, and his last fling came in 1997 when Hector Camacho became the only man to stop him.

SUGAR RAY LEONARD

BORN: MAY 17, 1956
Wilmington, South Carolina

WORLD TITLE FIGHTS:

Nov 30, 1979, w rsf 15
Wilfred Benitez, Las Vegas, NV
(WBC welterweigh)

Mar 31, 1980, w ko 4
Dave Green, Landover, MD (WBC)

Jun 20, 1980, l pts 15
Roberto Duran, Montreal (Can) (WBC)

Nov 25, 1980, w ret 8
Roberto Duran, New Orleans, (WBC)

Mar 28, 1981, w rsf 10
Larry Bonds, Syracuse, NY (WBC)

Jun 25, 1981, w ko 9
Ayub Kalule, Houston, TX
(WBA light-middleweight)

Sep 16, 1981, w rsf 14
Thomas Hearns, Las Vegas, NV
(undisputed welterweight)

Feb 15, 1982, w ko 3
Bruce Finch, Reno, NV
(undisputed welterweight)

Apr 6, 1987, w pts 12
Marvin Hagler, Las Vegas, NV
(WBC middleweight)

Nov 7, 1988 w rsf 9
Donny Lalonde, Las Vegas, NV
(WBC super-middleweight & light-heavyweight)

Jun 12, 1989, drew 12
Thomas Hearns, Las Vegas, NV
(WBC super-middleweight title)

Dec 7, 1989, w pts 12
Roberto Duran, Las Vegas, NV
(WBC super-middleweight)

Feb 9, 1991, l pts 12
Terry Norris, New York, NY
(WBC light-middleweight)

OVERALL RECORD:
40 contests
36 wins
1 draw
3 defeats

LEWIS

LENNOX LEWIS *graduated from Olympic gold medallist to world champion*

MISSION ACCOMPLISHED

It took most of his adult life to do it, but finally by outclassing Mike Tyson on a hot Memphis, Tennessee, night in the summer of 2002, Lennox Lewis had nothing left to prove: he had shown the world that he was the best heavyweight of his generation.

It completed a story that began when both were bright-eyed teenagers: one a recovering juvenile delinquent, attempting to find himself through boxing; the other a big kid who wasn't sure whether he was Canadian, English or Jamaican, but knew whichever it was, he could box. They sparred for a week in the gym of Cus D'Amato, Tyson's trainer, in the Catskill mountains in New York state. While Tyson exploded on to the heavyweight scene, and then crashed into the depths of disgrace and despair, Lewis matured quietly, building his legend piece by piece.

He learned to box after he moved from London to Canada, won a world junior title, a Commonwealth Games gold medal and in 1988 the Olympic super-heavyweight gold by stopping Riddick Bowe in two rounds. Lewis then returned to England to launch his professional career. In October 1992, a spectacular second-round knockout of Razor Ruddock earned him the right to box for the WBC heavyweight title.

However, two weeks later, Bowe dethroned Evander Holyfield and promptly reneged on an agreement to defend against Lewis. The WBC declared Lewis champion, although he was still far from the finished article. Nevertheless, he outpointed Tony Tucker, stopped Frank Bruno and knocked out Phil Jackson. In September 1994, Lewis casually walked on to a second-round right hand from a shut-eyed Oliver McCall, went down heavily, got up but was not allowed to go on. The sceptics, who had been waiting in the wings, rounded on him. No chin, they said. No defence. Over-rated.

By the summer of 1996 Lewis was the No.1 contender for the WBC title, held by Tyson. He should have boxed Tyson around September 1996, but the respective camps had differing ideas. Tyson switched to the WBA and was stopped by Holyfield in November 1996. Lewis had to wait until February 1997 for his chance to regain the WBC belt, ironically against McCall. The fifth-round victory over McCall in Las Vegas brought little genuine satisfaction. The American was led away weeping, having experienced some kind of emotional meltdown.

Lewis' first defence of this second reign brought another shambolic episode when Henry Akinwande was disqualified for holding. It wasn't until he blew away Andrew Golota in 95 seconds in Atlantic City in October 1997 that people really began to believe in him. Wins over Shannon Briggs and Zeljko Mavrovic followed and then, in 1999, Lewis twice outboxed Holyfield. The first fight, in New York, was scandalously judged a draw, a result that led to high-level investigations into boxing corruption. The rematch, in Las Vegas, was if anything slightly closer, but this time Lewis was awarded a unanimous decision. In beating Holyfield, he not only unified the three major titles (WBC, WBA and IBF) but he also proved his superiority over the man who had twice beaten Tyson.

Although he lost the WBA belt in a courtroom, Lewis remained the genuine champion. He knocked out WBC No.1 contender Michael Grant, a 6ft 7in, 250-lb American, in two rounds, stopped South African Frans Botha in his farewell appearance in London and then won a lop-sided decision over IBF No.1 David Tua.

Amazingly, for a man who had paid such attention to detail during his career, Lewis badly underestimated both opponent Hasim Rahman and the effects of boxing at altitude when he travelled late to South Africa for what was supposed to be a routine defence. He had taken time out to get involved in a movie, was overweight and under-trained, and in Brakpan, just outside Johannesburg, in April 2001, he paid a horrible price. A huge right hand laid him out in round five.

The shock galvanized him into getting into shape. He was embarrassed, his ego was hurt and he trained fiercely for the return in Las Vegas in November 2001. It paid off. A clean right hand flattened Rahman in round four. Lewis could have walked away. Certainly, he didn't need the money. What he did need was Tyson, the man he called "the last misfit of my era". A press conference to launch the fight in New York in January 2002 ended in mayhem. Boxing did not need the mess, and Nevada decided it didn't need Tyson. He was refused a licence.

The fight, originally planned for Las Vegas in April, was shunted around, until finally it settled on the Pyramid Arena, Memphis, on June 8. And there, three months short of his 37th birthday, Lewis turned on a masterclass. After a cautious opening round, he gave Tyson a systematic pounding, eventually knocking him out with a thunderous right hand in the eighth. Lewis knew it was the right time to retire, but whatever the future held inside the ring – and walking away from $6 million paydays is a tough call – after 13 years as a professional fighter, Lewis had completed his mission.

He did box once more, when he had an unexpectedly hard time in beating the big Ukrainian Vitali Klitschko in six rounds on cuts. Lewis announced his retirement in February 2004.

"I am on a mission."

Lewis explaining why he became a boxer.

LENNOX LEWIS

BORN: September 2, 1965
London, England.

WORLD TITLE FIGHTS:

May 8, 1993 w pts 12
Tony Tucker, Las Vegas, NV

Oct 1, 1993 2 rsf 7
Frank Bruno, Cardiff

May 6, 1994 w ko 8
Phil Jackson, Atlantic City, NJ

Sep 24, 1994 l ko 2
Oliver McCall, London

Feb 7, 1997 w rsf 5
Oliver McCall, Las Vegas, NV

Jul 12, 1997 w dis 5
Henry Akinwande, Lake Tahoe, CA

Oct 4, 1997 w ko 1
Andrew Golota, Atlantic City, NJ

Mar 28, 1998 w rsf 5
Shannon Briggs, Atlantic City, NJ

Sep,26 1998 w ko 8
Zeljko Mavrovic, Uncasville, CT

Mar 13, 1999 draw 12
Evander Holyfield, New York

Nov 13, 1999 w pts 12
Evander Holyfield, Las Vegas, NV

Apr 29, 2000 w ko 2
David Grant, New York

Jul 15, 2000 w rsf 2
Frans Botha, London

Nov 11, 2000 w pts 12
David Tua, Las Vegas, NV

Apr 22, 2001 l ko 5
Hasim Rahman, Johannesburg (South Africa)

Nov 17, 2001 w ko 4
Hasim Rahman, Las Vegas, NV

Jun 8, 2002 w ko 8
Mike Tyson, Memphis, TN

Jun 21, 2003 w rsf 6
Vitali Klitschko, Los Angeles, CA

OVERALL RECORD:
44 contests, 41 wins, 1 draw, 2 defeats

LENNOX LEWIS *beat all the best heavyweights of his generation*

LOUIS

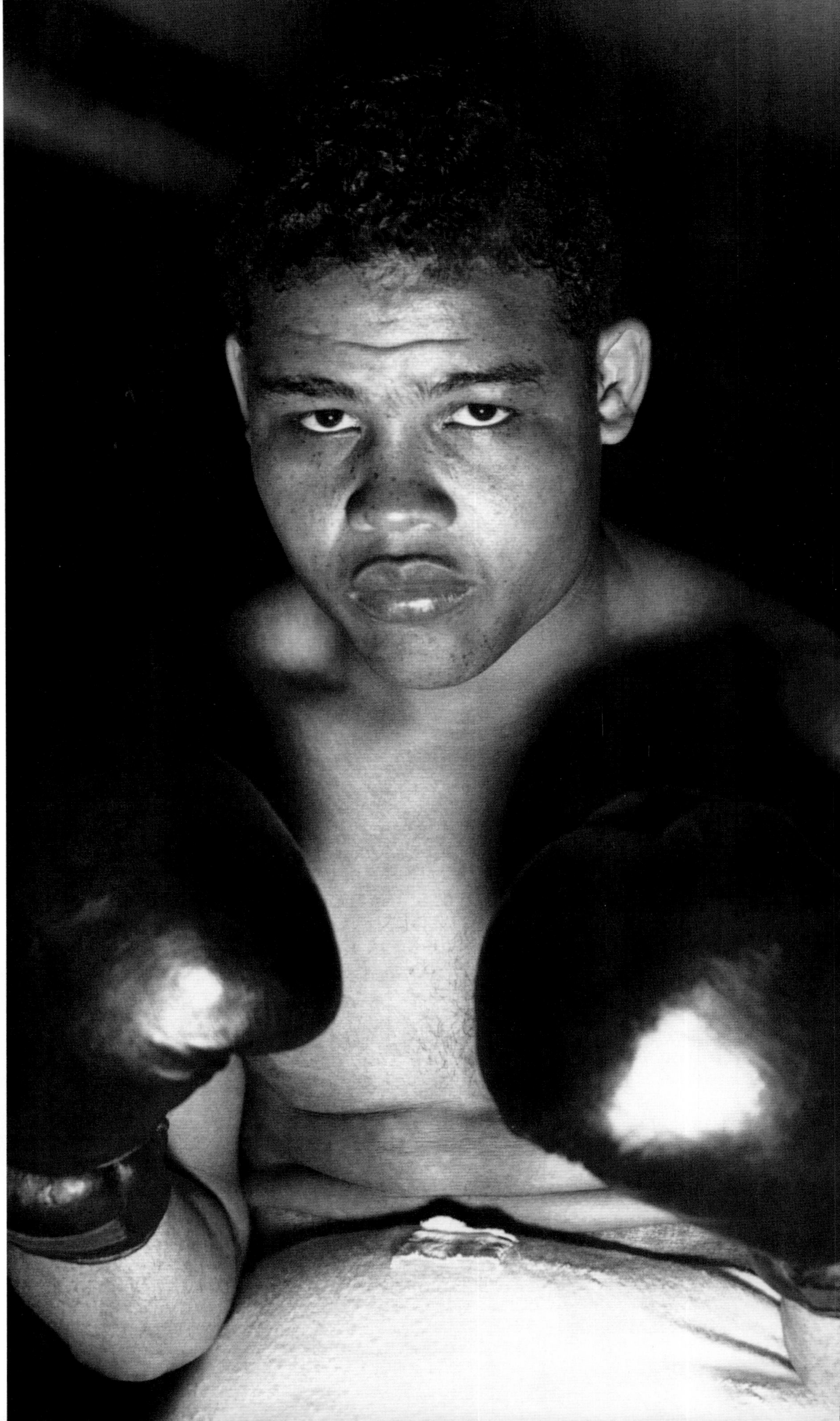

“He can run, but he can’t hide.”

Louis’ famous – and accurate – preview of his fight with Billy Conn.

EXPRESSIONLESS *and menacing, Joe Louis could demoralize opponents before the first bell*

BROWN BOMBER WHO BROKE THE COLOUR BAR

When Joe Louis served in the US Army during the Second World War, the authorities ordered him to perform to segregated crowds of American servicemen. He refused. When he died in 1981, the government had him buried in Arlington National Cemetery, which is reserved for American heroes. There can be few more striking illustrations of the changes in his country's society during his life, or of the importance of the role he played in bringing them about.

Louis led the quiet revolution, which helped erase the divisive memories of Jack Johnson and create a climate in which the talents of other great black performers like Ray Robinson, Archie Moore, and later Muhammad Ali could flourish. Judged by today's radical standards, Louis can sometimes seem obsequious, even servile, but that is a grossly unfair interpretation of who he was and what he did. Much of it is due to the way he was reported at the time, when all black men were quoted in American newspapers as if speaking in some sub-human "Nigger talk", full of "honeychiles", "Massas" and the like. The only roles open to black actors were either eye-rolling comic relief or mindless housemaids, while their music was ignored or else exploited and bastardized by white commercial interests.

Chris Mead, in his definitive biography *Champion – Joe Louis*, wrote: "Not only did (Louis) have to establish himself as a dominant athlete to get a shot at the heavyweight title; he also had to prove that blacks could compete on equal terms with dignity and without exacerbating racial antagonism. Louis accepted that responsibility and performed so well that he became a challenge to segregation, the challenge that began to crack the system."

Louis knew all about segregation. He was born Joe Louis Barrow in the Alabama cotton belt on May 13, 1914, and lived there until he was 12, when his stepfather moved the family north to Detroit. His mother paid for him to have violin lessons, but young Louis used the money to pay for boxing classes instead. In 1933, he reached the finals of the American championships at light-heavyweight, and the following year he won it.

Unusually, he opted to turn professional under a black manager, a gambler called John Roxborough, who recruited an old-time fighter, Jack Blackburn, as trainer. The trio hit it off from the start, and within three years the sensational youngster had beaten just about every heavyweight worth considering. The exception was Max Schmeling, who stunned the world – and particularly the world of black America – when he shattered Louis' unbeaten run with a 12th-round knockout in June 1934. But Louis put it down to experience, and two months later proved he was unaffected by beating ex-champion Jack Sharkey in three rounds.

ON TARGET *Walcott is ko'd in 1948*

Jim Braddock held the title, and he drove a hard bargain for a Louis defence, settling for a huge guarantee of $300,000 and a percentage of Louis' future earnings for the next ten years. It was a fabulous deal, but Braddock earned it by flooring the challenger in the opening round and fighting heroically until he was knocked out in the eighth.

As champion, Louis set new targets in excellence. He retained the title 25 times, and even if some of the opponents were what he cheerfully acknowledged to be "Bums of the Month", there was not a single worthwhile contender of his generation who was not accommodated as well.

On the night he touched perfection, Louis beat Schmeling in 124 seconds, to take revenge for his solitary defeat. Louis gave the champion such a beating that the Nazis ordered the commentary to be cut off because Schmeling's cries of pain were audible after Louis' right to the back had broken two vertebrae.

Louis retired in 1949 as undefeated champion, but tax problems forced him back into the ring. He lost to NBA champion Ezzard Charles, and retired for good after Rocky Marciano knocked him out in 1951. His money gone and debts spiralling, he went downhill fast until President Kennedy wrote off his tax bills as a gesture from the country he had served so well. Caesars Palace in Las Vegas gave him a well-paid sinecure as a greeter in their casino. He died in Las Vegas in April 1981.

JOE LOUIS

BORN: May 13, 1914
Lafayette, Alabama

WORLD TITLE FIGHTS:

Jun 22, 1937, w ko 8
James J. Braddock, Chicago, IL

Aug 30, 1937, w pts 15
Tommy Farr, New York, NY

Feb 23, 1938, w ko 3
Nathan Mann, New York, NY

Apr 1, 1938, w ko 5
Harry Thomas, Chicago, IL

Jun 22, 1938, w ko 1
Max Schmeling, New York, NY

Jan 25, 1939, w ko 1
John Henry Lewis, New York, NY

Apr 17, 1939, w ko 1
Jack Roper, Los Angeles, CA

Jun 28, 1939, w rsf 4
Tony Galento, New York, NY

Sep 20, 1939, w ko 11
Bob Pastor, Detroit, MI

Feb 9, 1940, w pts 15
Arturo Godoy, New York, NY

Mar 29, 1940, w ko 2
Johnny Paychek, New York, NY

Jun 20, 1940, w rsf 8
Arturo Godoy, New York, NY

Dec 16, 1940, w rsf 6
Al McCoy, Boston, MA

Jan 31, 1941, w ko 5
Red Burman, New York, NY

Feb 17, 1941, w ko 2
Gus Dorazio, Philadelphia, PA

Mar 21, 1941, w rsf 13
Abe Simon, Detroit, MI

Apr 8, 1941, w rsf 9
Tony Musto, St Louis, MO

May 23, 1941, w disq 7
Buddy Baer, Washington, DC

Jun 18, 1941, w ko 13
Billy Conn, New York, NY

Sep 29, 1941, w rsf 6
Lou Nova, New York, NY

Jan 9, 1942, w ko 1
Buddy Baer, New York, NY

Mar 27, 1942, w ko 6
Abe Simon, New York, NY

Jun 19, 1946, w ko 8
Billy Conn, New York, NY

Sep 18, 1946, w ko 1
Tami Mauriello, New York, NY

Dec 5, 1947, w pts 15
Jersey Joe Walcott, New York, NY

Jun 25, 1948, w ko 11
Jersey Joe Walcott, New York, NY

Sep 27, 1950, l pts 15
Ezzard Charles, New York, NY

OVERALL RECORD:
72 contests
69 wins
3 defeats

MARCIANO

ROCKY MARCIANO *(right) trailing on points, and with his left eye closing, knocks out Jersey Joe Walcott to win the world title*

WHIRLWIND PUNCHER WHO NEVER SAID DIE

By every known standard, Rocky Marciano lacked the equipment to be a successful fighter. He didn't take up the sport until he was 23, when most aspiring champions are well into their careers; he was short, a little over 5ft 10in; he was not a natural athlete, lacking co-ordination and balance; and he did not even particularly want to box, since his main ambition had been to make the grade in baseball. But he had two assets which, taken together, outweighed all the drawbacks: he was a concussive puncher, especially with the right, and he had unlimited courage and determination – what boxing writers called "bottom".

He was born Rocco Marchegiano, on September 1, 1923, the son of poor Italians who had settled in the Massachusetts town of Brockton where his father, Pasquale, worked in a shoe factory. Rocco did a little boxing in the Army, spending most of his service time in Britain, and only took it up seriously after failing in tryouts for a baseball club. His friend Allie Colombo, who stayed part of the team throughout Marciano's career, persuaded New York manager Al Weill to take him on, which Weill did after seeking advice from veteran trainer Charley Goldman. The 60-year-old Goldman, who had around 300 pro fights himself as a bantamweight, knew championship potential when he saw it. He worked hard with the raw heavyweight and, under Goldman's patient tuition, Marciano learned to channel his extraordinary punching power into short, destructive blows. In his first pro year, 1948, he flattened all 11 opponents, eight in the first round. In 1949 he was 13–0, with 11 knockouts, and the days of obscure venues and small purses were over.

> **"I was a strong guy who trained hard, but I didn't have the talent of Sugar Ray Robinson."**
>
> *Rocky Marciano.*

His breakthrough fight was against Roland LaStarza, a handsome New York-Italian who was unbeaten in 37 fights. They clashed at Madison Square Garden on March 24, 1950, and Marciano won a split decision in a desperately close fight which drew 13,658 fans. Marciano was big business, but Weill was in no rush. He kept him ticking over until he was ready, and then in July 1951 the drive for the title began in earnest. Rex Layne was beaten in six rounds, Freddie Beshore in four, and on October 26, Marciano ended the career of Joe Louis when he clubbed the ex-champion to defeat in nine rounds. Wins over contenders Lee Savold and Harry Matthews maintained the momentum, and Marciano finally fought for the title in Philadelphia on September 23, 1952. Champion Jersey Joe Walcott had been the oldest man to win the heavyweight title, and he did not relinquish it easily. Marciano was floored in the first minute and outboxed for round after round, until by the 13th Walcott had only to stand up to win. But then Marciano landed a single, devastating right, and Walcott crumpled to the floor. That punch took everything out of Walcott as a fighter. In the rematch he went out like a lamb in the first round, and never boxed again. Marciano removed the lingering doubts about the first LaStarza fight by hammering him to 11th-round defeat in September 1953. He boxed only twice in 1954, but his two wins over former champion Ezzard Charles were classics. In the first, on June 17, Charles defied him for the full 15 rounds, thrilling the crowd of almost 48,000 in Yankee Stadium with his spirited resistance. In the rematch, on September 17, Marciano's left nostril was cut clean in half, and his corner had to plead with the ringside doctor not to stop the fight. As ever, Marciano found the way out of the crisis: a stream of rights floored Charles in the eighth, and the follow-up attack knocked him cold.

There were only two fights after that, a foul-filled victory over England's Don Cockell and a ninth-round knockout of light-heavyweight champion Archie Moore. Rocky's retirement, announced on April 27, 1956, stunned the sporting world. He had a perfect record of 49–0, 43 inside the distance, and there were still large cheques to be earned. But he stuck to his decision, resisting all offers for a comeback. He was killed on August 31, 1969, when the Cessna light aircraft in which he was a passenger crashed near Des Moines. Sonny Liston, the least articulate of men, spoke an eloquent tribute. "This man was one of the greatest champions ever," he said. "He refused to accept defeat. And nobody beat him."

ROCKY MARCIANO: *a hard hitter, with a hero's heart*

ROCKY MARCIANO

BORN: September 1, 1923
Brockton, Massachusetts

WORLD TITLE FIGHTS:

Sep 23, 1952, w ko 13
Jersey Joe Walcott, Philadelphia, PA

May 15, 1953, w ko 1
Jersey Joe Walcott, Chicago, IL

Sep 24, 1953, w rsf 11
Roland LaStarza, New York, NY

Jun 17, 1954, w pts 15
Ezzard Charles, New York, NY

Sep 17, 1954, w ko 8
Ezzard Charles, New York, NY

May 16, 1955, w rsf 9
Don Cockell, San Francisco, CA

Sep 21, 1955, w ko 9
Archie Moore, New York, NY

OVERALL RECORD:
49 contests
49 wins

ROBINSON

SUGAR RAY ROBINSON *(right) took ten rounds to defeat Randolph Turpin in their 1951 rematch*

MASTER OF THE RING WITH A SENSE OF STYLE

There are not enough superlatives in a thesaurus to do justice to Sugar Ray Robinson, the ego-driven genius who was the greatest middleweight in history and, very probably, the greatest welterweight as well. He held the welterweight crown for four years, and won the middleweight championship an unmatched five times. In a fabulous 25-year career he boxed 202 times, losing only 19, the majority of them in his declining years. He faced 18 men who held world titles, at every weight from lightweight to light-heavyweight, and beat 14 of them, three in his first year as a pro. Some record: some fighter.

The only phony thing about Ray Robinson in the ring was his name. He was born Walker Smith in Detroit on May 3, 1921, and acquired the ring name when he turned up for his first amateur fight without having registered with the authorities and borrowed the card of another boxer. He won, of course – he was beaten only a few times in 85 amateur fights, 69 of which were knockouts, 40 in the first round – and won the featherweight Golden Gloves before turning pro in October 1940. The sheer statistics of what followed still defy belief. He reeled off 40 victories in a row, lost to Jake LaMotta for the only time in their six meetings, and then went unbeaten in his next 91 fights, a streak that brought him the welterweight title in December 1946 and the middleweight championship in February 1951.

RAY ROBINSON: *Glamour and glory*

“You are an artiste, like a musician or a dancer, and you will see, the people will react to you like an artiste.”

French promoter Charlie Michaelis, persuading Robinson to come to Paris in 1951.

But the figures alone do not convey his full impact. He was not just a boxer, but a megastar who, even when TV was in its early years, became known in every corner of the world for his dazzling talent and his astonishing lifestyle, which included pink Cadillacs, a staff barber, masseurs, a shoe-shiner and even a court jester dwarf. In the lean post-war years of his prime, such extravagance was startling. It also took some financing, which was why he maintained a busy programme of defences, non-title matches and exhibition tours.

By 1950 he had run out of opposition, and at 29 was finding it a strain to keep down to 147lb. He went after the middleweight title and, in a blistering 12-fight spell between June and December, trounced a string of contenders and won three contests that the Pennsylvania Commission recognized as being for the championship. The real champion was his old foe LaMotta, and Robinson hammered him to defeat in the 13th round in Chicago on St Valentine's Day 1951.

Ambitiously, he lined up a seven-fight European tour between May 21 and July 10, culminating in a £30,000 defence against British champion Randolph Turpin. The Continental leg of the trip went smoothly enough, but the awkward Englishman was a different proposition. Robinson had spent as much time partying as training in Europe, and it showed as Turpin outboxed him in round after round.

The rematch, just 64 days later, drew 61,370 to the Polo Grounds, New York, and again Robinson had problems with Turpin's style. There was nothing much in the first nine rounds, but then Robinson's left eyebrow, which had been cut in the first fight, split open again in the tenth. Referee Ruby Goldstein was poised to intervene when Robinson, wiping the blood away, set up a blistering attack that brought the referee's intervention in his favour with eight seconds left in the round.

Robinson made two quick defences in 1952, outpointing Carl "Bobo" Olson and knocking out Rocky Graziano, and then tried for Joey Maxim's light-heavyweight title. They fought in New York, in 104-degree heat so intense that the referee collapsed and had to be replaced. Robinson was ahead after 13 rounds, but was so drained by the heat that he could not come out for the 14th. He retired, but financial imperatives drove him back to the ring to regain the middleweight title from Olson in December 1955. He lost and regained the title twice more, in famous battles with Gene Fullmer and Carmen Basilio, and then lost it for the final time to Paul Pender in January 1960. He failed three times to regain it, and – the high-spending days now a memory – fought on until December 1965. He suffered Alzheimer's in later life, and died on April 12, 1989.

SUGAR RAY ROBINSON

BORN: May 3, 1921
Detroit, Michigan

WORLD TITLE FIGHTS:

Dec 20, 1946, w pts 15
Tommy Bell, New York, NY
(welterweight)

Jun 24, 1947, w rsf 8
Jimmy Doyle, Cleveland, OH

Dec 19, 1947, w rsf 6
Chuck Taylor, Detroit, MI

Jun 28, 1948, w pts 15
Bernard Docusen, Chicago, IL

Jul 11, 1949, w pts 15
Kid Gavilan, Philadelphia, PA

Aug 9, 1950, w pts 15
Charlie Fusari, Jersey City, NJ

Feb 14, 1951, w rsf 13
Jake LaMotta, Chicago, IL
(middleweight)

Jul 10, 1951, l pts 15
Randolph Turpin, London (Eng)

Sep 12, 1951, w rsf 10
Randolph Turpin, New York, NY

Mar 13, 1952, w pts 15
Carl "Bobo" Olson, San Francisco, CA

Apr 16, 1952, w ko 3
Rocky Graziano, Chicago, IL

Jun 25, 1952, l ret 14
Joey Maxim, New York, NY (light-heavyweight)

Dec 9, 1955, w ko 2
Carl "Bobo" Olson, Chicago, IL
(middleweight)

May 18, 1956, w ko 4
Carl "Bobo" Olson, Los Angeles, CA

Jan 2, 1957, l pts 15
Gene Fullmer, New York, NY

May 1, 1957, w ko 5
Gene Fullmer, Chicago, IL

Sep 23, 1957, l pts 15
Carmen Basilio, New York, NY

Mar 25, 1958, w pts 15
Carmen Basilio, Chicago, IL

Jan 22, 1960, l pts 15
Paul Pender, Boston, MA

Jun 10, 1960, l pts 15
Paul Pender, Boston, MA

Dec 3, 1960, drew 15
Gene Fullmer, Los Angeles, CA
(NBA middleweight)

Mar 4, 1961, l pts 15
Gene Fullmer, Las Vegas, NV
(NBA middleweight)

OVERALL RECORD:
202 contests
175 wins
6 draws
2 No Contests
19 defeats

TYSON

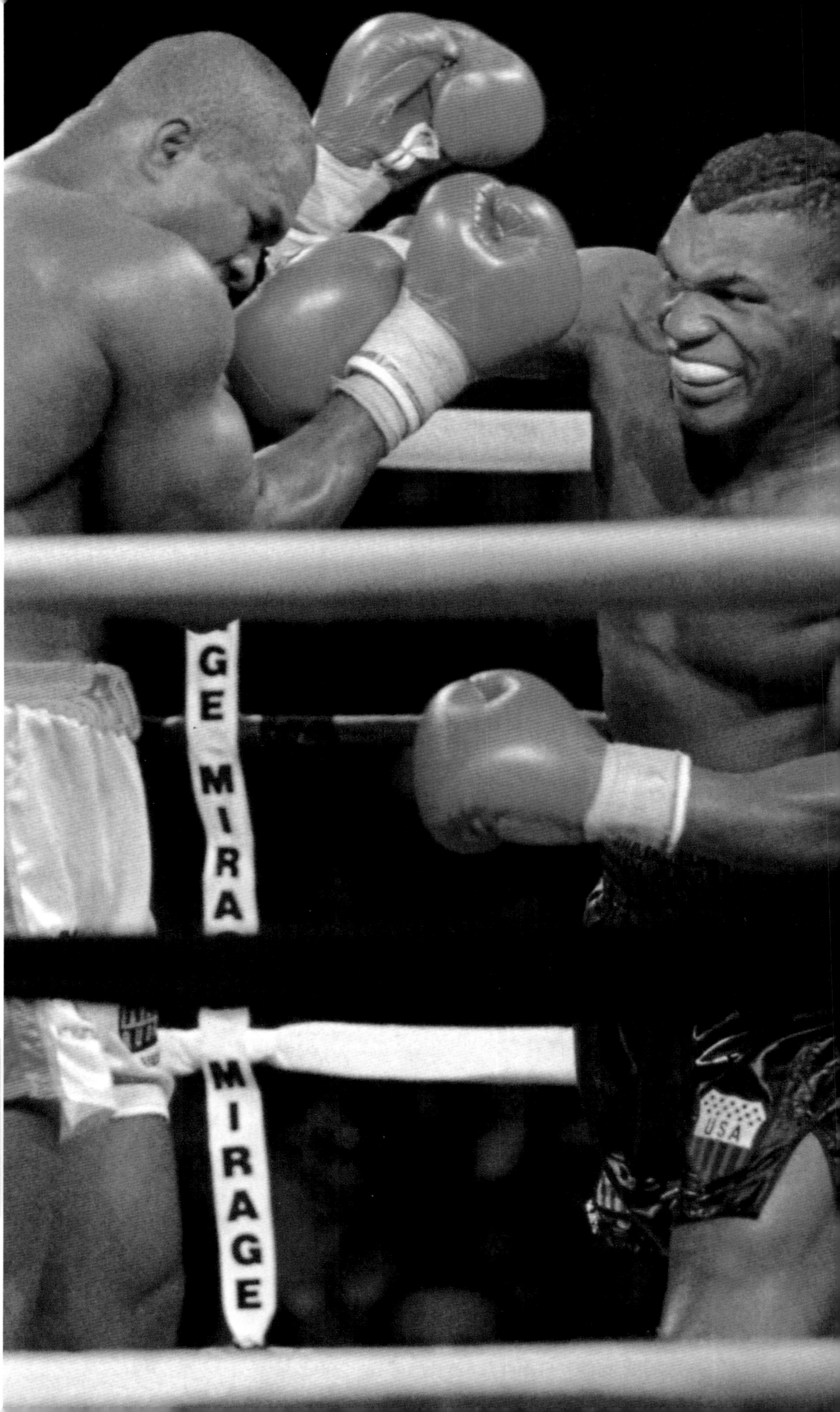

“I’m just a normal guy with heart.”

Mike Tyson, in 1990.

MIKE TYSON *(right) was not very impressive, but still too good for Donovan Ruddock in 1991*

TROUBLED MAN WITH IRON IN HIS SOUL

POWERHOUSE *The young Mike Tyson*

History will not be kind to Mike Tyson, who wasted the potential and the opportunity to be the greatest heavyweight of them all. But then Tyson always had the air of a man whose built-in self-destruct mechanism was ticking away. This was never more evident than in the 1997 WBA title fight against Evander Holyfield, when he was disqualified for biting Holyfield's ears in round three. Tyson lost his licence and, after winning it back he looked terrible in beating Frans Botha and was then jailed for a road rage assault.

Perhaps, considering his background, no one should have been surprised. He was born in Brooklyn, New York, on June 30, 1966, and grew up wild on the toughest streets of the Brownsville ghetto. His father had left even before he was born, and his mother, a drinker, struggled to cope with her four children on welfare. By the time he was ten, the boy was an accomplished mugger, a sociopath who beat up other children, and occasionally adults, for the sheer pleasure of doing so. He was incorrigible, in and out of a succession of juvenile detention centres and medium-security facilities until, at 13, he was sent to the Tryon School for Boys, a last-resort establishment where he could be detained until the age of 16.

An instructor there, Bobby Stewart, saw possibilities in the boy. He taught him the basics and referred him to Cus D'Amato, a 72-year-old manager and trainer who had steered Floyd Patterson to a world title. Tyson was released on his 14th birthday into D'Amato's care and his life began afresh.

He turned professional in May 1985, boxing mainly on small shows bankrolled by Jacobs and Cayton. The policy was deliberate, to keep him off national TV until public curiosity about the sensational heavyweight with the knockout record mounted to the right pitch of hysteria. Of his 15 fights in 1985, 11 finished in the first round. The pace continued in 1986, when 13 straight wins culminated in a second-round destruction of Trevor Berbick to win the WBC title. At 20 years and 145 days, he had broken Patterson's record as the youngest-ever heavyweight champion.

Within ten months, he had unified the championship, and in 1988 he reached his peak. Larry Holmes was taken apart in four rounds; Tony Tubbs in two, and the undefeated Mike Spinks in one with a performance of terrifying precision.

But Tyson's life was falling apart. D'Amato and Jacobs had died, and the ubiquitous Don King had ousted Cayton from the driving seat. There was a catastrophic marriage to actress Robin Givens, which ended in predictable but painful divorce, and a bitter split from trainer Kevin Rooney, who as D'Amato's protégé and professional heir had played such a significant part in the fighter's development. The champion looked vulnerable in stopping Frank Bruno, but more like the old Tyson in flattening Carl Williams in the first round. But it ended, shockingly, in Tokyo on February 11, 1990, when James "Buster" Douglas climbed off the floor to knock out an ill-prepared and unfocused Tyson in the tenth.

He came back with four wins of varying quality, struggling twice to beat Razor Ruddock, and then was jailed for six years for raping a beauty pageant contestant. He spent more than three years in prison before being released in 1995. By that time, his fortune had dwindled, but after two quick wins he took the WBC title from Frank Bruno in three rounds in Las Vegas in March 1996 and looked hungry again.

A one-round victory over WBA champion Bruce Seledon was almost effortless, but political machinations took over. He gave up the WBC belt, but lost the WBA version to Holyfield and began the familiar self-destruct process once again. Tyson plodded on, never far from controversy, and was wheeled out for one last world title shot against Lennox Lewis in Nevada. However, after a brawl between the two at a press conference in New York – instigated by Tyson, who had bitten Lewis' leg – the Nevada Boxing Commission refused to issue Tyson with a licence to box in the state. The upshot was that the fight was eventually consigned to Memphis, Tennessee, in June 2002. Tyson talked a big fight, but was outclassed and knocked out in eight rounds by a magnificent Lewis.

Tyson eventually retired in 2005 after shocking back-to-back defeats by Danny Williams and Kevin McBride. By then, just to add insult to injury, he was also declared bankrupt.

MIKE TYSON

BORN: June 30, 1966, Brooklyn,

WORLD TITLE FIGHTS:

Nov 22, 1986, w rsf 2
Trevor Berbick, Las Vegas, NV (WBC)

Mar 7, 1987, w pts 12
James "Bonecrusher" Smith, Las Vegas, NV (WBC and WBA)

Aug 1, 1987, w pts 12
Tony Tucker, Las Vegas, NV (undisputed)

Oct 16, 1987, w rsf 7
Tyrell Biggs, Atlantic City, NJ

Jan 22, 1988, w rsf 4
Larry Holmes, Atlantic City, NJ

Mar 21, 1988, w rsf 2
Tony Tubbs, Tokyo (Jap)

Jun 27, 1988, w ko 1
Mike Spinks, Atlantic City, NJ

Feb 25, 1989, w rsf 5
Frank Bruno, Las Vegas, NV

Jun 21, 1989, w rsf 1
Carl Williams, Atlantic City, NJ (WBC, WBA, IBF)

Feb 11, 1990, l ko 10
James "Buster" Douglas, Tokyo (Jap)

Mar 16, 1996, w rsf 3
Frank Bruno, Las Vegas, NV (WBC)

Sep 7, 1996, w rsf 1
Bruce Seldon, Las Vegas, NV (WBA)

Nov 9, 1996, l rsf 11
Evander Holyfield, Las Vegas NV (WBA)

Jun 28, 1997, l dis 3
Evander Holyfield, Las Vegas, NV (WBA)

Jun 8, 2002, l ko 8
Lennox Lewis, Memphis, TN (WBC/IBF)

OVERALL RECORD:
58 contests, 50 wins, 2 No Contests, 6 defeats

WILDE

JIMMY WILDE *(right) suffers a rare defeat by former bantam-weight champion Pete Herman*

THE GHOST WITH A HAMMER IN HIS HAND

Jimmy Wilde never scaled more than 102lb in his prime, yet he knocked out or stopped 101 of the 151 men he faced in his 12-year career, and lost to just four of them. Wilde claimed to have had 854 fights, but he was including hundreds in the booths and in the semi-professional fighting that was popular in Wales in the early part of the century. If those are included, then his figure may not be far short of the truth.

He was born into a mining family in Tylerstown on May 15, 1892, and as soon as he was old enough he, too, went down the pit. But he soon discovered he could fight, and with disproportionate punching power. When he was 18, his landlord, an old bare-knuckler called Dai Davies, encouraged him to join Jack Scarrott's travelling booth to gain experience. He was backed by Davies' daughter Elizabeth, whom he later married and who became, effectively, his manager and even, when necessary, his sparring partner.

His formal professional career began on December 26, 1910, and he set a hot pace. In 1911 he had 28 fights, winning 27 and drawing once. However, all but two of them were staged in Pontypridd. Even though he had won 22 by knockout, he couldn't seem to get noticed outside his home area. Eventually, he travelled to London and pestered Dick Burge, promoter at the Blackfriars Ring, for a booking. Burge matched him with a protégé of lightweight champion Matt Wells, and Wilde won in 45 seconds. But a second booking was not forthcoming, and after a trial at the National Sporting Club proved equally unproductive, he went back to Wales.

There, he compiled a further 54 straight wins, 33 inside the distance, to bring his tally to 81 wins (55 inside schedule), one draw and no defeats.

THE CHAMP'S *last fighting portrait, in June 1923*

Even so, London did not want to know. Peggy Bettinson, matchmaker at the NSC, explained that Wilde was simply too small, and would provoke complaints from his members about bad match-making. Eventually, though, they found a Frenchman who was actually lighter than Wilde, Eugene Husson. He scaled under 100lb for his fight with Wilde at the NSC on March 30, 1914, and while Wilde probably could have knocked him out quickly he chose instead to put on an exhibition of the full range of his boxing skills before disposing of Husson in the sixth.

Having convinced the game's most powerful promoters of his worth, Wilde was quickly moved ahead and, in January 1915, was matched with Tancy Lee for the British and European titles. Wilde went through with the fight despite a strength-sapping dose of flu, and took a shocking beating before his corner threw in the towel in the 17th round. Five months later, the little Welshman was back in action, and by early 1916 had earned a match with Joe Symonds for the world and British titles at the NSC on February 14; Wilde won on a 12th-round retirement after a gruelling battle that was settled in the end by a blow to the Englishman's Adam's Apple.

Symonds' world title claims were disputed by two Americans, Johnny Rosner and Giuseppe di Mefi, the latter who took his ring name of Young Zulu Kid, from the golliwog mascot he carried. Wilde stopped Rosner in 11 rounds, and while he waited for the match with the Zulu Kid to be finalized he stopped his old rival Tancy Lee, also in the 11th. The championship fight took place in London on December 18, 1916, Wilde yet again winning in 11 rounds to become the undisputed title-holder.

War service severely restricted his activity after that, and he spent 1920 on a well-paid tour of America and Canada. He came home to fight former bantamweight champion Pete Herman, but found the American much too big and strong for him and was rescued by the referee in the 17th round. After two years' inactivity he accepted a £13,000 offer to defend against Pancho Villa in New York, and took such a terrible beating that he later admitted that, for four months after the fight, he could not recognize anyone.

He never boxed again, but made a useful second career as a newspaper columnist. When he was 72 he was beaten up by a gang of thugs at Cardiff railway station, and lived out the last four years of his life unaware of who he was or what he had achieved. He died on March 10, 1969.

JIMMY WILDE

BORN: May 15, 1892
Tylerstown, Wales

WORLD TITLE FIGHTS:

Nov 16, 1914, w pts 15
Joe Symonds, London (Eng)

Dec 3, 1914, w ko 9
Sid Smith, Liverpool (Eng)

Jan 25, 1915, l rsf 17
Tancy Lee, London (Eng)

Feb 14, 1916, w rsf 12
Joe Symonds, London (Eng)

Apr 24, 1916, w rsf 11
Johnny Rosner, Liverpool (Eng)

Jun 26, 1916, w rsf 11
Tancy Lee, London (Eng)

Jul 31, 1916, w ko 10
Johnny Hughes, London (Eng)

Dec 18, 1916, w ko 11
Young Zulu Kid, London (Eng)

Mar 12, 1917, w rsf 4
George Clark, London (Eng)

Apr 29, 1918, w rsf 2
Dick Heasman, London (Eng)

Jun 18, 1923, l ko 7
Pancho Villa, New York, NY

OVERALL RECORD:
152 contests
133 wins
2 draws
13 No Decisions
4 defeats

"Give me a chance, Mr Burge – you won't regret it."

Wilde, pleading with promoter Dick Burge for his first London booking.

EVANDER HOLYFIELD *is on the back foot during the heavyweight title unification fight that only unified people in their condemnation of the drawn verdict*

THE GREAT FIGHTS

There have been many better fights than the ones chronicled here. Some were obscure six-rounders in tiny halls, or minor epics where area titles or just local pride were at stake. Others were multi-million-dollar encounters between the greatest fighters of their time: who can forget Julio Cesar Chavez stopping Meldrick Taylor with just two seconds to go in their classic clash at Caesars Palace in 1990?

It is impossible to condense 100 years of boxing history into so few fights, so inevitably your favourite fight may not be on our list. Chavez vs. Taylor didn't make it, but Jake LaMotta vs. Laurent Dauthuille did. That was also a last-gasp victory, but in its way it was even more impressive than Chavez's success because LaMotta had been so comprehensively outboxed for 14½ rounds. His win defined him as a fighter, a true triumph for heart, courage and simple refusal to acknowledge defeat. There was always a chance that Chavez could stop Taylor, but until it happened, there wasn't a hope that LaMotta could stop Dauthuille.

Other fights are included because of their social significance, such as Jack Johnson's defeat of James J. Jeffries in the most hate-laden fight in boxing history. Marvin Hagler's win over Thomas Hearns is there, since it was one of those special nights when two great talents collided at the peak of their powers. Muhammad Ali's win over George Foreman is included because it was the supreme moment of an unmatched career, while his triumph over Joe Frazier in Manila was simply one of the greatest fights of all time. It was not an easy shortlist to compile, but then that is yet another illustration of boxing's eternal appeal.

THE END OF AN ERA

JAMES J. CORBETT vs. JOHN L. SULLIVAN

It is one of the many ironies of boxing that the man who wins like a bullying lout will often lose with the chivalry and generosity of a Corinthian sportsman. So it was with John L. Sullivan, the Boston Strong Boy, terror of a thousand bar-rooms, when the time came for him to acknowledge that after 42 "official" fights and countless other short-lived brawls, he had met a better man than himself. Sullivan's grace in the moments after James J. Corbett had knocked him out in the 21st round of an embarrassingly one-sided fight served to cement his legend, and won him admirers who would have shunned him in the days when he was the old high-living, hard-drinking, rough-talking John L.

The result shocked the world as much as it stunned Sullivan. For a decade, ever since he knocked out Paddy Ryan to win the bare-knuckle championship of the world, Sullivan was the epitome of the fighting man, a brawler who battled for pleasure as much as for cash, and who had never even come close to defeat. Oddly, it was Sullivan who insisted that this fight be the first championship to be contested with gloves (five-ouncers), although Corbett, a skilled technician who relied on speed and skill rather than brawn, raised no objections – especially as his hands were known to be brittle.

Their clash was a landmark in boxing history. Louisiana had recently legalized decision fights under the Queensberry Rules, and the Sullivan-Corbett match, apart from being the first gloved heavyweight title fight of the modern era, would also be the climax of a boxing carnival at the New Orleans Olympic Club at 636 Royal Street. Boxing had become respectable, and the club celebrated the fact by organizing a series of championship fights. On the Monday, George Dixon and Jack Skelly met for the featherweight title; on Tuesday, Jack McAuliffe retained the lightweight crown against Billy Meyers, and on Wednesday John L. faced Corbett. McAuliffe, a close friend of Sullivan's who also acted as his chief second, bet his entire purse of $18,500 on Sullivan at 1–4.

FIGHT FACTS

DATE:	**September 7, 1892**
VENUE:	**New Orleans, LA**
TITLE:	**World Heavyweight**
RESULT:	**James J. Corbett won (K.O.,round 21)**

The first few rows were occupied by the Club members, all of them dinner-suited and wearing a white gardenia in their buttonholes, but the rest of the 10,000 crowd were more the traditional fight fans. Unusually, the champion was the first to enter the ring, and looked to be carrying more weight than was good for him at 212lb to Corbett's 180lb.

From the first bell, the outcome was painfully apparent. Corbett danced around the lumbering champion, seven years his senior at 33, and stabbed away with left jabs. Sullivan ploughed forward for round after round, swiping punches at a more elusive target than he had ever faced, and often missing so badly that he swung himself in a full circle. Even when he finally connected in the fourth round, Corbett shrugged it off and laughed as he broke away. The sustained punishment took its toll on the veteran: as early as the third round his nose was broken, his lips split, and all the while those relentless jabs were eroding his resistance.

By the 21st round, he was spent. Corbett floored him early in the round, and John L. only just beat the count. Corbett showed no mercy: another flurry of punches, and Sullivan crashed face first. Halfway through the count he rolled on to his right side, but he was finished. Afterwards, he raised his arm to silence the crowd who were applauding Corbett's victory. "All I have to say is that I came to the ring once too often," he said, before adding the sentence that confirmed him as an American folk hero: "If I had to get licked, I'm glad it was by an American."

JAMES J. CORBETT *(right) controlled every moment of their historic fight*

" Fighting under the new rules before gentlemen is a pleasure. "

John L. Sullivan, describing the difference between the sport he had dominated and boxing under the Marquess of Queensbury Rules.

BLACK POWER UNSETTLES WHITE AMERICA

FIGHT FACTS

DATE:	**July 4, 1910**
VENUE:	**Reno, NV**
TITLE:	**World Heavyweight**
RESULT:	**Jack Johnson won (stoppage, round 15)**

JACK JOHNSON vs. JAMES J. JEFFRIES

Squinting at the world through a white pointed hood must give a peculiar perspective on life, which may explain how otherwise sane people argued in 1910 that James J. Jeffries, who had not thrown a punch for money since 1904, was the rightful heavyweight champion of the world. Jeffries had retired as undefeated champion, and his title had passed to Marvin Hart, then to Tommy Burns and finally to Jack Johnson – the first black champion, and the object of an unprecedented out-pouring of hatred.

The cry went up for Jeffries to return to the ring and reclaim the title for the "white race". His advocates – led by the famous novelist Jack London – claimed that since Jeffries had never been beaten in the ring he remained the rightful champion. Johnson, more amused than insulted by the suggestion that a man who was now a fat and comfortable farmer had more right than he to regard himself as the world's best fighting man, encouraged speculation about the match, with one eye on the potential receipts.

"HOW DO YOU LIKE THIS, MR JEFF?" *Johnson taunts his challenger*

Jeffries proved initially unreceptive to the idea, at first claiming the right to draw the infamous "colour line" as laid down by his predecessor John L. Sullivan, who proclaimed that he had "never fought a Negro, and never will". Jeffries criticized Burns for defending the title against Johnson, and accused him of betraying his pride and the Caucasian race by doing so. Jeffries' father, a minister, threatened to disown his son if he fought Johnson, conveniently ignoring the fact that his other son, Jack, had fought and lost to Johnson eight years earlier.

Finally, the pressure on Jeffries to challenge Johnson became intolerable, and he agreed to the match. It was a troublesome affair from the start. Tex Rickard won an auction for the right to promote it, offering the then-staggering sum of $120,000 to be shared between the pair.

He initially planned to stage the fight in Salt Lake City, but then switched to San Francisco and built an arena there specially for the fight. But after $300,000 worth of tickets had been sold, the State Governor suddenly withdrew permission, costing Rickard $50,000.

He had offers from Goldfield, Reno and Ely, all in Nevada, to host the fight and made a theatrical tour of all three venues, being greeted each time by a brass band, before announcing that the fight – the first to be billed as "The Battle of the Century" – would take place in Reno on July 4, 1910.

It was scheduled for 45 rounds, and 15,710 paid to watch Jeffries attempt to reclaim the championship. The ex-champion, never beaten in 20 fights, had shed 70lb in training and looked drawn and haggard as he entered the ring under the blazing summer sun.

Johnson had split acrimoniously with his manager George Little in the weeks before the fight (in a dispute over a poker hand) and the disgruntled Little bet heavily on Jeffries and spread the rumour that the fight was fixed, which caused the odds to plummet and left the challenger a 5–2 favourite by fight time.

But when the action began, it was immediately apparent that the 35-year-old veteran had no business in the ring with a champion at the peak of his powers. Johnson taunted and tormented him unmercifully, just as he had done against Burns, landing at will with jabs and hooks and evading Jeffries' crude swings.

It was all so easy for Johnson that he later claimed he deliberately held off on Jeffries because he didn't want to cause him permanent damage, and certainly from the sixth round onwards the crowd were calling for Rickard (who doubled as referee) to stop the fight.

Jeffries was game and had his pride, though, and he kept trying his limited best, all the while walking into a bewildering barrage of punches from the quicksilver Johnson, who punctuated bursts of punches with sneers like "How do you like this jab then, Mr Jeff?"

It went on like that for 14 rounds, until the end came in the 15th. A succession of short punches to the head dropped Jeffries for the first time in his life, and when he rose he was immediately floored again by two hooks to the jaw. As he crawled across the ring on his hands and knees the crowd again called on Rickard to intervene, but when Jeffries got to his feet, Rickard waved him back into action.

Jeffries was defenceless, and sagged to the ground for the third time as Johnson rained punches on him. The challenger finished with one arm draped over the middle rope, and this time Rickard signalled the end without completing the count.

DAZED AND HURT *Tunney tries to haul himself upright in the seventh round*

THE BATTLE OF THE LONG COUNT

GENE TUNNEY vs. JACK DEMPSEY

There was deep and lasting respect between Jack Dempsey and Gene Tunney. Dempsey, the glamorous and charismatic heavyweight champion, was always the man in Tunney's sights from the day the former Marine, still only a light-heavyweight, decided to make boxing his career. He worked his way up to challenge for Dempsey's title, beat him then and in the rematch, and earned the old champ's undying esteem.

And yet Dempsey might have been excused a degree of bitterness towards his old rival, since half the world was convinced that he had been robbed of victory when they met for the second time in what history came to know as "The Battle of the Long Count". Dempsey never shared that view, acknowledging that he had been in breach of the rules by not immediately going to a neutral corner when Tunney was floored in the seventh round. Referee Dave Barry, quite properly, did not commence his count until Dempsey had obeyed the letter of the law, and Tunney took full advantage by remaining on one knee until Barry had reached "nine", by which point he had been on the floor for considerably longer than the traditional ten seconds.

The incident offered a telling insight into both men and their backgrounds... Dempsey, the hard nut who brawled his way out of the mining camps and hobo camps, the fighting animal who ignored the rules in his eagerness to get at his opponent; and Tunney, the cold and calculating professional who, even in his moment of supreme crisis, remained cool enough to exploit every angle to his maximum advantage.

Dempsey had grown complacent and soft during long spells of inactivity before facing Tunney for the first time in Philadelphia on September 23, 1926, and was easily outboxed by his fast-punching and clever challenger. But when they met again, a year all but a day later, Dempsey was a different man. The shock of defeat had concentrated his mind on his business. Tunney, too, was different. He wanted to knock Dempsey out this time and, uncharacteristically, missed with a whole stream of rights as Dempsey, boxing much more cagily than in their first encounter, slipped and ducked most of his efforts.

Tunney got through in the fourth and rocked the ex-champ to his heels, but Dempsey, ignoring blood from cuts over both eyes, came back strongly in the fifth. He had a tendency to rabbit punch, and time and again he crashed blows off the back of Tunney's neck until finally the champion's bodyguard, Sergeant Bill Smith of the Chicago Police, got onto the ring apron during the interval between the fifth and sixth rounds and yelled to Barry that if he didn't stop the rabbit punches he'd "be carried out of here dead".

A minute into the seventh, Dempsey crossed a right over Tunney's jab and shook him, following up with a barrage of six unanswered hooks that sent the champion into a crouch, almost sitting on the bottom rope before crumpling to the canvas for the first knockdown of his long career. His fighting instinct hauled him into a sitting position, and there he waited until Barry at last persuaded Dempsey to move to a neutral corner. Fourteen seconds had elapsed before Barry's count reached nine, time enough for Tunney's head to clear.

When he got up, Tunney met Dempsey's charge with a right to the heart so severe that Dempsey later described it as "the hardest blow I have ever received. It was not a question in my mind of being knocked out – I thought I was going to die." That punch turned the fight back Tunney's way, and he never lost control of it again. Dempsey was floored in the eighth, and when the final bell sounded at the end of the tenth round, he immediately acknowledged Tunney's superiority. The game's toughest competitor could also lose with style.

FIGHT FACTS

DATE:	**September 22, 1927**
VENUE:	**Soldier Field, Chicago, IL**
TITLE:	**World Heavyweight**
RESULT:	**Gene Tunney won (points decision, 10 rounds)**

BILLY CONN *full of confidence, has Joe Louis under severe pressure*

NO HIDING PLACE

JOE LOUIS vs. BILLY CONN

So many great fighters have had in-built flaws which prevented them from achieving their maximum potential. Billy Conn was one such, though in his case the flaw was in his temperament more than his technique. He was a brilliant boxer, but he was also of "fighting Irish" stock and, on the biggest night of his life, he allowed his Irish love of a punch-up to deny him the heavyweight championship of the world.

Conn was in his prime when he challenged Joe Louis for the title at the Polo Grounds, New York, on June 18, 1941. A huge crowd of 54,487 came out that Wednesday evening to watch Louis make his 18th title defence, and despite the weight disparity (174lb against Louis's 199½lb) there was plenty of support for the handsome Irish-American, the former light-heavyweight champion. The betting odds opened at 18–5, making him the shortest-priced challenger for three years, and by fight time they had come right down to 11–5.

Conn, at 23, was a veteran of 67 fights of which he had won 58 and drawn one. His skill was unquestioned, but it was not complemented by punching power: his 58 wins included only 12 inside the distance, although a run of four consecutive knockouts on the lead-in to the Louis fight was a major confidence-booster. It was widely accepted that if Conn were to win, it would have to be by exploiting his speed to outmanoeuvre the slow-footed champion. Louis, though, was unconcerned. "He can run, but he can't hide," he said, coining a phrase that passed into the language.

And running was all Conn did for the first two rounds, skipping around the ring as Louis plodded after him. The challenger took a more positive approach in the third, but did not have any real success until a left jab and two following rights to the jaw stopped Louis in his tracks early in the fourth. Conn switched on to the attack, driving Louis back with quick and well-placed jabs and hooks, but the champion took over again in the fifth when he staggered Conn with a left hook to the jaw and split open a cut over the right eye and another on the nose. At the bell, Conn was so dazed that he went to the wrong corner, and had to be revived with smelling salts between rounds.

But the fast pace was telling on Louis, and from the seventh onwards he was in pain from a damaged right wrist, which he'd jarred on the top of Conn's head. As Louis faded, Conn grew in self-belief, finding the confidence to step in with quick combinations and constantly stabbing left jabs into Louis' bewildered face.

The 12th was Conn's best round. Time and again he rocked Louis with left hooks and rights, which he seemed able to land at will. In the corner, Louis' trainer Jack Blackburn spelt it out to him between rounds. "You're losing on points," he told Louis. "You've got to knock him out." A knockout was on Conn's mind, too – his success in the 12th encouraged him to believe he could finish the exhausted champion in the 13th, and he came out looking for it.

Louis soaked up the first flurry, then suddenly caught Conn with a perfect right to the chin. Three more rights sent him into the ropes, but Conn rallied fiercely. But now he was fighting on Louis' terms, and that was what Joe had been waiting for all night. A right uppercut stunned Conn, and a burst of hooks, culminating in a right to the head which spun him in a half-circle, sent the challenger down and out. He was almost on his feet when referee Eddie Joseph reached "out" after 2:58 of the round. He'd been just six minutes away from the heavyweight championship of the world.

"Of all the times to be a wise guy, I had to pick it against him."

A rueful Billy Conn, years later.

FIGHT FACTS	
DATE:	**June 18, 1941**
VENUE:	**Polo Grounds, New York, NY**
TITLE:	**World Heavyweight**
RESULT:	**Joe Louis won (knockout in 2:58, round 13)**

RAGING BULL SEES RED . . .

JAKE LaMOTTA vs. LAURENT DAUTHUILLE

Laurent Dauthuille had every reason to feel confident when he ducked through the ropes in front of 11,424 fans at the Detroit Olympia on September 13, 1950, to challenge Jake LaMotta for the middleweight championship of the world. He had faced the champion before, on February 21, 1949 in Montreal, Canada, and stood head-to-head with the toughest man in the division for ten gory rounds. LaMotta finished the fight in a mess, his face smeared in his own blood, and Dauthuille got the unanimous verdict.

It was considered a huge upset. The Frenchman was regarded as, at best, a "fringe" contender, with a solid reputation in Europe but virtually unknown on the other side of the Atlantic. LaMotta, though, was the leading contender for the title, the Raging Bull who was the only man to beat Sugar Ray Robinson in Robinson's first 132 fights. He should have had a title chance years before, but it suited the shadowy figures who unofficially ran the business in those days to keep him waiting. LaMotta even threw a fight with the light-heavyweight Billy Fox, a Mob-controlled fighter, on the understanding that he would be rewarded with a crack at the middleweight title, but instead it was Marcel Cerdan who was matched with Tony Zale.

THE INDOMITABLE *Jake LaMotta completes the unlikeliest of comebacks*

Eventually, four months after losing to Dauthuille, LaMotta was paired with Cerdan and took the title when the Algerian retired with a damaged shoulder after nine punishing rounds. Success had come late in LaMotta's career, and when he lost his next fight, a non-title ten-rounder with yet another Frenchman, Robert Villemain, it looked as though his competitive fires were burning low. There was another problem; he was finding it increasingly hard to get down to the middleweight limit of 160lb, and had to lose more than 20lb in training. He did it the hard way, by starving himself and "drying out", denying himself liquid until his body was weakened and dehydrated.

The peak LaMotta might have been able to bulldoze his way through the Frenchman's defences, but instead the weight-drained champion tried to hang back and jab. Dauthuille, who had soaked up some severe punishment last time they met, couldn't believe his luck. He was able to back LaMotta up, scoring easily on the slow-moving and floundering target. Fighters hate having to box out of their usual style, rarely doing so with ease or grace, and LaMotta was no exception.

For round after round Dauthuille piled up points, landing with such ease that the suspicion grew – even in LaMotta's own corner – that there might be something "peculiar" about the fight. At times LaMotta was reduced to charging at the challenger with his left arm extended like a lance, but invariably Dauthuille avoided him easily and banged in counters.

Referee Lou Handler cautioned LaMotta in the sixth and seventh rounds that he had better start working, and for a while he did manage to string a few worthwhile attacks together. By the ninth, though, the quick-fisted challenger was once again scoring at will with bursts of combinations.

LaMotta had a habit of lying back on the ropes as if he was exhausted or badly hurt, then switching onto the attack when his opponent came in to finish him off. He tried it in the 12th round, and Dauthuille obligingly fell for the well-worn ploy, but LaMotta was too arm-weary to sustain the counter-attack for long enough to do any damage. By the end of the 14th round, he was hopelessly behind on points.

As he sat on his stool before the 15th round, his left eye bleeding and almost closed, the champion was told, "You've got to knock him out."

LaMotta came out for the final round throwing everything he had, but Dauthuille knew that he needed only to survive the last three minutes to be crowned champion. He covered up and clinched, and as the round wore on LaMotta's attacks became ever more desperate. And then, in the middle of a maul, the champion spotted an opening and fired the best left hook he'd ever thrown.

The blow landed perfectly on Dauthuille's jaw, and as the Frenchman sagged back into the ropes LaMotta stormed after him, clubbing blows to the head until the challenger finally slumped to the floor. Dauthuille was brave: he struggled to haul himself up by the ropes, and as the referee completed the count he was already on one knee. There were just 13 seconds left in the fight.

FIGHT FACTS

DATE:	**September 13, 1950**
VENUE:	**Detroit, MI**
TITLE:	**World Middleweight**
RESULT:	**Jake LaMotta won (knockout in 2:47, round 15)**

A DAMN CLOSE RUN THING

FIGHT FACTS	
DATE:	**September 23, 1952**
VENUE:	**Municipal Stadium, Philadelphia, PA**
TITLE:	**World Heavyweight**
RESULT:	**Rocky Marciano won (knockout in 43 seconds, round 13)**

ROCKY MARCIANO vs. JOE WALCOTT

It was the night Rocky Marciano won the heavyweight championship of the world and lost his trousers, stolen from his dressing room at the Municipal Stadium, Philadelphia, by a souvenir hunter with an eye for the offbeat. The list of suspects would have been lengthy, for it seemed that the entire population of Brockton, Mass., had crammed into the room to celebrate their hometown boy's success.

It had been a painfully won victory, achieved with perhaps the hardest single punch ever thrown in a heavyweight title fight. For the 29-year-old winner, the fight marked the launch of a fabulous championship reign, while the loser, Jersey Joe Walcott, earned more respect in defeat than he had ever done in victory.

Marciano, a rugged Italian-American, was a late starter, not making his pro debut until he was 23. He made it to a title fight in five years, but it had taken Walcott at least 17 – the champion's official record went back to 1930, but he was probably boxing even before then. Marciano had never been beaten in 42 fights, all but five of which he had won inside the distance. He was a 9–5 favourite, but the bookies' hearts (if that is not a contradiction in terms) must have been in their mouths in the opening round when the veteran landed a perfect left hook to drop Marciano for a count of four. He ignored his corner's calls to take an eight count, and charged at the champion. But Walcott's punches were infinitely more accurate and crisp, and by the end of a tumultuous round Marciano was bleeding from the lip and had a swelling over the left eye.

Walcott was 10lb heavier, two inches taller and had a seven-inch reach advantage, and he used all those assets brilliantly in the first five rounds. But however hard he landed, he could not reproduce that first-round success as Marciano ploughed forward, walking through the champion's punches in a futile bid to land his own clubbing blows. In the sixth, as the stocky challenger came up out of his customary crouch with the fighters at close range, their heads cracked together and blood spewed from a deep cut on Marciano's forehead and from a gash on Walcott's left eyelid. The champion's injury looked the worse, but in the succeeding rounds it was Marciano who suffered. A combination of blood from his own cut and some form of medication used on Walcott's wound found its way into Marciano's eyes, leaving him virtually blind and defenceless as Walcott ripped in hooks and uppercuts. Between rounds his corner team of Freddie Brown, Charlie Goldman and Allie Colombo worked frantically, rinsing their man's inflamed eyes with small sponges soaked in cold water.

By the ninth, the eyes had started to clear, but Walcott, boxing as one observer put it "with the legs of a 20-year-old", continued to out-manoeuvre and outpunch the increasingly ragged challenger. In the 11th, he landed a ferocious right to the heart which would have dropped a lesser man, and then opened a cut over Marciano's right eye. But Marciano's spirit was unbreakable, and he kept pressuring, pressuring, pressuring.

Finally, in the 13th round, it paid off. He hooked a left to the body, and as Walcott retreated to the ropes Marciano fired a short, six-inch right that exploded on Walcott's jaw with dramatic and instantaneous effect. The champion looked as though he had been filleted; he seemed to fold towards the floor in stages, ending up with his head and one knee on the canvas and his left arm hooked behind the middle rope. He had been ahead on all three cards (8–4, 7–4–1 and 7–5 in rounds), but that was academic now. After 43 seconds of the 13th round, the Marciano Era had begun.

ROCKY MARCIANO *doesn't need the left hook that followed that spectacular right – Walcott is already down and out*

YVON DURELLE *goes down for the final time in the 11th round*

THE STREET OF DREAMS

ARCHIE MOORE vs. YVON DURELLE

Take a world champion who is generally accepted as one of the best pound-for-pound fighters of his era, maybe even the best-ever in his weight division, and match him with a contender who's been beaten 20 times, six of them by knockout or stoppage, and what do you expect to happen? A one-sided mismatch? Well, that's what it looked like in the first round when Archie Moore faced Yvon Durelle in the Montreal Forum on December 10, 1958 – except that it was Moore, the veteran light-heavyweight champion, who fought like the sacrificial offering and Durelle, the rugged and unpolished French-Canadian from Baie Ste Anne, who seemed the champion-elect. Their fight is part of boxing legend, and became Moore's passport to immortality.

Moore was three days short of his 45th birthday, although his precise age was a matter of intense speculation. Much of that was mischievously fuelled by the man himself, who knew a good selling point when he saw one. He was a supreme salesman, principally of himself. He had talked, written and self-publicized his way into two cracks at the world heavyweight title, losing to Rocky Marciano in 1955 and Floyd Patterson a year later, and he still dreamt of a third chance.

Durelle, 29, had 11 years as a pro behind him when his big chance arrived. It hardly compared to Moore's 23 years in the business, but after 96 fights he was a seasoned, battle-hardened performer whose brawling style had carried him to the Canadian and British Empire titles. Moore, with an eye on the gate receipts, emphasized Durelle's ability. "Many regard him as just a rough club-fighter with no style or class," he said. "I fought another fellow who fitted this description – Rocky Marciano."

Moore should have heeded his own caution, because less than a minute into the fight Durelle electrified the 8,484 fans when he came up from a crouch with a booming right to the chin. Moore stood frozen by the impact, then pitched to the floor.

Somehow, he got up as referee Jack Sharkey (the former heavyweight champion) reached "nine", but Durelle was on him at once and half-punched, half-pushed him down again. This time Moore rose without a count and, adopting his familiar cross-arm defence, tried to ride out the storm. But Durelle kept firing, and another right put Moore down for the third time for a "nine" count.

Curiously, Durelle did not go all out for the knockout: he explained afterwards that he'd "forgotten this was a championship fight and that three knockdowns didn't halt the fight". Moore jabbed his way back into the fight in the second and third, though Durelle shook him in the third with a left-right to the head that made the veteran hold on briefly. After a brisk fourth round, in which the exchanges continued after the bell, Durelle found the range once more in the fifth and sent Moore sprawling with a sweeping right hook. He was up at six, and hung on frantically as Durelle went for the finish.

But in the closing moments of the round Moore hurt Durelle for the first time, and the momentum of the fight swung his way. The champion outboxed him in the sixth, and floored him for two in the seventh. The eighth and ninth were big rounds for Moore, whose left jab bloodied Durelle's nose and kept him off-balance. By the tenth, the challenger was spent: Moore battered him throughout the round, which finished with the Canadian on his knees with the count at seven.

The end came swiftly in the 11th. Durelle was floored for nine almost immediately, and Moore, who scored more knockouts than any man in history, completed the job with clinical efficiency. Another right stretched Durelle on the canvas, and he was still struggling to rise when, after 49 seconds of the round, Sharkey completed the count.

"I felt as if the top of my head was blown off. I walked the street of dreams."

Archie Moore, describing his first-round knockdown.

FIGHT FACTS

DATE:	**December 10, 1958**
VENUE:	**The Forum, Montreal (Canada)**
TITLE:	**World Light-heavyweight**
RESULT:	**Archie Moore won (knockout in 49 seconds of round 11)**

SLACKER TURNS UP THE HEAT

FIGHT FACTS	
DATE:	June 26, 1959
VENUE:	Yankee Stadium, New York, NY
TITLE:	World Heavyweight
RESULT:	Ingemar Johansson won (stoppage in 2:03, round 3)

INGEMAR JOHANSSON vs. FLOYD PATTERSON

Ingemar Johansson broke all the rules. That is not to say that the handsome, dimple-chinned Swede was a dirty fighter – his behaviour inside the ring was always impeccable. What outraged the purists and the traditionalists – and in those strait-laced pre-Ali days everybody was a traditionalist – was his attitude to training.

Roadwork was something best done on the dance floor, and as for abstinence, he showed what he thought of that by installing his gorgeous girlfriend Brigit in the training camp where he was ostensibly preparing to challenge Floyd Patterson for the heavyweight championship of the world at the Yankee Stadium, New York, on June 25, 1959. (Rain caused a 24-hour postponement until the 26th.) No wonder the American writers gave him no chance of dethroning even such a brittle-chinned champion as Patterson, who had been floored in one of his previous defences by Pete Rademacher, having his first professional fight.

Their opinions were largely based on the pair's respective performances in the 1952 Olympic Games in Helsinki. Patterson, a dazzlingly fast 17-year-old middleweight, won the gold medal, but Johansson suffered the ultimate indignity of being disqualified in the heavyweight final for "not trying" against the giant American Ed Sanders.

He tried to live down that disgrace by building an impressive unbeaten 21-fight run, winning the European title, which he retained against British challengers Henry Cooper and Joe Erskine. But the result that the Americans should have taken note of was dismissed as a fluke: his one-round, one-punch knockout of the top-ranked Eddie Machen in the fight before he faced Patterson. The bookies reckoned him a 4–1 shot, and the public showed their apathy by staying away – only 18,215 turned up. Curiously, though, the closed-circuit takings of over $1 million were the highest recorded to date for that relatively new medium.

For two rounds, there was little to cheer about. Johansson moved back behind a light, flicking left jab, never landing hard enough to inconvenience Patterson, who won both rounds on all three judges' cards.

But there was a subtle strategy at work, as Patterson later acknowledged. "Three times he shoved out the left hand, and three times I found myself moving straight towards the right hand," he wrote in his auto-biography *Victory Over Myself*. "I was directly in line with it, but three times he didn't do anything about throwing the right and I said to myself, 'He's not going to throw that right at all.'"

That proved a monumental miscalculation. Early in the third, Johansson showed him another jab and Patterson once more disregarded the right. This time, though, Johansson threw it hard and straight at the champion's jaw, and Patterson went down. He was so dazed when he rose at nine that he walked towards a neutral corner, having assumed that it was he who had knocked Johansson down.

Johansson moved after him and landed a left to the back of Patterson's head and a right to the jaw, sending him down again for nine. Referee Ruby Goldstein, a former top-class lightweight, could have stopped the fight at that point, but instead allowed the rout to continue. Johansson was merciless, firing right after right until Patterson dropped again. He was up at seven, down again for six, then for seven and finally for another count of nine. He tried gamely to fight back when he rose, but there was nothing left and Goldstein intervened as Johansson rocked the bewildered champion yet again with a left-right-left.

It had taken Johansson just eight minutes and three seconds of action to erase forever the stigma of his Olympic disgrace.

FLOYD PATTERSON *cannot believe what is happening to him as "Ingo's Bingo" floors him in the third round*

TOP OF THE WORLD *Muhammad Ali is champion again*

THE RUMBLE IN THE JUNGLE

MUHAMMAD ALI vs. GEORGE FOREMAN

FIGHT FACTS

DATE:	**October 30, 1974**
VENUE:	**Kinshasa (Zaire)**
TITLE:	**World Heavyweight**
RESULT:	**Muhammad Ali won (knockout, round 8)**

If you still don't understand why Muhammad Ali's knockout of George Foreman in the Stade du Mai, Kinshasa, on October 30, 1974 had such world-wide impact, look again at the famous photograph of Foreman as he waits for the first bell, tree-trunk arms thrust aloft into the African night. He looks carved from stone, omnipotent, unbeatable, and that's how he seemed to all but the most loyal Ali fans at the time. There was serious concern for the ex-champion's well-being, faced with this monster whose bearing in the ring made Sonny Liston seem benevolent. This, after all, was the man who had butchered Joe Frazier and Ken Norton in two rounds apiece – and Frazier and Norton had both beaten Ali.

Muhammad was 32, still clawing his way back from that shock, jaw-breaking defeat by Norton in March 1973. But, against all logic and visual evidence, Ali was convinced that he knew how to beat Foreman. Hugh McIlvanney, then writing for the London *Observer*, also knew how to beat Foreman. "First you shell him for three days, and then you send in the infantry," he wrote after watching George pulverize Norton in Caracas.

A confident Ali seemed unfazed by all the concern for his health. "I'm not scared of George," he said. "George ain't all that tough."

The match was originally scheduled for September 24, but had to be postponed when, a week before the fight, sparring partner Bill McMurray caught Foreman with his elbow and split open a cut over the champion's eye. The postponement seemed more likely to damage the challenger's chances than Foreman's: older fighters find it harder to reach peak condition twice in quick succession.

Instead, it was Ali who put the delay to better use. While the moody Foreman – who had wanted to go home to America while the cut healed – brooded in his quarters, Ali played the Zaire public like a politician running for office. By fight time, he was the most popular man in the country, and George didn't have a friend in the place.

Ali's arrival in the ring at 4 a.m. local time (to facilitate live TV coverage to America) was greeted with chants of "Ali, bomba-ya" ("Ali, kill him!"), and the uproar continued in the first two rounds as Ali, shooting out quick left jabs, frustrated Foreman and tied him up at close range. Foreman swung those mighty arms like a man chopping a tree, but hardly any got through. The challenger's corner, led by Angelo Dundee, were screaming at him to stay off the ropes and use his superior mobility, but Ali – alone in the stadium – knew what he was about.

In the third, Foreman drove a powerful right to Ali's heart. It was the hardest punch he had landed, but Ali merely retreated again to the ropes and covered up, allowing Foreman to pound away at his forearms and sides. Slowly, the champion was being revealed as a one-paced fighter with only one stratetgy in his head and not even the technical wizardry of former light-heavyweight champion Archie Moore in his corner could devise a way to prise open Ali's defences.

It was a whole new experience for Foreman, the archetypal ring bully, who was not accustomed to facing opponents who did not crumble when they sampled the big man's power.

By the sixth, Foreman looked sluggish and arm-weary, but Ali's sharp little jabs were as stingingly accurate as ever. Foreman's rare successes were received in silence, while every punch Ali landed was greeted ecstatically. It all served to erode Foreman's fighting spirit. He had minimal experience of long contests, as all but six of his 40 fights had finished inside four rounds, and had no concept of pacing himself. The power had left Foreman's blows in the seventh, and Ali taunted him with "Come on, George, show me something. Is that all you got?" Foreman tried to rush Ali in the eighth, knocking him backwards into a corner where he moved sideways along the ropes.

Foreman lunged after him, off-balance, and moved straight into a left and a long right to the head that sent him stumbling to the floor. He was fully conscious, but too exhausted and demoralized to beat referee Zack Clayton's count.

The Greatest had pulled off his most improbable win: after seven years, Ali was king again.

EARLY ACTION *Joe Frazier's left hand forces Muhammad Ali back in the opening round*

THE THRILLA IN MANILA

MUHAMMAD ALI vs. JOE FRAZIER

Great fights do not always involve boxers at their peak: sometimes they happen between men on the way down, like one last burst of bright sunlight before the dusk. That was the case when Muhammad Ali and Joe Frazier concluded their epic rivalry in Manila on October 1, 1975, in a clash so unrelentingly savage that neither was quite the same again.

Theirs was one of the ring's great feuds, and each time they met a classic ensued. Partly that was because of the happy blend of styles – the snarling, snorting aggression of Frazier against the inventive genius of Ali – but it was rooted too in their natures and their personalities. Frazier was born into poverty in the Deep South, and battled his way out of it when the family transplanted to Philadelphia. Ali had a comfortable upbringing in a family which, if never wealthy, at least had no experience of real deprivation.

Frazier's upbringing left its scar on his personality: he was abrasive and monosyllabic, at least in public, and Ali's fluency and wit often made Frazier seem dull and unintelligent, which did him less than justice. Frazier bitterly resented the way Ali used his glib tongue as a weapon to diminish and humiliate him in the build-up to their first fight in 1971, when Frazier defended the title Ali had never lost in the ring. With Ali, as always, it was just promotional hype, but Frazier took it all seriously and the hurt was real.

Even when he floored and outpointed Ali, the resentment still burned, and when Ali outscored him in the rematch in 1974 the scene was set for the dream fight, the one to settle the issue between them once and for all. The fight drew a crowd of 25,000, causing a three-hour traffic jam, and world-wide television revenue set new records

This time, there was no dancing from Ali. He set himself solidly in mid-ring and lashed hard punches at Frazier, who soaked them up impassively and kept firing those short, dazzling left hooks. Ali taunted and teased Frazier in the third, talking to him in the few clinches permitted by Filipino referee Carlos Padilla, but in the fourth the tide began to flow the challenger's way. Ali spent more time on the ropes in the fifth and sixth rounds, blocking a fair few of Frazier's hooks but being jarred to his boots by others. At the end of the sixth Ali, significantly, sat down for the first time between rounds. It was the clearest possible indication that he knew he was engaged in the fight of his life.

The seventh saw him on his toes, slamming jabs into Frazier's face, but Frazier, coming in close, buried his head on the champion's shoulder and drove home strength-draining body hooks. That was the pattern until the 12th round: a test of iron will and endurance as much as skill. Ali's title was in the balance, and he produced a champion's effort in the 12th. Frazier was driven back under a sustained barrage that left his face swollen and his left eye closing, and with restricted vision he was suddenly a vulnerable target for the revitalized Ali's sharp right hands.

In the 13th, it seemed that Frazier was on the brink of collapse. Ali's rights wobbled him, and once Joe did a crazy backwards dance, his legs out of control. But Ali too was in what he graphically called "the near room", the ante-room to death itself. It took a massive effort of will to haul himself off the stool for the 14th round, three minutes of hell as the two drained and barely conscious battlers flailed punches at each other. Frazier was in worse shape, though, and Ali scored with nine successive rights to his battered head.

At the bell, Padilla had to lead him to his corner. Trainer Eddie Futch had seen enough. "Sit down, son, it's all over," he told Joe. "But nobody will ever forget what you did here today."

Ali, ever gracious in victory, summed up his bitter-sweet relationship with Frazier when he said. "Without him I couldn't be who I am, and without me he couldn't be who he is. We've been a pretty good team."

FIGHT FACTS

DATE:	**October 1, 1975**
VENUE:	**Manila (Philippines)**
TITLE:	**World Heavyweight**
RESULT:	**Muhammad Ali won (retirement, after 14 rounds)**

BRIEF, BLOODY AND BRUTAL GRUDGE MATCH

MARVIN HAGLER vs. THOMAS HEARNS

When a great fighter produces his peak performance, those lucky enough to have been there count themselves blessed. But when two great fighters hit their peak against each other, something magical is in the air and their fight lives on in the memory, growing to epic proportions with each re-telling. When middleweight champion Marvin Hagler went up against his most dangerous challenger, Thomas "Hit Man" Hearns, at Caesars Palace on April 15, 1985, it was a match made in heaven, pitting the cold professionalism of Hagler against the explosive punching of Hearns, the former WBA welterweight and WBC light-middleweight champion.

The fight had been three years in the making, partly because of the genuine animosity that existed between these two proud champions, each of whom accused the other of ducking out of the match. It had taken Hagler seven years to prove what the trade had known for at least three years before then: that he was the best middleweight in the world. This was his 11th defence of the championship, and he looked absolutely invulnerable. Virtually all his challengers had been top-flight contenders, and only slippery old Roberto Duran had taken him the full 15-rounds championship course. But Duran, who won the WBA light-middleweight title in 1984 and relinquished it to challenge for Hearns' WBC version, was flattened by the Hit Man in two rounds; on that form-line, Hearns had a real chance of upsetting the shaven-skulled, muscular champion.

The Detroit puncher had lost just once in 41 fights, a welterweight unification match with Ray Leonard, and only six of his fights had gone the full distance. Hagler's record was equally impressive: 64 fights, two draws and two defeats, and all four men who blemished his record had been beaten inside the distance in rematches.

When they came together under the evening sky at Caesars' outdoor arena, there was no feeling-out period, no jabbing for distance or range. Instead they tore from their corners like greyhounds released from their traps, smashing hooks at each other with terminal intent. Every blow was designed to produce a knockout, and against other opponents they may well have succeeded.

It was, surely, only the adrenaline of the moment that kept them upright as they rocked each other with terrifying punches. Hearns was finally forced to concede the centre of the ring and retreated to the ropes, where he traded punches with the snarling Hagler for at least 30 seconds.

And then, with less than a minute to go in the round, blood suddenly spouted from a long vertical cut on the champion's forehead. He brushed the blood away with the irritated gesture of a man swatting at a fly, but he knew how serious the injury was. It was now a case of stopping Hearns quickly, or losing his title.

MARVIN HAGLER, *a relentless fighting, machine sets Hearns up for the finish*

He tried hard for the finish in the second, but Hearns sensed victory and he punched with him, splitting open a second, horrible cut under Hagler's right eye. With nothing to gain from caution, Hagler threw everything at his man in a blistering, sustained attack, but the deceptively spindly challenger soaked it up and punched back.

Referee Richard Steele, a former professional boxer himself, stopped the action to enquire of Hagler "Can you see him?" Hagler's response was unforgettable. "I'm hitting him, aren't I?"

It ended, abruptly, in the third as Hagler proved his right to be ranked alongside Robinson, Greb and Monzon with the middleweight greats. A right hook caught Hearns flush on the chin, and his legs went into spasm as he staggered back, turning almost a full circle.

Hagler literally ran after him, landing three clubbing rights which spread-eagled him. Hearns somehow beat the count, but was defenceless and Steele took the compassionate course, throwing his arms around the beaten fighter to signal the end of an epic encounter.

FIGHT FACTS

DATE:	**April 15, 1985**
VENUE:	**Caesars Palace, Las Vegas, NV**
TITLE:	**World Middleweight**
RESULT:	**Marvin Hagler won (stoppage, round 3)**

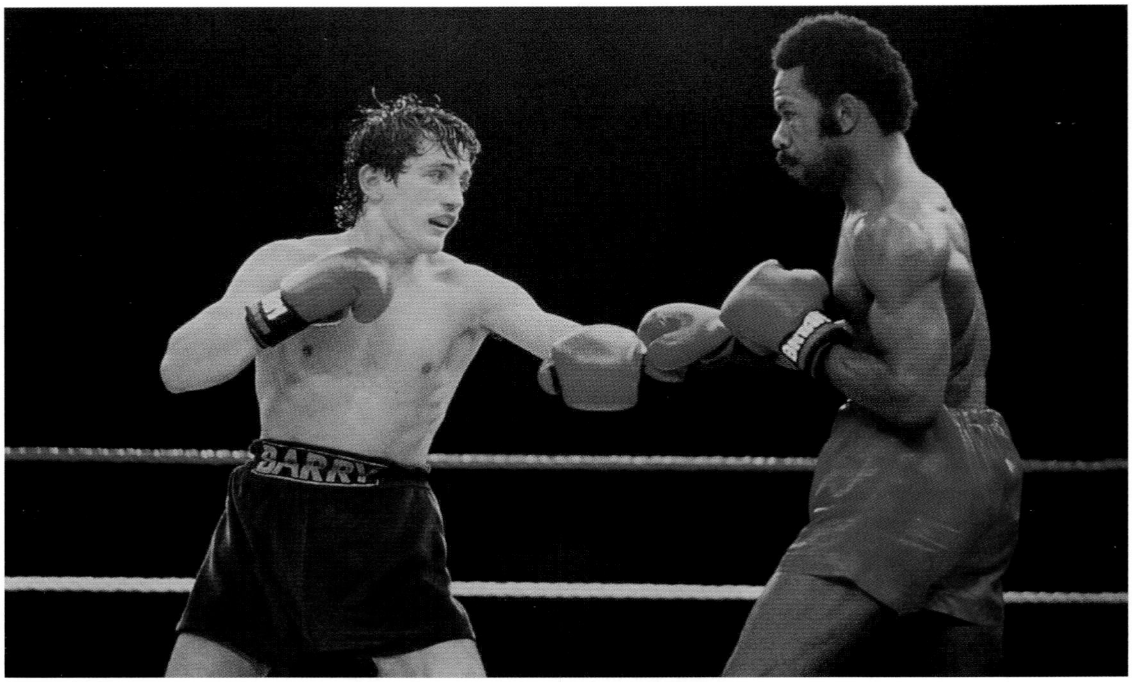

EUSEBIO PEDROZA *used all the craft acquired in 19 title defences, but could not keep McGuigan at bay*

BRILLIANT BARRY GETS THE PARTY GOING

BARRY McGUIGAN vs. EUSEBIO PEDROZA

Barry McGuigan's grip on the affections of the British sporting public in the mid-1980s was a unique product of the times and the circumstances. He was a Catholic from south of the Irish border, married to a Northern Protestant, and his Belfast manager Barney Eastwood marketed him brilliantly as a symbol of peace and unity at a time when the only images of Ireland being presented to the British was of soldiers sprawled dead in the streets, or bombed-out buildings, or hooded corpses in ditches. The concept of McGuigan as peace-maker was nonsense, but appealing none the less: the partisans came together in the King's Hall in Belfast to roar him up the world rankings, but when the fight was over they resumed business as usual.

It helped, of course, that McGuigan could fight better than any European of his era. He was a superb pressure fighter, whose hooks to the short ribs drew anguished gasps from ringsiders as often as opponents. He built his reputation and his rating on a series of victories over world-class opposition, including the former WBC featherweight champion Juan LaPorte.

The Puerto Rican came nearer than anyone else to spoiling the Irish script when he bounced two thunderous rights off McGuigan's chin at the King's Hall, but when his protégé took them unflinchingly and roared back to win on points, Eastwood knew that McGuigan was ready to go for glory.

The title was in dispute then as now, but there was little doubt that the real champion was Eusebio Pedroza. The lanky Panamanian veteran had been champion for seven years, making 19 defences around the world, including places like Papua New Guinea, where championship boxing had never been seen. He was, in the truest sense of the words, the world champion, and Eastwood paid him almost £1 million to risk his crown against McGuigan at Loftus Road football ground on a warm summer's evening on June 8, 1985.

English soccer grounds in the 1980s tended to be forbidding, threatening places, where violence always hung in the air, but the vast Irish contingent among the 26,000 crowd were concerned only with celebrations. Afterwards the police would record only two arrests, a tribute to the crowd's participation in a sporting event that is still recalled with a warm glow.

Pedroza had a well-deserved reputation as a rough handful who knew all the tricks in the book, while McGuigan's body punching had often brought him perilously close to disqualification. But for this night, they behaved with impeccable sportsmanship, as if sensing they were part of history in the making. Pedroza, tall and spindly, concentrated on his boxing in the early rounds, mixing sharp jabs with whipping right uppercuts. McGuigan was invariably slow to build an attacking rhythm, and it took him three or four rounds to force his way into contention against a masterly boxer who was having one of the best nights of an illustrious career.

But in the seventh, the Irishman surged ahead when he fired a perfect right through the gap as Pedroza's left hand dropped momentarily. The champion fell on his left side, rising at three and nodding reassurance to his corner as the referee Stanley Christodolou completed the mandatory eight count. He somehow got through the remainder of the round, mainly by holding and frustrating McGuigan, and raised his arms aloft in mock triumph at the bell.

The Panamanian rallied splendidly to win the eighth round, but another booming right knocked the defiance from him in the ninth. From then on it became a grim battle for survival, with the proud old champion using every ounce of experience to hold his boxing together as McGuigan launched attack after attack. Whatever doubts lingered about the outcome were vanquished in the 13th, when Pedroza tottered on the brink of defeat but kept going on pride alone.

At the final bell, the verdict was announced – unanimously in favour of McGuigan – and the biggest sporting party London had seen for years got under way.

FIGHT FACTS

DATE:	June 8, 1985
VENUE:	Loftus Road, London (England)
TITLE:	WBA Featherweight
RESULT:	Barry McGuigan won (unanimous decision, 15 rounds)

TOO CLOSE TO CALL

SUGAR RAY LEONARD vs. MARVIN HAGLER

There is a hoary old tradition in boxing that great champions shouldn't lose their titles on razor-thin calls, but somebody forgot to tell that to the judges when Marvin Hagler risked his WBC middleweight title against Sugar Ray Leonard at Caesars Palace on April 6, 1987. It was the fight the whole world wanted to see, even if it should have happened five years earlier before Leonard was driven into temporary retirement by an eye injury. He didn't deserve to leapfrog over the other contenders when he decided to return to action to challenge Hagler, but such con-siderations never worried the insufferably self-centred Sugarman. His ego was enormous, but then that was probably a large part of what made him such an outstanding performer.

Even those who were repelled by Leonard's cloyingly sweet public persona had to acknowledge that he was a rock-hard fighting man, while Hagler's worth had been proven in the furnace of more championship defences than any middleweight since Carlos Monzon, whose record he would equal were he to beat Leonard. The betting odds said he would, but the crowd's sympathies were with Leonard rather than the bleak, single-minded Hagler, who had never been able to capture the public's affection despite a magnificent seven-year reign.

Between them they secured a fabulous deal that guaranteed them a split of $23 million. Caesars Palace sold all 15,000 seats within weeks and an estimated 300 million watched world-wide on television. Leonard looked edgy and nervous when he ducked through the ropes in his short jacket-type gown, and he kept giving Hagler furtive glances during the preliminaries. He knew Hagler's strengths as well as he knew his own, and he spelt out his battle-plan from the opening bell, moving back and smothering Hagler's attacks. The champion, as ever, switched between orthodox and southpaw stances, but did not land effectively until a left hook in the second round made Leonard's eyes widen in apprehension.

Hagler's pressure took the third round, but there was an edge of frustration creeping into his work as the elusive challenger denied him a clean shot. Leonard's confidence was growing, to the point where he felt able to wind up a theatrical right and land it cleanly on Hagler's shaven skull. When Hagler tried to counter-attack, Leonard simply walked away with the unconcerned air of a man strolling in the park. It was sound psychological warfare and it was working: Hagler shouted in irritation at Leonard as they turned away at the end of the round.

But Hagler at last got on top in the fifth, hurting Leonard with a big left hook that drove the challenger to the ropes and forced him to duck and roll for survival. Leonard rallied well in the sixth with sharp counter-punching and clever defensive work on the ropes, but Hagler had him in trouble briefly again in the seventh.

Leonard's left eye looked swollen in the eighth, but he found the heart to stand, open-mouthed and weary, trading punches with Hagler in a wildly exciting ninth round. By the tenth the challenger was so tired that he stood flat-footed and missed crudely, something totally out of character for such a consummate stylist, but his heart hauled him back into the fight as he danced his way through the 11th.

There was nothing between them in a hard-fought final round, although Hagler had the last word with a left hook that sent Leonard spinning towards his own corner in the closing moments. And then there was the long wait for the verdict and the look of stunned disbelief on Hagler's face when it was announced. Dave Moretti scored 115–113 Leonard, Lou Filippo 115–113 Hagler, and Mexican Judge Jo Jo Guerra a ludicrous 118–110 for Leonard. Somehow, he had given Hagler just two rounds, rough justice indeed for a man who had proved himself one of the division's finest champions.

“If I were a betting man, I'd bet on Hagler. If I were a smart man, I'd bet on me.”

Leonard's fight prediction.

TWO WEARY BATTLERS *trade punches in a wildly exciting ninth round*

FIGHT FACTS

DATE:	**April 6, 1987**
VENUE:	**Caesars Palace, Las Vegas, NV**
TITLE:	**WBC Middleweight**
RESULT:	**Sugar Ray Leonard won (split points decision, 12 rounds)**

TURN UP FOR THE BOOKS

FIGHT FACTS

DATE:	**February 11, 1990**
VENUE:	**Tokyo (Japan)**
TITLE:	**World Heavyweight**
RESULT:	**Buster Douglas won (knockout in 1:23, round 10)**

JAMES DOUGLAS vs. MIKE TYSON

Journeymen professionals like James "Buster" Douglas are not supposed to topple ring legends like Mike Tyson, but occasionally they do: that is part of boxing's mystique, part of the unpredictability that is at the core of the sport's appeal. With hindsight, of course, it was not such a surprise when Douglas knocked out Tyson in the tenth round in the massive, domed Korakuen Stadium in Tokyo. The champion was self-destructing at an alarming rate. His life was in chaos, and the team that brought him to the title had been replaced by men whose lack of professional expertise was glaringly obvious.

The problem was that no one, least of all the bookies who installed Douglas as a 42–1 outsider, had understood the speed at which Tyson was unravelling. Great fighters do not become mediocre overnight, they reasoned, nor do mediocre fighters like Douglas become great. They were wrong, on both counts. On this one night, alone among the many mundane evenings of Douglas' undistinguished career, he touched the peaks and shattered the myth that had grown up around Iron Mike, the unbeatable monster who terrified a generation of heavyweight pretenders.

Douglas, though, was an improbable dragon-slayer, who seemed to have settled for life as a middle-ranking contender. There had been one previous title chance, when he fought Tony Tucker for the vacant IBF championship and quit in the tenth round. He had lost four of his 35 fights, and was considered such a sacrificial offering that promoter Don King refused him even a single complimentary ticket for the fight.

But he was a man with motivation, beset by so many griefs and upsets that he focused totally on the fight as a bolt-hole from his problems. Just 23 days before the fight his mother died of a stroke. His wife had left him, and the mother of his 11-year-old son was dying of cancer. Douglas sought distraction and comfort in the fight, and found it. He drove himself hard in training, and for the first time came to the ring as a superbly conditioned heavyweight rather than the blubbery slob who had gone through the motions for most of his career.

Tyson, by contrast, looked soft and ill-prepared: unlike Douglas, he had not been able to turn his problems into a plus. Douglas, trim and sharp at 231lb, outboxed Tyson easily with jabs in the opener and, in the second, introduced right uppercuts which were the perfect counter to the champion's crouching attacks. By the fourth Tyson's left eye had started to swell, and the injury progressively worsened until he was peering through a slit.

Douglas, virtually alone among the men Tyson had so far faced, was not intimidated by the champion's air of brooding menace. He stood toe-to-toe with him when he had to, but preferred to keep him on the end of those long jabs and whipping uppercuts. There was confusion, approaching panic, in the champion's inexperienced corner as the rounds went past and their man dropped further behind, but there was no one there with the tactical nous to devise a fight-winning strategy.

Thrown back on his own resources, Tyson almost rose to the challenge. A perfect right uppercut dropped Douglas on his back in the eighth round. Referee Octavio Meyran was slow to pick up the count, and Douglas – who had recovered by the count of "two", took full advantage of Meyran's indecision to stay on one knee until he had reached "nine", by which time Douglas had actually been down for 13 seconds.

It was Tyson's last chance, and the world watched in open-mouthed amazement as the once-formidable champion absorbed a merciless pounding throughout the ninth. The end, in the tenth, was almost a relief: a right uppercut and a four-punch combination sent Tyson to his knees, and he was counted out as he fumbled with his gumshield, cramming it lop-sidedly into his mouth as Meyran signalled the end of his reign.

MIKE TYSON *takes a pounding from Buster Douglas as the unthinkable becomes reality*

THE DRAW THAT NEVER WAS

LENNOX LEWIS *lands a left to the side of Evander Holyfield's head during their unsatisfactory fight*

LENNOX LEWIS vs. EVANDER HOLYFIELD

This was the opportunity boxing cast aside. For seven years, since Riddick Bowe cynically dumped the green WBC belt in a dustbin, the world heavyweight championship had been divided. Attempts to unify the three titles that mattered – the WBC, WBA and IBF – had come to nothing.

Finally, with the financial input of American cable giant Home Box Office, and at long last the will of promoters Don King, Dino Duva and Panos Eliades, the match boxing needed more than any other was made for Madison Square Garden in March 1999. King, representing the WBA and IBF champion Holyfield, was the major promoter, with Duva and Eliades representing WBC champion Lewis.

The 19,808 seats in the Garden were sold out well in advance. So too were around 1,000 others in luxury boxes overlooking the ring. Holyfield, the double champion and conqueror of Mike Tyson, was guaranteed $20.8 million. Lewis, whose claim to be the best heavyweight of the 1990s had not been put to the test because matches with Holyfield, Tyson, Bowe, George Foreman or even Michael Moorer had not materialized, was content with a guarantee of $9.5 million. He wanted the fight because his place in history depended on it. Holyfield, 36, with so many definitive moments behind him, fought because as a born warrior he could not duck the challenge.

Holyfield predicted boldly he would knock out Lewis in three rounds, but in the fight Lewis was 31lbs heavier (17st 8lbs, 246lbs; to 15st 5lbs, 215lbs). He towered above Holyfield and from the first round used that physical superiority to outbox him. Only in round three was Lewis under serious pressure. In the fifth he had Holyfield hurt and on the brink of defeat, but for some reason didn't let the punches fly. The rest of the way Lewis was content to box his way home, chipping away with short bursts and jabs to Holyfield's face.

He could have been, should have been, more decisive, and there were those who felt Holyfield's half-hearted hustling from rounds eight to 11 had brought him back into it. At the end the vast majority had no doubt: Lewis had won. Some had the margin as wide as nine rounds to three, while a few British writers saw it as a draw.

Nobody had Holyfield winning … except a judge from Atlantic City, appointed by the IBF, Eugenia Williams. Somehow she scored 115–113 for the WBA and IBF champ, including an incredible piece of scoring, a 10–9 round for Evander in round five when he was almost stopped. Larry O'Connell, for the WBC and from London, had it level at 115–115, while the WBA's Stanley Christodoulou of South Africa saw it 116–113 for Lewis. Lewis stalked angrily from the ring, his face a mask of fury and despair. "It was easier than I thought. I was in complete control," he said. His trainer, Emanuel Steward, said: "It was like Lennox was boxing a sparring partner. It was not even close. This hurts boxing. Every time we get a chance to move things forward, something like this happens."

King alone looked pleased. "What are you going to do, shoot the judges? When you have a dispute you resolve it. They can do it again."

However, within days the fury at the decision had increased to a level of intensity that amazed even hardened fight-watchers. A New York State investigation into the decision was launched and the media delved into the background of everyone concerned. Eugenia Williams, in particular, was put under severe scrutiny.

The ramifications went on and on. Coincidentally, the IBF were put under investigation by the FBI, who searched through papers from Don King's Florida office. The New York Commission introduced new rules over the appointment of judges, and both sides opened negotiations for the rematch. It took place in November 1999, and Lewis again proved he was the superior boxer – and this time was given the verdict to unify the titles.

FIGHT FACTS

DATE:	**March 13,1999**
VENUE:	**Madison Square Garden, New York City**
TITLE:	**World Heavyweight**
RESULT:	**Draw**

UNFORGETTABLE MEXICAN MAGIC

FIGHT FACTS

DATE:	**February 19, 2000**
VENUE:	**Mandalay Bay, Las Vegas, NV**
TITLES:	**WBC and WBO Super-bantamweight**
RESULT:	**Morales won (split points decision, 12 rounds)**

MARCO ANTONIO BARRERA vs. ERIK MORALES

Every so often, a fight comes along that keeps even the most jaundiced of observers on the edge of their seats. The first meeting of mind, body and soul between Erik Morales and Marco Antonio Barrera at the Mandalay Bay hotel and casino on the Las Vegas Strip was a masterclass; a pulsating, 12-round classic that those who saw it will never forget.

The bitter rivalry between these two Mexicans was not drummed up by publicists, and did not ease with time. They disliked each other before their first fight, and they still disliked each other five years on after they had taken each other to the limit three times.

Yet, apart, both men were dignified, honourable and generally good citizens. Morales, known as "El Terrible", was from the notorious north zone of the border city of Tijuana. For years he used the same gym attached to his family store. He remained a man of his people. The word was that he was the only man who could leave his car unlocked in those streets and know it would be untouched, such was the respect in which he was held. He grew up there, he remained in touch even when he became a world champion while still young and impressionable enough to have had his head turned by fame. He made it his business to provide computer technology for his local schools.

Barrera, who was called "The Baby Faced Assassin", was from a middle-class family in Mexico City. His father made a living designing television sets. Marco Antonio studied to be a lawyer and said, until he made his fortune in the ring, that he was quite prepared to go back to earn his living in the legal profession. He was dignified, gentlemanly... yet he sneered at Morales and is said to have called him *analfabeto*, illiterate. The feud between them grew as both won and defended rival versions of the super-bantamweight championship.

Barrera, two years older, won his title first, in March 1995, with a 12-round decision over Puerto Rican Daniel Jimenez in California. He had defended it eight times, then had a dip in form with two defeats by New Yorker Junior Jones. He worked his way back, regained the vacant title in 1998 and had made two more defences by the time he was matched in the unification fight with Morales. He was 26 years old, with more than 50 bouts behind him.

Morales, who like Barrera had been boxing professionally since he was at school, had held the WBC super-bantamweight title since 1997, when he dethroned the veteran Mexican Daniel Zaragoza. He had trounced Junior Jones in four rounds in one of his eight defences of his championship. He was 23 years old, had won all 35 of his professional contests and was the slightest of betting favourites.

So the stage was set, but nothing could have prepared us for the magnificence of what followed: for 12 rounds there was almost no let-up as they tested each other's skill, heart, pride and chin. They drilled in jabs, slammed home hooks, uppercuts, blocked, slipped, slid around in front of each other, and treated everyone in the arena to a breathtaking display of the art of boxing.

It was exhausting, draining to watch, but it also brought an involuntary smile of sheer admiration to the face. The exchanges were so close, but the impression was that Barrera was doing enough. Gradually he was inching his way in front, and by the end most at ringside felt it was his fight.

Judge Duane Ford thought so, too, with a 114–113 scoreline for Barrera. Carol Castellano went the other way, again 114–113... and the third Las Vegas judge Dalby Shirley saw it 115–112... for Morales!

Morales and his promoter Bob Arum celebrated; Barrera felt it was a bad decision. A few hours later he was chatting amiably with his fans in one of the Mandalay Bay bars, in a smart tracksuit, almost as if he had just come in from a stroll and not taken part in one of the greatest, most sustained 12 rounds of boxing ever seen.

They had to box again, of course, but Morales said he could no longer drill his body down to 122lb. Barrera moved up to featherweight, too, producing a masterclass to defuse the big-punching, extrovert from England, Naseem Hamed, in April 2001.

Eventually the return happened, with Morales' WBC featherweight crown at stake, at the MGM Grand, Las Vegas, in June 2002. This time, as if in reaction to their first meeting, each elected to box instead of trade punches. Most felt Morales had won... but this time the judges saw it unanimously for Barrera: 116–112 and 115–113 twice.

There was less of a clamour for a third meeting, but in the end it happened in November 2004 at super-featherweight. Morales, by his own admission, took too long to get started. It was a good fight, but not a great one. They let their punches go with greater venom than in the "chess match" second bout, but in turns. First one would let go with a burst; then the other would come back. This time, it seemed Morales had not managed to claw back the early deficit. Barrera did win, but it was desperately close again: one judge saw it level, the other two for Marco Antonio by 115–114 and 115–113.

Any thoughts that 36 rounds in three boxing rings had mellowed them were cast aside in an ugly exchange in the post-fight formalities.

They would not box again, but whether or not they would ever acknowledge it, these two wonderful fighters made each other's places in history secure.

ERIK MORALES *(right) and Marco Antonio Barrera trade blows in Las Vegas*

AS RAW AS IT GETS

IT'S MY TIME *Diego Corrales celebrates his tenth-round victory over Jose Luis Castillo*

JOSE LUIS CASTILLO vs. DIEGO CORRALES

Some say the definition of a great fight is one that swings one way, then the other, and perhaps back again, that keeps you guessing as to who has won until the very last minute. If that is so, the sensational world lightweight championship war between Jose Luis Castillo and Diego Corrales will endure as one of the legendary hours in boxing history.

These two fighters rose to greatness because they fought each other. Beforehand, both were respected, solidly appreciated champions with heart, attacking styles and power aplenty.

Nobody, but nobody, could have forecasted the heights they would reach at the Mandalay Bay hotel at the end of the Las Vegas strip in the late spring of 2005. Castillo was putting his WBC lightweight title on the line, while Corrales held the WBO version. There was a general welcoming of the fight, both for itself as a good match, and for the fact that it would unify two of the versions of the world title and go some way to establishing who was the genuine No.1.

They went straight down to business from the first bell, with Castillo a little bit quicker, more economical. He was shorter (5ft 8in to 5ft 11in) and so were his punches. Corrales, though, stayed with him every step. At the end of round two Castillo was the first to be seriously rocked. In the fourth Castillo was cut, but came back to stun Corrales in the sixth round. The seventh was a toe-to-toe war, but it ended with Castillo the more hurt. Both were in trouble at different times in the eighth. Castillo was shaken again in round nine, but by the bell it was Corrales, his eye closing, who looked near to exhaustion.

And in the tenth it was Corrales, the American, who crumbled. He walked into the path of a left hook that dropped him heavily. He spat out his gumshield to suck in air and referee Tony Weeks had it washed and replaced after Corrales struggled up at nine. Two more left hooks from Castillo and Corrales went down again. This time the spitting out of the gumshield looked a deliberate ploy to buy himself more time. Again, he was up at nine, and again Weeks had the mouthpiece rinsed and put back in. Corrales gained precious seconds and, when the action resumed, defied all of Castillo's efforts to finish it, then amazingly began to punch back.

Suddenly, almost out of nowhere, Corrales drove Castillo back to the ropes, landed clean, heavy punches and the Mexican reeled, his arms dropped and more shots rocked his head around. Referee Weeks jumped between them, held on to Castillo and waved it off.

The referee would be widely criticized for allowing Corrales to buy himself time, but in the wider picture these were hollow complaints. What we had witnessed was an extraordinary fight, one so sustained in its ferocity that we wondered if anyone would have the stomach to watch a return.

Of course, although Corrales' trainer Joe Goossen labelled even talk of a rematch "sadistic", money spoke.

They met again in October 2005. Again it was controversial, with Castillo apparently making little attempt to make lightweight. Corrales agreed to go on with the contest, but the titles were not at stake. Just as well for Diego as Castillo knocked him out with a big left hook in the fourth round.

Honour was not settled. They agreed a third fight for June 2006 at the Thomas and Mack Center. But again Castillo let himself down in preparations. He just couldn't do lightweight any more, and was 5lb over when he stepped on the scales. This time Corrales called it off and sued him. Castillo was also fined and suspended by the Nevada State Athletic Commission and officially moved up to light-welterweight.

While these events took the shine off the overall story, nothing could ever detract from the wonderful fight they staged on that magical night in May 2005.

FIGHT FACTS

DATE:	**May 7, 2005**
VENUE:	**Mandalay Bay, Las Vegas, NV**
TITLE:	**WBC and WBO Lightweight**
RESULT:	**Corrales won (referee stopped fight, round 10)**

THE NIGHT OF THE HIT MAN

FIGHT FACTS

DATE:	**June 4, 2005**
VENUE:	**MEN Arena, Manchester, England**
TITLE:	**IBF Light-welterweight**
RESULT:	**Hatton won (Tszyu retired after round 11)**

KOSTA TSZYU vs. RICKY HATTON

This was a British boxing party that was years in the making. Since he unified the three major light-welterweight belts in 2001, Kostya Tszyu was the undisputed king of the 140-lb division.

The Russian, who had settled in Australia after the 1991 world amateur championships, was cunning, quick-witted and had a lethal punch, particularly in his looping right hand. He made his reputation in 2001 when demolishing the undefeated and supposedly supreme Zab Judah in two rounds in Las Vegas to unify the WBC, IBF and WBA championships. Four years on, and although boxing's greedy politicians had taken away two of Tszyu's belts because he had a spell out with injuries, he was still the man and his reputation had grown to iconic status.

When Tsztu returned from his layoff at the end of 2004, he met old rival Sharmba Mitchell, the IBF's "interim" champion, and proved he had lost nothing during his absence by taking him out inside three rounds. He was the king, everyone else merely a pretender.

In December 2004, Ricky Hatton's promoter, Frank Warren, announced to British journalists in Las Vegas for the Danny Williams-Vitali Klitschko world heavyweight title fight, that Tszyu had agreed to defend against Hatton in England the following spring, and in his "fortress", the 22,000-seat MEN Arena in his home city of Manchester..

Hatton was a major attraction, but his aggressive, pressure-fighting style was not necessarily designed for longevity. He did not want to pass his peak before discovering how good he was. The only way to find out was to box the best – and that meant Tszyu.

The match was made for the night of Saturday, June 4 – actually it started just after 2 a.m. the following morning to suit the demands of Showtime, the American television company who paid for live rights – interest was huge. The fight could have been sold out four or five times over, perhaps at one of the Manchester soccer stadiums, had they been available.

Tszyu and Hatton were gentlemanly but contrasting figures: the champion, self-assured, smiling, apparently content; Hatton confident, but with an air of excitement about him, as if his moment of destiny was finally here.

The fight itself was one of those moments when, in Hatton's case, everything went to plan. He and trainer Billy Graham knew Tszyu's strengths all too well, and knew if he stood off too long, Hatton would be vulnerable. The only way, they decided, was to steam in, chin down, as fast as possible and draw the champion into a gruelling physical battle on the inside. It was a risky plan, but his entire dream was about gamble and challenge. Hatton knew he could have stayed in the cocoon that had been so cleverly wrapped around him. He also knew he couldn't have lived with himself if he had done only that.

From the moment he walked into the arena to his "Blue Moon" anthem, the crowd were singing and shouting him home. In the first four or five rounds, Hatton did what he said he wanted to do and walked into the champion and made him work. He had to absorb right hands and left hooks to the head that would have broken up most light-welterweights. He showed barely a flicker of reaction and kept working, working, working.

By the halfway point came the first signs that Tszyu was being forced to work at a pace he didn't like. The champion rallied, dragged everything out of himself, but Hatton, his face bruised and swollen, just kept up the momentum, drilling in more and more punches. Tszyu hit him low – Hatton hit him low back. On the inside Hatton clubbed the champion on the top of the head, sometimes around the back. By the tenth the almost ghostly pale Englishman was swarming all over the man who had dominated the light-welterweight scene for half a decade.

The tireless pressure continued into the 11th. Tszyu was still on his feet, but behind on points (107–102, 106–103 and 105–104). Only a huge last round could have saved his title, but he slumped on to his stool. His trainer, Johnny Lewis, knew his man had nothing left to give. He had been driven into a state of exhaustion. Referee Dave Parris walked across to Hatton's corner with the routine reminder that this was the last round coming up, then crossed to Tszyu's corner, bent over to them and looked as if he could not believe what he was hearing. "No more," said Lewis, and repeated it. "What are you going to do?" asked Parris, looking at Tszyu, then stood up and waved his arms to signal the end. The crowd let out an enormous roar.

It took a second or two to sink in, then Hatton, Graham and his whole corner team were embracing and bouncing around. Hatton lay on the canvas almost in disbelief that his moment had finally come. The boy next-door had taken the gamble, beaten the man who was the man, one who was the genuine champion of the world.

When he had calmed down and the world championship belt was around his waist, Hatton said: "To beat someone like Tszyu is end of the rainbow stuff." On the ring microphone he thanked his fans, told them the victory was theirs as well as his, and then Tszyu took the mike from him and said humbly: "I lost to the better fighter. I don't feel ashamed to say that today Ricky was better than me in every way."

Hatton moved on, winning the WBA titles at light-welterweight and welterweight, but eventually giving up all the belts because of the vagaries of the sanctioning bodies.

"I'm living my dream," he said, but remained essentially the same man he always was. "I don't feel I'm any different to anybody else," he said after beating Tszyu. The evidence would suggest that's not quite the case!

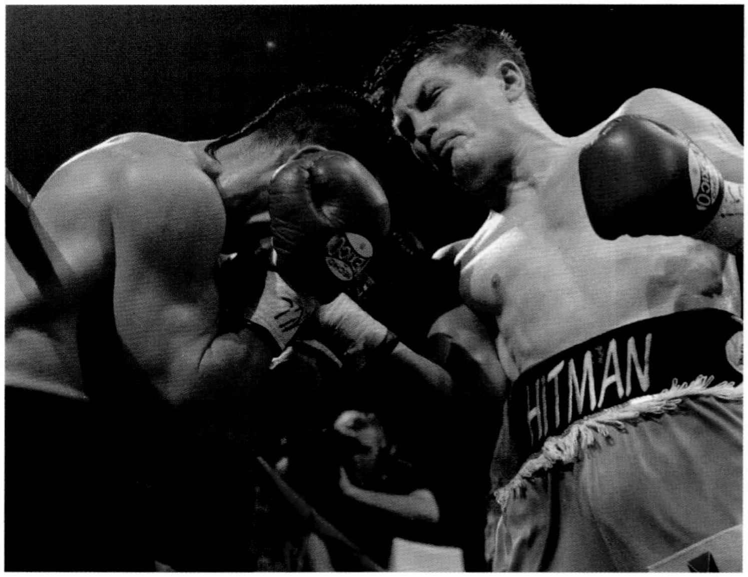

A STAR IS BORN *Ricky Hatton smashed the world light-welterweight title loose from Kostya Tszyu before 22,000 fans in Manchester*

CLASSIC CALZAGHE CRUISES

JOE CALZAGHE VS. MIKKEL KESSLER

Joe Calzaghe had held the World Boxing Organization super-middleweight title for ten years. He had destroyed the IBF champion Jeff Lacy, who had been considered the biggest threat to his domination, so utterly that it was unlikely Lacy would ever be the same boxer again.

Yet, until he boxed the undefeated Mikkel Kessler, there was something missing; that indefinable edge that separates the great champions from the good. Calzaghe was respected, acknowledged as the best in his weight division, yet was not adored.

Something changed when he fought Kessler – and it was not simply that the Dane held the WBC and WBA belts, and had replaced Lacy as the man most likely to topple Calzaghe.

It was something in the public response that began with Calzaghe's mismatch against the over-rated American Peter Manfredo in April 2007. Manfredo, who had made his name as a participant in the US boxing "reality" TV series *The Contender*, had no right sharing a ring with the far superior Welshman. Attention was deflected from that point by the intervention of referee Terry O'Connor in round three that some felt absurdly premature.

Yet in spite of the uncompetitive nature of the match, 37,000 people turned out to see it. Suddenly, at 35, Calzaghe was no longer the world champion who could walk through the streets of Cardiff without drawing more than a sideways glance. He was a national hero.

And so when, after protracted negotiations between respective promoters Frank Warren and Mogens Palle, Kessler agreed to fight at the Millennium Stadium, there were even suggestions that all kind of crowd records might be broken. In the end they were not, but still around 50,000 people paid to watch a fight that began in the early hours of the morning – as ever, to accommodate the interests of American television, in this case Home Box Office. Still, it was proof enough that in the 21st century this oft-maligned sport was alive and well.

By his own admission, after 20 defences of the WBO belt, Calzaghe needed an incentive to concentrate fully on the job, or in sporting parlance "to get up for it". This was everything he had ever dreamed of, and more.

"You can't knock Kessler," he said. "But he's never been in with a southpaw with my speed, my awkwardness, my slickness."

On this night, boxing, so often seen as innately corrupt and degenerate, became an uplifting sport again. From the beginning both men behaved like the champions they were: no crass bad-mouthing, no ugly confrontations at press conferences or weigh-ins, no egotistical ranting.

Rumours circulated, as they do, in the weeks before the fight. The most enduring one was that Kessler had damaged a hand in sparring. If it were true, it did nothing to crush his belief that he was going to win. For Calzaghe it was all about speed, about taking away the Dane's power and imposing the kind of masterclass on Kessler that he had on Lacy.

Over the first four rounds Kessler proved he was a far more complete operator than the talented but one-dimensional American, who had not won a minute of the 12 rounds, let alone a round.

Kessler gave Calzaghe plenty to think about. Although the Welshman was as quick as he promised to be, there were times when his head was knocked back by jabs, and in the fourth round he was momentarily dazed by a crunching right uppercut. At the halfway stage Calzaghe seemed ahead, but not by much.

Then over the second half his superiority established itself. Over ten years the one thing above all others that Calzaghe had learned was to adjust to what happened in a ring and to find a way to win. It had happened when his suspect hands had been broken, on the two occasions when he had been put down, when years before Robin Reid had repeatedly bounced right hands off the side of his head.

JOE CALZAGHE *(right) keeps Mikkel Kessler at bay with his southpaw jab*

And this was what he did against Kessler. The Dane, falling into the trap of believing he could turn the fight his way with one clean punch, kept looking for more single shots. Calzaghe sacrificed power and concentrated not only on accuracy, but also on fast combinations. In the past some had felt he slapped too much when he concentrated on speed. Not on this occasion, though. He was dazzling.

Kessler had no answer. Every so often he grew more competitive, but he was always struggling against the tide. Calzaghe's punches did not hurt him, but they confused and disorientated him to the point where his own attacks were nullified, or broken down before they built any rhythm.

By the end all but a few diehard Danish supporters and journalists knew Calzaghe's mastery was proven. The 28-year-old Kessler certainly knew. Once the decision had been announced – 117–111, 116–112 twice – and the fans had stood to roar their approval and applaud Calzaghe's victory, the fighters settled down to reflect.

"Mikkel's an excellent fighter," he said. "I'm getting old, man. He's going to come back when I'm gone, but tonight was my night. I'm going to chill out and have a rest now."

After acknowledging Calzaghe's performance Kessler then excused himself, because he wanted to visit Mogens Palle, who had been hospitalized throughout fight week because of heart problems.

Warren, who had promoted Calzaghe's career since before he was a world champion, was understandably effusive, calling him a "British boxing treasure".

"With Joe there is no entourage or bad behaviour. He's respectful, mature, and yes, he should get a knighthood."

Calzaghe's year was completed when he was voted the BBC Sports Personality of the Year, an award that reflected his long-sought-after, much-cherished status as a British boxing superstar.

FIGHT FACTS

DATE:	**November 3, 2007**
VENUE:	**Millennium Stadium, Cardiff, Wales**
TITLE:	**WBC, WBA, WBO Super-middleweight**
RESULT:	**Calzaghe won unanimous points decision, (12 rounds)**

HATTON MEETS HIS MATCH

FIGHT FACTS

DATE:	December 8, 2007
VENUE:	MGM Grand, Las Vegas, Nevada, USA
TITLE:	WBC welterweight
RESULT:	Mayweather won (stoppage, 1.35 of round 10)

FLOYD MAYWEATHER JR VS. RICKY HATTON

Floyd Mayweather's desire to be revered by future historians, coupled with Ricky Hatton's hunger to pit himself against the best fighter of his generation, led to a hugely lucrative showdown in Las Vegas as 2007 drew towards its close.

Mayweather's threats to retire after his two previous fights, against Carlos Baldomir and Oscar De La Hoya, suggested he might be reaching the limits of his interest in the business at which he had excelled since his teens. However, the chance to prove himself one more time was impossible to turn down once Hatton had knocked out Mayweather's old rival Jose Luis Castillo in Las Vegas in June. The Englishman was now 43-0, with an enormous following of proud British fans. Home Box Office were prepared to shell out millions of dollars one more time, and Mayweather knew it was a challenge he could not ignore.

In an otherwise low-key fight in Fresno, California, in 2003 Mayweather said: "I want people in 50 or 100 years' time who look into their history books to say: 'That Floyd Mayweather, he must have been a hell of a fighter.'"

Mayweather was pushed close enough by the bigger, stronger De La Hoya for some to question what might have been the outcome had they met when Oscar was in his prime, but the split decision had come down in his favour at the MGM Grand in May 2007.

In Hatton, he faced an entirely different opponent. The Englishman was short, strong, coming up from light-welterweight, and bringing a brand of aggression and ferocity that had kept him unbeaten in a ten-year professional career. Hatton, too, believed he was the best. And to prove it, he wanted to beat the best.

They tested each other psychologically in a long publicity tour, and by the time fight time came around they knew each other well. Hatton was as fit as it was possible for him to get, emotionally driven, unafraid. Far more British fans invaded Las Vegas for the week than could ever buy tickets to see the fight in the 17,000-capacity arena. For them the weigh-in was the only time they would see Hatton live. The noise they made just seemed to rattle Mayweather very slightly, while the worry was that it had fired up Hatton too much. He swore, when normally he would not.

Pre-fight Hatton seemed more pensive than usual; Mayweather had relaxed into his usual demeanour. His smile had a certainty to it. This was his territory, fight No. 39, a defence of one of the world championship belts he had won in five separate weight divisions from super-featherweight (130lb) to light-middleweight (154lb).

Once the bell rang Hatton attacked Mayweather, catching the dancing master a little by surprise with his light-welterweight's speed. Referee Joe Cortez, who was to be roundly criticized for his performance, was quickly on Hatton's case about infringements on the inside.

The cut-prone Hatton was damaged over the right eye in round three, but succeeded in closing the range over the first five rounds, which frustrated Mayweather, but did not hurt him. The Englishman's body punching wasn't as effective as it usually was, but his sheer intensity kept him in the fight. Gradually, though, Mayweather took control. His own body work was impressive and, little by little, he began to find more space to make his head shots more telling.

Hatton was deducted a point by Cortez for shoving Mayweather through the ropes and clubbing him on the back of the head and, as the fight went on, and the American took control, became increasingly reckless. Mayweather drew clear and then, in the tenth, exploited one rushing attack too many from Hatton, using his feet expertly to smash in a perfect left hook to the side of the jaw. Hatton fell heavily.

To his great credit Hatton got up, but Mayweather smashed him down again to force the stoppage.

Hatton admitted he lost his composure. "That's a cardinal sin for a boxer," he rued, adding: "It was a fight I was capable of winning, but I won't take anything away from him. He did what he said he was going to do. He's the best, the pound-for-pound best."

Mayweather was magnanimous in victory. "He [Hatton] has the heart of a lion," he said. "The crowd pumped him up, but the crowd didn't bother me. We decide who wins and who loses."

For Hatton there was no disgrace in losing to the best boxer in the world at this given moment; he had done what he had set out to do, from the moment he set foot in a professional ring back in the wilds of Widnes on a sweltering Saturday night in September 1997. He had lived out his dream, become the best light-welterweight in the world on that unforgettable night against Kostya Tszyu in 2005, and had then chased his American Dream.

It failed, in that he lost the biggest fight of his life, but along the way he made an army of British fans happy, won world titles in two weight divisions, and topped the bill in Las Vegas three times in 2007. There was also the not-insignificant sop of a payday said to finalize at somewhere in the region of £15 million.

For Mayweather, the Hatton fight was just one more stage upon which he had the opportunity to pound out his message. That – like him or loathe him – he was the best fighter of his generation, and one of the most naturally gifted of all time.

FLOYD MAYWEATHER *(left) picks apart Ricky Hatton in Las Vegas*

SCOTLAND CELEBRATES BURNS NIGHT

RICKY BURNS *(left) made it a rocky night for Roman Martinez at Glasgow's Kelvin Hall, winning a unanimous decision*

RICKY BURNS VS. ROMAN MARTINEZ

Nobody asked who would win the big fight. Just how long it would last. Sky Sports' commentator Adam Smith asked the opinion of his colleagues and they answered by holding up fingers. The most Smith counted was four. It was going to be an early night.

Twelve boxers from Scotland had won world titles and Ricky Burns didn't look like he was going to be the 13th. Put him in a line up and the chances are you wouldn't even pick him out as a prizefighter. Ricky had the wiry frame of a dieting pipe cleaner and a shy manner. Boxing – and his boyish enthusiasm for it – stripped away Ricky's natural shyness and he expressed himself through garish shorts, colourful hairstyles and a tattoo that revealed his love of the *Rocky* films. Burns said he watched *Rocky IV* before every fight for inspiration and 'There's No Easy Way Out' from the film's soundtrack was tattooed down his spine. To win the WBO super-featherweight championship, Burns would have to beat "Rocky."

Roman "Rocky" Martinez, that is.

For most who concern themselves with such things, Martinez was the best super-featherweight in the world in September 2010 and Burns possibly wasn't even No 1 in Britain. His two losses in 30 previous professional fights had come against Alex Arthur and Carl Johanneson. That loss to Johanneson in a challenge for the British title in February 2007 proved to be the pivotal moment in Ricky's career. He was floored three times and widely outpointed over 12 rounds and after that loss, he left trainer Rab Bannan for Billy Nelson. Nelson steered Burns to 13 straight wins and his world-title chance.

At the weigh-in, Burns laughed at Martinez's cut-throat gestures and the following night, "Rocky" just smiled while the crowd hissed and booed the 2/9 favourite. At 3/1, Burns was unfancied, but answered the opening bell by taking the centre of the ring and pumping out punches. His supporters cheered every blow that landed – and some that didn't. Martinez targeted Ricky's long, lean body, made him hold with a left hook and then in the final minute of the opening round, dumped Burns on the seat of his trunks with a right hand to hush even the most lubricated local.

Burns was not dazed, however, and Martinez didn't go in for the finish in the seconds that remained after the completion of the mandatory "eight" count.

Nelson remembered: "I told Ricky he had won the round apart from that punch. I just told him to keep boxing the same way."

Ricky kept his two-fisted combinations to body and head flowing and to the surprise of everyone, he outboxed and outpunched Martinez to send excitement crackling around the Kelvin Hall.

In the dying moments of the fifth, Burns responded to a spell of Martinez pressure with a chopping right hand that made the Puerto Rican's knees dip dramatically – and the Scottish supporters scream. Martinez got through the crisis, but went back to his stool on rubbery legs, while across the ring, Burns punched the air in recognition of his breakthrough.

Burns came through a tough seventh and was dazed again in the tenth, but whenever he was nailed, the Scot soon fired his fists straight back at Martinez.

As he got off his stool before the 11th, Ricky smiled. He later explained: "I was told: 'If you win these two rounds you will be world champion' and if that wouldn't put a smile on your face, nothing will."

But he still had another hurtful moment to endure in the final 30 seconds after Martinez landed a low blow. The referee gave Ricky time to recover, adding more suspense to a dramatic fight and giving Martinez the chance to drag together every bit of fighting resolve he had left in his aching, battered and bruised body for a final attack. But the knockout punch never came.

Zoltan Enyedi, from Hungary, and England's Paul Thomas both scored the bout 115–112 and Donald Trella, from America, had a two-round margin at 115–113. All for the winner and new WBO super-featherweight champion.

FIGHT FACTS

DATE:	**September 4, 2010**
VENUE:	**Kelvin Hall, Glasgow**
TITLE:	**WBO super-featherweight**
RESULT:	**Burns won (unanimous decision, 12 rounds)**

MARQUEZ GETS EVEN

FIGHT FACTS

DATE:	December 8, 2012
VENUE:	MGM Grand, Las Vegas, NV
TITLE:	N/A
RESULT:	Marquez won (knockout in 2.58, round 6)

JUAN MANUEL MARQUEZ VS. MANNY PACQUIAO

Manny Pacquiao had hit too fast, too hard, too often for the world's top fighters from flyweight to light-middleweight. The fabulous Filipino's flashing fists took him to world titles at six weights – thrashing pound-for-pound rivals Oscar De La Hoya, Ricky Hatton and Miguel Cotto along the way – but in Juan Manuel Marquez, he found a skilled, tough rival who could stay with him, make him miss and land counter punches. Nevertheless, the record books showed their three previous fights had ended in a draw and two razor-thin points wins for the Filipino.

Away from the ring, a bizarre singing competition screened on Mexican television in September 2011 was also keenly contested. Pacquiao sang 'Imagine', Marquez performed a Mexican tune and they teamed up for a duet of La Bamba. "I was more in key than he was," reckoned Pacquiao, previously unhappy to lose a darts match to Ricky Hatton in the countdown to their fight.

After each of their three previous fights – spread over eight years and three weight divisions – many of the public and press thought Marquez deserved better and the judges, not just the fighters, would be under the spotlight when he met the moustachioed "Mex-ecutioner" for a fourth time at the MGM Grand in Las Vegas in December 2012. The judges weren't always kind to Pacquiao either, however. His seven-year unbeaten run had been ended by a controversial points loss to Timothy Bradley earlier that year that cost him the WBO welterweight title and dealt another blow to any chance that he would ever meet Floyd Mayweather Jr.

Mayweather Jr's insistence on Pacquiao being drug tested had already made the fight unlikely. It was the fight the world wanted to see, the top two boxers in every pound-for-pound list meeting, but even that could not have matched the fourth clash between Pacquiao and Marquez for sheer excitement. The match was made at 147lb – above Marquez's best fighting weight – and all 20,000 tickets were sold. Marquez had the majority of the support in the MGM Grand Arena – and many millions more listened to radios on the streets of Mexico and the Philippines. Pacquiao had sold doughnuts on the streets of Manila to survive having run away from home when he was just 14 years old after watching his drunken father kill and eat his pet dog, and his rise to boxing superstardom made him an idol in his home country.

The opening two rounds of the fight had Filipinos cheering. Pacquiao appeared to win them clearly enough. He danced into range, unloaded rapid-fire two-fisted combinations, then danced out of range again, while Marquez kept his chin down and looked to pick clean counters. Marquez landed a clean right hand in the third round – and Pacquiao hit the deck. But he got up to floor Marquez in the fifth and by the end of a savage, give-and-take round, Pacquiao was a point ahead on all three judges' cards and the Mexican's nose was broken.

Pacquiao appeared to be winning the sixth as well. In the dying seconds of the round, he launched a southpaw left, but Marquez beat him to the punch with a short right-hand blast to the jaw. Pacquiao ran onto the punch and it took everything out of him. He landed flat on his face and lay there motionless for the "ten" count and beyond. Marquez had his revenge – and Mexico rejoiced. "I threw a perfect punch," he said afterwards. "This victory is justice for us, not just for me, but for Mexico." Reporters afterwards compared the fight's excitement to the classic Marvin Hagler-Thomas Hearns fight and within weeks, there was talk of a fifth fight between Pacquiao and Marquez.

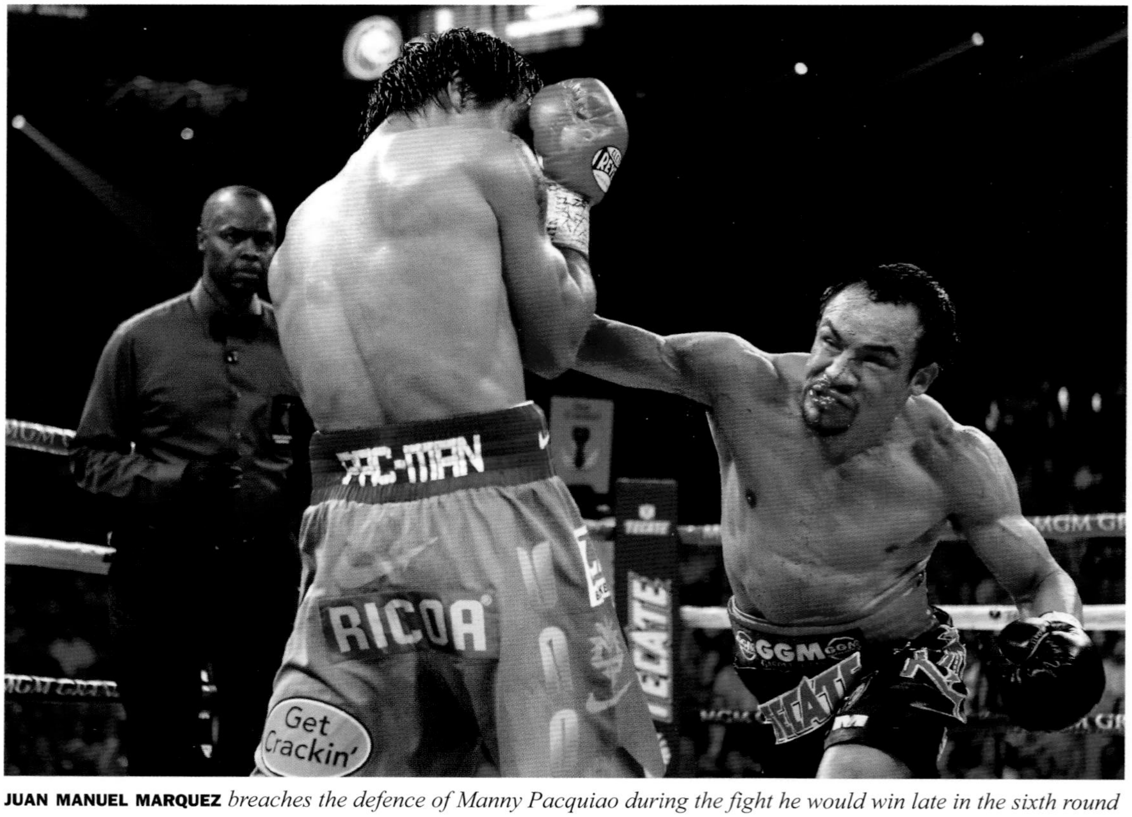

JUAN MANUEL MARQUEZ *breaches the defence of Manny Pacquiao during the fight he would win late in the sixth round*

MONEY CASHES IN

FLOYD MAYWEATHER JR. VS MANNY PACQUIAO

For years, Floyd Mayweather Jr. and Manny Pacquiao had been the top two – or thereabouts – in the pound-for-pound rankings, but it seemed the fight the world wanted to see may never happen.

The first negotiations for the fight had ended messily around Christmas 2009 when Mayweather insisted on random blood testing and, incensed at the implication he was a drugs cheat, Pacquiao ended talks and filed lawsuits for defamation.

Five years on, Pacquiao was in Florida as a judge for the Miss Universe contest and after his flight home to the Philippines was cancelled, he went to a Miami Heat basketball match. Mayweather was sitting across the court. At half-time, the fighters exchanged numbers, then met that evening at Pacquiao's hotel where a deal was agreed.

The richest fight in history – expected to gross more than $400 million – was on. The fight pitted a defensive master – Mayweather's fighting philosophy was: "The less you get hit, the longer you last," – against a southpaw whirlwind who threw punches in clusters.

Their characters were very different as well. Pacquiao, reportedly paid just $2 when he made his professional debut as a 16 year-old, declared he had turned his back on his womanizing, gambling past – he once bet the equivalent of $360,000 on a cock fight – and found God.

Mayweather, two years older at 38, worshipped only himself. "Me first," he once said. "Me first, then everyone else. But me first."

That was also how he ranked all-time greats. Muhammad Ali, he pointed out, was a great heavyweight, while his success spanned five weight divisions, from super-featherweight to light-middleweight, and his record was a perfect 47–0. He said: "Nobody's gonna brainwash me that Sugar Ray Leonard and Muhammad Ali are better than me, no way."

"TBE" – "The Best Ever" – was emblazoned on his baseball caps and T shirts and, whether you agreed or not, he was boxing's biggest draw.

Mayweather was the world's highest paid athlete in 2014 – earning $105 million – and stories of his wealth and extravagances were often told. But while Marvin Hagler, among others, had found it "hard to get out of bed to go for a run at five o'clock in the morning when you're wearing silk pyjamas," Mayweather kept his appetite, despite his wealth.

FLOYD MAYWEATHER JR. *did most of the attacking against Manny Pacquiao (right) and was a very clear points winner*

FIGHT FACTS

DATE:	**May 2, 2015**
VENUE:	**MGM Grand, Las Vegas**
TITLE:	**WBC, WBA Super and WBO welterweight**
RESULT:	**Mayweather won (unanimous decision, 12 rounds)**

"He trains like he's broke," said one gym mate. Mayweather Jr. trained at his own gym in Las Vegas, with father Floyd Sr., while Pacquiao was with Freddie Roach at his Wild Card gym in Hollywood.

Roach had come as close as any trainer to masterminding Mayweather's defeat when he trained Oscar de la Hoya for their fight in May 2007.

Mayweather grabbed a split verdict after pulling away in the second half of the fight, but in the opening rounds, de la Hoya had crowded him, attacked his body and led on the scorecards.

In other scares, Shane Mosley had Mayweather wobbly for a few seconds, and punch stats showed Jose Luis Castillo outpunched him, but Mayweather was troubled by a shoulder injury. In a later fight, Marcos Maidana hit him more often, 221 times, than any other opponent.

However, in rematches against Castillo and Maidana, Mayweather made adjustments and won more clearly. That Maidana rematch had been Mayweather's most recent fight, while Pacquiao had recorded a points win over Chris Algieri, an over-achieving light-welterweight who was dropped six times.

To beat Mayweather, the expectation was that Pacquaio had to start fast, because chasing a fight against Mayweather is inadvisable.

However, the opening three rounds belonged to Mayweather. He held the centre of the ring, scored with jabs and when Pacquiao got close, he held and smothered. There were boos from the crowd in the third.

Pacquiao had a better fourth, knocking Mayweather into the ropes with a southpaw left, but his follow-up attack hit only arms and gloves as Mayweather reorganized his defences. He found the target with lefts again in the sixth and though Mayweather wasn't badly shaken, at the bell he went back to an anxious corner.

Mayweather Sr., sensing the fight may be close on the scorecards, yelled: "They are going to take this away from you."

Mayweather Jr. got back to the centre of the ring from where he controlled the pace of the fight. The crowd chanted: "Manny! Manny!" when Pacquiao unloaded flurries in the eighth, but most of the punches missed and after Mayweather started drilling him with rights from the ninth round, the steam seemed to go out of Pacquiao's attacks.

There was a rally in the last round, but, as was the case for most of the fight, Pacquiao couldn't pin Mayweather down and hit him cleanly. All three judges scored it for Mayweather: Burt A Clements and Glenn Feldman both had it 116–112 – eight rounds to four – and Dave Moretti had it wider at 118–110. Punch stats showed Mayweather won that score 148–81.

The aftermath of the fight was unfortunate. Criticized for fighting without his usual fire, Pacquiao explained he had gone into the fight with a shoulder injury that would require surgery afterwards.

The public – and Mayweather – were unimpressed. Mayweather said he was "really upset" by Pacquiao's claim and added: "He's not at my level. He will never be at my level."

A MODERN-DAY CLASSIC

ANTHONY JOSHUA VS. WLADIMIR KLITSCHKO

ANTHONY JOSHUA *showed formidable strength and staying power in his impressive victory over Wladimir Klitschko*

British boxing fans had every reason to feel excited about Anthony Joshua. Since turning professional following his gold-medal success at the 2012 Olympic Games in London, the Watford-born heavyweight had produced a string of dynamic performances. He had won his first 14 fights as a professional inside three rounds (three of them by knockout), had proved he could go deeper into a fight with a seven-round victory over the experienced Dillian White, and had demolished American Charles Martin inside two rounds to win the IBF world heavyweight title. Critics might have pointed to a genuine lack of class among his opponents, but, as the adage goes, you can only beat what is placed in front of you, and Joshua had done so ruthlessly, showing fire in his fists in the process.

But just how good was he? What he needed was a sterner test; a chance to prove himself against someone who had been there and done it all in the ring. And that test came against 41-year-old Wladimir Klitschko in front of a packed, 90-000-strong crowd (a record in British boxing) at the iconic Wembley Stadium on April 29, 2017.

One of the reasons this fight will be remembered with such fondness by boxing fans all over the world is because of the classy manner in which both fighters conducted themselves in the build-up to the fight. There was no trash-talking or chest-thumping lunacy that seem to have become the disappointing and image-damaging norm here; instead, the pair had genuine respect for one another, and weren't afraid to express it. It was refreshing, and Klitschko endorsed it: "It's a great big message," he said. "If we compare it to many other big fights, it has never been done this way… And we didn't use the F-word. We were not throwing tables or glasses… The attitude and the respect to each other is being passed down to all the other young men down there in the gyms." But mild-manners don't make memories; the reason this fight will do down in heavyweight history is because it turned out to be an absolute classic.

FIGHT FACTS

DATE:	**April 29, 2017**
VENUE:	**Wembley Stadium, London**
TITLE:	**IBF, IBO, WBA Super heavyweight**
RESULT:	**Joshua won (TKO, round 11)**

After a tentative opening few rounds, the fight burst into life in the fifth round. Joshua produced a stinging punch to cut the giant Ukrainian over the left eye, and spotted his chance, going in for the kill. But Klitschko fought back: Joshua's desperate effort to finish the fight had left him blowing, and the veteran seized his opportunity, launching a blistering counter-attack. Joshua seemed to be out on his feet, and was ultimately saved by the bell.

The momentum continued to swing in the Ukrainian's favour. Joshua hit the canvas for the first time in his professional career in the sixth round. But he steadied himself, feeling his way through the eighth, ninth and tenth rounds. In the 11th, the Englishman's stinging, power-packed punches started to find their target once more, and it was Klitschko who was desperately trying to hang on. Joshua connected with a massive right uppercut and then sent his opponent sprawling to the canvas with a ferocious left-right-left combination. The giant Ukrainian stumbled uncertainly back to his feet, but the end was fast approaching. Joshua, roared on by the vocal, partisan crowd, launched another stinging attack, raining down punch after ferocious punch on his opponent who was propped up only by the ropes. Another left hook sent Klitschko sliding to the canvas once more. Showing supreme courage, the Ukrainian made it back onto his feet once again but, seemingly helpless and on the receiving end of yet another Joshua barrage, the referee stepped in to stop the fight.

Joshua saluted both the crowd and his opponent. Klitschko may have exposed vulnerabilities for the first time in his career, but the Englishman had come through his sternest test to date with flying colours. Both he, and the sport of boxing, were winners on this unforgettable night.

THE MONEY FIGHT

FLOYD MAYWEATHER JR VS. CONOR MCGREGOR

FLOYD MAYWEATHER JR *made millions from his overhyped bout with Conor McGregor*

Was this good for the sport? Was it the fight that everybody really wanted to see? Or was it simply two men and their respective camps exploiting a public only that seemed only too happy to fall for the hype and, what's more, pay for it?

By the beginning of 2017, only one thing seemed capable of dragging Floyd Mayweather out of retirement, money, and the promise of bag-fuls of cash seemingly on offer for a fight against MMA star Conor McGregor inevitably became too hard to turn down. After months of speculation, the fight was finally confirmed for August 26, 2017.

And then the hype spiralled into overdrive. The sums reputedly on offer to both fighters were staggering. Mayweather was guaranteed a disclosed pay cheque of $100 million; McGregor would pocket $30 million. When the dust finally settled after this extraordinary affair, it was estimated that both fighters received more than three times the disclosed estimate. It was no surprise, therefore, that the fight ultimately attracted the tag "The Money Fight".

For all the irritation of the pre-fight hype, there was still an element of curiosity for the purists. Could McGregor, a two-division mixed martial artist world champion who claimed he had always had an interest in boxing, really upstage Mayweather, an 11-time, five division boxing world champion who had gone into the ring on 49 occasions as a professional and emerged victorious on each and every occasion.

At the pre-fight press conference, McGregor certainly seemed to think so. He had won the battle to use heavier 8oz gloves for the fight and, outwardly at least, seemed was convinced he would go on to win the fight. "I believe he [Mayweather] will last one or two rounds," said the Irishman. "I just don't see him surviving. Really, I'm starting to think I will toy with him once he goes down."

The trouble was no one really believed him. Mayweather may well have passed 40, and he may have out of the ring for nearly two years, but, surely, he had enough ring craft, enough pure boxing skill, to see off McGregor, however hard the brash Dubliner claimed he could hit. Almost everyone agreed that Mayweather, the outstanding boxer of his era, would dominate the fight.

From the opening bell, McGregor shot from his corner and tried to swarm the American, landing a couple of bodyshots as Mayweather boxed largely on the back foot, perhaps waiting, along with the rest of us, to see exactly what the Irishman could bring to the ring. As McGregor swung wildly, desperate to find the bout-ending punch, Mayweater produced searching jabs to his opponent's body.

Mayweather finally burst into life in the fourth round, landing a right hook to McGregor's body, and the entire mood of the fight seemed to change. Now McGregor was in retreat and, fatally, by the middle of the fifth round he was visibly starting to tire. His chance had gone; now it was a question of survival. Mayweather reacted immediately, stepping up the pace and starting to land punches at will.

By the seventh, Mayweather was in total control: while his combinations continued to find their target, McGregor's counter-punches lacked the strength of the opening rounds. The punishment continued in the eighth round, as Mayweather rocked McGregor with a sparkling uppercut. It was now only a matter of time. Surprisingly, McGregor started brightly in the ninth before the American resumed control, landing punches freely, including one that left McGregor feeling for the ropes. The bell ultimately saved him.

The end finally came in the tenth round. Mayweather stunned McGregor with a stinging right-hand shot and when he landed another ten unanswered punches, the referee finally stepped in. Boxing mastery had overcome brawn: Mayweather had landed 170 of the 320 punches he threw; tellingly McGregor landed only 111 of 430.

Mayweather announced his retirement from boxing straight after the fight: his (and boxing's) reputation had been saved, his unbeaten record remained intact, and his bank balance had been significantly enhanced. From his point of view, it was mission well and truly accomplished.

FIGHT FACTS

DATE:	**August 26, 2017**
VENUE:	**T-Mobile Arena, Paradise, NV**
TITLE:	**No title**
RESULT:	**Mayweather won (rsf in 1.05, round 10)**

TRAINERS AND MANAGERS

Boxing is, at first sight, the most individual of sports, where a man stands or falls on his own merits. It is the classic one-on-one confrontation, and if things go wrong there is nowhere the man in trouble can look to for help except inside himself. That, at least, is the theory: in practice, a boxer depends as much on his back-up team of trainer, manager, cuts man and corner help as he does on his own resources. He may be good enough to win the fight, but if his training has been inadequate or the corner work is sloppy, or self-doubt is allowed to creep into his mind, then all the talent in the world may not be enough to see him through.

If that sounds an extravagant claim to make for men who may never have taken a punch in their lives, consider the number of times an important fight has been won because of what was done in the corner. Muhammad Ali (Cassius Clay, as he then was) gained vital extra seconds' recovery time after being floored by Henry Cooper at the end of the fourth round in 1963 because of the quick-wittedness of trainer Angelo Dundee, who stuck his finger into a slight tear in one of Ali's gloves, pulled it apart, and then called the referee's attention to the damage. By the time it was established that a replacement glove could not be found, Dundee's dazed fighter had regained control of himself and went on to stop Cooper in the next round.

Then there was Teddy Atlas, whose inspired pep-talk to Michael Moorer at the end of the eighth round of his world heavyweight title challenge against Evander Holyfield in April 1994 helped make Moorer world champion. The notoriously belligerent Atlas, a fireball who once held a gun to Mike Tyson's head during a row in the days when he trained the teenager, was becoming increasingly exasperated by the way the lethargic Moorer was allowing the fight to drift away from him against a man whom Atlas could see was not the fighter he had once been. (Holyfield was later diagnosed as having a heart condition which forced him to announce his retirement, later rescinded.)

When Moorer trudged back to his stool, Atlas leapt into the ring and, planting himself in front of the fighter with his face a couple of inches from Moorer's, gave a speech that has become, in its way, as famous as the "Coulda been a

TEDDY ATLAS *gives Michael Moorer that famous pep-talk*

contender" monologue from *On The Waterfront*. "Do you want me to fight, huh, do you?" he yelled at Moorer. "Do you want me to change places with you – do you? Listen, this guy is finished. There comes a time in a man's life when he makes a decision – makes a decision – to just live, survive. Or he wants to win. You're doing just enough to keep him off you and hope he leaves you alone.

"You're lying to yourself, but you're gonna cry tomorrow! You're lying to yourself and I'd lie to you if I let you get away with that! You're gonna cry tomorrow because of this. Do you want to cry tomorrow, huh? Then don't lie to yourself. There's something wrong with this guy. Back him up and fight a full round." Moorer took heed, and won on points.

Ironically, Holyfield himself contributed to his own defeat by making two false economies in training. He split with trainer Emanuel Steward (Moorer's former mentor) in an argument over $100,000 – a minuscule percentage of what he earned from the fight, and what the title was worth to him; and he was badly hampered by a cut left eye, after refusing to pay top cuts man Ace Marotta $25,000 to work in his corner.

HARD DAYS AT THE OFFICE

Famous gymnasia

For 40 years Stillman's was the most famous gymnasium in boxing – home to revered trainers like Ray Arcel, Charley Goldman, Whitey Bimstein and Chickie Ferrera, and the boxing academy to which Angelo Dundee came to listen, watch and learn. New York was the world capital of boxing then, in the decades before the Las Vegas casinos discovered the sport, and at one time or another all the fighters of any consequence would train either at Stillman's or at the nearby Gleason's.

EVANDER HOLYFIELD *in his state-of-the-art gym; not all gymnasia are so well-equipped*

Lou Stillman opened his gym, situated at 54th and Eighth, in 1920 and ran it with an autocratic hand until its closure in 1959. It was a large, long room up one flight of stairs, with a main floor 125 feet long and 50 feet wide, accommodating two rings. Up a spiral staircase, on the next level, was an area set aside for skipping and ground work. There was seating on the main floor for 200 spectators, and Stillman himself, seated on a high chair, would act as master of ceremonies, introducing the boxers who were sparring to the punters who paid their 50 cents to climb the stairs and watch the champions and contenders at work.

The closest modern equivalent to Stillman's was Johnny Tocco's, on Charleston Boulevard in downtown Las Vegas. It was small, dark, smelly and the air conditioning consisted of an open back door, but the fighters loved it. It had the feel and atmosphere of an old-time gym, and it was no coincidence that the boxers who felt most at home there, and who opted to train at Tocco's rather than in the casino facilities on the Strip, were the blue-collar champions like Marvin Hagler and, when he was younger, Mike Tyson. But gyms like this are hard to find. The modern gym is much more likely to be a state-of-the-art fitness centre, where computers play a bigger role than spit buckets and skipping ropes.

Evander Holyfield is the best-known product of such an establishment. He bulked up from cruiserweight (190lb) to heavyweight under the guidance of Tim Hallmark, a pioneer in the field who described himself as Holyfield's "Director Of Physical Build-up". Hallmark devised for him a programme combining diet control with cardiovascular exercise and resistance weight training, constantly monitoring his heart and pulse rates. Where old-time fighters strengthened their upper body by swinging an axe at a tree or hoisting barbells, Holyfield used something called a pec-deck machine, a weights-and-pulley arrangement which concentrated on the pectoral muscles.

Hallmark had Holyfield punch through water, and devised a 12-minute routine in which the boxer, feet together, jumped on and off a 2½ feet high block. He even had Holyfield taking ballet lessons, to improve his balance and movement. Somehow, one suspects Jack Dempsey or John L. Sullivan might have drawn the line there. But Hallmark's ideas worked, since Holyfield became a superbly muscled heavyweight good enough to beat George Foreman, Larry Holmes and Riddick Bowe.

His success has inspired many others to follow his example, but however much new technology and medical knowledge impacts on boxing, some things will never change. Boxers will still have to leave their beds for long runs in the early morning air, to strengthen their legs and improve their lung capacity; they will still have to do back-breaking, muscle-aching floor exercises, and they will still skip rope just as their predecessors were doing a century ago. (Sullivan, never an enthusiastic trainer, used a variation on road-work: rather than run, he used to walk a brisk eight miles every morning, doubling the distance on Saturdays.)

TRAINERS

Trainers traditionally get ten per cent of the purse, although in these days of seven or eight-figure purses, it is commonplace for a fee to be negotiated which is much less than that. But whatever he earns, a good trainer is worth the money. He fills any number of roles: conditioner, confidante, psychologist, motivator, and strategist. Brendan Ingle, the Sheffield-based Dubliner who developed talent like Naseem Hamed, Herol Graham and Johnny Nelson, defines himself as "a professor of boxing, a professor of psychology and a professor of kidology all rolled into one. You have to be."

Ingle has a better grasp than many of the importance of the psychological aspect of boxing. His fighters are trained to confuse and bewilder their opponents – in Ingle's phrase, to "Do their head in" rather than damage them physically. Herol Graham was the prime exponent of this kind of boxing, an artful dodger in the ring who could reduce opponents to tears of frustration by his evasive moves. Mark Kaylor, a brave and hard-hitting middleweight, retired on his stool after eight rounds of a European title fight with Graham, telling his corner "How can I beat a man I can't even hit?"

Because Ingle likes to start them young (Hamed was seven when he first came to the Sheffield gym) he gets to know his boxers inside out, and that is essential to a successful trainer-boxer relationship. The trainer must know his man so intimately that he can sense every change of mood, every nuance of expression. That way, he can be sure of getting the best out of his man, whereas the manager, whose role is primarily to negotiate the fee and hire the trainer, is a much more distant figure who, if he knows what is best for the boxer, will leave the corner work to the experts.

It is a two-way relationship, of course: the boxer must have absolute faith in the trainer, since he will entrust his future career to the trainer's judgement by implementing the strategies devised for him. Sometimes the trainer's art will be in kidding the fighter that a particular move or punch is the boxer's own creation, and then flattering him into constant repetition of the move until it has been mastered. Angelo Dundee, who used the ploy to great

THE 60-SECOND SURGEONS

The cuts man

The cuts man is an often unsung but vitally important member of the team, particularly with boxers who are cut-prone. By the time a bleeding fighter has made his way back to the corner, sat down, and the cuts man has climbed through the ropes to go to work on the injury, maybe 15 seconds of the allotted 60 have elapsed. That does not leave much time for treatment, and it is in those crucial moments that an expert cuts man comes into his own. First he will clean the cut with a cotton wool swab, taking care to change swabs between rounds to avoid the danger of dust or dirt gathering on a used swab. Hollywood films like to depict the cuts man working with a swab-stick in his mouth, but a good operator will be more hygiene-conscious than that.

Next he will soak a swab in the adrenaline solution and hold in on the wound, pressing down with his other hand. What he will never do – and here again Hollywood too often gets it wrong – is douse the man with water, since water serves to accelerate the blood flow. If there is a swelling developing, he will either use the Endswell – a small flat iron – to smooth down the lump, or else apply an ice-pack.

It is a specialized field, and the few top men working in it are always in demand. They tend to operate as freelancers, rather than commit themselves to one particular camp. In Britain, Paddy Byrne is much in demand, and his services are also used by anxious managers in South Africa and Denmark. In America, experts like Ace Marotta and Ralph Citro are highly paid, while some, like the late Freddie Brown (who treated Rocky Marciano's often horrible cuts) become the most valuable member of the fighter's entourage.

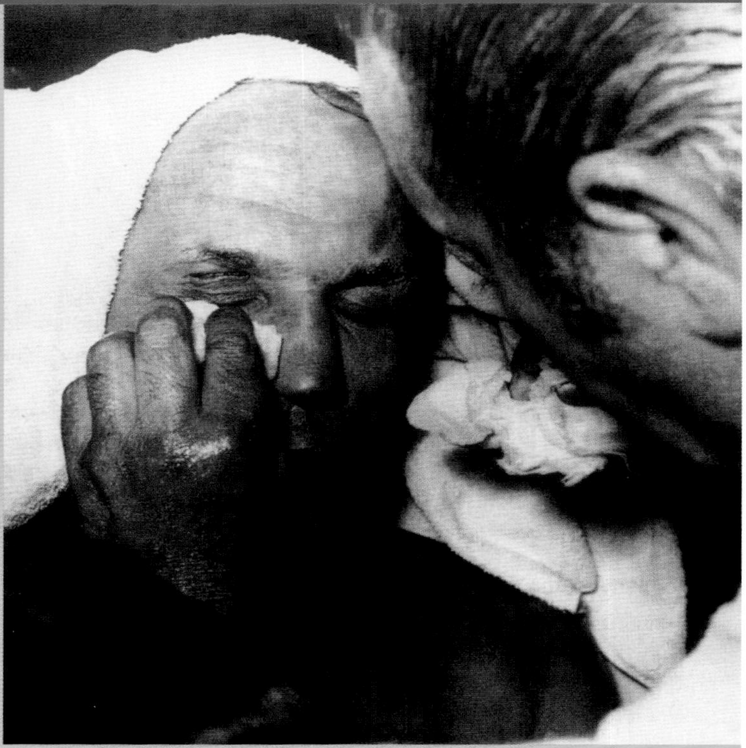

CUTS MAN *Danny Holland at work on Henry Cooper*

While the fight is underway, the trainer and his corner team will be watching closely, comparing notes and devising strategic changes, if such are needed. During the interval between rounds, in a well-run corner, only one man will be talking: too many voices distract a boxer, who has little enough time in which to absorb what may be complicated instructions. Usually, too, the trainer will not welcome comments from his boxer, who needs the recovery time and should not waste his breath and energy in talking.

The final service a good trainer will do for his man is to pull him out of the fight once it becomes unwinnable, as Eddie Futch memorably did for Joe Frazier in the "Thrilla in Manila" against Muhammad Ali in 1975 with the words: "Sit down, son, it's all over. But nobody will forget what you did here today." Dundee had to fight off his own corner helper, Bundini Brown, when he retired Ali against Larry Holmes in 1980. Brown grabbed Dundee's shirt, shouting for "One more round", but Dundee furiously shoved him away and yelled: "Take your hands off me. He can't take any more. Get the hell away from me. I'm the boss here. It's over."

effect with Muhammad Ali, explained: "What you have to do is make the fighter feel he's the innovator. I'd say to Ali, 'You're really putting your left hand into that jab. You're really snapping it,' or I'd say, 'I've never seen such a great left uppercut.' Then he'd throw it again, and again."

In the long build-up to a title fight, the trainer will be responsible for supervising his man's workouts, monitoring his weight and diet, shielding him from distractions, and devising tactics, often done nowadays by studying videotapes of the opponent to analyse his style and spot his flaws. He will hire sparring partners capable of imitating the opponent's style, and will study his own man's sparring to see how he copes. Either the trainer or his assistant will "work the pads", donning large pads like a baseball catcher's mitt and moving around the ring, hands up in a boxing stance, while the boxer throws punches in combinations at the pads. The routine is intended to develop timing and accuracy.

On fight night, the trainer will wrap his man's hands in the dressing room, under the supervision of a Board of Control official and a representative of the opponent's camp. Bandaging sounds a straightforward procedure, but is a skill in itself. Badly wrapped hands are prone to damage, and carelessness at this stage could have catastrophic consequences for a boxer's career. The human hand is a delicate piece of engineering, with a vast number of small bones which can be broken, splintered, or jarred by the impact of a punch. Good bandaging holds the bones firmly in place, and minimizes the risk of injury. When the procedure is complete, the Board official will rubber-stamp the bandages to certify that only the permitted 18 feet length of wrapping and 11 feet of zinc oxide sticky tape has been used, and that there has been no "skulduggery". (Jess Willard claimed that, in their 1919 fight, Jack Dempsey's bandages had been sprinkled with a type of powder which, when mixed with the sweat of his hands, hardened into a type of plaster of Paris, but that allegation was never substantiated and was always vehemently denied by Dempsey.)

He may then rub Vaseline over the boxer's face and body, the theory being that the opponent's punches will slide over the grease. So long as only a reasonable amount of Vaseline is used, the referee will permit it. But if he feels there is excessive grease on the man's face, he will call for a towel to wipe away the excess before allowing the action to commence. Before leaving the dressing room, the cuts man will have checked his tool box to ensure that nothing has been overlooked. The kit contains swab-sticks, scissors, sticking tape (used to secure the glove laces), cotton wool, and a solution of 1:1000 adrenaline and water solution, which in Britain is the only coagulant permitted by the Board of Control. Regulations vary in America, where some Commissions allow very much stronger solutions and other States have no Athletic Commission, so anything goes. The discrepancy between Britain and America in this area has often led to unseemly scenes in corners, with Board officials attempting to confiscate solutions which they suspect to be stronger than their permitted limits.

CHAIRMAN
Manager Roberto Alcazar provides a broad pair of shoulders for champion Oscar De La Hoya

RAY ARCEL *A legendary teacher of boxers*

The great trainers know their fighters as well as the fighters know themselves. They will sense when things are right, and when they are not, know when to talk, when a fighter needs encouragement or shaking out of lethargy, and know when even the Gettysburg Address wouldn't work. In those moments the good trainer will say everything with his eyes, with small gestures of reassurance, perhaps with just one short sentence of advice near the end of the minute's rest.

Ray Arcel was perhaps the greatest of them all. He saw Jack Dempsey fight way back in 1916. He was working corners from the 1920s, when he was with the legendary lightweight champion Benny Leonard, to the eighties, when he worked with Larry Holmes and Roberto Duran. It was Duran who once said: "When he is angry, he says nothing. He only gives me the look. Then I know it is time to go to work."

At one time Arcel tried to promote shows but fell foul of the Mob, who didn't like the fact that he had a (short-lived as it turned out) television contract.

Arcel said the most important thing he could teach his boxers was the need to be able to think inside the ring. He was a great tactician, but also had the intuitive sense when to change something in a fighter and when to leave well alone.

"Nobody had to teach Duran how to fight," he said. "The first day I saw him I told everybody around him: 'Don't change his style'... He knew how to fight."

Some say Joe Louis was never the same man once his trainer, Jack Blackburn, had died in 1942. While some say it was just the fact that Louis was in the US Army by then, and at 28 was naturally beginning to slow, others say while they were contributory factors, if Blackburn had lived, even with the enforced layoff, Louis would not have gone to seed so soon.

Some trainers were not boxers of any note, one or two were not boxers at all, but Blackburn had been a top-class lightweight in the early years of the century. He fought Joe Gans three times and Sam Langford, when it was said he conceded more than 40lb. He had been jailed for ten to fifteen years for killing a man and shooting two women. He was difficult to get to know and, some said, difficult to like. But Louis adored him. They did their real work behind closed doors. Blackburn sparred with him, taught him. He developed Louis from a tough, hard-hitting kid into a world champion with perhaps the best left jab of any heavyweight who walked.

As Jack Blackburn manufactured Joe Louis, so Charley Goldman turned Rocky Marciano from a wild brawler into a punching machine. Nobody was ever going to make Marciano a slick, cool stylist, but Goldman, who had been a clever bantamweight in his youth, improved The Rock's footwork, shortened his punches, made him explosive and able to use his strength and power at the highest level.

In a 1953 *Ring* interview, when Rocky was champion, Goldman said: "The part I like best is starting from the beginning with a green kid and watching him develop."

Marciano had his critics: not fast enough, took too many shots, cut too easily, too small, short arms, etc. etc. Goldman's answer was disarmingly simple. "He must be good. He always beats the other fella."

Eddie Futch sparred with Joe Louis at the red-brick Brewster Recreation Center in Detroit in the 1930s. He worked quietly with fighters for years, learning his job, and eventually took over as Joe Frazier's trainer when Yancey Durham, who made Smokin' Joe what he was, died.

Futch famously pulled Frazier out of the third fight with Muhammad Ali, with just one of the fifteen rounds to go. Ronald K Fried quoted the conversation in his book *Corner Men*.

Futch: Joe, I'm going to stop it.
Frazier: No, no, Eddie. You can't do that to me.
Futch: You couldn't see in the last two rounds. What makes you think you're gonna see in the fifteenth?
Frazier: I want him, boss.
Futch: Sit down, son. It's all over. No one will ever forget what you did here today.

Futch had trained Ken Norton for a while and, when in his eighties, he worked with another heavyweight champion, Riddick Bowe.

Dan Birmingham received acclaim, primarily for his work in Florida with the unfashionable Ronald "Winky" Wright, while James "Buddy" McGirt was one of the few world champions who became a top-class professional trainer.

Angelo Dundee, of course, was with Muhammad Ali from first to last, and also trained Sugar Ray Leonard. Dundee's brother Chris was a promoter in Miami for most of his life. Earlier on, Angelo had worked with Carmen Basilio, but he will always be remembered as the man who called the shots for Ali.

For three decades Emanuel Steward's Kronk Gym was home to generations of Detroit fighters, young and old. In the late 1970s and through the '80s, Steward concentrated on building his "army" of fighters, all of whom wore the "Kronk gold". His first star remained his greatest: Thomas Hearns, who won world titles

JACK BLACKBURN *(right) turned Joe Louis into a boxing great*

ENZO CALZAGHE *an individualist who ignored tradition to train his son*

in five weight divisions. Steward, however, developed a host of world champions and helped the careers of many others, one of whom, Dennis Andries, walked into the Kronk to better himself after losing his WBC light-heavyweight crown to Hearns. Under Steward, he got it back, not once, but twice.

By the 1990s Steward was diversifying and increasingly took well-paid "outside" jobs, principally with Lennox Lewis.

The Mayweather dynasty was also based in Michigan, across the state in Grand Rapids. Roger Mayweather was a two-weight world champion, and his brothers Floyd and Jeff were good class professionals. Roger took over as main trainer of the brilliant Floyd Jr, while Floyd Sr had what might be best described as an uneven relationship with his son.

Floyd Sr worked with other fighters – and at one point it looked as if he would work the corner of Oscar De La Hoya when the Golden Boy fought Floyd Jr in 2007. In the end, though, that didn't happen.

Not all trainers achieved their success in their home country. Charles Atkinson had an unremarkable amateur and pro boxing career, then learned his job training boxers under his father, Charles Sr. With his brother Mike, he also promoted boxing in Liverpool until the early 1980s, when an offer came to train fighters in Thailand.

His success was dramatic and quick. World champions rolled off a seemingly unending pipeline. Among them were: Sot Chitalada, who won the WBC flyweight title in only his eighth professional contest and went on to have 15 title bouts in two spells as champion; Samart Payakarun, who knocked out Mexican Lupe Pintor to become WBC super-bantamweight champ; at the mini-mum weight, strawweight, Napa Kiatwanchai; and, in 1995, not long before he returned to Britain for good, Saman Sorjatorung, who pulled off an upset seventh-round stoppage of WBC light-flyweight champion Humberto Gonzalez in Los Angeles.

In Britain, George Francis was the disciplinarian coach of light-heavyweight champion John Conteh as well as a string of Afro-Caribbean boxers who got few breaks. He was as proud of his work with British and European middleweight champion Bunny Sterling as he was of training Conteh. His famous early morning routines included a swim in the cold waters of the pond on Hampstead Heath.

Terry Lawless trained and managed world champions John H Stracey, Jim Watt, Maurice Hope, and Charlie Magri from his Royal Oak gym in London's East End.

Brendan Ingle, mentioned elsewhere in this section, had his own eccentric way of doing things: one of which included a sign on his gym wall in Wincobank, Sheffield, that read: "Boxing Can Damage Your Health!"

Ingle's safety-first techniques did not please everybody, but he helped take Herol Graham to the brink of a world title, then reached his own peak with the rise of Naseem Hamed in the early and mid-90s. They eventually fell out, and Ingle's greater pride came with the emergence of the once-ostracized cruiserweight Johnny Nelson in the late '90s. Nelson was virtually unpromoteable at one point because of his timid style, but he eventually held the WBO title for seven years and retired as undefeated champion in his mid-30s. Ingle still works corners, but has now passed on the day-to-day work to his son Dominic.

Of the other current trainers in Britain, Billy Graham cut his teeth under the late Phil Martin at the Champ's Camp gym in Manchester, and made his reputation by working with Ricky Hatton from the beginning of his career right through to his heady days as the best light-welterweight in the world.

Father-and-son relationships don't often work: it's hard for a man to get such things right as the timing of when, if it becomes necessary, to stop a fight; it is also true that offspring, as a matter of course, will listen to advice from anyone except their father!

The prime exception to the rule was Enzo Calzaghe, a former musician, who learned how to train a boxer from a few books and the rest by trial and error and intuition, it seems. Traditionalists sometimes scorned Calzaghe's homemade methods and his gym in Newbridge, which the polite described as "homely" and the impolite called "falling down". In the end Enzo did move his fighters out to more salubrious premises. His major triumph, of course, was guiding his son Joe to three consecutive Welsh ABA titles, then to the world super-middleweight championship… and then to ten years as the WBO king.

Calzaghe Sr's success did not end with his vastly talented son. He also made world champions of Enzo Maccarinelli and Gavin Rees, whose victory over WBA light-welterweight champion Souleymane M'baye was one of the upsets of 2007.

Scott Harrison, a strong, rugged fighter who twice held the WBO featherweight title, was also trained by his father, Peter, himself a former Scottish amateur international and national professional champion. The relationship worked well.

MANAGERS

The importance of good management is also one of the game's constants. The roles of promoter and manager are often blurred in the modern game, where old-style independent managers, negotiating fiercely with rival promoters to secure the best deal for their fighter, are the exception rather than the rule. In the era before TV cash attracted entrepreneurs like Don King and Bob Arum into the business, managers acted like theatrical agents, hustling their clients' talent around the industry and bargaining for their services. There were "front" managers then as now, the difference being that in America they would be fronting for the Mob, while in the modern era they front for big-name promoters, who have gained the exclusive services of the boxers by signing them to long-term, multi-fight contracts.

Some manage to avoid this form of commitment, but it takes enormous nerve and a lot of talent to maintain independence. Ray Leonard looked outside boxing for guidance, and placed his future in the hands of a lawyer, Mike Trainer, who was not hamstrung by the sport's customs or conventions and approached the idea of managing a fighter as he would have done any other business proposition. The pair were brilliantly successful, making Leonard enormously wealthy yet allowing him to dictate to the big promoters and TV networks rather than the other way round. Rock Newman did a similar service for Riddick Bowe, remaining stubbornly a free agent yet still managing to steer Bowe to the heavyweight championship. Roy Jones, the former IBF super-middleweight and WBC light-heavyweight champion, also consistently refused to grant any promoter options on his future fights, but his talent was so immense that, with the aid of two lawyers as advisers, he became one of the hottest properties in boxing.

Most managers, though, either double as promoters or else have close – often exclusive – links with a major promoter. Thus, for example, Lou Duva manages fighters, but his family group, Main Events, do the promoting. Carl King has been "manager of record" for a host of world champions, but the chances of any of them appearing on a show promoted by one of Don King's rivals are laughably slight.

In Britain, the main promoters – Frank Warren, Frank Maloney and Barry Hearn – also manage their own extensive stables of boxers, who appear on their shows or those of their provincial associates. It is rare indeed for boxers from one camp to appear on another's promotions, unless a championship is involved. The small-time managers tend to serve as "feeders" to the major operators, with their boxers generally used as "fodder" to fatten the record of the promoter's rising stars.

In the old days, the business was very different. Managers like Doc Kearns, who looked after a host of champions such as Jack Dempsey, Mickey Walker and Archie Moore, became major personalities in their own right, even if many of the business deals they struck either on their own behalf or for their clients would be considered wildly unethical today. Kearns was a larger-than-life character who worked his way through several fortunes, at least one of them his own. Jack Dempsey, his most successful fighter, recalled him in this way in his autobiography: "Jack Kearns was not the type of guy to sit still and watch the world go by. He tackled just about anything, whether it was acceptable or not. He was a crafty alligator, a real slicker, as expert at making a fortune as losing one. He was a man who connived for success, and any method was good enough just so long as it worked."

Kearns and Dempsey were at loggerheads as often as they were bosom pals, but overall Kearns did a good job for his man. So, too, did Billy Gibson, who steered Gene Tunney to the championship he acquired at Dempsey's expense. Tunney was an exceptionally bright and shrewd individual, and Gibson probably would not have been able to cheat him even had he wanted to.

Kearns took over Archie Moore's management at a time when Moore's career was apparently drifting towards its conclusion. Moore had been a top contender for years, first at middleweight and then at light-heavyweight, but was just too good for his own good: successive champions in both divisions gave him the cold shoulder. Kearns managed Joey Maxim, a competent but colourless performer who held the light-heavyweight title, and he saw Moore as a much more marketable commodity. He moved in on the fighter's then-manager, Charley Johnson, and bought his contract on exceptionally favourable terms, and then promptly matched him with Maxim. Whatever the outcome, Kearns would be a winner.

Not all managers were so mercenary. Cus D'Amato was never motivated primarily by money when he was developing the skills of Floyd Patterson, Jose Torres or the teenage Mike Tyson: he was searching for the perfect fighting machine, and it was his tragedy that, having discovered him in Tyson, he

Frank Maloney: *The British promoter's career will forever be linked with that of world heavyweight champion Lennox Lewis, whom he managed for 12 years*

MICKEY DUFF *and Lloyd Honeyghan had a volatile but very successful partnership, peaking with the world welterweight championship*

died before his protégé's talent had flowered. D'Amato cherished his independence above everything else, even at a time when the International Boxing Club under Jim Norris enjoyed a virtual monopoly on world championship fights. D'Amato refused to do business with the IBC, since he knew that there were more shadowy and sinister figures than Norris involved, and he performed an astonishing feat of managerial skill to bring Patterson through the ranks to the heavyweight championship.

He kept him champion by matching him with a selection of no-hopers in well-paid defences, which after all is a manager's first responsibility to his charge. When Sonny Liston emerged as leading contender, D'Amato opposed the match so strongly that Patterson, his professional pride stung, broke with his mentor and insisted on taking the fight anyway, with disastrous consequences.

In Britain, as in America, the contrast between caring and callous managers was striking. Ted Broadribb's daughter Chrissie married Freddie Mills, yet Broadribb matched Mills in one brutal fight after another until the fighter was spent. Perhaps the consequences of absorbing repeated poundings was not as widely understood then as it is now, but it remains hard to believe that Broadribb could watch his man take a merciless beating from Gus Lesnevich in a world light-heavyweight title challenge on May 14, 1946, and then put him in with British heavyweight champion Bruce Woodcock in a tough 12-rounder on June 4.

The other side of the coin was Jim "The Bishop" Wicks, who guided Henry Cooper throughout his long career. Wicks involved Cooper in every stage of the deals he made on his behalf, usually insisting that Cooper attend his meetings with the rival promoters who were bidding for his services. Wicks' concern was always to get the best deal going for "My 'Enery", as he always called him, and he did his job so well that Cooper retired a wealthy man and remained friends with his old manager until Wicks' death.

Such a close relationship between manager and boxer is unusual. Mickey Duff, himself a hugely successful manager and promoter, summed up his role perfectly when he was being quizzed by a reporter about yet another dispute with his world welterweight champion, Lloyd Honeyghan. "There's nothing in our contract that says we have to like each other," Duff said, and the shades of generations of harassed managers raised ghostly glasses in agreement.

THE FAMOUS PROMOTERS

Promotion is a multi-million pound business of companies usually headed by single promoters. Barry Hearn is promoter for Matchroom, Frank Warren for Sports Network and Frank Maloney for Panix Promotions. In the USA, the business is dominated by three groups: Don King, Bob Arum (Top Rank) and the Duva family's Main Events.

In bare-knuckle days bouts were promoted by agreement between the backers of the respective pugilists. Terms would usually be thrashed out in a tavern or "sporting house" when the fight was set up. Each side would then go away to train, the prize money having already been lodged with a trusted independent. Pugilism had its own society and largely looked after itself, with varying fortunes according to the social mood of the time.

Only towards the end of the 19th century did bouts become promoted by either a single entrepreneur or an organization. The most powerful organization in early British boxing was the National Sporting Club, which established what amounted to an autocratic grip on the championship scene. They allocated the Lonsdale Belts, which were the "badges" of the British champions, and they matched men accordingly.

Before the National Sporting Club was formed in 1891 boxing was illegal, except for sparring sessions and small-time competitions in amateur clubs. Anyone caught boxing, with gloves or bare-knuckle, in a discernible competition, was arrested as a common criminal. The Pelican Club existed from 1887 to 1892 more or less as a house for gambling on bare-knuckle fights, providing for the upper classes, and the National Sporting Club was formed with similar aims, for those who considered themselves respectable gentlemen but were not of sufficient social standing to gain admittance to the Pelican Club.

However, because of the dedication of two principal members, John Fleming and A.F. "Peggy" Bettinson, the club grew in stature and drew members from the City of London and the West End. Men went to the club's Covent Garden headquarters straight from work, ate a steak or chops in the grill room, downed it with a pint of beer or three, and then settled down to watch the boxing. It increased from a gambling alternative to the Pelican to a genuine "organizer" of all things appertaining to boxing. It gave British boxing a firm base, although gradually Fleming and Bettinson chased the favours of a wealthier clientele to add greater financial stability and so took it further away from its original supporters.

When the Pelican Club closed, the NSC moved "up-market". This, of course, took boxing away from the common man, but it did afford it a more powerful social standing. And this in turn enabled it to survive the death of Walter Croot of Leytonstone following a fight with Jimmy Barry of Chicago at the club in 1897. Calls for the club to be closed down were resisted, but the crisis deepened as four boxers died there in the space of four years. The arguments then were pretty much the same as they are now. Bettinson took the "accidents will happen" line, while the critics said such accidents could not happen if boxers didn't box. But the club was so well established that in a test case at the Old Bailey in 1901 boxing received the tacit backing of the law. The jury took only two minutes to decide that the death of a boxer named Billy Smith was an accident and the result of a legitimate boxing contest, not a prize-fight. By the time the National Sporting Club closed its doors in 1929, boxing was established as a national sport.

As boxing grew in popularity in the early years of the century, so its business expanded beyond the doors of the NSC. And try as they might, they could not control either the earning power of the boxers or the matches that were made.

By 1910 the old champion Dick Burge was promoting at the Blackfriars Ring, a former chapel in south London. He regularly drew packed houses and in 1914 was established enough to promote a huge fight between Georges Carpentier and Gunboat Smith at Olympia. Burge died of pneumonia in 1918 and his widow Bella continued promoting shows at The Ring until the Second World War broke out. In October 1940 the Ring was blown to rubble by a German bomb.

Solomons wisdom

Premierland and Manor Hall were popular venues in the 20s and in 1931 a fishmonger named Jack Solomons began promoting at an old church in Devonshire Street, Hackney, in north London. He called it the Devonshire Club. Solomons lost £275 – a small fortune in those days – on an over-ambitious first promotion at the Clapton Stadium when he staged a British bantamweight title fight between Johnny King and Dick Corbett.

Solomons went on to be one of the greatest boxing promoters in history, taking over from men like Jeff Dickson and Sydney Hulls, primarily because of his success with one of the greatest crowd pleasers of the day, the Chatteris lightweight Eric "Boy" Boon, who was so good he won a Lonsdale Belt outright before his 20th birthday.

Solomons fell out with the Board of Control at one point and handed back his licence, continuing to promote without one. The Board, as a self-appointed body, could do nothing to stop him. Solomons and Hulls worked together on major shows, and eventually he grew to be the dominant force in British, indeed European boxing, staging all the great outdoor shows in the post-war boom. His first major success was the Jack London-Bruce Woodcock British heavyweight title fight at White Hart Lane football ground in front of an official crowd of 26,479 in 1945.

"I made £400 profit," Solomons recalled in his autobiography. "Far, far more important to me was the fact that at long last I had laid the foundations of Solomons Promotions. I was in, and I meant to stay in."

Solomons saw off all rivals for the next decade and a half, putting on classics involving Woodcock, Freddie Mills and the greatest night in all those post-War years, the 1951 world middleweight title bout between Sugar Ray Robinson and Randy Turpin at Earls Court in London.

Eventually Solomons was challenged by Harry Levene in the 1960s and was superseded, retreating to the World Sporting Club, a dinner and boxing establishment at a Mayfair hotel, and branching out only occasionally with men like the British heavyweight champion Danny McAlinden.

Levene and his partners Mike Barrett, Mickey Duff, Jarvis Astaire and, later, Terry Lawless were in control by the late 1960s and established themselves as one of the major forces in world boxing in the 1970s. They promoted such world champions as John Conteh, Alan Minter, Jim Watt, Maurice Hope, John H. Stracey and, in the 1980s, Charlie Magri and Cornelius Boza-Edwards.

Frank Warren and ITV

Their dominance was such that they virtually monopolized boxing shows on BBC television. And because of that, they were able to hold all challengers to their supremacy at bay. That stranglehold was broken only by the interest shown by ITV in the early 1980s when they supported the brash young north London promoter Frank Warren, who had previously operated outside the British Board of Control.

Warren shook the boxing establishment to its core, challenging its rulings repeatedly and eventually forcing the Board to take out membership of the World Boxing Association. Since the formation of the World Boxing Council in 1962, the British Board had allied itself to the WBC and ignored the rival body, the WBA. No British boxer of the time was allowed to fight for a WBA belt.

Warren, however, challenged even that status quo – and, as always, with no legal standing, the Board were forced to accept not only him, but the WBA and any other world bodies that chose to introduce themselves. Eventually, this led to "world" title fights approved by the International Boxing Federation, the World Boxing Organization and even the virtually meaningless World Boxing Federation being staged in Britain.

Warren and ITV opened up British boxing in the 1980s until by the end of the decade it was more or less a free market. His first world champion was the IBF light-welterweight champion Terry Marsh

JACK SOLOMONS *was the leading British promoter in the 1940s and '50s*

THE FAMOUS BOXING ARENAS

White City

Boxing was big business in Britain in the years after the Second World War, and promoter Jack Solomons regularly drew crowds like this to his open-air shows at White City Stadium in west London. The stadium was home to the athletics events in the 1908 Olympic Games, and was used primarily for athletic meetings (many world records were broken there) and greyhound racing, although it also hosted some of the games in the 1966 football World Cup. It was demolished in the late 1980s.

THE FAMOUS BOXING ARENAS

Royal Albert Hall

Virtually every British world champion from the 1960s onwards boxed at the the Royal Albert Hall. It has always been a popular venue – Jack "Kid" Berg won his world light-welterweight title there in 1930. For nearly 20 years, from the mid-1960s to the mid-1980s, Mickey Duff and Mike Barrett had exclusive promotional rights, and ran shows there at least once a month.

and he went on to promote some of the biggest names in boxing: Nigel Benn, Frank Bruno, Steve Collins, Colin McMillan, Steve Robinson and Naseem Hamed were all world champions in the 1990s.

Meanwhile, snooker impresario Barry Hearn brought his Matchroom organization into boxing in the late 1980s, beginning with a stake in the lucrative 1987 fight between Bruno and veteran Joe Bugner. Hearn forged links with ITV and also branched out into the new satellite market, working with the ill-fated Screensport channel as well as Eurosport through his own series, Pro-Box.

Hearn's major success was in the shape of the eccentric but talented Chris Eubank, who was WBO middleweight and super-middleweight champion through more than 20 title fights, a record for a British boxer. Hearn and Eubank negotiated a 12-month deal worth a reported £10 million with the major satellite channel Sky Sports. Eubank's demise in 1995 sparked a split with Hearn, but the promoter continued to flourish, guiding WBO welterweight champion Eamonn Loughran and the former WBO heavyweight title holder Herbie Hide.

BSkyB became a major player as television's hold on boxing increased in the 1990s. Its Sky Sports channel and pay-per-view arm took over from 1996 as the leading outlet for the sport in the United Kingdom, with ITV losing interest not long after their leading promoter, Frank Warren, accepted an exclusive deal with Sky. For a while they had co-existed, with Warren working in association with Don King to produce some major championship nights for ITV, topped by the great but tragic contest between Nigel Benn and Gerald McClellan in 1995. It was Sky who had covered the world heavyweight championship fights of Lennox Lewis, with the exception of the night he lost it first time around to Oliver McCall in 1994. Sky broadcast Lewis' title defence against Frank Bruno in Cardiff Arms Park, and also Bruno's world title-winning display against McCall in 1995 and his defeat by Mike Tyson in 1996.

By the end of the decade Sky had effectively wiped out their opposition. Audley Harrison's Olympic gold medal win in Sydney in 2000 tempted the BBC to return to boxing, but the £1 million contract they gave the effectively self-promoted Harrison, which included the power to make his own matches, was not conducive to competitive sport. As Harrison's career went nowhere very slowly, the BBC's interest waned and they did not renew his contract.

When Warren's relationship with Sky broke down in 2005, he renewed his old relationship with ITV and took his fighters, the most important of which was Joe Calzaghe, with him. However, the prize catch, Ricky Hatton, who had been promoted by Warren since his professional debut in 1997, opted to leave him for a more independent life, with a new promoter, Dennis Hobson and his American partner Art Pelullo. Hatton remained with Sky, who began to spread their net. They had worked with Barry Hearn's Matchroom organization since the mid-90s, and then offered dates to other promoters.

By 2007 they were also providing opportunities for Frank Maloney, who had worked for Warren's Sports Network organiza-

BARRY HEARNS *celebrates Chris Eubank's victory over Henry Wharton in Manchester in 1994*

tion for some years, following his time as manager of Lennox Lewis, and also to a newer promoter, Mick Hennessy.

Tex Rickard

In the USA, where power transferred from Britain towards the end of the bare-knuckle era, promoters have often seemed larger-than-life figures. "Sunny Jim" Coffroth was the best of the promoters in the early years of the century. He was a Californian entrepreneur who staged the Jack Johnson-Stanley Ketchel world heavyweight title fight in Colma, just outside San Francisco, in 1909.

Coffroth was an opportunist, not above guiding a boxer to act in both of their interests. For example, he is said to have told Johnson to hold Ketchel up because he was having the fight filmed and didn't want it killed at the box office by a quick ending. Johnson was knocked down in the 12th round, and got up to flatten the middleweight Ketchel with his next attack. The film sold rapidly, giving Coffroth a lucrative bonus.

Coffroth and his arch rival "Tuxedo" Eddie Graney, the man who refereed the last three of Jim Jeffries' title defences in San Francisco, thought they had only each other to worry about when the Johnson-Jeffries bout was up for grabs in 1910. In those days negotiations were different to those of today. Jeffries and Johnson agreed to fight each other and then threw it open to offers from promoters, which were opened in a hotel in Hoboken, New Jersey.

TEX RICKARD *He became the world's best-known promoter*

Other promoters present apart from Coffroth and Graney were Tom McCarey, who had worked with Johnson in the past out of the Pacific Club in Los Angeles, Hugh McIntosh, the Australian who had staged the incredible Johnson-Tommy Burns fight in Rushcutter's Bay near Sydney, and a newcomer George Lewis (also known as Tex) Rickard. To general amazement when the bids were opened the winning bid was made by Rickard, who guaranteed the boxers $101,000 and two-thirds of the movie rights. Each fighter would also get a $10,000 bonus for just signing for the contest.

Rickard was backed by a Minnesota millionaire named Thomas Cole, who owned silver and gold mines in the USA and Alaska. Rickard had previously promoted a lightweight title fight between the great Joe Gans and Battling Nelson, which lasted 42 rounds in Goldfield, Nevada, where Tex had a gambling saloon at the time.

He was a gambler by nature and had already won and lost fortunes in gaming houses and business deals when he struck it rich with the Johnson-Jeffries fight (which he refereed himself), which became known as the Fight of the Century, even though the century was but a decade old. But it was Jack Dempsey and the Roaring Twenties that made Tex Rickard into one of the greatest, perhaps the greatest, boxing promoter in history.

Paul Gallico, who made his name as a sports writer before moving into "serious" literature, said Rickard understood how to make money work. "He knew how to exhibit it, use it, spend it..." Rickard knew that by paying out big money, he attracted big attention. If his fighters looked as if they were wealthy, then they drew the attention of the wealthy... and Rickard himself could feed off that and increase his business, and that of his fighters, by association alone.

Through Tex Rickard as much as through his own fists, Jack Dempsey became a "somebody". Other men before him had held the heavyweight championship of the world, but nobody had made it work for him the way Dempsey did. In his autobiography *Massacre In The Sun*, the world champ said: "We never had a contract. You didn't need one with Tex Rickard. He was the great man of my life. They don't make them like Rickard any more... I hadn't met a promoter before who gave a damn whether I lived or croaked."

Rickard promoted Dempsey's major fights from the day in the blazing sun of Toledo, Ohio, when he destroyed Jess Willard in three rounds to the night in the pouring rain of Philadelphia when 120,757 packed themselves into the Sesquicentennial Stadium to see Dempsey lose the title to Gene Tunney. Rickard promoted the first fight to gross $1 million, Dempsey's defence against Georges Carpentier at Boyle's Thirty Acres in Jersey City, New Jersey. Around 91,000 fans showed up and shelled out an official $1,626,580.

The only one of Dempsey's title defences not promoted by Rickard was the 15-rounder with Tommy Gibbons in Shelby, Montana, which was financed by a haphazard conglomerate of local businessmen. The town was more or less ruined and the challenger, Gibbons, went 15 rounds for nothing because hardly anyone turned up and most of those who did somehow omitted to pay at the gate. Rickard died of peritonitis in Miami in January 1929, leaving a

THE FAMOUS BOXING ARENAS

Madison Square Garden

The funeral cortege of Joe Humphreys, the best-known boxing MC of his time, pauses outside Madison Square Garden, New York, in July 1936. This was the second Garden: the original, built in 1882 and rebuilt only eight years later, occupied a site in Madison Square. It was pulled down in 1925, and Tex Rickard erected the building shown here on 8th Avenue. In 1968, the latest Garden opened at 7th and 31st, opposite Penn Station.

huge hole in boxing's finances.

The 1930s were a poor time for everybody. The Wall Street Crash ruined investment plans the world over. Money was scarce. Jimmy Johnston promoted men like Jack Sharkey and then became matchmaker at Madison Square Garden in 1931. But it fell to Mike Jacobs, a former ticket hustler and wheeler-dealer who used to work Rickard's fights to take boxing into a new era. Johnston was one of many who believed black fighters couldn't sell tickets. The bad publicity generated by Jack Johnson's seven-year reign had also prejudiced boxing promoters, Rickard included, against using black heavyweights in particular.

Consequently, when Joe Louis came along, Johnston didn't want to know. But Jacobs, already tipped off about his remarkable ability by the editor of *Ring* magazine, Nat Fleischer, showed no such bias. As Louis himself was to recall: "Mike had no prejudice about a man's colour so long as he could make a green buck for him." Louis' managers Julian Black and John Roxborough signed the young man over to Jacobs' Twentieth Century Sporting Club and the partnership lasted for the next decade and a half.

Jacobs staged all of Louis' title fights, eventually also working out of Madison Square Garden and establishing himself as the most powerful boxing figure in the world from the late 1930s all the way through to the end of the next decade. "Uncle Mike" was old and ill when Joe Louis switched his attention to the newly formed International Boxing Club owned by millionaires Jim Norris and Arthur Wirtz in 1949. They bought Louis' attention, and persuaded him to retire in return for an annual salary of $20,000. They also bought Jacobs out as Madison Square Garden matchmaker, then helped Louis launch his comeback and bought out all the major contenders. Eventually they persuaded Louis to take one last fight against Rocky Marciano, whom they were also pushing, and just as Rickard and Jacobs prospered because of Dempsey and Louis the IBC blossomed because of its control of Marciano, who reigned as world heavyweight champion from 1952 to 1956. However, when the US government won an anti-trust law case against the IBC it was forced to disband. Norris fought on to the end of the decade, but by then the IBC had faded as a viable promotional force.

New Governing Bodies

In 1962, the World Boxing Association was formed, quickly followed by its rival, the World Boxing Council, in what was at least partially an attempt to prevent any single promoter obtaining absolute power again. And for a while, at least, it looked as if it would work. The governing bodies controlled the championship bouts and ensured different promoters got a fair crack… or so it seemed.

However, the governing bodies fell some way short of the ideal. The weakness of the theory is simple – it relies on integrity and on a completely unbiased sense of fair play for it to work. If deep working relationships were formed between boxing promoters and the governing bodies, then the system becomes open to favouritism and prejudice. Some promoters, inevitably, become more powerful than others – and not simply because of their ability to conduct their businesses successfully. There was, of course, nothing to stop anybody setting up a world boxing authority, but it took until the early 1980s for a third organization to come into being.

The major promoters of the late 1970s were Bob Arum, a New York lawyer, and Don King, who had risen from the streets of Cleveland, Ohio, where he had once worked as a numbers man, and who had served time for killing a man. (He was later pardoned.) King formed a working relationship with WBC president Jose Sulaiman, who assumed a level of control within the organization that many perceived to be beyond the duties expected from a man in his position. But as undemocratic as the system appeared, it worked.

The WBA was accused of corruption by Arum in 1982 when, in an interview with *Ring* magazine, he admitted paying a bagman, a Puerto Rican named Pepe Cordero, to "get things done" in the WBA. The flaws in the governing body system became exposed, and the increased influence of television enabled a new authority, the International Boxing Federation, to grow out of foundations laid by a disenchanted number of WBA members who walked out of an annual convention in frustration at being unable to make changes they felt were necessary. Bobby Lee of New Jersey ran the IBF, with the help of his son Bobby Jnr. The hunger of television companies for world championships enabled first the IBF to obtain TV revenue and then, in 1988, for the WBO to do the same. The WBO was formed by none other than Pepe Cordero, who had himself become fed up with the WBA.

The proliferation of world title bouts in this time was quite staggering. In 1963 there were 20. In 1973 there were 40. In 1993 there were 140! By then the dominant world promoters were King and Arum and South African Cedric Kushner, who worked predominantly with the IBF. In 1993, Kushner promoted 21 world title fights either solely or in association with minor promoters. King and Arum promoted 20 and 17 respectively. Barry Hearn's Matchroom organization was a party to 14 championship bouts, while the Duvas' Main Events team had 12. This was a bad year for the Duvas. In the four-year period from 1990 to 1993, Kushner promoted 71, Dan Duva 69, Bob Arum 61, and Don King 47. King had business problems in this period following the controversial defeat of Mike Tyson by Buster Douglas in Tokyo in February 1990, and his figure was low because he was in a rebuilding period at the time.

Cedric Kushner is a South African who made his first significant money as a promoter of rock concerts. But, by 1985, he was firmly established as one of the rising stars in boxing and today,

THE FAMOUS BOXING ARENAS

Caesars Palace

Caesars Palace (the missing apostrophe is deliberate), in Las Vegas, has hosted some of the greatest fights of the last 30 years in its famous outdoor arena. Marvin Hagler battled Thomas Hearns, John Mugabi and Sugar Ray Leonard there, and Leonard won his epic welterweight title clash with Hearns at Caesars. Larry Holmes won his WBC title in the indoor arena behind the major stadium, and retained it against Muhammad Ali on an emotional night there. Caesars Palace also hosted all three of the Riddick Bowe vs Evander Holyfield classics.

DON KING *(left) rose to power on the back of Muhammad Ali, but stayed there on merit*

based in New York State, he is one of the most powerful men in the boxing business.

Main Events was the company of the Duva family led by extrovert patriarch Lou. They made their name with pay-per-view shows in the 1980s and by signing several of the members of the successful American team from the 1984 Olympic Games in Los Angeles. For many years they were linked with Evander Holyfield and Pernell Whitaker, and later Main Events became the American promoters of Lennox Lewis. The death of Lou's son, Dan, from a brain tumour at the age of 44, in January 1996 was a tragic loss. Eventually the business divided into Main Events and Duva Boxing.

Don King roadshow

Don King continues to carve his own path. "Jail was my school," he said of the four years he spent in prison from 1967 to 1971 for the manslaughter of a man named Sam Garrett, whom he had suspected of cheating him on a numbers deal. King managed heavyweight Earnie Shavers and, in 1974, worked as a consultant on the videoing of the George Foreman-Ken Norton fight. But he really launched himself because of his association with Muhammad Ali, which superseded that of Ali and Bob Arum, and he came to dominate the heavyweight division through Larry Holmes in the first half of the 1980s. He also bought up most of the top ten heavyweights and so controlled who fought for the championship. The WBC rarely, if ever, chose to work with another promoter as long as King wanted to be in on the fight. The relationship was perceived as unhealthy, but that was the way it was.

The arrival of Mike Tyson under co-managers Jim Jacobs and Bill Cayton threatened King's heavyweight supremacy, but Jacobs' untimely death altered the situation. Tyson and Cayton were never close and by 1988 the young champion had switched allegiance to King. His empire continued to prosper until Tyson's shocking defeat at the hands of James Buster Douglas in Tokyo. Douglas successfully bought himself out of his promotional contract with King in the courts, and promptly lost the title to the Main Events fighter, Evander Holyfield.

King was thus in the heavyweight wilderness for the first half of the 1990s and therefore was forced to concentrate his attentions on the lighter divisions, focusing in particular on the Mexican superstar Julio Cesar Chavez.

By the late 1990s, though, Tyson was out of jail and King was promoting Holyfield, too. He was the main promoter behind the lucrative 1999 drawn fight between Holyfield and Lennox Lewis, although the verdict once more brought King huge criticism. A state investigation into the decision produced a lot of accusations, but no firm evidence. King was associated with British promoter Frank Warren, and together they staged Frank Bruno's WBC heavyweight title win over Oliver McCall in 1995. But the partnership ended in court, with Warren being ordered to pay $12 million in settlement.

King survived wire fraud charges against an insurance company – the case was heard twice after the first attempt ended in a stalemate – and even in his late 60s remained one of the hardest-working, and certainly the noisiest, promoters in history.

Arum, the son of a New York accountant, graduated from Harvard Law School in 1956. He has been involved with boxing since 1962 when he was working for the United States Attorney's Office in New York and was involved when the Internal Revenue Service impounded the revenue from the closed circuit rights to the first Floyd Patterson-Sonny Liston fight. Arum liked what he saw and got involved, promoting several of Muhammad Ali's world championship bouts before Ali was stripped of the title in 1967 for refusing to fight in Vietnam.

Arum promoted Ali's comeback fights from 1970 and in the 1990s promoted the marketable Oscar De La Hoya. Eventually, after they fell out, De La Hoya, while still fighting, formed Golden Boy Promotions and used links with Bernard Hopkins and Ricky Hatton to build a network of fighters across the globe to emerge as possibly the major promoter in world boxing. HBO's decision to end their relationship in 2013 was a massive blow.

THE ADMINISTRATION OF BOXING

Boxing is one of the few major international sports that is not run by a simple, regulatory body – it has at least four, each of whom install their own "world champions". Anarchy rules, but then there's nothing new about that...

In the days before any so-called world governing bodies existed there were usually just eight world champions, acknowledged by their peers and by the fans as the best at their weight. Today, there are four widely accepted ruling bodies and a myriad of minor organizations each with their own champion in 17 weight divisions. At least half the names in any listing of the top ten in each division can claim to be "world champion" in their category, while the champions of some of the lunatic fringe organizations would struggle to command a place among an impartially assessed top 50 in their division, let alone the top ten. A state of near-anarchy prevails, and since it is profitable for all concerned, that is how it will remain.

By the 1990s only the purists, those with a feel for the history of the game, were offended by the proliferation of the titles, but gradually, as the picture grew increasingly confusing, the perception altered. In Britain, supposed world championship contests were allowed involving new private businesses like the World Boxing Union (run from a home in Norfolk, then Cambridgeshire), the World Boxing Federation, which changed its name to World Boxing Foundation after being sued by one of its former champions, and the International Boxing Organization, based in Florida. In the end, the signs were that the public, as well as media executives, were becoming fed up with the fare on offer, as promoters found it easier to do business with less-established "governing" bodies, who were keen to make their mark. While this was harsh on the IBO, who had sponsored computerized ratings in an effort to establish some kind of impartiality on the process of ranking boxers, it was perhaps inevitable. However, when Frank Warren and Sky parted company, he continued to promote WBU fights on the terrestrial, non-sports-dedicated ITV channel.

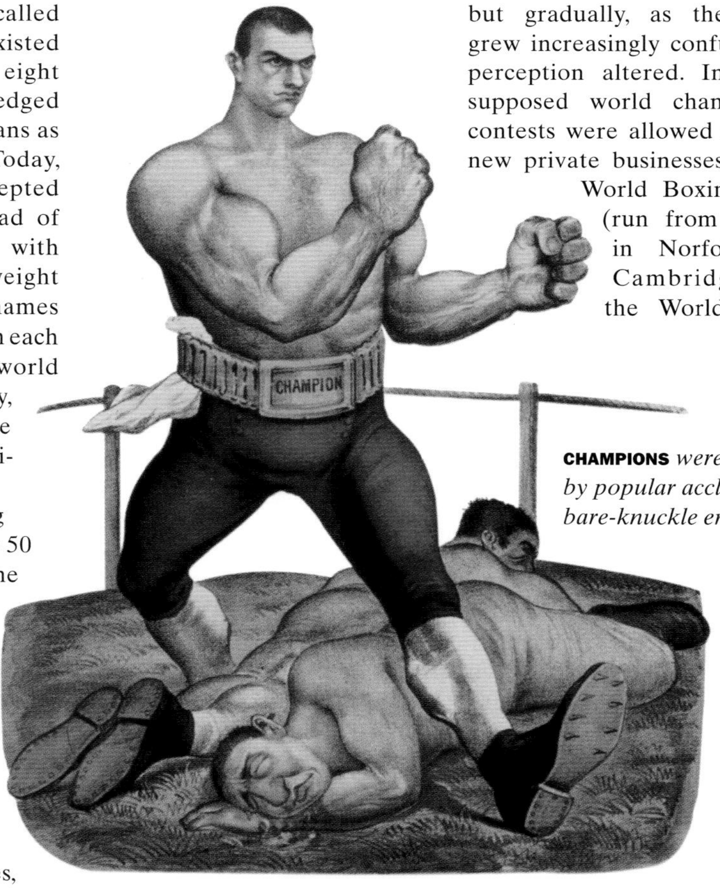

CHAMPIONS *were appointed by popular acclaim in the bare-knuckle era*

In the United States, in spite of the continuing vagaries of the so-called "Big Three" – the World Boxing Council, the World Boxing Association and the International Boxing Federation – there was no more energy available to deal

CHAOS DESCENDS *as cameramen, photographers and assorted nonentities pile in to the ring after Mike Tyson's defeat of Razor Ruddock in 1991*

with the situation of the sanctioning bodies. HBO, the major payer in American televised boxing, did its best to ignore them and concentrate on providing good value fights. Because of this, the crucial area of the USA was not open to advancement by one of the lesser organizations or to change. There was evidence aplenty that by the middle of the first decade of the 21st century the IBF, for example, had lost all credibility. (It had ended the 20th century with its founder and president Bobby Lee in disgrace after financial and corruption scandals). The IBF was forced by government watchdogs to apply its rules rigorously – but they seemed too quick to strip champions of the titles they had won in the ring. However, in spite of this loss of credibility, the IBF still clung on to power and there was insufficient flexibility to allow a newer, more rounded organization like, for example the IBO, to make its own mark and perhaps change the business for the better.

The Power of the Press

There is nothing new about the media influencing boxing, or the appointment of its champions. In the days before television, Commissions or Boards of Control, it was the print press who formed public opinion as to the merits of rival claimants. In bare-knuckle Britain Pierce Egan's *Boxiana* and, later, Henry Downes Miles' *Pugilistica* recorded their deeds and traced the course of the championships, while in America, in the last quarter of the 19th century, as prize-fighting grew in popularity there, Richard Kyle Fox's *Police Gazette* fulfilled the same function. Fox was a Dubliner who emigrated to America in 1871 when he was 29. Like so many of his countrymen, he brought nothing with him but an eagerness to work and a hunger for advancement, and within two years he had saved half of the $400 needed to buy a discredited and failing scandal sheet called the *National Police Gazette*.

Fox proved a publishing genius, and quickly turned the paper's fortunes around. He had a flair for imaginative sales gimmicks, designed to boost public awareness of his ten-cent product. In addition to giving away more than $250,000 in cash prizes, he awarded a whole range of belts, trophies and cups commemorating the most bizarre and obscure achievements of the type which today are chronicled in the *Guinness Book of Records*. But the real key to his success was that he was the first newspaper publisher to identify and service the public's craving for sports news. He introduced a full sports section, and the leap in circulation that followed convinced rival publishers to do likewise.

Fox appreciated that prize-fighting was among the most popular sports with his readership, even though it was still illegal in all the (then) 38 states of America. He concentrated his coverage on fights and races, and soon the *Gazette* had attained a position of influence and power in the sport unmatched by any other publication until *Ring* magazine was founded in 1922. It was so successful there was even a British edition, which was launched in 1896. In the same year he published the first of his annual record books, which continued until a fire in 1918 unfortunately destroyed the paper's offices and all its records.

Changing public tastes, coupled with the competition from *Ring,* finally killed the *Police Gazette* off in 1932. But it had served a worthwhile purpose, and in the years before boxing was legalized and the various states set up Athletic Commissions to regulate it, the *Gazette* effectively controlled the sport in America and had a large say in who the public regarded as champions.

Ring, under the editorship of its founder Nat Fleischer, became recognized as the sport's most authoritative voice, for two reasons. Fleischer made it his policy to record the result of every fight, however obscure, in tiny type at the back of the magazine, thus making it compulsory reading for the serious fan; and, more importantly, he introduced the first monthly ratings of the top ten in each division, which rapidly acquired quasi-official status and were enormously influential in determining a boxer's progress towards a title fight.

It is no exaggeration to say that, in the years before any of the present controlling bodies emerged, the *Ring* ratings effectively governed world championships. It was unheard of for a man to get a title fight if he was not in the magazine's top ten, and fans around the world would eagerly chart their favourite's progress up the lists month by month.

The early ratings were compiled by Tex Rickard, the leading promoter of the time. He was an odd choice by Fleischer, rather like the World Boxing Council entrusting their ratings to Don King, and Rickard would have needed to be a saint not to be swayed in his judgements by promotional considerations. Given a choice between advancing a fighter from, say, Nebraska, who was not under his control and a contender from New York who drew large crowds to his promotions, the New Yorker would get the vote every time. Fleischer eventually took over the ratings himself, and they retained a high level of accuracy and impartiality until his death in 1972.

HOW THE *POLICE GAZETTE*, *the most influential sports paper of its time, saw the Sullivan–Kilrain fight in 1889*

New York vs. The NBA

New York was ideally placed to dictate the course of world boxing. At the turn of the century it was the business and sporting capital of America, with a number of purpose-built arenas that were suitable to stage boxing. The original Madison Square Garden, whose name was to become synonymous with the sport, hosted its first prize-fight in 1882. It was rebuilt in 1890, and staged its last show (with Sid Terris beating Johnny Dundee over 12 rounds) on 5 May 1925. Tex Rickard built the new Garden, and opened it on 11 December 1925 with a world light-heavyweight title fight between Paul Berlanbach and Jack Delaney. In the following decades, notably under the promotional reign of Mike

Jacobs, the Garden was boxing's headquarters, and an appearance there was the summit of a fighter's career. The outdoor stadia, like the Polo Grounds and Yankee Stadium, would also become as well-known for boxing shows as for the sport which they were built to house.

There were other factors that helped make New York pre-eminent. The country's leading newspapers (and, later, its radio stations) were based there, as were most of the prominent promoters and managers. As the century progressed, the city's importance in boxing terms grew. Since it was the first point of entry to the United States, most of the prominent European boxers appeared there and some, like Englishman Jack "Kid" Berg, became major attractions.

Boxing was legalized in the state in 1900 when the Horton Law, permitting shows in members-only clubs, was passed. Predictably, the law proved unworkable, since membership would be granted to anyone purchasing a ticket for the fight. In 1911 it was replaced by the Frawley Law, permitting boxing to take place freely provided no points decision was awarded and the fights did not exceed ten rounds in duration. The New York State Athletic Commission also came into being in 1911, but did not take over the administration of boxing until 1920 when the Walker Law ended the No Decision era in the state (although various other states continued to enforce their own version of the Frawley Law until later in the decade.)

The New York Commission was the first of its kind in America, and soon established itself as a firm ruling body by stripping Johnny Kilbane of his featherweight title because of his failure to defend it, and by regularizing the weight limits for all the divisions to bring them into line with the rest of the world. They also approved a new weight class, the junior lightweight class (130lb) although this did not gain acceptance outside America. Other local controlling bodies around the world began to follow New York's leads, and whoever the NYSAC recognized as world champion was usually also regarded as such in Britain and, after the collapse of the International Boxing Union, in Europe generally.

But New York's domination was viewed with suspicion and envy in other states where the sport flourished, and in 1920 representatives of 13 states came together to establish the rival National Boxing Association. The choice of venue for the meeting was ironic, in several senses: they gathered at the Flatiron Building in New York. The meeting was called by an Englishman, William A. Gavin. He had his own agenda – he wanted to set up an International Sporting Club in the city to be run on the same lines as London's National Sporting Club, which was effectively the controlling body in British boxing at the time. Gavin's project never got off the ground, but the NBA did and over the next 40 years it grew in both strength and influence.

The NBA frequently opposed the New York choice as world champion, and (particularly in the 1930s) split titles were commonplace as the two organizations vied for supremacy. New York usually won, and when the European Boxing Union was formed in 1948 and allied itself with New York and Britain, the NBA struggled to keep pace. But the coming of the television age weakened New York's unique position. Now, fights could be staged anywhere, and when the Las Vegas casinos discovered boxing, or vice versa, the city's glory days were over. Suddenly, Las Vegas was the new hub of the sport, and New York, almost overnight, was reduced to the status of a fringe player.

Apart from a spurt of activity in the early 1970s (when, continuing Jack "Kid" Berg's tradition, Ken Buchanan of Scotland was the house favourite), the Garden ceased to host regular big-time boxing, and with the decline of the small fight clubs in the city, which in the 1940s and '50s staged four or five shows a week, boxing became a side show. The Felt Forum, a small arena in the basement of the latest Madison Square Garden, continued to stage regular minor shows, but the balance of power in American boxing had shifted, permanently, westwards to Nevada.

MIKE JACOBS, *boxing's top promoter in the 1930s and '40s*

The Rise of the Alphabet Boys

In August 1962, at its annual convention in Tacoma, Washington, the NBA renamed itself the World Boxing Association, although its officers remained American or Canadian for the next 12 years. The new body boasted affiliations from 51 state commissions and other organizations. This was the second attempt to establish a world controlling body: in 1957 a World Championship Committee was established consisting of a representative from the NBA, the NYSAC, the European Boxing Union, and the British Boxing Board of Control, but it was unsuccessful in its well-meaning attempt to end split titles. In 1959, the NBA broke ranks when it stripped Sugar Ray Robinson of the middleweight championship for his failure to defend it against Carmen Basilio, and matched Basilio with Gene Fullmer for its version of the vacant title.

The WBA started issuing its own monthly ratings and set up a Championship Committee, and by the late 1960s had succeeded in splitting almost all the world titles. In 1974, two Panamanians, Rodrigo Sanchez and Elias Cordova, engineered a voting coup that turned the WBA into a Latin-dominated organization and removed it from American control entirely. It was a well-planned operation. The WBA constitution offered voting rights at the annual convention to delegates who represented any body that controlled boxing at any level, be it national or regional. Cordova and Sanchez imported delegates by the busload for the 1974 convention, including three from the Virgin Islands (where no boxing commission existed), six from Venezuela, four from Panama and four from El Salvador. Cordova became the new president, and Sanchez took over from his successor in 1979.

Since then the WBA has remained predominately a Latin organization, although American promoters, notably Bob Arum, worked with it extensively. Arum revealed the extent of WBA corruption in memorable interviews with *Sports Illustrated* and *Ring* magazine, in which he detailed how he had to pay large amounts in bribes to a Puerto Rican, Pepe Cordero, who held no official position whatever in the organization. To get Ray Mancini a crack at the WBA lightweight title, Arum paid Cordero $10,000 and $25,000 from each of Mancini's first three defences, and had to agree to give Cordero's fighter Ernesto Espana a title fight for a purse of $250,000, of which Cordero took a third.

The status of the WBA improved somewhat when South Africans like Mike Mortimer and Judge Klopper were elected to office. South Africa at that time was an international sporting leper because of its apartheid policy, and the WBA was the only boxing organization that would grant it membership. There was plenty of South African money to inject into the WBA coffers, particularly when the Sun City gambling resort opened, but Mortimer and Klopper were men of high integrity who did their best to combat the financial excesses.

In 1983 an American group, headed by Robert Lee of the New Jersey State Athletic Commission, attempted to regain control of the WBA. When the coup failed, Lee and his associates walked out of the convention and announced the formation of their own organization, the International Boxing Federation. They succeeded in attracting strong support from American promoters who, like Arum, resented having to pay costly sanctioning fees to the WBA, as well as the additional under-the-table demands that had become routine. The IBF also drew support from the Orient, particularly from the rapidly expanding Korean market and from the Philippines.

The British Boxing Board of Control remained aloof from both the WBA and IBF, as they had been founder-members of the World Boxing Council in 1963. Sixteen countries took part in the WBC's inaugural meeting in Mexico City on 14 February 1963, and the new body sub-divided itself into seven federations representing North America, South America, Central America/Caribbean, Europe, Africa, Britain and the Orient. Unlike the WBA, it was Latin-dominated from the start. The United States shared North America's voting rights with Mexico and Canada, and so would always be outvoted by any combination of the South and Central American votes.

The driving force behind the rapid expansion of the WBC was Jose Sulaiman, a Mexican businessman who became its president in 1975 and who enjoyed a mutually rewarding friendship with the sport's most powerful promoter, Don King. Under Sulaiman's energetic presidency the WBC grew to embrace more than 100 countries, making it easily the most significant of the rival organizations. Despite the often-justified complaints about his dictatorial methods and his constant readiness to oblige King, Sulaiman cared passionately about the sport and worked hard to improve it, particularly in the safety area. He was responsible for the reduction in the number of championship rounds from 15 to 12, which the other bodies eventually adopted, and he also set up insurance schemes for boxers and initiated medical research programmes.

JOSE SULAIMAN *became the WBC's first president in 1975*

The British Board held out against the WBA for many years, even refusing permission in 1969 for the country's best-loved champion, Henry Cooper, to challenge for the WBA version of the heavyweight title held by Jimmy Ellis. Cooper was outraged by the lack of support from his own country, and gave up his British title in protest. The Board finally relented in the early 1980s, when they were under pressure from a new organization called the National Boxing Council, whose star promoter and standard-bearer was the young and hard-pushing Londoner, Frank Warren.

Warren aimed to steer the NBC into membership of the WBA, which would then put it on the same legal footing as the BBBC and force its acceptance as a properly constituted rival body. The WBA wanted the BBBC in their fold, but were being manoeuvred into a position where they would have to grant the NBC's application – and, since the WBA constitution barred membership by two bodies from the same country, that would have put the WBA and the British Board on a collision course. Through an intermediary, Mike Mortimer approached the Board and spelt out their predicament, which finally convinced the BBBC to take membership. Shrewdly, they invited Warren to apply for a Board licence at the same time and, deprived of its leading promoter and without the prospect of international recognition, the NBC faded from the British scene.

Warren, in turn, battled successfully for the right to stage IBF title fights in Britain, and because of his persistence the Board eventually affiliated to the IBF as well. The Warren-promoted Terry Marsh won the IBF light-welterweight title, and he also promoted the super featherweight champion Barry Michael, but when they departed Warren turned his attention elsewhere and an IBF title fight in Britain is now a rarity. In contrast, the World Boxing Organization has made giant strides in Britain.

The WBO was another breakaway from the WBA, and was set up by the former WBA "bag man" Pepe Cordero, although its president was an American lawyer, Ed Levine. The organization was banned from France and Denmark after initial acceptance, but has flourished in Germany and Britain where first Barry Hearn and then Warren promoted WBO title fights. Cordero died in 1995, but the headquarters remained in Puerto Rico under the control of his son. The WBO, despite its shaky start, has greatly enhanced its status over by the efforts of outstanding champions like Marco Antonio Barrera, Oscar De La Hoya, Riddick Bowe, Chris Eubank, Naseem Hamed, Joe Calzaghe and Manny Pacquiao.

Britain and Europe

The International Boxing Union, a loose alliance of interested parties from those European countries in which boxing took place, was formed in 1911 with a view to administering European championships, but immediately set about creating its own world champions as well. Those were chaotic times, with any number of boxers claiming world titles at whatever weight best suited them, there being in those days few universally recognized limits for any category. In those circumstances, the IBU had as much right to nominate its own champions as anybody else, and it continued to do so until the outbreak of the First World War in 1914.

The IBU reappeared between the wars, principally as a means of protecting the interests of European contenders like Marcel Thil, Valentin Angelmann, Maurice Holtzer and Gustav Roth. At a convention in Rome in May 1938 the delegates agreed to withdraw recognition from their own champions, to facilitate the reunification of the titles. The IBU was then overtaken by the Second World War in 1939, and its successor, the European Boxing Union, was not formed until 1948.

Claiming the affiliation of every European country in which boxing is staged, it is one of the strongest federations in the world and, in recent years, has increased its efficiency and impartiality after long years of Italian domination. The EBU now issues its own monthly ratings, which are compiled by consultation among the member countries, and titles can only be contested by rated boxers.

In Britain, the Pelican Club was the principal venue for boxing in the late 19th century, but it was eventually supplanted by the National Sporting Club, a much more up-market venture founded by John Fleming and A.F. "Peggy" Bettinson at 43 King Street, Covent Garden, in 1891. The NSC drew a titled clientele, and quickly became recognized as the sport's quasi-official governing body. It drew up its own set of boxing rules, and reinforced its position as boxing's administrator by introducing the Lonsdale Belts for British title fights. Since the belts could only be awarded for contests that took place at the Club, the NSC established a monopoly on British championships that endured until the 1920s, by which time the sport in Britain had outgrown the Club's 1,300-seat headquarters to become a major crowd-puller.

The NSC lacked the resources to run what was rapidly becoming a very big and lucrative business, and disputes mounted between the commercial promoters and the autocratic, self-appointed Club committee. A Board of Control was set up in 1921, but was largely under the direction of the NSC and did little to alleviate the tensions. Finally, in 1929, the Board was reconstituted, and this time it worked. The NSC was originally granted a permanent seat on the new Board, but had to relinquish that in 1936 when the Club set up as a commercial promoter in its own right.

The Board, composed almost entirely of men with no direct financial interest in the business, took on the responsibility for running every aspect of boxing, including licensing all participants, supervising tournaments, controlling championships and adjudicating on disputes between licence-holders. The Board is sub-divided into eight area councils, most of which contain representatives from local licence-holders in various capacities. It is funded by licence fees and by taxes on promotions and TV revenue, and has long been recognized as one of the world's most efficient boxing organizations. The Board was a founder member of the EBU, the WBC and the Commonwealth Championships Council, which controls the sport in British Commonwealth countries.

MARCO ANTONIO BARRERA, *an outstanding WBO champion, celebrates another victory*

BOXING RULES, CONVENTIONS AND SCORING

To the uninitiated, there is nothing very complicated about the scoring of boxing; if boxer A hits boxer B more frequently and harder than boxer B hits him, he wins the fight. But the reality is different, with wide variations in scoring methods, rules and conventions.

JACK BROUGHTON *drew up the first prize ring rules in 1743*

Fritzie Zivic, by popular consensus the dirtiest fighter ever to hold a world title, had a simple justification for his tactics in the ring. "I'd give 'em the head, choke 'em, hit 'em in the balls," he said. "You're fighting, not playing the piano, you know." Curiously, Zivic was never disqualified in 232 fights, which is either an indictment of the laxity of the referees who handled his fights, or a compliment to their common sense in adhering rigidly to the first rule of the ring, that a boxer must protect himself at all times.

Zivic would have been at home in the old days, before rules and referees got in the way of a straightforward fight to the finish. Just about anything was permissible, short of actually taking a weapon into the ring. Blows to the Adam's Apple (a target unreachable with a gloved fist) were a favourite, since they almost always incapacitated an opponent. Even grabbing a man by the hair or by the moustache was allowed, which was why fighters kept their heads shaven and forfeited their moustaches before a contest. A round ended when a man was floored, so in theory its duration could be ten minutes or ten seconds. Unscrupulous boxers would drop without taking a punch, to gain additional recovery time, and fights would often drag on interminably without many actual punches being landed.

It was not until Jack Broughton, the champion of England, drew up his own set of rules in 1743 that order began to be imposed on the chaotic world of the prize ring. Broughton did so in reaction to the death of an opponent, George Stevenson, and the rules he devised became the basis of boxing as we know it today. They were short and uncomplicated. Complete with eccentric punctuation and capitals, they read:

1 – That a square of a Yard be chalked in the middle of the Stage, and in each fresh set-to after a fall, or being from the rails, each second is to bring his Man to the side of the Square and place him opposite to the other, and until they are fairly set-to at the Lines, it shall not be lawful for one to strike at the other.

2 – That, in order to prevent any Disputes, the time a man lies after a fall if the Second does not bring his Man to the side of the square

within the space of half a minute, he shall be deemed a beaten Man.
3 – That in every Main Battle no person whatever shall be upon the Stage, except the Principals and their Seconds, the same rule to be observed in Bye-battles, except that in the latter Mr. Broughton is allowed to be upon the Stage to keep decorum and to assist Gentlemen in getting to their places, provided always he does not interfere in the Battle; and whoever pretends to infringe these Rules to be turned immediately out of the house. Everybody is to quit the Stage as soon as the Champions are stripped, before the set-to.
4 – That no Champion be deemed beaten, unless he fails coming up to the line in the limited time or that his own Second declares him beaten. No Second is to be allowed to ask his Man's adversary any questions or advise him to give out.
5 – That in Bye-battles the winning man have two-thirds of the Money given, which shall be publicly divided upon the Stage, not-withstanding private agreements to the contrary.
6 – That, to prevent Disputes, in every Main Battle the Principals shall, upon coming to the Stage, choose from among the Gentlemen present two Umpires, who shall absolutely decide all Disputes that may arise about the Battle; and if the two Umpires cannot agree, the said Umpires to choose a third, who is to determine it.
7 – That no person is to hit his Adversary when he is down or seize him by the ham, the breeches, or any part below the waist; a man on his knees to be reckoned down.

GENTLEMAN JOHN JACKSON *founded the Pugilistic Society in 1814, the sport's first regulatory body*

One of Broughton's successors, Gentleman John Jackson, founded an organization called the Pugilistic Society in 1814 in an attempt to regularize the sport, and Broughton's Rules were superseded in 1838 by the London Prize Rules (which were revised in 1853 and again in 1866). These provided for a 24-ft square ring, bounded with ropes. When a man was floored or thrown (wrestling was still an integral part of the developing sport) the round ended and the fighter was helped to his corner, being allowed a full 30 seconds to recover and a further eight seconds to "come up to scratch", which was a line scratched in the turf of the ring floor. Kicking, butting, biting and low blows were declared fouls, as was the previously common practice of going down without being hit, automatically finishing the round.

The London Rules did service until 1867, when John Graham Chambers of the London Amateur Athletic Club drew up another set of 12 rules which differed in four main aspects: contestants must wear padded gloves, rounds would be of three-minute duration with a minute's interval, wrestling throws would not be permitted, and a floored boxer had to rise within ten seconds or be declared the loser. Chambers devised the rules to cover amateur boxing, and persuaded the Marquess of Queensberry, John Sholto Douglas, to sponsor them and lend them his name. For a while the two sets of rules co-existed, but as boxing techniques developed the Queensberry Rules became the more popular. They suited fast boxers rather than slow brawlers, since without a minute's rest between rounds the style would be exhausting.

The introduction of the Queensberry Rules brought about another basic change: the classic "squaring up" posture adopted by bare-knucklers gave way to one more closely resembling the modern stance. In bare-knuckle fighting, the elbows and forearms were used to ward off punches, hence the peculiar stance the "knucklers" adopted. Under Queensberry Rules, the gloves could be used for the same purpose, and so the modern stance evolved.

Jem Mace won the championship under London Rules in 1861, but his technique (and particularly his defensive skills, not hitherto considered an important element of a fighter's art) was more at home under Queensberry Rules. Mace fought under both codes, but favoured Queensberry's and encouraged their adoption on his extensive travels around the world. In America, rapidly overtaking England as the home of prize-fighting, the Queensberry Rules took a long time to gain acceptance.

John L. Sullivan won and defended his title under London Prize Rules, but it was he who was responsible for the adoption of the Queensberry Rules. Because prize-fighting was illegal, the fighters and organizers constantly ran the risk of arrest and imprisonment, and Sullivan had frequent experience of both. The final straw was his arrest in 1889 for defending his title against Jake Kilrain, in the last bare-knuckle championship fight. Sullivan was fined $500, and Kilrain was given two months on an assault-and-battery charge.

Sullivan had had enough. "In all the fights I have been in under the London Prize Ring Rules I have not only lost money but have also had the care and worriment incidental to arrests, trials and penalties," he announced. "It has always cost me more money to get out of my fights under those rules than I have ever gained by them. Again, I have never seen a fight under the London Prize Ring Rules but what those present were of a rougher character than I have ever seen under Marquess of Queensberry Rules, and wherever the rowdy element predominates there is always sure to be trouble."

When he issued his famous challenge to Frank Slavin, Charlie Mitchell and James J. Corbett, he stipulated that "The Marquess of Queensberry Rules must govern this contest, as I want fighting, not foot racing." With that announcement, the Prize Ring era died and boxing entered the modern world.

JIMMY WALKER *(right, with President Roosevelt) was responsible for ending the "No Decision" era in New York*

The No-Decision Era

By the early 1900s America had replaced England as the world's leading boxing nation, but the sport was not universally welcomed by all the states. Fights under the old Prize Ring Rules were banned, and the unruly element that boxing attracted caused many authorities to outlaw gloved contests as well. In New York, the Horton Law was passed in 1900, which permitted only those fights that took place in a members-only club, but this proved near-impossible to enforce since the "membership requirements" were usually extremely elastic. In 1911, the state replaced it with the Frawley Law, which enabled boxing to take place openly, but restricted contests to ten rounds and prohibited points decisions.

This practice became commonplace across America, which is why the records of champions from that period contain so many "No Decision" entries. The only way a title could change hands was by a knockout or stoppage, provided both men were inside the weight limit for their division. The limits had evolved over the years, often with wildly differing standards on either side of the Atlantic, but by the century's second decade they had stabilized at their present limits: flyweight 112lb, bantam 118lb, featherweight 126lb, lightweight 135lb, welterweight 147lb, middleweight 160lb, light-heavyweight 175lb, and heavyweight over 175lb. There were only the eight categories, although two more (junior lightweight, 130lb and junior welterweight, 140lb) were introduced with limited success in the 1920s.

The No Decision law was designed also to curb betting on fights, but the ever-inventive punters found a way round that. The parties would agree to accept the opinion of a nominated newspaper reporter as to who had proved the better man. It was a system with obvious scope for corruption, but at least the so-called "Newspaper decisions" – assuming they were honest – gave the public some means of assessing a man's progress. This prevailed until the Walker Law (sponsored by New York's famous Mayor Jimmy Walker) legalized boxing completely in 1920. The rest of America took its lead from New York, whose State Athletic Commission became the sport's governing body there and, because most big fights now took place in that city, the Athletic Commission quickly established itself as one of the most influential controlling bodies in the world.

THE END *of the odious "colour bar" in British boxing as Dick Turpin (right) beats Vince Hawkins in 1948*

British Rules and Conventions

Boxing in Britain continued to be governed by the Marquess of Queensberry Rules until the emergence of the Pelican Club as the sport's quasi-official governing body in the late 19th century. In about 1890, the Club produced their own set of rules, modelled largely on Queensberry's. These restricted the maximum number of rounds to 20, and set the minimum weight for gloves at six ounces. When the Pelican faded from the scene to be replaced by the National Sporting Club as the sport's self-appointed administrator, the rules were revised in 1909 and again in 1923. The British Boxing Board Of Control used the NSC's rules when it took over the sport, and updated them in 1947. There have been occasional changes and variations since then, notably in the scoring system and, in 1948, the abolition of the obnoxious "colour bar" that restricted British championships to white boxers.

The colour bar, which prevented fine craftsmen, like the Manchester welterweight Len Johnson, from achieving their potential, was the legacy of what the NSC perceived to have been a slight inflicted on them by Jack Johnson, and at this distance it seems unbelievable that it took so long to get rid of it. Dick Turpin, whose brother Randolph went on to become world middleweight champion, was the first to benefit: he outpointed Vince Hawkins in 1948 to win the British middleweight title. Turpin's success led the way for black boxers to make their mark in the sport – although, curiously, one weight division, the bantamweight, has yet to produce a black champion.

With the wave of immigration from former colonies in the 1950s and 1960s, the Board relaxed the rules to permit immigrants to contest British titles after living in the country for ten years, and later reduced the qualifying period to six years. Bunny Sterling was the first immigrant to win a title, taking the middleweight championship from Mark Rowe in 1970 and, three years later, Des Morrison from Jamaica outpointed Joe Tetteh of Ghana for the light-welterweight title in the first championship match between immigrants.

Britain remains one of the few countries to leave the scoring of fights in the referee's sole hands. Most others employ three judges and a non-scoring referee, or two judges and a scoring referee, but the British Board has always resisted the change. Fights used to be scored on a fraction system with the winner of a round being awarded five points and the loser 4¾ or, if he clearly lost the round, 4½. This led to unnecessarily complicated arithmetic, not always easily done in the pressure of the moment, and finally Britain opted to fall in line with most other countries and adopt the ten-point must system, with the winner of the round getting ten points and the loser nine or less.

But because the rules also called for the referee to record, in the event of a knockout, ten points for the winner and none for the loser, a truly farcical situation developed in a British lightweight title fight in Derry in 1978 between champion Charlie Nash and London challenger Johnny Claydon. Nash was winning the fight clearly, but all the rounds were hard-fought and Claydon, who had not been hurt at any stage, was still firmly in contention. At the end of the 12th round the referee caused consternation by announcing that the fight was over: it transpired that Claydon was so far behind on points, having been edged out of most rounds by a 10–9 margin, that even if he scored a knockout and was awarded ten points against none for Nash, he would still have lost the fight on points! The rule was amended to avoid this happening again, with fights now being scored on a half-point basis.

There are other areas in which Britain remains stubbornly isolated. Foreign boxers are frequently confused by the absence of a mandatory eight count, which is in almost universal use elsewhere. Two-minute rounds, originally designed for novice professionals, are now commonplace in British rings but rare elsewhere. There is minimal co-operation between the amateur and professional governing bodies, although in many European countries relations between the two codes are so good that often they are administered by the same organization and amateurs are routinely featured on professional shows. France even has a special "in between" category called "independents", which allows boxers

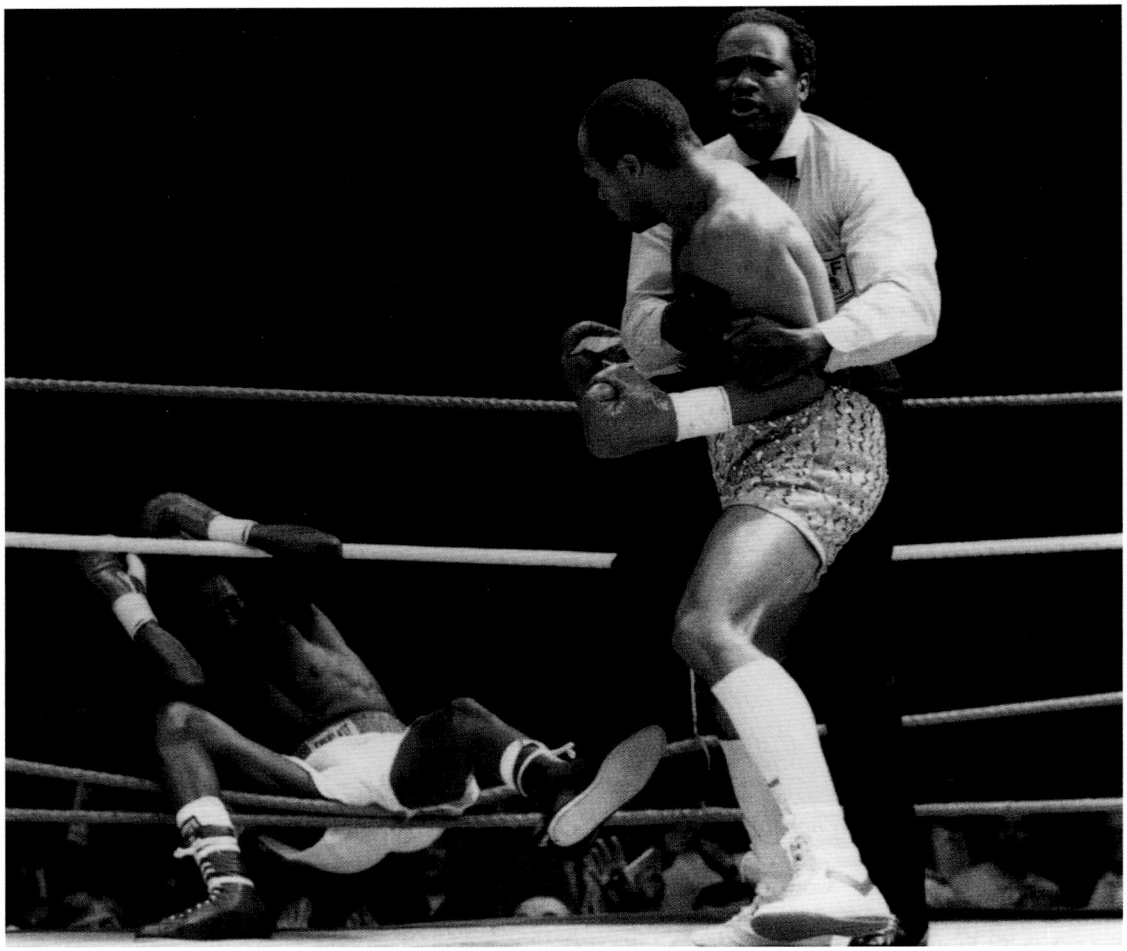

LLOYD HONEYGHAN *disposes of challenger Johnny Bumphus in one of his many controversial title fights*

to compete professionally for a maximum of two seasons and then, if they so choose, to be reinstated as amateurs. There are encouraging signs of a thaw between the amateur authorities and the British Board, and the fact that only two British boxers qualified to take part in the 1996 Olympic Games underlined the urgent need for change if the amateur sport is to survive.

Rules Disputes

Bob Arum, who shares the caustic wit of most fight promoters, once announced at a press conference before a championship fight that was taking place under the joint jurisdiction of the WBA and the New York State Athletic Commission: "The rules meeting for this fight as usual will be conducted in Spanish in order that nobody understands a word that is said." He was no doubt speaking from long experience of such terminally boring events, but the pre-fight rules meeting is now an inflexible part of the procedure. Given the variations in rules and practice between the many governing bodies, they are a necessary evil.

They are usually held on the evening before the fight, in the presence of the boxers, their representatives and the host Commission, under the chairmanship of the supervisor from the championship organization whose title is being contested.

The meeting affords an opportunity to clarify issues like whether there is a mandatory eight count; a standing count; a three-knockdown rule (under which three knockdowns in the same round automatically ends the fight); who is empowered to stop the fight (a doctor as well as the referee); what will happen in the event of an accidental cut that forces a stoppage (in some jurisdictions a technical points decision will be rendered, in others a No Contest will be ruled); whether the "no foul" rule is in operation (meaning that a man cannot be disqualified). These are all important issues, and it is preferable to settle any disputes at this stage rather than have arguments and confusion in the ring.

The No Foul rule is not applied in Britain, where it seems directly to contradict all the old-fashioned notions of sportsmanship and fair play, but it is in operation in most American states. Its most striking use was on an extraordinary afternoon in Atlantic City in July 1988, when Britain's Lloyd Honeyghan defended the WBC welterweight title against Yung-kil Chang of Korea and Marlon Starling risked the WBA version of the title against Tomas Molinares of Colombia. Chang was hit low, and finally refused to continue in the fifth round after being given time to recover from the latest low punch. Honeyghan was credited with a fifth-round retirement victory – and then Starling lost his title when he was knocked out by a punch thrown after the bell, but Molinares was nonetheless credited with a knockout win.

Honeyghan figured in some riotous and controversial title fights. He raced across the ring at Wembley to flatten Johnny Bumphus before the American challenger had got off the stool to answer the bell for the second round. He was perfectly within his rights to do so, since the bell had sounded and Bumphus, like all fighters, was obliged to protect himself at all times. "The bell went 'ding' and I went 'dong'," was Lloyd's laconic explanation.

He lost his title on a curious technical decision to Jorge Vaca in 1987, when after an accidental cut Vaca was unable to continue in the eighth round. A points total was called for, which included the eighth round even though it had not been completed, and Honeyghan was declared a narrow loser. That fight, incidentally, involved both the WBC and IBF titles, but Vaca was immediately stripped by the IBF as the fight had been scheduled for the WBC distance of 12 rounds, rather than the 15 which the IBF still regarded as the championship distance. (Since then the IBF, and all other governing bodies, have agreed to accept the 12 rounds limit, on safety grounds.)

How to Score

Boxing is probably the only competitive sport where the spectators don't know at any stage who is winning – where, in fact, that knowledge is restricted to four people in the arena (the three officials and the supervisor). In 2006, the World Boxing Council experimented with the idea of announcing the judges' scores to the crowd (without identifying them personally) at the end of rounds four and eight. By 2007 it was still a young idea, but had not had any discernible consequences. Opinion about its merits remained divided. And beyond that experiment, the situation remained that spectators could only speculate during a contest who was in front. In 2005, the British Boxing

Board of Control fell into line with the rest of the world in approving the use of three judges as well as a non-scoring referee for championship and eliminator contests, which was widely welcomed.

As to the scoring of the fight, so much depends upon personal interpretation, on which kind of boxing style you like. If Tony Zale or Gene Fullmer is your prototype fighting man, then you'll give points for aggression even if the aggression is not particularly effective. If you marvelled at the defensive artistry of Herol Graham, then you will reward the man who makes his opponent miss and counters him smartly. Quite a few referees and judges have been fighters themselves in their youth, but it does not automatically follow that they will lean towards the man whose style reminds them of their own. They may go the other way, and vote for the man whose style is the one they would have loved to have had in their days in the ring. After all, inside every Chris Eubank there may be a Nigel Benn bursting to get out.

In theory, scoring fights is a simple process. Points are awarded for punches landed on the target area (above the waist, on the front and sides of the body or head) with the front or the knuckle part of the closed glove. Open handed cuffs do not score, and back-handed blows are illegal. In world title fights, the principal governing bodies advise their judges to award a 10-8 score in a round in which a knockdown has occurred, but this is not always a fair or accurate reading of the round. For example, boxer A may have built up a big lead in the round, outscoring his opponent by a 3:1 ratio, and then boxer B scores a flash knockdown from which his opponent gets up almost at once, to carry on where he left off. Who then should win the round?

Where possible, good judges/referees try to avoid giving even rounds. It is barely conceivable that, in three minutes of sustained action, one man did not land at least a few more punches than the other, or show a wider range of skill. European judges are particularly prone to fence sit. When Britain's Dave Needham drew with Daniel Trioulaire of France in a European bantamweight title fight in 1975, one judge marked 11 of the 15 rounds even and another was unable to split them in ten of the rounds. Such scores suggest a worrying lack of confidence in their own ability to find a winner, and do an injustice to the boxers.

Even rounds often seem like a "cop-out", a case of the judge taking an easy way out. The late Chuck Minker, a forward-looking chairman of the Nevada State Athletic Commision, used to make his officials review with him the film of fights they had worked and explain to him precisely how and why they had scored each individual round as they did. While this was a commendable practice, it did little to dispel the notion that Las Vegas judges apply their own peculiar standards and often come up with verdicts which are, to put it mildly, controversial.

Marvin Hagler, who lost to Ray Leonard on such a verdict, gave a prophetic interview a month before the fight in which he said: "I'm not sure you can get a fair shake in Las Vegas. I mean, they've got very bad judges there, and it's a town where they'll bet on which cockroach will get across the sidewalk first." Larry Holmes was twice outscored by Mike Spinks in heavyweight title fights in Las Vegas, and after the second one expressed his opinion of the judges in succinct terms which later cost him a fine. "The referees and judges can kiss me where the sun don't shine – my big black behind."

Chris Eubank figured in many close calls during his reign as WBO super-middleweight champion. He had mastered an art of which old-timers like Archie Moore were prime exponents: fine-judging the time remaining in the round so that judges will be swayed by a fast finishing burst and forget what had gone on before. Muhammad Ali, too, tended to fight in well-judged spurts rather than sustained action.

There is a case that the referee is the only man well-enough placed to score a fight, since he can move around with the boxers and see virtually all punches, while judges, seated in a fixed position at ringside, only see the action that is within their eye-line. By the same token, it is often possible to watch a fight on television, with the benefit of multi-angled camera shots that show you all the action, and find a different winner than you did at ringside. For once, arguably, the armchair experts can get it right.

OUT FOR THE COUNT *the referee signals the end of a fight*

CULTURE AND CONTROVERSY

Boxing's appeal crosses all barriers of class, race, religion and sex. Gangsters and cabinet ministers sit elbow-by-elbow at ringside; Popes and princes are equally fascinated by its indefinable, sometimes seedy glamour. It has a culture all of its own, and a history littered with scandals and controversy.

Let's face it, boxing never has been politically correct. It is a macho world, in which violence is venerated and rewarded, and where (with a few exceptions) women are little more than attractive set-dressings. Men who are hard inside the ring draw the admiration of men who are hard outside it: the biggest gangster in London will defer to the lowliest six-rounder, because the boxer has asserted his masculinity in a way that a gunman never could. The underworld has always flirted with the fight game, and the sometimes sleazy, slightly raffish glamour of the ring is part of its attraction.

That was certainly true in the old days, when bare-knuckle fights were illegal and attending them offered otherwise law-abiding citizens a little *frisson* of naughtiness. Prize-fights and public executions drew much the same range of spectators. Contemporary accounts such as in Pierce Egan's *Boxiana* or William Hazlitt's famous essay *The Fight* paint a vivid picture of a sport patronized by obscenely wealthy and worthless aristocrats who gambled fortunes on the outcome, and who travelled to the fights accompanied by ladies of spectacularly less than the highest moral standards. Prize-fights were no place for a "proper" lady to be seen, but they afforded a busy market-place for whores and camp-followers. Pickpockets, too, thrived among the vast throngs who were drawn to the spectacle – 30,000 watched Tom Spring beat Bill Neat in 1823, and gatherings of 20,000 or more were not unusual. "Fences" were always on hand to buy the stolen items, which would then be sold on again in the same afternoon.

Fixed fights were commonplace especially in the latter part of the 18th century when the sport was in decline and the rewards for "straight" fights had diminished. Given the amounts that were staked, it was always worth a fighter's while to oblige a gambler in return for a slice of his winnings. Maybe, in a variation on the scene so beloved of

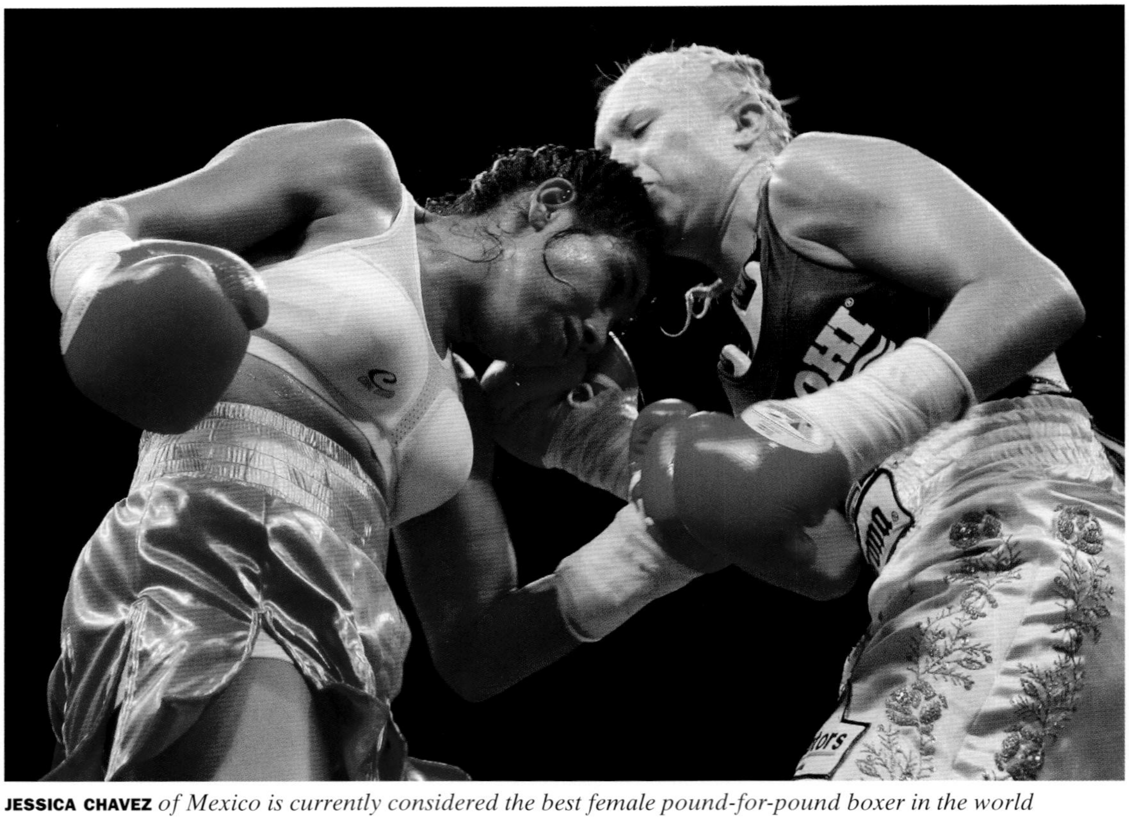

JESSICA CHAVEZ *of Mexico is currently considered the best female pound-for-pound boxer in the world*

Hollywood film makers of the 1930s and 1940s, a sinister-looking character would open the door of the carriage in which the fighter was changing and hiss: "The boss says you go in the 17th."

Bill Stevens, a notorious "fixer", won the championship in dubious circumstances from Jack Slack in 1760 and lost it to George Meggs a year later in a blatantly pre-arranged affair. Stevens justified himself to an outraged friend by saying: "I got 50 guineas more than I should otherwise have done by letting George beat me, and damme, ain't I the same man still?" Peter Corcoran and Jem Ward, who presumably shared Stevens' cheerful pragmatism, also figured in their share of fixed fights.

Many prize-fighters turned to the pub business when they retired, a tradition which endures. Nineteenth-century gin palaces were a far cry from the discreet and orderly modern pub, and it helped to have a respected fighting man behind the bar. Since the upper levels of society did not patronize such places, the links between boxing and the underworld were strengthened. Pubs were gathering places for criminals and their associates, and even Tom Cribb, a figure of legendary propriety while a fighter, set up his pub in Panton Street just off the Haymarket in London, right in the heart of what was then the city's red-light district.

There were close links too between boxing and the theatre, or more specifically the music hall. Champions like John L. Sullivan, James J. Corbett and Bob Fitzsimmons earned more on the boards than they did in the ring, either in touring melodramas or by giving sparring and training exhibitions. Sullivan took that a stage further: he would offer $50 to any man in the audience who thought he could beat the champion, and never had to pay out. According to Sullivan's biographer Donald Barr Chidsey his 11 theatrical tours earned a total of $83,000, a staggering total for the time. By comparison, his fight purses were meagre – $11,000 for the first Charlie Mitchell fight, $8,500 for the rematch with Dominick McCaffrey, and $10,000 for his last bare-knuckle championship defence against Jake Kilrain.

JACK DEMPSEY *(with wife Estelle Taylor in 1927) was one of the many boxing champions who flirted with the movies. His films included* Damn Citizen *(1958),* Off Limits *(1953) and* Prizefighter and the Lady *(1933)*

When moving pictures came in, the champions of the day found themselves in demand. Jack Dempsey – who married several actresses – and Max Baer both starred in a number of decidedly lightweight films. (Baer's nephew, Buddy Baer Jr., became well known in the 1960s playing Jed Clampett's affable but slow-thinking son in the long-running TV series *The Beverly Hillbillies.*) It became fashionable for film stars to be seen with fighters, even to manage them: George Raft and Al Jolson, for example, were both involved in Henry Armstrong's management, with the Mob-connected Eddie Mead actually doing the business deals for the triple champion.

In Europe, too, boxing and show-business shared the same clientele and often the same bed. The long-running affair between Marcel Cerdan and Edith Piaf entranced the French public for years (with the possible exception of Madame Cerdan), while in Britain the heavyweight sensation Jack Doyle earned well on the music halls and eventually married the film actress Movita, who

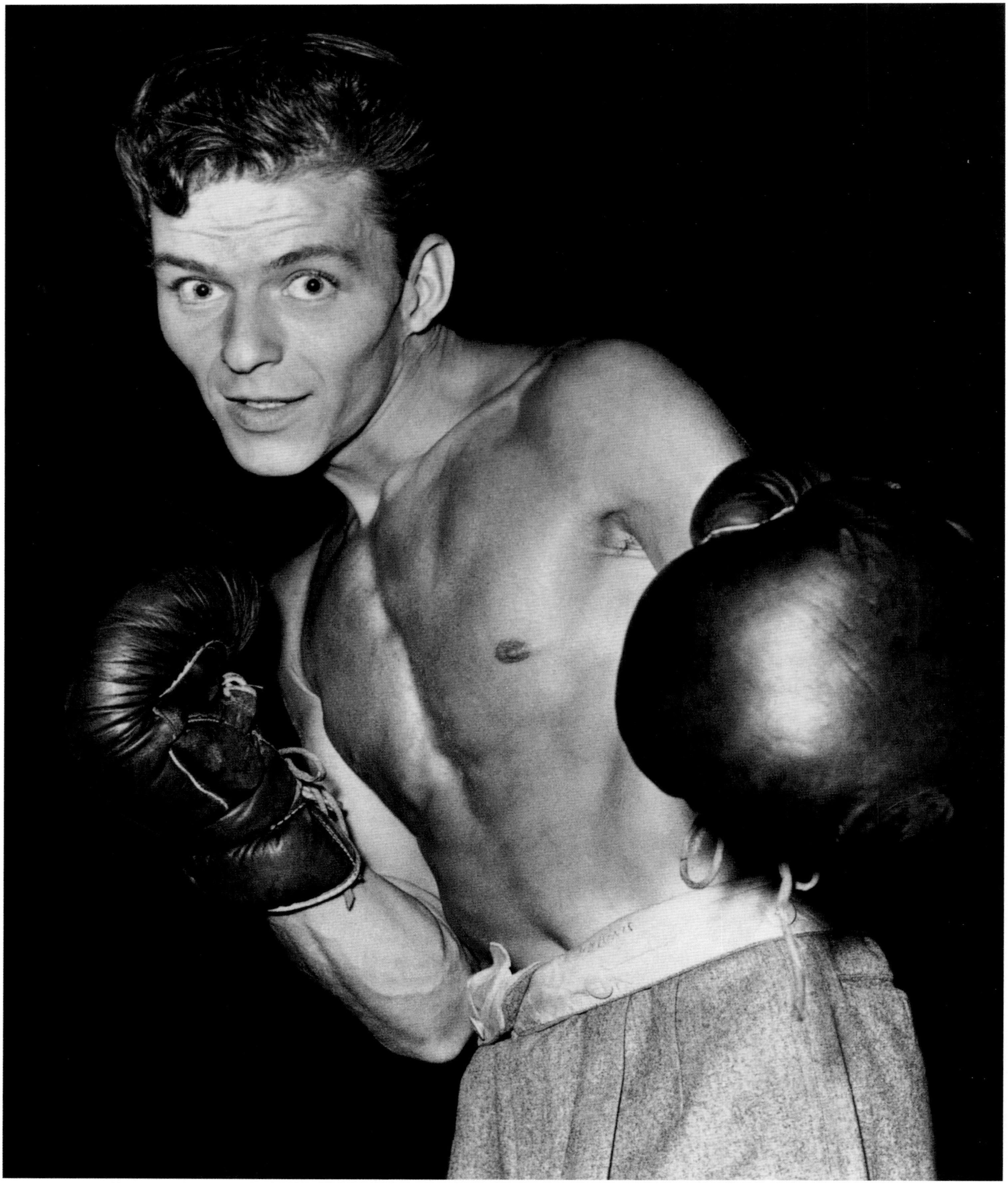

subsequently divorced him and married Marlon Brando instead. Brando, to complete the circle, used boxing as his vehicle to stardom with his unforgettable portrayal of the broken-down ex-fighter Terry Malloy in *On The Waterfront.*

Paul Newman and Robert DeNiro had huge successes playing former middleweight champions Rocky Graziano and Jake LaMotta in, respectively, *Somebody Up There Likes Me* and *Raging Bull.* The Graziano role was Newman's first big break, and – as did DeNiro – he prepared for it by immersing himself in the world of boxing and learning enough of the basic moves to look convincing in the ring. Other stars, notably Jon Voight in *The Champ* and, oddly, Elvis Presley in *Kid Galahad*, did this so well that they might even have won a couple of fights in the professional ring. Mickey Rourke, who cherishes his screen "tough guy" image, believed his own publicity to the extent of actually taking out a professional licence and winning a handful of four-rounders, although sceptical observers noted that the opponents may have been better actors than he was.

Boxing is such a colourful world that film makers have always been fascinated by it. Apart from tear-jerkers like *The Champ* or ludicrous yarns like the *Rocky* series there have been cinema classics made about the game. *The Harder They Fall* is a bleak and moving retelling of the Primo Carnera story with Humphrey Bogart – an inveterate fight fan – outstanding as the world-weary press hack who knows what is going on but lacks the moral courage to do anything about it. John Huston's *Fat City* has never been bettered for its accurate depiction of the other side of the boxing coin, the life of a down-the-bill "opponent" who is always just a Greyhound Bus ride away from another defeat.

A few such fighters manage a twist in the story by turning to movies themselves and becoming stars. Bob Hope was a woefully inept boxer who later worked his ring experiences into his stage act.

(ABOVE) ROBERT DENIRO *played Jake LaMotta in* Raging Bull
(OPPOSITE) FRANK SINATRA *a lifetime boxing fan, claimed to have had ten fights and looks the part in a 1947 publicity picture*

("I was called Rembrandt Hope because I was on the canvas so much. My last fight, a guy hit me so hard I bounced right into dancing school.") Jack Palance and Dean Martin were competent performers in the ring, as was Martin's former drinking partner Frank Sinatra. The son of a fighter, Sinatra had ten fights himself and enjoyed a life-long affinity with the sport and its stars. He even claimed his own little corner of boxing immortality. One of the most famous fight photographs ever taken shows Muhammad Ali snarling over the prostrate Sonny Liston in their rematch in Lewiston, Maine, in 1965. Note the picture credit: Frank Sinatra.

Fixes, Scandals and the Mob

The popular perception of boxing as a crooked business dominated by sinister men in camel-hair overcoats who talk out of the sides of their mouths owes everything to Hollywood and little to reality, or at least to reality in the modern game. Fifty or 60 years ago, of course, it was very different: then, the Mob virtually ran big-time boxing in America, and since America dominated the world championship scene, it followed that titles were at their disposal and in their gift. It took a US Senate investigation, the Kefauver Commission, to expose the extent of organized crime involvement and eradicate it.

Britain has always run a cleaner operation, partly because the sport has been rigorously controlled first by the National Sporting Club and, since 1929, by the British Boxing Board of Control. Many American states lack an effective Commission to regulate the business, and the absence of a national controlling body has resulted in conditions of near-anarchy which made it easy for the criminal element to infiltrate and take over boxing there. British criminals would no doubt have relished those kind of opportunities, but simple geography worked against them. The country is too small to allow, for instance, a phoney record like Primo Carnera's to be compiled in out-of-the-way places where opponents could swan-dive without attracting unwelcome attention from either Commission Inspectors or national newspapermen.

British gangsters have always loved to be seen around fighters and at ringside, but the strict licensing procedures operated by the Board of Control make it difficult for them to pursue any active involvement in the sport. Applications for managerial or promotional licences are carefully vetted, and any hint of criminality is usually enough to guarantee rejection. Similarly, a boxer who breaks the law risks forfeiture of his licence, however prominent he may be. Chic Calderwood was British light-heavyweight champion and a world-ranked contender when his licence was suspended following his conviction on an assault charge in the 1960s, and there have been many similar cases.

The Kray brothers, acknowledged bosses of London gangland in the early 1960s, were all former pros who were also genuine *aficionados,* as were their arch-rivals the Richardsons. Any world champion or ex-champion visiting London in the early 1960s would sooner or later find a Kray arm around his shoulders and a photographer on hand to record the moment, and the twins relished these encounters like wide-eyed fans. London villains like Frankie Fraser, Joey Pyle and Freddie

THE KRAY TWINS *Ronnie and Reggie at Klein's Gym in London in 1952*

Foreman were all regular big-fight patrons (Her Majesty's Pleasure permitting), and their provincial counterparts shared their enthusiasm for the sport.

Many former boxers, even some ex-champions, turned to crime when their ring careers ended. It is easy to understand why they would do so: generally they were ill-educated men whose only trade was boxing, and who had grown accustomed to the lifestyle their ring earnings brought them. When the income ceased abruptly on retirement, they had to look elsewhere for sources of revenue – and crime offered a quick and easy way of maintaining their living standards. Happily, that does not happen so often today. Educational standards are higher, and television has helped make people more aware and sophisticated than their parents' generation were. The modern British boxer knows that he needs top-class lawyers and accountants just as much as he needs a good cuts man, and the emergence of the Professional Boxers' Association has served to make fighters more aware of their rights and of the need to safeguard their financial future.

Despite the tight control exercised by the Board of Control, there have been occasional scandals in British boxing. One such was Bruce Woodcock's fourth-round knockout of American Lee Oma, in London in September 1948. Woodcock was European and British heavyweight champion, and his promoter Jack Solomons was trying to bring him back from a catastrophic defeat by another American, Joe Baksi. Oma had beaten Baksi, as well as top men like Lou Nova, Tami Mauriello and light-heavyweight champion Gus Lesnevich. He looked a tough proposition for Woodcock and the fight generated so much interest that all 10,600 seats at Harringay Arena were sold out nearly a fortnight before the show.

The rumours began when Oma was seen to be lackadaisical in training and soon they hardened to a specific allegation: that he had been paid £5,000 to take a dive. When the fight got under way, the American was strangely lethargic, scarcely throwing a punch for three rounds. At the end of the third, boos came from all around the arena as the fans showed their displeasure with his lack of effort. Oma made a slight show of aggression early in the fourth, but then crashed for the full count when Woodcock landed a right to the jaw. The press were scathing, and the result produced one of the great headlines in British sports journalism: "Oma Coma Aroma".

Woodcock vigorously denied that anything improper had occurred. In his autobiography, he wrote: "So far as I am concerned, I can honestly say that I have never taken part in a fixed fight in my life." And then he added, perhaps significantly, "It would, I suppose, be possible for one man to have agreed to lose without the other knowing about it, but such is the bush-telegraph system of the training camps of boxing that even that possibility is remote."

The truth of the Oma affair will never be ascertained. If the fight was fixed, then only Oma and Solomons need have known about it. Woodcock was a fighter of blazing honesty and exemplary courage, who would never knowingly have allowed himself to be a part of such a shoddy deal, but it would be naive to pretend that such arrangements did not occasionally happen. British libel laws are so strict that they prohibit discussion of other possible fixes involving boxers who are still living, but the number of questionable results in the last 40 years is reassuringly low.

There have been instances where perhaps a man may not have tried as hard as he should have done, or where he neglected his training to such an extent that he left himself with little chance of victory. But outright prearrangements are rare and almost impossible to prove, since they require only two men to know in advance – the fixer and the diver, and as they have each committed a criminal act, they are unlikely to admit it. Only the man on the receiving end of a punch knows for certain whether the punch is of knockout quality or not. What looks an innocuous blow from the safe side of the ropes can have a dramatic effect on the recipient, with the second Muhammad Ali vs. Sonny Liston "phantom punch" knockdown being the best-known case in point.

As television became ever more involved in boxing, the incentive to fix fights lessened. This was partly because, with TV revenue underwriting the show, more money could be made legitimately from purses and receipts than from gambling, which had always been the prime reason for fixing results. Another factor was that TV

BRUCE WOODCOCK *(right) and Lee Oma weigh in for their 1948 fight*

companies, ever eager for spectacular knockouts, were perfectly happy to settle for blatantly one-sided matches in which the fighter they were projecting, the audience-puller, had at least an 80 per cent chance of success. In the absence of any kind of quality control on televised matches, promoters were able to build long winning records for their protégés against imported losers, while the Board of Control – who had the power to veto unsuitable opponents – too often turned a blind eye to mismatches.

The explosion in purse levels in recent years makes it simply uneconomic for a boxer to "throw" a title fight. The heavyweight championship, conservatively, is worth at least $50 million to the holder: how much, then, would Michael Moorer have needed to be paid to give the title away to George Foreman, or how large a bribe would Lennox Lewis have required to lose to Oliver McCall? Fixing a title fight is just too expensive to contemplate and, given the hundreds of millions of people watching the fight around the world, too public a spectacle to get away with a prearranged result.

No such inhibitions applied in the wild, anything-goes days of boxing's early development. Barry Hugman's outstanding research on world title history for his *British Boxing Yearbook* has unearthed some gems, such as the match in San Francisco in April 1904 between Joe Walcott, defending his claim to the welterweight title, and Dixie Kid. Walcott was winning easily when, for no apparent reason, he was disqualified in the 20th round. It later transpired that the referee had backed the Kid, and disqualified Walcott to protect his investment. (Traditionally, a disqualification meant that all bets were off.) Walcott continued to be regarded as champion.

Dixie Kid was involved in another scandalous decision seven years later to the very day, though this time he was the injured party. France was effectively the capital of world boxing in those pre-war years, and matches between American stars were big attractions. Kid (whose real name was Aaron Brown) boxed Willie Lewis in a 20-rounder and, in what was suspected to be a betting coup, was adjudged to have lost when in fact he had outboxed Lewis convincingly. The verdict caused such an uproar that a jury of leading Parisian sportsmen was convened to reconsider it, and they duly reversed the decision in the Kid's favour.

Lewis was appointed to referee Dixie Kid's defence of his International Boxing Union version of the championship against George Bernard of France in Paris in April 1912, and disqualified his old opponent when Bernard fell to the canvas in the 11th round, writhing in apparent pain and claiming a foul. Three doctors examined the Frenchman and found no trace of injury, and the decision was overturned with the Kid being declared the winner by retirement.

This tradition of French fair play was maintained when Battling Siki took the light-heavyweight title from Georges Carpentier in 1922. Carpentier had agreed to a fixed fight, in which he would hold up the challenger for at least four rounds to give the fight film some sale value, and then knock him out in the fifth. But Siki double-crossed him, and gave the out-of-condition Frenchman a bad beating before Carpentier's corner threw in the towel in the sixth round. The referee, however, disregarded their action and instead disqualified Siki for tripping the champion, which caused such an uproar that the French Boxing Federation went into a hurried conference and, an hour later, declared Siki the new champion.

Only eight months after the Lewis debacle, Bernard figured in the most blatant case of "nobbling" a fighter on record when, challenging Billy Papke for the middleweight title, he fell sound asleep in his corner between the sixth and seventh rounds and could not be roused in time to answer the bell. There was an echo of that affair 43 years on when Harold Johnson, working his way back from a light-heavyweight title loss to Archie Moore, was surprisingly knocked out in two rounds by Julio Mederos, whom he had previously outpointed. Johnson claimed afterwards that he had been given a drugged orange to eat before the fight, which had the effect of slowing his reflexes drastically. The episode seriously damaged Johnson's career: he did not get another fight for 19 months, and had to wait until 1961 for a second championship chance.

Benny Leonard is rightly remembered as one of the greatest lightweight champions of all time, but he took part in a contest which, if not actually fixed, he at least contrived deliberately to lose. Challenging Jack Britton for the welterweight title in New York in June 1922, Leonard was comfortably outboxing the veteran until, having floored Britton in the 13th round, he struck the champion while he was down, incurring instant disqualification. In this case, at least, it seems that betting was not involved. Leonard was really only a lightweight, and did not particularly want the burden of winning the welterweight title and having to concede weight every time he defended it, so he opted for a disqualification as a means of losing the fight without forfeiting any of his status or prestige.

It was normal practice in those days for champions to insist that their favourite referees handle their fights, to give them every possible edge. It was often a wise precaution. Mike McTigue, who took the light-heavyweight title from Battling Siki, needed a little help from the referee when he faced Young Stribling, the "Georgia

YOUNG STRIBLING, *who figured in a riotous affair against Mike McTigue in 1923*

THE TRUTH *about his knockout by Primo Carnera (above) died with Jack Sharkey in 1994*

championship weight, which upset him greatly as he had done a deal to go to Philadelphia and lose the title there for $50,000.

Battling Battalino lost his featherweight title in 1931 following a fixed fight with Freddie Miller, whose contract Battalino and his manager Pete Reilly had bought for $3,500. Battalino came in three pounds overweight, but the fight went ahead as a non-title match. Battalino made no effort, and laid down in the third round. "I stretched out," he recalled years later. "The referee says for me to get up. I told him to count. He says 'No Contest'." The title was immediately declared vacant, and was eventually won by Miller two years later.

One of the best-known fixes involved Jake LaMotta, who took a dive against the Mob-controlled Blackjack Billy Fox in 1947 in return for the promise of a crack at the middleweight title. Fox was an undefeated light-heavyweight, and LaMotta reasoned that losing to him would not affect his status as a middleweight contender. But he had his pride: he refused to be counted out, and stood against the ropes in the fourth round allowing Fox to land at will until the referee stopped it. Even then, he had to wait almost two years for his chance, and pay a "fee" of $20,000 for the privilege.

LaMotta told the story to the Kefauver Commission, a US Senate body investigating organized crime in 1960, and his evidence was instrumental in breaking the stranglehold that gangsters like Frankie Carbo and Blinky Palermo had on the business. They were actual or undercover managers of a host of champions. They decided who won and who lost, and through their manipulation of James Norris' International Boxing Club, which enjoyed an effective monopoly on world championship shows, they controlled the promotional side of the business as well. The power of the IBC was eventually broken by an anti-trust (monopoly) action brought against it at the instigation of Cus D'Amato, the manager of the heavyweight champion Floyd Patterson.

Through an organization called

Peach", in 1923. It was, even by the standards of the time, a chaotic affair. McTigue broke his hand and wanted to retire, but was "persuaded" at gun-point to complete the ten rounds, of which Stribling had won eight. The referee saved the Irishman's title by declaring a draw, but then hastily changed that to a win for Stribling when the crowd, which included Ku Klux Klansmen in full regalia, threatened to string him up. Once he was safely out of the state, the official announced that his original drawn decision stood.

Controversy endures about the heavyweight title fight in which Jack Johnson lost to Jess Willard in 1915. Johnson insisted that a deal had been done for him to surrender the title in exchange for the dropping of outstanding criminal charges against him, and pointed as evidence to a famous photograph of him on his back in the 26th round, his forearm apparently shielding his eyes from the glare of the Havana sun. Yet the fight film showed that as the count was completed both of Johnson's arms were lying on the scorching canvas. Willard offered the most convincing refutation of Johnson's story when he remarked that: "If he was going to throw the fight, I sure wish he hadn't waited until the 26th round to do it – it was hotter 'n' Hell out there."

Jack Sharkey's sixth-round knockout by Primo Carnera in 1933, which cost the American the heavyweight title, is still viewed with suspicion, given the fact that so many of the challenger's previous fights had been blatant fixes and that Sharkey had been much too smart for Carnera when they first boxed, in 1931. Accounts vary of how the fight finished. Some described the finishing blow as "a phantom punch", while the *New York Times* wrote of "a tremendous right uppercut". Sharkey claimed that as the sixth round began he had seen a vision of Ernie Schaaf, a protégé of his who had recently died in the ring, which threw his mind into such turmoil that he could not concentrate on the fight. But, as he conceded to author Peter Heller in a 1971 interview, "Even my wife has her doubts," and the truth died with Sharkey in 1994.

Charley Phil Rosenberg, a bantamweight contemporary of Sharkey's, was dogged by scandal throughout his championship career. He was suspended indefinitely by the New York Commission, and his opponent Eddie Shea banned for life, after Shea went down for the count in the fourth round in July 1925. Shea had reportedly been threatened with death unless he threw the fight, and armed gangsters were said to be at ringside to ensure that he obliged. The story may be true: Rosenberg was friendly with Al Capone, whom he described to Heller in *In This Corner* as: "A fine man. I don't know what he done on the outside. He may have had hundreds of people killed. I don't know. I'm not interested. To me, he was a fine person."

Rosenberg's suspension was lifted to allow him to defend against Bushy Graham, whom he outpointed, but he was then suspended again when a secret agreement was unearthed concerning the purse split. He was finally stripped of the title after failing to make the

the Boxing Guild, the Mob kept recalcitrant fighters in line. The Guild was a kind of managers' union, and any boxer who tried to leave his manager was blackballed by the Guild and denied work. Not even Ike Williams, NBA lightweight champion at the time, could beat the Guild. He was blackballed, until he agreed to sign contracts with Palermo, who promptly got him a match with Bob Montgomery, which he won, for the undisputed title.

Carbo and his like, once omnipotent, would struggle to survive in the modern game. Today, contracts are hammered out by corporate lawyers in boardrooms rather than haggled over in smoky bars or sweaty changing rooms, and a length of lead pipe won't get you as far in the negotiating process as a degree in business administration or law. The game is unquestionably cleaner than it was in the bad old days, but to the uninvolved and uncommitted outside observer, it's also a lot duller.

Death in the Ring

Tragedy is never far from the ring. This is a violent sport, and only the ignorant or incurably naive would argue that it leaves its participants unscathed. Every punch to the head inflicts a degree of irreversible brain damage, since it kills off cells which do not regenerate. Some men are lucky, and can walk away from a long career with their faculties intact, but most will be affected to some extent. Boxers understand the risks they take, and weigh them against the potential rewards. As Barry McGuigan, a perceptive and articulate former featherweight champion, said: "This is the price we pay, and we budget for it."

But for some, mercifully few, the price is too high. Every year, a handful of men die in the ring. Some are killed in obscure corners of the world, fighting for small purses in primitive arenas in Latin America or the Philippines. Others die or suffer lasting injury fighting for world titles with millions watching around the world. When that happens, as it did when Gerald McClellan was dreadfully injured against Nigel Benn in London in 1995, the calls to outlaw boxing are heard loud and clear and the sport is forced on to the defensive.

For the present, at least, the law is on boxing's side. Two prosecutions at the turn of the 20th century, each arising from ring deaths at the National Sporting Club in London, established the principle that deaths resulting from a properly organized and controlled boxing contest, as opposed to an unregulated prize fight, were accidental. The first was in 1897 when Walter Croot of Leytonstone died after being knocked out by Jimmy Barry of Chicago in a world bantamweight title fight. In that instance, the magistrate found there was no case to answer, and that position was reinforced in 1901 when Jack Roberts was acquitted on a charge of "feloniously killing and slaying Murray Livingstone" (boxing as Billy Smith), who died in a fight with Roberts at the Club. Smith's death was the fourth in as many years at the NSC, following Croot (1897), Tom Turner (1898) and Mike Riley (1900).

The first to die in a championship ring this century was welterweight Jimmy Doyle, who never regained consciousness after Ray Robinson knocked him out in the eighth round at Cleveland in 1947. Robinson had dreamt the precise circumstances of Doyle's death the night before the fight, and had to be persuaded to go through with it by Doyle's parish priest.

Benny Paret died following his 12th-round stoppage by Emile Griffith in a welterweight title defence in New York in 1962: he had been unable to extricate himself from the ropes and was defenceless as Griffith pounded him, a tragedy which led to the introduction of the four-roped ring. Just under a year later, featherweight champion Davey Moore lost his life against Sugar Ramos in Los Angeles, which was also the scene of a bizarre, tragic coincidence. Welsh bantamweight Johnny Owen was fatally injured when challenging Lupe Pintor for the WBC title there in September 1980, dying 46 days later, and in 1983 Kiko Bejines died of a blood clot on the brain three days after losing to Albert Davila in the same ring, for the same title. Both fights ended in the same round, the 12th.

Four sometime-world heavyweight champions have been involved in ring fatalities: Jess Willard against Bull Young (1913), Max Baer against Frankie Campbell (1930), Primo Carnera against Ernie Schaaf (1933) and Ezzard Charles against Sam Baroudi (1948.) Other world champions who went through that trauma included Barry McGuigan, Alan Minter, Ray Mancini, Brian Mitchell and Lou Ambers, who echoed the experiences of many fighters in those circumstances when he described how, after Tony Scarpati died when Ambers knocked him out in 1936: "Every once in a while I'd look in that corner and I'd see like a picture of Tony, God rest his soul." McGuigan, too, spoke movingly of the death of his opponent, Young Ali of Nigeria. "It was as though the world had stopped for me. I never thought something like this could happen. I had always thought boxing was just a sport, just a game."

But it isn't, and as long as men compete in a ring, the casualty list will grow. That is the real price of boxing's transient glory.

MOMENT OF TRAGEDY: *Benny Paret, trapped on the ropes, is battered into a coma by Emile Griffith in 1962*

THE WORLD CHAMPIONSHIPS

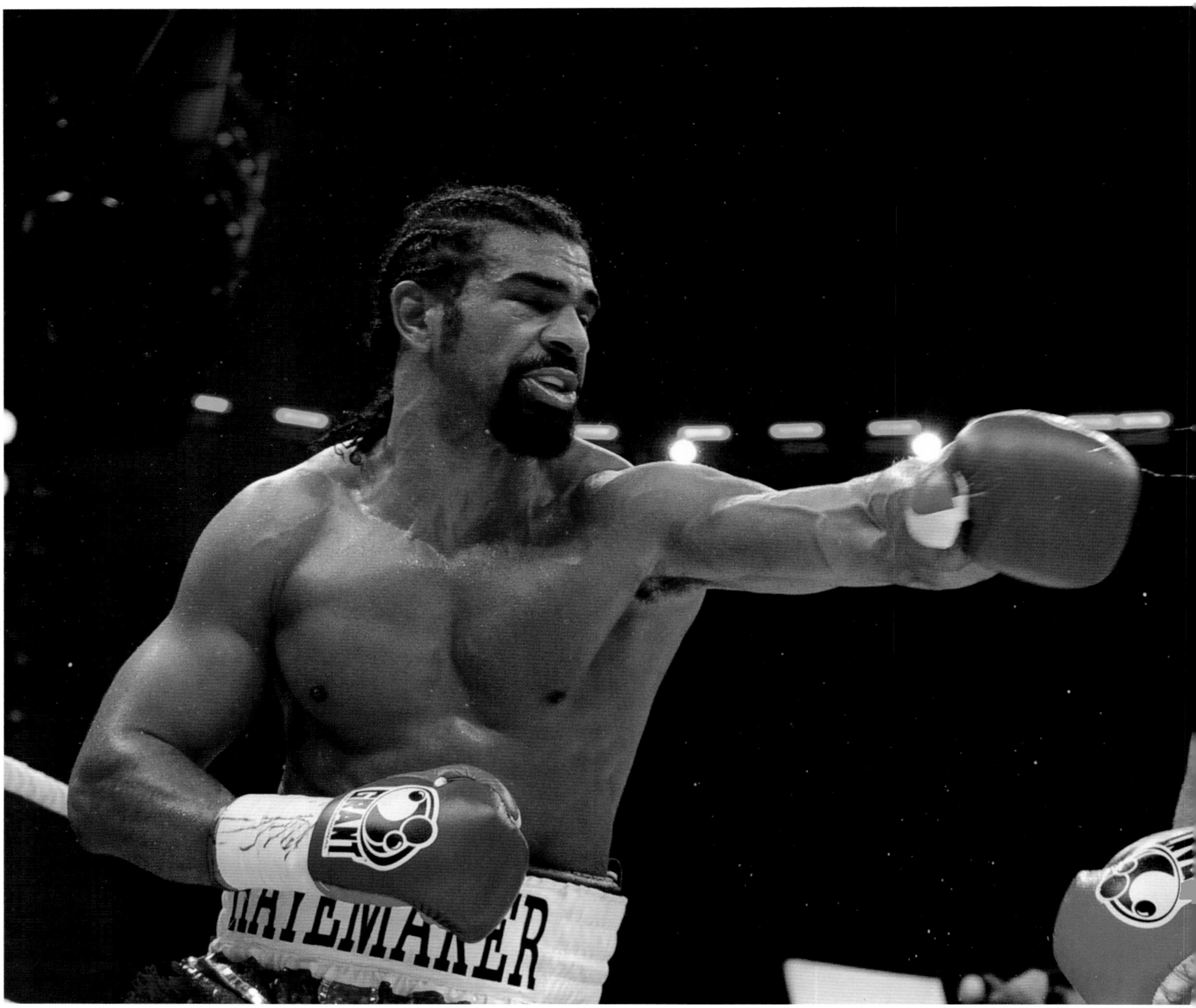

The history of each weight division from heavyweight down to minimumweight, tracing how the world championship has passed from boxer to boxer from the start of each division to the present day.

RARE SUCCESS *WBA champion David Haye snaps back the head of WBO and IBF title-holder Wladimir Klitschko with a vicious left during their July 2011 World Heavyweight championship unification bout, but it was the Ukrainian who won a unanimous points decision*

For reasons of sanity as much as space, this list of world championship fights has been restricted to those involving the four major organizations: the World Boxing Council (WBC), World Boxing Association (WBA), International Boxing Federation (IBF) and World Boxing Organization (WBO). There are any number of other would-be governing bodies, including the World Boxing Union, the Intercontinental Boxing Council, the International Boxing Organization and so on *ad nauseam*, but they lack even the limited credibility of their more established rivals.

The chaos which reigns today in world boxing is deplorable but inevitable, given the close association which the various organizations enjoy with individual promoters and power groups within the sport. The bulk of their income derives from fees for sanctioning championships: the more title fights, the greater the cash flow. The simple days of eight weight divisions and eight champions have gone forever, and it is startling to realize just how far back in history they are.

The last time an undisputed world championship was contested in each of the 17 weight categories was:

Heavyweight: February 25, 1989: Mike Tyson vs. Frank Bruno
Cruiserweight: April 9, 1988: Evander Holyfield vs. Carlos DeLeon
Light-heavyweight: June 6, 1985: Mike Spinks vs. Jim MacDonald
Super-middleweight: July 26, 1987 Chang-Pal Park vs. Emmanuel Otti
Middleweight: March 10, 1986: Marvin Hagler vs. John Mugabi
Light-middle: January 21, 1975: Koichi Wajima vs. Oscar Albarado
Welterweight: September 27, 1986: Lloyd Honeyghan vs. Don Curry
Light-welterweight: November 16, 1967: Paul Fuji vs. Willi Quator
Lightweight: January 21, 1978: Roberto Duran vs. Esteban DeJesus
Super-featherweight: October 6, 1968: Hiroshi Kobayashi vs. Jaime Valladeres
Featherweight: October 14, 1967: Vicente Saldivar vs. Howard Winstone
Super-bantamweight: July 11, 1977: Wilfredo Gomez vs. Raul Tirado
Bantamweight: July 30, 1972: Enrique Pinder vs. Rafael Herrera
Super-flyweight: July 29, 1981: Chul-Ho Kim vs. Willie Jensen
Flyweight: April 23, 1965: Salvatore Burruni vs. Pone Kingpetch
Light-flyweight: April 4, 1975: Franco Udella vs. Valentin Martinez
Strawweight: June 14, 1987: Kyung-Yun Lee vs. Masaharu Kawakami

In several of those cases, the championship was "undisputed" only in so far as the other organizations had not yet followed the lead of the body which inaugurated the division. To be strictly accurate, none of the men who have styled themselves world champions since the dates shown above was anything more than the champion of the particular organization he represented – and that includes magnificent fighters like Julio Cesar Chavez, Azumah Nelson or Sot Chitalada, who would have won titles in any era.

For ease of reference, the various strands of each title have been disentangled rather than merely listing them all in indiscriminate chronological order. The history of the championships in the early days is cloudy, and there were often several versions of a title in circulation: nothing changes. The situation is further complicated by the sketchy records of the period, and the fact that many American states permitted boxing matches only on condition that no decision was given.

Barry Hugman, compiler of the estimable *British Boxing Yearbook*, has scoured newspaper files on both sides of the Atlantic in an effort to clarify the story, and future historians will be in his debt.

Heavyweight

Some historians' researches lead them to take the controversial view that the distinction of being the first world heavyweight champion in the modern sense belongs to the Australian Frank Slavin rather than to John L. Sullivan, who was the last of the bare-knuckle champions. Slavin stopped Jake Kilrain in nine rounds in June 1891 in a match made with four-ounce gloves, and was then knocked out by his compatriot Peter Jackson in the National Sporting Club, London, a year later.

But Jackson was black, and Sullivan, to his lasting discredit, put up the so-called "colour bar" which would remain in place until Jack Johnson's victory over Tommy Burns in 1908. When Sullivan finally came out of semi-retirement to fight James J. Corbett in September 1892, the gloved era had truly begun.

World Heavyweight Championship Bouts

Feb 7,	1882*	**John L. Sullivan** (US) w ko 9 Paddy Ryan (US)	Mississippi City, MS
Mar 10,	1888*	John L. Sullivan drew 39 Charlie Mitchell (Eng)	Chantilly (Fra)
Aug 8,	1889*	John L. Sullivan w rsf 75 Jake Kilrain (US)	Richburg, MS
		** Under London Prize Ring rules (bare-knuckle)*	
Sep 7,	1892	**James J. Corbett** (US) w ko 21 John L. Sullivan	New Orleans, LA
Jan 25,	1894	James J. Corbett w ko 3 Charlie Mitchell	Jacksonville, FL
Mar 17,	1897	**Bob Fitzsimmons** (Eng) w ko 14 James J. Corbett	Carson City, NV
Jun 9,	1899	**James J. Jeffries** (US) w ko 11 Bob Fitzsimmons	Coney Island, NY
Nov 3,	1899	James J. Jeffries w pts 25 Tom Sharkey (Ire)	Coney Island, NY
Apr 6,	1900	James J. Jeffries w ko 1 Jack Finnegan (US)	Detroit, MI
May 11,	1900	James J. Jeffries w ko 23 James J. Corbett	Coney Island, NY
Nov 15,	1901	James J. Jeffries w rtd 5 Gus Ruhlin (US)	San Francisco, CA
Jul 25,	1902	James J. Jeffries w ko 8 Bob Fitzsimmons	San Francisco, CA
Aug 14,	1903	James J. Jeffries w ko 10 James J. Corbett	San Francisco, CA
Aug 26,	1904	James J. Jeffries w ko 2 Jack Munroe (US)	San Francisco, CA
		Jeffries announced retirement	
Jul 3,	1905	**Marvin Hart** (US) w rsf 12 Jack Root (US)	Reno, NV
Feb 23,	1906	**Tommy Burns** (Can) w pts 20 Marvin Hart	Los Angeles, CA
Oct 2,	1906	Tommy Burns w ko 15 Jim Flynn (US)	Los Angeles, CA
Nov 28,	1906	Tommy Burns drew 20 Philadelphia Jack O'Brien (US)	Los Angeles, CA
May 8,	1907	Tommy Burns w pts 20 Philadelphia Jack O'Brien	Los Angeles, CA
Jul 4,	1907	Tommy Burns w ko 1 Bill Squires (Aus)	Colma, CA
Dec 2,	1907	Tommy Burns w ko 10 Gunner Moir (Eng)	London (Eng)
Feb 10,	1908	Tommy Burns w ko 4 Jack Palmer (Eng)	London (Eng)
Mar 17,	1908	Tommy Burns w ko 1 Jem Roche (Ire)	Dublin (Ire)
Apr 18,	1908	Tommy Burns w ko 5 Jewey Smith (Eng)	Paris (Fra)
Jun 13,	1908	Tommy Burns w ko 13 Bill Squires	Paris (Fra)
Aug 24,	1908	Tommy Burns w ko 13 Bill Squires	Sydney (Aus)
Sep 2,	1908	Tommy Burns w ko 6 Bill Lang (Aus)	Melbourne (Aus)
Dec 26,	1908	**Jack Johnson** (US) w rsf 14 Tommy Burns	Sydney (Aus)
Oct 16,	1909	Jack Johnson w ko 12 Stanley Ketchel (US)	Colma, CA
Jul 4,	1910	Jack Johnson w rsf 15 James J. Jeffries	Reno, NV
Jul 4,	1912	Jack Johnson w rsf 9 Jim Flynn	Las Vegas, NM
Dec 19,	1913	Jack Johnson drew 10 Jim Johnson (US)	Paris (Fra)
Jun 27,	1914	Jack Johnson w pts 20 Frank Moran (US)	Paris (Fra)
Apr 5,	1915	**Jess Willard** (US) w ko 26 Jack Johnson	Havana (Cub)
Mar 25,	1916	Jess Willard no dec 10 Frank Moran	New York, NY
Jul 4,	1919	**Jack Dempsey** (US) w rtd 3 Jess Willard	Toledo, OH
Sep 6,	1920	Jack Dempsey w ko 3 Billy Miske (US)	Benton Harbor, MI
Dec 14,	1920	Jack Dempsey w ko 12 Bill Brennan (US)	New York, NY
Jul 2,	1921	Jack Dempsey w ko 4 Georges Carpentier (Fra)	Jersey City, NJ
Jul 4,	1923	Jack Dempsey w pts 15 Tommy Gibbons (US)	Shelby, MT
Sep 14,	1923	Jack Dempsey w ko 2 Luis Angel Firpo (Arg)	New York, NY
Sep 23,	1926	**Gene Tunney** (US) w pts 10 Jack Dempsey	Philadelphia, PA
Sep 22,	1927	Gene Tunney w pts 10 Jack Dempsey	Chicago, IL
Jul 23,	1928	Gene Tunney w rsf 11 Tom Heeney (NZ)	New York, NY
		Tunney announced retirement	
Jun 12,	1930	**Max Schmeling** (Ger) w dis 4 Jack Sharkey (US)	New York, NY
Jul 3,	1931	Max Schmeling w rsf 15 Young Stribling (US)	Cleveland, OH
Jun 21,	1932	**Jack Sharkey** w pts 15 Max Schmeling	Long Island, NY
Jun 29,	1933	**Primo Carnera** (Ita) w ko 6 Jack Sharkey	Long Island, NY
Oct 22,	1933	Primo Carnera w pts 15 Paulino Uzcudun (Sp)	Rome (Ita)
Mar 1,	1934	Primo Carnera w pts 15 Tommy Loughran (US)	Miami, FL
Jun 14,	1934	**Max Baer** (US) w rsf 11 Primo Carnera	Long Island, NY
Jun 13,	1935	**James J. Braddock** (US) w pts 15 Max Baer	Long Island, NY
Jun 22,	1937	**Joe Louis** (US) w ko 8 James J. Braddock	Chicago, IL
Aug 30,	1937	Joe Louis w pts 15 Tommy Farr (Wal)	New York, NY
Feb 23,	1938	Joe Louis w ko 3 Nathan Mann (US)	New York, NY
Apr 1,	1938	Joe Louis w ko 5 Harry Thomas (US)	Chicago, IL
Jun 22,	1938	Joe Louis w ko 1 Max Schmeling	New York, NY
Jan 25,	1939	Joe Louis w rsf 1 John Henry Lewis (US)	New York, NY
Apr 17,	1939	Joe Louis w ko 1 Jack Roper (US)	Los Angeles, CA
Jun 28,	1939	Joe Louis w rsf 4 Tony Galento (US)	New York, NY
Sep 20,	1939	Joe Louis w ko 11 Bob Pastor (US)	Detroit, MI
Feb 9,	1940	Joe Louis w pts 15 Arturo Godoy (Ch)	New York, NY
Mar 29,	1940	Joe Louis w rsf 2 Johnny Paycheck (US)	New York, NY
Jun 20,	1940	Joe Louis w rsf 8 Arturo Godoy	New York, NY
Dec 16,	1940	Joe Louis w rtd 6 Al McCoy (US)	Boston, MA
Jan 31,	1941	Joe Louis w ko 5 Red Burman (US)	New York, NY
Feb17,	1941	Joe Louis w ko 2 Gus Dorazio (US)	Philadelphia, PA
Mar 21,	1941	Joe Louis w rsf 13 Abe Simon (US)	Detroit, MI
Apr 8,	1941	Joe Louis w rsf 9 Tony Musto (US)	St Louis, MO
May 23,	1941	Joe Louis w dis 7 Buddy Baer (US)	Washington, DC
Jun 18,	1941	Joe Louis w ko 13 Billy Conn (US)	New York, NY
Sep 29,	1941	Joe Louis w rsf 6 Lou Nova (US)	New York, NY
Jan 9,	1942	Joe Louis w ko 1 Buddy Baer	New York, NY
Mar 27,	1942	Joe Louis w ko 6 Abe Simon	New York, NY
Jun 19,	1946	Joe Louis w ko 8 Billy Conn	New York, NY
Sep 18,	1946	Joe Louis w ko 1 Tami Mauriello (US)	New York, NY
Dec 5,	1947	Joe Louis w pts 15 Jersey Joe Walcott (US)	New York, NY
Jun 25,	1948	Joe Louis w ko 11 Jersey Joe Walcott	New York, NY
		Louis announced retirement	
Jun 22,	1949	**Ezzard Charles** (US) w pts 15 Jersey Joe Walcott	Chicago, IL
		For vacant NBA title	
Aug 10,	1949	Ezzard Charles w rsf 7 Gus Lesnevich (US)	New York, NY
Oct 14,	1949	Ezzard Charles w ko 8 Pat Valentino (US)	San Francisco, CA
Aug 15,	1950	Ezzard Charles w rsf 14 Freddy Beshore (US)	Buffalo, NY
Sep 27,	1950	Ezzard Charles w pts 15 Joe Louis	New York, NY
		(Undisputed title)	
Dec 5,	1950	Ezzard Charles w ko 11 Nick Barone (US)	Cincinnati, OH
Jan 12,	1951	Ezzard Charles w rsf 10 Lee Oma (US)	New York, NY
Mar 7,	1951	Ezzard Charles w pts 15 Jersey Joe Walcott	Detroit, MI
May 30,	1951	Ezzard Charles w pts 15 Joey Maxim (US)	Chicago, IL
Jul 18,	1951	**Jersey Joe Walcott** w ko 7 Ezzard Charles	Pittsburgh, PA
Jun 5,	1952	Jersey Joe Walcott w pts 15 Ezzard Charles	Philadelphia, PA
Sep 23,	1952	**Rocky Marciano** (US) w ko 13 Jersey Joe Walcott	Philadelphia, PA
May 15,	1953	Rocky Marciano w ko 1 Jersey Joe Walcott	Chicago, IL
Sep 24,	1953	Rocky Marciano w rsf 11 Roland La Starza (US)	New York, NY
Jun 17,	1954	Rocky Marciano w pts 15 Ezzard Charles	New York, NY
Sep 17,	1954	Rocky Marciano w ko 8 Ezzard Charles	New York, NY
May 16,	1955	Rocky Marciano w rsf 9 Don Cockell (Eng)	San Francisco, CA
Sep 21,	1955	Rocky Marciano w ko 9 Archie Moore (US)	New York, NY
		Marciano announced retirement	
Nov 30,	1956	**Floyd Patterson** (US) w ko 5 Archie Moore	Chicago, IL
Jul 29,	1957	Floyd Patterson w rsf 10 Tommy Jackson (US)	New York, NY
Aug 22,	1957	Floyd Patterson w ko 6 Pete Rademacher (US)	Seattle, WA
Aug 18,	1958	Floyd Patterson w rtd 12 Roy Harris (US)	Los Angeles, CA
May 1,	1959	Floyd Patterson w ko 11 Brian London (Eng)	Indianapolis, IN
Jun 26,	1959	**Ingemar Johansson** (Swe) w rsf 3 Floyd Patterson	New York, NY
Jun 20,	1960	**Floyd Patterson** w ko 5 Ingemar Johansson	New York, NY
Mar 13,	1961	Floyd Patterson w ko 6 Ingemar Johansson	Miami, FL
Dec 4,	1961	Floyd Patterson w ko 4 Tom McNeeley (US)	Toronto (Can)
Sep 25,	1962	**Sonny Liston** (US) w ko 1 Floyd Patterson	Chicago, IL
Jul 22,	1963	Sonny Liston w ko 1 Floyd Patterson	Las Vegas, NV
Feb 25,	1964	**Cassius Clay** (US) w rtd 6 Sonny Liston	Miami, FL
		Clay announced he would henceforth be known as Muhammad Ali	
Sep 14,	1964	*WBA withdrew recognition of Ali because he signed for return bout with Sonny Liston*	
Mar 5,	1965	**Ernie Terrell** (US) w pts 15 Eddie Machen (US)	Chicago, IL
		For vacant WBA title	
May 25,	1965	Muhammad Ali w ko 1 Sonny Liston	Lewiston, ME
Nov 1,	1965	Ernie Terrell w pts 15 George Chuvalo (Can)	Toronto (Can)
		WBA title	
Nov 22,	1965	Muhammad Ali w rsf 12 Floyd Patterson	Las Vegas, NV
Mar 29,	1966	Muhammad Ali w pts 15 George Chuvalo	Toronto (Can)
May 21,	1966	Muhammad Ali w rsf 6 Henry Cooper (Eng)	London (Eng)
Jun 28,	1966	Ernie Terrell w pts 15 Doug Jones	Houston, TX
		WBA title	
Aug 6,	1966	Muhammad Ali w ko 3 Brian London	London (Eng)
Sep 10,	1966	Muhammad Ali w rsf 12 Karl Mildenberger (Ger)	Frankfurt (Ger)
Nov 14,	1966	Muhammad Ali w rsf 3 Cleveland Williams (US)	Houston, TX
Feb 6,	1967	Muhammad Ali w pts 15 Ernie Terrell	Houston, TX
		(Undisputed title)	
Mar 22,	1967	Muhammad Ali w ko 7 Zora Folley (US)	New York, NY
Apr 28,	1967	*Ali stripped of title by WBA and New York State Athletic Commission for refusing to join US Army*	

JOHN L. SULLIVAN *and Jake Kilrain in the last championship fight staged under London Prize Ring rules*

New York title

Mar 4, 1968	**Joe Frazier** (US) w rsf 11 Buster Mathis (US)	New York, NY
	For vacant title	
Jun 24, 1968	Joe Frazier w rtd 2 Manuel Ramos (Mex)	New York, NY
Dec 10, 1968	Joe Frazier w pts 15 Oscar Bonavena (Arg)	Philadelphia, PA
Apr 22, 1969	Joe Frazier w ko 1 Dave Zyglewicz (US)	Houston, TX
Jun 23, 1969	Joe Frazier w rsf 7 Jerry Quarry (US)	New York, NY
Feb 16, 1970	Joe Frazier w rtd 4 Jimmy Ellis (US)	New York, NY
	Undisputed title	

Undisputed title

Nov 18, 1970	Joe Frazier w ko 2 Bob Foster (US)	Detroit, MI
Mar 8, 1971	Joe Frazier w pts 15 Muhammad Ali	New York, NY
Jan 15, 1972	Joe Frazier w rsf 4 Terry Daniels (US)	New Orleans, LA
May 25, 1972	Joe Frazier w rsf 4 Ron Stander (US)	Omaha, NE
Jan 22, 1973	**George Foreman** (US) w rsf 2 Joe Frazier	Kingston (Jam)
Sep 1, 1973	George Foreman w ko 1 Joe Roman (PR)	Tokyo (Jap)
Mar 26, 1974	George Foreman w rsf 2 Ken Norton (US)	Caracas (Ven)
Oct 30, 1974	**Muhammad Ali** w ko 8 George Foreman	Kinshasa (Za)
Mar 24, 1975	Muhammad Ali w rsf 15 Chuck Wepner (US)	Cleveland, OH
May 16, 1975	Muhammad Ali w rsf 11 Ron Lyle (US)	Las Vegas, NV
Jul 1, 1975	Muhammad Ali w pts 15 Joe Bugner (Eng)	Kuala Lumpur (Mal)
Oct 1, 1975	Muhammad Ali w rtd 14 Joe Frazier	Manila (Phil)
Feb 10, 1976	Muhammad Ali w ko 5 Jean-Pierre Coopman (Bel)	San Juan, CA
Apr 30, 1976	Muhammad Ali w pts 15 Jimmy Young (US)	Landover, MD
May 25, 1976	Muhammad Ali w rsf 5 Richard Dunn (Eng)	Munich (Ger)
Sep 28, 1976	Muhammad Ali w pts 15 Ken Norton	New York, NY
May 16, 1977	Muhammad Ali w pts 15 Alfredo Evangelista (Sp)	Landover, MD
Sep 29, 1977	Muhammad Ali w pts 15 Earnie Shavers (US)	New York, NY
Feb 15, 1978	**Leon Spinks** (US) w pts 15 Muhammad Ali	Las Vegas, NV
Mar 18, 1978	*Spinks stripped by the WBC for his failure to defend against Ken Norton. The WBC then proclaimed Norton champion on the basis of his 15-rounds points win over Jimmy Young in their final eliminator in Las Vegas on November 5, 1977*	

WBC title

Jun 10, 1978	**Larry Holmes** (US) w pts 15 Ken Norton	Las Vegas, NV
Nov 10, 1978	Larry Holmes w ko 7 Alfredo Evangelista	Las Vegas, NV
Mar 24, 1979	Larry Holmes w rsf 7 Osvaldo Ocasio (PR)	Las Vegas, NV
Jun 22, 1979	Larry Holmes w rsf 12 Mike Weaver (US)	New York, NY
Sep 28, 1979	Larry Holmes w rsf 11 Earnie Shavers	Las Vegas, NV
Feb 3, 1980	Larry Holmes w ko 6 Lorenzo Zanon (Ita)	Las Vegas, NV
Mar 31, 1980	Larry Holmes w pts 15 Trevor Berbick (Jam)	Las Vegas, NV
Jul 7, 1980	Larry Holmes w rsf 7 Scott LeDoux (US)	Bloomington, MN
Oct 2, 1980	Larry Holmes w rtd 10 Muhammad Ali	Las Vegas, NV
Apr 11, 1981	Larry Holmes w pts 15 Trevor Berbick	Las Vegas, NV
Jun 12, 1981	Larry Holmes w rsf 3 Leon Spinks	Detroit, MI
Nov 6, 1981	Larry Holmes w rsf 11 Renaldo Snipes (US)	Pittsburgh, PA
Jun 11, 1982	Larry Holmes w dis 13 Gerry Cooney (US)	Las Vegas, NV
Nov 26, 1982	Larry Holmes w pts 15 Randy "Tex" Cobb (US)	Houston, TX

RINGSIDE VIEW

Leon Spinks vs Muhammad Ali

DO THE HUSTLE

Upsets are the life-blood of boxing, and there has rarely been a bigger one than when Leon Spinks, a seven-fight novice, outhustled Muhammad Ali for 15 rounds in Las Vegas in February 1979. Spinks, the former Olympic champion, fought with an inspired intensity which the jaded Ali could not match.

Mar 27, 1983	Larry Holmes w pts 12 Lucien Rodriguez (Fra)	Scranton, PA
May 20, 1983	Larry Holmes w pts 12 Tim Witherspoon (US)	Las Vegas, NV
Sep 10, 1983	Larry Holmes w rsf 5 Scott Frank (US)	Atlantic City, NJ
Dec 1983	*Holmes relinquished WBC title and accepted recognition from the newly formed International Boxing Federation*	
Mar 9, 1984	**Tim Witherspoon** w pts 12 Greg Page (US) *For vacant title*	Las Vegas, NV
Aug 31, 1984	**Pinklon Thomas** (US) w pts 12 Tim Witherspoon	Las Vegas, NV
Jun 15, 1985	Pinklon Thomas w ko 8 Mike Weaver	Las Vegas, NV
Mar 22, 1986	**Trevor Berbick** w pts 12 Pinklon Thomas	Las Vegas, NV
Nov 22, 1986	**Mike Tyson** (US) w rsf 2 Trevor Berbick	Las Vegas, NV
Mar 7, 1987	Mike Tyson w pts 12 James "Bonecrusher" Smith (US) *Tyson won Smith's WBA title*	Las Vegas, NV
May 30, 1987	Mike Tyson w rsf 6 Pinklon Thomas	Las Vegas, NV
Aug 1, 1987	Mike Tyson w pts 12 Tony Tucker (US) *For unified and undisputed world title.*	Las Vegas, NV
May 8, 1993	**Lennox Lewis** (Eng) w pts 12 Tony Tucker	Las Vegas, NV
Oct 1, 1993	Lennox Lewis w rsf 7 Frank Bruno	Cardiff (Wal)
May 6, 1994	Lennox Lewis w rsf 8 Phil Jackson (US)	Atlantic City, NJ
Sep 24, 1994	**Oliver McCall** (US) w rsf 2 Lennox Lewis	London (Eng)
Apr 8, 1995	Oliver McCall w pts 12 Larry Holmes	Las Vegas, NV
Sep 2, 1995	**Frank Bruno** w pts 12 Oliver McCall	Wembley (Eng)
Mar 16, 1996	**Mike Tyson** w rsf 3 Frank Bruno	Las Vegas, NV
Sep 1996	*Tyson forfeited the title for his failure to defend against Lennox Lewis*	
Feb 7, 1997	Lennox Lewis w rsf 5 Oliver McCall *For vacant title*	Las Vegas, NV
July 12, 1997	**Lennox Lewis** w dis 5 Henry Akinwande (Eng)	Lake Tahoe, NV
Oct 4, 1997	Lennox Lewis w ko 1 Andrew Golota (Pol)	Atlantic City, NJ
Mar 28, 1998	Lennox Lewis w rsf 5 Shannon Briggs (US)	Atlantic City, NJ
Sep 26, 1998	Lennox Lewis w pts 12 Zeljko Mavrovic (Cro)	Uncasville, CT

WBA title

Apr 27, 1968	**Jimmy Ellis** w pts 15 Jerry Quarry *For vacant title*	Oakland, CA
Sep 14, 1968	Jimmy Ellis w pts 15 Floyd Patterson	Stockholm (Swe)
Feb 16, 1970	**Joe Frazier** w rtd 4 Jimmy Ellis *Undisputed title*	New York, NY
Sep 15, 1978	**Muhammad Ali** w pts 15 Leon Spinks *Muhammad Ali announced his retirement as WBA champion*	New Orleans, LA
Oct 20, 1979	**John Tate** (US) w pts 15 Gerrie Coetzee (SA) *For vacant title*	Pretoria (SA)
Mar 31, 1980	**Mike Weaver** w ko 15 John Tate	Knoxville, TN
Oct 25, 1980	Mike Weaver w ko 13 Gerrie Coetzee	Sun City (Bop)
Oct 3, 1981	Mike Weaver w pts 15 James Tillis (US)	Rosemount, IL
Dec 10, 1982	**Mike Dokes** (US) w rsf 1 Mike Weaver	Las Vegas, NV
May 20, 1983	Mike Dokes drew 15 Mike Weaver	Las Vegas, NV
Sep 23, 1983	**Gerrie Coetzee** w ko 10 Mike Dokes	Richfield, OH
Dec 1, 1984	**Greg Page** w ko 8 Gerrie Coetzee	Sun City (Bop)
Apr 29, 1985	**Tony Tubbs** (US) w pts 15 Greg Page	Buffalo, NY
Jan 17, 1986	**Tim Witherspoon** w pts 15 Tony Tubbs	Atlanta, GA
Jul 19, 1986	Tim Witherspoon w rsf 11 Frank Bruno (Eng)	Wembley (Eng)
Dec 12, 1986	**James "Bonecrusher" Smith** w rsf 1 Tim Witherspoon	New York, NY
Mar 7, 1987	**Mike Tyson** w pts 12 James Smith	Las Vegas, NV
May 30, 1987	Mike Tyson w rsf 6 Pinklon Thomas	Las Vegas, NV
Aug 1, 1987	Mike Tyson w pts 12 Tony Tucker *For unified and undisputed world title*	Las Vegas, NV

IBF title

Dec 1983	*The IBF proclaimed Holmes champion after he had given up the WBC title*	
Nov 9, 1984	**Larry Holmes** w rsf 12 James "Bonecrusher" Smith	Las Vegas, NV
Mar 15, 1985	Larry Holmes w rsf 10 David Bey (US)	Las Vegas, NV
May 20, 1985	Larry Holmes w pts 15 Carl Williams (US)	Reno, NV
Sep 21, 1985	**Mike Spinks** (US) w pts 15 Larry Holmes	Las Vegas, NV
Apr 19, 1986	Mike Spinks w pts 15 Larry Holmes	Las Vegas, NV
Sep 6, 1986	Mike Spinks w rsf 4 Steffen Tangstad (Nor)	Las Vegas, NV
Feb 1987	*Spinks was stripped for signing to fight Gerry Cooney rather than the IBF No. 1, Tony Tucker*	
May 30, 1987	**Tony Tucker** (US) w rsf 10 James "Buster" Douglas (US) *For vacant title*	Las Vegas, NV
Aug 1, 1987	**Mike Tyson** w pts 12 Tony Tucker *For unified and undisputed world title*	Las Vegas, NV
Apr 22, 1995	**George Foreman** w pts 12 Axel Schulz (Ger)	Las Vegas, NV
Jul 1995	*Foreman vacated title rather than face Schulz in a rematch in Germany*	
Dec 9, 1995	**Frans Botha** w pts 12 Axel Schulz *For vacant title*	Stuttgart, (Ger)
Mar 1996	*Botha was stripped of the title for failing a drugs test after beating Schulz*	
Jun 22, 1996	**Michael Moorer** (US) w pts 12 Axel Schulz *For vacant title*	Dortmund, (Ger)
Nov 9, 1996	Michael Moorer w rsf 12 Frans Botha	Las Vegas, NV
Mar 29, 1997	Michael Moorer w pts 12 Vaughn Bean (US)	Las Vegas, NV

Undisputed title

Oct 16, 1987	**Mike Tyson** w rsf 7 Tyrell Biggs (US)	Atlantic City, NJ
Jan 22, 1988	Mike Tyson w rsf 4 Larry Holmes	Atlantic City, NJ
Mar 21, 1988	Mike Tyson w rsf 2 Tony Tubbs	Tokyo (Jap)
Jun 27, 1988	Mike Tyson w ko 1 Mike Spinks	Atlantic City, NJ
Feb 25, 1989	Mike Tyson w rsf 5 Frank Bruno	Las Vegas, NV

The newly formed WBO announced that they would recognize the winner between Francesco Damiani and Johnny Du Plooy as champion, rather than Tyson, a decision which set new standards in eccentricity

WBC/WBA/IBF titles

Jul 21, 1989	**Mike Tyson** w rsf 1 Carl Williams	Atlantic City, NJ
Feb 11, 1990	**James "Buster" Douglas** w ko 10 Mike Tyson	Tokyo (Jap)
Oct 25, 1990	**Evander Holyfield** (US) w ko 3 James "Buster" Douglas	Las Vegas, NV
Apr 19, 1991	Evander Holyfield w pts 12 George Foreman	Atlantic City, NJ
Nov 23, 1991	Evander Holyfield w rsf 7 Bert Cooper (US)	Atlanta, GA
Jun 19, 1992	Evander Holyfield w pts 12 Larry Holmes	Las Vegas, NV
Nov 14, 1992	**Riddick Bowe** (US) w pts 12 Evander Holyfield	Las Vegas, NV
Dec 1992	*Bowe relinquished the WBC title rather than defend against Britain's Lennox Lewis, who was awarded the championship retrospectively on the basis of his second-round stoppage of Razor Ruddock in London on October 31, 1992 in an official WBC final eliminator*	

WBA/IBF titles

Feb 6, 1993	**Riddick Bowe** w rsf 1 Mike Dokes	New York, NY
May 22, 1993	Riddick Bowe w rsf 2 Jesse Ferguson (US)	Washington, DC
Nov 6, 1993	**Evander Holyfield** w pts 12 Riddick Bowe	Las Vegas, NV
Apr 22, 1994	**Michael Moorer** (US) w pts 12 Evander Holyfield	Las Vegas, NV
Nov 5, 1994	**George Foreman** w ko 10 Michael Moorer	Las Vegas, NV
Mar 1995	*Foreman stripped of the WBA title for failing to defend*	
Nov 8, 1997	**Evander Holyfield** w rsf 8 Michael Moorer	Las Vegas, NV
Sep 19, 1998	Evander Holyfield w pts 12 Vaughn Bean	Atlanta, GA

WBA title

Apr 8, 1995	**Bruce Seldon** (US) w rtd 7 Tony Tucker (US) *For vacant title*	Las Vegas, NV
Aug 19, 1995	Bruce Seldon w rsf 10 Joe Hipp (US)	Las Vegas, NV
Sep 7, 1996	**Mike Tyson** w rsf 1 Bruce Seldon	Las Vegas, NV
Nov 9, 1996	**Evander Holyfield** w rsf 11 Mike Tyson	Las Vegas, NV
Jun 28, 1997	Evander Holyfield w dis 3 Mike Tyson	Las Vegas, NV

WBC/WBA/IBF titles

Mar 13, 1999	Lennox Lewis drew 12 Evander Holyfield	New York, NY
Nov 13, 1999	Lennox Lewis w pts 12 Evander Holyfield	Las Vegas, NV
Apr 2000	*Lewis was stripped of the WBA title by a US court decision for failing to honour a commitment to box the WBA No. 1 next.*	

WBC/IBF titles

Apr 29, 2000	**Lennox Lewis** w ko 2 Michael Grant (US)	New York, NY
Jul 15, 2000	Lennox Lewis w rsf 2 Frans Botha (SA)	London (Eng)
Nov 11, 2000	Lennox Lewis w pts 12 David Tua (NZ)	Las Vegas, NV
Apr 22, 2001	**Hasim Rahman** (US) w ko 5 Lennox Lewis	Brakpan (SA)
Nov 17, 2001	**Lennox Lewis** w ko 4 Hasim Rahman	Las Vegas, NV
Jun 8, 2002	Lennox Lewis w ko 8 Mike Tyson	Memphis, TN

WBA title

Aug 12, 2000	**Evander Holyfield** w pts 12 John Ruiz (US)	Las Vegas, NV
	For vacant title	
Mar 2, 2001	**John Ruiz** w pts 12 Evander Holyfield	Las Vegas, NV
Dec 15, 2001	John Ruiz drew 12 Evander Holyfield	Uncasville, CT
Jul 27, 2002	John Ruiz w dis 10 Kirk Johnson (Can)	Las Vegas, NV
Mar 1, 2003	**Roy Jones** (US) w pts 12 John Ruiz	Las Vegas, NV
	Jones relinquished title to move back to light-heavyweight	
Dec 13, 2003	**John Ruiz** w pts 12 Hasim Rahman	Atlantic City, NJ
Apr 17, 2004	John Ruiz w rsf 11 Fres Oquendo (PR)	New York, NY
Nov 13, 2004	John Ruiz w pts 12 Andrew Golota (Pol)	New York, NY
Apr 30, 2005	John Ruiz nc 12* James Toney (US)	New York, NY
	** Toney won on points but tested positive for a banned substance. The result was changed to a no contest, which meant Ruiz retained the title.*	
Dec 17, 2005	**Nikolay Valuev** w (Rus) pts 12 John Ruiz	Berlin (Ger)
Jun 3, 2006	Nikolay Valuev w rsf 3 Owen Beck (Jam)	Hannover (Ger)
Oct 7, 2006	Nikolay Valuev w rsf 11 Monte Barrett (US)	Rosemont, IL
Jan 20, 2007	Nikolay Valuev w rsf 3 Jameel McCline (US)	Basel (Swi)
Apr 14, 2007	**Ruslan Chagaev** (Uzb) w pts 12 Nikolay Valuev (US)	Stuttgart (Ger)
Jan 19, 2008	Ruslan Chagaev w pts 12 Matt Skelton (Eng)	Dusseldorf (Ger)
	Ruslan Chagaev was declared Champion In Recess after injury forced a cancellation of a defence against Nikolay Valuev on July 5, 2008. Valuev boxed John Ruiz for the vacant world title, but when Chagaev was fit, he was also recognized as champion when he boxed Carl Davis Drummond. However, when Chagaev failed a medical before another fight with Valuev on May 30, 2009, Valuev was recognised as the sole WBA champion.	
Aug 30, 2008	**Nikolay Valuev** w pts 12 John Ruiz	Berlin (Ger)
Dec 20, 2008	Nikolay Valuev w pts 12 Evander Holyfield	Zurich (Swi)
Feb 7, 2009	**Ruslan Chagaev** w tdec 6 Carl Davis Drummond (CR)	Rostock (Ger)
Nov 7, 2009	**David Haye** w pts 12 Nikolay Valuev	Nuremberg (Ger)
Apr 3, 2010	David Haye w rsf 9 John Ruiz	Manchester (Eng)
Nov 13, 2010	David Haye w rsf 3 Audley Harrison (Eng).	Manchester (Eng)
Mar 2011	The WBA upgraded Haye to Super champion	
Aug 27, 2011	**Alexander Povetkin** (Rus) w pts Ruslan Chagaev	Erfut (Ger)
	For vacant title	
Dec 3, 2011	Alexander Povetkin w ko 8 Cedric Boswell (US)	Helsinki (Fin)
Feb 25, 2012	Alexander Povetkin w pts 12 Marco Huck (Ger)	Stuttgart (Ger)
Sep 29, 2012	Alexander Povetkin w rsf 2 Hasim Rahman	Hamburg (Ger)

WBO title

May 6, 1989	**Francesco Damiani** (Ita) w ko 3 Johnny Du Plooy (SA)	Syracuse, NY
	For vacant title	
Dec 16, 1989	Francesco Damiani w rtd 2 Daniel Netto (Arg)	Cesena (Ita)
Jan 11, 1991	**Ray Mercer** (US) w ko 9 Francesco Damiani	Atlantic City, NJ
Oct 18, 1991	Ray Mercer w rsf 5 Tommy Morrison (US)	Atlantic City, NJ
Jan 1992	*Mercer was stripped for failing to defend against Michael Moorer*	
May 15, 1992	**Michael Moorer** w rsf 5 Bert Cooper	Atlantic City, NJ
Feb 1993	*Moorer relinquished the WBO title because it was "retarding his career"*	
Jun 7, 1993	**Tommy Morrison** w pts 12 George Foreman	Las Vegas, NV
	For vacant title	
Oct 29, 1993	**Michael Bentt** (US) w rsf 1 Tommy Morrison	Tulsa, OK
Mar 19, 1994	**Herbie Hide** (Eng) w ko 7 Michael Bentt	London (Eng)
Mar 11, 1995	**Riddick Bowe** w ko 6 Herbie Hide	Las Vegas, NV
Jun 17, 1995	Riddick Bowe w ko 6 Jorge Luis Gonzalez (Cub)	Las Vegas, NV
Jul 1995	*Bowe vacated title*	
Oct 1995	*Bowe requested reinstatement as champion, although his third fight with Evander Holyfield in Las Vegas on November 4, 1995, which Bowe won on an eighth-round stoppage, was not billed as a title defence*	
Jun 29, 1996	**Henry Akinwande** (Eng) w ko 3 Jeremy Williams (US)	Indio, CA
	For vacant title	
Nov 9 1996	Henry Akinwande w rsf 10 Alexander Zolkin (Rus)	Las Vegas, NV
Jan 11, 1997	Henry Akinwande w pts 12 Scott Welch (Eng)	Nashville, Tenn.
Feb 1997	*Akinwande relinquished the WBO title to challenge for the WBC version*	
Jun 28, 1997	**Herbie Hide** (Eng) w rsf 2 Tony Tucker (US)	Norwich (Eng)
Apr 18, 1998	Herbie Hide w rsf 1 Damon Reed (US)	Manchester (Eng)
Sep 26, 1998	Herbie Hide w rsf 2 Willi Fischer (Ger)	Norwich (Eng)
Jun 26, 1999	**Vitaly Klitschko** (Ukr) w ko 2 Herbie Hide	London (Eng)
Oct 9, 1999	Vitaly Klitschko w rsf 3 Ed Mahone (US)	Oberhausen (Ger)
Dec 11, 1999	Vitaly Klitschko w rtd 9 Obed Sullivan (US)	Phoenix, AZ
Apr 1, 2000	**Chris Byrd** (US) w rtd 9 Vitaly Klitschko	Berlin (Ger)
Oct 14, 2000	**Wladimir Klitschko** (Ukr) w pts 12 Chris Byrd	Cologne (Ger)
Mar 24, 2001	Wladimir Klitschko w rsf 2 Derrick Jefferson (US)	Munich (Ger)
Aug 4, 2001	Wladimir Klitschko w rsf 6 Charles Shufford (US)	Las Vegas, NV
Mar 16, 2002	Wladimir Klitschko w rsf 8 Frans Botha (SA)	Stuttgart (Ger)
Jun 29, 2002	Wladimir Klitschko w rsf 6 Ray Mercer (US)	Atlantic City, NJ
Dec 7, 2002	Wladimir Klitschko w rsf 10 Jameel McCline (US)	Las Vegas, NV
Mar 8, 2003	**Corrie Sanders** (SA) w rsf 2 Wladimir Klitschko	Hannover (Ger)
	Sanders announced his retirement	
Apr 10, 2004	**Lamon Brewster** (US) w rsf 5 Wladimir Klitschko	Las Vegas, NV
	For vacant title	
Sep 4, 2004	Lamon Brewster w pts 12 Kali Meehan (NZ)	Las Vegas, NV
May 21, 2005	Lamon Brewster w rsf 1 Andrew Golota (Pol)	Chicago, IL
Sep 28, 2005	Lamon Brewster w rsf 9 Luan Krasniqi (Ger)	Hamburg (Ger)
Apr 1, 2006	**Sergei Lyakhovich** (Blr) w pts 12 Lamon Brewster	Cleveland, OH
Nov 4, 2006	**Shannon Briggs** (US) w ko 12 Sergei Lyakhovich	Phoenix, AZ
Jun 2, 2007	**Sultan Ibragimov** (Rus) w pts 12 Shannon Briggs	Atlantic City, NJ
Oct 13, 2007	Sultan Ibragimov w pts 12 Evander Holyfield	Moscow (Rus)

THE BEAST FROM THE EAST *Nikolay Valuev, all 7ft and 23st of him, in full flow, sends Monte Barrett staggering into the ropes during their WBA title fight*

WBC title

Jun 21, 2003	Lennox Lewis w rsf 6 Vitali Klitschko (Ukr)	Los Angeles, CA
	Lewis announced his retirement in Feb 2004.	
Apr 24, 2004	**Vitali Klitschko** w rsf 8 Corrie Sanders (SA)	Los Angeles, CA
	For vacant title	
Dec 11, 2004	Vitali Klitschko w rsf 8 Danny Williams (Eng)	Las Vegas, NV
	Klitschko announced his retirement. Hasim Rahman declared interim champ.	
Mar 18, 2006	**Hasim Rahman** (US) drew 12 James Toney (US)	Atlantic City, NJ
Aug 12, 2006	**Oleg Maskaev** (Rus) w rsf 12 Hasim Rahman	Las Vegas, NV
Dec 10, 2006	Oleg Maskaev w pts 12 Peter Okhello (Ug)	Moscow (Rus)
Mar 8, 2008	**Samuel Peter** (Nig) w rsf 6 Oleg Maskaev	Cancun (Mex)
Oct 11, 2008	**Vitali Klitschko** w rtd 8 Samuel Peter	Berlin (Ger)
Mar 21, 2009	Vitali Klitschko w rsf 9 Juan Carlos Gomez (Cub)	Stuttgart (Ger)
Sep 26, 2009	Vitali Klitschko w rtd 10 Chris Arreola (US)	Los Angeles, CA
Dec 12, 2009	Vitali Klitschko w pts 12 Kevin Johnson (US)	Berne (Swi)
May 29, 2010	Vitali Klitschko w ko 10 Albert Sosnowski (Pol)	Gelsenkirchen (Ger)
Oct 16, 2010	Vitali Klitschko w pts 12 Shannon Briggs	Hamburg (Ger)
Mar 19, 2011	Vitali Klitschko w ko 1 Odlanier Solis (Cub)	Cologne (Ger)
Sep 10, 2011	Vitali Klitschko w rsf 10 Tomasz Adamek	Wroclaw (Pol)
Feb 18, 2012	Vitali Klitschko w pts 12 Dereck Chisora (Eng)	Munich (Ger)
Sep 8, 2012	Vitali Klitschko w rsf 4 Manuel Charr (Ger)	Moscow (Rus)
Dec 2013	*Vitali Klitschko announced he was vacating title*	
May 10, 2014	**Bermane Stiverne** (Hai) w rsc 6 Chris Arreola (US)	Los Angeles, CA
	For vacant title	
Jan 17, 2015	**Deontay Wilder** (US) w pts 12 Bermane Stiverne	Las Vegas, NV
Jun 13, 2015	Deontay Wilder w ko 9 Eric Molina (US)	Birmingham, AL
Sep 26, 2015	Deontay Wilder w rsf 11 Johann Duhaupas (Fra)	Birmingham, AL
Jan 16, 2016	Deontay Wilder w ko 9 Artur Szpilka (Pol)	New York, NY
Jul 16, 2016	Deontay Wilder w rtd 8 Chris Arreola (US)	Birmingham, AL
Feb 25, 2017	Deontay Wilder w rsf 5 Gerald Washington (US)	Birmingham, AL
Nov 4, 2017	Deontay Wilder w ko 1 Bermane Stiverne (Can)	New York, NY

IBF title

Dec 14, 2002	**Chris Byrd** (US) w pts 12 Evander Holyfield	Atlantic City, NJ
	For vacant title after Lennox Lewis had been stripped of the championship	
Sep 20, 2003	Chris Byrd w pts 12 Fres Oquendo (PR)	Uncasville, CT
Apr 17, 2004	Chris Byrd drew 12 Andrew Golota (Pol)	New York, NY
Nov 13, 2004	Chris Byrd w pts 12 Jameel McCline (US)	New York, NY
Oct 1, 2005	Chris Byrd w pts 12 DaVarryl Williamson (US)	Reno, NV
Apr 22, 2006	**Wladimir Klitschko** w rsf 7 Chris Byrd	Mannheim (Ger)

WLADIMIR KLITSCHKO *made light work of the Bulgarian Kubrat Pulev in the November 2014 fight in Hamburg, knocking him out in five rounds*

ANTHONY JOSHUA *overpowered American champion Charles Martin in April 2016 to claim the IBF heavyweight title*

Nov 11, 2006	Wladimir Klitschko w rsf 7 Calvin Brock (US)	New York, NY
Mar 10, 2007	Wladimir Klitschko w rsf 2 Ray Austin (US)	Mannheim, (Ger)
Jul 7, 2007	Wladimir Klitschko w rtd 6 Lamont Brewster (US)	Cologne, (Ger)r

IBF/WBO titles

Feb 23, 2008	**Wladimir Klitschko** w pts 12 Sultan Ibragimov	New York, NY
Feb 23 2008	Wladimir Klitschko w pts 12 Sultan Ibragimov	New York, NY
Jul 12, 2008	Wladimir Klitschko w ko 11 Tony Thompson (US)	Hamburg (Ger)
Dec 13, 2008	Wladimir Klitschko w rsf 7 Hasim Rahman	Mannheim (Ger)
Jun 20, 2009	Wladimir Klitschko w rtd 9 Ruslan Chagaev	Gelsenkirchen (Ger)
Mar 20, 2010	Wladimir Klitschko w ko 12 Eddie Chambers (US)	Dusseldorf (Ger)
Sep 11, 2010	Wladimir Klitschko w pts 12 Samuel Peter	Frankfurt (Ger)

IBF/WBO/WBA super titles

Jul 2, 2011	**Wladimir Klitschko** w pts 12 David Haye	Hamburg (Ger)
Mar 3, 2012	Wladimir Klitschko w ko 4 Jean-Marc Mormeck (Fr)	Dusseldorf (Ger)
Jul 7, 2012	Wladimir Klitschko w rsf 6 Tony Thompson (US)	Berne (Swi)
Nov 10, 2012	Wladimir Klitschko w pts 12 Mariusz Wach (Pol)	Hamburg (Ger)
Apr 5, 2013	Wladimir Klitschko w rsf 6 Francesco Pianeta (It)	Mannheim, Ger
Oct 5, 2013	Wladimir Klitschko w pts 12 Alexander Povetkin	Moscow, Russia
Apr 26, 2014	Wladimir Klitschko w rsc 5 Alex Leapai (Australia)	Oberhausen, Ger
Apr 25, 2015	Wladimir Klitschko w pts 12 Bryant Jennings (USA)	New York, USA
Nov 28, 2015	**Tyson Fury (Eng)** w pts 12 Wladimir Klitschko	Dusseldorf (Ger)

IBF title

Nov 15, 2014	Wladimir Klitschko w ko 5 Kubrat Pulev (Bul)	Hamburg, Ger

WBA title

May 17, 2013	**Alexander Povetkin** w rsc 3 Andrzej Wawrzyk (Pol)	Myakinino, Russia
	Povetkin stripped of title following loss to Wladimir Klitschko	
Jul 6, 2014	**Ruslan Chagaev** w pts 12 Fres Oquendo (PR)	Grozny, Russia
	For vacant title	
	The WBA sanctioned the following for their Interim title	
Sep 11, 2014	Luis Ortiz (Cub) nc 1 Lateef Kayode (Nig)	Las Vegas,NV

IBF title

Jan 16, 2016	**Charles Martin (US)** w rsf 3 Vyacheslav Glazkov (Ukr)	New York, NY
Apr 9, 2016	**Anthony Joshua (Eng)** w ko 2 Charles Martin	London (Eng)
Jun 25, 2016	Anthony Joshua w rsf 7 Dominic Breazeale (US)	London (Eng)
Dec 10, 2016	Anthony Joshua w rsf 3 Eric Molina (US)	Manchester (Eng)

IBF/WBA titles

Apr 29, 2017	Anthony Joshua w rsf 11 Wladimir Klitschko	London (Eng)
Oct 28, 2017	Anthony Joshua w rsf 10 Carlos Takam (Fra)	Cardiff (Wal)

WBO title

Dec 10, 2016	**Joseph Parker (NZ)** w pts 12 Andy Ruiz Jr (US)	Auckland (NZ)
Jun 5, 2017	Joseph Parker w pts 12 Razvan Cojanu (Rom)	Manukau City (NZ)
Sep 23, 2017	Joseph Parker w pts 12 Hughie Fury (Eng)	Manchester (Eng)

IBF/WBA/WBO titles

Mar 30, 2018	Anthony Joshua w pts 12 Joseph Parker	Cardiff (Wal)

Cruiserweight

In the near-20 years which separated the reigns of Floyd Patterson and George Foreman, the physical dimensions of the average heavyweight boxer changed dramatically. Patterson was little more than a light-heavyweight, as was his great British contemporary Henry Cooper, and in their era a heavyweight scaling over 210lb would have been considered exceptional. By the time the massive Foreman was champion, 210-lb heavyweights would have looked undernourished.

Yet there were still a substantial number of good fighters who were too heavy for the 175lb light-heavyweight division but who would have been hopelessly overmatched against genuine heavyweights. There was an urgent need for an in-between division, and in 1979 the WBC instituted the cruiserweight class with a weight limit of 190lb. Three years later, they raised the limit to 195lb, while the WBA and IBF – who set up their own champions in 1982 and 1983 respectively – stayed with the original limit. It was not until Evander Holyfield unified the titles in 1988 that the limit was standardized at 190lb.

The division, which the WBA call "junior heavyweight", has struggled for acceptance, with Holyfield its sole champion of real quality and the only man to have held the undisputed title.

World Cruiserweight Championship Bouts

WBC title

Dec 8, 1979	Marvin Camel (US) drew 15 Mate Parlov (Yug)	Split (Yug)
	For vacant title	
Mar 31, 1980	**Marvin Camel** w pts 15 Mate Parlov	Las Vegas, NV
	For vacant title	
Nov 26, 1980	**Carlos DeLeon** (PR) w pts 15 Marvin Camel	New Orleans, LA
Feb 24, 1982	Carlos DeLeon w rsf 7 Marvin Camel	Atlantic City, NJ
Jun 27, 1982	**S.T. Gordon** (US) w rsf 2 Carlos De Leon	Cleveland, OH
Feb 16, 1983	S.T. Gordon w rsf 2 Jesse Burnett (US)	East Rutherford, NJ
Jul 17, 1983	**Carlos DeLeon** w pts 12 S.T. Gordon	Las Vegas, NV
Sep 21, 1983	Carlos DeLeon w rsf 4 Alvaro Lopez (US)	San Jose, CA
Mar 9, 1984	Carlos DeLeon w pts 12 Anthony Davis (US)	Las Vegas, NV
Jun 2, 1984	Carlos DeLeon w pts 12 Bashiru Ali (Nig)	Oakland, CA
Jun 6, 1985	**Alfonso Ratliff** (US) w pts 12 Carlos DeLeon	Las Vegas, NV
Sep 21, 1985	**Bernard Benton** (US) w pts 12 Alfonso Ratliff	Las Vegas, NV
Mar 22, 1986	**Carlos DeLeon** w pts 12 Bernard Benton	Las Vegas, NV
Aug 10, 1986	Carlos DeLeon w rsf 8 Michael Greer (US)	Giardini Naxos (Ita)
Feb 21, 1987	Carlos DeLeon w rsf 5 Angelo Rottoli (Ita)	Bergamo (Ita)
Jan 22, 1988	Carlos DeLeon w pts 12 Jose Maria Flores Burlon (Uru)	Atlantic City, NJ
Apr 9, 1988	**Evander Holyfield** w ko 8 Carlos DeLeon	Las Vegas, NV
	Undisputed title	

WBA title

Feb 9, 1982	**Ossie Ocasio** (PR) w pts 15 Robbie Williams (SA)	Johannesburg (SA)
	For vacant title	
Dec 16, 1982	Ossie Ocasio w pts 15 Young Joe Louis (US)	Chicago, IL
May 20, 1983	Ossie Ocasio w pts 15 Randy Stephens (US)	Las Vegas, NV
May 5, 1984	Ossie Ocasio w rsf 15 John Odhiambo (Ken)	San Juan, CA
Dec 1, 1984	**Piet Crous** (SA) w pts 15 Ossie Ocasio	Sun City (Bop)
Mar 29, 1985	Piet Crous w pts 15 Ossie Ocasio	Sun City (Bop)
Jul 27, 1985	**Dwight Muhammad Qawi** (US) w ko 11 Piet Crous	Sun City (Bop)
Mar 23, 1986	Dwight Muhammad Qawi w rsf 6 Leon Spinks (US)	Reno, NV
Jul 12, 1986	**Evander Holyfield** (US) w pts 15 Dwight Muhammad Qawi	Atlanta, GA
Feb 14, 1987	Evander Holyfield w rsf 7 Henry Tillman (US)	Reno, NV

IBF title

May 21, 1983	**Marvin Camel** w ko 9 Rick Sekorski (US)	Billings, MT
Dec 13, 1983	Marvin Camel w ko 5 Roddy McDonald (Can)	Halifax (Can)
Oct 6, 1984	**Lee Roy Murphy** (US) w rsf 14 Marvin Camel	Billings, MT
Dec 20, 1984	Lee Roy Murphy w rsf 12 Young Joe Louis (US)	Chicago, IL
Oct 19, 1985	Lee Roy Murphy w ko 12 Chisanda Mutti (Zam)	Monte Carlo (Mon)
Apr 19, 1986	Lee Roy Murphy w ko 9 Dorcey Gaymon (US)	San Remo (Ita)
Oct 25, 1986	**Rickey Parkey** (US) w rsf 10 Lee Roy Murphy	Marsala (Ita)
May 15, 1987	**Evander Holyfield** w rsf 3 Rickey Parkey	Las Vegas, NV

WBA/IBF titles

Aug 15, 1987	**Evander Holyfield** w rsf 11 Ossie Ocasio	St Tropez (Fra)
Dec 6, 1987	Evander Holyfield w ko 4 Dwight Muhammad Qawi	Atlantic City, NJ

Undisputed title

Apr 9, 1988	**Evander Holyfield** w ko 8 Carlos DeLeon	Las Vegas, NV
Nov 1988	*Holyfield relinquished the title to box at heavyweight*	

WBC title

May 17, 1989	**Carlos DeLeon** w rsf 9 Sammy Reeson (Eng)	London (Eng)
	For vacant title	
Jan 27, 1990	Carlos DeLeon drew 12 Johnny Nelson (Eng)	Sheffield (Eng)
Jul 27, 1990	**Masimiliano Duran** (Ita) w dis 11 Carlos DeLeon	Capo D'Orlando (Ita)
Dec 8, 1990	Masimiliano Duran w dis 12 Anaclet Wamba (Fra)	Ferrera (Ita)
Jul 20, 1991	**Anaclet Wamba** w rsf 11 Masimiliano Duran	Palermo (Ita)
Dec 13, 1991	Anaclet Wamba w rsf 11 Masimiliano Duran	Paris (Fra)
Jun 13, 1992	Anaclet Wamba w rsf 5 Andrei Rudenko (Rus)	Paris (Fra)
Oct 16, 1992	Anaclet Wamba w pts 12 Andrew Maynard (US)	Paris (Fra)
Mar 6, 1993	Anaclet Wamba w pts 12 David Vedder (US)	Paris (Fra)
Oct 16, 1993	Anaclet Wamba w rtd 7 Akim Tafer (Fra)	Paris (Fra)
Jul 14, 1994	Anaclet Wamba drew 12 Adolpho Washington (US)	Monte Carlo (Mon)
Dec 3, 1994	Anaclet Wamba w pts 12 Marcelo Dominguez (Arg)	Salta (Arg)
Apr 20, 1996	***Marcelo Dominguez*** *(Arg) was proclaimed champion after Wamba had failed to make the weight for defence against Dominguez, who had won the WBC "interim" title during Wamba's prolonged spell of inactivity*	
Jul 5, 1996	Marcelo Dominguez w rtd 9 Patrice Aouissi (Fra)	Hyères, (Fra)
Dec 7, 1996	Marcelo Dominguez w rtd 7 Jose Arimateia Da Silva (Bra)	Buenos Aires (Arg)
Aug 16, 1997	Marcelo Dominguez w pts 12 Akim Tafer (Fra)	Le Cannet (Fra)
Feb 21, 1998	**Juan Carlos Gomez** (Cub) w pts 12 Marcelo Dominguez	Mar Del Plata (Arg)
Jun 5, 1998	Juan Carlos Gomez w rsf 6 Guy Waters (Aus)	Hamburg (Ger)
Oct 3, 1998	Juan Carlos Gomez w rsf 2 Alexei Iliin (Rus)	Augsburg (Ger)
Dec 12, 1998	Juan Carlos Gomez w ko 2 Rodney Gordon (US)	Frankfurt (Ger)
Mar 13, 1999	Juan Carlos Gomez w pts 12 Marcelo Dominguez	Lubeck (Ger)
Jul 17, 1999	Juan Carlos Gomez w rsf 6 Bruce Scott (Jam)	Düsseldorf (Ger)
Dec 11, 1999	Juan Carlos Gomez w rsf 9 Napoleon Tagoe (Gha)	Hamburg (Ger)
Mar 11, 2000	Juan Carlos Gomez w rsf 2 Jo Siluvangi (Fra)	Lubeck (Ger)
May 6, 2000	Juan Carlos Gomez w ko 3 Imamu Mayfield (US)	Neuss (Ger)
Dec 16, 2000	Juan Carlos Gomez w rsf 10 Jorge Castro (Arg)	Essen (Ger)
Nov 3, 2001	Juan Carlos Gomez w rsf 6 Pietro Aurino (Ita)	Lubeck (Ger)
	Gomez relinquished his title to compete at heavyweight	
Oct 11, 2002	**Wayne Braithwaite** (Guy) w rsf 10 Vincenzo Cantatore (Ita)	C. d'Italia (Ita)
	For vacant title	
Feb 21, 2003	Wayne Braithwaite w rsf 4 Ravea Springs (US)	Miami, FL
Dec 13, 2003	Wayne Braithwaite w rsf 1 Luis Pineda (Pan)	Atlantic City, NJ
Apr 17, 2004	Wayne Braithwaite w pts 12 Louis Azille (DR)	New York, NY
	Braithwaite then fought a WBC/WBA unification bout against Jean Marc Mormeck on Apr 2, 2005 in Worcester, MA	

WBA title

Mar 25, 1989	**Taoufik Belbouli** (Fra) w rsf 8 Michael Greer	Casablanca (Mor)
	For vacant title, which Belbouli then relinquished in August 1989 because of a knee injury	
Nov 28, 1989	**Robert Daniels** (US) w pts 12 Dwight Muhammad Qawi	Nogent-Sur-Marne (Fra)
	For vacant title	
Jul 19, 1990	Robert Daniels w pts 12 Craig Bodzianowski (US)	Seattle, WA
Nov 22, 1990	Robert Daniels drew 12 Taoufik Belbouli (Fra)	Madrid (Sp)
Mar 9, 1991	**Bobby Czyz** (US) w pts 12 Robert Daniels	Atlantic City, NJ
Aug 9, 1991	Bobby Czyz w pts 12 Bash Ali (Nig)	Atlantic City, NJ
May 8, 1992	Bobby Czyz w pts 12 Donny Lalonde (Can)	Las Vegas, NV
Sep 1993	*Czyz stripped for failure to defend*	
Nov 6, 1993	**Orlin Norris** (US) w rsf 6 Marcelo Figueroa (Arg)	Paris (Fra)
	For vacant title	
Mar 4, 1994	Orlin Norris w pts 12 Arthur Williams (US)	Las Vegas, NV
Jul 2, 1994	Orlin Norris w ko 3 Arthur Williams	Las Vegas, NV
Nov 12, 1994	Orlin Norris w ko 2 James Heath (US)	Mexico City (Mex)
Mar 17, 1995	Orlin Norris w pts 12 Adolpho Washington	Worcester, MA
Jul 22, 1995	**Nate Miller** (US) w ko 8 Orlin Norris	London (Eng)
Jan 13, 1996	Nate Miller w rsf 4 Reynaldo Giminez (Arg)	Miami, FL
Mar 23, 1996	Nate Miller w rsf 9 Brian LaSpada (US)	Miami, FL
Aug 31, 1996	Nate Miller w rsf 7 James Heath (US)	Dublin (Ire)
Feb 22, 1997	Nate Miller w rsf 2 Alexander Gurov (Ukr)	Ft. Lauderdale, FL
Nov 8, 1997	**Fabrice Tiozzo** (Fra) w pts 12 Nate Miller	Las Vegas, NV
May 2, 1998	Fabrice Tiozzo w ko 1 Terry Ray (US)	Villeurbanne (Fra)
Nov 14 1998	Fabrice Tiozzo w rsf 2 Ezequiel Paixao (Bra)	Mont-de-Marsan (Fra)
Nov 13, 1999	Fabrice Tiozzo w rtd 7 Ken Murphy (US)	Las Vegas, NV
Apr 8, 2000	Fabrice Tiozzo w rsf 6 Valery Vikhor (Ukr)	Paris (Fra)

Dec 9,	2000	**Virgil Hill** (US) w rsf 1 Fabrice Tiozzo	Villeurbanne (Fra)
Feb 23,	2002	**Jean-Marc Mormeck** (Fra) w rtd 8 Virgil Hill	Marseille (Fra)
Aug 10,	2002	Jean Marc Mormeck w rsf 9 Virgil Hill	Marseille (Fra)
Mar 1,	2003	Jean Marc Mormeck w rsf 8 Alexander Gurov (Ukr)	Las Vegas, NV
May 22,	2004	Jean Marc Mormeck w pts 12 Virgil Hill	Brakpan (SA)
		Mormeck unified the WBC & WBA titles, but lost WBA recognition when he lost to O'Neil Bell in January 2006. When he beat Bell in a return, however, the WBA recognized him once again as a "unified WBA" champion. Meanwhile, the WBA simultaneously ran their "world" championship as follows	
Jan 27,	2006	**Virgil Hill** w pts 12 Valery Brudov (Rus)	Atlantic City, NJ
		Hill stripped for failing to defend	
Dec 2,	2006	**Valery Brudov** w rsf 11 Luis Andres Pineda (Pan)	Paris (Fra)
		For vacant title	
Jun 16,	2007	**Firat Arslan** (Ger) w pts 12 Valery Brudov	Budapest (Hun)
Nov 24,	2007	Firat Arslan w pts 12 Vrigil HillDresden (Ger)	

WBC & WBA titles

Apr 2,	2005	**Jean Marc Mormeck** w pts 12 Wayne Braithwaite	Worcester, MA
Mar 17,	2007	Jean-Marc Mormeck w pts 12 O'Neil Bell	Paris (Fra)
Nov 10,	2007	**David Haye** (Eng) w rsf 7 Jean-Marc Mormeck	Paris (Fra)

WBC, WBA & IBF titles

Jan 7	2006	**O'Neil Bell** w ko 10 Jean Marc Mormeck	New York

IBF title

Jun 3,	1989	**Glenn McCrory** (Eng) w pts 12 Patrick Lumumba (Ken)	Stanley (Eng)
		For vacant title	
Oct 21,	1989	Glenn McCrory w ko 11 Siza Makhathini (SA)	Middlesbrough (Eng)
Mar 22,	1990	**Jeff Lampkin** (US) w ko 3 Glenn McCrory	Gateshead (Eng)
Jul 29,	1990	Jeff Lampkin w ko 8 Sika Makhatini	St Petersburg (Rus)
Jul	1991	*Lampkin relinquished title*	
Sep 6,	1991	**James Warring** (US) w ko 1 James Pritchard (US)	Salemi (Ita)
		For vacant title	
Nov 15,	1991	James Warring w ko 5 Donnell Wingfield (US)	Roanoke, VA
May 16,	1992	James Warring w pts 12 Johnny Nelson (Eng)	Fredericksburg, VA
Jul 30,	1992	**Al Cole** (US) w pts 12 James Warring	Stanhope, NJ
Feb 28,	1993	Al Cole w pts 12 Uriah Grant (Jam)	Atlantic City, NJ
Jul 16,	1993	Al Cole w pts 12 Glenn McCrory	Moscow (Rus)
Nov 17,	1993	Al Cole w rsf 5 Vince Boulwaire (US)	Atlantic City, NJ
Jul 23,	1994	Al Cole w pts 12 Nate Miller (US)	Bismark, ND
Jun 24,	1995	Al Cole w pts 12 Uriah Grant	Atlantic City, NJ
Aug 31,	1996	**Adolpho Washington** (US) w pts 12 Torsten May (Ger)	Palma (Sp)
		For vacant title. Cole relinquished championship for weight reasons.	
Jun 21,	1997	**Uriah Grant** (Jam) w pts 12 Adolpho Washington	Tampa, FL
Nov 8,	1997	**Imamu Mayfield** (US) w pts 12 Uriah Grant	Las Vegas, NV
Oct 30,	1998	**Arthur Williams** (Eng) w rsf 9 Imamu Mayfield	Biloxi, MS
Jun 5,	1999	**Vassily Jirov** (Kaz) w rsf 7 Arthur Williams	Biloxi MS
Sep 18,	1999	Vassily Jirov w ko 10 Dale Brown (Can)	Las Vegas NV
Feb 12,	2000	Vassily Jirov w rsf 9 Saul Montana (Mex)	Boise, ID
Feb 6,	2001	Vassily Jirov w ko 1 Alex Gonzales (PR)	Almaty (Kaz)
Mar 24,	2001	Vassily Jirov w ko 1 Terry McGroom (US)	Las Vegas NV
Sep 8,	2001	Vassily Jirov w rsf 8 Julian Letterlough (US)	Las Vegas NV
Feb 1,	2002	Vassily Jirov w pts 12 Jorge Castro (Arg)	Phoenix AZ
Apr 26,	2003	**James Toney** (US) w pts 12 Vassily Jirov (Kaz)	Mashantucket, CT
		Toney relinquished the title to box at heavyweight	
May 1,	2004	**Kelvin Davis** (US) w rsf 8 Ezra Sellers (US)	Miami, CL
		Davis was stripped of the IBF title.	
May 20,	2005	**O'Neil Bell** (US) w pts 12 Dale Brown (Can)	Hollywood, FL
		For vacant title	
Aug 26,	2005	O'Neil Bell w ko 11 Sebastiaan Rothmann (SA)	Hollywood, FL
		After Bell unified the WBC, WBA and IBF titles, he was stripped of the IBF title	
Nov 25,	2006	**Krzysztof Wlodarczyk** (Pol) w pts 12 Steve Cunningham (US)	Warsaw (Pol)
		For vacant title	
May 26,	2007	**Steve Cunningham** w pts 12 Krzysztof Wlodarczyk	Katowice (Pol)
Dec 29,	2007	Steve Cunningham w pts 12 Marco Huck (Ger)	Bielefeld (Ger)
Dec 11,	2008	**Tomasz Adamek** (Pol) w pts 12 Steve Cunningham	Newark, NJ
Feb 27,	2009	Tomasz Adamek w rsf 8 Johnathon Banks (US)	Newark, NJ
Jul 11,	2009	Tomasz Adamek w rtd 4 Bobby Gunn (US),	Newark, NJ
Oct 18,	2009	*Adamek relinquished the title to box at heavyweight.*	
Jun 5,	2010	Steve Cunningham w rsf 5 Troy Ross (Can)	Neubrandenburg (Ger
		For vacant title	
Feb 12,	2011	Steve Cunningham w pts 12 Enad Licina (Ger	Muelheim (Ger)
Oct 1,	2011	Yoan Pablo Hernandez (Cuba) w pts 12 Steve Cunningham	Neubrandenburg (Ger)
Feb 4,	2012	Yoan Pablo Hernandez w pts 12 Steve Cunningham	Frankfurt (Ger)
Sep 15,	2012	Yoan Pablo Hernandez w pts 12 Troy Ross	Bamberg (Ger)
Nov 23,	2013	Yoan Pablo Hernandez w ko 10 Alexander Alekseev (Uzbek)	Bamberg (Ger)
Aug 16,	2014	Yoan Pablo Hernandez w pts 12 Firat Arslan	Erfurt (Ger)
		The IBF also sanctioned the following for their Interim title	
Apr 10,	2015	Victor Emilio Ramirez (Arg) w pts 12 Ola Afolabi	Buenos Aires (Arg)
Oct 2,	2015	**Victor Emilio Ramirez** w pts 12 Ovill McKenzie (Eng)	Buenos Aires (Arg)
		For the IBF title	

WBO title

Dec 3,	1989	**Boone Pultz** (US) w pts 12 Magne Havnaa (Nor)	Copenhagen (Den)
		For vacant title	
May 17,	1990	**Magne Havnaa** w rsf 5 Boone Pultz	Aars (Den)
Dec 8,	1990	Magne Havnaa w pts 12 Daniel Netto (Arg)	Aalborg (Den)
Feb 15,	1991	Magne Havnaa w pts 12 Tyrone Booze (US)	Randers (Den)
Feb	1992	*Havnaa relinquished the title because of weight problems*	
Jul 25,	1992	**Tyrone Booze** (US) w ko 7 Derek Angol (Eng)	Manchester (Eng)
		For vacant title	
Oct 2,	1992	Tyrone Booze w pts 12 Ralf Rocchigiani (Ger)	Berlin (Ger)
Feb 13,	1993	**Marcus Bott** (Ger) w pts 12 Tyrone Booze	Hamburg (Ger)
Mar 26,	1993	**Nestor Giovannini** (Arg) w pts 12 Marcus Bott	Hamburg (Ger)
Nov 20,	1993	Nestor Giovannini w pts 12 Marcus Bott	Hamburg (Ger)
Oct 1,	1994	Nestor Giovannini w rtd 6 Larry Carlisle (US)	Buenos Aires (Arg)
Dec 17,	1994	**Dariusz Michalczewski** (Ger) w rsf 10 Nestor Giovannini	Hamburg (Ger)
Mar	1995	*Michalczewski relinquished the cruiserweight title to concentrate on defending his WBO light-heavyweight championship*	
Jun 10,	1995	**Ralf Rocchigiani** (Ger) w rsf 11 Carl Thompson (Eng)	Manchester (Eng)
		For vacant title	
Sep 30,	1995	Ralf Rocchigiani w pts 12 Mark Randazzo (US)	Hanover (Ger)
Nov 25,	1995	Ralf Rocchigiani w ko 8 Dan Ward (US)	Brunswick (Ger)
Mar 16,	1996	Ralf Rocchigiani w rsf 4 Jay Snyder (US)	Berlin (Ger)
Jul 13,	1996	Ralf Rocchigiani w pts 12 Bashiru Ali (Nig)	Essen (Ger)
Dec 14,	1996	Ralf Rocchigiani w pts 12 Stefan Anghern (Swi)	Hanover (Ger)
Apr 26,	1997	Ralf Rocchigiani w pts 12 Stefan Anghern	Zurich (Swi)
Oct 4	1997	**Carl Thompson** w pts 12 Ralf Rocchigiani	Hanover (Ger)
Apr 18	1998	Carl Thompson w pts 12 Chris Eubank (Eng)	Manchester (Eng)
July 18	1998	Carl Thompson w rsf 9 Chris Eubank	Sheffield (Eng)
Mar 27	1999	**Johnny Nelson** (Eng) w rsf 5 Carl Thompson	Derby (Eng)
May 15	1999	Johnny Nelson w pts 12 Bruce Scott (Jam)	Sheffield (Eng)
Aug 7,	1999	Johnny Nelson w rtd 4 Willard Lewis (Can)	Dagenham (Eng)
Sep 18,	1999	Johnny Nelson w pts 12 Sione Asipeli (Ton)	Las Vegas NV
Nov 6,	1999	Johnny Nelson w ko 4 Christophe Girard (Fra)	Widnes (Eng)
Apr 8,	2000	Johnny Nelson w rtd 7 Pietro Aurino (Ita)	London (Eng)
Oct 7,	2000	Johnny Nelson w rsf 5 Adam Watt (Aus)	Doncaster (Eng)
Jan 27,	2001	Johnny Nelson w pts 12 George Arias (Bra)	London (Eng)
Jul 21,	2001	Johnny Nelson w pts 12 Marcelo Dominguez (Arg)	Sheffield (Eng)
Apr 6,	2002	Johnny Nelson w ko 8 Ezra Sellers (US)	Copenhagen (Den)
Nov 23,	2002	Johnny Nelson drew 12 Guillermo Jones (Pan)	Derby (Eng)
Nov 15,	2003	Johnny Nelson w pts 12 Alexander Petkovic (Ger)	Bayreuth (Ger)
Sep 4,	2004	Johnny Nelson w rsf 7 Rudiger May (Ger)	Essen (Ger)
Nov 26,	2005	Johnny Nelson w pts 12 Vincenzo Cantatore (Ita)	Rome (Ita)
		Nelson announced his retirement because of recurring knee injury. Enzo Maccarinelli declared interim champion	
Oct 14,	2006	Enzo Maccarinelli (Wal) w rsf 1 Mark Hobson (Eng)	Manchester (Eng)
Apr 7,	2007	Enzo Maccarinelli (Wal) w rsf 1 Bobby Gunn (US)	Cardiff (Wal)
Jul 21,	2007	Enzo Maccarinelli (Wal) w pts 12 Wayne Braithwaite (Guy)	Cardiff (Wal)
Nov 3,	2007	Enzo Maccarinelli (Wal) w rsf 4 Mohamed Azzaoui (Fra)	Cardiff (Wal)

WBC/WBA/WBO titles

Mar 8,	2008	**David Haye** w rsf 2 Enzo Maccarinelli	London (Eng)
		Haye relinquished the titles to box at heavyweight	

WBC title

Oct 24,	2008	**Giacobbe Fragomeni** (Ita) w tdec 8 Rudolf Kraj (Cz)	Milan (Ita)
		For vacant title	
May 16,	2009	Giacobbe Fragomeni drew 12 Krzysztof Wlodarczyk (Pol)	Rome (Ita)
Nov 21,	2009	**Zsolt Erdei** (Hun) w pts 12 Giacobbe Fragomeni	Kiel (Ger)
		Erdei relinquished the title in January 2010 to return to light-heavyweight	
May 15,	2010	**Krzysztof Wlodarczyk** (Pol) w rsf 8 Giacobbe Fragomeni	Ludz (Pol)
Sep 25,	2010	Krzysztof Wlodarczyk w pts 12 Jason Robinson (US)	Warsaw (Pol)
Apr 2,	2011	Krzysztof Wlodarczyk w pts 12 Francisco Palacios (PR)	Bydgoszcz (Pol)
Nov 30,	2011	Krzysztof Wlodarczyk w pts 11 Danny Green (Aus)	Mt Claremont (Aus)
Sep 22,	2012	Krzysztof Wlodarczyk w pts 12 Francisco Palacios	Wroclaw (Pol)
Jun 21,	2013	Krzysztof Wlodarczyk w rsf 8 Rakhim Chakhkiev	Moscow (Rus)
Dec 6,	2013	Krzysztof Wlodarczyk w rtd 6 Giacobbe Fragomeni	Chicago, IL
Sep 27,	2014	Grigory Drozd (Rus) w pts 12 Krzysztof Wlodarczyk	Moscow (Rus)
May 22,	2015	Grigory Drozd w rsf 9 Lukasz Janik (Pol)	Moscow (Rus)
May 29,	2016	**Tony Bellew (Eng)** w rsf 3 Ilunga Makabu (DR Con)	Liverpool (Eng)
Oct 15,	2016	Tony Bellew w rsf 3 BJ Flores (US)	Liverpool (Eng)
Apr 1,	2017	**Mairis Briedis (Lat)** w pts 12 Marco Huck (Ger)	Dortmund (Ger)
Sep 30,	2017	Mairis Briedis w pts 12 Mike Perez (Cub)	Riga (Lat)

WBA title

When David Haye beat Jean-Marc Mormeck for the WBC & WBA titles in November 2007 he was, as Mormeck had been, recognized as Super Champion by the WBA. Firat Arslan retained recognition as World Champion.

May 3, 2008	Firat Arslan w pts 12 Darnell Wilson (US)	Stuttgart (Ger)
Sep 27, 2008	**Guillermo Jones** (Pan) w rsf 10 Firat Arslan	Hamburg (Ger)
Oct 2, 2010	Guillermo Jones w rsf 11 Valery Brudov (Rus)	Panama City (Pan)
Nov 5, 2011	Guillermo Jones w rsf 6 Michael Marrone (US).	Hollywood, CA
	Jones stripped of WBA title for refusing to box Denis Lebedev and he was upgraded from Interim to full champion	
Dec 17, 2011	**Denis Lebedev** (Rus) w ko 4 Santander Silgado (Col)	Myakinino (Rus)
	The WBA sanctioned the following for the Interim title	
Jul 3, 2010	Steve Herelius (Fra) w ret 11 Firat Arslan (Ger)	Stuttgart (Ger)
Feb 12, 2011	Yoan Pablo Hernandez w ko 7 Steve Herelius	Muelheim (Ger)
Nov 4, 2011	Denis Lebedev w pts 12 James Toney	Moscow (Rus)
Apr 4, 2012	Denis Lebedev w ko 2 Shawn Cox (Barbados)	Myakinino (Rus)
Dec 17, 2012	Denis Lebedev w ko 4 Santander Silgado (Col)	Myakinino (Rus)
May 17, 2013	Guillermo Jones w ko 11 Denis Lebedev	Myakinino (Rus)
	Jones failed drug test and Lebedev reinstated as WBA champion	
Sep 27, 2014	Denis Lebedev w ko 2 Pawel Kolodziej (Pol)	Moscow (Rus)
Apr 10, 2015	Denis Lebedev w pts 12 Youri Kayembre Kalenga (Fra)	Moscow (Rus)
	The WBA also sanctioned the following for their Interim title	
Jun 21, 2014	Youri Kayembre Kalenga w pts 12 Mateusz Masternak (Pol)	Monte Carlo (Mon)
Nov 15, 2014	Youri Kayembre Kalenga w rsf 12 Denton Daley (Can)	Mississauga (Can)
Apr 10, 2015	Denis Lebedev (Rus) w pts 12 Youri Kayembre Kalenga (DR Con)	Moscow (Rus)
Nov 4, 2015	Denis Lebedev w rsf 8 Lateef Kayode (Nig)	Kazan (Rus)
May 21, 2016	**Beibut Shumenov (Kaz)** w rsf 10 Junior Anthony Wright (US)	Las Vegas, NV
Sep 23, 2017	**Yunier Dorticos (Cub)** w rsf 2 Dmitry Kudryashov (Rus)	San Antonio, TX

WBO titles

After David Haye moved up to heavyweight, the WBO approved two Interim title fights as follows:

Jan 17, 2009	**Victor Emilio Ramirez** (Arg) w rtd 9 Alexander Alexeev (Rus)	Dusseldorf (Ger)
Mar 14, 2009	**Ola Afolabi** (Nig) w rsf 9 Enzo Maccarinelli	Manchester (Eng)
	However, then the WBO recognised Ramirez as champion.	
May 16, 2009	Victor Emilio Ramirez w pts 12 Ali Ismailov (Aze)	Buenos Aires (Arg)
Aug 29, 2009	**Marco Huck** (Ger) w pts 12 Victor Emilio Ramirez	Halle (Ger)
Dec 5, 2009	Marco Huck w pts 12 Ola Alofabi (US)	Ludwigsburg (Ger)
Mar 13, 2010	Marco Huck w ko 3 Adam Richards (US)	Berlin (Ger)
May 1, 2010	Marco Huck w ret 9 Brian Minto (US)	Oldenburg (Ger)
Aug 21, 2010	Marco Huck w rsf 5 Matt Godfrey (US)	Erfut (Ger)
Dec 18, 2010	Marco Huck w pts 12 Denis Lebedev	Berlin (Ger)
Apr 2, 2011	Marco Huck w pts 12 Ran Nakash (Isr).	Halle (Ger)
Jul 16, 2011	Marco Huck w ko 10 Hugo Hernan Garay (Arg)	Munich (Ger)
Oct 22, 2011	Marco Huck w ko 6 Rogelio Omar Rossi (Arg).	Ludwigsburg (Ger)
	Marco Huck moved up to heavyweight and the WBO ordered a match between Ola Afolabi and Valery Brudov for the Interim belt.	
Mar 3, 2012	Ola Afolabi w ret 5 Valery Brudov	Dusseldorf (Ger)
	For Interim title	
May 5, 2012	Marco Huck drew 12 Ola Afolabi	Erfut (Ger)
Nov 3, 2012	Marco Huck w pts 12 Firat Arslan	Halle (Ger)
Jun 8, 2013	Marco Huck w pts 12 Ola Afolabi	Berlin (Ger)
Jan 25, 2014	Marco Huck w rsf 6 Firat Arslan (Ger)	Stuttgart (Ger)
Aug 30, 2014	Marco Huck w pts 12 Mirko Larghetti (Ita)	Halle (Ger)
Aug 14, 2015	**Krzysztof Glowacki (Pol)** w ko 11 Marco Huck	Newark, NJ
Apr 16, 2016	Krzysztof Glowacki w pts 12 Steve Cunningham (US)	Brooklyn, NY
Sep 17, 2016	**Oleksandr Usyk (Ukr)** w pts 12 Krzysztof Glowacki	Gdansk (Pol)
Dec 17, 2016	Oleksandr Usyk w ko 9 Thabiso Mchunu (SA)	Inglewood, CA
Apr 8, 2017	Oleksandr Usyk w pts 12 Michael Hunter (US)	Oxon Hill, MD
Sep 9, 2017	Oleksandr Usyk w rsf 10 Marco Huck	Berlin (Ger)

IBF/WBA Super titles

May 21, 2016	Denis Lebedev (Rus) w rsf 2 Victor Emilio Ramirez	Moscow (Rus)

IBF title

Dec 3, 2016	Murat Gassiev (Rus) w pts 12 Denis Lebedev	Moscow (Rus)
Oct 21, 2017	Murat Gassiev w ko 3 Krzysztof Wlodarczyk (Pol)	Newark, NJ

IBF/WBA Super titles

Feb 3, 2018	Murat Gassiev w rsf 12 Yunier Dorticos (Cub)	Adler (Rus)

WBC/WBO titles

Jan 27, 2017	**Oleksandr Usyk (Ukr)** w pts 12 Mairis Briedis (Lat)	Riga (Lat)

DENIS LEBEDEV *connects solidly with Shawn Cox during their brief fight for the interim WBA cruiserweight title in April 2012; Lebedev won in two rounds*

Light-Heavyweight

Although it is one of the eight "classic" divisions in boxing, the light-heavyweight category took a long time to become established. It was the brainchild of a Chicago newspaperman, Lou Houseman, who steered his own protégé, Jack Root, to the title in 1903. The weight limit fluctuated between 165lb and 170lb before settling at the present 175lb.

Before the introduction of the cruiserweight class it was seen as a launchpad into the heavyweight division, but although light heavyweight champions Carpentier, Loughran, Lewis, Billy Conn, Gus Lesnevich, Joey Maxim, Archie Moore and Bob Foster all tried for the heavyweight crown, none succeeded until Mike Spinks beat Larry Holmes in 1985.

World Light-Heavyweight Championship Bouts

Apr 22,	1903	**Jack Root** (US) w pts 10 Kid McCoy (US)	Detroit, MI
Jul 4,	1903	**George Gardner** (Ire) w ko 12 Jack Root	Fort Erie (Can)
Nov 25,	1903	**Bob Fitzsimmons** (Eng) w pts 20 George Gardner	San Francisco, CA
Dec 20,	1905	**Philadelphia Jack O'Brien** (US) w ko 13 Bob Fitzsimmons	San Francisco, CA
Nov 28,	1906	Philadelphia Jack O'Brien drew 20 Tommy Burns (Can)	Los Angeles, CA
		The title fell into disuse for five years	
May 28,	1912	**Jack Dillon** (US) w ko 3 Hugo Kelly (US)	Indianapolis, IN
Apr 14,	1914	Jack Dillon w pts 12 Battling Levinsky (US)	Butte, MT
Apr 28,	1914	Jack Dillon w pts 10 Al Norton (US)	Kansas City, KS
Jun 15,	1914	Jack Dillon w pts 12 Bob Moha (US)	Butte, MT
Jul 3,	1914	Jack Dillon w pts 10 Sailor Petroskey (US)	Kansas City, KS
Apr 25,	1916	Jack Dillon w pts 15 Battling Levinsky	Kansas City, KS
Oct 24,	1916	**Battling Levinsky** w pts 12 Jack Dillon	Boston, MA
Oct 12,	1920	**Georges Carpentier** (Fra) w ko 4 Battling Levinsky	New York, NY
May 11,	1922	Georges Carpentier w ko 1 Ted "Kid" Lewis (Eng)	London (Eng)
Sep 24,	1922	**Battling Siki** (Sen) w ko 6 Georges Carpentier	Paris (Fra)
Mar 17,	1923	**Mike McTigue** (Ire) w pts 20 Battling Siki	Dublin (Ire)
Oct 4,	1923	Mike McTigue drew 10 Young Stribling (US)	Columbus, OH
May 30,	1925	**Paul Berlenbach** (US) w pts 15 Mike McTigue	New York, NY
Sep 11,	1925	Paul Berlenbach w rsf 11 Jimmy Slattery (US)	New York, NY
Dec 11,	1925	Paul Berlenbach w pts 15 Jack Delaney (Can)	New York, NY
Jun 10,	1926	Paul Berlenbach w pts 15 Young Stribling	New York, NY
Jul 16,	1926	**Jack Delaney** w pts 15 Paul Berlenbach	Brooklyn, NY
Dec 10,	1926	Jack Delaney w ko 3 Jamaica Kid (US)	Waterbury, CT
June	1927	*Delaney relinquished title to box at heavyweight*	
Aug 30,	1927	**Jimmy Slattery** w pts 10 Maxie Rosenbloom (US)	Hartford, CT
		For vacant NBA title	
Oct 7,	1927	**Tommy Loughran** (US) w pts 15 Mike McTigue	New York, NY
		For vacant New York title	
Dec 12,	1927	Tommy Loughran w pts 15 Jimmy Slattery	New York, NY
		For undisputed title	
Jan 6,	1928	Tommy Loughran w pts 15 Leo Lomski (US)	New York, NY
Jun 1,	1928	Tommy Loughran w pts 15 Pete Latzo (US)	New York, NY
Jul 16,	1928	Tommy Loughran w pts 10 Pete Latzo	Wilkes-Barre, PA
Mar 28,	1929	Tommy Loughran w pts 10 Mickey Walker (US)	Chicago, IL
Jul 18,	1929	Tommy Loughran w pts 15 James J. Braddock (US)	New York, NY
Sep	1929	*Loughran relinquished title to box at heavyweight*	
Feb 10,	1930	**Jimmy Slattery** w pts 15 Lou Scozza (US)	Buffalo, NY
		For vacant New York title	
Jun 25,	1930	**Maxie Rosenbloom** w pts 15 Jimmy Slattery	New York, NY
		For undisputed title	
Oct 22,	1930	Maxie Rosenbloom w rsf 11 Abe Bain (US)	New York, NY
Jun 6,	1931	*NBA withdrew recognition from Rosenbloom for failing to defend within a stipulated period*	
Aug 5,	1931	Maxie Rosenbloom w pts 15 Jimmy Slattery	New York, NY
Mar 18,	1932	**George Nichols** (US) w pts 10 Dave Maier (US)	Chicago, IL
		For vacant NBA title	
Jul 14,	1932	Maxie Rosenbloom w pts 15 Lou Scozza	Buffalo, NY
Dec	1932	*NBA vacated Nichols' title*	
Mar 1,	1933	**Bob Godwin** (US) w pts 10 Joe Knight (US)	Palm Beach, FL
		For vacant NBA title	
Mar 10,	1933	Maxie Rosenbloom w pts 15 Adolf Heuser (Ger)	New York, NY
Mar 24,	1933	Maxie Rosenbloom w ko 4 Bob Godwin	New York, NY
		For undisputed title	
Nov 3,	1933	Maxie Rosenbloom w pts 15 Mickey Walker	New York, NY
Feb 5,	1934	Maxie Rosenbloom drew 15 Joe Knight	Miami, FL
Nov 16,	1934	**Bob Olin** (US) w pts 15 Maxie Rosenbloom	New York, NY
Aug	1935	*The European-based IBU withdrew recognition from Olin and matched Hein Lazek with Merlo Preciso for their version of the title.*	

RINGSIDE VIEW

Mike McTigue vs Battling Siki

EXPLOSIVE ATMOSPHERE

Gunfire and grenade explosions were audible in the street outside the Dublin cinema where Mike McTigue from Co. Clare, boxing on St Patrick's Day 1923 during the height of the Irish Civil War, was challenging Battling Siki for the light-heavyweight title ... but there was little excitement in the ring as McTigue won a dull points decision.

IBU title

Sep 17,	1935	**Hein Lazek** (Aut) w dis 13 Merlo Preciso (Ita)	Vienna (Aut)
		For vacant title	
Feb 25,	1936	Hein Lazek w ko 6 Reinus de Boer (Hol)	Vienna (Aut)
Aug 3,	1936	Hein Lazek w ko 9 Emil Olive (Fra)	Vienna (Aut)
Sep 1,	1936	**Gustav Roth** (Bel) w pts 15 Hein Lazek	Vienna (Aut)
Oct 29,	1936	Gustav Roth w pts 15 Adolph Witt (Ger)	Berlin (Ger)
Jan 12,	1937	Gustav Roth drew 15 Antonio Rodriguez (Br)	Rio de Janeiro (Br)
Mar 24,	1937	Gustav Roth w pts 15 Merlo Preciso	Brussels (Bel)
May 1,	1937	Gustav Roth w pts 15 John Andersson (Swe)	Antwerp (Bel)
Dec 1,	1937	Gustav Roth drew 15 Karel Sys (Bel)	Brussels (Bel)
Jan 21,	1938	Gustav Roth w pts 15 Josef Besselmann (Ger)	Berlin (Ger)
Mar 25,	1938	**Adolf Heuser** w ko 7 Gustav Roth	Berlin (Ger)
May	1938	*The IBU, in an effort to unify the title, withdrew recognition from Heuser*	

New York/NBA titles

Oct 31,	1935	**John Henry Lewis** (US) w pts 15 Bob Olin	St Louis, MO
Mar 30,	1936	John Henry Lewis w pts 15 Jock McAvoy (Eng)	New York, NY
Nov 9,	1936	John Henry Lewis w pts 15 Len Harvey (Eng)	London (Eng)
Jun 3,	1937	John Henry Lewis w rsf 8 Bob Olin	St Louis, MO
Apr 25,	1938	John Henry Lewis w ko 4 Emilio Martinez (US)	Minneapolis, MN
Jul 27,	1938	*The New York Commission withdrew recognition from Lewis*	
Oct 28,	1938	John Henry Lewis w pts 15 Al Gainer (US)	New Haven, CT
Feb 23,	1939	**Melio Bettina** (US) w rsf 9 Tiger Jack Fox (US)	New York, NY
		For vacant New York title	
Jun 19,	1939	*Lewis announced his retirement*	
Jul 13,	1939	**Billy Conn** (US) w pts 15 Melio Bettina	Pittsburgh, PA
		For New York and NBA titles: the British Board decided instead to recognize Len Harvey's 15-rounds points win over Jock McAvoy in London on July 10, 1939 as being for the vacant world title	
Sep 25,	1939	Billy Conn w pts 15 Melio Bettina	Pittsburgh, PA
Nov 17,	1939	Billy Conn w pts 15 Gus Lesnevich (US)	New York, NY
Jun 5,	1940	Billy Conn w pts 15 Gus Lesnevich	Detroit, MI
Dec	1940	*The NBA withdrew recognition from Conn, who had moved into the heavyweight division*	
Jan 13,	1941	**Anton Christoforidis** (Gr) w pts 15 Melio Bettina	Cleveland, OH
		For vacant NBA title	
Mar	1941	*New York stripped Conn of the title*	
May 22,	1941	**Gus Lesnevich** w pts 15 Anton Christoforidis	New York, NY
		For NBA and NY titles	
Aug 26,	1941	Gus Lesnevich w pts 15 Tami Mauriello (US)	New York, NY
Nov 14,	1941	Gus Lesnevich w pts 15 Tami Mauriello	New York, NY
Jun 20,	1942	**Freddie Mills** (Eng) w ko 2 Len Harvey	London (Eng)
		For British version of title	
May 14,	1946	Gus Lesnevich w rsf 10 Freddie Mills	London (Eng)
		For undisputed title	
Feb 8,	19247	Gus Lesnevich w ko 10 Billy Fox (US)	New York, NY
Mar 5,	1948	Gus Lesnevich w ko 1 Billy Fox New York, NY	
Jul 26,	1948	**Freddie Mills** w pts 15 Gus Lesnevich	London (Eng)

Jan 24, 1950 Joey Maxim (US) w ko 10 Freddie Mills .... London (Eng)
Aug 22, 1951 Joey Maxim w pts 15 Bob Murphy (US) .... New York, NY
Jun 25, 1952 Joey Maxim w rtd 14 Sugar Ray Robinson (US) .... New York, NY
Dec 17, 1952 **Archie Moore** (US) w pts 15 Joey Maxim .... St Louis, MO
Jun 24, 1953 Archie Moore w pts 15 Joey Maxim .... Ogden, UT
Jan 27, 1954 Archie Moore w pts 15 Joey Maxim .... Miami, FL
Aug 11, 1954 Archie Moore w rsf 14 Harold Johnson (US) .... New York, NY
Jun 22, 1955 Archie Moore w ko 3 Carl "Bobo" Olson (US) .... New York, NY
Jun 5, 1956 Archie Moore w rsf 10 Yolande Pompey (Tr) .... London (Eng)
Sep 20, 1957 Archie Moore w rsf 7 Tony Anthony (US) .... Los Angeles, CA
Dec 10, 1958 Archie Moore w ko 11 Yvon Durelle (Can) .... Montreal (Can)
Aug 12, 1959 Archie Moore w ko 3 Yvon Durelle .... Montreal (Can)
Oct 1960 *The NBA stripped Moore for failing to defend*
Feb 7, 1961 **Harold Johnson** w rsf 9 Jesse Bowdrey (US) .... Miami, FL
For vacant NBA title
Apr 24, 1961 Harold Johnson w rsf 2 Von Clay (US) .... Philadelphia, PA
The New York Commission and EBU continued to recognize Moore as champion
Jun 10, 1961 **Archie Moore** w pts 15 Guilio Rinaldi (Ita) .... New York, NY
Aug 29, 1961 **Harold Johnson** w pts 15 Eddie Cotton (US) .... Seattle, WA
Feb 1962 *The New York Commission and the EBU withdrew recognition from Moore because of his failure to meet Johnson*
May 12, 1962 Harold Johnson w pts 15 Doug Jones (US) .... Philadelphia, PA
For vacant undisputed title
Jun 23, 1962 Harold Johnson w pts 15 Gustav Scholz (Ger) .... Berlin (Ger)
Jun 1, 1963 **Willie Pastrano** (US) w pts 15 Harold Johnson .... Las Vegas, NV
Apr 10, 1964 Willie Pastrano w rsf 5 Gregorio Peralta (Arg) .... New Orleans, LA
Nov 30, 1964 Willie Pastrano w rsf 11 Terry Downes (Eng) .... Manchester (Eng)
Mar 30, 1965 **Jose Torres** (PR) w rsf 9 Willie Pastrano .... New York, NY
May 21, 1966 Jose Torres w pts 15 Wayne Thornton (US) .... New York, NY
Aug 15, 1966 Jose Torres w pts 15 Eddie Cotton .... Las Vegas, NV
Oct 15, 1966 Jose Torres w ko 2 Chic Calderwood (Sco) .... San Juan, CA
Dec 16, 1966 **Dick Tiger** (Nig) w pts 15 Jose Torres .... New York, NY
May 16, 1967 Dick Tiger w pts 15 Jose TorresNew York, NY
Nov 17, 1967 Dick Tiger w rsf 12 Roger Rouse (US) .... Las Vegas, NV
May 24, 1968 **Bob Foster** (US) w ko 4 Dick Tiger .... New York, NY
Jan 22, 1969 Bob Foster w ko. 1 Frank DePaula (US) .... New York, NY
May 24, 1969 Bob Foster w rsf 4 Andy Kendall (US) .... Springfield, MA
Apr 4, 1970 Bob Foster w rsf 4 Roger Rouse .... Missoula, MT
Jun 27, 1970 Bob Foster w ko 10 Mark Tessman (US) .... Baltimore, MD
Dec 9, 1970 *Foster stripped of title by WBA for refusing to meet their deadline for defence against No. 1 WBA challenger, Jimmy Dupree*

WBA title

Feb 27, 1971 **Vicente Rondon** (Ven) w rsf 6 Jimmy Dupree (US) .... Caracas (Ven)
For vacant title
Jun 5, 1971 Vicente Rondon w ko 1 Piero Del Papa (Ita) .... Caracas (Ven)
Aug 21, 1971 Vicente Rondon w pts 15 Eddie Jones (US) .... Caracas (Ven)
Oct 26, 1971 Vicente Rondon w ko 13 Gomeo Brennan (Bah) .... Miami, FL
Dec 15, 1971 Vicente Rondon w ko 8 Doyle Baird (US) .... Cleveland, OH
Apr 7, 1972 **Bob Foster** w ko 2 Vicente Rondon .... Miami Beach, FL
Undisputed title

WBC title

Mar 2, 1971 **Bob Foster** w ko 4 Hal Carroll (US) .... Scranton, PA
Apr 24, 1971 Bob Foster w pts 15 Ray Anderson (US) .... Tampa, FL
Oct 29, 1971 Bob Foster w rsf 8 Tommy Hicks (US) .... Scranton, PA
Dec 16, 1971 Bob Foster w rsf 3 Brian Kelly (US) .... Oklahoma City, OK
Apr 7, 1972 Bob Foster w ko 2 Vicente Rondon .... Miami Beach, FL
Undisputed title

Undisputed title

Jun 27, 1972 **Bob Foster** w ko 4 Mike Quarry (US) .... Las Vegas, NV
Sep 26, 1972 Bob Foster w ko 14 Chris Finnegan (Eng) .... Wembley (Eng)
Aug 21, 1973 Bob Foster w pts 15 Pierre Fourie (SA) .... Albuquerque, NM
Dec 1, 1973 Bob Foster w pts 15 Pierre Fourie .... Johannesburg (SA)
Jun 17, 1974 Bob Foster drew 15 Jorge Ahumada (Arg) .... Albuquerque, NM
Aug 1974 *World Boxing Council withdrew recognition of Foster as world champion for failure to sign for a title defence against John Conteh or Jorge Ahumada*

WBC title

Oct 1, 1974 **John Conteh** (Eng) w pts 15 Jorge Ahumada .... Wembley (Eng)
For vacant title
Mar 11, 1975 John Conteh w rsf 5 Lonnie Bennett (US) .... Wembley (Eng)
Oct 9, 1976 John Conteh w pts 15 Alvaro "Yaqui" Lopez (US) .... Copenhagen (Den)
Mar 5, 1977 John Conteh w rsf 3 Len Hutchins (US) .... Liverpool (Eng)
May 1977 *Conteh stripped of his title by the WBC for failure to go through with a contracted defence against Miguel Angel Cuello*
May 21, 1977 **Miguel Cuello** (Arg) w ko 9 Jesse Burnett (US) .... Monte Carlo (Mon)
For vacant title
Jan 7, 1978 **Mate Parlov** (Yug) w ko 9 Miguel Cuello .... Milan (Ita)
Jun 17, 1978 Mate Parlov w pts 15 John Conteh .... Belgrade (Yug)
Dec 2, 1978 **Marvin Johnson** (US) w rsf 10 Mate Parlov .... Marsala (Ita)
Apr 22, 1979 **Matthew Saad Muhammad** *[formerly known as Matt Franklin]* (US) w rsf 8 Marvin Johnson .... Indianapolis, IN
Aug 18, 1979 Matthew Saad Muhammad w pts 15 John Conteh .... Atlantic City, NJ
Mar 29, 1980 Matthew Saad Muhammad w rsf 4 John Conteh .... Atlantic City, NJ
May 11, 1980 Matthew Saad Muhammad w rsf 5 Louis Pergaud (Fra) .... Halifax (Can)
Jul 13, 1980 Matthew Saad Muhammad w rsf 14 Alvaro Lopez .... McAfee, NJ
Nov 28, 1980 Matthew Saad Muhammad w ko 4 Lotte Mwale (Zam) .... San Diego, CA
Feb 28, 1981 Matthew Saad Muhammad w rsf 11 Vonzell Johnson (US) .... Atlantic City, NJ
Apr 25, 1981 Matthew Saad Muhammad w ko 9 Murray Sutherland (Sco) .... Atlantic City, NJ
Sep 26, 1981 Matthew Saad Muhammad w rsf 11Jerry Martin (US) .... Atlantic City, NJ
Dec 19, 1981 **Dwight Braxton** (US) w rsf 10 Matthew Saad Muhammad ..... Atlantic City, NJ
Mar 21, 1982 Dwight Braxton w rsf 6 Jerry Martin .... Las Vegas, NV
Aug 7, 1982 Dwight Braxton w rsf 6 Matthew Saad Muhammad .... Philadelphia, PA
Nov 28, 1982 Dwight Muhammad Qawi *[formerly known as Dwight Braxton]* w rsf 11 Eddie Davis (US) .... Atlantic City, NJ
Mar 18, 1983 **Michael Spinks** (US) w pts 15 Dwight Muhammad Qawi .... Atlantic City, NJ
Undisputed title

WBA title

Dec 7, 1974 **Victor Galindez** (Arg) w rtd 12 Len Hutchins .... Buenos Aires (Arg)
For vacant title
Apr 7, 1975 Victor Galindez w pts 15 Pierre Fourie .... Johannesburg (SA)
Jun 30, 1975 Victor Galindez w pts 15 Jorge Ahumada .... New York, NY
Sep 13, 1975 Victor Galindez w pts 15 Pierre Fourie .... Johannesburg (SA)
Mar 28, 1976 Victor Galindez w rtd 3 Harald Skog (Nor) .... Oslo (Nor)
May 22, 1976 Victor Galindez w ko 15 Richie Kates (US) .... Johannesburg (SA)
Oct 5, 1976 Victor Galindez w pts 15 Kosie Smith (SA) .... Johannesburg (SA)
Jun 18, 1977 Victor Galindez w pts 15 Richie Kates .... Rome (Ita)
Sep 17, 1977 Victor Galindez w pts 15 Alvaro "Yaqui" Lopez (US) .... Rome (Ita)
Nov 20, 1977 Victor Galindez w pts 15 Eddie Mustafa Muhammad *[formerly known as Eddie Gregory]* (US) .... Turin (Ita)
May 6, 1978 Victor Galindez w pts 15 Alvaro "Yaqui" Lopez .... Reggio (Ita)
Sep 15, 1978 **Mike Rossman** (US) w rsf 13 Victor Galindez .... New Orleans, LA
Dec 5, 1978 Mike Rossman w rsf 6 Aldo Traversaro (Ita) .... Philadelphia, PA
Apr 14, 1979 **Victor Galindez** w rtd 9 Mike Rossman .... New Orleans, LA
Nov 30, 1979 **Marvin Johnson** (US) w rsf 11 Victor Galindez .... New Orleans, LA
Mar 31, 1980 **Eddie Mustafa Muhammad** w rsf 11 Marvin Johnson .... Knoxville, TN
Jul 20, 1980 Eddie Mustafa Muhammad w rsf 10 Jerry Martin (US) .... McAfee, NJ
Nov 29, 1980 Eddie Mustafa Muhammad w rsf 3 Rudi Koopman (Hol) .... Los Angeles, CA
Jul 18, 1981 **Michael Spinks** (US) w pts 15 Eddie Mustafa Muhammad ...... Las Vegas, NV
Nov 7, 1981 Michael Spinks w rsf 7 Vonzell Johnson .... Atlantic City, NJ
Feb 13, 1982 Michael Spinks w pts 15 Mustapha Wassaja (Ug) .... Atlantic City, NJ
Apr 11, 1982 Michael Spinks w rsf 8 Murray Sutherland .... Atlantic City, NJ
Jun 12, 1982 Michael Spinks w rsf 8 Jerry Celestine (US) .... Atlantic City, NJ
Sep 18, 1982 Michael Spinks w rsf 9 Johnny Davis (US) .... Atlantic City, NJ
Mar 18, 1983 Michael Spinks w pts 15 Dwight Muhammad Qawi .... Atlantic City, NJ
For undisputed title

Undisputed title

Nov 25, 1983 **Michael Spinks** w rsf 11 Oscar Rivadeneyra (Peru) .... Vancouver (Can)
Feb 25, 1984 Michael Spinks w pts 12 Eddie Davis .... Atlantic City, NJ
Feb 23, 1985 Michael Spinks w rsf 3 David Sears (US) .... Atlantic City, NJ
Jun 6, 1985 Michael Spinks w rsf 8 Jim MacDonald (US) .... Las Vegas, NV
Sep 1985 *Spinks relinquished the title when he became IBF heavyweight champion*

WBC title

Dec 10, 1985 **J. B. Williamson** (US) w pts 12 Mama Muhammad (Gha) .... Los Angeles, CA
Apr 30, 1986 **Dennis Andries** (Eng) w pts 12 J. B. Williamson .... London (Eng)
Sep 10, 1986 Dennis Andries w rsf 9 Tony Sibson (Eng) .... London (Eng)
Mar 7, 1987 **Thomas Hearns** (US) w rsf 10 Dennis Andries .... Detroit, MI
Aug 1987 *Hearns gave up the title to fight for the WBC middleweight championship*
Nov 27, 1987 **Donny Lalonde** (Can) w rsf 2 Eddie Davis .... Port of Spain (Trin)
For vacant title
May 29, 1988 Donny Lalonde w rsf 5 Leslie Stewart (Trin) .... Port of Spain (Trin)
Nov 7, 1988 **Sugar Ray Leonard** (US) w rsf 9 Donny Lalonde .... Las Vegas, NV
Also for the vacant WBC super-middleweight title.
Leonard immediately relinquished this one.

Feb 21, 1989	**Dennis Andries** w rsf 5 Tony Willis (US)	Tucson, AZ
	For vacant title	
Jun 24, 1989	**Jeff Harding** (Aus) w rsf 12 Dennis Andries	Atlantic City, NJ
Oct 24, 1989	Jeff Harding w rtd 2 Tom Collins (Eng)	Brisbane (Aus)
Mar 18, 1990	Jeff Harding w rsf 11 Nestor Giovannini (Arg)	Atlantic City, NJ
Jul 28, 1990	**Dennis Andries** w ko 7 Jeff Harding	Melbourne (Aus)
Oct 10, 1990	Dennis Andries w rtd 4 Sergio Merani (Arg)	London (Eng)
Jan 10, 1991	Dennis Andries w pts 12 Guy Waters (Aus)	Adelaide (Aus)
Sep 11, 1991	**Jeff Harding** w pts 12 Dennis Andries	London (Eng)
Jun 5, 1992	Jeff Harding w rsf 8 Christophe Tiozzo (Fra)	Marseilles (Fra)
Dec 3, 1992	Jeff Harding w pts 12 David Vedder (US)	St-Jean-de-Luz (Fra)
Jul 23, 1994	**Mike McCallum** (Jam) w pts 12 Jeff Harding	Bismark, ND
Feb 25, 1995	Mike McCallum w rsf 7 Carl Jones (US)	London (Eng)
Jun 16, 1995	**Fabrice Tiozzo** (Fra) w pts 12 Mike McCallum	Lyon (Fra)
Jan 13, 1996	Fabrice Tiozzo w pts 12 Eric Lucas (Can)	St. Etienne (Fra)
Feb 1997	*Roy Jones crowned champion; Tiozzo stripped of title for failing to defend it*	
Mar 21, 1997	**Montell Griffin** (US) w dis 9 Roy Jones (US)	Atlantic City, NJ
Aug 7, 1997	**Roy Jones** w ko 1 Montell Griffin	Ledyard, CT

WBA title

Feb 9, 1986	**Marvin Johnson** (US) w rsf 7 Leslie Stewart (Tr)	Indianapolis, IN
	For vacant title	
Sep 20, 1986	Marvin Johnson w rsf 13 Jean-Marie Emebe (Cam)	Indianapolis, IN
May 23, 1987	**Leslie Stewart** w rtd 8 Marvin Johnson	Port of Spain (Trin)
Sep 5, 1987	**Virgil Hill** (US) w rsf 4 Leslie Stewart	Atlantic City, NJ
Nov 21, 1987	Virgil Hill w pts 12 Rufino Angulo(Fr)	Paris (Fra)
Apr 3, 1988	Virgil Hill w rsf 11 Jean-Marie Emebe	Bismark, ND
Jun 6, 1988	Virgil Hill w pts 12 Ramzi Hassan (US)	Las Vegas, NV
Nov 11, 1988	Virgil Hill w rsf 10 Willie Featherstone (Can)	Bismark, ND
Mar 4, 1989	Virgil Hill w pts 12 Bobby Czyz (US)	Bismark, ND
May 27, 1989	Virgil Hill w rsf 7 Joe Lasisi (Nig)	Bismark, ND
Oct 24, 1989	Virgil Hill w rsf 1 James Kinchen (US)	Bismark, ND
Feb 25, 1990	Virgil Hill w pts 12 David Vedder	Bismark, ND
Jul 7, 1990	Virgil Hill w pts 12 Tyrone Frazier (US)	Bismark, ND
Jan 6, 1991	Virgil Hill w pts 12 Mike Peak (US)	Bismark, ND
Jun 3, 1991	**Thomas Hearns** w pts 12 Virgil Hill	Las Vegas, NV
Mar 20, 1992	**Iran Barkley** (US) w pts 12 Thomas Hearns	Las Vegas, NV
Apr 1992	*Barkley vacated title to concentrate on defending IBF super-middleweight title*	
Sep 29, 1992	**Virgil Hill** w pts 12 Frank Tate (US)	Bismark, ND
	For vacant title	
Feb 20, 1993	Virgil Hill w rtd 11 Adolfo Washington (US)	Fargo, ND
Nov 9, 1993	Virgil Hill w rsf 10 Saul Montana (US)	Bismark, ND
Dec 17, 1993	Virgil Hill w pts 12 Guy Waters (US)	Minot, ND
Jul 23, 1994	Virgil Hill w pts 12 Frank Tate	Bismark, ND
Apr 1, 1995	Virgil Hill w pts 12 Crawford Ashley (Eng)	Stateline, NV
Sep 2, 1995	Virgil Hill w pts 12 Drake Thadzi (Mlw)	London (Eng)
Apr 20, 1996	Virgil Hill w pts 12 Lou Del Valle (US)	Grand Forks, ND
Nov 23, 1996	Virgil Hill w pts 12 Henry Maske	Munich (Ger)
	Hill unified WBA and IBF titles	
Jun 13, 1997	**Dariusz Michalczewski** w pts 12 Virgil Hill	Oberhausen (Ger)
Jun 1997	*Michalczewski relinquished WBA title one day later, IBF title three days later*	
Sept 20 1997	Lou Del Valle w rsf 8 Eddy Smulders (Hol)	Bremen (Ger)

IBF title

Dec 12, 1985	**Slobodan Kacar** (Yug) w pts 15 Eddie Mustafa Muhammad	Pesaro (Ita)
	For vacant title	
Sep 6, 1986	**Bobby Czyz** (US) w rsf 5 Slobodan Kacar	Las Vegas, NV
Dec 26, 1986	Bobby Czyz w rsf 1 David Sears (US)	West Orange, NJ
Feb 21, 1987	Bobby Czyz w ko 2 Willie Edwards (US)	Atlantic City, NJ
May 3, 1987	Bobby Czyz w rsf 6 Jim MacDonald	Atlantic City, NJ
Oct 29, 1987	**Prince Charles Williams** (US) w rtd 9 Bobby Czyz	Las Vegas, NV
Jun 10, 1988	Prince Charles Williams w rtd 11 Richard Caramanolis (Fra)	Annecy (Fra)
Oct 21, 1988	Prince Charles Williams w rsf 3 Rufino Angulo (Fra)	Bordeaux (Fra)
Jun 25, 1989	Prince Charles Williams w rtd 10 Bobby Czyz	Atlantic City, NJ
Jan 7, 1990	Prince Charles Williams w rtd 8 Frankie Swindell (US)	Atlantic City, NJ
Jan 12, 1991	Prince Charles Williams w pts 12 Mwehu Beya (Ita)	St Vincent (Ita)
Apr 20, 1991	Prince Charles Williams w rsf 2 James Kinchen	Atlantic City, NJ
Jul 20, 1991	Prince Charles Williams w ko 3 Vince Boulaire (US)	San Remo (Ita)
Oct 19, 1991	Prince Charles Williams w rsf 2 Freddie Delgado (PR)	Williamsburg, VA
Mar 20, 1993	**Henry Maske** (Ger) w pts 12 Prince Charles Williams	Dusseldorf (Ger)
Dec 11, 1993	Henry Maske w pts 12 David Vedder	Dusseldorf (Ger)
Mar 26, 1994	Henry Maske w rsf 9 Ernesto Magdelano (US)	Dortmund (Ger)
Jun 4, 1994	Henry Maske w pts 12 Andrea Magi	Dortmund (Ger)
Oct 8, 1994	Henry Maske w rtd 9 Iran Barkley (US)	Halle (Ger)
Feb 11, 1995	Henry Maske w pts 12 Egerton Marcus (Can)	Frankfurt (Ger)
May 27, 1995	Henry Maske w pts 12 Graciano Rocchigiani (Ger)	Dortmund (Ger)
Oct 14, 1995	Henry Maske w pts 12 Graciano Rocchigiani (Ger)	Munich (Ger)
Feb 17, 1996	Henry Maske w pts 12 Duran Williams (Jam)	Dortmund (Ger)
May 25, 1996	Henry Maske w pts 12 John Scully (US)	Leipzig (Ger)
Nov 23, 1996	**Virgil Hill** w pts 12 Henry Maske	Munich (Ger)
	Hill retained WBA title and won Maske's IBF title	
Jun 13, 1997	**Dariusz Michalczewski** (Ger) w pts 12 Virgil Hill	Oberhausen (Ger)
Jun 16, 1997	*Michalczewski unified WBA, IBF & WBO titles; kept only latter. Title vacant*	
Jul 19, 1997	**William Guthrie** (US) w rsf 3 Darrin Allen (US)	Indio, CA
	For vacant title	
Feb 6, 1998	**Reggie Johnson** (US) w ko 5 William Guthrie	Uncasville, CT
May 29, 1998	Reggie Johnson w pts 12 Ole Klemetsen (Nor)	Pesaro (Ita)
Feb 27, 1999	Reggie Johnson w pts 12 Will Taylor (US)	Miami, FL

WBO/WBA/IBF titles

Jun 13, 1997	**Dariusz Michalczewski** w pts 12 Virgil Hill	Oberhausen (Ger)

(Michalczewski relinquished the WBA and IBF titles on June 14 and June 16 respectively)

WBC/WBA titles

Jul 18, 1998	**Roy Jones** w pts 12 Lou Del Valle	New York, NY
Nov 14, 1998	Roy Jones w rsf 10 Otis Grant (Can)	Mashantucket, CT
Jan 9, 1999	Roy Jones w rsf 2 Ricky Frazier (US)	Pensacola, FL

WBO title

Dec 3, 1988	**Michael Moorer** (US) w rsf 5 Ramzi Hassan	Cleveland, OH
Jan 14, 1989	Michael Moorer w rsf 2 Victor Claudio (PR)	Detroit, MI
Feb 19, 1989	Michael Moorer w rsf 6 Frankie Swindell (US)	Monessen, PA
Apr 22, 1989	Michael Moorer w rsf 1 Freddie Delgado (PR)	Detroit, MI
Jun 25, 1989	Michael Moorer w rsf 8 Leslie Stewart	Atlantic City, NJ
Nov 16, 1989	Michael Moorer w rsf 1 Jeff Thompson (US)	Atlantic City, NJ
Dec 22, 1989	Michael Moorer w rsf 6 Mike Sedillo (US)	Detroit, MI
Feb 3, 1990	Michael Moorer w rsf 9 Marcellus Allen (US)	Atlantic City, NJ
Apr 28, 1990	Michael Moorer w ko 1 Mario Melo (Arg)	Atlantic City, NJ
Dec 15, 1990	Michael Moorer w ko 8 Danny Lindstrom (Can)	Pittsburgh, PA
Apr 1991	*Moorer relinquished the title to box at heavyweight*	
May 9, 1991	**Leeonzer Barber** (US) w rtd 5 Tom Collins	Leeds (Eng)
	For vacant title	
Jan 7, 1992	Leeonzer Barber w pts 12 Anthony Hembrick (US)	Detroit, MI
Feb 27, 1993	Leeonzer Barber w pts 12 Mike Sedillo	Bejing (Chn)
Sep 29, 1993	Leeonzer Barber w pts 12 Andrea Magi (Ita)	Pesaro (Ita)
Jan 29, 1994	Leeonzer Barber w rsf 9 Nicky Piper (Wal)	Cardiff (Wal)
Sep 10, 1994	**Dariusz Michalczewski** (Ger) w pts 12 Leeonzer Barber	Hamburg (Ger)
Mar 11, 1995	Dariusz Michalczewski w rsf 2 Roberto Dominguez (Sp)	Cologne (Ger)
May 20, 1995	Dariusz Michalczewski w ko 4 Paul Carlo (US)	Hamburg (Ger)
Aug 19, 1995	Dariusz Michalczewski w ko 5 Everardo Armenta (Mex)	Dusseldorf (Ger)
Oct 7, 1995	Dariusz Michalczewski w pts 12 Philippe Michel (Fra)	Frankfurt (Ger)
Apr 6, 1996	Dariusz Michalczewski w ko 5 Asluddin Umarov (Kaz)	Hannover (Ger)
Jun 8, 1996	Dariusz Michalczewski w pts 12 Christophe Girard (Fra)	Cologne (Ger)
Aug 10, 1996	Dariusz Michalczewski w dis 7 Graciano Rocchigiani (Ita)	Hamburg (Ger)
Dec 14, 1996	Dariusz Michalczewski w rsf 8 Christophe Girard	Hannover (Ger)
Oct 4, 1997	Dariusz Michalczewski w rsf 8 Nicky Piper (Wal)	Hannover (Ger)
Dec 13, 1997	Dariusz Michalczewski w rsf 7 Darren Zenner (US)	Hamburg (Ger)
Mar 20, 1998	Dariusz Michalczewski w rsf 4 Andrea Magi (Ita)	Frankfurt (Ger)
Sep 19, 1998	Dariusz Michalczewski w rsf 8 Mark Prince (Eng)	Oberhausen (Ger)
Dec 12, 1998	Dariusz Michalczewski w rsf 9 Drake Thadzi (Mlw)	Frankfurt (Ger)
Aug 28, 1999	Dariusz Michalczewski w rsf 4 Montell Griffin (US)	Bremen (Ger)
Apr 15, 2000	Dariusz Michalczewski w rtd 9 Graciano Rocchigiani	Hanover (Ger)
Dec 16, 2000	Dariusz Michalczewski w rsf 7 Ka-Dy King (US)	Essen (Ger)
May 5, 2001	Dariusz Michalczewski w ko 9 Venti Lakatus (Rom)	Braunchsweig (Ger)
Dec 15, 2001	Dariusz Michalczewski w rsf 11 Richard Hall (US)	Berlin (Ger)
Apr 20, 2002	Dariusz Michalczewski w ko 2 Joey DeGrandis (US)	Gdansk (Pol)

WBA/WBC/IBF titles

Jun 5, 1999	**Roy Jones** w pts 12 Reggie Johnson (US)	Biloxi, MS
Jan 15, 2000	Roy Jones w pts 12 David Telesco (US)	New York, NY
May 13, 2000	Roy Jones w rsf 11 Richard Hall (Jam)	Indianapolis, IN
Sep 9, 2000	Roy Jones w rtd 10 Eric Harding (US)	New Orleans, LA
Feb 24, 2001	Roy Jones w rtd 10 Derrick Harmon (US)	Tampa, FL
Jul 28, 2001	Roy Jones w pts 12 Julio Gonzalez (US)	Los Angeles, CA
Feb 2, 2002	Roy Jones w ko 7 Glen Kelly (Aus)	Miami, FL
Sep 7, 2002	Roy Jones w rsf 6 Clinton Woods (Eng)	Portland, OR
	Jones relinquished the world titles to box at heavyweight	

WBC/IBF titles

Apr 26, 2003	**Antonio Tarver** (US) w pts 12 Montell Griffin (US)	Mashantucket, CT

BERNARD HOPKINS *(left) outpointed Tavoris Cloud to win the IBF light-heavyweight world championship at Brooklyn, New York, in March 2013 and, at the age of 48 years and 53 days, broke his own world record as the oldest man to ever win a world title belt*

WBC title

Nov 8,	2003	**Roy Jones** w pts 12 Antonio Tarver	Las Vegas, NV
May 15,	2004	**Antonio Tarver** w ko 2 Roy Jones	Las Vegas, NV
		Tarver stripped of WBC title.	
May 21,	2005	**Tomasz Adamek** (Pol) w pts 12 Paul Briggs (Aus)	Chicago, IL
Oct 15,	2005	Tomasz Adamek w ko 6 Thomas Ulrich (Ger)	Dusseldorf (Ger)
Oct 7,	2006	Tomasz Adamek w pts 12 Paul Briggs	Rosemont, IL
Feb 3,	2007	**Chad Dawson** (US) w pts 12 Tomasz Adamek	Kissimmee, FL
Jun 9,	2007	Chad Dawson w rsf 6 Jesus Ruiz (Mex)	Hartford,CT
Sep 29,	2007	Chad Dawson w rsf 4 Epifanio Mendoza (Col)	Sacramento, CA
Apr 12,	2008	Chad Dawson w pts 12 Glen Johnson	Tampa, FL
		Chad Dawson vacated the title. The WBC recognized the following fight between Adrian Diaconu and Chris Henry as for the Interim title	
Apr 19,	2008	**Adrian Diaconu** (Rom) w pts 12 Chris Henry (Bar)	Montreal (Can)
Jun 19,	2009	**Jean Pascal** (Can) w pts 12 Adrian Diaconu	Montreal (Can)
Sep 25,	2009	Jean Pascal w rsf 10 Silvio Branco (Ita)	Montreal (Can)
Dec 11,	2009	Jean Pascal w pts 12 Adrian Diaconu	Montreal (Can)
		The WBC also recognised the following fight for the Interim title	
Nov 7,	2009	Chad Dawson w pts 12 Glen Johnson	Hartford, CT
		The WBC upgraded Chad Dawson to World Champion	
Aug 14,	2010	**Jean Pascal** (Can) w tdec 11 Chad Dawson	Montreal (Can)
Dec 18,	2010	Jean Pascal drew 12 Bernard Hopkins	Quebec City (Can)
May 21,	2011	**Bernard Hopkins** w pts 12 Jean Pascal	Montreal (Can)
Oct 15,	2011	Bernard Hopkins nc 2 Chad Dawson	Los Angeles, CA
Apr 28,	2012	**Chad Dawson** w pts 12 Bernard Hopkins	Atlantic City, NJ
Jun 8,	2013	**Adonis Stevenson** (Hai) w ko 1 Chad Dawson	Montreal (Can)
Sep 28,	2013	Adonis Stevenson w ret 7 Tavoris Cloud (USA)	Montreal (Can)
Nov 30,	2013	Adonis Stevenson w rsc 6 Tony Bellew (Eng)	Quebec City (Can)
May 24,	2014	Adonis Stevenson w pts 12 Andrzej Fonfara (Pol)	Montreal (Can)
Dec 19,	2014	Adonis Stevenson w ko 5 Dmitriy Sukhotsky (Russia)	Quebec City (Can)
Apr 4,	2015	Adonis Stevenson w pts 12 Sakio Bika (Australia)	Quebec City (Can)

WBA title

When Roy Jones held the WBC, WBA and IBF titles, the WBA declared him a "super" champion and installed Bruno Girard as "world" champion

May 23,	2002	**Bruno Girard** (Fra) w pts 12 Thomas Hansvoll (Nor)	Paris (Fra)
Jul 13,	2002	Bruno Girard w pts 12 Lou Del Valle (US)	Palavas-les-Flots (Fra)
Mar 8,	2003	**Mehdi Sahnoune** (Fr) w rsf 7 Bruno Girard	Marseille (Fra)
Oct 10,	2003	**Silvio Branco** (Ita) w rsf 11 Mehdi Sahnoune	Marseille (Fra)
Mar 20,	2004	**Fabrice Tiozzo** (Fra) w pts 12 Silvio Branco	Lyon (Fra)
Feb 26	2005	Fabrice Tiozzo w rsf 6 Dariusz Michalczewski	Hamburg (Ger)
		Tiozzo suffered injuries that led to a long layoff. He returned with a non-title fight in the autumn of 2006 but then retired. Meanwhile the WBA installed Silvio Branco as interim champion, following a points win over Manny Siaca in Milan in July 2006. Branco then received retrospective recognition	
Jul 27,	2006	**Silvio Branco** w pts 12 Manny Siaca (PR)	Milan (Ita)
Apr 28,	2007	**Stipe Drews** (Cro) w pts 12 Silvio Branco	Oberhausen (Ger)
Dec 16,	2007	**Danny Green** (Aus) w pts 12 Stipe Drews	Perth (Aus)
Mar 25,	2008	*Danny Green announced his retirement*	
Jul 3,	2008	**Hugo Garay** (Arg) w pts 12 Yuri Barashian (Ukr)	Buenos Aires (Arg)
		For vacant title	
Nov 22,	2008	Hugo Garay w pts 12 Jurgen Brahmer (Ger)	Rostock (Ger)
Jun 20,	2009	**Gabriel Campillo** (Spa) w pts 12 Hugo Garay	Santa Fe (Arg)
Aug 15,	2009	Gabriel Campillo w pts 12 Beibut Shumenov (Kaz)	Astana (Kaz)
Jan 29,	2010	**Beibut Shumenov** w pts 12 Gabriel Campillo	Las Vegas, NV
Jul 23,	2010	Beibut Shumenov w pts 12 Vyacheslav Uzelkov (Ukr)	Lemoore, CA
Jan 8,	2011	Beibut Shumenov w ko 6 William Joppy (US)	Shymkent (Kaz)
Jul 29,	2011	Beibut Shumenov w rsf 9 Danny Santiago (US)	Las Vegas, NV
Jun 2,	2012	Beibut Shumenov w pts 12 Enrique Ornelas (US)	Las Vegas, NV
		Beibut Shumenov upgraded to WBA super champion	

WBA super title

Dec 14, 2013	**Beibut Shumenov** w rsc 3 Tamas Kovacs (Slovakia)	San Antonio, TX

IBF title

	Roy Jones was stripped of the IBF title when he boxed John Ruiz for the WBA heavyweight crown in March 2003. Antonio Tarver won the WBC and IBF titles in April 2003 against Montell Griffin, but was stripped by the IBF	
Nov 7, 2003	Glen Johnson (Jam) drew 12 Clinton Woods (Eng)	Sheffield (Eng)
Feb 6, 2004	**Glen Johnson** w pts 12 Clinton Woods	Sheffield (Eng)
Sep 25, 2004	Glen Johnson w ko 9 Roy Jones	Memphis, TN
	Johnson stripped of IBF title for agreeing to box Antonio Tarver.	
Mar 4, 2005	**Clinton Woods** w rsf 5 Rico Hoye (US)	Rotherham (Eng)
Sep 9, 2005	Clinton Woods w pts 12 Julio Cesar Gonzalez (Mex)	Sheffield (Eng)
May 13, 2006	Clinton Woods w rsf 6 Jason DeLisle (Aus)	Sheffield (Eng)
Sep 2, 2006	Clinton Woods w pts 12 Glen Johnson	Bolton (Eng)
Sep 29, 2007	Clinton Woods w pts 12 Julio Cesar Gonzalez	Sheffield (Eng)
Apr 12, 2008	**Antonio Tarver** w pts 12 Clinton Woods	Tampa, FL
Oct 11, 2008	**Chad Dawson** w pts 12 Antonio Tarver	Las Vegas, NV
May 9, 2009	Chad Dawson w pts 12 Antonio Tarver	Las Vegas, NV
	Chad Dawson relinquished the title	
Aug 28, 2009	**Tavoris Cloud** (US) w pts 12 Clinton Woods	Hollywood, FL
	For vacant title	
Aug 7, 2010	Tavoris Cloud w pts 12 Glen Johnson	St Louis, MS
Dec 17, 2010	Tavoris Cloud w pts 12 Fulgencio Zuniga (Col)	Miami, FL
Jun 25, 2011	Tavoris Cloud w rsf 8 Yusaf Mack (US)	Saint Charles, MO
Feb 18, 2012	Tavoris Cloud w pts 12 Gabriel Campillo (Spain)	Corpus Christi, TX
Mar 9, 2013	**Bernard Hopkins** w pts 12 Tavoris Cloud	Brooklyn, NY
Oct 26, 2013	Bernard Hopkins w pts 12 Karo Murat (Ger)	Atlantic City, NJ

WBA super/IBF titles

Apr 19, 2014	**Bernard Hopkins** w pts 12 Beibut Shumenov	Washington, DC

WBO title

Sep 14, 2002	Dariusz Michalczewski w rsf 10 Richard Hall (Jam)	Braunschweig (Ger)
Mar 29, 2003	Dariusz Michalczewski w kioo 9 Derrick Harmon (US)	Hamburg (Ger)
Oct 18, 2003	**Julio Cesar Gonzalez** (Mex) w pts 12 Dariusz Michalczewski	Hamburg (Ger)
Jan 17, 2004	**Zsolt Erdei** (Hun) w pts 12 Julio Cesar Gonzalez	Karlsruhe (Ger)
May 8, 2004	Zsolt Erdei w pts 12 Hugo Garay (Arg)	Dortmund (Ger)
Sep 11, 2004	Zsolt Erdei w pts 12 Alejandro Lakatus (Rom)	Budapest (Hun)
Feb 26, 2005	Zsolt Erdei w pts 12 Hugo Garay	Hamburg (Ger)
Oct 22, 2005	Zsolt Erdei w rsf 12 Mehdi Sahnoune	Halle Ger)
May 6, 2006	Zsolt Erdei w rsf 10 Paul Murdoch (Aus)	Dusseldorf (Ger)
Jul 29, 2006	Zsolt Erdei w pts 12 Thomas Ulrich (Ger)	Oberhausen (Ger)
Jan 27, 2007	Zsolt Erdei w rsf 8 Danny Santiago (US)	Dusseldorf (Ger)
Jun 16, 2007	Zsolt Erdei w rsf 11 George Blades (US)	Budapest (Hun)
Nov 24, 2007	Zsolt Erdei w pts 12 Tito Mendoza (Pan)	Dresden (Ger)
Apr 26, 2008	Zsolt Erdei w pts 12 DeAndrey Abron (US)	Dresden (Ger)
Jan 10, 2009	Zsolt Erdei w pts 12 Yuri Barashian	Magdeburg (Ger)
	Zsolt Erdei relinquished the title to box at cruiserweight	
Aug 22, 2009	Jurgen Brahmer w rsf 11 Aleksy Kuziemski (Pol)	Budapest (Hun)
	For vacant title	
Dec 19, 2009	Jurgen Brahmer w pts 12 Dmitry Sukhotsky (Rus)	Schwerin (Ger)
Apr 24, 2010	Jurgen Brahmer w rsf 5 Mariano Nicolas Plotinsky (Arg)	Hamburg (Ger)
	Brahmer was set to appear in court and Nathan Cleverly and Nadjib Mohammedi were matched for the Interim title	
Dec 11, 2010	Nathan Cleverly (Wal) w pts 12 Nadjib Mohammedi (Fra)	Liverpool (Eng)
	Brahmer stripped of title for pulling out of defence against Cleverly, who was upgraded to WBO champion	
May 21, 2011	Nathan Cleverly w rsf 4 Aleksy Kuziemski (Pol)	London (Eng)
Oct 15, 2011	Nathan Cleverly w pts 12 Tony Bellew (Eng)	Liverpool (Eng)
Feb 25, 2012	Nathan Cleverly w pts 12 Tommy Karpency (US)	Cardiff (Wal)
Nov 10, 2012	Nathan Cleverly w rsf 8 Shawn Hawk (US)	Los Angeles, CA
Apr 20, 2013	Nathan Cleverly w pts 12 Robin Krasniqi (Ger)	Wembley (Eng)
Aug 17, 2013	**Sergey Kovalev** (Rus) w rsf 4 Nathan Cleverly	Cardiff (Wal)
Nov 30, 2013	Sergey Kovalev w ko 2 Ismayl Sillah (Ukr)	Quebec City (Can)
Mar 29, 2014	Sergey Kovalev w ko 7 Cedric Agnew (USA)	Atlantic City, NJ
Aug 2, 2014	Sergey Kovalev w rsc 2 Blake Caparello (Australia)	Atlantic City, NJ

WBO/IBF/WBA super titles

Nov 8, 2014	**Sergey Kovalev** w pts 12 Bernard Hopkins	Atlantic City, NJ
Mar 14, 2015	Sergey Kovalev w rsf 8 Jean Pascal (Can)	Montreal (Can)
Jul 25, 2015	Sergey Kovalev w ko 3 Nadjib Mohammedi (Fra)	Las Vegas, NV
Jan 30, 2016	Sergey Kovalev w rtd 7 Jean Pascal	Montreal (Can)
Jul 11, 2016	Sergey Kovalev w pts 12 Isaac Chilemba (Mal)	Ekaterinburg (Rus)
Nov 19, 2016	**Andre Ward (US)** w pts 12 Sergey Kovalev	Las Vegas, NV
Jun 17, 2017	Andre Ward w rsf 8 Sergey Kovalev	Las Vegas, NV

WBO title

Nov 25, 2017	Sergey Kovalev w rsf 2 Vyacheslav Shabranskyy (Ukr)	New York, NY

IBF title

Nov 11, 2017	Artur Beterbiev (Rus) w ko 12 Enrico Koelling (Ger)	Fresno, CA

SERGEY KOVALEV *on his way to his 12-round points victory over Bernard Hopkins in Atlantic City*

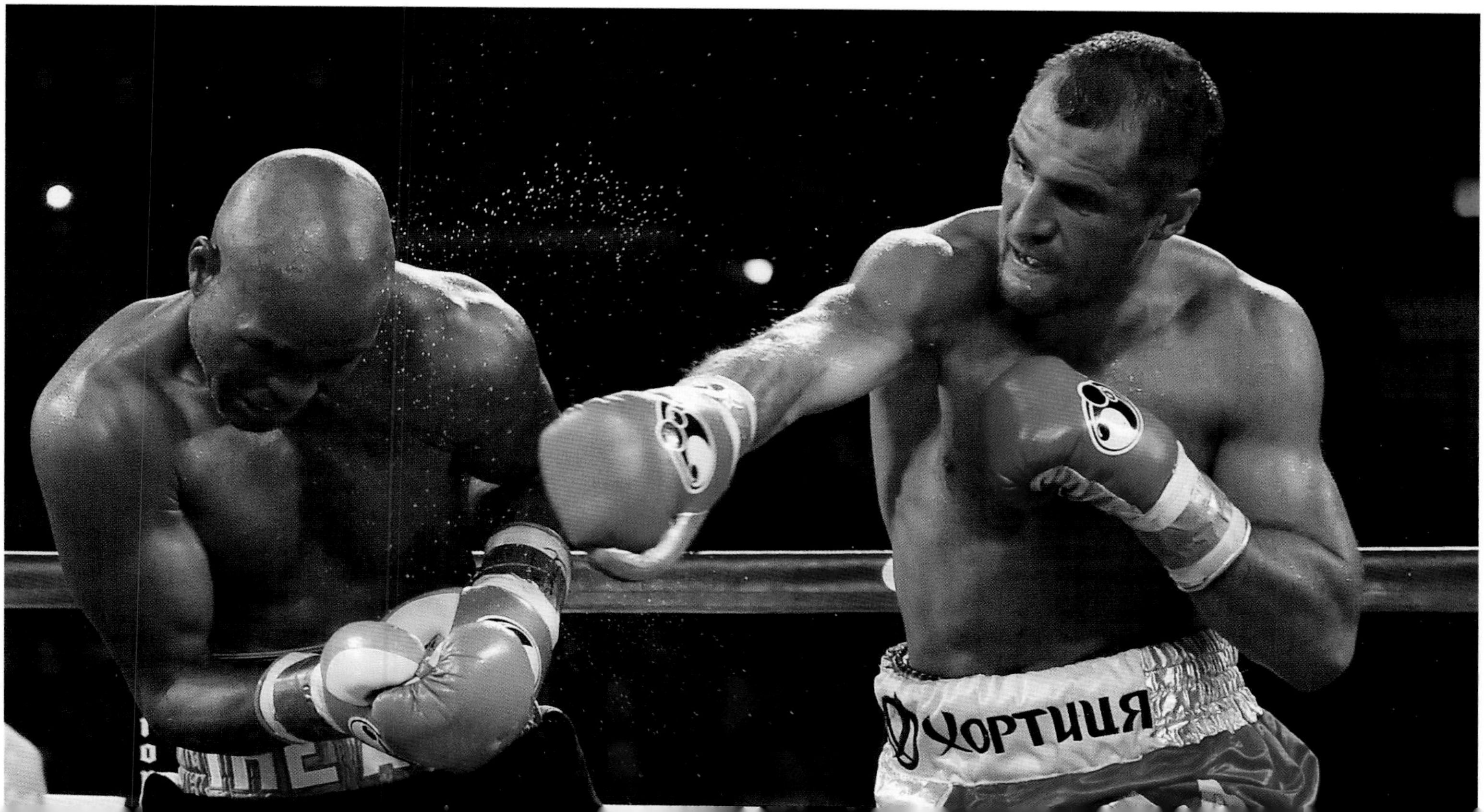

Super-Middleweight

One of Scottish boxing's unsung heroes, Murray Sutherland, holds the distinction of being the first generally accepted champion of the super-middleweight division (weight limit 168lb). Sutherland was born in Edinburgh, but the family emigrated to Canada. Sutherland made his name in the "Tough Guy" free-for-all contests in America in the late 1970s before he became a well-respected professional, operating between the middleweight and light-heavyweight classes.

There had been sporadic attempts to cater for men of his weight, but the category did not become officially recognized until the IBF matched Sutherland with Ernie Singletary for the vacant title. The new category was clearly needed, since the gulf between middleweight (160lb) and light-heavyweight (175 lb) was the biggest in boxing, and the WBA followed suit in 1987. The WBC, unusually, were slowest off the mark – their first championship was not contested until Ray Leonard stopped Donny Lalonde in 1988.

Since then the class has become one of boxing's busiest and most popular, due in large measure to the efforts of the rival British title-holders Chris Eubank (WBO) and Nigel Benn (WBC).

World Super-Middleweight Championship Bouts

IBF title

Mar 28,	1984	**Murray Sutherland** (Sco) w pts 15 Ernie Singletary (US)	Atlantic City, NJ
		For inaugural title	
Jul 22,	1984	**Chong-Pal Park** (Kor) w ko 11 Murray Sutherland	Seoul (Kor)
Jan 2,	1985	Chong-Pal Park w ko 2 Roy Gumbs (Eng)	Seoul (Kor)
Jun 30,	1985	Chong-Pal Park w pts 15 Vinnie Curto (US)	Seoul (Kor)
Apr 11,	1986	Chong-Pal Park w ko 15 Vinnie Curto	Los Angeles, CA
Jul 6,	1986	Chong-Pal Park tech draw 2 Lindell Holmes (US)	Chungju (Kor)
Sep 14,	1986	Chong-Pal Park w pts 15 Marvin Mack (US)	Pusan (Kor)
Jan 25,	1987	Chong Pal-Park w rsf 15 Doug Sam (Aus)	Seoul (Kor)
May 3,	1987	Chong-Pal Park w pts 15 Lindell Holmes	Inchon (Kor)
Jul 26,	1987	Chong-Pal Park w rsf 4 Emmanuel Otti (Ug)	Kwangju (Kor)
Dec	1987	*Park relinquished IBF title to box for vacant WBA version*	
Mar 12,	1988	**Graciano Rocchigiani** (Ger) w rsf 8 Vince Boulware (US)	Dusseldorf (Ger)
		For vacant title	
Jun 3,	1988	Graciano Rocchigiani w pts 15 Nicky Walker (US)	Berlin (Ger)
Oct 7,	1988	Graciano Rocchigiani w rsf 11 Chris Reid (US)	Berlin (Ger)
Jan 27,	1989	Graciano Rocchigiani w pts 12 Sugar Boy Malinga (SA)	Berlin (Ger)
Sep	1989	*Rocchigani relinquished the title because of weight problems*	
Jan 27,	1990	**Lindell Holmes** w pts 12 Frank Tate (US)	New Orleans, LA
		For vacant title	
Jul 19,	1990	Lindell Holmes w rsf 9 Carl Sullivan (US)	Seattle, WA
Dec 16,	1990	Lindell Holmes w pts 12 Sugar Boy Malinga	Marino (Ita)
Mar 7,	1991	Lindell Holmes w pts 12 Antoine Byrd (US)	Madrid (Sp)
May 18,	1991	**Darrin Van Horn** (US) w ko 11 Lindell Holmes	Verbania (Ita)
Aug 17,	1991	Darrin Van Horn w ko 3 John Jarvis (US)	Irvine, CA
Jan 10,	1992	**Iran Barkley** (US) w rsf 2 Darrin Van Horn	New York, NY
Feb 13,	1993	**James Toney** (US) w rtd 9 Iran Barkley	Las Vegas, NV
Oct 29,	1993	James Toney w pts 12 Tony Thornton (US)	Tulsa, OK
Mar 5,	1994	James Toney w rsf 4 Tim Littles (US)	Los Angeles, CA
Jul 29,	1994	James Toney w ko 12 Prince Charles Williams (US)	Las Vegas, NV
Nov 18,	1994	**Roy Jones** (US) w pts 12 James Toney	Las Vegas, NV
Mar 18,	1995	Roy Jones w rsf 1 Antoine Byrd (US)	Pensacola, FL
Jun 24,	1995	Roy Jones w rsf 6 Vinny Pazienza (US)	Atlantic City, NJ
Sep 30,	1995	Roy Jones w rsf 3 Tony Thornton	Pensacola, FL
Jun 15,	1996	Roy Jones w rtd 11 Eric Lucas (Can)	Jacksonville, FL
Oct 4,	1996	Roy Jones w rsf 2 Bryant Brannon (US)	Shreveport, LA
Mar 97 Jones relinquished title after being recognized as WBC light-heavyweight champion			
Jun 21,	1998	**Charles Brewer** (US) w rsf 5 Gary Ballard (SA)	Tampa, FL
Dec 2,	1997	Charles Brewer w pts 12 Joey De Grandis (US)	Philadelphia, PA
Mar 28,	1998	Charles Brewer w rsf 10 Herol Graham (Eng)	Atlantic City, NJ
Aug 22,	1998	Charles Brewer w rsf 3 Antoine Byrd (US)	Leipzig (Ger)
Oct 24,	1998	**Sven Ottke** (Ger) w pts 12 Charles Brewer	Dusseldorf (Ger)
Feb 27,	1999	Sven Ottke w ko 3 Giovanni Nardiello (Ita)	Berlin (Ger)
May 8,	1999	Sven Ottke w pts 12 Gabriel Hernandez (Dr)	Dusseldorf (Ger)
Sep 4,	1999	Sven Ottke w tdec 11 Thomas Tate (US)	Magdeburg (Ger)
Nov 27,	1999	Sven Ottke w pts 12 Glencoffe Johnson (Jam)	Dusseldorf (Ger)
Mar 11,	2000	Sven Ottke w pts 12 Lloyd Bryan (Jam)	Magdeburg (Ger)
Jun 3,	2000	Sven Ottke w pts 12 Tocker Pudwill (US)	Karlsruhe (Ger)
Sep 2,	2000	Sven Ottke w pts 12 Charles Brewer (US)	Magdeburg (Ger)
Dec 16,	2000	Sven Ottke w pts 12 Silvio Branco (Ita)	Karlsruhe (Ger)
Mar 24,	2001	Sven Ottke w rsf 8 James Crawford (US)	Magdeburg (Ger)
Jun 9,	2001	Sven Ottke w rsf 11 Ali Ennebati (Fra)	Nuremberg (Ger)
Sep 1,	2001	Sven Ottke w pts 12 James Butler	Magdeburg (Ger)
Dec 1,	2001	Sven Ottke w ko 10 Anthony Mundine (Aus)	Dortmund (Ger)
Mar 16,	2002	Sven Ottke w pts 12 Rick Thornberry (Aus)	Magdeburg (Ger)
Jun 1,	2002	Sven Ottke w pts 12 Thomas Tate (US)	Nuremburg (Ger)

WBA title

Dec 6,	1987	**Chong-Pal Park** w rsf 2 Jesus Gallardo (Mex)	Seoul (Kor)
		For vacant title	
Mar 1,	1988	Chong Pal-Park w ko 5 Polly Pasieron (Indo)	Chungju (Kor)
May 23,	1988	**Fulgencio Obelmejias** (Ven) w pts 12 Chong-Pal Park	Chungju (Kor)
May 27,	1989	**Inchul Baek** (Kor) w rsf 11 Fulgencio Obelmejias	Seoul (Kor)
Oct 8,	1989	Inchul Baek w rsf 11 Ron Essett (US)	Seoul (Kor)
Jan 13,	1990	Inchul Baek w rtd 7 Yoshiaki Tajima (Jap)	Ulsan (Kor)
Mar 30,	1990	**Christophe Tiozzo** (Fra) w rsf 6 Inchul Baek	Lyon (Fra)
Jul 20,	1990	Christophe Tiozzo w rsf 8 Paul Whittaker (US)	Arles (Fra)
Nov 23,	1990	Christophe Tiozzo w rsf 2 Danny Morgan (US)	Cergy Pontoise (Fra)
Apr 9,	1991	**Victor Cordoba** (Pan) w rsf 9 Christophe Tiozzo	Marseilles (Fra)
Dec 13,	1991	Victor Cordoba w rsf 11 Vincenzo Nardiello (Ita)	Paris (Fra)
Sep 12,	1992	**Michael Nunn** (US) w pts 12 Victor Cordoba	Las Vegas, NV
Jan 30,	1993	Michael Nunn w pts 12 Victor Cordoba	Memphis, TN
Feb 20,	1993	Michael Nunn w ko 1 Danny Morgan (US)	Mexico City (Mex)
Apr 23,	1993	Michael Nunn w rsf 6 Crawford Ashley (Eng)	Memphis, TN
Dec 18,	1993	Michael Nunn w pts 12 Merqui Sosa (DR)	Puebla (Mex)
Feb 26,	1904	**Steve Little** (US) w pts 12 Michael Nunn	London (Eng)
Aug 12,	1994	**Frank Liles** (US) w pts 12 Steve Little	Tucuman (Arg)
Dec 16,	1994	Frank Liles w pts 12 Michael Nunn	Quito (Ecu)
May 27,	1995	Frank Liles w rsf 6 Frederic Seillier (Fra)	Fort Lauderdale, FL
Dec 9,	1995	Frank Liles w pts 12 Mauricio Amaral (Bra)	Stuttgart (Ger)
Jun 8,	1996	Frank Liles w rsf 3 Tim Littles (US)	Newcastle (Eng)
Apr 19,	1997	Frank Liles w rsf 5 Segundo Mercado (Ecu)	Shreveport, LA
Jul 19,	1997	Frank Liles w pts 12 Zafarou Ballogou (Tog)	Nashville, TN
Apr 3,	1998	Frank Liles w pts 12 Andrei Shkalkov (Rus)	Bayamon (PR)
Jun 12,	1999	**Byron Mitchell** (US) w rsf 11 Frank Liles	Wilmington OH
Dec 11,	1999	Byron Mitchell drew 12 Bruno Girard (Fra)	Tunica MS
Apr 8,	2000	**Bruno Girard** w pts 12 Byron Mitchell	Paris (Fra)
Sep 16,	2000	Bruno Girard w pts 12 Manuel Siaca (PR)	Chateauroux (Fra)
Feb	2001	*Girard relinquished title due to contractual problems*	
Mar 3,	2001	**Byron Mitchell** w rsf 12 Manuel Siaca (PR)	Las Vegas NV
Sep 29,	2001	Byron Mitchell w pts 12 Manuel Siaca	New York NY
Jul 27,	2002	Byron Mitchell w rsf 4 Julio Cesar Green (DR)	Las Vegas NV

WBC title

Nov 7,	1988	Sugar Ray Leonard (US) w rsf 9 Donny Lalonde (Can)	Las Vegas, NV
		For vacant title: Lalonde's WBC light-heavyweight title was also at stake, even though he scaled only 167 lb	
Jun 12,	1989	Sugar Ray Leonard drew l2 Thomas Hearns	Las Vegas, NV
Dec 7,	1989	Sugar Ray Leonard w pts 12 Roberto Duran (Pan)	Las Vegas, NV
Aug	1990	*Leonard relinquished the title to pursue the light-middleweight championship*	
Dec 15,	1990	**Mauro Galvano** (Ita) w pts 12 Dario Matteoni (Arg)	Monte Carlo (Mon)
		For vacant title	
Jul 27,	1991	Mauro Galvano w pts 12 Ron Essett (US)	Capo D'Orlando (Ita)
Feb 6,	1992	Mauro Galvano w pts 12 Juan Carlos Giminez (Par)	Marino (Ita)
Oct 3,	1992	**Nigel Benn** (Eng) w rtd 3 Mauro Galvano	Marino (Ita)
Dec 12,	1992	Nigel Benn w rsf 11 Nicky Piper	Muswell Hill (Eng)
Mar 6,	1993	Nigel Benn w pts 12 Mauro Galvano	Glasgow (Sco)
Jun 26,	1993	Nigel Benn w rsf 4 Lou Gent (Eng)	London (Eng)
Oct 9,	1993	Nigel Benn drew 12 Chris Eubank (Eng)	Manchester (Eng)
		WBC/WBO unification match	
Feb 26,	1994	Nigel Benn w pts 12 Henry Wharton (Eng)	London (Eng)
Sep 10,	1994	Nigel Benn w pts 12 Juan Carlos Gimenez (Par)	Birmingham (Eng)
Feb 25,	1995	Nigel Benn w ko 10 Gerald McClellan (US)	London (Eng)
Jul 22,	1995	Nigel Benn w rsf 8 Vincenzo Nardiello (Ita)	London (Eng)
Sep 2,	1995	Nigel Benn w ko 7 Danny Ray Perez (US)	London (Eng)
Mar 2,	1996	**Sugarboy Malinga** (SA) w pts 12 Nigel Benn	Newcastle (Eng)
Jul 6,	1996	**Vincenzo Nardiello** w pts 12 Sugarboy Malinga	Manchester (Eng)

Oct 12,	1996	**Robin Reid** (Eng) w ko 7 Vincenzo Nardiello	Milan (Ita)
Feb 8,	1997	Robin Reid w ko 7 Giovanni Pretorius (SA)	Millwall (Eng)
May 3,	1997	Robin Reid w pts 12 Henry Wharton	Manchester (Eng)
Sep 11,	1997	Robin Reid w pts 12 Hassine Cherifi (Fra)	Widness (Eng)
Dec 19,	1997	**Sugarboy Malinga** w pts 12 Robin Reid	London (Eng)
Mar 27,	1998	**Richie Woodhall** (Eng) w pts 12 Sugarboy Malinga	Telford (Eng)
Sept 5,	1998	Richie Woodhall w pts 12 Glenn Catley (Eng)	Telford (Eng)
Feb 13,	1999	Richie Woodhall w rsf 6 Vincenzo Nardiello	Newcastle (Eng)
Oct 23,	1999	**Markus Beyer** (Ger) w pts 12 Richie Woodhall	Telford (Eng)
Jan 29,	2000	Markus Beyer w ko 7 Leif Keiski (Swe)	Riesa (Ger)
May 6,	2000	**Glenn Catley** (Eng) w rsf 12 Markus Beyer	Frankfurt (Ger)
Sep 1,	2000	**Dingaan Thobela** (SA) w ko 12 Glenn Catley	Brakpan (SA)
Dec 15,	2000	**Dave Hilton** (Can) w pts 12 Dingaan Thobela	Montreal (Can)
Apr	2001	*Hilton forfeited title because of a jail sentence*	
Jul 10,	2001	**Eric Lucas** (Can) w rsf 7 Glenn Catley	Montreal (Can)
Nov 30,	2001	Eric Lucas w rsf 8 Dingaan Thobela	Montreal (Can)
Mar 1,	2002	Eric Lucas w pts 12 Vinny Pazienza (US)	Mashantucket, CT
Sep 6,	2002	Eric Lucas w pts 12 Omar Sheika (US)	Montreal (Can)
Apr 5,	2003	**Markus Beyer** (Ger) w pts 12 Eric Lucas	Leipzig (Ger)
Aug 16,	2003	Markus Beyer w dis 5 Danny Green (Aus)	Nuremberg (Ger)
Feb 28,	2004	Markus Beyer w pts 12 Andre Thysse (SA)	Dresden (Ger)
Jun 5,	2004	**Cristian Sanavia** (Ita) w pts 12 Markus Beyer	Chemnitz (Ger)
Oct 9,	2004	**Markus Beyer** w ko 6 Cristian Sanavia	Erfurt (Ger)
Dec 18,	2004	Markus Beyer w pts 12 Yoshinori Nishizawa (Jap)	Bayreuth (Ger)
Mar 12,	2005	Markus Beyer w pts 12 Danny Green	Zwickau (Ger)
Sep 3,	2005	Markus Beyer w pts 12 Omar Sheika	Berlin (Ger)
Jan 28,	2006	Markus Beyer w rsf 12 Alberto Colajanni (Ita)	Berlin (Ger)
May 13,	2006	Markus Beyer tec. draw 4 Sakio Bika (Cam)	Zwickau (Ger)

WBO title

Nov 4,	1988	**Thomas Hearns** (US) w pts 12 James Kinchen (US)	Las Vegas, NV
		For vacant title	
Apr 28,	1990	Thomas Hearns w pts 12 Michael Olajide (Can)	Atlantic City, NJ
Apr	1991	*Hearns relinquished the title to box at light-heavyweight*	
Sep 21,	1991	**Chris Eubank** (Eng) w rsf 12 Michael Watson (Eng)	London (Eng)
		For vacant title	
Feb 1,	1992	Chris Eubank w pts 12 Sugar Boy Malinga	Birmingham (Eng)
Apr 25,	1992	Chris Eubank w ko 3 John Jarvis	Manchester (Eng)
Jun 27,	1992	Chris Eubank w pts 12 Ron Essett	Quinto do Lago (Por)
Sep 19,	1992	Chris Eubank w pts 12 Tony Thornton	Glasgow (Sco)
Nov 28,	1992	Chris Eubank w pts 12 Juan Carlos Giminez	Manchester (Eng)
Feb 20,	1993	Chris Eubank w pts 12 Lindell Holmes	London (Eng)
May 15,	1993	Chris Eubank drew 12 Ray Close (Ire)	Glasgow (Sco)
Oct 9,	1993	Chris Eubank drew 12 Nigel Benn	Manchester (Eng)
		(WBC/WBO unification match)	
Feb 5,	1994	Chris Eubank w pts 12 Graciano Rocchigiani	Berlin (Ger)
May 21,	1994	Chris Eubank w pts 12 Ray Close	Belfast (N. Ire)
Jul 9,	1994	Chris Eubank w pts 12 Mauricio Amaral (Bra)	London (Eng)
Aug 27,	1994	Chris Eubank w rsf 7 Sam Storey (Ire)	Cardiff (Wal)
Oct 25,	1994	Chris Eubank w pts 12 Dan Schommer (US)	Sun City (Bop)
Dec 10,	1994	Chris Eubank w pts 12 Henry Wharton	Manchester (Eng)
Mar 18,	1995	**Steve Collins** (Ire) w pts 12 Chris Eubank	Millstreet (Ire)
Sep 9,	1995	Steve Collins w pts 12 Chris Eubank	Cork (Ire)
Nov 25,	1995	Steve Collins w pts 12 Cornelius Carr (Eng)	Dublin (Ire)
Mar 9,	1996	Steve Collins w rsf 11 Neville Brown (Eng)	Millstreet (Ire)
Jul 6,	1996	Steve Collins w rsf 4 Nigel Benn	Manchester (Eng)
Nov 9,	1996	Steve Collins w rtd 6 Nigel Benn	Manchester (Eng)
Feb 8,	1997	Steve Collins w rsf 5 Frederic Seillier (Fra)	London (Eng)
July 5,	1997	Steve Collins w rsf 3 Craig Cummings (US)	Glasgow (Sco)
Sep	1997	*Collins relinquished title and retired*	
Jan 24,	1998	**Joe Calzaghe** (Wal) w rsf 3 Branco Sobot (Cro)	Cardiff (Wal)
		For vacant title	
Apr 25,	1998	Joe Calzaghe w rtd 9 Juan Carlos Gimenez (Par)	Cardiff (Wal)
Feb 13,	1999	Joe Calzaghe w pts 12 Robin Reid	Newcastle (Eng)
Jun 5,	1999	Joe Calzaghe w pts 12 Rick Thornberry (Aus)	Cardiff (Wal)
Jan 29,	2000	Joe Calzaghe w pts 12 David Starie (Eng)	Manchester (Eng)
Aug 12,	2000	Joe Calzaghe w rsf 5 Omar Sheika (US)	London (Eng)
Dec 16,	2000	Joe Calzaghe w rsf 10 Richie Woodhall	Sheffield (Eng)
Apr 28,	2001	Joe Calzaghe w rsf 1 Mario Veit (Ger)	Cardiff (Wal)
Oct 13,	2001	Joe Calzaghe w rsf 4 Will McIntyre (US)	Copenhagen (Den)
Apr 20,	2002	Joe Calzaghe w pts 12 Charles Brewer (US)	Cardiff (Wal)
Aug 17,	2002	Joe Calzaghe w pts 12 Miguel Angel Jimenez (PR)	Cardiff (Wal)
Dec 14,	2002	Joe Calzaghe w rsf 2 Tocker Pudwill (US)	Newcastle (Eng)
Jun 28,	2003	Joe Calzaghe w rsf 2 Byron Mitchell (US)	Cardiff (Wal)
Feb 21,	2004	Joe Calzaghe w rsf 7 Mger Mkrtchian (Arm)	Cardiff (Wal)
Oct 22,	2004	Joe Calzaghe w pts 12 Kabary Salem (Egy)	Edinburgh (Sco)
May 7,	2005	Joe Calzaghe w rsf 6 Mario Veit (Ger)	Braunschweig (Ger)
Sep 10,	2005	Joe Calzaghe w pts 12 Evans Ashira (Ken)	Cardiff (Wal)
		Calzaghe unified the WBO & IBF titles, then was stripped of the IBF belt	
Apr 7,	2007	Joe Calzaghe w rsf 3 Peter Manfredo (US)	Cardiff (Wal)

WBA & IBF titles

Mar 15,	2003	**Sven Ottke** (Ger) w pts 12 Byron Mitchell (US)	Berlin (Ger)
Jun 14,	2003	Sven Ottke w pts 12 David Starie (Eng)	Magdeburg (Ger)
Sep 6,	2003	Sven Ottke w pts 12 Mads Larsen (Den)	Erfurt (Ger)
Dec 13,	2003	Sven Ottke w pts 12 Robin Reid (Eng)	Nuremburg (Ger)
Mar 27,	2004	Sven Ottke w pts 12 Armand Krajnk (Svk)	Magdeburg (Ger)
		Ottke announced his retirement	

WBA title

	2003	*Sven Ottke was declared a "super" champion and when he retired recognition passed to the world champion*	
Sep 3,	2003	**Anthony Mundine** (Aus) w pts 12 Antwun Echols (US)	Sydney (Aus)
Jan 19,	2004	Anthony Mundine w rsf 5 Yoshinori Nishizawa (Jap)	Wollongong (Aus)
May 5,	2004	**Manny Siaca** (PR) w pts 12 Anthony Mundine	Sydney (Aus)
Nov 12,	2004	**Mikkel Kessler** (Den) w rsf 8 Manny Siaca	Copenhagen (Den)
Jun 8,	2005	Mikkel Kessler w pts 12 Anthony Mundine	Sydney (Aus)
Jan 14,	2006	Mikkel Kessler w rsf 10 Eric Lucas (Can)	Copenhagen (Den)
		When Mikkel Kessler beat Markus Beyer, the WBA recognized him as "unified" champion, transferring that status to Joe Calzaghe when he beat Kessler. To keep the sanction fees flowing in, they installed Anthony Mundine as "world" champion	
Mar 7,	2007	**Anthony Mundine** (Aus) w ko 9 Sam Soliman (Aus)	Sydney (Aus)
Jun 27,	2007	Anthony Mundine w pts 12 Pablo Zamora (Arg)	Broadbeach (Aus)
Dec 10,	2007	Anthony Mundine w ko 4 Jose Alberto Clavero (Arg)	Sydney (Aus)

RINGSIDE VIEW

Sugar Ray Leonard vs Thomas Hearns

LAS VEGAS STALEMATE

Ray Leonard and Thomas Hearns provided one of the greatest contests in boxing history when they met for the welterweight title in Las Vegas in 1981, but their rematch in the same ring eight years later, in which Leonard scraped a draw to retain his WBC super-middleweight title, was a sad echo of past glories.

Leonard, never the most gracious of men, at least had the class to acknowledge that the draw favoured him more than Hearns, although he soon retracted that view and claimed, against all the evidence, that he had deserved to win. When he produced another low-key display to win his next defence, a third meeting with Roberto Duran, the signs were clear to all but him that it was to get out of the game.

But the fighter is always the last to know, and it took a beating by Terry Norris in a bid for the light-middleweight title to convince Leonard that his fabulous career was over.

WBC/WBA titles

Oct 14, 2006 **Mikkel Kessler** w ko 3 Markus Beyer ... Copenhagen (Den)
A WBC/WBA unification fight
Mar 24, 2007 **Mikkel Kessler** w pts 12 Librado Andrade (Mex) ... Copenhagen (Den)

IBF title

Aug 24, 2002 Sven Ottke w rsf 9 Joe Gatti (Can) ... Leipzig (Ger)
Nov 16, 2002 Sven Ottke w pts 12 Rudy Markussen (Den) ... Nuremberg (Ger)
Ottke then unified the IBF and WBA titles and retired in 2004
Oct 2, 2004 **Jeff Lacy** (US) w rsf 8 Syd Vanderpool (Can) ... Las Vegas, NV
For vacant title
Dec 4, 2004 Jeff Lacy w pts 12 Omar Sheika (US) ... Las Vegas, NV
Mar 5, 2005 Jeff Lacy w rsf 7 Rubin Williams (US) ... Las Vegas, NV
Aug 6, 2005 Jeff Lacy w rtd 7 Robin Reid (Eng) ... Tampa, FL
Nov 5, 2005 Jeff Lacy w ko 2 Scott Pemberton (US) ... Stateline, NV
Mar 3, 2007 **Alejandro Berrio** (Col) w rsf 3 Robert Stieglitz (Ger) ... Rostock (Ger)
Oct 19, 2007 **Lucian Bute** (Can) w rsf 11 Alejandro Berrio ... Montreal (Can)
Feb 29, 2008 Lucian Bute w rsf 10 William Joppy (US) ... Montreal (Can)
Oct 24, 2008 Lucian Bute w pts 12 Librado Andrade (Mex) ... Montreal (Can)
Mar 13, 2009 Lucian Bute w rsf 4 Fulgencio Zuniga (Col) ... Montreal (Can)
Nov 28, 2009 Lucian Bute w ko 4 Librado Andrade ... Montreal (Can)
Apr 17, 2010 Lucian Bute w rsf 3 Edison Miranda ... Montreal (Can)
Oct 15, 2010 Lucian Bute w ko 9 Jesse Brinkley ... Montreal (Can)
Mar 19, 2011 Lucian Bute w rsf 10 Brian Magee ... Montreal (Can)
Jul 9, 2011 Lucian Bute w ko 4 Jean-Paul Mendy (Fra) ... Bucharest (Rom)
Nov 5, 2011 Lucian Bute w pts 12 Glen Johnson ... Quebec (Can)
May 26, 2012 Carl Froch w rsf 5 Lucian Bute ... Nottingham (Eng)
Nov 17, 2012 Carl Froch w ko 3 Yusaf Mack (US) ... Nottingham (Eng)

IBF & WBO titles

Mar 4, 2006 **Joe Calzaghe** w pts 12 Jeff Lacy (US) ... Manchester (Eng)
Oct 14, 2006 Joe Calzaghe w pts 12 Sakio Bika (Cmr) ... Manchester (Eng)
Dec 2006 *Calzaghe stripped of IBF title, December 2006*

WBC/WBA/WBO titles

Nov 3, 2007 **Joe Calzaghe** w pts 12 Mikkel Kessler ... Cardiff (Wal)

WBC title

Joe Calzaghe moved up to the light-heavyweight division
Dec 6, 2008 **Carl Froch** (Eng) w pts 12 Jean Pascal ... Nottingham (Eng)
Apr 25, 2009 Carl Froch w rsf 12 Jermain Taylor (US) ... Mashantucket, CT
Oct 17, 2009 Carl Froch w pts 12 Andre Dirrell (US) ... Nottingham (Eng)
Apr 24, 2010 **Mikkel Kessler** w pts 12 Carl Froch ... Herning (Den)
Kessler suffered elbow injury and vacated title
Nov 27, 2010 Carl Froch w pts 12 Arthur Abraham ... Helsinki (Fin)
For vacant title
Jun 4, 2011 Carl Froch w pts 12 Glen Johnson ... Atlantic City, NJ

WBA title

Joe Calzaghe moved up to the light-heavyweight division.
Feb 27, 2008 **Anthony Mundine** w pts 12 Nader Hamdan (Aus) ... Sydney (Aus)
For vacant title
May 28, 2008 Anthony Mundine w pts 12 Sam Soliman (Aus) ... Melbourne (Aus)
Mundine relinquished the title and moved down to middleweight
Jun 21, 2008 Mikkel Kessler w ko 12 Dmitri Sartison (Ger) ... Copenhagen (Den)
For vacant title
Oct 25, 2008 Mikkel Kessler w ko 3 Danilo Haussler (Ger) ... Oldenberg (Ger)
Sep 12, 2009 Mikkel Kessler w rsf 4 Gusmyr Perdomo (Ven) ... Herning (Den)
Nov 21, 2009 **Andre Ward** (US) w tdec 11 Mikkel Kessler ... Oakland, CA
The WBA recognized the Ward-Kessler fight as for their Super Championship and on the same day sanctioned another fight for their world title as follows:
Nov 21, 2009 **Dimitri Sartison** w rsf 6 Stjepan Bozic (Cro) ... Kiel (Ger)
Jul 31, 2010 Dimitri Sartison (Ger) w pts 12 Khoren Gevor ... Hamburg (Ger)
Sartison stripped of the WBA title
Aug 26, 2011 **Karoly Balzsay** (Hun) w rsf 12 Stanyslav Kashtanov (Ukr) ... Donetsk (Ukr)
For vacant title
Apr 21, 2012 Karoly Balzsay (Hun) w rsf 12 Dimitri Sartison ... Schwerin (Ger)
The WBA also sanctioned the following for the Interim title
Jul 30, 2011 Brian Magee (Ire) w pts 12 Jaime Barboza (CR) ... San Jose (Costa Rica)
Feb 18, 2012 Brian Magee w ko 5 Rudy Markussen (Den) ... Brondby (Den)
Oct 11, 2012 Stanyslav Kashtanov w pts 12 Server Yemurlayev (Ukr) ... Donetsk (Ukr)
Dec 8, 2012 Mikkel Kessler w ko 3 Brian Magee ... Herning (Den)

WBC/WBA super titles

Dec 17, 2011 Andre Ward w pts 12 Carl Froch ... Atlantic City, NJ
Sep 8, 2012 Andre Ward w pts 12 Chad Dawson ... Atlantic City, NJ

WBO title

Joe Calzaghe moved up to light-heavyweight
Sep 27, 2008 **Denis Inkin** (Rus) w pts 12 Fulgencio Zuniga ... Hamburg (Ger)
For vacant title
Jan 10, 2009 **Karoly Balzsay** (Hun) w pts 12 Denis Inkin ... Magdeburg (Ger)
Apr 25, 2009 Karoly Balzsay w ko 11 Maselino Masoe (NZ) ... Krefeld (Ger)
Aug 22, 2009 **Robert Stieglitz** (Ger) w rsf 11 Karoly Balzsay ... Budapest (Hun)
Jan 9, 2010 Robert Stieglitz w rsf 5 Ruben Eduardo Acosta (Arg) ... Magdeburg (Ger)
Apr 17, 2010 Robert Stieglitz w pts 12 Eduard Gutknecht (Ger) ... Magdeburg (Ger)
Nov 26, 2010 Robert Stieglitz w pts 12 Enrique Ornelias (Mex) ... Dresden (Ger)
Apr 9, 2011 Robert Stieglitz w dq 10 Khoren Gevor (Arm) ... Magdeburg (Ger)
Jan 14, 2012 Robert Stieglitz w pts 12 Henry Weber (Ger) ... Offenburg (Ger)
May 5, 2012 Robert Stieglitz w pts 12 Nader Hamdan (Aus) ... Erfut (Ger)
Aug 25, 2012 Arthur Abraham (Ger) w pts 12 Robert Stieglitz ... Berlin (Ger)
Dec 15, 2012 Arthur Abraham w rsf 8 Mehdi Bouadla (Fra) ... Nuremberg (Ger)
Mar 23, 2013 **Robert Stieglitz** w tko 4 Arthur Abraham ... Magdeburg (Ger)
Jul 13, 2013 Robert Stieglitz w rsf 10 Yuzo Kiyota (Jap) ... Dresden (Ger)
Oct 19, 2013 Robert Stieglitz w pts 12 Isaac Ekpo (Nig) ... Leipzig (Ger)
Robert Stieglitz vacated title
May 3, 2014 **Arthur Abraham** w pts 12 Nikola Sjekloca ... Berlin (Ger)
For vacant title
Sep 27, 2014 Arthur Abraham w pts 12 Paul Smith (Eng) ... Kiel (Ger)
Feb 21, 2015 Arthur Abraham w pts 12 Paul Smith ... Berlin (Ger)
Nov 21, 2015 Arthur Abraham w pts 12 Martin Murray (Eng) ... Niedersachsen (Ger)
Apr 9, 2016 **Gilberto Ramirez (Mex)** w pts 12 Arthur Abraham ... Las Vegas, NV
Apr 22, 2017 Gilberto Ramirez w pts 12 Max Bursak (Ukr) ... Carson, CA
Sep 22, 2017 Gilberto Ramirez w pts 12 Jesse Hart (US) ... Tucson, AZ
Feb 3, 2018 Gilberto Ramirez w rsf 6 Habib Ahmed (Gha) ... Corpus Christi, TX

WBC title

Andre Ward stripped of title
Jun 22, 2013 Sakio Bika w pts 12 Marco Antonio Periban (Mex) ... New York, NY
For vacant title
Dec 7, 2013 Sakio Bika drew 12 Anthony Dirrell (USA) ... New York, NY
Aug 16, 2014 **Anthony Dirrell** w pts 12 Sakio Bika ... Carson, CA
Apr 24, 2015 **Badou Jack** (Swe) w pts 12 Anthony Dirrell ... Chicago, IL
Sep 12, 2015 Badou Jack w pts 12 George Groves (Eng) ... Las Vegas, NV
Apr 30, 2016 Badou Jack w dis 12 Lucian Bute (Rom) ... Washington, DC

IBF/WBA titles

May 25, 2013 **Carl Froch** w pts 12 Mikkel Kessler ... London (Eng)
Nov 23, 2013 Carl Froch w rsf 9 George Groves (Eng) ... Manchester (Eng)
May 31, 2014 Carl Froch w rsf 8 George Groves ... London (Eng)

IBF title

Carl Froch stripped of title
May 23, 2015 **James DeGale** (Eng) w pts 12 Andre Dirrell ... Boston, MA
For vacant title
Nov 28, 2015 James DeGale w pts 12 Lucian Bute (Can) ... Quebec (Can)
Apr 30, 2016 James DeGale w pts 12 Rogelio Medina (Mex) ... Washington, DC

WBA title

Carl Froch vacated title
May 9, 2015 **Fedor Chudinov** (Russia) w pts 12 Felix Sturm ... Frankfurt (Ger)
For vacant title
Sep 26, 2015 Fedor Chudinov w pts 12 Frank Buglioni (Eng) ... London (Eng)
Jan 9, 2016 **Giovanni De Carolis (Ita)** w rsf 11 Vincent Feigenbutz (Ger) . Baden-Wurtt. (Ger)
Jul 16, 2016 Giovanni De Carolis w pts 12 Tyron Zeuge (Ger) ... Berlin (Ger)
Nov 5, 2016 **Tyron Zeuge** w ko 12 Giovanni De Carolis ... Brandenburg (Ger)
Mar 25, 2017 Tyron Zeuge w td 5 Isaac Ekpo (Nig) ... Brandenburg (Ger)
Jun 17, 2017 Tyron Zeuge w pts 12 Paul Smith (Eng) ... Hessen (Ger)

IBF/WBC titles

Jan 14, 2017 James DeGale drew 12 Badou Jack ... New York, NY

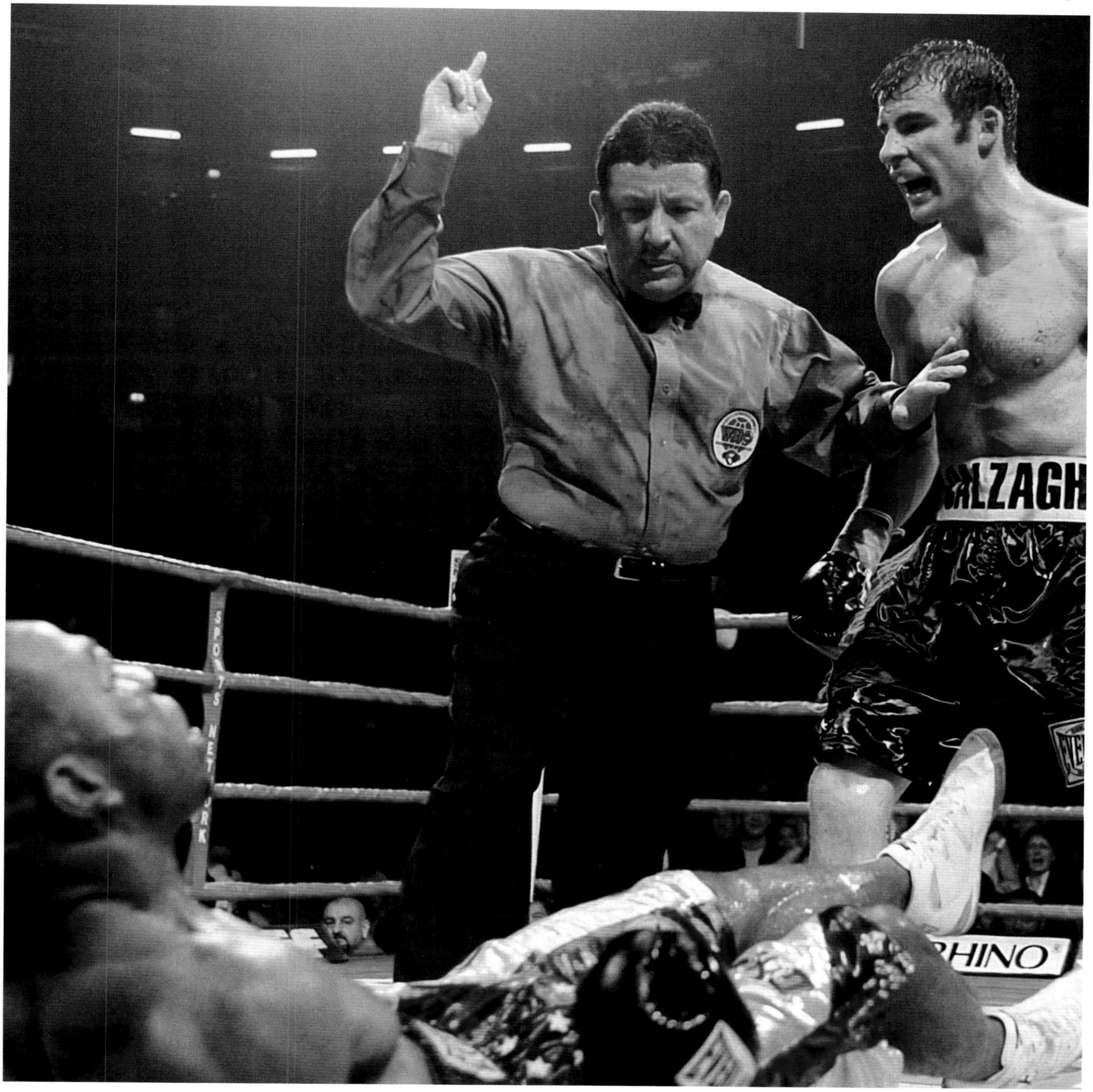

CROWNING GLORY *Joe Calzaghe takes his career to a new level as he beats a bruised and battered Jeff Lacy in their unification fight in 2006*

WBC title

Sep 8, 2017	**David Benavidez (US)** w pts 12 Ronald Gavrill (Rom)	Las Vegas, NV
Feb 17, 2017	David Benavidez w pts 12 Ronald Gavrill	Las Vegas, NV

IBF title

Dec 9, 2017	**Caleb Truax (US)** w pts 12 James DeGale	London (Eng)

WBA Super title

Nov 16, 2013	Andre Ward (US) w pts 12 Edwin Rodriguez (Dom Rep)	Ontario, CA
Feb 20, 2016	**Felix Sturm (Ger)** w pts 12 Fedor Chudinov (Rus)	Nordrhein-Westfalen (Ger)
May 27, 2017	**George Groves (Eng)** w rsf 6 Fedor Chudinov	Sheffield (Eng)
Oct 14, 2017	George Groves w ko 4 Jamie Cox (Eng)	London (Eng)
Feb 17, 2018	George Groves w pts 12 Chris Eubank Jr.	Manchester (Eng)

Middleweight

The Irish-born Jack Dempsey – the original, "Nonpareil" Dempsey – earns his place in boxing history as the man who bridged the eras from bare-knuckles to gloves to become the first world middleweight champion. Dempsey had been accepted as the American champion at the new weight (154 lb), and his win over Billy McCarthy (English-born but Australian based) was the first proper international contest in the division.

Dempsey was dethroned by Bob Fitzsimmons, who, in keeping with the practice of the time, named a new weight limit of 158 lb, since he could no longer make 154 lb. The limit crept up to the modern 160 lb in stages. It was first accepted in Europe, where France hosted a series of famous middleweight matches in the years immediately before the First World War, but America did not adopt the new poundage until 1921.

Middleweight has produced more of boxing's legendary champions than any other: Harry Greb, Sugar Ray Robinson, Carlos Monzon and Marvin Hagler each became international superstars. Perhaps because they combine speed, skill and power so perfectly, the middleweights are properly regarded as the sport's thoroughbreds.

World Middleweight Championship Bouts

Feb 3,	1886	**"Nonpareil" Jack Dempsey** (Ire) w ko 27 Jack Fogarty (US)	New York, NY
Mar 4,	1886	"Nonpareil" Jack Dempsey w ko 13 George LaBlanche (Can)	Larchmont, NY
Dec 13,	1887	"Nonpareil" Jack Dempsey w ko 15 Johnny Reagan (US)	Long Island, NY
Feb 18,	1890	"Nonpareil" Jack Dempsey w rsf 28 Billy McCarthy (Aus)	San Francisco, CA
Jan 14,	1891	**Bob Fitzsimmons** (Eng) w ko 12 "Nonpareil" Jack Dempsey	New Orleans, LA
Sep 26,	1894	Bob Fitzsimmons w ko 2 Dan Creedon (NZ)	New Orleans, LA
		Fitzsimmons gave up the title to pursue the heavyweight championship. There was no clear-cut successor, but Kid McCoy (US) established a solid claim to the title by beating welterweight champion Tommy Ryan	
Mar 2,	1896	**Kid McCoy** w ko 15 Tommy Ryan (US)	Long Island, NY
May 18,	1896	Kid McCoy w dis 6 Mysterious Billy Smith (US)	Boston, MA
Dec 26,	1896	Kid McCoy w ko 9 Billy Doherty (Aus)	Johannesburg (SA)
Dec 17,	1897	Kid McCoy w ko 15 Dan Creedon	Long Island, NY
		Creedon had gained recognition in England as the world champion. McCoy subsequently relinquished the title, which was claimed by Tommy Ryan	
Oct 24,	1898	**Tommy Ryan** w pts 20 Jack Bonner (US)	Coney Island, NY
Aug 31,	1899	Tommy Ryan w pts 20 Jack Moffatt (US)	Dubuque, IA
Mar 4,	1901	Tommy Ryan w rtd 17 Tommy West (US)	Louisville, KY
Jun 24,	1902	Tommy Ryan w ko 3 Johnny Gorman (US)	London (Eng)
Sep 15,	1902	Tommy Ryan w ko 6 Kid Carter (US)	Fort Erie (Can)
		Ryan retired, and once more confusion reigned. Hugo Kelly, Jack "Twin" Sullivan, Stanley Ketchel and Billy Papke all claimed the title. Ketchel's wins over the other three established him as the rightful champion	
May 9,	1908	**Stanley Ketchel** (US) w ko 20 Jack "Twin" Sullivan (US)	Colma, CA
Jun 4,	1908	Stanley Ketchel w pts 10 Billy Papke (US)	Milwaukee, WI
Jul 31,	1908	Stanley Ketchel w ko 3 Hugo Kelly (US)	San Francisco, CA
Sep 7,	1908	**Billy Papke** w ko 12 Stanley Ketchel	Los Angeles, CA
Nov 26,	1908	**Stanley Ketchel** w ko 11 Billy Papke	Colma, CA
Jul 5,	1909	Stanley Ketchel w pts 20 Billy Papke	Colma, CA
Jan	1910	*Ketchel announced that he could no longer make the weight (then 158 lb) and Papke and Willie Lewis were matched for the vacant title*	
Mar 19,	1910	**Billy Papke** w ko 3 Willie Lewis (US)	Paris (Fra)
Mar	1910	*Ketchel reclaimed the title*	
May 27,	1910	**Stanley Ketchel** w ko 2 Willie Lewis	New York, NY
Oct 15,	1910	*Ketchel was shot to death, and Papke reclaimed the title. Various other claimants emerged during the next couple of years, including Frank Mantell, Frank Klaus and Georges Carpentier, but Papke's claim was generally regarded as the strongest*	
Jun 8,	1911	**Billy Papke** w rtd 9 Jim Sullivan (Eng)	London (Eng)
Jun 29,	1912	Billy Papke w rsf 6 Marcel Moreau (Fra)	Paris (Fra)
Dec 4,	1912	Billy Papke w rtd 7 George Bernard (Fra)	Paris (Fra)
Mar 5,	1913	**Frank Klaus** (US) w dis 15 Billy Papke	Paris (Fra)
Oct 11,	1913	**George Chip** (US) w ko 6 Frank Klaus	Pittsburgh, PA
Dec 23,	1913	George Chip w ko 5 Frank Klaus	Pittsburgh, PA
		With these two wins over Klaus, Chip earned recognition in America as champion, even though he had been over the division limit on each occasion. Meanwhile, the Australians set up their own version of the title	

Australian version of world title

Jan 1,	1914	**Eddie McGoorty** (US) w ko 1 Dave Smith (US)	Sydney (Aus)
Feb 7,	1914	Eddie McGoorty w pts 20 Pat Bradley (Aus)	Sydney (Aus)
Mar 14,	1914	**Jeff Smith** (US) w pts 20 Eddie McGoorty	Sydney (Aus)
Apr 13,	1914	Jeff Smith w ko 16 Pat Bradley	Sydney (Aus)
Jun 6,	1914	Jeff Smith w pts 20 Jimmy Clabby (US)	Sydney (Aus)
Nov 28,	1914	**Mick King** (Aus) w pts 20 Jeff Smith	Sydney (Aus)
Dec 26,	1914	**Jeff Smith** w pts 20 Mick King	Sydney (Aus)
Jan 23,	1915	Jeff Smith w dis 5 Les Darcy (Aus)	Sydney (Aus)
Feb 20,	1915	Jeff Smith w pts 20 Mick King	Melbourne (Aus)
May 22,	1915	**Les Darcy** w dis 2 Jeff Smith	Sydney (Aus)
Jun 12,	1915	Les Darcy w ko 10 Mick King	Sydney (Aus)
Jul 31,	1915	Les Darcy w rsf 15 Eddie McGoorty	Sydney (Aus)
Sep 4,	1915	Les Darcy w pts 20 Billy Murray (US)	Sydney (Aus)
Oct 9,	1915	Les Darcy w rtd 6 Fred Dyer (Eng)	Sydney (Aus)
Oct 23,	1915	Les Darcy w pts 20 Jimmy Clabby	Sydney (Aus)
Jan 15,	1916	Les Darcy w pts 20 George "KO" Brown (US)	Sydney (Aus)
May 15,	1916	Les Darcy w ko 4 Alex Costica (Rom)	Sydney (Aus)
Sep 9,	1916	Les Darcy w pts 20 Jimmy Clabby	Sydney (Aus)
Sep 30,	1916	Les Darcy w ko 9 George Chip Sydney (Aus)	
		Darcy went to America to pursue his claim to the championship, but died in Memphis on May 27, 1917	

World title

Apr 6,	1914	**Al McCoy** (US) w ko 1 George Chip	Brooklyn, NY
Nov 14,	1917	**Mike O'Dowd** (US) w ko 6 Al McCoy	Brooklyn, NY
Nov 6,	1919	Mike O'Dowd w ko 2 Billy Kramer (US)	Paterson, NJ
Mar 1,	1920	Mike O'Dowd w ko 2 Jack McCarron (US)	Philadelphia, PA
Mar 31,	1920	Mike O'Dowd w ko 5 Joe Eagan (US)	Boston, MA
May 6,	1920	**Johnny Wilson** (US) w pts 12 Mike O'Dowd	Boston, MA
Mar 17,	1921	Johnny Wilson w pts 15 Mike O'Dowd	New York, NY
		The division limit was now set at 160 lb	
Jul 27,	1921	Johnny Wilson w dis 7 Bryan Downey (US)	Cleveland, OH
		Although this was not a title fight, Wilson scaling 165 lb, the result was so controversial that the New York Commission declared the title vacant	
Aug 14,	1922	**Dave Rosenburg** (US) w pts 15 Phil Krug (US)	New York, NY
		For vacant New York title	
Nov 30,	1922	**Mike O'Dowd** w dis 8 Dave Rosenburg	New York, NY
Mar 16,	1923	*O'Dowd retired after being knocked out in the first round of a non-title fight against Jock Malone in St Paul. Harry Greb was universally recognized as champion after his wins over Johnny Wilson and Bryan Downey in 1923*	
Aug 31,	1923	**Harry Greb** (US) w pts 15 Johnny Wilson	New York, NY
Dec 3,	1923	Harry Greb w pts 10 Bryan Downey (US)	Pittsburgh, PA
Jan 18,	1924	Harry Greb w pts 15 Johnny Wilson	New York, NY
Mar 24,	1924	Harry Greb w ko 12 Fay Kaiser (US)	Baltimore, MD
Jul 2,	1925	Harry Greb w pts 15 Mickey Walker (US)	New York, NY
Jun 26,	1924	Harry Greb w pts 15 Ted Moore (Eng)	New York, NY
Feb 26,	1926	**Tiger Flowers** (US) w pts 15 Harry Greb	New York, NY
Aug 19,	1926	Tiger Flowers w pts 15 Harry Greb	New York, NY
Dec 3,	1926	**Mickey Walker** (US) w pts 10 Tiger Flowers	Chicago, IL
Jun 30,	1927	Mickey Walker w ko 10 Tommy Milligan (Sco)	London (Eng)
Jun 21,	1928	Mickey Walker w pts 10 Ace Hudkins (US)	Chicago, IL
Oct 29,	1929	Mickey Walker w pts 10 Ace Hudkins	Los Angeles, CA
June	1931	*Walker relinquished the title, and the division again became chaotic, with various versions of the championship on offer*	

RINGSIDE VIEW

Harry Greb vs Johnny Wilson

THE GREAT PRETENDER

Harry Greb (right), one of the legendary middleweight champions, "conned" the title away from Johnny Wilson (left) in 1922 when he led Wilson to believe that he had done his training in nightclubs and speakeasies. Wilson thought he would be a pushover, but instead the superbly fit Greb – in his 234th fight – won easily.

National Boxing Association (NBA) title

Jan 25, 1932	**Gorilla Jones** (US) w ko 6 Oddone Piazza (Ita)	Milwaukee, WI
	For vacant title	
Apr 26, 1932	Gorilla Jones w pts 12 Young Terry (US)	Trenton, NJ
	The NBA withdrew recognition from Jones after his loss to Marcel Thil	
Aug 9, 1933	**Lou Brouillard** (Can) w ko 7 Ben Jeby	New York, NY
	For NBA and New York versions	

International Boxing Union (IBU) title

Jun 11, 1932	**Marcel Thil** (Fra) w dis 11 Gorilla Jones	Paris (Fra)
	Thil was recognized as champion following this result, even though the NBA did not regard it as a championship defence by Jones	
Jul 4, 1932	Marcel Thil w pts 15 Len Harvey (Eng)	London (Eng)
Oct 2, 1933	Marcel Thil w pts 15 Kid Tunero (Cub)	Paris (Fra)
Feb 26, 1934	Marcel Thil w pts 15 Ignacio Ara (Sp)	Paris (Fra)
May 3, 1934	Marcel Thil w pts 15 Gustave Roth (Bel)	Paris (Fra)
Oct 15, 1934	Marcel Thil drew 15 Carmelo Candel (Fra)	Paris (Fra)
May 4, 1935	Marcel Thil w rtd 14 Vilda "Kid" Jaks (Cze)	Paris (Fra)
Jun 1, 1935	Marcel Thil w pts 15 Ignacio Ara (Sp)	Madrid (Sp)
Jan 20, 1936	Marcel Thil w dis 4 Lou Brouillard	Paris (Fra)
Feb 15, 1937	Marcel Thil w dis 6 Lou Brouillard	Paris (Fra)
	Thil retired after being stopped in ten rounds by Fred Apostoli (US) in New York on September 23, 1937. Although they fought under championship conditions, both men had to sign a pre-fight agreement that the world title would not be at stake, so as to protect the position of New York's champion Freddie Steele	
Apr 7, 1938	**Edouard Tenet** (Fra) w rtd 12 Josef Besselmann (Ger)	Berlin (Ger)
	For vacant title	
May 1938	*The IBU withdrew recognition from Tenet (and their other champions) in an effort to reunite the world titles*	

New York title

Jan 13, 1933	**Ben Jeby** (US) w rsf 12 Frank Battaglia (Can)	New York, NY
	For vacant title	
Mar 17, 1933	Ben Jeby drew 15 Vince Dundee (US)	New York, NY
Jul 10, 1933	Ben Jeby w pts 15 Young Terry Newark, NJ	
Aug 9, 1933	**Lou Brouillard** w ko 7 Ben Jeby	New York, NY
	For NY and NBA recognition	

NY/NBA titles

Oct 30, 1933	**Vince Dundee** (US) w pts 15 Lou Brouillard	Boston, MA
Dec 8, 1933	Vince Dundee w pts 15 Andy Callahan (US)	Boston, MA
May 1, 1934	Vince Dundee w pts 15 Al Diamond (US)	Paterson, NJ
Sep 11, 1934	**Teddy Yarosz** (US) w pts 15 Vince Dundee	Pittsburgh, PA
Sep 19, 1935	**Ed "Babe" Risko** (US) w pts 15 Teddy Yarosz	New York, NY
Feb 10, 1936	Ed "Babe" Risko w pts 15 Tony Fisher (US)	Newark, NJ
Jul 11, 1936	**Freddie Steele** (US) w pts 15 Ed "Babe" Risko	New York, NY
Jan 1, 1937	Freddie Steele w pts 10 Gorilla Jones	Milwaukee, WI
Feb 19, 1937	Freddie Steele w pts 15 Ed "Babe" Risko	New York, NY
May 11, 1937	Freddie Steele w ko 3 Frank Battaglia (Can)	Seattle, WA
Sep 11, 1937	Freddie Steele w ko 4 Ken Overlin (US)	Seattle, WA
Feb 19, 1938	Freddie Steele w ko 7 Carmen Barth (US)	Cleveland, OH
May 1938	*The NY Commission vacated Steele's title for his failure to defend against Fred Apostoli*	

New York title

Nov 18, 1938	**Fred Apostoli** (US) w ko 8 Young Corbett III (US)	New York, NY
	For vacant title	
Oct 2, 1939	**Ceferino Garcia** (Phil) w rsf 7 Fred Apostoli	New York, NY
Dec 23, 1939	Ceferino Garcia w ko 13 Glen Lee (US)	Manila (Phil)
Mar 1, 1940	Ceferino Garcia drew 10 Henry Armstrong (US)	Los Angeles, CA
May 23, 1940	**Ken Overlin** w pts 15 Ceferino Garcia	New York, NY
Nov 1, 1940	Ken Overlin w pts 15 Steve Belloise (US)	New York, NY
Dec 13, 1940	Ken Overlin w pts 15 Steve Belloise	New York, NY
May 9, 1941	**Billy Soose** (US) w pts 15 Ken Overlin	New York, NY
	Soose was stripped for failing to defend the title	

NBA title

Jul 26, 1938	**Al Hostak** (US) w ko 1 Freddie Steele	Seattle, WA
	For vacant title	
Nov 1, 1938	**Solly Kreiger** (US) w pts 15 Al Hostak	Seattle, WA
Jun 27, 1939	**Al Hostak** w ko 4 Solly Kreiger	Seattle, WA
Dec 11, 1939	Al Hostak w ko 1 Eric Seelig (Ger)	Cleveland, OH
Jul 19, 1940	**Tony Zale** (US) w rtd 13 Al Hostak	Chicago, IL
Feb 21, 1941	Tony Zale w ko 14 Steve Mamakos (US)	Chicago, IL
May 28, 1941	Tony Zale w ko 2 Al Hostak Chicago, IL	
Nov 28, 1941	Tony Zale w pts 15 Georgie Abrams (US)	New York, NY
	For undisputed title	

Undisputed title

Sep 27, 1946	**Tony Zale** w ko 6 Rocky Graziano (US)	New York, NY
Jul 16, 1947	**Rocky Graziano** (US) w rsf 6 Tony Zale	Chicago, IL
Jun 10, 1948	**Tony Zale** w ko 3 Rocky Graziano	Newark, NJ
Sep 21, 1948	**Marcel Cerdan** (Fra) w rtd 11 Tony Zale	Jersey City, NJ
Jun 16, 1949	**Jake LaMotta** (US) w rtd 10 Marcel Cerdan	Detroit, MI
Jul 12, 1950	Jake LaMotta w pts 15 Tibero Mitri (Ita)	New York, NY
Sep 13, 1950	Jake LaMotta w ko 15 Laurent Dauthuille (Fra)	Detroit, MI
Feb 14, 1951	**Sugar Ray Robinson** (US) w rsf 13 Jake LaMotta	Chicago, IL
Jul 10, 1951	**Randolph Turpin** (Eng) w pts 15 Sugar Ray Robinson	London (Eng)
Sep 12, 1951	**Sugar Ray Robinson** w rsf 10 Randolph Turpin	New York, NY
Mar 13, 1952	Sugar Ray Robinson w pts 15 Carl "Bobo" Olson (US)	San Francisco, CA
Apr 16, 1952	Sugar Ray Robinson w ko 3 Rocky Graziano	Chicago, IL
Dec 18, 1952	*Robinson announced his retirement*	
Oct 21, 1953	**Carl "Bobo" Olson** (US) w pts 15 Randolph Turpin	New York, NY
	For vacant title	
Apr 2, 1954	Carl "Bobo" Olson w pts 15 Kid Gavilan (Cub)	Chicago, IL
Aug 20, 1954	Carl "Bobo" Olson w pts 15 Rocky Castellani (US)	San Francisco, CA
Dec 15, 1954	Carl "Bobo" Olson w rsf 11 Pierre Langlois (Fra)	San Francisco, CA
Dec 9, 1955	**Sugar Ray Robinson** w ko 2 Carl "Bobo" Olson	Chicago, IL
May 18, 1956	Sugar Ray Robinson w ko 4 Carl "Bobo" Olson	Los Angeles, CA
Jan 2, 1957	**Gene Fullmer** (US) w pts 15 Sugar Ray Robinson	New York, NY
May 1, 1957	**Sugar Ray Robinson** w ko 5 Gene Fullmer	Chicago, IL
Sep 23, 1957	**Carmen Basilio** (US) w pts 15 Sugar Ray Robinson	New York, NY
Mar 25, 1958	**Sugar Ray Robinson** w pts 15 Carmen Basilio	Chicago, IL
May 1959	*The NBA stripped Robinson for his failure to defend against Basilio*	

NBA title

Aug 28, 1959	**Gene Fullmer** w rsf 14 Carmen Basilio	San Francisco, CA
	For vacant title	
Dec 4, 1959	Gene Fullmer w pts 15 Spider Webb (US)	Logan (Can)
Apr 20, 1960	Gene Fullmer drew 15 Joey Giardello (US)	Bozeman, MT
Jun 29, 1960	Gene Fullmer w rsf 12 Carmen Basilio	Salt Lake City, UT
Dec 3, 1960	Gene Fullmer drew 15 Sugar Ray Robinson	Los Angeles, CA
Mar 4, 1961	Gene Fullmer w pts 15 Sugar Ray Robinson	Las Vegas, NV
Aug 5, 1961	Gene Fullmer w pts 15 Florentino Fernandez (Cub)	Ogden, UT
Oct 9, 1961	Gene Fullmer w ko 10 Benny "Kid" Paret (Cub)	Las Vegas, NV
Oct 23, 1962	**Dick Tiger** (Nig) w pts 15 Gene Fullmer	San Francisco, CA
Feb 23, 1963	Dick Tiger drew 15 Gene Fullmer	Las Vegas, NV
Aug 10, 1963	Dick Tiger w rtd 7 Gene Fullmer	Ibadan (Nig)
	For undisputed title	

New York and European versions

Jan 22, 1960	**Paul Pender** (US) w pts 15 Sugar Ray Robinson	Boston, MA
Jun 10, 1960	Paul Pender w pts 15 Sugar Ray Robinson	Boston, MA
Jan 14, 1961	Paul Pender w rsf 7 Terry Downes (Eng)	Boston, MA
Apr 22, 1961	Paul Pender w pts 15 Carmen Basilio	Boston, MA
Jul 11, 1961	**Terry Downes** w rtd 9 Paul Pender	London (Eng)
Apr 7, 1962	**Paul Pender** w pts 15 Terry Downes	Boston, MA
Nov 9, 1962	*Pender forfeited the title for failing to defend it within a stipulated period*	

Undisputed title

Dec 7, 1963	**Joey Giardello** (US) w pts 15 Dick Tiger	Atlantic City, NJ
Dec 14, 1964	Joey Giardello w pts 15 Rubin Carter (US)	Philadelphia, PA
Oct 21, 1965	**Dick Tiger** w pts 15 Joey Giardello	New York, NY
Apr 25, 1966	**Emile Griffith** (VI) w pts 15 Dick Tiger	New York, NY
Jul 13, 1966	Emile Griffith w pts 15 Joey Archer (US)	New York, NY
Jan 23, 1967	Emile Griffith w pts 15 Joey Archer	New York, NY
Apr 17, 1967	**Nino Benvenuti** (Ita) w pts 15 Emile Griffith	New York, NY
Sep 29, 1967	**Emile Griffith** w pts 15 Nino Benvenuti	New York, NY
Mar 4, 1968	**Nino Benvenuti** w pts 15 Emile Griffith	New York, NY
Dec 14, 1968	Nino Benvenuti w pts 15 Don Fullmer (US)	San Remo (Ita)
Oct 4, 1969	Nino Benvenuti w dis 7 Fraser Scott (US)	Naples (Ita)
Nov 22, 1969	Nino Benvenuti w ko 11 Luis Rodriguez (Cub)	Rome (Ita)
May 23, 1970	Nino Benvenuti w ko 8 Tom Bethea (US)	Umag (Yug)
Nov 7, 1970	**Carlos Monzon** (Arg) w ko 12 Nino Benvenuti	Rome (Ita)
May 8, 1971	Carlos Monzon w rsf 3 Nino Benvenuti	Monte Carlo (Mon)
Sep 25, 1971	Carlos Monzon w rsf 14 Emile Griffith	Buenos Aires (Arg)
Mar 4, 1972	Carlos Monzon w rsf 5 Denny Moyer (US)	Rome (Ita)
Jun 17, 1972	Carlos Monzon w rtd 12 Jean-Claude Bouttier (Fra)	Paris (Fra)

CARLOS MONZON *(left) embraces Rodrigo Valdes after their 1976 battle*

Aug 19,	1972	Carlos Monzon w rsf 5 Tom Bogs (Den)	Copenhagen (Den)
Nov 11,	1972	Carlos Monzon w pts 15 Bennie Briscoe (US)	Buenos Aires (Arg)
Jun 2,	1973	Carlos Monzon w pts 15 Emile Griffith	Monte Carlo (Mon)
Sep 29,	1973	Carlos Monzon w pts 15 Jean-Claude Bouttier	Paris (Fra)
Feb 9,	1974	Carlos Monzon w rtd 6 Jose Napoles (Cub)	Paris (Fra)
Apr	1974	*WBC stripped Monzon for failing to defend against their official contender*	

WBC title

May 25,	1974	**Rodrigo Valdez** (Col) w ko 7 Bennie Briscoe (US) *For vacant title*	Monte Carlo (Mon)
Nov 13,	1974	Rodrigo Valdez w ko 11 Gratien Tonna (Fra)	Paris (Fra)
May 31,	1975	Rodrigo Valdez w rsf 8 Ramon Mendez (Arg)	Cali (Col)
Aug 16,	1975	Rodrigo Valdez w pts 15 Rudy Robles (Mex)	Cartagena (Col)
Mar 28,	1976	Rodrigo Valdez w rtd 4 Max Cohen (Fra)	Paris (Fra)
Jun 26,	1976	**Carlos Monzon** w pts 15 Rodrigo Valdez	Monte Carlo (Mon)

WBA title

Oct 5,	1974	**Carlos Monzon** w ko 7 Tony Mundine (Aus)	Buenos Aires (Arg)
Jun 30,	1975	Carlos Monzon w ko 10 Tony Licata (US)	New York, NY
Dec 13,	1975	Carlos Monzon w ko 5 Gratien Tonna	Paris (Fra)
Jun 26,	1976	Carlos Monzon w pts 15 Rodrigo Valdez	Monte Carlo (Mon)

Undisputed title

Jul 30,	1977	**Carlos Monzon** w pts 15 Rodrigo Valdez	Monte Carlo (Mon)
Aug	1977	*Monzon retired*	
Nov 5,	1977	**Rodrigo Valdez** w pts 15 Bennie Briscoe *For vacant undisputed title*	Campione d'Italia (Ita)
Apr 22,	1978	**Hugo Corro** (Arg) w pts 15 Rodrigo Valdez	Buenos Aires (Arg)
Aug 5,	1978	Hugo Corro w pts 15 Ronnie Harris (US)	Buenos Aires (Arg)
Nov 11,	1978	Hugo Corro w pts 15 Rodrigo Valdez	Buenos Aires (Arg)
Jun 30,	1979	**Vito Antuofermo** (Ita) w pts 15 Hugo Corro	Monte Carlo (Mon)
Nov 30,	1979	Vito Antuofermo drew 15 Marvin Hagler (US)	Las Vegas, NV
Mar 16,	1980	**Alan Minter** (Eng) w pts 15 Vito Antuofermo	Las Vegas, NV
Jun 28,	1980	Alan Minter w rtd 8 Vito Antuofermo	Wembley (Eng)
Sep 27,	1980	**Marvin Hagler** (US) w rsf 3 Alan Minter	Wembley (Eng)
Jan 17,	1981	Marvin Hagler w rsf 8 Fulgencio Obelmejias (Ven)	Boston, MA
Jun 13,	1981	Marvin Hagler w rtd 4 Vito Antuofermo	Boston, MA
Oct 3,	1981	Marvin Hagler w rsf 11 Mustafa Hamsho (Syr)	Rosemount, IL
Mar 7,	1982	Marvin Hagler w rsf 1 William "Caveman" Lee (US)	Atlantic City, NJ
Oct 31,	1982	Marvin Hagler w rsf 5 Fulgencio Obelmejias	San Remo (Ita)
Feb 11,	1983	Marvin Hagler w rsf 6 Tony Sibson (Eng)	Worcester, MA
May 27,	1983	Marvin Hagler w ko 4 Wilford Scypion (US)	Providence, RI
Nov 10,	1983	Marvin Hagler w pts 15 Roberto Duran (Pan)	Las Vegas, NV
Mar 30,	1984	Marvin Hagler w rsf 10 Juan Domingo Roldan (Arg)	Las Vegas, NV
Oct 19,	1984	Marvin Hagler w rsf 3 Mustafa Hamsho	New York, NY
Apr 15,	1985	Marvin Hagler w rsf 3 Thomas Hearns (US)	Las Vegas, NV
Mar 10,	1986	Marvin Hagler w ko 11 John Mugabi (Ug)	Las Vegas, NV
Feb	1987	*WBA stripped Hagler for his failure to defend against Herol Graham*	

WBC/IBF titles

Apr 6,	1987	**Sugar Ray Leonard** (US) w pts 12 Marvin Hagler	Las Vegas, NV
Apr	1987	*IBF vacated the title because they felt unable to recognize Leonard as*	

champion. And in June Leonard relinquished the WBC title, leaving all versions of the title vacant

IBF title

Oct 10, 1987	**Frank Tate** (US) w pts 15 Michael Olajide (Can) *For vacant title*	Las Vegas, NV
Feb 7, 1988	Frank Tate w ko 10 Tony Sibson	Stafford (Eng)
Jul 28, 1988	**Michael Nunn** (US) w rsf 9 Frank Tate	Las Vegas, NV
Nov 4, 1988	Michael Nunn w ko 8 Juan Domingo Roldan	Las Vegas, NV
Mar 25, 1989	Michael Nunn w ko 1 Sumbu Kalambay (Zai)	Las Vegas, NV
Aug 14, 1989	Michael Nunn w pts 12 Iran Barkley (US)	Reno, NV
Apr 14, 1990	Michael Nunn w pts 12 Marlon Starling (US)	Las Vegas, NV
Oct 18, 1990	Michael Nunn w rsf 10 Don Curry (US)	Paris (Fra)
May 10, 1991	**James Toney** (US) w rsf 11 Michael Nunn	Davenport, IA
Jun 29, 1991	James Toney w pts 12 Reggie Johnson (US)	Las Vegas, NV
Oct 12, 1991	James Toney w rsf 4 Francisco Dell'Aquila (Ita)	Monte Carlo (Mon)
Dec 13, 1991	James Toney drew 12 Mike McCallum (Jam)	Atlantic City, NJ
Feb 8, 1992	James Toney w pts 12 Dave Tiberi (US)	Atlantic City, NJ
Apr 11, 1992	James Toney w pts 12 Glenn Wolfe (US)	Las Vegas, NV
Aug 29, 1992	James Toney w pts 12 Mike McCallum	Reno, NV
Feb 1993	*Toney relinquished title on becoming IBF super-middleweight champion*	
May 22, 1993	**Roy Jones** (US) w pts 12 Bernard Hopkins (US) *For vacant title*	Washington, DC
May 27, 1994	Roy Jones w rsf 2 Thomas Tate (US) *Jones relinquished the title to box at super-middleweight*	Las Vegas, NV
Dec 16, 1994	**Bernard Hopkins** drew 12 Segundo Mercado (Ecu) *For vacant title*	Quito (Ecu)
Apr 29, 1995	Bernard Hopkins w rsf 7 Segundo Mercado *For vacant title*	Landover, MD
Jan 27, 1996	Bernard Hopkins w rsf 1 Steve Frank (US)	Phoenix, AZ
Mar 16, 1996	Bernard Hopkins w rsf 4 Joe Lipsey (US)	Las Vegas, NV
Jul 16, 1996	Bernard Hopkins w rsf 11 William James (US)	Atlantic City, NJ
Apr 19, 1997	Bernard Hopkins w rsf 7 John David Jackson	Shreveport, LA
Jul 29, 1997	Bernard Hopkins w rsf 11 Glen Johnson (US)	Indio, CA
Nov 18, 1997	Bernard Hopkins w pts 12 Andrew Council (US)	Upper Marlboro, MD
Jan 31, 1998	Bernard Hopkins w rsf 6 Simon Brown (Jam)	Atlantic City, NJ
Aug 28, 1998	Bernard Hopkins nc 4 Robert Allen (US)	Las Vegas, NV
Feb 6, 1999	Bernard Hopkins w rsf 7 Robert Allen	Wasington, DC
Dec 12, 1999	Bernard Hopkins w pts 12 Antwun Echols (US)	Miami, FL
May 13, 2000	Bernard Hopkins w pts 12 Syd Vanderpool (Can)	Indianapolis, IN
Dec 1, 2000	Bernard Hopkins w rsf 10 Antwun Echols	Las Vegas, NV

WBA title

Oct 23, 1987	**Sumbu Kalambay** (Zai) w pts 15 Iran Barkley *For vacant title*	Livorno (Ita)
Mar 5, 1988	Sumbu Kalambay w pts 12 Mike McCallum	Pesaro (Ita)
Jun 12, 1988	Sumbu Kalambay w pts 12 Robbie Sims (US)	Ravenna (Ita)
Nov 8, 1988	Sumbu Kalambay w ko 7 Doug De Witt (US)	Monte Carlo (Mon)
Mar 1989	*Kalambay was stripped for failing to defend against Herol Graham*	
May 10, 1989	**Mike McCallum** w pts 12 Herol Graham (Eng) *For vacant title*	London (Eng)
Feb 3, 1990	Mike McCallum w pts 12 Steve Collins (Ire)	Boston, MA
Apr 14, 1990	Mike McCallum w ko 11 Michael Watson (Eng)	London (Eng)
Apr 1, 1991	Mike McCallum w pts 12 Sumbu Kalambay	Monte Carlo (Mon)
Dec 1991	*The WBA stripped McCallum for agreeing to box for James Toney's IBF title*	
Apr 22, 1992	**Reggie Johnson** w pts 12 Steve Collins *For vacant title*	East Rutherford, NJ
Oct 27, 1992	Reggie Johnson w pts 12 Lamar Parks (US)	Houston, TX
Jan 19, 1993	Reggie Johnson w rsf 8 Ki-Yun Song (Kor)	Boise, ID
May 4, 1993	Reggie Johnson w pts 12 Wayne Harris (US)	Denver, CO
Oct 1, 1993	**John David Jackson** (US) w pts 12 Reggie Johnson	Buenos Aires (Arg)
May 1994	*Jackson was stripped by the WBA for taking a non-title fight without having first sought their permission*	
Aug 12, 1994	**Jorge Castro** (Arg) w pts 12 Reggie Johnson *For vacant title*	Tucuman (Arg)
Nov 5, 1994	Jorge Castro w ko 2 Alex Ramos (US)	Caleta Olivia (Arg)
Dec 10, 1994	Jorge Castro w rsf 9 John David Jackson	Monterrey (Mex)
May 27, 1995	Jorge Castro w rsf 12 Anthony Andrews (Guy)	Fort Lauderdale, FL
Oct 14, 1995	Jorge Castro w pts 12 Reggie Johnson	Comodoro Rivadavoa (Arg)
Dec 19, 1995	**Shinji Takehara** (Jap) w pts 12 Jorge Castro	Tokyo (Jap)
Jun 24, 1996	**William Joppy** (US) w rsf 9 Shinji Takehara	Yokohama (Jap)
Oct 19, 1996	William Joppy w rsf 6 Ray McElroy (US)	Upper Marlboro, MD
May 10, 1997	William Joppy w pts 12 Peter Venancio (Bra)	Coconut Grove, FL
Aug 23, 1997	**Julio Cesar Green** (DR) w pts 12 William Joppy	New York, NY
Jan 31, 1998	**William Joppy** w pts 12 Julio Cesar Green	Tampa, FL
Aug 28, 1998	William Joppy w rsf 3 Roberto Duran (Pan)	Las Vegas, NV
Sep 24, 1999	William Joppy w rsf 7 Julio Cesar Green (DR)	Washington, DC
May 20, 2000	William Joppy w rsf 1 Rito Ruvalcaba (Mex)	Tunica, MS
Sep 16, 2000	William Joppy w pts 12 Hassine Cherifi (Fra)	Las Vegas, NV
Dec 2, 2000	William Joppy w rsf 4 Jonathan Reid (US)	Las Vegas, NV
May 12, 2001	**Felix Trinidad** (PR) w rsf 5 William Joppy *Felix Trinidad then fought Bernard Hopkins in a WBA/WBC/IBF unification fight on Sep 29, 2001 in New York*	New York, NY

WBC title

Oct 29, 1987	**Thomas Hearns** w ko 4 Juan Domingo Roldan *For vacant title*	Las Vegas, NV
Jun 6, 1988	**Iran Barkley** w rsf 3 Thomas Hearns	Las Vegas, NV
Feb 24, 1989	**Roberto Duran** w pts 12 Iran Barkley	Atlantic City, NJ
Jan 1990	*Duran stripped for failing to give a written undertaking to defend the title*	
Nov 24, 1990	**Julian Jackson** (VI) w ko 4 Herol Graham *For vacant title*	Benalmadena (Sp)
Sep 14, 1991	Julian Jackson w ko 1 Dennis Milton (US)	Las Vegas, NV
Feb 15, 1992	Julian Jackson w ko 1 Ismael Negron (US)	Las Vegas, NV
Apr 10, 1992	Julian Jackson w rsf 5 Ron Collins (US)	Mexico City (Mex)
Aug 1, 1992	Julian Jackson w pts 12 Thomas Tate	Las Vegas, NV
May 8, 1993	**Gerald McClellan** (US) w rsf 5 Julian Jackson	Las Vegas, NV
Aug 6, 1993	Gerald McClellan w ko 1 Jay Bell (US)	Bayamon (PR)
Mar 4, 1994	Gerald McClellan w rsf 1 Gilbert Baptist (US)	Las Vegas, NV
May 7, 1994	Gerald McClellan w ko 1 Julian Jackson *McClellan relinquished the title to box at super-middleweight*	Las Vegas, NV
Mar 7, 1995	**Julian Jackson** w rsf 2 Agostino Cardamone (Ita) *For vacant title*	Worcester, MA
Aug 19, 1995	**Quincy Taylor** (US) w rsf 6 Julian Jackson	Las Vegas, NV
Mar 16, 1996	**Keith Holmes** (US) w rsf 9 Quincy Taylor	Las Vegas, NV
Oct 19, 1996	Keith Holmes w rsf 12 Richie Woodhall (Eng)	Upper Marlboro, ML
Dec 5, 1997	Keith Holmes w rsf 11 Paul Vaden (US)	Pompano Beach, FL
May 2, 1998	**Hassine Cherifi** (Fra) w pts 12 Keith Holmes	Villeurbanne (Fra)
Apr 24, 1999	**Keith Holmes** w rsf 7 Hassine Cherifi	Washington, DC
Sep 24, 1999	Keith Holmes w pts 12 Andrew Council (US)	Washington, DC
Apr 29, 2000	Keith Holmes w rsf 11 Robert McCracken (Eng)	London (Eng)

WBO title

Apr 18, 1989	**Doug DeWitt** w pts 12 Robbie Sims *For vacant title*	Atlantic City, NJ
Jan 15, 1990	Doug DeWitt w rtd 11 Matthew Hilton (Can)	Atlantic City, NJ
Apr 29, 1990	**Nigel Benn** (Eng) w rsf 8 Doug DeWitt	Atlantic City, NJ
Aug 18, 1990	Nigel Benn w rsf 1 Iran Barkley	Las Vegas, NV
Nov 18, 1990	**Chris Eubank** (Eng) w rsf 9 Nigel Benn	Birmingham (Eng)
Feb 23, 1991	Chris Eubank w tech dec 10 Dan Sherry (Can)	Brighton (Eng)
Apr 18, 1991	Chris Eubank w rsf 6 Gary Stretch (Eng)	London (Eng)
Jun 22, 1991	Chris Eubank w pts 12 Michael Watson	London (Eng)
Jul 1991	*Eubank vacated the title to box for the WBO super-middleweight title*	
Nov 20, 1991	**Gerald McClellan** w rsf 1 John Mugabi *For vacant title*	London (Eng)
Mar 1993	*McClellan relinquished the WBO title to box for the WBC version*	
May 19, 1993	**Chris Pyatt** (Eng) w pts 12 Sumbu Kalambay *For vacant title*	Leicester (Eng)
Sep 18, 1993	Chris Pyatt w ko 6 Hugo Corti (Arg)	Leicester (Eng)
Feb 9, 1994	Chris Pyatt w ko 1 Mark Cameron (SA)	Brentwood (Eng)
May 11, 1994	**Steve Collins** (Ire) w rsf 5 Chris Pyatt	Sheffield (Eng)
Mar 1995	*Collins relinquished title on becoming WBO super-middleweight champion*	
May 19, 1995	**Lonnie Bradley** (US) w rsf 12 David Mendez (Mex) *For vacant title*	Jean (Sp)
Jul 15, 1995	Lonnie Bradley w rsf 1 Dario Galindez (Arg)	Inglewood, CA
Feb 6, 1996	Lonnie Bradley w rsf 2 Randy Smith (US)	New York, NY
May 10, 1996	Lonnie Bradley w pts 12 Lonnie Beasley	Steubenville, OH
Aug 30, 1996	Lonnie Bradley w pts 12 Simon Brown (Jam)	Reading, PA
Mar 4, 1997	Lonnie Bradley drew 12 Otis Grant (Can)	Las Vegas, NV
Jun 28, 1997	Lonnie Bradley w rsf 8 John Williams *Bradley relinquished the title because of eye injuries*	Las Vegas, NV
Dec 13, 1997	**Otis Grant** w pts 12 Ryan Rhodes (Eng) *For vacant title*	Sheffield (Eng)
May 12, 1998	Otis Grant w tdec 9 Ernesto Sena (Arg) *Grant relinquished the title to fight Roy Jones for WBA/WBC light-heavyweight titles*	Kanata (Can)
Jan 30, 1999	**Bert Schenk** (Ger) w ko 4 Freeman Barr (Bah) *For vacant title*	Cottbus (Ger)
May 22, 1999	Bert Schenk w pts 12 Juan Ramon Medina (Dr)	Budapest (Hun)
Jul 1999	*Bert Schenk stripped of the WBO title because of injury*	
Jul 17, 1999	**Jason Matthews** (Eng) w ko 2 Ryan Rhodes (Eng) *Schenk reinstated, but withdrew from Matthews bout because of injury and lost claim*	Doncaster (Eng)
Nov 27, 1999	**Armand Krajnc** (Swe) w rsf 8 Jason Matthews	Lubeck (Ger)
Mar 11, 2000	Armand Krajnc w rsf 2 Jonathan Corn (US)	Lubeck (Ger)
Oct 7, 2000	Armand Krajnc w rsf 6 Bert Schenk *Krajnc reportedly gave up the title, then reclaimed it after Harry Simon had outpointed Hassine Cherifi, supposedly for the vacant championship. Krajnc was, however, reinstated*	Berlin (Ger)

Nov 3, 2001 Armand Krajnc w pts 12 Paolo Roberto (Swe) .... Lubeck (Ger)

Apr 6, 2002 **Harry Simon** (Nam) w pts 12 Armand Krajnc .... Copenhagen (Den)
Harry Simon was forced to retire following a road crash in Namibia

May 10, 2003 **Hector Velazco** (Arg) w rsf 8 Andras Galfi (Un)............. Buenos Aires (Arg)
For vacant title

Sep 13, 2003 **Felix Sturm** (Ger) w pts 12 Hector Velazco .... Berlin (Ger)

Dec 20, 2003 Felix Sturm w pts 12 Ruben Varon Fernandez (Spa)................ Kiel (Ger)

Jun 5, 2004 **Oscar De La Hoya** (US) w pts 12 Felix Sturm .... Las Vegas, NV
Oscar De La Hoya then fought Bernard Hopkins in a WBA/WBC/WBO/IBF unification fight on Sep 18, 2004 in Las Vegas

IBF/WBC titles

Apr 14, 2001 **Bernard Hopkins** w pts 12 Keith Holmes .... New York, NY
IBF/WBC unification fight

IBF/WBC/WBA titles

Sep 29, 2001 **Bernard Hopkins** w rsf 12 Felix Trinidad .... New York, NY
IBF/WBA/WBC unification fight

Feb 2, 2002 Bernard Hopkins w rsf 10 Carl Daniels .... Reading, PA

Mar 29, 2003 Bernard Hopkins w rtd 8 Morrade Hakkar (Fra) .... Philadelphia, PA

Dec 13, 2003 Bernard Hopkins w pts 12 William Joppy (US) .... Atlantic City, NJ

Jun 5, 2004 Bernard Hopkins w pts 12 Robert Allen (US).................. Las Vegas, NV

WBC/WBA/IBF/WBO titles

Sep 18, 2004 **Bernard Hopkins** w ko 9 Oscar De La Hoya (US) .... Las Vegas, NV
IBF/WBA/WBC/WBO unification fight

Feb 19, 2005 Bernard Hopkins w pts 12 Howard Eastman (Guy)........... Los Angeles, CA

Jul 16, 2005 **Jermain Taylor** (US) w pts 12 Bernard Hopkins .... Las Vegas, NV
Taylor stripped of the IBF title

WBC/WBA/WBO titles

Dec 3, 2005 **Jermain Taylor** w pts 12 Bernard Hopkins................... Las Vegas, NV
Taylor lost recognition as WBA champion

WBC/WBO titles

Jun 17, 2006 Jermain Taylor drew 12 Ronald Wright (US) .... Memphis, TN

Dec 9, 2006 **Jermain Taylor** w pts 12 Kassim Ouma (Uga) .... Little Rock, AK

May 19, 2007 Jermain Taylor w pts 12 Cory Spinks (US) .... Memphis, TN

Sep 29, 2007 **Kelly Pavlik** (US) w rsf 7 Jermain Taylor.................... Atlantic City, NJ

Jun 7, 2008 Kelly Pavlik w rsf 3 Gary Lockett (Wal) .... Atlantic City, NJ

Feb 21, 2009 Kelly Pavlik w rtd 9 Marco Antonio Rubio (Mex) .... Youngstown, OH

Dec 19, 2009 Kelly Pavlik w rsf 5 Miguel Angel Espino (US)............... Youngstown, OH
The WBC sanctioned interim title fights as follows:

Jul 11, 2009 **Sebastian Zbik** (Ger) w pts 12 Domenico Spada (Ita)......... Nuremberg (Ger)

Dec 19, 2009 Sebastian Zbik w pts 12 Emanuele Della Rosa (Ita) .... Schwerin (Ger)

Apr 17, 2010 Sergio Martinez w pts 12 Kelly Pavlik...................... Atlantic City, NJ
Martinez was stripped of the WBO title while he decided which weight division to campaign in. He also held the WBC light-middleweight title

WBA title

Nov 20, 2010 Sergio Martinez w ko 2 Paul Williams...................... Atlantic City, NJ
The WBC sanctioned the Interim title fight as follows

Jul 31, 2010 Sebastian Zbik w pts 12 Sebastian Heiland (Arg).............. Hamburg (Ger)
In January 2011, WBC made Martinez their Champion in Emeritus and Zbik was upgraded to full champion

Jun 4, 2011 Julio Cesar Chavez Jr. (Mex) w pts 12 Sebastian Zbik .... Los Angeles, CA

Nov 19, 2011 Julio Cesar Chavez Jr. w rsf 5 Peter Manfredo (US).............. Houston, TX

Feb 4, 2012 Julio Cesar Chavez Jr. w pts 12 Marco Antonio Rubio .... San Antonio, TX

Jun 16, 2012 Julio Cesar Chavez Jr. w rsf 7 Andy Lee (Ire) .... El Paso, TX

Sep 15, 2012 Sergio Martinez w pts 12 Julio Cesar Chavez................. Las Vegas, NV
The WBC sanctioned the following for the WBC Diamond belt

Mar 12, 2011 Sergio Martinez w rsf 8 Sehiy Dzinziruk.................. Mashantucket, CN

Oct 1, 2011 Sergio Martinez w ko 11 Darren Barker (Eng) .... Atlantic City, NJ

Mar 17, 2012 Sergio Martinez w rtd 11 Matthew Macklin .... New York, NY

WBO title

Martinez was stripped of the WBO title

Jul 7, 2010 Dmitry Pirog (Rus) w rsf 5 Daniel Jacobs .... Las Vegas, NV

Mar 26, 2011 Dmitry Pirog w pts 12 Javier Francisco Maciel (Arg)....... Ekaterinburg (Rus)

Sep 25, 2011 Dmitry Pirog w rtd 10 Gennady Martirosyan (Rus) .... Krasnodar (Rus)

May 1, 2012 Dmitry Pirog w pts 12 Nobuhiro Ishida (Jap) .... Moscow (Rus)
The WBO sanctioned the following for the vacant Interim title

May 4, 2012 Hassan N'Dam N'Jikam (Fra) w pts Max Bursak (Ukr) ..... Levallois-Perret (Fra)
Pirog was stripped for boxing WBA champion Gennady Golovkin and Hassan D'Dam N'Jikam was upgraded to full champion

Oct 20, 2012 **Peter Quillin** (US) w pts Hassan N'Dam N'Jikam .... New York, NY

Apr 27, 2013 Peter Quillin w rsc 7 Fernando Guerrero (DR).................. Brooklyn, NY

Oct 26, 2013 Peter Quillin w rsf 10 Gabriel Rosado (USA).................. Atlantic City, NJ

Apr 19, 2014 Peter Quillin w pts 12 Lukas Konecny (CR).................. Washington, DC
Quillin vacated title

Dec 13, 2014 Andy Lee (Ire) w rsf 6 Matt Korobov (Rus) .... Las Vegas, NV
For vacant title

WBA title

The WBA installed Bernard Hopkins as "super" champion and recognized William Joppy as "world" champion. When Hopkins beat Joppy in December 2003, they sanctioned a "world" title fight between Maselino Mahoe and Evans Ashira, as below, then in 2005 withdrew recognition of Hopkins' successor Jermain Taylor as "super" champion.

May 1, 2004 **Maselino Mahoe** (Sam) w rsf 2 Evans Ashira (Ken) .... Miami, FL

Mar 11, 2006 **Felix Sturm** (Ger) w pts 12 Maselino Mahoe.................. Hamburg (Ger)

Jul 15, 2006 **Javier Castillejo** (Spa) w rsf 10 Felix Sturm.................. Hamburg (Ger)

Dec 2, 2006 Javier Castillejo nd 11 Mariano Carrera (Arg)................... Berlin (Ger)
Carrera won the bout in the 11th round but tested positiive for a banned substance. Castillejo was reinstated and the verdict changed to a no decision

Apr 28, 2007 **Felix Sturm** w pts 12 Javier Castillejo .... Oberhausen (Ger)

Jun 30, 2007 Felix Sturm w pts 12 Noe Gonzalez (Uru) .... Stuttgart (Ger)

Oct 20, 2007 Felix Sturm drew 12 Randy Griffin (US) .... Halle (Ger)

Apr 5, 2008 Felix Sturm w rsf 7 Jamie Pittman (Aus) .... Dusseldorf (Ger)

Jul 5, 2008 Felix Sturm w pts 12 Randy Griffin (US) .... Halle (Ger)

Nov 1, 2008 Felix Sturm w pts 12 Sebastian Sylvester (Ger) .... Oberhausen (Ger)

Apr 25, 2009 Felix Sturm w rsf 7 Koji Sato (Jap) .... Krefeld (Ger)

Jul 11, 2009 Felix Sturm w pts 12 Khoren Gevor (Arm).................. Nuremberg (Ger)
The WBA sanctioned the following for their Interim title

Aug 14, 2010 Gennady Golovkin (Kaz) w ko 1 Milton Nunez (Col).......... Panama City (Pan)
Golovkin was upgraded to full champion after Felix Sturm elevated to Super champion

Dec 16, 2010 Gennady Golovkin w ko 3 Nilson Julio Tapia (Col)............... Astana (Kaz)

Jun 17, 2011 Gennady Golvkin w rsf 10 Kassim Ouma .... Panama City (Pan)

Dec 9, 2011 Gennady Golovkin w ko 1 Lajuan Simon (US) .... Dusseldorf (Ger)

May 12, 2012 Gennady Golovkin w rsf 3 Makoto Fuchigami (Jap) .... Borvari (Ukr)

Sep 1, 2012 Gennady Golovkin w rsf 5 Gregorz Proksa (Pol) .... New York, NY

Jan 19, 2013 Gennady Golovkin w rsf 7 Gabriel Rosado (US)................ New York, NY

Mar 30, 2013 Gennady Golovkin w ko 3 Nobuhiro Ishida (Jap)........... Monte Carlo (Mon)

Jun 29, 2013 Gennady Golovkin w ko 3 Matthew Macklin.............. Mashantucket, CN

Feb 1, 2014 Gennady Golovkin w rtd 8 Curtis Stevens (USA)............... New York, NY

Jul 26, 2014 Gennady Golovkin w rsf 3 Daniel Geale .... New York, NY
Golovkin upgraded to super champion

Aug 9, 2014 **Daniel Jacobs** (USA) w rsf 5 Jarrod Fletcher (Aus) .... Brooklyn, NY
For vacant title

Apr 24, 2015 Daniel Jacobs w rsf 12 Caleb Truax (USA) .... Chicago, IL
The WBA sanctioned the following for their Super title

Sep 4, 2010 **Felix Sturm** (Ger) w pts 12 Giovanni Lorenzo (Dom)............ Cologne (Ger)
For vacant title

Feb 2, 2011 Felix Sturm w pts 12 Ronald Hearns (US). .... Stuttgart (Ger)

Jun 25, 2011 Felix Sturm w pts 12 Matthew Macklin (Eng)................. Cologne (Ger)

Dec 2, 2011 Felix Sturm drew 12 Martin Murray (Eng)................. Mannheim (Ger)

Apr 13, 2012 Felix Sturm w rtd 9 Sebastian Zbik.......................... Cologne (Ger)
The WBA sanctioned the following for their Interim title

Apr 2, 2011 Hassan N'Dam N'Jikam w pts 12 Giovanni Lorenzo .... Le Cannet (Fra)

Nov 24, 2011 Martin Murray (Eng) w rsf 6 Jorge Navarro (Col) .... Manchester (Eng)

Dec 21, 2013 Dmitriy Chudinov (Rus) w rsf 6 Juan Camilo Novoa (Col)........ Moscow (Rus)

Jun 1, 2014 Dmitriy Chudinov w pts 12 Patrick Nielsen (Den)............ Mytishchi (Rus)

Aug 9, 2014 Dmitriy Chudinov w rsc 3 Mehdi Bouadia (Fra)................ Crimea (Rus)

Feb 28, 2015 Chris Eubank Jr (Eng) w rsf 12 Dmitry Chudinov .... London (Eng)

Dec 5, 2015 Daniel Jacobs (US) w rsf 1 Peter Quillin (US) .... New York, NY

Sep 9, 2016 Daniel Jacobs w rsf 7 Sergio Mora (US) .... Reading, PA

Dec 17, 2016 Hassan N'Dam N'Jikam (Fra) w ko 1 Alfonso Blanco (Ven) Saint-Denis (Réunion)

May 20, 2017 Hassan N'Dam N'Jikam w pts 12 Ryota Murata (Jap) .... Tokyo (Jap)

Oct 22, 2017 Ryota Murata w rtd 7 Hassan N'Dam N'Jikam .... Tokyo (Jap)

IBF/WBA super titles

Sep 1, 2012 Daniel Geale (Aus) w pts 12 Felix Sturm.................. Oberhausen (Ger)

IBF title

Dec 10, 2005 **Arthur Abraham** (Arm) w ko 5 Kingsley Ikeke (Nig) .... Leipzig (Ger)
For vacant title

Mar 4,	2006	Arthur Abraham w pts 12 Shannan Taylor (Aus)	Oldenberg (Ger)
May 13,	2006	Arthur Abraham w pts 12 Kofi Jantuah (Gha)	Zwickau (Ger)
Sep 23,	2006	Arthur Abraham w pts 12 Edison Miranda (Col)	Wetzlar (Ger)
May 26,	2007	Arthur Abraham w ko 3 Sebastian Demers (Can)	Bamber (Ger)
Aug 18,	2007	Arthur Abraham w ko 11 Koren Ghevor (Arm)	Berlin (Ger)
Dec 8,	2007	Arthur Abraham w rsf 5 Wayne Elcock (Eng)	Basel (Swi)
Mar 29,	2008	Arthur Abraham w ko 12 Elvin Ayala (US)	Kiel (Ger)
Nov 8,	2008	Arthur Abraham w rtd 6 Raul Marquez (US)	Bamberg (Ger)
Mar 14,	2009	Arthur Abraham w pts 12 Lajuan Simon (US)	Kiel (Ger)
Jun 27,	2009	Arthur Abraham w rsf 10 Mahir Oral (Ger)	Berlin (Ger)
		Arthur Abraham relinquished the title to box at super-middleweight	
Sep 19,	2009	**Sebastian Sylvester** w pts 12 Giovanni Lorenzo (DR),	Neubrandenberg (Ger)
		For vacant title	
Jan 30,	2010	Sebastian Sylvester w rsf 10 Billy Lyell (US)	Neubrandenberg (Ger)
Jun 5,	2010	Sebastian Sylvester drew 12 Roman Karmazin	Neubrandenburg (Ger)
Oct 30,	2010	Sebastian Sylvester w pts 12 Mahir Oral (Ger)	Rostock (Ger)
May 7,	2011	Daniel Geale (Aus) w pts 12 Sebastian Sylvester	Neubrandenburg (Ger)
Aug 31,	2011	Daniel Geale w pts 12 Eromosele Albert (Nig)	Hobart (Aus)
May 7,	2012	Daniel Geale w pts 12 Osumanu Adama (Gha)	Hobart (Aus)
Jan 30,	2013	Daniel Geale w pts 12 Anthony Mundine	Sydney (Aus)
Aug 17,	2013	**Darren Barker** (Eng) w pts 12 Daniel Geale	Atlantic City, NJ
Dec 7,	2013	**Felix Sturm** w rsc 2 Darren Barker	Stuttgart (Ger)
May 31,	2014	**Sam Soliman** (Aus) w pts 12 Felix Sturm	Krefeld (Ger)
Oct 8,	2014	**Jermain Taylor** (USA) w pts Sam Soliman	Biloxi, MI
		Taylor stripped of title	
Jun 20,	2015	**David Lemieux** (Can) w pts 12 Hassan N'Dam N'Jikam	Montreal (Can)
		For vacant title	

WBA super/WBC interim titles

Oct 18,	2014	**Gennady Golovkin** w ko 2 Marco Antonio Rubio (Mex)	Carson, CA
Feb 21,	2015	Gennady Golovkin w rsf 11 Martin Murray	Monte Carlo (Mon)
May 16,	2015	Gennady Golovkin w rsf 6 Willie Monore jr (USA)	Inglewood, CA

WBC title

Nov 20,	2010	**Sergio Martinez** w ko 2 Paul Williams (US)	Atlantic City, NJ
		Martinez upgraded to Emeritus champion. Sebastian Zbik upgraded to full champion	
Jun 4,	2011	**Julio Cesar Chavez Jr** (Mex) w pts 12 Sebastian Zbik	Los Angeles, CA
Nov 19,	2011	Julio Cesar Chavez Jr w rsf 5 Peter Manfredo jr (USA)	Houston, TX
Apr 2,	2012	Julio Cesar Chavez jr w pts 12 Marco Antonio Rubio	San Antonio, TX
Jun 6,	2012	Julio Cesar Chavez jr w rsf 7 Andy Lee	El Paso, TX
Sep 15,	2012	**Sergio Martinez** w pts 12 Julio Cesar Chavez jr.	Las Vegas, NV
Apr 27,	2013	Sergio Martinez w pts 12 Martin Murray	Buenos Aires (Arg)
Jun 7,	2014	**Miguel Cotto** w ret 10 Sergio Martinez.	New York, NY
Jun 6,	2015	Miguel Cotto w rsc 4 Daniel Geale	Brooklyn, NY

IBF/IBO/WBC titles

Oct 17,	2015	Gennady Govolkin w rsf 8 David Lemieux	New York, NY
Apr 23,	2016	Gennady Govolkin w ko 2 Dominic Wade (US)	Inglewood, CA
Sep 10,	2016	Gennady Govolkin w rsf 5 Kell Brook (Eng)	London (Eng)

IBF/IBO/WBC/WBA Super titles

Mar 18,	2017	Gennady Govolkin w pts 12 Daniel Jacobs (US)	New York, NY
Sep 16,	2017	Gennady Govolkin drew Saul Alvarez (Mex)	Las Vegas, NV

GENNADY GOVOLKIN, *the class act of the middleweight division, beat Daniel Jacob on points in March 2018*

Light-Middleweight

Sugar Ray Robinson would have been unbeatable in the 154 lb division had it been around in his day, but instead Robinson had to move up from 147 to 160 lb to become a double champion. Emile Griffith, who made the same leap in the 1960s, at least managed to get a fingerhold on the first light-middleweight world championship. The Austrian Board of Control, which existed mainly to facilitate the career of the great Hungarian Laszlo Papp, approved a match in 1962 between Griffith and Teddy Wright. They billed it as a world title fight, but three days later the WBA staged the first "real" world championship at the new weight. Griffith made one attempt to win the WBC light-middleweight title, 13 years later, but was outpointed by Eckhard Dagge.

The division, which the Americans prefer to call "junior middleweight" took a long time to become accepted. The WBC did not create its own championship until 1975, with the first IBF champion being crowned nine years later.

World Light-Middleweight Championship Bouts

WBA title

Oct 20, 1962	**Denny Moyer** (US) w pts 15 Joey Giambra (US)	Portland, OR
	For vacant title	
Feb 19, 1963	Denny Moyer w pts 15 Stan Harrington (US)	Honolulu, HI
Apr 29, 1963	**Ralph Dupas** (US) w pts 15 Denny Moyer	New Orleans, LA
Jun 17, 1963	Ralph Dupas w pts 15 Denny Moyer	Baltimore, MD
Sep 7, 1963	**Sandro Mazzinghi** (Ita) w ko 9 Ralph Dupas	Milan (Ita)
Dec 2, 1963	Sandro Mazzinghi w rsf 13 Ralph Dupas	Sydney (Aus)
Dec 11, 1964	Sandro Mazzinghi w pts 15 Fortunato Manca (Ita)	Rome (Ita)
Jun 18, 1965	**Nino Benvenuti** (Ita) w ko 6 Sandro Mazzinghi	Milan (Ita)
Dec 17, 1965	Nino Benvenuti w pts 15 Sandro Mazzinghi	Rome (Ita)
Jun 25, 1966	**Kim Ki-Soo** (Kor) w pts 15 Nino Benvenuti	Seoul (Kor)
Dec 17, 1966	Kim Ki-Soo w pts 15 Stan Harrington	Seoul (Kor)
Oct 3, 1967	Kim Ki-Soo w pts 15 Freddie Little (US)	Seoul (Kor)
May 26, 1968	**Sandro Mazzinghi** w pts 15 Kim Ki-Soo	Milan (Ita)
Oct 25, 1968	Sandro Mazzinghi no contest 9 Freddie Little	Rome (Ita)
	Mazzinghi was unable to come out for the ninth because he was badly cut. The referee ruled a no contest. Mazzinghi refused a rematch, and the WBA declared his title vacant in January 1969	
Mar 17, 1969	**Freddie Little** w pts 15 Stan Hayward (US)	Las Vegas, NV
	For vacant title	
Sep 9, 1969	Freddie Little w ko 2 Hisao Minami (Jap)	Osaka (Jap)
Mar 20, 1970	Freddie Little w pts 15 Gerhard Piaskowy (Ger)	Berlin (Ger)
Jul 9, 1970	**Carmelo Bossi** (Ita) w pts 15 Freddie Little	Monza (Ita)
Apr 29, 1971	Carmelo Bossi drew 15 Jose Hernandez (Sp)	Madrid (Sp)
Oct 31, 1971	**Koichi Wajima** (Jap) w pts 15 Carmelo Bossi	Tokyo (Jap)
May 7, 1972	Koichi Wajima w ko 1 Domenico Tiberia (Ita)	Tokyo (Jap)
Oct 3, 1972	Koichi Wajima w ko 3 Matt Donovan (Tr)	Tokyo (Jap)
Jan 9, 1973	Koichi Wajima drew 15 Miguel DeOliveira (Bra)	Tokyo (Jap)
Apr 19, 1973	Koichi Wajima w pts 15 Ryu Sorimachi (Jap)	Osaka (Jap)
Aug 14, 1973	Koichi Wajima w rsf 13 Silvani Bertini (Ita)	Sapporo (Jap)
Feb 5, 1974	Koichi Wajima w pts 15 Miguel DeOliveira (Bra)	Tokyo (Jap)
Jun 4, 1974	**Oscar Albarado** (US) w ko 15 Koichi Wajima	Tokyo (Jap)
Oct 8, 1974	Oscar Albarado w rsf 7 Ryu Sorimachi (Jap)	Tokyo (Jap)
Jan 21, 1975	**Koichi Wajima** w pts 15 Oscar Albarado	Tokyo (Jap)
	The WBC withdrew recognition from Wajima and set up their own title	

WBC title

May 7, 1975	**Miguel DeOliveira** w pts 15 Jose Duran (Sp)	Monte Carlo (Mon)
	For vacant title	
Nov 13, 1975	**Elisha Obed** (Bah) w rtd 10 Miguel DeOliveira	Paris (Fra)
Feb 28, 1976	Elisha Obed w ko 2 Tony Gardner (US)	Nassau (Bah)
Apr 25, 1976	Elisha Obed w pts 15 Sea Robinson (IC)	Abidjan (IC)
Jun 18, 1976	**Eckhard Dagge** (Ger) w rtd 10 Elisha Obed	Berlin (Ger)
Sep 18, 1976	Eckhard Dagge w pts 15 Emile Griffith (VI)	Berlin (Ger)
Mar 15, 1977	Eckhard Dagge drew 15 Maurice Hope (Eng)	Berlin (Ger)
Aug 6, 1977	**Rocky Mattioli** (Ita) w ko 5 Eckhard Dagge	Berlin (Ger)
Mar 11, 1978	Rocky Mattioli w ko 7 Elisha Obed	Melbourne (Aus)
May 14, 1978	Rocky Mattioli w rsf 5 Jose Duran	Pescara (Ita)
Mar 4, 1979	**Maurice Hope** w rtd 8 Rocky Mattioli	San Remo (Ita)
Sep 25, 1979	Maurice Hope w rsf 7 Mike Baker (US)	Wembley (Eng)
Jul 12, 1980	Maurice Hope w rsf 11 Rocky Mattioli	Wembley (Eng)
Nov 26, 1980	Maurice Hope w pts 15 Carlos Herrera (Arg)	Wembley (Eng)
May 24, 1981	**Wilfred Benitez** (PR) w ko 12 Maurice Hope	Las Vegas, NV
Nov 14, 1981	Wilfred Benitez w pts 15 Carlos Santos (PR)	Las Vegas, NV
Jan 30, 1982	Wilfred Benitez w pts 15 Roberto Duran (Pan)	Las Vegas, NV
Dec 3, 1982	**Thomas Hearns** (US) w pts 15 Wilfred Benitez	New Orleans, LA
Feb 11, 1984	Thomas Hearns w pts 12 Luigi Minchillo (Ita)	Detroit, MI
Jun 15, 1984	Thomas Hearns w ko 2 Roberto Duran	Las Vegas, NV
Sep 15, 1984	Thomas Hearns w rsf 3 Fred Hutchings (US)	Saginaw, MI
Jun 23, 1986	Thomas Hearns w rsf 8 Mark Medal (US)	Las Vegas, NV
	Thomas Hearns moved out of the light-middleweight division	
Dec 5, 1986	**Duane Thomas** (US) w rsf 3 John Mugabi (Ug)	Las Vegas, NV
	For vacant title	
Jul 12, 1987	**Lupe Aquino** (Mex) w pts 12 Duane Thomas	Bordeaux (Fra)
Oct 2, 1987	**Gianfranco Rosi** (Ita) w pts 12 Lupe Aquino	Perugia (Ita)
Jan 3, 1988	Gianfranco Rosi w ko 7 Duane Thomas	Genoa (Ita)
Jul 8, 1988	**Don Curry** (US) w rtd 9 Gianfranco Rosi	San Remo (Ita)
Feb 11, 1989	**Rene Jacquot** (Fra) w pts 12 Don Curry	Grenoble (Fra)
Jul 9, 1989	**John Mugabi** w rsf 1 Rene Jacquot	Paris (Fra)
Mar 31, 1990	**Terry Norris** (US) w ko 1 John Mugabi	Tampa, FL
Jul 13, 1990	Terry Norris w pts 12 Rene Jacquot	Annecy (Fra)
Feb 9, 1991	Terry Norris w pts 12 Sugar Ray Leonard (US)	New York, NY
Jun 1, 1991	Terry Norris w ko 8 Don Curry	Palm Springs, CA
Aug 16, 1991	Terry Norris w rsf 1 Brett Lally (US)	San Diego, CA
Dec 13, 1991	Terry Norris w pts 12 Jorge Castro (Arg)	Paris (Fra)
Feb 22, 1992	Terry Norris w rsf 9 Carl Daniels (US)	San Diego, CA
May 9, 1992	Terry Norris w rsf 4 Meldrick Taylor (US)	Las Vegas, NV
Feb 20, 1993	Terry Norris w rsf 2 Maurice Blocker (US)	Mexico City (Mex)
Jun 19, 1993	Terry Norris w rtd 3 Troy Waters (Aus)	San Diego, CA
Sep 10, 1993	Terry Norris w rsf 1 Joe Gatti (US)	San Antonio, TX
Dec 18, 1993	**Simon Brown** (Jam) w ko 4 Terry Norris	Puebla (Mex)
Jan 29, 1994	Simon Brown w pts 12 Troy Waters	Las Vegas, NV
May 7, 1994	**Terry Norris** w pts 12 Simon Brown	Las Vegas, NV
Nov 12, 1994	**Luis Santana** (DR) w dis 5 Terry Norris	Mexico City (Mex)
Apr 8, 1995	Luis Santana w dis 3 Terry Norris	Las Vegas, NV
Aug 19, 1995	**Terry Norris** w rsf 2 Luis Santana	Las Vegas, NV
Sep 16, 1995	Terry Norris w rsf 9 David Gonzales (US)	Las Vegas, NV
Dec 16, 1995	Terry Norris w pts 12 Paul Vaden (US)	Philadelphia, PA
	Norris retained WBC title and won Vaden's IBF Championship	
Dec 6, 1997	**Keith Mullings** (US) rsf 9 Terry Norris	Atlantic City, NJ
Mar 14, 1998	Keith Mullings w rsf 5 Davide Ciarlante (Ita)	Atlantic City, NJ
Jan 29, 1999	**Javier Castillejo** (Spa) w pts 12 Keith Mullings	Madrid (Spa)
May 15, 1999	Javier Castillejo w rsf 4 Humberto Aranda (CR)	Madrid (Spa)
Sep 10, 1999	Javier Castillejo w rsf 7 Paolo Roberto (Swe)	Madrid (Spa)
Dec 17, 1999	Javier Castillejo w rsf 7 Mikael Rask (Den)	Madrid (Spa)
Jul 21, 2000	Javier Castillejo w pts 12 Tony Marshall (US)	Madrid (Spa)
Oct 21, 2000	Javier Castillejo w rsf 4 Javier Martinez (Spa)	Mexico City (Mex)
Jun 23, 2001	**Oscar De La Hoya** (US) w pts 12 Javier Castillejo	Las Vegas, NV
	De La Hoya then fought a WBC/WBA unification fight with Fernando Vargas on Sep 14, 2002 in Las Vegas	

WBA title

Jun 7, 1975	**Jae Do Yuh** (Kor) w ko 7 Koichi Wajima	Kitakyushu (Jap)
Nov 11, 1975	Jae-Do Yuh w rsf 6 Masahiro Masaki (Jap)	Shizuoka (Jap)
Feb 17, 1976	**Koichi Wajima** w ko 15 Jae Do Yuh	Tokyo (Jap)
May 18, 1976	**Jose Duran** (Sp) w ko 14 Koichi Wajima	Tokyo (Jap)
Oct 8, 1976	**Miguel Angel Castellini** (Arg) w pts 15 Jose Duran	Madrid (Sp)
Mar 5, 1977	**Eddie Gazo** (Nic) w pts 15 Miguel Angel Castellini	Managua (Nic)
Jun 7, 1977	Eddie Gazo w rsf 11 Koichi Wajima	Tokyo (Jap)
Sep 13, 1977	Eddie Gazo w pts15 Kenji Shibata (Jap)	Tokyo (Jap)
Dec 18, 1977	Eddie Gazo w pts 15 Chae-Keun Lim (Kor)	Inchon (Kor)
Aug 9, 1978	**Masashi Kudo** (Jap) w pts 15 Eddie Gazo	Akita (Jap)
Dec 13, 1978	Masashi Kudo w pts 15 Ho-In Joo (Kor)	Osaka (Jap)
Mar 14, 1979	Masashi Kudo w pts 15 Manuel Ricardo Gonzalez (Arg)	Tokyo (Jap)
Jun 20, 1979	Masashi Kudo w rsf 12 Manuel Ricardo Gonzalez	Yokkaichi (Jap)
Oct 24, 1979	**Ayub Kalule** (Ug) w pts 15 Masashi Kudo	Akita (Jap)
Dec 6, 1979	Ayub Kalule w pts 15 Steve Gregory (US)	Copenhagen (Den)
Apr 17, 1980	Ayub Kalule w rtd 11 Emiliano Villa (Col)	Copenhagen (Den)
Jun 12, 1980	Ayub Kalule w pts 15 Marijan Benes (Yug)	Randers (Den)
Sep 6, 1980	Ayub Kalule w pts 15 Bushy Bester (SA)	Aarhus (Den)
Jun 25, 1981	**Sugar Ray Leonard** w rsf 9 Ayub Kalule	Houston, TX
Nov 7, 1981	**Tadashi Mihara** (Jap) w pts 15 Rocky Fratto (US)	Rochester, NY
	For vacant title	

Feb 2,	1982	**Davey Moore** (US) w rsf 6 Tadashi Mihara	Tokyo (Jap)
Apr 26,	1982	Davey Moore w ko 5 Charlie Weir (SA)	Johannesburg (SA)
Jul 17,	1982	Davey Moore w rsf 10 Ayub Kalule	Atlantic City, NJ
Jan 29,	1983	Davey Moore w ko 4 Gary Guiden (US)	Atlantic City, NJ
Jun 16,	1983	**Roberto Duran** w rsf 8 Davey Moore	New York, NY
Jun	1984	*Duran relinquished the title to challenge Thomas Hearns for the WBC version*	
Oct 19,	1984	**Mike McCallum** (Jam) w pts 15 Sean Mannion (Ire)	New York, NY
		For vacant title	
Dec 1,	1984	Mike McCallum w rsf 14 Luigi Minchillo (Ita)	Milan (Ita)
Jul 28,	1985	Mike McCallum w rsf 8 David Braxton (US)	Miami, FL
Aug 23,	1986	Mike McCallum w rsf 2 Julian Jackson (VI)	Miami, FL
Oct 25,	1986	Mike McCallum w rsf 9 Said Skouma (Alg)	Paris (Fra)
Apr 19,	1987	Mike McCallum w rsf 10 Milton McCrory (US)	Phoenix, AZ
Jul 18,	1987	Mike McCallum w ko 5 Don Curry (US)	Las Vegas, NV
		Mike McCallum moved up to the middleweight division	
Nov 21,	1987	**Julian Jackson** w rsf 3 In-Chul Baek (Kor)	Las Vegas, NV
		For vacant title	
Jul 30,	1988	Julian Jackson w rsf 3 Buster Drayton (US)	Atlantic City, NJ
Feb 25,	1989	Julian Jackson w ko 8 Francisco DeJesus (Bra)	Las Vegas, NV
Jul 30,	1989	Julian Jackson w rsf 2 Terry Norris (US)	Atlantic City, NJ
		Julian Jackson moved up to the middleweight division	
Feb 23,	1991	**Gilbert Dele** (Fra) w rsf 7 Carlos Elliott (US)	Point-à-Pitre (Guad)
		For vacant title	
May 5,	1991	Gilbert Dele w pts 12 Jun-Suk Hwang (Kor)	Paris (Fra)
Oct 3,	1991	**Vinny Pazienza** (US) w rsf 12 Gilbert Dele	Providence, RI
		Vinny Pazienza relinquished the title	
Dec 21,	1992	**Julio Cesar Vasquez** (Arg) w rsf 1 Hitoshi Kamiyama (Jap)	Buenos Aires (Arg)
		For vacant title	
Apr 24,	1993	Julio Cesar Vasquez w pts 12 Javier Castillejos (Sp)	Madrid (Sp)
Jul 10,	1993	Julio Cesar Vasquez w pts 12 Alejandro Ugueto (Ven)	Tucuman (Arg)
Aug 21,	1993	Julio Cesar Vasquez w pts 12 Aaron Davis (US)	Monte Carlo (Mon)
Jan 22,	1994	Julio Cesar Vasquez w pts 12 Juan Medina Padilla (Sp)	Alma Ata (Kaz)
Mar 4,	1994	Julio Cesar Vasquez w rsf 2 Armand Picar (Phil)	Las Vegas, NV
Apr 8,	1994	Julio Cesar Vasquez w pts 12 Ricardo Nunez (Arg)	Tucuman (Arg)
May 21,	1994	Julio Cesar Vasquez w rsf 10 Ahmet Dottuev (Rus)	Belfast (N. Ire)
Aug 21,	1994	Julio Cesar Vasquez w pts 12 Ronald Wright (US)	St-Jean-de-Luz (Fra)
Nov 11,	1994	Julio Cesar Vasquez w pts 12 Tony Marshall (US)	Tucuman (Arg)
Mar 4,	1995	**Pernell Whitaker** (US) w pts 12 Julio Cesar Vasquez	Atlantic City, NJ
		Pernell Whitaker relinquished the title the day after winning it	
Jun 16,	1995	**Carl Daniels** (US) w pts 12 Julio Cesar Green (US)	Lyon (Fra)
		For vacant title	
Dec 16,	1995	**Julio Cesar Vasquez** w rsf 11 Carl Daniels	Philadelphia, PA

IBF title

Mar 11,	1984	**Mark Medal** (US) w rsf 5 Earl Hargrove (US)	Atlantic City, NJ
		For vacant title	
Nov 2,	1984	**Carlos Santos** w pts 15 Mark Medal	New York, NY
Jun 1,	1985	Carlos Santos w pts 15 Louis Acaries (Fra)	Paris (Fra)
Feb	1986	*IBF withdrew recognition from Santos for failure to defend v Davey Moore*	
Jun 4,	1986	**Buster Drayton** w pts 15 Carlos Santos	East Rutherford, NJ
		For vacant title	
Aug 24,	1986	Buster Drayton w rsf 10 Davey Moore	Juan-les-Pins (Fra)
Mar 27,	1987	Buster Drayton w rtd 10 Said Skouma (Alg)	Cannes (Fra)
Jun 27,	1987	**Matthew Hilton** (Can) w pts 15 Buster Drayton	Montreal (Can)
Oct 16,	1987	Matthew Hilton w rsf 2 Jack Callahan (US)	Atlantic City, NJ
Nov 4,	1988	**Robert Hines** (US) w rsf 12 Matthew Hilton	Las Vegas, NV
Feb 5,	1989	**Darrin van Horn** (US) w pts 12 Robert Hines	Atlantic City, NJ
Jul 15,	1989	**Gianfranco Rosi** w pts 12 Darrin van Horn	Atlantic City, NJ
Oct 27,	1989	Gianfranco Rosi w pts 12 Troy Waters (Aus)	St Vincent (Ita)
Apr 14,	1990	Gianfranco Rosi w rsf 7 Kevin Daigle	Monte Carlo (Mon)
Jul 21,	1990	Gianfranco Rosi w pts 12 Darrin Van Horn	Marino (Ita)
Nov 30,	1990	Gianfranco Rosi w pts 12 Rene Jacquot	Marsala (Ita)
Mar 16,	1991	Gianfranco Rosi w pts 12 Ron Amundsen (US)	St Vincent (Ita)
Jul 13,	1991	Gianfranco Rosi w pts 12 Glenn Wolfe (US)	Avezzano (Ita)
Nov 21,	1991	Gianfranco Rosi w pts 12 Gilbert Baptist (US)	Perugia (Ita)
Apr 9,	1992	Gianfranco Rosi w rsf 6 Angel Hernandez (Sp)	Celano (Ita)
Jul 11,	1992	Gianfranco Rosi w pts 12 Gilbert Dele	Monte Carlo (Mon)
Jan 20,	1993	Gianfranco Rosi w pts 12 Gilbert Dele	Avoriaz (Ita)
Mar 4,	1994	Gianfranco Rosi tech draw 6 Vincent Pettway (US)	Las Vegas, NV
Sep 17,	1994	**Vincent Pettway** w ko 4 Gianfranco Rosi	Las Vegas, NV
Apr 29,	1995	Vincent Pettway w ko 6 Simon Brown	Landover, MD
Aug 12,	1995	**Paul Vaden** w rsf 12 Vincent Pettway	Las Vegas, NV
Dec 16,	1995	**Terry Norris** w pts 12 Paul Vaden	Philadelphia, PA
Jan 27,	1996	Terry Norris w rsf 2 Jose Luis Vado (Nic)	Phoenix, AZ
		Only IBF belt at stake. Norris relinquished IBF title to make title vacant	
Apr 12,	1997	**Raul Marquez** (US) w rsf 9 Anthony Stephens (US)	Las Vegas, NV
Jul 5,	1997	Raul Marquez w rsf 4 Romallis Ellis (US)	Lake Charles, LA
Sep 13,	1997	Raul Marquez w pts 12 Keith Mullings	Las Vegas, NV
Dec 6,	1997	**Luis Ramon Campas** (Mex) w rsf 8 Raul Marquez	Atlantic City, NJ
Mar 23,	1998	Luis Ramon Campas w rsf 3 Anthony Stephens	Mashantucket, CT
Jun 6,	1998	Luis Ramon Campas w rsf 11 Pedro Ortega (Mex)	Tijuana (Mex)
Sep 18,	1998	Luis Ramon Campas w rsf 3 Larry Barnes (US)	Las Vegas, NV
Dec 12,	1998	**Fernando Vargas** (US) w rsf 7 Luis Ramon Campas	Atlantic City, NJ
Mar 13,	1999	Fernando Vargas w rsf 4 Howard Clarke (Engl)	New York, NY
Jul 17,	1999	Fernando Vargas w rsf 11 Raul Marquez (US)	Lake Tahoe, NV
Dec 4,	1999	Fernando Vargas w pts 12 Ronald Wright (US)	Lincoln City, NB
Apr 15,	2000	Fernando Vargas w pts 12 Ike Quartey (Gha)	Las Vegas, NV
Aug 26,	2000	Fernando Vargas w rsf 4 Ross Thompson (US)	Las Vegas, NV

WBC/IBF titles

Feb 24,	1996	Terry Norris w rsf 8 Vincent Pettway (US)	Richmond, VA
Sep 7,	1996	Terry Norris w rsf 5 Alex Rios (US)	Las Vegas, NV
Jan 11	1997	Terry Norris w rsf 10 Nick Rupa (Can)	Nashville, TN
Mar	1997	*Norris relinquished IBF title*	

WBA title

Aug 21,	1996	**Laurent Boudouani** (Fra) w rsf 5 Julio Cesar Vasquez	Le Cannet (Fra)
Mar 29,	1997	Laurent Boudouani w pts 12 Carl Daniels	Las Vegas, NV
Feb 13,	1998	Laurent Boudouani drew 12 Guillermo Jones (Pan)	Albuquerque, NM
May 30,	1998	Laurent Boudouani w pts 12 Guillermo Jones	Las Vegas, NV
Nov 30,	1998	Laurent Boudouani w rsf 9 Terry Norris	Paris (Fra)
Mar 6,	1999	**David Reid** (US) w pts 12 Laurent Boudouani	Atlantic City, NJ
Jul 16,	1999	David Reid w pts 12 Kevin Kelly (Aus)	Atlantic City, NJ
Aug 28,	1999	David Reid w pts 12 Keith Mullings (US)	Las Vegas, NV
Mar 3,	2000	**Felix Trinidad** (PR) w pts 12 David Reid	Las Vegas, NV
Jul 22,	2000	Felix Trinidad w rsf 3 Mamadou Thiam (Fra)	Miami, FL

IBF/WBA titles

Dec 2,	2000	**Felix Trinidad** (PR) w rsf 12 Fernando Vargas	Las Vegas, NV

IBF title

Oct 12,	2001	**Ronald Wright** (US) w pts 12 Robert Frazier (US)	Indio, CA
Feb 2,	2002	Ronald Wright w rsf 5 Jason Papillion (US)	Miami, FL

WBA title

Sep 22,	2001	**Fernando Vargas** (US) w ko 7 Jose Flores (Mex)	Las Vegas, NV

WBO title

Dec 8,	1988	**John David Jackson** (US) w rtd 7 Lupe Aquino	Detroit, MI
		For vacant title	
Apr 22,	1989	John David Jackson w rsf 8 Steve Little (US)	Detroit, MI
Feb 17,	1990	John David Jackson no contest 11 Martin Camara (Fra)	Deauville (Fra)
		This decision caused such a scandal that the French Federation prohibited any further WBO championships from taking place under their jurisdiction	
Nov 23,	1990	John David Jackson w pts 12 Chris Pyatt (Eng)	Leicester (Eng)
Jul 20,	1991	John David Jackson w pts 12 Tyrone Trice (US)	McKee, NJ
Jun 9,	1992	John David Jackson w rtd 9 Pat Lawlor (US)	San Francisco, CA
Dec 19,	1992	John David Jackson w rtd 10 Michele Mastrodonato (Ita)	San Severo (Ita)
Oct 30,	1993	**Verno Phillips** (US) w rsf 7 Lupe Aquino	Phoenix, AZ
		For vacant title	
Jul 25,	1994	Verno Phillips w rsf 7 Jaime Llanes (Mex)	Inglewood, CA
Nov 9,	1994	Verno Phillips w pts 12 Santos Cardona (PR)	New Orleans, LA
Feb 3,	1995	Verno Phillips w pts 12 Santos Cardona	Bushkill, PA
May 17,	1995	**Gianfranco Rosi** (Ita) w pts 12 Verno Phillips	Perugia (Ita)
		Rosi failed a post-fight drugs test and Phillips was reinstated as champion	
Nov 22,	1995	**Paul Jones** (Eng) w pts 12 Verno Phillips	Sheffield (Eng)
Feb	1996	*Jones stripped for failing to make mandatory defence against Bronco McKart*	
Mar 1,	1996	**Bronco McKart** (US) w rsf 9 Santos Cardona (PR)	Indio, CA
		For vacant title	
May 17,	1996	**Ronald Wright** (US) w pts 12 Bronco McKart	Monroe, MI
Nov 9,	1996	Ronald Wright w pts 12 Ensley Bingham (Eng)	Manchester (Eng)
May 3,	1997	Ronald Wright w rsf 6 Steve Foster (Eng)	Manchester (Eng)
Dec 19,	1997	Ronald Wright w rtd 6 Adrian Dodson (Guy)	London (Eng)
Aug 22,	1998	**Harry Simon** (Nam) w pts 12 Ronald Wright	Hammanskraal (SA)
May 1,	1999	Harry Simon w rsf 3 Kevin Lueshing (Eng)	London (Eng)
Feb 19,	2000	Harry Simon w rtd 10 Enrique Areco (Arg)	Dagenham (Eng)
Sep 23,	2000	Harry Simon w pts 12 Rodney Jones (US)	Rama, Ontario (Can)
Feb 10,	2001	Harry Simon w rsf 5 Wayne Alexander (Eng)	Widnes (Eng)
Mar 16,	2002	**Daniel Santos** (PR) w rsf 11 Luis Ramon Campas (Mex)	Las Vegas, NV

Aug 17, 2002 Daniel Santos w pts 12 Mehrdud Takalobigashi (Irn) .... Cardiff (Wal)
Jun 28, 2003 Daniel Santos w pts 12 Fulgencio Zuniga (Ecu) .... Bayamon (PR)
Apr 17, 2004 Daniel Santos w pts 12 Michael Lerma (US)..................... Tampa, FL
Sep 11, 2004 Daniel Santos w tdec 10 Antonio Margarito (Mex) .... Hato Rey (PR)
Dec 3, 2005 **Sergei Dzindziruk** (Ukr) w pts 12 Daniel Santos .... Magdeburg (Ger)
May 27, 2006 Sergei Dzindziruk w pts 12 Sebastian Lujan (Arg) .... Munich (Ger)
Oct 21, 2006 Sergei Dzindziruk w pts 12 Alisultan Nadirbegov (Rus) .... Halle (Ger)
May 19, 2007 Sergei Dzindziruk w ko 11 Carlos Nascimento (Bra) ....Hamburg (Ger)
Apr 26, 2008 Sergey Dzindziruk w pts 12 Lukas Konecny (CZ) .... Dresden (Ger)
Nov 1, 2008 Sergey Dzindziruk w pts 12 Joel Julio (Col) .... Oberhausen (Ger)
The WBO sanctioned the following Interim title fights:
Nov 29, 2008 **Paul Williams** w rsf 8 Verno Phillips.......................... Ontario, CA
Nov 7, 2009 **Alfredo Angulo** (Mex) w ko 3 Harry Joe Yorgey (US) ....Hartford, CT
May 14, 2010 Sergey Dzinziruk w rsf 10 Daniel Dawson (Aus).............. Santa Ynez, CA
Dzinziruk stripped of the title
Apr 5, 2012 Zaurbek Baysangurov (Ukr) w pts 12 Michel Soro (Fra) .... Borvari (Ukr)
Oct 6, 2012 Zaurbek Baysangurov w pts 12 Lukas Konecny (Czech).............Kiev (Ukr)
Baysangurov stripped of title
Nov 9, 2013 **Demetrius Andrade** (USA) w pts 12 Vanes Martirosyan (USA) ... Corpus Christi, TX
For vacant title
Jun 14, 2014 Demetrius Andrade w rsf 7 Brian Rose (Eng) .... Brooklyn, NY
The WBO also sanctioned the following for the Interim title
Apr 24, 2010 Alfredo Angulo w ko 11 Joel Julio (Col)........................ Ontario, CA
Angulo was stripped of the title
Jul 30, 2011 **Zaurbek Baysangurov** w ko 1 Mike Miranda.................. Odessa (Ukr)
Apr 5, 2012 **Lukas Konecny** w ko 7 Salim Larbi (Fra) .... Brno (Czech)

WBC/WBA titles

Sep 14, 2002 Oscar De La Hoya w rsf 11 Fernando Vargas (US) .... Las Vegas, NV
WBA/WBC unification fight
May 3, 2003 Oscar De La Hoya w rtd 7 Luis Ramon Campas (Mex) .... Las Vegas, NV
Sep 13, 2003 **Shane Mosley** (US) w pts 12 Oscar De La Hoya............... Las Vegas, NV

WBC/WBA/IBF titles

Mar 13, 2004 **Ronald Wright** (US) w pts 12 Shane Mosley.................. Las Vegas, NV
Wright was stripped of IBF title

WBC/WBA titles

Nov 20, 2004 Ronald Wright w pts 12 Shane Mosley .... Las Vegas, NV
Wright relinquished titles to move up to middleweight

WBC title

The WBC recognized Javier Castillejo as interim champion in 2002–03 for a short while
Aug 13, 2005 **Ricardo Mayorga** (Nic) w pts 12 Michele Piccirillo (Ita)...........Chicago, IL
For vacant title
May 6, 2006 **Oscar De La Hoya** w rsf 6 Ricardo Mayorga (Nic) .... Las Vegas, NV
May 5, 2007 **Floyd Mayweather Jr** (US) w pts 12 Oscar De La Hoya .... Las Vegas, NV
Mayweather Jr relinquished the title to return to welterweight
Jul 28, 2007 **Vernon Forrest** (US) w pts 12 Carlos Baldomir (Mex).............Tacoma, WA
For vacant title
Dec 1, 2007 Vernon Forrest w pts 12 Michele Piccirillo (Ita) .... Mashantucket, CT
Jun 7, 2008 Sergio Mora (US) w pts 12 Vernon Forrest .... Uncasville, CT
Sep 13, 2008 Vernon Forrest w pts 12 Sergio Mora....................... Las Vegas, NV
Jul 25, 2008 *Vernon Forrest was shot dead in Atlanta, Georgia. The WBC sanctioned the following Interim title fights:*
Oct 4, 2008 **Sergio Martinez** (Arg) w rtd 8 Alex Bunema (US) ....Temecula, CA
Feb 14, 2009 Sergio Martinez drew 12 Kermit Cintron (PR)....................Sunrise, FL
Sergio Martinez relinquished title
Nov 13, 2010 **Manny Pacquiao** (Phi) w pts 12 Antonio Margarito (Mex) .... Arlington, TX
For vacant title
Pacquiao relinquished title
Mar 5, 2011 **Saul Alvarez** (Mex) w pts 12 Matthew Hatton (Eng)............. Anaheim, CA
Jun 18, 2011 Saul Alvarez w rsf 12 Ryan Rhodes (Eng).....................Jalisco (Mex)
Sep 17, 2011 Saul Alvarez w rsf 6 Alfonso Gomez (Mex) ....Los Angeles, CA
Nov 26, 2011 Saul Alvarez w rsf 5 Kermit Cintron .... Mexico City (Mex)
May 5, 2012 Saul Alvarez w pts 12 Shane Mosley .... Las Vegas, NV
Sep 15, 2012 Saul Alvarez w rsf 5 Josesito Lopez (US) .... Las Vegas, NV

WBA title

The WBA recognized Oscar De La Hoya only as a "super" champion, followed by Mosley and Wright, and continued to sanction "world" title fights
Mar 1, 2003 **Alejandro Garcia** (Mex) w rsf 3 Santiago Samaniego (Pan) ...... Las Vegas, NV
For vacant title
Sep 20, 2003 Alejandro Garcia w rsf 10 Rhoshii Wells (US) .... Uncasville, CT
Dec 13, 2003 **Travis Simms** (US) w ko 5 Alejandro Garcia ....Atlantic City, NJ
Oct 2, 2004 Travis Simms w pts 12 Bronco McKart (IS)....................New York, NY
Simms was stripped of the title for inactivity
May 21, 2005 **Alejandro Garcia** w rsf 9 Rhoshii Wells ....Chicago, IL
For vacant title
Aug 13, 2005 Alejandro Garcia w pts 12 Luca Messi (Ita)......................Chicago, IL
May 6, 2006 **Jose Rivera** (US) w pts 12 Alejandro Garcia.................. Worcester, MA
Jan 6, 2007 Travis Simms w rsf 9 Jose Rivera.......................... Hollywood, FL
Jul 7, 2007 **Joachim Alcine** (Hai) w pts 12 Travis Simms .... Bridgeport, CT
Dec 7, 2007 Joachim Alcine (Hai) w rsf 12 Alfonso Mosquera (Pan) ....Montreal (Can)
Jul 11, 2008 **Daniel Santos** w ko 6 Joachim Alcine ....Montreal (Can)
Nov 14, 2009 Yuri Foreman (Bel) w pts 12 Daniel Santos.................. Las Vegas, NV
The WBA also sanctioned the following Interim title fights:
Aug 30, 2009 Nobuhiro Ishida (Jap) w pts 12 Marco Antonio Avendano (Ven)..... Osaka (Jap)
The WBA sanctioned the following for the Interim title
Oct 9, 2010 Rigoberto Alvarez (Mex) w pts 12 Nobuhiro Ishida............... Tepic (Mex)
For the WBA title
Dec 29, 2009 Nobuhiro Ishida w pts 12 Oney Valdez (Col) .... Osaka (Jap)
Jun 5, 2010 **Miguel Cotto** w rsf 9 Yuri Foreman..........................New York, NY
Miguel Cotto was promoted to Super champion
Feb 5, 2011 **Austin Trout** (US) w pts 12 Rigoberto Alvarez (Mex)......... Guadalajara (Mex)
For vacant title
Jun 11, 2011 Austin Trout w pts 12 David Alonso Lopez (Mex) .... San Luis Potosi (Mex)
The WBA sanctioned the following for the Interim title
Oct 19, 2011 Anthony Mundine (Aus) w pts 12 Rigoberto Alvarez.......... Newcastle (Aus)
For the WBA title
Nov 11, 2011 Austin Trout w rsf 6 Frank LoPorto (Aus)........................El Paso, TX
Jun 2, 2012 Austin Trout w pts 12 Delvin Rodriguez (Dom) ....Carson, CA
Dec 1, 2012 Austin Trout w pts 12 Miguel Cotto..........................New York, NY

WBA super title

Mar 12, 2011 Miguel Cotto w rsf 12 Ricardo Mayorga .... Las Vegas, NV
Dec 3, 2012 Miguel Cotto w rtd 10 Antonio Margarito ....New York, NY
May 5, 2012 Floyd Mayweather Jr. w pts 12 Miguel Cotto .... Las Vegas, NV

IBF title

Sep 7, 2002 **Ronald Wright** (US) w dis 8 Bronco McKart (US) .... Portland, OR
Mar 1, 2003 Ronald Wright w pts 12 Juan Carlos Candelo (Col)............. Las Vegas, NV
Nov 8, 2003 Ronald Wright w pts 12 Angel Hernandez (Mex)............... Las Vegas, NV
Wright unified the WBC, WBA and IBF titles, then was stripped of the IBF belt
Jun 5, 2004 **Verno Phillips** (US) w rsf 6 Carlos Bojorquez (Mex) ....Joplin, MO
For vacant title
Oct 2, 2004 **Kassim Ouma** (Uga) w pts 12 Verno Phillips.................. Las Vegas, NV
Jan 29, 2005 Kassim Ouma w pts 12 Kofi Jantuah (Gha).................Atlantic City, NJ
Jul 14, 2005 **Roman Karmazin** (Rus) w pts 12 Kassim Ouma............... Las Vegas, NV
Jul 8, 2006 **Cory Spinks** (US) w pts 12 Roman Karmazin .... St Louis, MO
Feb 3, 2007 Cory Spinks w pts 12 Rodney Jones (US)....................Kissimmee, FL
Mar 27, 2008 **Verno Phillips** w pts 12 Cory Spinks......................... St Louis, MO
Nov, 2008 *Title vacated when Phillips lost to Paul Williams in a match not sanctioned by the IBF*
Apr 24, 2009 **Cory Spinks** w pts 12 Deandre Latimore (US) .... St Louis, MO
For vacant title
Aug 7, 2010 Cornelius Bundrage (US) v Cory Spinks ....Saint Louis, MO
Jun 25, 2011 Cornelius Bundrage w pts 12 Sechew Powell (US).......... Saint Charles, MO
Jun 30, 2012 Cornelius Bundrage w rsf 7 Cory Spinks .... Indio, CA
Feb 23, 2013 Ishe Smith w pts 4 Cornelius Bundrage .... Detroit, MI
Sep 9, 2013 **Carlos Molina** (Mex) w pts 12 Ishe Smith................... Las Vegas, NV
Oct 11, 2014 **Cornelius Bundrage** w pts 12 Carlos Molina .... Cancun (Mex)

WBC/WBA titles

Apr 20, 2013 **Saul Alvarez** w pts 12 Austin Trout.......................San Antonio, TX
Sep 14, 2013 **Floyd Mayweather Jr** w pts 12 Saul Alvarez .... Las Vegas, NV
For WBA Super-welterweight Super title

IBO/WBO titles

May 12, 2012 Zaurbek Baysangurov w pts 12 Michel Soro (Fra) ....Brovari (Ukraine)

WBO title

Oct 6, 2012 Zaurbek Baysangurov w pts 12 Lukas Konecny (Cze) .... Kiev (Ukraine)
Nov 9, 2013 **Demetrius Andrade (US)** w pts 12 Vanes Martirosyan (US)... Corpus Christi, TX
For the vacant title
Jun 14, 2014 Demetrius Andrade w rsf 7 Brian Rose (Eng) ....New York, NY
For vacant title
Oct 10, 2015 **Liam Smith (Eng)** w rsf 7 John Thompson (US) .... Manchester (Eng)

SADAM ALI *beat Miguel Cotto on points in a hard-fought bout in New York, USA, in December 2017*

Dec 19, 2015	Liam Smith w rsf 7 "Jimmy" Kilrain Kelly (Eng)	Manchester (Eng)
Jun 4, 2016	Liam Smith w ko 2 Predrag Radoseciv (Mon)	Liverpool (Eng)
Sep 17, 2016	**Saul Alvarez** w ko 9 Liam Smith	Arlington, TX
	WBO sanctioned the following fight for the interim title	
Apr 18, 2017	Liam Smith w rtd 9 Liam Williams (Wal)	Manchester (Eng)
	For the vacant title	
Aug 26, 2017	**Miguel Cotto (PR)** w pts 12 Yoshihiro Kamegai (Jap)	Carson, CA
Dec 2, 2017	**Sadam Ali (US)** w pts 12 Miguel Cotto	New York, NY

WBA Super/WBC/WBO titles

Sep 13, 2014	Floyd Mayweather Jr w pts 12 Marcos Maidana (Arg)	Las Vegas, NV

WBC title

	For the vacant title	
May 21, 2016	**Jermell Charlo (US)** w ko 8 John Jackson (US VI)	Las Vegas, NV
Apr 22, 2017	Jermell Charlo w ko 6 Charles Hatley (US)	New York, NY
Oct 14, 2017	Jermell Charlo w ko 1 Erickson Lubin (US)	New York, NY

WBA/WBC titles

Apr 20, 2013	Saul Alvarez w pts 12 Austin Trout	San Antonio, TX

WBA title

	WBA sanctioned the following fights for the interim title	
Jun 8, 2013	Erislandy Lara (US) w rsf 10 Alfredo Angulo (Mex)	Carson, CA
	For the WBA title	
Dec 7, 2013	**Erislandy Lara** w pts 12 Austin Trout	Brooklyn, NY
Dec 12, 2014	Erislandy Lara w pts 12 Ishe Smith (US)	San Antonio, TX
	WBA sanctioned the following fight for the interim title	
May 9, 2015	Jack Culcay (Ecu) w pts 12 Maurice Weber (Ger)	Frankfurt (Ger)

WBO/WBA Super titles

Jun 12, 2015	Erislandy Lara w pts 12 Delvin Rodriguez (DR)	Chicago, IL

IBO/WBA Super titles

Nov 25, 2015	Erislandy Lara w rsf 3 Jan Zaveck (Slo)	Hialeah, FL
May 21, 2016	Erislandy Lara w pts 12 Venes Martirosyan (US)	Las Vegas, NV
Jan 13, 2017	Erislandy Lara w ko 4 Yuri Foreman (Bls)	Hialeah, FL
Oct 14, 2017	Erislandy Lara w pts 12 Terrell Gausha (US)	Brooklyn, NY

WBA title

	WBA sanctioned the following fights for the interim title	
Dec 5, 2015	Jack Culcay w pts 12 Dennis Hogan (Ire)	Hamburg (Ger)
Apr 9, 2016	Jack Culcay w rtd 9 Jean Carlos Prada (Ven)	Brandenburg (Ger)
Nov 26, 2016	Brian Carlos Castano (Arg) w ko 6 Emmanuel de Jesus	Buenos Aires (Arg)
	For the WBA title	
Mar 11, 2017	**Demetrius Andrade (US)** w pts 12 Jack Culcay	Ludwigshafen (Ger)
	WBA sanctioned the following fights for the interim title	
Jul 1, 2017	Brian Carlos Castano w pts 12 Michel Soro (Fra)	Evian les Bains (Fra)

Welterweight

Paddy Duffy, an Irish-American from Boston, was the first cross-over champion of the welterweight division; he won the 142lb championship (as the limit then was) under London Prize Ring rules and then knocked out Billy McMillan under Queensberry Rules in the first gloved championship match, even if the gloves were only skin-tight. His disqualification win over the Australian-based Englishman Tom Meadows is generally accepted as the inaugural international match of the gloved era in thewelterweight class, which Duffy had helped to popularize in the Prize Ring.

Sadly, it was his last fight: he died of tuberculosis a year later, and set off one of the periodic scrambles for recognition to which the division was particularly prone in its first 30 years. His successors included colourful characters like Joe Walcott, the Barbados Demon, and the gloriously named Mysterious Billy Smith. (A disgruntled ex-opponent of his explained that Smith was so called because "He was always doing something mysterious in the ring".) That larger-than-life tradition has been maintained by great champions like Ted "Kid" Lewis, Mickey Walker, Henry Armstrong, Jose Napoles and Emile Griffith.

The championship limit fluctuated between 142 and 145lb for the first two decades of the last century, until the present poundage was universally accepted in 1920 during Jack Britton's second spell as champion.

World Welterweight Championship Bouts

Oct 30,	1888	**Paddy Duffy** (US) w ko 17 Billy McMillan (US)	Fort Foote, VA
Mar 29,	1889	Paddy Duffy w dis 45 Tom Meadows (Eng)	San Francisco, CA
Jul 19,	1890	*Duffy died, and the title was claimed by Tommy Ryan and Mysterious Billy Smith*	
Aug 9,	1891	**Tommy Ryan** (US) w ko 3 Billy McMillan	Richardson (Can)
Dec 13,	1891	Tommy Ryan w ko 14 Frank Howson (Eng)	Chicago, IL
Dec 14,	1892	**Mysterious Billy Smith** (US) w ko 14 Danny Needham (US)	San Francisco, CA
Apr 17,	1893	Mysterious Billy Smith w ko 2 Tom Williams (Aus)	Brooklyn, NY
Jul 26,	1894	**Tommy Ryan** w pts 20 Mysterious Billy Smith	Minneapolis, MN
Jan 18,	1895	Tommy Ryan w rsf 3 "Nonpareil" Jack Dempsey (Ire)	New York, NY
May 27,	1895	Tommy Ryan no contest 18 Mysterious Billy Smith	New York, NY
		Ryan was subsequently unable to make the championship weight, then 142lb, although he continued to style himself champion until 1898	
Mar 17,	1897	**George Green** (US) w ko 12 Mysterious Billy Smith	Carson City, NV
Aug 26,	1897	**Joe Walcott** (Bar) w ko 18 George Green	San Francisco, CA
		Joe Walcott dropped back down to the lightweight division	
Aug 27,	1898	**Mysterious Billy Smith** w pts 25 Matty Matthews (US)	New York, NY
		With this victory Smith, who had outpointed Green in an overweight match a month earlier, was generally accepted as champion	
Oct 7,	1898	Mysterious Billy Smith w pts 25 Charley McKeever (US)	New York, NY
Dec 6,	1898	Mysterious Billy Smith w pts 20 Joe Walcott	New York, NY
		Although the match was made at 145lb, Smith's victory helped consolidate his claim to the title	
Mar 10,	1899	Mysterious Billy Smith w rsf 14 George Lavigne (US)	San Francisco, CA
Apr 17,	1900	**Matty Matthews** w ko 19 Mysterious Billy Smith	New York, NY
Jun 5,	1900	**Eddie Connolly** (Can) w pts 25 Matty Matthews	Brooklyn, NY
Aug 13,	1900	**Jim "Rube" Ferns** (US) w rtd 15 Eddie Connolly	Buffalo, NY
Oct 16,	1900	**Matty Matthews** w pts 15 Jim "Rube" Ferns	Detroit, MI
Apr 20,	1901	Matty Matthews w pts 20 Tom Couhig (US)	Louisville, KY
May 24,	1901	**Jim "Rube" Ferns** w ko 10 Matty Matthews	Toronto (Can)
Sep 23,	1901	Jim "Rube" Ferns w ko 9 Frank Erne (US)	Fort Erie (Can)
Dec 18,	1901	**Joe Walcott** w rsf 5 Jim "Rube" Ferns	Fort Erie (Can)
Sep 5,	1904	Joe Walcott drew 15 Sam Langford (US)	Manchester, NH
Sep 30,	1904	Joe Walcott drew 20 Joe Gans (US)	San Francisco, CA
Jul 10,	1906	Joe Walcott w ko 8 Jack Dougherty (US)	Chelsea, MA
Sep 29,	1906	Joe Walcott drew 20 Billy Rhodes (US)	Kansas City, KS
Nov 29,	1906	**Honey Mellody** (US) w rsf 12 Joe Walcott	Chelsea, MA
Apr 23,	1907	**Mike "Twin" Sullivan** w pts 20 Honey Mellody	Los Angeles, CA
		The title was in dispute during this period with Sullivan, Frank Mantell and Harry Lewis calling themselves champion, with varying degrees of authenticity. Sullivan relinquished his claim in April 1908 because of weight problems, and Lewis, who had beaten Mellody and Mantell, became accepted as champion at the division's new limit of 147lb	
Feb 19,	1910	**Harry Lewis** (US) drew 25 Willie Lewis (US)	Paris (Fra)
Apr 23,	1910	Harry Lewis drew 25 Willie Lewis	Paris (Fra)
May 4,	1910	Harry Lewis w ko 3 Peter Brown (Eng)	Paris (Fra)
Jun 27,	1910	Harry Lewis w rtd 7 Harry "Young" Joseph (Eng)	London (Eng)
Feb	1911	*Lewis gave up the title to box at middleweight*	
Nov 9,	1911	**Dixie Kid** (US) w ko 2 Johnny Summers (Eng)	Liverpool (Eng)
Apr 24,	1912	Dixie Kid w rtd 11 George Bernard (Fra)	Paris (Fra)
Oct 4,	1912	**Marcel Thomas** (Fra) w pts 15 Dixie Kid	Paris (Fra)
		For IBU version of title	
Jul 22,	1913	**Mike Glover** (US) w rsf 4 Marcel Thomas	Boston, MA
		Glover was widely accepted in America and Europe as champion, but a separate version of the title was contested in Australia	

Australian version

Jan 1,	1914	**Waldemar Holberg** (Den) w pts 20 Ray Bronson (US)	Melbourne (Aus)
Jan 24,	1914	**Tom McCormick** (Eng) w dis 6 Waldemar Holberg	Melbourne (Aus)
Mar 21,	1914	**Matt Wells** (Eng) w pts 20 Tom McCormick	Sydney (Aus)

World title

Jun 1,	1915	**Mike Glover** w pts 12 Matt Wells	Boston, MA
		Glover lost his claim to the title when he was outpointed over 12 rounds by Jack Britton (US) in Boston on June 26, 1915, although the fight was not billed as for the championship and no weights were announced. The title was variously claimed by Britton, Ted "Kid" Lewis and Eddie Moha (US), with Britton finally gaining acceptance by beating Lewis	
Apr 24,	1916	**Jack Britton** w pts 20 Ted "Kid" Lewis (Eng)	New Orleans, LA
Oct 17,	1916	Jack Britton w pts 12 Ted "Kid" Lewis	Boston, MA
Nov 21,	1916	Jack Britton w pts 12 Charlie White (US)	Boston, MA
Jun 25,	1917	**Ted "Kid" Lewis** w pts 20 Jack Britton	Dayton, OH
May 17,	1918	Ted "Kid" Lewis w pts 20 Johnny Tillman (US)	Denver, CO
Mar 17,	1919	**Jack Britton** w ko 9 Ted "Kid" Lewis	Canton, OH
Aug 23,	1920	Jack Briton drew 12 Lou Bogash (US)	Bridgeport, CT
Feb 7,	1921	Jack Britton w pts 15 Ted "Kid" Lewis	New York, NY
Feb 17,	1922	Jack Britton drew 15 Dave Shade (US)	New York, NY
Jun 26,	1922	Jack Britton w dis 13 Benny Leonard (US)	New York, NY
Oct 10,	1922	Jack Britton w pts 12 Jimmy Kelly (US)	Havana (Cub)
Nov 1,	1922	**Mickey Walker** (US) w pts 15 Jack Britton	New York, NY
Jun 6,	1923	*The New York Commission stripped Walker for his failure to defend against Dave Shade, whom they proclaimed champion*	
Jul 27,	1923	**Jimmy Jones** (US) w pts 10 Dave Shade	Boston, MA
		For New York title	
Oct 11,	1923	*The NY Commission withdrew recognition from Jones, after he and Mickey Walker had both been disqualified for "not trying" in their overweight match in Newark three days earlier*	
Jun 2,	1924	**Mickey Walker** w pts 10 Lew Tendler (US)	Philadelphia, PA
Oct 1,	1924	Mickey Walker w ko 6 Bobby Barrett (US)	Philadelphia, PA
Sep 21,	1925	Mickey Walker w pts 15 Dave Shade	New York, NY
May 20,	1926	**Pete Latzo** (US) w pts 10 Mickey Walker	Scranton, PA
Jul 9,	1926	Pete Latzo w dis 4 George Levine (US)	New York, NY
Jun 3,	1927	**Joe Dundee** (US) w pts 15 Pete Latzo	New York, NY
Jul 13,	1927	Joe Dundee w pts 10 Billy Drako (US)	Cincinnati, OH
Sep	1928	*Dundee was stripped by the NBA for failing to defend against Young Jack Thompson (who had stopped him in two rounds in an overweight match on August 30, 1928) or Jackie Fields*	
Mar 25,	1929	**Jackie Fields** (US) w pts 10 Young Jack Thompson (US)	Chicago, IL
		For vacant NBA title	
Jul 25,	1929	Jackie Fields w dis 2 Joe Dundee	Detroit, MI
		For undisputed title	
May 9,	1930	**Young Jack Thompson** w pts 15 Jackie Fields	Detroit, MI
Sep 5,	1930	**Tommy Freeman** (US) w pts 15 Young Jack Thompson	Cleveland, OH
Apr 14,	1931	**Young Jack Thompson** w rtd 12 Tommy Freeman	Cleveland, OH
Oct 23,	1931	**Lou Brouillard** (Can) w pts 15 Young Jack Thompson	Boston, MA
Jan 28,	1932	**Jackie Fields** w pts 10 Lou Brouillard	Chicago, IL
Feb 22,	1933	**Young Corbett III** (US) w pts 10 Jackie Fields	San Francisco, CA
May 29,	1933	**Jimmy McLarnin** (Ire) w ko 1 Young Corbett III	Los Angeles, CA
May 28,	1934	**Barney Ross** (US) w pts 15 Jimmy McLarnin	New York, NY
Sep 17,	1934	**Jimmy McLarnin** w pts 15 Barney Ross	New York, NY
May 28,	1935	**Barney Ross** w pts 15 Jimmy McLarnin	New York, NY
Nov 27,	1936	Barney Ross w pts 15 Izzy Jannazzo (US)	New York, NY
Sep 23,	1937	Barney Ross w pts 15 Ceferino Garcia (Phil)	New York, NY
Jan	1938	*The IBU withdrew recognition from Ross in favour of Felix Wouters (Bel) who outpointed Gustav Eder (Ger) over 15 rounds in Brussels on February 16, 1938*	
May	1938	*The IBU agreed to recognize Ross again, in the interests of unity*	
May 31,	1938	**Henry Armstrong** (US) w pts 15 Barney Ross	New York, NY
Nov 25,	1938	Henry Armstrong w pts 15 Ceferino Garcia	New York, NY

Dec 5, 1938	Henry Armstrong w rsf 3 Al Manfredo (US)	Cleveland, OH
Jan 10, 1939	Henry Armstrong w pts 10 Baby Arizmendi (Mex)	Los Angeles, CA
Mar 4, 1939	Henry Armstrong w rsf 4 Bobby Pacho (US)	Havana (Cub)
Mar 16, 1939	Henry Armstrong w ko 1 Lew Feldman (US)	St Louis, MO
	Armstrong's lightweight title was also at stake	
Mar 31, 1939	Henry Armstrong w ko 12 Davey Day (US)	New York, NY
May 25, 1939	Henry Armstrong w pts 15 Ernie Roderick (Eng)	London (Eng)
Oct 9, 1939	Henry Armstrong w rsf 4 Al Manfredo	Des Moines, IA
Oct 13, 1939	Henry Armstrong w ko 2 Howard Scott (US)	Minneapolis, MN
Oct 20, 1939	Henry Armstrong w ko 3 Richie Fontaine (US)	Seattle, WA
Oct 24, 1939	Henry Armstrong w pts 10 Jimmy Garrison (US)	New York, NY
Oct 30, 1939	Henry Armstrong w rsf 4 Bobby Pacho	Denver, CO
Dec 11, 1939	Henry Armstrong w ko 7 Jimmy Garrison	Cleveland, OH
Jan 4, 1940	Henry Armstrong w ko 5 Joe Ghnouly (US)	St Louis, MO
Jan 24, 1940	Henry Armstrong w rsf 9 Pedro Montanez (PR)	New York, NY
Apr 26, 1940	Henry Armstrong w rsf 7 Paul Junior (Can)	Boston, MA
May 24, 1940	Henry Armstrong w rsf 5 Ralph Zanelli (US)	Boston, MA
Jun 21, 1940	Henry Armstrong w rsf 3 Paul Junior	Portland, ME
Sep 23, 1940	Henry Armstrong w ko 4 Phil Furr (US)	Washington, DC
Oct 4, 1940	**Fritzie Zivic (US)** w pts 15 Henry Armstrong	New York, NY
Jan 17, 1941	Fritzie Zivic w rsf 12 Henry Armstrong	New York, NY
Jul 21, 1941	**Freddie (Red) Cochrane** (US) w pts 15 Fritzie Zivic	Newark, NJ
Feb 1, 1946	**Marty Servo** w ko 4 Freddie (Red) Cochrane	New York, NY
Sep 25, 1946	*Servo retired*	
Dec 20, 1946	**Sugar Ray Robinson** (US) w pts 15 Tommy Bell (US)	New York, NY
	For vacant title	
Jun 24, 1947	Sugar Ray Robinson w rsf 8 Jimmy Doyle (US)	Cleveland, OH
Dec 19, 1947	Sugar Ray Robinson w rsf 6 Chuck Taylor (US)	Detroit, MI
Jun 28, 1948	Sugar Ray Robinson w pts 15 Bernard Docusen (US)	Chicago, IL
Jul 11, 1949	Sugar Ray Robinson w pts 15 Kid Gavilan (Cub)	Philadelphia, PA
Aug 9, 1950	Sugar Ray Robinson w pts 15 Charlie Fusari (US)	Jersey City, NJ
Feb 15, 1951	*Robinson gave up welterweight title on becoming middleweight champion*	
Mar 14, 1951	**Johnny Bratton** (US) w pts 15 Charlie Fusari	Chicago, IL
	For vacant NBA title	
May 18, 1951	**Kid Gavilan** w pts 15 Johnny Bratton	New York, NY
	For undisputed title	
Aug 29, 1951	Kid Gavilan w pts 15 Billy Graham (US)	New York, NY
Feb 4, 1952	Kid Gavilan w pts 15 Bobby Dykes (US)	Miami, FL
Jul 7, 1952	Kid Gavilan w rsf 11 Gil Turner (US)	Philadelphia, PA
Oct 5, 1952	Kid Gavilan w pts 15 Billy Graham	Havana (Cub)
Feb 11, 1953	Kid Gavilan w rtd 9 Chuck Davey (US)	Chicago, IL
Sep 18, 1953	Kid Gavilan w pts 15 Carmen Basilio (US)	Syracuse, NY
Nov 13, 1953	Kid Gavilan w pts 15 Johnny Bratton	Chicago, IL
Oct 20, 1954	**Johnny Saxton** (US) w pts 15 Kid Gavilan	Philadelphia, PA
Apr 1, 1955	**Tony DeMarco** (US) w rsf 14 Johnny Saxton	Boston, MA
Jun 10, 1955	**Carmen Basilio** w rsf 12 Tony DeMarco	Syracuse, NY
Nov 30, 1955	Carmen Basilio w rsf 12 Tony DeMarco	Boston, MA
Mar 14, 1956	**Johnny Saxton** w pts 15 Carmen Basilio	Chicago, IL
Sep 12, 1956	**Carmen Basilio** w rsf 9 Johnny Saxton	Syracuse, NY
Feb 22, 1957	Carmen Basilio w ko 2 Johnny Saxton	Cleveland, OH
Sep 1957	*Basilio relinquished the title on winning the middleweight championship*	
Jun 6, 1958	**Virgil Akins** (US) w rsf 4 Vince Martinez (US)	St Louis, MO
	For vacant title	
Dec 5, 1958	**Don Jordan** (US) w pts 15 Virgil Akins	Los Angeles, CA
Apr 24, 1959	Don Jordan w pts 15 Virgil Akins	St Louis, MO
Jul 10, 1959	Don Jordan w pts 15 Denny Moyer (US)	Portland, ME
May 27, 1960	**Benny (Kid) Paret** (Cub) w pts 15 Don Jordan	Las Vegas, NV
Dec 10, 1960	Benny (Kid) Paret w pts 15 Federico Thompson (Pan)	New York, NY
Apr 1, 1961	**Emile Griffith** (VI) w ko 13 Benny (Kid) Paret	Miami, FL
Jun 3, 1961	Emile Griffith w rsf 12 Gaspar Ortega (Mex)	Los Angeles, CA
Sep 30, 1961	**Benny (Kid) Paret** w pts 15 Emile Griffith	New York, NY
Mar 24, 1962	**Emile Griffith** w rsf 12 Benny (Kid) Paret	New York, NY
Jul 13, 1962	Emile Griffith w pts 15 Ralph Dupas (US)	Las Vegas, NV
Dec 8, 1962	Emile Griffith w rtd 9 Jorge Fernandez (Arg)	Las Vegas, NV
Mar 21, 1963	**Luis Rodriguez** (Cub) w pts 15 Emile Griffith	Los Angeles, CA
Jun 8, 1963	**Emile Griffith** w pts 15 Luis Rodriguez	New York, NY
Jun 12, 1964	Emile Griffith w pts 15 Luis Rodriguez	Las Vegas, NV
Sep 22, 1964	Emile Griffith w pts 15 Brian Curvis (Wal)	London (Eng)
Mar 30, 1965	Emile Griffith w pts 15 Jose Stable (Cub)	New York, NY
Dec 10, 1965	Emile Griffith w pts 15 Manny Gonzalez (US)	New York, NY
Apr 1966	*Griffith relinquished the title on winning the middleweight championship*	
Aug 24, 1966	**Curtis Cokes** (US) w pts 15 Manny Gonzalez	New Orleans, LA
	For vacant WBA title	
Nov 28, 1966	Curtis Cokes w pts 15 Jean Josselin (Fra)	Dallas, TX
	For undisputed title	
May 19, 1967	Curtis Cokes w rsf 10 Francois Pavilla (Fra)	Dallas, TX
Oct 2, 1967	Curtis Cokes w rsf 8 Charlie Shipes (US)	Oakland, CA
Apr 16, 1968	Curtis Cokes w rsf 5 Willie Ludick (SA)	Dallas, TX
Oct 21, 1968	Curtis Cokes w pts 15 Ramon La Cruz (Arg)	New Orleans, LA
Apr 18, 1969	**Jose Napoles** (Cub) w rsf 13 Curtis Cokes	Inglewood, CA
Jun 29, 1969	Jose Napoles w rtd 10 Curtis Cokes	Mexico City (Mex)
Oct 17, 1969	Jose Napoles w pts 15 Emile Griffith	Inglewood, CA
Feb 15, 1970	Jose Napoles w rsf 15 Ernie Lopez (US)	Los Angeles, CA
Dec 3, 1970	**Billy Backus** (US) w rsf 4 Jose Napoles	Syracuse, NY
Jun 4, 1971	**Jose Napoles** w rsf 8 Billy Backus	Inglewood, CA
Dec 14, 1971	Jose Napoles w pts 15 Hedgemon Lewis (US)	Inglewood, CA
Mar 28, 1972	Jose Napoles w ko 7 Ralph Charles (Eng)	Wembley (Eng)
Jun 10, 1972	Jose Napoles w rsf 2 Adolph Pruitt (US)	Monterrey (Mex)
May 1972	*The NY Commission stripped Napoles for refusing to meet Backus again*	
Jun 16, 1972	**Hedgemon Lewis** w pts 15 Billy Backus	Syracuse, NY
	For vacant NY version of title	
Dec 8, 1972	Hedgemon Lewis w pts 15 Billy Backus	Syracuse, NY
Feb 28, 1973	Jose Napoles w ko 7 Ernie Lopez	Inglewood, CA
Jun 23, 1973	Jose Napoles w pts 15 Roger Menetrey (Fra)	Grenoble (Fra)
Sep 22, 1973	Jose Napoles w pts 15 Clyde Gray (Can)	Toronto (Can)
Aug 3, 1974	Jose Napoles w rsf 9 Hedgemon Lewis	Mexico City (Mex)
	For undisputed title	
Dec 14, 1974	Jose Napoles w ko 3 Horacio Saldano (Arg)	Mexico City (Mex)
Mar 30, 1975	Jose Napoles w tech dec 12 Armando Muniz (US)	Acapulco (Mex)
May 14, 1975	*Napoles announced he would relinquish WBA title to concentrate on defending the WBC version*	

WBC title

Jul 12, 1975	**Jose Napoles** w pts 15 Armando Muniz	Mexico City (Mex)
Dec 6, 1975	**John H. Stracey** (Eng) w rsf 6 Jose Napoles	Mexico City (Mex)
Mar 20, 1976	John H. Stracey w rsf 10 Hedgemon Lewis	Wembley (Eng)
Jun 22, 1976	**Carlos Palomino** (US) w rsf 12 John H. Stracey	Wembley (Eng)
Jan 22, 1977	Carlos Palomino w rsf 15 Armando Muniz	Los Angeles, CA
Jun 14, 1977	Carlos Palomino w ko 11 Dave Green (Eng)	Wembley (Eng)
Sep 13, 1977	Carlos Palomino w pts 15 Everaldo Costa Azevedo (Bra)	Los Angeles, CA
Dec 10, 1977	Carlos Palomino w ko 13 Jose Palacios (Mex)	Los Angeles, CA
Feb 11, 1978	Carlos Palomino w ko 7 Ryu Sorimachi (Jap)	Las Vegas, NV
Mar 18, 1978	Carlos Palomino w rsf 9 Mimoun Mohatar (Mor)	Las Vegas, NV
May 27, 1978	Carlos Palomino w pts 15 Armando Muniz	Los Angeles, CA
Jan 14, 1979	**Wilfred Benitez** (PR) w pts 15 Carlos Palomino	San Juan, CA
Mar 25, 1979	Wilfred Benitez w pts 15 Harold Weston (US)	San Juan, CA
Nov 30, 1979	**Sugar Ray Leonard** (US) w rsf 15 Wilfred Benitez	Las Vegas, NV
Mar 31, 1980	Sugar Ray Leonard w ko 4 Dave Green	Landover, MD
Jun 20, 1980	**Roberto Duran** (Pan) w pts 15 Sugar Ray Leonard	Montreal (Can)
Nov 25, 1980	**Sugar Ray Leonard** w rtd 8 Roberto Duran	New Orleans, LA
Mar 28, 1981	Sugar Ray Leonard w rsf 10 Larry Bonds (US)	Syracuse, NY
Sep 16, 1981	Sugar Ray Leonard w rsf 14 Thomas Hearns (US)	Las Vegas, NV
	For undisputed title	

WBA title

Jun 28, 1975	**Angel Espada** (PR) w pts 15 Clyde Gray	San Juan, CA
	For vacant title	
Oct 11, 1975	Angel Espada w pts 15 Johnny Gant (US)	San Juan, CA
Jul 17, 1976	**Jose Pipino Cuevas** (Mex) w rsf 2 Angel Espada	Mexicali (Mex)
Oct 27, 1976	Jose Pipino Cuevas w ko 2 Shoji Tsujimoto (Jap)	Kanazawa (Jap)
Mar 12, 1977	Jose Pipino Cuevas w ko 2 Miguel Campanino (Arg)	Mexico City (Mex)
Aug 6, 1977	Jose Pipino Cuevas w ko 2 Clyde Gray	Los Angeles, CA
Nov 19, 1977	Jose Pipino Cuevas w rsf 11 Angel Espada	San Juan, CA
Mar 4, 1978	Jose Pipino Cuevas w rsf 9 Harold Weston (US)	Los Angeles, CA
May 20, 1978	Jose Pipino Cuevas w rsf 1 Billy Backus	Los Angeles, CA
Sep 9, 1978	Jose Pipino Cuevas w rsf 2 Pete Ranzany (US)	Sacramento, CA
Jan 29, 1979	Jose Pipino Cuevas w rsf 2 Scott Clark (US)	Los Angeles, CA
Jul 30, 1979	Jose Pipino Cuevas w pts 15 Randy Shields (US)	Chicago, IL
Dec 8, 1979	Jose Pipino Cuevas w rsf 10 Angel Espada	Los Angeles, CA
Apr 6, 1980	Jose Pipino Cuevas w ko 5 Harold Volbrecht (SA)	Houston, TX
Aug 2, 1980	**Thomas Hearns** w rsf 2 Jose Pipino Cuevas	Detroit, MI
Dec 6, 1980	Thomas Hearns w ko 6 Luis Primera (Ven)	Detroit, MI
Apr 25, 1981	Thomas Hearns w rsf 12 Randy Shields	Phoenix, AZ
Jun 25, 1981	Thomas Hearns w rsf 4 Pablo Baez (US)	Houston, TX
Sep 16, 1981	**Sugar Ray Leonard** w rsf 14 Thomas Hearns	Las Vegas, NV
	For undisputed title	

Undisputed title

Feb 5, 1982	**Sugar Ray Leonard** w rsf 3 Bruce Finch (US)	Reno, NV
Nov 1982	*Leonard retired as undisputed champion*	

WBA title

Feb 13, 1983	**Don Curry** (US) w pts 15 Junsok Hwang (Kor)	Fort Worth, TX
Sep 3, 1983	Don Curry w rsf 1 Roger Stafford (US)	Marsala (Ita)

Feb 4,	1984	Don Curry w pts 15 Marlon Starling (US)	Atlantic City, NJ
Apr 21,	1984	Don Curry w rtd 7 Elio Diaz (Ven)	Fort Worth, TX
Sep 22,	1984	Don Curry w rsf 6 Nino LaRocca (Ita)	Monte Carlo (Mon)
Jan 19,	1985	Don Curry w rsf 4 Colin Jones (Wal)	Birmingham (Eng)
Dec 6,	1985	Don Curry w ko 2 Milton McCrory (US)	Las Vegas, NV
		For undisputed title	

WBC title

Mar 19,	1983	**Milton McCrory** drew 12 Colin Jones	Reno, NV
Aug 13,	1983	Milton McCrory w pts 12 Colin Jones	Las Vegas, NV
Jan 14,	1984	Milton McCrory w rsf 6 Milton Guest (US)	Detroit, MI
Apr 15,	1984	Milton McCrory w rsf 6 Gilles Ebilia (Fra)	Detroit, MI
Mar 9,	1985	Milton McCrory w pts 12 Pedro Villela (PR)	Paris (Fra)
Jul 14,	1985	Milton McCrory w rsf 3 Carlos Trujillo (Pan)	Monte Carlo (Mon)
Dec 6,	1985	**Don Curry** w ko 2 Milton McCrory	Las Vegas, NV
		For undisputed title	

Undisputed title

Mar 9,	1986	**Don Curry** w ko 2 Eduardo Rodriguez (Pan)	Fort Worth, TX
Sep 27,	1986	**Lloyd Honeyghan** (Eng) w rtd 6 Don Curry	Atlantic City, NJ
Dec	1986	*Honeyghan relinquished the WBA title rather than defend against the official challenger, Harold Volbrecht of South Africa. He continued to be recognized by the WBC and the IBF*	

WBC/IBF titles

Feb 22,	1987	**Lloyd Honeyghan** w rsf 2 Johnny Bumphus (US)	Wembley (Eng)
Apr 18,	1987	Lloyd Honeyghan w pts 12 Maurice Blocker (US)	London (Eng)
Aug 30,	1987	Lloyd Honeyghan w rsf 1 Gene Hatcher (US)	Marbella (Sp)
Oct 28,	1987	**Jorge Vaca** (Mex) w tech dec 8 Lloyd Honeyghan	Wembley (Eng)
		The IBF withdrew recognition from Vaca as the bout had been scheduled for 12 rounds rather than their championship distance, which was still 15 rounds	

WBA title

Feb 6,	1987	**Mark Breland** (US) w ko 7 Harold Volbrecht	Atlantic City, NJ
		For vacant title	
Aug 22,	1987	**Marlon Starling** (US) w ko 11 Mark Breland	Columbia, SC
Feb 5,	1988	Marlon Starling w pts 12 Fujio Ozaki (Jap)	Atlantic City, NJ
Apr 16,	1988	Marlon Starling drew 12 Mark Breland	Las Vegas, NV
Jul 29,	1988	**Thomas Molinares** (Col) w ko 6 Marlon Starling	Atlantic City, NJ
Jan	1989	*Molinares was stripped of the title because of his inability to make the weight*	
Feb 5,	1989	**Mark Breland** w rsf 1 Seung-Soon Lee (Kor)	Las Vegas, NV
		For vacant title	
Apr 22,	1989	Mark Breland w rsf 5 Rafael Pineda (Col)	Atlantic City, NJ
Oct 13,	1989	Mark Breland w rsf 2 Mauro Martelli (Swi)	Geneva (Swi)
Dec 10,	1989	Mark Breland w rsf 4 Fujio Ozaki	Tokyo (Jap)
Mar 3,	1990	Mark Breland w rsf 3 Lloyd Honeyghan	Wembley (Eng)
Jul 8,	1990	**Aaron Davis** w ko 9 Mark Breland	Reno, NV
Jan 19,	1991	**Meldrick Taylor** (US) w pts 12 Aaron Davis	Atlantic City, NJ
Jun 1,	1991	Meldrick Taylor w pts 12 Luis Garcia (Ven)	Palm Springs, CA
Jan 18,	1992	Meldrick Taylor w pts 12 Glenwood Brown (US)	Atlantic City, NJ
Oct 31,	1992	**Crisanto Espana** (Ven) w rsf 8 Meldrick Taylor	London (Eng)
May 5,	1993	Crisanto Espana w pts 12 Rodolfo Aguilar (Pan)	Belfast (N. Ire)
Oct 9,	1993	Crisanto Espana w rsf 10 Donovan Boucher (Can)	Manchester (Eng)
Jun 4,	1994	**Ike Quartey** (Gha) w rsf 11 Crisanto Espana	Levallois Perret, Paris (Fra)
Oct 1,	1994	Ike Quartey w ko 5 Alberto Cortes (Arg)	Carpentras (Fra)
Mar 4,	1995	Ike Quartey w rsf 4 Jung-Oh Park (Kor)	Atlantic City, NJ
Aug 23,	1995	Ike Quartey w rsf 4 Andrew Murray (Guy)	Le Cannet (Fra)
Apr 12,	1996	Ike Quartey w rsf 3 Vince Phillips (US)	St Maarten, Netherlands Antilles
Oct 4,	1996	Ike Quartey w pts 12 Oba Carr (US)	New York, NY
Apr 18,	1997	Ike Quartey w rsf 5 Ralph Jones (US)	Las Vegas, NV
Oct 17,	1997	Ike Quartey drew 12 Jose Luis Lopez (Mex)	Ledyard, CT
		Quartey stripped of WBA title for taking fight with Oscar De La Hoya for WBC title	
Oct 10,	1998	**James Page** w ko 2 Andrei Pestraiev (Rus)	Paris (Fra)
		For vacant title	
Dec 5,	1998	James Page w pts 12 Jose Luis Lopez	Atlantic City, NJ
Mar 13,	1999	James Page w pts 12 Sam Garr (US)	New York, NY
Jul 24,	1999	James Page w rsf 11 Freddie Pendleton (US)	Las Vegas, NV
Sep	2000	*Page was stripped of the title because of contractual problems.*	
Feb 17,	2001	**Andrew Lewis** (Guy) w rsf 7 James Page (US)	Las Vegas, NV
Apr 28,	2001	Andrew Lewis w pts 12 Larry Marks (US)	New York, NY
Jul 28,	2001	Andrew Lewis nc 2 Ricardo Mayorga (Nic)	Los Angeles, CA
Mar 30,	2002	**Ricardo Mayorga** w rsf 5 Andrew Lewis	Reading, PA
Jan 25,	2003	Ricardo Mayorga w rsf 3 Vernon Forrest (US)	Temecula, CA
Jul 12,	2003	Ricardo Mayorga w pts 12 Vernon Forrest	Las Vegas, NV

WBC title

Mar 29,	1988	**Lloyd Honeyghan** w ko 3 Jorge Vaca	Wembley (Eng)
Jul 29,	1988	Lloyd Honeyghan w rtd 5 Yung-Kil Chang (Kor)	Atlantic City, NJ
Feb 5,	1989	**Marlon Starling** w rsf 9 Lloyd Honeyghan	Las Vegas, NV
Aug 15,	1989	Marlon Starling w pts 12 Yung-Kil Chung (Kor)	Hartford, CT
Aug 19,	1990	**Maurice Blocker** w pts 12 Marlon Starling	Reno, NV
Mar 18,	1991	**Simon Brown** (Jam) w rsf 10 Maurice Blocker	Las Vegas, NV
Nov 29,	1991	**James "Buddy" McGirt** (US) w pts 12 Simon Brown	Las Vegas, NV
Jun 25,	1992	James "Buddy" McGirt w pts 12 Patrizio Oliva (Ita)	Naples (Ita)
Jan 12,	1993	James "Buddy" McGirt w pts 12 Genaro Leon (Mex)	New York, NY
Mar 6,	1993	**Pernell Whitaker** (US) w pts 12 James "Buddy" McGirt	New York, NY
Sep 10,	1993	Pernell Whitaker drew 12 Julio Cesar Chavez (Mex)	San Antonio, TX
Apr 9,	1994	Pernell Whitaker w pts 12 Santos Cardona (PR)	Norfolk, VA
Oct 1,	1994	Pernell Whitaker w pts 12 James "Buddy" McGirt	Norfolk, VA
Aug 26,	1995	Pernell Whitaker w pts 12 Gary Jacobs (Sco)	Atlantic City, NJ
Nov 17,	1995	Pernell Whitaker w ko 6 Jake Rodriguez (US)	Atlantic City, NJ
Apr 12	1996	Pernell Whitaker w pts 12 Wilfredo Rivera (PR)	St Maarten, (Neth. Ant)
Sep 20,	1996	Pernell Whitaker w pts 12 Wilfredo Rivera	Miami, FL
Jan 24,	1997	Pernell Whitaker w rsf 11 Diobelys Hurtado (Cub)	Atlantic City, NJ
Apr 12,	1997	**Oscar De La Hoya** (US) w pts 12 Pernell Whitaker	Las Vegas, NV
Jun 14,	1997	Oscar De La Hoya w ko 2 David Kamau (Ken)	San Antonio, TX
Sep 13,	1997	Oscar De La Hoya w pts 12 Hector Camacho (PR)	Las Vegas, NV
Dec 6,	1997	Oscar De La Hoya w rsf 8 Wilfredo Rivera	Atlantic City, NJ
Jun 13,	1998	Oscar De La Hoya w rsf 3 Patrick Charpentier (Fra)	El Paso, TX
Sep 18,	1998	Oscar De La Hoya w rtd 8 Julio Cesar Chavez	Las Vegas, NV
Feb 13,	1999	Oscar De La Hoya w pts 12 Ike Quartey (Gha)	Las Vegas, NV
May 22,	1999	Oscar De La Hoya w rsf 11 Oba Carr (US)	Las Vegas, NV
		De La Hoya went on to fight in an IBF/WBC unification bout against Felix Trinidad on Sep 18, 1999 in Las Vegas	

IBF title

Apr 23,	1988	**Simon Brown** (Jam) w rsf 14 Tyrone Trice (US)	Berck-sur-Mer (Fra)
		For vacant title	
Jul 16,	1988	Simon Brown w rsf 3 Jorge Vaca	Kingston (Jam)
Oct 14,	1988	Simon Brown w pts 12 Mauro Martelli	Lausanne (Swi)
Feb 18,	1989	Simon Brown w rsf 3 Jorge Maysonet (PR)	Budapest (Hun)
Apr 27,	1989	Simon Brown w ko 7 Al Long (US)	Washington, DC
Sep 20,	1989	Simon Brown w rsf 2 Bobby Joe Young (US)	Rochester, NY
Nov 9,	1989	Simon Brown w pts 12 Luis Santana (DR)	Springfield, MA
Apr 1,	1990	Simon Brown w rsf 10 Tyrone Trice	Washington, DC
Mar	1991	*Brown relinquished the IBF title to challenge for the WBC version*	
Oct 4,	1991	**Maurice Blocker** w pts 12 Glenwood Brown (US)	Atlantic City, NJ
		For vacant title	
Aug 28,	1992	Maurice Blocker w pts 12 Luis Garcia (Ven)	Atlantic City, NJ
Jun 19,	1993	**Felix Trinidad** (PR) w ko 2 Maurice Blocker	San Diego, CA
Aug 6,	1993	Felix Trinidad w rsf 1 Luis Garcia	Bayamon (PR)
Oct 23,	1993	Felix Trinidad w ko 10 Anthony Stephens (US)	Fort Lauderdale, FL
Jan 20,	1994	Felix Trinidad w pts 12 Hector Camacho (PR)	Las Vegas, NV
Sep 17,	1994	Felix Trinidad w rsf 4 Luis Ramon "Yori Boy" Campas (Mex)	Las Vegas, NV
Dec 10,	1994	Felix Trinidad w rsf 8 Oba Carr (US)	Monterrey (Mex)
Apr 8,	1995	Felix Trinidad w rsf 2 Roger Turner (US)	Las Vegas, NV
Nov 17,	1995	Felix Trinidad w ko 4 Larry Barnes (US)	Atlantic City, NJ
Feb 10,	1996	Felix Trinidad w rtd 4 Rodney Moore (US)	Las Vegas, NV
May 18,	1996	Felix Trinidad w ko 5 Freddie Pendleton (US)	Las Vegas, NV
Sep 7,	1996	Felix Trinidad w rsf 6 Ray Lovato (US)	Las Vegas, NV
Jan 11,	1997	Felix Trinidad w rsf 3 Kevin Lueshing (Eng)	Nashville, TN
Apr 3,	1998	Felix Trinidad w ko 4 Mahenge Zulu (Zai)	Bayamon (PR)
Feb 20,	1999	Felix Trinidad w pts 12 Pernell Whitaker	New York, NY
May 29,	1999	Felix Trinidad w rsf 4 Hugo Pineda (Col)	San Juan (PR)
		Trinidad then fought Oscar De La Hoya in an IBF/WBC unification bout	

IBF/WBC titles

Sep 18,	1999	**Felix Trinidad** w pts 12 Oscar De La Hoya	Las Vegas, NV
		IBF/WBC unification bout	
Mar	2000	*Trinidad moved up to light-middleweight and relinquished titles*	

WBC title

Sep	1999	*After losing the unification bout with Felix Trinidad, De La Hoya was reinstated as WBC champion when Trinidad moved up to light-middleweight*	
Jun 17,	2000	**Shane Mosley** (US) w pts 12 Oscar De La Hoya	Los Angeles, CA
Nov 4,	2000	Shane Mosley w rsf 6 Antonio Diaz (US)	New York, NY
Mar 10,	2001	Shane Mosley w rtd 5 Shannan Taylor (Aus)	Las Vegas, NV
Jul 21,	2001	Shane Mosley w ko 3 Adrian Stone (Eng)	Las Vegas, NV
Jan 26,	2002	**Vernon Forrest** w pts 12 Shane Mosley	New York, NY
Jul 20,	2002	Vernon Forrest w pts 12 Shane Mosley	Indianapolis, IN

Vernon Forrest lost the WBC title to Ricardo Mayorga in the Jan 2003 WBA/WBC unification fight. Mayorga then lost the titles to Cory Spinks

IBF title

Aug 26, 2000	**Vernon Forrest** nc 3 Raul Frank (US)	Las Vegas, NV
May 12, 2001	Vernon Forrest w pts 12 Raul Frank	New York, NY
	Forrest was stripped of the title for agreeing to a unification fight with Shane Mosley instead of boxing the No.1 contender	
Apr 13, 2002	**Michele Piccirillo** (Ita) w pts12 Cory Spinks (US)	Campione d'Italia (Ita)
	For vacant title	

WBO title

May 8, 1989	**Genaro Leon** (Mex) w ko 1 Danny Garcia (PR)	Santa Ana, CA
	For vacant title	
Oct 1989	*Leon gave up the WBO title*	
Dec 15, 1989	**Manning Galloway** (US) w pts 12 Al Hamza (US)	Yabucoa
	For vacant title	
Aug 25, 1990	Manning Galloway w pts 12 Nike Khumalo (SA)	Lewiston, MT
Feb 15, 1991	Manning Galloway w rtd 8 Gert Bo Jacobsen (Den)	Randers (Den)
May 17, 1991	Manning Galloway w rtd 7 Racheed Lawal (Den)	Copenhagen (Den)
Sep 15, 1991	Manning Galloway w pts 12 Jeff Malcolm (Aus)	Broadbeach (Aus)
Dec 14, 1991	Manning Galloway w pts 12 Nike Khumalo	Cape Town (SA)
Jul 25, 1992	Manning Galloway w pts 12 Pat Barrett (Eng)	Manchester (Eng)
Nov 27, 1992	Manning Galloway no contest 1 Gert Bo Jacobsen	Randers (Den)
Feb 12, 1993	**Gert Bo Jacobsen** w pts 12 Manning Galloway	Randers (Den)
Oct 1993	*Jacobsen relinquished the title*	
Oct 16, 1993	**Eamonn Loughran** (Ire) w pts 12 Lorenzo Smith (US)	Belfast (N. Ire)
	For vacant title	
Jan 22, 1994	Eamonn Loughran w pts 12 Alessandro Duran (Ita)	Belfast (N. Ire)
Dec 10, 1994	Eamonn Loughran w tech dec 5 Manning Galloway	Manchester (Eng)
May 27, 1995	Eamonn Loughran no contest 3 Angel Beltre (DR)	Belfast (N. Ire)
Aug 26, 1995	Eamonn Loughran w rsf 6 Tony Ganarelli (US)	Belfast (N. Ire)
Oct 7, 1995	Eamonn Loughran w pts 12 Angel Beltre	Belfast (N. Ire)
Apr 13, 1996	**Jose Luis Lopez** (Mex) w rsf 1 Eamonn Loughran	Liverpool (Eng)
Oct 6, 1996	Jose Luis Lopez w rtd 6 Yori Boy Campos	Los Angeles, CA
	Lopez was subsequently stripped of the title after failing a drugs test	
Feb 22, 1997	**Michael Loewe** (Rom) w pts 12 Santiago Samaniego (Pan)	Hamburg (Ger)
Sep 20, 1997	Michael Loewe w pts 12 Michael Carruth (Ire)	Aachen (Ger)
	Loewe relinquished title because of injury	
Feb 14, 1998	**Ahmed Katajev** (Rus) w pts 12 Leonard Townsend (US)	Stuttgart (Ger)
May 23, 1998	Ahmed Katajev w pts 12 Paulo Sanchez (Arg)	Offenburg (Ger)
Nov 28, 1998	Ahmed Katajev w pts 12 Santos Cardona (PR)	Lubeck (Ger)
Apr 24, 1999	Ahmed Katajev w ko 3 Peter Malinga (SA)	Munich (Ger)
	Katajev's surname changed to Kotiev	
Nov 27, 1999	Ahmed Kotiev w pts 12 Daniel Santos (PR)	Lubeck (Ger)
May 6, 2000	**Daniel Santos** w ko 5 Ahmed Kotiev	Neuss (Ger)
Jul 29, 2000	Daniel Santos w rsf 4 Giovanni Parisi (Ita)	Reggio Calabria (Ita)
Dec 16, 2000	Daniel Santos w ko 2 Neil Sinclair (NI)	Sheffield (Eng)
Jul 21, 2001	Daniel Santos nc 1 Antonio Margarito (Mex)	Bayamon (PR)
	Santos relinquished the title to box at light-middleweight	
Mar 16, 2002	**Antonio Margarito** (Mex) w rsf 10 Antonio Diaz (US)	Las Vegas, NV
Oct 12, 2002	Antonio Margarito w pts 12 Danny Perez (US)	Anaheim, CA
Feb 8, 2003	Antonio Margarito w rsf 2 Andrew Lewis (Guy)	Las Vegas, NV
Jan 31, 2004	Antonio Margarito w rsf 2 Hercules Kyvelos (Can)	Phoenix, AZ
Feb 18, 2005	Antonio Margarito w rsf 10 Sebastian Lujan (Arg)	Atlantic City, NJ
Apr 23, 2005	Antonio Margarito w rsf 5 Kermit Cintron (PR)	Las Vegas, NV
Feb 18, 2006	Antonio Margarito w rsf 1 Manuel Gomez (Mex)	Las Vegas, NV
Dec 2, 2006	Antonio Margarito w pts 12 Joshua Clottey (Gha)	Atlantic City, NJ
Jul 14, 2007	**Paul Williams** (US) w pts 12 Antonio Margarito	Carson, CA
Feb 9, 2008	**Carlos Quintana** (PR) w pts 12 Paul Williams	Temecula, CA
Jun 7, 2008	**Paul Williams** w rsf 1 Carlos Quintana	Uncasville, CT
	Williams relinquished the title to box at light-middleweight	
Feb 21, 2009	**Miguel Cotto** w rsf 5 Michael Jennings (Eng)	New York, NY
	For vacant title	
Jun 13, 2009	Miguel Cotto w pts 12 Joshua Clottey	New York, NY

PERNELL WHITAKER *(left) was the victim of a rank injustice when Julio Cesar Chavez was given a draw in their 1993 WBC title clash*

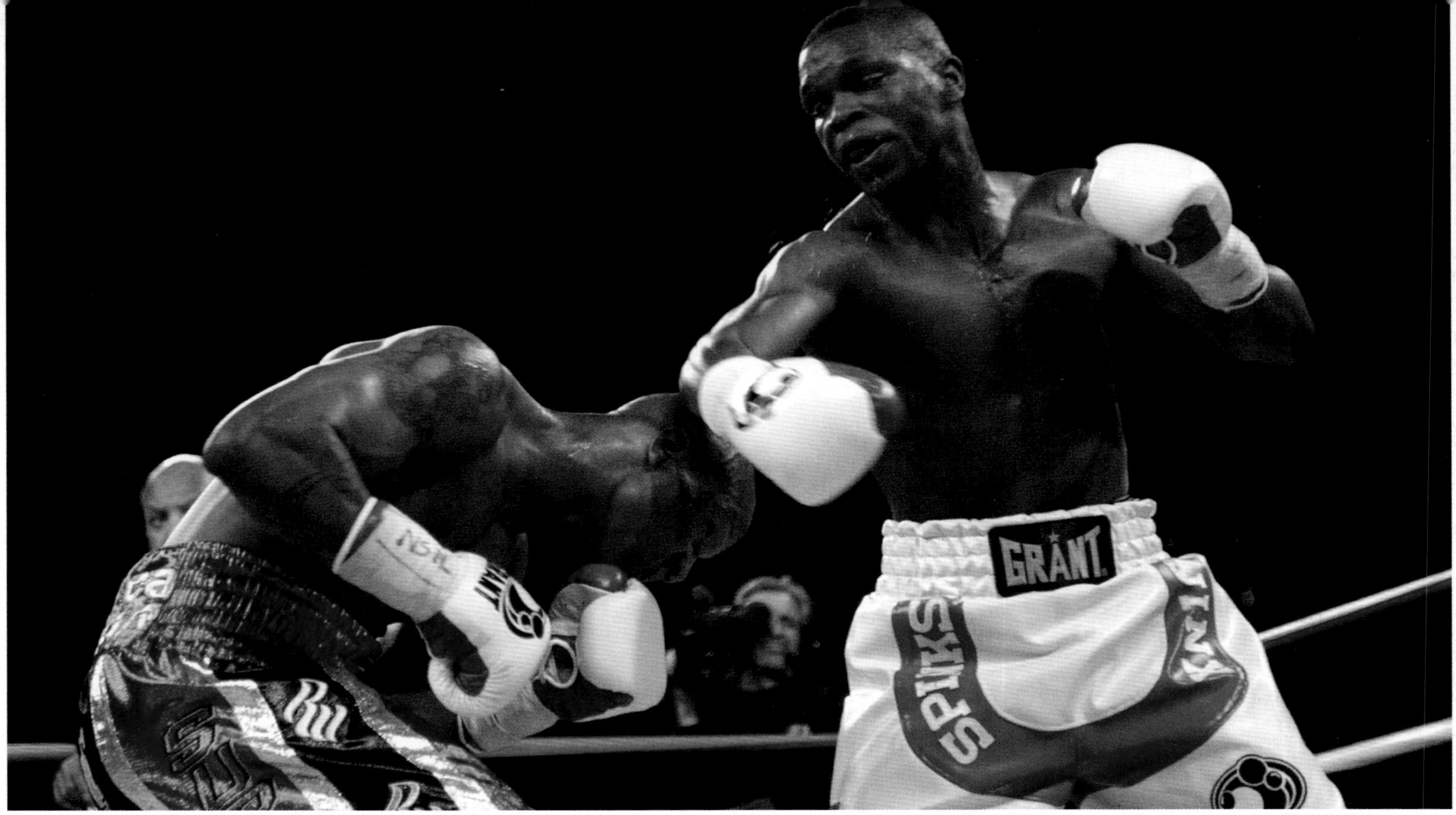

NEW GENERATION *Cory Spinks, whose father Leon and uncle Michael both were world heavyweight champs, defends his welterweight crown against Zab Judah*

Nov 14,	2009	**Manny Pacquiao** (Phi) w rsf 12 Miguel Cotto	Las Vegas, NV
Mar 13,	2010	Manny Pacquiao w pts 12 Joshua Clottey	Arlington, TX
May 7,	2011	Manny Pacquiao w pts 12 Shane Mosley	Las Vegas, NV
Nov 12,	2011	Manny Pacquiao w pts 12 Juan Manuel Marquez (Mex)	Las Vegas, NV
Jun 9,	2012	**Timothy Bradley** w pts 12 Manny Pacquiao	Las Vegas, NV
Mar 16,	2013	Timothy Bradley w pts 12 Ruslan Provodnikov (Rus)	Carson, CA
Oct 12,	2013	Timothy Bradley w pts 12 Juan Manuel Marquez	Las Vegas, NV
Apr 12,	2014	**Manny Pacquia**o w pts 12 Timothy Bradley	Las Vegas, NV
Nov 23,	2014	Manny Pacquiao w pts 12 Chris Algieri (US)	Macao (Chi)
		The WBO sanctioned the following for their Interim title	
Jun 27,	2015	Timothy Bradley w pts 12 Jessie Vargas (US)	Carson, CA

WBC/WBA/IBF titles

Dec 13,	2003	**Cory Spinks** (US) w pts 12 Ricardo Mayorga	Atlantic City, NJ
		WBC/WBA/IBF unification bout	
Apr 10,	2004	Cory Spinks w pts 12 Zab Judah (US)	Las Vegas, NV
Sep 4,	2004	Cory Spinks w pts 12 Miguel Angel Gonzalez (Mex)	Las Vegas, NV
Feb 5,	2005	**Zab Judah** w rsf 9 Cory Spinks	St Louis, MO
May 14,	2005	Zab Judah w rsf 3 Cosme Rivera (Mex)	Las Vegas, NV
	2005	*Judah stripped of WBA recognition*	

WBC/IBF titles

Jan 7,	2006	**Carlos Baldomir** (Arg) w pts 12 Zab Judah	New York, NY
		The IBF ignored this result and continued to recognize Judah	

WBC title

Jul 22,	2006	Carlos Baldomir w rsf 9 Arturo Gatti (Can)	Atlantic City, NJ
Nov 4,	2006	**Floyd Mayweather** Jr (US) w pts 12 Carlos Baldomir	Las Vegas, NV
Dec 8,	2007	Floyd Mayweather Jr w rsf 10 Ricky Hatton (Eng)	Las Vegas, NV
		Floyd Mayweather Jr announced his retirement	
Jun 21,	2008	**Andre Berto** (US) w rsf 7 Miguel Angel Rodriguez (Mex)	Memphis, TN
		For vacant title	
Sep 27,	2008	Andre Berto w pts 12 Steve Forbes (US)	Carson, CA
Jan 17,	2009	Andre Berto w pts 12 Luis Collazo	Biloxi, MS
May 30,	2009	Andre Berto w pts 12 Juan Urango (Col)	Hollywood, FL
Apr 10,	2010	Andre Berto w rsf 8 Carlos Quintana (PR)	Sunrise, FL
Nov 27,	2010	Andre Berto w rsf 1 Freddy Hernandez (Mex)	Las Vegas, NV
Apr 16,	2011	Victor Ortiz (US) w pts 12 Andre Berto	Mashantucket, CN
Sep 17,	2011	Floyd Mayweather Jr w ko 4 Victor Ortiz	Las Vegas, NV
		The WBC sanctioned the following for the Interim title	
Jul 28,	2012	Robert Guerrero w pts 12 Selcuk Aydin (Tur)	San Jose, CA
Nov 24,	2012	Robert Guerrero w pts 12 Andre Berto	Ontario, CA

WBA title

The WBA elevated Ricardo Mayorga to "super" champion, succeeded by Cory Spinks and Zab Judah, but continued to sanction world title fights

Sep 13,	2003	**Jose Rivera** (US) w pts 12 Michel Trabant (Ger)	Berlin (Ger)
Apr 2,	2005	**Luis Collazo** (US) w pts 12 Jose Rivera	Worcester, MA
Aug 13,	2005	Luis Collazo w rtd 8 Miguel Angel Gonzalez (Mex)	Chicago, IL
		For vacant title – Judah stripped of title in May 2005	
May 13,	2006	**Ricky Hatton** (Eng) w pts 12 Luis Collazo	Boston, MA
		Hatton relinquished the title to box at light-welterweight	
Dec 2,	2006	**Miguel Cotto** (PR) w rtd 5 Carlos Quintana (PR)	Atlantic City, NJ
		For vacant title	
Mar 3,	2007	Miguel Cotto w rsf 11 Oktay Urkal (Ger)	San Juan (PR)
Jun 9,	2007	Miguel Cotto w rsf 11 Zab Judah	New York, NY
Nov 10	2007	Miguel Cotto w pts 12 Shane Mosley	New York, NY
		The WBA elevated Miguel Cotto to Super Champion status and recognized Yuri Nuzhnenko as World Champion	
Dec 8,	2007	**Yuri Nuzhnenko** (Ukr) w pts 12 Frederic Klose (Fra)	Le Cannet (Fra)
Apr 12,	2008	**Miguel Cotto** w rtd 5 Alfonso Gomez (Mex)	Atlantic City, NJ
Apr 19,	2008	Yuri Nuzhnenko drew 12 Irving Garcia (PR)	Kiev (Ukr)
Jul 26,	2008	**Antonio Margarito** w rsf 11 Miguel Cotto	Las Vegas, NV
Jan 24,	2009	**Shane Mosley** w rsf 9 Antonio Margarito	Los Angeles, CA
Apr 10,	2009	**Vyacheslav Senchenko** (Ukr) w pts 12 Yuri Nuzhnenko	Donetsk (Ukr)
Jun 3,	2009	Vyacheslav Senchenko w pts 12 Motoki Sasaki (Jap)	Donetsk (Ukr)
Aug 30,	2010	Vyacheslav Senchenko w pts 12 Charlie Navarro (Ven)	Donetsk (Ukr)
Aug 26,	2011	Vyacheslav Senchenko w rsf 6 Marco Antonio Avendano (Ven)	Donetsk (Ukr)
Apr 29,	2012	Paul Malignaggi w rsf 9 Vyacheslav Senchenko	Donetsk (Ukr)
Oct 20,	2012	Paul Malignaggi w pts 12 Pablo Cesar Cano (Mex)	New York, NY
Jun 22,	2013	**Adrien Broner** (US) w pts 12 Paul Malignaggi	New York, NY
Dec 14,	2013	**Marcos Rene Maidana** (Arg) w pts 12 Adrien Broner	San Antonio, TX
		Maidana lost to Floyd Mayweather Jr for WBA super title and interim champion Keith Thurman upgraded to full champion	
Mar 7,	2015	Keith Thurman (US) w pts 12 Robert Guerrero US)	Las Vegas, NV
		The WBA also sanctioned the following for the Interim title	
May 28,	2010	Souleymane M'Baye (Fra) w pts 12 Antonin Decarie (Can).	Levallois-Perret (Fra)
Jul 7,	2011	Ismael El Massoudi (Fra) w rsf 12 Souleymane M'Baye	Marrakech (Morr)
Jul 21,	2012	Diego Gabriel Chaves (Arg) w ko 2 Ismael El Massoudi (Mor)	Buenos Aires (Arg)
Sep 22,	2012	Diego Gabriel Chaves w rsf 2 Joe Miranda (Pan)	Buenos Aires (Arg)
Jul 27,	2013	Keith Thurman w ko 10 Diego Gabriel Chaves (Arg)	San Antonio, TX
Dec 14,	2013	Keith Thurman w rsf 9 Jesus Soto Karass (Mex)	San Antonio, TX

Apr 26, 2014	Keith Thurman w rtd 3 Julio Diaz (Mex)	Carson, CA
Dec 13, 2014	Keith Thurman w pts 12 Leonard Bundu (Ita)	Las Vegas, NV
Mar 13, 2015	Andre Berto w rsf 6 Josesito Lopez (Mex)	Ontario, CA
	For the interim title	
July 11, 2015	Keith Thurman w rtd 7 Luis Collazo (US)	Tampa, FL
	The WBA sanctioned the following fights for the interim title	
Nov 7, 2015	David Avenesyan (Rus) w rsf 9 Charlie Navarro (Ven)	Monte Carlo (Mon)
May 28, 2016	David Avenesyan w pts 12 Shane Mosley (US)	Glendale, AZ
Jun 25, 2016	Keith Thurman w pts 12 Shawn Porter (US)	New York, NY
	For the title	
Feb 18, 2017	**Lamont Peterson (US)** w pts 12 David Avenesyan	Cincinnati, OH
Jan 27, 2018	**Lucas Martin Matthysse (Arg)** w ko 8 Tewa Kiram (Tha)	Inglewood, CA
	For the vacant title	

IBF title

	The IBF continued to recognize Zab Judah despite his defeat by Carlos Baldomir	
Apr 8, 2006	**Floyd Mayweather Jr** w pts 12 Zab Judah	Las Vegas, NV
	Mayweather Jr relinquished the title to box WBC champion Baldomir	
Oct 28, 2006	**Kermit Cintron** (PR) w rsf 6 Mark Suarez (US)	Palm Beach, FL
	For vacant title	
Jul 14, 2007	Kermit Cintron w ko 2 Walter Matthysse (Arg)	Atlantic City, NJ
Nov 23, 2007	Kermit Cintron w rsf 10 Jesse Feliciano (US)	Los Angeles, CA
Apr 12, 2008	**Antonio Margarito** (Mex) w ko 6 Kermit Cintron	Atlantic City, NJ
July 2008	*Margarito relinquished the title to fight Miguel Cotto in a WBA-sanctioned bout*	
Aug 2, 2008	**Joshua Clottey** (Gha) w tdec 9 Zab Judah	Las Vegas, NV
June 2009	*Clottey relinquished the title to fight Miguel Cotto in a WBO-sanctioned bout*	
Aug 1, 2009	**Isaac Hlatshwayo** (SA) w pts 12 Delvin Rodriguez (PR)	Uncasville, CT
	For vacant title	
Dec 11, 2009	**Jan Zaveck** (Slv) w rsf 3 Isaac Hlatshwayo	Johannesburg (SA)
Apr 9, 2010	Jan Zaveck w rsf 2 Rodolfo Ezequiel Martinez (Arg)	Ljubljana (Slov)
Sep 4, 2010	Jan Zaveck w pts 12 Rafal Jackiewicz (Pol)	Ljubljana (Slov)
Feb 18, 2011	Jan Zaveck w ko 5 Paul Delgado (US)	Ljubljana (Slov)
Sep 3, 2011	Andre Berto w rtd 5 Jan Zaveck	Biloxi, MS
	Berto tested positive for a banned substance in May 2012 and was stripped	
Jun 9, 2012	**Randall Bailey** (US) w ko 11 Mike Jones (US)	Las Vegas, NV
	For vacant title	
Oct 20, 2012	**Devon Alexander** (US) w pts 12 Randall Bailey	New York, NY
Dec 7, 2013	**Shawn Porter** (US) w pts 12 Devon Alexander	New York, NY
Apr 19, 2014	Shawn Porter w rsf 4 Paul Malignaggi (US)	Washington, DC
Aug 16, 2014	**Kell Brook** (Eng) w pts 12 Shawn Porter	Carson, CA
Mar 28, 2015	Kell Brook w rtd 4 Ionut Dan Ion (Rom)	Sheffield (Eng)
May 30, 2015	Kell Brook w rsf 6 Frankie Gavin (Eng)	London (Eng)
Mar 26, 2016	Kell Brook w rsf 2 Kevin Bizier (Can)	Sheffield (Eng)
May 27, 2017	**Errol Spence Jr (US)** w ko 11 Kell Brook	Sheffield (Eng)
Jan 20, 2018	Errol Spence Jr w rtd 7 Lamont Peterson	New York, NY

WBC title

Sep 17, 2011	Floyd Mayweather Jr w ko 4 Victor Ortiz	Las Vegas, NV

WBC/WBA Super titles

Sep 14, 2013	Floyd Mayweather Jr w pts 12 Saul Alvarez (Mex)	Las Vegas, NV
May 3, 2014	Floyd Mayweather Jr w pts 12 Marcos Rene Maidana (Arg)	Las Vegas, NV
	Fight was also for WBC light-middleweight title	

WBC/WBA Super/WBO titles

May 2, 2015	Floyd Mayweather Jr w pts 12 Manny Pacquiao	Las Vegas, NV
July 2015	*WBO stripped Mayweather Jr for failing to pay a fee*	

WBC/WBA Super titles

Sep 12, 2015	Floyd Mayweather Jr w pts 12 Andre Berto (US)	Las Vegas, NV

WBC title

Jan 23, 2016	**Danny Garcia (US)** w pts 12 Robert Guerrero (US)	Los Angeles, CA
	For the vacant title	

WBC/WBA Super titles

Mar 4, 2017	**Keith Thurman** w pts 12 Danny Garcia	New York, NY

WBO title

	The WBO sanctioned the following for the interim title	
Jun 27, 2015	Timothy Bradley Jr (US) w pts 12 Jessie Vargas (US)	Carson, CA
Nov 7, 2015	**Timothy Bradley Jr** w rsf 9 Brandon Rios (US)	Las Vegas, NV
	For the title	
Mar 5, 2016	**Jessie Vargas** w rsf 9 Sadam Ali (US)	Washington, DC
	For the vacant title	
Nov 5, 2016	**Manny Pacquiao** w pts 12 Jessie Vargas	Las Vegas, NV
July 2, 2017	**Jeff Horn (Aus)** w pts 12 Manny Pacquiao	Brisbane (Aus)
Dec 13, 2017	Jeff Horn w rsf 11 Gary Corcoran (Eng)	Brisbane (Aus)

KEITH THURMAN *connects with a left-hand uppercut during his points victory over Danny Garcia in March 2017*

Light-Welterweight

The light-welterweight or "junior welterweight" class had an uncertain beginning when its first champion, Pinkey Mitchell, was elected to the title by the readers of a weekly boxing magazine called the *Boxing Blade*, which was published in Minneapolis. Since the owner of *Boxing Blade,* Mike Collins, was also Mitchell's manager the outcome of the poll astonished nobody. Mitchell lost his title at the first defence and sub-sequently won only three of his remaining 35 fights.

Controversy dogged the new division, weight limit 140lb. The New York Commission withdrew recognition in 1930, and the British Board would not even accept their own Jack "Kid" Berg as world cham-pion when he beat Mushy Callahan at the Albert Hall in 1930. The category fell out of favour in 1935 when champion Barney Ross opted to defend his welterweight title instead, and there were sporadic unsuccessful efforts to revive it before Carlos Ortiz at last got it up and running in 1959. At first the weight was accepted only by the NBA and their successors, the WBA, but the WBC set up their own champion in 1968.

World Light-Welterweight Championship Bouts

Sep 21,	1926	**Mushy Callahan** (US) w pts 10 Pinkey Mitchell (US)	Vernon, CA
		For NBA title	
Jan 22,	1926	Mushy Callahan w ko 2 Charlie Pitts (Aus)	Los Angeles, CA
Mar 14,	1927	Mushy Callahan w ko 2 Andy Divodi (US)	New York, NY
		For NBA and New York recognition	
May 31,	1927	Mushy Callahan w pts 10 Spug Myers (US)	Chicago, IL
May 28,	1929	Mushy Callahan w ko 3 Fred Mahan (US)	Los Angeles, CA
Jan 1,	1930	*The NY Commission decided not to recognize so-called "junior" weight classes*	
Jan 30,	1930	*The NBA withdrew recognition of Callahan on signing to defend title in London*	
Feb 18,	1930	**Jack "Kid" Berg** (Eng) w rtd 10 Mushy Callahan	London (Eng)
Apr 4,	1930	Jack "Kid" Berg w pts 10 Joe Glick (US)	New York, NY
May 29,	1930	Jack "Kid" Berg w rsf 4 Al Delmont (US)	Newark, NJ
Jun 12,	1930	Jack "Kid" Berg w pts 10 Herman Perlick (US)	New York, NY
Aug 7,	1930	Jack "Kid" Berg w pts 10 Kid Chocolate (Cub)	New York, NY
Sep 3,	1930	Jack "Kid" Berg w pts 10 Buster Brown (US)	Newark, NJ
Sep 18,	1930	Jack "Kid" Berg w pts 10 Joe Glick	Long Island, NY
Oct 10,	1930	Jack "Kid" Berg w pts 10 Billy Petrolle (US)	New York, NY
Jan 23,	1931	Jack "Kid" Berg w pts 10 Goldie Hess (US)	Chicago, IL
		Berg won NBA recognition as champion	
Jan 30,	1931	Jack "Kid" Berg w pts 10 Herman Perlick	New York, NY
Apr 10,	1931	Jack "Kid" Berg w pts 10 Billy Wallace (US)	Detroit, MI
Apr 24,	1931	**Tony Canzoneri** (US) w ko 3 Jack "Kid" Berg	Chicago, IL

Billed as a lightweight title defence by Canzoneri, but as both were within the light-welterweight limit that title was automatically at stake. Berg refused to accept this, and continued to bill himself as world champion even though only Ring *magazine supported his claim*

Jun 25,	1931	Tony Canzoneri w pts 10 Herman Perlick	New Haven, CT
Jul 13,	1931	Tony Canzoneri w pts 10 Cecil Payne (US)	Los Angeles, CA
Sep 10,	1931	Tony Canzoneri w pts 15 Jack "Kid" Berg	New York, NY
		Billed as lightweight title defence	
Oct 29,	1931	Tony Canzoneri w pts 10 Phillie Griffin (US)	Newark, NJ
Nov 20,	1931	Tony Canzoneri w pts 15 Kid Chocolate (Cub)	New York, NY
		Billed as lightweight title defence	
Jan 18,	1932	**Johnny Jadick** (US) w pts 10 Tony Canzoneri	Philadelphia, PA
Jul 18,	1932	Johnny Jadick (US) w pts 10 Tony Canzoneri	Philadelphia, PA
Sep 20,	1932	*The NBA withdrew recognition from the division*	
Feb 20,	1933	**Battling Shaw** (Mex) w pts 10 Johnny Jadick	New Orleans, LA
May 21,	1933	**Tony Canzoneri** w pts 10 Battling Shaw	New Orleans, LA
Jun 23,	1933	**Barney Ross** (US) w pts 10 Tony Canzoneri	Chicago, IL
		Canzoneri's lightweight title was also at stake	
Jul 26,	1933	Barney Ross w rsf 6 Johnny Farr (US)	Kansas City, KS
Sep 12,	1933	Barney Ross w pts 15 Tony Canzoneri	New York, NY
		Billed as lightweight title defence	
Nov 17,	1933	Barney Ross w pts 10 Sammy Fuller (US)	Chicago, IL
Feb 7,	1934	Barney Ross w pts 12 Pete Nebo (US)	Kansas City, KS
Mar 5,	1934	Barney Ross drew 10 Frankie Klick (US)	San Francisco, CA
Mar 27,	1934	Barney Ross w pts 10 Bobby Pacho (US)	Los Angeles, CA
Dec 10,	1934	Barney Ross w pts 12 Bobby Pacho	Cleveland, OH
Jan 28,	1935	Barney Ross w pts Frankie Klick	Miami, FL
Apr 9,	1935	Barney Ross w pts 12 Harry Woods (US)	Seattle, WA
Jun	1935	*Ross relinquished the title on regaining the welterweight championship*	
Jul 5,	1939	**Maxie Berger** (Can) w pts 10 Wes Ramey (US)	Montreal (Can)
		Recognized in Canada as being for the vacant title, which Berger never defended	
Oct 28,	1940	**Harry Weekly** (US) w pts 15 Jerome Conforto (US)	New Orleans, LA
		Recognized by the Louisiana Commission as a title fight	
Jun 27,	1941	Harry Weekly w pts 10 Carmelo Fenoy (US)	Birmingham, AL
Jul 28,	1941	Harry Weekly w pts 15 Baby Breese (US)	New Orleans, LA
Oct 20,	1941	Harry Weekly w ko 5 Ervin Berlier (US)	New Orleans, LA

The title fell into disuse when Weekly joined the Army, and was not contested again until the Massachusetts Commission approved the first Tippy Larkin v Willie Joyce fight. The New York Commission agreed to recognize their second fight as involving the world title

Apr 29,	1946	**Tippy Larkin** w pts 12 Willie Joyce	Boston, MA
Sep 13,	1946	Tippy Larkin w pts 12 Willie Joyce	New York, NY

The New York and Massachusetts Commissions withdrew recognition from Larkin in June 1947 after his fourth-round knockout by lightweight champion Ike Williams, and the title was not revived again until 1959

Jun 12,	1959	**Carlos Ortiz** (PR) w rtd 2 Kenny Lane (US)	New York, NY
Feb 4,	1960	Carlos Ortiz w ko 10 Battling Torres (Mex)	Los Angeles, CA
Jun 15,	1960	Carlos Ortiz w pts 15 Duilio Loi (Ita)	San Francisco, CA
Sep 1,	1960	**Duilio Loi** w pts 15 Carlos Ortiz	Milan (Ita)
May 10,	1961	Duilio Loi w pts 15 Carlos Ortiz	Milan (Ita)
Oct 21,	1961	Duilio Loi drew 15 Eddie Perkins (US)	Milan (Ita)
Sep 14,	1962	**Eddie Perkins** w pts 15 Duilio Loi	Milan (Ita)
Dec 15,	1962	**Duilio Loi** w pts 15 Eddie Perkins	Milan (Ita)
		Loi announced retirement in January 1963	
Mar 21,	1963	**Roberto Cruz** (Phil) w ko 1 Battling Torres	Los Angeles, CA
		For vacant title	
Jun 15,	1963	**Eddie Perkins** w pts 15 Roberto Cruz	Manila (Phil)
Jan 4,	1964	Eddie Perkins w rsf 13 Yoshinori Takahashi (Jap)	Tokyo (Jap)
Apr 18,	1964	Eddie Perkins w pts 15 Bunny Grant (Jam)	Kingston (Jam)
Jan 18,	1965	**Carlos Hernandez** (Ven) w pts 15 Eddie Perkins	Caracas (Ven)
May 15,	1965	Carlos Hernandez w rsf 4 Mario Rossito (Col)	Maracaibo (Ven)
Jul 10,	1965	Carlos Hernandez w ko 3 Percy Hayles (Jam)	Kingston (Jam)
Apr 29,	1966	**Sandro Lopopolo** (Ita) w pts 15 Carlos Hernandez	Rome (Ita)
Oct 21,	1966	Sandro Lopopolo w rsf 7 Vicente Rivas (Ven)	Rome (Ita)
Apr 30,	1967	**Paul Fuji** (US) w rtd 2 Sandro Lopopolo	Tokyo (Jap)
Nov 16,	1967	Paul Fuji w ko 4 Willi Quator (Ger)	Tokyo (Jap)

The WBC stripped Fuji of title for failure to defend against the No. 1 challenger Pedro Adigue, and set up their own version of the title. The WBA continued to recognize Fuji as the champion

WBA title

Dec 12,	1968	**Nicolino Loche** (Arg) w rtd 9 Paul Fuji	Tokyo (Jap)
May 3,	1969	Nicolino Loche w pts 15 Carlos Hernandez	Buenos Aires (Arg)
Oct 11,	1969	Nicolino Loche w pts 15 Joao Henrique (Bra)	Buenos Aires (Arg)
May 16,	1970	Nicolino Loche w pts 15 Adolph Pruitt (US)	Buenos Aires (Arg)
Apr 3,	1971	Nicolino Loche w pts 15 Domingo Barrera (Sp)	Buenos Aires (Arg)
Dec 11,	1971	Nicolino Loche w pts 15 Antonio Cervantes (Col)	Buenos Aires (Arg)
Mar 10,	1972	**Alfonso Frazer** (Pan) w pts 15 Nicolino Loche	Panama City (Pan)
Jun 17,	1972	Alfonso Frazer w rtd 4 Al Ford (Can)	Panama City (Pan)
Oct 28,	1972	**Antonio Cervantes** w ko 10 Alfonso Frazer	Panama City (Pan)
Feb 16,	1973	Antonio Cervantes w pts 15 Josua Marquez (PR)	San Juan, CA
Mar 17,	1973	Antonio Cervantes w rtd 9 Nicolino Loche	Maracay (Ven)
May 19,	1973	Antonio Cervantes w rsf 5 Alfonso Frazer	Panama City (Pan)
Sep 8,	1973	Antonio Cervantes w rsf 5 Carlos Giminez (Arg)	Bogota (Col)
Dec 4,	1973	Antonio Cervantes w pts 15 Lion Furuyama (Jap)	Panama City (Pan)
Mar 2,	1974	Antonio Cervantes w ko 6 Chang-Kil Lee (Kor)	Cartagena (Col)
Jul 27,	1974	Antonio Cervantes w ko 2 Victor Ortiz (PR)	Cartagena (Col)
Oct 26,	1974	Antonio Cervantes w ko 8 Shinchi Kadota (Jap)	Tokyo (Jap)
May 17,	1975	Antonio Cervantes w pts 15 Esteban De Jesus (PR)	Panama City (Pan)
Nov 15,	1975	Antonio Cervantes w rtd 7 Hector Thompson (Aus)	Panama City (Pan)
Mar 6,	1976	**Wilfredo Benitez** (PR) w pts 15 Antonio Cervantes	San Juan, CA
May 31,	1976	Wilfredo Benitez w pts 15 Emiliano Villa (Col)	San Juan, CA
Oct 16,	1976	Wilfredo Benitez w rsf 3 Tony Petronelli (US)	San Juan, CA
Dec 1976		*WBA stripped Benitez for failing to defend against Antonio Cervantes*	
Jun 25,	1977	**Antonio Cervantes** w rsf 5 Carlos Gimenez	Maracaibo (Ven)
Nov 5,	1977	Antonio Cervantes w pts 15 Adriano Marrero (DR)	Maracay (Ven)
Apr 28,	1978	Antonio Cervantes w ko 6 Tonga Kiatvayupakdi (Thai)	Udon (Thai)
Aug 26,	1978	Antonio Cervantes w rsf 9 Norman Sekgapane (SA)	Mabatho (Bots)
Jan 18,	1979	Antonio Cervantes w pts 15 Miguel Montilla (DR)	New York, NY
Aug 25,	1979	Antonio Cervantes w pts 15 Kwang-Min Kim (Kor)	Seoul (Kor)

Mar 29,	1980	Antonio Cervantes w rsf 7 Miguel Montilla	Cartagena (Col)
Aug 2,	1980	**Aaron Pryor** (US) w ko 4 Antonio Cervantes	Cincinnati, OH
Nov 22,	1980	Aaron Pryor w rsf 6 Gaetan Hart (Can)	Cincinnati, OH
Jun 27,	1981	Aaron Pryor w rsf 2 Lennox Blackmoore (Guy)	Las Vegas, NV
Nov 14,	1981	Aaron Pryor w rsf 7 Dujuan Johnson (US)	Cleveland, OH
Mar 21,	1982	Aaron Pryor w rsf 12 Miguel Montilla	Atlantic City, NJ
Jul 4,	1982	Aaron Pryor w rsf 6 Akio Kameda (Jap)	Cincinnati, OH
Nov 12,	1982	Aaron Pryor w rsf 14 Alexis Arguello (Nic)	Miami, FL
Apr 2,	1983	Aaron Pryor w rsf 3 Kim Sang Hyun (Kor)	Atlantic City, NJ
Sep 9,	1983	Aaron Pryor w ko 10 Alexis Arguello	Las Vegas, NV
		Pryor gave up the WBA title and was proclaimed champion by the IBF	
Jan 22,	1984	**Johnny Bumphus** (US) w pts.15 Lorenzo Garcia (Arg)	Atlantic City, NJ
		For vacant title	
Jun 1,	1984	**Gene Hatcher** (US) w rsf 11 Johnny Bumphus	Buffalo, NY
Dec 15,	1984	Gene Hatcher w pts 15 Ubaldo Sacco (Arg)	Fort Worth, TX
Jul 21,	1985	**Ubaldo Sacco** w rsf 9 Gene Hatcher	Campione (Ita)
Mar 15,	1986	**Patrizio Oliva** (Ita) w pts 15 Ubaldo Sacco	Monte Carlo (Mon)
Sep 6,	1986	Patrizio Oliva w rsf 3 Brian Brunette (US)	Naples (Ita)
Jan 10,	1987	Patrizio Oliva w pts 15 Rodolfo Gonzalez (Mex)	Agrigento (Ita)
Jul 4,	1987	**Juan Martin Coggi** (Arg) w ko 3 Patrizio Oliva	Ribera (Sp)
May 7,	1988	Juan Martin Coggi w ko 2 Sang-Ho Lee (Kor)	Roseto (Ita)
Jan 21,	1989	Juan Martin Coggi w pts 12 Harold Brazier (US)	Vasto (Ita)
Apr 29,	1989	Juan Martin Coggi w pts 12 Akinobu Hiranaka (Jap)	Vasto (Ita)
Mar 24,	1990	Juan Martin Coggi w pts 12 Jose Luis Ramirez (Mex)	Arjaccio (Arg)
Aug 17,	1990	**Loreto Garza** (US) w pts 12 Juan Martin Coggi	Nice (Fra)
Dec 1,	1990	Loreto Garza w dis 11 Vinny Pazienza (US)	Sacramento, CA
Jun 14,	1991	**Edwin Rosario** (PR) w rsf 3 Loreto Garza	Sacramento, CA
Apr 10,	1992	**Akinobu Hiranaka** (Jap) w rsf 1 Edwin Rosario	Mexico City (Mex)
Sep 9,	1992	**Morris East** (Phil) w rsf 11 Akinobu Hiranaka	Tokyo (Jap)
Jan 13,	1993	**Juan M. Coggi** w rsf 8 Morris East	Mar del Plata (Arg)
Apr 10,	1993	Juan Martin Coggi w rsf 7 Jose Rivera (PR)	Mar del Plata (Arg)
Jun 23,	1993	Juan Martin Coggi w ko 5 Hiroyuki Yoshino (Jap)	Tokyo (Jap)
Aug 13,	1993	Juan Martin Coggi w pts 12 Jose Barboza (Ven)	Buenos Aires (Arg)
Sep 24,	1993	Juan Martin Coggi w rsf 10 Guillermo Cruz (Mex)	Tucuman (Arg)
Dec 17,	1993	Juan Martin Coggi w rsf 7 Eder Gonzalez (Col)	Tucuman (Arg)
Mar 18,	1994	Juan Martin Coggi w rsf 3 Eder Gonzalez	Las Vegas, NV
Sep 17,	1994	**Frankie Randall** (US) w pts 12 Juan Martin Coggi	Las Vegas, NV
Dec 10,	1994	Frankie Randall w rsf 7 Rodney Moore (US)	Monterrey (Mex)
Jun 16,	1995	Frankie Randall w pts 12 Jose Barboza	Lyon (Fra)
Jan 13,	1996	**Juan Martin Coggi** w tdec 5 Frankie Randall	Miami, FL
Aug 16,	1996	**Frankie Randall** w pts 12 Juan Martin Coggi	Buenos Aires (Arg)
Jan 11,	1997	**Khalid Rahilou** (Fra) w rsf 11 Frankie Randall	Nashville, TN
July 5,	1997	Khalid Rahilou w rsf 7 Marty Jakubowski (US)	Casablanca (Mor)
Feb 21	1998	Khalid Rahilou w pts 12 Jean Baptiste Mendy (Fra)	Paris (Fra)
Oct 10,	1998	**Sharmba Mitchell** (US) w pts 12 Khalid Rahilou	Paris (Fra)
Feb 6,	1999	Sharmba Mitchell w pts 12 Pedro Saiz (US)	Washington, DC
Apr 24,	1999	Sharmba Mitchell w pts 12 Reggie Green (US)	Washington, DC
Nov 13,	1999	Sharmba Mitchell w pts 12 Elio Ortiz (Ven)	Las Vegas, NV
Sep 16,	2000	Sharmba Mitchell w pts 12 Felix Flores (PR)	Las Vegas, NV

New York title

The New York Commission continued to regard Benitez as champion until he announced in August 1977 that he could no longer make the weight

Aug 3,	1977	**Wilfredo Benitez** w rsf 15 Guerrero Chavez (Can)	New York, NY

WBC title

Dec 14,	1968	**Pedro Adigue** (Phil) w pts 15 Adolph Pruitt	Manila (Phil)
		For vacant title	
Jan 31,	1970	**Bruno Arcari** (Ita) w pts 15 Pedro Adigue	Rome (Ita)
Jul 10,	1970	Bruno Arcari w dis 6 Rene Roque (Fra)	Lignano (Ita)
Oct 30,	1970	Bruno Arcari w ko 3 Raimundo Dias (Bra)	Genoa (Ita)
Mar 6,	1971	Bruno Arcari w pts 15 Joao Henrique	Rome (Ita)
Jun 26,	1971	Bruno Arcari w rsf 9 Enrique Jana (Arg)	Palermo (Ita)
Oct 10,	1971	Bruno Arcari w ko 10 Domingo Barrera	Genoa (Ita)
Jun 10,	1972	Bruno Arcari w ko 12 Joao Henrique	Genoa (Ita)
Dec 2,	1972	Bruno Arcari w pts 15 Everaldo Costa Azevedo (Bra)	Turin (Ita)
Feb 16,	1974	Bruno Arcari w dis 8 Tony Ortiz (Sp)	Turin (Ita)
Aug	1974	*Arcari relinquished the title because of weight problems*	
Sep 21,	1974	**Perico Fernandez** (Sp) w pts 15 Lion Furuyama	Rome (Ita)
		For vacant title	
Apr 19,	1975	Perico Fernandez w ko 9 Joao Henrique	Barcelona (Sp)
Jul 15,	1975	**Saensak Muangsurin** (Thai) w rtd 8 Perico Fernandez	Bangkok (Thai)
Jan 25,	1976	Saensak Muangsurin w pts 15 Lion Furuyama	Tokyo (Jap)
Jun 30,	1976	**Miguel Velasquez** (Sp) w dis 4 Saensak Muangsurin	Madrid (Sp)
Oct 29,	1976	**Saensak Muangsurin** w rsf 2 Miguel Velasquez	Segovia (Sp)
Jan 5,	1977	Saensak Muangsurin w rsf 15 Monroe Brooks (US)	Chiang (Thai)
Apr 2,	1977	Saensak Muangsurin w ko 6 Guts Ishimatsu (Jap)	Tokyo (Jap)
Jun 17,	1977	Saensak Muangsurin w pts 15 Perico Fernandez	Madrid (Sp)
Aug 20,	1977	Saensak Muangsurin w rsf 6 Mike Everett (US)	Roi-Et (Thai)
Oct 22,	1977	Saensak Muangsurin w pts 15 Saoul Mamby (US)	Korat (Thai)
Dec 29,	1977	Saensak Muangsurin w rtd 13 Jo Kimpuani (Zai)	Chanthabun (Thai)
Apr 8,	1977	Saensak Muangsurin w ko 13 Francisco Moreno (Ven)	Hat Yai (Thai)
Dec 30,	1978	**Kim Sang Hyun** w rsf 13 Saensak Muangsurin	Seoul (Kor)
Jun 3,	1979	Kim Sang Hyun w pts 15 Fitzroy Guiseppe (Tr)	Seoul (Kor)
Oct 4,	1979	Kim Sang Hyun w ko 11 Masahiro Yokai (Jap)	Tokyo (Jap)
Feb 23,	1980	**Saoul Mamby** w ko 14 Kim Sang Hyun	Seoul (Kor)
Jul 7,	1980	Saoul Mamby w rsf 13 Esteban De Jesus	Bloomington, MN
Oct 2,	1980	Saoul Mamby w pts 15 Maurice "Termite" Watkins (US)	Las Vegas, NV
Jun 12,	1981	Saoul Mamby w pts 15 Jo Kimpuani	Detroit, MI
Aug 29,	1981	Saoul Mamby w pts 15 Thomas Americo (Indo)	Jakarta (Indo)
Dec 20,	1981	Saoul Mamby w pts 15 Obisia Nwankpa (Nig)	Lagos (Nig)
Jun 26,	1982	**Leroy Haley** (US) w pts 15 Saoul Mamby	Cleveland, OH
Oct 20,	1982	Leroy Haley w pts 15 Juan Jose Giminez (Arg)	Cleveland, OH
Feb 13,	1983	Leroy Haley w pts 15 Saoul Mamby	Cleveland, OH
May 18,	1983	**Bruce Curry** (US) w pts 12 Leroy Haley	Las Vegas, NV
Jul 7,	1983	Bruce Curry w rsf 7 Hidekazu Akai (Jap)	Osaka (Jap)
Oct 19,	1983	Bruce Curry w pts 12 Leroy Haley	Las Vegas, NV
Jan 29,	1984	**Bill Costello** (US) w rsf 10 Bruce Curry	Beaumont, TX
Jul 15,	1984	Bill Costello w pts 12 Ronnie Shields (US)	Kingston, NY
Nov 3,	1984	Bill Costello w pts 12 Saoul Mamby	Kingston, NY
Feb 16,	1985	Bill Costello w pts 12 Leroy Haley	Kingston, NY
Aug 21,	1985	**Lonnie Smith** (US) w rsf 8 Bill Costello	New York, NY
May 5,	1986	**Rene Arredondo** (Mex) w rsf 5 Lonnie Smith	Los Angeles, CA
Jul 24,	1986	**Tsuyoshi Hamada** (Jap) w ko 1 Rene Arredondo	Tokyo (Jap)
Dec 2,	1986	Tsuyoshi Hamada w pts 12 Ronnie Shields	Tokyo (Jap)
Jul 22,	1987	**Rene Arredondo** w rsf 6 Tsuyoshi Hamada	Tokyo (Jap)
Nov 12,	1987	**Roger Mayweather** (US) w rsf 6 Rene Arredondo	Los Angeles, CA
Mar 24,	1988	Roger Mayweather w ko 3 Maurico Aceves (Mex)	Los Angeles, CA
Jun 6,	1988	Roger Mayweather w pts 12 Harold Brazier	Las Vegas, NV
Sep 22,	1988	Roger Mayweather w rsf 12 Rodolfo Gonzalez (Mex)	Los Angeles, CA
Nov 7,	1988	Roger Mayweather w pts 12 Vinny Pazienza	Las Vegas, NV
May 13,	1989	**Julio Cesar Chavez** (Mex) w rtd 10 Roger Mayweather	Los Angeles, CA
Nov 18,	1989	Julio Cesar Chavez w rsf 10 Sammy Fuentes (PR)	Las Vegas, NV
Dec 16,	1989	Julio Cesar Chavez w ko 3 Alberto Cortes (Arg)	Mexico City (Mex)
Mar 17,	1990	Julio Cesar Chavez w rsf 12 Meldrick Taylor (US)	Las Vegas, NV
		For WBC and IBF titles	

IBF title

Jun 22,	1984	**Aaron Pryor** w pts 15 Nicky Furlano (Can)	Toronto (Can)
Mar 2,	1985	Aaron Pryor w pts 15 Gary Hinton (US)	Atlantic City, NJ
Dec	1985	*The IBF stripped Pryor for inactivity*	
Apr 26,	1986	**Gary Hinton** w pts 15 Antonio Reyes Cruz (DR)	Lucca (Ita)
		For vacant title	
Oct 30,	1986	**Joe Manley** (US) w ko 10 Gary Hinton	Hartford, CT
Mar 4,	1987	**Terry Marsh** (Eng) w rsf 10 Joe Manley	Basildon (Eng)
Jul 1,	1987	Terry Marsh w rtd 6 Akio Kameda	London (Eng)
Sep	1987	*Marsh retired*	
Feb 14,	1988	**James "Buddy" McGirt** (US) w rsf 12 Frankie Warren (US)	Corpus Christi, TX
		For vacant title	
Jul 31,	1988	James "Buddy" McGirt w ko 1 Howard Davis (US)	New York, NY
Sep 3,	1988	**Meldrick Taylor** w rsf 12 James "Buddy" McGirt	Atlantic City, NJ
Jan 21,	1989	Meldrick Taylor w rsf 7 John Meekins (US)	Atlantic City, NJ
Sep 11,	1989	Meldrick Taylor w pts 12 Courtney Hooper (US)	Atlantic City, NJ
Mar 17,	1990	**Julio Cesar Chavez** w rsf 12 Meldrick Taylor	Las Vegas, NV
		For WBC and IBF titles	

WBC/IBF titles

Dec 8,	1990	**Julio Cesar Chavez** w rsf 3 Kyung-Duk Ahn (Kor)	Atlantic City, NJ
Mar 18,	1991	Julio Cesar Chavez w rsf 4 John Duplessis (US)	Las Vegas, NV
Apr	1991	*Chavez relinquished the IBF title*	

WBC title

Sep 14,	1991	**Julio Cesar Chavez** w pts 12 Lonnie Smith	Las Vegas, NV
Apr 10,	1992	Julio Cesar Chavez w ko 5 Angel Hernandez (PR)	Mexico City (Mex)
Aug 1,	1992	Julio Cesar Chavez w rsf 4 Frankie Mitchell (US)	Las Vegas, NV
Sep 12,	1992	Julio Cesar Chavez w pts 12 Hector Camacho (PR)	Las Vegas, NV
Feb 20,	1993	Julio Cesar Chavez w rsf 5 Greg Haugen (US)	Mexico City (Mex)
May 8,	1993	Julio Cesar Chavez w rsf 6 Terrence Alli (Guy)	Las Vegas, NV
Dec 18,	1993	Julio Cesar Chavez w rtd 5 Andy Holligan (Eng)	Mexico City (Mex)
Jan 29,	1994	**Frankie Randall** (US) w pts 12 Julio Cesar Chavez	Las Vegas, NV
May 7,	1994	**Julio Cesar Chavez** w tech dec 8 Frankie Randall	Las Vegas, NV
Sep 17,	1994	Julio Cesar Chavez w rsf 8 Meldrick Taylor	Las Vegas, NV
Dec 10,	1994	Julio Cesar Chavez w rsf 10 Tony Lopez (US)	Monterrey (Mex)

Apr 8,	1995	Julio Cesar Chavez w pts 12 Giovanni Parisi (Ita)	Las Vegas, NV
Sep 16,	1995	Julio Cesar Chavez w pts 12 David Kamau (Ken)	Las Vegas, NV
Jun 7,	1996	**Oscar De La Hoya** w rsf 4 Julio Cesar Chavez	Las Vegas, NV
Jan 18,	1997	Oscar De La Hoya w pts 12 Miguel Angel Gonzalez (Mex)	Las Vegas, NV
Apr	1997	*De La Hoya relinquished title when he won WBC welterweight belt*	
Mar 7,	1998	Miguel Angel Gonzalez drew 12 Julio Cesar Chavez	Mexico City (Mex)
Nov 28,	1998	**Kostya Tszyu** (Rus) w rsf 5 Diobelys Hurtado (Cub)	Indio, CA
Aug 21,	1999	Kostya Tszyu w rsf 10 Miguel Angel Gonzalez	Miami, FL
Feb 12,	2000	Kostya Tszyu w rsf 8 Ahmed Santos (Mex)	Uncasville, CT
Jul 29,	2000	Kostya Tszyu w rsf 6 Julio Cesar Chavez	Phoenix, AZ

WBA/WBC titles

Feb 3,	2001	**Kostya Tszyu** (Rus) w rtd 7 Sharmba Mitchell	Las Vegas, NV
		WBA/WBC unification bout	
Jun 23,	2001	Kostya Tszyu w pts 12 Oktay Urkal (Ger)	Uncasville, CT

IBF title

Dec 7,	1991	**Rafael Pineda** (Col) w rsf 9 Roger Mayweather	Reno, NV
		For vacant title	
May 22,	1992	Rafael Pineda w rsf 7 Clarence Coleman (US)	Mexico City (Mex)
Jul 18,	1992	**Pernell Whitaker** (US) w pts 12 Rafael Pineda	Las Vegas, NV
Mar	1993	*Whitaker relinquished the title on becoming WBC welterweight champion*	
May 15,	1993	**Charles Murray** (US) w pts 12 Rodney Moore	Atlantic City, NJ
		For vacant title	
Jul 24,	1993	Charles Murray w pts 12 Juan LaPorte (PR)	Atlantic City, NJ
Nov 19,	1993	Charles Murray w rtd 5 Courtney Hooper	Atlantic City, NJ
Feb 13,	1994	**Jake Rodriguez** (US) w pts 12 Charles Murray	Atlantic City, NJ
Apr 21,	1994	Jake Rodriguez w pts 12 Ray Oliveira (US)	Ledyard, CT
Aug 27,	1994	Jake Rodriguez w rsf 9 George Scott (Swe)	Bushkill
Jan 28,	1995	**Kostya Tszyu** (Rus) w rsf 6 Jake Rodriguez	Las Vegas, NV
Jun 25,	1995	Kostya Tszyu w pts 12 Roger Mayweather	Newcastle (Aus)
Jan 20,	1996	Kostya Tszyu w rsf 11 Hugo Pineda (Col)	Sydney (Aus)
May 24,	1996	Kostya Tszyu w rsf 4 Corey Johnson (US)	Sydney (Aus)
Sep 14,	1996	Kostya Tszyu w ko 6 Jan Bergman (SA)	Newcastle (Aus)
Jan 18,	1997	Kostya Tszyu tdraw 1 Leonardo Mas (PR)	Las Vegas, NV
		Mas was judged "unable to continue because of an unintentional illegal blow"	
May 31,	1997	**Vincent Phillips** (US) w rsf 10 Konstantin Tszyu	Atlantic City, NJ
Aug 9,	1997	Vincent Phillips w rsf 3 Mickey Ward (US)	Boston ,MA
Dec 13,	1997	Vincent Phillips w rsf 10 Freddie Pendleton	Pompano Beach, FL
Mar 14,	1998	Vincent Philips w ko 1 Alfonso Sanchez (Mex)	Atlantic City, NJ
Feb 20,	1999	**Terron Millett** (US) w rsf 5 Vincent Phillips	New York, NY
Jul 24,	1999	Terron Millett w rsf 12 Virgil McClendon (US)	Las Vegas, NV
Aug 5,	2000	**Zab Judah** (US) w rsf 4 Terron Millett	Uncasville, CT
Oct 20,	2000	Zab Judah w rsf 8 Hector Quiroz (US)	Auburn Hills, MI
Jan 13,	2001	Zab Judah w rsf 10 Reggie Green (US)	Uncasville, CT
Jun 23,	2001	Zab Judah w ko 3 Allan Vester (Den)	Uncasville, CT

WBC/WBA/IBF titles

Nov 3,	2001	**Kostya Tszyu** (Rus) w rsf 2 Zab Judah	Las Vegas, NV
May 18,	2002	Kostya Tszyu w pts 12 Ben Tackie (Gha)	Las Vegas, NV
Jan 19,	2003	Kostya Tszyu w rsf 6 James Leija (US)	Melbourne (Aus)

The WBC & WBA "elevated" Tszyu to the role of "champion emeritus" and "super" champion respectively, while during his injury layoff in 2004, the IBF installed Sharmba Mitchell as interim champion. During his layoff, Tszyu lost recognition by the WBC and WBA

WBO title

Mar 6,	1989	**Hector Camacho** w pts 12 Ray Mancini (US)	Reno, NV
		For vacant title	
Feb 3,	1990	Hector Camacho w pts 12 Vinny Pazienza	Atlantic City, NJ
Aug 11,	1990	Hector Camacho w pts 12 Tony Baltazar (US)	Stateline, NV
Feb 23,	1991	**Greg Haugen** w pts 12 Hector Camacho	Las Vegas, NV
Mar	1991	*Haugen was stripped of the title for failing a post-fight drugs test*	
May 18,	1991	**Hector Camacho** w pts 12 Greg Haugen	Reno, NV
Mar	1992	*Camacho was stripped of the title for failure to defend it*	
Jun 30,	1992	**Carlos Gonzalez** (Mex) w rsf 2 Jimmy Paul (US)	Los Angeles, CA
		For vacant title	
Nov 9,	1992	Carlos Gonzalez w rtd 6 Lorenzo Smith (US)	Los Angeles, CA
Dec 14,	1992	Carlos Gonzalez w rsf 1 Rafael Ortiz (DR)	Mexico City (Mex)
Mar 22,	1993	Carlos Gonzalez w rsf 1 Tony Baltazar	Los Angeles, CA
Jun 7,	1993	**Zack Padilla** (US) w pts 12 Carlos Gonzalez	Las Vegas, NV
Nov 19,	1993	Zack Padilla w rtd 7 Efrem Calamati (Ita)	Arezzo (Ita)
Dec 16,	1993	Zack Padilla w pts 12 Ray Oliveira	Ledyard, CT
Apr 18,	1994	Zack Padilla w rtd 6 Harold Miller (US)	Rotterdam (Hol)
Jul 24,	1994	Zack Padilla w rtd 11 Juan LaPorte	Los Angeles, CA
		Padilla was forced to retire on medical grounds	
Feb 20,	1995	**Sammy Fuentes** w rsf 2 Fidel Avendano (Mex)	Inglewood, CA
		For vacant title	
Jun 10,	1995	Sammy Fuentes w pts 12 Hector Lopez (US)	Las Vegas, NV
Mar 9,	1996	**Giovanni Parisi** (Ita) w rsf 8 Sammy Fuentes	Milan (Ita)
Jun 20,	1996	Giovanni Parisi drew 12 Carlos Gonzalez	Milan (Ita)
Oct 12,	1996	Giovanni Parisi w rsf 4 Sergio Rey Revilla (Spa)	Milan (Ita)
Apr 19,	1997	Giovanni Parisi w rsf 8 Harold Miller (US)	Milan (Ita)
Oct 4,	1997	Giovanni Parisi w rsf 8 Nigel Wenton (Eng)	Vibo Valentia (Ita)
Dec 6,	1997	Giovanni Parisi w pts 12 Jose Manuel Berdonce (Spa)	Catanzaro (Ita)
May 29,	1998	**Carlos Gonzalez** w rsf 9 Giovanni Parisi	Pesaro (Ita)
May 15,	1999	**Randall Bailey** (US) w ko 1 Carlos Gonzalez	Miami FL
Dec 11,	1999	Randall Bailey w rsf 9 Hector Lopez (US)	Tunica MS
Apr 8,	2000	Randall Bailey w rtd 6 Rocky Martinez (US)	Paris (Fra)
Jul 22,	2000	**Ener Julio** (Col) w pts 12 Randall Bailey	Miami FL
Jun	2001	*Julio relinquished the title because of cataracts in both eyes*	
Jun 30,	2001	**DeMarcus Corley** (US) w rsf 1 Felix Flores	Las Vegas NV
Jan 19,	2002	DeMarcus Corley w pts 12 Ener Julio	Miami FL
Jan 4,	2003	DeMarcus Corley w pts 12 Randall Bailey	Washington, DC
Jul 12,	2003	Zab Judah w pts 12 DeMarcus Corley	Las Vegas, NV
Dec 13,	2003	Zab Judah w ko 1 Jaime Rangel (US)	Atlantic City, NJ
		Judah relinquished title to box at welterweight	
Sep 11,	2004	**Miguel Angel Cotto** (PR) w rsf 6 Kelson Pinto (Bra)	Hato Rey (PR)
		For vacant title	
Dec 11,	2004	Miguel Angel Cotto w rsf 6 Randall Bailey	Las Vegas, NV
Feb 26,	2005	Miguel Angel Cotto w rsf 5 DeMarcus Corley	Bayamon, (PR)
Jun 11,	2005	Miguel Angel Cotto w rsf 9 Mohamed Abdulaev (Uzb)	New York, NY
Sep 24,	2005	Miguel Angel Cotto w ko 7 Ricardo Torres (Col)	Atlantic City, NJ
Mar 4,	2006	Miguel Angel Cotto w rsf 8 Gianluca Branco (Ita)	Bayamon (PR)
Jun 10,	2006	Miguel Angel Cotto w pts 12 Paulie Malignaggi (US)	New York, NY
		Cotto relinquished title to box at welterweight	
Nov 18,	2006	**Ricardo Torres** w pts 12 Mike Arnaoutis (Gre)	Las Vegas, NV
		For vacant title	
Apr 28,	2007	Ricardo Torres w pts 12 Arturo Morua (Mex)	Barranquilla (Col)
Sep 1,	2007	Ricardo Torres w rsf 11 Kendall Holt (US)	Barranquilla (Col)
Jul 3,	2008	**Kendall Holt** w ko 1 Ricardo Torres	Las Vegas NV
Dec 13,	2008	Kendall Holt w pts 12 Demetrius Hopkins (US)	Atlantic City NJ

WBC title

Jan 24,	2004	**Arturo Gatti** (Can) w pts 12 Gianluca Branco (Ita)	Atlantic City, NJ
		For vacant title	
Jul 24,	2004	Arturo Gatti w ko 2 Leonard Dorin (Rom)	Atlantic City, NJ
Jan 29,	2005	Arturo Gatti w ko 5 James Leija (US)	Atlantic City, NJ
Jun 25,	2005	**Floyd Mayweather** (US) w rtd 6 Arturo Gatti	Atlantic City, NJ
		Mayweather relinquished the title to box at welterweight	
Sep 15,	2006	**Junior Witter** (Eng) w pts 12 DeMarcus Corley (US)	London (Eng)
		For vacant title	
Jan 20,	2007	Junior Witter w rsf 9 Arturo Morua	London (Eng)
Sep 7,	2007	Junior Witter w ko 7 Vivian Harris	Doncaster (Eng)
May 10,	2008	**Timothy Bradley** (US) w pts 12 Junior Witter	Nottingham (Eng)
Sep 13,	2008	Timothy Bradley w pts 12 Edner Cherry (US)	Biloxi MS

WBA title

Oct 19,	2002	**Vivian Harris** (Guy) w rsf 2 Diosbelys Hurtado (Cub)	Houston, TX
Jul 12,	2003	Vivian Harris w pts 12 Souleymane M'baye (Fra)	Las Vegas, NV
Apr 17,	2004	**Vivian Harris** w pts 12 Oktay Urkal (Ger)	Berlin (Ger)
Oct 23,	2004	Vivian Harris w rsf 11 Oktay Urkal	Berlin (Ger)
Jun 25,	2005	**Carlos Maussa** (Arg) w rsf 7 Vivian Harris	Atlantic City, NJ
		Maussa then fought a WBA/IBF unification bout against Ricky Hatton	

WBA/IBF titles

Nov 26,	2005	**Ricky Hatton** (Eng) w ko 9 Carlos Maussa	Sheffield (Eng)
		Hatton relinquished the titles to box at welterweight	

WBA title

Sep 2,	2006	**Souleymane M'baye** (Fra) w rsf 4 Raul Balbi (Arg)	Bolton (Eng)
		For vacant title	
Mar 10,	2007	Souleymane M'Baye drew 12 Andreas Kotelnik (Ukr)	Liverpool (Eng)
Jul 21,	2007	**Gavin Rees** (Wal) w pts 12 Souleymane M'baye	Cardiff (Wal)
Mar 22,	2008	**Andriy Kotelnik** (Ukr) w rsf 12 Gavin Rees	Cardiff (Wal)
Feb 7,	2009	Andriy Kotelnik w pts 12 Marcos Maidana (Arg)	Rostock (Ger)
Jul 18,	2009	**Amir Khan** (Eng) w pts 12 Andriy Kotelnik	Manchester (Eng)
Dec 5,	2009	Amir Khan w rsf 1 Dimitry Salita (Ukr)	Newcastle (Eng)
		The WBA also sanctioned the following Interim title fights:	
Jun 27,	2009	Marcos Maidana w rsf 6 Victor Ortiz (US)	Los Angeles, CA
Nov 21,	2009	Marcos Maidana w ko 3 William Gonzalez (Pan)	Santa Fe (Arg)
May 15,	2010	Amir Khan w rsf 11 Paul Malignaggi (US)	New York, NY

Dec 11,	2010	Amir Khan w pts 12 Marcos Maidana	Las Vegas, NV
Apr 16,	2011	Amir Khan w tdec 6 Paul McCloskey (Ire)	Manchester (Eng)
		Amir Khan promoted to WBA Super champion and Interim champion Marcos Maidana upgraded to full champion	
Sep 23,	2011	Marcos Maidana w ko 4 Petr Petrov (Rus)	Buenos Aires (Arg)
		Marcos Maidana vacated WBA title to box at welterweight	
Nov 30,	2012	**Khabib Allakhvediev** (Rus) w tdec 8 Joan Guzman (DR)	Sunrise, FL
		For vacant title	
Jul 13,	2013	Khabib Allakhverdiev w rsf 11 Souleymane M'baye	Monte Carlo (Mon)
Apr 12,	2014	**Jessie Vargas** (US) w pts 12 Khabib Allakhverdiev	Las Vegas, NV
Aug 2,	2014	Jessie Vargas w pts 12 Anton Novikov (Rus)	Las Vegas, NV
Nov 23,	2014	Jessie Vargas w pts 12 Antonio DeMarco (Mex)	Macao (Chi)
		The WBA also sanctioned the following for the Interim title	
Mar 27,	2010	Marcos Maidana w ko 6 Victor Manuel Cayo (Dom)	Las Vegas, NV
Aug 28,	2010	Marcos Maidana w pts 12 DeMarcus Corley	Buenos Aires (Arg)
Apr 9,	2011	Marcos Maidana w pts 12 Erik Morales (US)	Las Vegas, NV
Oct 22,	2011	Alberto Mosquera (Pan) drew 12 Brunet Zamora (It)	Panama City (Pan)
Dec 10,	2011	Johan Perez (Ven) w rsf 4 Fernando Castaneda (Mex)	Tepic (Mex)
Jul 21,	2012	Pablo Cesar Cano w tdec 7 Johan Perez	Cancun (Mex)
Nov 30,	2013	Johan Perez w pts 12 Paul Spadafora (US)	Chester, WV
May 10,	2014	Johan Perez w rtd 10 Fernando Monte de Oca (DR)	La Guaira (Ven)
Dec 13,	2014	Jose Benavidez (US) w pts 12 Mauricio Herrera (US)	Las Vegas, NV
May 15,	2015	Jose Benavidez w rsf 12 Jorge Paez Jr (Mex)	Phoenix, AZ
Oct 3,	2015	**Adrien Broner (US)** w rsf 12 Khabib Allakhverdiev (Rus)	Cincinnati, OH
		For the vacant title	
Apr 1,	2016	Adrien Broner w rsf 9 Ashley Theophane (Eng)	Washington, DC
May 28,	2016	**Ricky Burns (Sco)** w rsf 8 Michele Di Rocco (Ita)	Glasgow (Sco)
		For the vacant title	
Oct 7,	2016	Ricky Burns w pts 12 Kiryl Relikh (Brs)	Glasgow (Sco)

WBC title/WBA super title

Jul 14,	2012	Danny Garcia w rsf 4 Amir Khan	Las Vegas, NV
Apr 27,	2013	Danny Garcia w pts 12 Zab Judah	Brooklyn, NY
Sep 14,	2013	Danny Garcia w pts 12 Lucas Martin Matthysse	Las Vegas, NV
Mar 15,	2014	Danny Garcia w pts 12 Mauricio Herrera (USA)	Bayamon (PR)

IBF title

Feb 7,	2004	**Sharmba Mitchell** w pts 12 Lovemore Ndou (Aus)	Atlantic City, NJ
Apr 3,	2004	Sharmba Mitchell w pts 12 Michael Stewart (US)	Manchester (Eng)
Nov 6,	2004	**Kostya Tszyu** w rsf 3 Sharmba Mitchell	Phoenix, AZ
Jun 4,	2005	**Ricky Hatton** w rtd 11 Kostya Tszyu	Manchester (Eng)
		Hatton unified the WBA and IBF titles, then relinquished them	
Jun 30,	2006	**Juan Urango** (Col) w pts 12 Naoufel Ben Rabah (Tun)	Hollywood, FL
		For vacant title	
Jan 20,	2007	**Ricky Hatton** w pts 12 Juan Urango	Las Vegas, NV
		Hatton relinquished title because IBF would not accept Jose Luis Castillo as his next challenger. Lovemore Ndou was installed as champion	
Feb 4,	2007	Lovemore Ndou w rtd 11 Naoufel Ben Rabah	Sydney (Aus)
		For vacant title	
Jun 16,	2007	**Paulie Malignaggi** (US) w pts 12 Lovemore Ndou	Uncasville, CT
Jan 5,	2008	Paulie Malignaggi w pts Herman Ngoudjo (Cam)	Atlantic City, NJ
May 24,	2008	**Paulie Malignaggi** w pts 12 Lovemore Ndou	Manchester (Eng)
		Malignaggi relinquished the title to box Ricky Hatton in an IBO title fight	
Jan 30,	2009	**Juan Urango** w pts 12 Herman Ngoudjo	Montreal (Can)
		For vacant title	
Aug 28,	2009	Juan Urango w rsf 11 Randall Bailey	Hollywood, FL
Mar 6,	2010	Devon Alexander w rsf 8 Juan Urango	Uncasville, CN
Aug 7,	2010	Devon Alexander w pts 12 Andriy Kotelnik	Saint Louis, MO
		The IBF stripped Devon Alexander for refusing to box mandatory challenger Kaizer Mabuza	
Mar 5,	2011	**Zab Judah** w rsf 7 Kaizer Mabuza (SA)	Newark, NJ
		For vacant title	

WBA super title/IBF title

Jul 23,	2011	Amir Khan w ko 5 Zab Judah	Las Vegas, NV
Dec 10,	2011	**Lamont Peterson** w pts 12 Amir Khan	Washington, DC
		Peterson stripped of WBA belt for failing a drugs test	

IBF title

Feb 22,	2013	Lamont Peterson w rsf 8 Kendall Holt	Washington, DC
Jan 25,	2014	Lamont Peterson w pts 12 Dierry Jean (Can)	Washington, DC
Aug 9,	2014	Lamont Peterson w rsf 10 Edgar Santana (PR)	New York, NY
Jul 18,	2015	**Cesar Rene Cuenca (Arg)** w pts 12 Ik Yang (Chi)	Macau (Chi)
		For vacant title	
Nov 4,	2015	**Eduard Troyanovsky (Rus)** w rsf 6 Cesar Rene Cuenca	Kazan (Rus)
Apr 8,	2016	Eduard Troyanovsky w rsf 7 Cesar Rene Cuenca	Moscow (Rus)
Sep 9,	2016	Eduard Troyanovsky w rsf 2 Keita Obara (Jap)	Moscow (Rus)
Dec 3,	2016	**Julius Indongo (Nam)** w ko 1 Eduard Troyanovsky	Moscow (Rus)

WBC/WBO titles

Apr 4,	2009	**Timothy Bradley** w pts 12 Kendall Holt	Montreal (Can)
		Bradley elected to keep the WBO title and relinquished the WBC title	
Jan 29,	2011	Timothy Bradley w tdec 10 Devon Alexander	Pontiac, MI

WBC title

Aug 1,	2009	**Devon Alexander** (US) w rtd 8 Junior Witter	Rancho Mirage, CA
		For vacant title	
Mar 6,	2010	Devon Alexander w rsf 8 Juan Urango	Uncasville, CA
Aug 7,	2010	Devon Alexander w pts 12 Andriy Kotelnik	Saint Louis, MO
		Timothy Bradley won WBC title from Devon Alexander and retained WBO title. The WBC stripped Timothy Bradley for refusing to box Amir Khan	
Sep 17,	2011	**Erik Morales** w rtd 10 Pablo Cesar Cano (Mex)	Las Vegas, NV
		For vacant title	
Mar 23,	2012	**Danny Garcia** (US) w pts Erik Morales	Houston, TX
Oct 20,	2012	Danny Garcia w ko 4 Erik Morales	Brooklyn, NY
		The WBC also sanctioned the following for the Interim title	
Sep 8,	2012	Lucas Martin Matthysse (Arg) w rsf 10 Ajose Olusegun (Nig)	Las Vegas, NV
Jan 26,	2013	Lucas Martin Matthysse w ko 1 Mike Dallas Jr (US)	Las Vegas, NV

WBO title

Aug 1,	2009	Timothy Bradley nc 3 Nate Campbell (US)	Rancho Mirage, CA
Dec 12,	2009	**Timothy Bradley** w pts 12 Lamont Peterson (US)	Rancho Mirage, CA
		The WBO had sanctioned an Interim title fight as follows:	
Apr 25,	2009	**Lamont Peterson** w rsf 7 Willy Blain (Fra)	Bayamon (PR)
Dec 11,	2011	Timothy Bradley w rsf 8 Joel Casamayor	Las Vegas, NV
		The WBO sanctioned the following for the Interim title	
Apr 14,	2012	Juan Manuel Marquez w pts 12 Serhiy Fedchenko (Ukr)	Mexico City (Mex)
		Interim champion Mike Alvarado upgraded to full champion	
Oct 19,	2013	**Ruslan Provodnikov** (Rus) w pts 12 Mike Alvarado	Denver, CO
Jun 14,	2014	**Chris Algieri** (US) w pts 12 Ruslan Provodnikov	New York, NY
		Algieri stripped of title after taking non-title fight with Manny Pacquiao	
Apr 18,	2015	**Terence Crawford** w rsf 6 Thomas Dulorme (PR)	Arlington, TX
		For vacant title	

WBC title

Oct 3,	2015	**Viktor Postol (Ukr)** w ko 10 Lucas Martin Matthysse (Arg)	Carson, CA
		For the vacant title	

WBC/WBO titles

Jul 23,	2016	**Terence Crawford** w pts 12 Viktor Postol	Las Vegas, NV
Dec 10,	2016	Terence Crawford w rsf 8 John Molina Jr (US)	Omaha, NE
May 20,	2016	Terence Crawford w rtd 10 Felix Diaz (Dom Rep)	New York, NY

IBF/WBA titles

Apr 15,	2017	**Julius Indongo** w pts 12 Rickie Burns	Glasgow (Sco)

IBF/WBA Super/WBC/WBO titles

Aug 19,	2017	**Terence Crawford** w ko 3 Julius Indongo (Nam)	Lincoln, NE

Lightweight

The lightweight division had a long and colourful history under Prize Ring rules, but the scandal which surrounded the outcome of an international match between Jack McAuliffe and English champion Jem Carney in 1887 was so great that it was nine years before the first gloved championship could be staged between American champion George Lavigne and his British counterpart Dick Burge.

The weight limit then was 133lb in America and 134lb in Britain, although Freddie Welsh had it increased to 135lb in 1912 and Willie Ritchie, who was also claiming the title at the time, raised the American limit by a pound. A year later Ritchie again increased the limit to bring it into line with the British mark, at which it has remained ever since.

Racism was rampant in the division's early years, to the extent that because the black Joe Gans dominated the weight so thoroughly his rivals had to set up a "white lightweight championship". Gans was the first major figure the category produced, but his successors have included Benny Leonard, Tony Canzoneri, Barney Ross, Henry Armstrong, Joe Brown and Roberto Duran.

World Lightweight Championship Bouts

Jun 1,	1896	**George "Kid" Lavigne** (US) w ko 17 Dick Burge (Eng)	London (Eng)
Feb 8,	1897	George "Kid" Lavigne w pts 25 Kid McPartland (US)	New York, NY
Apr 30,	1897	George "Kid" Lavigne w rsf 11 Eddie Connolly (Can)	New York, NY
Sep 28,	1898	George "Kid" Lavigne drew 25 Frank Erne (US)	Coney Island, NY
Jul 3,	1899	**Frank Erne** w pts 20 George "Kid" Lavigne	Buffalo, NY
Dec 4,	1899	Frank Erne drew 25 Jack O'Brien (US)	Coney Island, NY
Mar 23,	1900	Frank Erne w rtd 12 Joe Gans (US)	New York, NY
May 12,	1902	**Joe Gans** w ko 1 Frank Erne	Fort Erie (Can)
Sep 17,	1902	Joe Gans w ko 5 Gus Gardner (US)	Baltimore, MD
Oct 31,	1904	Joe Gans w dis 5 Jimmy Britt (US)	San Francisco, CA
Sep 3,	1906	Joe Gans w dis 42 Battling Nelson (Den)	Goldfield, NV
Jan 1,	1907	Joe Gans w ko 8 Kid Herman (US)	Tonopah, NV
Sep 27,	1907	Joe Gans w pts 20 George Memsic (US)	Los Angeles, CA
May 14,	1908	Joe Gans w rsf 11 Rudy Unholz (US)	San Francisco, CA
Jul 4,	1908	**Battling Nelson** w ko 17 Joe Gans	San Francisco, CA
Sep 9,	1908	Battling Nelson w ko 21 Joe Gans	San Francisco, CA
May 29,	1909	Battling Nelson w ko 23 Dick Hyland (US)	San Francisco, CA
Feb 22,	1910	**Ad Wolgast** (US) w rsf 40 Battling Nelson	Port Richmond, CA
Mar 17,	1911	Ad Wolgast w rsf 9 George Memsic	Los Angeles, CA
Mar 31,	1911	Ad Wolgast w rtd 5 Antonio la Grave (US)	San Francisco, CA
May 27,	1911	Ad Wolgast w rtd 16 Frankie Burns (US)	San Francisco, CA
Jul 4,	1911	Ad Wolgast w ko 13 Owen Moran (Eng)	San Francisco, CA
Jul 4,	1912	Ad Wolgast w ko 13 Joe Rivers (Mex)	Los Angeles, CA
Nov 28,	1912	**Willie Ritchie** (US) w dis 16 Ad Wolgast	Daly City, CA
Jul 4,	1913	Willie Ritchie w ko 11 Joe Rivers	San Francisco, CA
Apr 17,	1914	Willie Ritchie w pts 20 Tommy Murphy (US)	San Francisco, CA
Jul 7,	1914	**Freddie Welsh** (Wal) w pts 20 Willie Ritchie	London (Eng)
Sep 4,	1916	Freddie Welsh w pts 20 Charlie White (US)	Colorado Springs, CO
May 28,	1917	**Benny Leonard** (US) w rsf 9 Freddie Welsh	New York, NY
		Leonard was recognized as champion, even though Welsh was overweight and the fight, like most of Leonard's subsequent contests, was a "no decision" affair	
Nov 26,	1920	Benny Leonard w rsf 14 Joe Welling (US)	New York, NY
Oct 14,	1921	Benny Leonard w rsf 6 Richie Mitchell (US)	New York, NY
Feb 10,	1922	Benny Leonard w pts 15 Rocky Kansas (US)	New York, NY
Jan	1925	*Leonard relinquished title*	
Jul 3,	1925	**Jimmy Goodrich** (US) w rsf 2 Stanislaus Loayza (Cze)	Long Island, NY
		For vacant title	
Dec 7,	1925	**Rocky Kansas** w pts 15 Jimmy Goodrich	Buffalo, NY
Jul 3,	1926	**Sammy Mandell** (US) w pts 10 Rocky Kansas	Chicago, IL
May 21,	1928	Sammy Mandell w pts 15 Jimmy McLarnin (Ire)	New York, NY
Aug 2,	1929	Sammy Mandell w pts 10 Tony Canzoneri (US)	Chicago, IL
Jul 17,	1930	**Al Singer** (US) w ko 1 Sammy Mandell	New York, NY
Nov 14,	1930	**Tony Canzoneri** w ko 1 Al Singer	New York, NY
Apr 24,	1931	Tony Canzoneri w ko 3 Jack "Kid" Berg (Eng)	Chicago, IL
Sep 10,	1931	Tony Canzoneri w pts 15 Jack "Kid" Berg	New York, NY
Nov 20,	1931	Tony Canzoneri w pts 15 Kid Chocolate (Cub)	New York, NY
Nov 4,	1932	Tony Canzoneri w pts 15 Billy Petrolle	New York, NY
Jun 23,	1933	**Barney Ross** (US) w pts 10 Tony Canzoneri	Chicago, IL
Sep 12,	1933	Barney Ross w pts 15 Tony Canzoneri	New York, NY
Apr	1935	*Ross relinquished title*	
May 10,	1935	**Tony Canzoneri** w pts 15 Lou Ambers (US)	New York, NY
		For vacant title	
Oct 4,	1935	Tony Canzoneri w pts 15 Al Roth (US)	New York, NY
Sep 3,	1936	**Lou Ambers** w pts 15 Tony Canzoneri	New York, NY
May 7,	1937	Lou Ambers w pts 15 Tony Canzoneri	New York, NY
Sep 23,	1937	Lou Ambers w pts 15 Pedro Montanez (PR)	New York, NY
Aug 17,	1938	**Henry Armstrong** (US) w pts 15 Lou Ambers	New York, NY
Mar 16,	1939	Henry Armstrong w ko 1 Lew Feldman (US)	St Louis, MO
		Billed as a welterweight title defence by Armstrong, but both were inside the lightweight limit	
Aug 22,	1939	**Lou Ambers** w pts 15 Henry Armstrong	New York, NY
		The NBA withdrew recognition from Ambers for his failure to defend against Davey Day	
May 3,	1940	**Sammy Angott** (US) w pts 15 Davey Day (US)	Louisville, KY
		For vacant NBA title	
May 10,	1940	**Lew Jenkins** (US) w rsf 3 Lou Ambers	New York, NY
Nov 22,	1940	Lew Jenkins w rsf 2 Pete Lello (US)	New York, NY
Dec 19,	1941	Sammy Angott w pts 15 Lew Jenkins	New York, NY
		For undisputed title	
May 15,	1942	Sammy Angott w pts 15 Allie Stolz (US)	New York, NY
		Angott retired and relinquished the title in November 1942, although he changed his mind in 1943 and was installed as the challenger for the vacant NBA version of the title	

New York title

Dec 18,	1942	**Beau Jack** (US) w ko 3 Tippy Larkin (US)	New York, NY
		For vacant title	
May 21,	1943	**Bob Montgomery** (US) w pts 15 Beau Jack (US)	New York, NY
Nov 19,	1943	**Beau Jack** w pts 15 Bob Montgomery	New York, NY
Mar 3,	1944	**Bob Montgomery** w pts 15 Beau Jack	New York, NY
Jun 28,	1946	Bob Montgomery w ko 13 Allie Stolz	New York, NY
Nov 26,	1946	Bob Montgomery w ko 8 Wesley Mouzon (US)	Philadelphia, PA
Aug 4,	1947	**Ike Williams** (US) w ko 6 Bob Montgomery	Philadelphia, PA
		For undisputed title	

NBA title

Oct 27,	1943	**Sammy Angott** w pts 15 Slugger White (US)	Los Angeles, CA
		For vacant title	
Mar 8,	1944	**Juan Zurita** (Mex) w pts 15 Sammy Angott	Hollywood, CA
Apr 18,	1945	**Ike Williams** w ko 2 Juan Zurita	Mexico City (Mex)
Apr 30,	1946	Ike Williams w rsf 8 Enrique Bolanos (US)	Los Angeles, CA
Sep 4,	1946	Ike Williams w ko 9 Ronnie James (Wal)	Cardiff (Wal)
Aug 4,	1947	Ike Williams w ko 6 Bob Montgomery	Philadelphia, PA
		For undisputed title	

Undisputed title

May 25,	1948	**Ike Williams** w pts 15 Enrique Bolanos	Los Angeles, CA
Jul 12,	1948	Ike Williams w rsf 6 Beau Jack Philadelphia, PA	
Sep 23,	1948	Ike Williams w ko 10 Jesse Flores (US)	New York, NY
Jul 21,	1949	Ike Williams w rsf 4 Enrique Bolanos	Los Angeles, CA
Dec 5,	1949	Ike Williams w pts 15 Freddie Dawson (US)	Philadelphia, PA
May 25,	1951	**Jimmy Carter** (US) w rsf 14 Ike Williams	New York, NY
Nov 14,	1951	Jimmy Carter w pts 15 Art Aragon (US)	Los Angeles, CA
Apr 1,	1952	Jimmy Carter w pts 15 Lauro Salas (Mex)	Los Angeles, CA
May 14,	1952	**Lauro Salas** w pts 15 Jimmy Carter	Los Angeles, CA
Oct 15,	1952	**Jimmy Carter** w pts 15 Lauro Salas	Chicago, IL
Apr 24,	1953	Jimmy Carter w rsf 4 Tommy Collins (US)	Boston, MA
Jun 12,	1953	Jimmy Carter w rsf 13 George Araujo (US)	New York, NY
Nov 11,	1953	Jimmy Carter w ko 5 Armand Savoie (Can)	Montreal (Can)
Mar 5,	1954	**Paddy DeMarco** (US) w pts 15 Jimmy Carter	New York, NY
Nov 17,	1954	**Jimmy Carter** w rsf 15 Paddy DeMarco	San Francisco, CA
Jun 29,	1955	**Wallace (Bud) Smith** (US) w pts 15 Jimmy Carter	Boston, MA
Oct 19,	1955	Wallace (Bud) Smith (US) w pts 15 Jimmy Carter	Cincinnati, OH
Aug 24,	1956	**Joe Brown** (US) w pts 15 Wallace (Bud) Smith	New Orleans, LA
Feb 13,	1957	Joe Brown w rsf 10 Wallace (Bud) Smith	Miami, FL
Jun 19,	1957	Joe Brown w rsf 15 Orlando Zulueta (Cub)	Denver, CO
Dec 4,	1957	Joe Brown w rsf 11 Joey Lopes (US)	Chicago, IL
May 7,	1958	Joe Brown w rsf 8 Ralph Dupas (US)	Houston, TX
Jul 23,	1958	Joe Brown w pts 15 Ralph Dupas	Houston, TX
Feb 11,	1959	Joe Brown w pts 15 Johnny Busso (US)	Houston, TX
Jun 3,	1959	Joe Brown w rtd 8 Paolo Rosi (Ita)	Washington, DC
Dec 2,	1959	Joe Brown w rtd 5 Dave Charnley (Eng)	Houston, TX
Oct 28,	1960	Joe Brown w pts 15 Cisco Andrade (US)	Los Angeles, CA
Apr 18,	1961	Joe Brown w pts 15 Dave Charnley	London (Eng)
Oct 28,	1961	Joe Brown w pts 15 Bert Somodio (Phil)	Quezon City (Phil)
Apr 21,	1962	**Carlos Ortiz** (PR) w pts 15 Joe Brown	Las Vegas, NV
Dec 3,	1962	Carlos Ortiz w ko 5 Teruo Kosaka (Jap)	Tokyo (Jap)
Apr 7,	1963	Carlos Ortiz w rsf 13 Doug Vaillant (Cub)	San Juan, CA
Feb 15,	1964	Carlos Ortiz w rsf 14 Flash Elorde (Phil)	Manila (Phil)

Apr 11, 1964 Carlos Ortiz w pts 15 Kenny Lane (US) . . . . San Juan, CA
Apr 10, 1965 **Ismael Laguna** (Pan) w pts 15 Carlos Ortiz . . . . Panama City (Pan)
Nov 13, 1965 **Carlos Ortiz** w pts 15 Ismael Laguna . . . . San Juan, CA
Jun 20, 1966 Carlos Ortiz w rsf 12 Johnny Bizzaro (US). Pittsburgh, PA
Oct 22, 1966 Carlos Ortiz w rsf 5 Sugar Ramos (Cub) . . . . Mexico City (Mex)
A riot ensued when Ramos was stopped because of a cut eye. He was ordered to resume the fight, and he refused. Two days later, the WBC vacated his title
Nov 28, 1966 Carlos Ortiz w ko 14 Flash Elorde . . . . New York, NY
For WBA title
Jul 1, 1967 Carlos Ortiz w rsf 4 Sugar Ramos . . . . San Juan, CA
For undisputed title
Aug 16, 1967 Carlos Ortiz w pts 15 Ismael Laguna . . . . New York, NY
Jun 29, 1968 **Carlos Teo Cruz** (DR) w pts 15 Carlos Ortiz . . . . Santo Domingo (DR)
Sep 28, 1968 Carlos Teo Cruz w pts 15 Mando Ramos (US). . . . . Los Angeles, CA
Feb 18, 1969 **Mando Ramos** w rsf 11 Carlos Teo Cruz. Los Angeles, CA
Oct 4, 1969 Mando Ramos w rsf 6 Yoshiaki Numata (Jap) . . . . Los Angeles, CA
Mar 3, 1970 **Ismael Laguna** w rtd 9 Mando Ramos . . . . Los Angeles, CA
May 1970 *WBC stripped Laguna of title for allegedly breaking a contract to make first defence for promoter Aileen Eaton. The following two fights involved only the WBA title*
Jun 7, 1970 Ismael Laguna w rsf 13 Guts Ishimatsu (Jap). . . . . Panama City (Pan)
Sep 26, 1970 **Ken Buchanan** (Sco) w pts 15 Ismael Laguna . . . . San Juan, CA
Feb 12, 1971 Ken Buchanan w pts 15 Ruben Navarro (US) . . . . Los Angeles, CA
For undisputed title WBC stripped Buchanan in June 1971 for signing to meet Laguna instead of their No. 1 challenger, Pedro Carrasco. The British Boxing Board upheld Buchanan as world champion

WBA title

Sep 13, 1971 **Ken Buchanan** w pts 15 Ismael Laguna. . . . . New York, NY
Jun 26, 1972 **Roberto Duran** (Pan) w rsf 13 Ken Buchanan. . . . . New York, NY
For WBA, New York and British recognition
Jan 20, 1973 Roberto Duran w ko 5 Jimmy Robertson (US). . . . . Panama City (Pan)
Jun 2, 1973 Roberto Duran w rsf 8 Hector Thompson (Aus). . . . . Panama City (Pan)
Britain and New York withdrew recognition of Duran in September 1973 for failing to honour a contract with Madison Square Garden to defend against Ken Buchanan
Sep 8, 1973 Roberto Duran w rsf 10 Guts Ishimatsu . . . . Panama City (Pan)
Mar 16, 1974 Roberto Duran w rsf 11 Esteban De Jesus (PR) . . . . Panama City (Pan)
Dec 21, 1974 Roberto Duran w rsf 1 Masataka Takayama (Jap) . . . . San Jose, CA
Mar 2, 1975 Roberto Duran w ko 14 Ray Lampkin (US) . . . . Panama City (Pan)
Dec 14, 1975 Roberto Duran w ko 15 Leoncio Ortiz (Mex) . . . . San Juan, CA
May 22, 1976 Roberto Duran w ko 14 Lou Bizzaro (US) . . . . Fort Erie (Can)
Oct 15, 1976 Roberto Duran w ko 1 Alvaro Rojas (CR). . . . . Los Angeles, CA
Jan 29, 1977 Roberto Duran w ko 13 Vilomar Fernandez (DR). . . . . Miami, FL
Sep 17, 1977 Roberto Duran w pts 15 Edwin Viruet (PR) . . . . Philadelphia, PA
Jan 21, 1978 Roberto Duran w ko 12 Esteban De Jesus . . . . Las Vegas, NV
For undisputed title Duran relinquished the title in January 1979 because of difficulty in making the weight
Jun 16, 1979 **Ernesto Espana** (Ven) w ko 13 Claude Noel (Tr) . . . . San Juan, CA
For vacant WBA title
Aug 4, 1979 Ernesto Espana w rsf 9 Johnny Lira (US) . . . . Chicago, IL
Mar 2, 1980 **Hilmer Kenty** (US) w rsf 9 Ernesto Espana . . . . Detroit, MI
Aug 2, 1980 Hilmer Kenty w rsf 9 Yong-Ho Oh (Kor). . . . . Detroit, MI
Sep 20, 1980 Hilmer Kenty w rsf 4 Ernesto Espana . . . . San Juan, CA
Nov 8, 1980 Hilmer Kenty w pts 15 Vilomar Fernandez . . . . Detroit, MI
Apr 12, 1981 **Sean O'Grady** (US) w pts 15 Hilmer Kenty . . . . Atlantic City, NJ
August 1981 T*he WBA vacated O'Grady's title because of a contractual dispute*
Sep 12, 1981 **Claude Noel** w pts 15 Rodolfo Gonzalez (Mex). . . . . Atlantic City, NJ
For vacant title
Dec 5, 1981 **Arturo Frias** (US) w ko 8 Claude Noel. . . . . Las Vegas, NV
Jan 30, 1982 Arturo Frias w tech dec 9 Ernesto Espana . . . . Atlantic City, NJ
May 8, 1982 **Ray Mancini** (US) w rsf 1 Arturo Frias . . . . Las Vegas, NV
Jul 24, 1982 Ray Mancini w rsf 6 Ernesto Espana. . . . . Warren, OH
Nov 13, 1982 Ray Mancini w rsf 14 Deuk-Koo Kim (Kor) . . . . Las Vegas, NV
Sep 15, 1983 Ray Mancini w ko 9 Orlando Romero (Peru) . . . . Atlantic City, NJ
Jan 14, 1984 Ray Mancini w rsf 3 Bobby Chacon (US). . . . . Reno, NV
Jun 1, 1984 **Livingstone Bramble** (VI) w rsf 14 Ray Mancini . . . . Buffalo, NY
Feb 16, 1985 Livingstone Bramble w pts 15 Ray Mancini . . . . Reno, NV
Feb 16, 1986 Livingstone Bramble w rsf 13 Tyrone Crawley (US) . . . . Reno, NV
Sep 26, 1986 **Edwin Rosario** (PR) w ko 2 Livingstone Bramble . . . . Miami, FL
Aug 11, 1987 Edwin Rosario w ko 8 Juan Nazario (PR) . . . . Chicago, IL
Nov 21, 1987 **Julio Cesar Chavez** (Mex) w rsf 11 Edwin Rosario. . . . . Las Vegas, NV
Apr 16, 1988 Julio Cesar Chavez w rsf 6 Rodolfo Aguilar (Pan). . . . . Las Vegas, NV
Oct 29, 1988 Julio Cesar Chavez w tech dec 11 Jose Luis Ramirez (Mex) . . . . . Las Vegas, NV
For WBA and WBC titles, both of which Chavez relinquished in May 1989
Jul 9, 1989 **Edwin Rosario** w rsf 6 Anthony Jones (US) . . . . Atlantic City, NJ
For vacant WBA title
Apr 4, 1990 **Juan Nazario** w rsf 8 Edwin Rosario . . . . New York, NY
Aug 11, 1990 **Pernell Whitaker** w ko 1 Juan Nazario. . . . . Stateline, NV
For WBC, IBF and WBA titles

WBC title

Nov 5, 1971 **Pedro Carrasco** (Sp) w dis 11 Mando Ramos . . . . Madrid (Sp)
For vacant title. Because of controversy surrounding Ramos' disqualification, the verdict was declared "null and void" at a WBC meeting in Mexico City on November 20
Feb 18, 1972 **Mando Ramos** w pts 15 Pedro Carrasco . . . . Los Angeles, CA
WBC later withdrew recognition of fight as the decision was "locally influenced"
Jun 28, 1972 Mando Ramos w pts 15 Pedro Carrasco. . . . . Madrid (Sp)
For vacant title
Sep 15, 1972 **Chango Carmona** (Mex) w rsf 8 Mando Ramos . . . . Los Angeles, CA
Nov 10, 1972 **Rodolfo Gonzalez** (Mex) w rtd 12 Chango Carmona. . . . . Los Angeles, CA
Mar 17, 1973 Rodolfo Gonzalez w rsf 9 Ruben Navarro . . . . Los Angeles, CA
Oct 27, 1973 Rodolfo Gonzalez w rtd 10 Antonio Puddu (Ita). . . . . Los Angeles, CA
Apr 11, 1974 **Guts Ishimatsu** w ko 8 Rodolfo Gonzalez. . . . . Tokyo (Jap)
Sep 13, 1974 Guts Ishimatsu drew 15 Turi Pineda (Mex) . . . . Nagoya (Jap)
Nov 28, 1974 Guts Ishimatsu w ko 12 Rodolfo Gonzalez . . . . Osaka (Jap)
Feb 21, 1975 Guts Ishimatsu w pts 15 Ken Buchanan . . . . Tokyo (Jap)
Jun 5, 1975 Guts Ishimatsu w pts 15 Turi Pineda. . . . . Osaka (Jap)
Dec 4, 1975 Guts Ishimatsu w ko 14 Alvaro Rojas . . . . Tokyo (Jap)
May 8, 1976 **Esteban De Jesus** w pts 15 Guts Ishimatsu . . . . San Juan, CA
Sep 10, 1976 Esteban De Jesus w ko 7 Hector Medina (DR) . . . . Bayamon (PR)
Feb 12, 1977 Esteban De Jesus w rsf 6 Buzzsaw Yamabe (Jap) . . . . Bayamon (PR)
Jun 25, 1977 Esteban De Jesus w ko 11 Vicente Mijares (Mex) . . . . Bayamon (PR)
Jan 21, 1978 **Roberto Duran** w ko 12 Esteban De Jesus. . . . . Las Vegas, NV
For undisputed title Duran relinquished the title in January 1979 because of difficulty making the weight
Apr 17, 1979 **Jim Watt** (Sco) w rsf 12 Alfredo Pitalua (Col) . . . . Glasgow (Sco)
For vacant WBC title
Nov 3, 1979 Jim Watt w rsf 9 Roberto Vasquez (US). . . . . Glasgow (Sco)
Mar 14, 1980 Jim Watt w rsf 4 Charlie Nash (Ire) . . . . Glasgow (Sco)
Jun 7, 1980 Jim Watt w pts 15 Howard Davis (US). . . . . Glasgow (Sco)
Nov 1, 1980 Jim Watt w rsf 12 Sean O'Grady . . . . Glasgow (Sco)
Jun 20, 1981 **Alexis Arguello** (Nic) w pts 15 Jim Watt. . . . . Wembley (Eng)
Oct 3, 1981 Alexis Arguello w rsf 14 Ray Mancini . . . . Atlantic City, NJ
Nov 21, 1981 Alexis Arguello w ko 7 Roberto Elizondo (US). . . . . Las Vegas, NV
Feb 13, 1982 Alexis Arguello w rsf 6 James "Bubba" Busceme (US). . . . . Beaumont, TX
May 22, 1982 Alexis Arguello w ko 5 Andy Ganigan (US) . . . . Las Vegas, NV
Arguello relinquished WBC title in February 1983
May 1, 1983 **Edwin Rosario** (PR) w pts 12 Jose Luis Ramirez . . . . San Juan, CA
For vacant title
Mar 17, 1984 Edwin Rosario w rsf 1 Roberto Elizondo. . . . . San Juan, CA
Jun 23, 1984 Edwin Rosario w pts 12 Howard Davis . . . . San Juan, CA
Nov 3, 1984 **Jose Luis Ramirez** w rsf 4 Edwin Rosario . . . . San Juan, CA
Aug 10, 1985 **Hector Camacho** (PR) w pts 12 Jose Luis Ramirez . . . . New York, NY
Jun 13, 1986 Hector Camacho w pts 12 Edwin Rosario. . . . . New York, NY
Sep 26, 1986 Hector Camacho w pts 12 Cornelius Boza-Edwards (Eng) . . . . Miami, FL
Camacho relinquished the title because of weight problems in May 1987
Jul 19, 1987 **Jose Luis Ramirez** w pts 12 Terrence Alli (Guy). . . . . St Tropez (Fra)
For vacant title
Oct 10, 1987 Jose Luis Ramirez w ko 5 Cornelius Boza-Edwards. . . . . Paris (Fra)
Mar 12, 1988 Jose Luis Ramirez w pts 12 Pernell Whitaker. Paris (Fra)
Oct 29, 1988 **Julio Cesar Chavez** w tech dec 11 Jose Luis Ramirez. . . . . Las Vegas, NV
For WBA and WBC titles, both of which Chavez relinquished in May 1989
Aug 20, 1989 **Pernell Whitaker** w pts 12 Jose Luis Ramirez . . . . Norfolk, VA
For IBF and vacant WBC titles

IBF title

Jan 30, 1984 **Charlie "Choo Choo" Brown** (US) w pts 15 Melvin Paul (US) . . . . Atlantic City, NJ
Apr 15, 1984 **Harry Arroyo** (US) w rsf 14 Charlie "Choo Choo" Brown . . . . Atlantic City, NJ
Sep 1, 1984 Harry Arroyo w rsf 8 Charlie "White Lightning" Brown (US) . . . . Youngstown, OH
Jan 12, 1985 Harry Arroyo w rsf 11 Terrence Alli . . . . Atlantic City, NJ
Apr 6, 1985 **Jimmy Paul** (US) w pts 15 Harry Arroyo . . . . Atlantic City, NJ
Jun 30, 1985 Jimmy Paul w rsf 14 Robin Blake (US) . . . . Las Vegas, NV
Jun 4, 1986 Jimmy Paul w pts 15 Irleis Perez (Cub) . . . . East Rutherford, NJ
Aug 15, 1986 Jimmy Paul w pts 15 Darryl Tyson (US) . . . . Detroit, MI
Dec 5, 1986 **Greg Haugen** (US) w pts 15 Jimmy Paul. . . . . Las Vegas, NV
Jun 7, 1987 **Vinny Pazienza** (US) w pts 15 Greg Haugen . . . . Providence, RI
Feb 6, 1988 **Greg Haugen** w pts 15 Vinny Pazienza . . . . Atlantic City, NJ
Apr 11, 1988 Greg Haugen w tech dec 11 Miguel Santana (PR) . . . . Tacoma, WA
Oct 28, 1988 Greg Haugen w rtd 10 Gert Bo Jacobsen (Den) . . . . Copenhagen (Den)
Feb 18, 1989 **Pernell Whitaker** w pts 12 Greg Haugen . . . . Hampton, VA
Apr 30, 1989 Pernell Whitaker w rsf 3 Louie Lomeli (US). . . . . Norfolk, VA
Aug 20, 1989 Pernell Whitaker (US) w pts 12 Jose Luis Ramirez. . . . . Norfolk, VA
For IBF and vacant WBC titles

WBC/IBF titles

Feb 3, 1990 **Pernell Whitaker** w pts 12 Fred Pendleton (US). . . . . Atlantic City, NJ
May 19, 1990 Pernell Whitaker w pts 12 Azumah Nelson (Gha) . . . . Las Vegas, NV

Aug 11,	1990	Pernell Whitaker w ko 1 Juan Nazario	Stateline, NV
		For WBC, IBF and WBA titles	

WBC/WBA/IBF titles

Feb 23,	1991	**Pernell Whitaker** w pts 12 Anthony Jones	Las Vegas, NV
Jul 27,	1991	Pernell Whitaker w pts 12 Poli Diaz (Sp)	Norfolk, VA
Oct 5,	1991	Pernell Whitaker w pts 12 Jorge Paez (Mex)	Reno, NV
Feb	1992	*Whitaker relinquished the lightweight titles to box at light-welterweight*	

WBA title

Jun 12,	1992	**Joey Gamache** (US) w rtd 8 Chil-Sung Chun (Kor)	Portland, ME
		For vacant title	
Oct 24,	1992	**Tony Lopez** (US) w rsf 11 Joey Gamache	Portland, ME
Feb 12,	1993	Tony Lopez w pts 12 Dingaan Thobela (SA)	Sacramento, CA
Jun 26,	1993	**Dingaan Thobela** w pts 12 Tony Lopez	Sun City (Bop)
Oct 30,	1993	**Orzoubek Nazarov** (Rus) w pts 12 Dingaan Thobela	Johannesburg (SA)
Mar 19,	1994	Orzoubek Nazarov w pts 12 Dingaan Thobela	Hammanskraal
Dec 10,	1994	Orzoubek Nazarov w ko 2 Joey Gamache	Portland, ME
May 15,	1995	Orzoubek Nazarov w ko 2 Won Park (Kor)	Tokyo (Jap)
Nov 15,	1995	Orzoubek Nazarov w pts 12 Dindo Canoy (Phil)	Iwaki (Jap)
Apr 15,	1996	Orzoubek Nazarov w ko 4 Adrianus Taroe (Indo)	Tokyo (Jap)
May 10,	1997	Orzoubek Nazarov w rsf 7 Leveander Johnson (US)	Coconut Grove, FL
May 16,	1998	**Jean Baptiste Mendy** w pts 12 Orzoubek Nazarov	Paris (Fra)
Jan 25,	1999	Jean Baptiste Mendy w pts 12 Alberto Sicurella (Arg)	Paris (Fra)
Apr 10,	1999	**Julien Lorcy** (Fra) w rsf 6 Jean Baptiste Mendy	Paris (Fra)
Aug 7,	1999	**Stefano Zoff** (Ita) w pts 12 Julien Lorcy	Le Cannet (Fra)
Nov 13,	1999	**Gilberto Serrano** (Ven) w rsf 10 Stefano Zoff	Las Vegas, NV
Mar 12,	2000	Gilberto Serrano w rsf 5 Hiroyuki Sakamoto (Jap)	Tokyo (Jap)
Jun 11,	2000	**Takanori Hatakeyama** (Jap) w rsf 8 Gilberto Serrano	Tokyo (Jap)
Oct 11,	2000	Takanori Hatakeyama w rtd 10 Hiroyuki Sakamoto	Yokohama (Jap)
Feb 17,	2001	Takanori Hatakeyama drew 12 Rick Roberts Yoshimura	Tokyo (Jap)
Jul 7,	2001	**Julien Lorcy** w pts 12 Takanori Hatakeyama	Saitama (Jap)
Oct 8,	2001	**Raul Balbi** (Arg) w pts 12 Julien Lorcy	Paris (Fra)
Jan 5,	2002	**Leonard Dorin** (Rom) w pts 12 Raul Balbi	San Antonio, TX
May 31,	2002	Leonard Dorin w pts 12 Raul Balbi	Bucharest (Rom)
		Dorin then fought a WBA/IBF unification bout against Paul Spadafora	

WBC title

Aug 24,	1992	**Miguel Angel Gonzalez** (Mex) w rtd 9 Wilfredo Rocha (Col)	Mexico City (Mex)
Dec 5,	1992	Miguel Angel Gonzalez w pts 12 Darryl Tyson	Mexico City (Mex)
Apr 26,	1993	Miguel Angel Gonzalez w pts 12 Hector Lopez (Mex)	Aguascalientes (Mex)
Aug 13,	1993	Miguel Angel Gonzalez w pts 12 David Sample (US)	Guadalajara (Mex)
Nov 27,	1993	Miguel Angel Gonzalez w rsf 10 Wilfredo Rocha	Mexico City (Mex)
Mar 29,	1994	Miguel Angel Gonzalez w rsf 5 Jean Baptiste Mendy (Fra)	Paris (Fra)
Aug 6,	1994	Miguel Angel Gonzalez w rsf 8 Leavander Johnson (US)	Ciudad Juarez (Mex)
Dec 13,	1994	Miguel Angel Gonzalez w rtd 5 Calvin Grove (US)	Albuquerque, NM
Apr 25,	1995	Miguel Angel Gonzalez w pts 12 Ricardo Silva (Arg)	South Padre Island, TX
Jun 2,	1995	Miguel Angel Gonzalez w pts 12 Marty Jakubowski (US)	Ledyard, CT
Aug 19,	1995	Miguel Angel Gonzalez w pts 12 Lamar Murphy (US)	Las Vegas, NV
Feb	1996	*Miguel Angel Gonzalez relinquished the title to box at light-welterweight*	
Apr 20,	1996	**Jean-Baptiste Mendy** (Fra) w pts 12 Lamar Murphy	Paris (Fra)
		For vacant title	
Mar 1,	1997	**Steve Johnston** (US) w pts 12 Jean-Baptiste Mendy	Paris (Fra)
Jul 27	1997	Steve Johnston w pts 12 Hiroyuki Sakamato (Jap)	Yokohama (Jap)
Sep 12,	1997	Steve Johnston w pts 12 Saul Duran (Mex)	Las Vegas, NV
Feb 28,	1998	Steve Johnston w pts 12 George Scott (Lib)	Atlantic City, NJ
Jun 13,	1998	**Cesar Bazan** (Mex) w pts 12 Steve Johnston	El Paso, TX
Aug 23,	1998	Cesar Bazan w pts 12 Hiroyuki Sakamato	Yokohama (Jap)
Oct 30,	1998	Cesar Bazan w pts 12 Mauro Lucero (Mex)	Juarez (Mex)
Feb 27,	1999	**Steve Johnston** w pts 12 Cesar Bazan	Miami, FL
Jun 26,	1999	Stevie Johnston w pts 12 Aldo Rios (Arg)	Las Vegas, NV
Aug 14,	1999	Stevie Johnston w pts 12 Angel Manfredy (US)	Ledyard, CT
Nov 29,	1999	Stevie Johnston w pts 12 Billy Schwer (Eng)	London (Eng)
Mar 17,	2000	Stevie Johnston w rsf 2 Julio Alvarez (Mex)	Denver, CO
Jun 17,	2000	**Jose Luis Castillo** (Mex) w pts 12 Stevie Johnston	Bell Gdns, CA
Sep 15,	2000	Jose Luis Castillo drew 12 Stevie Johnston	Denver, CO
Jan 20,	2001	Jose Luis Castillo w rsf 6 Cesar Bazan (Mex)	Las Vegas, NV
Jun 16,	2001	Jose Luis Castillo w rsf 1 Sung-ho Yuh (SK)	Hermosillo, MX
Apr 20,	2002	**Floyd Mayweather** (US) w pts 12 Jose Luis Castillo	Las Vegas, NV
Dec 7,	2002	Floyd Mayweather w pts 12 Jose Luis Castillo	Las Vegas, NV
Apr 19,	2003	Floyd Mayweather w pts 12 Victoriano Sosa (DR)	Fresno, CA
Nov 1,	2003	Floyd Mayweather w rsf 7 Philip Ndou (SA)	Grand Rapids, MI
		Mayweather relinquished title to box at light-welterweight	
Jun 5,	2004	**Jose Luis Castillo** w pts 12 Juan Lazcano (US)	Las Vegas, NV
		For vacant title	
Dec 4,	2004	Jose Luis Castillo w pts 12 Joel Casamayor (Cub)	Las Vegas, NV
Mar 5,	2005	Jose Luis Castillo w rsf 10 Julio Diaz (Mex)	Las Vegas, NV
		Castillo then fought a WBC/WBO unification fight against Diego Corrales	

IBF title

Aug 29,	1992	**Fred Pendleton** tech draw 2 Tracy Spann (US)	Reno, NV
		For vacant title	
Jan 10,	1993	Fred Pendleton w pts 12 Tracy Spann	Atlantic City, NJ
Jul 17,	1993	Fred Pendleton w pts 12 Jorge Paez	Las Vegas, NV
Feb 19,	1994	**Rafael Ruelas** (US) w pts 12 Fred Pendleton	Inglewood, CA
May 27,	1994	Rafael Ruelas w rsf 3 Mike Evgen (US)	Las Vegas, NV
Jan 28,	1995	Rafael Ruelas w rsf 8 Billy Schwer (Eng)	Las Vegas, NV
May 6,	1995	**Oscar De La Hoya** (US) w rsf 2 Rafael Ruelas	Las Vegas, NV
		For both the WBO and IBF titles. In July 1995, De La Hoya vacated IBF title	
Aug 19,	1995	**Phillip Holiday** (SA) w rtd 11 Miguel Julio (Col)	Sun City (Bop)
		For vacant title	
Sep 9,	1995	Phillip Holiday w pts 12 Ray Martinez (US)	Sun City (Bop)
Feb 17,	1996	Philip Holiday w rsf 10 John Lark (US)	Hammanskraal (SA)
May 18,	1996	Philip Holiday w rsf 2 Jeff Fenech (Aus)	Melbourne (Aus)
Oct 19,	1996	Philip Holiday w pts 12 Joe Diaz (Mex)	Johannesburg (SA)
Dec 21,	1996	Philip Holiday w pts 12 Ivan Robinson (US)	Uncasville, CT
May 16,	1997	Philip Holiday w pts 12 Pete Taliaferro (US)	Hammanskraal (SA)
Aug 2,	1997	**Shane Mosley** w pts 12 Philip Holiday	Uncasville, CT
Nov 25,	1997	Shane Mosley w ko 11 Manuel Gomez (Mex)	El Paso, TX
Feb 6,	1998	Shane Mosley w rsf 8 Demetrius Ceballos (Pan)	Uncasville, CT
May 9,	1998	Shane Mosley w rsf 8 Juan Molina (PR)	Atlantic City, NJ
June 27,	1998	Shane Mosley w rsf 5 Wilfredo Ruiz (Col)	Philadelphia, PA
Sept 22,	1998	Shane Mosley w rsf 5 Eduardo Morales (Arg)	New York, NY
Nov 14,	1998	Shane Mosley w rtd 9 Jesse James Leija (US)	Ledyard, CT
April 17,	1999	Shane Mosley w rsf 8 John Brown (US)	Indio, CA
		Mosley vacated the title to box at welterweight	
Aug 20,	1999	**Paul Spadafora** (US) w pts 12 Israel Cardona (PR)	Chester, WV
Dec 17,	1999	Paul Spadafora w rsf 11 Renato Cornett (Aug)	Pittsburgh, PA
Mar 3,	2000	Paul Spadafora w pts 12 Victoriano Sosa (DR)	Verona, NY
May 6,	2000	Paul Spadafora w tdec 11 Mike Griffith (US)	Pittsburgh, PA
Dec 16,	2000	Paul Spadafora w pts 12 Billy Irwin (Can)	Pittsburgh, PA
May 8,	2001	Paul Spadafora w pts 12 Joel Perez (US)	Pittsburgh, PA
Mar 9,	2002	Paul Spadafora w pts 12 Angel Manfredy	Pittsburgh, PA

WBO title

Jan 21,	1989	**Mauricio Aceves** (Mex) drew 12 Amancio Castro (Col)	Monteria (Col)
		For vacant title	
May 8,	1989	Mauricio Aceves w pts 12 Amancio Castro	Santa Ana, CA
Aug 30,	1989	Mauricio Aceves w rsf 10 Oscar Bejines (Mex)	Los Angeles, CA
Sep 22,	1990	**Dingaan Thobela** w pts 12 Mauricio Aceves	Brownsville, TX
Feb 2,	1991	Dingaan Thobela w pts 12 Mario Martinez (Mex)	San Jose, CA
Sep 14,	1991	Dingaan Thobela w pts 12 Antonio Rivera (PR)	Johannesburg (SA)
Jul	1992	*Thobela relinquished the WBO title to box for the WBA version*	
Sep 25,	1992	**Giovanni Parisi** (Ita) w rsf 10 Javier Altamirano (Mex)	Voghera (Ita)
		For vacant title	
Apr 16,	1993	Giovanni Parisi w pts 12 Michael Ayers (Eng)	Rome (Ita)
Sep 24,	1993	Giovanni Parisi w pts 12 Antonio Rivera (PR)	Rome (Ita)
Apr	1994	*Parisi relinquished the title to box at light-welterweight*	
Jul 29,	1994	**Oscar De La Hoya** w ko 2 Jorge Paez	Las Vegas, NV
		For vacant title	
Nov 18,	1994	Oscar De La Hoya w rsf 3 Carl Griffith (US)	Las Vegas, NV
Dec 10,	1994	Oscar De La Hoya w rsf 9 Johnny Avila (US)	Los Angeles, CA
Feb 18,	1995	Oscar De La Hoya w pts 12 Juan "John-John" Molina (PR)	Las Vegas, NV
May 6,	1995	Oscar De La Hoya w rsf 2 Rafael Ruelas	Las Vegas, NV
		For WBO and IBF titles. La Hoya vacated IBF title in July 1995	
Sep 9,	1995	Oscar De La Hoya w rtd 6 Genaro Hernandez (US)	Las Vegas, NV
Dec 15,	1995	Oscar De La Hoya w rsf 2 Jesse James Leija (US)	New York, NY
Jul	1996	*De La Hoya relinquished title on becoming WBC light-welterweight champion*	
Sep 24,	1996	**Artur Grigorian** (Arm) w ko 2 Gene Reed (US)	Berlin (Ger)
		For vacant title	
Nov 16,	1996	Artur Grigorian w pts 12 Marty Jakubowski	Hamburg (Ger)
Feb 22,	1997	Artur Grigorian w rsf 11 Raul Horacio Balbi (Arg)	Hamburg (Ger)
Oct 11,	1997	Artur Grigorian w pts 12 David Armstrong (US)	Cottbus (Ger)
Mar 14,	1998	Artur Grigorian w rsf 6 Marco Rudolph (Ger)	Hamburg (Ger)
Oct 24,	1998	Artur Grigorian w rsf 10 Giorgio Ccampanella (Ita)	Hamburg (Ger)
Mar 13,	1999	Artur Grigorian w pts 13 Oscar Garcia Cano (Spa)	Lubeck (Ger)
Oct 9,	1999	Artur Grigorian w ko 5 Michael Clark (US)	Oberhausen (Ger)
Nov 27,	1999	Artur Grigorian w rsf 10 Wilson Galli (Ur)	Lubeck (Ger)
Feb 19,	2000	Artur Grigorian w rtd 9 Sandro Casamonica (Ita)	Berlin (Ger)
Jun 23,	2000	Artur Grigorian w rsf 10 Zoltan Kalocsai (Hun)	Budapest (Hun)
Nov 25,	2000	Artur Grigorian w pts 12 Antonio Pitalua (Col)	Hanover (Ger)
Feb 24,	2001	Artur Grigorian w rsf 6 Jose Angel Perez (Sp)	Hamburg (Ger)
Jun 16,	2001	Artur Grigorian w pts 12 Aldo Rios	Budapest (Hun)
Jan 5,	2002	Artur Grigorian w rsf 7 Rocky Martinez (US)	Magdeburg (Ger)
Sep 14,	2002	Artur Grigorian w pts 12 Stefano Zoff (Ita)	Braunschweig (Ger)

Jan 18, 2003	Artur Grigorian w pts 12 Matt Zegan (Pol) .... Essen (Ger)	
Jan 3, 2004	**Acelino Freitas** (Bra) w pts 12 Artur Grigorian .... Mashantucket, CT	
Aug 7, 2004	**Diego Corrales** (US) w rtd 10 Acelino Freitas .... Mashantucket, CT *Corrales unified the WBO and WBC titles against Jose Luis Castillo*	
Apr 29, 2006	**Acelino Freitas** w pts 12 Zahir Raheem (US) .... Mashantucket *For vacant title*	

WBC/WBO titles

May 7, 2005 — **Diego Corrales** w rsf 10 Jose Luis Castillo (Mex)............. Las Vegas, NV
WBC/WBO unification bout. Corrales later relinquished the WBO title

WBC title

Oct 7, 2006 — **Joel Casamayor** (Cub) w pts 12 Diego Corrales............... Las Vegas, NV
Joel Casamayor stripped of title for failing to defend. David Diaz was recognized as Interim champion after stopping Jose Armando Santa Cruz in August 2006
Aug 4, 2007 — **David Diaz** (US) w pts 12 Erik Morales (Mex)................. Rosemont, IL
While recognising Joel Casamayor as world champion, the WBC sanctioned the following two matches for an Interim title:
May 20, 2006 — **Jose Armando Santa Cruz** (Mex) w rsf 6 Chikashi Inada (Jap) . .Los Angeles, CA
Aug 12, 2006 — **David Diaz** (US) w rsf 10 Jose Armando Santa Cruz .... Las Vegas, NV
Then the WBC resumed recognition of Casamayor.
Nov 10, 2007 — **Joel Casamayor** w pts 12 Jose Armando Santa Cruz............New York, NY
WBC stripped Casamayor of recognition, and recognised David Diaz as champion
Jun 28, 2008 — **Manny Pacquiao** w rsf 9 David Diaz....................... Las Vegas, NV
Manny Pacquiao relinquished the title to move up to light-welterweight
Apr 4, 2009 — **Edwin Valero** (Ven) w rsf 2 Antonio Pitalua (Col) .... Austin, TX
For vacant title
The WBC then recognised an Interim fight, as follows:
Oct 31, 2009 — **Antonio De Marco** (Mex) w rsf 10 Jose Alfaro (Nic)............ Las Vegas, NV
Dec 19, 2009 — Edwin Valero w rtd 7 Hector Velasquez (Mex)................ La Guaira (Ven)
Feb 6, 2010 — Edwin Valero w rtd 9 Antonio DeMarco.................... Monterrey (Mex)
Edwin Valero vacated title on medical grounds
Mar 13, 2010 — Humberto Soto w pts 12 David Diaz .... Arlington, TX
For vacant title
May 15, 2010 — Humberto Soto w pts 12 Ricardo Dominguez (Mex) .... Los Mochis (Mex)
Sep 18, 2010 — Humberto Soto w pts 12 Fidel Monterrosa Munoz (Mex) ....Culiacan (Mex)
Dec 4, 2010 — Humberto Soto w pts 12 Urbano Antillon .... Anaheim, CA
Jun 25, 2011 — Humberto Soto w tdec 11 Motoki Sasaki (Jap)................Cozumel (Mex)
Soto relinquished title to box at light-welterweight
Oct 15, 2011 — Antonio DeMarco w rsf 11 Jorge Linares ....Los Angeles, CA
For vacant title
Mar 17, 2012 — Antonio DeMarco w ko 5 Miguel Roman (Mex)............ Los Mochis (Mex)
Sep 8, 2012 — Antonio DeMarco w rsf 1 John Molina (US) ....Oakland, CA
Nov 17, 2012 — Adrien Broner (US) w rsf 8 Antonio DeMarco ....Atlantic City, NJ
Feb 16, 2013 — Adrien Broner w ret 5 Gavin Rees (Wal) .... Newark, NJ
Adrien Broner stripped of title.
Interim champion Omar Figueroa Jr upgraded to full champion
Jul 27, 2013 — Omar Figueroa Jr (USA) w pts 12 Nihito Arakawa (Jap)........San Antonio, TX
Apr 26, 2014 — Omar Figueroa Jr w pts 12 Jerry Belmontes (USA) ....Carson, CA
Aug 16, 2014 — Omar Figueroa Jr w ko 9 Daniel Estrada (Mex) ....Carson, CA
Omar Figueroa Jr vacated title
Dec 30, 2014 — **Jorge Linares** (Ven) w ko 4 Javier Prieto (Mex) .... Tokyo (Jap)
For vacant title
May 30, 2015 — Jorge Linares w rsf 10 Kevin Mitchell........................London (Eng)

WBA/IBF title

May 17, 2003 — Leonard Dorin drew 12 Paul Spadafora .... Pittsburgh, PA
WBA/IBF unification bout. Dorin relinquished WBA title to move up to light-welterweight

WBA title

Apr 10, 2004 — **Lavka Sim** (Mng) w rsf 5 Miguel Callist (Pan)................. Las Vegas, NV
For vacant title
Jul 17, 2004 — **Juan Diaz** (US) w pts 12 Lavka Sim .... Houston, TX
Nov 4, 2004 — Juan Diaz w pts 12 Julien Lorcy (Fra)...................... San Antonio, TX
Jan 21, 2005 — Juan Diaz w rsf 9 Billy Irwin (Can) .... Houston, TX
Apr 8, 2006 — Juan Diaz w pts 12 Jose Miguel Cotto (PR) .... Las Vegas, NV
Jul 15, 2006 — Juan Diaz w rsf 9 Randy Suico (Phi)........................ Las Vegas, NV
Nov 4, 2006 — Juan Diaz w pts 12 Fernando Angulo (Ecu) .... Phoenix, TX

IBF title

Nov 9, 2002 — Paul Spadafora w pts 12 Dennis Holbaek Pedersen (Den) .... Chester, WV
Spadafora drew a unification fight with WBA champion Leonard Dorin, then was stripped of the IBF title because of legal problems
Nov 22, 2003 — **Javier Jauregui** (Mex) w rsf 11 Leavander Johnson (US).......Los Angeles, CA
May 13, 2004 — **Julio Diaz** (Mex) w pts 12 Javier Jauregui .... San Diego, CA
Diaz relinquished the title to box WBC champion Jose Luis Castillo
Jun 17, 2005 — **Leavander Johnson** w rsf 7 Stefano Zoff (Ita) .... Milan (Ita)
For vacant title
Sep 17, 2005 — **Jesus Chavez** (Mex) w rsf 11 Leavander Johnson............ Las Vegas, NV
Feb 3, 2007 — **Julio Diaz** w ko 3 Jesus Chavez .... Kissimmee, FL

WBA/WBO title

Apr 28, 2007 — **Juan Diaz** w rtd 8 Acelino Freitas....................... Mashantucket, CT

WBA/WBO/IBF titles

Oct 13, 2007 — **Juan Diaz** w rsf 9 Julio Diaz.......................... Mashantucket, CT
Mar 8, 2008 — **Nate Campbell** w pts 12 Juan Diaz......................... Cancun (Mex)
Feb 14, 2009 — Nate Campbell w pts 12 Ali Funeka (SA)........................ Sunrise FL
Campbell failed to make the weight and so the titles were vacated

WBA super title/WBO title

Jul 31, 2010 — Juan Manuel Marquez w pts 12 Juan Diaz.................. Las Vegas, NV
Nov 21, 2010 — Juan Manuel Marquez w rsf 9 Michael Katsidis............... Las Vegas, NV

WBA title

When Juan Diaz unified the WBA and WBO titles, the WBA recognized him as a "unified" champion, so freeing up their "world" title as follows:
May 11, 2007 — Jose Miguel Cotto (PR) drew 12 Prawet Singwancha (Tha) ....Salinas (PR)
Dec 29, 2007 — **Jose Alfaro** (Nic) w pts 12 Prawet Singwancha .... Bielefeld (Ger)
May 19, 2008 — **Yusuke Kobori** (Jap) w rsf 3 Jose Alfaro .... Tokyo (Jap)
Jan 3, 2009 — **Paulus Moses** (Nam) w pts 12 Yusuke Kobori ....Yokohama (Jap)
Jul 25, 2009 — Paulus Moses w pts 12 Takehiro Shimada (Jap)............. Windhoek (Nam)
The WBA also declared the following fight for the Interim championship:
Jul 25, 2009 — **Miguel Acosta** (Ven) w ko 9 Urbano Antillon (Mex) ....Nuevo Vallerta (Mex)
May 29, 2010 — Miguel Acosta w ko 6 Paulus Moses (Nam) .... Windhoek (Nam)
Feb 26, 2011 — **Brandon Rios** (US) w rsf 10 Miguel Acosta.................. Las Vegas, NV
Jul 9, 2011 — Brandon Rios w pts 12 Urbano Antillon.........................Carson, CA
Dec 3, 2011 — Brandon Rios w rsf 11 John Murray (Eng) ....New York, NY
Apr 14, 2012 — Brandon Rios w pts 12 Richard Abril......................... Las Vegas, NV
For vacant title. Rios failed to make the weight and only Abril could win the title
The WBA sanctioned the following for the Interim title
Apr 9, 2011 — Robert Guerrero w pts 12 Michael Katsidis .... Las Vegas, NV
Oct 22, 2011 — Richard Abril (US) w pts 12 Miguel Acosta ....Panama City (Pan)
Abril upgraded to full champion
Mar 2, 2013 — Richar Abril w pts 12 Sharif Bogere (Uganada)................ Las Vegas, NV
Sep 20, 2014 — Richar Abril w pts 12 Edis Tatli (Fin) .... .Helsinki (Fin)
The WBA sanctioned the following for the Interim title
Jun 8, 2013 — Yuriorkis Gamboa w pts 12 Darleys Perez (Col) ....Montreal (Can)
Jun 28, 2014 — Darleys Perez w pts 12 Argenis Lopez (DR) .... Santo Domingo (DR)
Oct 24, 2014 — Darleys Perez w ko 6 Jaider Parra (Ven)..................Barranquilla (Col)
Jan 19, 2015 — Darleys Perez w pts 12 Jonathan Maicelo (Peru)............. Santa Ynez, CA
Apr 18, 2015 — Derry Mathews (Eng) w pts 12 Tony Luis (Can) .... Liverpool (Eng)
Jul 18, 2015 — Darleys Perez drew Anthony Crolla (Eng) .... Manchester (Eng)
Nov 21, 2015 — **Anthony Crolla** w ko 5 Darleys Perez........................London (Eng)
The WBO sanctioned the following fight for the interim title
Dec 12, 2015 — Ismael Barroso (Ven) w rsf 5 Kevin Mitchell (Eng) ....London (Eng)
May 7, 2016 — Anthony Crolla w ko 7 Ismael Barroso .... Manchester (Eng)
Sep 24, 2016 — **Jorge Linares (Ven)** w pts Anthony Crolla .... Manchester (Eng)
Mar 25, 2017 — Jorge Linares w pts 12 Anthony Crolla .... Manchester (Eng)
Sep 23, 2017 — Jorge Linares w pts 12 Luke Campbell (Eng) .... Inglewood, CA
Jan 27, 2018 — Jorge Linares w pts 12 Mercito Gesta (Phi) .... Inglewood, CA

WBO title

The WBO recognized the following fights as for the Interim title:
Feb 17, 2007 — **Michael Katsidis** (Aus) w rtd 5 Graham Earl (Eng)............... London (Eng)
Jul 21, 2007 — Michael Katsidis w pts 12 Czar Amonsot (Phi)..................Las Vegas NV
Mar 22, 2008 — **Joel Casamayor** w rsf 10 Michael Katsidis .... Cabazon CA
Casamayor forfeited the interim title when he lost a non-title fight to Juan Manuel Marquez in September 2008. After the unification fights involving Acelino Freitas, Juan Diaz, Nate Campbell, Ali Funeka and Juan Manuel Marquez, as stated earlier, the title became vacant. Another interim title fight was sanctioned as follows.
Sep 19, 2009 — **Michael Katsidis** w pts 12 Vicente Escobedo (US) .... Las Vegas, NV
Ricky Burns was upgraded from Interim champion to full champion in January 2012 after Juan Manuel Marquez vacated.
Mar 10, 2012 — Ricky Burns w pts 12 Paulus Moses........................ Glasgow (Sco)
Sep 22, 2012 — Ricky Burns w rsf 4 Kevin Mitchell .... Glasgow (Sco)
The WBO sanctioned the following for the Interim title
May 15, 2010 — Michael Katsidis w rsf 3 Kevin Mitchell (Eng)................West Ham (Eng)

Apr 9,	2011	Robert Guerrero w pts 12 Michael Katsidis	Las Vegas, NV
Nov 5,	2011	Ricky Burns w pts 12 Michael Katsidis	Wembley (Eng)
May 11,	2013	Ricky Burns w rtd 9 Jose A Gonzalez (PR)	Glasgow (Sco)
Sep 7,	2013	Ricky Burns drew 12 Ryamundo Beltran (USA)	Glasgow (Sco)
Mar 1,	2014	**Terence Crawford** (USA) w pts 12 Ricky Burns	Glasgow (Sco)
Jun 28,	2014	Terence Crawford w rsf 9 Yuriorkis Gamboa	Omaha, NE
Nov 29,	2014	Terence Crawford w pts 12 Raymundo Beltran *Terence Crawford vacated title*	Omaha, NE
May 1,	2015	Raymundo Beltran w rsf 2 Takahiro Ao (Jap) *For vacant title. Beltran weighed in heavy, so title only at stake for Ao*	Las Vegas, NV
Jul 11,	2015	**Terry Flanagan (Eng)** w rtd 2 Jose Zepeda (US) *For vacant title*	Manchester (Eng)
Oct 10,	2015	Terry Flanagan w rsf 2 Diego Magdaleno (US)	Manchester (Eng)
Mar 12,	2016	Terry Flanagan w pts 12 Derry Matthews (Eng)	Liverpool (Eng)
Jul 16,	2016	Terry Flanagan w pts 12 Mzonke Fana (SA)	Cardiff (Wal)
Nov 26,	2016	Terry Flanagan w rsf 8 Orlando Cruz (PR)	Cardiff (Wal)
April 8,	2017	Terry Flanagan w pts 12 Petr Petrov (Rus)	Manchester (Eng)
Feb 16,	2018	**Raymundo Beltran (Mex)** w pts 12 Paulus Moses (Nam) *For vacant title*	Reno, NV

IBF title

Nov 28,	2009	**Joan Guzman** (DR) drew 12 Ali Funeka	Quebec City (Can)
Mar 27,	2010	Joan Guzman w pts 12 Ali Fuenka *For vacant title. Guzman failed to make the 135lb weight limit*	Las Vegas, NV
Aug 14,	2010	Miguel Vazquez (Mex) w pts 12 Ji-Hoon Kim (South Korea)	Laredo, TX
Nov 27,	2010	Miguel Vazquez w pts 12 Ricardo Dominguez (Mex)	Tijuana, CA
Mar 12,	2011	Miguel Vazquez w pts 12 Leonardo Zappavigna (Aus)	Las Vegas, NV
Apr 21,	2012	Miguel Vazquez w pts 12 Ammeth Diaz (Pan)	Guadalajara (Mex)
Oct 27,	2012	Miguel Vazquez w pts 12 Marvin Quintero (Mex)	Verona, NY
Dec 8,	2012	Miguel Vazquez w pts 12 Mercito Gesta (Phil)	Las Vegas, NV
Feb 22,	2014	Miguel Vazquez w pts 12 Denis Shafikov (Rus)	Macao (Chi)
Sep 13,	2014	**Mickey Bey** (USA) w pts 12 Miguel Vazquez	Las Vegas, NV
Dec 18,	2015	**Rances Barthelemy (Cub)** w pts 12 Denis Shafikov (Rus) *For vacant title*	Las Vegas, NV
Jun 3,	2016	Rances Barthelemy w pts 12 Mickey Bey	Hollywood, FL
Sep 9,	2016	**Robert Easter Jr (US)** w pts 12 Richard Commey (Gha) *For vacant title*	Reading, PA
Feb 10,	2017	Robert Easter Jr w pts 12 Luis Cruz (PR)	Toledo, OH
Jun 30,	2017	Robert Easter Jr w pts 12 Denis Shafikov	Toledo, OH
Jan 20,	2018	Robert Easter Jr w pts 12 Javier Fortuna (Dom Rep) *Fortuna overweight; title not on the line for him*	

TERRY FLANAGAN *stopped American Jose Zepeda in two rounds to claim the vacant WBO lightweight title in July 2015*

Super-Featherweight

The super-featherweight or junior lightweight class was popularized by the promoter Tex Rickard, who put up a $2,500 championship belt in 1921 which prompted the New York Commission to approve the new division, which can be considered to have been launched by Johnny Dundee and George Chaney's fight in New York in November 1921.

The NBA added their blessing in 1923, and when Tod Morgan became champion between 1925 and 1929, the category's future looked assured. But Morgan's reign ended in scandal, when both he and Benny Bass had their purses suspended on suspicion of a betting coup after Bass knocked him out in two rounds. The evidence was inconclusive, but in January 1930 New York withdrew recognition from the division. The NBA did likewise two years later, and although the 130lb class stumbled on for a few more years it effectively went out of business from 1933 until 1949, when Sandy Saddler briefly revived it.

There was an eight-year break between 1951, when Saddler ceased to claim the title, and 1959, when the NBA brought it back. This time, due mainly to the outstanding Filipino champion Flash Elorde, the category flourished. The inevitable split came in 1968, when the WBC stripped Hiroshi Kobayashi, and not even outstanding performers like Julio Cesar Chavez, Alexis Arguello or Brian Mitchell were able to reunite the championship.

World Super-Featherweight Championship Bouts

Nov 18,	1921	**Johnny Dundee** (US) w dis 5 George "KO" Chaney (US)	New York, NY
		For vacant title	
Jul 6,	1922	Johnny Dundee w pts 15 Jackie Sharkey (US)	New York, NY
Aug 28,	1922	Johnny Dundee w pts 15 Vincent "Pepper" Martin (US)	New York, NY
Feb 2,	1923	Johnny Dundee w pts 15 Elino Flores (Phil)	New York, NY
May 30,	1923	**Jack Bernstein** (US) w pts 15 Johnny Dundee	New York, NY
Dec 17,	1923	**Johnny Dundee** w pts 15 Jack Bernstein	New York, NY
Jun 20,	1924	**Steve "Kid" Sullivan** (US) w pts 10 Johnny Dundee	Brooklyn, NY
Aug 18,	1924	Steve "Kid" Sullivan w pts 15 Pepper Martin	New York, NY
Oct 15,	1924	Steve "Kid" Sullivan w ko 5 Mike Ballerino (US)	New York, NY
Apr 1,	1925	**Mike Ballerino** w pts 10 Steve "Kid" Sullivan	Philadelphia, PA
Jul 6,	1925	Mike Ballerino w pts 15 Vincent "Pepper" Martin	Long Island, NY
Dec 2,	1925	**Tod Morgan** (US) w rtd 10 Mike Ballerino	Los Angeles, CA
Jun 3,	1926	Tod Morgan w rtd 6 Steve "Kid" Sullivan	Brooklyn, NY
Sep 30,	1926	Tod Morgan w pts 15 Joe Glick (US)	New York, NY
Oct 19,	1926	Tod Morgan w pts 10 Johnny Dundee	San Francisco, CA
Nov 19,	1926	Tod Morgan w pts 15 Carl Duane (US)	New York, NY
May 28,	1927	Tod Morgan w pts 12 Vic Foley (US)	Vancouver (Can)
Dec 16,	1927	Tod Morgan w dis 14 Joe Glick	New York, NY
May 24,	1928	Tod Morgan w pts 15 Eddie Martin (US)	New York, NY
Jul 18,	1928	Tod Morgan w pts 15 Eddie Martin	Brooklyn, NY
Dec 3,	1928	Tod Morgan drew 10 Santiago Zorilla (Pan)	San Francisco, CA
Apr 5,	1929	Tod Morgan w pts 10 Santiago Zorilla	Los Angeles, CA
May 20,	1929	Tod Morgan w pts 10 Sal Sorio (US)	Los Angeles, CA
Dec 19,	1929	**Benny Bass** (Rus) w ko 2 Tod Morgan	New York, NY
NY Commission withdrew recognition of the weight class, leaving Bass recognized only by the NBA			
Jan 5,	1931	Benny Bass w pts 10 Lew Massey (US)	aPhiladelphia, PA
Jul 15,	1931	**Kid Chocolate** (Cub) w rsf 7 Benny Bass	Philadelphia, PA
Apr 10,	1932	Kid Chocolate w pts 15 Davey Abad (Pan)	Havana (Cub)
Aug 4,	1932	Kid Chocolate w pts 10 Eddie Shea (US)	Chicago, IL
Sep 20,	1932	*The NBA also withdrew recognition from the division, although individual commissions were free to authorize title fights in their jurisdiction*	
Oct 13,	1932	Kid Chocolate w rsf 12 Lew Feldman (US)	New York, NY
Dec 9,	1932	Kid Chocolate w pts 15 Fidel la Barba (US)	New York, NY
Both the above contests were billed as featherweight title defences by Chocolate, but as the boxers were inside the 130lb limit that title was automatically at stake also			
May 1,	1933	Kid Chocolate w pts 10 Johnny Farr (US)	Philadelphia, PA
May 19,	1933	Kid Chocolate w pts 15 Seaman Tommy Watson (Eng)	New York, NY
		Billed as a featherweight title defence	
Dec 4,	1933	Kid Chocolate w pts 10 Frankie Wallace (US)	Cleveland, OH
Dec 26,	1933	**Frankie Klick** (US) w rsf 7 Kid Chocolate	Philadelphia, PA
		Klick never defended the title. Sandy Saddler revived it briefly in 1949	
Dec 6,	1949	**Sandy Saddler** (US) w pts 10 Orlando Zulueta (Cub)	Cleveland, OH
Apr 18,	1950	Sandy Saddler w rsf 9 Lauro Salas (Mex)	Cleveland, OH
Feb 28,	1951	Sandy Saddler w ko 2 Diego Sosa (Cub)	Havana (Cub)
		Saddler then fought only at featherweight. The division was inactive until 1959	
Jul 20,	1959	**Harold Gomes** (US) w pts 15 Paul Jorgensen (US)	Providence, RI
		For vacant titile	
Mar 16,	1960	**Gabriel "Flash" Elorde** (Phil) w ko 7 Harold Gomes	Quezon City (Phil)
Aug 17,	1960	Gabriel "Flash" Elorde w ko 1 Harold Gomes	San Francisco, CA
Mar 19,	1961	Gabriel "Flash" Elorde w pts 15 Joey Lopes (US)	Manila (Phil)
Dec 16,	1961	Gabriel "Flash" Elorde w rsf 1 Sergio Caprari (Ita)	Manila (Phil)
Jun 23,	1962	Gabriel "Flash" Elorde w pts 15 Auburn Copeland (US)	Manila (Phil)
Feb 16,	1963	Gabriel "Flash" Elorde w pts 15 Johnny Bizzaro (US)	Manila (Phil)
Nov 16,	1963	Gabriel "Flash" Elorde w dis 11 Love Allotey (Gha)	Quezon City (Phil)
Jul 27,	1964	Gabriel "Flash" Elorde w rsf 12 Teruo Kosaka (Jap)	Tokyo (Jap)
Jun 5,	1965	Gabriel "Flash" Elorde w ko 15 Teruo Kosaka	Quezon City (Phil)
Dec 4,	1965	Gabriel "Flash" Elorde w pts 15 Kang-Il Suh (Kor)	Quezon City (Phil)
Oct 22,	1966	Gabriel "Flash" Elorde w pts 15 Vicente Derado (Arg)	Quezon City (Phil)
Jun 15,	1967	**Yoshiaki Numata** (Jap) w pts 15 Gabriel "Flash" Elorde	Tokyo (Jap)
Dec 14,	1967	**Hiroshi Kobayashi** (Jap) w ko 12 Yoshiaki Numata	Tokyo (Jap)
Mar 30,	1968	Hiroshi Kobayashi drew 15 Rene Barrientos (Phil)	Tokyo (Jap)
Oct 6,	1968	Hiroshi Kobayashi w pts 15 Jaime Valladeres (Ecu)	Tokyo (Jap)
		The WBC vacated Kobayashi's title for his failure to defend against Rene Barrientos	

WBA title

Apr 6,	1969	**Hiroshi Kobayashi** w pts 15 Antonio Amaya (Pan)	Tokyo (Jap)
Nov 9,	1969	Hiroshi Kobayashi w pts 15 Carlos Canete (Arg)	Tokyo (Jap)
Aug 23,	1970	Hiroshi Kobayashi w pts 15 Antonio Amaya	Tokyo (Jap)
Mar 3,	1971	Hiroshi Kobayashi w pts 15 Ricardo Arredondo (Mex)	Tokyo (Jap)
Jul 29,	1971	**Alfredo Marcano** (Ven) w rtd 10 Hiroshi Kobayashi	Aomari (Jap)
Nov 7,	1971	Alfredo Marcano w rsf 4 Kenji Iwata (Jap)	Caracas (Ven)
Apr 25,	1972	**Ben Villaflor** (Phil) w pts 15 Alfredo Marcano	Honolulu, HI
Sep 5,	1972	Ben Villaflor drew 15 Victor Echegaray (Arg)	Honolulu, HI
Mar 12,	1973	**Kuniaki Shibata** (Jap) w pts 15 Ben Villaflor	Honolulu, HI
Jun 19,	1973	Kuniaki Shibata w pts 15 Victor Echegaray	Tokyo (Jap)
Oct 17,	1973	**Ben Villaflor** w ko 1 Kuniaki Shibata	Honolulu, HI
Mar 14,	1974	Ben Villaflor drew 15 Apollo Yoshio (Jap)	Toyama (Jap)
Aug 24,	1974	Ben Villaflor w rsf 2 Yasutsune Uehara (Jap)	Honolulu, HI
Mar 13,	1975	Ben Villaflor w pts 15 Hyun-Chi Kim (Kor)	Quezon City (Phil)
Jan 12,	1976	Ben Villaflor w rsf 13 Morito Kashiwaba (Jap)	Tokyo (Jap)
Apr 13,	1976	Ben Villaflor drew 15 Sam Serrano (PR)	Honolulu, HI
Oct 16,	1976	**Sam Serrano** w pts 15 Ben Villaflor	San Juan, CA
Jan 15,	1977	Sam Serrano w rsf 11 Alberto Herrera (Ecu)	Guayaquil (Ecu)
Jun 26,	1977	Sam Serrano w pts 15 Leonel Hernandez (Ven)	Puerta La Cruz (Ven)
Aug 27,	1977	Sam Serrano w pts 15 Apollo Yoshio	San Juan, CA
Nov 19,	1977	Sam Serrano w rsf 10 Tae-Ho Kim (Kor)	San Juan, CA
Feb 18,	1978	Sam Serrano w pts 15 Mario Martinez (Nic)	San Juan, CA
Jul 8,	1978	Sam Serrano w rsf 9 Yong-Ho Oh (Kor)	San Juan, CA
Nov 29,	1978	Sam Serrano w pts 15 Takas Maruki (Jap)	Nagoya (Jap)
Feb 18,	1979	Sam Serrano w pts 15 Julio Valdez (DR)	San Juan, CA
Apr 14,	1979	Sam Serrano w rsf 8 Nkosana Mgxaji (SA)	Cape Town (SA)
Apr 3,	1980	Sam Serrano w rsf 13 Kiyoshi Kazama (Jap)	Nara (Jap)
Aug 2,	1980	**Yasutsune Uehara** (Jap) w ko 6 Sam Serrano	Detroit, MI
Nov 20,	1980	Yasutsune Uehara w pts 15 Leonel Hernandez	Tokyo (Jap)
Apr 9,	1981	**Sam Serrano** w pts 15 Yasutsune Uehara	Wakayama (Jap)
Jun 29,	1981	Sam Serrano w pts 15 Leonel Hernandez	Caracas (Ven)
Dec 10,	1981	Sam Serrano w rsf 12 Hikaru Tomonari (Jap)	San Juan, CA
Jun 5,	1982	Sam Serrano no contest 11 Benedicto Villablanca (Ch)	Santiago (Ch)
Jan 19,	1983	**Roger Mayweather** (US) w ko 8 Sam Serrano	San Juan, CA
Apr 20,	1983	Roger Mayweather w rsf 8 Jorge Alvarado (PR)	San Jose, CA
Aug 17,	1983	Roger Mayweather w ko 1 Benedicto Villablanca	Las Vegas, NV
Feb 26,	1984	**Rocky Lockridge** (US) w ko 1 Roger Mayweather	Beaumont, TX
Jun 12,	1984	Rocky Lockridge w rsf 11 Taej-In Moon (Kor)	Anchorage, AK
Jan 27,	1985	Rocky Lockridge w rsf 6 Kamel Bou-Ali (Tun)	Riva del Garda (Ita)
May 19,	1985	**Wilfredo Gomez** (PR) w pts 12 Rocky Lockridge	San Juan, CA
May 24,	1986	**Alfredo Layne** (Pan) w rsf 9 Wilfredo Gomez	San Juan, CA
Sep 27,	1986	**Brian Mitchell** (SA) w rsf 10 Alfredo Layne	Sun City (Bop)
Mar 27,	1987	Brian Mitchell drew 15 Jose Rivera (PR)	San Juan, CA
Jul 31,	1987	Brian Mitchell w rsf 14 Francisco Fernandez (Pan)	Panama City (Pan)
Oct 3,	1987	Brian Mitchell w pts 15 Daniel Londas (Fra)	Gravelines (Fra)
Dec 19,	1987	Brian Mitchell w rsf 8 Salvatore Curcetti (Ita)	Capo D'Orlando (Ita)
Apr 26,	1988	Brian Mitchell w pts 12 Jose Rivera	Madrid (Sp)
Nov 2,	1988	Brian Mitchell w pts 12 Jim McDonnell (Eng)	London (Eng)
Feb 10,	1989	Brian Mitchell w rsf 8 Salvatore Bottiglieri (Ita)	Capo D'Orlando (Ita)
Jul 1,	1989	Brian Mitchell w tech dec 9 Jackie Beard (US)	Crotone (Ita)
Sep 28,	1989	Brian Mitchell w rsf 7 Irving Mitchell (US)	Lewiston, ME
Mar 14,	1990	Brian Mitchell w pts 12 Jackie Beard	Grossetto (Ita)

Sep 29, 1990	Brian Mitchell w pts 12 Frankie Mitchell (US)	Aosta (Ita)
Mar 15, 1991	Brian Mitchell drew 12 Tony Lopez (US)	Sacramento, CA
	For WBA and IBF titles. Mitchell relinquished the WBA title to challenge again for the IBF version	
Jun 28, 1991	**Joey Gamache** (US) w rsf 10 Jerry N'Gobeni (SA)	Lewiston, ME
	For vacant title. Gamache relinquished the title because of weight problems	
Nov 22, 1991	**Genaro Hernandez** (US) w rtd 9 Daniel Londas	Epernay (Fra)
	For vacant title	
Feb 24, 1992	Genaro Hernandez w pts 12 Omar Catari (Ven)	Los Angeles, CA
Jul 15, 1992	Genaro Hernandez w pts 12 Masuaki Takeda (Jap)	Fukuoka (Jap)
Nov 20, 1992	Genaro Hernandez w rsf 6 Yuji Watanabe (Jap)	Tokyo (Jap)
Apr 26, 1993	Genaro Hernandez tech draw 1 Raul Perez (Mex)	Los Angeles, CA
Jun 28, 1993	Genaro Hernandez w ko 8 Raul Perez	Los Angeles, CA
Oct 11, 1993	Genaro Hernandez w pts 12 Harold Warren (US)	Inglewood, CA
Jan 31, 1994	Genaro Hernandez w rsf 8 Jorge Ramirez (Mex)	Inglewood, CA
Nov 12, 1994	Genaro Hernandez w pts 12 Jimmy Garcia (Col)	Mexico City (Mex)
Aug 1995	*Hernandez relinquished the title*	
Oct 21, 1995	**Yong Soo Choi** (Kor) w rsf 10 Victor Hugo Paz (Arg)	Salta (Arg)
	For vacant title	
Jan 27, 1996	Yong Soo Choi w pts 12 Yamato Mitani (Jap)	Tokyo (Jap)
May 11, 1996	Yong Soo Choi w rsf 8 Orlando Soto (Pan)	Chejudo (Kor)
Oct 13, 1996	Yong Soo Choi w pts 12 Yamato Mitani	Tokyo (Jap)
Feb 1, 1997	Yong Soo Choi w pts 12 Lavka Sim (Mon)	Seoul (Kor)
May 24, 1997	Yong Soo Choi w pts 12 Koji Matsumoto (Jap)	Suwon (Kor)
Oct 4, 1997	Yong Soo Choi drew 12 Takanori Hatakeyama (Jap)	Tokyo (Jap)
Apr 18, 1998	Yong Soo Choi w rsf 9 Gilberto Serrano (Ven)	Seoul (Kor)
Sep 5, 1998	**Takanori Hatakeyama** w pts 12 Yong Soo Choi	Tokyo (Jap)
Feb 13, 1999	Takanori Hatakeyama drew 12 Saul Duran (Mex)	Tokyo (Jap)
Jun 27, 1999	**Lavka Sim** (Mon) w rsf 5 Takenori Hatakeyama	Tokyo (Jap)
Oct 31, 1999	**Jong-kwon Baek** (SK) w pts 12 Lavka Sim	Pusan (SK)
Jan 30, 2000	Jong-kwon Baek drew 12 Kyun-chul Choi (SK)	Pohang (SK)
May 21, 2000	**Joel Casamayor** (Cub) w rsf 5 Jong-kwon Baek	Kansas City, MS
Sep 16, 2000	Joel Casamayor w rsf 5 Radford Beasley (US)	Las Vegas, NV
Jan 6, 2001	Joel Casamayor w rsf 9 Roberto Garcia	Las Vegas, NV
May 5, 2001	Joel Casamayor w pts 12 Edwin Santana (DR)	Philadelphia, PA
Sep 29, 2001	Joel Casamayor w rsf 8 Joe Morales (US)	Miami, FL

WBC title

Feb 15, 1969	**Rene Barrientos** w pts 15 Ruben Navarro (US)	Manila (Phil)
	For vacant WBC title	
Apr 5, 1970	**Yoshiaki Numata** (Jap) w pts 15 Rene Barrientos	Tokyo (Jap)
Sep 27, 1970	Yoshiaki Numata w ko 5 Raul Rojas (US)	Tokyo (Jap)
Jan 3, 1971	Yoshiaki Numata w pts 15 Rene Barrientos	Shizuoka (Jap)
May 3, 1971	Yoshiaki Numata w pts 15 Lionel Rose (Aus)	Hiroshima (Jap)
Oct 10, 1971	**Ricardo Arredondo** w ko 10 Yoshiaki Numata	Sendai (Jap)
Jan 29, 1972	Ricardo Arredondo w pts 15 Jose Marin (CR)	San Jose, CA
Apr 22, 1972	Ricardo Arredondo w ko 5 William Martinez (Nic)	Mexico City (Mex)
Sep 15, 1972	Ricardo Arredondo w ko 12 Susumu Okabe (Jap)	Tokyo (Jap)
Mar 6, 1973	Ricardo Arredondo w pts 15 Apollo Yoshio	Fukuoka (Jap)
Sep 1, 1973	Ricardo Arredondo w rsf 6 Morito Kashiwaba (Jap)	Tokyo (Jap)
Feb 28, 1974	**Kuniaki Shibata** w pts 15 Ricardo Arredondo	Tokyo (Jap)
Jun 27, 1974	Kuniaki Shibata w pts 15 Antonio Amaya	Tokyo (Jap)
Aug 3, 1974	Kuniaki Shibata w rsf 15 Ramiro Clay Bolanos (Ecu)	Tokyo (Jap)
Mar 27, 1975	Kuniaki Shibata w pts 15 Ould Makloufi (Alg)	Fukuoka (Jap)
Jul 5, 1975	**Alfredo Escalera** (PR) w ko 2 Kuniaki Shibata	Mito (Jap)
Sep 20, 1975	Alfredo Escalera drew 15 Leonel Hernandez (Ven)	Caracas (Ven)
Dec 12, 1975	Alfredo Escalera w rsf 9 Sven-Erik Paulsen (Nor)	Oslo (Nor)
Feb 20, 1976	Alfredo Escalera w rsf 13 Jose Fernandez (DR)	San Juan, CA
Apr 1, 1976	Alfredo Escalera w rsf 6 Buzzsaw Yamabe (Jap)	Nara (Jap)
Jul 1, 1976	Alfredo Escalera w pts 15 Buzzsaw Yamabe	Nara (Jap)
Sep 18, 1976	Alfredo Escalera w rtd 12 Ray Lunny (US)	San Juan, CA
Nov 30, 1976	Alfredo Escalera w pts 15 Tyrone Everett (US)	Philadelphia, PA
Mar 17, 1977	Alfredo Escalera w rsf 6 Ronnie McGarvey (US)	San Juan, CA
May 16, 1977	Alfredo Escalera w ko 8 Carlos Becerril (Mex)	Landover, MD
Sep 10, 1977	Alfredo Escalera w pts 15 Sigfredo Rodriguez (Mex)	San Juan, CA
Jan 28, 1978	**Alexis Arguello** (Nic) w rsf 13 Alfredo Escalera	San Juan, CA
Apr 29, 1978	Alexis Arguello w rsf 5 Rey Tam (Phil)	Los Angeles, CA
Jun 3, 1978	Alexis Arguello w ko 1 Diego Alcala (Pan)	San Juan, CA
Nov 10, 1978	Alexis Arguello w pts 15 Arturo Leon (Mex)	Las Vegas, NV
Feb 4, 1979	Alexis Arguello w ko 13 Alfredo Escalera	Rimini (Ita)
Jul 8, 1979	Alexis Arguello w rsf 1 Rafael Limon (Mex)	New York, NY
Nov 16, 1979	Alexis Arguello w rtd 7 Bobby Chacon (US)	Los Angeles, CA
Jan 20, 1980	Alexis Arguello w rsf 11 Ruben Castillo (US)	Tucson, AZ
Apr 27, 1980	Alexis Arguello w rsf 4 Rolando Navarette (Phil)	San Juan, CA
Oct 1980	*Arguello relinquished WBC title to box as a lightweight*	
Dec 11, 1980	**Rafael Limon** w rsf 15 Idelfonso Bethelmi (Ven)	Los Angeles, CA
	For vacant title	
Mar 8, 1981	**Cornelius Boza-Edwards (Eng)** w pts 15 Rafael Limon	Stockton, CA
May 30, 1981	Cornelius Boza-Edwards w rtd 13 Bobby Chacon (US)	Las Vegas, NV
Aug 29, 1981	**Rolando Navarette** w ko 5 Cornelius Boza-Edwards	Via Reggio (Ita)
Jan 16, 1982	Rolando Navarette w ko 11 Chung-Il Choi (Kor)	Manila (Phil)
May 29, 1982	**Rafael Limon** w ko 12 Rolando Navarette	Las Vegas, NV
Sep 18, 1982	Rafael Limon w rsf 7 Chung-Il Choi	Los Angeles, CA
Dec 11, 1982	**Bobby Chacon** w pts 15 Rafael Limon	Sacramento, CA
May 15, 1983	Bobby Chacon w pts 12 Cornelius Boza-Edwards	Las Vegas, NV
June 1983	*The WBC stripped Chacon of the title because of a contractual dispute*	
Aug 7, 1983	**Hector Camacho** (PR) w rsf 5 Rafael Limon	San Juan, CA
	For vacant title	
Nov 18, 1983	Hector Camacho w ko 5 Rafael Solis (PR)	San Juan, CA
June 1984	*Camacho relinquished WBC title to box as a lightweight*	
Sep 13, 1984	**Julio Cesar Chavez** (Mex) w rsf 8 Mario Martinez (Mex)	Los Angeles, CA
	For vacant title	
Apr 19, 1985	Julio Cesar Chavez w rsf 6 Ruben Castillo	Los Angeles, CA
Jul 7, 1985	Julio Cesar Chavez w rsf 2 Roger Mayweather	Las Vegas, NV
Sep 22, 1985	Julio Cesar Chavez w pts 12 Dwight Pratchett (US)	Las Vegas, NV
May 15, 1986	Julio Cesar Chavez w rsf 5 Faustino Barrios (Arg)	Paris (Fra)
Jun 13, 1986	Julio Cesar Chavez w rsf 7 Refugio Rojas (US)	New York, NY
Aug 3, 1986	Julio Cesar Chavez w pts 12 Rocky Lockridge	Monte Carlo (Mon)
Dec 12, 1986	Julio Cesar Chavez w pts 12 Juan LaPorte (PR)	New York, NY
Apr 18, 1987	Julio Cesar Chavez w rsf 3 Francisco Tomas Da Cruz (Bra)	Nimes (Fra)
Aug 21, 1987	Julio Cesar Chavez w pts 12 Danilo Cabrera (DR)	Tijuana (Mex)
Nov 21, 1987	*Chavez relinquished the title on becoming WBA lightweight champion*	
Feb 29, 1988	**Azumah Nelson** (Gha) w pts 12 Mario Martinez (Mex)	Los Angeles, CA
	For vacant title	
Jun 25, 1988	Azumah Nelson w rsf 9 Lupe Suarez (US)	Atlantic City, NJ
Dec 10, 1988	Azumah Nelson w ko 3 Sydnei dal Rovere (Bra)	Accra (Gha)
Feb 25, 1989	Azumah Nelson w rsf 12 Mario Martinez (Mex)	Las Vegas, NV
Nov 5, 1989	Azumah Nelson w ko 12 Jim McDonnell	London (Eng)
Oct 13, 1990	Azumah Nelson w pts 12 Juan LaPorte	Sydney (Aus)
Jun 28, 1991	Azumah Nelson drew 12 Jeff Fenech (Aus)	Las Vegas, NV
Mar 1, 1992	Azumah Nelson w rsf 8 Jeff Fenech	Melbourne (Aus)
Nov 7, 1992	Azumah Nelson w pts 12 Calvin Grove (US)	Lake Tahoe, NV
Feb 20, 1993	Azumah Nelson w pts 12 Gabriel Ruelas (Mex)	Mexico City (Mex)
Sep 10, 1993	Azumah Nelson drew 12 Jesse James Leija (US)	San Antonio, TX
May 7, 1994	**Jesse James Leija** w pts 12 Azumah Nelson	Las Vegas, NV
Sep 17, 1994	**Gabriel Ruelas** w pts 12 Jesse James Leija	Las Vegas, NV
Jan 28, 1995	Gabriel Ruelas w rtd 2 Freddie Liberatore (US)	Las Vegas, NV
May 6, 1995	Gabriel Ruelas w rsf 11 Jimmy Garcia	Las Vegas, NV
Dec 1, 1995	**Azumah Nelson** w rsf 5 Gabriel Ruelas	Indio Springs, CA
Jun 1, 1996	Azumah Nelson w rsf 6 Jesse James Leija	Las Vegas, NV
Mar 22, 1997	**Genaro Hernandez** w pts 12 Azumah Nelson	Corpus Christi, TX
Jun 14, 1997	Genaro Hernandez w pts 12 Anatoly Alexandrov (Rus)	San Antonio, TX
Nov 20, 1997	Genaro Hernandez w pts 12 Carlos Hernandez (US)	Los Angeles, CA
May 16, 1998	Genaro Hernandez w pts 12 Carlos Gerena (Pan)	Indio, CA
Oct 3, 1998	**Floyd Mayweather** (US) w rtd 8 Genaro Hernandez	Las Vegas, NV
Dec 18, 1998	Floyd Mayweather w rsf 2 Angel Manfredy (US)	Miami, FL
Feb 17, 1999	Floyd Mayweather w pts 12 Carlos Rios (Arg)	Grand Rapids, MI
May 22, 1999	Floyd Mayweather w ko 9 Justin Juuko (Uga)	Las Vegas, NV
Sep 11, 1999	Floyd Mayweather w rtd 7 Carlos Gerena	Las Vegas, NV
Mar 18, 2000	Floyd Mayweather w pts 12 Gregorio Vargas (Mex)	Las Vegas, NV
Jan 20, 2001	Floyd Mayweather w rsf 10 Diego Corrales	Las Vegas, NV
May 26, 2001	Floyd Mayweather w pts 12 Carlos Hernandez (US	Grand Rapids, MI
Nov 10, 2001	Floyd Mayweather w rtd 9 Jesus Chavez (US)	San Francisco, CA
	Mayweather moved up to the lightweight division	

IBF title

Apr 22, 1984	**Hwan-Kil Yuh** (Kor) w pts 15 Rod Sequenan (Phil)	Seoul (Kor)
	For vacant title	
Sep 16, 1984	Hwan-Kil Yuh w ko 6 Sak Galexi (Thai)	Pohang (Kor)
Feb 15, 1985	**Lester Ellis** (Aus) w pts 15 Hwan-Kil Yuh	Melbourne (Aus)
Apr 26, 1985	Lester Ellis w ko 13 Rod Sequenan	Melbourne (Aus)
Jul 12, 1985	**Barry Michael** (Aus) w pts 15 Lester Ellis	Melbourne (Aus)
Oct 18, 1985	Barry Michael w rsf 4 Jin-Shik Choi (Kor)	Darwin (Aus)
May 23, 1986	Barry Michael w rsf 4 Mark Fernandez (US)	Melbourne (Aus)
Aug 23, 1986	Barry Michael w pts 12 Najib Daho (Eng)	Manchester (Eng)
Aug 9, 1987	**Rocky Lockridge** w rtd 8 Barry Michael	Windsor (Eng)
Oct 25, 1987	Rocky Lockridge w rsf 10 Johnny De La Rosa (DR)	Tucson, AZ
Apr 2, 1988	Rocky Lockridge w pts 15 Harold Knight (US)	Atlantic City, NJ
Jul 27, 1988	**Tony Lopez** (US) w pts 12 Rocky Lockridge	Sacramento, CA
Oct 27, 1988	Tony Lopez w pts 12 Juan "John-John" Molina (PR)	Sacramento, CA
Mar 5, 1989	Tony Lopez w pts 12 Rocky Lockridge	Sacramento, CA
Jun 18, 1989	Tony Lopez w rsf 8 Tyrone Jackson (US)	Stateline, NV
Oct 7, 1989	**Juan "John-John" Molina** w rsf 10 Tony Lopez	Sacramento, CA
Jan 28, 1990	Juan "John-John" Molina w rsf 6 Lupe Suarez	Atlantic City, NJ
May 20, 1990	**Tony Lopez** w pts 12 Juan "John-John" Molina	Reno, NV
Sep 22, 1990	Tony Lopez w pts 12 Jorge Paez (Mex)	Sacramento, CA
Mar 15, 1991	Tony Lopez drew 15 Brian Mitchell	Sacramento, CA
	For IBF and WBA titles	
Jul 12, 1991	Tony Lopez w rsf 6 Lupe Guttierez (US)	Lake Tahoe, NV
Sep 13, 1991	**Brian Mitchell** w pts 12 Tony Lopez	Sacramento, CA
Jan 1992	*Mitchell announced his retirement*	

Feb 22, 1992	**Juan "John-John" Molina** w rsf 4 Jackie Gunguluza (SA)	Sun City (Bop)
	For vacant title	
Aug 22, 1992	Juan "John-John" Molina w rsf 4 Fernando Caicedo (Col)	Bayamon (PR)
Feb 13, 1993	Juan "John-John" Molina w rsf 8 Francisco Segura (Mex)	Bayamon (PR)
Jun 26, 1993	Juan "John-John" Molina w pts 12 Manuel Medina (Mex)	Atlantic City, NJ
Oct 9, 1993	Juan "John-John" Molina w ko 8 Bernard Taylor (US)	San Juan, CA
Jan 22, 1994	Juan "John-John" Molina w rtd 6 Floyd Havard (Wal)	Cardiff (Wal)
Apr 22, 1994	Juan "John-John" Molina w pts 12 Gregorio Vargas (Mex)	Las Vegas, NV
Nov 26, 1994	Juan "John-John" Molina w ko 10 Wilson Rodriguez (DR)	Bayamon (PR)
Jan 1995	*Molina vacated the title to move up to lightweight*	
Apr 22, 1995	**Eddie Hopson** (US) w ko 7 Moises Pedroza (Col)	Atlantic City, NJ
	For vacant title	
Jul 9, 1995	**Tracy Harris Patterson** (US) w rsf 2 Eddie Hopson	Reno, NV
Dec 15, 1995	**Arturo Gatti** (Can) w rsf 2 Tracy Harris Patterson	New York, NY
Mar 23, 1996	Arturo Gatti w ko 6 Wilson Rodriguez (DR)	New York, NY
Feb 22, 1997	Arturo Gatti w pts 12 Tracy Harris Patterson	Atlantic City, NJ
Oct 4, 1997	Arturo Gatti w rsf 5 Gabriel Ruelas (Mex)	Atlantic City, NJ
Feb 1998	*Gatti relinquished title because he could no longer make the weight..*	
Mar 13, 1998	**Roberto Garcia** (US) w pts 12 Harold Warren (US)	Miami, FL
	For vacant title	
Oct 24, 1998	Roberto Garcia w rsf 5 Ramon Ledon (Cub)	Atlantic City, NJ
Jan 16, 1999	Roberto Garcia w pts 12 Juan Molina	Las Vegas, NV
Oct 23, 1999	**Diego Corrales** (US) w rsf 7 Roberto Garcia	Las Vegas, NV
Dec 4, 1999	Diego Corrales w pts 12 John Brown (US)	Lincoln City, NB
Mar 18, 2000	Diego Corrales w rsf 3 Derrick Gainer (US)	Las Vegas, NV
Jun 17, 2000	Diego Corrales w rsf 10 Justin Juuko (Uga)	Los Angeles, CA
Sep 2, 2000	Diego Corrales w rsf 3 Angel Manfredy	El Paso, TX
Oct 2000	*Corrales relinquished the title to move up to lightweight*	
Dec 3, 2000	**Steve Forbes** (US) w rsf 8 John Brown	Miami, FL
	For vacant title	
Sep 29, 2001	Steve Forbes w pts 12 John Brown	Miami, FL
	Forbes was stripped for failing to make weight for defence against David Santos	
Feb 1, 2003	**Carlos Hernandez** w tdec 8 David Santos (US)	Las Vegas, NV
	For vacant title	
Oct 4, 2003	Carlos Hernandez w tdec 10 Steve Forbes	Los Angeles, CA

WBO title

Apr 29, 1989	**Juan "John-John" Molina** (PR) w pts 12 Juan LaPorte (PR)	San Juan, CA
	For vacant title. Molina relinquished title in Sept to challenge for the IBF belt	
Dec 9, 1989	**Kamel Bou-Ali** (Tun) w ko 8 Antonio Rivera (PR)	Terano
	For vacant title	
Oct 20, 1990	Kamel Bou-Ali no contest 2 Pedro Villegas (Arg)	Cesena (Ita)
Jun 1, 1991	Kamel Bou-Ali w ko 3 Joey Jacobs (Eng)	Ragusa (Ita)
Mar 21, 1992	**Daniel Londas** w pts 12 Kamel Bou-Ali	San Rufo
Sep 4, 1992	**Jimmi Bredahl** (Den) w pts 12 Daniel Londas	Copenhagen (Den)
Sep 17, 1993	Jimmi Bredahl w pts 12 Renato Cornett (Aus)	Copenhagen (Den)
Mar 5, 1994	**Oscar De La Hoya** (US) w rtd 10 Jimmi Bredahl	Los Angeles, CA
May 27, 1994	Oscar De La Hoya w rsf 3 Giorgio Campanella (Ita)	Las Vegas, NV
June 1994	*De La Hoya vacated title to box at lightweight*	
Sep 24, 1994	**Regilio Tuur** (Hol) w pts 12 Eugene Speed (US)	Rotterdam (Hol)
	For vacant title	
Mar 9, 1995	Regilio Tuur w pts 12 Tony Pep (Can)	Groningen (Hol)
Jun 17, 1995	Regilio Tuur w rsf 5 Pete Taliefero (US)	New Orleans, LA
Sep 17, 1995	Regilio Tuur w rtd 10 Luis Mendoza (Col)	Arnhem (Hol)
Dec 23, 1995	Regilio Tuur w rsf 12 Giorgio Campanella	Amsterdam (Hol)
Apr 1, 1996	Regilio Tuur w pts 12 Narciso Valenzuela (Mex)	Hertogenbosch (Hol)
Sep 6, 1996	Regilio Tuur w ko 1 Jose Vida Ramos (DR)	Atlantic City, NJ
Jan 1997	*Tuur announced his retirement*	
Mar 1, 1997	Arnulfo Castillo (Mex) drew 12 Julien Lorcy (Fra)	Paris (Fra)
	For vacant title	
Oct 4, 1997	Arnulfo Castillo drew 12 Julien Lorcy	Villebon sur Yvette (Fra)
Dec 19, 1997	**Barry Jones** (Wal) w pts 12 Wilson Palacios (Col)	London (Eng)
Apr 1998	*Jones stripped of title on medical grounds*	
May 16, 1998	**Anatoly Alexandrov** (Rus) w pts 12 Julien Lorcy	Paris (Fra)
	For vacant title	
Jan 25, 1999	Anatoly Alexandrov w rsf 8 Arnulfo Castillo	Paris (Fra)
Aug 7, 1999	**Acelino Freitas** (Bra) w ko 1 Anatoly Alexandrov	Le Cannet (Fra)
Oct 26, 1999	Acelino Freitas w rsf 3 Anthony Martinez (CR)	Salvador (Bra)
Jan 15, 2000	Acelino Freitas w rsf 8 Barry Jones (Wal)	Doncaster (Eng)
Mar 18, 2000	Acelino Freitas w rsf 1 Javier Jauregui (Mex)	Sao Paulo (Bra)
Jun 10, 2000	Acelino Freitas w rsf 2 Lemuel Nelson (US)	Detroit MI
Sep 23, 2000	Acelino Freitas w rsf 9 Carlos Rios (Arg)	Rama (Can)
Jan 27, 2001	Acelino Freitas w rsf 1 Orlando Soto (Pan)	Brasilia (Bra)

WBO/WBA titles

Jan 12, 2002	**Acelino Freitas** w pts 12 Joel Casamayor	Las Vegas, NV
Aug 3 2002	Acelino Freitas w pts 12 Daniel Attah (Gha)	Phoenix, AZ
Mar 15 2003	Acelino Freitas w rsf 4 Juan Carlos Ramirez (Mex)	Chicago, IL
Aug 9, 2003	Acelino Freitas w rsf 12 Jorge Barrios (Arg)	Miami, FL
	Freitas relinquished titles to box at lightweight.	

WBC title

Aug 24, 2002	**Sirimongkol Singwangcham** (Tha) w ko 2 Kengo Nagashima (Jap)	Tokyo (Jap)
	For vacant title	
Jan 13, 2003	Sirimongkol Singwangcha w pts 12 Yong-soo Choi (Kor)	Tokyo (Jap)
Aug 15, 2003	**Jesus Chavez** (Mex) w pts 12 Sirimongkol Singwangcham	Austin, TX
Feb 28, 2004	**Erik Morales** (Mex) w pts 12 Jesus Chavez	Las Vegas, NV

WBC/IBF titles

Jul 31, 2004	**Erik Morales** w pts 12 Carlos Hernandez (El Sal)	Las Vegas, NV
	Morales was stripped of the IBF title	

IBF title

Feb 23, 2005	**Robbie Peden** (Aus) w rsf 8 Nate Campbell (US)	Melbourne (Aus)
	Peden lost a unification fight with Marco Antonio Barrera, who gave up the IBF title	
May 31, 2006	**Cassius Baloyi** (SA) w rsf 11 Manuel Medina (Mex)	Airway Hts, WA
	For vacant title	
Jul 29, 2006	**Gairy St Clair** (Guy) w pts 12 Cassius Baloyi	Kempton Park (SA)
Nov 4, 2006	**Malcolm Klassen** (SA) w pts 12 Gairy St Clair	Kempton Park (SA)
Apr 20, 2007	**Mzonke Fana** (SA) w pts 12 Malcolm Klassen	Khayelitsha (SA)
Aug 31, 2007	Mzonke Fana w ko 9 Javier Alvarez (Arg)	Klerksdrop (SA)
Apr 12, 2008	**Cassius Baloyi** (SA) w pts 12 Mzonke Fana	Mafikeng (SA)
Sep 13, 2008	Cassius Baloyi w rsf 3 Javier Alvarez (Arg)	Kempton Park (SA)
Apr 18, 2009	**Malcolm Klassen** (SA) w rsf 7 Cassius Baloyi	Mafikeng (SA)
Aug 22, 2009	**Robert Guerrero** (US) w pts 12 Malcolm Klassen	Houston TX
	Robert Guerrero vacated title	
Sep 1, 2010	**Mzonke Fana** (SA) w pts 12 Cassius Baloyi (SA)	Brakpan (SA)
	For vacant title	
	Fana relinquished title	
Sep 10, 2011	**Juan Carlos Salgado** (Mex) w pts 12 Argenis Mendez (DR)	Zapopan (Mex)
Dec 10, 2011	Juan Carlos Salgado nc 2 Miguel Beltran Jr. (Mex)	Los Mochis (Mex)
Apr 28, 2012	Juan Carlos Salgado w pts 12 Martin Honorio (Mex)	Cancun (Mex)
Aug 18, 2012	Juan Carlos Salgado w pts 12 Jonathan Victor Barros (Arg)	Los Angeles, CA
Mar 9, 2013	**Argenis Mendez** (Dom rep) w ko 4 Juan Carlos Salgado	Costa Mesa, CA
Aug 23, 2013	Argenis Mendez drew 12 Arash Usmanee (Can)	Verona, NY
Jan 3, 2014	Argenis Mendez nc 2 Rances Barthelemy (Cub)	Minneapolis, MN
Jul 10, 2014	**Rances Barthelemy** w pts 12 Argenis Mendez	Miami, FL
Oct 4, 2014	Rances Barthelemy w pts 12 Fernando David Saucedo (Arg)	Mashantucket, CN
	Rances Barthelemy vacated title	
Jun 13, 2015	**Jose Pedraza** (Puerto Rico) w pts 12 Andrey Klimov (Russia)	Birmingham, AL
	For vacant title	

WBC title

Nov 27, 2004	**Marco Antonio Barrera** w pts 12 Erik Morales	Las Vegas, NV
Apr 9, 2005	Marco Antonio Barrera w ko 2 Mzonke Fana (SA)	El Paso, TX

WBC/IBF titles

Sep 17, 2005	Marco Antonio Barrera w pts 12 Robbie Peden	Las Vegas, NV
	Barrera relinquished the IBF title	

WBC title

May 20, 2006	**Marco Antonio Barrera** w pts 12 Rocky Juarez (US)	Los Angeles, CA
Sep 16, 2006	Marco Antonio Barrera w pts 12 Rocky Jaurez	Las Vegas, NV
Mar 17, 2007	**Juan Manuel Marquez** (Mex) w pts 12 Marco Antonio Barrera	Las Vegas, NV
Nov 30, 2007	Juan Manuel Marquez w pts 12 Rocky Juarez	Tucson, AZ
Mar 15, 2008	**Manny Pacquiao** w pts 12 Juan Manuel Marquez	Las Vegas NV
	Pacquiao relinquished the title to box at lightweight	
Oct 11, 2008	**Humberto Soto** (Mex) w rtd 11 Gamaliel Diaz (Mex)	Torreon (Mex)
	For vacant title	
Dec 20, 2008	Humberto Soto w rsf 2 Francisco Lorenzo (DR)	Cozumel (Mex)
Mar 28, 2009	Humberto Soto w rsf 4 Antonio Davis (US)	Tijuana (Mex)
May 2, 2009	Humberto Soto w rsf 9 Benoit Gaudet (Can)	Las Vegas NV
Sep 15, 2009	Humberto Soto w rsf 2 Aristides Perez (Col)	Cancun (Mex)
	The WBC also recognized the following fights for the Interim title:	
Aug 22, 2009	**Humberto Gutierrez** (Mex) w pts 12 Sergey Gulyakevich (Blr)	Los Labos (Mex)
Nov 21, 2009	**Vitali Tajbert** (Ger) w pts 12 Humberto Gutierrez	Kiel (Ger)
	Humberto Soto vacated the WBC title and Vitali Tajbert was upgraded to full champion	
May 22, 2010	**Vitali Tajbert** w tdec 9 Hector Velazquez (Mex)	Rostock (Ger)
Nov 26, 2010	**Takahiro Ao** (Jap) w pts 12 Vitali Tajbert	Nagoya (Jap)
Apr 8, 2011	Takahiro Ao w ko 4 Humberto Mauro Gutierrez (Mex)	Kobe (Jap)
Nov 6, 2011	Takahiro Ao w pts 12 Devis Boschiero (Ita)	Tokyo (Jap)
Apr 6, 2012	Takahiro Ao w pts 12 Terdsak Kokietgym (Thai)	Tokyo (Jap)

Oct 27, 2012 **Gamaliel Diaz** w pts 12 Takahiro Ao .... Tokyo (Jap)
Apr 8, 2013 **Takashi Miura** w rsf 9 Gamaliel Diaz .... Tokyo (Jap)
Aug 17, 2013 Takashi Miura w pts 12 Sergio Thompson (Mex) .... Cancun (Mex)
Dec 31, 2013 Takashi Miura w rsf 9 Dante Jardon (Mex) .... Tokyo (Jap)
Nov 22, 2014 Takashi Miura w rsf 6 Edgar Puerta (Mex) .... Yokohama (Jap)
May 1, 2015 Takashi Miura w rsf 3 Billy Dib (Aus) .... Tokyo (Jap)
Nov 21, 2015 **Francisco Vargas (Mex)** w rsf 9 Takashi Miura .... Las Vegas, NV
Jun 4, 2016 Francisco Vargas drew 12 Orlando Salido (Mex) .... Carson, CA
Jan 28, 2017 **Miguel Berchelt (Mex)** w ko 11 Francisco Vargas .... Indio, CA
Jul 15, 2017 Miguel Berchelt w pts 12 Takashi Miura .... Inglewood, CA
Feb 10, 2018 Miguel Berchelt w rsf 3 Maxwell Awuku (Gha) .... Cancun (Mex)

WBA title

Freitas was considered "super" champion by the WBA following his win over Casamayor. "World" championships continued to be sanctioned

Apr 13, 2002 **Yodsanan Nanthachai** (Tha) w pts 12 Lavka Sim .... Nakornrachasima (Tha)
Dec 5, 2002 Yodsanan Nanthachai w rsf 7 Lamont Pearson (US) .... Bangkok (Tha)
Feb 8, 2004 Yodsanan Nanthachai rsf 7 Ryuhai Sugita (Jap) .... Gifu (Jap)
Aug 7 2004 Yodsanan Nanthachai w pts 12 Steve Forbes (US) .... Mashantucket, CT
Apr 30, 2005 **Vicente Mosquera** (Pan) w pts 12 Yodsanan Nanthachai .... New York, NY
May 12, 2006 Vicente Mosquera w pts 12 Jose Estrella (Arg) .... Cordoba (Arg)
Aug 5, 2006 **Edwin Valero** (Ven) w rsf 10 Vicente Mosquera .... Panama City (Pan)
Jan 3, 2007 Edwin Valero w rsf 1 Michael Lozada (Mex) .... Tokyo (Jap)
May 3, 2007 Edwin Valero w rsf 8 Nobuhito Honmo (Jap) .... Tokyo (Jap)
Dec 15, 2007 Edwin Valero w rsf 3 Zaid Zavaleta (Mex) .... Cancun (Mex)
Jun 12, 2008 Edwin Valero w rsf 7 Takehiro Shimada (Jap) .... Tokyo (Jap)
Valero relinquished the title to box at lightweight
Nov 28, 2008 **Jorge Linares** (Ven) w rsf 5 Whyber Garcia (Pan) .... Panama City (Pan)
For vacant title
Jun 27, 2009 Jorge Linares w rsf 8 Josafat Perez (Mex) .... Nuevo Laredo (Mex)
Oct 10, 2009 **Juan Carlos Salgado** (Mex) w rsf 1 Jorge Linares .... Tokyo (Jap)
WBA sanctioned the following fight for the interim title
Nov 19, 2009 Likar Ramos (Col) w pts 12 Angel Granados (Ven) .... Medellin (Col)
Jan 11, 2010 **Takashi Uchiyama (Jap)** w rsf 12 Juan Carlos Salgado (Mex) .... Tokyo (Jap)
For WBA title
WBA sanctioned the following fights for the interim title
Feb 6, 2010 Jorge Solis (Mex) w ko 7 Likar Ramos .... Merida (Mex)
May 8, 2010 Jorge Solis w pts 12 Mario Santiago (PR) .... Aguascalientes (Mex)
May 17, 2010 Takashi Uchiyama w rsf 6 Angel Granados .... Saitama (Jap)
For WBA title
WBA sanctioned following fight for the interim title
Sep 4, 2010 Jorge Solis w rsf 6 Francisco Cordero (Col) .... Guadalajara (Mex)
Sep 20, 2010 Takashi Uchiyama w rsf 5 Roy Mukhlis (Indonesia) .... Saitama (Jap)
For WBA title
Jan 31, 2011 Takashi Uchiyama w rtd 8 Takashi Miura (Jap) .... Tokyo (Jap)
WBA sanctioned the following fight for the interim title
Nov 3, 2011 Bryan Vasquez (Costa R) w pts 12 Santos Benavides (Nic) .... Zapota (Costa R)
Dec 31, 2011 Takashi Uchiyama w rsf 11 Jorge Solis .... Yokohama (Jap)
For WBA title
Jul 16, 2012 Takashi Uchiyama w disq 3 Michael Farenas (Phi) .... Saitama (Jap)
WBA sanctioned the following fights for the interim title
Jul 21, 2012 Bryan Vasquez (Costa R) w rsf 9 Jorge Lacierva (Mex) .... Tijuana (Mex)
Dec 8, 2012 Yuriorkis Gamboa (Cub) w pts 12 Michael Farenas .... Las Vegas, NV
Dec 31, 2012 Takashi Uchiyama w rsf 8 Bryan Vasquez .... Tokyo (Jap)
For the WBA title
May 6, 2013 Takashi Uchiyama w ko 5 Jaider Parra (Ven) .... Tokyo (Jap)
WBA sanctioned the following fight for the interim title
Oct 26, 2013 Bryan Vasquez w td 5 Rene Gonzalez (Nic) .... San Jose (Costa R)
Dec 31, 2013 Takashi Uchiyama w pts 12 Daiki Kaneko (Jap) .... Tokyo (Jap)
For the WBA title
WBA sanctioned the following fights for the interim title
Apr 12, 2014 Bryan Vasquez w pts 12 Jose Felix Jr (Mex) .... Las Vegas, NV
Dec 20, 2014 Bryan Vasquez w rtd 9 Sergio Thompson (Mex) .... Cancun (Mex)
Vasquez lost his interim title belt on the scales
Dec 31, 2014 Takashi Uchiyama w rtd 9 Israel Hector Enrique Perez (Arg) .... Tokyo (Jap)
For WBA title
WBA sanctioned the following fight for the interim title
Mar 21, 2015 Emanuel Lopez (Mex) w rsf 9 Carlos Padilla (Col) .... Tapachula (Mex)
May 29, 2015 **Javier Fortuna** w pts 12 Bryan Vasquez .... New York, NY
For vacant WBA title
WBA sanctioned the following fight for the interim title
Jun 20, 2015 Emanuel Lopez w rsf 10 Rolando Giono (Pan) .... Comitan (Mex)
Sep 29, 2015 Javier Fortuna w rsf 10 Carlos Ivan Velasquez (PR) .... Las Vegas, NV
For WBA title
WBA sanctioned the following fight for the interim title
Dec 17, 2015 Jezreel Corrales (Pan) w rsf 10 Juan Antonio Rodriguez (Mex) .... Panama City (Pan)
Jun 24, 2016 **Jason Sosa (US)** w rsf 11 Javier Fortuna .... Beijing (Chi)
For WBA title
Nov 12, 2016 Jason Sosa w pts 12 Stephen Smith (Eng) .... Monte Carlo (Mon)
Oct 21, 2017 **Alberto Machado (PR)** w ko 8 Jezreel Corrales .... Verona, NY
For vacant WBA title

WBO title

Mar 6, 2004 Diego Corrales w pts 12 Joel Casamayor .... Mashantucket, CT
For vacant title. Corrales relinquished title to box at lightweight
Jul 15, 2004 **Mike Anchondo** (US) w pts 12 Julio Pablo Chacon (Arg) .... Miami, FL
For vacant title
Apr 8, 2005 **Jorge Barrios** (Arg) w rsf 4 Mike Anchondo .... Miami, FL
Aug 12, 2005 Jorge Barrios w rsf 2 Victor Santiago (PR) .... Cordoba (Arg)
May 20, 2006 Jorge Barrios w ko 1 Janos Nagy (Hun) .... Los Angeles, CA
Sep 16, 2006 **Joan Guzman** (DR) w pts 12 Jorge Barrios .... Las Vegas, NV
Dec 18, 2006 Joan Guzman w pts 12 Antonio Davis (US) .... Santo Domingo (DR)
Nov 17, 2007 Joan Guzman w pts 12 Humberto Soto (Mex) .... Atlantic City, NJ
The WBO sanctioned the following fight for the Interim title
Dec 15, 2007 **Alex Arthur** (Sco) w pts 12 Stephen Foster Jr (Eng) .... Edinburgh (Sco)
Joan Guzman relinquished the title to move up to lightweight
Sep 6, 2008 **Nicky Cook** (Eng) w pts 12 Alex Arthur .... Manchester (Eng)
Mar 14, 2009 **Roman Martinez** (PR) w rsf 4 Nicky Cook .... Manchester (Eng)
Sep 12, 2009 Roman Martinez w ko 9, Feider Viloria (Col) .... Hato Rey (PR)
Sep 4, 2010 **Ricky Burns** (Sco) w pts 12 Roman Martinez .... Glasgow (Sco)
Dec 4, 2010 Ricky Burns w pts 12 Andreas Evensen (Nor) .... Glasgow (Sco)
Mar 12, 2011 Ricky Burns w pts 12 Joseph Laryea (Gha) .... Glasgow (Sco)
Jul 16, 2011 Ricky Burns w rsf 1 Nicky Cook (Eng) .... Liverpool (Eng)
Burns relinquished title to box at lightweight
Nov 26, 2011 **Adrien Broner** w ko 3 Vicente Martin Rodriguez (Arg) .... Cincinnati, OH
For vacant title
Feb 25, 2011 Adrien Broner w rsf 4 Eloy Perez (US) .... Saint Louis, MO
Jul 21, 2011 Adrien Broner w rsf 5 Vicente Escobedo (US) .... Cincinnati, OH
For vacant title. Broner failed to make weight; so title only at stake for Escobedo
Sep 15, 2012 **Roman Martinez** w pts 12 Miguel Beltran Jr .... Las Vegas, NV
For vacant title.
Jan 19, 2013 Roman Martinez drew 12 Juan Carlos Burgos (Mex) .... New York, NY
Apr 6, 2013 Roman Martinez w pts 12 Diego Magdaleno (USA) .... Macao (Chi)
Nov 9, 2013 **Mikey Garcia** (USA) w ko 8 Roman Martinez .... Corpus Christi,TX
Jan 25, 2014 Mikey Garcia w pts 12 Juan Carlos Burgos .... New York, NY
Garcia stripped of WBA title
Sep 20, 2014 **Orlando Salido** w ko 11 Terdsak Kokietgym (Thai) .... Tijuana (Mex)
For vacant title
Apr 11, 2015 **Roman Martinez** w pts 12 Orlando Salido .... San Juan, PR
Sep 12, 2015 Roman Martinez drew 12 Orlando Salido (Mex) .... Las Vegas, NV
WBO sanctioned the following fight for the interim title
Mar 12, 2016 Miguel Berchelt (Mex) w rsf 6 George Jupp (Eng) .... Merida (Mex)
Jun 11, 2016 **Vasyl Lomachenko (Ukr)** w ko 5 Roman Martinez .... New York, NY
For the WBO title
WBO sanctioned the following fight for the interim title
Jul 16, 2016 Miguel Berchelt w ko 4 Suriya Tatakhun (Tha) .... Los Reyes La Paz (Mex)
Nov 26, 2016 Vasyl Lomachenko w rtd 7 Nicholas Walters (Jam) .... Los Angeles, CA
For the WBO title
Apr 8, 2017 Vasyl Lomachenko w rtd 9 Jason Sosa (US) .... Oxon Hill, MD
Aug 5, 2017 Vasyl Lomachenko w rtd 7 Miguel Marriaga (Col) .... Los Angeles, CA
Dec 9, 2017 Vasyl Lomachenko w rtd 6 Guillermo Rigondeaux (Cub) .... New York, NY

WBA Super title

May 6, 2015 **Takashi Uchiyama (Jap)** w rsf 2 Tanakorn Phawachart (Tha) .... Tokyo (Jap)
Dec 31, 2015 Takashi Uchiyama w rsf 3 Oliver Flores (Nic) .... Tokyo (Jap)
Apr 27, 2016 **Jezreel Corrales (Pan)** w ko 2 Takashi Uchiyama .... Tokyo (Jap)
Dec 31, 2016 Jezreel Corrales w pts 12 Takashi Uchiyama .... Tokyo (Jap)
Jul 15, 2017 Jezreel Corrales w td 10 Robinson Castellanos (Mex) .... Inglewood, CA

Featherweight

The featherweight class first became active in the Prize Ring around 1860, but did not gain widespread acceptance until the Irishman with the English name, Ike Weir, fought the Englishman with the Irish name, Frank Murphy, to a draw in 1889. Weir was generally considered to be getting on top when the police intervened, but when he got a second chance at the title he was knocked out by "Torpedo" Billy Murphy of New Zealand. There was at this time a wide gap between the division limits in Britain and America. The British regarded it as being anywhere from 122 to 126lb, while the Americans favoured 112 to 114lb.

The pick of the early champions was George Dixon, a black Canadian who was known as "Little Chocolate". He was responsible for moving the American limit first to 117, then 120, and finally 122lb. It was not until 1920 that the Americans accepted the British figure of 126lb at which it has remained.

As the list below shows, the story of the featherweight class is complicated, with the title frequently in dispute. That is still the case: the last time there was just one champion was almost 30 years ago, in 1967. But the featherweights have always had a place in the public's affections, and champions of the quality of Willie Pep, Eusbeio Pedroza, Sandy Saddler and Salvador Sanchez stand pound-for-pound comparison with the best in the game.

World Featherweight Championship Bouts

Mar 31, 1889	Ike Weir (Ire) drew 80 Frank Murphy (Eng)	Kouts, IN
Jan 13, 1890	**Billy Murphy** (NZ) w ko 14 Ike Weir	San Francisco, CA
Sep 2, 1890	**Young Griffo** (Aus) w rsf 15 Billy Murphy	Sydney (Aus)
	Griffo outgrew the division	
Jun 27, 1892	**George Dixon** (Can) w ko 14 Fred Johnson (Eng)	Coney Island, NY
Sep 6, 1892	George Dixon w ko 8 Jack Skelly (US)	New Orleans, LA
Aug 7, 1893	George Dixon w ko 3 Eddie Pierce (US)	Coney Island, NY
Sep 25, 1893	George Dixon w ko 7 Solly Smith (US)	Coney Island, NY
Jun 29, 1894	George Dixon drew 20 Young Griffo	Boston, MA
Nov 27, 1896	**Frank Erne** (US) w pts 20 George Dixon	New York, NY
Mar 24, 1897	**George Dixon** w pts 25 Frank Erne	New York, NY
Oct 4, 1897	**Solly Smith** (US) w pts 20 George Dixon	San Francisco, CA
	Dixon argued that as Smith was two pounds over the agreed weight of 118lb, the title was not at stake. Smith was widely regarded as the new champion, but in Britain, a rival version of the championship (limit 122lb) was claimed by Ben Jordan of Bermondsey, London, who outpointed Dixon over 25 rounds in New York on July 1, 1898	
Aug 1, 1898	Solly Smith drew 25 Tommy White (US)	Coney Island, NY
Sep 26, 1898	**Dave Sullivan** (US) w rtd 5 Solly Smith	Coney Island, NY
Nov 11, 1898	**George Dixon** w dis 10 Dave Sullivan	New York, NY
Nov 29, 1898	George Dixon w pts 25 Oscar Gardner (US)	New York, NY
Jan 17, 1899	George Dixon w ko 10 Young Pluto (Aus)	New York, NY
May 29, 1899	**Ben Jordan** (Eng) w ko 9 Harry Greenfield	London (Eng)
Oct 10, 1899	**Eddie Santry** w ko 15 Ben Jordan	New York, NY
	Above two were for British version of title	
Nov 2, 1899	George Dixon w pts 25 Will Curley (Eng)	New York, NY
Nov 21, 1899	George Dixon w pts 25 Eddie Lenny (US)	New York, NY
Jan 9, 1900	**Terry McGovern** (US) w rsf 8 George Dixon	New York, NY
Feb 1, 1900	Terry McGovern w ko 5 Eddie Santry (US)	Chicago, IL
	For undisputed title	
Mar 9, 1900	Terry McGovern w ko 3 Oscar Gardner	New York, NY
Nov 2, 1900	Terry McGovern w ko 7 Joe Bernstein (US)	Louisville, KY
Nov 28, 1901	**Young Corbett II** (US) w ko 2 Terry McGovern	Hartford, CT
	Corbett could no longer make the championship limit and Abe Attell, who had drawn with and beaten George Dixon in 1901, was regarded as the best man at the weight	
Sep 3, 1903	**Abe Attell** (US) w pts 25 Johnny Reagan (US)	St Louis, MO
Feb 1, 1904	Abe Attell w ko 5 Harry Forbes (US)	St Louis, MO
Feb 22, 1906	Abe Attell w pts 15 Jimmy Walsh (US)	Chelsea, MA
May 11, 1906	Abe Attell drew 20 Kid Herman (US)	Los Angeles, CA
Jul 4, 1906	Abe Attell w pts 20 Frankie Neil (US)	Los Angeles, CA
Oct 30, 1906	Abe Attell w pts 20 Harry Baker (US)	Los Angeles, CA
Nov 16, 1906	Abe Attell w pts 15 Billy de Coursey (US)	San Diego, CA
Dec 7, 1906	Abe Attell w ko 8 Jimmy Walsh Los Angeles, CA	
Jan 18, 1907	Abe Attell w ko 8 Harry Baker	Los Angeles, CA
May 24, 1907	Abe Attell w pts 20 Kid Solomon (US)	Los Angeles, CA
Oct 29, 1907	Abe Attell w ko 4 Freddie Weeks (US)	Los Angeles, CA
Jan 1, 1908	Abe Attell drew 25 Owen Moran (Eng)	San Francisco, CA
Jan 31, 1908	Abe Attell w rtd 13 Frankie Neil	San Francisco, CA
Feb 28, 1908	Abe Attell w rsf 7 Eddie Kelly (US)	San Francisco, CA
Sep 7, 1908	Abe Attell drew 23 Owen Moran	San Francisco, CA
Dec 29, 1908	Abe Attell w ko 8 Biz Mackey (US)	New Orleans, LA
Jan 14, 1909	Abe Attell w ko 10 Freddie Weeks	Goldfield, NV
Feb 4, 1909	Abe Attell w rtd 7 Eddie Kelly	New Orleans, LA
Feb 19, 1909	**Jim Driscoll (Wal)** no decision 10 Abe Attell	New York, NY
	Driscoll was clearly the better man, but Attell refused to give him a rematch for the championship. However, on the basis of this performance Driscoll was recognized as world champion by Britain and the IBU	
Oct 24, 1910	Abe Attell w pts 10 Johnny Kilbane (US)	Kansas City, KS
Feb 22, 1912	**Johnny Kilbane** w pts 20 Abe Attell	Vernon, CA
Jun 3, 1912	Jim Driscoll w ko 12 Jean Poesy (Fra)	London (Eng)
Jan 27, 1913	Jim Driscoll drew 20 Owen Moran	London (Eng)
Feb 1913	*Driscoll retired*	
Apr 29, 1913	Johnny Kilbane drew 20 Johnny Dundee (US)	Los Angeles, CA
Sep 6, 1913	Johnny Kilbane w pts 12 Jimmy Walsh	Boston, MA
Sep 4, 1916	Johnny Kilbane w ko 3 Kid Chaney (US)	Cedar Point, OH
Sep 17, 1921	Johnny Kilbane w ko 7 Danny Frush (Eng)	Cleveland, OH
	New York Commission stripped Kilbane of the title for failing to defend against Johnny Dundee, and matched Dundee and Danny Frush for the vacant title	
Aug 15, 1922	**Johnny Dundee** w ko 9 Danny Frush	Brooklyn, NY
Jun 2, 1923	**Eugene Criqui** (Fra) w ko 6 Johnny Kilbane	New York, NY
Jul 26, 1923	**Johnny Dundee** w ko 6 Eugene Criqui	New York, NY
	For undisputed title Dundee relinquished title because of weight problems in August 1923	
Jan 2, 1925	**Louis "Kid" Kaplan** (US) w rtd 9 Danny Kramer (US)	New York, NY
	For vacant title	
Aug 27, 1925	Louis "Kid" Kaplan drew 15 Babe Herman (US)	Waterbury, CT
Dec 18, 1925	Louis "Kid" Kaplan w pts 15 Babe Herman	New York, NY
July 1927	*Kaplan relinquished the title because of weight problems*	
Sep 19, 1927	**Benny Bass** (Rus) w pts 10 Red Chapman (US)	Philadelphia, PA
	For vacant NBA title	
Oct 24, 1927	**Tony Canzoneri** (US) w pts 15 Johnny Dundee	New York, NY
	NY version of vacant title	
Feb 10, 1928	Tony Canzoneri w pts 15 Benny Bass	New York, NY
	For undisputed title	
Sep 28, 1928	**Andre Routis** (Fra) w pts 15 Tony Canzoneri	New York, NY
May 27, 1929	Andre Routis w rsf 3 Buster Brown (US)	Baltimore, MD
Sep 23, 1929	**Battling Battalino** (US) w pts 15 Andre Routis	Hartford, CT
Jul 15, 1930	Battling Battalino w ko 5 Ignacio Fernandez (Phil)	Hartford, CT
Dec 12, 1930	Battling Battalino w pts 15 Kid Chocolate (Cub)	New York, NY
May 22, 1931	Battling Battalino w pts 15 Fidel LaBarba (US)	New York, NY
Jul 23, 1931	Battling Battalino w pts 10 Freddie Miller (US)	Cincinnati, OH
Nov 4, 1931	Battling Battalino w pts 10 Earl Mastro (US)	Chicago, IL
Jan 1932	*The NBA and NY Commission declared the title vacant after Battalino had been three pounds overweight for a scheduled defence against Freddie Miller*	

NBA title

May 26, 1932	**Tommy Paul** (US) w pts 15 Johnny Pena (PR)	Detroit, MI
	For vacant title	
Jan13, 1933	**Freddie Miller** w pts 10 Tommy Paul	Chicago, IL
Feb 28, 1933	Freddie Miller w pts 10 Baby Arizmendi (Mex)	Los Angeles, CA
Mar 21, 1933	Freddie Miller w pts 10 Speedy Dado (Phil)	Los Angeles, CA
Jul 11, 1933	Freddie Miller w ko 4 Abie Israel (US)	Seattle, WA
Jan 1, 1934	Freddie Miller w pts 10 Jackie Sharkey (US)	Cincinnati, OH
Jul 13, 1934	Freddie Miller w ko 8 Gene Espinosa (US)	Watsonville, CA
Sep 21, 1934	Freddie Miller w pts 15 Nel Tarleton (Eng)	Liverpool (Eng)
Feb 17, 1935	Freddie Miller w ko 1 Jose Girones (Sp)	Barcelona (Sp)
Jun 12, 1935	Freddie Miller w pts 15 Nel Tarleton	Liverpool (Eng)
Oct 22, 1935	Freddie Miller w pts 15 Vernon Cormier (US)	Boston, MA
Feb 18, 1936	Freddie Miller w pts 12 Johnny Pena	Seattle, WA
Mar 2, 1936	Freddie Miller w pts 15 Petey Sarron (US)	Miami, FL
May 11, 1936	**Petey Sarron** w pts 15 Freddie Miller	Washington, DC
Jul 22, 1936	Petey Sarron w pts 15 Baby Manuel (US)	Dallas, TX
Sep 4, 1937	Petey Sarron w pts 12 Freddie Miller	Johannesburg (SA)
Oct 29, 1937	**Henry Armstrong** (US) w ko 6 Petey Sarron	New York, NY
	For NBA and vacant NY titles, which Armstrong relinquished in August 1938	
Dec 29, 1938	**Leo Rodak** (US) w pts 10 Leone Efrati (US)	Chicago, IL
	Although this was an overweight match, the NBA agreed to recognize Rodak as champion	
Apr 18, 1939	**Joey Archibald** (US) w pts 15 Leo Rodak	Providence, RI
	For undisputed title	

New York title

Oct 13, 1932	**Kid Chocolate** w rsf 12 Lew Feldman (US)	New York, NY
	For vacant title	
Dec 9, 1932	Kid Chocolate w pts 15 Fidel LaBarba	New York, NY
May 19, 1933	Kid Chocolate w pts 15 Tommy Watson (Eng)	New York, NY
	NY Commission stripped Chocolate in May 1934 for failing to defend against Frankie Klick	
May 1936	*NY Commission recognized Mike Belloise as champion*	
Sep 3, 1936	**Mike Belloise (US)** w ko 9 Dave Crowley (Eng)	New York, NY
Oct 27, 1936	**Henry Armstrong** w pts 10 Mike Belloise	Los Angeles, CA
	Armstrong was defending the California version of the title, which he had won by outpointing Baby Arizmendi over ten rounds in Los Angeles on August 4, 1936. The NY Commission did not regard it as involving Belloise's title, and it continued to recognize him as champion until Belloise was forced to give up the title because of injury	
Aug 10, 1937	*Belloise relinquished title*	
Oct 29, 1937	Henry Armstrong w ko 6 Petey Sarron	New York, NY
	For NBA and vacant NY titles which Armstrong relinquished in August 1938	
Oct 17, 1938	**Joey Archibald** (US) w pts 15 Mike Belloise	New York, NY
	For vacant title	
Apr 18, 1939	Joey Archibald w pts 15 Leo Rodak	Providence, RI
	For undisputed title	

IBU title

Oct 5, 1937	**Maurice Holtzer** (Fra) w pts 15 Phil Dolhem (Bel)	Algiers (Alg)
	For vacant title	
Feb 19, 1938	Maurice Holtzer drew 15 Maurice Dubois (Swi)	Geneva (Swi)
	The IBU agreed to recognize Armstrong in May 1938, in an effort to promote unity	

Undisputed title

Sep 28, 1939	**Joey Archibald** w pts 15 Harry Jeffra (US)	Washington, DC
	The NBA withdrew recognition from Archibald in May 1940 for his failure to defend against Petey Scalzo, who they declared champion	

New York title

May 20, 1940	**Harry Jeffra** w pts 15 Joey Archibald	Baltimore, MD
Jul 29, 1940	Harry Jeffra w pts 15 Spider Armstrong (Can)	Baltimore, MD
May 12, 1941	**Joey Archibald** w pts 15 Harry Jeffra	Washington, DC
Sep 11, 1941	**Chalky Wright** (Mex) w ko 11 Joey Archibald	Washington, DC
Jun 19, 1942	Chalky Wright w rsf 10 Harry Jeffra	Baltimore, MD
Sep 25, 1942	Chalky Wright w pts 15 Lulu Constantino (US)	New York, NY
Nov 20, 1942	**Willie Pep** (US) w pts 15 Chalky Wright	New York, NY
Jun 8, 1943	Willie Pep w pts 15 Sal Bartolo (US)	Boston, MA
Sep 29, 1944	Willie Pep w pts 15 Chalky Wright	New York, NY
Feb 19, 1945	Willie Pep w pts 15 Phil Terranova (US)	New York, NY
Jun 7, 1946	Willie Pep w ko 12 Sal Bartolo	New York, NY
	For undisputed title	

NBA title

Jul 10, 1940	**Petey Scalzo** (US) w rsf 15 Bobby "Poison" Ivy (US)	Hartford, CT
May 19, 1941	Petey Scalzo w pts 15 Phil Zwick (US)	Milwaukee, WI
Jul 1, 1941	**Richie Lemos** (US) w ko 5 Petey Scalzo	Los Angeles, CA
Nov 18, 1941	**Jackie Wilson** (US) w pts 12 Richie Lemos	Los Angeles, CA
Dec 16, 1941	Jackie Wilson w pts 12 Richie Lemos	Los Angeles, CA
Jan 18, 1943	**Jackie Callura** (Can) w pts 15 Jackie Wilson	Providence, RI
Mar 18, 1943	Jackie Callura w pts 15 Jackie Wilson	Boston, MA
Aug 16, 1943	**Phil Terranova** (US) w ko 8 Jackie Callura	New Orleans, LA
Dec 27, 1943	Phil Terranova w rsf 6 Jackie Callura	New Orleans, LA
Mar 10, 1944	**Sal Bartolo** w pts 15 Phil Terranova	Boston, MA
May 5, 1944	Sal Bartolo w pts 15 Phil Terranova	Boston, MA
Dec 15, 1944	Sal Bartolo w pts 15 Willie Roache (US)	Boston, MA
May 3, 1946	Sal Bartolo w ko 6 Spider Armstrong (Can)	Boston, MA
Jun 7, 1946	**Willie Pep** w ko 12 Sal Bartolo New York, NY	
	For undisputed title	

Undisputed title

Aug 22, 1947	**Willie Pep** w ko 12 Jock Leslie (US)	Flint, MI
Feb 24, 1948	Willie Pep w rsf 10 Humberto Sierra (Cub)	Miami, FL
Oct 29, 1948	**Sandy Saddler** (US) w ko 4 Willie Pep	New York, NY
Feb 11, 1949	**Willie Pep** w pts 15 Sandy Saddler	New York, NY
Sep 20, 1949	Willie Pep w rsf 7 Eddie Compo (US)	Waterbury, CT
Jan 16, 1950	Willie Pep w ko 5 Charlie Riley (US)	St Louis, MO
Mar 17, 1950	Willie Pep w pts 15 Ray Famechon (Fra)	New York, NY
Sep 8, 1950	**Sandy Saddler** w rtd 7 Willie Pep	New York, NY
Sep 26, 1951	Sandy Saddler w rtd 9 Willie Pep	New York, NY
Feb 25, 1955	Sandy Saddler w pts 15 Teddy Davis (US)	New York, NY
Jan 18, 1956	Sandy Saddler w rsf 13 Gabriel "Flash" Elorde (Phil)	San Francisco, CA
Jan 1957	*Saddler retired because of injuries sustained in a car crash*	
Jun 24, 1957	**Hogan Bassey** (Nig) w rsf 10 Cherif Hamia (Fra)	Paris (Fra)
	For vacant title	
Apr 1, 1958	Hogan Bassey w ko 3 Ricardo Moreno (Mex)	Los Angeles, CA
Mar 18, 1959	**Davey Moore** (US) w rtd 13 Hogan Bassey	Los Angeles, CA
Aug 19, 1959	Davey Moore w rtd 10 Hogan Bassey	Los Angeles, CA
Aug 29, 1960	Davey Moore w pts 15 Kazuo Takayama (Jap)	Tokyo (Jap)
Apr 8, 1961	Davey Moore w ko 1 Danny Valdez (US)	Los Angeles, CA
Nov 13, 1961	Davey Moore w pts 15 Kazuo Takayama	Tokyo (Jap)
Aug 17, 1962	Davey Moore w rsf 2 Olli Maki (Fin)	Helsinki (Fin)
Mar 21, 1963	**Sugar Ramos** (Cub) w rtd 10 Davey Moore	Los Angeles, CA
Jul 13, 1963	Sugar Ramos w pts 15 Rafiu King (Nig)	Mexico City (Mex)
Feb 28, 1964	Sugar Ramos w rtd 6 Mitsunori Seki (Jap)	Tokyo (Jap)
May 9, 1964	Sugar Ramos w pts 15 Floyd Robertson (Gha)	Accra (Gha)
Sep 26, 1964	**Vicente Saldivar** (Mex) w rtd 11 Sugar Ramos	Mexico City (Mex)
Dec 6, 1964	Vicente Saldivar w rsf 11 Delfino Rosales (Mex)	Guanajuato (Mex)
May 7, 1965	Vicente Saldivar w rsf 15 Raul Rojas (US)	Los Angeles, CA
Sep 7, 1965	Vicente Saldivar w pts 15 Howard Winstone (Wal)	London (Eng)
Feb 12, 1966	Vicente Saldivar w ko 2 Floyd Robertson	Mexico City (Mex)
Aug 7, 1966	Vicente Saldivar w pts 15 Mitsunori Seki	Mexico City (Mex)
Jan 29, 1967	Vicente Saldivar w rsf 7 Mitsunori Seki	Mexico City (Mex)
Jun 15, 1967	Vicente Saldivar w pts 15 Howard Winstone	Cardiff (Wal)
Oct 14, 1967	Vicente Saldivar w rtd 12 Howard Winstone	Mexico City (Mex)
	Saldivar announced his retirement in the ring immediately after the fight	

WBC title

Jan 23, 1968	**Howard Winstone** w rsf 9 Mitsunori Seki	London (Eng)
	For vacant title	
Jul 24, 1968	**Jose Legra** (Cub) w rsf 5 Howard Winstone	Porthcawl (Wal)
Jan 21, 1969	**Johnny Famechon** (Aus) w pts 15 Jose Legra	London (Eng)
Jul 28, 1969	Johnny Famechon w pts 15 Fighting Harada (Jap)	Sydney (Aus)
Jan 6, 1970	Johnny Famechon w ko 14 Fighting Harada	Tokyo (Jap)
May 9, 1970	**Vicente Saldivar** w pts 15 Johnny Famechon	Rome (Ita)
Dec 11, 1970	**Kuniaki Shibata** (Jap) w rsf 12 Vicente Saldivar	Tijuana (Mex)
Jun 3, 1971	Kuniaki Shibata w ko 1 Raul Cruz (Mex)	Tokyo (Jap)
Nov 11, 1971	Kuniaki Shibata drew 15 Ernesto Marcel (Pan)	Matsuyama (Jap)
May 19, 1972	**Clemente Sanchez** (Mex) w ko 3 Kuniaki Shibata	Tokyo (Jap)
Dec 16, 1972	**Jose Legra** w rsf 10 Clemente Sanchez	Monterrey (Mex)
	Sanchez was overweight, but Legra was recognized as champion by the WBC	
May 5, 1973	**Eder Jofre** (Bra) w pts 15 Jose Legra	Brasilia (Bra)
Oct 21, 1973	Eder Jofre w ko 4 Vicente Saldivar	Salvador (Bra)
	WBC withdrew recognition of Jofre in June 1974 for failing to defend against Alfredo Marcano	
Sep 7, 1974	**Bobby Chacon** (US) w rsf 9 Alfredo Marcano (Ven)	Los Angeles, CA
	For vacant title	
Mar 1, 1975	Bobby Chacon w ko 2 Jesus Estrada (Mex)	Los Angeles, CA
Jun 20, 1975	**Ruben Olivares** (Mex) w rsf 2 Bobby Chacon	Inglewood, CA
Sep 20, 1975	**David Kotey** (Gha) w pts 15 Ruben Olivares	Inglewood, CA
Mar 6, 1976	David Kotey w rsf 12 Flipper Uehara (Jap)	Accra (Gha)
Jul 16, 1976	David Kotey w rsf 3 Shigeo Fukuyama (Jap)	Tokyo (Jap)
Nov 5, 1976	**Danny Lopez** (US) w pts 15 David Kotey	Accra (Gha)
Sep 13, 1977	Danny Lopez w rsf 7 Jose Torres (Mex)	Los Angeles, CA
Feb 15, 1978	Danny Lopez w rsf 6 David Kotey	Las Vegas, NV
Apr 23, 1978	Danny Lopez w rsf 6 Jose de Paula (Bra)	Los Angeles, CA
Sep 15, 1978	Danny Lopez w ko 2 Juan Malvarez (Arg)	New Orleans, LA
Oct 21, 1978	Danny Lopez w dis 4 Fel Clemente (Phil)	Pesaro (Ita)
Mar 10, 1979	Danny Lopez w ko 2 Roberto Castanon (Sp)	Salt Lake City, UT
Jun 17, 1979	Danny Lopez w ko 15 Mike Ayala (US)	San Antonio, TX
Sep 25, 1979	Danny Lopez w rsf 3 Jose Caba (DR)	Los Angeles, CA
Feb 2, 1980	**Salvador Sanchez** (Mex) w rsf 13 Danny Lopez	Phoenix, AZ
Apr 12, 1980	Salvador Sanchez w pts 15 Ruben Castillo (US)	Tucson, AZ
Jun 21, 1980	Salvador Sanchez w rsf 14 Danny Lopez	Las Vegas, NV
Sep 13, 1980	Salvador Sanchez w pts 15 Pat Ford (Guy)	San Antonio, TX
Dec 13, 1980	Salvador Sanchez w pts 15 Juan LaPorte (PR)	El Paso, NM
Mar 22, 1981	Salvador Sanchez w rsf 10 Roberto Castanon (Sp)	Las Vegas, NV
Aug 21, 1981	Salvador Sanchez w rsf 8 Wilfredo Gomez (PR)	Las Vegas, NV
Dec 12, 1981	Salvador Sanchez w pts 15 Pat Cowdell (Eng)	Houston, TX
May 8, 1982	Salvador Sanchez w pts 15 Rocky Garcia (US)	Dallas, TX
Jul 21, 1982	Salvador Sanchez w rsf 15 Azumah Nelson (Gha)	New York, NY
	Sanchez was killed in a car crash in August 1982	
Sep 15, 1982	**Juan LaPorte** w rtd 10 Mario Miranda (Col)	New York, NY
	For vacant title	
Feb 20, 1983	Juan LaPorte w pts 12 Ruben Castillo	San Juan, CA
Jun 25, 1983	Juan LaPorte w pts 12 Johnny De La Rosa (DR)	San Juan, CA

Mar 31, 1984	**Wilfredo Gomez** w pts 12 Juan LaPorte	San Juan, CA
Dec 8, 1984	**Azumah Nelson** w rsf 11 Wilfredo Gomez	San Juan, CA
Sep 6, 1985	Azumah Nelson w ko 5 Juvenal Ordenes (Ch)	Miami, FL
Oct 12, 1985	Azumah Nelson w ko 1 Pat Cowdell	Birmingham (Eng)
Feb 25, 1986	Azumah Nelson w pts 12 Marcos Villasana (Mex)	Los Angeles, CA
Jun 22, 1986	Azumah Nelson w rsf 10 Danilo Cabrera (DR)	San Juan, CA
Mar 7, 1987	Azumah Nelson w ko 6 Mauro Gutierrez (Mex)	Las Vegas, NV
Aug 29, 1987	Azumah Nelson w pts 12 Marcos Villasana	Los Angeles, CA
	Nelson relinquished the title in January 1988 to box at super-featherweight	
Mar 7, 1988	**Jeff Fenech** (Aus) w rsf 10 Victor Callejas (PR)	Sydney (Aus)
	For vacant title	
Aug 12, 1988	Jeff Fenech w rsf 5 Tyrone Downes (Bar)	Melbourne (Aus)
Nov 30, 1988	Jeff Fenech w rsf 5 George Navarro (US)	Melbourne (Aus)
Apr 8, 1989	Jeff Fenech w pts 12 Marcos Villasana	Melbourne (Aus)
	Fenech relinquished the title because of weight problems	
Jun 2, 1990	**Marcos Villasana** w rsf 8 Paul Hodkinson (Eng)	Manchester (Eng)
	For vacant title	
Sep 30, 1990	Marcos Villasana w rsf 8 Javier Marquez (Mex)	Mexico City (Mex)
Apr 11, 1991	Marcos Villasana w rsf 6 Rafael Zuniga (Col)	Mexico City (Mex)
Aug 16, 1991	Marcos Villasana w pts 12 Ricardo Cepeda (PR)	Marbella (Sp)
Nov 13, 1991	**Paul Hodkinson** w pts 12 Marcos Villasana	Belfast (N. Ire)
Apr 25, 1992	Paul Hodkinson w rsf 3 Steve Cruz (US)	Belfast (N. Ire)
Sep 12, 1992	Paul Hodkinson w rsf 10 Fabrice Benichou (Fra)	Blagnac (Fra)
Feb 3, 1993	Paul Hodkinson w rtd 4 Ricardo Cepeda	London (Eng)
Apr 28, 1993	**Gregorio Vargas** (Mex) w rtd 7 Paul Hodkinson	Dublin (Ire)
Dec 4, 1993	**Kevin Kelley** (US) w pts 12 Gregorio Vargas	Reno, NV
May 6, 1994	Kevin Kelley w pts 12 Jesse Benavides (US)	Atlantic City, NJ
Jan 7, 1995	**Alejandro Gonzalez** (Mex) w rtd 11 Kevin Kelley	San Antonio, TX
Mar 31, 1995	Alejandro Gonzalez w pts 12 Louie Espinosa (US)	Anaheim, CA
Jun 2, 1995	Alejandro Gonzalez w rsf 9 Tony Green (US)	Ledyard, CT
Sep 23, 1995	**Manuel Medina** (Mex) w pts 12 Alejandro Gonzalez	Sacramento, CA
Dec 11, 1995	**Luisito Espinosa** (Phil) w pts 12 Manuel Medina	Tokyo (Jap)
Mar 1, 1996	Luisito Espinosa w ko 4 Alejandro Gonzalez	Guadalajara (Mex)
Jul 6, 1996	Luisito Espinosa w pts 12 Cesar Soto (Mex)	Manila (Phil)
Nov 2, 1996	Luisito Espinosa w rsf 8 Nobutoshi Hiranaka (Jap)	Fukuoka (Jap)
May 17, 1997	Luisito Espinosa w tdec 8 Manuel Medina	Manila (Phil)
Dec 5, 1997	Luisito Espinosa w rsf 6 Carlos Rios (Arg)	Koronadal (Phil)
Aug 15, 1998	Luisito Espinosa w tdec 11 Juan Carlos Ramirez (Mex)	El Paso, TX
Nov 28, 1998	Luisito Espinosa w rsf 2 Kennedy McKinney (US)	Indio, CA
May 15, 1999	**Cesar Soto** w pts 12 Luisito Espinosa	El Paso, TX

WBA title

Mar 28, 1968	**Raul Rojas** w pts 15 Enrique Higgins (Col)	Los Angeles, CA
	For vacant title	
Sep 27, 1968	**Shozo Saijo** (Jap) w pts 15 Raul Rojas	Los Angeles, CA
Feb 9, 1969	Shozo Saijo w pts 15 Pedro Gomez (Ven)	Tokyo (Jap)
Sep 7, 1969	Shozo Saijo w ko 2 Jose Luis Pimental (Mex)	Sapporo (Jap)
Feb 8, 1970	Shozo Saijo w pts 15 Godfrey Stevens (Ch)	Tokyo (Jap)
Jul 5, 1970	Shozo Saijo w pts 15 Frankie Crawford (US)	Sendai (Jap)
Feb 28, 1971	Shozo Saijo w pts 15 Frankie Crawford	Utsonomija (Jap)
Sep 2, 1971	**Antonio Gomez** (Ven) w rsf 5 Shozo Saijo	Tokyo (Jap)
Feb 6, 1972	Antonio Gomez w ko 7 Raul Martinez (Mex)	Maracay (Ven)
Aug 19, 1972	**Ernesto Marcel** w pts 15 Antonio Gomez	Maracay (Ven)
Dec 3, 1972	Ernesto Marcel w rsf 6 Enrique Garcia (Mex)	Panama City (Pan)
Jul 14, 1973	Ernesto Marcel w rtd 11 Antonio Gomez	Panama City (Pan)
Sep 8, 1973	Ernesto Marcel w ko 9 Spider Nemoto (Jap)	Panama City (Pan)
Feb 16, 1974	Ernesto Marcel w pts 15 Alexis Arguello (Nic)	Panama City (Pan)
May 1974	*Marcel retired*	
Jul 9, 1974	**Ruben Olivares** w ko 7 Zensuke Utagawa (Jap)	Inglewood, CA
	For vacant title	
Nov 23, 1974	**Alexis Arguello** w ko 13 Ruben Olivares	Inglewood, CA
Mar 15, 1975	Alexis Arguello w rsf 8 Leonel Hernandez (Ven)	Caracas (Ven)
May 31, 1975	Alexis Arguello w rsf 2 Rigoberto Riasco (Pan)	Managua (Nic)
Oct 12, 1975	Alexis Arguello w ko 5 Royal Kobayashi (Jap)	Tokyo (Jap)
Jun 19, 1976	Alexis Arguello w ko 3 Salvatore Torres (Mex)	Los Angeles, CA
Jun 1976	*Arguello gave up WBA title in due to weight problems*	
Jan 15, 1977	**Rafael Ortega** (Pan) w pts 15 Francisco Coronado (Nic)	Panama City (Pan)
	For vacant title	
May 29, 1977	Rafael Ortega w pts 15 Flipper Uehara	Okinawa (Jap)
Dec 17, 1977	**Cecilio Lastra** (Sp) w pts 15 Rafael Ortega	Torrelavega (Sp)
Apr 15, 1978	**Eusebio Pedroza** (Pan) w ko 13 Cecilio Lastra	Panama City (Pan)
Jul 2, 1978	Eusebio Pedroza w rsf 12 Ernesto Herrera (Mex)	Panama City (Pan)
Nov 27, 1978	Eusebio Pedroza w pts 15 Enrique Solis (PR)	San Juan, CA
Jan 9, 1979	Eusebio Pedroza w rtd 13 Royal Kobayashi	Tokyo (Jap)
Apr 8, 1979	Eusebio Pedroza w rsf 11 Hector Carrasquilla (Pan)	Panama City (Pan)
Jul 21, 1979	Eusebio Pedroza w rsf 12 Ruben Olivares	Houston, TX
Nov 17, 1979	Eusebio Pedroza w rsf 11 Johnny Aba (PNG)	Port Moresby (PNG)
Jan 22, 1980	Eusebio Pedroza w pts 15 Spider Nemoto (Jap)	Tokyo (Jap)
Mar 29, 1980	Eusebio Pedroza w ko 9 Juan Malvarez (Arg)	Panama City (Pan)
Jul 20, 1980	Eusebio Pedroza w ko 9 Sa-Wang Kim (Kor)	Seoul (Kor)
Oct 4, 1980	Eusebio Pedroza w pts 15 Rocky Lockridge (US)	McAfee, NJ
Feb 14, 1981	Eusebio Pedroza w ko 13 Pat Ford (Guy)	Panama City (Pan)
Aug 1, 1981	Eusebio Pedroza w ko 7 Carlos Pinango (Ven)	Caracas (Ven)
Dec 5, 1981	Eusebio Pedroza w ko 5 Bashew Sibaca (SA)	Panama City (Pan)
Jan 24, 1982	Eusebio Pedroza w pts 15 Juan LaPorte	Atlantic City, NJ
Oct 16, 1982	Eusebio Pedroza drew 15 Bernard Taylor (US)	Charlotte, NC
Apr 24, 1983	Eusebio Pedroza w pts 15 Rocky Lockridge	San Remo (Ita)
Oct 22, 1983	Eusebio Pedroza w pts 15 Jose Caba	St Vincent (Ita)
May 27, 1984	Eusebio Pedroza w pts 15 Angel Mayor (Ven)	Maracaibo (Ven)
Feb 2, 1985	Eusebio Pedroza w pts 15 Jorge Lujan (Pan)	Panama City (Pan)
Jun 8, 1985	**Barry McGuigan** (Ire) w pts 15 Eusebio Pedroza	London (Eng)
Sep 28, 1985	Barry McGuigan w rtd 8 Bernard Taylor	Belfast (Ire)
Feb 15, 1986	Barry McGuigan w rsf 14 Danilo Cabrera	Dublin (Ire)
Jun 23, 1986	**Steve Cruz** w pts 15 Barry McGuigan	Las Vegas, NV
Mar 6, 1987	**Antonio Esparragoza** (Ven) w rsf 12 Steve Cruz	Fort Worth, TX
Jul 26, 1987	Antonio Esparragoza w ko 10 Pascual Aranda (Mex)	Houston, TX
Jun 23, 1988	Antonio Esparragoza drew 12 Marcos Villasana	Los Angeles, CA
Nov 5, 1988	Antonio Esparragoza w ko 8 Jose Marmolejo (Pan)	Marsala (Ita)
Mar 25, 1989	Antonio Esparragoza w ko 10 Mitsuri Sugiya (Jap)	Kawasaki Jap)
Jun 2, 1989	Antonio Esparragoza w ko 6 Jean Marc Renard (Bel)	Namur (Bel)
Sep 22, 1989	Antonio Esparragoza w ko 5 Eduardo Montoya (Mex)	Mexicali (Mex)
May 12, 1990	Antonio Esparragoza w pts 12 Chan-Mok Park (Kor)	Seoul (Kor)
Mar 30, 1991	**Kyun-Yung Park** (Kor) w pts 12 Antonio Esparragoza	Kwangju (Kor)
Jun 15, 1991	Kyun-Yung Park w rsf 6 Masuaki Takeda (Jap)	Seoul (Kor)
Sep 14, 1991	Kyun-Yung Park w pts 12 Eloy Rojas (Ven)	Mokpo (Kor)
Jan 25, 1992	Kyun-Yung Park w ko 9 Seiji Asakawa (Jap)	Seoul (Kor)
Apr 25, 1992	Kyun-Yung Park w rsf 11 Koji Matsumoto (Jap)	Ansan (Kor)
Aug 29, 1992	Kyun-Yung Park w pts 12 Giovanni Neves (Ven)	Taeju (Kor)
Dec 19, 1992	Kyun-Yung Park w pts 12 Ever Beleno (Col)	Changwon (Kor)
Mar 20, 1993	Kyun-Yung Park w rsf 4 Thanomchit Kiatkriengkrai (Thai)	Cheju Do (Kor)
Sep 3, 1993	Kyun-Yung Park w pts 12 Tae-Shik Chun (Kor)	Damyang (Kor)
Dec 4, 1993	**Eloy Rojas** w pts 12 Kyun-Yung Park	Kwangmong (Kor)
Mar 19, 1994	Eloy Rojas w ko 5 Seiji Asakawa (Jap)	Kobe (Jap)
Sep 11, 1994	Eloy Rojas w rsf 8 Samart Payakaroon (Thai)	Trang (Thai)
Dec 3, 1994	Eloy Rojas w pts 12 Luis Mendoza (Col)	Bogota (Col)
May 27, 1995	Eloy Rojas w pts 12 Kyun-Yung Park	Soeul (Kor)
Aug 13, 1995	Eloy Rojas w pts 12 Nobutoshi Hiranaka (Jap)	Tagawa
Jan 27, 1996	Eloy Rojas w pts 12 Miguel Arrozal (Phil)	Phoenix, AZ
May 18, 1996	**Wilfredo Vasquez** (PR) w rsf 11 Eloy Rojas	Las Vegas, NV
Dec 7, 1996	Wilfredo Vasquez w rsf 5 Bernardo Mendoza (Chi)	Indio, CA
Mar 30, 1997	Wilfredo Vasquez w rsf 5 Yuji Watanabe (Jap)	Tokyo (Jap)
Aug 23, 1997	Wilfredo Vasquez w pts 12 Roque Cassiani (Col)	New York, NY
Nov 8, 1997	Wilfredo Vasquez w pts 12 Genaro Rios (Nic)	Las Vegas, NV
Mar 1998	*Vasquez stripped of title for failing to meet mandatory contender*	
Apr 3, 1998	**Freddie Norwood** (US) w pts 12 Antonio Cermeno (Ven)	Bayamon (PR)
	For vacant title	
Jun 13, 1998	Freddie Norwood w rsf 8 Genaro Rios	Atlantic City, NJ
Jul 10, 1998	Freddie Norwood w pts 12 Luis Mendoza (Col)	Miami, FL
Sep 1998	*Norwood stripped for failing to make weight for defence against Matsumato*	
Oct 3, 1998	**Antonio Cermeno** w ko 4 Genaro Rios	Caracas (Ven)
	For vacant title	
Feb 5, 1999	Antonio Cermeno w ko 2 Eddy Saenz (Nic)	Miami, FL
May 29, 1999	**Freddie Norwood** w pts 12 Antonio Cermeno	San Juan (PR)
Sep 11, 1999	Freddie Norwood w pts 12 Juan Manuel Marquez (Mex)	Las Vegas, NV
Jan 30, 2000	Freddie Norwood w ko 8 Takashi Koshimoto (Jap)	Fukuoka (Jap)
May 25, 2000	Freddie Norwood w pts 12 Julio Pablo Chacon (Arg)	Mendoza (Arg)
Sep 9, 2000	**Derrick Gainer** (US) w rsf 11 Freddie Norwood	New Orleans, LA
Feb 24, 2001	Derrick Gainer w pts 12 Victor Polo (Col)	Tampa, FL
Aug 24, 2002	Derrick Gainer tdraw 2 Daniel Seda (PR)	Carolina (PR)
Apr 12, 2003	Derrick Gainer w pts 12 Oscar Leon (Col)	Las Vegas, NV
	Gainer went on to fight a WBA/IBF unification bout against Juan Manuel Marquez	

IBF title

Mar 4, 1984	**Min-Keun Oh** (Kor) w ko 2 Joko Arter (Phil)	Seoul (Kor)
	For vacant title	
Jun 10, 1984	Min-Keun Oh w pts 15 Kelvin Lampkin (US)	Seoul (Kor)
Apr 7, 1985	Min-Keun Oh w pts 15 Irving Mitchell (US)	Pusan (Kor)
Nov 29, 1985	**Ki-Yung Chung** (Kor) w rsf 15 Min-Keun Oh	Chonju (Kor)
Feb 16, 1986	Ki-Yung Chung w rtd 6 Tyrone Jackson (US)	Ulsan (Kor)
May 18, 1986	Ki-Yung Chung w pts 15 Richard Savage (US)	Taegu (Kor)
Aug 30, 1986	**Antonio Rivera** (PR) w rtd 10 Ki-Yung Chung	Osan (Kor)
Jan 23, 1988	**Calvin Grove** (US) w rsf 4 Antonio Rivera	Gamaches (Fra)
May 17, 1988	Calvin Grove w pts 15 Myron Taylor (US)	Atlantic City, NJ
Sep 4, 1988	**Jorge Paez** (Mex) w pts 15 Calvin Grove	Mexicali (Mex)
Mar 30, 1989	Jorge Paez w ko 11 Calvin Grove	Mexicali (Mex)

May 21,	1989	Jorge Paez drew 12 Louie Espinosa	Phoenix, AZ
Aug 6,	1989	Jorge Paez w pts 12 Steve Cruz	El Paso, NM
Sep 16,	1989	Jorge Paez w rsf 2 Jose Mario Lopez (Arg)	Mexico City (Mex)
Dec 9,	1989	Jorge Paez w rsf 6 Lupe Guttierez (US)	Reno, NV
Feb 4,	1990	Jorge Paez w pts 12 Troy Dorsey (US)	Las Vegas, NV
Apr 7,	1990	Jorge Paez w pts 12 Louie Espinosa	Las Vegas, NV
		For IBF and WBO titles	

WBO title

Jan 28,	1989	**Maurizio Stecca** (Ita) w rsf 6 Pedro Nolasco (DR)	Milan (Ita)
		For vacant title	
Jun 16,	1989	Maurizio Stecca w rsf 9 Angel Mayor	Milan (Ita)
Nov 11,	1989	**Louie Espinosa** (US) w rsf 7 Maurizio Stecca	Rimini (Ita)
Apr 7,	1990	**Jorge Paez** w pts 12 Louie Espinosa	Las Vegas, NV
		For IBF and WBO titles	

IBF/WBO titles

Jul 8,	1990	**Jorge Paez** drew 12 Troy Dorsey	Las Vegas, NV
		Paez relinquished both titles in April 1991 to box at lightweight	
May 3,	1997	Naseem Hamed w rsf 1 Billy Hardy (Eng)	Manchester (Eng)
Sep	1997	*Hamed relinquished IBF title to concentrate on WBO championship*	

IBF title

Jun 3,	1991	**Troy Dorsey** w ko 1 Alfred Rangel (US)	Las Vegas, NV
		For vacant title	
Aug 12,	1991	**Manuel Medina** (Mex) w pts 12 Troy Dorsey	Los Angeles, CA
Nov 18,	1991	Manuel Medina w tech dec 9 Tom Johnson (US)	Los Angeles, CA
Mar 14,	1992	Manuel Medina w pts 12 Fabrice Benichou	Antibes (Fra)
Jul 22,	1992	Manuel Medina w rtd 10 Fabrizio Cappai (Ita)	Capo D'Orlando (Ita)
Oct 23,	1992	Manuel Medina w pts 12 Moussa Sangare (Fra)	Gravelines (Fra)
Feb 26,	1993	**Tom Johnson** w pts 12 Manuel Medina	Melun (Fra)
Sep 11,	1993	Tom Johnson w pts 12 Sugar Baby Rojas (Col)	Miami, FL
Nov 30,	1993	Tom Johnson w rsf 9 Stephane Haccoun (Fra)	Marseilles (Fra)
Feb 12,	1994	Tom Johnson w pts 12 Orlando Soto (Pan)	St Louis, MO
Jun 11,	1994	Tom Johnson w rsf 12 Benny Amparo (DR)	Atlantic City, NJ
Oct 22,	1994	Tom Johnson w pts 12 Francisco Segura (US)	Atlantic City, NJ
Jan 28,	1995	Tom Johnson w pts 12 Manuel Medina	Atlantic City, NJ
May 28,	1995	Tom Johnson w pts 12 Eddie Croft (US)	South Padre Island, TX
Dec 9,	1995	Tom Johnson w pts 12 Jose Badillo (PR)	Stuttgart (Ger)
Mar 2,	1996	Tom Johnson w rsf 12 Ever Beleno (Col)	Newcastle (Eng)
Apr 22,	1996	Tom Johnson w ko 7 Claudio Martinet (Arg)	Antibes (DWI)
Aug 31,	1996	Tom Johnson w pts 12 Ramon Guzman (Ven)	Dublin (Ire)
Feb 8,	1997	**Naseem Hamed** w rsf 8 Tom Johnson	Millwall (Eng)
Sept	1997	*Hamed relinquished the IBF title, having unified IBF/WBO championships*	
Dec 13,	1997	**Hector Lizarraga** (Mex) w rsf 11 Welcome Ncita (SA)	Pompano Beach, FL
		For vacant title	
Apr 24,	1998	**Manuel Medina** w pts 12 Hector Lizarraga	San Jose, CA
Apr 16,	1999	Manuel Medina w tdec 9 Victory Polo (Col)	Las Vegas, NV
Nov 13,	1999	**Paul Ingle** (Eng) w pts 12 Manuel Medina	Hull (Eng)
Apr 29,	2000	Paul Ingle w rsf 11 Junior Jones (US)	New York, NY
Dec 16,	2000	**Mbulelo Botile** (SA) w rsf 12 Paul Ingle	Sheffield (Eng)
Apr 6,	2001	**Frankie Toledo** (US) w pts 12 Mbulelo Botile	Las Vegas, NV
Nov 16,	2001	**Manuel Medina** w rsf 6 Frankie Toledo	Las Vegas, NV
Apr 27,	2002	**Johnny Tapia** (US) w pts 12 Manuel Medina	New York, NY
		Johnny Tapia vacated the title	

WBO title

Jan 26,	1991	**Maurizio Stecca** w rsf 5 Armando Reyes (DR)	Sassari (Ita)
		For vacant title	
Jun 15,	1991	Maurizio Stecca w pts 12 Fernando Ramos (Mex)	Mantichiari (Ita)
Nov 9,	1991	Maurizio Stecca w rtd 9 Tim Driscoll (Eng)	Campione d'Italia (Ita)
May 16,	1992	**Colin McMillan** (Eng) w pts 12 Maurizio Stecca	London (Eng)
Sep 26,	1992	**Ruben Palacio** (Col) w rtd 8 Colin McMillan	London (Eng)
Apr	1993	*Palacio forfeited the title on medical grounds*	
Apr 17,	1993	**Steve Robinson** (Wal) w pts 12 John Davison (Eng)	Washington (Eng)
		For vacant title	
Jul 10,	1993	Steve Robinson w rsf 9 Sean Murphy (Eng)	Cardiff (Wal)
Oct 23,	1993	Steve Robinson w pts 12 Colin McMillan	Cardiff (Wal)
Mar 12,	1994	Steve Robinson w ko 12 Paul Hodkinson (Eng)	Cardiff (Wal)
Jun 4,	1994	Steve Robinson w pts 12 Freddy Cruz (DR)	Cardiff (Wal)
Oct 1,	1994	Steve Robinson w ko 9 Duke McKenzie (Eng)	Cardiff (Wal)
Feb 4,	1995	Steve Robinson w pts 12 Domingo Damigella (Arg)	Cardiff (Wal)
Jul 7,	1995	Steve Robinson w rsf 7 Pedro Ferradas (Sp)	Cardiff (Wal)
Sep 30,	1995	**Naseem Hamed** (Eng) w rsf 8 Steve Robinson	Cardiff (Wal)
Mar 16,	1996	Naseem Hamed w rsf 1 Said Lawal (Nig)	Glasgow (Sco)
June 8,	1996	Naseem Hamed w rsf 2 Daniel Alicea (PR)	Newcastle (Eng)
Aug 31,	1996	Naseem Hamed w rtd 11 Manuel Medina	Dublin (Ire)
Nov 9,	1996	Naseem Hamed w rsf 2 Remegio Molina (Arg)	Manchester (Eng)
Feb 8,	1997	Naseem Hamed w rsf 8 Tom Johnson	Millwall (Eng)
		Hamed retained the WBO title and won Johnson's IBF championship	
Jul 19,	1997	Naseem Hamed w rsf 2 Juan Cabrera (Arg)	London (Eng)
		IBF did not recognize this fight	
Oct 11,	1997	Naseem Hamed w rsf 7 Jose Badillo (PR)	Sheffield (Eng)
Dec 19,	1997	Naseem Hamed w ko 4 Kevin Kelley (US)	New York, NY
Apr 18,	1998	Naseem Hamed w rsf 7 Wilfredo Vasquez	Manchester (Eng)
Oct 31,	1998	Naseem Hamed w pts 12 Wayne McCullough (Ire)	Atlantic City, NJ
Apr 10,	1999	Naseem Hamed w rsf 11 Paul Ingle (Eng)	Manchester (Eng)

WBC/WBO titles

Oct 22,	1999	Naseem Hamed w pts 12 Cesar Soto	Detroit, MI
Jan	2001	*Hamed relinquished the WBC title for business reasons.*	

WBC title

Apr 14,	2000	**Guty Espadas Jnr** (Mex) w tdec 11 Luisito Espinosa	Merida (Mex)
		For vacant title	
Jun 23,	2000	Guty Espadas Jnr w pts 12 Wethya Sakuangklang (Tha)	Merida (Mex)
Feb 17,	2001	**Erik Morales** (Mex) w pts 12 Guty Espadas Jnr	Las Vegas, NV
Jul 28,	2001	Erik Morales w pts 12 In-jin Chi (Kor)	Los Angeles, CA
Jun 22,	2002	**Marco Antonio Barrera** (Mex) w pts 12 Erik Morales	Las Vegas, NV
		Barrera refused to accept the WBC title, which was then declared vacant	
Nov 16,	2002	**Erik Morales** w pts 12 Paulie Ayala (US)	Las Vegas, NV
		For vacant title	
Feb 22,	2003	Erik Morales w rsf 3 Eddie Croft (US)	Mexico City (Mex)
May 3,	2003	Erik Morales w rsf 5 Fernando Velardez (USi)	Las Vegas, NV
		Morales relinquished title to box at super-featherweight	
Oct 18,	2003	**In-jin Chi** drew 12 Michael Brodie (Eng)	Manchester (Eng)
		For vacant title	
Apr 10,	2004	In-jin Chi w ko 7 Michael Brodie	Manchester (Eng)
Jul 24,	2004	In-jin Chi w rsf 10 Eiichi Sugama (Jap)	Seoul (Kor)
Jan 30,	2005	In-jin Chi w pts 12 Tommy Browne (Aus)	Seoul (Kor)
Jan 29,	2006	**Takashi Koshimoto** (Jap) w pts 12 In-jin Chi	Fukuoka (Jap)
Jul 30,	2006	**Rudy Lopez** (Mex) w rsf 7 Takashi Koshimoto	Fukuoka (Jap)
Dec 17,	2006	In-jin Chi w pts 12 Rudy Lopez Seoul (Kor)	
		In-jin Chi retired	
Jul 21,	2007	**Jorge Linares** (Ven) w rsf 10 Oscar Larios (Mex)	Las Vegas, NV
		For vacant title	
Dec 15,	2007	Jorge Linares w ko 8 Gamaliel Diaz (Mex)	Cancun (Mex)
		The WBC sanctioned the following fights for the Interim title:	
May 31,	2008	**Oscar Larios** w rsf 5 Feider Viloria	Chetumal (Mex)
Aug 2,	2008	Oscar Larios wko 7 Marlon Aguilar (Nic)	Zapotan (Mex)
		Jorge Linares relinquished the title to move up to super-featherweight	
Oct 16,	2008	**Oscar Larios** w pts 12 Takahiro Aoh (Jap)	Tokyo (Jap)
		For vacant title	
Mar 12,	2009	**Takahiro Aoh** w pts 12 Oscar Larios	Tokyo (Jap)
Jul 14,	2009	**Elio Rojas** (DR) w pts 12 Takahiro Aoh	Tokyo (Jap)
Feb 20,	2010	Elio Rojas w pts 12 Guty Espadas Jr (Mex)	Merida (Mex)
		Rojas relinquished title	
Nov 26,	2010	**Hozumi Hasegawa** (Jap) w pts 12 Juan Carlos Burgos (Mex)	Nagoya (Jap)
Apr 8,	2011	**Jhonny Gonzalez** (Mex) w rsf 4 Hozumi Hasegawa	Kobe (Jap)
Jul 9,	2011	Jhonny Gonzalez w rsf 4 Tomas Villa (Mex)	Atlantic City, NJ
Sep 15,	2011	Jhonny Gonzalez w rsf 2 Rogers Mtagwa	El Paso, TX
Dec 3,	2011	Jhonny Gonzalez w ko 2 Roinet Caballero (Pan)	Mexico City (Mex)
Apr 28,	2012	Jhonny Gonzalez w pts 12 Elio Rojas	Cancun (Mex)
Sep 15,	2012	**Daniel Ponce De Leon** w tdec 8 Jhonny Gonzalez	Las Vegas, NV
May 4,	2013	**Abner Mares** w rsf 9 Daniel Ponce De Leon	Las Vegas, NV
Aug 24,	2013	**Jhonny Gonzalez** w ko 1 Abner Mares	Carson, CA
May 24,	2014	Jhonny Gonzalez w tech pts 10 Clive Atwell (Guyana)	Acapulco (Mex)
Oct 4,	2014	Jhonny Gonzalez w rsf 11 Jorge Arce	Los Mochis (Mex)
Mar 28,	2015	**Gary Russell Jr** w rsf 4 Jhonny Gonzalez	Las Vegas, NV
		WBC sanctioned the following fight for the interim title	
Mar 5,	2016	Oscar Escandon (Col) w ko 7 Robinson Castellanos (Mex)	Washington, DC
Apr 16,	2016	Gary Russell Jr w rsf 2 Patrick Hyland (Ire)	Mashantucket, CT
		For the WBC title	
May 20,	2017	Gary Russell Jr w rsf 7 Oscar Escandon	Oxon Hill, MD

WBO title

Mar 11,	2000	Naseem Hamed w ko 4 Vuyani Bungu (SA)	London (Eng)
Aug 19,	2000	Naseem Hamed w ko 4 Augie Sanchez (US)	Uncasville CT
Oct	2000	*Hamed relinquished the title rather than meet No. 1 contender Istvan Kovacs.*	
Jan 27,	2001	**Istvan Kovacs** (Hun) w rsf 12 Antonio Diaz (DR)	Munich (Ger)
Jun 16,	2001	**Julio Pablo Chacon** (Arg) w rsf 6 Istvan Kovacs	Budapest (Hun)

Aug 11, 2001	Julio Pablo Chacon w rsf 5 Eduardo Barrios (Col)	Mendoza (Arg)
Jan 19, 2002	Julio Pablo Chacon w pts 12 Victor Polo	London (Eng)
Oct 19, 2002	**Scott Harrison** (Sco) w pts 12 Julio Pablo Chacon	Glasgow (Sco)
Mar 22, 2003	Scott Harrison w pts 12 Wayne McCullough (Ire)	Glasgow (Sco)
Jul 12, 2003	**Manuel Medina** (Mex) w pts 12 Scott Harrison	Glasgow (Sco)
Nov 29, 2003	**Scott Harrison** w rsf 11 Manuel Medina	Glasgow (Sco)
Mar 6, 2004	Scott Harrison w rsf 5 Walter Estrada (Col)	Glasgow (Sco)
Jun 19, 2004	Scott Harrison w rsf 3 William Abelyan (Arm)	Glasgow (Sco)
Oct 29, 2004	Scott Harrison w rsf 1 Samuel Kebede (Eth)	Glasgow (Sco)
Jan 28, 2005	Scott Harrison drew 12 Victor Polo (Col)	Glasgow (Sco)
Jun 3, 2005	Scott Harrison w ko 4 Michael Brodie (Eng)	Glasgow (Sco)
Nov 5, 2005	Scott Harrison w pts 12 Nedal Hussein (Aus) *Juan Manuel Marquez was installed as interim champion, when Harrison was unable to box because of injuries and legal problems*	Glasgow (Sco)
Nov 25, 2006	**Juan Manuel Marquez** (Mex) w ko 9 Jimrex Jaca (Phi) *For vacant title. Marquez vacated the title when he won the WBC super-featherweight championship*	Hidalgo, TX
Jul 14, 2007	**Steven Luevano** (US) w ko 11 Nicky Cook (Eng) *For vacant title*	London (Eng)
Oct 6, 2007	Steven Luevano w pts 12 Antonio Davis (US)	Las Vegas, NV
Mar 15, 2008	Steven Luevano w pts 12 Terdsak Jandaeng (Tha)	Las Vegas, NV
Jun 28, 2008	Steven Luevano drew 12 Mario Santiago (PR)	Las Vegas, NV
Oct 18, 2008	Steven Luevano w pts 12 Billy Dib (Aus)	Atlantic City, NV
Aug 15, 2009	Steven Luevano w dis 7 Bernabe Concepcion (Phi)	Las Vegas, NV
Jan 23, 2010	**Juan Manuel Lopez** (PR) w rsf 7 Steven Luevano	New York, NY
Jul 10, 2010	Juan Manuel Lopez w rsf 2 Bernabe Concepcion (Phil)	San Miguel (PR)
Nov 6, 2010	Juan Manuel Lopez w rtd 8 Rafael Marquez (Mex)	Las Vegas, NV
Apr 16, 2011	Orlando Salido w rsf 8 Juan Manuel Lopez	Bayamon (PR)

ONE EYE ON THE FUTURE *His right eye swollen shut, Juan Manuel Marquez is lifted high by his cornermen after a non-title win over Thailand's Terdsak Jandaeng*

Date	Bout	Venue
Jul 23, 2011	Orlando Salido w rsf 11 Kenichi Yamaguchi (Jap)	Ciudad Obregon (Mex)
Mar 10, 2012	Orlando Salido w rsf 10 Juan Manuel Lopez	San Juan (PR)
Jan 19, 2013	**Mikey Garcia** (US) w tdec 8 Orlando Salido	New York, NY
Jun 15, 2013	Mikey Garcia w rsf 4 Juan Manuel Lopez	Dallas, TX
	For vacant title. Garcia failed to make weight, so title only at stake for Lopez	
Oct 12, 2013	**Orlando Salido** w ko 7 Orlando Cruz (Puerto Rico)	Las Vegas, NV
	For vacant title	
Mar 1, 2014	Orlando Salido w pts 12 Vasyl Lomachenko (Ukr)	San Antonio, TX
	For vacant title. Salido failed to make weight, so title only at stake for Lomachenko	
Jun 21, 2014	**Vasyl Lomachenko** w pts 12 Gary Russell jr	Carson, CA
	For vacant title.	
Nov 23, 2014	Vasyl Lomachenko w pts 12 Chonlatarn Piriyapinyo	Macao (Chi)
May 2, 2015	Vasyl Llomachenko w ko 9 Gamalier Rodriguez (Puerto Rico)	Las Vegas, NV
Nov 7, 2015	Vasyl Lomachenko w ko 10 Romulo Koasicha (Mex)	Las Vegas, NV
Jul 23, 2016	**Oscar Valdez (Mex)** w rsf 2 Matias Carlos Adrian Rueda (Arg)	Las Vegas, NV
	For vacant WBO title	
Nov 5, 2016	Oscar Valdez w rsf 7 Hiroshige Osawa (Jap)	Las Vegas, NV
Apr 22, 2017	Oscar Valdez w pts 12 Miguel Marriaga (Col)	Carson, CA
Sep 22, 2017	Oscar Valdez w pts 12 Genesis Servania (Phi)	Tucson, AZ

WBA /IBF titles

Date	Bout	Venue
Feb 1, 2003	**Juan Manuel Marquez** (Mex) w rsf 7 Manuel Medina	Las Vegas, NV
	Marquez unified the WBA & IBF titles	
Nov 1, 2003	Juan Manuel Marquez w tdec 7 Derrick Gainer (US)	Grand Rapids, MI
May 8, 2004	Juan Manuel Marquez drew 12 Manny Pacquiao (Phi)	Las Vegas, NV
Sep 1, 2004	Juan Manuel Marquez w pts 12 Orlando Salido (Mex)	Las Vegas, NV
May 7, 2005	Juan Manuel Marquez w pts 12 Victor Polo	Las Vegas, NV
	Marquez, who had been made a "super" champion when he beat Gainer, was stripped of the WBA title when no promoter wanted to stage a fight with the "world" champion Chris John, who was installed as interim champion in 2003. He was also stripped of the IBF title in 2005	

WBA title

Date	Bout	Venue
Jun 4, 2004	**Chris John** (Indo) w pts 12 Osamu Soto (Jap)	Tokyo (Jap)
	For vacant title	
Dec 3, 2004	Chris John tdraw 4 Jose Rojas (Ven)	Teggarong (Borneo)
Apr 22, 2005	Chris John w pts 12 Derrick Gainer	Jakarta (Indo)
Aug 7, 2005	Chris John w rsf 10 Tommy Browne (Aus)	Penrith (Aus)
Mar 4, 2006	Chris John w pts 12 Juan Manuel Marquez	Tenggarong (Aus)
Sep 9, 2006	Chris John w pts 12 Renan Acosta (Pan)	Jakarta (Indo)
Mar 3, 2007	Chris John w pts 12 Jose Rojas	Jakarta (Indo)
Aug 19, 2007	Chris John w rtd 9 Zaiki Takemoto (Jap)	Kobe (Jap)
Jan 26, 2008	Chris John w rtd 7 Roinet Caballero (Pan)	Jakarta (Ind)
Jan 26, 2008	Chris John w rtd 7 Roinet Caballero (Pan)	Jakarta (Ind)
Oct 24, 2008	Chris John w pts 12 Hiroyuki Enoki (Jap)	Tokyo (Jap)
Feb 28, 2009	Chris John drew 12 Rocky Juarez (US)	Houston, TX
	The WBA sanctioned the following Interim title fight	
Apr 17, 2009	**Yuriorkis Gamboa** (Cub) w rsf 10 Jose Rojas (Ven)	Primm, NV
	The WBA awarded Chris John status of Super Champion	
Sep 19, 2009	Chris John w pts 12 Rocky Juarez	Las Vegas, NV
	The WBA recognized the winner of the following bout as World Champion:	
Oct 10, 2009	Yuriorkis Gamboa w rsf 4 Whyber Garcia (Pan)	New York, NY
Jan 23, 2010	Yuriorkis Gamboa w rsf 2 Rogers Mtagwa (Tan)	New York, NY
Mar 27, 2010	Yuriorkis Gamboa w pts 12 Jonathan Victor Barros (Arg)	Hamburg (Ger)
	Gamboa upgraded to WBA Super champion	
Dec 4, 2010	**Jonathan Victor Barros** w rsf 7 Irving Berry (Pan)	Las Heras (Arg)
	For vacant title	
Mar 12, 2011	Jonathan Victor Barros w pts 12 Miguel Roman (Mex)	Junin (Arg)
Jul 2, 2011	Jonathan Victor Barros w pts 12 Celestino Caballero	Junin (Arg)
Oct 14, 2011	**Celestino Caballero** w pts 12 Jonathan Victor Barros	Buenos Aires (Arg)
Dec 31, 2011	Celestino Caballero w pts 12 Satoshi Hosono (Jap)	Yokohama (Jap)
	Caballerro relinquished title	
Dec 8, 2012	Nicholas Walters (Jam) w rsf 7 Daulis Prescott (Col)	Kingston (Jam)
	For the vacant title	
	WBA sanctioned the following fights for the interim title	
Dec 8, 2012	Javier Fortuna (DR) w pts 12 Patrick Hyland (Ire)	Las Vegas, NV
Apr 19, 2013	Javier Fortuna w ko 1 Miguel Zamudio (Mex)	Atlantic City, NJ
	Fortuna lost the interim title on the scales	
Aug 23, 2013	Jesus Andres Cuellar (Arg) w pts 12 Claudio Marrero (DR)	Verona, NY
Nov 9, 2013	**Nicholas Walters** w rsf 4 Alberto Garza (Mex)	Corpus Christi (Mex)
	For the WBA title	
	WBA sanctioned the following fight for the interim title	
May 2, 2014	Jesus Andres Cuellar w pts 12 Rico Ramos (US)	Las Vegas, NV
May 31, 2014	Nicholas Walters w ko 5 Vic Darchinyan (Arm)	Macao (Chi)
	WBA sanctioned the following fights for the interim title	
Sep 11, 2014	Jesus Andres Cuellar w ko 2 Juan Manuel Lopez (PR)	Las Vegas, NV
Dec 20, 2014	Jesus Andres Cuellar w rsf 5 Ruben Tamayo (Mex)	Shelton, WA
Mar 28, 2015	Carlos Zambrano (Per) w pts 12 Daniel Ramirez (DR)	Lima (Peru)
Jun 6, 2015	Jesus Andres Cuellar w rsf 8 Vic Darchinyan	Carson, CA
	For the WBA title	
	WBA sanctioned the following fight for the interim title	
Aug 1, 2015	Carlos Zambrano w pts 12 Jose Sanmartin (Col)	Chincha (Peru)
Dec 5, 2015	Jesus Andres Cuellar w pts 12 Jonathan Oquendo (PR)	New York, NY
Dec 10, 2016	Abner Mares (Mex) w pts 12 Jesus Andres Cuellar	Los Angeles, CA
	The following fight was for the vacant WBA interim title and the vacant WBO title	
Apr 29, 2017	**Claudio Marrero (DR)** w ko 1 Carlos Zambrano	Las Vegas, NV
	WBA sanctioned the following fight for the interim title	
Sep 15, 2017	Jesus M Rojas (PR) w ko 7 Claudio Marrero	Las Vegas, NV
Oct 14, 2017	Abner Mares w td 10 Andres Gutierrez (Mex)	Carson, CA

WBA super title

Date	Bout	Venue
Dec 5, 2010	**Chris John** w pts 12 Fernando David Saucedo (Arg)	Jakarta (Indo)
Apr 17, 2011	Chris John w pts 12 Daud Cino Yordan (Indo)	Jakarta (Indo)
Nov 30, 2011	Chris John w pts 12 Stanyslav Merdov (Ukr)	Mt Claremont (Aus)
May 5, 2012	Chris John w pts 12 Shoji Kimura (Jap)	Singapore (Si)
Nov 9, 2012	Chris John w pts 12 Chonlatam Piriyapinyo (Tha)	Singapore (Si)
Apr 14, 2013	Chris John tech drew 3 Satoshi Hosono	Jakarta (Ind)
Dec 6, 2013	**Simpiwe Vetyeka** (South Africa) w rtd 6 Chris John	Northbridge (Aus)
May 31, 2014	**Nonito Donaire** w tech pts 5 Simpiwe Vetyeka	Macao (Chi)
Oct 18, 2014	**Nicholas Walters** w rsf 6 Nonito Donaire	Carson, CA
Jun 13, 2015	Nicholas Walters w pts 12 Miguel Marriaga (Col)	New York, NY
	For vacant title. Walters failed to make weight, so title only at stake for Marriaga.	
Aug 29, 2015	**Leo Santa Cruz (Mex)** w pts 12 Abner Mares (Mex)	Los Angeles, CA
Feb 27, 2016	Leo Santa Cruz w rsf 5 Kiko Martinez (Spa)	Anaheim, CA
Jul 30, 2016	**Carl Frampton (N Ire)** w pts 12 Leo Santa Cruz	New York, NY
Jan 28, 2017	**Leo Santa Cruz** w pts 12 Carl Frampton	Las Vegas, NV
Oct 14, 2017	Leo Santa Cruz w ko 8 Chris Avalos (US)	Carson, CA

WBA super title/IBF title

Date	Bout	Venue
Sep 11, 2010	Yuriorkis Gamboa w pts 12 Orlando Salido (Mex)	Las Vegas, NV
Mar 26, 2011	Yuriorkis Gamboa w rsf 4 Jorge Solis	Atlantic City, NJ
	Gamboa failed to make the weight and was stripped of IBF title before the fight. Only Solis could win the belt	

IBF title

Date	Bout	Venue
Jan 20, 2006	**Valdemir Pereira** (bra) w pts 12 Fahprakorb Rakkiatgym (Tha)	Mashantucket, CT
	For vacant title	
May 13, 2006	**Eric Aiken** (US) w dis 8 Valdemir Pereira	Boston, MA
Sep 2, 2006	**Robert Guerrero** (US) w rtd 8 Eric Aiken	Los Angeles, CA
Nov 4, 2006	Robert Guerrero nc 12 Orlando Salido (Mex)	Las Vegas, NV
	Orlando Salido won on points, but tested positive for a banned substance and the title was declared vacant	
Feb 23, 2007	**Robert Guerrero** w rtd 8 Spend Abazi (Den)	Copenhagen (Den)
	For vacant title	
Nov 3, 2007	Robert Guerrero w ko 1 Martin Honorio (Mex)	Tucson, AZ
Feb 29, 2008	Roberto Guerrero w ko 8 Jason Litzau (US)	Lemoore, CA
	Guerrero relinquished the title to move up to super-featherweight	
Oct 23, 2008	**Cristobal Cruz** (Mex) w pts 12 Orlando Salido	Airway Heights, WA
	For vacant title	
Feb 14, 2009	Cristobal Cruz w pts 12 Cyril Thomas (Fra)	St Quentin (Fra)
Jul 11, 2009	Cristobal Cruz w pts 12 Jorge Solis (Mex)	Tuxtla Gutierrez (Mex)
Dec 19, 2009	Cristobal Cruz tdraw 3 Ricardo Castillo (Mex)	Tuxtla Gutierrez (Mex)
May 15, 2010	**Orlando Salido** (Mex) w pts 12 Cristobal Cruz	Ciudad Obregon (Mex)
	Yuriorkis Gamboa took the title from Orlando Salido, then failed to make the weight when he defended WBA Super title and IBF belt against Jorge Solis	
Jul 29, 2011	**Billy Dib** (Aus) w pts 12 Jorge Lacierva	Homebush (Aus)
	For vacant title	
Nov 19, 2011	Billy Dib w pts 12 Alberto Servidei (Ita)	Sydney (Aus)
Mar 7, 2012	Billy Dib w pts 12 Eduardo Escobedo (Mex)	Hobart (Aus)
Mar 1, 2013	**Evgeny Gradovich** (Rus) w pts 12 Billy Dib	Mashantucket, CN
Jul 27, 2013	Evgeny Gradovich w pts 12 Mauricio Javier Munoz (Arg)	Macao (Chi)
Nov 24, 2013	Evgeny Gradovich w rsf 9 Billy Dib	Macao (Chi)
May 31, 2014	Evgeny Gradovich w pts 12 Alex Miskirtchian (Bel)	Macao (Chi)
Nov 29, 2014	Evgeny Gradovich drew 12 Jayson Vlez (Puerto Rico)	Omaha, NE
May 30, 2015	**Lee Selby** (Wales) w tech pts 8 Evgeny Gradovich	London (Eng)
Oct 14, 2015	Lee Selby w pts 12 Fernando Montiel (Mex)	Glandale, AZ
April 9, 2016	Lee Selby w pts 12 Eric Hunter (US)	London (Eng)
July 15, 2017	Lee Selby w pts 12 Jonathan Victor Barros (Arg)	London (Eng)
Dec 9, 2017	Lee Selby w pts 12 Eduardo Ramirez (Mex)	London (Eng)

Super-Bantamweight

There was sporadic championship activity in the 122lb class in the early 1920s, but the promoters who were trying to establish the new division could not get any organization to give it official sanction and, without that status, the super-bantams slipped back into obscurity. A long-forgotten body called the American Federation of Boxing failed to revive the category in the early 1940s, but the WBC were more successful in 1976. The phenomenal Wilfredo Gomez defended the WBC title 17 times before relinquishing it, became a major star and thus established the division with the fans. The WBA set up their own title in 1977, but have yet to produce a champion of Gomez's stature.

World Super-Bantamweight Championship Bouts

WBC title

Apr 3, 1976	**Rigoberto Riasco** (Pan) w rtd 8 Waruinge Nakayama (Ken)	Panama City (Pan)
Jun 12, 1976	Rigoberto Riasco w ko 10 Livio Nolasco (DR)	Panama City (Pan)
Aug 1, 1976	Rigoberto Riasco w pts 15 Dong-Kyun Yum (Kor)	Pusan (Kor)
Oct 10, 1976	**Royal Kobayashi** (Jap) w rsf 8 Rigoberto Riasco	Tokyo (Jap)
Nov 24, 1976	**Dong Kyun Yum** w pts 15 Royal Kobayashi	Seoul (Kor)
Feb 13, 1977	Dong Kyun Yum w pts 15 Jose Cervantes (Col)	Seoul (Kor)
May 21, 1977	**Wilfredo Gomez** (PR) w ko 12 Dong Kyun Yum	San Juan, CA
Jul 11, 1977	Wilfredo Gomez w ko 5 Raul Tirado (Mex)	San Juan, CA
Jan 19, 1978	Wilfredo Gomez w ko 3 Royal Kobayashi	Kitakyushu (Jap)
Apr 8, 1978	Wilfredo Gomez w rsf 7 Juan Antonio Lopez (Mex)	Bayamon (PR)
Jun 2, 1978	Wilfredo Gomez w rsf 3 Sakad Petchyindee (Thai)	Korat (Thai)
Sep 9, 1978	Wilfredo Gomez w rsf 13 Leonardo Cruz (DR)	San Juan, CA
Oct 28, 1978	Wilfredo Gomez w rsf 5 Carlos Zarate (Mex)	San Juan, CA
Mar 9, 1979	Wilfredo Gomez w rsf 5 Nestor Jiminez (Col)	New York, NY
Jun 16, 1979	Wilfredo Gomez w rsf 5 Jesus Hernandez (Nic)	San Juan, CA
Sep 28, 1979	Wilfredo Gomez w rsf 10 Carlos Mendoza (Pan)	Las Vegas, NV
Oct 26, 1979	Wilfredo Gomez w rsf 5 Nicky Perez (US)	New York, NY
Feb 3, 1980	Wilfredo Gomez w rtd 6 Ruben Valdez (Col)	Las Vegas, NV
Aug 22, 1980	Wilfredo Gomez w rsf 5 Derrick Holmes (US)	Las Vegas, NV
Dec 13, 1980	Wilfredo Gomez w ko 3 Jose Cervantes	Miami, FL
Mar 27, 1982	Wilfredo Gomez w rsf 6 Juan Meza (Mex)	Atlantic City, NJ
Jun 11, 1982	Wilfredo Gomez w ko 10 Juan Antonio Lopez	Las Vegas, NV
Aug 18, 1982	Wilfredo Gomez w rtd 7 Roberto Rubaldino (Mex)	San Juan, CA
Dec 3, 1982	Wilfredo Gomez w rsf 14 Lupe Pintor (Mex)	New Orleans, LA
	Wllfredo Gomez outgrew the super-bantamweight division	
Jun 15, 1983	**Jaime Garza** (US) w rsf 2 Bobby Berna (Phil)	Los Angeles, CA
	For vacant title	
May 26, 1984	Jaime Garza w ko 3 Felipe Orozco (Col)	Miami, FL
Nov 3, 1984	**Juan Meza** (Mex) w ko 1 Jaime Garza	Kingston, NY
Apr 19, 1985	Juan Meza w rsf 6 Mike Ayala (US)	Los Angeles, CA
Aug 18, 1985	**Lupe Pintor** (Mex) w pts 12 Juan Meza	Mexico City (Mex)
Jan 18, 1986	**Samart Payakarun** (Thai) w ko 5 Lupe Pintor	Bangkok (Thai)
	Pintor forfeited the title by being three pounds overweight, but the WBC agreed to recognize Payakarun as the new champion if he won	
Dec 10, 1986	**Samart Payakarun** w ko 12 Juan Meza	Bangkok (Thai)
May 8, 1987	**Jeff Fenech** (Aus) w rsf 4 Samart Parakarun	Sydney (Aus)
Jul 10, 1987	Jeff Fenech w rsf 5 Greg Richardson (US)	Sydney (Aus)
Oct 16, 1987	Jeff Fenech w tech dec 4 Carlos Zarate	Sydney (Aus)
Jan 1988	*Fenech relinquished the title to challenge for the WBC featherweight title*	
Feb 29, 1988	**Daniel Zaragoza** (Mex) w rsf 10 Carlos Zarate	Los Angeles, CA
	For vacant title	
May 29, 1988	Daniel Zaragoza drew 12 Seung-Hoon Lee (Kor)	Youchan (Kor)
Nov 21, 1988	Daniel Zaragoza w ko 5 Valerio Nati (Ita)	Forli (Ita)
Jun 22, 1989	Daniel Zaragoza w pts 12 Paul Banke (US)	Los Angeles, CA
Sep 1, 1989	Daniel Zaragoza w rsf 10 Frankie Duarte (US)	Los Angeles, CA
Dec 3, 1989	Daniel Zaragoza w pts 12 Chan-Young Park (Kor)	Seoul (Kor)
Apr 23, 1990	**Paul Banke** w rsf 9 Daniel Zaragoza	Los Angeles, CA
Aug 17, 1990	Paul Banke w rsf 12 Ki-Jun Lee (Kor)	Seoul (Kor)
Nov 5, 1990	**Pedro Decima** (Arg) w rsf 4 Paul Banke	Los Angeles, CA
Feb 3, 1991	**Kiyoshi Hatanaka** (Jap) w rsf 8 Pedro Decima	Nagoya (Jap)
Jun 14, 1991	**Daniel Zaragoza** w pts 12 Kiyoshi Hatanaka	Tokyo (Jap)
Aug 24, 1991	Daniel Zaragoza w pts 12 Huh Chin (Kor)	Seoul (Kor)
Dec 9, 1991	Daniel Zaragoza w pts 12 Paul Banke	Los Angeles, CA
Mar 20, 1992	**Thierry Jacob** (Fra) w pts 12 Daniel Zaragoza	Calais (Fra)
Jun 23, 1992	**Tracy Harris Patterson** (US) w rsf 2 Thierry Jacob	Albany, NY
Dec 5, 1992	Tracy Harris Patterson drew 12 Daniel Zaragoza	Berck-sur-Mer (Fra)
Mar 13, 1993	Tracy Harris Patterson w pts 12 Jesse Benavides (US)	Poughkeepsie, NY
Apr 9, 1994	Tracy Harris Patterson w pts 12 Richard Duran (US)	Reno, NV
Aug 26, 1994	**Hector Acero Sanchez** (DR) w pts 12 Tracy Harris Patterson	Atlantic City, NJ
Mar 11, 1995	Hector Acero-Sanchez w pts 12 Julio Gervacio (PR)	Atlantic City, NJ
Jun 2, 1995	Hector Acero-Sanchez drew 12 Daniel Zaragoza	Ledyard, CT
Nov 6, 1995	**Daniel Zaragoza** w pts 12 Hector Acero-Sanchez	Inglewood, CA
Mar 3, 1996	Daniel Zaragoza w rsf 11 Joichiro Tatsuyoshi (Jap)	Yokohama (Jap)
July 20, 1996	Daniel Zaragoza w rsf 7 Tsuyoshi Harada (Jap)	Osaka (Jap)
Jan 11, 1997	Daniel Zaragoza w pts 12 Wayne McCullough (Ire)	Boston, MA
Apr 14, 1997	Daniel Zaragoza w pts 12 Joichiro Tatsuyoshi	Osaka (Jap)
Sep 6, 1997	**Erik Morales** (Mex) w rsf 11 Daniel Zaragoza	El Paso, TX
Dec 12, 1997	Erik Morales w rtd 8 John Lowey (Ire)	Tijuana (Mex)
Apr 3, 1998	Erik Morales w rsf 6 Remigio Molina (Arg)	Tijuana (Mex)
May 16, 1998	Erik Morales w ko 2 Jose Luis Bueno (Mex)	Indio, CA
Sep 12, 1998	Erik Morales w rsf 4 Junior Jones (US)	Tijuana (Mex)
Feb 13, 1999	Erik Morales w ko 2 Angel Chacon (PR)	Las Vegas, NV
May 8, 1999	Erik Morales w rsf 9 Juan Carlos Ramirez (Mex)	Las Vegas, NV
Jul 31, 1999	Erik Morales w rsf 6 Reynante Jamili (Phi)	Tijuana (Mex)
Oct 22, 1999	Erik Morales w pts 12 Wayne McCullough (NI)	Detroit MI

WBA title

Nov 26, 1977	**Soo Hwan Hong** (Kor) w ko 3 Hector Carasquilla (Pan)	Panama City (Pan)
	For vacant title	
Feb 1, 1978	Soo Hwan Hong w pts 15 Yu Kasahara (Jap)	Tokyo (Jap)
May 6, 1978	**Ricardo Cardona** (Col) w rsf 12 Soo Hwan Hong	Seoul (Kor)
Sep 2, 1978	Ricardo Cardona w pts 15 Ruben Valdez (Col)	Cartagena (Col)
Nov 12, 1978	Ricardo Cardona w pts 15 Soon-Hyun Chung (Kor)	Seoul (Kor)
Jun 23, 1979	Ricardo Cardona w pts 15 Soon-Hyun Chung	Seoul (Kor)
Sep 6, 1979	Ricardo Cardona w pts 15 Yukio Segawa (Jap)	Hachinhoe (Jap)
Dec 15, 1979	Ricardo Cardona w pts 15 Sergio Palma (Arg)	Barranquilla (Col)
May 4, 1980	**Leo Randolph** (US) w rsf 15 Ricardo Cardona	Seattle, WA
Aug 9, 1980	**Sergio Palma** w ko 6 Leo Randolph	Spokane, WA
Nov 8, 1980	Sergio Palma w rsf 9 Ulisses Morales (Pan)	Buenos Aires (Arg)
Apr 4, 1981	Sergio Palma w pts 15 Leonardo Cruz (DR)	Buenos Aires (Arg)
Aug 15, 1981	Sergio Palma w rsf 12 Ricardo Cardona	Buenos Aires (Arg)
Oct 3, 1981	Sergio Palma w pts 15 Vichit Muangroi-et (Thai)	Buenos Aires (Arg)
Jan 15, 1982	Sergio Palma w pts 15 Jorge Lujan (Pan)	Cordoba (Arg)
Jun 12, 1982	**Leonardo Cruz** w pts 15 Sergio Palma	Miami Beach, FL
Nov 13, 1982	Leonardo Cruz w ko 8 Benito Badilla (Ch)	San Juan, CA
Mar 16, 1983	Leonardo Cruz w pts 15 Soon-Hyun Chung	San Juan, CA
Aug 26, 1983	Leonardo Cruz w pts 15 Cleo Garcia (Nic)	Santo Domingo (Bah)
Feb 22, 1984	**Loris Stecca** (Ita) w rsf 12 Leonardo Cruz	Milan (Ita)
May 26, 1984	**Victor Callejas** (PR) w rsf 8 Loris Stecca	Guaynabo (PR)
Feb 2, 1985	Victor Callejas w pts 15 Seung-Hoon Lee	San Juan, CA
Nov 8, 1985	Victor Callejas w rtd 6 Loris Stecca	Rimini (Ita)
Dec 1986	*The WBA stripped Callejas for failing to defend against Louie Espinosa*	
Jan 16, 1987	**Louie Espinosa** (US) w rsf 4 Tommy Valoy (DR)	Phoenix, AZ
	For vacant title	
Jul 15, 1987	Louie Espinosa w rsf 15 Manuel Vilchez (Ven)	Phoenix, AZ
Aug 15, 1987	Louie Espinosa w ko 9 Mike Ayala (US)	San Antonio, TX
Nov 28, 1987	**Julio Gervacio** (DR) w pts 12 Louie Espinosa	San Juan, CA
Feb 27, 1988	**Bernardo Pinango** (Ven) w pts 12 Julio Gervacio	San Juan, CA
May 28, 1988	**Juan Jose Estrada** (Mex) w pts 12 Bernardo Pinango	Tijuana (Mex)
Oct 15, 1988	Juan Jose Estrada w rsf l1 Takuya Muguruma (Jap)	Osaka (Jap)
Apr 4, 1989	Juan Jose Estrada w rsf 10 Jesus Poll (Ven)	Los Angeles, CA
Jul 10, 1989	Juan Jose Estrada w pts 12 Luis Mendoza (Col)	Tijuana (Mex)
Dec 11, 1989	**Jesus Salud** (US) w dis 9 Juan Jose Estrada	Los Angeles, CA
Apr 1990	*The WBA stripped Salud for failing to defend against Luis Mendoza*	
May 25, 1990	**Luis Mendoza** drew 12 Ruben Palacio (Col)	Cartagena (Col)
	For vacant title	
Sep 11, 1990	Luis Mendoza w rsf 3 Ruben Palacio	Miami, FL
Oct 18, 1990	Luis Mendoza w pts 12 Fabrice Benichou	Paris (Fra)
Jan 19, 1991	Luis Mendoza w rsf 8 Noree Jockygym (Thai)	Bangkok (Thai)
Apr 21, 1991	Luis Mendoza w pts 12 Carlos Uribe (Ch)	Cartagena (Col)
May 30, 1991	Luis Mendoza w ko 7 Jose Cardosa de Oliveira (Bra)	Madrid (Sp)
Oct 7, 1991	**Raul Perez** (Mex) w pts 12 Luis Mendoza	Los Angeles, CA
Mar 27, 1992	**Wilfredo Vasquez** (PR) w rsf 3 Raul Perez	Mexico City (Mex)
Jun 27, 1992	Wilfredo Vasquez w pts 12 Freddy Cruz (DR)	Gorle (Ita)
Dec 5, 1992	Wilfredo Vasquez w rsf 8 Thierry Jacob (Fra)	Berck- sur-Mer (Fra)
Mar 6, 1993	Wilfredo Vasquez w pts 12 Luis Mendoza	Paris (Fra)
Jun 24, 1993	Wilfredo Vasquez w ko 10 Thierry Jacob	Bordeaux (Fra)

Nov 18,	1993	Wilfredo Vasquez w pts 12 Horoaki Yokota (Jap)	Tokyo (Jap)
Mar 2,	1994	Wilfredo Vasquez w rsf 1 Yuichi Kasai (Jap)	Tokyo (Jap)
Jul 2,	1994	Wilfredo Vasquez w rsf 2 Jae-Won Choi (Kor)	Las Vegas, NV
Oct 13,	1994	Wilfredo Vasquez w pts 12 Juan Polo-Perez (Col)	Paris (Fra)
Jan 7,	1995	Wilfredo Vasquez w pts 12 Orlando Canizales (US)	San Antonio, TX
May 13,	1995	**Antonio Cermeno** (Ven) w pts 12 Wilfredo Vasquez	Bayamon (PR)
Nov 26,	1995	Antonio Cermeno w pts 12 Jesus Salud	Caracas (Ven)
Mar 23,	1996	Antonio Cermeno w pts 12 Yober Ortega (Ven)	Miami, FL
Nov 9,	1996	Antonio Cermeno w rtd 5 Eddie Saenz (Nic)	Las Vegas, NV
Dec 21,	1996	Antonio Cermeno w pts 12 Yuichi Kasai (Jap)	Las Vegas, NV
May 10,	1997	Antonio Cermeno w pts 12 Angel Chacon (PR)	Coconut Grove, FL
Jul 26,	1997	Antonio Cermeno w ko 12 Yuichi Kasai	Yokohama (Jap)
Sep 17,	1997	Antonio Cermeno w pts 12 Jose Rojas (Ven)	Caracas (Ven)
Sep 28,	1997	*Cermeno relinquished his title to move up in weight*	
Feb 8,	1998	**Enrique Sanchez** (Mex) w pts Rafael Del Valle (PR)	Lake Charles, LA
		For vacant title	
Dec 12,	1998	**Nestor Garza** (Mex) w pts 12 Enrique Sanchez	Indio, CA
May 8,	1999	Nestor Garza w rsf 8 Carlos Barreto (Ven)	Las Vegas, NV
Nov 21,	1999	Nestor Garza w rsf 12 Kozo Ishi (Jap)	Nagoya (Jap)
Mar 4,	2000	**Clarence Adams** (US) w pts 12 Nestor Garza	Las Vegas, NV
Aug 5,	2000	Clarence Adams w rsf 6 Andres Fernanez (US)	Madison, WI
Mar 23,	2001	Clarence Adams w pts 12 Ivan Alvarez (Col)	Owensboro, KY
		Adams was stripped of the title when he lost on points to Paulie Ayala for the IBO championship in August 2001	
Nov 17,	2001	**Yober Ortega** (Ven) w ko 4 Jose Rojas (Ven)	Las Vegas, NV
		For vacant title	
Feb 21,	2002	**Yoddamrong Sithyodthong** (Thai) w pts 12 Yober Ortega	Nakhon Ratchasima (Thai)
May 18,	2002	**Osamu Sato** (Jap) w ko 8 Yoddamrong Sithyodthong	Saitama (Jap)
Oct 9,	2002	**Salim Medjkoune** (Fra) w pts 12 Osamu Sato	Tokyo (Jap)
Apr 4,	2003	Salim Medjkoune w pts 12 Vincenzo Gigliotti (Ita)	Clermont Ferrand (Fra)
Jul 4,	2003	**Mahyar Monshipour** (Irn) w ko 12 Salim Medjkoune	Poitiers (Fra)
Dec 16,	2003	Mahyar Monshipour w rsf 7 Jairo Tagliaferro (Ven)	Paris (Fra)
May 27,	2004	Mahyar Monshipour w rsf 8 Salim Medjkoune	Clermont Ferrand (Fra)
Nov 8,	2004	Mahyar Monshipour w rsf 6 Yoddamrong Sithyodthong (Tha)	Paris (Fra)
Apr 29,	2005	Mahyar Monshipour w rsf 6 Shigeru Nakazato (Jap)	Marseille (Fra)
Jun 25,	2005	Mahyar Monshipour w rsf 9 Julio Zarate (Mex)	Poitiers (Fra)
Jun 18,	2006	**Somsak Sithchatchawal** (Tha) w rsf 10 Mahyar Monshipour	Paris (Fr)
Oct 4,	2006	**Celestino Caballero** (Pan) w rsf 3 Somsak Sithchatchawal	Nakornratchasima (Kor)
Mar 16,	2007	Celestino Caballero w dis 9 Ricardo Castillo (Mex)	Hollywood, FL
Aug 4,	2007	Celestino Caballero w pts 12 Jorge Lacierva (Mex)	Hidalgo TX
Dec 1,	2007	Celestino Caballero w rsf 8 Mauricio Pastrana (Col)	Panama City (Pan)
Jun 7,	2008	Celestino Caballero w rsf 12 Lorenzo Parra (Ven).	San Juan de Los Morros (Ven)
Sep 18,	2008	Celestino Caballero w rsf 1 Elvis Meija (Col)	Panama City (Pan)
		Incredibly, the WBA sanctioned an Interim title fight on the same day – and on the same show, as follows:	
Sep 18,	2008	Ricardo Cordoba (Pan) w pts 12 Luis Alberto Perez (Nic)	Panama City (Pan)

IBF title

Dec 14,	1983	**Bobby Berna** (Phi) w rtd 11 Seung-In Suh (Kor)	Seoul (Kor)
		For vacant title	
Apr 15,	1984	**Seung-In Suh** w ko 10 Bobby Berna	Seoul (Kor)
Jul 8,	1984	Seung-In Suh w ko 4 Cleo Garcia	Seoul (Kor)
Jan 3,	1985	**Ji-Won Kim** (Kor) w ko 10 Seung-In Sun	Seoul (Kor)
Mar 30,	1985	Ji-Won Kim w pts 15 Dario Palacio (Col)	Suwon (Kor)
Jun 28,	1985	Ji-Won Kim w ko 4 Bobby Berna	Pusan (Kor)
Oct 9,	1985	Ji-Won Kim w ko 1 Seung-In Suh	Chungju (Kor)
Jun 1,	1986	Ji-Won Kim w ko 2 Rudy Casicas (Phil)	Inchon (Kor)
		Ji-Won Kim retired an undefeated champion	
Jan 18,	1987	**Seung-Hoon Lee** w ko 9 Prayoonsak Muangsurin (Thai)	Pohang (Kor)
		For vacant title	
Apr 5,	1987	Seung-Hoon Lee w ko 10 Jorge Urbina Diaz (Mex)	Seoul (Kor)
Jul 19,	1987	Seung-Hoon Lee w ko 5 Lion Collins (Phil)	Seoul (Kor)
Dec 27,	1987	Seung-Hoon Lee w pts 15 Jose Sanabria (Ven)	Pohang (Kor)
Mar	1988	*Lee relinquished the title to challenge for the WBC version*	
May 21,	1988	**Jose Sanabria** w ko 5 Moises Fuentes (Col)	Bucaramanga (Col)
		For vacant title	
Aug 21,	1988	Jose Sanabria w pts 12 Vincenzo Belcastro (Ita)	Capo D'Orlando (Ita)
Sep 26,	1988	Jose Sanabria w rsf 10 Fabrice Benichou	Paris (Fra)
Nov 11,	1988	Jose Sanabria w rsf 6 Thierry Jacob	Gravelines (Fra)
Mar 10,	1989	**Fabrice Benichou** w pts 12 Jose Sanabria	Limoges (Fra)
Jun 10,	1989	Fabrice Benichou w ko 5 Franie Badenhorst (SA)	Frasnone (Ita)
Oct 7,	1989	Fabrice Benichou w pts 12 Ramon Cruz (PR)	Bordeaux (Fra)
Mar 10,	1990	**Welcome Ncita** (SA) w pts 12 Fabrice Benichou	Tel Aviv (Is)
Jun 2,	1990	Welcome Ncita w rsf 7 Ramon Cruz (DR)	Rome (Ita)
Sep 29,	1990	Welcome Ncita w rsf 8 Gerardo Lopez (Pan)	Aosta (Ita)
Feb 27,	1991	Welcome Ncita w pts 12 Jesus Rojas (Col)	St Vincent (Ita)
Jun 15,	1991	Welcome Ncita w pts 12 Hurley Snead (US)	San Antonio, TX
Sep 28,	1991	Welcome Ncita w pts 12 Jesus Rojas	Sun City (Bop)
Apr 18,	1992	Welcome Ncita w pts 12 Jesus Salud	Treviola (Ita)
Dec 2,	1992	**Kennedy McKinney** (US) w ko 11 Welcome Ncita	Tortoli (Ita)
Apr 17,	1993	Kennedy McKinney w pts 12 Richard Duran (US)	Sacramento, CA
Oct 17,	1993	Kennedy McKinney w pts 12 Jesus Salud	Lake Tahoe, CA
Apr 16,	1994	Kennedy McKinney w pts 12 Welcome Ncita	South Padre Island, TX
Aug 20,	1994	**Vuyani Bungu** (SA) w pts 12 Kennedy McKinney	Hammanskraal (SA)
Nov 19,	1994	Vuyani Bungu w pts 12 Felix Camacho (PR)	Hammanskraal (SA)
Mar 4,	1995	Vuyani Bungu w pts 12 Mohammed Al Haji Nurhuda (Ind)	Hammanskraal (SA)
Apr 29,	1995	Vuyani Bungu w pts 12 Victor Llerena (Col)	Johannesburg (SA)
Sep 26,	1995	Vuyani Bungu w pts 12 Laureano Ramirez (DR)	Hammanskraal (SA)
Jan 23,	1996	Vuyani Bungu w pts 12 Johnny Lewus (US)	Biloxi, MS
Apr 15,	1996	Vuyani Bungu w ko 2 Pablo Osuna (Col)	Hammanskraal (SA)
Aug 20,	1996	Vuyani Bungu w pts 12 Jesus Salud (Phi)	Hammanskraal (SA)
Apr 5,	1997	Vuyani Bungu w pts 12 Kennedy McKinney	Hammanskraal (SA)
Aug 16,	1997	Vuyani Bungu w pts 12 Enrique Jupiter (Mex)	Hammanskraal (SA)
Nov 15,	1997	Vuyani Bungu w pts 12 Arnel Barotillo (Phi)	Hammanskraal (SA)
May 16,	1998	Vuyani Bungu w pts 12 Ernesto Grey (Col)	Hammanskraal (SA)
Oct 31,	1998	Vuyani Bungu w pts 12 Danny Romero (US)	Atlantic City, NJ
Feb 6,	1999	Vuyani Bungu w rtd 7 Victory Llerena (Col)	Hammanskraal (SA)
Mar	1999	*Bungu relinquished title to box at featherweight*	
May 29,	1999	**Lehlohonolo Ledwaba** (SA) w pts 12 John Michael Johnson (US)	Hammanskraal (SA)
		For vacant title	
Sep 25,	1999	Lehlohonolo Ledwaba w rsf 5 Edison Valencia (Col)	Tunica MS
Apr 7,	2000	Lehlohonolo Ledwaba w rsf 8 Ernesto Grey (Col)	Bristol (Eng)
Oct 6,	2000	Lehlohonolo Ledwaba w ko 8 Eduardo Alvarez (Arg)	Maidstone (Eng)
Feb 17,	2001	Lehlohonolo Ledwaba w rsf 9 Arnel Barotillo (Phi)	Brakpan (SA)
Apr 22,	2001	Lehlohonolo Ledwaba w pts 12 Carlos Contreras (Mex)	Brakpan (SA)
Jun 23,	2001	**Manny Pacquiao** (Phi) w rsf 6 Lehlohonolo Ledwaba	Las Vegas, NV
		After his technical draw with WBO champion Agapito Sanchez, Pacquiao continued as IBF champion	
Jun 8,	2002	Manny Pacquiao w rsf 2 Jorge Julio (Col)	Memphis, TN
Oct 26,	2002	Manny Pacquiao w ko 1 Fahprakorb Rakkiatgym (Tha)	Davao (Phi)
Jul 26,	2003	Manny Pacquiao w rsf 3 Emmanuel Lucero (Mex)	Los Angeles, CA
		Pacquaio relinquished title to box at featherweight	
Mar 28,	2004	**Israel Vazquez** (Mex) w rsf 12 Jose Luis Valbuena (Mex)	Los Angeles, CA
		For vacant title	
Dec 28,	2004	Israel Vazquez w rsf 5 Artyom Simonyan (Arm)	El Cajon, CA
May 31,	2005	Israel Vazquez w pts 12 Armando Guerrero (Mex)	Lynwood, IL
		Vazquez unified the WBC & IBF titles, then relinquished the IBF title	
Nov 10,	2006	**Steve Molitor** (Can) w ko 5 Michael Hunter (Eng)	Hartlepool (Eng)
		For vacant title	
Jul 14,	2007	**Steve Molitor** w rsf 9 Takalani Ndlovu (SA)	Rama (Can)
		For vacant title	
Oct 27,	2007	Steve Molitor w pts 12 Fahsan 3K-Battery (Tha)	Rama (Can)
Jan 19,	2008	Steve Molitor w pts 12 Ricardo Castillo (Mex)	Rama (Can)
Apr 5,	2008	Steve Molitor w pts 12 Fernando Beltran jr. (Mex)	Rama (Can)
Aug 28,	2008	Steve Molitor w rsf 10 Ceferino Dario Labarda (Arg)	Rama (Can)

WBO title

Apr 29,	1989	**Kenny Mitchell** (US) w pts 12 Julio Gervacio	San Juan, CA
Sep 9,	1989	Kenny Mitchell w pts 12 Simon Skosana (SA)	San Juan, CA
Dec 9,	1989	**Valerio Nati** w dis 4 Kenny Mitchell	Teramo (Ita)
May 12,	1990	**Orlando Fernandez** (PR) w rsf 10 Valerio Nati	Sassari (Ita)
May 24,	1991	**Jesse Benavides** w pts 12 Orlando Fernandez	Corpus Christi, TX
Aug 31,	1991	Jesse Benavides w rsf 5 Fernando Ramos (Mex)	Corpus Christi, TX
Oct 15,	1992	**Duke McKenzie** (Eng) w pts 12 Jesse Benavides	London (Eng)
Jun 9,	1993	**Daniel Jiminez** (PR) w pts 12 Duke McKenzie	London (Eng)
Oct 29,	1993	Daniel Jiminez w rsf 5 Felix Garcia Losada (Sp)	Zaragoza (Sp)
Jan 7,	1994	Daniel Jimenez w pts 12 Felix Garcia Losada	Palma, Majorca (Sp)
Jun 25,	1994	Daniel Jimenez w pts 12 Cristobal Pascual (Sp)	Utrera, Seville (Sp)
Sep 3,	1994	Daniel Jimenez w ko 1 Harald Geier (Aut)	Wiener Neustadt (Aut)
Mar 31,	1995	**Marco Antonio Barrera** (Mex) w pts 12 Daniel Jimenez	Anaheim, CA
Jun 2,	1995	Marco Antonio Barrera w rsf 2 Frankie Toledo (US)	Ledyard, CT
Jul 15,	1995	Marco Antonio Barrera w rsf 1 Mauri Diaz (US)	Inglewood, CA
Aug 22,	1995	Marco Antonio Barrera w pts 12 Agapito Sanchez (DR)	S Padre Island, TX
Nov 4,	1995	Marco Antonio Barrera w rsf 7 Eddie Croft (US)	Las Vegas, NV
Feb 3,	1996	Marco Antonio Barrera w rsf 12 Kennedy McKinney	Los Angeles, CA
May 4,	1996	Marco Antonio Barrera w ko 3 Jesse Benavides	Anaheim, CA
July 14,	1996	Marco Antonio Barrera w rsf 7 Orlando Fernandez	Denver, CO
Sep 14,	1996	Marco Antonio Barrera w rsf 10 Jesse Magana (US)	Los Angeles, CA
Nov 22,	1996	**Junior Jones** (US) w dis 5 Marco Antonio Barrera	Tampa, FL
Apr 18,	1997	Junior Jones w pts 12 Marco Antonio Barrera	Las Vegas, NV
Dec 19,	1997	**Kennedy McKinney** w rsf 4 Junior Jones	New York, NY
Oct 31,	1998	**Marco Antonio Barrera** w rtd 3 Richie Wenton (Eng)	Atlantic City, NJ
		For vacant title	
Apr 3,	1999	Marco Antonio Barrera w rtd 1 Paul Lloyd (Eng)	London (Eng)
Aug 7,	1999	Marco Antonio Barrera w pts 12 Pastor Maurin (Arg)	Atlantic City, NJ

WBC/WBO titles

Feb 19, 2000 **Erik Morales** w pts 12 Marco Antonio Barrera (Mex) . . . . Las Vegas, NV
WBO refused to accept the result of the fight and reinstated Barrera as champion. Morales relinquished WBC title to box at featherweight

WBO title

Feb 2000 *Barrera lost to Erik Morales (see WBC/WBO) but was reinstated as champion.*
Jun 17, 2000 Marco Antonio Barrera w ko 1 Luiz Claudio Freitas (Bra) . . . . Mexico City (Mex)
Sep 9, 2000 Marco Antonio Barrera w pts 12 Jose Luis Valbuena (Ven) . . . . New Orleans, LA
Dec 1, 2000 Marco Antonio Barrera w rtd 6 Jesus Salud (US) . . . . Las Vegas, NV
May 2001 *Barrera vacated the title after outpointing Naseem Hamed for the vacant IBO featherweight belt, which he then refused to accept*
Jun 23, 2001 **Agapito Sanchez** (DR) w rsf 7 Jorge Monsalvo (Col) . . . . Las Vegas, NV

IBF/WBO titles

Nov 10, 2001 Manny Pacquiao tdraw 6 Agapito Sanchez. . . . . Las Vegas, NV
Thus Pacquiao kept the IBF title and Sanchez remained WBO champion

WBC title

Sep 9, 2000 **Willie Jorrin** (US) w pts 12 Michael Brodie (Eng) . . . . .Manchester (Eng)
Jan 19, 2001 Willie Jorrin w pts 12 Oscar Larios (Mex) . . . . Sacramento CA
Feb 5, 2002 Willie Jorrin drew 12 Osamu Sato (Jap) . . . . Tokyo (Jap)
Nov 1, 2002 **Oscar Larios** w rsf 1 Willie Jorrin . . . . .Sacramento, CA
Apr 26, 2003 Oscar Larios w pts 12 Shigeru Nakazato (Jap) . . . . Tokyo (Jap)
Sep 7, 2003 Oscar Larios w rsf 2 Kozo Ishii (Jap). . . . . .Nagoya (Jap)
Nov 22, 2003 Oscar Larios w rsf 10 Napapol Kiatisakchokchai (Tha). . . . . .Los Angeles, CA
Mar 6, 2004 Oscar Larios w pts 12 Shigeru Nakazato . . . . Saitama (Jap)
Nov 27, 2004 Oscar Larios w pts 12 Nedal Hussein (Aus) . . . . Las Vegas, CA
Feb 10, 2005 Oscar Larios w pts 12 Wayne McCullough (Ire). . . . . Lemoore, CA
Jul 16, 2005 Oscar Larios w rsf 10 Wayne McCullough. Las Vegas, CA

WBC/IBF titles

Dec 3, 2005 **Israel Vazquez** (Mex) w rsf 3 Oscar Larios. . . . . Las Vegas, NV
The IBF withdrew recognition of Vazquez

WBC title

Jun 10, 2006 Israel Vazquez w rtd 4 Ivan Hernandez (Mex). . . . . .Atlantic City, NJ
Sep 16, 2006 Israel Vazquez w rsf 10 Jhonny Gonzalez (Mex). . . . . Las Vegas, NV
Mar 3, 2007 **Rafael Marquez** (Mex) w rtd 7 Israel Vazquez . . . . .Carson, CA
Aug 4, 2007 **Israel Vazquez** w rsf 6 Rafael Marquez . . . . Hidalgo, TX
Mar 1, 2008 Israel Vazquez w pts 12 Rafael Marquez . . . . Carson, CA
The WBC sanctioned the following fight as for the Interim title
Sep 15, 2008 **Toshiaki Nishioka** (Jap) w pts 12 Napapol Kiatisakchokchoi (Tha). . Yokohama (Jap)
Jan, 2009 *WBC stripped Vazquez of his title because a detached retina left him unable to box*
Jan 3, 2009 Toshiaki Nishioka w rsf 12 Genaro Garcia (Mex). . . . . .Yokohama (Jap)
For vacant title
May 23, 2009 Toshiaki Nishioka w rsf 3 Jhonny Gonzalez (Mex) . . . . Monterrey (Mex)
Oct 10, 2009 Toshiaki Nishioka w rtd 3 Ivan Hernandez (Mex) . . . . Tokyo (Jap)
Apr 30, 2010 Toshiaki Nishioka (Jap) w rsf 5 Balweg Bangoyan (Phil) . . . . Tokyo (Jap)
Oct 24, 2010 Toshiaki Nishioka w pts 12 Rendall Munroe (Eng) . . . . Tokyo (Jap)
Apr 8, 2011 Toshiaki Nishioka w ko 9 Mauricio Javier Munoz (Arg) . . . . .Kobe (Jap)
Oct 1, 2011 Toshiaki Nishioka w pts 12 Rafael Marquez (Mex). . . . . Las Vegas, NV
Nishioka relinquished WBA title due to personal reasons and named Champion In Emeritus
Apr 21, 2012 Abner Mares (US) w pts 12 Eric Morel (PR) . . . . .El Paso, TX
For vacant title
Nov 10, 2012 Abner Mares w pts 12 Anselmo Moreno (Pan) . . . . .Los Angeles, CA
Abner Mares vacated title
Apr 20, 2013 **Victor Terrazas** (Mex) w pts 12 Cristian Mijares (Mex). . . . . . . Mexico City (Mex)
For vacant title
Aug 24, 2013 **Leo Santa Cruz** (Mex) w ko 3 Victor Terrazas. . . . . .Carson, CA
Dec 14, 2013 Leo Santa Cruz w pts 12 Cesar Seda (PR) . . . . San Antonio, TX
Mar 8, 2014 Leo Santa Cruz w pts 12 Cristian Mijares. Las Vegas, NV
Sep 13, 2014 Leo Santa Cruz w rsf 2 Manuel Roman (Mex). . . . . Las Vegas, NV
Jan 17, 2015 Leo Santa Cruz w rsf 8 Jesus Ruiz (Mex) . . . . Las Vegas, NV
WBC sanctioned the following fight for the interim title
Aug 29, 2015 Julio Ceja (Mex) w rsf 5 Hugo Ruiz (Mex) . . . . .Los Angeles, CA
Feb 27, 2015 **Hugo Ruiz** w ko 1 Julio Ceja . . . . Anaheim, CA
For the WBC title
Sep 16, 2015 **Hozumi Hasegawa (Jap)** w rtd 9 Hugo Ruiz . . . . Osaka (Jap)
Feb 25, 2016 Ray Vargas (Mex) w pts 12 Gavin McDonnell (Eng). . . . . Hull (Eng)
For the vacant WBC title
Aug 26, 2017 Ray Vargas w pts 12 Ronny Rios (US). . . . . .Carson, CA
Dec 2, 2017 Ray Vargas w pts 12 Oscar Negrete (US) . . . . .New York, NY

WBO title

Aug 17, 2002 **Joan Guzman** (DR) w ko 3 Fabio Oliva (Arg). . . . . Cardiff (Wal)
For vacant title
Feb 26, 2004 Joan Guzman w rsf 7 Agapito Sanchez (DR). . . . . San Diego, CA
Apr 22, 2005 Joan Guzman w pts 12 Fernando Beltran (Mex). . . . . Hidalgo, TX
Guzman relinquished title to box at featherweight
Oct 29, 2005 **Daniel Ponce de Leon** (Mex) w pts 12 Sod Looknongyangtoy (Tha) . . . . . .Tucson, AZ
For vacant title
May 27, 2006 Daniel Ponce de Leon w ko 2 Gerson Guerrero (Mex). . . . . .Carson, CA
Jul 15, 2006 Daniel Ponce de Leon w ko 1 Sod Looknongyangtoy . . . . Las Vegas, NV
Oct 21, 2006 Daniel Ponce de Leon w rsf 8 Al Seeger (US) . . . . .El Paso, TX
Mar 17, 2007 Daniel Ponce de Leon w pts 12 Gerry Penalosa (Phi). . . . . Las Vegas, NV
Aug 11, 2007 Daniel Ponce de Leon w rsf 1 Rey Bautista (Phi) . . . . .Sacramento, CA
Dec 8, 2007 Daniel Ponce de Leon w pts 12 Eduardo Escobedo (Mex) . . . . Las Vegas, NV
Jun 7, 2008 **Juan Manuel Lopez** (PR) w rsf 1 Daniel Ponce de Leon. . . . . . . .Atlantic City, NJ
Oct 4, 2008 Juan Manuel Lopez w ko 1 Cesar Figueroa (Mex) . . . . Hato Rey (PR)
Dec 6, 2008 Juan Manuel Lopez w rsf 1 Sergio Medina (Arg) . . . . Las Vegas, NV
Apr 25, 2009 Juan Manuel Lopez w rtd 10 Gerry Penalosa (Phi). . . . . Bayamon (PR)
Jun 27, 2009 Juan Manuel Lopez w rtd 9 Olivier Lontchi (Cmr). . . . . .Atlantic City, NJ
Oct 10, 2009 Juan Manuel Lopez w pts 12 Rogers Mtagwa (Tan) . . . . .New York, NY
Juan Manuel Lopez relinquished the title to box at featherweight
Feb 27, 2010 **Wilfredo Vazquez Jr.** (PR) w ko 4 Marvin Sonsona (Phil) . . . . Bayamon (PR)
For vacant title
May 29, 2010 Wilfredo Vazquez Jr. w rsf 10 Zsolt Bedak (Hun) . . . . Bayamon (PR)
Oct 16, 2010 Wilfredo Vazquez Jr. w rsf 11 Ivan Hernandez (Mex) . . . . .Kissimmee, FL
May 7, 2011 **Jorge Arce** (Mex) w rsf 12 Wilfredo Vazquez Jr.. . . . . Las Vegas, NV
Sep 24, 2011 Jorge Arce w rsf 4 Simphiwe Nongqayi (SA) . . . . .Mexicali (Mex)
Arce relinquished WBO title to box for WBO bantamweight title
Feb 4, 2012 Nonito Donaire (Phi) w pts 12 Wilfredo Vazquez Jr. . . . . San Antonio, TX
Jul 7, 2012 Nonito Donaire w pts 12 Jeffrey Mathebula . . . . .Carson, CA
Oct 13, 2012 Nonito Donaire w rsf 9 Tishioka Nishioka . . . . .Carson, CA
Dec 15, 2012 Nonito Donaire w ko 3 Jorge Arce. . . . . .Houston, TX

IBF/WBO titles

Jul 7, 2012 Nonito Donaire w pts 12 Jeffrey Mathebula . . . . Baja (Mex)

WBA/IBF titles

Nov 21, 2008 **Celestino Caballero** w rsf 4 Steve Molitor (Can) . . . . Rama (Can)
Apr 30, 2009 Celestino Caballero w pts 12 Jeffrey Mathebula (SA). . . . . . . .Panama City (Pan)
Aug 29, 2009 Celestino Caballero w rtd 8 Francisco Leal (Mex). . . . . .Mexicali (Mex)

IBF title

Celestino Caballero relinquished title
Mar 27, 2010 Steve Molitor w pts 12 Takalani Ndlovu (SA) . . . . Rama (Can)
Sep 11, 2010 Steve Molitor w pts 12 Jason Booth (Eng) . . . . Houghton-le-Spring (Eng)
Mar 26, 2011 **Takalani Ndlovu** w pts 12 Steve Molitor. . . . . Johannesburg (SA)
Oct 29, 2011 Takalani Ndlovu w pts 12 Giovanni Caro (Mex). . . . . Colima (Mex)
Mar 24, 2012 **Jeffrey Mathebula** w pts 12 Takalani Ndlovu. . . . . Brakpan (SA)
Nonito Donaire vacated after unifiying IBF/WBO titles beating Jeffrey Mathebula
Feb 16, 2013 **Jhonatan Romero** (Col) w pts 12 Alejandro Lopez (Mex) . . . . .Tijuana (Mex)
For vacant title
Aug 17, 2013 **Kiko Martinez** (Sp) w rsf 6 Jhonatan Romero . . . . .Atlantic City, NJ
Dec 21, 2013 Kiko Martinez w pts 12 Jeffrey Mathebula . . . . Elche (Spain)
Apr 23, 2014 Kiko Martinez w rsf 7 Hozumi Hasegawa . . . . Osaka (Jap)
Sep 6, 2014 **Carl Frampton** (NI) w pts 12 Kiko Martinez . . . . .Belfast (NI)
Feb 28, 2015 Carl Frampton w rsf 5 Chris Avalos (USA). . . . . .Belfast (NI)
Jul 18, 2015 Carl Frampton w pts 12 Alejandro Gonzalez Jr (Mex). . . . . .El Paso, TX

WBA title

The WBA declared Celestino Caballero to be Unified Champion upon his victory over Steve Molitor and sanctioned the following fight as for the World title:
Mar 21, 2009 **Bernard Dunne** (Ire) w rsf 11 Ricardo Cordoba . . . . .Dublin (Ire)
The WBA also sanctioned the following fight as an Interim title fight, the winner to challenge Dunne for the world title:
Apr 30, 2009 **Poonsawat Kratingdaengym** (Tha) w rsf 9 Rafael Hernandez (Ven). . .Patumthanee (Tha)
Sep 26, 2009 Poonsawat Kratingdaengym w ko 3 Bernard Dunne. . . . . .Dublin (Ire)
Jan 11, 2010 Poonsawat Kratingdaengym w pts 12 Satoshi Hosono (Jap) . . . . Tokyo (Jap)
May 20, 2010 Poonsawat Kratingdaengym w ko 4 Shoji Kimura (Jap). . .Maha Sarakham (Tha)
Oct 2, 2010 **Ryo Li Lee** (Jap) w pts 12 Poonsawat Kratingdaengym . . . . Tokyo (Jap)
Jan 31, 2011 **Akifumi Shimoda** (Jap) w pts 12 Ryo Li Lee . . . . Tokyo (Jap)
Jul 9, 2011 **Rico Ramos** (US) w ko 7 Akifumi Shimoda. . . . . .Atlantic City, NJ
Jan 20, 2012 **Guillermo Rigondeaux** (Cub) w ko 6 Rico Ramos. . . . . Las Vegas, NV
Jun 9, 2012 Guillermo Rigondeaux w rsf 5 Teon Kennedy (US) . . . . Las Vegas, NV
Sep 15, 2012 Guillermo Rigondeaux w pts 12 Robert Marroquin (US) . . . . Las Vegas, NV

The WBA sanctioned the following for the Interim title

Nov 13, 2010 Guillermo Rigondeaux w pts 12 Ricardo Cordoba (Pan) .... Arlington, TX
Mar 19, 2011 Guillermo Rigondeaux w rsf 1 Willie Casey (Ire) .... Dublin (Ire)
Jun 6, 2012 Scott Quigg (Eng) tdraw 3 Rendall Munroe (Eng) .... Manchester (Eng)
Nov 24, 2012 Scott Quigg w rsf 6 Rendall Munroe .... Manchester (Eng)
Scott Quigg upgraded to full champion
Oct 5, 2013 Scott Quigg drew 12 Yoandris Salinas (Cuba) .... London (Eng)
Nov 23, 2013 Scott Quigg w rsf 2 Diego Oscar Silva (Arg) .... Manchester (Eng)
Apr 19, 2014 Scott Quigg w rsf 2 Tshifhiwa Munyai (SA) .... Manchester (Eng)
Sep 13, 2014 Scott Quigg w rsf 3 Stephane Jamoye (Bel) .... Manchester (Eng)
Nov 22, 2014 Scott Quigg w pts 12 Hidenori Otake (Jap) .... Liverpool (Eng)
The WBA sanctioned the following for their Interim belt
Dec 11, 2014 Oscar Escandon (Col) w pts 12 Tyson Cave (Can) .... Temecula, CA
Apr 18, 2015 Moises Flores (Mex) w pts 12 Oscar Escandon .... Carson, CA
Jul 18, 2015 Scott Quigg w rsf 2 Kiko Martinez (Spa) .... Manchester (Eng)
For the WBA title
WBA sanctioned the following fight for the interim title
Sep 22, 2015 Moises Flores w rsf 12 Luis Emmanuel Cusolito (Arg) .... Bethlehem, PA

WBO/WBA Super titles

Apr 13, 2013 **Guillermo Rigondeaux** w pts 12 Nonito Donaire .... New York, NY
Dec 7, 2013 Guillermo Rigondeaux w pts 12 Joseph Agbeko .... Atlantic City, NJ
Jul 19, 2014 Guillermo Rogondeaux w ko 1 Sod Kokietgym (Thai) .... Macao (Chi)
Dec 31, 2014 Guillermo Rigondeaux w rtd 11 Hisashi Amagasa (Jap) .... Osaka (Jap)
Jul 16, 2016 Guillermo Rigondeaux w rtd 2 James Dickens (Eng) .... Cardiff (Wal)
Jun 17, 2017 Guillermo Rigondeaux w nc 1 Moises Flores (Mex) .... Las Vegas, NV

IBF/WBA titles

Feb 27, 2016 Carl Frampton w pts 12 Scott Quigg (Eng) .... Manchester (Eng)

IBF title

Jul 20, 2016 **Jonathan Guzman (DR)** w rsf 11 Shingo Wake (Jap) .... Osaka (Jap)
For the vacant IBF title
Dec 31, 2016 **Yukinori Oguni (Jap)** w pts 12 Jonathan Guzman .... Kyoto (Jap)
Sep 13, 2017 **Ryosuke Iwasa (Jap)** w rsf 6 Yukinori Oguni .... Osaka (Jap)

WBA title

WBC sanctioned the following fight for the interim title
Jun 11, 2016 Moises Flores w pts 12 Paulus Ambunda (Nam) .... Windhoek (Nam)
Jun 24, 2016 **Nehomar Cermeno (Ven)** w rsf 12 Xiaojun Qiu (Chi) .... Beijing (Chi)
For the vacant WBA title
Sep 30, 2016 Nehomar Cermeno w ko 3 Anurak Thisa (Tha(................ Wenzhou (Chi)
Dec 17, 2016 Nehomar Cermeno w pts 12 Xiaojun Qiu .... Hangzhou (Chi)
Apr 9, 2017 **Shun Kubo (Jap)** w rtd 10 Nehomar Cermeno .... Osaka (Jap)
Sep 3, 2017 **Daniel Roman (US)** w rsf 9 Shun Kubo .... Kyoto (Jap)

CARL FRAMPTON *finds his range during his points victory over Scott Quigg in Manchester in February 2016.*

Bantamweight

The bantamweight gloved era began when Chappie Moran from Manchester beat Tommy Kelly in 1889. The weight limit in America at that time was 110lb, but it crept up pound by pound from 112 to 114, 115, and 116lb until finally settling in 1915 at the present 118lb, which the British had introduced in 1910.

The early history of the division is even more confused than most, with the championship almost continuously in dispute until the 1920s, sometimes with parallel versions on offer on either side of the Atlantic. Since the record-breaking eight-year reign of the Mexican-American Manuel Ortiz, who made 19 successful defences, the bantamweight class has been dominated by Mexicans like Joe Becerra, Ruben Olivares, Carlos Zarate, Lupe Pintor and Alfonso Zamora, while Eder Jofre (Brazil) and Jorge Lujan (Panama) both made their mark.

Champions Jeff Chandler, Richard Sandoval and Orlando Canizales from America revived interest there in the division, with Canizales – whose brother Gaby held the WBO title at the same time – enjoying a remarkable run as IBF champion.

World Bantamweight Championship Bouts

Jun 5,	1889	**Chappie Moran** (Eng) w pts 10 Tommy Kelly (US)	Brooklyn, NY
Jan 31,	1890	**Tommy Kelly** w ko 10 Chappie Moran	New York, NY
May 9,	1892	**Billy Plimmer** (Eng) w pts 10 Tommy Kelly	Coney Island, NY
Dec 28,	1892	Billy Plimmer w rsf 8 Joe McGrath (US)	Coney Island, NY
May 28,	1895	Billy Plimmer w ko 7 George Corfield (Eng)	London (Eng)
Nov 25,	1895	**Pedlar Palmer** (Eng) w dis 14 Billy Plimmer	London (Eng)
Oct 12,	1896	Pedlar Palmer w pts 20 Johnny Murphy (US)	London (Eng)
Jan 25,	1897	Pedlar Palmer w rsf 14 Ernie Stanton (US)	London (Eng)
Dec 12,	1898	Pedlar Palmer w rsf 17 Billy Plimmer	London (Eng)
Apr 17,	1899	Pedlar Palmer w rsf 3 Billy Rotchford (US)	London (Eng)
Sep 12,	1899	**Terry McGovern** (US) w ko 1 Pedlar Palmer	Tuckahoe, NY
Sep 6,	1900	Harry Forbes (US) drew 20 Caspar Leon (US) *For vacant title*	St Joseph, MO
Mar 18,	1901	**Harry Harris** (US) w pts 20 Pedlar Palmer *Harris claimed the vacant title, but soon relinquished it to box at featherweight*	London (Eng)
Apr 2,	1901	**Harry Forbes** w pts 15 Casper Leon *For vacant title*	Memphis, TN
Nov 11,	1901	Harry Forbes w ko 2 Dan Dougherty (US)	St Louis, MO
Jan 23,	1902	Harry Forbes w ko 4 Dan Dougherty	St Louis, MO
Feb 27,	1902	Harry Forbes w pts 15 Tommy Feltz (US)	St Louis, MO
May 1,	1902	Harry Forbes drew 20 Johnny Reagan (US)	St Louis, MO
Dec 23,	1902	Harry Forbes w rsf 7 Frankie Neil (US)	Oakland, CA
Feb 27,	1903	Harry Forbes w pts 10 Andy Tokell (Eng)	Detroit, MI
Aug 13,	1903	**Frankie Neil** w ko 2 Harry Forbes	San Francisco, CA
Sep 4,	1903	Frankie Neil w ko 15 Billy de Coursey (US)	Los Angeles, CA
Oct 16,	1903	Frankie Neil drew 20 Johnny Reagan	Los Angeles, CA
Oct 17,	1904	**Joe Bowker** (Eng) w pts 20 Frankie Neil	London (Eng)
May 29,	1905	Joe Bowker w pts 20 Pinky Evans (US) *Bowker relinquished the title, which was claimed for America by Jimmy Walsh and for Britain by Digger Stanley*	London (Eng)
Oct 20,	1905	**Jimmy Walsh** (US) w pts 15 Digger Stanley (Eng) *Walsh relinquished the title due to weight problems. There followed a most confused period, with several claimants including Johnny Coulon, Digger Stanley, Monte Attell, Frankie Conley, and Walsh (on his comeback)*	Chelsea, MA

British/IBU version of title

Jan 20,	1906	**Digger Stanley** w pts 20 Ike Bradley (Eng)	Newcastle (Eng)
Dec 13,	1906	Digger Stanley w pts 20 Ike Bradley	Liverpool (Eng)
May 24,	1909	Digger Stanley drew 15 Jimmy Walsh	London (Eng)
Oct 17,	1910	Digger Stanley w ko 8 Joe Bowker	London (Eng)
Dec 5,	1910	Digger Stanley w pts 20 Johnny Condon (Eng)	London (Eng)
Sep 14,	1911	Digger Stanley w pts 20 Ike Bradley	Liverpool (Eng)
Apr 22,	1912	Digger Stanley w pts 20 Charles Ledoux (Fra) *The IBU recognized this as a title fight*	London (Eng)
Jun 23,	1912	**Charles Ledoux** w ko 7 Digger Stanley	Dieppe (Fra)
Jun 24,	1913	**Eddie Campi** (US) w pts 20 Charles Ledoux	Vernon, CA
Oct 10,	1913	Eddie Campi drew 15 Frankie Burns (US)	Denver, CO
Jan 31,	1914	**Kid Williams** (US) w ko 12 Eddie Campi	Los Angeles, CA
Jun 9,	1914	Kid Williams w ko 3 Johnny Coulon (Can) *For undisputed title*	Los Angeles, CA

American versions

Jun 26,	1908	**Jimmy Walsh** w ko 11 Jimmy Carroll	San Francisco, CA
Oct 9,	1908	Jimmy Walsh w pts 15 Young Britt (US)	Baltimore, MD
Dec 21,	1908	Jimmy Walsh drew 15 Monte Attell (US)	San Francisco, CA
May 24,	1909	Jimmy Walsh drew 15 Digger Stanley *Walsh moved back to featherweight again*	London (Eng)
Jun 19,	1909	**Monte Attell** w rsf 18 Frankie Neil	San Francisco, CA
Dec 17,	1909	Monte Attell drew 20 Danny Webster (US)	San Francisco, CA
Feb 22,	1910	**Frankie Conley** (US) w rtd 42 Monte Attell	Vernon, CA
Mar 6,	1910	**Johnny Coulon** w ko 19 Jim Kendrick (Eng)	New Orleans, LA
Feb 26,	1911	Johnny Coulon w pts 20 Charles Ledoux	New Orleans, LA
Feb 3,	1912	Johnny Coulon w pts 20 Frankie Conley	Los Angeles, CA
Feb 18,	1912	Johnny Coulon w pts 20 Frankie Burns	New Orleans, LA
Jun 9,	1914	**Kid Williams** w ko 3 Johnny Coulon *For undisputed title*	Los Angeles, CA

Undisputed title

Dec 6,	1915	**Kid Williams** drew 20 Frankie Burns	New Orleans, LA
Feb 7,	1916	Kid Williams drew 20 Pete Herman (US)	New Orleans, LA
Jan 9,	1917	**Pete Herman** w pts 20 Kid Williams	New Orleans, LA
Nov 5,	1917	Pete Herman w pts 20 Frankie Burns	New Orleans, LA
Dec 22,	1920	**Joe Lynch** (US) w pts 15 Pete Herman	New York, NY
Jul 25,	1921	**Pete Herman** w pts 15 Joe Lynch	New York, NY
Sep 23,	1921	**Johnny Buff** (US) w pts 15 Pete Herman	New York, NY
Nov 10,	1921	Johnny Buff w pts 15 Jackie Sharkey (US)	New York, NY
Jul 10,	1922	**Joe Lynch** w rtd 14 Johnny Buff	New York, NY
Dec 22,	1922	Joe Lynch w pts 15 Midget Smith (US)	New York, NY
Mar 21,	1924	**Abe Goldstein** (US) w pts 15 Joe Lynch	New York, NY
Jul 17,	1924	Abe Goldstein w pts 15 Charles Ledoux	New York, NY
Sep 9,	1924	Abe Goldstein w pts 15 Tommy Ryan (US)	Long Island, NY
Dec 19,	1924	**Eddie Martin** (US) w pts 15 Abe Goldstein	New York, NY
Mar 20,	1925	**Charlie Rosenberg** (US) w pts 15 Eddie Martin	New York, NY
Jul 23,	1925	Charlie Rosenberg w ko 4 Eddie Shea (US) *Rosenberg was suspended indefinitely by the NY Commission because of suspicion that the fight was fixed*	New York, NY
Feb	1927	*Rosenberg's suspension was lifted to allow him to defend against Bushy Graham in New York on February 4, 1927. Rosenberg lost his title on the scales when he came in at 122½lb, although he won a 15-round decision. He was then suspended again for making a secret agreement with Graham concerning the percentage split of the purse money*	
Feb 24,	1927	**Bud Taylor** (US) w pts 10 Eddie Shea *Taylor won recognition in four States as champion*	Chicago, IL
Mar 26,	1927	Bud Taylor drew 10 Tony Canzoneri (US) *For vacant NBA title*	Chicago, IL
May 5,	1927	**Teddy Baldock** (Eng) w pts 15 Archie Bell (US) *British version of vacant title*	London (Eng)
Jun 24,	1927	Bud Taylor w pts 10 Tony Canzoneri *For vacant NBA title*	Chicago, IL
Oct 6,	1927	**Willie Smith** (SA) w pts 15 Teddy Baldock *For British version of title. Smith never defended it, and moved up to featherweight*	London (Eng)
May 23,	1928	**Bushy Graham** (US) w pts 15 Cpl Izzy Schwarz (US) *For vacant New York title*	New York, NY
Aug	1928	*Taylor relinquished the NBA title to box at featherweight*	
Jan	1929	*Graham gave up the NY title because of weight problems*	
Jun 18,	1929	**Al Brown** (Pan) w pts 15 Vidal Gregorio (Sp) *For vacant title*	New York, NY
Feb 8,	1930	Al Brown w dis 4 Johnny Erickson (US)	New York, NY
Oct 4,	1930	Al Brown w pts 15 Eugene Huat (Fra)	Paris (Fra)
May 20,	1931	**Pete Sanstol** (Nor) w pts 10 Archie Bell *Recognized in Canada as being for the title*	Montreal (Can)
Jun 17,	1931	Pete Sanstol w pts 15 Art Giroux (Can)	Montreal (Can)
Aug 25,	1931	Al Brown w pts 15 Pete Sanstol *For undisputed title*	Montreal (Can)
Oct 27,	1931	Al Brown w pts 15 Eugene Huat	Montreal (Can)
Jul 10,	1932	Al Brown w pts 15 Kid Francis (Ita)	Marseilles (Fra)
Sep 19,	1932	Al Brown w ko 1 Emile Pladner (Fra)	Toronto (Can)
Mar 18,	1933	Al Brown w pts 12 Dom Bernasconi (Ita)	Milan (Ita)
Jul 3,	1933	Al Brown w pts 15 Johnny King (Eng)	Manchester (Eng)
Feb 19,	1934	Al Brown w pts 15 Young Perez (Tun)	Paris (Fra)
May	1934	*The NBA stripped Brown for his failure to defend against Baby Casanova*	

NBA title

Jun 26, 1934	**Sixto Escobar** (PR) w ko 9 Baby Casanova (Mex)	Montreal (Can)
	For vacant title	
Aug 8, 1934	Sixto Escobar w pts 15 Eugene Huat	Montreal (Can)

New York/IBU titles

Nov 1, 1934	**Al Brown** w ko 10 Young Perez	Tunis (Tun)
Jun 1, 1935	**Baltazar Sangchilli** (Sp) w pts 15 Al Brown	Valencia (Sp)
	The NY Commission and the NBA decided to recognize the winner between Lou Salica and Sixto Escobar as champion	

NY/NBA titles

Aug 26, 1935	**Lou Salica** (US) w pts 15 Sixto Escobar	New York, NY
Nov 15, 1935	**Sixto Escobar** w pts 15 Lou Salica	New York, NY

IBU title

Jun 29, 1936	**Tony Marino** (US) w ko 14 Baltazar Sangchilli	New York, NY
Aug 31, 1936	**Sixto Escobar** w rsf 13 Tony Marino	New York, NY
	For undisputed title	

Undisputed title

Oct 13, 1936	**Sixto Escobar** w ko 1 Carlos Quintana (Pan)	New York, NY
Feb 21, 1937	Sixto Escobar w pts 15 Lou Salica	New York, NY
Sep 23, 1937	**Harry Jeffra** (US) w pts 15 Sixto Escobar	New York, NY
Feb 20, 1938	**Sixto Escobar** w pts 15 Harry Jeffra	San Juan, CA
	The IBU withdrew recognition from Escobar	

IBU title

Mar 4, 1938	**Al Brown** w pts 15 Baltazar Sangchilli	Paris (Fra)
	For vacant title	
May 1938	*The IBU, in the interests of unity, withdrew recognition from Brown*	

Undisputed title

Apr 2, 1939	**Sixto Escobar** w pts 15 Kayo Morgan (US)	San Juan, CA
Oct 1939	*Escobar relinquished the title because of difficulty in making the weight*	
	The NBA nominated Georgie Pace as champion	

NBA title

Mar 4, 1940	**Georgie Pace** (US) drew 15 Lou Salica	Toronto (Can)
Sep 24, 1940	**Lou Salica** w pts 15 Georgie Pace	New York, NY
Dec 2, 1940	Lou Salica w rsf 3 Small Montana (Phi)	Toronto (Can)
Jan 13, 1941	Lou Salica w pts 15 Tommy Forte (US)	Philadelphia, PA
Apr 25, 1941	Lou Salica w pts 15 Lou Transparenti (US)	Baltimore, MD
	For undisputed title	

Undisputed title

Jun 16, 1941	**Lou Salica** w pts 15 Tommy Forte	Philadelphia, PA
Aug 7, 1942	**Manuel Ortiz** (Mex) w pts 12 Lou Salica	Hollywood, CA
	The NY Commission refused to accept this as a title fight because it had been contested over 12 rounds rather than their 15, and they continued to regard Salica as champion	

NBA title

Jan 1, 1943	**Manuel Ortiz** w pts 10 Kenny Lindsay (Can)	Portland, OR
Jan 27, 1943	Manuel Ortiz w rsf 10 George Freitas (US)	Oakland, CA
Mar 10, 1943	Manuel Ortiz w rsf 11 Lou Salica	Oakland, CA
	For undisputed title	

Undisputed title

Apr 28, 1943	**Manuel Ortiz** w ko 6 Lupe Cordoza (US)	Fort Worth, TX
May 26, 1943	Manuel Ortiz w pts 15 Joe Robelto (US)	Los Angeles, CA
Jul 12, 1943	Manuel Ortiz w ko 7 Joe Robelto	Seattle, WA
Oct 1, 1943	Manuel Ortiz w ko 4 Leonardo Lopez (US)	Los Angeles, CA
Nov 23, 1943	Manuel Ortiz w pts 15 Benny Goldberg (US)	Los Angeles, CA
Mar 14, 1944	Manuel Ortiz w pts 15 Ernesto Aguilar (Mex)	Los Angeles, CA
Apr 4, 1944	Manuel Ortiz w pts 15 Tony Olivera (US)	Los Angeles, CA
Sep 12, 1944	Manuel Ortiz w ko 4 Luis Castillo (Mex)	Los Angeles, CA
Nov 14, 1944	Manuel Ortiz w rsf 9 Luis Castillo	Los Angeles, CA
Feb 25, 1946	Manuel Ortiz w ko 13 Luis Castillo	San Francisco, CA
May 26, 1946	Manuel Ortiz w ko 5 Kenny Lindsay (Can)	Los Angeles, CA
Jun 10, 1946	Manuel Ortiz w ko 11 Jackie Jurich (US)	San Francisco, CA
Jan 6, 1947	**Harold Dade** (US) w pts 15 Manuel Ortiz	San Francisco, CA
Mar 11, 1947	**Manuel Ortiz** w pts 15 Harold Dade	Los Angeles, CA
May 30, 1947	Manuel Ortiz w pts 15 Kui Kong Young (Haw)	Honolulu, HI
Dec 20, 1947	Manuel Ortiz w pts 15 Tirso del Rosario (Phi)	Manila (Phi)
Jul 4, 1948	Manuel Ortiz w rsf 8 Memo Valero (Mex)	Mexicali (Mex)
Mar 1, 1949	Manuel Ortiz w pts 15 Dado Marino (Haw)	Honolulu, HI
May 31, 1950	**Vic Toweel** (SA) w pts 15 Manuel Ortiz	Johannesburg (SA)
Dec 2, 1950	Vic Toweel w rtd 10 Danny O'Sullivan (Eng)	Johannesburg (SA)
Nov 17, 1951	Vic Toweel w pts 15 Luis Romero (Sp)	Johannesburg (SA)
Jan 26, 1952	Vic Toweel w pts 15 Peter Keenan (Sco)	Johannesburg (SA)
Nov 15, 1952	**Jimmy Carruthers** (Aus) w ko 1 Vic Toweel	Johannesburg (SA)
Mar 21, 1953	Jimmy Carruthers w ko 10 Vic Toweel	Johannesburg (SA)
Nov 13, 1953	Jimmy Carruthers w pts 15 Henry "Pappy" Gault (US)	Sydney (Aus)
May 2, 1954	Jimmy Carruthers w pts 15 Chamrern Songkitrat (Tha)	Bangkok (Tha)
May 16, 1954	*Carruthers retired as undefeated champion*	
Sep 18, 1954	**Robert Cohen** (Alg) w pts 15 Chamrern Songkitrat	Bangkok (Tha)
	For vacant title	
Jan 1955	*The NBA stripped Cohen because of his failure to defend against Raton Macias*	

JIMMY CARRUTHERS *(right) the Australian challenger rips the bantamweight title away from Vic Toweel, whom he knocked out in the first round*

NY/EBU title

Sep 3, 1955	**Robert Cohen** drew 15 Willie Toweel (SA)	Johannesburg (SA)
Jun 29, 1956	**Mario D'Agata** (Ita) w rtd 6 Robert Cohen	Rome (Ita)
Apr 1, 1957	**Alphonse Halimi** (Fra) w pts 15 Mario D'Agata	Paris (Fra)
Nov 6, 1957	Alphonse Halimi w pts 15 Raton Macias (Mex)	Los Angeles, CA
	For undisputed title	

NBA title

Mar 9, 1955	**Raton Macias** w ko 11 Chamrern Songkitrat	San Francisco, CA
	For vacant title	
Mar 25, 1956	Raton Macias w ko 10 Leo Espinosa (Phi)	Mexico City (Mex)
Jun 15, 1957	Raton Macias w rsf 11 Dommy Ursua (Phi)	San Francisco, CA
Nov 6, 1957	**Alphonse Halimi** w pts 15 Raton Macias	Los Angeles, CA
	For undisputed title	

Undisputed title

Jul 8, 1959	**Joe Becerra** (Mex) w ko 8 Alphonse Halimi	Los Angeles, CA
Feb 4, 1960	Joe Becerra w ko 9 Alphonse Halimi	Los Angeles, CA
May 23, 1960	Joe Becerra w pts 15 Kenji Yonekura (Jap)	Tokyo (Jap)
Aug 30, 1960	*Becerra retired as undefeated champion*	

European version of title

Oct 25, 1960	**Alphonse Halimi** w pts 15 Freddie Gilroy (Ire)	Wembley (Eng)
	For vacant title	
May 30, 1961	**John Caldwell** (Ire) w pts 15 Alphonse Halimi	Wembley (Eng)
Oct 31, 1961	John Caldwell w pts 15 Alphonse Halimi	Wembley (Eng)
Jan 18, 1962	**Eder Jofre** (Bra) w rtd 10 John Caldwell	Sao Paulo (Bra)
	For undisputed title	

NBA title

Nov 18, 1960	**Eder Jofre** (Bra) w ko 6 Eloy Sanchez (Mex)	Los Angeles, CA
	For vacant title	
Mar 25, 1961	Eder Jofre w rtd 9 Piero Rollo (Ita)	Rio de Janiro (Bra)
Aug 19, 1961	Eder Jofre w rsf 7 Ramon Arias (Ven)	Caracas (Ven)
Jan 18, 1962	Eder Jofre w rtd 10 John Caldwell	Sao Paulo (Bra)
	For undisputed title	

Undisputed title

May 4, 1962	**Eder Jofre** w rsf 10 Herman Marquez (US)	San Francisco, CA
Sep 11, 1962	Eder Jofre w ko 6 Joe Medel (Mex)	Sao Paulo (Bra)
Apr 4, 1963	Eder Jofre w ko 3 Katsutoshi Aoki (Jap)	Tokyo (Jap)
May 18, 1963	Eder Jofre w rtd 11 Johnny Jamito (Phi)	Quezon City (Phi)
Nov 27, 1964	Eder Jofre w ko 7 Bernardo Caraballo (Col)	Bogota (Col)
May 18, 1965	**Masahiko "Fighting" Harada** (Jap) w pts 15 Eder Jofre	Nagoya (Jap)
Nov 30, 1965	Masahiko "Fighting" Harada w pts 15 Alan Rudkin (Eng)	Tokyo (Jap)
Jun 1, 1966	Masahiko "Fighting" Harada w pts 15 Eder Jofre	Tokyo (Jap)
Jan 3, 1967	Masahiko "Fighting" Harada w pts 15 Joe Medel	Nagoya (Jap)
Jul 4, 1967	Masahiko "Fighting" Harada w pts 15 Bernardo Caraballo	Tokyo (Jap)
Feb 27, 1968	**Lionel Rose** (Aus) w pts 15 Masahiko "Fighting" Harada	Tokyo (Jap)
Jul 2, 1968	Lionel Rose w pts 15 Takao Sakuri (Jap)	Tokyo (Jap)
Dec 6, 1968	Lionel Rose w pts 15 Jesus "Chuchu" Castillo (Mex)	Los Angeles, CA
Mar 8, 1969	Lionel Rose w pts 15 Alan Rudkin	Melbourne (Aus)
Aug 22, 1969	**Ruben Olivares** (Mex) w ko 5 Lionel Rose	Inglewood, CA
Dec 12, 1969	Ruben Olivares w rsf 2 Alan Rudkin	Inglewood, CA
Apr 18, 1970	Ruben Olivares w pts 15 Jesus "Chuchu" Castillo	Los Angeles, CA
Oct 16, 1970	**Jesus "Chuchu" Castillo** w rsf 14 Ruben Olivares	Mexico City (Mex)
Apr 3, 1971	**Ruben Olivares** w pts 15 Jesus "Chuchu" Castillo	Inglewood, CA
Oct 25, 1971	Ruben Olivares w rsf 14 Katsutoshi Kanazawa (Jap)	Nagoya (Jap)
Dec 14, 1971	Ruben Olivares w rsf 11 Jesus Pimentel (Mex)	Los Angeles, CA
Mar 19, 1972	**Rafael Herrera** (Mex) w ko 8 Ruben Olivares	Mexico City (Mex)
Jul 30, 1972	**Enrique Pinder** (Pan) w pts 15 Rafael Herrera	Panama City (Pan)
Dec 1972	*The WBC stripped Pinder for signing to defend against Romeo Anaya, whom they considered to be an unsuitable challenger*	

WBA title

Jan 20, 1973	**Romeo Anaya** (Mex) w ko 3 Enrique Pinder	Panama City (Pan)
Apr 28, 1973	Romeo Anaya w pts 15 Rogelio Lara (Mex)	Los Angeles, CA
Aug 18, 1973	Romeo Anaya w ko 3 Enrique Pinder	Los Angeles, CA
Nov 3, 1973	**Arnold Taylor** (SA) w ko 14 Romeo Anaya	Johannesburg (SA)
Jul 3, 1974	**Soo Hwan-Hong** (Kor) w pts 15 Arnold Taylor	Durban (SA)
Dec 28, 1974	Soo Hwan-Hong w pts 15 Fernando Canabela (Phi)	Seoul (Kor)
Mar 14, 1975	**Alfonso Zamora** (Mex) w ko 4 Soo Hwan Hong	Inglewood, CA
Aug 30, 1975	Alfonso Zamora w ko 4 Thanomjit Sukhothai (Tha)	Los Angeles, CA
Dec 6, 1975	Alfonso Zamora w ko 1 Socrates Batoto (Phi)	Mexico City (Mex)
Apr 3, 1976	Alfonso Zamora w ko 2 Eusebio Pedroza (Col)	Mexicali (Mex)
Jul 10, 1976	Alfonso Zamora w ko 3 Gilberto Illueca (Pan)	Juarez (Mex)
Oct 16, 1976	Alfonso Zamora w rsf 12 Soo-Hwan Hong	Inchon (Kor)
Nov 19, 1977	**Jorge Lujan** (Pan) w ko 10 Alfonso Zamora	Los Angeles, CA
Mar 18, 1978	Jorge Lujan w rtd 11 Roberto Rubaldino (Mex)	San Antonio, TX
Sep 15, 1978	Jorge Lujan w pts 15 Albert Davila	New Orleans, LA
Apr 8, 1979	Jorge Lujan w rsf 15 Cleo Garcia	Las Vegas, NV
Oct 6, 1979	Jorge Lujan w ko 15 Roberto Rubaldino	McAllen, TX
Apr 2, 1980	Jorge Lujan w rsf 9 Shuichi Isogami (Jap)	Tokyo (Jap)
Aug 29, 1980	**Julian Solis** (PR) w pts 15 Jorge Lujan	Miami, FL
Nov 14, 1980	**Jeff Chandler** (US) w rsf 14 Julian Solis	Miami Beach, FL
Jan 31, 1981	Jeff Chandler w pts 15 Jorge Lujan	Philadelphia, PA
Apr 5, 1981	Jeff Chandler drew 15 Eijiro Murata (Jap)	Tokyo (Jap)
Jul 25, 1981	Jeff Chandler w ko 7 Julian Solis	Atlantic City, NJ
Dec 10, 1981	Jeff Chandler w rsf 13 Eijiro Murata	Atlantic City, NJ
Mar 27, 1982	Jeff Chandler w rsf 6 Johnny Carter (US)	Philadelphia, PA
Oct 27, 1982	Jeff Chandler w rsf 9 Miguel Iriale (Pan)	Atlantic City, NJ
Mar 13, 1983	Jeff Chandler w pts 15 Gaby Canizales (US)	Atlantic City, NJ
Sep 11, 1983	Jeff Chandler w rsf 10 Eijiro Murata	Tokyo (Jap)
Dec 17, 1983	Jeff Chandler w rsf 7 Oscar Muniz (US)	Atlantic City, NJ
Apr 7, 1984	**Richard Sandoval** (US) w rsf 15 Jeff Chandler	Atlantic City, NJ
Sep 22, 1984	Richard Sandoval w pts 15 Edgar Roman (Ven)	Monte Carlo (Mon)
Dec 15, 1984	Richard Sandoval w rsf 8 Cardenio Ulloa (Ch)	Miami, FL
Mar 10, 1986	**Gaby Canizales** w rsf 7 Richard Sandoval	Las Vegas, NV
Jun 4, 1986	**Bernardo Pinango** (Ven) w pts 15 Gaby Canizales	East Rutherford, NJ
Oct 4, 1986	Bernardo Pinango w rsf 10 Ciro De Leva (Ita)	Turin (Ita)
Nov 22, 1986	Bernardo Pinango w rsf 15 Simon Skosana (SA)	Johannesburg (SA)
Feb 3, 1987	Bernardo Pinango w pts 15 Frankie Duarte (US)	Los Angeles, CA
	Pinango immediately relinquished the title because of weight problems	
Mar 29, 1987	**Takuya Muguruma** (Jap) w ko 5 Azael Moran (Pan)	Moriguchi (Jap)
	For vacant title	
May 24, 1987	**Chan-Yong Park** (Kor) w rsf 11 Takuya Muguruma	Moriguchi (Jap)
Oct 4, 1987	**Wilfredo Vasquez** (PR) w rsf 10 Chan-Yong Park	Seoul (Kor)
Jan 17, 1988	Wilfredo Vasquez drew 12 Takuya Muguruma	Osaka (Jap)
May 9, 1988	**Kaokor Galaxy** (Tha) w pts 12 Wilfredo Vasquez	Bangkok (Tha)
Aug 14, 1988	**Sung-Il Moon** (Kor) w tech dec 6 Kaokor Galaxy	Pusan (Kor)
Nov 27, 1988	Sung-Il Moon w ko 7 Edgar Monserrat (Pan)	Seoul (Kor)
Feb 19, 1989	Sung-Il Moon w rsf 5 Chaiki Kobayashi (Jap)	Taejon (Kor)
Jul 8, 1989	**Kaokor Galaxy** w pts 12 Sung-Il Moon	Bangkok (Tha)
Oct 18, 1989	**Luisito Espinosa** (Phi) w rsf 1 Kaokor Galaxy	Bangkok (Tha)
May 30, 1990	Luisito Espinosa w rtd 8 Hurley Snead (US)	Bangkok (Tha)
Oct 12, 1990	Luisito Espinosa w ko 1 Yong-Man Chung (Kor)	Manila (Phi)
Nov 29, 1990	Luisito Espinosa w pts 12 Thalerngsak Sitbobay (Tha)	Bangkok (Tha)
Oct 19, 1991	**Israel Contrerras** (Ven) w ko 5 Luisito Espinosa	Manila (Phi)
Mar 15, 1992	**Eddie Cook** (US) w ko 5 Israel Contrerras	Las Vegas, NV
Oct 9, 1992	**Jorge Elicier Julio** (Col) w pts 12 Eddie Cook	Cartagena (Col)
Jul 8, 1993	Jorge Elicier Julio w pts 12 Ricardo Vargas (Mex)	Tijuana (Mex)
Oct 23, 1993	**Junior Jones** (US) w pts 12 Jorge Elicier Julio	Atlantic City, NJ
Jan 8, 1994	Junior Jones w pts 12 Elvis Alvarez (Col)	Catskill, NY
Apr 22, 1994	**John Michael Johnson** (US) w rsf 11 Junior Jones	Las Vegas, NV
Jul 16, 1994	**Daorung Chuvatana** [*aka MP Petroleum*] (Tha) w rsf 1 John Michael Johnson	Bangkok (Tha)
Nov 20, 1994	Daorung MP Petroleum w rsf 5 Koh In Sik (Kor)	Bangkok (Tha)
May 27, 1995	Daorung MP Petroleum drew 12 Lakhin CP Gym (Tha)	Bangkok (Tha)
Sep 17, 1995	**Veeraphol Sahaprom** (Tha) (*aka Verraphol Nakornluang*) w pts 12 Daorung MP Petroleum	Nongtha Buri (Tha)
Jan 27, 1996	**Nana Yaw Konadu** (Gha) w rsf 2 Veeraphol Sahaprom	Kanchunburi (Tha)
Oct 27, 1996	**Daorung Chuvatana** w tdec 10 Nana Yaw Konadu	Uttaradit (Tha)
	(formerly known as MP Petroleum, Chuvatana was billed for this fight as Daorung Chorsiriwat)	
Mar 15, 1997	Daorung Chuvatana w pts 12 Felix Machado (Ven)	Bangkok (Tha)
Jun 21, 1997	**Nana Yaw Konadu** w rsf 7 Daorung Chuvatana	Tampa, FL
Feb 21, 1997	Nana Yaw Konadu w ko 2 Abraham Torres (Ven)	Mar Del Plata (Arg)
Dec 5, 1998	**Johnny Tapia** (US) w pts 12 Nana Yaw Konadu	Atlantic City, NJ
Jun 26, 1999	**Paulie Ayala** (US) w pts 12 Johnny Tapia	Las Vegas, NV
Oct 23, 1999	Paulie Ayala w pts 12 Saohin Sorthanikul (Tha)	Fort Worth, TX
Mar 4, 2000	Paulie Ayala w pts 12 Johnny Bredahl (Den)	Las Vegas, NV
Mar 30, 2001	Paulie Ayala w pts 12 Hugo Dianza (Mex)	Fort Worth, TX
	Ayala relinquished the title to box at super-bantamweight	
Oct 14, 2001	**Eidy Mora** (Ven) w ko 11 Adan Vargas (Mex)	McAllen, TX
	For vacant title	
Apr 19, 2002	**Johnny Bredahl** (Den) w ko 9 Eidy Mora	Copenhagen (Den)
Nov 8, 2002	Johnny Bredahl w pts 12 Leo Gamez (Ven)	Copenhagen (Den)
Oct 24, 2003	Johnny Bredahl w pts 12 David Guerault (Fra)	Copenhagen (Den)
Mar 13, 2004	Johnny Bredahl w pts 12 Nobuaki Naka (Jap)	Copenhagen (Den)
	Bredahl announced his retirement	
Feb 26, 2005	**Wladimir Sidorenko** (Ukr) w pts 12 Julio Zarate (Mex)	Hamburg (Ger)
	For vacant title	
Nov 26, 2005	Wladimir Sidorenko w pts 12 Jose de Jesus Lopez (Ven)	Leverkusen (Ger)
Mar 11, 2006	Wladimir Sidorenko drew 12 Ricardo Cordoba (Pan)	Hamburg (Ger)
Jul 15, 2006	Wladimir Sidorenko w pts 12 Poonsawat Kratingdaengym (Tha)	Hamburg (Ger)
Mar 17, 2007	Wladimir Sidorenko drew 12 Ricardo Cordoba (Pan)	Stuttgart (Ger)
Jun 29, 2007	Wladimir Sidorenko w ko 7 Jerome Arnould (Fra)	Marseille (Fra)
Jan 10, 2008	Wladimir Sidorenko w pts 12 Nobuto Ikehara (Jap)	Osaka (Jap)
May 31, 2008	**Anselmo Moreno** (Pan) w pts 12 Wladimir Sidorenko	Dusseldorf (Ger)
Sep 18, 2008	Anselmo Moreno w tdec 7 Cecilio Santos (Mex)	Panama City (Pan)
Oct 30, 2008	Anselmo Moreno w pts 12 Roly Matsushita (Jap)	Panama City (Pan)
May 2, 2009	Anselmo Moreno w pts 12 Wladimir Sidorenko	Bremen (Ger)
Jul 4, 2009	Anselmo Moreno w pts 12 Mahyar Monshipour (Fra)	Vienne (Fra)
Dec 4, 2009	Anselmo Moreno w rsf 11 Frederic Patrac (Fra)	Agde (Fra)
	T*he WBA sanctioned Interim title fights, as follows:*	
Mar 14, 2009	**Nehomar Cermeno** (Ven) w pts 12 Cristian Mijares (Mex)	Torreon (Mex)
Sep 12, 2009	Nehomar Cermeno w pts 12 Cristian Mijares	Monterrey (Mex)
Dec 19, 2009	Nehomar Cermeno w ko 11 Alejandro Valdez (Mex)	Ciudad Obregon (Mex)
Mar 27, 2010	**Anselmo Moreno** (Pan) w pts 12 Nehomar Cermeno	La Guaira (Ven)
Aug 14, 2010	Anselmo Moreno w pts 12 Nehomar Cermeno	Panama City (Pan)
	Moreno was upgraded to Super champion	
Dec 26, 2010	Koki Kameda (Jap) w pts 12 Alexander Munoz (Ven)	Saitama (Jap)
May 7, 2011	Koki Kameda w rtd 11 Daniel Diaz (Nic)	Osaka (Jap)
Aug 31, 2011	Koki Kameda w pts 12 David De La Mora (Mex)	okyo (Jap)
Dec 7, 2011	Koki Kameda w ko 4 Mario Macias (Mex)	Osaka (Jap)
Apr 4, 2012	Koki Kameda w pts 12 Nouldy Manakane (Indo)	Yokohama (Jap)

Dec 4, 2012 Koki Kameda w pts 12 Hugo Ruiz ... Osaka (Jap)
Apr 7, 2013 Koki Kameda w pts 12 Panomroonglek Kaiyanghadaogym (Thai) ... Osaka (Jap)
Jul 23, 2013 Koki Kameda w pts John Mark Apolinario (Phi) ... Tokyo (Jap)
Nov 19, 2013 Koki Kameda w pts 12 Jung-Oh Son (South Korea) ... Jeju (South Korea)
Kameda vacated title
May 31, 2014 **Jamie McDonnell** (Eng) w rsf 10 Tabtimdaeng Na Rachawat (Thai) ... Wembley (Eng)
Nov 22, 2014 Jamie McDonnell w rsf 10 Javier Nicolas Chacon (Arg) ... Liverpool (Eng)
May 9, 2015 Jamie McDonnell w pts Tomoki Kameda (Jap) ... Hidalgo, TX
The WBA sanctioned the following for their Interim belt
Aug 30, 2014 Yonfrez Parejo (Ven) w rsf 11 Luis Hinojosa (DR) ... Caracas (Ven)
Nov 22, 2014 Jamie McDonnell w rsf 10 Javier Nicholas Chacon (Arg) ... Liverpool (Eng)
May 9, 2015 Jamie McDonnell w pts 12 Tomoki Kameda (Jap) ... Hidalgo, TX
Sep 6, 2015 Jamie McDonnell w pts 12 Tomoki Kameda ... Corpus Christi, TX
The WBA sanctioned the following fight for the interim title
Nov 7, 2015 Zhanat Zhalyanov (Kaz) w pts 12 Yonfrez Parejo (Ven) ... Monte Carlo (Mon)
Apr 9, 2016 Jamie McDonnell w rsf 9 Fernando Vargas (Mex) ... London (Eng)
Nov 12, 2016 Jamie McDonnell w pts 12 Liborio Solis (Ven) ... Monte Carlo (Mon)

WBA super title

Jun 17, 2011 Anselmo Moreno w rsf 8 Lorenzo Parra (Ven) ... Panama City (Pan)
Dec 3, 2011 Anselmo Moreno w pts 12 Vic Darchinyan ... Anaheim, CA
Apr 21, 2012 Anselmo Moreno w rsf 9 David De La Mora ... El Paso, TX
Aug 10, 2013 Anselmo Moreno w pts 12 William Urina (Col) ... Panama City (Pan)
Mar 22, 2014 Anselmo Moreno w pts 12 Javier Nicolas Chacon (Arg) ... Panama City (Pan)
Sep 26, 2014 **Juan Carlos Payano (DR)** w td 6 Anselmo Moreno ... Mesquite, TX

WBC title

Apr 14, 1973 **Rafael Herrera** w rsf 12 Rodolfo Martinez (Mex) ... Monterrey (Mex)
For vacant title
Oct 13, 1973 Rafael Herrera w pts 15 Venice Borkorsor (Tha) ... Los Angeles, CA
May 25, 1974 Rafael Herrera w ko 6 Romeo Anaya ... Mexico City (Mex)
Dec 7, 1974 **Rodolfo Martinez** w rsf 4 Rafael Herrera ... Merida (Mex)
May 31, 1975 Rodolfo Martinez w rsf 7 Nestor Jiminez (Col) ... Bogota (Col)
Oct 8, 1975 Rodolfo Martinez w pts 15 Hisami Numata (Jap) ... Sendai (Jap)
Jan 30, 1976 Rodolfo Martinez w pts 15 Venice Borkorsor ... Bangkok (Tha)
May 8, 1976 **Carlos Zarate** (Mex) w ko 9 Rodolfo Martinez ... Inglewood, CA
Aug 28, 1976 Carlos Zarate w rsf 12 Paul Ferreri (Aus) ... Los Angeles, CA
Nov 13, 1976 Carlos Zarate w ko 4 Waruinge Nakayama (Ken) ... Culiacan (Mex)
Feb 5, 1977 Carlos Zarate w rsf 3 Fernando Cabanela ... Mexico City (Mex)
Oct 29, 1977 Carlos Zarate w rsf 6 Danilo Batista (Bra) ... Los Angeles, CA
Dec 2, 1977 Carlos Zarate w rsf 5 Juan Francisco Rodriguez (Spa) ... Madrid (Sp)
Feb 25, 1978 Carlos Zarate w rsf 8 Albert Davila (US) ... Los Angeles, CA
Apr 22, 1978 Carlos Zarate w rsf 13 Andres Hernandez (PR) ... San Juan, CA
Jun 9, 1978 Carlos Zarate w ko 4 Emilio Hernandez (Ven) ... Las Vegas, NV
Mar 10, 1979 Carlos Zarate w ko 3 Mensah Kpalongo (Togo) ... Los Angeles, CA
Jun 2, 1979 **Lupe Pintor** (Mex) w pts 15 Carlos Zarate ... Las Vegas, NV
Feb 9, 1980 Lupe Pintor w rsf 12 Alberto Sandoval (US) ... Los Angeles, CA
Jun 11, 1980 Lupe Pintor drew 15 Ejiro Murata (Jap) ... Tokyo (Jap)
Sep 19, 1980 Lupe Pintor w ko 12 Johnny Owen (Wal) ... Los Angeles, CA
Dec 19, 1980 Lupe Pintor w pts 15 Albert Davila ... Las Vegas, NV
Feb 22, 1981 Lupe Pintor w pts 15 Jose Uziga (Arg) ... Houston, TX
Jul 26, 1981 Lupe Pintor w rsf 8 Jovio Rengifo (Ven) ... Las Vegas, NV
Sep 22, 1981 Lupe Pintor w ko 15 Hurricane Teru (Jap) ... Nagoya (Jap)
Jun 3, 1982 Lupe Pintor w rsf 11 Seung-Hoon Lee (Kor) ... Los Angeles, CA
Jul 1983 *Pintor relinquished the title because of injuries sustained in a motor bike accident*
Sep 1, 1983 **Albert Davila** w ko 12 Francisco "Kiko" Bejines (Mex) ... Los Angeles, CA
For vacant title
May 26, 1984 Albert Davila w rsf 11 Enrique Sanchez (DR) ... Miami, FL
Feb 1985 *The WBC stripped Davila for his failure to defend*
May 4, 1985 **Daniel Zaragoza** (Mex) w dis 7 Freddie Jackson (US) ... Aruba (Neth Ant)
For vacant title
Aug 9, 1985 **Miguel Lora** (Col) w pts 12 Daniel Zaragoza ... Miami, FL
Feb 8, 1986 Miguel Lora w pts 12 Wilfredo Vasquez (PR) ... Miami, FL
Aug 23, 1986 Miguel Lora w rsf 6 Enrique Sanchez (DR) ... Miami, FL
Nov 15, 1986 Miguel Lora w pts 12 Albert Davila ... Barranquilla (Col)
Jul 25, 1987 Miguel Lora w rsf 4 Antonio Avelar (Mex) ... Miami, FL
Nov 27, 1987 Miguel Lora w pts 12 Ray Minus (Bah) ... Miami, FL
Apr 30, 1988 Miguel Lora w pts 12 Lucio Lopez (Arg) ... Cartagena (Col)
Aug 1, 1988 Miguel Lora w pts 12 Albert Davila ... Los Angeles, CA
Oct 29, 1988 **Raul Perez** (Mex) w pts 12 Miguel Lora ... Las Vegas, NV
Mar 9, 1989 Raul Perez w pts 12 Lucio Lopez ... Los Angeles, CA
Aug 26, 1989 Raul Perez w rtd 7 Cardenio Ulloa ... Santiago (Ch)
Oct 23, 1989 Raul Perez w pts 12 Diego Avila (Mex) ... Los Angeles, CA
Jan 22, 1990 Raul Perez w pts 12 Gaby Canizales ... Los Angeles, CA
May 7, 1990 Raul Perez w rsf 9 Gerardo Martinez (US) ... Los Angeles, CA
Dec 17, 1990 Raul Perez w ko 8 Chanquito Carmona (Mex) ... Tijuana (Mex)
Feb 25, 1991 **Greg Richardson** (US) w pts 12 Raul Perez ... Los Angeles, CA
May 20, 1991 Greg Richardson w pts 12 Victor Rabanales (Mex) ... Los Angeles, CA
Sep 19, 1991 **Joichiro Tatsuyushi** (Jap) w rtd 10 Greg Richardson ... Tokyo (Jap)
March 1992 *Tatsuyushi relinquished the title because of injury*
Mar 30, 1992 **Victor Rabanales** w tech dec 9 Yong-Hoon Lee (Kor) ... Los Angeles, CA
For vacant title
May 16, 1992 Victor Rabanales w rsf 4 Luis Ocampo (Arg) ... Tuxtla Gutierrez (Mex)
Jul 27, 1992 Victor Rabanales w pts 12 Chang-Kyun Oh (Kor) ... Los Angeles, CA
Sep 17, 1992 Victor Rabanales w rsf 9 Joichiro Tatsuyoshi ... Osaka (Jap)
Jan 25, 1993 Victor Rabanales w pts 12 Dio Andujar (Phi) ... Los Angeles, CA
Mar 28, 1993 **Jung-Il Byun** (Kor) w pts 12 Victor Rabanales ... Kyungju
May 28, 1993 Jung-Il Byun w pts 12 Josefino Suarez (Mex) ... Seoul (Kor)
Dec 23, 1993 **Yasuei Yakushiji** (Jap) w pts 12 Jung-Il Byun ... Nagoya (Jap)
Apr 16, 1994 Yasuei Yakushiji (Jap) w ko 10 Josefino Suarez ... Nagoya (Jap)
Aug 1, 1994 Yasuei Yakushiji w rsf 11 Jung-Il Byun (Kor) ... Nagoya (Jap)
Dec 4, 1994 Yasuei Yakushiji w pts 12 Joichiro Tatsuyoshi ... Nagoya (Jap)
Apr 2, 1995 Yasuei Yakushiji w pts 12 Cuauhtemoc Gomez (Mex) ... Nagoya (Jap)
Jul 30, 1995 **Wayne McCullough** (Ire) w pts 12 Yasuei Yakushiji ... Nagoya (Jap)
Dec 4, 1995 Wayne McCullough w rsf 8 Johnny Bredhal (Den) ... Belfast (Ire)
Mar 30, 1996 Wayne McCullough w pts 12 Jose Luis Bueno (Mex) ... Dublin (Ire)
Feb 1997 *McCullough relinquished the title to move up in weight*
***Sirimongkol Singmanassak** (Tha), won "interim" WBC title, 10 Aug 1996, ko 6 Jose Luis Bueno in Phitsanulok, (Tha), confirmed as new champion*
Feb 15, 1997 Sirimongkol Singmanassak w pts 12 Jesus Sarabia (Mex) ... Nakorn Phakon (Tha)
Apr 26, 1997 Sirimongkol Singmanassak w ko 4 Javier Campanario (Spa) ... Phuket (Tha)
Jul 4, 1997 Sirimongkol Singmanassak w pts 12 Victor Rabanales ... Pattani (Tha)
Nov 22, 1997 **Joichiro Tatsuyoshi** (Jap) w rsf Sirimongkol Singmanassak ... Osaka (Jap)
Mar 8, 1998 Joichiro Tatsuyoshi w pts 12 Jose Sosa (Arg) ... Yokohama (Jap)
Aug 22, 1998 Joichiro Tatsuyoshi w tdec 7 Paulie Ayala (US) ... Yokohama (Jap)
Dec 31, 1998 **Veeraphol Sahaprom** (Tha) w ko 6 Joichiro Tatsuyoshi ... Osaka (Jap)
May 21, 1999 Veerapol Sahaprom w rtd 5 Mauro Blanc (Uru) ... Sara Buri (Tha)
Aug 29, 1999 Veerapol Sahaprom w rsf 7 Joichiro Tatsuyoshi ... Osaka (Jap)
Mar 10, 2000 Veerapol Sahaprom w pts 12 Adan Vargas (Mex) ... Bangkok (Tha)
Jun 25, 2000 Veerapol Sahaprom w pts 12 Toshiaki Nishioka (Jap) ... Takasago (Jap)
Dec 5, 2000 Veerapol Sahaprom w rsf 5 Oscar Arciniega (Mex) ... Bangkok (Tha)
May 14, 2001 Veerapol Sahaprom w ko 3 Ricardo Barajas (Mex) ... Paris (Fra)
Jan 11, 2002 Veerapol Sahaprom w pts 12 Sergio Perez (Mex) ... Thanyaburi (Tha)
May 1, 2002 Veerapol Sahaprom w pts 12 Julio Coronet (Col) ... Nonthaburi (Tha)
May 1, 2003 Veeraphol Sahaprom w pts 12 Hugo Dianzo (Mex) ... Bangkok (Tha)
Oct 4, 2003 Veeraphol Sahaprom drew 12 Toshiaki Nishioka (Jap) ... Tokyo (Jap)
Mar 6, 2004 Veeraphol Sahaprom w pts 12 Toshiaki Nishioka ... Saitama (Jap)
May 1, 2004 Veeraphol Sahaprom w rsf 12 Julio Cesar Avila (Mex) ... Nongkhai (Jap)
Sep 11, 2004 Veeraphol Sahaprom w pts 12 Cecilio Santos (Mex) ... Chainart (Jap)
Apr 16, 2005 **Hozumi Hasegawa** (Jap) w pts 12 Veeraphol Sahaprom ... Tokyo (Jap)
Sep 25, 2005 Hozumi Hasegawa w rsf 7 Gerardo Martinez (Mex) ... Yokohama (Jap)
Mar 25, 2006 Hozumi Hasegawa w rsf 9 Veeraphol Sahaprom ... Kobe (Jap)
Nov 13, 2006 Hozumi Hasegawa w pts 12 Genaro Garcia (Mex) ... Tokyo (Jap)
May 3, 2007 Hozumi Hasegawa w pts 12 Simpiwe Vetyeka (SA) ... Tokyo (Jap)
Jan 10, 2008 Hozumi Hasegawa w pts 12 Simone Maludrottu (Ita) ... Osaka (Jap)
Jun 12, 2008 Hozumi Hasegawa w rsf 2 Cristian Faccio (Uru) ... Tokyo (Jap)
Oct 16, 2008 Hozumi Hasegawa w rsf 2 Alejandro Valdez (Mex) ... Tokyo (Jap)
Mar 12, 2009 Hozumi Hasegawa w rsf 1 Vusi Malinga (SA) ... Kobe (Jap)
Jul 14, 2009 Hozumi Hasegawa w rsf 1 Nestor Rocha (USA) ... Kobe (Jap)
Dec 18, 2009 Hozumi Hasegawa w rsf 4 Alvaro Perez (Nic) ... Kobe (Jap)
Apr 30, 2010 **Fernando Montiel** (Mex) w rsf 4 Hozumi Hasegawa ... Tokyo (Jap)
Jul 17, 2010 Fernando Montiel w ko 3 Rafael Concepcion (Pan) ... Tuxtla Gutierrez (Mex)
WBO champion Donaire beat Montiel in a unification match and then relinquished WBC and WBO titles to box at super-bantamweight
Nov 6, 2011 Shinsuke Yamanaka (Jap) w rsf 11 Christian Esquivel (Mex) ... Tokyo (Jap)
Apr 6, 2012 Shinsuke Yamanaka w pts 12 Vic Darchinyan (Aus) ... Tokyo (Jap)
Nov 3, 2012 Shinsuke Yamanaka w ko 7 Tomas Rojas (Mex) ... Sendai (Jap)
Apr 8, 2013 Shinsuke Yamanaka w rsf 12 Malcolm Tunacao (Phi) ... Tokyo (Jap)
Aug 12, 2013 Shinsuke Yamanaka w ko 1 Jose Nieves (PR) ... Tokyo (Jap)
Nov 10, 2013 Shinsuke Yamanaka w ko 9 Alberto Guevara (Mex) ... Tokyo (Jap)
Apr 23, 2014 Shinsuke Yamanaka w rsf 9 Stephane Jamoye (Bel) ... Osaka (Jap)
Oct 22, 2014 Shinsuke Yamanaka w pts 12 Suriyan Sor Rungvisai (Thai) ... Tokyo (Jap)
Apr 16, 2015 Shinsuke Yamanaka w ko 7 Diego Ricardo Santillan (Arg) ... Osaka (Jap)
Sep 22, 2015 Shinsuke Yamanaka w pts 12 Anselmo Moreno (Pan) ... Tokyo (Jap)
Mar 4, 2016 Shinsuke Yamanaka w pts 12 Liborio Solis (Ven) ... Kyoto (Jap)
Sep 16, 2016 Shinsuke Yamanaka w rsf 7 Anselmo Moreno ... Osaka (Jap)
Mar 2, 2017 Shinsuke Yamanaka w rsf 7 Carlos Carlson (Mex) ... Tokyo (Jap)
Aug 15, 2017 **Luis Nery (Mex)** w rsf 4 Shinsuke Yamanaka ... Kyoto (Jap)

WBC/WBO titles

Feb 19, 2011 **Nonito Donaire** w rsf 2 Fernando Montiel ... Las Vegas, NV
Oct 22, 2011 Nonito Donaire w pts 12 Omar Andres Narvaez (Arg) ... New York, NY

LUPE PINTOR *(left) was the controversial points winner of the clash with defending champion, Mexican compatriot Carlos Zarate*

IBF title

Apr 16,	1984	**Satoshi Shingaki** (Jap) w rsf 8 Elmer Magallano (Phi)	Kashiwa (Jap)
		For vacant title	
Aug 4,	1984	Satoshi Shingaki w pts 15 Joves de la Puz (Phi)	Kashiwa (Jap)
Apr 26,	1985	**Jeff Fenech** (Aus) w rsf 9 Satoshi Shingaki	Sydney (Aus)
Aug 23,	1985	Jeff Fenech w ko 3 Satoshi Shingaki	Sydney (Aus)
Dec 2,	1985	Jeff Fenech w pts 15 Jerome Coffee (US)	Sydney (Aus)
Jul 18,	1986	Jeff Fenech w rsf 14 Steve McCrory (US)	Sydney (Aus)
Feb	1987	*Fenech relinquished the title to challenge for the WBC super-bantamweight championship*	
May 15,	1987	**Kelvin Seabrooks** (US) w ko 5 Miguel Maturana (Col)	Cartagena (Col)
		For vacant title	
Jul 4,	1987	Kelvin Seabrooks No Contest 9 Thierry Jacob (Fra)	Calais (Fra)
Nov 18,	1987	Kelvin Seabrooks w rsf 4 Ernie Cataluna (Phi)	San Cataldo (Ita)
Feb 6,	1988	Kelvin Seabrooks w rsf 2 Fernando Beltran (Mex)	Paris (Fra)
Jul 9,	1988	**Orlando Canizales** (US) w rsf 15 Kelvin Seabrooks	Atlantic City, NJ
Nov 29,	1988	Orlando Canizales w ko 1 Jimmy Navarro (US)	San Antonio, TX
Jun 24,	1989	Orlando Canizales w rsf 11 Kelvin Seabrooks	Atlantic City, NJ
Jan 24,	1990	Orlando Canizales w pts 12 Billy Hardy (Eng)	Sunderland (Eng)
Jun 10,	1990	Orlando Canizales w rsf 2 Paul Gonzalez (US)	El Paso, NM
Aug 14,	1990	Orlando Canizales w rsf 5 Eddie Rangel (US)	Saratoga Springs, NY
May 4,	1991	Orlando Canizales w rsf 8 Billy Hardy	Laredo, TX
Sep 22,	1991	Orlando Canizales w pts 12 Fernie Morales (US)	Indio, CA
Dec 21,	1991	Orlando Canizales w rsf 11 Ray Minus	Laredo, TX
Apr 23,	1992	Orlando Canizales w pts 12 Francisco Alvarez (Col)	Paris (Fra)
Sep 18,	1992	Orlando Canizales w pts 12 Samuel Duran (Phi)	Bozeman, MT
Mar 27,	1993	Orlando Canizales w rtd 11 Clarence Adams (US)	Evian les Bains (Fra)
Jun 19,	1993	Orlando Canizales No Contest 3 Derrick Whiteboy (SA)	Houston, TX
Nov 20,	1993	Orlando Canizales w pts 12 Juvenal Berrio (Col)	Hammanskraal
Feb 26,	1994	Orlando Canizales w rsf 4 Gerardo Martinez (US)	San Jose, CA
Jun 7,	1994	Orlando Canizales w ko 5 Rolando Bohol (Phi)	South Padre Island, TX
Oct 15,	1994	Orlando Canizales w pts 12 Sergio Reyes (US)	Laredo, TX
Dec	1994	*Canizales relinquished the title*	
Jan 21,	1995	**Harold Mestre** (Col) w rsf 8 Juvenal Berrio (Col)	Cartagena (Col)
		For vacant title	
Apr 29,	1995	**Mbulelo Botile** (SA) w ko 2 Harold Mestre	Johannesburg (SA)
Jul 4,	1995	Mbulelo Botile w pts 12 Sam Stewart (Lib)	Hammanskraal (SA)
Nov 25,	1995	Mbulelo Botile w ko 2 Reynaldo Hurtado (Col)	East London (SA)
Apr 2,	1996	Mbulelo Botile w ko 11 Ancee Gedeon (Hai)	Providence, RI
Jun 29,	1996	Mbulelo Botile w rsf 8 Marion Arlos (Phi)	Alice (SA)
Nov 29,	1996	Mbulelo Botile w pts 12 Aristead Clayton (US)	Baton Rouge, LA
Jul 19,	1997	**Tim Austin** (US) w rsf 8 Mbulelo Botile	Nashville, TN
Mar 28,	1998	Tim Austin w rsf 2 Paul Lloyd (Eng)	Hull (Eng)
May 30,	1998	Tim Austin w rsf 3 Adrian Kaspari (Ind)	Las Vegas, NV
Mar 27,	1999	Tim Austin w ko 9 Sergio Aguila (Mex)	Miami, FL
Dec 18,	1999	Tim Austin w rsf 1 Bernardo Mendoza (Chi)	Robinsonville, MS
Aug 11,	2000	Tim Austin w pts 12 Arthur Johnson (US)	Las Vegas, NV
Mar 3,	2001	Tim Austin w rsf 6 Jesus Perez (Col)	Las Vegas, NV
Jun 16,	2001	Tim Austin w rsf 6 Steve Dotse (Gha)	Cincinnati, OH
Dec 15,	2001	Tim Austin w pts 12 Ratanachai Sorvorapin (Tha)	Uncasville, CT
Jul 27,	2002	Tim Austin w rsf 10 Adan Vargas (Mex)	Las Vegas, NV
Feb 15,	2003	**Rafael Marquez** (Mex) w rsf 8 Tim Austin	Las Vegas, NV
Oct 4,	2003	Rafael Marquez w pts 12 Mauricio Pastrana (Col)	Los Angeles, CA
Jan 31,	2004	Rafael Marquez w rsf 2 Peter Frissina (US)	Phoenix, AZ
Jul 31,	2004	Rafael Marquez w ko 3 Heriberto Ruiz (Mex)	Las Vegas, NV
Nov 27,	2004	Rafael Marquez w rsf 8 Mauricio Pastrana	Las Vegas, NV
May 29,	2005	Rafael Marquez w pts 12 Ricardo Vargas (Mex)	Los Angeles, CA
Nov 5,	2005	Rafael Marquez w rsf 4 Silence Mabuza (SA)	Stateline, NV
Aug 5,	2006	Rafael Marquez w rtd 9 Silence Mabuza	Stateline, NV
		Marquez relinquished title on becoming WBC super-bantamweight champion	
Jul 7,	2007	**Luis Alberto Perez** (Nic) w rsf 7 Genaro Garcia (Mex)	Bridgeport, CT
		For vacant title.	
Sep 29,	2007	**Joseph Agbeko** (Gha) w rsf 7 Luis Alberto Perez	Sacramento, CA
Dec 11,	2008	Joseph Agbeko w pts 12 William Gonzalez (Nic)	Newark NJ
Jul 11,	2009	Joseph Agbeko w pts 12 Vic Darchinyan (Arm)	Sunrise FL
Oct 31,	2009	**Yonnhy Perez** (Col) w pts 12 Joseph Agbeko	Las Vegas NV
May 22,	2010	Yonnhy Perez drew 12 Abner Mares (Mex)	Los Angeles, CA
Dec 11,	2010	**Joseph Agbeko** (Gha) w pts 12 Yonnhy Perez	Tacoma, WA
Aug 13,	2011	**Abner Mares** w pts 12 Joseph Agbeko	Las Vegas, NV
Dec 3,	2011	Abner Mares w pts 12 Joseph Agbeko	Anaheim, CA
		Mares relinquished title to box at super-bantamweight	
Jun 2,	2012	**Leo Santa Cruz** (Mex) w pts 12 Vusi Malinga (SA)	Carson, CA
Sep 15,	2012	Leo Santa Cruz w rsf 5 Eric Morel	Las Vegas, NV
Nov 10,	2012	Leo Santa Cruz w rsf 9 Victor Zaleta (Mex)	Los Angeles, CA
Dec 15,	2012	Leo Santa Cruz w pts 12 Alberto Guevara (Mex)	Los Angeles, CA
		Leo Santa Cruz vacated	

May 11,	2013	**Jamie McDonnell** w pts 12 Julio Ceja (Mex)	Doncaster (Eng)
		McDonnell stripped of title	
Dec 21,	2013	**Stuart Hall** (Eng) w pts 12 Vusi Malinga (SA)	Leeds (Eng)
		For vacant title	
Mar 29,	2014	Stuart Hall tech draw 3 Martin Ward (Eng)	Newcastle (Eng)
Jun 7,	2014	**Paul Butler** (Eng) w pts 12 Stuart Hall	Newcastle (Eng)
		Paul Butler vacated his title	
Oct 25,	2014	**Randy Caballero** (USA) w pts 12 Stuart Hall.	Monte Carlo (Mon)
		For vacant title	
		The IBF sanctioned the following for their Interim title	
Jun 13,	2015	Lee Haskins (Eng) w rsf 6 Ryosuke Iwasa (Jap)	Bristol (Eng)
May 14,	2016	**Lee Haskins** w pts 12 Ivan Morales (Mex)	Cardiff (Wal)
		For the IBF title	
Sep 10,	2016	Lee Haskins w pts 12 Stuart Hall (Eng)	London (Eng)
Jun 10,	2017	**Ryan Burnett (NI)** w pts 12 Lee Haskins	Belfast (NI)

WBO title

Feb 3,	1989	**Israel Contrerras** (Ven) w ko 1 Maurizio Lupino (Ita)	Caracas (Ven)
		For vacant title	
Sep 2,	1990	Israel Contrerras w rsf 9 Ray Minus	Nassau (Bah)
Jan	1991	*Contrerras relinquished the WBO title to challenge for the WBA version*	
Mar 12,	1991	**Gaby Canizales** w ko 2 Miguel Lora	Detroit, MI
		For vacant title	
Jun 30,	1991	**Duke McKenzie** (Eng) w pts 12 Gaby Canizales	London (Eng)
Sep 12,	1991	Duke McKenzie w pts 12 Cesar Soto (Mex)	London (Eng)
Mar 25,	1992	Duke McKenzie w rsf 8 Wilfredo Vargas (PR)	London (Eng)
May 13,	1992	**Rafael Del Valle** (PR) w ko 1 Duke McKenzie	London (Eng)
Mar 24,	1993	Rafael Del Valle w rsf 5 Wilfredo Vargas	Conado (PR)
Jun 19,	1993	Rafael Del Valle w pts 12 Miguel Lora.	Hato Rey (PR)
Jul 30,	1994	**Alfred Kotey** (Gha) w pts 12 Rafael Del Valle	London (Eng)
Oct 25,	1994	Alfred Kotey w pts 12 Armando Castro (Mex)	Middlesbrough (Eng)
Feb 17,	1995	Alfred Kotey w rsf 4 Drew Docherty (Sco)	Cumbernauld (Sco)
Oct 21,	1995	**Daniel Jimenez** (PR) w pts 12 Alfred Kotey	London (Eng)
Jan 20,	1996	Daniel Jimenez w pts 12 Drew Docherty	Mansfield (Eng)
Apr 26,	1996	**Robbie Regan** (Wales) w pts 12 Daniel Jimenez	Cardiff (Wal)
Jan	1997	*Regan retired on medical grounds*	
Jul 28,	1997	**Jorge Julio** (Col) w pts 12 Oscar Maldonado (Mex)	Los Angeles, CA
		For vacant title	
Apr 3,	1998	Jorge Julio w rsf 9 Daniel Jimenez	Bayamon (PR)
Sep 19,	1998	Jorge Julio w pts 12 Adonis Cruz (Nic)	Atlanta, GA
Mar 27,	1999	Jorge Julio w pts 12 Julio Gamboa (Nic)	Miami, FL
Jan 8,	2000	**Johnny Tapia** (US) w pts 12 Jorge Julio (Col)	Albuquerque, NM
May 6,	2000	Johnny Tapia w pts 12 Pedro Torres (Arg)	Las Cruces, NM
Aug	2000	*Tapia relinquished the title to box at super-bantamweight*	
Sep 4,	2000	**Mauricio Martinez** (Pan) w rsf 5 Lester Fuentes (Nic)	Manchester (Eng)
Dec 16,	2000	Mauricio Martinez w rsf 1 Esham Pickering (Eng)	Sheffield (Eng)
Mar 15,	2002	**Cruz Carbajal** (Mex) w ko 9 Mauricio Martinez	Veracruz (Mex)
Sep 27,	2002	Cruz Carbajal w rsf 4 Danny Romero (US)	Albuquerque, NM
Oct 4,	2003	Cruz Carbajal w rsf 8 Gerardo Espinoza (Mex)	Las Vegas, NV
May 7,	2004	**Ratanachai Sorvorapin** (Tha) w pts 12 Cruz Carbajal	Bangkok (Tha)
Aug 5,	2005	Ratanachai Sorvorapin w pts 12 Mauricio Martinez	Phuket (Tha)
Oct 29,	2005	**Jhonny Gonzalez** (Mex) w rsf 7 Ratanachai Sorvorapin	Tucson, AZ
May 27,	2006	Jhonny Gonzalez w pts 12 Fernando Montiel (Mex)	Carson, CA
Mar 30,	2007	Jhonny Gonzalez w rsf 9 Irene Pacheco (Ven)	Tucson, AZ
Aug 11,	2007	**Gerry Penalosa** (Phi) w ko 7 Jhonny Gonzalez	Sacramento, CA
Apr 6,	2008	Gerry Penalosa w rsf 8 Ratanachai Sor Vorapin (Tha)	Quezon City (Phi)
		The WBO sanctioned an Interim title fight as follows:	
Mar 28,	2009	**Fernando Montiel** (Mex) w ko 3 Diego Oscar Silva (Arg)	Tijuana (Mex)
		Fernando Montiel was promoted from Interim champion to full champion	
Feb 13,	2010	Fernando Montiel w rsf 1 Ciso Morales (Phil	Las Vegas, NV
		Montiel lost WBO title to WBC champion Nonito Donaire in a unification match.	
		Donaire relinquished the WBO and WBC belts to box at super-bantamweight.	
Nov 26,	2011	**Jorge Arce** (Mex) w pts 12 Angky Angotta (Indo)	Mazatlan (Mex)
		For vacant title	
		Arce relinquished the title to box at super-bantamweight	
Oct 20,	2012	**Pungluang Sor Singyu** (Thai) w rsf 9 AJ Banal (Phil)	Pasay City (Phil)
Mar 12,	2013	**Paulus Ambunda** (Nam) w pts 12 Pungluang Sor Singyu	Windhoek (Nam)
Aug 1,	2013	**Tomoki Kameda** (Jap) w pts 12 Paulus Ambunda	Cebu City (Phi)
Dec 3,	2013	Tomoki Kameda w pts 12 Immanuel Naidjala (Nam)	Osaka (Jap)
Jul 12,	2014	Tomoki Kameda w ko 7 Pungluang Sor Singyu.	Las Vegas, NV
Nov 1,	2014	Tomoki Kameda w pts 12 Alejandro Hernadez (Mex)	Chicago, IL
		The WBO sanctioned the following for the Interim title	
Feb 13,	2010	Eric Morel w pts 12 Gerry Penalosa (Phil)	Las Vegas, NV
Jun 14,	2014	Alejandro Hernandez w pts 12 Daniel Rosas (Mex)	Chiapas (Mex)
Jul 12,	2014	**Tomoki Kameda** w ko 7 Panya Uthok (Tha)	Las Vegas, NV
		For the WBO title	
Nov 1,	2014	Tomoki Kameda w pts 12 Alejandro Hernandez (Mex)	Chicago, IL
Aug 7,	2015	**Panya Uthok** w ko 2 Ryo Akaho (Jap)	Ratchaburi (Tha)
		For the vacant WBO title	
Feb 12,	2016	Panya Uthok w td 7 Jetro Pabustan (Phi)	Soongnern (Tha)
Jul 27,	2016	**Marlon Tapales (Phi)** w ko 11 Panya Uthok	Ayutthaya (Tha)
		The WBO sanctioned the following fight for the interim title	
Apr 22,	2017	Zolani Tete (SA) w pts 12 Arthur Villaueva (Phi)	Leicester (Eng)
Apr 23,	2017	**Marlon Tapales** w ko 1 Shohei Omori (Jap)	Osaka (Jap)
		For the vacant WBO title	
Nov 18,	2017	**Zolani Tete** w ko 1 Sinboniso Gonya (SA)	Belfast (NI)
		For the WBO title	

IBO/WBA Super titles

Aug 2,	2015	**Juan Carlos Payano** w pts 12 Rau'shee Warren (US)	Winter Park, FL
		For the vacant IBF title and the WBA Super title	
Jun 18,	2016	**Rau'shee Warren** w pts 12 Juan Carlos Payano	Chicago, IL
Feb 10,	2017	**Zhanat Zhaklyanov (Kaz)** w pts 12 Rau'shee Warren	Toldeo, OH

IBF/WBA titles

Oct 21,	2017	**Ryan Burnett (NI)** w pts 12 Zhanat Zhaklyanov	Belfast (NI)

RYAN BURNETT *took the IBF and WBA bantamweight titles with a points victory over Zhanat Zhaklyanov in Belfast in October 2017*

Super-Flyweight

The super-flyweight division, weight limit 115lb, was introduced by the World Boxing Council in 1979, in response particularly to pressure from their Latin and Oriental members who felt that the gap from flyweight (112lb) to bantamweight (118lb) was too great. The first champion, Rafael Orono, had been a professional for less than a year when he won a split decision over Seung-Hoon Lee in 1980, but he soon established himself as a worthwhile performer. In fact, the division has been blessed with a high proportion of outstanding champions, including Jiro Watanabe, Gilberto Roman and Kaosai Galaxy.

The WBA were slow to recognize the potential of what quickly became one of boxing's brighter innovations: they did not establish their own championship until 1981, with the IBF following in 1983.

World Super-Flyweight Championship Bouts

WBC title

Feb 2,	1980	**Rafael Orono** (Ven) w pts 15 Seung-Hoon Lee (Kor)	Caracas (Ven)
Apr 14,	1980	Rafael Orono w pts 15 Ramon Soria (Arg)	Caracas (Ven)
Jul 28,	1980	Rafael Orono drew 15 Willie Jensen (US)	Caracas (Ven)
Sep 15,	1980	Rafael Orono w rsf 3 Jovito Rengifo (Ven)	Barquisimeto (Ven)
Jan 24,	1981	**Chul-Ho Kim** (Kor) w ko 9 Rafael Orono	San Cristobal (Ven)
Apr 22,	1981	Chul-Ho Kim w pts 15 Jiro Watanabe (Jap)	Seoul (Kor)
Jul 29,	1981	Chul-Ho Kim w ko 12 Willie Jensen	Pusan (Kor)
Nov 18,	1981	Chul-Ho Kim w rsf 9 Jackal Maruyama (Jap)	Pusan (Kor)
Feb 10,	1982	Chul-Ho Kim w ko 8 Koki Ishii (Jap)	Taegu (Kor)
Jul 4,	1982	Chul-Ho Kim drew 15 Raul Valdez (Mex)	Daejon (Kor)
Nov 28,	1982	**Rafael Orono** w ko 6 Chul-Ho Kim	Seoul (Kor)
Jan 30,	1983	Rafael Orono w ko 4 Pedro Romero (Pan)	Caracas (Ven)
May 9,	1983	Rafael Orono w pts 15 Raul Valdez	Caracas (Ven)
Oct 29,	1983	Rafael Orono w rsf 5 Orlando Maldonado (PR)	Caracas (Ven)
Nov 27,	1983	**Payao Poontarat** (Tha) w pts 12 Rafael Orono	Pattaya (Tha)
Mar 28,	1984	Payao Poontarat w rsf 10 Guty Espadas (Mex)	Bangkok (Tha)
Jul 5,	1984	**Jiro Watanabe** w pts 12 Payao Poontarat	Osaka (Jap)
		The fight was for the WBC title, Watanabe was immediately stripped by the WBA	
Nov 29,	1984	**Jiro Watanabe** w rsf 11 Payao Poontarat	Kumamoto (Jap)
May 9,	1985	Jiro Watanabe w pts 12 Julio Solano (DR)	Tokyo (Jap)
Sep 17,	1985	Jiro Watanabe w rsf 7 Katsuo Katsuma (Jap)	Osaka (Jap)
Dec 13,	1985	Jiro Watanabe w ko 5 Yun-Sok Hwang (Kor)	Taegu (Kor)
Mar 30,	1986	**Gilberto Roman** (Mex) w pts 12 Jiro Watanabe	Osaka (Jap)
May 15,	1986	Gilberto Roman w pts 12 Edgar Monserrat (Pan)	Paris (Fra)
Jul 18,	1986	Gilberto Roman w pts 12 Ruben Condori (Mex)	Salta (Arg)
Aug 30,	1986	Gilberto Roman drew 12 Santos Laciar (Arg)	Cordoba (Arg)
Dec 15,	1986	Gilberto Roman w pts 12 Kongtoranee Payakarun (Tha)	Bangkok (Tha)
Jan 31,	1987	Gilberto Roman w rsf 9 Antoine Montero (Fra)	Montpelier (Fra)
Mar 19,	1987	Gilberto Roman w pts 12 Frank Cedeno (Phi)	Mexicali (Mex)
May 16,	1987	**Santos Laciar** w rsf 11 Gilberto Roman	Reims (Fra)
Aug 8,	1987	**Sugar Baby Rojas** (Col) w pts 12 Santos Laciar	Miami, FL
Oct 24,	1987	Sugar Baby Rojas w rsf 4 Gustavo Ballas (Arg)	Miami, FL
Apr 8,	1988	**Gilberto Roman** w pts 12 Sugar Baby Rojas	Miami, FL
Jul 9,	1988	Gilberto Roman w rsf 5 Yoshiyuki Uchida (Jap)	Kawagoe (Jap)
Sep 3,	1988	Gilberto Roman w pts 12 Kiyoshi Hatanaka (Jap)	Nagoya (Jap)
Nov 7,	1988	Gilberto Roman w pts 12 Sugar Baby Rojas	Las Vegas, NV
Jun 5,	1989	Gilberto Roman w pts 12 Juan Carazo (PR)	Los Angeles, CA
Sep 12,	1989	Gilberto Roman w pts 12 Santos Laciar	Los Angeles, CA
Nov 7,	1989	**Nana Yaw Konadu** (Gha) w pts 12 Gilberto Roman	Mexico City (Mex)
Jan 20,	1990	**Sung-Il Moon** (Kor) w pts 12 Nana Yaw Konadu	Seoul (Kor)
Jun 9,	1990	Sung-Il Moon w rtd 8 Gilberto Roman	Seoul (Kor)
Oct 20,	1990	Sung-Il Moon w tech dec 5 Kenji Matsumara (Jap)	Seoul (Kor)
Mar 16,	1991	Sung-Il Moon w rsf 4 Nana Yaw Konadu	Zaragoza (Sp)
Jul 20,	1991	Sung-Il Moon w ko 5 Ernesto Ford (Pan)	Seoul (Kor)
Dec 22,	1991	Sung-Il Moon w rsf 6 Torsak Pongsupa (Tha)	Inchon (Kor)
Jul 4,	1992	Sung-Il Moon w rsf 8 Armando Salazar (Mex)	Inchon (Kor)
Oct 31,	1992	Sung-Il Moon w pts 12 Greg Richardson (US)	Seoul (Kor)
Feb 27,	1993	Sung-Il Moon w rsf 1 Hilario Zapata (Pan)	Seoul (Kor)
Jul 3,	1993	Sung-Il Moon w pts 12 Carlos Salazar (Arg)	Seoul (Kor)
Nov 13,	1993	**Jose Luis Bueno** (Mex) w pts 12 Sung-Il Moon	Seoul (Kor)
May 4,	1994	**Hiroshi Kawashima** (Jap) w pts 12 Jose Luis Bueno	Yokohama (Jap)
Aug 7,	1994	Hiroshi Kawashima w pts 12 Carlos Salazar	Tokyo (Jap)
Jan 18,	1995	Hiroshi Kawashima w pts 12 Jose Luis Bueno	Yokohama (Jap)
May 24,	1995	Hiroshi Kawashima w pts 12 Seung Koo Lee (Kor)	Yokohama (Jap)
Nov 8,	1995	Hiroshi Kawashima w rsf 3 Boy Aruan (Indo)	Tokyo (Jap)
Apr 27,	1996	Hiroshi Kawashima w pts 12 Cecilio Espino (Mex)	Tokyo (Jap)
Oct 12,	1996	Hiroshi Kawashima w ko 2 Domingo Sosa (Arg)	Tokyo (Jap)
Feb 20,	1997	**Gerry Penalosa** (Phi) w pts 12 Hiroshi Kawashima	Tokyo (Jap)
Jun 14,	1997	Gerry Penalosa w ko 9 Seung-Koo Lee (Kor)	Lapu City (Phi)
Nov 23,	1997	Gerry Penalosa w ko 10 Yung-Joo Choo (Kor)	Songham (Kor)
Apr 25,	1998	Gerry Penalosa tdraw 2 Joel Luna Zarate (Mex)	Manila (Phi)
Aug 29,	1998	**In-joo Choo** (Kor) w pts 12 Gerry Penalosa	Seoul (Kor)
Jan 10,	1999	In-joo Cho w pts 12 Joel Luna Zarate (Mex)	Seoul (SK)
Jun 13,	1999	In-joo Cho w ko 8 Pone Saengmorakot (Tha)	Seoul (SK)
Sep 5,	1999	In-joo Cho w pts 12 Keiji Yamaguchi (Jap)	Tokyo (Jap)
Jan 2,	2000	In-joo Cho w pts 12 Gerry Penalosa	Seoul (SK)
May 14,	2000	In-joo Cho w pts 12 Julio Cesar Avila (Mex)	Seoul (SK)
Aug 27,	2000	**Masamori Tokuyama** (Jap) w pts 12 In-joo Cho	Osaka (Jap)
Dec 12,	2000	Masamori Tokuyama w pts 12 Akihiko Nago (Jap)	Osaka (Jap)
May 20,	2001	Masamori Tokuyama w ko 5 In-joo Cho	Seoul (SK)
Sep 24,	2001	Masamori Tokuyama w pts 12 Gerry Penalosa	Yokohama (Jap)
Mar 23,	2002	Masamori Tokuyama w rsf 9 Kazuhiro Ryuko (Jap)	Yokohama (Jap)
Aug 26,	2002	Masamori Tokuyama w rtd 6 Erik Lopez (Mex)	Saitama (Jap)
Dec 20,	2002	Masamori Tokuyama w pts 12 Gerry Penalosa	Osaka (Jap)
Jun 23,	2003	Masamori Tokuyama w pts 12 Katsushige Kawashima (Jap)	Yokohama (Jap)
Jan 3,	2004	Masamori Tokuyama w pts 12 Dmitry Kirilov (Rus)	Osaka (Jap)
Jun 28,	2004	**Katsushige Kawashima** w rsf 1 Masamori Tokuyama	Yokohama (Jap)
Sep 20,	2004	Katsushige Kawashima w pts 12 Raul Juarez (Mex)	Yokohama (Jap)
Jan 3,	2005	Katsushige Kawashima w pts 12 Jose Navarro (US)	Tokyo (Jap)
Jul 18,	2005	**Masamori Tokuyama** w pts 12 Katsushige Kawashima	Osaka (Jap)
Feb 27,	2006	Masamori Tokuyama w pts 12 Jose Navarro	Osaka (Jap)
		Tokuyama relinquished title and decided to retire	
Sep 18,	2006	**Cristian Mijares** (Mex) w pts 12 Katsushige Kawashima	Yokohama (Jap)
		For vacant title	
Nov 17,	2006	Cristian Mijares w pts 12 Reynaldo Lopez (Col)	Torreon (Mex)
Jan 3,	2007	Cristian Mijares w rsf 10 Katsushige Kawashima	Tokyo (Jap)
Apr 14,	2007	Cristian Mijares w pts 12 Jorge Arce (Mex)	San Antonio, TX
Jul 13,	2007	Cristian Mijares w rsf 10 Teppei Kikui (Jap)	Durango (Mex)
Oct 20,	2007	Cristian Mijares w rsf 1 Franck Gorjux (Fra)	Cancun (Mex)
Feb 16,	2008	Cristian Mijares w pts 12 Jose Navarro (US)	Las Vegas, NV

WBA title

Sep 12,	1981	**Gustavo Ballas** w rsf 8 Sok-Chul Baek (Kor)	Buenos Aires (Arg)
Dec 5,	1981	**Rafael Pedroza** (Pan) w pts 15 Gustavo Ballas	Panama City (Pan)
Apr 8,	1982	**Jiro Watanabe** (Jap) w pts 15 Rafael Pedroza	Osaka (Jap)
Jul 29,	1982	Jiro Watanabe w rsf 9 Gustavo Ballas	Osaka (Jap)
Nov 11,	1982	Jiro Watanabe w rtd 12 Shoji Oguma (Jap)	Hamamatsu (Jap)
Feb 24,	1983	Jiro Watanabe w ko 8 Luis Ibanez (Per)	Tsu City (Jap)
Jun 23,	1983	Jiro Watanabe w pts 15 Roberto Ramirez (Mex)	Sendai (Jap)
Oct 6,	1983	Jiro Watanabe w tech dec 11 Soon-Chun Kwon (Kor)	Osaka (Jap)
Mar 15,	1984	Jiro Watanabe w rsf 15 Celso Chavez (Pan)	Osaka (Jap)
Jul 5,	1984	Jiro Watanabe w pts 12 Payao Poontarat	Osaka (Jap)
		The fight was for the WBC title. Watanabe was immediately stripped by the WBA for failing to defend against their leading contender, Kaosai Galaxy	
Nov 21,	1984	**Kaosai Galaxy** (Tha) w ko 6 Eusebio Espinal (DR)	Bangkok (Tha)
		For vacant title	
Mar 6,	1985	Kaosai Galaxy w ko 7 Dong-Chun Lee (Kor)	Bangkok (Tha)
Jul 17,	1985	Kaosai Galaxy w rsf 5 Rafael Orono	Bangkok (Tha)
Dec 23,	1985	Kaosai Galaxy w rsf 2 Edgar Monserrat	Bangkok (Tha)
Nov 1,	1986	Kaosai Galaxy w ko 5 Israel Contreras (Ven)	Willemstad (Curacao)
Feb 28,	1987	Kaosai Galaxy w ko 13 Elly Pical (Indo)	Jakarta (Indo)
Oct 12,	1987	Kaosai Galaxy w rsf 3 Byong-Kwan Chung (Kor)	Bangkok (Tha)
Jan 26,	1988	Kaosai Galaxy w pts 12 Kongtoranee Payakarun (Tha)	Bangkok (Tha)
Oct 9,	1988	Kaosai Galaxy w ko 8 Chang-Ho Choi (Kor)	Seoul (Kor)
Jan 15,	1989	Kaosai Galaxy w ko 2 Tae-Il Chang (Kor)	Bangkok (Tha)
Apr 8,	1989	Kaosai Galaxy w pts 12 Kenji Matsumura (Jap)	Yokohama (Jap)
Jul 29,	1989	Kaosai Galaxy w rsf 10 Alberto Castro (Col)	Surin (Tha)
Oct 31,	1989	Kaosai Galaxy w ko 12 Kenji Matsumara	Kobe (Jap)
Mar 29,	1990	Kaosai Galaxy w ko 5 Ari Blanca (Phi)	Bangkok (Tha)
Jun 30,	1990	Kaosai Galaxy w rsf 8 Schunichi Kakajima (Jap)	Chiang Mai (Tha)
Dec 9,	1990	Kaosai Galaxy w ko 6 Ernesto Ford	Petchabun (Tha)
Apr 6,	1991	Kaosai Galaxy w rsf 5 Jae-Suk Park (Kor)	Samut Songkhram (Tha)
Jul 20,	1991	Kaosai Galaxy w rsf 5 David Griman (Ven)	Bangkok (Tha)
Dec 22,	1991	Kaosai Galaxy w pts 12 Armando Castro (Mex)	Bangkok (Tha)
Jan	1992	*Galaxy retired*	
Apr 10,	1992	**Katsuya Onizuka** (Jap) w pts 12 Thalerngsak Sithbaobey (Tha)	Tokyo (Jap)

		For vacant title	
Sep 11,	1992	Katsuya Onizuka w rsf 5 Kenji Matsumara	Tokyo (Jap)
May 21,	1993	Katsuya Onizuka w pts 12 Jae-Shin Lim (Kor)	Tokyo (Jap)
Nov 5,	1993	Katsuya Onizuka w pts 12 Thalerngsak Sithbaobey	Tokyo (Jap)
Apr 3,	1994	Katsuya Onizuka w pts 12 Seungkoo Lee (Kor)	Tokyo (Jap)
Sep 18,	1994	**Hyung-Chul Lee** (Kor) w rsf 9 Katsuya Onizuka	Tokyo (Jap)
Feb 25,	1995	Hyung-Chul Lee w ko 12 Tamonori Tamura (Jap)	Pusan (Kor)
Jul 22,	1995	**Alimi Goitia** (Ven) w ko 4 Hyung-Chul Lee	Seoul (Kor)
Nov 25,	1995	Alimi Goitia w rsf 5 Aquiles Guzman (Ven)	Porlama (Ven)
Feb 24,	1996	Alimi Goitia w rsf 12 Hyung-Chul Lee (Kor)	Kwangyan (Kor)
Apr 29,	1996	Alimi Goitia w rsf 5 Satoshi Iida (Jap)	Nagoya (Jap)
Aug 24,	1996	**Yokthai Sit-Oar** (Tha) w rsf 8 Alimi Goitia	Kampaengpetch (Tha)
Nov 10,	1996	Yokthai Sit-Oar w ko 2 Jack Siahaya (Indo)	Pichit (Tha)
Mar 1,	1997	Yokthai Sit-Oar w pts 12 Aquiles Guzman (Ven)	Chachengsao (Tha)
Apr 29,	1997	Yokthai Sit-Oar drew 12 Satoshi Iida (Jap)	Nagoya (Jap)
Aug 7,	1997	Yokthai Sit-Oar w pts 12 Jesus Rojas (Ven)	Bangkok (Tha)
Dec 23,	1997	**Satonshi Iida** w pts 1 Yokthai Sit-Oar	Nagoya (Jap)
Apr 29,	1998	Satoshi Iida w pts 12 Hiroki Ioka (Jap)	Nagoya (Jap)
Jul 26,	1998	Satoshi Iida w pts 12 Julio Gamboa (Nic)	Nagoya (Jap)
Dec 23,	1998	**Jesus Rojas** w pts 12 Satoshi Iida	Nagoya (Jap)
Mar 28,	1999	Jesus Rojas tdraw 4 Hedeki Todaka (Jap)	Miyazaki (Jap)
Jul 31,	1999	**Hideki Todaka** (Jap) w pts 12 Jesus Rojas	Nagoya (Jap)
Nov 7,	1999	Hideki Todaka w pts 12 Akihiko Nago (Jap)	Tokyo (Jap)
Apr 23,	2000	Hideko Todaka w rsf 11 Yokthai Sith-Oar (Tha)	Nagoya (Jap)
Oct 9,	2000	**Leo Gamez** (Ven) w rsf 7 Hideki Todaka	Nagoya (Japa)
Mar 11,	2001	**Celes Kobayashi** (Jap) w rsf 10 Leo Gamez	Yokohama (Jap)
Sep 1,	2001	Celes Kobayashi w pts 12 Jesus Rojas	Yokohama (Jap)
Mar 9,	2002	**Alexander Munoz** (Ven) w rsf 8 Celes Kobayashi	Tokyo (Jap)
Jul 31,	2002	Alexander Munoz w ko 2 Eiji Kojima (Jap)	Osaka (Jap)
Oct 4,	2003	Alexander Munoz w pts 12 Hidenobu Honda (Jap)	Tokyo (Jap)
Jan 3,	2004	Alexander Munoz w rsf 10 Eiji Kojima	Osaka (Jap)
Dec 8,	2004	**Martin Castillo** (Mex) w pts 12 Alexander Munoz	Laredo, TX
Mar 19,	2005	Martin Castillo w pts 12 Eric Morel (PR)	Las Vegas, NV
Jun 26,	2005	Martin Castillo w pts 12 Hideyasu Ishihara (Jap)	Nagoya (Jap)
Jan 21,	2006	Martin Castillo w pts 12 Alexander Munoz	Las Vegas, NV
Jul 22,	2006	**Nobuo Nashiro** (Jap) w rsf 10 Martin Castillo	Higashiosaka (Jap)
Dec 2,	2006	Nobuo Nashiro w pts 12 Eduardo Garcia (Mex)	Osaka (Jap)
May 3,	2007	**Alexander Munoz** w pts 12 Nobuo Nashiro	Tokyo (Jap)
Sep 24,	2007	Alexander Munoz w pts 12 Kuniyuki Aizawa (Jap)	Tokyo (Jap)
Jan 14,	2008	Alexander Munoz w pts 12 Katsushige Kawashima (Jap)	Tokyo (Jap)

IBF title

Dec 10,	1983	**Joo-Do Chun** (Kor) w ko 5 Ken Kasugai (Jap)	Osaka (Jap)
Jan 28,	1984	Joo-Do Chun w ko 12 Prayoonsak Muangsurin (Tha)	Seoul (Kor)
Mar 17,	1984	Joo-Do Chun w ko 1 Diego de Villa (Phi)	Kwangju (Kor)
May 26,	1984	Joo-Do Chun w rsf 6 Felix Marques (PR)	Wonju (Kor)
Jul 20,	1984	Joo-Do Chun w ko 7 William Develos (Phi)	Pusan (Kor)
Jan 6,	1985	Joo-Do Chun w ko 15 Kwang-Gu Park (Kor)	Ulsan (Kor)
May 3,	1985	**Elly Pical** w rsf 8 Joo-Do Chun	Jakarta (Indo)
Aug 25,	1985	Elly Pical w rsf 3 Wayne Mulholland (Aus)	Jakarta (Indo)
Feb 15,	1986	**Carlos Cesar Polanco** (DR) w pts 15 Elly Pical	Jakarta (Indo)
Jul 5,	1986	**Elly Pical** w ko 3 Carlos Cesar Polanco	Jakarta (Indo)
Dec 3,	1986	Elly Pical w ko 10 Dong-Chun Lee (Kor)	Jakarta (Indo)
Mar	1987	*Pical forfeited his title by challenging for the WBA version*	
May 17,	1987	**Tae-Il Chang** w pts 15 Soon-Chun Kwan (Kor)	Pusan (Kor)
		For vacant title	
Oct 17,	1987	**Elly Pical** w pts 15 Tae-Il Chang	Jakarta (Indo)
Feb 20,	1988	Elly Pical w pts 15 Raul Diaz (Col)	Pontianak (Indo)
Sep 3,	1988	Elly Pical w pts 12 Chang-Ki Kim (Kor)	Surubaya (Indo)
Feb 25,	1989	Elly Pical w pts 12 Mike Phelps (US)	Singapore
Oct 14,	1989	**Juan Polo Perez** (Col) w pts 12 Elly Pical	Roanoke, VA
Apr 21,	1990	**Robert Quiroga** (US) w pts 12 Juan Polo Perez	Sunderland (Eng)
Oct 6,	1990	Robert Quiroga w rtd 3 Vuyani Nene (SA)	Benevento (Ita)
Jan 26,	1991	Robert Quiroga w pts 12 Vincenzo Belcastro (Ita)	Capo D'Orlando (Ita)
Jun 15,	1991	Robert Quiroga w pts 12 Akeem Anifowashe (Nig)	San Antonio, TX
Feb 15,	1992	Robert Quiroga w pts 12 Carlos Mercardo (Col)	Salerno (Ita)
Jul 11,	1992	Robert Quiroga w pts 12 Jose Ruiz (PR)	Las Vegas, NV
Jan 16,	1993	**Julio Cesar Borboa** (Mex) w rsf 12 Robert Quiroga	San Antonio, TX
May 22,	1993	Julio Cesar Borboa w pts 12 Joel Luna Zarate (Mex)	Mexico City (Mex)
Aug 21,	1993	Julio Cesar Borboa w ko 3 Carlos Mercardo	Kalispell, MT
Nov 26,	1993	Julio Cesar Borboa w rsf 5 Rolando Pascua (Phi)	Hermosillo (Mex)
Apr 25,	1994	Julio Cesar Borboa w rsf 4 Jorge Luis Roman (Mex)	Inglewood, CA
May 21,	1994	Julio Cesar Borboa w rsf 9 Jaji Sibali (SA)	Hammanskraal
Aug 29,	1994	**Harold Grey** (Col) w pts 12 Julio Cesar Borboa	Inglewood, CA
Dec 17,	1994	Harold Grey w pts 12 Vincenzo Belcastro	Cagliari (Ita)
Mar 18,	1995	Harold Grey w pts 12 Orlando Tobon (Col)	Cartagena (Col)
Jun 24,	1995	Harold Grey w pts 12 Julio Cesar Borboa	Cartagena (Col)
Oct 7,	1995	**Carlos Salazar** w pts 12 Harold Grey	Mar del Plata (Arg)
Feb 10,	1996	Carlos Salazar w rsf 6 Antonella Melis (Ita)	Rome (Ita)
Apr 27,	1996	**Harold Grey** w pts 12 Carlos Salazar	Cartagena (Col)
Aug 24,	1996	**Danny Romero** (US) w ko 2 Harold Grey	Albuquerque, NM
Nov 1,	1996	Danny Romero w rsf 12 Paulo Saucedo (US)	Indio, CA
Mar 8,	1997	Danny Romero w ko 6 Jaji Sibali (SA)	Albuquerque, NM

WBO title

Sep 9,	1989	**Jose Ruiz** (PR) w rsf 1 Juan Carazo (PR)	San Juan, CA
Oct 21,	1989	Jose Ruiz w rsf 12 Angel Rosario (PR)	San Juan, CA
Aug 18,	1990	Jose Ruiz w rsf 8 Wilfredo Vargas (PR)	Ponce (PR)
Nov 3,	1990	Jose Ruiz w pts 12 Armando Velasco (Mex)	Acapulco (Mex)
Feb 22,	1992	**Jose Quirino** (Mex) w pts 12 Jose Ruiz	Las Vegas, NV
Sep 4,	1992	**Johnny Bredahl** (Den) w pts 12 Jose Quirino	Copenhagen (Den)
Mar 26,	1993	Johnny Bredahl w pts 12 Rafael Caban (PR)	Copenhagen (Den)
Oct 29,	1993	Johnny Bredahl w dis 4 Eduardo Nazario (PR)	Korsör (Den)
Mar 25,	1994	Johnny Bredahl w pts 12 Eduardo Nazario	Barnholme
Aug 19,	1994	*Bredahl relinquished title because of problems making the weight*	
Oct 12,	1994	**Johnny Tapia** (US) w rsf 11 Henry Martinez (US)	Albuquerque, NM
		For vacant title	
Feb 10,	1995	Johnny Tapia w pts 12 Jose Rafael Sosa (Arg)	Albuquerque, NM
May 6,	1995	Johnny Tapia tech draw 8 Ricardo Vargas (Mex)	Las Vegas, NV
Jul 2,	1995	Johnny Tapia w pts 12 Arthur Johnson (US)	Albuquerque, NM
Dec 1,	1995	Johnny Tapia w rtd 9 Willy Salazar (Mex)	Indio Springs, CA
Feb 3,	1996	Johnny Tapia w rsf 2 Giovanni Andrade (Bra)	Inglewood, CA
Jun 7,	1996	Johnny Tapia w rsf 8 Ivan Alvarez (Col)	Las Vegas, NV
Aug 17,	1996	Johnny Tapia w pts 12 Hugo Soto (Arg)	Albuquerque, NM
Oct 11,	1996	Johnny Tapia w rsf 7 Sammy Stewart (Lib)	Las Vegas, NV
Nov 30,	1996	Johnny Tapia w pts 12 Adonis Cruz (Nic)	Albuquerque, NM
Mar 8,	1997	Johnny Tapia w rsf 3 Jorge Barrera (Mex)	Albuquerque, NM

IBF/WBO titles

Jul 18,	1997	Johnny Tapia w pts 12 Danny Romero	Las Vegas, NV
		An IBF/WBO unification bout	
Dec 13,	1997	Johnny Tapia w pts 12 Andy Agosto (PR)	Pompano Beach, FL
Feb 13,	1998	Johnny Tapia w pts 12 Rodolfo Blanco (Col)	Albuquerque, NM
		Tapia vacated both titles to move up to bantamweight	

IBF title

Apr 24,	1999	**Marc Johnson** (US) w pts 12 Ratanachai Sorvoraphin (Tha)	Washington, DC
		For vacant title	
Aug 13,	1999	Marc Johnson w pts 12 Jorge Lacierva (Mex)	Ledyard, CT
Nov 19,	1999	Marc Johnson nc 4 Raul Juarez (Mex)	Washington, DC
Feb	2000	*Johnson stripped of the title because of a jail sentence*	
May 20,	2000	**Felix Machado** (Ven) drew 12 Julio Gamboa (Nic)	Tunica, MS
Jul 22,	2000	Felix Machado w pts 12 Julio Gamboa	Miami, FL
Dec 16,	2000	Felix Machado w rsf 3 William De Souza (Pan)	Maracay (Ven)
Jun 16,	2001	Felix Machado w pts 12 Mauricio Pastrana (Col)	Cincinnati, OH
Mar 30,	2002	Felix Machado tec draw 3 Martin Castillo (Mex)	Reading, PA
Jan 4,	2003	**Luis Perez** (Nic) w pts 12 Felix Machado	Washington, DC
Dec 13,	2003	Luis Perez w pts 12 Felix Machado	Atlantic City, NJ
Apr 30,	2005	Luis Perez w rsf 6 Luis Bolano (Col)	New York, NY
May 6,	2006	Luis Perez w pts 12 Dmitry Kirilov (Rus)	Worcester, MA
		Luis Perez relinquished title to fight at and become bantamweight champion	
Oct 13,	2007	**Dimitry Kirilov** w pts 12 Jose Navarro (US)	Moscow (Rus)
		For vacant title	
Feb 28,	2008	Dmitry Kirilov drew 12 Cecilio Santos (Mex)	New York, NY
		For vacant title	
Feb 28,	2008	Dmitry Kirilov drew 12 Cecilio Santos (Mex)	New York, NY
Aug 2,	2008	**Vic Darchinyan** (Arm) w ko 5 Dmitry Kirilov	Tacoma WA

WBO titles

Nov 7,	1998	**Victor Godoi** (Arg) w pts 12 Pedro Morquecho (Mex)	Chubut (Arg)
Jun 7,	1999	**Diego Morales** (Mex) w rtd 10 Victor Godoi	Tijuana (Mex)
Jul 31,	1999	Diego Morales w rsf 8 Ysaias Zamudio (Mex)	Tijuana (Mex)
Nov 20,	1999	**Adonis Rivas** (Nic) w pts 12 Diego Morales	Las Vegas NV
Mar 25,	2000	Adonis Rivas (Nic) w tdec 11 Pedro Morquecho (Mex)	Managua (Nic)
Sep 2,	2000	Adonis Rivas w pts 12 Joel Luna Zarate	Managua (Nic)
Jun 16,	2001	**Pedro Alcazar** (Pan) w pts 12 Adonis Rivas	Panama City (Pan)
Oct 5,	2001	Pedro Alcazar w pts 12 Jorge Otero (Col)	Panama City (Pan)
Jun 22,	2002	**Fernando Montiel** (Mex) w rsf 6 Pedro Alcazar	Las Vegas NV
Jan 18,	2003	Fernando Montiel w rsf 2 Ray Doliguez (Phi)	Los Mochis (Mex)
Aug 16,	2003	**Marc Johnson** (US) w pts 12 Felix Montiel	Uncasville, CT
Mar 6,	2004	Marc Johnson w ko 4 Luis Bolano	Mashantucket, NM
Sep 25,	2004	**Ivan Hernandez** (Mex) w ko 8 Marc Johnson	Memphis, TN
Apr 9,	2005	**Fernando Montiel** w ko 7 Ivan Hernandez	El Paso, NM

Jul 16, 2005 Fernando Montiel w pts 12 Evert Briceno (Nic) .... Las Vegas, NV
Oct 29, 2005 Fernando Montiel w pts 12 Pramuansak Posuwan (Tha) .... Tucson, AZ
Feb 24, 2007 Fernando Montiel w pts 12 Z Gorres (Phi) .... Cebu (Phi)
Jul 14, 2007 Fernando Montiel w rsf 10 Cecilio Santos (Mex) ....Obregon (Mex)
Oct 4, 2007 Fernando Montiel w rsf 12 Luis Melendez (Col) .... Las Vegas, NV
Feb 16, 2008 Fernando Montiel w ko 4 Martin Castillo (Mex) .... Las Vegas, NV
May 31, 2008 Fernando Montiel w rsf 3 Luis Maldonado (Mex) .... San Luis Potosi (Mex)
Montiel vacated the title by moving up to bantamweight
Mar 28, 2009 **Jose Lopez** (PR) w pts 12 Pramansuak Posuwan (Tha) .... Bayamon (PR)
For vacant title
Sep 4, 2009 **Marvin Sonsona** (Phi) w pts 12 Jose Lopez .... Rama (Can)
Nov 21, 2009 Marvin Sonsona drew 12 Alejandro Hernandez (Mex) .... Rama (Can)
Sonsona failed to make the weight and the title was declared vacant
Jan 30, 2010 **Jorge Arce** w tdec 7 Angky Angkota (Ind) .... Mexico City (Mex)
For vacant title
Jorge Arce relinquished title to box at bantamweight
May 15, 2010 **Omar Narvaez** w pts 12 Everth Briceno (Nic).............Buenos Aires (Arg)
For vacant title
May 15, 2010 Omar Narvaez w pts 12 Victor Saleta ....Buenos Aires (Arg)
Apr 15, 2011 Omar Narvaez w pts 12 Cesar Seda (PR) ....Buenos Aires (Arg)
Jun 11, 2011 Omar Narvaez w pts 12 William Urina (Col) ....Buenos Aires (Arg)
The WBO sanctioned the following for the Interim title
Oct 15, 2011 Daniel Rosas drew 12 Jose Cabrera .... Los Mochis (Mex)
Apr 21, 2012 Omar Narvaez w pts 12 Jose Cabrera (Mex)..................San Juan (Arg)
For the WBA title
Oct 20, 2012 Omar Narvaez w ko 11 Johnny Garcia (Mex) ....Buenos Aires (Arg)
Dec 15, 2012 Omar Narvaez w pts 12 David Quijano (PR) .... San Miguel (Arg)
May 25, 2013 Omar Narvaez w pts 12 Felipe Orucuta (Mex) ....Buenos Aires (Arg)
Aug 24, 2013 Omar Narvaez w rsf 10 Hiroyuki Hisataka (Jap)................ Chubut (Arg)
Dec 21, 2013 Omar Narvaez w rsf 7 David Carmona (Mex) ....Buenos Aires (Arg)
May 17, 2014 Omar Narvaez w ko 4 Antonio Tostado Garcia (Mex) .... Cordoba (Arg)
Sep 19, 2014 Omar Narvaez w pts 12 Felipe Orucuta .... Cordoba (Arg)
Dec 30, 2014 **Naoya Inoue** w ko 2 Omar Narvaez .... Tokyo (Jap)
WBO sanctioned the following fight for the interim title
Jul 7, 2015 David Carmona (Mex) drew 12 Warlito Parrenas (Phi) ....Hermosillo (Mex)
Sec 29, 2015 Naoya Inoue w rsf 2 Warlito Parrenas......................... Tokyo (Jap)
For the WBO title
May 8, 2016 Naoya Inoue w pts 12 David Carmona .... Tokyo (Jap)
Sep 4, 2016 Naoya Inoue w ko 10 Karoon Jarupianlerd (Tha) .... Kanagawa (Jap)
Dec 30, 2016 Naoya Inoue w rsf 6 Kohei Kono (Jap) .... Tokyo (Jap)
May 21, 2017 Naoya Inoue w ko 3 Ricardo Rodriguez (US).................... Tokyo (Jap)
Sep 9, 2017 Naoya Inoue w rtd 6 Antonio Nieves (US) ....Carson, CA
Dec 30, 2017 Naoya Inoue w rsf 3 Yoann Boyeaux (Fra).................. Kanagawa (Jap)

WBC/WBA titles

May 17, 2008 **Cristian Mijares** w pts 12 Alexander Munoz (Ven) ....Gomez Palacio (Mex)
Unification contest
Aug 30, 2008 Cristian Mijares w rsf 3 Chatchai Sasakul (Tha)............. Monterrey (Mex)

WBC/WBA/IBF titles

Nov 1, 2008 **Vic Darchinyan** w ko 9 Cristian Mijares ....Carson, CA
Feb 7, 2009 Vic Darchinyan w rtd 11 Jorge Arce (Mex) .... Anaheim, CA

WBA title

The WBA recognized Cristian Mijares and then Vic Darchinyan as Super Champions
Sep 15, 2008 **Nobuo Nashiro** (Jap) w pts 12 Kohei Kono (Jap) ....Yokohama (Jap)
Apr 11, 2009 Nobuo Nashiro w rsf 8 Kunosuke Tomiyama (Jap)............... Osaka (Jap)
Sep 30, 2009 Nobuo Nashiro w pts 12 Hugo Cazares (Mex)................... Osaka (Jap)
The WBA also recognized the following fights as Interim titles:
Jul 26, 2008 **Rafael Concepcion** (Pan) w ko 10 A J Banal (Phi) .... Cebu (Phi)
Sep 15, 2008 **Jorge Arce** w rtd 9 Rafael Concepcion................... Mexico City (Mex)
Nov 1, 2008 Jorge Arce w rsf 4 Isidro Garcia (Mex),...................... Las Vegas, NV
The WBA withdrew recognition of Arce as Interim champion after he lost to WBA Super Champion Vic Darchinyan, as above. They sanctioned the following fight for the Interim title
Aug 15, 2009 **Nonito Donaire** (Phi) w pts 12 Rafael Concepcion .... Las Vegas, NV
Sep 9, 2009 **Hugo Fidel Cazares** (Mex) w pts 12 Nobu Nashiro............... Osaka (Jap)
Jul 3, 2010 Hugo Fidel Cazares w rsf 7 Everardo Morales (Mex) ....Tlalnepantla (Mex)
WBA sanctioned the following fight for the interim title
Jul 10, 2010 Nonito Donaire (Phi) w rsf 8 Hernan Marquez (Mex)....... San Juan (Puerto R)
For the WBA title
Oct 9, 2010 Hugo Fidel Cazares w rsf 9 Alberto Rossel (Per)...........Tialnepantla (Mex)
WBA sanctioned the following fight for the interim title
Nov 30, 2010 Drian Francisco (Phi) w rsf 10 Duangpetch Kokietgym (Tha) . . . Bueng Kan (Tha)
For the WBA title
Dec 23, 2010 Hugo Fidel Cazares w pts 12 Hiroyuki Kudaka (Jap) ....Osaka (Jap)
WBA sanctioned the following fight for the interim title
May 1, 2011 Panthep Mullipoom (Tha) w pts 12 Drian Francisco.......... Petchaburi (Tha)
For the WBA title
Jul 9, 2011 Hugo Fidel Cazares w ko 3 Arturo Badillo (Mex).............. Mazatlan (Mex)
Aug 31, 2011 **Tomonobu Shimizu (Jap)** w pts 12 Hugo Fidel Cazares .... Tokyo (Jap)
Dec 7, 2011 **Panthep Mullipoom** w pts 12 Daiki Kameda (Jap)...............Osaka (Jap)
WBA sanctioned the following fight for the interim title
Dec 10, 2011 Liborio Solis (Ven) w pts 12 Jose Salgado (Mex) .... Tepic (Mex)
For the WBA title
Apr 4, 2012 Panthep Mullipoom w rsf 9 Tomonobu Shimizu .... Kanagawa (Jap)
WBA sanctioned the following fight for the interim title
Apr 28, 2012 Liborio Solis w pts 12 Santiago Ivan Acosta (Arg).............. Maracay (Ven)
For the WBA title
Sep 1, 2012 Panthep Mullipoom w pts 12 Nobuo Nashiro (Jap)...............Osaka (Jap)
Dec 31, 2012 **Kohei Kono (Jap)** w ko 4 Panthep Mullipoom .... Tokyo (Jap)
May 6, 2013 **Liborio Solis** w pts 12 Kohei Kono .... Tokyo (Jap)
WBA sanctioned the following fight for the interim title
Sep 3, 2013 Sutep Wangmuk (Tha) w pts 12 Nobuo Nashiro (Jap) ....Nakhon (Tha)
For IBF and vacant WBA titles. Solis failed to make weight, so titles at stake for Kameda only
Dec 3, 2013 Liborio Solis w pts 12 Daiki Kameda..........................Osaka (Jap)
For the vacant WBA title
Mar 26, 2014 **Kohei Kono** w ko 8 Sutep Wangmuk .... Tokyo (Jap)
WBA sanctioned the following fight for the interim title
May 24, 2014 David Sanchez (Mex) w pts 12 Breilor Teran (Ven) ....Tijuana (Mex)
For the WBA title
Dec 31, 2014 Kohei Kono drew 12 Norberto Jimenez (DR).................... Tokyo (Jap)
WBA sanctioned the following fights for the interim title
Feb 14, 2015 David Sanchez w rsf 10 Juan Alberto Rosas (Mex)...........Hermosillo (Mex)
Sep 19, 2015 Luis Concepcion (Pan) w rtd 10 David Sanchez ....Hermosillo (Mex)
For the WBA title
Oct 16, 2015 Kohei Kono w pts 12 Koki Kameda (Jap) ....Chicago, IL
The WBA sanctioned the following fight for the interim title
Dec 17, 2015 Luis Concepcion w pts 12 Hernan Marquez (Mex) ....Panama City (Pan)
For the WBA title
Apr 27, 2016 Kohei Kono w pts 12 Tanawat Phonnaku (Tha).................. Tokyo (Jap)

Vic Darchinyan The first Armenian to win a world title

Aug 31, 2016	**Luis Concepcion** w pts 12 Kohei Kono	Tokyo (Jap)
Dec 10, 2016	**Khalid Yafai (Eng)** w pts 12 Luis Concepcion	Manchester (Eng)
May 13, 2017	Khalid Yafai w pts 12 Suguru Maranaka (Jap)	Birmingham (Eng)
Oct 28, 2017	Khalid Yafai w pts 12 Sho Ishida (Jap)	Cardiff (Wal)

WBC title

The WBC sanctioned the following bouts for the Interim title:

Jul 18, 2009	**Tomas Rojas** w rsf 9 Everardo Morales (Mex)	Puerto Vallarta (Mex)
Oct 24, 2009	Tomas Rojas w pts 12 Evans Mbamba (SA)	Veracruz (Mex)
Sep 20, 2010	Tomas Rojas w pts 12 Kohei Kono (Jap)	Saitama (Jap)
Feb 5, 2011	Tomas Rojas w pts 12 Nobuo Nashiro (Jap)	Osaka (Jap)
May 21, 2011	Tomas Rojas w rtd 11 Juan Jose Montes (Mex)	Tuxtla Gutierrez (Mex)
Aug 18, 2011	**Suriyan Sor Rungvisai** (Thai) w pts 12 Tomas Rojas	Mueang Noi (Thai)
Nov 4, 2011	Suriyan Sor Rungvisai w pts 12 Nubuo Nashiro	Bangkok (Thai)
Mar 27, 2012	**Yota Sato** (Jap) w pts 12 Suriyan Sor Rungvisai	Tokyo (Jap)
Jul 8, 2012	Yota Sato w pts 12 Sylvester Lopez (Phil)	Kangawa (Jap)
Dec 31, 2012	Yota Sato w pts 12 Ryo Akaho (Jap)	Tokyo (Jap)
May 3, 2013	**Srisaket Sor Rungvisai** (Thai) w rsf 8 Yota Sato	Si Sa Ket (Thai)
Nov 15, 2013	Srisaket Sor Rungvisai w rsf 9 Hirofumi Mukai (Jap)	Nakhon Ratchasima (Thai)
May 31, 2014	**Carlos Cuadras** (Mex) w tech pts 8 Srisaket Sor Rungvisai	Iztacalco (Mex)
Sep 20, 2014	Carlos Cuadras drew 12 Jose Salgado (Mex)	Guamuchil (Mex)
Nov 13, 2014	Carlos Cuadras w rsf 6 Marvin Mabait (Phi)	Washington, DC
Apr 4, 2015	Carlos Cuadras w pts 12 Luis Concepcion (Pan)	Metepec (Mex)
Aug 15, 2015	Carlos Cuadras w rsf 5 Dixon Flores (Nic)	Guamuchil (Mex)
Nov 28, 2015	Carlos Cuadras w pts 12 Koki Eto	Sendai (Jap)
Apr 23, 2016	Carlos Cuadras w rtd 8 Richie Mapranum (Phi)	Los Mochis (Mex)
Sep 10, 2016	**Roman Gonzalez (Nic)** w pts 12 Carlos Cuadras	Inglewood, CA
Mar 18, 2017	**Wisaksil Wangek (Tha)** w pts 12 Roman Gonzalez	New York, NY
Sep 9, 2017	Wisaksil Wangek w pts 12 Roman Gonzalez	Carson, CA
Feb 24, 2018	Wisaksil Wangek w pts 12 Juan Francisco Estrada (Mex)	Ingelwood, CA

IBF title

IBF withdrew recognition of Vic Darchinyan when he boxed at bantamweight.

Sep 15, 2009	**Simphiwe Nongzayi** (SA) w pts 12 Jorge Arce	Cancun (Mex)
	For vacant title	
Apr 9, 2010	Simphiwe Nongzayi drew 12 Malik Bouziane (Fra)	Massy (Fra)
Jul 31, 2010	**Juan Alberto Rosas** (Mex) w rsf 6 Simphiwe Nongzayi	Tepic (Mex)
Dec 11, 2010	**Mijares** w pts 12 Juan Alberto Rosas	Torreon (Mex)
May 14, 2011	Cristian Mijares w pts 12 Carlos Rueda (Nic)	Victoria de Durango (Mex)
	Mijares relinquished the title	
Oct 8, 2011	**Rodrigo Guerrero** (Mex) w tdec 6 Raul Martinez (US)	Tijuana (Mex)
	For vacant title	
Feb 11, 2012	**Juan Carlos Sanchez Jr.** (Mex) w pts 12 Rodrigo Guerrero	Los Mochis (Mex)
May 19, 2012	Juan Carlos Sanchez Jr. w pts 12 Juan Alberto Rosas	Puerto Vallarta (Mex)
Sep 22, 2012	Juan Carlos Sanchez Jr. w ko 9 Rodel Mayol (Phil)	Los Mochis (Mex)

WBC/WBA titles

Dec 12, 2009	**Vic Darchinyan** w ko 2 Tomas Rojas (Mex)	Rancho Mirage, CA
Mar 6, 2010	Victor Darchinyan w pts 12 Rodrigo Guerrero (Mex)	Rancho Mirage, CA
	Darchinyan relinquished WBC and WBA Super titles to box at bantamweight	

WBA/IBF titles

Dec 3, 2013	Liborio Solis w pts 12 Daiki Kameda (Jap)	Osaka (Jap)
	For vacant WBA title. Solis weighed in heavy, so title only at stake for Kameda	

IBF title

Jun 8, 2013	Juan Carlos Sanchez jr w pts 12 Roberto Domingo Sosa (Arg)	Las Vegas, NV
	For vacant IBF title. Sanchez weighed in heavy, so title only at stake for Sosa	
Sep 3, 2013	**Daiki Kameda** w pts 12 Rodrigo Guerrero (Mex)	Takamatsu (Jap)
	Title declared vacant after Kameda lost unification fight with WBA champion Liborio Solis	
Jul 18, 2014	**Zolani Tete** (SA) w pts 12 Teiru Kinoshita (Jap)	Kobe (Jap)
	For vacant title	
Mar 6, 2015	Zolani Tete w rsf 8 Paul Butler (Eng)	Liverpool (Eng)
	For vacant IBF title	
Jul 18, 2015	McJoe Arroyo (PR) w td 12 Arthur Villanueva (Phi)	El Paso, TX
Sep 3, 2016	Jerwin Ancajas (Phi) w pts 12 McJoe Arroyo	Taguig City (Phi)
Jan 29, 2017	Jerwin Ancajas w rsf 7 Jose Alfredo Rodriguez (Mex)	Macao (Chi)
July 2, 2017	Jerwin Ancajas w rsf 7 Teiru Kinoshita (Jap)	Brisbane (Aus)
Nov 18, 2017	Jerwin Ancajas w rsf 6 Jamie Conlan (NI)	Belfast (NI)
Feb 3, 2018	Jerwin Ancajas w rsf 10 Israel Gonzalez (Mex)	Corpus Christi, TX

JERWIN ANCAJAS *stopped Northern Ireland's Jamie Conlan in six rounds in Belfast in November 2017 to retain his IBF super-flyweight title*

Flyweight

Flyweight (112lb) was the last of boxing's eight "classic" divisions to be established. Until the National Sporting Club introduced it in 1909, anyone below featherweight was regarded as a bantamweight. At that time the bantamweight limit was fluctuating at anything from 105 to 118lb, depending on which "champion" was involved, and the position clearly needed to be regularized.

The NSC, the predecessors of the British Boxing Board of Control, held the first British championship at the weight in 1911. In America Johnny Coulon had claimed the world bantamweight championship at 112lb, but he had moved up to 116lb by the time the category became official.

The Americans did not accept Wilde as champion until 1916, when he knocked out their representative, Giuseppe di Melfi, who boxed as Young Zulu Kid. Wilde did not defend his title between 1918 and his last contest in 1923, but thereafter the division became active and popular on both sides of the Atlantic – and when boxing took hold in the Orient after the Second World War, the contribution of Japanese, Filipinos and Thais was immense.

World Flyweight Championship Bouts

Apr 11, 1913	**Sid Smith** (Eng) w pts 20 Eugene Criqui (Fra)	Paris (Fra)
Jun 2, 1913	**Bill Ladbury** (Eng) w rsf 11 Sid Smith	London (Eng)
Jan 26, 1914	**Percy Jones** (Wal) w pts 20 Bill Ladbury	London (Eng)
Mar 26, 1914	Percy Jones w pts 20 Eugene Criqui	Liverpool (Eng)
May 15, 1914	**Joe Symonds** (Eng) w ko 18 Percy Jones	Plymouth (Eng)
	Jones came in overweight but Symonds claimed the title	
Nov 16, 1914	**Jimmy Wilde** (Wal) w pts 15 Joe Symonds	London (Eng)
Dec 3, 1914	Jimmy Wilde w ko 9 Sid Smith Liverpool (Eng)	
	A match between Wilde and Tancy Lee, who had stopped Percy Jones, was accepted as being for the championship	
Jan 25, 1915	**Tancy Lee** (Sco) w rsf 17 Jimmy Wilde	London (Eng)
Oct 18, 1915	**Joe Symonds** w rsf 16 Tancy Lee	London (Eng)
Feb 14, 1916	**Jimmy Wilde** w rsf 12 Joe Symonds	London (Eng)
Apr 24, 1916	Jimmy Wilde w rtd 11 Johnny Rosner (US)	Liverpool (Eng)
Jun 26, 1916	Jimmy Wilde w rsf 11 Tancy Lee	London (Eng)
Jul 31, 1916	Jimmy Wilde w ko 10 Johnny Hughes (Eng)	London (Eng)
Dec 18, 1916	Jimmy Wilde w ko 11 Young Zulu Kid (US)	London (Eng)
Mar 12, 1917	Jimmy Wilde w rtd 4 George Clark (Eng)	London (Eng)
Apr 29, 1918	Jimmy Wilde w rsf 2 Dick Heasman (Eng)	London (Eng)
Jun 18, 1923	**Pancho Villa** (Phi) w ko 7 Jimmy Wilde	New York, NY
Oct 13, 1923	Pancho Villa w pts 15 Benny Schwartz (US)	Baltimore, MD
May 30, 1924	Pancho Villa w pts 15 Frankie Ash (Eng)	New York, NY
May 1, 1925	Pancho Villa w pts 15 Jose Senica (Phi)	Manila (Phi)
Jul 14, 1925	*Villa died, and Frankie Genaro claimed the title*	
Aug 22, 1925	**Fidel LaBarba** (US) w pts 10 Frankie Genaro (US)	Los Angeles, CA
	For American recognition as champion	
Jul 8, 1926	Fidel LaBarba w pts 10 Georgie Rivers (US)	Los Angeles, CA
Jan 21, 1927	Fidel LaBarba w pts 12 Elky Clark (Sco)	New York, NY
	For undisputed title	

NBA title

Oct 22, 1927	**Pinky Silverburg** (US) w dis 7 Ruby Bradley (US)	Bridgeport, CT
	For vacant title, which Silverburg forfeited a month later for failing to meet Ernie Jarvis within the stipulated period	
Dec 19, 1927	**Albert "Frenchy" Belanger** (Can) w pts 12 Ernie Jarvis (Eng)	Toronto (Can)
	For vacant title	
Feb 6, 1928	**Frankie Genaro** w pts 10 Albert "Frenchy" Belanger	Toronto (Can)
Oct 15, 1928	Frankie Genaro w pts 10 Albert "Frenchy" Belanger	Toronto (Can)
Mar 2, 1929	**Emile Pladner** (Fra) w ko 1 Frankie Genaro	Paris (Fra)
	For NBA title. Pladner's win also earned him recognition by the International Boxing Union	

British version

Aug 29, 1928	**Johnny Hill** (Sco) w pts 15 Newsboy Brown (Rus)	London (Eng)
	Brown had been recognized as champion in California after outpointing Johnny McCoy over ten rounds in Los Angeles on January 3,1928	
Mar 21, 1929	Johnny Hill w pts 15 Ernie Jarvis	London (Eng)
Jun 29, 1929	Johnny Hill w dis 10 Ernie Jarvis	Glasgow (Sco)
Sep 27, 1929	*Hill died*	

NBA/IBU titles

Apr 18, 1929	**Frankie Genaro** w dis 5 Emile Pladner	Paris (Fra)
Oct 17, 1929	Frankie Genaro w pts 15 Ernie Jarvis	London (Eng)
Jan 18, 1930	Frankie Genaro w rtd 12 Yvon Trevidic (Fra)	Paris (Fra)
Jun 10, 1930	Frankie Genaro w pts 10 Albert "Frenchy" Belanger	Toronto (Can)
Dec 26, 1930	Frankie Genaro drew 15 Midget Wolgast (US)	New York, NY
	For undisputed title	
Mar 25, 1931	Frankie Genaro drew 15 Victor Ferrand (Sp)	Madrid (Sp)
	Ferrand was four points ahead, but IBU rules required a challenger to have at least a five-point lead for the title to change hands	
Jul 30, 1931	Frankie Genaro w ko 6 Jackie Harmon (US)	Waterbury, CT
Oct 3, 1931	Frankie Genaro w pts 15 Valentin Angelmann (Fra)	Paris (Fra)
Oct 27, 1931	**Victor "Young" Perez** (Tun) w ko 2 Frankie Genaro	Paris (Fra)
Oct 31, 1932	**Jackie Brown** (Eng) w rsf 13 Victor "Young" Perez	Manchester (Eng)
Jun 12, 1933	Jackie Brown w pts 15 Valentin Angelmann	Manchester (Eng)
Sep 11, 1933	Jackie Brown w pts 15 Valentin Angelmann	Manchester (Eng)
Dec 11, 1933	Jackie Brown w pts 15 Ginger Foran (Eng)	Manchester (Eng)
Jun 18, 1934	Jackie Brown drew 15 Valentin Angelmann	Manchester (Eng)
Sep 1936	*Brown was stripped by the IBU for failing to give Angelmann a rematch*	

IBU title

Jan 6, 1936	**Valentin Angelmann** w rtd 5 Kid David (Bel)	Paris (Fra)
	For vacant title	
Dec 12, 1936	Valentin Angelmann w pts 15 Ernst Weiss (Aut)	Paris (Fra)
Jan 1937	*The IBU withdrew recognition from Angelmann after Peter Kane had outpointed him over 12 rounds in Paris on January 18, 1937*	

NBA title

Sep 9, 1935	**Benny Lynch** (Sco) w rtd 2 Jackie Brown	Manchester (Eng)
Sep 16, 1936	Benny Lynch w ko 8 Pat Palmer (Eng)	Glasgow (Sco)
Jan 19, 1937	Benny Lynch w pts 15 Small Montana (Phi)	Wembley (Eng)
	For undisputed title	

NY title

Dec 16, 1927	**Cpl Izzy Schwartz** (US) w pts 15 Newsboy Brown	New York, NY
	For vacant title	
Apr 9, 1928	Cpl Izzy Schwartz w pts 15 Routier Parra (Ch)	New York, NY
Jul 20, 1928	Cpl Izzy Schwartz w dis 4 Frisco Grande (Phi)	Rockaway, NY
Aug 3, 1928	Cpl Izzy Schwartz w ko 4 Little Jeff Smith (US)	Rockaway, NY
Mar 12, 1929	Cpl Izzy Schwartz w pts 12 Albert "Frenchy" Belanger	Toronto (Can)
Aug 22, 1929	**Willie La Morte** (US) w pts 15 Cpl Izzy Schwartz	Newark, NJ
	New York did not recognize La Morte as champion, but withdrew recognition from Schwartz and instituted a tournament in which the finalists were Midget Wolgast and Black Bill	
Mar 21, 1930	**Midget Wolgast** w pts 15 Black Bill (Cub)	New York, NY
	For vacant title	
May 16, 1930	Midget Wolgast w rtd 5 Willie La Morte	New York, NY
Dec 26, 1930	Midget Wolgast drew 15 Frankie Genaro	New York, NY
	For undisputed title	
Jul 13, 1931	Midget Wolgast (US) w pts 15 Ruby Bradley	Brooklyn, NY
Sep 16, 1935	**Small Montana** w pts 10 Midget Wolgast	Oakland, CA
Dec 16, 1935	Small Montana w pts 10 Tuffy Pierpoint (US)	Oakland, CA
Jan 19, 1937	**Benny Lynch** w pts 15 Small Montana	Wembley (Eng)
	For undisputed title	

Undisputed title

Oct 13, 1937	**Benny Lynch** w ko 13 Peter Kane (Eng)	Glasgow (Sco)
Jun 29, 1938	*Lynch forfeited the title by scaling 118½lb for a scheduled defence against Jackie Jurich*	
Sep 22, 1938	**Peter Kane** w pts 15 Jackie Jurich (US)	Liverpool (Eng)
	For vacant title	

NBA title

Dec 14, 1939	*The NBA proclaimed Little Dado champion*	
Feb 21, 1941	**Little Dado** (Phi) w pts 10 Jackie Jurich	Honolulu, HI
1942	*Dado relinquished the title because of his inability to make the weight, and the NBA reinstated Kane as champion*	
Jun 19, 1943	**Jackie Paterson** (Sco) w ko 1 Peter Kane	Glasgow (Sco)
Jul 10, 1946	Jackie Paterson w pts 15 Joe Curran (Eng)	Glasgow (Sco)
Jul 31, 1947	*The NBA and BBBC stripped Paterson of the title because of his inability*	

YOUNG MARTIN *goes the way of most of Pascual Perez's title challengers, the Spanish flyweight knocked out in the third round in December 1957*

	to make the weight for a planned defence against Dado Marino	
Oct 20, 1947	**Rinty Monaghan** (Ire) w pts 15 Dado Marino (Haw)	London (Eng)
	For NBA and Irish Board recognition as champion. Paterson obtained a court injunction restraining the BBBC from recognizing anyone else as world champion or from recognizing as a title fight any contest not involving him	
Mar 23, 1948	Rinty Monaghan w ko 7 Jackie Paterson	Belfast (N. Ire)
	For undisputed title	

Undisputed title

Apr 5, 1949	**Rinty Monaghan** w pts 15 Maurice Sandeyron (Fra)	Belfast (N. Ire)
Sep 30, 1949	Rinty Monaghan drew 15 Terry Allen (Eng)	Belfast (N. Ire)
	Rinty Monoghan retired as undefeated champion.	
Apr 25, 1950	**Terry Allen** w pts 15 Honore Pratesi (Fra)	London (Eng)
	For vacant title	
Aug 1, 1950	**Dado Marino** w pts 15 Terry Allen	Honolulu, HI
Nov 1, 1951	Dado Marino w pts 15 Terry Allen	Honolulu, HI
May 19, 1952	**Yoshio Shirai** (Jap) w pts 15 Dado Marino	Tokyo (Jap)
Nov 15, 1952	Yoshio Shirai w pts 15 Dado Marino	Tokyo (Jap)
May 18, 1953	Yoshio Shirai w pts 15 Tanny Campo (Phi)	Tokyo (Jap)
Oct 27, 1953	Yoshio Shirai w pts 15 Terry Allen	Tokyo (Jap)
May 23, 1954	Yoshio Shirai w pts 15 Leo Espinosa (Phi)	Tokyo (Jap)
Nov 26, 1954	**Pascual Perez** (Arg) w pts 15 Yoshio Shirai	Tokyo (Jap)
May 30, 1955	Pascual Perez w ko 5 Yoshio Shirai	Tokyo (Jap)
Jan 11, 1956	Pascual Perez w pts 15 Leo Espinosa	Buenos Aires (Arg)
Jun 30, 1956	Pascual Perez w rtd 11 Oscar Suarez (Cub)	Montevideo (Uru)
Mar 30, 1957	Pascual Perez w ko 1 Dai Dower (Wal)	Buenos Aires (Arg)
Dec 7, 1957	Pascual Perez w ko 3 Young Martin (Sp)	Buenos Aires (Arg)
Apr 19, 1958	Pascual Perez w pts 15 Ramon Arias (Ven)	Caracas (Ven)
Dec 15, 1958	Pascual Perez w pts 15 Dommy Ursua (Phi)	Manila (Phi)
Aug 10, 1959	Pascual Perez w pts 15 Kenji Yonekura (Jap)	Tokyo (Jap)
Nov 5, 1959	Pascual Perez w ko 13 Sadao Yaoita (Jap)	Osaka (Jap)
Apr 16, 1960	**Pone Kingpetch** (Tha) w pts 15 Pascual Perez	Bangkok (Tha)
Sep 22, 1960	Pone Kingpetch w rsf 8 Pascual Perez	Los Angeles, CA
Jun 27, 1961	Pone Kingpetch w pts 15 Mitsunori Seki (Jap)	Tokyo (Jap)
May 30, 1962	Pone Kingpetch w pts 15 Kyo Noguchi (Jap)	Tokyo (Jap)
Oct 10, 1962	**Masahiko "Fighting" Harada** (Jap) w ko 11 Pone Kingpetch	Tokyo (Jap)
Jan 12, 1963	**Pone Kingpetch** w pts 15 Masahiko "Fighting" Harada	Bangkok (Tha)
Sep 18, 1963	**Hiroyuki Ebihara** (Jap) w ko 1 Pone Kingpetch	Tokyo (Jap)
Jan 23, 1964	**Pone Kingpetch** w pts 15 Hiroyuki Ebihara	Bangkok (Tha)

Apr 23, 1965 **Salvatore Burrini** (Ita) w pts 15 Pone Kingpetch . . . . Rome (Ita)
Nov 1965 *The WBA stripped Burruni for his failure to defend against Horacio Accavallo*

WBC title

Dec 2, 1965 **Salvatore Burrini** w ko 13 Rocky Gattellari (Aus) . . . . Sydney (Aus)
Jun 14, 1966 **Walter McGowan** (Sco) w pts 15 Salvatore Burruni . . . . Wembley (Eng)
Dec 30, 1966 **Chartchai Chionoi** (Tha) w rsf 9 Walter McGowan . . . . Bangkok (Tha)
Jul 26, 1967 Chartchai Chionoi w ko 3 Puntip Keosuriya (Tha) . . . . Bangkok (Tha)
Sep 19, 1967 Chartchai Chionoi w rsf 7 Walter McGowan . . . . Wembley (Eng)
Jan 28, 1968 Chartchai Chionoi w rsf 13 Efren Torres (Mex) . . . . Mexico City (Mex)
Nov 10, 1968 Chartchai Chionoi w pts 15 Bernabe Villacampo (Phi) . . . . Bangkok (Tha)
Feb 23, 1969 **Efren Torres** w rsf 8 Chartchai Chionoi . . . . Mexico City (Mex)
Nov 28, 1969 Efren Torres w pts 15 Susumu Hanagata (Jap) . . . . Guadalajara (Mex)
Mar 20, 1970 **Chartchai Chionoi** w pts 15 Efren Torres . . . . Bangkok (Tha)
Dec 7, 1970 **Erbito Salavarria** (Phi) w rsf 2 Chartchai Chionoi . . . . Bangkok (Tha)
Apr 30, 1971 Erbito Salavarria w pts 15 Susumu Hanagata . . . . Manila (Phi)
Nov 20, 1971 Erbito Salavarria drew 15 Betulio Gonzalez (Ven) . . . . Maracaibo (Ven)
The WBC named Gonzalez champion after Salavarria used an illegal stimulant
Jun 3, 1972 **Betulio Gonzalez** w ko 4 Socrates Batoto (Phi) . . . . Caracas (Ven)
Sep 29, 1972 **Venice Borkorsor** (Tha) w rtd 10 Betulio Gonzalez . . . . Bangkok (Tha)
Feb 9, 1973 Venice Borkorsor w pts 15 Erbito Salavarria . . . . Bangkok (Tha)
Venice Borkorsor relinquished his title to box at bantamweight
Aug 4, 1973 **Betulio Gonzalez** w pts 15 Miguel Canto (Mex) . . . . Maracaibo (Ven)
For vacant title
Nov 17, 1973 Betulio Gonzalez w rsf 11 Alberto Morales (Mex) . . . . Caracas (Ven)
Oct 1, 1974 **Shoji Oguma** (Jap) w pts 15 Betulio Gonzalez . . . . Tokyo (Jap)
Jan 8, 1975 **Miguel Canto** w pts 15 Shoji Oguma . . . . Sendai (Jap)
May 24, 1975 Miguel Canto w pts 15 Betulio Gonzalez . . . . Monterrey (Mex)
Aug 23, 1975 Miguel Canto w rsf 11 Jiro Takada (Jap) . . . . Merida (Mex)
Dec 13, 1975 Miguel Canto w pts 15 Ignacio Espinal (DR) . . . . Merida (Mex)
May 15, 1976 Miguel Canto w pts 15 Susumu Hanagata . . . . Merida (Mex)
Oct 3, 1976 Miguel Canto w pts 15 Betulio Gonzalez . . . . Caracas (Ven)
Nov 19, 1976 Miguel Canto w pts 15 Orlando Javierta (Phi) . . . . Los Angeles, CA
Apr 24, 1977 Miguel Canto w pts 15 Reyes Arnal (Ven) . . . . Caracas (Ven)
Jun 15, 1977 Miguel Canto w pts 15 Kimio Furesawa (Jap) . . . . Tokyo (Jap)
Sep 17, 1977 Miguel Canto w pts 15 Martin Vargas (Ch) . . . . Merida (Mex)
Nov 30, 1977 Miguel Canto w pts 15 Martin Vargas . . . . Santiago (Ch)
Jan 4, 1978 Miguel Canto w pts 15 Shoji Oguma . . . . Tokyo (Jap)
Apr 18, 1978 Miguel Canto w pts 15 Shoji Oguma . . . . Tokyo (Jap)
Nov 20, 1978 Miguel Canto w pts 15 Tacomron Vibonchai (Tha) . . . . Houston, TX
Feb 10, 1979 Miguel Canto w pts 15 Antonio Avelar (Mex) . . . . Merida (Mex)
Mar 18, 1979 **Chan Hee Park** (Kor) w pts 15 Miguel Canto . . . . Pusan (Kor)
May 19, 1979 Chan Hee Park w pts 15 Tsutomo Igarishi (Jap) . . . . Seoul (Kor)
Sep 9, 1979 Chan Hee Park drew 15 Miguel Canto . . . . Seoul (Kor)
Dec 16, 1979 Chan Hee Park w ko 2 Guty Espadas . . . . Pusan (Kor)
Feb 9, 1980 Chan Hee Park w pts 15 Arnel Arrozal (Pan) . . . . Seoul (Kor)
Apr 13, 1980 Chan Hee Park w pts 15 Alberto Morales (Mex) . . . . Taegu (Kor)
May 18, 1980 **Shoji Oguma** w ko 9 Chan Hee Park . . . . Seoul (Kor)
Jul 28, 1980 Shoji Oguma w pts 15 Sung-Jun Kim (Kor) . . . . Tokyo (Jap)
Oct 18, 1980 Shoji Oguma w pts 15 Chan Hee Park . . . . Sendai (Jap)
Feb 3, 1981 Shoji Oguma w pts 15 Chan Hee Park . . . . Tokyo (Jap)
May 12, 1981 **Antonio Avelar** w ko 7 Shoji Oguma . . . . Mito (Jap)
Aug 30, 1981 Antonio Avelar w ko 2 Taeshik Kim . . . . Seoul (Kor)
Mar 20, 1982 **Prudencio Cardona** (Col) w ko 1 Antonio Avelar . . . . Tampico (Mex)
Jul 24, 1982 **Freddie Castillo** (Mex) w pts 15 Prudencio Cardona . . . . Merida (Mex)
Nov 6, 1982 **Eleoncio Mercedes** (DR) w pts 15 Freddie Castillo . . . . Los Angeles, CA
Mar 15, 1983 **Charlie Magri** (Eng) w rsf 7 Eleoncio Mercedes . . . . Wembley (Eng)
Sep 27, 1983 **Frank Cedeno** (Phi) w rsf 6 Charlie Magri . . . . Wembley (Eng)
Jan 18, 1984 **Koji Kobayashi** (Jap) w rsf 2 Frank Cedeno . . . . Tokyo (Jap)
Apr 9, 1984 **Gabriel Bernal** (Mex) w ko 2 Koji Kobayashi . . . . Tokyo (Jap)
Jun 1, 1984 Gabriel Bernal w rsf 11 Antoine Montero (Fra) . . . . Nimes (Fra)
Oct 8, 1984 **Sot Chitalada** (Tha) w pts 12 Gabriel Bernal . . . . Bangkok (Tha)
Feb 20, 1985 Sot Chitalada w rtd 4 Charlie Magri . . . . London (Eng)
Jun 22, 1985 Sot Chitalada drew 12 Gabriel Bernal . . . . Bangkok (Tha)
Feb 22, 1986 Sot Chitalada w pts 12 Freddie Castillo . . . . Kuwait City (Ku)
Dec 10, 1986 Sot Chitalada w pts 12 Gabriel Bernal . . . . Bangkok (Tha)
Sep 5, 1987 Sot Chitalada w ko 4 Rae-Ki Ahn (Kor) . . . . Bangkok (Tha)
Jan 31, 1988 Sot Chitalada w rsf 7 Hideaki Kamishiro (Jap) . . . . Osaka (Jap)
Jul 23, 1988 **Yong-Kang Kim** (Kor) w pts 12 Sot Chitalada . . . . Pohang (Kor)
Nov 13, 1988 Yung-Kang Kim w pts 12 Emil Romano (Phi) . . . . Chungju (Kor)
Mar 5, 1989 Yung-Kang Kim w pts 12 Yukhito Tamakuma (Jap) . . . . Aomori (Jap)
Jun 3, 1989 **Sot Chitalada** w pts 12 Yung-Kang Kim . . . . Trang (Tha)
Jan 30, 1990 Sot Chitalada w pts 12 Ric Siodoro (Phi) . . . . Bangkok (Tha)
May 1, 1990 Sot Chitalada w pts 12 Carlos Salazar (Arg) . . . . Bangkok (Tha)
Sep 9, 1990 Sot Chitalada w ko 1 Richard Clark (Jam) . . . . Kingston (Jam)
Nov 24, 1990 Sot Chitalada w pts 12 Jung-Koo Chang (Kor) . . . . Seoul (Kor)
Feb 15, 1991 **Muangchai Kitikasem** (Tha) w rsf 6 Sot Chitalada . . . . Ayuthaya (Tha)
May 18, 1991 Muangchai Kitikasem w rsf 12 Jung-Koo Chang . . . . Seoul (Kor)
Oct 25, 1991 Muangchai Kitikasem w pts 12 Alberto Jiminez (Mex) . . . . Bangkok (Tha)
Feb 28, 1992 Muangchai Kitikasem w rsf 9 Sot Chitalada . . . . Samut Prakan (Tha)
Jun 23, 1992 **Yuri Arbachakov** (Arm) w ko 8 Muangchai Kitikasem . . . . Tokyo (Jap)
Oct 20, 1992 Yuri Arbachakov w pts 12 Yun-Un Chin (Kor) . . . . Tokyo (Jap)
Mar 20, 1993 Yuri Arbachakov w rsf 9 Muangchai Kitikasem . . . . Lop Buri (Tha)
Jul 16, 1993 Yuri Arbachakov w pts 12 Ysias Zamudio (Mex) . . . . Kobe (Jap)
Dec 13, 1993 Yuri Arbachakov w pts 12 Nam-Hook Cha (Kor) . . . . Kyoto (Jap)
Aug 1, 1994 Yuri Arbachakov w ko 8 Hugo Rafael Soto (Arg) . . . . Tokyo (Jap)
Jan 30, 1995 Yuri Arbachakov w pts 12 Oscar Arciniega (Mex) . . . . Sapporo (Jap)
Sep 25, 1995 Yuri Arbachakov w pts 12 Chatchai Elite-Gym (Tha) . . . . Tokyo (Jap)
Feb 5, 1996 Yuri Arbachakov w pts 12 Raul Juarez (Mex) . . . . Osaka (Jap)
Aug 26, 1996 Yuri Arbachakov w rsf 9 Takoto Toguchi (Jap) . . . . Tokyo (Jap)
Nov 12, 1997 **Chatchai Sasakul** (Tha) w pts 12 Yuri Arbachakov . . . . Sapporo (Jap)
NB: Chatchai is also known as Chatchai Elitegym and Chatchai Dutchboygym
Feb 27, 1998 Chatchai Sasakul w pts 12 Yong-Jin Kim (Kor) . . . . Koh Sumai (Tha)
May 1, 1998 Chatchai Sasakul w ko 5 Yong-Soon Chang (Kor) . . . . Bangkok (Tha)
Dec 3, 1998 **Manny Pacquaio** (Phi) w rsf 8 Chatchai Sasakul . . . . Phuttamonthon (Tha)
Apr 24, 1999 Manny Pacquaio w ko 4 Gabriel Mira (Mex) . . . . Manila (Phi)
Sep 17, 1999 **Medgoen Singsurat** (Tha) w ko 3 Manny Pacquiao . . . . Nakhon (Tha)
Pacquiao lost the title on the scales
Feb 25, 2000 Medgoen Singsurat w pts 12 Masaki Kawabata (Jap) . . . . . Samut Sakorn (Tha)
May 19, 2000 **Malcolm Tunacao** (Phi) w rsf 7 Medgoen Singsurat . . . . Udon Thani (Tha)
Aug 20, 2000 Malcolm Tunacao (Phi) drew 12 Celes Kobayashi . . . . Tokyo (Jap)
Mar 2, 2001 **Pongsaklek Wonjongkam** (Tha) w rsf 1 Malcolm Tunacao . . . . Pichit (Tha)
Jun 15, 2001 Pongsaklek Wonjongkam w rsf 5 Hayato Asai (Jap) . . . . Nagoya (Jap)
Oct 26, 2001 Pongsaklek Wonjongkam w tdec 8 Alex Baba (Gha) . . . . Hat Yai (Tha)
Dec 6, 2001 Pongsaklek Wonjongkam w rsf 2 Luiz Lazarte (Arg) . . . . Pattaya (Tha)
Apr 19, 2002 Pongsaklek Wonjongkam w ko 1 Daisuke Naito (Jap) . . . . Khonkaen (Tha)
Sep 6, 2002 Pongsaklek Wonjongkam w pts 12 Jesus Martinez (Mex) . . . . Rangsit (Tha)
Nov 26, 2002 Pongsaklek Wonjongkam w pts 12 Hidenobu Honda (Jap) . . . . Osaka (Jap)
Jun 6, 2003 Pongsaklek Wonjongkam w pts 12 Randy Mangubat (Phi) . . . . Songkla (Jap)
Nov 14, 2003 Pongsaklek Wonjongkam w pts 12 Hussein Hussein (Aus) . . . . Bangkok (Tha)
Jan 3, 2004 Pongsaklek Wonjongkam w pts 12 Trash Nakanuma (Jap) . . . . . Yokohama (Jap)
Jul 15, 2004 Pongsaklek Wonjongkam w rsf 5 Luis Angel Martinez (Mex) . . . . Khonkaen (Tha)
Jan 29, 2005 Pongsaklek Wonjongkam w rsf 5 Noriyuko Komatsu (Jap) . . . . Osaka (Jap)
Oct 10, 2005 Pongsaklek Wonjongkam w tdec 7 Daisuke Naito . . . . Tokyo (Jap)
Feb 16, 2006 Pongsaklek Wonjongjam w pts 12 Gilberto Keb Baas (Mex) . . . . . . Chainart (Jap)
May 1, 2006 Pongsaklek Wonjongkam w pts 12 Daigo Nakahiro (Jap) . . . . Bangkok (Tha)
Jun 30, 2006 Pongsaklek Wonjongkam w rsf 4 Everardo Morales (Mex) . . . . Bangkok (Tha)
Nov 17, 2006 Pongsaklek Wonjongkam w pts 12 Monelisi Mhikiza Myekeni (SA) . . . . . N'chasima (Tha)
Apr 6, 2007 Pongsaklek Wonjongkam w rsf 7 Tomono Shimizu (Jap) . . . . Saraburi (Tha)
Jul 18, 2007 **Daisuke Naito** w pts 12 Pongsaklek Wonjongkam . . . . Tokyo (Jap)
Oct 17, 2007 Daisuke Naito w pts 12 Daiki Kameda (Jao) . . . . Tokyo (Jap)
Mar 8, 2008 Daisuke Naito drew 12 Pongsaklek Wonjongkam . . . . Tokyo (Jap)
Jul 30, 2008 Daisuke Naito w ko 10 Tomonobu Shimizu (Jap) . . . . Tokyo (Jap)
Dec 23, 2008 Daisuke Naito w rsf 11 Shingo Yamaguchi (Jap) . . . . Tokyo (Jap)
May 26, 2009 Daisuke Naito w pts 12 Xiong Zhao Zhong (Chi) . . . . Tokyo (Jap)
Nov 29, 2009 **Koki Kameda** (Jap) w pts 12 Daisuke Naito . . . . Saitama (Jap)
The WBC also sanctioned Interim title fights as follows:
Apr 24, 2009 Pongsaklek Wonjongkam w pts 12 Julio Cesar Miranda (Mex) . . Chachoengsao (Tha)
Aug 28, 2009 Pongsaklek Wonjongkam w rsf 6 Takahisa Masuda (Jap) . . . . . Chiangmai (Tha)
Mar 27, 2010 **Ponsgsaklek Wonjongkam** w pts 12 Koki Kameda . . . . Tokyo (Jap)
For full WBC title
Oct 8, 2010 Ponsgsaklek Wonjongkam w pts 12 Suriyan Sor Rungvisai . . . Mueang Noi (Thai)
Jul 1, 2011 Ponsgsaklek Wonjongkam w pts 12 Takuya Kogawa (Jap) . . . . Hat Yai (Thai)
Oct 21, 2011 Ponsgsaklek Wonjongkam w pts 12 Edgar Sosa (Mex) . . . . Bangkok (Thai)
Dec 23, 2011 Ponsgsaklek Wonjongkam drew 12 Hirofumi Mukai (Jap) . . . . . . Bangkok (Thai)
Mar 2, 2012 **Sonny Boy Jaro** (Phil) w rsf 6 Ponsgsaklek Wonjongkam . . . . Chonburi (Thai)
Jul 16, 2012 **Toshiyuki Igarashi** (Jap) w pts 12 Sonny Boy Jaro . . . . Kasukabe (Jap)
Nov 3, 2012 Toshiyuki Igarashi w pts 12 Nestor Daniel Narvaes (Arg) . . . . Sendai (Jap)
Apr 8, 2013 **Akira Yaegashi** (Jap) w pts 12 Toshiyuki Igarashi . . . . Tokyo (Jap)
Aug 12, 2013 Akira Yaegashi w pts 12 Ocsar Blanquet (Mex) . . . . Tokyo (Jap)
Apr 6, 2014 Akira Yaegashi w ko 9 Odilon Zaleta (Mex) . . . . Tokyo (Jap)
Sep 5, 2014 **Roman Gonzalez** (Nic) w rsf 9 Akira Yaegashi . . . . Tokyo (Jap)
Nov 22, 2014 Roman Gonzalez w rsf 6 Rocky Fuentes (Phi) . . . . Yokohama (Jap)
May 16, 2015 Roman Gonzalez w rsf 2 Edgar Sosa (Mex) . . . . Inglewood, CA
Oct 17, 2015 Roman Gonzalez w rsf 9 Brian Viloria (US) . . . . New York, NY
Apr 23, 2016 Roman Gonzalez w pts 12 McWilliams Arroyo (PR) . . . . Inglewood, CA
Mar 4, 2017 **Juan Hernandez Navarrete (Mex)** w rsf 3 Nawaphon Kaikanga (Tha) Bangkok (Tha)
For vacant WBC title
May 20, 2017 **Daigo Higa (Jap)** w rsf 6 Juan Hernandez Navarrete . . . . Tokyo (Jap)
Oct 22, 2017 Daigo Higa w rsf 7 Thomas Masson (Fra) . . . . Tokyo (Jap)
Feb 4, 2018 Daigo Higa w ko 1 Moises Fuentes (Mex) . . . . Naha (Jap)

WBA title

Mar 1, 1966 **Horacio Accavallo** (Arg) w pts 15 Katsutoshi Takayama (Jap) . . . . . . Tokyo (Jap)
For vacant title
Jul 15, 1966 Horacio Accavallo w pts 15 Hiroyuki Ebihara . . . . Buenos Aires (Arg)
Dec 10, 1966 Horacio Accavallo w pts 15 Efren Torres . . . . Buenos Aires (Arg)

Aug 13,	1967	Horacio Accavallo w pts 15 Hiroyuki Ebihara	Buenos Aires (Arg)
		Horacio Accavallo retired as undefeated champion	
Mar 30,	1969	**Hiroyuki Ebihara** w pts 15 Jose Severino (Bra)	Sapporo (Jap)
		For vacant title	
Oct 19,	1969	**Bernabe Villacampo** w pts 15 Hiroyuki Ebihara	Osaka (Jap)
Apr 6,	1970	**Berkrerk Chartvanchai** (Tha) w pts 15 Bernabe Villacampo	Bangkok (Tha)
Oct 21,	1970	**Masao Ohba** (Jap) w rsf 13 Berkrerk Chartvanchai	Tokyo (Jap)
Apr 1,	1971	Masao Ohba w pts 15 Betulio Gonzalez	Tokyo (Jap)
Oct 23,	1971	Masao Ohba w pts 15 Fernando Cabanela (Phi)	Tokyo (Jap)
Mar 4,	1972	Masao Ohba w pts 15 Susumu Hanagata	Tokyo (Jap)
Jun 20,	1972	Masao Ohba w ko 5 Orlando Amores (Pan)	Tokyo (Jap)
Jan 2,	1973	Masao Ohba w rsf 12 Chartchai Chionoi	Tokyo (Jap)
Jan 25,	1973	*Ohba was killed in a road crash*	
May 17,	1973	**Chartchai Chionoi** w rsf 4 Fritz Chervet (Swi)	Bangkok (Tha)
		For vacant title	
Oct 27,	1973	Chartchai Chionoi w pts 15 Susumu Hanagata	Bangkok (Tha)
Apr 27,	1974	Chartchai Chionoi w pts 15 Fritz Chervet	Zurich (Swi)
Oct 18,	1974	**Susumu Hanagata** w rsf 6 Chartchai Chionoi	Yokohama (Jap)
		Chionoi forfeited the title on the scales when he weighed in 3½lb over the limit. Hanagata was awarded the championship when he won the fight	
Apr 1,	1975	**Erbito Salavarria** w pts 15 Susumu Hanagata	Toyama (Jap)
Oct 7,	1975	Erbito Salavarria w pts 15 Susumu Hanagata	Yokohama (Jap)
Feb 27,	1976	**Alfonso Lopez** (Pan) w rsf 15 Erbito Salavarria	Manila (Phi)
Apr 21,	1976	Alfonso Lopez w pts 15 Shoji Oguma	Tokyo (Jap)
Oct 2,	1976	**Guty Espadas** w rsf 13 Alfonso Lopez	Los Angeles, CA
Jan 1,	1977	Guty Espadas w rtd 7 Jiro Takada	Tokyo (Jap)
Apr 30,	1977	Guty Espadas w rsf 13 Alfonso Lopez	Merida (Mex)
Nov 19,	1977	Guty Espadas w ko 8 Alex Santana (Nic)	Los Angeles, CA
Jan 2,	1978	Guty Espadas w rsf 7 Kimio Furesawa	Tokyo (Jap)
Aug 13,	1978	**Betulio Gonzalez** w pts 15 Guty Espadas	Maracay (Ven)
Nov 4,	1978	Betulio Gonzalez w rsf 12 Martin Vargas	Maracay (Ven)
Jan 29,	1979	Betulio Gonzalez drew 15 Shoji Oguma	Hamamatsu (Jap)
Jul 6,	1979	Betulio Gonzalez w ko 12 Shoji Oguma	Utsunomiya (Jap)
Nov 16,	1979	**Luis Ibarra** (Pan) w pts 15 Betulio Gonzalez	Maracay (Ven)
Feb 16,	1980	**Taeshik Kim** (Kor) w ko 2 Luis Ibarra	Seoul (Kor)
Jun 29,	1980	Taeshik Kim w pts 15 Arnel Arrozal	Seoul (Kor)
Dec 13,	1980	**Peter Mathebula** (SA) w pts 15 Taeshik Kim	Los Angeles, CA
Mar 28,	1981	**Santos Laciar** (Arg) w ko 7 Peter Mathebula	Soweto (SA)
Jun 6,	1981	**Luis Ibarra** w pts 15 Santos Laciar	Buenos Aires (Arg)
Sep 26,	1981	**Juan Herrera** (Mex) w ko 11 Luis Ibarra	Merida (Mex)
Dec 26,	1981	Juan Herrera w rsf 7 Betulio Gonzalez	Maracaibo (Ven)
May 1,	1982	**Santos Laciar** w rsf 13 Juan Herrera	Merida (Mex)
Aug 14,	1982	Santos Laciar w pts 15 Betulio Gonzalez	Maracaibo (Ven)
Nov 5,	1982	Santos Laciar w rsf 13 Steve Muchoki (Ken)	Copenhagen (Den)
Mar 4,	1983	Santos Laciar w ko 9 Ramon Neri (DR)	Cordoba (Arg)
May 5,	1983	Santos Laciar w rsf 2 Suichi Hozumi (Jap)	Shizuoka (Jap)
Jul 17,	1983	Santos Laciar w ko 1 Hi-Sup Shin (Kor)	Cheju Do (Kor)
Jan 28,	1984	Santos Laciar w pts 15 Juan Herrera	Marsala (Ita)
Sep 15,	1984	Santos Laciar w ko 10 Prudencio Cardona (Col)	Cordoba (Arg)
Dec 8,	1984	Santos Laciar w pts 15 Hilario Zapata (Pan)	Buenos Aires (Arg)
May 6,	1985	Santos Laciar w pts 15 Antoine Montero	Grenoble (Fra)
Jul	1985	*Laciar relinquished the title to box at super-flyweight*	
Oct 5,	1985	**Hilario Zapata** w pts 15 Alonzo Gonzalez (US)	Panama City (Pan)
		For vacant title	
Jan 31,	1986	Hilario Zapata w pts 15 Javier Lucas (Mex)	Panama City (Pan)
Apr 7,	1986	Hilario Zapata w pts 15 Suichi Hozumi (Jap)	Nirasaki (Jap)
Jul 5,	1986	Hilario Zapata w pts 15 Dodie Penalosa (Phi)	Manila (Phi)
Sep 13,	1986	Hilario Zapata w pts 15 Alberto Castro (Col)	Panama City (Pan)
Dec 6,	1986	Hilario Zapata w pts 15 Claudemir Dias (Bra)	Salvador (Bra)
Feb 13,	1987	**Fidel Bassa** (Col) w pts 15 Hilario Zapata	Barranquilla (Col)
Apr 25,	1987	Fidel Bassa w ko 13 Dave McAuley (Ire)	Belfast (Ire)
Aug 15,	1987	Fidel Bassa drew 15 Hilario Zapata	Panama City (Pan)
Dec 18,	1987	Fidel Bassa w pts 12 Felix Marty (DR)	Cartagena (Col)
Mar 26,	1988	Fidel Bassa w pts 12 Dave McAuley	Belfast (Ire)
Oct 2,	1988	Fidel Bassa w pts 12 Ray Medel (US)	San Antonio, TX
Apr 15,	1989	Fidel Bassa w rsf 6 Julio Gudino (Pan)	Barranquilla (Col)
Sep 30,	1989	**Jesus Rojas** (Ven) w pts 12 Fidel Bassa	Barranquilla (Col)
Mar 10,	1990	**Yul-Woo Lee** (Kor) w pts 12 Jesus Rojas	Taejon (Kor)
Jul 28,	1990	**Yukihito Tamakuma** (Jap) w rsf 10 Yul-Woo Lee	Mito (Jap)
Dec 6,	1990	Yukihito Tamakuma drew 12 Jesus Rojas	Aomori (Jap)
Mar 14,	1991	**Elvis Alvarez** (Col) w pts 12 Yukihito Tamakuma	Tokyo (Jap)
Jun 1,	1991	**Yong-Kang Kim** (Kor) w pts 12 Elvis Alvarez	Seoul (Kor)
Oct 5,	1991	Yong-Kang Kim w pts 12 Silvio Gamez (Ven)	Inchon (Kor)
Mar 24,	1992	Yong-Kang Kim w ko 6 Jon Penalosa (Phi)	Inchon (Kor)
Sep 26,	1992	**Aquiles Guzman** (Ven) w pts 12 Yong-Kang Kim	Pohang (Kor)
Dec 15,	1992	**David Griman** (Ven) w pts 12 Aquiles Guzman	Caracas (Ven)
Jun 21,	1993	David Griman w rsf 8 Hiroki Ioka (Jap)	Osaka (Jap)
Oct 4,	1993	David Griman w pts 12 Alvaro Mercardo (Col)	Puerto La Cruz (Ven)
Feb 13,	1994	**Saensor Ploenchit** (Tha) w pts 12 David Griman	Bangkok (Tha)
Apr 10,	1994	Saensor Ploenchit w pts 12 Jesus Rojas	Bangkok (Tha)
Jun 12,	1994	Saensor Ploenchit w pts 12 Aquiles Guzman	Bangkok (Tha)
Sep 25,	1994	Saensor Ploenchit w pts 12 Yong-Kang Kim (Kor)	Kanchanaburi (Tha)
Dec 26,	1994	Saensor Ploenchit w ko 11 Danny Nunez (DR)	Rayong (Tha)
May 7,	1995	Saensor Ploenchit w pts 12 Evangelio Perez (Pan)	Songkhla (Tha)
Oct 17,	1995	Saensor Ploenchit w ko 10 Hioki Ioka	Osaka (Jap)
Jan 14,	1996	Saensor Ploenchit w pts 12 Young-Soon Chang (Kor)	Nonsaburi (Tha)
Mar 23,	1996	Saensor Ploenchit w pts 12 Leo Gamez (Ven)	Rangsit (Tha)
Sep 8,	1996	Saensor Ploenchit w pts 12 Alexander Mahmutov	Nakhon Phanom (Tha)
Nov 24,	1996	**Jose Bonilla** (Ven) w pts 12 Saensor Ploenchit	Ubon Ratchatani (Tha)
Feb 25,	1997	Jose Bonilla w rsf 7 Hiroki Ioka (Jap)	Osaka (Jap)
Aug 23,	1997	Jose Bonilla w pts 12 Evangelio Perez (Pan)	Cumana (Ven)
Nov 22,	1997	Jose Bonilla w rsf 6 Keiji Yamaguchi (Jap)	Osaka (Jap)
May 29,	1998	**Hugo Soto** (Arg) w pts 12 Jose Bonilla	Las Vegas, NV
Mar 13,	1999	**Leo Gamez** w ko 3 Hugo Soto	New York, NY
Sep 3,	1999	**Sornpichai Pisanurachan** (Tha) w ko 8 Leo Gamez	Mukdaham (Tha)
Apr 8,	2000	Sornpichai Pisanurachan w rsf 5 Gilberto Gonzalez (Ven)	Bangkok (Tha)
Aug 5,	2000	**Eric Morel** (PR) w pts 12 Sornpichai Pisanurachan	Madison, WI
Oct 7,	2000	Eric Morel w pts 12 Alberto Ontiveros (Mex)	Las Vegas, NV
Dec 15,	2000	Eric Morel w pts 12 Gilberto Keb-Baas (Mex)	Madison, WI
Jun 8,	2001	Eric Morel w rtd 8 Jose de Jesus (Ven)	Baraboo, WI
Oct 12,	2002	Eric Morel w rsf 11 Denkaosan Kaovichit (Tha)	Anaheim, CA
Jun 28,	2003	Eric Morel w pts 12 Isidro Garcia (Mex)	Bayamon (PR)
Dec 6,	2003	**Lorenzo Parra** (Ven) w pts 12 Eric Morel	Bayamon (PR)
Jun 4,	2004	Lorenzo Parra w pts 12 Takefumi Sakata (Jap)	Tokyo (Jap)
Sep 9,	2004	Lorenzo Parra w pts 12 Yo-sam Choi (Kor)	Seoul (Kor)
Jan 3,	2005	Lorenzo Parra w pts 12 Trash Nakanumba (Jap)	Tokyo (Jap)
Sep 19,	2005	Lorenzo Parra w pts 12 Takefumi Sakati (Jap)	Tokyo (Jap)
Dec 5,	2005	Lorenzo Parra w pts 12 Brahim Asloum (Fra)	Paris (Fra)
		Parra was stripped of the title because of unavailability, but reinstated only to fail to make the weight for a defence in March 2007.	
Dec 2,	2006	**Roberto Vasquez** (Pan) w pts 12 Takefumi Sakata	Paris (Fra)
		Originally was for vacant title, then reduced to Interim title fight as Parra was reinstated.	
Mar 19,	2007	**Takefumi Sakata** w rsf 3 Lorenzo Parra	Tokyo (Jap)
Jul 1,	2007	Takefumi Sakata w pts 12 Roberto Vasquez	Tokyo (Jap)
Nov 4,	2007	Takefumi Sakata drew 12 Dekaosan Kaovichit (Tha)	Saitama (Jap)
Mar 29,	2008	Takefumi Sakata w pts 12 Shingo Yamaguchi	Chiba City (Jap)
Jul 30,	2008	Takefumi Sakata w pts 12 Hiroyuki Hisataka (Jap)	Tokyo (Jap)
Dec 31,	2008	**Denkaosan Kaovichit** (Tha) w ko 2 Takefumi Sakata	Hiroshima (Jap)
May 26,	2009	Denkaosan Kaovichit w pts 12 Hiroyuki Hisataka	Uttaradit (Tha)
Oct 6,	2009	Denkaosan Kaovichit w pts 12 Daiki Kameda (Jap)	Osaka (Jap)
		The WBA also sanctioned Interim title fights as follows:	
Sep 5,	2009	**Luis Concepcion** (Pan) w rsf 12 Omar Salado (Mex)	Panama City (Pan)
Nov 27,	2009	Luis Concepcion w ko 4 Roberto Leyva (Mex)	Panama City (Pan)
Feb 7,	2010	**Daiki Kameda** (Jap) w pts 12 Denkaosan Kavoichit	Kobe (Jap)
Sep 25,	2010	Daiki Kameda w pts 12 Takefumi Sakata (Jap)	Tokyo (Jap)
Dec 26,	2010	Daiki Kameda w pts 12 Silvio Olteanu (Spa)	Saitama (Jap)
		Kameda relinquished title to box at super-flyweight and Luis Concepcion upgraded to full champion	
Apr 2,	2011	**Hernan Marquez** (Mex) w rsf 11 Luis Concepcion (Pan)	Panama City (Pan)
Jul 2,	2011	Hernan Marquez w rsf 3 Edrin Dapudong (Phil)	Hermosillo (Mex)
Oct 29,	2011	Hernan Marquez w rsf 1 Luis Concepcion	Hermosillo (Mex)
		Marquez lost unification match to WBO champion Brian Viloria when WBA super title was also at stake	
		The WBA sanctioned the following for the Interim title	
Jan 29,	2011	**Juan Piero Perez** (Ven) w pts 12 Jesus Jimenez (Mex)	Guadalajara (Mex)
Jun 10,	2011	**Juan Carlos Reveco** (Arg) w ko 2 Jean Piero Perez	Las Heras (Arg)
May 11,	2012	Juan Carlos Reveco w pts 12 Karim Guerfi (Fra)	Cordoba (Arg)
Nov 10,	2012	Juan Carlos Reveco w pts 12 Julian Rivera (Mex)	Malargue (Arg)
		The following were for the full title	
Feb 27,	2013	**Juan Carlos Reveco** w pts 12 Masayuki Kuroda (Jap)	Kawaski (Jap)
Jun 22,	2013	Juan Carlos Reveco w rsf 8 Ulises Lara (Mex)	Mendoza (Arg)
		The WBA sanctioned the following for the Interim title	
Aug 1,	2013	Koki Eto (Jap) w pts 12 Kompayak Porpramook (Thai)	Bangkok (Thai)
Oct 12,	2013	Juan Carlos Reveco w tech pts 8 Ricardo Nunez (Pan)	Mendoza (Arg)
		For the WBA title	
		The WBA sanctioned the following for the Interim title	
Nov 29,	2013	Yodmongkol Vor Saengthep (Thai) w rsf 12 Koki Eto	Chonburi (Thai)
Mar 4,	2014	Yodmongkol Vor Saengthep w pts 12 Takuya Kogawa (Jap)	Nakhon Ratchasima (Thai)
		For the WBA title	
Mar 21,	2014	Juan Carlos Reveco w ko 2 Manuel Vides (Pan)	Buenos Aires (Arg)
Jun 6,	2014	Juan Carlos Reveco w pts 12 Felix Alvarado (Nic)	Buenos Aires (Arg)
Dec 19,	2014	Juan Carlos Reveco w rsf 5 Yodmongkol Vor Saengthep (Thai).	Mendoza (Arg)
Apr 22,	2015	**Kazuto Ioka** (Jap) w pts 12 Juan Carlos Reveco	Osaka (Jap)
		WBA sanctioned the following for the interim title	
Jul 29,	2015	Yutthana Kaensa (Tha) w pts 12 Gregorio Lebron (DR)	Loei (Tha)
Sep 27,	2015	Kazuto Ioka w pts 12 Roberto Domingo Sosa (Arg)	Osaka (Jap)
		For WBA title	

Dec 31, 2015 Kazuto Ioka w rsf 11 Juan Carlos Reveco (Arg)............... Osaka (Jap)
WBA sanctioned the following for the interim title
Feb 9, 2016 Yutthana Kaensa w pts 12 Gregorio Lebron (DR)............ Bangkok (Tha)
Jul 20, 2016 Kazuto Ioka w ko 11 Keyvin Lara (Nic)...................... Osaka (Jap)
For WBA title
Dec 31, 2016 Kazuto Ioka w rsf 7 Yutthana Kaensa........................Kyoto (Jap)
Apr 23, 2017 Kazuto Ioka w pts 12 Noknoi Sitthiprasert (Tha).............. Osaka (Jap)
Feb 24, 2018 **Artem Dalaklan (Ukr)** w pts 12 Brian Viloria (US)........... Inglewood, CA
For vacant WBA title

IBF title

Dec 24, 1983 **Soon-Chun Kwon** (Kor) w ko 5 Rene Busayong (Phi).............Seoul (Kor)
Feb 25, 1984 Soon-Chun Kown w tech dec 2 Roger Castillo (Phi)..............Seoul (Kor)
May 19, 1984 Soon-Chun Kwon w pts 15 Ian Clyde (Can)....................Daejon (Kor)
Sep 7, 1984 Soon-Chun Kwon w rsf 12 Joaquin Caraballo (Phi) .... Chungju (Kor)
Jan 25, 1985 Soon-Chun Kwon drew 15 Chong-Kwang Chung (Kor)...........Daejon (Kor)
Apr 14, 1985 Soon-Chun Kwon w ko 3 Shinobu Kawashima (Jap) .... Pohang (Kor)
Jul 17, 1985 Soon-Chun Kwon drew 15 Chong-Kwang Chung ....Masan (Kor)
Dec 20, 1985 **Chong-Kwang Chung** w rsf 4 Soon-Chun Kwon .... Taegu (Kor)
Apr 27, 1986 **Bi-Won Chung** (Kor) w pts 15 Chong-Kwang Chung .... Pusan (Kor)
Aug 2, 1986 **Hi-Sup Shin** w rsf 15 Bi-Won Chung..........................Inchon (Kor)
Nov 22, 1986 Hi-Sup Shin w rsf 13 Henry Brent (US)..................... Chunchon (Kor)
Feb 22, 1987 **Dodie Penalosa** w ko 5 Hi-Sup Shin..........................Inchon (Kor)
Sep 5, 1987 **Chang-Ho Choi** (Kor) w ko 11 Dodie Penalosa..................Manila (Phi)
Jan 16, 1988 **Rolando Bohol** (Phi) w pts 15 Chang-Ho Choi ....Manila (Phi)
May 6, 1988 Rolando Bohol w pts 15 Cho-Woon Park.......................Manila (Phi)
Oct 5, 1988 **Duke McKenzie** (Eng) w ko 11 Rolando Bohol .... Wembley (Eng)
Mar 8, 1989 Duke McKenzie w rsf 4 Tony DeLuca (US).....................London (Eng)
Jun 7, 1989 **Dave McAuley** w pts 12 Duke McKenzie .... Wembley (Eng)
Nov 8, 1989 Dave McAuley w pts 12 Dodie Penalosa.................... Wembley (Eng)
Mar 17, 1990 Dave McAuley w pts 12 Louis Curtis (US)...................... Belfast (Ire)

OMAR NARVAEZ *(right) held the WBO flyweight title for six years, turning back tough challengers such as the Frenchman Brahim Asloum in March 2007*

Sep 15,	1990	Dave McAuley w pts 12 Rodolfo Blanco (Col)	Belfast (Ire)
May 11,	1991	Dave McAuley w pts 12 Pedro Feliciano (PR)	Belfast (Ire)
Sep 7,	1991	Dave McAuley w ko 9 Jake Matlala (SA)	Belfast (Ire)
Jun 11,	1992	**Rodolfo Blanco** w pts 12 Dave McAuley	Bilbao (Sp)
Nov 29,	1992	**Pichit Sitbangprachan** (Tha) w ko 3 Rodolfo Blanco	Bangkok (Tha)
Mar 6,	1993	Pichit Sitbangprachan w rsf 4 Antonio Perez (Mex)	Uttaradit (Tha)
Oct 3,	1993	Pichit Sitbangprachan w rsf 9 Miguel Martinez (Mex)	Chaiyaphum (Tha)
Jan 23,	1994	Pichit Sithbangprachan w pts 12 Arthur Johnson (US)	Surat Thani (Tha)
May 8,	1994	Pichit Sithbangprachan w pts 12 Jose Luis Zepeda (Mex)	Rajaburi Province
Nov	1994	*Sithbangprachan relinquished the title rather than defend it against Jose Luis Zepeda*	
Feb 18,	1995	**Francisco Tejedor** (Col) w rsf 7 Jose Luis Zepeda *For vacant title*	Cartagena (Col)
Apr 22,	1995	**Danny Romero** (US) w pts 12 Francisco Tejedor	Las Vegas, NV
Jul 29,	1995	Danny Romero w ko 6 Miguel Martinez	San Antonio, TX
Jan	1996	*Romero vacated the title to box at super-flyweight*	
May 4,	1996	**Marc Johnson** (US) w ko 1 Francisco Tejedor *For vacant title*	Anaheim, CA
Aug 5,	1996	Marc Johnson w rsf 8 Raul Juarez (Mex)	Inglewood, CA
Feb 10,	1997	Marc Johnson w pts 12 Alejandro Montiel (Mex)	Inglewood, CA
Jun 1,	1997	Marc Johnson w ko 2 Cecilio Espino (Mex)	Uncasville, CT
Sep 16,	1997	Marc Johnson w pts 12 Angel Almena (PR)	Nashville, TN
Feb 22,	1998	Marc Johnson w ko 1 Arthur Johnson (US)	Washington, DC
Jul 26,	1998	Marc Johnson w pts 12 Luis Rolon (PR)	Oneida, NY
Sep 4,	1998	Marc Johnson w rtd 7 Jose Laureano (PR)	Atlantic City, NJ
Oct	1998	*Johnson relinquished title to box at super-flyweight*	
Apr 10,	1999	**Irene Pacheco** (Col) w rsf 9 Luis Cox (Per) *For vacant title*	Barranquilla (Col)
Oct 16,	1999	Irene Pacheco w rsf 4 Ferid Ben Jeddou (Tun)	Barranquilla (Col)
Jan 14,	2000	Irene Pacheco w ko 11 Pedro Pena (US)	El Paso, TX
Nov 10,	2000	Irene Pacheco w pts 12 Hawk Makepula (SA)	Las Vegas, NV
Nov 9,	2001	Irene Pacheco w rsf 4 Mike Trejo (US)	San Antonio, TX
Nov 29,	2002	Irene Pacheco w pts 12 Alejandro Montiel (Mex)	El Paso, TX
Sep 27,	2003	Irene Pacheco w rtd 6 Damaen Kelly (Ire)	Barranquilla (Col)
Dec 16,	2004	**Vic Darchinyan** (Arm) w rsf 11 Irene Pacheco	Hollywood, FL
Mar 27,	2005	Vic Darchinyan w rsf 8 Mzukisi Sikali (SA)	Homebush Bay (Aus)
Aug 24,	2005	Vic Darchinyan w rsf 5 Jair Jimenez (Mex)	Sydney (Aus)
Mar 3,	2006	Vic Darchinyan w rsf 8 Diosdado Gabi (Phi)	Santa Ynez, CA
Jun 3,	2006	Vic Darchinyan w rsf 8 Luis Maldonado (Mex)	Las Vegas, NV
Oct 7,	2006	Vic Darchinyan w tdec 6 Glenn Donaire (Phi)	Las Vegas, NV
Mar 3,	2007	Vic Darchinyan w rsf 12 Victor Burgos (Mex)	Carson, CA
Jul 7,	2007	**Nonito Donaire** (Phi) w rsf 5 Vic Darchinyan	Bridgeport, CT
Dec 1,	2007	Nonito Donaire w rsf 8 Luis Maldonado (Mex)	Mashantucket, CT
Nov 1,	2008	Nonito Donaire w rsf 6 Moruti Mthalane (SA)	Las Vegas NV
Apr 19,	2009	Nonito Donaire w rsf 4 Raul Martinez (US) *Donaire relinquished the title to move up to super-flyweight*	Quezon City (Phi)
Nov 20,	2009	**Moruti Mthalane** w pts 12 Julio Cesar Miranda *For vacant title*	Johannesburg (SA)
Sep 1,	2010	Moruti Mthalane w rsf 5 Zolani Tete (SA)	Brakpan (SA)
Mar 26,	2011	Moruti Mthalane w rsf 5 John Riel Casimero (Phil)	Johannesburg (SA)
Oct 28,	2011	Moruti Mthalane w rsf 7 Andreas Sarritzu (It)	Cagliari (It)
Sep 1,	2012	Moruti Mthalane w rsf 8 Ricardo Nunez (Pan) *Moruti Mthalane vacated*	Panama City (Pan)
Jan 22, (Thai)	2014	**Amnat Ruenroeng** (Thai) w pts 12 Rocky Fuentes (Phi) *For vacant title*	Nakhon Ratchasima
May 7,	2014	Amnat Ruenroeng w pts 12 Kazuto Ioka (Jap)	Osaka (Jap)
Sep 10,	2014	Amnat Ruenroeng w pts 12 McWilliams Arroyo (PR)	Nakhon Ratchasima (Thai)
Mar 7,	2015	Amnat Ruenroeng w pts 12 Zou Shiming (Chi)	Macao (Chi)
Jun 27,	2015	Amnat Ruenroeng w pts 12 John Riel Casimero	Bangkok (Thai)
Dec 7,	2015	Amnat Ruenroeng w pts 12 Myung Ho Lee (Jap)	Hua Hin (Tha)
May 25,	2016	**John Riel Casimero (Phi)** w ko 4 Amnat Ruenroeng	Beijing (Chi)
Sep 10,	2016	John Riel Casimero w rsf 10 Charlie Edwards (Eng)	London (Eng)
Apr 29,	2017	**Donnie Nietes (Phi)** w pts 12 Komgrich Nantapech (Tha) *For vacant title*	Cebu City (Phi)
Feb 24,	2018	Donnie Nietes w ko 7 Juan Carlos Reveco (Arg)	Inglewood, CA

WBO title

Mar 3,	1989	**Elvis Alvarez** w pts 12 Miguel Mercedes (DR) *Alvarez relinquished the WBO title in October 1989*	Medellin (Col)
Aug 18,	1990	**Isidro Perez** (Mex) w rsf 12 Angel Rosario (PR) *For vacant title*	Ponce (PR)
Nov 3,	1990	Isidro Perez w pts 12 Alli Galvez (Ch)	Acapulco (Mex)
Aug 10,	1991	Isidro Perez w pts 12 Alli Galvez	Santiago (Ch)
Mar 18,	1992	**Pat Clinton** (Sco) w pts 12 Isidro Perez	Glasgow (Sco)
Sep 19,	1992	Pat Clinton w pts 12 Danny Porter (Eng)	Glasgow (Sco)
May 15,	1993	**Jake Matlala** w rsf 8 Pat Clinton	Glasgow (Sco)
Dec 4,	1993	Jake Matlala w rtd 8 Luigi Camputaro (Ita)	Sun City (Bop)
Jun 11,	1994	Jake Matlala w rtd 9 Francis Ampofo (Eng)	London (Eng)
Oct 15,	1994	Jake Matlala w pts 12 Domingo Lucas (Phi)	Sun City (Bop)
Feb 11,	1995	**Alberto Jimenez** (Mex) w rsf 8 Jake Matlala	Hammanskraal (SA)
Jun 17,	1995	Alberto Jimenez w rtd 9 Robbie Regan (Wal)	Cardiff (Wal)
Oct 9,	1995	Alberto Jimenez w rsf 2 Zolili Mbityi (SA)	Tijuana (Mex)
Mar 23,	1996	Alberto Jimenez w rsf 5 Miguel Martinez	Las Vegas, NV
Jun 1,	1996	Alberto Jimenez w pts 12 Jose Lopez (PR)	Lake Tahoe, NV
Sep 6,	1996	Alberto Jimenez drew 12 Carlos Salazar (Arg)	Villa Ballester (Arg)
Dec 13,	1996	**Carlos Salazar** w rsf 10 Alberto Jimenez	Buenos Aires (Arg)
Mar 8,	1997	Carlos Salazar drew 12 Antonio Ruiz (Mex)	Mexicali (Mex)
May 23,	1997	Carlos Salazar w pts 12 Antonio Gonzalez (Mex)	Roque Saenz Pena (Arg)
Jul 19,	1997	Carlos Salazar w pts 12 Salvatore Fanni (Ita)	Porto Rotundo (Ita)
Oct 10,	1998	Carlos Salazar w pts 12 Everardo Morales (Mex)	Resistencia (Arg)
Mar 21,	1998	Carlos Salazar w pts 12 Jose Lopez (PR)	Roque Saenz Pena (Arg)
Aug 14,	1998	**Ruben Sanchez** (Mex) w tdec 8 Carlos Salazar	Mexicali (Mex)
Dec 18,	1998	Ruben Sanchez w pts 12 Savatore Fanni	Cagliari (Ita)
Apr 23,	1999	**Jose Antonio Lopez** (Spa) w ko 3 Ruben Sanchez	Zaragoza (Spa)
Jun 4,	1999	Jose Antonio Lopez w rsf 7 Igor Gerasimov (Rus)	Malaga (Spa)
Dec	1999	*Lopez stripped of the title following motor cycle accident, but then took part in vacant title fight the same month!*	
Dec 18,	1999	Isidro Garcia (Mex) w pts 12 Jose Antonio Lopez	Indio, CA
Aug 12,	2000	Isidro Garcia w rsf 6 Jose Sosa (Arg)	Cordoba (Arg)
Dec 15,	2000	**Fernando Montiel** (Mex) w rsf 7 Isidro Garcia	Obregon (Mex)
Mar 24,	2001	Fernando Montiel w rsf 7 Zoltan Lunka (Rom)	Munich (Ger)
May 25,	2001	Fernando Montiel w ko 1 Juan Domingo Cordoba (Arg)	Acapulco (Mex)
Sep 8,	2001	Fernando Montiel w pts 12 Jose Lopez (PR) *Montiel relinquished title when he became WBO super-flyweight champion*	Reno NV
Jul 13,	2002	**Oscar Narvaez** (Arg) w pts 12 Adonis Rivas (Nic)	Buenos Aires (Arg)
Sep 13,	2002	Omar Narvaez w dis 10 Luis Lazarte (Arg)	Chubut (Arg)
Dec 14,	2002	Omar Narvaez w pts 12 Andrea Sarritzu (Ita)	Quarto Santa Elena (Arg)
Jun 7,	2003	Omar Narvaez w rsf 5 Everardo Morales (Mex)	Buenos Aires (Arg)
Aug 9,	2003	Omar Narvaez drew 12 Andrea Sarritzu	Cagliari (Ita)
Nov 14,	2003	Omar Narvaez w rsf 11 Alexander Mahmutov (Rus)	Paris (Fra)
Mar 6,	2004	Omar Narvaez w rsf 3 Reginaldo Martins Carvalho (Bra)	Buenos Aires (Arg)
Dec 5,	2005	Omar Narvaez w rsf 11 Bernard Inom (Fra)	Paris (Fra)
Aug 5,	2006	Omar Narvaez w pts 12 Rexon Flores (Phi)	Cordoba (Arg)
Oct 14,	2006	Omar Narvaez w pts 12 Walberto Ramos (Col)	Buenos Aires (Arg)
Mar 10,	2007	Omar Narvaez w pts 12 Brahim Asloum (Fra)	Le Cannet (Fra)
Sep 14,	2007	Omar Narvaez w rsf 4 Marlon Marquez (Nic)	Trelew (Arg)
Jan 25,	2008	Omar Narvaez w pts 12 Carlos Tamara (Col)	Puerto Madryn (Arg)
May 9,	2008	Omar Narvaez w rtd 7 Ivan Pozo (Spa)	Vigo (Spa)
Sep 20,	2008	Omar Narvaez w pts 12 Alejandro Hernandez (Mex)	Puerto Madryn (Arg)
Feb 7,	2009	Omar Narvaez w rsf 10 Rayonta Whitfield (US)	Puerto Madryn (Arg)
Jun 26,	2009	Omar Narvaez w ko 11 Omar Soto (Mex) *Omar Narvaez relinquished title to box at super-flyweight*	Buenos Aires (Arg)
Jun 12,	2010	**Julio Cesar Miranda** (Mex) w rsf 5 Richie Mepranum (Phil)	Puebla (Mex)
Sep 4,	2010	Julio Cesar Miranda w rtd 8 Ronald Ramos (Col)	Monterrey (Mex)
Oct 16,	2010	Julio Cesar Miranda w rsf 2 Michael Arango (Col)	Monterrey (Mex)
Feb 26,	2011	Julio Cesar Miranda w rsf 4 Ardin Diale (Phil)	Queretaro (Mex)
Jul 17,	2011	**Brian Viloria** w pts 12 Julio Cesar Miranda	Honolulu, HI
Dec 11,	2011	Brian Viloria w rsf 8 Giovani Segura (Mex)	Pasig City (Phil)
May 13,	2012	Brian Viloria w rsf 9 Omar Nino Romero (Mex)	Pasig City (Phil)

WBO/WBA super title

Nov 17,	2012	Brian Viloria (US) w rsf 10 Hernan Marquez	Los Angeles, CA
Apr 16,	2013	**Juan Francisco Estrada** (Mex) w pts 12 Brian Viloria	Macao (Chi)
Jul 27,	2013	Juan Francisco Estrada w pts 12 Milan Melindo (Phi)	Macao (Chi)
Apr 26,	2014	Juan Francisco Estrada w rsf 10 Richie Mepranum (Phi)	Puerto Penasco (Mex)
Sep 6,	2014	Juan Francisco Estrada w rsf 11 Giovani Segura (Mex)	Mexico City (Mex)
Mar 28,	2015	Juan Francisco Estrada w rsf 3 Rommel Asenjo (Phi)	Merida (Mex)
Sep 26,	2015	Juan Francisco Estrada w ko 10 Hernan Marquez	Puerto Penasco (Mex)

WBO title

Nov 5,	2016	**Shiming Zou (Chi)** w pts 12 Prasitsak Phaprom (Tha) *For vacant WBO title*	Las Vegas, NV
Jul 28,	2017	**Sho Kimura (Jap)** w rsf 11 Shiming Zou	Shanghai (Chi)
Dec 31,	2017	Sho Kimura w rsf 9 Toshiyuki Igarashi (Jap)	Tokyo (Jap)

Light-Flyweight

The WBC introduced the light-flyweight division (weight limit 108lb) in 1975, and must have immediately regretted it as the second fight for their championship proved an embarrassing fiasco. Rafael Lovera, a Paraguayan with an extremely persuasive manager, was installed as No. 1 contender for the title and, when the inaugural champion Franco Udella failed to defend against him, Udella forfeited the championship and Lovera faced Luis Estaba, a 34-year-old grandfather from Panama, for the vacant title. Estaba won easily, prompting the WBC to investigate the impressive record which Lovera's manager had used to manoeuvre his man into the No. 1 spot. It transpired that Lovera had never had a professional fight in his life! Despite the inauspicious start to his reign, Estaba went on to make 11 successful defences, a reign which earned the new division some degree of credibility.

The WBA crowned their first champion within four months of the WBC, and soon produced one of the outstanding champions of the decade in the Japanese Yoko Gushiken. As expected, the division has been dominated by Mexican and Oriental fighters, with the American Michael Carbajal being a notable exception.

World Light-Flyweight Championship Bouts

WBC title

Apr 4, 1975	**Franco Udella** (Ita) w dis 12 Valentin Martinez (Mex)	Milan (Ita)
	For vacant WBC title	
Aug 1975	*The WBC withdrew recognition of Udella for failing to defend against Rafael Lovera*	
Sep 13, 1975	**Luis Estaba** (Ven) w ko 4 Rafael Lovera (Par)	Caracas (Ven)
	For vacant title	
Dec 17, 1975	Luis Estaba w rsf 10 Takenobu Shimabakuro (Jap)	Okinawa (Jap)
Feb 14, 1976	Luis Estaba w pts 15 Leo Palacios (Mex)	Caracas (Ven)
May 2, 1976	Luis Estaba w pts 15 Juan Alvarez (Mex)	Caracas (Ven)
Jul 17, 1976	Luis Estaba w ko 3 Franco Udella	Maracay (Ven)
Sep 26, 1976	Luis Estaba w rtd 10 Rodolfo Rodriguez (Arg)	Caracas (Ven)
Nov 21, 1976	Luis Estaba w rsf 10 Valentin Martinez (Mex)	Caracas (Ven)
May 15, 1977	Luis Estaba w pts 15 Rafael Pedroza (Pan)	Caracas (Ven)
Jul 17, 1977	Luis Estaba w pts 15 Ricardo Estupinan (Col)	Puerto la Cruz (Ven)
Aug 21, 1977	Luis Estaba w rsf 11 Juan Alvarez	Puerto la Cruz (Ven)
Sep 18, 1977	Luis Estaba w ko 15 Orlando Hernandez (CR)	Caracas (Ven)
Oct 30, 1977	Luis Estaba w pts 15 Netrnoi Vorasingh (Tha)	Caracas (Ven)
Feb 19, 1978	**Freddie Castillo** (Mex) w rsf 14 Luis Estaba	Caracas (Ven)
May 6, 1978	**Netrnoi Vorasingh** w pts 15 Freddie Castillo	Bangkok (Tha)
Jul 29, 1978	Netrnoi Vorasingh w rtd 5 Luis Estaba	Caracas (Ven)
Sep 30, 1978	**Sung-Jun Kim** (Kor) w ko 3 Netrnoi Vorasingh	Seoul (Kor)
Mar 31, 1979	Sung-Jun Kim drew 15 Hector Melendez (DR)	Seoul (Kor)
Jul 28, 1979	Sung-Jun Kim w pts 15 Stony Carupo (Phi)	Seoul (Kor)
Oct 21, 1979	Sung-Jun Kim w pts 15 Hector Melendez	Seoul (Kor)
Jan 3, 1980	**Shigeo Nakajima** (Jap) w pts 15 Sung-Jun Kim	Tokyo (Jap)
Mar 24, 1980	**Hilario Zapata** (Pan) w pts 15 Shigeo Nakajima	Tokyo (Jap)
Jun 7, 1980	Hilario Zapata w pts 15 Chi-Bok Kim (Kor)	Seoul (Kor)
Aug 4, 1980	Hilario Zapata w pts 15 Hector Melendez	Caracas (Ven)
Sep 17, 1980	Hilario Zapata w rsf 11 Shigeo Nakajima	Gifu (Jap)
Dec 1, 1980	Hilario Zapata w pts 15 Reynaldo Becerra (Ven)	Caracas (Ven)
Feb 8, 1981	Hilario Zapata w rsf 13 Joey Olivo (US)	Panama City (Pan)
Apr 24, 1981	Hilario Zapata w pts 15 Rudy Crawford (US)	San Francisco, CA
Aug 15, 1981	Hilario Zapata w pts 15 German Torres (Mex)	Panama City (Pan)
Nov 6, 1981	Hilario Zapata w rsf 10 Netrnoi Vorasingh	Korat (Tha)
Feb 6, 1982	**Amado Ursua** (Mex) w ko 2 Hilario Zapata	Panama City (Pan)
Apr 13, 1982	**Tadashi Tomori** (Jap) w pts 15 Amado Ursua	Tokyo (Jap)
Jul 20, 1982	**Hilario Zapata** w pts 15 Tadashi Tomori	Kanazawa (Jap)
Sep 18, 1982	Hilario Zapata w pts 15 Jung Koo Chang (Kor)	Chonju (Kor)
Mar 26, 1983	**Jung Koo Chang** w ko 3 Hilario Zapata	Daejon (Kor)
Jun 11, 1983	Jung Koo Chang w rsf 2 Masaharu Iha (Jap)	Taegu (Kor)
Sep 10, 1983	Jung Koo Chang w pts 12 German Torres	Daejon (Kor)
Mar 31, 1984	Jung Koo Chang w pts 15 Sot Chitalada (Tha)	Pusan (Kor)
Aug 18, 1984	Jung Koo Chang w rsf 9 Katsuo Tokashiki (Jap)	Sapporo (Jap)
Dec 15, 1984	Jung Koo Chang w pts 12 Tadashi Kuramochi (Jap)	Pusan (Kor)
Aug 3, 1985	Jung Koo Chang w pts 15 Francisco Montiel (Mex)	Seoul (Kor)
Nov 10, 1985	Jung Koo Chang w pts 12 Jorge Cano (Mex)	Daejon (Kor)
Apr 13, 1986	Jung Koo Chang w pts 12 German Torres	Kwangju (Kor)
Sep 13, 1986	Jung Koo Chang w pts 12 Francisco Montiel	Seoul (Kor)
Dec 14, 1986	Jung Koo Chang w rsf 5 Hideyuki Ohashi (Jap)	Inchon (Kor)
Apr 19, 1987	Jung Koo Chang w rsf 6 Efren Pinto (Mex)	Seoul (Kor)
Jun 28, 1987	Jung Koo Chang w rsf 10 Augustin Garcia (Col)	Seoul (Kor)
Dec 13, 1987	Jung Koo Chang w pts 12 Isidro Perez (Mex)	Seoul (Kor)
Jun 27, 1988	Jung Koo Chang w rsf 8 Hideyuki Ohashi	Tokyo (Jap)
Oct 1988	*Chang relinquished the title for health reasons*	
Dec 11, 1988	**German Torres** w pts 12 Soon-Jung Kang (Kor)	Seoul (Kor)
	For vacant title	
Mar 19, 1989	**Yul-Woo Lee** (Kor) w ko 9 German Torres	Taejon (Kor)
Jun 25, 1989	**Humberto Gonzalez** (Mex) w pts 12 Yul-Woo Lee	Seoul (Kor)
Dec 9, 1989	Humberto Gonzalez w pts 12 Jung Koo Chang	Seoul (Kor)
Mar 24, 1990	Humberto Gonzalez w ko 3 Francisco Tejedor (Col)	Mexico City (Mex)
Jun 4, 1990	Humberto Gonzalez w rsf 3 Luis Monzote (Cub)	Los Angeles, CA
Jul 24, 1990	Humberto Gonzalez w rsf 5 Jung-Keun Lim (Kor)	Los Angeles, CA
Aug 26, 1990	Humberto Gonzalez w ko 8 Jorge Rivera (Mex)	Cancun (Mex)
Dec 19, 1990	**Rolando Pascua** (Phi) w ko 6 Humberto Gonzalez	Inglewood, CA
Mar 25, 1991	**Melchor Cob Castro** (Mex) w rsf 10 Rolando Pascua	Inglewood, CA
Jun 3, 1991	Humberto Gonzalez w pts 12 Melchor Cob Castro	Las Vegas, NV
Jan 27, 1992	Humberto Gonzalez w pts 12 Domingo Sosa (DR)	Los Angeles, CA
Jun 7, 1992	Humberto Gonzalez w rsf 12 Kwang-Sun Kim (Kor)	Seoul (Kor)
Sep 14, 1992	Humberto Gonzalez w rsf 2 Napa Kiatwanchai (Tha)	Los Angeles, CA
Dec 7, 1992	Humberto Gonzalez w pts 12 Melchor Cob Castro	Los Angeles, CA
Mar 13, 1993	**Michael Carbajal** w ko 7 Humberto Gonzalez	Las Vegas, NV
	For WBC and IBF titles	

WBA title

Aug 23, 1975	**Jaime Rios** (Pan) w pts 15 Rigoberto Marcano (Ven)	Panama City (Pan)
	For vacant title	
Jan 3, 1976	Jaime Rios w pts 15 Kazunori Tenryu (Jap)	Kagoshima (Jap)
Jul 1, 1976	**Juan Guzman** (DR) w pts 15 Jaime Rios	Santo Domingo (DR)
Oct 10, 1976	**Yoko Gushiken** (Jap) w ko 7 Juan Guzman	Kofu (Jap)
Jan 30, 1977	Yoko Gushiken w pts 15 Jaime Rios	Tokyo (Jap)
May 22, 1977	Yoko Gushiken w pts 15 Rigoberto Marcano (Ven)	Sapporo (Jap)
Oct 9, 1977	Yoko Gushiken w rsf 4 Montsayarm Mahachai (Tha)	Oita (Jap)
Jan 29, 1978	Yoko Gushiken w rsf 14 Aniceto Vargas (Phi)	Nagoya (Jap)
May 7, 1978	Yoko Gushiken w rsf 13 Jaime Rios	Hiroshima (Jap)
Oct 15, 1978	Yoko Gushiken w ko 4 Sang-Il Chung (Kor)	Tokyo (Jap)
Jan 7, 1979	Yoko Gushiken w ko 7 Rigoberto Marcano	Kawasaki (Jap)
Apr 8, 1979	Yoko Gushiken w rsf 7 Alfonso Lopez (Pan)	Tokyo (Jap)
Jul 29, 1979	Yoko Gushiken w pts 15 Rafael Pedroza	Kitakyushi (Jap)
Oct 28, 1979	Yoko Gushiken w rsf 7 Tito Abella (Phi)	Tokyo (Jap)
Jan 27, 1980	Yoko Gushiken w pts 15 Yong-Hyun Kim (Kor)	Osaka (Jap)
Jun 1, 1980	Yoko Gushiken w rsf 8 Martin Vargas (Ch)	Kochi City (Jap)
Oct 12, 1980	Yoko Gushiken w pts 15 Pedro Flores (Mex)	Kanazawa (Jap)
Mar 8, 1981	**Pedro Flores** w rtd 12 Yoko Gushiken	Okinawa (Jap)
Jul 19, 1981	**Hwan-Jin Kim** (Kor) w rsf 13 Pedro Flores	Taegu (Kor)
Oct 11, 1981	Hwan-Jin Kim w pts 15 Alfonso Lopez	Daejon (Kor)
Dec 16, 1981	**Katsuo Tokashiki** (Jap) w pts 15 Hwan-Jin Kim	Sendai (Jap)
Apr 4, 1982	Katsuo Tokashiki w pts 15 Lupe Madera (Mex)	Sendai (Jap)
Jul 7, 1982	Katsuo Tokashiki w ko 8 Masahara Inami (Jap)	Tokyo (Jap)
Oct 10, 1982	Katsuo Tokashiki w pts 15 Sung-Nam Kim (Kor)	Tokyo (Jap)
Jan 9, 1983	Katsuo Tokashiki w pts 15 Hwan-Jin Kim	Kyoto (Jap)
Apr 10, 1983	Katsuo Tokashiki drew 15 Lupe Madera	Tokyo (Jap)
Jul 10, 1983	**Lupe Madera** w tech dec 4 Katsuo Tokashiki	Tokyo (Jap)
Oct 23, 1983	Lupe Madera w pts 12 Katsuo Tokashiki	Sapporo (Jap)
May 19, 1984	**Francisco Quiroz** (DR) w ko 9 Lupe Madera	Maracaibo (Ven)
Aug 18, 1984	Francisco Quiroz w ko 2 Victor Sierra (Pan)	Panama City (Pan)
Mar 29, 1985	**Joey Olivo** (US) w pts 15 Francisco Quiroz	Miami, FL
Jul 28, 1985	Joey Olivo w pts 15 Moon-Jin Choi (Kor)	Seoul (Kor)
Dec 8, 1985	**Myung-Woo Yuh** (Kor) w pts 15 Joey Olivo	Seoul (Kor)
Mar 9, 1986	Myung-Woo Yuh w pts 15 Jose De Jesus (PR)	Suwon (Kor)
Jun 14, 1986	Myung-Woo Yuh w rsf 12 Tomohiro Kiyuna (Jap)	Inchon (Kor)
Nov 30, 1986	Myung-Woo Yuh w pts 15 Mario de Marco (Arg)	Seoul (Kor)
Mar 1, 1987	Myung-Woo Yuh w rsf 1 Eduardo Tunon (Pan)	Seoul (Kor)
Jun 7, 1987	Myung-Woo Yuh w rsf 15 Benedicto Murillo (Pan)	Pusan (Kor)
Sep 20, 1987	Myung-Woo Yuh w ko 8 Rodolfo Blanco (Col)	Inchon (Kor)
Feb 7, 1988	Myung-Woo Yuh w pts 12 Wilibaldo Salazar (Mex)	Seoul (Kor)
Jun 12, 1988	Myung-Woo Yuh w pts 12 Jose De Jesus	Seoul (Kor)
Aug 28, 1988	Myung-Woo Yuh w ko 6 Putt Ohyuthanakorn (Tha)	Pusan (Kor)
Nov 6, 1988	Myung-Woo Yuh w ko 7 Bahar Udin (Indo)	Seoul (Kor)
Feb 12, 1989	Myung-Woo Yuh w rsf 10 Katsumi Komiyama (Jap)	Chongju (Kor)
Jun 11, 1989	Myung-Woo Yuh w pts 12 Mario de Marco	Seoul (Kor)

Sep 24,	1989	Myung-Woo Yuh w ko 11 Kenbun Taiho (Jap)	Suanbo (Kor)
Jan 14,	1990	Myung-Woo Yuh w rsf 7 Hitashi Takashima (Jap)	Seoul (Kor)
Apr 29,	1990	Myung-Woo Yuh w pts 12 Silvio Gamez (Ven)	Seoul (Kor)
Nov 10,	1990	Myung-Woo Yuh w pts 12 Silvio Gamez	Seoul (Kor)
Apr 28,	1991	Myung-Woo Yuh w rsf 10 Kajkong Danphoothai (Tha)	Masan (Kor)
Dec 17,	1991	**Hiroki Ioka** (Jap) w pts 12 Myung-Woo Yuh	Osaka (Jap)
Mar 31,	1992	Hiroki Ioka w pts 12 Noel Tunacao (Phi)	Osaka (Jap)
Jun 15,	1992	Hiroki Ioka w pts 12 Bong-Jun Kim (Kor)	Osaka (Jap)
Nov 18,	1992	**Myung-Woo Yuh** w pts 12 Hiroki Ioka	Osaka (Jap)
Jul 25,	1993	Myung-Woo Yuh w pts 12 Yuichi Hosono (Jap)	Seoul (Kor)
Sep	1993	*Yuh retired*	
Oct 21,	1993	**Leo Gamez** (Ven) w rsf 9 Shiro Yahiro (Jap)	Tokyo (Jap)
		For vacant title	
Feb 6,	1994	Leo Gamez w rsf 7 Juan Torres (Pan)	Panama City (Pan)
Jun 27,	1994	Leo Gamez drew 12 Kaj Ratchabandit (Tha)	Bangkok (Tha)
Oct 9,	1994	Leo Gamez w rsf 6 Pichitnoi Sithbangprachan (Tha)	Bangkok (Tha)
Feb 4,	1995	**Hiyong Choi** (Kor) w pts 12 Leo Gamez	Ulsan (Kor)
Feb 4,	1995	Hiyong Choi w pts 12 Keji Yamaguchu (Jap)	Osaka (Jap)
Jan 13,	1996	**Carlos Murillo** (Pan) w pts 12 Hiyong Choi	Miami, FL
Mar 15,	1996	Carlos Murillo w rsf 10 Jose Garcia Bernal (Col)	Panama City (Pan)
May 21,	1996	**Keiji Yamaguchi** (Jap) w pts 12 Carlos Murillo	Osaka (Jap)
Dec 3,	1996	**Pichitnoi Sithbangprachan** (Tha) w rsf 2 Keiji Yamaguchi	Osaka (Jap)
Jun 28,	1997	Pichitnoi Sithbangprachan w pts 12 Sang-Chul Lee (Kor)	Ratchaburi (Tha)
Mar 1,	1998	Pichitnoi Sithbangprachan w pts 12 Kaj Chartbandit (Tha)	Bangkok (Tha)
		Chartbandit also boxed as Hadao CP Gym	
Oct 17,	1998	Pichitnoi Sithbangprachan w rtd 8 Tae-Kil Lee (Kor)	Bangkok (Tha)
Feb 20,	1999	Pichitnoi Sithbangprachan w pts 12 Joma Gamboa (Phi)	Samui (Tha)
Feb 5,	2000	Pichitnoi Sithbangprachan w pts 12 Sang-il Yang (Kor)	Bangkok (Tha)
Jul	2000	*Pichitnoi stripped of title for failing to meet No.1 contender*	
Aug 12,	2000	**Beibis Mendoza** (Col) w dis 7 Rosendo Alvarez (Nic)	Las Vegas, NV
		For vacant title	
Mar 3,	2001	**Rosendo Alvarez** w pts 12 Beibis Mendoza	Las Vegas, NV
Jan 19,	2002	Rosendo Alvarez w rsf 12 Pichitnoi Sithbangprachan	Miami, FL
Mar 31	2003	Rosendo Alvarez w pts 12 Beibis Mendoza (Col)	Little Rock, AR

IBF title

Dec 10,	1983	**Dodie Penalosa** (Phi) w rsf 11 Satoshi Shingaki (Jap)	Osaka (Jap)
		For vacant title	
May 13,	1984	**Dodie Penalosa** w rsf 9 Jae-Hong Kim (Kor)	Seoul (Kor)
Nov 16,	1984	Dodie Penalosa w pts 15 Jum-Hwan Choi (Kor)	Manila (Phi)
Oct 12,	1985	Dodie Penalosa w ko 3 Yani "Hagler" Dokolamo (Indo)	Jakarta (Indo)
July	1986	*The IBF stripped Penalosa for challenging for the WBA flyweight title*	
Dec 7,	1986	**Jum-Hwan Choi** (Kor) w pts 15 Cho-Woon Park (Kor)	Pusan (Kor)
		For vacant title	
Mar 29,	1987	Jum-Hwan Choi w pts 15 Tacy Macalos (Phi)	Seoul (Kor)
Jul 5,	1987	Jum-Hwan Choi w rsf 4 Toshihiko Matsuta (Jap)	Seoul (Kor)
Aug 9,	1987	Jum-Hwan Choi w rsf 3 Azadin Anhar (Indo)	Jakarta (Indo)
Nov 5,	1988	**Tacy Macalos** w pts 12 Jum-Hwan Choi	Manila (Phi)
May 2,	1989	**Muangchai Kitkasem** (Tha) w pts 12 Tacy Macalos	Bangkok (Tha)
Oct 6,	1989	Muangchai Kitkasem w rsf 7 Tacy Macalos	Bangkok (Tha)
Jan 19,	1990	Muangchai Kitkasem w rsf 3 Chung-Jae Lee (Kor)	Bangkok (Tha)
Apr 10,	1990	Muangchai Kitkasem w pts 12 Abdy Pohan (Indo)	Bangkok (Tha)
Jul 29,	1990	**Michael Carbajal** (US) w rsf 7 Muangchai Kitkasem	Phoenix, AZ
Dec 8,	1990	Michael Carbajal w ko 4 Leon Salazar (Pan)	Scottsdale, AZ
Feb 17,	1991	Michael Carbajal w ko 2 Nacario Santos (Mex)	Las Vegas, NV
Mar 17,	1991	Michael Carbajal w pts 12 Javier Varquez (Mex)	Las Vegas, NV
May 10,	1991	Michael Carbajal w pts 12 Hector Patri (Arg)	Davenport, IA
Feb 15,	1992	Michael Carbajal w pts 12 Marcos Pancheco (Mex)	Phoenix, AZ
Dec 12,	1992	Michael Carbajal w rsf 8 Robinson Cuestas (Pan)	Phoenix, AZ
Mar 13,	1993	Michael Carbajal w ko 7 Humberto Gonzalez	Las Vegas, NV
		For WBC and IBF titles	

IBF/WBC titles

Jul 17,	1993	**Michael Carbajal** w ko 7 Kwang-Sun Kim	Las Vegas, NV
Oct 30,	1993	Michael Carbajal w rsf 5 Domingo Sosa (DR)	Phoenix, AZ
Feb 19,	1994	**Humberto Gonzalez** w pts 12 Michael Carbajal	Inglewood, CA
Sep 10,	1994	Humberto Gonzalez w rtd 7 Juan Cordoba (Arg)	Lake Tahoe, CA
Nov 12,	1994	Humberto Gonzalez w pts 12 Michael Carbajal	Mexico City (Mex)
Mar 31,	1995	Humberto Gonzalez w ko 5 Jesus Zuniga (Col)	Anaheim, CA
Jul 15,	1995	**Saman Sorjaturong** (Tha) w rsf 7 Humberto Gonzalez	Inglewood, CA
Nov 12,	1995	Saman Sorjaturong w ko 4 Yuichi Hosono (Jap)	Ratchaburi (Tha)
Jan	1996	*Sorjaturong relinquished the IBF version*	

WBO title

May 19,	1989	**Jose de Jesus** (PR) w rsf 9 Fernando Martinez (Mex)	San Juan, CA
		For vacant title	
Oct 21,	1989	Jose de Jesus w pts 12 Isidro Perez (Mex)	San Juan, CA
May 6,	1990	Jose de Jesus w ko 5 Alli Galvez (Ch)	Talcahuano (Ch)
Nov 10,	1990	Jose de Jesus w rsf 7 Abdy Pohan	Medan (Indo)
May	1992	*De Jesus stripped of the title for failure to defend it*	
Jul 31,	1992	**Josue Camacho** (PR) w ko 6 Eduardo Vallejo (Mex)	San Juan, CA
		For vacant title	
Feb 2,	1994	Josue Camacho w pts 12 Paul Weir (Sco)	Glasgow (Sco)
Jul 15,	1994	**Michael Carbajal** w pts 12 Josue Camacho	Phoenix, AZ
Oct	1994	*Carbajal vacated the title to challenge for the IBF/WBC championships*	
Nov 23,	1994	**Paul Weir** w pts 12 Paul Oulden (SA)	Irvine, CA
		For vacant title	
Apr 5,	1995	Paul Weir w pts 12 Ric Magramo (Phi)	Irvine, CA
Jul 15,	1995	**Jake Matlala** (SA) w tech dec 5 Paul Weir	Glasgow (Sco)
Apr 13,	1996	Jake Matlala w rsf 10 Paul Weir	Liverpool (Eng)
Feb 8,	1997	Jake Matlala w pts 12 Mickey Cantwell (Eng)	Millwall (Eng)
May	1997	*Matlala relinquished title when denied a defence against Michael Carbajal*	
May 31,	1997	**Jesus Chong** (Mex) w rsf 2 Eric Griffin (US)	Las Vegas, NV
		For vacant title	
Aug 25,	1997	**Melchor Cob Castro (Mex)** w pts 12 Jesus Chong	Los Angeles, CA
Jan 17,	1998	**Juan Cordoba** w pts 12 Melchor Cob Castro	Santiago del Estero (Arg)
May 9,	1998	Juan Cordoba w pts 12 Sandro Oviedo (Arg)	Santiago del Estero (Arg)
Dec 5,	1998	**Jorge Arce** (Mex) w pts 12 Juan Cordoba	Tijuana (Mex)
Apr 17,	1999	Jorge Arce w rsf 6 Salvatore Fanni (Ita)	Sassari (Ita)
Jul 31,	1999	**Michael Carbajal** w rsf 11 Jorge Arce	Tijuana (Mex)
Jan	2000	*Carbajal retired*	
Feb 19,	2000	**Hawk Makepula** (SA) w pts 12 Jacob Matlala (SA)	Brakpan (SA)
Mar	2000	*For vacant title after Makepula relinquished it for business reasons*	
Jul 22,	2000	**Will Grigsby** w pts 12 Nelson Dieppa (PR)	Miami, FL
Oct	2000	*For vacant title. Grigsby stripped of title for failing dope test*	
Feb 3,	2001	Andy Tabanas (Phi) drew 12 Fahlan Sakkiren (Tha)	Las Vegas, NV
		For vacant title	
Apr 14,	2001	**Nelson Dieppa** (PR) w rsf 11 Andy Tabanas	New York, NY
Sep 29,	2001	Nelson Dieppa w pts 12 Fahlan Sakkiren	New York, NY
Aug 24,	2002	Nelson Dieppa tdraw 2 John Molina (Col)	Carolina, PR
Mar 20,	2004	Nelson Dieppa w ko 1 Kermin Guardia (Col)	Guaynabo (PR)
Jul 30,	2004	Nelson Dieppa w pts 12 Ulises Solis (Mex)	Louisville, KN
Jan 29,	2005	Nelson Dieppa w ko 11 Alex Sanchez (PR)	Bayamon (PR)
Apr 30,	2005	**Hugo Cazares** (Mex) w tdec 10 Nelson Dieppa	Hato Rey (PR)
Aug 20,	2005	Hugo Cazares w rsf 8 Alex Sanchez	Ponce (PR)
Oct 29,	2005	Hugo Cazares w ko 6 Kaichon Sorvorapin (Tha)	Tucson, AZ
Jun 30,	2006	Hugo Cazares w ko 1 Domingo Guillen (DR)	Tucson, AZ
Sep 30,	2006	Hugo Cazares w rsf 10 Nelson Dieppa	Caguas (PR)
May 4,	2007	Hugo Cazares w rsf 2 Wilfrido Valdez (Col)	Las Vegas, NV
Aug 25,	2007	**Ivan Calderon** (PR) w pts 12 Hugo Cazares	Bayamon (PR)
Dec 1,	2007	Ivan Calderon w pts 12 Juan Esquer (Mex)	Albuquerque, NM
Apr 5,	2008	Ivan Calderon w pts 12 Nelson Dieppa	San Juan (PR)
Aug 30,	2008	Ivan Calderon w tdec 7 Hugo Cazares	Bayamon (PR)
Jun 13,	2009	Ivan Calderon t.draw 6 Rodel Mayol	New York, NY
Sep 12,	2009	Ivan Calderon w tdec 7 Rodel Mayol	Hato Rey (PR)
		The WBO also sanctioned an Interim title fight:	
Dec 19,	2009	**Johnriel Casimero** (Phi) w rsf 11 Cesar Canchila	Managua (Nic)
Jun 12,	2010	Ivan Calderon w pts 12 Jesus Iribe (Mex)	New York, NY
		WBA super champion Giovani Segura took the WBO belt from Ivan Calderon in a unification match	
		The WBO sanctioned the following for the Interim title	
Jul 24,	2010	Ramon Garcia Hirales w pts 12 John Riel Casimero	Los Mochis (Mex)
Sep 25,	2010	Ramon Garcia Hirales w pts 12 Manuel Vargas (Mex)	Tijuana (Mex)
Oct 30,	2010	Jesus Geles w pts 12 Omar Soto	Cartagena (Col)
Dec 18,	2010	Ramon Garcia Hirales w pts 12 Omar Soto	Campeche (Mex)
Feb 5,	2011	Jesus Geles w pts 12 Ramon Garcia Hirales	Cartagena (Col)
Apr 2,	2011	Giovani Segura w ko 3 Ivan Calderon	Mexicali (Mex)
		Segura vacated and Interim champion Jesus Geles was upgraded to full champion	
Apr 30,	2011	**Ramon Garcia Hirales** (Mex) w ko 4 Jesus Geles (Col)	Mexico City (Mex)
Oct 8,	2011	**Donnie Nietes** (Phil) w pts 12 Ramon Garcia Hirales	Bacolod City (Phil)
Jun 2,	2012	Donnie Nietes w pts 12 Felipe Salguero (Mex)	Pasay City (Phil)
Mar 2,	2013	Donnie Nietes drew 12 Moises Fuentes (Mex)	Cebu (Phi)
		The WBO sanctioned the following for the Interim title	
Sep 7,	2013	Moises Fuentes w rsf 1 Luis De la Rosa (Mex)	Tapachula (Mex)
		For WBO title	
Nov 30,	2013	Donnie Nietes w rsf 3 Sammy Gutierrez (Mex)	Quezon City (Phi)
May 10,	2014	Donnie Nietes w ko 9 Moises Fuentes	Pasay City (Phi)
Nov 15,	2014	Donnie Nietes w rtd 7 Carlos Velarde (Mex)	Cebu City (Phi)
Mar 28,	2015	Donnie Nietes w rtd 9 Gilberto Parra (Mex)	Quezon City (Phi)
Jul 11,	2015	Donnie Nietes w pts 8 Francisco Rodriguez Jr (Mex)	Cebu City (Phi)
Oct 17,	2015	Donnie Nietes w pts 12 Juan Alejo (Mex)	Carson, CA
May 28,	2016	Donnie Nietes w rtd 5 Raul Garcia (Mex)	Bacolod City (Phi)
Dec 31,	2016	**Kosei Tanaka (Jap)** w rsf 5 Moises Fuentes (Mex)	Gifu (Jap)
		For vacant WBO title	
May 20,	2017	Kosei Tanaka w pts 12 Angel Acosta (PR)	Nagoya (Jap)

Sep 13, 2017	Kosei Tanaka w rsf 9 Rangsan Chayanram (Tha)	Osaka (Jap)
Dec 2, 2017	Kosei Tanaka w ko 10 Juan Alejo	New York, NY

IBF title

Jan 1996	*Sorjaturong relinquished the IBF version*	
Mar 16, 1996	**Michael Carbajal** w pts 12 Melchor Cob Castro	Las Vegas, NV
	For vacant title	
Sep 13, 1996	Michael Carbajal w rsf 8 Julio Coronel (Col)	Des Moines, IA
Oct 12, 1996	Michael Carbajal w ko 5 Tomas Rivera (Mex)	Anaheim, CA
Jan 18, 1997	**Mauricio Pastrana** (Col) w pts 12 Michael Carbajal	Las Vegas, NV
May 1997	*Pastrana stripped for failing to make weight for defence against Manuel Herrera*	
Aug 30, 1997	Manuel Herrera (DR) tdraw 9 Anis Roga (Indo)	Surabaya (Indo)
Dec 13, 1997	**Mauricio Pastrana** w ko 3 Manuel Herrera	Pompano Beach, FL
	For vacant title	
Apr 30, 1998	Mauricio Pastrana w ko 4 Anis Roga	Fort Lauderdale, FL
Aug 29, 1998	*Pastrana stripped for failing to make weight for defence against Carlos Murillo*	
Dec 16, 1998	**Will Grigsby** (US) w pts 12 Ratanopol Sorvoraphin (Tha)	Fort Lauderdale, FL
	For vacant title	
Mar 6, 1999	Will Grigsby w pts 12 Carmelo Caceres (Phi)	St Paul, MN
Oct 2, 1999	**Ricardo Lopez** (Mex) w pts 12 Will Grigsby	Las Vegas, NV
Dec 2, 2000	Ricardo Lopez w rsf 3 Ratanapol Sorvoraphin (Tha)	Las Vegas, NV
Sep 29, 2001	Ricardo Lopez w ko 8 Zolani Petelo (SA)	New York, NY
Nov 2002	*Ricardo Lopez announced his retirement*	

WBC title

Feb 24, 1996	Saman Sorjaturong w rsf 4 Antonio Perez (Mex)	Chachengsao (Tha)
Apr 27, 1996	Saman Sorjaturong w rsf 7 Joma Gamboa (Phi)	Maha Sarakham (Tha)
Aug 10, 1996	Saman Sorjaturong w rsf 9 Shiro Yahiro (Jap)	Phitsanulok (Tha)
Oct 19, 1996	Saman Sorjaturong w ko 2 Ali Galvez (Chi)	Samut Prakhan (Tha)
Dec 14, 1996	Saman Sorjaturong w pts 12 Manuel Herrera (DR)	Chiang Rai (Tha)
Apr 13, 1997	Saman Sorjaturong w rsf 7 Julio Coronel (Col)	Chaiyaphum (Tha)
May 31, 1997	Saman Sorjaturong w rsf 4 Mzukisi Marali (SA)	Petchabun (Tha)
Mar 8, 1998	Saman Sorjaturong w rsf 4 Shiro Yahiro	Yokohama (Jap)
Nov 26, 1998	Saman Sorjaturong w pts 12 Ladislao Vazquez (Mex)	Pathum Thani (Tha)
Oct 17, 1999	**Yo-sam Choi** (Kor) w pts 12 Saman Sorjaturong	Seoul (Kor)
Jun 17, 2000	Yo-sam Choi w ko 5 Chart Kiatpetch (Tha)	Seoul (Kor)
Jan 30, 2001	Yo-sam Choi w ko 7 Saman Sorjatorung	Seoul (Kor)
Feb 23, 2002	Yo-sam Choi w rsf 10 Shingo Yamaguchi (Jap)	Chiba (Jap)
Jul 6, 2002	**Jorge Arce** (Mex) w rsf 6 Yo-sam Choi	Seoul (Kor)
Nov 16, 2002	Jorge Arce w rsf 3 Agustin Luna (Mex)	Las Vegas, NV
Feb 22, 2003	Jorge Arce w ko 1 Ernesto Castro (Nic)	Mexico City (Mex)
May 3, 2003	Jorge Arce w tdec 6 Melchor Cob Castro (Mex)	Las Vegas, NV
Jan 10, 2004	Jorge Arce w ko 2 Joma Gambon (Phi)	Mexico City (Mex)
Apr 24, 2004	Jorge Arce w rsf 5 Melchor Cob Castro	Tuxtla Gutierrez (Mex)
Sep 4, 2004	Jorge Arce w pts 12 Juanito Rubillar (Phi)	Tijuana (Mex)
Dec 18, 2004	Jorge Arce w rsf 3 Juan Francisco Cesteno Roque (Nic)	Culiacan (Mex)
	Arce relinquished title to box at flyweight	
Mar 11, 2005	**Eric Ortiz** (Mex) w rsf 7 Jose Antonio Aguirre (Mex)	Mexico City (Mex)
	For vacant title	
Sep 10, 2005	**Brian Viloria** (Haw) w ko 1 Eric Ortiz	Los Angeles, CA
Feb 18, 2006	Brian Viloria w pts 12 Jose Antonio Aguirre	Las Vegas, NV
Aug 10, 2006	**Omar Nino** (Mex) w pts 12 Brian Viloria	Las Vegas, NV
Nov 18, 2006	Omar Nino nd 12 Brian Viloria	Las Vegas, NV
	Nino tested positive for a banned substance and was stripped of the title	
Apr 14, 2007	**Edgar Sosa** (Mex) w pts 12 Brian Viloria	San Antonio, TX
	For vacant title	
Jul 28, 2007	Edgar Sosa w dis 10 Luis Alberto Lazarte (Arg)	Cancun (Mex)
Sep 16, 2007	Edgar Sosa w rsf 9 Lorenzo Trejo (Mex)	Las Vegas, NV
Nov 24, 2007	Edgar Sosa w rsf 4 Roberto Leyva (Mex)	Veracruz (Mex)
Feb 9, 2008	Edgar Sosa w pts 12 Jesus Iribe (Mex)	Leon (Mex)
Jun 14, 2008	Edgar Sosa w rsf 8 Takashi Kunishige (Jap)	Mexico City (Mex)
Sep 27, 2008	Edgar Sosa w pts 12 Sonny Boy Jaro (Phi)	Mexico City (Mex)
Nov 29, 2008	Edgar Sosa w rsf 7 Juanito Rubillar (Phi)	Mexico City (Mex)
Apr 4, 2009	Edgar Sosa w rsf 4 Pornsawan Porpramook (Tha)	Tamaulipas (Mex)
Jun 20, 2009	Edgar Sosa w rsf 5 Carlos Melo (Pan)	Mexico City (Mex)
Sep 15, 2009	Edgar Sosa w rsf 6 Omar Soto (PR)	Puebla (Mex)
Nov 21, 2009	**Rodel Mayol** (Phi) w rsf 2 Edgar Sosa	Tuxtla Gutierrez (Mex)
Feb 27, 2010	Rodel Mayol tdraw 3 Omar Nino Romero (Mex)	Guadalajara (Mex)
Jun 9, 2010	**Omar Nino Romero** w pts 12 Rodel Mayol	San Juan del Rio (Mex)
Sep 4, 2010	Omar Nino Romero w rtd 7 Ronald Barrera (Col)	Guadalajara (Mex)
Nov 6, 2010	**Gilberto Keb Baas** (Mex) w pts 12 Omar Nino Romero	Merida (Mex)
Feb 26, 2011	Gilberto Keb Baas w rtd 9 Jose Antonio Aguirre (Mex)	Merida (Mex)
Apr 30, 2011	**Adrian Hernandez** (Mex) w rtd 11 Gilberto Keb Baas	Texcoco (Mex)
Sep 24, 2011	Adrian Hernandez w ko 2 Gideon Buthelezi (SA)	Mexico City (Mex)
Dec 23, 2011	**Kompayak Porpramook** (Thai) w ko 10 Adrian Hernandez	Bangkok (Thai)
May 3, 2012	Kompayak Porpramook w tdec 5 Adrian Taconing (Phil)	Buriram (Thai)
Oct 6, 2012	**Adrian Hernandez** w ko 6 Kompayak Porpramook	Toluca (Mex)
Jan 12, 2013	Adrian Hernandez w pts 12 Dirceu Cabarca (Pan)	Toluca (Mex)
May 11, 2013	Adrian Hernandez w pts 12 Yader Cardoza (Nic)	Toluca (Mex)
Aug 31, 2013	Adrian Hernandez w rsf 4 Atsushi Katutani (Jap)	Mexico City (Mex)
Apr 6, 2014	**Naoya Inoue** (Jap) w rsf 6 Adrian Hernandez	Tokyo (Jap)
Sep 5, 2014	Naoya Inoue w rsc 11 Samartlek Kokietgym (Thai)	Tokyo (Jap)
	Naoya Inoue vacated to box at super-flyweight	
Dec 30, 2014	**Pedro Guevara** (Mex) w ko 7 Akira Yaegashi (Jap)	Tokyo (Jap)
	For vacant title	
Apr 11, 2015	Pedro Guevara w rsf 1 Richard Claveras (Phi)	Mazatlan (Mex)
Jul 4, 2015	Pedro Guevara w pts 12 Ganigan Lopez (Mex)	Mazatlan (Mex)
Nov 28, 2015	**Yu Kimura (Jap)** w pts 12 Pedro Guevara	Sendai (Jap)
Mar 4, 2016	**Ganigan Lopez** w pts 12 Yu Kimura	Kyoto (Jap)
Jul 2, 2016	Ganigan Lopez w pts 12 Jonathan Taconing (Phi)	Mexico City (Mex)
May 20, 2017	**Ken Shiro (Jap)** w pts 12 Ganigan Lopez	Tokyo (Jap)
Oct 22, 2017	Ken Shiro w pts 12 Pedro Guevara	Tokyo (Jap)
Dec 30, 2017	Ken Shiro w rsf 4 Gilberto Pedroza (Pan)	Yokohama (Jap)

WBA/IBF title

Dec 13, 2003	Rosendo Alvarez drew 12 Victor Burgos (Mex)	Atlantic City, NJ
	A WBA/IBF unification bout	

WBA title

	Rosendo Alvarez relinquished title in 2005 because of weight problems	
Apr 29, 2005	**Roberto Vasquez** (Pan) w ko 10 Beibis Mendoza (Col)	Panama City (Pan)
	For vacant title	
Aug 20, 2005	Roberto Vasquez w rsf 4 Jose Antonio Aguirre (Mex)	Panama City (Pan)
Nov 19, 2005	Roberto Vasquez w pts 12 Nerys Espinoza (Nic)	Panama City (Pan)
May 20, 2006	Roberto Vasquez w pts 12 Noel Arambulet (Ven)	Panama City (Pan)
	Vasquez relinquished title to box at flyweight	
Aug 2, 2006	**Koki Kameda** (Jap) w pts 12 Juan Jose Landaerta (Ven)	Yokohama (Jap)
	For vacant title	
Dec 20, 2006	Koki Kameda w pts 12 Juan Jose Landaerta	Tokyo (Jap)
	Koki Kameda relinquished title because of weight-making difficulties	
Jun 22, 2007	**Juan Carlos Reveco** (Arg) w ko 8 Nethra Sasiprapa (Tha)	Las Heras (Arg)
	For vacant title	
Oct 13, 2007	Juan Carlos Reveco w ko 5 Humberto Pool (Mex)	Buenos Aires (Arg)
Dec 8, 2007	**Brahim Asloum** (Fra) w pts 12 Juan Carlos Reveco	Le Cannet (Fra)
	In July 2008, the WBA proclaimed Asloum Champion In Recess. He was inactive, he said, because of a dispute with a French television station over coverage of his fights. Asloum announced his retirement in 2009	
Jul 26, 2008	**Cesar Canchila** (Col) w pts 12 Giovanni Segura (Mex)	Las Vegas, NV
	For vacant title	
Mar 14, 2009	**Giovani Segura** w rsf 4 Cesar Canchila	Mexicali (Mex)
Jul 25, 2009	Giovani Segura w rsf 6 Juanito Rubillar	Nuevo Vallarta (Mex)
Nov 21, 2009	Giovani Segura w ko 1 Sonny Boy Jaro	Merida (Mex)
	The WBA also sanctioned the following Interim fights:	
Aug 15, 2009	Juan Carlos Reveco w pts 12 Francisco Rosas (Mex)	Cozumel (Mex)
Dec 18, 2009	Juan Carlos Reveco w ko 3 Ronald Barrera (Col)	Junin (Arg)
Feb 20, 2010	Giovani Segura w rsf 3 Walter Tello (Pan)	Acapulco (Mex)
	Roman Gonzalez upgraded from Interim champion to full champion in February 2011 with Giovani Segura the Super champion after his win over WBO champion Ivan Calderon in their unification match	
Mar 19, 2011	**Roman Gonzalez** (Nic) w pts 12 Manuel Vargas (Mex)	San Pedro Cholula (Mex)
Jul 17, 2011	Roman Gonzalez w rsf 7 Omar Salado (Mex)	Cancun (Mex)
Oct 1, 2011	Roman Gonzalez w ko 2 Omar Soto (Mex)	Las Vegas, NV
Nov 17, 2011	Roman Gonzalez w pts 12 Juan Francisco Estrada (Mex)	Los Angeles, CA
Apr 28, 2012	Roman Gonzalez w ko 4 Ramon Garcia Hirales (Mex)	Pomona, CA
Nov 17, 2012	Roman Gonzalez w pts 12 Juan Francisco Estrada	Los Angeles, CA
	Gonzalez upgraded to Super champion	
Dec 31, 2012	**Kazuto Ioka** (Jap) w rsf 6 Jose Alfredo Rodriguez	Osaka (Jap)
May 8, 2013	Kazuto Ioka w ko 9 Wisanu Kokietgym (Thai)	Osaka (Jap)
Sep 11, 2013	Kazuto Ioka w ko 7 Kwanthai Sithmorseng (Thai)	Osaka (Jap)
Dec 31, 2013	Kazuto Ioka w pts 12 Felix Alvarado (Nic)	Osaka (Jap)
	The WBA sanctioned the following for their Interim title	
Jul 17, 2010	Juan Carlos Reveco w rsf 5 Armando Torres (Mex)	Las Heras (Arg)
Oct 24, 2010	Roman Gonzalez w ko 2 Francisco Rosas (Mex)	Tokyo (Jap)
Nov 19, 2011	Jose Alfredo Rodriguez w pts 12 Nethra Sasiprapa (Thai)	Mazatlan (Mex)
Apr 14, 2012	Alberto Rossel (Peru) w pts 12 Jose Alfredo Rodriguez	Lima (Peru)
Aug 18, 2012	Alberto Rossel w pts 12 Karluis Diaz (Col)	Callao (Peru)
Mar 16, 2013	Alberto Rossel w pts 12 Walter Tello (Pan)	Callao (Peru)
Sep 28, 2013	Alberto Rossel w pts 12 Jose Alfredo Zuniga (Mex)	Lima (Peru)
	Kazuto Ioka vacated. Alberto Rossel upgraded to full champion	
Dec 31, 2014	**Ryoichi Taguchi** (Jap) w pts 12 Alberto Rossel (Peru)	Tokyo (Jap)
	The WBA sanctioned the following for their Interim title	
Apr 24, 2015	Randy Petalcorin (Phi) w rsf 1 Ma Yi Ming (Chi)	Beijing (Chi)
May 6, 2015	Ryoichi Taguchi w rsc 8 Kwanthai Sithmorseng w rsc 8	Tokyo (Jap)
Dec 12, 2015	Ryoichi Taguchi w rtd 9 Luis de la Rosa (Col)	Tokyo (Jap)

Apr 27, 2016 Ryoichi Taguchi w rtd 11 Juan Jose Landaeta (Ven) .... Tokyo (Jap)
Aug 31, 2016 Ryoichi Taguchi w pts 12 Ryo Miyazaki (Jap) .... Tokyo (Jap)
Dec 31, 2016 Ryoichi Taguchi drew 12 Carlos Canizales (Ven) .... Tokyo (Jap)
Jul 23, 2017 Ryoichi Taguchi w rsf 9 Robert Barrera (Col) .... Tokyo (Jap)

WBO/WBA super titles

Aug 28, 2010 Giovani Segura w ko 8 Ivan Calderon .... Guaynabo (PR)

IBF title

Feb 15, 2003 Victor Burgos w rsf 12 Alex Sanchez (PR) .... Las Vegas, NV
May 15, 2004 Victor Burgos w rsf 6 Fahlan Sakkreerin (Tha) .... Las Vegas, NV
May 14, 2005 **Will Grigsby** (US) w pts 12 Victor Burgos .... Las Vegas, NV
Jan 7, 2006 **Ulises Solis** (Mex) w pts 12 Will Grigsby .... New York, NY
Mar 25, 2006 Ulises Solis w rsf 9 Eric Ortiz (Mex) .... Guadalajara (Mex)
Aug 4, 2006 Ulises Solis drew 12 Omar Salado (Mex) .... Tijuana (Mex)
Jan 25, 2007 Ulises Solis w rtd 8 Will Grigsby .... Las Vegas, NV
May 19, 2007 Ulises Solis w rsf 9 Jose Antonio Aguirre (Mex) .... Guadalajara (Mex)
Aug 4, 2007 Ulises Solis w rsf 8 Rodel Mayol (Phi) .... Rosemont, IL
Dec 15, 2007 Ulises Solis w rsf 9 Bert Batawang (Phi) .... Guadalajara (Mex)
Jul 12, 2008 Ulises Solis w pts 12 Glenn Donaire .... Hermosillo (Mex)
Nov 2, 2008 Ulises Solis w pts 12 Nerys Espinoza (Nic) .... Aguascalientes (Mex)
Apr 19, 2009 **Brian Viloria** (Haw) w ko 11 Ulises Solis .... Quezon City (Phi)
Aug 29, 2009 Brian Viloria w pts 12 Jesus Iribe (Mex) .... Honolulu (Haw)
Jan 23, 2010 **Carlos Tamara** (Col) w rsf 12 Brian Viloria .... Pasay City (Phi)
May 29, 2010 **Luis Alberto Lazarte** (Arg) w pts 12 Carlos Tamara .... Buenos Aires (Arg)
Sep 4, 2010 Luis Alberto Lazarte w pts 12 Nerys Espinoza (Nic) .... Buenos Aires (Arg)
Dec 18, 2010 Luis Alberto Lazarte drew 12 Ulises Solis (Mex) .... Buenos Aires (Arg)
Apr 30, 2011 **Ulises Solis** w pts 12 Luis Alberto Lazarte .... Buenos Aires (Arg)
Aug 27, 2011 Ulises Solis w pts 12 Jether Oliva (Phil) .... Guadalajara (Mex)
Solis was stripped of the title in July 2012 and John Riel Casimero upgraded from Interim to full champion
Aug 4, 2012 **John Riel Casimero** w pts 12 Pedro Guevara (Mex) .... Mazatlan (Mex)
The IBF sanctioned the following for the Interim title
Feb 10, 2012 John Riel Casimero w rsf 10 Luis Alberto Lazarte .... Buenos Aires (Arg)
Mar 16, 2013 John Riel Casimero w pts 12 Luis Alberto Rios (Pan) .... Panama City (Pan)
Oct 26, 2013 John Riel Casimero w rsf 11 Felipe Salguero .... Makati City (Phi)
May 3, 2014 John Riel Casimero w ko 1 Mauricio Fuentes (Col) .... Cebu City (Phi)
Caismero weighed in heavy, so title only at stake for Fuentes
Sep 20, 2014 **Javier Mendoza** (Mex) w pts 12 Ramon Garcia Hirales (Mex) .... Tijuana (Mex)
For vacant title
May 30, 2015 Javier Mendoza w tech pts 5 Milan Melindo (Phi) .... Ensenada (Mex)
Dec 29, 2015 **Akira Yaegashi (Jap)** w pts 12 Javier Mendoza .... Tokyo (Jap)
May 8, 2016 Akira Yaegashi w pts 12 Martin Tecuapetia (Mex) .... Tokyo (Jap)
IBF sanctioned the following fight for the interim title
Nov 26, 2016 Milan Melindo (Phi) w pts 12 Teeraphong Utaida (Tha) .... Cebu City (Phi)
Dec 30, 2016 Akira Yaegashi w rsf 12 Wittawas Basapean (Tha) .... Tokyo (Jap)
For IBF title
May 21, 2017 **Milan Melindo** w rsf 1 Akira Yaegashi .... Tokyo (Jap)
Sep 16, 2017 Milan Melindo w pts 12 Hekkie Budler (SA) .... Cebu City (Phi)

IBF/WBA Super titles

Dec 31, 2017 **Ryoichi Taguchi (Jap)** w pts 12 Milan Melindo (Phi) .... Tokyo (Jap)

RYOICHI TAGUCHI *proved too strong for the Philippine's Milan Melindo when they fought for the IBF and WBA Super light-flyweight titles in Tokyo in December 2017, winning on points*

Minimumweight

The IBF were first off the mark with the minimumweight division, which is also known as the mini-flyweight (weight limit 105lb). They crowned their inaugural champion in June 1987, and within six months there were rival champions from the WBC and WBA. The division has proved especially popular in the Orient, although the only truly outstanding champion so far produced has been the Mexican Ricardo Lopez.

World Minimumweight Championship Bouts

IBF title

Jun 14,	1987	**Kyung-Yun Lee** (Kor) w ko 2 Masaharu Kawakami (Jap)	Bujok (Kor)
Lee vacated IBF title in December 1987 to challenge for the WBC version			
Mar 24,	1988	**Samuth Sithnaruepol** (Tha) w rsf 11 Domingo Lucas (Phi). *For vacant title*	Bangkok (Tha)
Aug 29,	1988	Samuth Sithanruepol w pts 15 In-Kyu Hwang (Kor)	Bangkok (Tha)
Mar 23,	1989	Samuth Sithanruepol drew 12 Nico Thomas (Indo)	Jakarta (Indo)
Jun 17,	1989	**Nico Thomas** w pts 12 Samuth Sithanruepol	Jakarta (Indo)
Sep 21,	1989	**Eric Chavez** (Phi) w ko 5 Nico Thomas	Jakarta (Indo)
Feb 22,	1990	**Fahlan Lukmingkwan** (Tha) w rsf 7 Eric Chavez	Bangkok (Tha)
Jun 14,	1990	Fahlan Lukmingkwan w pts 12 Joe Constantino (Phi)	Bangkok (Tha)
Aug 15,	1990	Fahlan Lukmingkwan w pts 12 Eric Chavez	Bangkok (Tha)
Dec 20,	1990	Fahlan Lukmingkwan drew 12 Domingo Lucas	Bangkok (Tha)
Jul 2,	1991	Fahlan Lukmingkwan w pts 12 Abdy Pohan (Indo)	Bangkok (Tha)
Oct 21,	1991	Fahlan Lukmingkwan w pts 12 Andy Tabanas (Phi)	Bangkok (Tha)
Feb 23,	1992	Fahlan Lukmingkwan w ko 2 Felix Naranjo (Col)	Bangkok (Tha)
Jun 14,	1992	Fahlan Lukmingkwan w rsf 8 Said Iskander (Indo)	Bangkok (Tha)
Sep 6,	1992	**Manny Melchor** (Phi) w pts 12 Fahlan Lukmingkwan	Bangkok (Tha)
Dec 10,	1992	**Ratanapol Sorvoraphin** (Tha) w pts 12 Manny Melchor. *Sorvoraphin also boxed as Ratanal (Ratanapol) Dutchboygym*	Bangkok (Tha)
Mar 14,	1993	Ratanapol Sorvoraphin w rsf 7 Nico Thomas	Nakhon (Tha)
Jun 27,	1993	Ratanapol Sorvoraphin w rtd 7 Ala Villamor (Phi)	Bangkok (Tha)
Sep 26,	1993	Ratanapol Sorvoraphin w rsf 4 Dominguez Siwalette (Indo)	Bangkok (Tha)
Dec 10,	1993	Ratanapol Sorvoraphin w rsf 2 Felix Naranjo (Col)	Suphan Buri (Tha)
Feb 27,	1994	Ratanapol Sorvoraphin w pts 12 Ronnie Magrama (Phi)	Bangkok (Tha)
May 14,	1994	Ratanapol Sorvoraphin w rsf 6 Roger Espanola (Phi)	Bangkok (Tha)
Aug 13,	1994	Ratanapol Sorvoraphin w rsf 4 Marcelino Bolivar (Ven)	Buriram (Tha)
Nov 12,	1994	Ratanapol Sorvoraphin w ko 3 Carlos Rodriguez (Ven)	Khon Kaen (Tha)
Feb 25,	1995	Ratanapol Sorvoraphin w rsf 3 Jerry Pahayahay (Phi)	Bangkok (Tha)
May 20,	1995	Ratanapol Sorvoraphin w rsf 2 Oscar Flores (Col)	Chiang Mai (Tha)
Oct 29,	1995	Ratanapol Sorvoraphin w ko 2 Jack Russell (Aus)	Suphan Buri (Tha)
Dec 30,	1995	Ratanapol Sorvoraphin w rsf 6 Osvaldo Guerrero (Mex)	Bangkok (Tha)
Mar	1986	*IBF stripped Sorvoraphin for failing to make the weight for a defence against Lee Castillo, but they allowed him to fight for the title immediately*	
May 18,	1996	**Ratanapol Sorvoraphin** w pts 12 Jun Arlos (Phi)	Yala (Tha)
Jul 13,	1996	Ratanapol Sorvoraphin w ko 3 Joseph Orgaliza (Phi)	Chiangmai (Tha)
Sep 28,	1996	Ratanapol Sorvoraphin w ko 5 Oscar Andrade	Prajuabkirkhan (Tha)
Nov 24,	1996	Ratanapol Sorvoraphin w ko 2 Gustavo Vera (Ven)	Udonthani (Tha)
Mar 22,	1997	Ratanapol Sorvoraphin w rsf 4 Luis Doria (Col)	Saraburi (Tha)
Jun 14,	1997	Ratanapol Sorvoraphin w pts 12 Juanito Herrera (Mex)	Bangkok (Tha)
Aug 30,	1997	Ratanapol Sorvoraphin w rsf 2 Wellington Vicente (Bra)	Nogkhai (Tha)
Dec 27,	1997	**Zolani Petelo** (SA) w Ratanapol Sorvoraphin	Songkhla (Tha)
Mar 21,	1998	Zolani Petelo w pts 12 Raisol Akbar (Indo)	Hammanskraal (SA)
Jul 4,	1998	Zolani Petelo w rsf 7 Carmelo Caceres (Phi)	Hammanskraal (SA)
May 29,	1999	Zolani Petelo w ko 1 Eric Jamili (Phi)	Hammanskraal (SA)
Dec 3,	1999	Zolani Petelo w pts 12 Juanito Rubillar (Phi)	Peterborough (Eng)
Jun 2,	2000	Zolani Petelo w rsf 8 Mickey Cantwell (Eng)	Ashford (Eng)
Dec	2000	*Petelo relinquished title because of weight problems*	
Apr 29,	2001	**Roberto Leyva** (Mex) w pts 12 Daniel Reyes (Col). *For vacant title*	New York, NY
Sep 29,	2001	Roberto Leyva tec.draw 3 Miguel Barrera (Col)	Ensenada (Mex)
Aug 9,	2002	**Miguel Barrera** (Col) w pts 12 Roberto Leyva	Las Vegas, NV
Mar 22,	2003	Miguel Barrera w ko 3 Roberto Leyva	Las Vegas, NV
May 31,	2003	**Edgar Cardenas** (Mex) w ko 10 Miguel Barrera	Tijuana (Mex)
Oct 4,	2004	**Daniel Reyes** (Col) w rsf 6 Edgar Cardenas	Los Angeles, CA
Sep 14,	2005	**Muhammad Rachman** (Indo) w pts 12 Daniel Reyes	Jakarta (Indo)
Apr 5,	2006	Muhammad Rachman tdraw 3 Fahlan Sakkreerin (Tha)	Merauke (Indo)
May 6,	2006	Muhammad Rachman w ko 6 Omar Soto (Mex)	Jakarta (Indo)
Dec 23,	2006	Muhammad Rachman w rsf 7 Benjie Sorolla (Phi)	Jakarta (Indo)
Jul 7,	2007	**Florante Condes** (Phi) w pts 12 Muhammad Rachman	Jakarta (Indo)
Jun 14,	2008	**Raul Garcia** (Mex) w pts 12 Florante Condes	La Paz (Mex)
Sep 13,	2008	Raul Garcia w pts 12 Jose Luis Varela (Ven)	La Paz (Mex)
Dec 13,	2008	Raul Garcia w pts 12 Jose Luis Varela	Loreto (Mex)
Apr 11,	2009	Raul Garcia w rsf 6 Ronald Barrera (Col)	La Paz (Mex)
Aug 22,	2009	Raul Garcia w pts 12 Sammy Gutierrez (Mex)	Los Cabas (Mex)
Mar 26,	2010	**Nkosinathi Joyi** (SA) w pts 12 Raul Garcia	East London (SA)
Jan 29,	2011	Nkosinathi Joyi nc 3 Katsunari Takayama (Jap)	Brakpan (SA)
Mar 20,	2012	Nkosinathi Joyi w pts 12 Katsunari Takayama	East London (SA)
Sep 1,	2012	**Mario Rodriguez** (Mex) w ko 7 Nkosinathi Joyi	Guasave (Mex)
Mar 30,	2013	**Katsunari Takayama** (Jap) w pts 12 Mario Rodriguez	Guasave (Mex)
Dec 3,	2013	Katsunari Takayama w pts 12 Vergilio Silvano (Phi)	Osaka (Jap)
May 7,	2014	Katsunari Takayama w pts 12 Shin Ono (Jap)	Osaka (Jap)
Apr 22,	2015	Katsunari Takayama w tech pts 9 Fahlan Sakkreerin (Thai)	Osaka (Jap)

WBC title

Oct 18,	1987	**Hiroki Ioka** (Jap) w pts 12 Mai Thornburifarm (Tha)	Osaka (Jap)
Jan 31,	1988	Hiroki Ioka w rsf 12 Kyung-Yung Lee (Kor)	Osaka (Jap)
Jun 5,	1988	Hiroki Ioka drew 12 Napa Kiatwanchai (Tha)	Osaka (Jap)
Nov 13,	1988	**Napa Kiatwanchai** w pts 12 Hiroki Ioka	Osaka (Jap)
Feb 11,	1989	Napa Kiatwanchai w pts 12 John Arief (Indo)	Bangkok (Tha)
Jun 10,	1989	Napa Kiatwanchai w rsf 11 Hiroki Ioka	Osaka (Jap)
Nov 12,	1989	**Jum-Hwan Choi** (Kor) w rsf 12 Napa Kiatwanchai	Seoul (Kor)
Feb 7,	1990	**Hideyuki Ohashi** (Jap) w ko 9 Jum-Hwan Choi	Tokyo (Jap)
Jun 8,	1990	Hideyuki Ohashi w pts 12 Napa Kiatwanchai	Tokyo (Jap)
Oct 25,	1990	**Ricardo Lopez** (Mex) w rsf 5 Hideyuki Ohashi	Tokyo (Jap)
May 19,	1991	Ricardo Lopez w rsf 8 Kimio Hirano (Jap)	Shizoka (Jap)
Dec 22,	1991	Ricardo Lopez w pts 12 Kyung-Yun Lee (Kor)	Inchon (Kor)
Mar 16,	1992	Ricardo Lopez w pts 21 Domingo Lucas	Mexico City (Mex)
Aug 22,	1992	Ricardo Lopez w ko 5 Singpraset Kitkasem (Tha)	Ciudad Madero (Mex)
Oct 11,	1992	Ricardo Lopez w ko 2 Rocky Lim (Jap)	Tokyo (Jap)
Mar 31,	1993	Ricardo Lopez w rsf 9 Kwang-Soo Oh (Kor)	Seoul (Kor)
Jul 3,	1993	Ricardo Lopez w rsf 2 Saman Sorjaturong (Tha)	Nuevo Laredo (Mex)
Dec 18,	1993	Ricardo Lopez w ko 11 Manny Melchor	Lake Tahoe, CA
May 7,	1994	Ricardo Lopez w pts 12 Kermin Guardia (Col)	Las Vegas, NV
Sep 17,	1994	Ricardo Lopez w rsf 1 Yodsing Au Saenmorokot (Tha)	Las Vegas, NV
Nov 12,	1994	Ricardo Lopez w rsf 8 Javier Varguez (Mex)	Mexico City (Mex)
Dec 10,	1994	Ricardo Lopez w ko 1 Yamil Caraballo (Col)	Monterrey (Mex)
Apr 1,	1995	Ricardo Lopez w rsf 12 Andy Tabanas	Stateline, NV
Mar 16,	1996	Ricardo Lopez w ko 8 Ala Villamor (Phi)	Las Vegas, NV
Jun 29,	1996	Ricardo Lopez w ko 3 Kitichai Preecha (Tha)	Indio, CA
Nov 9,	1996	Ricardo Lopez w rsf 6 Morgan Nduma (SA)	Las Vegas, NV
Dec 7,	1996	Ricardo Lopez w rsf 1 Myung-Sup Park (Kor)	Indio, CA
Mar 29,	1997	Ricardo Lopez w pts 12 Mongkil Chareon (Tha)	Las Vegas, NV

WBA title

Jan 18,	1988	**Luis Gamez** (Ven) w pts 12 Bong-Jun Kim (Kor)	Pusan (Kor)
Apr 24,	1988	Luis Gamez w rsf 3 Kenji Yokozawa (Jap)	Tokyo (Jap)
Feb	1988	*Gamez vacated the title to box at light-flyweight*	
Apr 16,	1989	**Bong-Jun Kim** w rsf 7 Augustin Garcia (Col). *For vacant title*	Seoul (Kor)
Aug 6,	1989	Bong-Jun Kim w pts 12 Sam-Jung Lee (Kor)	Seoul (Kor)
Oct 22,	1989	Bong-Jun Kim w rsf 9 John Arief	Pohang (Kor)
Feb 10,	1990	Bong-Jun Kim w rsf 3 Petchai Chuwatana (Tha)	Seoul (Kor)
May 13,	1990	Bong-Jun Kim w tech dec 5 Silverio Barcenas (Pan)	Seoul (Kor)
Nov 3,	1990	Bong-Jun Kim w pts 12 Silverio Barcenas (Pan)	Seoul (Kor)
Feb 2,	1991	**Hi-Yon Choi** (Kor) w pts 12 Bong-Jun Kim	Seoul (Kor)
Jun 15,	1991	Hi-Yon Choi w pts 12 Sugar Ray Mike (Phi)	Seoul (Kor)
Oct 26,	1991	Hi-Yon Choi w pts 12 Bong-Jun Kim	Seoul (Kor)
Feb 22,	1992	Hi-Yon Choi w rsf 10 Ryuichi Hosono (Jap)	Seoul (Kor)
Jun 13,	1992	Hi-Yon Choi w ko 3 Rommel Lawas (Phi)	Inchon (Kor)
Oct 14,	1992	**Hideyuki Ohashi** w pts 12 Hi-Yon Choi	Tokyo (Jap)
Feb 10,	1993	**Chana Porpaoin** (Tha) w pts 12 Hideyuki Ohashi	Tokyo (Jap)
May 9,	1993	Chana Porpaoin w pts 12 Carlos Murillo (Pan)	Bangkok (Tha)
Aug 22,	1993	Chana Porpaoin w pts 12 Ronnie Magramo (Phi)	Bangkok (Tha)
Nov 28,	1993	Chana Porpaoin w ko 4 Rafael Torres (DR)	Pichit (Tha)
Mar 27,	1994	Chana Porpaoin w pts 12 Carlos Murillo (Pan)	Chon Buri (Tha)
Aug 27,	1994	Chana Porpaoin w pts 12 Keunyoung Kang (Kor)	Petchaboon (Tha)
Nov 5,	1994	Chana Porpaoin w pts 12 Manuel Herrera (DR)	Hatyai (Tha)
Jan 28,	1995	Chana Porpaoin w pts 12 Jiu Ho Kim (Kor)	Bangkok (Tha)
Aug 5,	1995	Chana Porpaoin w ko 6 Ernesto Rubillar Jr (Phi)	Bangkok (Tha)
Dec 2,	1995	**Rosendo Alvarez** (Nic) w pts 12 Chana Porpaoin	Bangkok (Tha)
Mar 30,	1996	Rosendo Alvarez w ko 3 Kermin Guardia (Col)	Managua (Nic)
Jun 15,	1996	Rosendo Alvarez w pts 12 Kenta Sato (*aka Eric Chavez*) (Jap)	Sendai (Jap)
Oct 1,	1996	Rosendo Alvarez w ko 8 Takashi Shiohama (Jap)	Kitakyushi (Jap)
Jan 11,	1997	Rosendo Alvarez w rsf 11 Songkram Porpaoin (Tha)	Sakaew (Tha)
Nov	1998	*Alvarez stripped of WBA title in November 1998 before unification bout against WBC champion Ricardo Lopez. On Mar 7, 1998, they fought a technical draw*	

Jan 31,	1999	**Songkram Porpaoin** (Tha) w tdec 9 Ronnie Magramo (Phi)	Pattaya (Tha)

WBO title

Aug 31,	1989	**Rafael Torres** (DR) w pts 12 Yamil Caraballo (Col)	Santo Domingo (Bah)
Jul 31,	1990	Rafael Torres w pts 12 Husni Ray (Indo)	Jakarta (Indo)
May	1992	*Torres was stripped of the title for failure to defend*	
May 15,	1993	**Paul Weir** (Sco) w rsf 7 Fernando Martinez (Mex)	Glasgow (Sco)
		For vacant title	
Oct 25,	1993	Paul Weir w pts 12 Lindi Memani (SA)	Glasgow (Sco)
Dec	1993	*Weir vacated title in to box at light-flyweight*	
Dec 22,	1993	**Alex Sanchez** (PR) w rsf 1 Orlando Malone (US)	San Juan, CA
		For vacant title	
Jan 7,	1994	Alex Sanchez w rsf 1 Arturo Garcia Mayen (US)	Palma (Sp)
Aug 13,	1994	Alex Sanchez w ko 1 Carlos Juan Rodriguez (DR)	Bayamon (PR)
Sep 10,	1994	Alex Sanchez w ko 4 Oscar Andrade (Mex)	Hamburg (Ger)
Jan 28,	1995	Alex Sanchez w pts 12 Rafael Orozco (Mex)	Las Vegas, NV
Jul 29,	1995	Alex Sanchez w pts 12 Tomas Rivera (Mex)	San Antonio, TX
Mar 29,	1997	Alex Sanchez w pts 12 Victor Burgos (Mex)	Las Vegas, NV

WBO/WBC title

Aug 23,	1997	Ricardo Lopez w rsf 4 Alex Sanchez	New York, NY
Mar	1998	*Lopez stripped of WBO title*	

WBA/WBC title

Mar 7,	1998	Ricardo Lopez tdraw 7 Rosendo Alvarez	Mexico City (Mex)
Nov 13,	1998	Ricardo Lopez w pts 12 Rosendo Alvarez	Las Vegas, NV
		Alvarez failed to make the weight. The fight was allowed to go ahead, although it was recognized only by the WBC. With the WBA title not at stake, technically it was not a unification bout	

WBO title

May 30,	1998	**Kermin Guardia** (Col) w rtd 5 Eric Jamili (Phi)	Las Vegas, NV
		For vacant title	
Mar 27,	1999	Kermin Guardia w pts 12 Eric Jamili (Phi)	Miami FL
Oct 30,	1999	Kermin Guardia w pts 12 Luis Lazarate (Arg)	Mar del Plata (Arg)
Apr 6,	2001	Kermin Guardia w pts 12 Juan Alfonso Keb-Baas (Mex)	Merida (Mex)
		Kermin Guardia was stripped of his title because of inactivity	
Jun 29,	2002	**Jorge Mata** (Spa) w rsf 9 Reynaldo Frutos (Pan)	Palma (Spa)
Nov 22,	2002	Jorge Mata w pts 12 Jairo Arango (Pan)	Leon (Fra)
Mar 28,	2003	**Eduardo Marquez** (Nic) w rsf 11 Jorge Mata	Madrid (Spa)
May 3,	2003	**Ivan Calderon** (Mex) w tdec 9 Eduardo Marquez	Las Vegas, NV
Sep 5,	2003	Ivan Calderon w pts 12 Lorenzo Trejo (Mex)	Caguas (Mex)
Dec 6,	2003	Ivan Calderon w pts 12 Alex Sanchez (PR)	Bayamon (PR)
Jul 31,	2004	Ivan Calderon w pts 12 Roberto Leyva (Mex)	Las Vegas, NV
Nov 27,	2004	Ivan Calderon w pts 12 Carlos Fajardo (Nic)	Las Vegas, NV
May 30,	2005	Ivan Calderon w rsf 8 Noel Tunacao (Phi)	Hato Rey (PR)
Jun 25,	2005	Ivan Calderon w pts 12 Gerardo Verde (Mex)	Atlantic City, NJ
Dec 10,	2005	Ivan Calderon w pts 12 Daniel Reyes (Col)	San Juan (PR)
Feb 18,	2006	Ivan Calderon w pts 12 Isaac Bustos (Mex)	Las Vegas, NV
Apr 29,	2006	Ivan Calderon w rsf 9 Miguel Tellez (Nic)	Guaynabo (Mex)
Oct 21,	2006	Ivan Calderon w pts 12 Jose Luis Varela (Ven)	Barranquilla (Mex)
Apr 28,	2007	Ivan Calderon w pts 12 Ronald Barrera (Col)	Barranquilla (Col)
		Calderon relinquished title when he moved up to fight for and become light-flyweight champion	
Sep 30,	2007	**Donnie Nietes** (Phi) w pts 12 Pornsawan Kratingdaenggym (Tha)	Cebu (Phi)
		For vacant title	
Aug 30,	2008	Donnie Nietes w ko 2 Eddy Castro (Nic)	Cebu City (Phi)
Feb 28,	2009	Donnie Nietes w pts 12 Erik Ramirez (Mex)	Oaxaca (Mex)
Sep 12,	2009	Donnie Nietes w pts 12 Manuel Vargas (Mex)	Tepic (Mex)
Aug 14,	2010	Donnie Nietes w pts 12 Mario Rodriguez	Guasave (Mex)
		Nietes relinquished WBO title. The WBO had previously sanctioned the following Interim fights:	
Sep 26,	2008	**Daniel Reyes** (Col) w pts 12 Luis Alberto Lazarte (Arg)	Buenos Aires (Arg)
Dec 6,	2008	**Manuel Vargas** w ko 4 Daniel Reyes	Lagos de Moreno (Mex)
Feb 14,	2009	Manuel Vargas w pts 12 Walter Tello (Pan)	Hermosillo (Mex)
Oct 30,	2010	Raul Garcia w pts 12 Luis De la Rosa (Col)	Cartagena (Col)
		Raul Garcia upgraded from Interim to full champion	
Apr 30,	2011	**Raul Garcia** (Mex) w rsf 3 Rommel Asenjo (Phil)	Mexico City (Mex)
Aug 27,	2011	**Moises Fuentes** (Mex) w pts 12 Raul Garcia	Guadalajara (Mex)
Jun 2,	2012	Moises Fuentes w ko 1 Julio Cesar Felix (Mex)	Tijuana (Mex)
Oct 6,	2012	Moises Fuentes w rsf 5 Ivan Calderon	Bayamon (PR)
		Moises *Fuentes vacated. Merlito Sabillo upgraded from Interim to full champion*	
Jul 13,	2013	**Merlito Sabillo** (Phi) w ko 9 Jorle Estrada (Col)	Manila (Phi)
Nov 30,	2013	Merlito Sabillo drew 12 Carlos Buitrago (Nic)	Manila (Phi)
Mar 22,	2014	Francisco Rodriguez Jr (Mex) w rsf 10 Merlito Sabillo	Monterrey (Mex)
		Francisco Rodriguez Jr vacated title	
May 30,	2015	**Kosei Tanaka** (Jap) w pts 12 Julian Yedras (Mex)	Komaki (Jap)
		The WBO had previously sanctioned the following Interim fight:	
Mar 9,	2013	Merlito Sabillo w rsf 8 Luis De La Rosa (Col)	Cerete (Col)

WBC title

Sep	1999	*Lopez relinquished title, Wandee Chor Chareon declared champion*	
Feb 11,	2000	**Jose Antonio Aguirre** (Mex) w pts 12 Wandee Chor Chareon	Samut Sakorn (Tha)
Jul 7,	2000	Jose Antonio Aguirre w ko 5 Jose Luis Zepeda (Mex)	Villahermosa (Mex)
Oct 21,	2000	Jose Antonio Aguirre w rsf 4 Erdene Chuluun (Mon)	Mexico City (Mex)
Feb 2,	2001	Jose Antonio Aguirre w pts 12 Manny Melchor (Phi)	Tijuana (Mex)
Nov 10,	2001	Jose Antonio Aguirre w rsf 3 Wolf Tokimitsu (Jap)	Okayama (Jap)
Oct 19,	2002	Jose Antonio Aguirre w pts 12 Juan Palacios (Nic)	Villahermosa (Mex)
Feb 22,	2003	Jose Antonio Aguirre w rsf 7 Juan Alfonso Keb Baas (Mex)	Mexico City (Mex)
Jun 23,	2003	Jose Antonio Aguirre w rsf 12 Keitaro Hoshino (Jap)	Yokohama (Jap)
Jan 10,	2004	**Eagle Kyowa** (Jap) w pts 12 Jose Antonio Aguirre	Tokyo (Jap)
Jun 28,	2004	Eagle Kyowa w tdec 8 Jatoshi Kogumazaka (Jap)	Yokohama (Jap)
Dec 18,	2004	**Isaac Bustos** (Mex) w rsf 4 Eagle Kyowa	Tokyo (Jap)
Apr 4,	2005	**Katsunari Takayama** (Jap) w pts 12 Isaac Bustos	Osaka (Jap)
Aug 6,	2005	**Eagle Kyowa** w pts 12 Katsunari Takayama	Tokyo (Jap)
Jan 9,	2006	Eagle Kyowa w rsf 7 Ken Nakajima (Jap)	Yokohama (Jap)
May 6,	2006	Eagle Kyowa w pts 12 Rodel Mayol (Phi)	Tokyo (Jap)
Nov 13,	2006	Eagle Kyowa w pts 12 Lorenzo Trejo (Mex)	Tokyo (Jap)
Jun 4,	2007	Eagle Kyowa w pts 12 Akira Yaegashi (Jap)	Yokohama (Jap)
Nov 29,	2007	**Oleydong Sithsamerchai** (Tha) w pts 12 Eagle Kyowa	Bangkok (Thai)
Jun 18,	2008	Oleydong Sithsamerchai w ko 9 Junichi Ebisuoka (Jap)	Phuket (Tha)
Nov 27,	2008	Oleydong Sithsamerchai w pts 12 Pornsawan Porpramood (Tha)	Phitsanulok (Tha)
May 29,	2009	Oleydong Sithsamerchai w tdec 11 Muhammad Rachman (Ind)	Phuket (Tha)
Nov 27,	2009	Oleydong Sithsamerchai w pts 12 Juan Palacios (Nic)	Rangsit (Tha)
		The WBC had previously sanctioned Interim title fights as follows:	
Aug 2,	2008	**Juan Palacios** w rsf 10 Omar Soto (PR)	Ponce (PR)
Nov 7,	2008	Juan Palacios w rsf 7 Teruo Misawa (Jap)	Chengdu (Chi)
Jun 13,	2009	Juan Palacios w rsf 10 Erik Ramirez (Mex)	Mexico City (Mex)
Mar 27,	2010	Oleydong Sithsamerchai w pts 12 Yasutaka Kuroki (Jap)	Tokyo (Jap)
Sep 3,	2010	Olyedong Sithsamerchai drew 12 Pornsawan Popramook	Chiang Mai (Thai)
Feb 11,	2011	**Kazuto Ioka** (Jap) w rsf 5 Oleydong Sithsamerchai	Kobe (Jap)
Aug 10,	2011	Kazuto Ioka w pts 12 Juan Hernandez (Mex)	Tokyo (Jap)
Dec 31,	2011	Kazuto Ioka w rsf 1 Yodngoen Tor Chalermchai (Thai)	Osaka (Jap)
		Ioka relinquished title after winning unification match with WBA champion Akira Yaegashi	
Nov 24,	2012	**Xiong Zhao Zhong** (Chi) w pts 12 Javier Martinez Resendiz (Mex).	Kunming (Chi)
		For vacant title	
Jun 28,	2013	Xiong Zhao Zhong w pts 12 Denver Cuello (Phi)	Dubai (UAE)
Nov 30,	2013	Xiong Zhao Zhong w rsc 5 Lookrak Kiatmungmee (Tha)	Maguan (Chi)
Feb 5,	2014	**Oswaldo Novoa** (Mex) w rsf 5 Xiong Zhao Zhong	Haikou (Chi)
Nov 6,	2014	**Chayaphon Moonsri** (Thai) w rtd 9 Oswaldo Novoa	Chonburi (Thai)
Feb 5,	2015	Chayaphon Moonsri w pts 12 Jeffrey Galero (Phi)	Nakhon Sawan (Thai)
Jun 2,	2015	Chayaphon Moonsri w ko 9 Jerry Tomogdan (Phi)	Bangkok (Thai)
Nov 24,	2015	Chayaphon Moosri w rsf 9 Young Gil Bae (S Kor)	Chonburi (Tha)
Mar 3,	2016	Chayaphon Moosri w rsf 5 Go Odaira (Jap)	Nakhon Ratchasima (Tha)
Aug 2,	2016	Chayaphon Moosri w pts 12 Saul Juarez (Mex)	Chonburi (Tha)
Jan 25,	2017	Chayaphon Moosri w pts 12 Melvin Jerusalem (Phi)	Phitsanulok (Tha)
Jun 3,	2017	Chayaphon Moosri w pts 12 Omari Kimweri (Aus)	Rayong (Tha)
Nov 25,	2017	Chayaphon Moosri w pts 12 Tatsuya Fukuhara (Jap)	Nakhon Ratchasima (Tha)

WBC/WBA titles

Jun 20,	2012	Kazuto Ioka w pts 12 Akira Yaegashi	Osaka (Jap)

WBA title

Oct 9,	1999	**Noel Arambulet** (Ven) w pts 12 Jomo Gamboa	Caracas (Ven)
Mar 4,	2000	Noel Arambulet w pts 12 Jose Garcia (Col)	Caracas (Ven)
Aug 20,	2000	**Jomo Gamboa** w pts 12 Noel Arambulet	Tokyo (Jap)
Dec 6,	2000	**Keitaro Hoshino** (Jap) w pts 12 Jomo Gamboa	Yokohama (Jap)
Apr 16,	2001	**Chana Porpaoin** (Tha) w pts 12 Keitaro Hoshino	Yokohama (Jap)
Aug 25,	2001	**Yutaka Niida** (Jap) w pts 12 Chana Porpaoin	Yokohama (Jap)
		Niida retired	
Jan 29,	2002	**Keitaro Hoshino** w pts 12 Jomo Gamboa	Yokohama (Jap)
		For vacant title	
Jul 29,	2002	**Noel Arambulet** (Ven) w pts 12 Kataro Hoshino	Yokohama (Jap)
Dec 20,	2002	Noel Arambulet w pts 12 Kataro Hoshino	Yokohama (Jap)
Jul 12,	2003	Noel Arambulet w pts 12 Yutaka Niida	Yokohama (Jap)
Jul 3,	2004	**Yutaka Niida** w pts 12 Noel Arambulet	Tokyo (Jap)
Oct 30,	2004	Yutaka Niida w pts 12 Juan Jose Landaerta (Ven)	Tokyo (Jap)
Apr 16,	2005	Yutaka Niida w pts 12 Jae-won Kim (Kor)	Tokyo (Jap)
Sep 25,	2005	Yutaka Niida w tdec 10 Eriberto Gejon (Phi)	Yokohama (Jap)
Mar 4,	2006	Yutaka Niida w pts 12 Ronald Barrera (Col)	Tokyo (Jap)
Apr 7,	2007	Yutaka Niida w pts Katsunari Takayama (Jap)	Tokyo (Jap)

Sep 1,	2007	Yutaka Niida w pts 12 Eriberto Gejon (Phi)	Tokyo (Jap)
Mar 1,	2008	Yutaka Niida w ko 6 Jose Luis Varela (Ven)	Tokyo (Jap)
Sep 15,	2008	**Roman Gonzalez** (Nic) w rsf 4 Yutaka Niida	Yokohama (Jap)
Feb 28,	2009	Roman Gonzalez w pts 12 Francisco Rojas (Mex)	Oaxaca (Mex)
Jul 14,	2009	Roman Gonzalez w pts 12 Katsunari Takayama (Jap)	Kobe (Jap)
Jan 30,	2010	Roman Gonzalez w rtd 4 Ivan Meneses (Mex)	Puebla (Mex)
		Roman Gonzalez relinquished title to box at light-flyweight	
Nov 5,	2010	**Kwanthai Sithmorseng** (Thai) w pts 12 Pigmy Kokietgym (Thai).	Bangkok (Thai)
		For vacant title	
Apr 19,	2011	**Muhammad Rachman** (Indo) w ko 9 Kwanthai Sithmorseng	Bangkok (Thai)
Jul 30,	2011	**Pornsawan Popramook** w pts 12 Muhammad Rachman	Jakarta (Indo)
Oct 24,	2011	**Akira Yaegashi** w rsf 10 Pornsawan Popramook	Tokyo (Jap)
		Yaegashi lost WBA title to WBC champion Kazuto Ioka in unification match. Ioka then relinquished title to box at light-flyweight	
Dec 31,	2012	**Ryo Miyazaki** (Jap) w pts 12 Pornsawan Popramook	Osaka (Jap)
		For vacant title	
May 8,	2013	Ryo Miyazaki w rsf 5 Carlos Velarde (Mex)	Osaka (Jap)
Sep 11,	2013	Ryo Miyazaki w pts 12 Jesus Silvestre (Mex)	Osaka (Jap
		Miyazaki vacates title	
Mar 1,	2014	**Hekkie Budler** (RSA) w ko 1 Karluis Diaz (Col)	Kempton Park (SA)
		For vacant title	
Jun 21,	2014	Hekkie Budler w ko 8 Pigmy Kokietgym (Thai)	Monte Carlo (Mon)
Oct 1,	2014	Hekkie Budler w pts 12 Xiong Zhao Zhong	Monte Carlo (Mon)
Feb 21,	2015	Hekkie Budler w pts 12 Jesus Silvestre	Monte Carlo (Mon)
		The WBA sanctioned the following for their Interim title	
Oct 23,	2010	Sammy Gutierrez (Mex) w pts 12 Luis Carillo (Col)	Puebla (Mex)
Feb 12,	2011	Sammy Gutierrez (Mex) w rsf 6 Renan Trongco (Phil)	Buenos Aires (Arg)
May 21,	2011	Juan Palacios (Nic) w pts 12 Sammy Gutierrez	Puebla (Mex)
Aug 13,	2011	Juan Palacios w rsf 9 Armando Torres (Mex)	Acapulco (Mex)
Nov 7,	2011	Paipharob Kokietgym (Thai) w pts 12 Jesus Silvestre (Mex)	Nong Khai (Thai)
Jul 14,	2012	Jesus Silvestre w pts 12 Edwin Diaz (Pan)	Tepic (Mex)
Oct 6,	2012	Jesus Silvestre w rsf 4 Takuya Mitamura (Jap)	Tepic (Mex)
Nov 9,	2013	Hekkie Budler w rsf 4 Hugo Hernan Verchelli (Arg)	Kempton Park (SA)
		The WBA sanctioned the following fights for their Interim title	
Oct 1,	2014	Thammanoon Niyomtrong (Thai) w pts 12 Carlos Buitrago	Buriram (Thai)
Mar 5,	2015	Thammanoon Niyomtrong w pts 12 Muhammad Rachman (Indo)	Chonburi (Thai)
Jul 2,	2015	Thammanoon Niyomtrong w rsf 4 Alexis Diaz (Ven)	Nakhon Ratchasima (Tha)
Oct 25,	2015	Hekkie Budler w pts 12 Simphiwe Khonco (SA)	Kempton Park (SA)
		For WBA and IBO titles	
		WBA sanctioned the following fight for the interim title	
Feb 4,	2016	Thammanoon Niyomtrong w pts 12 Carlos Buitrago (Nic)	Chonburi (Tha)
Jun 29,	2016	**Thammanoon Niyomtrong** w pts 12 Bryon Rojas (Nic)	Khon Kaen (Tha)
		For WBA title	
Dec 14,	2016	Thammanoon Niyomtrong w pts 12 Shin Ono (Jap)	Nakhon Ratchasima (Tha)
Mar 1,	2016	Thammanoon Niyomtrong w ko 5 Go Odaira (Jap)	Chonburi (Tha)
Jul 15,	2017	Thammanoon Niyomtrong w pts 12 Rey Loreto (Phi)	Chonburi (Tha)

IBF/WBO titles

Aug 9,	2014	**Francisco Rodriguez Jr** (Mex) w pts 12 Katsunari Takayama.	Neuvo Leon (Mex)
		Rodriguez vacated title	
Dec 31,	2014	**Katsunari Takayama** w pts 12 Shin Ono (Jap)	Osaka (Jap)
		Takayama vacated WBO title	

IBF title

Dec 31,	2014	Katsunari Takayama w rsf 7 Go Adaira (Jap)	Osaka (Jap)
Apr 22,	2015	Katsunari Takayama w td 9 Teeraphong Utaida (Tha)	Osaka (Jap)
Sep 27,	2015	Katsunari Takayama w rsf 8 Ryuji Hara (Jap)	Osaka (Jap)
Dec 31,	2015	**Jose Argumedo (Mex)** w td 9 Katsunari Takayama	Osaka (Jap)
Jul 1,	2016	Jose Argumedo w pts 12 Julio Mendoza (Nic)	Tepic (Mex)
Nov 12,	2016	Jose Argumedo w rsf 3 Jose Antonio Jimenez (Mex)	Ciudad Valles (Mex)
May 27,	2017	Jose Argumedo w rsf 8 Gabriel Mendoza (Col)	Monterrey (Mex)
Jul 23,	2017	**Hiroto Kyoguchi (Jap)** w pts 12 Jose Argumedo	Tokyo (Jap)
Dec 31,	2017	Hiroto Kyoguchi w rsf 8 Carlos Buitrago (Nic)	Tokyo (Jap)

WBA Super title

Mar 19,	2016	**Byron Rojas (Nic)** w pts 12 Hekkie Budler (SA)	Kempton Park (SA)

BYRON ROJAS *finds his range on his way to a points victory over Hekkie Budler for the WBA Super minimum weight title in March 2016*

CHRONOLOGY

Who, what, where and when ... an at-a-glance guide to some of the pivotal events in boxing history.

1681
(Jan) First known newspaper report of a prize-fight appears in the Protestant Mercury.

1743
Jack Broughton introduces the first set of formal rules to govern prize-fights.

1810
(Dec 18) Tom Cribb beats Tom Molineaux in the first major international match.

1838
London Prize Ring Rules are established.

1860
(Apr 17) Tom Sayers fights with John Carmel Heenan of America in the last great prize-fight to be staged in England.

1867
The Queensberry Rules are published.

1882
(Feb 7) John L. Sullivan beats Paddy Ryan to become the last bare-knuckle heavyweight champion.

1889
(July 8) Sullivan stops Jake Kilrain in 75 rounds in the last bare-knuckle title fight.

1891
The National Sporting Club is formed in London: it will administer the sport in Britain until 1929.

1892
(Sept 7) James J. Corbett knocks out Sullivan in 21 rounds in the first gloved heavyweight title fight.

1897
(Mar 17) Bob Fitzsimmons becomes the first English-born world heavyweight champion by knocking out James J. Corbett in the first filmed fight.

1907
(Dec 2) The world heavyweight title is contested outside America for the first time as Tommy Burns beats Gunner Moir in London.

1908
(Dec 26) Jack Johnson becomes the first black heavyweight champion. Race riots ensue across America, and the hunt begins for a Great White Hope to beat him.

1909
(Sept) *Boxing*, a weekly paper, makes its first appearance. It survives today as *Boxing News*.

1910
(July 4) Jack Johnson stops James J. Jeffries in a much-publicized "black vs. white" battle.

1911
The Frawley Law legalizes boxing in New York.

The International Boxing Union (IBU) is formed.

1913
(Oct 6) Ted "Kid" Lewis wins the first of his many titles.

1920
The New York State Athletic Commission takes over the running of boxing in the state. The National Boxing Association is also formed at a meeting in New York.

1921
(July 2) Jack Dempsey knocks out Georges Carpentier in the first fight to draw a million dollars.

1923
(Mar 17) Mike McTigue outpoints Battling Siki over 20 rounds to win the world light-heavyweight title in the last world title bout to go more than 15 rounds.

1926
(Oct 22) Harry Greb, former middleweight champion, dies following an eye operation.

1927
(Sept 22) Jack Dempsey fails to regain the heavyweight title from Gene Tunney.

1929
The British Boxing Board of Control is formed.

1931
(Apr 24) Tony Canzoneri wins his third world title.

Jack Solomons, the most flamboyant and successful British promoter, stages his first show. He loses £275.

1933
(June 23) Barney Ross wins the first of his three world titles;

(June 29) The Mob's proudest achievement: Primo Carnera takes the heavyweight title from Jack Sharkey.

1935
(June 13) James J. Braddock wins the heavyweight title, outpointing Max Baer.

1937
(Aug 30) Tommy Farr of Wales defies Joe Louis for the full 15 rounds in Louis' first defence of the heavyweight title.

1938
(Apr 4) Len Harvey

vs. Jock McAvoy fight becomes the first to be shown on TV.

(Aug 17) Henry Armstrong beats Lou Ambers to become the only man in history to hold three titles simultaneously.

1939
(Sept 30) The last scheduled 20-rounds world title fight takes place.

1941
(June 18) Joe Louis scores his finest victory, knocking out Billy Conn in the 13th round to retain the heavyweight title.

1948
(July 26) Freddie Mills ends Gus Lesnevich's long spell as light-heavyweight champion.

(Oct 29) Willie Pep's fabulous reign as featherweight champion is ended by Sandy Saddler.

The European Boxing Union is formed.

1949
(Oct 27) Marcel Cerdan dies in a plane crash on his way to America for a title rematch with Jake LaMotta.

1951
(Feb 14) Ray Robinson wins the first of his five middleweight titles, stopping Jake LaMotta in 14 rounds.
(July 10) Randolph Turpin dethrones Robinson in London. His reign is shortlived, lasting only 64 days, losing the title back to Robinson in September.

1952
(Sept 23) Rocky Marciano wins the heavyweight title.

(Nov 15) Australia's first undisputed world champion, Jimmy Carruthers, knocks out Vic Toweel in the first round to win the bantamweight title.

1956
(Apr 27) Rocky Marciano retires as heavyweight champion, the only one to remain undefeated.

1959
(June 26) Ingemar Johanason brings the heavyweight title back to Europe.

1960
(Mar 16) Gabriel "Flash" Elorde wins the recently revived 130 lb title;

(Apr 16) Thailand's first champion, Pone Kingpetch, takes the flyweight title;

(June 20) Floyd Patterson becomes the first to regain the heavyweight title, knocking out Ingemar Johansson in five rounds.

1961
(Oct 28) Joe Brown sets a lightweight record by retaining the title for the 11th and final time.

1962
(Apr 2) Benny Paret dies after being stopped in a welterweight title defence by Emile Griffith.
(Aug) The National Boxing Association changes its name to the World Boxing Association.

CASSIUS CLAY *(Muhammad Ali) forced Sonny Liston to retire on his seat to win the world heavyweight title in February 1964*

1963
(Feb 14) The World Boxing Council is formed in Mexico City.

(July 22) Sonny Liston and Floyd Patterson become the first to earn over $1m for a fight.

1964
(Feb 25) Cassius Clay (Muhammad Ali) shocks the world by beating Sonny Liston for the heavyweight title.

1971
(Mar 8) Muhammad Ali loses for the first time as Joe Frazier retains the heavyweight title in New York.
(Mar 16) Henry Cooper, Britain's longest-serving heavyweight champion and the only boxer to win three Lonsdale Belts outright, retires after a controversial loss to Joe Bugner.

1972
(June 26) Roberto Duran wins his first world title, beating lightweight champion Ken Buchanan in 13 rounds in New York.

1976
(Mar 6) Wilfred Benitez of Puerto Rico becomes the youngest world champion in history when, aged 17 years and six months, he takes the WBA light-welterweight title from Antonio Cervantes.

1977
(Aug 29) Carlos Monzon, the most successful middle-weight champion in history with 14 defences, retires as undefeated champion

1978
(June 9) Larry Holmes launches one of the great championship reigns by beating Ken Norton for the WBC heavyweight title.

1981
(June 20) Nicaraguan Alexis Arguello wins his third world title, outpointing Scotland's Jim Watt for the WBC lightweight title.

1982
(Aug 12) Featherweight champion Salvador Sanchez, a brilliant Mexican, dies in a car crash just weeks after retaining his WBC title against future champion Azumah Nelson.

1983
The International Boxing Federation is formed by a breakaway group from the WBA.

(Apr) Wilfredo Gomez relinquishes the WBC super-bantamweight title after a record 17 defences, all inside the distance.

1985
(June 8) Ireland's most successful fighter, Barry McGuigan, wins the WBA featherweight title from Eusebio Pedroza, making his 20th defence.

1986
(Nov 22) Mike Tyson becomes the youngest heavyweight champion by taking the WBC title from Trevor Berbick at the age of 20 years and five months.

1987
(Apr 6) Ray Leonard ends Marvin Hagler's reign as middleweight champion after 12 successful defences.

1988
(Apr 9) Evander Holyfield unifies the cruiserweight titles for the only time in the division's history;

(Nov 4) Thomas Hearns becomes the first to win titles in five divisions, beating his arch-rival Ray Leonard to the record by three days.

1990
(Feb 11) Buster Douglas knocks out Mike Tyson in the biggest shock in boxing history.

(July 28) Dennis Andries makes British boxing history by winning the WBC light-heavyweight title for the third time, knocking out Jeff Harding in seven rounds.

1992
(Oct 15) Duke McKenzie takes the WBO super-bantamweight title from Jesse Benavides to become the first British boxer to claim world titles in three divisions.

1993
(Nov 6) Evander Holyfield regains the heavyweight title from Riddick Bowe, in an epic fight interrupted by the arrival in the ring of a para-glider.

1994
(Jan 29) Julio Cesar Chavez, world champion at three weights and the greatest fighter of his time, loses the WBC light-welterweight title to Frankie Randall. It is his first defeat in 91 fights.

(Nov 5) George Foreman becomes the oldest-ever world champion at any weight when, aged 45 years and 10 months, he takes the heavyweight title from Michael Moorer.

1995
(Mar 18) Steve Collins wins WBO title, and ends Chris Eubank's 43-fight unbeaten record, to become super-middleweight champ.

(Sept 2) Frank Bruno wins a heavyweight title at the fourth attempt, outpointing Oliver McCall to become WBC champion.

1996
(Mar 16) Mike Tyson regains the WBC title by stopping Frank Bruno.

1997
(Apr 12) Oscar De La Hoya wins 4th world title.

1999
(March 13) Lennox Lewis and Evander Holyfield draw their unification heavyweight title fight.

(Nov 13) Lennox Lewis unifies heavyweight division by outpointing Evander Holyfield.

2000
(Feb 19) Erik Morales edges out Marco Antonio Barrera on a controversial points decision after one of the most thrilling contests of the era. It sets up a compelling three-fight series between the two great Mexicans.

2003
(Mar 1) Roy Jones Jr makes the leap from light-heavyweight to heavyweight and outboxes John Ruiz for the WBA belt, but relinquishes it without making a defence.

(Jun 21) Lennox Lewis beats Vitali Klitschko in six bloody rounds in Los Angeles in his final world title defence;

(Sep 13) Shane Mosley beats Oscar De La Hoya for the second time and becomes WBC light-middleweight champion in Las Vegas, but the decision of the judges is heavily criticized and brings the business of scoring fights under scrutiny once again.

2004
(Feb) Lennox Lewis announces his retirement at a London hotel.

(Sep 18) At the age of 39 Bernard Hopkins knocks out Oscar De La Hoya with a ninth-round body shot to unify the four main world middleweight championship belts.

2005
(May 7) Diego Corrales wins the WBC lightweight title, recovering from two heavy knockdowns in the tenth round to stop Jose Luis Castillo. It is widely regarded as one of the best fights in world title history;

(June 4) Ricky Hatton rips the world light-welterweight crown from Kostya Tszyu in 11 rounds before a 20,000-plus crowd in Manchester.

(Dec 17) The 7st 2in, 320lb giant from St Petersburg, Nikolay Valuev, becomes the biggest ever heavyweight champion by outpointing John Ruiz for the WBA title in Berlin.

2006
(May 6) Oscar De La Hoya returns to the ring, stops Ricardo Mayorga with a classy display to regain the WBC light-middleweight title – and sets up a $50 million showdown with Floyd Mayweather.

(May 13) Ricky Hatton joins the elite band of British boxers who have won world titles abroad with a gruelling 12-round decision over welterweight Luis Collazo in Boston.

(Nov 4) Floyd Mayweather, now a four-weight champion, defeats Carlos Baldomir to establish himself as welterweight No.1.

2007
(May 5) Floyd Mayweather edges out Oscar De La Hoya on a split decision in one of the richest fights in history.

(Nov 3) Joe Calzaghe holds three of the four main belts after beating Mikkel Kessler before 50,000 fans in Cardiff.

(Dec 8) Ricky Hatton loses in ten rounds to pound-for-pound no.1 Floyd Mayweather.

2008
(Mar 5) David Haye destroys Enzo Maccarinelli in two rounds of cruiserweight unification fight.

(Apr 19) Joe Calzaghe overcomes a first round knockdown in his American debut to beat 43-year-old Bernard Hopkins on a split decision in Las Vegas.

2009
(Jul 18) Amir Khan comes of age by dethroning Andriy Kotelnik for the WBA light-welter crown.

(Nov 7) The fight's dull, but the result is all that matters for David Haye as he outwits Nikolay Valuev in Nuremberg for the WBA heavyweight belt.

(Nov 14) Manny Pacquiao wins a world title in his fifth weight division by stopping Miguel Cotto.

2010
(May 1) Floyd Mayweather extends his winning record to 41 fights with a unanimous decision over Shane Mosley. in Las Vegas.

(Nov 13) Manny Pacquiao becomes a six-weight world champion by outpointing Antonio Margarito to win the vacant WBC light-middleweight title in Arlington, Texas.

2011
(May 21) Bernard Hopkins becomes boxing's oldest world champion when, aged 46 years and 126 days, he took the WBC light-heavyweight title from Jean Pascal in Montreal, Canada.

THREE BELT FAMILY *New IBF super-flyweight champion Daiki Kameda. centre, poses with brothers WBA bantanmweight champion Koki, left, and WHO bantamweight champion Tomoki, right, after defeating Rodrigo Guerrero*

2012
(Nov 24) Xiong Zhao Zhong becomes China's first world professional champion beating Javier Martinez Resendez in Kunming, China.

2013
(Mar 9) Aged 48 years, 53 days, Bernard Hopkins breaks his own record as the oldest world champion with a points win over Tavoris Cloud.

(Sep 3) Daiki Kameda outpoints Rodrigo Guerrero for the vacant IBF super-flyweight title and for the first time in boxing history, three brothers hold world titles simultaneously. Koki held the WBA bantamweight title and Tomoki was the WBO bantamweight champion.

2014
(Dec 30) In just his eighth professional fight, Naoya Inoue becomes a two-weight world champion by stopping Omar Narvaez for the WBO super-flyweight title

2015
(May 2) Floyd Mayweather Jr. and Manny Pacquiao split a $300 million purse 60/40 in what was called "The Fight of the Century". Mayweather wins unanimously on points.

2016
(Jun 3) The boxing world is in mourning when Muhammad Ali dies after a 32-year battle with Parkinson's Disease.

(Dec 10) New Zealander Joseph Parker wins vacant WBO heavyweight title after controversial points win over Andy Ruiz.

2017
(Apr 29) Anthony Joshua outguns Wladimir Klitschko at Wembley to become IBF, IBO and WBA Super heavyweight champion.

(Aug 26) Floyd Mayweather Jr beats MMA world champion Conor McGregor in a much-hyped contest in Nevada and immediately announces his retirement from the sport with a perfect record (50 wins from 50 fights).

BOXING FACTS AND FEATS

Lovers of the esoteric will find much to engage and amuse them in boxing's long and colourful history. Here, to settle some arguments and start others, is an entirely random selection of Fight Game trivia.

CURIOSITIES

Largest paid attendance
132,247 to watch Julio Cesar Chavez stop Greg Haugen in five rounds at the Estadio Azteca, Mexico City on February 20, 1993.

Largest attendance (free admission)
135,132 for Tony Zale vs. Billy Pryor at Milwaukee on August 18, 1941.

Boxers whose first fight was for the world title
Jack Skelly, knocked out in eight by George Dixon for the featherweight title in New Orleans, on September 6, 1892.

Pete Rademacher, knocked out in six by Floyd Patterson for the heavyweight title in Seattle, on August 22, 1957.

Rafael Lovera, knocked out in four by Luis Estaba for the vacant WBC light-flyweight title in Caracas on September 13, 1975.

Longest spell between championships
George Foreman lost the heavyweight title on October 30, 1974, knocked out by Muhammad Ali. He regained it on November 5, 1994, by knocking out Michael Moorer.

Last scheduled 20-rounds world title fight
Joe Louis' 13th round knockout of Abe Simon for the heavyweight title in Detroit on March 21, 1941. The last title fight to go more than 15 rounds was Mike McTigue's 20-rounds points win over Battling Siki for the light-heavyweight title in Dublin on March 17, 1923.

Novice champions
Vasyl Lomachenko equalled the record of Thailand's WBC light-welterweight champion Saensak Muangsurin when he won the WBO featherweight title in just his third professional fight. In his previous fight, he lost a challenge for the same belt. Naoya Inoue won the WBA light-flyweight title in his sixth fight and, two fights later, he added the WBO super-flyweight title.

Record number of world title fights
Julio Cesar Chavez (37)

Champions who had 25 or more title fights
Oscar De La Hoya, Virgil Hill (29) Joe Louis (27) Wladimir Klitschko (27) Henry Armstrong, Ricardo Lopez (26) Muhammad Ali, Larry Holmes, Terry Norris, Bernard Hopkins, Roy Jones, Marco Antonio Barrera (25).

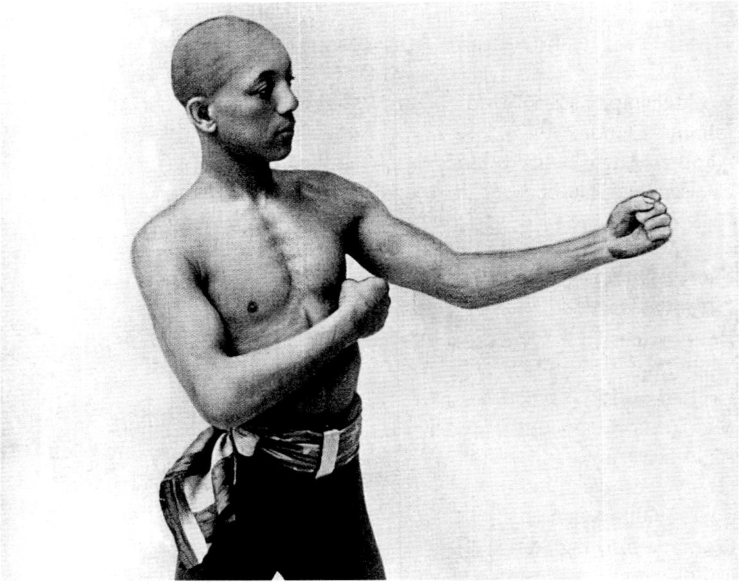

GEORGE DIXON *featherweight legend*

Most championship rounds fought
George Dixon (350), Emile Griffith (320), Julio Cesar Chavez (302).

Famous series
Ted Kid Lewis vs. Jack Britton (20 meetings); Sam Langford vs. Sam McVey (15), Langford vs. Harry Wills (18), Joe Jeanette (14), Jeff Clark (13) and Jim Barry (12).

Most knockdowns
Sam McVey vs. Joe Jeanette, Paris, April 1909: Jeanette was floored 27 times, McVey 19. Jeanette won when McVey collapsed at the start of the 49th round, after 3 hours and 122 minutes.

Highest (verifiable) number of fights
Len Wickwar of Leicester, England, had 466 between 1928 and 1947. The highest of the modern day professionals is the journeyman Reggie Strickland who had 363 between 1987 and 2005.

UNUSUAL ENDINGS

On January 13, 1995 the 12-rounder for the vacant NABF light-heavyweight title between former IBF champion Prince Charles Williams and Merqui Sosa in Atlantic City was declared a technical draw after seven rounds when the ringside doctor, Frank B. Doggett, decided they had each taken too much punishment for them safely to continue.

On the only other similar occasion, when Eddie Woods and Al Milone were too severely cut to continue their fight in Philadelphia in 1959, the result was recorded as a stoppage loss for both men.

There was a double knockout in the world lightweight title fight between champion Ad Wolgast and Mexican Joe Rivers in Los Angeles on July 4, 1912. Both were knocked down simultaneously in the 13th round, and with neither looking likely to beat the count the referee picked up the champion and, holding him under the arm, carried on counting out Rivers.

But the most peculiar ending ever to a championship fight was when challenger George Bernard of France fell asleep in his corner during the interval between the sixth and seventh rounds of his middleweight title fight with Billy Papke in Paris on December 4, 1912. He could not be woken in time for the seventh round, and the ending was recorded as a retirement. He claimed he had been drugged, and was probably right.

World champions Jack Britton 349 and Johnny Dundee 342 came next. Another Englishman, Billy Bird of Chelsea, had 330 between 1920 and 1948.

First southpaw champions

Heavyweight: (see over)
Michael Moorer (1992)
Cruiserweight:
Marvin Camel (1980)
Light-heavyweight:
George Nichols (1932)
Super-middleweight:
Graciano Rocchigiani (1988)
Middleweight:
Al McCoy (1914)
Light-middleweight:
Maurice Hope (1979)
Welterweight:
Young Corbett III (1933)
Light-welterweight:
Sandro Lopopolo (1966)
Lightweight:
Juan Zurita (1944)
Super-featherweight:
Flash Elorde (1960)
Featherweight:
Freddie Miller (1933)
Super-bantamweight:
Bobby Berna (1983)
Bantamweight:
Jimmy Carruthers (1952)
Super-flyweight:
Jiro Watanabe (1982)
Flyweight:
Jackie Paterson (1943)
Light-flyweight:
Yoko Gushiken (1976)
Strawweight:
Ratanapol Sorvoraphin (1992)

THE BIGGEST

Heaviest men to fight for the title

1. Nikolai Valuev (328lb) w rsf 11 Monte Barrett, Rosemont. October 7, 2006
2. Shannon Briggs (273lb) l pts 12 Sultan Ibragimov, Atlantic City, June 2, 2007
3. Primo Carnera (270lb) w pts 15 Tommy Loughran, Miami, March 1, 1934
4. Jameel McCline (270lb) l pts 12 Chris Byrd, New York, November 13, 2004
5. Danny Williams (270lb) l rsf 8 Vitali Klitschko, Las Vegas, December 11, 2004
6. Derrick Jefferson (260lb) l rsf 2 Wladimir Klitschko, Munich, March 24, 2001
7. George Foreman (257lb) l pts 12 Evander Holyfield, Atlantic City, April 19, 1991
8. Lennox Lewis (256 ½lb) w rsf 6 Vitali Klitschko, Los Angeles, June 21, 2003
9. Abe Simon (255lb) l ko 6 Joe Louis, New York, March 27 1942.
10. Matt Skelton (254 3/4lbs) l pts 12 Ruslan Chagaev, Dusseldorf, January 19, 2008

THE BEST

The multiple champions

NB: WBC, WBA, IBF, WBO only in modern era

Six weights: Oscar De La Hoya, Manny Pacquiao
Five weights: Thomas Hearns, Sugar Ray Leonard, Floyd Mayweather
Four weights: Roberto Duran, Pernell Whitaker, Roy Jones, Erik Morales, Miguel Cotto
Three weights: Bob Fitzsimmons, Tony Canzoneri, Barney Ross, Henry Armstrong, Wilfred Benitez, Alexis Arguello, Wilfredo Gomez, Jeff Fenech, Julio Cesar Chavez, Mike McCallum, Wilfredo Vazquez, Duke McKenzie, James Toney, Marco Antonio Barrera, Shane Mosley, Felix Trinidad, Nonito Donaire

Only Fitzsimmons, Canzoneri, Ross and Armstrong were undisputed champions of three divisions. Armstrong is the only man to hold three titles simultaneously. Emile Griffith won a version of the light-middleweight title, recognized only in Austria, to go with his welterweight and middleweight titles. Leonard's claim to five titles includes two won in the same fight, against the WBC light-heavyweight champion Donny Lalonde of Canada, under artificial conditions. Lalonde, was forced to fight under the super-middleweight limit so that the vacant WBC version of that title could also be at stake.

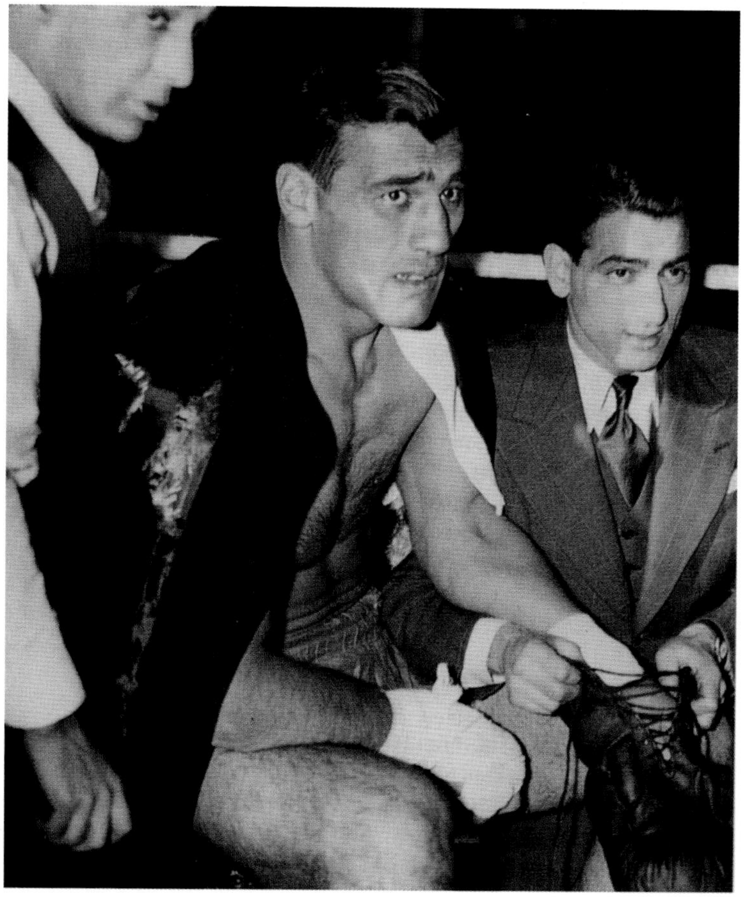

MAN MOUNTAIN *Primo Carnera, the giant of the 20th century*

WINNERS ...

Famous come-from-behind victories in world title fights

Julio Cesar Chavez w rsf 12 (2 min 58 sec) Meldrick Taylor to retain the WBC and win the IBF light-welterweight titles in Las Vegas on March 17, 1990.

Jake LaMotta w ko 15 (2:47) Laurent Dauthuille to retain the middleweight title in Detroit, September 13, 1950.

Paul Vaden w ko 12 Vince Pettway (2:33) to win the IBF light-middleweight title in Las Vegas on August 12, 1995.

Mike Weaver w ko 15 (2:15) John Tate to win the WBA heavyweight title in Tennessee on March 31, 1980.

Oscar Albarado w ko 15 (1:57) Koichi Wajima to win the WBA light-middleweight title in Tokyo on June 4, 1974.

Jeff Harding w rsf 12 (1:23) Dennis Andries to win the WBC light-heavyweight title in Atlantic City on June 24, 1989.

Humberto Gonzalez w rsf 12 (55 sec) Kwang-Sun Kim to retain the WBC light-flyweight title in Seoul on June 7, 1992.

Diego Corrales w rsf 10 Jose Luis Castillo to win the WBC lightweight title, Las Vegas, 7 May 2005.

Shannon Briggs w rsf 12 (2:59) Siarhei Liakhovich to win the WBO heavyweight title in Phoenix, Arizona on November 4, 2006

Carl Froch w rsf 12 (2:46) Jermain Taylor to retain the WBC super-middleweight title in Mashantucket, Connecticut, April 25, 2009.

Highest number of inside-schedule wins

Archie Moore, with 145 between 1936 and 1963. Young Stribling is second with 126 (1921–33) and Billy Bird third with 125 (1920–48).

Most consecutive quick wins

Heavyweight Lamar Clark, who scored 44 (mostly against very poor opposition) between 1958 and 1960. Blackjack Billy Fox is second with 43 between 1943 and 1946, but at least one – the notorious stoppage of Jake LaMotta – was fixed, and it may safely be assumed that this was not the first time it had happened in his career. No such suspicion attaches to the third-highest, Ghanaian bantamweight Bob Allotey, who scored 33 between 1957 and 1963, or to the brilliant Wilfredo Gomez, who had 32 between 1974 and 1981.

Longest unbeaten streak

183 Hal Bagwell (1938–48)
97 Packey McFarland (1905–15)
94 Fred Dyer (1908–12)
93 Pedro Carrasco (1964–71)
91 Ray Robinson (1943–51)
90 Julio Cesar Chavez (1980–94)

Olympic champions who won professional world titles

1920 Frankie Genaro (flyweight)
1924 Jackie Fields (featherweight) Willie Smith (bantamweight) Fidel LaBarba (flyweight)
1948 Pascual Perez (flyweight)
1952 Floyd Patterson (middleweight)
1960 Cassius Clay (light-heavy); Nino Benvenuti (welterweight)
1964 Joe Frazier (heavyweight)
1968 George Foreman (heavy)
1972 Mate Parlov (light-heavy)
1976 Leon Spinks (light-heavy); Mike Spinks (middleweight); Ray Leonard (light-welter); Leo Randolph (flyweight)
1980 Slobodan Kacar (light-heavy); Patrizio Oliva (light-welter)
1984 Frank Tate (light-middle); Mark Breland (welterweight); Pernell Whitaker (lightweight); Meldrick Taylor (featherweight); Maurizio Stecca (bantamweight)
1988 Lennox Lewis (super-heavy); Ray Mercer (heavyweight); Henry Maske (middleweight); Giovanni Parisi (featherweight); Kennedy McKinney (bantamweight)
1992 Oscar De La Hoya (lightweight); Joel Casamayor (bantamweight)
1996 David Reid (light-middle); Istvan Kovacs (bantam-weight); Vassily Jirov (light-heavy); Wladimir Klitschko (super-heavy)
2000 Guillermo Rigondeaux
2004 Guillermo Rigondeaux, Andre Ward, Yuriorkis Gamboa, Alexander Povetkin
2008 Vasyl Lomachenko (featherweight); James DeGale (super-middleweight)

... AND LOSERS

World champions who were unsuccessful in five or more world title fights (losses, unless otherwise specified)

10 Tony Canzoneri (9 losses, 1 draw)
9 Betulio Gonzalez (7 losses, 2 draws)
8 Emile Griffith, Shoji Oguma (7 losses, 1 draw), Sugar Ray Robinson (7 losses, 1 draw)
7 Susumu Hanagata, Juan LaPorte, Daniel Zaragoza (4 losses, 3 draws) Leo Gamez (6 losses, 1 draw), Hiroki Ioka (6 losses, 1 draw)
6 Iran Barkley, Carmen Basilio, Rocky Lockridge, Jersey Joe Walcott, Jack Britton (4 losses, 2 draws), Roberto Duran, Gene Fullmer (3 losses, 3 draws), Luis Mendoza (5 losses, 1 draw), Jorge Paez (4 losses, 2 draws), Hilario Zapata (5 losses, 1 draw), Azumah Nelson (4 losses, 2 draws)
5 Fabrice Benichou, Don Curry, Albert Davila, Larry Holmes, Thierry Jacob, Roger Mayweather, Ruben Olivares, Floyd Patterson, Jose Luis Ramirez, Sugar Baby Rojas, German Torres, Terry Allen (4 losses, 1 draw), Sot Chitalada (4 losses, 1 draw), Carlos De Leon (4 losses, 1 draw), Harry Forbes (4 losses, 1 draw), Frankie Genaro (3 losses, 2 draws), Thomas Hearns (4 losses, 1 draw), Soo-Chun Kwon (3 losses, 2 draws), Tony Lopez (4 losses, 1 draw), Freddie Miller (4 losses, 1 No Contest), Raul Perez (3 losses, 1 draw, 1 technical draw), Lou Salica (4 losses, 1 draw), Marlon Starling (3 losses, 1 draw, 1 No Contest), Ishimatsu Susuki (4 losses, 1 draw), Ben Villamor (2 losses, 3 draws), Marcos Villasana (4 losses, 1 draw), Koichi Wajima (4 losses, 1 draw)

World champions with more than 50 defeats

65 Fritzie Zivic
55 Johnny Jadick
53 Lauro Salas

Statistics can be misleading: Zivic was a famously tough and durable fighter who beat many outstanding performers, including Henry Armstrong, in a 232-fight career.

Most knockdowns suffered in a title challenge

14, by English bantamweight Danny O'Sullivan against South African champion Vic Toweel in Johannesburg on December 2, 1950. O'Sullivan was down eight times in the fifth round, but somehow kept going until the 10th, when he retired.

THE LONGEST

Longest fight

110 rounds (7 hours 19 minutes) Andy Bowen drew with Jack Burke, New Orleans, April 6, 1893.

Longest bare-knuckle fight

6 hours 15 minutes, James Kelly vs. Jack Smith at Melbourne, Australia, October 19, 1856.

Longest title reigns in each division

Heavyweight: Joe Louis (11 years, eight months, 18 days)
Cruiser: Johnny Nelson (7 years 5 months)
Light-heavyweight: Archie Moore (9 years 2 months)
Super-middleweight: Joe Calzaghe (10 years 4 months)
Middleweight: Bernard Hopkins (10 years 3 months)
Light-middleweight: Gianfranco Rosi (5 years 2 months)
Welterweight: Felix Trinidad (6 years)
Light-welterweight: Kostya Tszyu (5 years 10 months)
Lightweight: Roberto Duran (6 years 7 months)
Super-featherweight: Flash Elorde (7 years 3 months)
Featherweight: Eusebio Pedroza (7 years 2 months)
Super-bantamweight: Wilfredo Gomez (5 years 10 months)
Bantamweight: Orlando Canizales (6 years 5 months)

Super-flyweight: Kaosai Galaxy (7 years 1 month)
Flyweight: Jimmy Wilde (7 years 4 months)
Light-flyweight: Myung Woo Yuh (6 years)
Strawweight: Ricardo Lopez (8 years 7 months)

THE SHORTEST

Shortest fight on record
Ever Beleno vs. Alfredo Lugo, April 21, 1995, five seconds.

Shortest world championship reign
Technically the distinction belongs to Pernell Whitaker, who relinquished the WBA light-middleweight title immediately after winning it from Julio Cesar Vasquez in Atlantic City on March 4, 1995.

There have also been cases where a man has won a title but then been stripped of it after failing a drugs test, but flyweight Emile Pladner, whose 47-day reign extended from March 2, 1929 to April 18, 1929, was the quickest to lose it in the ring.

Shortest-reigning European champion
Featherweight Ernst Weiss of Austria, whose 31-day reign lasted from May 30 to June 30, 1941.

Shortest-reigning British champion
Frank Goddard, who was heavyweight champion for just 24 days from May 25 to June 17, 1919.

Shortest-reigning Commonwealth champion
Heavyweight Richard Dunn, who won the title on September 30, 1975, and lost it 36 days later, on November 4.

NOTABLE FIRSTS

First Lonsdale Belt outright winners
Heavyweight: Billy Wells (1916).
Cruiserweight: Johnny Nelson (1991).
Light-heavyweight: Dick Smith (1918).
Super-middle: Sam Storey (1995).
Middleweight: Len Harvey (1930).
Light-middleweight: Maurice Hope (1976).
Welterweight: Johnny Basham (1916).
Light-welterweight: Joey Singleton (1975).
Lightweight: Freddie Welsh (1912).
Junior-light/Super-featherweight: Jimmy Anderson (1969).
Featherweight: Jim Driscoll (1911).
Super-bantamweight: Richie Wenton (1996)
Bantamweight: Digger Stanley (1913).
Flyweight: Jimmy Wilde (1917).

First to win three world titles
Bob Fitzsimmons – middleweight 1891, heavyweight 1897 and light-heavyweight 1903.

First (and only man) to hold three weight titles simultaneously
Henry Armstrong – featherweight 1937, welterweight 1938, and lightweight 1938.

First world heavyweight title fight outside America
Tommy Burns vs. Gunner Moir in London on December 2, 1907.

First judges in a world heavyweight title bout
Tex Rickard and Anthony Drexel Biddle, for the Jack Dempsey vs. Jess Willard fight on July 4, 1919.

First woman to judge a title fight
Eva Shain (Muhammad Ali vs. Earnie Shavers in New York on September 29, 1977).

First to win a world title on disqualification
Pedlar Palmer, against Billy Plimmer in London on November 25, 1895.

First black referee in a world title bout
Zack Clayton, who handled Jersey Joe Walcott vs. Ezzard Charles on June 5, 1952.

GIRL POWER: *Nicola Adams squares up en route to Boxing gold*

First million-dollar gate
Jack Dempsey vs. Georges Carpentier, at Rickard's Oval, Jersey City on July 2, 1921. 80,183 fans paid $1,789,238. It was the first of the five million-dollar gates Dempsey drew, the others being against Luis Firpo, Gene Tunney (twice) and Jack Sharkey.

First brothers to retain world titles on the same show
Rafael and Gabriel Ruelas, in Las Vegas on January 28, 1995. Rafael stopped Billy Schwer in eight rounds to retain the IBF lightweight title. Gabriel kept his WBC super-featherweight crown by stopping Fred Liberatore in the second round.

First use of a motion picture camera
Exhibition between James J. Corbett and Peter Courtney over six rounds at Edison Laboratories, Llewellyn, NJ, in 1897. Corbett knocked him out in the final round.

First movie of a fight
Bob Fitzsimmons vs. James J. Corbett, Carson City, Nevada, March 17, 1897.

First movie of a fight in Britain
Jack Johnson vs. Ben Taylor at the Cosmopolitan Gymnasium, Plymouth on July 31, 1908

First radio transmisson of a fight result
Jack Dempsey vs. Jess Willard at Toledo, Ohio on July 4, 1919.

First radio commentary
Packey O'Gatty vs. Frankie Burns at Boyle's Thirty Acres, Jersey City on July 2, 1921, a preliminary on the Dempsey vs. Carpentier card. This was also the fight in which, for the first time, the ring MC used a microphone.

First radio commentary in Britain
Johnny Curley vs. Harry Corbett at the National Sporting Club, London on March 29, 1926.

First televised boxing
Exhibition between Archie Sexton and Laurie Raiteri at Broadcasting House, London on August 22, 1933.

First televised fight
Len Harvey vs. Jock McAvoy at Harringay Arena, April 4, 1938.

First televised fight to be publicly screened
Eric Boon vs. Arthur Danahar at Harringay Arena, February 23, 1939.

First closed-circuit screening
Joe Louis vs. Lee Savold in New York on June 15, 1951.

First female boxer to win Olympic gold
Nicola Adams, from England, outpointed China's Ren Cancan to win gold in the 51kgs weight category at the London Olympics in 2012.

First million-dollar purse

Sonny Liston and Floyd Patterson were each paid $1,434,000 for their heavyweight title rematch in Las Vegas on July 22, 1963.

First use of a four-roped ring in title fight

Emile Griffith vs. Luis Rodriguez for the welterweight title in New York on June 8, 1963. The fourth rope was introduced as a safety measure following Benny Paret's death in a fight with Griffith the previous year, when he became entangled in the ropes and was unable to avoid Griffith's punches.

First champion from each country

Algeria – Marcel Cerdan (1948)
America – Paddy Duffy (1888)
Antigua – Maurice Hope (1979)
Argentina – Pascual Perez (1954)
Armenia – Vic Darchinyan (2004)
Australia – Jimmy Carruthers (1952)
Austria – Jack Root (1903)
Bahamas – Elisha Obed (1975)

CHARLES LEDOUX *first French champ*

MIKE McCALLUM *Jamaica's first*

Barbados – Joe Walcott (1901)
Belarus – Sergey Lyakhovich (2006)
Belgium – Gustav Roth (1936)
Brazil – Eder Jofre (1960)
Canada – George Dixon (1890)
China – Xiong Zhao Zhong (2012)
Colombia – Antonio Cervantes (1972)
Cuba – Kid Chocolate (1931)
Congo – Anaclet Wamba (1991)
Denmark – Battling Nelson (1905)
Dominican Republic – Carlos Teo Cruz (1968)
England – Bob Fitzsimmons (1891)
France – Charles Ledoux (1912)
Germany – Frank Mantell (1907)
Ghana – David Kotey (1975)
Greece – Anton Christoforidis (1941)
Guadaloupe – Gilbert Dele (1991)
Guyana – Dennis Andries (1986)
Haiti – Joachim Aleine (2007)
Hawaii – Dado Marino (1952)
Hungary – Istvan Kovacs (2001)
Indonesia – Elly Pical (1985)
Iran – Mahyar Monshipour (2003)
Ireland – "Nonpareil" Jack Dempsey (1884)
Italy – Frankie Conley (1910)
Jamaica – Mike McCallum (1984)
Japan – Yoshio Shirai (1952)
Kazakhstan – Anatoly Alexandrov (1998)
Korea – Kim Ki-Soo (1966)
Kyrgyzstan – Orzubek Nazarov (1993)
Martinique – Daniel Londas (1992)
Mauritania – Taoufik Belbouli (1989)
Mongolia – Lavka Sim (1999)
Mexico – Battling Shaw (1933)
Namibia – Harry Simon (1998)
New Zealand – Billy Murphy (1890)
Nicaragua – Alexis Arguello (1974)
Nigeria – Hogan Bassey (1957)
Norway – Pete Sanstol (1931)
Panama – Panama Al Brown (1929)
Philippines – Pancho Villa (1923)
Poland – Darius Michalszewski (1994).
Puerto Rico – Sixto Escobar (1934)
Romania – Michael Loewe (1997)
Russia – Louis Kid Kaplan (1925)
Scotland – Tancy Lee (1915)
Senegal – Battling Siki (1922)
Slovenia – Armand Krajnc (1999)
South Africa – Willie Smith (1927)
Spain – Baltazar Sangchilli (1935)
Sweden – Ingemar Johansson (1959)
Switzerland – Frank Erne (1899)
Thailand – Pone Kingpetch (1960)
Trinidad – Claude Noel (1981)
Tunisia – Victor Young Perez (1931)
Uganda – Ayub Kalule (1979)
Ukraine – Vitali Klitschko (1999)
Uzbekistan – Artur Grigorian (1996)
Venezuela – Carlos Hernandez (1965)
Virgin Islands – Emile Griffith (1961)
Wales – Jim Driscoll (1912)
Yugoslavia – Mate Parlov (1978)
Zaire – Sumbu Kalambay (1987)

THE FASTEST

Fastest one-round finish to a title fight in each division (winner named first)

Heavyweight: James J Jeffries vs Jack Finnegan, 55 seconds, April 6, 1900. NB: Herbie Hide beat Damon Reed in 52 seconds in a WBO title fight on April 18, 1998, but this version is not usually accepted. Lamon Brewster also beat Andrew Golota in 52 seconds in a WBO title fight in Chicago on May 21, 2005.
Cruiserweight: James Warring v James Pritchard, 36 seconds, September 6, 1991
Light-heavyweight: Bobby Cruz v David Sears, 61 seconds, December 12, 1986
Super-middleweight: Joe Calzaghe v Mario Veit, 112 seconds, March 28, 2001
Middleweight: Bernard Hopkins vs. Steve Frank, 24 seconds, January 27, 1996.
Light-middleweight: Julio Cesar Vasquez vs. Aquilino Asprilla, 47 seconds, February 22, 1993.
Welterweight: Lloyd Honeyghan vs. Gene Hatcher, 45 seconds, August 30, 1987.
Light-welterweight: Randall Bailey v Carlos Gonzalez, 41 seconds, May 15, 1999.
Lightweight: Tony Canzoneri vs. Al Singer, 66 seconds, November 14, 1930.
Super-featherweight: Genaro Hernandez vs. Raul Perez (tech draw) 28 seconds, April 26, 1993.
Featherweight: Naseem Hamed v Said Lawal, 35 seconds, March 16, 1996.
Super-bantamweight: Daniel Jimenez v Harald Geier, 19 seconds, September 3, 1994.
Bantamweight: Mauricio Martinez vs Esham Pickering, 72 seconds, December 16, 2000.
Super-flyweight: Katsushige Kawashima vs Masamori Tokuyama, 107 seconds, June 28, 2004.
Flyweight: Pongsaklek Wonjongkam vs Daisuke Naito, 34 seconds, April 19, 2002.
Light-flyweight: Jorge Arce vs Ernesto Castro, 100 seconds, February 22, 2003.
Strawweight: Ricardo Lopez vs. Yamil Caraballo, 70 seconds, December 10, 1994.

Fastest world title fight

Daniel Jimenez's 19-second knockout of Harald Geier of Austria to retain the WBO super-bantamweight title at Wiener Neustadt on September 3, 1994.

Fastest British title fight

Dave Charnley w ko 1 Darkie Hughes for the European, British and Empire lightweight title in 40 seconds at Nottingham on November 20, 1961. This fight also holds the record for the quickest finish to both a British and Empire (later Commonwealth) championship.

THE OLDEST

Oldest to win title

Heavyweight: George Foreman (45 years, 10 months, 25 days)

GOLDEN OLDIE *Stuart Hall*

Cruiserweight: Virgil Hill (42 years, 9 days)
Light-heavyweight: Bernard Hopkins (48 years, 1 month, 22 days)
Super-middleweight: Sugarboy Malinga (38 years)
Middleweight: Javier Castillejo (38 years, 4 months)
Light-middleweight: Cornelius Bundrage (41 years, 5 months, 16 days)
Welterweight: Carlos Baldomir (34 years, 8 months, 7 days)
Light-welterweight Frankie Randall (34 years, 11 months)
Lightweight: Jean-Baptiste Mendy (35 years, 2 months)
Super-featherweight: Azumah Nelson (37 years, 4 months)
Featherweight: Eder Jofre (37 years, 1 month, 10 days)
Super-bantamweight: Daniel Zaragoza (37 years, 11 months)
Bantamweight: Stuart Hall (33 years, 9 months, 25 days)
Super-flyweight: Leo Gamez (37 years, 2 months)
Flyweight: Leo Gamez (35 years, 7 months)
Light-flyweight: Luis Estaba (34 years, 1 month)
Strawweight: Daniel Reyes (31 years, 5 months)

THE YOUNGEST

Youngest to win title

Heavyweight: Mike Tyson (20 years, four months, 22 days)
Cruiserweight: Carlos DeLeon (21 years, 6 months, 20 days)
Light-heavyweight: Michael Moorer (21 years, 21 days)
Super-middleweight: Darrin Van Horn (22 years, 8 months, 11 days)
Middleweight: Al McCoy (19 years, 5 months, 14 days)
Light-middleweight: Darrin Van Horn (20 years, 4 months, 28 days)
Welterweight: Pipino Cuevas (18 years, 6 months, 20 days)
Light-welterweight: Wilfred Benitez (17 years, 5 months, 24 days)
Lightweight: Edwin Rosario (20 years, 1 month, 17 days)
Super-featherweight: Ben Villaflor (19 years, 5 months, 15 days)
Featherweight: Tony Canzoneri (18 years, 11 months, 18 days)
Super-bantamweight: Julio Gervacio (20 years, 1 month, 11 days)
Bantamweight: Teddy Baldock (18 years, 11 months, 15 days)
Super-flyweight: Cesar Polanco (18 years, 2 months, 17 days)
Flyweight: Joe Symonds (19 years, 4 months, 18 days)
Light-flyweight: Netrnoi Vorasingh (19 years, 14 days)
Strawweight: Hiroki Ioka (18 years, 9 months, 10 days)

THE HEAVYWEIGHTS

Shortest-reigning heavyweight champion

Tony Tucker (two months, one day).

Longest unbeaten run en route to the heavyweight title

44 Nikolay Valuev (one No Contest)
43 Rocky Marciano
38 George Foreman
35 Tony Tucker (one No Contest)
32 Riddick Bowe

Heavyweight champion with the fewest fights when winning title

8 Leon Spinks

Heavyweight champion with the most fights

Ezzard Charles (122). Charles also had the most defeats (25), but many occurred after he had lost the title.

Smallest attendance at a heavyweight title fight

2,434 to watch the rematch between Muhammad Ali and Sonny Liston at a High School arena in Lewiston, Maine on May 25, 1965.

Greatest combined weight in a title fight

590½ lb, when Nikolay Valuev met Jameel McCline in Basel, Switzerland on January 20, 2007.

BAD STARTS

World champions who lost professional debut

Bruno Arcari, Alexis Arguello, Henry Armstrong, Rodolfo Blanco, Jack Britton, Joe Brown, Victor Callejas, Miguel Canto, Freddie Castillo, Jesus Castillo, Frank Cedeno, Chang-Ho Choi, Billy Conn, Roberto Cruz, Carlos Teo Cruz, Pipino Cuevas, Joe Dundee, Harry Forbes, Nestor Giovanni, S.T. Gordon, Bernard Hopkins, Daniel Jimenez, Sung Jun Kim, Tae-Shik Kim, Pone Kingpetch, Tippy Larkin, Alfredo Layne, Benny Leonard, Benny Lynch, Tacy Macalos, Eddie Martin, Manny Melchor, Johnny Nelson, Manuel Ortiz, Freddie Pendleton, Eddie Perkins, James "Bonecrusher" Smith, Seung-Il Suk, Wilfredo Vasquez, Mike Weaver, Prince Charles Williams.

World champions held to a draw on debut

Pedro Adigue, Rolando Bohol, Jeff Chandler, Tae-Il Chung, Victor Cordoba, Jack Dempsey, Jack Dillon, Ralph Dupas, Angel Espada, Johnny Famechon, Perico Fernandez, Ceferino Garcia, Wilfredo Gomez, Pete Herman, Soo Hwan Hong, Beau Jack, Matty Matthews, Dave McAuley, Tod Morgan, Billy Papke, Young Perez, Bernardo Pinango, Dwight Muhammad Qawi, Rigoberto Riasco, Arnold Taylor, Aquiles Guzman, Buddy McGirt, Jake Rodriguez, Gabriel Ruelas, Johnny Tapia.

KINGS OF THE DRAW

World champions who fought 10 or more draws

41 George Dixon
37 Young Griffo
31 Tod Morgan
30 Joe Walcott
28 Mysterious Billy Smith
23 Harry Forbes
22 Maxie Rosenbloom
20 Jack Britton, Bob Godwin, Jimmy Goodrich, Solly Smith, Johnny Thompson
19 Torpedo Billy Murphy, Battling Nelson
18 Abe Attell, Johnny Dundee, Matty Matthews, Jimmy Walsh
16 Philadelphia Jack O'Brien, Midget Wolgast
15 Perico Fernandez, Ceferino Garcia, Benny Lynch, Young Perez, Dave Sullivan, Chalky Wright
14 Mike Ballarino, Jack Dillon, Dixie Kid, Nicolino Locche, Honey Mellody, Marcel Thil, Ad Wolgast
13 Baby Arizmendi, Joe Brown, Young Corbett III, Vince Dundee, Gorilla Jones, Battling Levinsky, Ted Kid Lewis, Joe Lynch
12 Miguel Angel Castellini, Frank Erne, Tommy Freeman, Louis Kid Kaplan, Frankie Klick, Al McCoy, Willie Ritchie, Lauro Salas, Lou Salica, Cpl. Izzy Schwartz, Young Jack Thompson
11 Panama Al Brown, Jackie Callura, Paddy Duffy, Jack Johnson, Santos Laciar, Leo Rodak, Phil Terranova
10 Tony Canzoneri, Young Corbett II, Eugene Criqui, Joe Dundee, George Gardner, Al Hostak, George Lavigne, Small Montana, George Nichols, Emile Pladner, Ed Babe Risko, Petey Sarron.

INDEX

A

B

C

D

E

F

G

H

I

J

K

L

M

N

OP

Q

R

S

T

U

V

W

Y

Z

PICTURE CREDITS

The publishers would like to thank the following sources for their kind permission to reproduce the pictures in this book.

Action Images: /Lee Smith: 249; /Paul Thomas: 119

AP: / Christian Alminana/AP: 231; /Simon Dawson/AP: 129; /Spencer Green/AP: 163; /Brad Horn/AP: 211; /Eric Jamison: 26; /Carlos Osorio/AP: 192; /Eckehard Schulz: 28; /Jon Super: 116; /Tim Larsen: 24R

Boxing News

EPA: /Sergei Ilnitsky: 168

Getty Images: /Takashi Aoyama: 236; /Al Bello: 33, 42B, 49T, 118, 120, 121, 173, 187; /Jeff Bottari: 4, 48, 55; /Tom Briglia: 63; /Chris Brunskill: 202; /Ramsey Cardy/Sportsfile: 183, 226; /Rob Casey: 19; /Central Press: 241; /Douglas DeFelice/Eclipse Sportswire: 193; /Kevork Djansezian: 58; /Stephen Dunn: 18; /Johannes Eisele/AFP: 158-159; /Alfred Eisenstaedt/Time & Life Pictures: 71; /Elsa/Golden Boy: 5BL, 172; /Jonathan Ferrey: 225; /Stuart Franklin/Bongarts: 42T; /John Gichigi: 20, 36, 117; /John Gurzinsku/AFP: 6; /Richard Heathcote: 3, 41, 122; /Harry How: 27; /Jed Jacobsohn: 70, 114; /Jiji Press/AFP: 69, 243; /Keystone: 57; /Toshifumi Kitamura/AFP: 34T, 39T; /Jens-Ulrich Koch/AFP: 54; /Nick Laham: 31, 67, 115; /Bob Levey: 32; /Alex Livesey: 216; /Juan Mabromata/AFP: 52; /Steve Marcus: 68; /Stephen McCarthy/Sportsfile: 123; /Charles McQuillan: 222; /Ethan Miller: 34B, 44T; /Jonathan Moore: 66; /Chris Polk: 38; /Mark Ralston/AFP: 14; /Martin Rose/Bongarts: 164; /Mark Runnacles: 25; /Nancy R. Schiff: 128T; /William C. Shrout/Time & Life Pictures: 128B; /Justin Tallis/AFP: 165; /Hector Vivas/Jam Media/LatinContent: 150; /Bob Thomas/Popperfoto: 244

Nick Lourens: 239

PA Images: /Nick Potts: 177

Special thanks are due to *Boxing News* for allowing us to decimate their photographic archive.

Every effort has been made to acknowledge correctly and contact the source and/or copyright holder of each picture and Carlton Books Limited apologises for any unintentional errors or omissions, which will be, corrected in future editions of this book.